AMBIGUOUS REPUBLIC

ALSO BY DIARMAID FERRITER

The Transformation of Ireland 1900–2000
Judging Dev: A reassessment of the life and legacy of Éamon de Valera
Occasions of Sin: Sex and Society in Modern Ireland

AMBIGUOUS REPUBLIC

IRELAND IN THE 1970s

DIARMAID FERRITER

PROFILE BOOKS

First published in Great Britain in 2012 by
Profile Books Ltd
3A Exmouth House
Pine Street
Exmouth Market
London EC1R 0JH
www.profilebooks.com

1 3 5 7 9 10 8 6 4 2

Typeset in Garamond by MacGuru Ltd
info@macguru.org.uk

Printed and bound in Great Britain by
Clays, Bungay, Suffolk

A CIP catalogue record for this book is available from the British Library.

ISBN 978 1 84668 468 5
eISBN 978 1 84765 856 2

The paper this book is printed on is certified by the © 1996 Forest Stewardship Council A.C. (FSC). It is ancient-forest friendly. The printer holds FSC chain of custody SGS-COC-2061

For Catriona Crowe

CONTENTS

Acknowledgements xi
Timeline xiii

Introduction: Old Moulds Broken? 1

Part I: Irish Political and Administrative Culture 13
1 Ballymagash Style Politics 23
2 How to Win the Next Election 32
3 Identifying the Problems 40
4 Servants of the Minister 51
5 Political Soul-Searching 58
6 Leaders and Aspirants 74
7 Shuffling the Traditional Ranks 89
8 Status, Perception and the Press 100
9 A Tedious Honour? 109

Part II: The Impact of the Troubles on the Republic 119
10 A Post-1916 Mood 127
11 Studied Indifference or Generous Tolerance? 135
12 Lost Reputations and Suppressed Truth 141
13 Green America and Blue Britain 153
14 Reporting and Broadcasting the Conflict 162

15 Possibilities, Encounters and Institutions to Trust 168
16 Visitors from the North 180
17 A More Tolerant Republic? 188
18 Trouble Spills Over the Border 197
19 A Passion for Unity? 215

Part III: Commemoration, Memory, Cultural Life and Entertainment 221
20 Remembering the Fight for Freedom 231
21 History Wars 243
22 Irish Identity on Stage 255
23 Music and Language: Redeploying Tradition 266
24 Artistic Creativity and Challenges 279
25 Expanding the Broadcasting Horizons 289
26 Screening and Reporting Ireland 302
27 The Sporting Irish 314

Part IV: Rights, Responsibilities and Justice 325
28 Troubling Times for the Guardians of the Peace 333
29 A Discredited Force? 339
30 The Terror of Urban Decay? 348
31 Controversial Custodies and Contemptuous Judges 358
32 Reforming the Law 367
33 Inalienable Rights of the Child? 374

Part V: Foreign Affairs 385
34 Taking the European Plunge 393
35 Brittany Reunions, Public Apathy and Thinking European 403
36 Negotiating the Benefits and the Dilemmas 409
37 Fear of Enlargement and Striving for Sex Appeal after the Honeymoon Ends 415
38 Garret's Wider Mission 427
39 Leverage with Washington 436
40 Ireland of the Welcomes? 442
41 Marketing Ireland 449

Part VI: The Economy 457
42 The Irish Economic Dilemma 465

43 The Cost of Living, Poverty and Giving Up Meat 474
44 Local Finance, Economic Patriotism, Competitiveness and Employment 486
45 Spending, Planning and Pleading 494
46 Taxing, Dodging, Negotiating and Protesting 502
47 Strikes Raging, Babies Howling 512
48 Hoping to Strike It Rich 525

Part VII: Social Change 539
49 The Urban/Rural Divide 547
50 Taking Responsibility for the Irish Abroad? 554
51 Living on the Edge 561
52 The Broader Social Outlook 565
53 Eating and Drinking through the Seventies 573
54 A New Affluence 585
55 Fatal Lifestyles and the Health System Challenge 597
56 Protecting the Purity of the Republic 612

Part VIII: New Horizons: Education, Religion and the Status of Women 617
57 Democratising Education? 625
58 Practising Lapsed Catholics 641
59 Breaking the Shackles 657

Bibliography 681
Notes 699
List of Illustrations 783
Index 785

ACKNOWLEDGEMENTS

The research and writing of this book would not have been possible without the generous assistance of family, friends, UCD colleagues and those working in a variety of libraries and archives. I am indebted to my colleagues in the School of History and Archives at UCD and the two Heads of School there in recent years, Edward James and John McCafferty, for their collegiality and generosity in facilitating me in completing another research-intensive project. To all those working in the UCD archives, the UCD James Joyce and Richview libraries, the National Archives of Ireland and the National Library of Ireland I extend my deep and sincere gratitude for all their generous assistance. Thanks also to those who have helped, with friendship, advice, information, assistance and stimulation in recent years: Hugh Brady, Kate Breslin, Carla, Melanie, Tom and Anna Briggs, Aisling Caden, Peter and Olivia Casey, Stephen Cullinane, Fergus D'Arcy, Mairín de Burca, Mark Duncan, Adrienne Egan, Liza Finnegan, Roy Foster, Carmel, Ronan, Karen and Rachel Furlong, Tom Garvin, Gráinne Gavigan, Brian Hanley, David Heron, Lucy Hogan, Anthony Hyland, Gareth Ivory, Anne Marie Kearney, Seán Kearns, Jimmy Kelly, Philip King, Cormac Kinsella, Michael Laffan, Georgina Laragy, Margaret Mac Curtain, Peter Mooney, Paul Murphy, William Murphy, Joe Nugent, Nuala O'Connor, Fiona Poole, Greg Prendergast, Antoinette Prout, Mary Raftery, Yetti Redmond, Declan d'Estelle Roe, Paul Rouse, James Ryan, Rob Savage, Jean Smith, Gerry Stembridge,

Richard Stokes, Tony and Catherine Sweeney, Colm Tóibín, Caroline Walsh, Martin Walsh and David Whelan. Peter Carson, Andrew Franklin, Penny Daniel and Ruth Killick at Profile Books have been generous, patient and supportive, and Trevor Horwood copy-edited with precision, flair and insight. Particular best wishes on his retirement to Peter Carson, and thanks for the wisdom and help over the past twelve years. My parents, Nollaig and Vera, siblings, Cian, Tríona, Muireann, and in-laws, soulmate Kevin Maher, Tom, Anne, Lucy, Rose and Catherine Maher, Lar Joyce and Deirdre Mulligan, once again deserve my deepest generosity for all they give; I am truly grateful. I could fill much space with superlatives to sing the praises of Sheila Maher. I have done so before; this time, a simple but profound thank you from the heart, for everything you have done and endured to help me finish this book. As with the others, it belongs to you too. You are beyond marvellous. Our cherished daughters, Enya, Ríona and Saorla, majestic madams, continue to remind us of what is important; it is a pleasure and a privilege to watch them grow, enthral and torment. As in the past, my thanks to Deirdre McMahon, who was, again, a generous, insightful and engaged reader of the first draft, as was Catríona Crowe, to whom this book is dedicated, for years of valued friendship, humanity, history and archive talk, insight, irreverence and humour.

TIMELINE

1970

January

6 Tribunal of inquiry into RTÉ *Seven Days* television programme about moneylending

10 Anti-apartheid demonstrations in Dublin as Ireland's rugby team plays host to South Africa

11 Split develops between the Official and Provisional wings of Sinn Féin after a disagreement at the party's annual meeting in Dublin over taking seats in Dublin and Belfast parliaments

18 Dr Thekla Beere appointed to chair the Commission on the Status of Women

February

24 Health Act provides for the establishment of eight regional health boards and a hospitals authority

March

12 Private Member's Bill from the Labour Party calls for voting age to be lowered to eighteen from twenty-one

21 Ireland's entry, 'All Kinds of Everything', sung by Dana, wins the Eurovision Song Contest in Amsterdam

April

3 Garda Richard Fallon murdered during a bank robbery in Dublin

21 A White Paper 'Membership of the European Communities: Implications for Ireland', is published

30 Bank workers strike in pursuit of higher wages; the Industrial Development Authority becomes an autonomous state-sponsored body

May

4 Minister for Justice Micheál Ó Móráin resigns from office due to ill health

6 Charles Haughey, Minister for Finance, and Neil Blaney, Minister for Agriculture, are asked to resign by the Taoiseach Jack Lynch; Kevin Boland, Minister for Local Government, resigns in sympathy

22 Employer-Labour Conference established

27 Captain James Kelly, a former army intelligence officer, arrested to face charges of conspiracy to import arms to Ireland

28 Charles Haughey and Neil Blaney arrested and charged with conspiracy to import arms

June

1 Announcement of a new Department of Public Service

4 Fianna Fáil withdraws the whip from Kevin Boland

7 Demolition workers begin to strip the roofs of four Georgian houses in Hume Street, Dublin city, after protestors are removed; Owen Sheehy Skeffington, independent senator and liberal, dies aged sixty-one

10 Taoiseach Jack Lynch opens the Electricity Supply Board's generating station at Tarbert, County Kerry

22 Kevin Boland resigns from Fianna Fáil

25 The Catholic Hierarchy's ban on Catholic attendance at Trinity College, Dublin is lifted

26 Unity MP Bernadette Devlin imprisoned in Armagh

28 Extra British troops flown to Belfast after five people shot dead by the IRA in Northern Ireland

30 Negotiations for Ireland's membership of EEC open in Brussels

July

2 Neil Blaney discharged after district justice at his trial rules there is insufficient evidence to justify the conspiracy charge against him

August

21 Social Democratic and Labour Party (SDLP) formed in Belfast

September

22 The Arms Trial opens in Dublin's Four Courts; the jury is discharged seven days later following allegations of bias

29 President Eamon de Valera opens a new Arts block at the Belfield Campus of University College, Dublin

October

5 American president Richard Nixon visits Ireland

6 A new Arms Trial opens in Dublin

22 Taoiseach Jack Lynch addresses the general assembly of the United Nations in New York

23 Charles Haughey is found not guilty at the Arms Trial and calls on Jack Lynch to resign

November

4 Irish School of Ecumenics established in Dublin

13 Declan Costello, author of Fine Gael's 'Just Society' document, announces his return to politics

17 Commercial banks reopen to the public

20 At the United Nations, Ireland abstains on the issue of the admission of China

21 Ireland's largest Protestant primary school opens in Dundrum in Dublin

26 Minister for Finance George Colley announces the establishment of a radio station for the Gaeltacht (Irish language-speaking districts)

December

13 The Labour Party agrees to negotiate with Fine Gael to form a coalition government if no party has an overall majority after the next general election

21 National Wage Agreement concluded

1971

January

23 The Official sports body COSAC is established by the Minister for Education, Pádraig Faulkner

February

6 The first British soldier to be killed in the modern Troubles is shot in Belfast

8 The Theobald Wolfe Tone statue in Dublin is shattered by an explosion

11 A White Paper 'Local Government Reorganisation' is published

15 The Irish currency officially changes to a decimal system

March

1 An experimental traffic lane for buses is introduced in Dublin

3 Aer Lingus, the state airline, becomes one of the first major employers in Ireland to offer equal pay

15 The Gate Theatre in Dublin reopens after its reconstruction due to the dangerous condition of the previous structure

19 David Lean's film *Ryan's Daughter* opens in Dublin

20 James Chichester Clark resigns as prime minister of Northern Ireland

21 120 acres of land in Navan, County Meath being prospected by the Canadian mining company Tara are sold by the owner to Bula, a three-man Irish company; Brian Faulkner becomes prime minister of Northern Ireland; six Irish players selected for the British Lions rugby team

April

1 The eight regional health boards become operable

3 RTÉ television first broadcasts in colour, as it films the Eurovision Song Contest in Dublin

11 The Gaelic Athletic Association (GAA) deletes Rule 27, prohibiting its members from playing soccer, rugby, hockey and cricket

18 Census of Population reveals the Republic has a population of 2,978,248, an increase of 3.3 per cent from 1966

20 The first North/South talks on cross-border co-operation begin in Dublin

May

11 Former Taoiseach Seán Lemass dies aged seventy-one

22 Members of the Irish Women's Liberation Movement (IWLM) bring in contraceptives to the Republic from Northern Ireland to protest against the law banning their importation

June

1 Safety belts become compulsory in certain kinds of vehicles

July

1 The first meeting of the Broadcasting Review Committee to examine progress of state broadcaster RTÉ and recommend developments in radio and television

5 The Nuclear Energy Act provides for the establishment of a Nuclear Energy Board

8 Mary Robinson's bill to liberalise the law on contraceptives is refused a reading in the Senate

9 Forty refugees from Northern Ireland arrive in the Republic

16 SDLP announces it will boycott the Northern Ireland parliament at Stormont

27 The Higher Education Act provides statutory authority for the Higher Education Authority

28 The Central Bank Act gives the Central Bank greater control over the country's banking system

August

9 At least fifteen die in violence in Northern Ireland after internment without trial is introduced; more than 300 are arrested

11 Nearly 4,500 refugees from Northern Ireland in refugee camps in the Republic

12 Taoiseach Jack Lynch calls for the abolition of the Stormont regime

September

1 Prohibition of Forcible Entry and Occupation Act introduced to combat squatting

4 Tipperary win a record twenty-second All-Ireland hurling final

6 Taoiseach Jack Lynch meets the British prime minister Edward Heath at Chequers for talks on Northern Ireland

19 Aontacht Éireann, the new Republican Unity Party, is launched by Kevin Boland
27 Tripartite talks at Chequers between Jack Lynch, Edward Heath and Brian Faulkner

October

1 Gerry Collins, Minister for Posts and Telegraphs, invokes Section 31 of the Broadcasting Authority Act 1960 for the first time to prevent RTÉ from broadcasting material which could promote the aims or activities of an organisation which seeks 'any political objective by violent means'
3 Composer and musician Seán Ó Riada dies aged forty
5 Ian Paisley and three other MPs take their seats in Stormont as the Democratic Unionist Party (DUP)
27 Commission on the Status of Women Report is published

November

1 Marathon Petroleum announces the discovery of gas off the coast of Kinsale

December

4 Fifteen killed in an explosion at a public house in Belfast
10 Unemployment in the Republic rises to 69,462, the highest figure in two decades
16 General Richard Mulcahy, the former leader of Fine Gael, dies aged eighty-five

1972

January

15 Publication of the White Paper 'The Accession to the European Communities'
22 Taoiseach Jack Lynch and Minister for Foreign Affairs Patrick Hillery sign the Treaty of Accession to the European Communities in Brussels; the United Kingdom and Denmark also sign
27 The Ardmore Film Studios in County Wicklow are sold; one of the directors of a new company, Ardmore Studios International, is film director John Huston
28 Irish Congress of Trade Unions decides to oppose entry to the EEC

30 'Bloody Sunday', during which thirteen unarmed people are shot dead in Derry by British paratroopers at a banned civil rights march
31 Huge protests after the killings in Derry; Ireland's ambassador to Britain is recalled

February
2 British Embassy in Dublin burned down after a large demonstration
12 Irish rugby team defeat England at Twickenham
13 Dr Dermot Ryan ordained as the new Archbishop of Dublin
17 Scotland calls off its rugby international with Ireland owing to the Troubles
22 Bomb in Aldershot kills seven people; official IRA claims responsibility

March
9 It is announced that between August 1969 and March 1972, 262 people died as a result of the Troubles in Northern Ireland
24 Direct rule from Westminster imposed on Northern Ireland; William Whitelaw appointed Secretary of State for Northern Ireland
30 Last meeting of the Northern Ireland parliament takes place

April
2 Radio na Gaeltachta inaugurated
12 Electricity Supply Board shift-workers strike; almost 90 per cent of the country's industries have to be closed down
19 Report by Lord Chief Justice Widgery into Bloody Sunday published; it places the responsibilities for the deaths on the organisers of the civil rights march; Minister for Finance George Colley proposes a current budget deficit to be met by borrowing, the first time such a deficit is used as a deliberate policy instrument
27 Poet Thomas Kinsella's *Butcher's Dozen*, a response to the Widgery Report, is published

May
10 Referendum on Ireland's membership of the EEC finds almost five to one in favour (1,041,890 to 211,891); a new £7 million terminal at Dublin airport comes into partial service

19 Nearly 200 prisoners removed from the riot-damaged Mountjoy Jail in Dublin
23 Quinnsworth supermarkets come into operation
26 Special Criminal Court established
31 President of Sinn Féin Ruairí O Brádaigh and Belfast Republican Joe Cahill arrested and detained

June

8 Mary McGee, a twenty-seven-year-old mother of four, seeks a declaration in the High Court that the procedures under which customs officers seized her contraceptives were illegal
18 Twelve leading Irish businessmen among 118 killed in air crash at Staines, Middlesex
26 Neil Blaney expelled from Fianna Fáil

July

1 School-leaving age raised from fourteen to fifteen
3 Announced that three government departments – Health, Industry and Commerce, and Transport and Power – will be reorganised
19 Muhammad Ali beats Al Lewis in the eleventh round of their boxing bout at Croke Park in Dublin
21 Bombs in Belfast kill eleven people

August

7 Death toll in Northern Ireland since 1969 rises to 500
15 Justice Cearbhall Ó Dálaigh, the Chief Justice appointed the Irish member of the European Community's Court of Justice
23 Lord Killanin elected president of the International Olympic Committee; Committee of Public Accounts reports that more than £76,000 of a £100,000 grant-in-aid voted in 1969 by the government for the relief of distress in Northern Ireland has not been accounted for

September

8 Ernest Blythe retires from the board of the Abbey Theatre after a thirty-year membership
12 Solicitor Michael Corkery becomes the first Irishman to be appointed to the European Commission

27 National Institute of Higher Education (NIHE) opened in Limerick

October

1 European Court of Human Rights admits for investigation charges brought against Britain by the Irish government that will determine whether measures taken under the Special Powers Act, including internment, were justified

7 At Ringaskiddy in Cork Taoiseach Jack Lynch opens the Pfizer chemical plant, which contains the largest citric acid unit in the world

24 A bill to amend the law on the sale of contraceptives is published by senators Mary Robinson, Trevor West and John Horgan

27 Thousands of university students protest against the higher education grants scheme

November

1 VAT comes into effect, replacing wholesale tax and turnover tax

5 Dr Dermot Ryan attends a service in Dublin's Anglican Christ Church Cathedral, the first time a Catholic archbishop has done so since the Reformation

19 Seán Mac Stiofáin, the leader of the Provisional IRA, arrested in Dublin

24 The government dismisses the RTÉ Authority after RTÉ broadcasts the content of an interview with Mac Stiofáin

December

1 Two bombs explode in the centre of Dublin, killing two and injuring 127; Offences Against the State (Amendment) Bill passed in the Dáil

7 Referenda to lower the voting age to eighteen and to delete the reference in the constitution to the 'special position' of the Catholic Church are passed

1973

January

1 Ireland joins the EEC along with Denmark and the UK

6 Dr Patrick Hillery appointed Commissioner for Social Affairs at the European Community

11 Special Criminal Court sentences Ruairí O Brádaigh to six months' imprisonment for IRA membership

20 Car bomb in Dublin kills one and injures thirteen; Ralph Nader, the American consumer advocate, meets parents of Irish thalidomide children to discuss ways of obtaining increased compensation

February

5 19th Dáil dissolved and general election called for 28 February, five weeks before 140,000 new voters between the age of eighteen and twenty-one are entitled to vote; Kenneth Griffith's documentary on the life of Michael Collins is banned from British screens

28 General election brings victory for Fine Gael and Labour, who had agreed a programme for coalition government: seats won: FF 69, FG 54, Labour 19, Others 2

March

9 Broadcasting Review Committee recommends establishment of a second RTÉ channel

14 20th Dáil assembles and Liam Cosgrave appointed Taoiseach; coalition cabinet includes nine Fine Gael and five Labour ministers

16 Tony O'Reilly takes control of Independent Newspapers

20 British government publishes its White Paper 'Northern Ireland: Constitutional Proposals', proposing a unicameral eighty-seat assembly with an executive that will include members of Catholic minority

April

5 Minister for Education Richard Burke announces Irish is no longer required for a pass in state examinations but remains a compulsory subject

7 Dr John Charles McQuaid, former archbishop of Dublin (1940–72), dies aged seventy-seven

26 First issue of the *Education Times*, edited by John Horgan

May

3 Northern Ireland Assembly Act establishes an assembly of seventy-eight members

5 Erskine Childers of Fianna Fáil begins his campaign for the presidency

15 Minister for Health Brendan Corish announces government will give help to Irish thalidomide victims
16 Minister for Finance Richie Ryan introduces his first budget
30 Erskine Childers defeats Tom O'Higgins in the presidential election

June

1 3,000 women in the civil service receive their first wages based on equal pay
22 Freedom of the City of Dublin conferred on legendary theatre figures Hilton Edwards and Micheál MacLiammóir
26 Minister for Industry and Commerce Justin Keating caps prices on certain basic foodstuffs

July

25 Government buys Ardmore Studios, intending to establish an Irish film industry there
31 First meeting of the Northern Ireland Assembly ends in chaos; civil service abolishes its bar against the continued employment of women who marry

August

30 Minister for Health Brendan Corish announces that from April 1974 everyone in the country will be entitled to all hospital services without direct charge

September

17 Taoiseach Liam Cosgrave and Edward Heath meet in County Dublin, the first official visit of a British prime minister since the foundation of the state
24 RTÉ begins broadcasting from its new radio centre in Donnybrook, Dublin
29 Minister for Foreign Affairs Garret FitzGerald announces that Ireland and Russia will exchange diplomatic missions

October

2 Attorney General Declan Costello opens the government's case before the European Commission of Human Rights accusing Britain of torturing internees in Northern Ireland

3 A new record for Dublin property established at auction when a 0.9-acre plot at Sydney Parade in Dublin sells for £115,000
8 Fianna Fáil appoints Séamus Brennan as the party's general secretary
26 Minister for Industry and Commerce Justin Keating announces the appointment of a National Consumer Advisory Council
30 240 Irish troops are dispatched to serve with the UN peacekeeping force in the Middle East
31 Hijacked helicopter used to snatch three Northern Provisionals from Mountjoy Jail

November
3 Petrol prices increase due to Middle East oil crisis
9 All prisoners convicted of IRA-related offences are moved to Portlaoise Prison
19 Garages introduce petrol rationing
22 Announcement of eleven-man Northern Ireland Executive under Brian Faulkner and his deputy Gerry Fitt
26 Government obtains £7.5 million loan to finance the expansion of Ireland's telephone service
28 National Economic and Social Council hosts its first meeting

December
1 Tomás Mac Anna becomes artistic director of the Abbey Theatre
9 Sunningdale Agreement proposes to establish, in addition to the power-sharing executive in Northern Ireland, a Council of Ireland with representatives from North and South and an Anglo-Irish Law Commission; Irish government agrees to accept there will be no change in the status of Northern Ireland until a majority there desire such change
19 Supreme Court decides the ban on the importation of contraceptives is unconstitutional
20 Thirteen letter bombs discovered in post offices and businesses in Dublin

1974

January
1 Northern Ireland Executive takes office
7 Brian Faulkner resigns as leader of the Unionist Party

21 Minister for Local Government James Tully announces proposed civic offices in Dublin will not be built at the controversial Wood Quay Viking site
23 Official, Democratic and Vanguard Unionist parties withdraw from the Northern Ireland Assembly
26 The Kenny Report on the cost of building land is published

February

7 The McCormick Report, recommending a comprehensive state health service, is published
27 Seven thousand students march through Dublin to demand a comprehensive higher education grants system
28 In the British general election, anti-Sunningdale Unionists win eleven out of the twelve seats in Northern Ireland; Gerry Fitt of the SDLP holds his seat in West Belfast

March

7 New National Wage Agreement accepted by the Irish Congress of Trade Unions (ICTU)
11 Fine Gael senator Billy Fox murdered in Monaghan; Kenneth Littlejohn, one of two brothers convicted of an armed robbery in Dublin in August 1972, escapes from Mountjoy Jail; at his trial he claimed he was spying on the IRA for British military intelligence
20 Poet Austin Clarke dies in Dublin aged seventy-seven
27 The Senate refuses the second reading of Mary Robinson's Family Planning Bill

April

4 A trust is established to maintain the *Irish Times* as 'a serious and independent newspaper'
6 A new automatic telephone exchange comes in to operation in Ballsbridge, Dublin
10 Sister Stanislaus Kennedy of the Kilkenny Social Service Centre announced as chair of an advisory committee to initiate schemes to combat poverty
21 Dublin Corporation refuse-collection dispute ends after two months

May

1 Trans World Airlines opens its new Atlantic service to Dublin

9 Plans announced for a 900-seat concert hall in Dublin to be home to the RTÉ symphony orchestra

14 Ulster Council declares a general strike

17 31 killed and 150 injured by bombs in Dublin and Monaghan

22 284 Irish troops on duty with the UN in the Middle East return to Ireland to augment the army's border controls

24 First official strike in the history of Guinness's brewery in Dublin

28 Northern Ireland Executive collapses

June

3 Michael Gaughan, a Republican prisoner on hunger strike in Parkhurst Prison, dies; he is buried in Mayo six days later

25 Dr Rose Dugdale sentenced to nine years in prison at the Special Criminal Court in Dublin for receiving nineteen stolen paintings from the home of Sir Alfred Beit

July

8 Dublin bus strike ends after nine weeks

16 Taoiseach Liam Cosgrave helps defeat his own government's bill for the control, sale and manufacture of contraceptives, by 75 votes to 61

August

18 Nineteen Provisional IRA prisoners escape from Portlaoise Prison, prompting the biggest manhunt in the history of the state

September

7 Centenary celebrations of the Irish Rugby Football Union

16 Attorney General Declan Costello announces the formation of a Law Reform Commission

October

3 Bord Fáilte Éireann, the Irish Tourist Board, opens its first office in Belgium

8 Seán Mac Bride, former Minister for External Affairs, shares the 1974 Nobel Peace Prize, the first Irishman to achieve the honour

21 Gulf Oil spillage in Bantry Bay

30 Ireland's soccer team defeats the Soviet Union at Dalymount Park in Dublin

November

7 Minister for Finance Richie Ryan announces knowledge of Irish will no longer be obligatory for entry to the civil service or promotion within it
17 President Erskine Childers dies suddenly in Dublin aged sixty-nine
21 Bombs in two Birmingham pubs kill 19 and injure 182
28 The Irish Export Board, Córas Tráchtála, announces Ireland's yearly exports have exceeded £1 billion for the first time

December

3 Cearbhall Ó Dálaigh elected unopposed as the fifth president of Ireland
4 Petrol prices increase by 30 per cent in an attempt to curb the country's oil imports
6 Students march in Dublin city campaigning for more government spending on higher education
8 Eighty delegates break away from the Official IRA to form the Irish Republican Socialist Party
29 Twenty-seven prison officers are overpowered and held captive after a riot in Portlaoise Prison

1975

January

1 Ireland assumes presidency of the EEC for six months
7 Six fishermen drown off the coast of Donegal
8 Eamon Barnes appointed the state's first Director of Public Prosecutions
28 Colm O Briain appointed first full-time director of the newly constituted Arts Council
30 Jack Lynch announces that Charles Haughey (Health) and James Gibbons (Agriculture) have returned to the Fianna Fáil front bench
31 Unemployment exceeds 100,000 for the first time since 1942

February

3 Brendan Corish, Minister for Health, sets up the Health Education Bureau

March

3 EEC Regional Fund designates £35 million for Ireland
10 Taoiseach Liam Cosgrave presides over summit of EEC heads of government at Dublin Castle
13 Irish horse Ten Up, ridden by Tommy Carberry, wins the Cheltenham Gold Cup
17 A prisoner is shot dead while attempting to escape from Portlaoise Prison

April

2 Community Law Centre opened in Coolock in Dublin, run by the Free Legal Advice Centre (FLAC)
5 Irish horse L'Escargot, ridden by Tommy Carberry, wins the Aintree Grand National
15 Ireland's first day centre for children in trouble with the law is opened in Cork
27 Petrol and oil distribution strike ends after twelve days
29 Minister for Industry and Commerce Justin Keating announces the licensing terms for offshore drilling and gas

May

3 High Court in Belfast rules that the Republic has no jurisdiction over Northern Ireland's coastal waters
10 Dr Rose Dugdale enters the seventeenth day of her hunger strike

June

4 State sponsored company set up to run Ardmore Studios in Wicklow
22 Unsuccessful attempt to blow up a train carrying 300 Official Republicans to Wolfe Tone Commemoration ceremony

July

7 Robert Molloy resigns as a member of the Fianna Fáil front bench after apologising for allegations of corruption made against Minister for Local Government James Tully

9 IRA leader Dáithí Ó Conaill arrested in Dublin
16 Edmund Garvey appointed Garda Commissioner
24 Ireland becomes the first of the nine EEC members to apply for aid from EEC Regional Fund
26 Newly built gallery at the Chester Beatty library in Dublin opens to house oriental art collection
31 Three members of the Miami Showband killed in ambush in County Down

August

5 Capital Gains Tax provides for taxes on gifts and inheritance to replace death duties
10 Two children killed during gun battles in Belfast on the fourth anniversary of internment
15 Six Irishmen convicted of the Birmingham pub murders are jailed for life at Lancaster Crown Court
16 Wealth Tax Act introduced
28 A psychiatric research unit opens at St Patrick's Hospital, Dublin
29 Former president, Taoiseach and leader of Fianna Fáil Eamon de Valera dies, aged ninety-two, in Dublin

September

11 Garda Michael Reynolds shot dead after a bank raid in Dublin
16 Hortense Allende, widow of former president of Chile, visits Dublin to thank the Irish government for accepting 100 Chilean refugees after Chilean coup
25 Henry Kenny, parliamentary secretary to the Minister for Finance, dies aged sixty-two

October

2 Eleven people killed after a wave of UVF violence in Northern Ireland
3 Dr Tiede Herrema, managing director of the Ferenka Plant at Limerick, is kidnapped
12 Taoiseach Liam Cosgrave leads an Irish delegation to Rome for the canonisation of Oliver Plunkett
20 Law Reform Commission meets for the first time

November

6 For the first time Egon Ronay's *Guide to Hotels* gives its Gold Plate award to an Irish hotel – Ashford Castle in Cong, County Mayo

7 Dr Tiede Herrema released after the siege of Monasterevin

29 Two bombs planted by Loyalist paramilitaries kill one and injure five at Dublin airport

December

3 Annual Report of Garda Commissioner reveals that the number of murders committed in Ireland in 1974, at fifty-one, is the highest since the foundation of the state

4 Irish Planning Institute inaugurated

5 Detention without trial ends in Northern Ireland

10 Taoiseach Liam Cosgrave declares a pay freeze for some workers

12 Supreme Court allows an appeal by Mairín de Burca and Mary Anderson against a High Court decision regarding the exemption of women from jury service

1976

January

5 Former Taoiseach John A. Costello dies in Dublin aged eighty-four; ten Protestants shot dead at Kingmills, County Armagh

28 Minister for Finance Richie Ryan presents a severe budget, which imposes an extra £107 million in taxes

February

1 Minister for Industry and Commerce Justin Keating confirms oil and gas finds thirty miles south of Kinsale, County Cork

12 Frank Stagg, a member of the Provisional IRA, dies in Wakefield Prison after a sixty-day hunger strike

16 *Conquest of Light*, a documentary film by Louis Marcus on the making of Waterford Crystal, is nominated for an Oscar

21 Frank Stagg buried near Ballina, County Mayo

March

1 Charles Murray, former secretary of the Department of Finance, succeeds Dr T. K. Whitaker as governor of the Central Bank

3 EEC rejects Irish government's application for derogation from Community's directive on equal pay for men and women
11 Eddie Gallagher and Marion Coyle sentenced to twenty and fifteen years, respectively, for kidnap of Dr Tiede Herrema; National Institute of Higher Education recognised as a college of the National University of Ireland
14 Córas Tráchtála announces that half of Irish exports worldwide are manufactured goods; in 1975, markets outside the UK represented 50 per cent of total exports for the first time
17 Taoiseach Liam Cosgrave addresses both houses of US Congress
31 Cork–Dublin mail train robbed of over £150,000 near Sallins, County Kildare

April
13 It is estimated that 1,497 people have died in violence in Northern Ireland since 1969
25 Provisional Republican ceremonies to commemorate the sixtieth anniversary of the 1916 Rising
28 Labour Party expels David Thornley TD for appearing on a provisional Sinn Féin platform during a banned Rising commemoration

May
5 Eight SAS members arrested south of the border
10 James Tully, Minister for Local Government, rejects an appeal to build an oil refinery in Dublin Bay

June
9 Noel and Marie Murray sentenced to death by the Special Criminal Court for the capital murder of Garda Michael Reynolds, subsequently commuted to life imprisonment
28 Banks close nationwide due to a strike by bank officials

July
3 ICTU rejects National Wage Agreement
13 Adoption Act allows adoptions in which natural and adoptive parents of children are not of the same religion

21 Christopher Ewart-Biggs, Britain's ambassador to Ireland assassinated in Dublin
30 Minister for Education announces that University College Cork, University College Galway and St Patrick's College Maynooth are to become independent universities

August
10 Three children killed in Belfast when hit by a car driven by a Provisional IRA member
14 Women's Peace Movement, led by Máiréad Corrigan and Betty Williams, holds its first rally in Belfast
28 Thousands march in Dublin in support of Women's Peace Movement

September
1 The Dáil and Senate declare 'a national emergency' due to conflict in Northern Ireland
2 Report of the European Commission of Human Rights concludes British troops were guilty of torture during their interrogation of Northern internees
5 Protest by Irish Women United against 'Gentlemen only' bathing in Sandycove, County Dublin
10 Roy Mason replaces Merlyn Rees as Secretary of State for Northern Ireland
16 Second RTÉ radio channel announced
24 President Ó Dálaigh refers the Emergency Powers Bill to the Supreme Court to test its constitutionality
26 For the first time since 1934, Dublin defeat Kerry in an all-Ireland football final; European Commission limits the national fishing zone to twelve miles

October
8 National Economic and Social Council publishes *A Prelude to Planning*, investigating policy options open to the Irish economy
15 Garda Michael Clarkin killed in an explosion in County Laois
16 President Ó Dálaigh signs the Emergency Powers Bill after the Supreme Court affirms its constitutionality
18 Minister for Justice Patrick Donegan refers to President Ó Dálaigh as a 'thundering disgrace'

22 President Ó Dálaigh resigns
27 Female Aer Lingus employees allege sexual discrimination in the matter of promotion, the first case of its kind in the public sector

November

2 Fianna Fáil nominates Patrick Hillery for the presidency
3 EEC report reveals that Ireland's inflation rate, at 18.9 per cent, is the highest in the EEC
9 Patrick Hillery returned unopposed as president
16 Poet Seamus Heaney receives the W. H. Smith Literary award in London for his collection *North*; Abbey Players tour of the United States begins
23 Five fishermen drown off the Donegal coast

December

10 Major James Quinn from Tipperary is appointed commander of the UN peacekeeping force in Cyprus
14 Garret FitzGerald begins a six-day visit to the Soviet Union, the first by an Irish foreign minister
21 Fund launched to finance a legal challenge to the banning of a family planning booklet by the Censorship of Publications Board

1977

January

5 First meeting of the new Planning Appeals Board
6 Richard Burke, Ireland's new EEC commissioner, attends the inaugural meeting of the new Commission
23 Sinn Féin The Workers Party replaces Official Sinn Féin as the party's name

February

4 Government announces the setting up of a Department of Fisheries
5 Gemma Hussey, a member of the Women's Political Association, announces her intention to seek a Senate seat
21 National Wage Agreement ratified by ICTU

March

16 Minister for Foreign Affairs Garret FitzGerald meets US president Jimmy Carter to discuss Irish-American funding for the IRA
31 The Broadcasting Complaints Commission is established

April

6 The Unfair Dismissals Act is enacted
17 Cardinal William Conway dies in Armagh aged sixty-four
22 A forty-seven-day hunger strike by Provisional IRA prisoners in the Curragh is called off

May

19 Declan Costello retires as Attorney General to become a High Court judge
25 The twentieth Dáil is dissolved
26 Fianna Fáil publishes its election manifesto

June

1 The Employment Equality Act outlaws employment discrimination on grounds of sex or marital status
16 Fianna Fáil wins the general election (FF 84, FG 43, Labour 17, Others 4)
23 Liam Cosgrave announces his retirement as leader of Fine Gael
26 Brendan Corish announces he is stepping down from the leadership of the Labour Party

July

1 Garret FitzGerald elected leader of Fine Gael; Frank Cluskey elected leader of the Labour Party
5 Twenty-first Dáil assembles; Jack Lynch elected Taoiseach; a new Department of Economic Planning, headed by Dr Martin O'Donoghue is announced
7 Josie Airey brings her case regarding legal aid to the European Commission of Human Rights
14 European Court of Justice orders the Irish government to suspend its unilateral fisheries conservation measures
27 Announcement that the system of marriage differentiation in public service pay is to be eliminated

August

26 Minister for Justice Gerry Collins announces increased funds for Garda overtime

30 US president Jimmy Carter releases a statement recognising the role of the Irish government in any Northern Ireland settlement and commits his government to a political solution achieved by peaceful means

31 Paddy Devlin of the SDLP is stripped of his positions within the party following his criticism of its leadership and policies

September

18 Conor Cruise O'Brien claims at a conference in Oxford that a majority of Irish people do not want Irish unity

19 Minister for Health and Social Welfare, Charles Haughey, announces a new social welfare system based on a pay-related contribution

28 Taoiseach Jack Lynch meets British prime minister James Callaghan to discuss Northern Ireland

October

2 Dr Tomás Ó Fiaich is ordained as Archbishop of Armagh

3 A strike begins at Dr Tiede Herrema's Ferenka factory in Limerick

5 Séamus Costello, chairman of the Irish Republican Socialist Party, shot dead in Dublin

7 A three-member commission of inquiry is established to investigate the treatment of suspects in Garda custody

November

16 Announcement of a National Board for Science and Technology

28 Ferenka plant shut down, with the loss of 1,400 jobs

1978

January

8 In an RTÉ interview, Taoiseach Jack Lynch suggests the government might consider an amnesty for Republican prisoners in the event of a ceasefire

12 Minister for Economic Planning and Development Martin O'Donoghue issues the White Paper 'National Development 1977–1980'

18 European Court of Human Rights finds the British government guilty of 'inhuman and degrading treatment' but not torture in Northern Ireland
19 Garda Commissioner Edmund Garvey dismissed by the government
24 IRA members Eddie Gallagher and Rose Dugdale marry in Limerick prison

February
13 Edmund Garvey issues a summons against the government in the High Court
17 Sixteen people killed in an explosion at the La Mon Hotel in Down
21 Consumer Protection Act introduced

March
6 Micheál MacLiammóir, co-founder of the Gate Theatre, dies in Dublin
22 ICTU votes in favour of the National Wage Agreement

April
4 Irish Catholic Hierarchy reiterates its opposition to artificial contraception but maintains it does not follow that the state is bound to prohibit the sale of contraceptives
24 Queen Margrethe of Denmark arrives in Dublin for a state visit

May
8 Post Office and Aer Lingus workers return to work after two long-running strikes
23 Minister for Justice Gerry Collins confirms that Garda experts made wrong fingerprint identifications in four murder cases

June
16 The government publishes a Green Paper on the economy
18 David Thornley, former Labour TD, historian and broadcaster, dies aged forty-two
28 Conservation activist and historian F. X. Martin seeks a declaration in the High Court that part of the Wood Quay site in Dublin is a national monument

July

27 The government publishes a discussion document on energy, advocating the advantages of nuclear power to generate electricity

30 Dr Tomás Ó Fiaich, Archbishop of Armagh, visits the Maze Prison

August

18 Thousands gather at Carnsore Point in Wexford to protest against nuclear power

24 The first programme on RTÉ 2 television is broadcast

25 Minister for Foreign Affairs Michael O'Kennedy embarks on a tour of Africa; Office of Public Works announces excavations on the Wood Quay site will continue for six more weeks but building of civic offices would then begin, barring an exceptional archaeological find

September

1 A new constitution for Fine Gael comes into effect

12 The government rejects the main recommendations of the O'Briain Committee on safeguards for people in Garda custody

October

10 Minister for Industry and Commerce Desmond O'Malley announces that Ireland's licensing and royalty system will be liberalised for oil companies

12 Minister for Education John Wilson announces that elections to management boards of national schools will go ahead, despite Irish National Teachers Organisation boycott

31 High Court finds in relation to the Garvey case that the government does not have unrestricted powers to dismiss the Garda Commissioner and must apply the concept of justice

December

22 Dr James White, director of the National Gallery, is appointed chairman of the Arts Council

1979

January

6 Government White Paper 'Programme for National Development 1979–1981' is published

8 Explosion at Whiddy Island oil terminal in Bantry Bay, kills fifty
19 National bus strike ends after two weeks

February

1 Wearing of seat belts becomes compulsory
12 Minister for Education John Wilson announces that university fees for new students will rise by 25 per cent and that grants will also rise
19 National postal strike begins
27 Thousands of farmers protest against a 2 per cent levy on farm produce

March

2 Christy Ring, the renowned Cork hurler, dies aged fifty-eight
7 Dublin Corporation start excavation work in Wood Quay
13 European Monetary System comes into operation; Ireland breaks its link with sterling
20 An estimated 200,000 PAYE taxpayers march to demand tax reform

April

1 The 1979 Census is taken
26 Aer Lingus's first female pilot flies on her first scheduled flight

May

3 Margaret Thatcher leads the Conservative Party to victory in the British general election
11 Final episode of RTÉ's popular soap opera *The Riordans*
31 Minister for Posts and Telegraphs Pádraig Faulkner opens RTÉ Radio 2

June

7 Elections to the European Parliament take place at the same time as local elections
15 Oisín Kelly's memorial to Jim Larkin unveiled in O'Connell Street, Dublin
30 Dr Tomás Ó Fiaich created a cardinal in Rome

July

5 Referenda on adoption and university representation in the Senate; both amendments carried

16 Minister for Industry, Commerce and Energy Desmond O'Malley announces the establishment of a state oil company, Irish National Petroleum Corporation Ltd

17 Charles Haughey's Health (Family Planning) Bill passed

18 Taoiseach Jack Lynch addresses the European Parliament as current president of the European Council

25 ICTU votes to accept the revised National Understanding for economic and social development

August

9 Fifty-eight Vietnamese refugees arrive in Ireland

10 The Irish show-jumping team wins the Aga Khan Cup at the Dublin Horse Show for the third year running

14 Seventeen yachtsmen die in storms during the Fastnet round-the-world yacht race

27 Lord Louis Mountbatten killed when his boat is destroyed by a bomb in Donegal Bay

September

9 Fianna Fáil TD Síle de Valera makes a speech critical of Jack Lynch's leadership and policy on Northern Ireland

10 Dublin Corporation refuse dispute resolved after months of disruption to city collections

18 The government bans the proposed visit to Ireland of the South African rugby team

23 John Hume of the SDLP demands that Irish and British governments act together to take a decisive initiative on Northern Ireland

29 Pope John Paul II arrives in Dublin for a three-day visit and says Mass in Dublin before a crowd of one million

October

2 The Provisional IRA rejects the Pope's call for an end to violence

9 In the Josey Airey case regarding legal aid, the European Court of Justice rules that Ireland has violated the Human Rights Convention

15 West German Chancellor Helmut Schmidt arrives in Ireland for a two-day visit

November

7 Taoiseach Jack Lynch begins an eight-day visit to the US
8 Fine Gael wins both seats in the Cork by-elections
17 Taoiseach Jack Lynch announces a free legal-aid scheme will be introduced by the end of the year
22 Gerry Fitt resigns as leader of the SDLP; John Hume replaces him
29 EEC heads of government meet in Dublin

December

5 Jack Lynch announces his resignation as Taoiseach and leader of Fianna Fáil
7 Charles Haughey becomes leader of Fianna Fáil
11 Charles Haughey becomes Taoiseach
28 It is reported that 1979 was the worst year for industrial disputes in the history of the state*

---

* Some of the information in this timeline is reproduced from Jim O'Donnell (ed), *Ireland, the past twenty years: an illustrated chronology* (Dublin, Institute of Public Administration, 1986)

INTRODUCTION: OLD MOULDS BROKEN?

'Promise ... fury and danger'

In a contribution to the short-lived literary and political magazine *Atlantis*, published from University College Dublin between 1971 and 1973, archaeologist, historian and writer Liam de Paor addressed the theme of the contemporary ambiguity of the Irish Republic: 'The myths with which – whether we accepted them or not – we have lived for many decades have suddenly ceased to have the appearance of life ... It is not only in the North that old moulds are broken.'[1]

De Paor's reference to the breaking of moulds came directly from the opening line of a 1970 poem by John Montague, 'The Rough Field', one of a number of poems that sought to encapsulate the sense of bewilderment, but perhaps also opportunity, that the Troubles in Northern Ireland which erupted in 1969 might present. As his fellow poet Seamus Heaney was to remark of the early 1970s, 'there was promise in the air as well as fury and danger'.[2] But in Northern Ireland, any nervous sense of hopeful expectation quickly soured; as Heaney recalled: 'soon enough it all went rancid',[3] or as the second line of Montague's poem announced, 'In the dark streets, firing starts.'[4]

The consequences of the firing, of the rottenness, were monumental, particularly in terms of loss of life, and the 1970s on the island of Ireland was to be marked by death and destruction, reprisal and counter reprisal. Nor was there any sense of an end in sight by the close of the decade, by which time 1,900 people had been killed. If anything, there was even more of a sense of entrenchment. In many respects, the Troubles in Northern Ireland defined the island of Ireland in the 1970s, not just internally, but in terms of how Ireland was viewed by the rest of the world, a case of 'old arguments' but 'new deaths'.[5]

Throughout the decade the conflict continued to prompt poems, some reflective, some angry, immediate and blunt, with little attempt to disguise outrage. At a reading in the Clonard Monastery in the Ardoyne area of Belfast in the aftermath of Bloody Sunday in Derry on 30 January 1972, when thirteen unarmed civilians were shot dead by British paratroopers, Thomas Kinsella read 'steadily and carefully' from his poem 'Butcher's Dozen':

And when I came where thirteen died
It shrivelled up my heart. I sighed
And looked about that brutal place
Of rage and terror and disgrace.[6]

Rage and terror abounded at various stages throughout the 1970s, ensuring that, as suggested by Mary Holland, one of the most gifted journalistic chroniclers of the Troubles, 'The 1970s were a period of simple – deadly – certainties in both parts of the island.'[7] That was certainly true in terms of loss of life; as a result of the Troubles, there were 496 deaths in 1972, 252 in 1973, 303 in 1974 and 308 in 1976. Given such carnage, the view that a united Ireland was attainable and even desirable to solve the Troubles and the partition of Ireland, separating the six Northern counties from the rest of the island, that had been a reality since 1920, had significant currency, not just among Republicans in the North but privately, in British government circles.

Many Republicans also believed that a Fianna Fáil government under the leadership of Taoiseach (the Republic's prime minister) Jack Lynch from 1969 to 1973 would and should intervene to protect them against Loyalist attack by those committed to the UK and determined to resist the onslaught of the Irish Republican Army (IRA), and that the attitude of many politicians south of the border was equivocal. Both the British and Irish governments, however, underestimated the determination of Unionists, dedicated to keeping Northern Ireland in the United Kingdom, to resist a unitary state or a power-sharing solution accompanied by a Council of Ireland. Such an initiative – the doomed Sunningdale Agreement of

There was also an evident determination to subject inequality to greater scrutiny; it was a decade during which there was more awareness of poverty and poor housing – conservative estimates suggested one-quarter of the population could be classified as poor – and an increased public discourse about social, economic and cultural opportunities offered and denied, facilitated or avoided. It was also a decade that inspired much cynicism about continuity; although there was a net inflow of population recorded in the census of 1979, emigration was still a reality for those from marginalised districts; and those in underdeveloped communities, or traditionally neglected parts of the country, sometimes felt little had changed when it came to political and social priorities, but they also had emerging champions. Individualism and sexuality were still quite rigorously repressed and access to university education was still the preserve of an elite. Educating children and students was deemed to be a priority, and the numbers at schools increased, but the distribution of power within the education system was much contested.

Debate in relation to all these areas expanded and was frequently presented as a response to a crisis of authority. Some of the institutions that had enjoyed unchallenged supremacy in previous decades, including the Catholic Church, in a state where 94 per cent of the population were Catholic and only 4 per cent Protestant, were subjected to more criticism. While the Catholic religion appeared on the surface to be robust in terms of outward convention and obedience, fault lines were beginning to appear that would create questions about its capacity to survive the decade with an assurance of continued deference to and respect for its teachings and personnel.

Those intent on pressing for significant change displayed much courage and there was a maturation of sorts as well as increased tolerance. Journalists, broadcasters and economists sought to ask more searching questions, demanded more engaged and honest answers and created new outlets. Radio and television faced new challenges, and while public service broadcasting had much to recommend it, the monopoly of the state broadcaster, Radio Telefís Éireann (RTÉ), came in for some stinging criticism. Culturally, artists broke new ground in giving poetic, theatrical and visual representation to Irelands old and new, and Irish musicians were vibrant and productive.

As well as economically lean years, there were periods during the decade of significantly increased spending and consumption. Food that had rarely if ever reached the Irish palate began to appear; holiday destinations that had previously seemed beyond Irish aspirations became more accessible and a noisy youth culture, expressed through music, writing, oratory, dancing and experimenting with new substances and new modes of sexual behaviour, made itself felt. The beginning of modern Irish consumerism was facilitated by increased exposure to the outside world and there was reason to celebrate the achievements of athletes and other sporting greats who made their presence felt on the world stage.

Not all of these stirrings came without protest. They prompted warnings that Ireland was losing its soul and its national, defining characteristics. A transitional decade also made for a bad-tempered decade, and not due solely to the despair created by paramilitary violence, which prompted censorship and rough justice. Improvements in the economy and indulgent consumerism were apparent and real but frequently faltering and too dependent on borrowed money; the oil crises bit hard and the cost of living became intolerable for some. Many of the attempts to bring a modern infrastructure to the country made agonisingly slow progress. Roads and transport assumed a new significance, but the increase in traffic created dilemmas and vastly increased the risk of road death. The first experience of a significant increase in house prices created tension and concern about sustainability. Discarding an older Ireland amounted in some cases to a reckless disregard for heritage in the rush to expand, adapt and modernise.

Strikes proliferated and raised serious questions about productivity, management and the role of trade unions. Foreign investors saw many opportunities in Ireland, but were also conscious and blunt about its deficiencies as a modern industrial economy. The balance to be struck between spending and taxes raised questions about equality among the workforce. Public sector workers complained of unfair budgets and a failure to distribute the burden of taxation fairly. While EEC membership provided significant opportunities for agriculturists in terms of new and bigger markets, the quest to get farmers to pay more – or indeed, any – income taxes met with stubbornness, and the notion of a European identity was curiously ill defined. The 1970s also saw some semblance of an engagement with the theme of the environment; issues around pollution and natural resources were sometimes tentatively probed and, given the shortage of oil during the decade, it was inevitable that questions of alternative fuel and energy supplies would be raised, though goals that were set in that regard were far short of ambitious.

Given the threat from subversives and new outlets for protesting, there were new challenges for law enforcers and it proved to be a difficult decade for the Gardaí (the Irish police force). How and indeed whether the policing and legal systems were working, and the extent to which the administration of justice was fair and transparent created new questions about civil liberties and human rights. In terms of individual welfare and health, there were attempts to tackle shortcomings, administrative and physical, and a new awareness of dangers to mental health. The role of the state in catering for the vulnerable was raised in different ways, often without demonstrable or impressive results.

In other European countries, including West Germany, there was a sense that 'the bubbling reform atmosphere of the late 1960s and early 1970s rapidly lost its fizz',[12] flattened by international recession and mass unemployment, with, as in France, the main impulse being one of damage limitation and consolidation rather than grandeur, and complications in reconciling a desire for individual freedom with social justice.[13] In the United States in the 1970s, the decade has also been regarded by historians as representing the end of an era when a 'new sense of limits struck home' and abuse of trust was manifest in the political establishment. Identifying the crisis of confidence, as President Jimmy Carter sought to do, did not necessarily translate into consensus, as Conservatism reached a new power with the rise of the 'New Right' that denounced a society built on secularism.[14]

These issues, or local versions of them, were raised in the Irish Republic in the 1970s: in parliament, within the civil service, in newspapers, at public meetings, by protest groups, on radio and television and in private writings. The challenges of increased modernisation, secularisation, Europeanisation and consumerism have to be placed in the context of a republic that, after Ireland's precocious politicisation in the early twentieth century and the civil war of 1922–3, had ultimately created a conservative, authoritarian governing culture, that seemed to prize the stability and endurance of the institutions of state and created a very wide definition of dissent. The Troubles and the fear that they would spill over the border further entrenched those traits, but it was clear that not all the dissent and challenges to authority could be contained.

The questions of governance and the distribution of power are of central relevance to any assessment of the decade and go to the heart of what changed, how and why, but also what remained the same. The 1960s was justly regarded as a decade of progress in the Republic; the failed economic policies of previous decades had been reversed as protection gave way to free trade and created new employment and improved living standards. The emigration that had characterised the 1950s, when half a million people left the country, had been vastly reduced; there was investment in education, the arrival of television, exposure to outside influences and a relaxation of the censorship mentality.

But history, of course, does not fall neatly into decades; the Republic was still a state and society in transition in the 1970s and the way in which power – economic, social, political and cultural – was being exercised prompted much criticism. After a half-century of self-rule, there was much focus on what was not working and what might, could or should change for the better. The questions were searching and pointed – why was the political culture still so dominated by clientelism and localism? Could there be parliamentary reform and a truly representative Senate? Were state institutions viewed as the property of the politicians and how much reform of the civil service was necessary? Why were Irish natural resources not cherished and better used for the common good? Would Europe be the solution to doubts about Irish competence and potential or would it create even more problems? What was the answer to Ireland's economic woes: a self-sufficient narrowly focused approach to commerce or subjecting the economy to market forces with all the attendant risks? Was the public sector too big and too expensive or one of the country's greatest strengths? Was the Irish social and cultural identity truly distinctive or just a second-rate version of what was manifesting itself elsewhere? Were the children and women of the Republic cherished? Did Ireland share in the sense of an end to a 'golden age' thought to have terminated in Britain, for example, in 1973, giving way to 'an age of relative confusion',[15] or had Ireland even made it to a 'golden age' in the first place? Did both countries discover that modernisation required political resources which British prime ministers Ted Heath, Harold Wilson and their counterparts in Ireland were 'ill-equipped to mobilize?'[16]

There were valiant attempts to address some of these questions, but many of them were responded to ambiguously or simply ignored, or put on the long finger. A number of them, particularly those relating to leadership, political culture, economic management, status in Europe, natural resources, public service reform, and the status of children, are still relevant and very obviously unanswered forty years later in a Republic much more peaceful and stable since the end of the Troubles in Northern Ireland, but bankrupt and shorn of much of its sovereignty due to a disastrous government decision to guarantee the entire Irish banking system in 2008 and the subsequent International Monetary Fund and European Union bailout of the economy.

Historians are now in a position to research and assess many aspects of the 1970s from primary sources as a result of the release of state documents, under the 1986 National Archives Act, which allows for the release of such papers after thirty years has lapsed, and the growing number of private collections being released relating to those active across many fronts during the decade. This book seeks to exploit them to the full to provide a window for understanding the decade, its governance, controversies and personalities.

In particular, this book draws heavily on the files of the Department of the Taoiseach in the National Archives, through which came an abundance of policy papers, discussions and assessments from all government departments and their civil servants. These files underline the strong centralised nature of government in Ireland and also the crucial role played by a generation of civil servants who feature prominently in the narrative, including T. K. Whitaker, governor of the Central Bank, Frank Murray, Richard Stokes, Dermot Nally, Bertie O'Dowd and Walter Kirwan in the Department of the Taoiseach, Charles Murray in the Department of Finance, Seán O'Connor in the Department of Education, and Seán Donlon, Noel Dorr and Paul Keating in the Department of Foreign Affairs. These formulated their opinions and thoughts at great length and were indispensable to the running of their respective departments. As observed by former Irish civil servant Martin Mansergh in 2011, 'Anonymous civil servants can achieve a degree of immortality on file ... with the passage of time and the release of archives, particular civil servants stand out, as much as ministers.'[17] The Department of the Taoiseach also became a repository for a multitude of correspondence from the public, reflecting the extent to which it was a forum for expressions of anxiety, and approval or disapproval of the way in which various contemporary controversies were dealt with.

Some of the personal papers of two Taoisigh, Jack Lynch and Liam Cosgrave, also housed in the National Archives, reveal much about their styles of leadership and their relationships with departmental staff as they grappled with some of the difficulties of the 1970s, most obviously the stability of the state and the various threats to it. Some of their younger colleagues proved to be impatient to develop new ways of doing business, nationally and internationally. The papers of Ireland's foremost constitutional expert, UCD law professor and Fine Gael TD (member of parliament) John Kelly, and the first batch of the archival papers of Garret FitzGerald, Minister for Foreign Affairs from 1973–7 and future Taoiseach, are instructive and revealing in this regard and give a strong sense of some of the internal difficulties within Fine Gael. Correspondence across all these collections sheds light on the activities of some of the dominant Labour Party personalities and intellects of the decade, including historian and diplomat Conor Cruise O'Brien and historian and broadcaster David Thornley, both first elected as TDs in 1969.

Likewise, the papers of the Fianna Fáil parliamentary party, in the archives of University College Dublin, detail the strategies and attention to organisation that made it one of the most successful political parties in the world but also the tensions that arose in relation to its structures and large membership and the convulsions within the party after disagreements over how to relate to the Troubles in Northern Ireland. The issue of senior members' involvement with the importation of arms led to the sacking of two of its most ambitious cabinet members, Charles Haughey, another future Taoiseach, and Donegal's Neil Blaney in 1970 and the subsequent 'Arms Trial'. The young general secretary of the party, Séamus Brennan, who took on that job in 1973, played a key role in attempting to manage the internal party fallout as the decade progressed. The papers of another key office holder, president of Ireland from 1974–6, Cearbhall Ó Dálaigh, who resigned after being insulted by Fine Gael's Minister for Defence Patrick Donegan, have also been used to detail another memorable controversy of the decade, while the neglected papers of the Irish Council of the European Movement (ICEM) also held in the UCD archives, have been drawn on to look at how one of the key challenges of the 1970s – to inform and enlighten people about the implications of EEC membership – was faced.

Valuable insights have also been obtained through the lens of contemporary newspapers, magazines and the personal memoirs and documents generated by those who lived through this decade. A host of sociological, religious, political, literary, educational and administrative journals have also been used in the introductory sections to each part to set the scene for each theme and underline the degree to which the 1970s was a decade of debate about governance, identity and social change. Also of particular value, because of their intensive coverage of politics, culture and economics, are two current affairs magazines. *Hibernia*, a conservative organ which had existed since 1937, was acquired in 1968 by journalist John Mulcahy, who revamped and transformed it into a high-quality crusading publication with in-depth coverage of politics and business, while investigative current affairs magazine *Magill* was launched in 1977 by Vincent Browne, Mary Holland and Noel Pearson. In the same year *Hot Press*, a music magazine, was established by Niall Stokes and its value lies in the extent to which it highlighted the burgeoning youth culture of the era as well as new musical departures and a determination to embrace international influences.

This book does not offer a chronology of the decade or give another history of the Troubles, about which a voluminous library already exists.[18] Instead, it brings to light new sources of information on the emergence and persistence of the political, social and cultural issues that go to the heart of the nature of the Irish Republic, and in particular its governance, in one of its most challenging and defining decades. It reflects on its contemporary concerns, its successes and failures, and elaborates on 'trends and tendencies, the evolution of ideas, the striving to new values'.[19] Ultimately, it underlines the extent to which, in the Republic of Ireland in the 1970s, while some old moulds were broken, ambiguities still abounded.

PART I

IRISH POLITICAL AND ADMINISTRATIVE CULTURE

'The tepid quality of our democratic passion'

Fifty years after a generation of Irish revolutionaries had succeeded in creating a twenty-six-county dominion state, subsequently declared a republic in 1949, there were aspects of Irish political culture that could be both admired and lamented. The stability of the Irish political system was striking but such robustness also served as a barrier to embracing widespread reform of governance, a dominant theme of the 1970s as various intellectuals began to subject aspects of Irish political culture and structures to systematic, detailed studies. In his influential The Government and Politics of Ireland *(1970), Basil Chubb sought to be more analytical and conceptual than had previously been the case. One of the Republic's best-known political scientists, and one of a number of British academics recruited by Trinity College Dublin in the post-war years, Chubb held the Chair of Political Science and transformed the approach to his chosen discipline. He identified the themes central to the evolution and character of Irish politics: the legacy of British rule and influence, Irish nationalism, Catholicism, the social system and land ownership, the notion of loyalty to people rather than ideas and a certain anti-intellectualism. But he also highlighted the achievements of the survival of the state, a political system robust enough to generate support and adaptable enough to contain dissent while providing stable government.*

But just how democratic was the Republic? If democracy was defined as facilitating fair elections and free voting, and easy access to politicians for the citizens, it was something of a model, but if it meant the influence of both politicians and people on policy, it fell short: 'For generations, Irish people saw that to get the benefits that public authorities bestow, the help of a man with connections and influence was necessary. All that democracy has meant is that such a man has been laid on officially as it were, and is now no longer a master but a servant.'[1] There was little meaningful commitment to embracing reform of that system throughout the decade, despite many criticisms of it. What the characteristics of Irish politics identified by Chubb meant in practice was underlined by an interview broadcast on Irish television in the early 1970s. It featured two political activists, one each from the two dominant Irish political parties, Fianna Fáil and Fine Gael, both of which dated from the civil war divisions of the 1920s, standing on a hill surveying a district in County Donegal. They discussed each of the individual houses visible from the hill and could identify how members of each household voted. This was 'personalism exemplified'.[2] It remained that way; party infighting and personal links with voters were prioritised over ideas and policies, with candidates chosen on the basis of the votes they could garner due to their association with geographical areas rather than ideological positions.[3]

It was undoubtedly a challenging decade for politics and politicians, given the security situation and the extent to which the Troubles in Northern Ireland permeated decision-making and transformed the political environment. The talk in 1969, when a general election saw Labour predicting the 1970s would be socialist, had been of change and watersheds, with a predicted increase in Labour representation, a generation change and a different quality of representation. But, as observed by UCD political scientist and RTÉ broadcaster Brian Farrell, 'the move from the so-called revolutionary generation of original Irish political leaders to a more professional political elite does not appear likely to lead to any substantial adjustments in the structure, whatever about the style of Irish politics in the seventies. In the face of entrenched and increasing executive power, the real legislative influence of deputies is marginal.'[4]

As the civil-war generation passed away, younger politicians replaced them, many possessing inherited loyalties. In the case of Fine Gael this also involved, for some, reaffirming their traditional association with a strong, authoritarian state and the upholding of law and order, most obviously exemplified by Liam Cosgrave's tenure as Taoiseach from 1973–7. His father, William T., had led the governments of the 1920s through the prism of the civil war. Notwithstanding such continuity, the legacy of the 1960s tensions within the party over the pursuit of a 'Just Society' favoured by some younger members, was still relevant and ultimately was manifest in the rise to the top of Garret FitzGerald, one of the towering personalities of the party in the 1970s, whose father, Desmond, had also served as a government minister in the 1920s. Others, like legal academic John Kelly, first elected to the Senate in 1969, devoted much thought, not just to the essence of what Fine Gael stood for, but also to the status and functions of politicians generally.

For Fianna Fáil, it was a turbulent decade; the party's stance on Northern Ireland wreaked havoc on traditional discipline and defined the leadership of the underwhelming Jack Lynch, as hungry aspiring leaders, most obviously Dublin TD Charles Haughey, a talented Minister for Justice in the 1960s, eyed the party leadership. Given the release of archival material, it is now also possible for the historian to reach into the heart of why Fianna Fáil continued to dominate electoral contests and to get a sense of how this remarkable political organisation – one of the most successful in the world and in power from 1932 to 1973 except for two short periods of coalition government from 1948–51 and 1954–7 – was able to endure and persist, despite the tumult.

Its success highlighted the continuing importance of something that guided the political career of its founder and patriarch, Eamon de Valera, leader from 1926 to 1959; the devotion to 'the essential dull details of how the bottom rung of the ladder to power is hammered into place'.[5] *In relation to support for the party according to social class, it was not until 1969 that detailed data became available, when Gallup carried out the first major opinion poll. It revealed that in the 1969 general election, Fianna Fáil achieved virtually identical levels of support among the three main social categories: middle class (45 per cent), working class (42 per cent) and farmers (42 per cent). In contrast, the figures for Fine Gael were: middle class 28 per cent, working class 16 per cent and farmers 20 per cent. The figures for the Labour Party were 13, 14 and 15 per cent, respectively, making it clear they were dependent on the same middle- and working-class support base as Fianna Fáil, but received little support from farmers.*[6] *The 1969 figures made clear the extent to which Fianna Fáil successfully became a 'catch-all' political party.*

But there was a new interest in social and economic issues that affected politics and it was significant that the victors in the 1973 general election won on the basis of a commitment to social and economic reform; there was no precedent for two parties coming to power on the basis of an agreed programme for government. The Labour Party, the oldest of the dominant Irish political parties, had reversed its 1960s stance of refusing to countenance coalition, and got to serve in government with Fine Gael, but it too faced searching questions about its identity and appeal. As recalled by writer and actor Desmond Hogan, who began to make his mark in the early 1970s, in 1975 the Non Stop Connolly Show was performed in Dublin, a twenty-four-hour extravaganza of the life and time of iconic socialist and 1916 revolutionary James Connolly involving actors, socialists, playwrights and musicians. The central question it raised was, 'What is the position of a socialist in the face of an overwhelmingly nationalist sense of history?'[7]

The Labour Party's alternative to capitalism remained largely verbal, 'and does not really get rooted in the practice of the party ... the totality of reference remains the capitalist society'.[8] One of the fascinating developments of the decade was the potential and limitations that the intellectual stars and personalities of the Labour Party such as former diplomat and historian Conor Cruise O'Brien and historian and broadcaster David Thornley demonstrated in politics. Dismissive of traditional machine politics, they could not and did not last in Irish politics, suggesting the continuance of an innate caution.

There was talk of political reform, more accountability and increasing professionalism, but much of it came to nought; what did change were questions about the status and perception of politicians, and the development of a political journalism that was more combative. As identified by television director Lelia Doolan, more and more journalists were 'thinking on the job and presenting questions about politics; what was the government at, what were we supposed to be doing'.[9]

The writer and socialist James Plunkett, whose hugely successful novel Strumpet City (1969) detailed the tensions between political and socialist awakening, and family and personal concerns in the second decade of the twentieth century, lamented in 1980 that when he was growing up (he was born in 1920), too many politicians were devoid of ideas and 'managed to get through their political careers without any hint of a visitation from any abstraction whatsoever'.[10] Much the same conclusion could be reached about most politicians in the 1970s, but again, one can detect those voices within seeking reform, decrying the machine, clientelist politics and conceiving of both politics and the welfare state in a different way.

There is no doubt that individuals of dignity and probity were among those involved in politics, and the row over the treatment of Irish president Cearbhall Ó Dálaigh in 1976, when he was insulted by a government *minister, highlighted that many still attached a premium to decorum, but the political soul-searching did not go far enough. For all the volubility of the Irish feminist movement, for example, it found itself disappointed in its attempts to weaken the ingrained macho roots of Irish politics and in many respects, as identified by one of the leading lights of the feminist movement, lawyer and senator Mary Robinson, 'the Oireachtas (Irish parliament) is still basically a nineteenth century debating forum'.*[11] *As Robinson recalled at a later stage about Irish politics; there were politicians to admire in the respective political parties, 'but the party system did not really commit itself to real change'; as the civil society became more critical and aware, it forced change from the outside.*[12] *Another noted feminist who made an impact in the 1970s was historian and pioneer of women's history Margaret Mac Curtain, who observed tartly in 1974 the speeches of men in the Dáil that were 'magnificently condescending in their appreciation of the little women'. She suggested 'at this point in time it would seem commonsense for the feminist and socialist viewpoints to arrive at a consensus',*[13] *but given the endurance of the conservative political culture throughout the decade, such a marriage was by no means likely to succeed.*

Another vocal, and often colourful and trenchant contributor to debates about the governing culture was Tom Barrington. A senior civil servant in the Department of Local Government in the 1950s, he was instrumental in the creation of the Institute of Public Administration (IPA) and the journal Administration *which became an important forum for discussion on public administration from the late 1950s and which throughout the decade of the 1970s was dominated by the theme of reform. Barrington aired his criticisms of the over-centralisation of Irish government and the lack of effective local government throughout the decade. He wondered if there was any future for local government in Ireland as its powers had been progressively weakened since the foundation of the state. As he declared in 1971, 'we have the unsystematic local administration of a dwindling number of services. It is not a system, it is not local and it is not self government.'*[14] *Two years later, he was adamant, 'We are trying to tackle new, extremely difficult tasks with inadequate instruments.'*[15] *But in truth, citizens of the Republic were more preoccupied with the issue of paying rates than reform and it was to this instinct that politicians shamelessly played by crystallising the discussion on local government into the issue of rates abolition.*

The courts were independent of government, and discrimination on political, religious or class grounds was forbidden, but there were many negative aspects of Irish bureaucracy. These were identified by trade unionist and former president of the Irish Congress of Trade Unions (ICTU) Charles McCarthy in his 1968 book The Distasteful Challenge, *a harsh indictment of the static nature of Irish society in areas such as the civil service, local government and education. He identified the attitude of many public servants as being authoritarian and small-minded and crucially, in terms of areas mentioned for reform in the 1970s, characterised the public service as prioritising control rather than initiative.*

The tensions between the perceived noble achievements of stability and continuity and the need to adapt and change characterised debate about political culture and public service during the decade. Given the terror and tension that existed as a result of the Troubles in Northern Ireland and some of the economic fluctuations, it was perhaps understandable that the more cautious could effectively stymie change. But there was no shortage of manifestos for reform as the civil service, which had doubled in size from the foundation of the state from 21,000 in 1922 to 41,000 in 1973, along with an increase in the number of government departments during the same period from eleven to sixteen, came under increased scrutiny. To its credit, it placed itself under some intense examination while also (as was happening in Britain with the Fulton Report into its civil service) debating the 1969 Report of the Public Services Organisation Review Group *(The Devlin Report), which had highlighted that 'a serious feature of the present system is its built-in resistance to change'.*

There had been an increase in the function of government departments but no radical change in departmental organisation; the Devlin Report was also critical that the top levels of departments were so involved in daily business that they had little time to participate in the formulation of overall policy and it recommended a centralised ministry with responsibility for policy-making and satellite bodies for its execution. These were elite debates; the Higher Civil Service, for example, was a relatively small group in the mid 1970s consisting of about 2,000 officers and, on paper, they were a homogeneous group; an analysis in the late 1960s of the sixty-four secretaries of government departments since 1923 revealed that 98 per cent had been born in Ireland, 82 per cent were from urban areas and 97 per cent were Catholic. Nor, historically, did they have a high level of formal education; only 26 per cent had university degrees.

This had changed by the early 1970s; in April 1972, nine of the twenty-one departmental secretaries in office (43 per cent) had a university degree.

Informal contact between civil servants was not that common, the idea persisting that 'because in law the minister is the department, the civil servant must be anonymous'. There were traditions of reticence and secrecy (and they were forbidden from engaging in politics),[16] *but things were also changing in this regard, as civil servants became more vocal in the 1970s. It was apparent that the distinction between policy creation and execution was not always a clear one and civil service influence in the decisional process continued to grow as the legacy of the late 1950s initiative of T. K. Whitaker, the secretary of the Department of Finance from 1956–69, and his contemporaries, who had been instrumental in reframing economic policy away from protection, endured.*

There was an ongoing relevance to the assertion made by Taoiseach Seán Lemass (who served from 1959–66) that he wanted to see government departments become 'development corporations', as opposed to waiting 'for new ideas to walk in the door', in contrast to the sentiment established by the Ministries and Secretaries Act of 1924 which had established the concept of the Minister as 'Corporation sole' and the only effective authority in his area, though in practice he delegated powers. Thomas P. O'Connor, a civil servant in the Department of Finance, noted in 1970 that 'the moral for the 1970s is to exploit to the full this concept ... it is not sufficient for administrators to be passive, though well-informed advisers on policy proposals ... the civil service must of itself be an active and creative agency in policy matters' in relation to areas such as health, education and welfare.[17]

Overall, the Irish civil service could be characterised as one of the successes of Irish independence, and what is striking about the 1970s state papers is the degree to which key civil servants in individual departments, who feature throughout this book, acted as influential advisers, admonishers and initiators. But structural problems persisted; Noel Whelan, the deputy secretary of the Department of Public Service, noted the over-reliance on state-sponsored bodies. Public service reform, as he identified it in 1975, remained 'urgent'; the same year a new Public Service Advisory Council met for the first time. As Irish Times *journalist James Downey noted, its first report was written in very cautious language, 'but it added up to a fairly severe criticism of the slow pace of reform'.*[18] *As Whelan noted two years later, however, there was very little 'enthusiastic interest' from the public about such reform.*[19]

There seemed to be a deflation in expectation by the end of the decade at a time when there were 54,000 civil servants (of whom 22,000 were employed in the Department of Posts and Telegraphs) but 65,000 employed by state sponsored bodies. In 1978, Colm O'Nualláin, the director of the IPA, concluded mournfully that there was 'so relatively little advance in the key areas of reorganisation that there is some apathy and perhaps even cynicism abroad'. Others decried the lack of unity in the civil service, pointing to two key developments of the 1970s – the creation of the Department of Public Service in 1973 and the Department of Economic Planning and Development in 1977 – that were being treated as separate entities for the purposes of staffing and promotion; there was no increased mobility and a continued over-reliance on state sponsored bodies.[20] *What was not found in this decade was sufficient solution to what Tom Barrington called 'the disease of congestion of government'.*[21]

– ONE –

BALLYMAGASH STYLE POLITICS

Throughout the decade of the 1970s, a programme called *Hall's Pictorial Weekly* was broadcast on Irish television. Written and presented by Frank Hall, it also included actors Frank Kelly and Eamon Morrissey and had a 'level of penetrative satire' that was unmatched. Some of the show's catch phrases entered the national lexicon, such as 'Ballymagash style politics', a reference to the programme's infamous Ballymagash urban district councillors. Eamon Morrissey remembered 'once being down the country on a theatre run and going to a pub to watch the show one night – and every single person was watching it'. One of the abiding images of the series was a caricature of Liam Cosgrave, who served as Taoiseach from 1973–7, as a shivering mitten-clad 'Minister for Hardship' (a term also applied to Richie Ryan, the Minister for Finance in that government) who used to say, 'If you think it's bad now ... it's only going to get worse.'[1]

It was maintained by some critics that Hall 'only got away with it and rose to such glorious heights because to a great extent he was lampooning the worst aspects of parochial life'.[2] Irish politics, it appeared, was ripe for satire because of its excessively local and myopic focus and could be depicted as quite backward. While some councillors laughed, 'many more passed resolutions complaining that it belittled their efforts'.[3] It was easy to present local and national politics as lacking sophistication, as, on the surface, the political system functioned in a primitive way. In an interview to mark his retirement from politics in 2011, Fine Gael TD Paul

Connaughton recalled his early days in the Irish Senate, to which he was elected in 1977: 'When I was elected to the Seanad first, there was no such thing as secretaries for either TDs or senators. There were six of us in one room and one phone between us. Depending on your hunger for the job, you had to be in very early or very late at night to get your crack at the phone. For most of the queries to government departments, the writing was in longhand.'[4]

As can be gleaned from Connaughton's recollections, for most public representatives at this time the daily graft of Irish politics was unsophisticated in terms of communications and function. TDs and senators could indeed have great 'hunger for the job', but much of it was about frustrating waits for questions to be posed and answered and then delivered to constituents. This was a reflection of a style and approach to politics that centred on 'clientelism'. Another retiree from party politics in 2011, Labour Party TD Michael D. Higgins, elected president of Ireland the same year, and who first entered the Senate in 1973, was less benign than Connaughton when reflecting on his experience in politics since 1969: 'I believe no real republic has been created in Ireland.' Along with administrative and communications shortcomings, he suggested there had been a failure either to make political power Republican or to distribute it sufficiently widely. Instead, he had witnessed a system where power was confined solely to the exercise of parliamentary democracy; excessive power was concentrated in cabinet, specifically in a hegemonic Department of Finance: 'If one wanted to effect radical change one would break the connection between the monopoly enjoyed by the government of the day and parliament.'[5]

What both Connaughton and Higgins acknowledged, however, was the kindness and courtesy of colleagues and the opportunity to meet so many people that came with politics. Undoubtedly, political representatives of all shades were also brought closer by the reality that they were attempting to stay elected in multi-seat constituencies with an electoral system based on the single transferable vote. Sometimes the most intense rivalry was actually between candidates of the same party.

But the issue Higgins alluded to was bigger; the evolution and triumph of the centralisation of power had profound consequences for the character of Irish politics and government. Political scientist Tom Garvin makes the observation that a political culture that had been characterised by Basil Chubb in the late 1960s as post-British, Nationalist, 'just about post peasant', Catholic, loyal and anti-intellectual, may have been undergoing some change in the 1970s but it was a culture that was also 'authoritarian and secretive. Power holders were commonly control freaks, to use modern terminology.'[6]

In April 1976, historian John A. Murphy, appointed Professor of Irish History in University College Cork in 1971 and whose book *Ireland in the Twentieth Century* (1975) was one of the first surveys of contemporary history, addressed the American Committee for Irish Studies in Missouri. Murphy, who the following year was elected an independent senator and who was an advocate of increased political and cultural pluralism, suggested one of the consequences for the Republic of the Troubles in Northern Ireland was the halting of a drive towards social progress: 'There is evidence of a backlash against radical change of whatever nature and the religious and cultural homogeneity of the South has been underlined.' But he also argued that the formative influence of statehood and citizenship on the Irish had been profound (and perhaps not always appreciated as such by the Irish-Americans); that surviving civil war, the dangers of the 1930s, the experience of neutrality and the despair of the 1950s meant that 'the state has emerged as a sophisticated polity, no longer troubled even in recession by doubts about the worthwhileness of its existence (as it was in the 1950s) and at the same time having outgrown emotional manifestations of nationalism'. He further suggested there was 'an intense political interest and awareness' but that 'we no longer have immortal longings in us. Nor the arrogance to think that we can be, in [Patrick Pearse's] phrase, "the saviours of idealism". After the tragedy of recent years, Irishness is a matter of sober acceptance rather than of pride.'[7]

In 1975, Tom Barrington of the IPA predicted that the centralised system would result in a drift 'towards a bureaucratic neo feudalism' where the elected government would not be in effective control of the process of government. He maintained that government was growing too big and the task of policy-making was being impeded because so much decision-making was sucked into the centre; what was needed was a programme for the decentralisation of executive work. He lamented that there was no teasing out of the roles specific to central, functional and local geographical government.[8] As a result of the gradual stripping away of the political and economic autonomy of local government over the course of the twentieth century, there was widespread resentment at the cultivation of a centralised and functionalist approach to local administration, but although local government did not have much power, it was still seen as an essential part of the Irish political fabric.

Election to local authorities was frequently seen as a route or stepping stone to national politics; others stood for more local reasons, but the reality was that even in pre-election campaigns, the expected role of the prospective office holder remained largely undefined, with candidates holding conflicting ideas as to their function. Some saw their role as watchdogs for the ratepayers or conveying the views and needs of constituents, or providing services, as opposed to playing a role in the formulation of policy, which did not feature prominently. In 1976 a survey carried out by American political scientist Joseph Zimmerman suggested that policy as a 'role orientation' figured poorly among respondents, with only four of the forty-nine councillors he interviewed making a direct reference to policy-making.[9] The same could be said of many national politicians, who saw their role in terms of serving the needs of constituents. As the makers of *Hall's Pictorial Weekly* realised, such a clientelist system at local and national level was ripe for satirical send-up, particularly as politicians of the 1970s had to get used to the exposure that television brought, which often highlighted what could be portrayed as their embarrassingly local preoccupations.

Michael D. Higgins, as an academic sociologist at University College Galway, had professional reasons to be particularly alert to the local political phenomenon, sometimes also referred to as Irish 'gombeenism'. When studying at Manchester, he had met Peter Gibbon; they co-authored a 1974 study of clientelism and the phenomenon of the Irish 'gombeen' man.[10] What it clearly demonstrated was how a brokerist politics privatised what should have been a state activity and, in the process, in the words of Declan Kiberd, who in the 1970s emerged as one of Ireland's leading literary critics and cultural commentators, succeeded in 'preventing the poor from organising themselves or articulating a shared programme'. Higgins gave the example of many women looking for housing, who had to 'wait in the same queue for the same politician about the same needs. Their presentation of their case will be an individual one about their needs and not about the principle of the gap between the number of houses needed and those provided. Being without adequate housing is perceived as an individual problem that might be resolved by the mediation of the politician.'

It also involved the pulling of 'strokes', which amounted to engineering special access to confidential information. Higgins cited an example from 1976 where a former member of the cabinet visited the housing office of one of the local authorities being studied by Higgins, 'and by a mixture of cajolery and subtle intimidation secured a list of housing allocations before the local representatives had received their list … he was able to congratulate all the "lucky" recipients of houses three days in advance of his political rivals and even his fellow party councillor henchmen'. Because of the existence of the dual mandate, where individuals could serve as both TDs and councillors, it seemed imperative to them not to take their eye off the local ball, but as a result, 'every action of the state, of the local authority and of related agencies generates a source of clientelist communication. They help create the illusion of assistance.' Decisions were thus presented as the outcome of personal interventions, rather than policies put forward and debated.[11]

In short, Irish politicians were obsessed with getting the credit for what were, in effect, fictional prizes, which secured the collusion of local and national bureaucracy, damaged the legitimacy of the state and ensured a legislature dominated by clientelist politicians 'ill-equipped in educational or motivational terms for the drafting or scrutiny of legislation and the achievement of accountability in public finances'.[12]

Mary Robinson, a senator for Trinity College from 1969, observed in 1974 that getting medical cards and agricultural grants was more important for the advancement of a TD's career than the research of legislative proposals or examining governmental activity in detail; and yet, as she was to discover, getting elected to the Dáil on the basis of her political principles proved impossible. The irrelevance of the national legislature was also something that exercised Dublin Labour TD Barry Desmond, who suggested in 1975, in appealing for administrative reform, that 'successive Fianna Fáil cabinets regarded the Dáil and the Seanad as wearisome intrusions into the routine of implementing cabinet and departmental decisions, the two areas of real parliamentary power.'[13]

Senator John Kelly, a law professor at UCD and subsequently a Fine Gael TD for Dublin, was even more blunt in 1971 when addressing a party meeting in Cavan: 'The reality of political power has shifted out of the reach of parliamentary debate and into the hands of virtually professional administrators and manipulators – we are left with a ghost parliament.'[14] One of his colleagues, John Bruton, a future Taoiseach, while regarded by some as having an undistinguished career as a junior minister from 1973 to 1977, did devote a lot of attention to 'a radical policy statement on the reform of parliamentary institutions', emphasising the need for the Dáil to have much greater control over public expenditure.[15] It also did not sit frequently enough, as far as some TDs were concerned; Desmond noted caustically in a letter to a colleague in August 1970, in relation to a resumption of the parliament, 'Dáil Éireann, to our disgrace, resumes on 28 October.'[16]

Most politicians in the 1970s were not thinking in such grandiose terms, however. Ironically, given his criticisms and observations, Michael D. Higgins eventually won a Dáil seat after four attempts through 'arduous constituency work'.[17] Another new recruit to Irish politics in the 1970s was Bertie Ahern, also a future Taoiseach, who won a seat in the landslide general election victory of Fianna Fáil in 1977. From the outset he was an unashamedly locally focused politician who was surrounded by a group nicknamed the 'Drumcondra Mafia' after his constituency base in Dublin Central. Most of them were not 'natural political animals', but just 'Bertie men, first, last and always'. Ahern and his mafia divided the constituency into twenty-five wards (groups of streets) and a 'boss' was appointed in each ward

> who would be in charge of up to ten people whose job it was to canvass each of those streets at least three or four times a year. The ward bosses were Ahern's eyes and ears in that section of the constituency. They would know everything that was going on – births, deaths, football games, sales of work – and would notify him of events he should attend and accompany him. While out canvassing it was their job to know each house and ascertain how long should be spent at each door ... the ward system later evolved to include parish leaders, based around the churches and local schools. Knowledge was power. Every opportunity was used – collecting the kids from school or football, going to mass – to build information, to get to know people in the locality and crucially, the area's problems. Everybody connected to the Drumcondra machine was involved in intelligence gathering. If the children of a canvasser saw a light missing on a road, they would go home and tell their parents. A letter would be typed stating that the matter would be addressed and put through the doors on the road in question. When the light was fixed, another letter would be dispatched pointing it out. It was time consuming and unglamorous work, but it meant Ahern's name was always out there in Dublin Central.[18]

The same was true of some rural politicians; by 1978 Chub O'Connor was a seventy-five-year-old Fianna Fáil TD for South Kerry who had entered the Dáil in 1961 and won his seat in each subsequent election. He was such an assiduous constituency worker that he was known locally as 'Dole' or 'Pension Book' O'Connor: 'He maintains files on all communications and where positive results are achieved the names are entered in his "favourite book". Those who are so honoured get a personal reminder at election time that they are expected to reciprocate ... his ability to predict closely the results in Dáil elections is legendary in Kerry.'[19] In 1971 Jackie Fahey, parliamentary secretary (in effect, junior minister) to the Minister for Agriculture, was reputed to have sent a Christmas card to each of the 37,000 names on the voting list in his south Tipperary constituency at a cost to the taxpayer of £500.[20]

Getting the credit and being seen to react was also, it seemed, crucial at local level in politics. Perhaps this was precisely because of the limits to local power, even though, by the end of the 1970s, local authorities in the twenty-six counties had a combined budget of over £400 million a year. Journalist Brian Trench observed, in advance of the local elections in 1979, that there were a total of 3,500 candidates seeking election to the twenty-seven county councils (Tipperary has two county councils due to historic boundary issues), four county borough corporations, forty-nine urban district councils and twenty-eight town commissions. They were under no illusions, he suggested, that they would have, if elected, a decisive influence over the spending of the budget.[21]

Expenditure on housing and roads accounted for half of the budget, and decisions in this regard were being made at central level. And yet, local politics could not be ignored, even if there were admissions from senior politicians like the leader of Fine Gael after 1977, Garret FitzGerald, that he was bored by local politics. As Trench observed, 'other leading politicians would admit it too, if they dared, but for all the comments that the Irish voters are becoming increasingly sophisticated, the principal route to national office still goes through the local authorities ... over 60 per cent of those returned two years ago to the present Dáil and Seanad [in the 1977 general election] were sitting councillors', though it was also pointed out that ministers when appointed now had to resign from local authority membership. But the reality was that up to a quarter of all parliamentary questions were distinctly local, there being a particular preoccupation with questions about the grading of local roads, how many houses had been built in specific locations, the siting of telephone kiosks and the quality of television reception. As Trench caustically observed: 'On such stirring stuff is the cut and thrust of Irish representative politics founded.'[22]

Many young journalists in provincial newspapers were charged with the task of covering local authority proceedings; the kind of scenes they frequently witnessed bordered on farce, as Nell McCafferty discovered in 1978, when she observed the proceedings of Cork County Council for *Magill* magazine. The first item on the agenda was the rosary, 'cited in full by the assembled councillors, the manager, the secretary and the pious press under the sorrowful gaze of a crucified Christ, nailed to the wall above them'. The proceedings of the council, peopled by thirty-nine male councillors and just one woman, were dominated by complaints about bad telephone services in isolated areas and crossed lines ('Everyone gets word of my private information over the lines,' complained one), roads and parking spaces. But the greatest scramble was to be associated with good news: '"I move that!!" they all shout at once.'[23]

Those who were critical of the 'parish pump' mentality frequently felt they were fighting a losing battle. John Kelly, for example, thought deeply and wrote extensively about the character of Irish politics in the 1970s and corresponded in a frank way with his Fine Gael colleagues about the nature of their political mission. An exceptionally gifted academic, he was a graduate in Classics from UCD and went on to earn a doctorate in Roman law, publishing three highly regarded books on this subject as well as writing a thesis on the Irish constitution, subsequently acclaimed when published in 1980. A Fellow of Oxford in the 1960s, he was later appointed Professor of Roman Law and Jurisprudence at UCD. Keenly interested in politics, he joined Fine Gael in 1966. Kelly narrowly missed out on election to the Dáil in 1969, but was subsequently elected to the Senate; draft notes of his from that era relating to constituency work made clear his view that 'a good deal of it [is] work which there should be no need for a public representative to do, but which, under the existing system he cannot possibly decline without incurring unpopularity'.[24] Kelly was elected to the Dáil in 1973 and in running successfully for re-election in 1977, his constituency notes reveal that ultimately it was the individual problems of residents that would need to be addressed: 'will talk for hours', 'asks very demanding questions', 'upset about letter to dead husband', 'unwilling to vote – visit needed', 'schooling difficulty for mentally handicapped child', 'tax; teachers pay etc.', 'fault with sewer outside no. 13'.[25]

Kelly was a caustic critic of jobbery and patronage; he suggested in 1970 that Fianna Fáil depended for much of its strength 'on a continuance of the degrading system of patronage; if that party was really interested in giving the Irish people moral leadership it would sweep that system away as FG intend to do as soon as the people give us their mandate'. He admitted that his own party 'has not been free of patronage', but pointed out that it was Fine Gael's predecessor party in the 1920s, Cumann na nGaedheal, that had created the Civil Service Commission and the Local Appointments Commission to ensure appointments were decided on merit alone and independent of political influence. But what he had witnessed as a barrister suggested that 'nearly all' state legal work was given to Fianna Fáil supporters and that the party was hostile to the idea of public advice centres or the creation of an office of Ombudsman because it would 'relieve them [the people] of abject dependence on politicians'.[26] But at a later stage, he also admitted, 'It is true that Fine Gael representatives exercise patronage and intercession whenever they can', even though 'it's wrong and degrading'. One of Kelly's main concerns was that public representatives should not be able to make individual private representations to government departments, suggesting 'we will have to lay the axe to the root of this gigantic and absurd system'.[27]

Political scientist John Whyte, who lectured at Queen's University Belfast in the 1970s and published a groundbreaking work on church–state relations in 1971, also highlighted this problem, suggesting 'there are too many deputies who seem to derive their interest and satisfaction in politics from running innumerable errands on behalf of their constituents. Some positively invent work for themselves, by implying that benefits which their constituents should get by right will not be forthcoming unless they (the deputies) interest themselves in the matter. The fact that some deputies lay so much stress on constituency service means that others, whose personal interests would be more wide ranging have to follow suit'. One of the responses to this issue within Fine Gael was, 'I thought we had all agreed that any TD who complains about being changed from an errand boy to a legislator should not be a TD.'[28]

The difficulty for Kelly and those who shared his misgivings about the functions of the parliamentarian was underlined within his own party by the appearance in 1970 of a new Fine Gael magazine published by the parliamentary party. It suggested that a local branch keeping the Oireachtas members up to date with local issues was the most important cog in the party wheel: 'Local news is the real machine which wins elections. The branches are our eyes and ears.'[29]

– TWO –

HOW TO WIN THE NEXT ELECTION

As Brian Trench recognised, the Irish electorate facilitated this type of politics by reserving their votes for the politicians who had 'delivered' for them; in that sense, in enjoying the satire of 'Ballymagash' style politics, they were laughing at themselves. And yet, as a people who had a long history of politicisation, they were also living in what was a very stable democracy, with a strong attachment to the institutions of political power and the established political parties. Despite the grubbiness of the local machine and clientelist politics in Ireland, fifty years after independence there was a strong attachment to it and its practitioners and there was little significant upheaval in established political attachments.

Fianna Fáil, which had won the 1969 general election, having been in power since 1957, and before that from 1951–4 and 1932–48, received something of a shock when unseated by a coalition of Fine Gael and Labour in 1973, but only had to wait four years before an emphatic return to power in 1977. Despite the other upheavals of the decade, it was business as usual with central politics; the choices were Fianna Fáil as a majority power or a Fine Gael/Labour coalition and there were few serious ideological differences between the main parties. Although the Labour Party was the oldest, established in 1912, it had never broken the dominance of Fine Gael and Fianna Fáil, which represented the two sides of the civil war divide that resulted from the Anglo-Irish Treaty with Britain in 1921, creating dominion status for the twenty-six counties of southern Ireland (a republic was declared in 1949). Fine Gael, Labour and some smaller parties had previously served in coalitions between 1948–51 and 1954–7, while Fine Gael had not experienced single-party government since the 1920s, when its predecessor party Cumann na nGaedheal governed during the first ten years of the new Free State's existence.

On one level, this combination of a clientelist system dominated by local concerns and a national parliament peopled by mostly conservative representatives could be seen as staid and unimaginative, and as convenient during a decade when there were considerable challenges to the stability and legitimacy of the state due to the situation in Northern Ireland (see Part II). But the mechanics underpinning the dominance of Fianna Fáil were anything but unsophisticated. There is a reason why Fianna Fáil established itself as one of the most successful political parties in the world and it can be found in the party's archive. It was always a political movement that devoted itself to control, discipline, centralisation and obedience and this involved the expending of an effort that was layered, energetic and exceptionally focused. It was also canny about public relations and publicity; in 1976, a Fine Gael strategist wrote to Liam Cosgrave to point out that Fianna Fáil, then in opposition, was getting headlines for weekend speeches and concluded that Fine Gael ministers needed to start making speeches at weekends.[1]

One of the reasons Fianna Fáil was so shaken in the 1970s, particularly after the Arms Trial of 1970, when a number of ministers were sacked or resigned over a plot to import arms to assist Republicans in Northern Ireland (see Part II), was precisely because its legendary discipline and control was seen to break down for the first time in its history. Right up to the end of the decade Jack Lynch, leader of the party from 1966 to 1979 and Taoiseach 1966–73 and 1977–9, was struggling with that aspect of breakdown; his criticism of 'further breaches of confidentiality' of the proceedings of parliamentary party meetings as late as November 1979 and his appeal for 'a united party' reflected the consequences of a decade of inner turmoil.[2] Four years earlier it had been maintained at another of those meetings that those responsible for leaking information 'would bring about the downfall of the party'. The following year, Lynch was uncharacteristically emotional at a party meeting: 'I will no longer tolerate in the party generally, any more ambivalence in relation to the North of Ireland policy. If we are to win the next general election this has to stop now and also all this cloak and dagger messing about party leadership.'[3]

The party did win the next general election but it did not heal the fractures; if anything it gave them added depth, but that the party was able to win so decisively after eight years of internal strife was a reflection of the endurance and effectiveness of its electoral machine and its internal disciplinary procedures, evidence of which is littered throughout its archive. The 'expulsion' of 'offenders' was common; great importance was attached to its national collection fundraising and renewal of registration – 'the close of the Ard Fheis [annual party conference] marks the opening of a new organisation year'[4] – procedures and rules had to be adhered to. The party built its organisation from the smallest local unit, a *cumann* (branch) area could be defined by a church or an area with 1,000 people, an area which could give a minimum of ten active members or a clearly defined housing area, but no new *cumainn* could be accepted until a scheme of organisation for the constituency had been lodged and accepted by party headquarters.[5]

Patrick Smith, chairman of the Organisation Committee of the party, excoriated a member of a *cumann* who wrote directly to Jack Lynch in June 1973 about skulduggery at local level and what he regarded as the wrongful convening of a meeting. Smith informed the upstart that the way to deal with complaints was to adhere resolutely to the party structure from the ground up – the Comhairle Ceantair (district executive), the Dáil Ceantair (constituency executive), the National Executive and the Organisation Committee: 'A voluntary Organisation cannot be expected to be perfect but if those who have talent do not use it for the purpose of improving it, no reasonable person could expect that this could be done from the top.'[6]

Throughout the 1970s there was a large volume of correspondence sent to Fianna Fáil headquarters about local disagreements, dissidents, threatened resignations, accusations of victimisation, and the failure of the party's National Executive to respond to branch resolutions. Some resorted to sending solicitors' letters.[7] Lynch was contacted by a *cumann* in 1973 which demanded 'that the grassroots opinion in Fianna Fáil be listened to over and above that which the National Executive try to dictate'.[8] Séamus Brennan, who had been appointed general secretary of the party at the age of just twenty-five in 1973, needed all his patience, noting laconically after six years in the job that 'one gets more abuse than encouragement in politics generally'.[9]

He also had to deal with complaints about aggressive politicians in their personal fiefdoms throwing their weight about; from Swords, for example, came a letter about the behaviour of the dominant local (and later proven to be very corrupt) TD Ray Burke, who at a Comhairle meeting 'ranted and raved and completely domineered the chairman, therefore effectively taking control of the meeting with the conclusions prearranged and a personal vendetta against certain people'. These sorts of complaints were common, and in this case the person making the complaint resigned from the party.[10] In another part of Dublin, complaints were made in 1973 about irregular procedures, 'disrespect and abuse', meetings ending in disarray and the idea that the party was 'on its very knees in the public estimation'.[11] Another correspondent plaintively asked, in a dispute over membership, that Brennan 'prove to me that Fianna Fáil is after all democratic'.[12]

Skulduggery at local level could be nasty and dangerous; in May 1970, a party stalwart who looked after election rallies for the party in Donegal was injured after he fell from a lorry which was being used as a speaker's platform during the 1969 general election where there was a challenge to Fianna Fáil from an independent candidate. He fell four feet to the tarmac and 'another member of the platform party fell on top of him ... it was generally felt that the lynchpins had been maliciously removed so that an accident would occur'. Compensation was sought from the party as 'his injuries flow directly from his political activity on behalf of the party'.[13]

But the party's archive also reveals how and why it was able to overcome such internal difficulties and triumph electorally. The Organising Committee of Fianna Fáil met twice a month to discuss strategy, covering every aspect of election campaigns – 'one poster for every seven voters' – and assessments of morale and feedback that was regarded in 1973 as initially 'too good'.[14] It also oversaw forensic dissections of election results and had to deal with the fallout from internal rows. In March 1970 Fianna Fáil minister Erskine Childers wrote to the committee noting that the party had lost a seat in Monaghan in the general election of 1969 and as a result 'allegations would be hurled from one part of the constituency representation to the other' but that it was essential that these divisions did not become public as it would 'discredit the party'.[15]

In December 1975, its post-mortem on the loss of the by-election in West Mayo, won by Enda Kenny, another future Taoiseach and the son of the deceased TD Henry Kenny, concluded that, while sympathy and Kenny's youth were big factors, there was a lesson to be learned for Fianna

Fáil: 'We must be more positive in our approach and refrain from just reacting to government speeches.'[16] There was also a concern about dormant, or 'paper' *cumainn* and a suggestion that special visiting committees were needed to kick neglectful *cumainn* into shape and a necessity for election schemes to be in place for all parts of the country.[17] Quite simply, these kinds of issues were approached with military precision and there was a constant vigilance about organisational review. Constituency directors were also required to submit their reports, though in the aftermath of the successful 1977 general election, Lynch was regarded as having taken his eye off the ball: 'Disappointment was expressed at the failure of a Taoiseach to send messages of appreciation and thanks to all directors as had been the practice down through the years.'[18] Maybe Lynch thought they had done their job too well; he was, after all, wary of the size of his majority and what it might mean in terms of backbench discontent and ambition.

Fianna Fáil was also a voluntary organisation that excelled at fundraising but not without plenty of pressure being applied and reminders issued about the national collection. As was recorded at a meeting of the parliamentary party in February 1970, 'we must have funds to remain the premier party'.[19] The fundraising results were significant, as revealed by the minutes of the Finance Committee; the total of the 1970 collection was £49,000; in 1971, £55,000, while by 1976 the figure was £126,000 and for the following year £154,000. In 1978, the collection by October of that year was £193,000; almost the same figure was raised the following year, and this was separate from other donations. The total income for the party between May and September 1977 – during which period the general election was held – was £133,000 while total expenditure was £52,000.[20] *Cumainn* did not qualify for a ballot paper to choose constituency delegates for annual general meetings unless their national collection returns were deemed bona fide and included a list of subscribers.[21]

According to Tom Mullins, the former TD and senator who was involved in the foundation of the party in 1926 and who served as its general secretary from 1954–73, in the aftermath of electoral defeat in 1973, the challenge had been to have 'the state of the organisation examined in every constituency with the aim of achieving 100 per cent for the task of restoring Fianna Fáil to power'. In relation to the national collection any 'sheer carelessness on the part of treasurers' would not be tolerated. George Colley, Minister for Finance and director of elections for the party in 1973, wanted information on subscriptions raised by each *cumann* in order to 'show up the *cumann* who are not doing their work and there are very many of them' while in relation to those whose names were not on the National Register of Voters, 'the time to get them is now'.[22] There were also 'constituency collection awards'; in 1977 a member of the Roundwood *cumann* in Wicklow wrote to Séamus Brennan informing him of fundraising of £200 'from the tiny village ... I wonder if you could let me know whether they are in line for a plaque.'[23]

The Fianna Fáil fundraising money trail was shrouded in secrecy; Des Hanafin, a senator and county councillor from Tipperary, had been asked to take over control of fundraising from Taca (a group formed by Fianna Fáil fundraisers to raise money by giving businessmen access to ministers at regular dinners and private functions in return for a yearly contribution of £100 to party coffers). Taca had been disbanded at the end of the 1960s because of negative publicity about the association of FF with the construction industry. These links had perturbed Lynch; it was maintained by Hanafin that Lynch had no problem with returning donations that might compromise the party.[24] But in March 1976, the firm of accountants charged with auditing the party's financial affairs wrote to Lynch pointing out that 'subscription income is now being collected directly by Mr Hanafin through his office in the Burlington Hotel ... the Burlington Hotel fund is operating under the FF name although it would appear that the Trustees have no control over its activities or the disposal of its fund', therefore it could not be audited.[25] The following year it was pointed out to Lynch that there were three groups 'working in isolation of one another' in relation to fundraising and overseeing accounts – the Trustees of the party, those in charge of election funds and the party's official finance committee: 'I am concerned that there is no overall supervision and correlation between these sources.'[26] That same month, Lynch, at a FF National Executive meeting dismissed the 'antics' of Liam Cosgrave over party funding and pointed out that 'FF was the only political party that had to furnish its accounts'.[27] But which accounts were these and did they cover all donations and were they all audited? Hardly, on the basis of the above correspondence.

In relation to individual constituencies and elections, there was not only a constituency director of elections but also separate directors of publicity, canvass, transport and finance as well as sub-directors in all those areas, and even in the aftermath of a by-election victory in 1974 there was frankness in condemning 'a few weak spots'.[28] But Fianna Fáil was still not used to opposition politics, prompting internal criticisms of its 'lamentable lack of attack' on the coalition from 1973–7.[29]

At meetings of the parliamentary party there were also frequent criticisms that the backbenchers did not have 'a more effective role' in contributing to discussions about legislation; Lynch insisted he would do his 'utmost to see that the party worked in a democratic way'.[30]

By the time of the first elections to the European Parliament in 1979, Fianna Fáil, with its total number of *cumainn* at 2,669, was once again determined to run a centralised, disciplined campaign: 'No Fianna Fáil candidate has hired or will hire a PR agency on a professional basis. HQ will use PR firms ... no personal literature is allowed ... all literature produced locally is to be cleared by HQ', including 'matches, biros and pencils', and television training would be given by Carr Communications, a Dublin based company.[31]

The historic electoral success of Fianna Fáil inevitably generated resentment on the part of its opponents. Relief was expressed by many of them in the aftermath of the 1973 general election that sixteen years of unbroken Fianna Fáil power had been brought to an end. For example the *Irish Times* journalist Maeve Binchy, then reporting from London, was moved to write to Fine Gael's Garret FitzGerald, who was appointed Minister for Foreign Affairs in the new government ('this is the first time I ever wrote to a politician in my life') to express 'how delighted we all are ... I have lived all my life under a Fianna Fáil government and it is now a great joy to be going back to a change'. With this new era, she expressed the hope that 'people will be considered and that the party machine may take a second place'.[32] None had exemplified the importance of the party machine more than Fianna Fáil throughout its existence. Some of the letters expressing relief at the change of government underlined the visceral dislike of Fianna Fáil and its dominance; one supporter wrote to FitzGerald: 'My God, it is great to be able to smile again after 16 years ... delighted we have a nation once again.'[33] Many wedded to Fine Gael support would have echoed the views of writer John Waters's father, that the party 'maintained the holy grail of principled and God-given leadership'.[34] James Downey, then working as a political correspondent with the *Irish Times*, suggested that with a new government in 1973, 'the fervour of its supporters bordered on delirium'; his colleague Michael McInerney referred to it as 'the government of all the talents'.[35] It was suggested that Liam Cosgrave, at the outset of leading a new government, would be assisted 'by perhaps the most talented cabinet to have assumed office since the war' and that 'few, if any Irish administrations come to office with such an amount of goodwill from journalists as the national coalition'.[36] It was not an affection that would last.

– THREE –

IDENTIFYING THE PROBLEMS

Despite the endurance of traditional ways of doing political business and reinforcing political hegemony, there were suggestions throughout the 1970s as to how things might be reformed. In the main, such initiatives were not followed through. Parliamentary secretaries (subsequently given the title junior ministers) did not have to resign from local authorities; the general practice was that they did but some, including Fianna Fáil's Bobby Molloy, a member of Galway Corporation, did not, while Fine Gael's Henry Kenny, when appointed parliamentary secretary to the Minister for Finance, made it clear in March 1973 that he had 'no intention of resigning his position on Mayo County Council'.[1] A government memorandum that same month questioned the wisdom of this; it was apparent, for example, that the parliamentary secretaries 'come on deputations to ministers' and in doing so 'do not feel themselves bound by the collective responsibility of the government'.[2]

A cynical approach to misusing power was not the monopoly of any one party; given the Irish voting system, the preoccupation with constituencies, the extent of their boundaries and the number of representatives, they had remained a paramount concern. In November 1973 the Minister for Local Government, the Labour Party's James Tully, was accused, in presenting his Constituency Revision Bill, of engineering 'the most ruthless gerrymander in the history of this country, north or south'. In relation to Dublin, where most of the constituencies were now going to consist of three seats, Tully was regarded as having condemned Fianna Fáil to long-term opposition; it was even predicted that on current levels of support it would get just 66 seats, and the coalition 80, out of a Dáil of 144 seats.[3] This turned out to be a misplaced fear on Fianna Fáil's part and Tully's attempt to minimise proportionately any swing towards the opposition failed miserably. In the event there was a massive vote in favour of the Fianna Fáil election manifesto in 1977; the adjustments of the constituencies actually caused a disproportionate increase in the party's representation in the Dáil, and secured the largest majority in its history. Tully's 'stroke' also backfired because the coalition's vote did not hold up, but some also regarded his initiative as a form of revenge for the previous government's constituency revision that had been denounced as 'Boland's gerrymander' after the Fianna Fáil Minister for Local Government Kevin Boland.[4]

Questions were also raised as to the appropriateness of ministers' involvement in activities that could raise a conflict of interest. The new Fine Gael Minister for Agriculture and Fisheries, Mark Clinton, resigned his company directorships in 1973, while that same year the new Minister for Foreign Affairs, Garret FitzGerald, suggested he was 'happy to terminate' his involvement with, inter alia, the Irish Council of the European Movement, the Institute of Public Administration and his position as governor of Holles Street Maternity Hospital. Cosgrave believed some of these posts 'have the possibility of conflict with your position'. With regard to fees paid by BBC and RTÉ for interviews – FitzGerald had wondered if there was 'some way we can give them away without being liable for tax' – Cosgrave's tone was somewhat irritated: 'I think that ministers should make their own decisions on questions of this nature and involve me only when they are in doubt in an important instance. I do not agree that it was agreed by the government that there should be reference to me in all cases.'[5] With regard to the holding of company shares and whether or not this had the capacity to lead to a conflict of interest or compromise the position of a politician, it was made clear on legal advice that this in some cases could be 'inconsistent with the government decision' and that ministers would be honour bound to respect this, but that 'there is no monitoring procedures or record in this matter'.[6]

This was a situation that seemed to bother the Attorney General Declan Costello, a former Fine Gael TD, after his appointment in 1973; as far as he was concerned the law relating to conflict of interest of local authority and Oireachtas members was 'completely inadequate' and needed to be changed. His misgivings, as outlined the following year, arose not just from newspaper reports 'but from the existence of a more widespread public disquiet at the manner in which public affairs are conducted in this country. Legislative action is required not merely to dispel this public unease but also for the purpose of protecting the reputation of this country's public representatives.' It was pointed out that an 1898 enactment order that stipulated local authority members could not vote or take part in a discussion on matters before the council in which the member had 'a direct or indirect pecuniary interest' had been repealed by the Local Government Act of 1946 and not re-enacted.

There was a limited 'conflict of interest' section included in the Housing Act of 1966 but it was not brought into operation. English law, it was argued, provided for a much stricter code of conduct; in Ireland, however, there was disquiet concerning the operation of planning acts and it was maintained that a register of TD's interests was also needed.[7] The reality was that there was no legislation in force that would prohibit a member of a local authority from taking part in a discussion or voting on a matter in which they had an interest: 'Members of local authorities are, however, subject to the provisions of the Public Bodies Corrupt Practices Act, 1889' (which made it an offence 'corruptly to solicit or receive any gift or award or advantage as an inducement to or a reward for doing or forbearing to do anything in respect of a transaction in which the public body is concerned'). The difficulties of proving an offence under this Act were obvious, according to Costello, and 'the existence of this section has not hindered the development of practices which have given rise to the present public disquiet',[8] including politicians voting in favour of land re-zoning from which they could benefit. A cabinet committee was established to consider changing the law, which begs the question as to why proposed legislation could not just be considered in the normal way. It was patently obvious and reported in the media – and the *Sunday Independent* was particularly vocal in this regard in the summer of 1974 – that councillors, legally, were able to profit at a later date from motions which they originally voted on as public representatives. Councillors who were auctioneers, for example, could freely vote to have land re-zoned with a resulting steep rise in its value.

Auctioneer Ray Burke, as a Fianna Fáil councillor, seconded a motion in Dublin County Council in February 1971 which increased the value of a site there by almost £400,000, and he was subsequently allocated £15,000 from the sale of the land under a contract registered in November 1973. The following year, the accounts of a building firm in Dublin recorded a payment of £15,000 to Burke under the heading 'planning'; the accountant told Gardaí he had made an 'error'.[9] Fianna Fáil's Niall Andrews, when a member of the same council, brought a motion before it in 1973 to have representatives declare their business interests; it failed because he could not get a seconder from among his twenty-four fellow councillors. He subsequently lost his seat in the 1974 local elections.[10] All of this suggested rottenness at the core of local government in Ireland and little appetite to tackle it.

In 1975, two Fianna Fáil TDs, Bobby Molloy and Brendan Crinion, were found by the Dáil Committee on Procedure and Privilege to be 'in grave breach of privilege', after erroneously alleging that the Minister for Local Government, James Tully, had been given a cheque by a building contractor in relation to the re-zoning of land in Dublin. The minister had denied the allegation and challenged Molloy to repeat it outside the Dáil, where he would be devoid of parliamentary privilege. Molloy subsequently withdrew the allegation and said he was acting on false information given by third parties. Liam Cosgrave castigated the Fianna Fáil TDs, pointing out that the allegations had even made the news on the BBC. A tribunal of inquiry found there was absolutely no evidence to support the allegations.[11]

Molloy handwrote his version of how he obtained follow-up information after he had made his allegations and passed it on to Jack Lynch; he had received an 'anonymous phone call from person who said he was a banker ... he informed me that everything I had said about Tully in the Dáil was correct ... he said he was not in that end of banking where he would see these cheques but assured me that he knew enough to know that I was absolutely right.' The informant would not put his allegations in writing and Molloy asked him to ring him again 'as I needed as much information as I could to make the allegations stick'.[12] He clearly did not get it.

This obviously raised the issue of the use and abuse of privilege in the Dáil, and whatever the truth about the allegations against Tully – Molloy 'wanted to believe the allegations so he accepted them at face value' – it was pointed out in the current affairs magazine *Hibernia* that 'the public has every reason to be wary of political influence in land deals'. Ironically, the case of Molloy himself was deemed worthy of significance in this regard, as the magazine questioned his sale of land near his house in Salthill in Galway, a popular holiday spot, given that his decisions as Minister for Local Government in the early 1970s had 'shaped the growth of that resort'.[13]

John Boland of Fine Gael, who was chairman of Dublin County Council from 1971–2 and again from 1976–7, had taken out an auctioneer's licence in the early 1970s and was the subject of a Garda fraud investigation regarding the sale of land he was instrumental in getting re-zoned and subsequently profiting from. The Director of Public Prosecutions (DPP) decided to take no action and there was no internal inquiry by Fine Gael regarding the propriety of what he had done. Ray Burke was also investigated, it being suggested the Fraud Squad interviewed him on more than twenty occasions regarding his land deals, but again, there was no action taken by the DPP. As pointed out in the *Magill Book of Irish Politics*, 'the ethical aspects of the case were never explored. Such an exploration might have dealt with the propriety of elected public representatives earning considerable fees from ventures whose profitability they are in a position to enhance through their activities as public representatives.'[14]

There had also been 'blatant political jobbery' in the appointment of rate collectors. In 1972, *Hibernia* magazine reported that Dublin county councillors had taken on six rate collectors, three appointed by Fine Gael members and three appointed by Fianna Fáil members. The six were chosen out of 279 applicants and of the six, two were brothers of sitting councillors and another two were highly connected with the political parties. From the perspective of politicians, rate collectors were in a vital strategic position in getting to know large numbers of voters and their preferences.[15]

Were contemporary journalists and other observers and commentators aware of the shortcomings of Irish political life? Or was corruption exaggerated? In September 1972, it was argued in *Hibernia*: 'By and large, the degree of personal integrity in Irish public life compares very favourably with international standards ... for one thing, the smaller size of our society limits the scale of the temptations; for another its intimacy is an effective antidote to close intrigue. Too, the high standard in the civil service is a constant check on the designs of public men and favour seekers alike.'[16]

Is this really a conclusion that can withstand serious scrutiny, even by the standards of what was being reported in *Hibernia*'s own pages? And what were popular attitudes in that regard? Was it true, as suggested by journalist Mary Kenny, one of the leading members of the Irish Women's Liberation Movement, in relation to the defeat of Fianna Fáil in the general election of 1973, that the 'old corrupt razzmatazz ... offended one's high principles but delighted one's baser soul?'[17] Perhaps she had identified an important and ultimately destructive ambiguity in relation to the toleration by the electorate of corruption.

John Kelly had been correct in identifying the continued importance of patronage to Fine Gael when it was in power; there are numerous letters in the papers of Garret FitzGerald from the time he was Minister for Foreign Affairs, for example, which contain representations by senior party figures seeking his assistance in getting people they knew jobs in Europe. In March 1977, the Minister for Transport and Power made such representations about a woman he knew who had applied for a clerical position in the European Parliament: 'perhaps you will convey my recommendation to the proper quarter'. FitzGerald subsequently asked the permanent Irish representative at Brussels 'to make inquiries'.[18] In April 1975 the Minister for Defence, Fine Gael's Patrick Donegan, also made representations to FitzGerald about a woman seeking work with the Court of Justice in Luxembourg; her father 'was a cousin of mine', while to emphasise that she came from good stock he stressed that her mother 'is a daughter of ex deputy commissioner of the Garda Síochána' (her hobbies included 'casting horoscopes').[19]

Frank Cluskey of the Labour Party, parliamentary secretary to the Minister for Health and Social Welfare (his party leader Brendan Corish), was also active in this regard, making representations to get clerical work for people.[20] Politicians were also promised special service from some quarters; after his appointment as a minister in 1973, Garret FitzGerald received a letter from the manager of Allied Irish Bank (AIB) in Grafton Street, suggesting that he would have little time in his new position for the 'routine chores' of banking and that 'if you require any banking services you can ring me on my private line and I will be only too pleased to do what I can for you'.[21] AIB, it seemed, remained for a very long time pleased to do what it could for FitzGerald; twenty years later, after he had exhausted all efforts to pay them, it wrote off debts he had incurred with the bank of up to £200,000 which arose out of the aborted flotation of the aircraft leasing group GPA.[22] FitzGerald had borrowed money to buy GPA shares and had hoped to honour the debt through future earnings from his writing or a recovery in the share price of GPA, but in the event had to sell his house and use the proceeds left after settlement of the mortgage to offer just a portion (£40,000) of the debt, an offer the bank accepted.

In relation to parliamentary procedures, aspects of possible political reform were being discussed in the early 1970s by the Fianna Fáil government. An informal inter-departmental committee was established in April 1971 chaired by the Minister for Justice, Fianna Fáil's Desmond O'Malley; it held nineteen meetings and looked at comparisons with the UK and European systems. It suggested the broadcasting of parliamentary debates should be 'specially examined'; it also highlighted the need to delegate business to parliamentary committees due to lack of time for debate and asserted that more time was needed for private members' business and that the Dáil 'should sit on Church holidays'. O'Malley suggested to Lynch: 'Many of the proposals are not as far reaching as I would wish and as I think are necessary', but thought that compromise in the committee was necessary 'from the point of view of getting the changes accepted'. By May 1973 it was noted there was 'no action on this report'.[23]

This issue was raised by the new Attorney General Declan Costello in June 1973; he also suggested reform of the Senate electoral system was necessary; that more frequent debates on matters of urgent pubic importance were essential; that joint committees should look at European affairs and the activities of state sponsored bodies, and that if the broadcasting on radio of Dáil debates was successful they should be televised.[24] The Minister for Posts and Telegraphs, Conor Cruise O'Brien, insisted in correspondence with Liam Cosgrave that the broadcasting of Dáil proceedings 'should be supported by all deputies on the government side', pointing out that Cosgrave himself had said he was in favour;[25] televising of Dáil proceedings, however, did not happen until 1991.

There was a degree of cynicism about the usefulness of the Senate and the manner in which its representatives were chosen. This upper house of the Irish parliament, consisting of sixty members, supposedly representing different vocational interests, had a very restricted electorate and very restricted powers (it could delay but not veto legislation). The Taoiseach of the day was entitled to appoint eleven nominees to ensure a government majority; a small number were elected by university graduates and the rest by fellow senators, TDs and councillors. On the back of the publication of a book by a young political scientist, Tom Garvin, in 1970, journalist John Horgan, later a Labour Party TD, suggested 'the chief and quite probably the only justification for retaining the Senate is because it's there', and he wondered if 'the absurdities of vocationalism' could be 'dispensed with in the method of election'.[26] In July 1969 John Kelly, having failed to win a Dáil seat, captured the somewhat ambiguous approach to the Senate by asserting that 'I am not seeking election to the Senate merely as a decoration', but he also told Fine Gael members that he wanted a Senate seat 'to strengthen my position for capturing a second seat for Fine Gael in the Dublin constituency'.[27]

Capturing a Senate seat, due to the need for county councillors' votes, was also about criss-crossing the country (as Kelly wrote, 'since my nomination I have been travelling almost non-stop ... to visit you all in a limited time is not easy') and horse trading; as one TD suggested to Kelly in offering support: 'you deserve a break now ... on a quid pro quo basis I will expect you to use your influence with your own colleagues for me on the Administration panel. That's only fair.'[28] In 1974, Minister for Defence Patrick Donegan reflected on the time he had served there from 1957–61: 'I must admit that during that period I regarded the Senate, and I am sure the hallowed walls will not fall in when I say this, as a place or state of punishment where I must suffer until I returned to the Dáil.'[29]

The refreshing honesty of Donegan reflected a widely held view and was the political reality for many. After he lost his seat in the 1977 general election, the Labour Party's Conor Cruise O'Brien was elected to the Senate, but left before his term was up and subsequently described it as 'my useless seat in the Senate' because he could not debate Northern Ireland in the way he desired in a Fianna Fáil dominated Senate.[30] But there were others who had used it effectively. A genuinely radical voice in Irish politics, Trinity College Dublin (TCD) academic Owen Sheehy Skeffington, died in 1970; writer Seán O'Faoláin regarded him as 'rich in moral courage' and 'a giant of honesty'. It was argued that he had used the Senate effectively to attack 'the entrenched, arrogant religion, politics and outlook that kept Irishmen at each other's throats and did it without a party or a book'. He had also championed women's rights, advocated the primacy of private conscience, railed against corporal punishment and violence, opposed apartheid and advocated separation of church and state and a national health plan. More familiar to his students as simply 'Skeff', he was a brilliant orator, and the son of Francis Skeffington, journalist and pacifist campaigner killed in 1916 during the Rising, and Hanna Sheehy, suffragist and Nationalist. He was also regarded as having brought TCD into 'the liberal front line of Irish national debate' and as a result of his contributions was dubbed 'Man of the Senate' by the *Irish Times*. As the chairman of the Senate said at the time of his death, 'He was never dismayed if his point of view was a minority one and indeed seemed at times to revel in a position of isolation ... though few senators have not crossed swords with him at one time or another, no one could withhold admiration for his honesty, integrity and moral courage.'[31]

The question of amending the constitution on the issue of Senate representation from just TCD and the National University of Ireland graduates to include members of other third-level institutions was addressed, but despite the endorsement of the electorate, a referendum result of 1979 was not acted upon, another illustration of reform of Irish politics being raised in the 1970s but deliberately placed on the long finger.

In relation to the lower house, just how useful was the Dáil and did it adequately represent the interests of the Irish people? The Devlin Report, reviewing public service organisation and published in 1969, had recommended an Irish Ombudsman, but the government's view seemed to be that 'there is no need for an ombudsman here' (Britain had got one in 1967). The Devlin Report had made it clear that 'the parliamentary question, whatever its merit, is not an effective way of remedying all but a handful of grievances'. The Irish instead were dependent on the Free Legal Advice Centres and the Citizens Advice Bureau. In relation to an Ombudsman, Anthony Butler, a journalist with the *Evening Press* newspaper, suggested in January 1970 that 'no politician is strongly opposed to the concept or – on the other hand – seriously enthusiastic for it. This could well be an indication of the tepid quality of our democratic passion. In any event, the vast extension of power to bureaucrats in our administrative state suggests that it should be balanced by some major and formal protection for the citizens'. Six months later, Brian Lenihan, Fianna Fáil Minister for Transport and Power, effectively dismissed this contention by asserting in the Dáil that 'we have here a very democratic system in which there is a total availability of local and national representatives where the people are concerned and the rights are remedied ... through questions here in the house ... representatives are readily available to the public'.[32]

There was a smugness, if not arrogance, about such assertions that suggested a satisfaction with clientelism and it is again striking the degree to which proposals in the 1970s about changes, transparencies and representation were kicked to touch and ultimately took so long to bring to fruition. In 1976 Minister for Finance Richie Ryan of Fine Gael addressed the first meeting of an all-party informal committee on the administration of justice at Leinster House and made the frank observation that 'It is indeed possible that our success as spokesmen for aggrieved individuals has led us, and the people we represent into complacency about our arrangements for administrative justice. People are aware that public representatives will generally take up individual grievances.' He suggested the onus was on politicians to 'fund a cheap, informal and expeditious means of having grievances examined by an impartial authority'. The report of this committee recommended the establishment of an Ombudsman,[33] but there was no legislation catering for the office of Irish Ombudsman until 1980 and none appointed until 1984, when former political journalist Michael Mills took up the position.

Questions were also raised in the 1970s as to whether there were enough government departments to cater for the modern era. In the Dáil in May 1973 the Taoiseach Liam Cosgrave was pressed as to whether he would create new Departments of the Environment, Regional Development and Culture; he responded negatively in relation to all three. There were various proposals throughout the 1970s about the abolition of the Departments of Land, Gaeltacht [Irish-speaking districts] and Transport and Power and the possible creation of Departments for the EEC, Transport and Communications, Consumer Affairs and a separate Ministry of Public Service. But while a new Department of Public Service was created in 1973 on the back of the Devlin Report's recommendations, it was in effect an appendage of the Department of Finance, and 'a caricature of the department proposed by Devlin. Instead of being a primarily creative department concerned with implementing Devlin, its main responsibility was to control staff numbers throughout the public service' and it was abolished and reincorporated into the Department of Finance in 1987.[34] An indication of a continuing commitment to centralisation at government level was that one of Cosgrave's main concerns was to strengthen his own department. He dismissed the need for a Department of Consumer Affairs and would merely see if the environment 'could be given more prominence'.

In 1973 a memorandum from the Office of the Minister for the Public Service insisted 'a primary goal for each department is self-maintenance; redistribution will not, therefore originate with single departments. From the centre there has been, apart from the review group's study [the Devlin Report] no overall examination of the distribution of the functions of government'. It was also pointed out that 'in the field of commerce, the questions of consumer protection and price control are among the most important issues facing the government'. In the view of Richie Ryan, 'In many ways, this fundamental matter of whether or not existing ministerial portfolio areas have the correct functions, because of duties and responsibilities is in need of very careful thought and consideration.'[35] Such thought and consideration, however, was rarely translated into bold action. While Fianna Fáil's Martin O'Donoghue was given responsibility for implementing the economic promises in Fianna Fáil's 1977 election manifesto by being appointed as Minister for Economic Planning and Development, a new department, on his first day as TD, it was an initiative criticised by T. K. Whitaker, whom Jack Lynch had nominated to the Senate and 'whose warnings of a paralysing tension with George Colley and his officials in Finance were soon vindicated'.[36] That same year, the Department of Local Government became the Department of the Environment, but there was no Department of Communications until 1984.

– FOUR –

SERVANTS OF THE MINISTER

Questions were also being asked about the function of civil servants in the political process. As noted earlier, an expanded civil service was achieving more visibility and influence and frequently debating the merits of reform and restructuring in the pages of its journal *Administration.* But these were elite debates that did not necessarily enthuse all those working at the coalface. Richard Stokes, for example, who was promoted from higher executive officer to principal officer in the Department of the Taoiseach in 1972, and subsequently assistant secretary, felt the arguments for reform, while having merit, did not have much of an influence in disturbing the degree of 'placidity' in the civil service and were seen as largely 'academic'. Many focused civil servants just continued to work hard in what were fairly sheltered environments. The staff of the Department of the Taoiseach during this decade – including assistant secretary (later secretary) Dan O'Sullivan, assistant secretaries Dermot Nally and Bertie O'Dowd and principal officers Frank Murray and Walter Kirwan – was small, Stokes pointing out that in 1972 he was the only principal officer in the department, in contrast to the situation ten years later when there were ten such officers.

Stokes, a native of Limerick city, whose father had been a clerk for CIÉ (Córas Iompair Éireann, the state-run national transport company), before dying in his mid fifties, joined the civil service on his nineteenth birthday, beginning his career in the Office of Public Works before moving to the Department of the Taoiseach. Given the relatively small staff there, he engaged with a great variety of issues as evidenced by the huge amount of memoranda he authored. He also remembered that this was an era when there was a premium placed on ethics and a discouragement of waste (a prevailing 'parsimony') or indulgence in the service, recalling that after a work trip to Belfast, he and colleagues alighted from the train at night and when one suggested they get a taxi home, he was told in no uncertain terms they would be using public transport – the bus.[1] There was much preoccupation with hierarchy within the service and a sense that there would be little encouragement for autonomous thinking unless a particular grade had been reached. Ideas from those 'only a wet day in the place' often received short shrift, but there was a strong sense of camaraderie. In dealing with the many issues that came through the department, those in the higher grades expressed themselves trenchantly when they felt such a tone was required.[2]

But there was adverse comment early in the decade about the role of civil servants in deputising for ministers at official openings. Liam Tobin, secretary of the Department of the Gaeltacht, for example, opened a factory in the Donegal Gaeltacht in place of George Colley, the Minister for Industry and Commerce, in April 1970. The following week Richard Foley, Chief Inspector of Secondary Schools, opened the new Holy Ghost Fathers' College at Templeogue in Dublin, representing the Minister for Education. It was pointed out stoutly by the Departments of Justice and Finance that this was unacceptable; a decision of government in November 1969 declared the 'undesirability of civil servants deputising for their ministers ... at public functions'. Furthermore, as pointed out by the Department of Finance, under its regulations, not only were civil servants forbidden from becoming TDs or councillors or supporting same, but they were also prohibited from 'speaking publicly or contributing articles for publication conveying information, comment or criticism on political matters'.[3]

There was further controversy, however, the following year when public meetings convened to discuss proposals for community schools involved civil servants; this was criticised in the Dáil by Labour TD Noel Browne as inappropriate, 'particularly when such policy is politically controversial and involves important social and religious issues'. George Colley defended the practice, on the grounds that the civil servants were there to 'explain, clarify and listen', while the *Irish Press* editorialised about the important role played by civil servants in drawing up legislation and their need for feedback. Former Fine Gael Taoiseach John A. Costello, who had served from 1948–51 and 1954–7, was, however, unimpressed with such arguments: 'Civil servants, in my view, are getting too much control. The FF government have landed themselves into the hands of civil servants. Their policies are now civil service policies.'[4]

In May 1978, *Magill* magazine reported that in the interregnum between the election and the change of government in 1977, Liam Cosgrave had made several senior civil service appointments, including Thomas Coffey as head of the Department of Finance. It was asserted that, traditionally, outgoing governments had deferred all pending appointments until a new government had taken up office and that 'Jack Lynch was furious about the matter but opted to keep quiet lest further damage be done to the civil service'.[5] Ted Nealon, who was head of the Government Information Services from 1975–7, contested the 1977 general election for Fine Gael and, when defeated, rejoined the civil service again in his old job 'in a move which raised a lot of questions about its propriety'; the new government removed him from that position and compensated him.[6]

Individual civil servants in senior positions undoubtedly remained exceptionally powerful. It was observed that when Richie Ryan was appointed Minister for Finance in 1973 he was regarded as 'something of an unknown quantity in Finance' (in contrast to FitzGerald, who, as Fine Gael's spokesman on Finance, was on record as decrying 'intolerable levels of poverty') but his appointment was seen as Cosgrave's attempt to suggest that the new coalition would be orthodox on matters of finance: 'In other words, Charlie Murray [secretary of the Department of Finance] will continue in control.'[7]

There were also frequent concerns about status in the civil service throughout the decade in terms of functions, seniority, rank and promotions. The Civil Service Executive Association pointed out to Garret FitzGerald in May 1973 that it had 'for some time been greatly concerned about the irrational manner in which promotions are made in government departments', arguing that there was no openness or information about the criteria used.[8] In January 1974 Richie Ryan found himself in disagreement with the Minister for Posts and Telegraphs, Conor Cruise O'Brien, who had requested that private secretaries to ministers were deserving of the rank of assistant principal grade instead of higher executive officer; he pointed out that a private secretary, who was paid an allowance of £628 a year in addition to normal salary, was 'in no way concerned with the content of any matter he deals with', also suggesting that 'the reality is that private secretaries to ministers form a closely knit corps who meet frequently at Leinster House and, naturally, compare notes about a lot of things, including the idiosyncrasies of ministers'.[9] There was certainly much to discuss in that regard in relation to Cruise O'Brien.

Given the degree of centralisation of government, civil servants in the Department of the Taoiseach were highly influential. In November 1978, H. J. [Bertie] O'Dowd, assistant secretary in the Department of the Taoiseach, in a letter to Richard Stokes, expressed the view that there was in fact too much information coming through the Department of the Taoiseach and a growing tendency for that department to 'comment on matters that, strictly speaking, are not for us at all', including the legal basis of circulars issued by the Department of Public Service which should have gone to the Attorney General's office.[10] The concern persisted that public service reform was urgently needed in the context of planning and finance in each government department and the concept of 'specialist staff' support to line management. It was maintained that all departments needed to be reorganised because of the absence of a specialised approach as 'the old generalist tradition still persists'.[11] There were mixed views on this; and tensions between the Department of the Taoiseach and Department of Public Service. Stokes, for example, acknowledged the need for reform but decried overspecialisation and maintained that, 'Far from specialisation being needed, I would say that it is good and enlightening for personnel people to have a mix of experience in the various divisions of their department.'

A few months later, assistant secretary in the Department of the Taoiseach, Dermot Nally, who went on to become secretary to the government the following decade, wrote to Lynch urging caution, arguing that what was needed was not new forms of organisation, but detailed training in particular skills and services inter-departmentally. He suggested that if civil servants overspecialised, 'an unnecessary rigidity will be built into the service. This trend is totally contrary to what has been happening in what is, I think, one of the most capable public services in the world – that of the British. In the late 1960s there, the Fulton Committee recommended measures to break down barriers between professional grades within the civil service and administrative and executive grades. In other words their recommendations were the opposite of what is now proposed for the Irish service.'[12]

Despite these occasional tensions, the relationship between governing politicians and civil servants remained tight-knit and dependent and there was a caution about disturbing that mutual dependence and the hierarchies it created. But there were some concerns expressed about its restrictiveness. The formulation of policy was believed by Garret FitzGerald, for example, to be something that required advice and assistance. When reflecting on his appointment as a minister in 1973 he recalled that as he was abroad so often he was 'falling behind' in studying the whole range of cabinet memorandums which he believed had to be read by all ministers in the interests of collective responsibility. Civil servants in individual departments, he surmised, should not have been expected to provide an input on matters that lay outside the scope of their responsibilities, so he appointed an economist, Brendan Dowling, 'to study cabinet documentation to ensure I would be fully briefed'. Other ministers in that government also arranged to have this kind of advice available to them and FitzGerald pointed out that in the late 1960s he had visited the Treasury in London with Jim Dooge (one of Ireland's foremost engineers and later a Fine Gael senator and briefly Minister for Foreign Affairs in 1981) to discuss with its permanent secretary the possible role of such expert advisers in a cabinet system.[13] FitzGerald, however, felt that in the long term, not enough use of advisers was made in the Irish political system; it did not bring in enough people of calibre to influential positions as the localism, clientelism and 'cronyism' of the system won out.

Likewise, when interviewed in the 1980s, Tom Barrington talked about a book that had influenced his thinking from the 1960s onwards in relation to the nature of governance, *Beyond the Welfare State*, by renowned Swedish economist Gunnar Myrdal. In Barrington's estimation the book effectively demonstrated how, as people became better educated and more self-conscious, central government would shed a lot of 'the detailed things and these would be looked after by small groups instead'; that central government would gradually devolve power. This remained a vision for him, but an unfulfilled one.[14]

Decentralisation of civil servants was also an issue that arose periodically in the 1970s in the context of discussions about moving state and semi-state administrative organisations out of Dublin. Between 1967 and 1974 some civil servants from the Departments of Education, Lands and the Gaeltacht had moved voluntarily, an initiative designed to facilitate the social and economic advancement of less developed or favoured areas. But a proposal by the Department of Public Service in 1978 to move 1,500 more in general service grades was regarded by the Department of the Taoiseach as 'entirely unrealistic'. It was rubbished as ill-thought out and ill planned in the context of the unavailability of facilities and education services for staffs' children:

> It took ten years to transfer 160 officers of the former Department of Lands to Castlebar and ten years to transfer a hundred officers of the Department of Education to Athlone ... in this context, the suggested figures of 1,500 officers and the proposed time scale – a period of four years beginning in two years' time – seem entirely unrealistic. Not alone do they seem unrealistic, but if they are adopted they will become known publicly either by way of political decision or by way of leaks through civil service organisations and the government will be stuck with a target figure which probably could only be met, if it could be met at all, by half-baked arrangements.

A compromise arrangement was reached regarding the decentralisation of between 160 and 180 civil servants from the Department of Defence.[15]

There was, it seemed, by the end of the 1970s, increased consultation between civil servants and concern was expressed about the resulting tendency, 'probably due to the ease with which papers can be reproduced, of giving documents very wide circulation'. This increased concerns about the dangers of breaches of confidentiality or secrecy. There were circulars about official secrecy, integrity and the need not to make 'unauthorised communications'. There was also mounting alarm during the decade about deliberate leaks. In May 1978, disquiet was expressed about the fact that the National Flat Dwellers' Association (NFDA) appeared to be in possession of leaked local government financial provisions from the Department of the Environment; the issue at stake was the bill to abolish rates on private houses.

When, in the Dáil, Lynch was asked about details of the provisions being published in the *Irish Independent*, having seemingly been given them by the NFDA, Lynch replied nonchalantly, 'I was always taught that one should believe only half what one reads' (to which Fine Gael TD

Paddy Harte replied: 'Is the Taoiseach talking again about the Fianna Fáil manifesto?'), but it was erroneously asserted that he was moved by the gravity of it to order an inquiry. The NFDA said it was leaked to it by 'an anonymous sympathiser' in the Department of the Environment; it was also suggested that almost half of the association's membership was made up of civil servants.[16]

At a cabinet meeting it was agreed informally that the Minister for the Environment should ask the Garda Commissioner to have the matter investigated 'on the basis that a *prima facie* breach of the Official Secrets Act had occurred. Taoiseach mentioned that he had not ordered an inquiry as reported in today's newspapers.'[17] The subsequent report of the Garda investigation was removed from the file.

– FIVE –

POLITICAL SOUL-SEARCHING

Leaks were not just emanating from the civil service; Fine Gael senator John Kelly found himself in an uncomfortable position in September 1972 when the *Sunday Independent* newspaper referred to a document seemingly sent to the paper anonymously by a Fine Gael party member. It suggested Kelly had referred to the Labour Party as 'baboons'; that he and FitzGerald were in a minority in looking for a coalition with the Labour Party and that there was a resentment in the party towards lawyers 'since these people are regarded as impractical political theorists who only devote their spare time to politics. Senator Kelly in particular is deeply resented. He is forever talking about doing something but then disappears back to the university in the middle of a meeting.'[1]

Kelly suggested the piece was written by some 'hatchet man' and thought the culprit was a front bench member because of the reference to Kelly 'forever saying something must be done ... I admit I have this habit, but I confine it to the front bench for the most part and do not inflict broad generalities on the party at party meetings – which indeed I am frequently unable to attend.' Kelly was concerned about the suggestion that the party needed to bring in a private detective to investigate the issue as the party might face jibes in the Dáil 'about whether our Sherlock Holmes had found anything yet'.

But it was ultimately Kelly who became the Sherlock Holmes; he believed that the document had been typed on a Hume Street typewriter [where the party offices were] and he went to the office and retyped the document's content using the machine he suspected. With Cosgrave's permission, the typewriter was taken from head office and brought to the makers, who confirmed the document was typed on that machine. Cosgrave, at this stage, feared that the issue had gone far enough and insisted that under no circumstances were staff to be questioned, but Kelly persuaded him otherwise. Internally, Kelly apologised for his 'irritable tone' at the original party meeting; he did not deny that he had called the Labour Party 'baboons', but apologised for saying things that were 'needlessly offensive'.[2]

This episode was one of many which caused Kelly to reflect on Fine Gael's internal divisions and its struggle to define itself. Years later, in an extraordinary letter to Fine Gael leader Alan Dukes in 1989 (Dukes had succeeded Garret FitzGerald in 1987), he explained where he felt Fine Gael had gone wrong since 1977 and why he believed it should disband and reintegrate with either Fianna Fáil or the Labour Party, depending on the individual members' preferences: 'The core of the problem is what do we stand for that no one else stands for, or what justifies our separate existence now that (unlike earlier times) it is not possible to fault Fianna Fáil convincingly on any of the old grounds.'

Retrospectively, Kelly seemed to regard the mid 1970s as the golden age for Fine Gael, precisely because it had what he regarded as a completely different identity: 'When Liam Cosgrave was leader it was easy to see Fine Gael, sincerely, as the one rational and moderate and more or less honest political option for the country and correspondingly easy to detest and oppose Fianna Fáil. In 1973 and thereafter they were arrogant, bullying, often corrupt, opportunistic, irresponsible about both the North and the economy. When Liam went out in 1977 his party could hold its head high.'[3]

Kelly's letter to Dukes was the culmination of twenty years of soul searching about the nature and identity of Fine Gael. He had been disarmingly frank after the 1969 general election, which returned Fianna Fáil with an overall majority, about Fine Gael's weaknesses and the sense that the party was anything but united. He had even published an article in the *Sunday Independent* on the dilemmas facing the party, which provoked a divided response within it. Peter Barry for example, elected a Fine Gael TD representing Cork in 1969, wrote to him: 'I agree with about three-quarters of what you said in yesterday's Independent ... FG needs a policy about the place of policies.'[4] An older stalwart of the party and one hostile to the 'Just Society' notions of the younger advocates that had emerged in the 1960s, Gerard Sweetman, a former Minister for Finance, agreed with 'a very great deal' of what he suggested but 'what appals me, however, is that you would give your lecture in public … it makes quite nonsense of a party to have the discussion in public'. Sweetman also suggested articles being written by Kelly and Garret FitzGerald 'can only have the effect of dividing and not unifying the party'.[5]

Kelly's frankness extended to acknowledging a perception of Fine Gael by the public as 'a party of essentially conservative people, somewhat old fashioned in attitude, thinking themselves (perhaps rightly) more "decent" and "respectable" than their opponents but lacking the necessary vigour and aggressiveness and possibly even the will to beat Fianna Fáil and uneasily containing within itself a progressive wing which is at loggerheads with the old Guard'.[6] What Kelly did not want to suggest was 'a cynical imitation of Fianna Fáil's ambiguity', but he insisted that this was a major part of Fianna Fáil's appeal, along with its perceived commitment to redistribution of wealth and its determination to eschew labels:

> Fianna Fáil fought the 1969 election in the shadow of conditions which could hardly have been less favourable and still won. Its referendum disaster [when its proposal to get rid of proportional representation was defeated] its bad relations with teachers, farmers, the unions, the guards, the rows about Taca, about interference in RTÉ, about the place of Irish in schools, about land prices, about planning decisions and about the Criminal Justice Bill and its general reputation for arrogance. It emerged from all this apparent unpopularity with 602,227 first preference votes.[7]

This was after a general election during a year in which political correspondent Michael Mills suggested there was 'a quiet revolution' going on in Irish politics; that more young people were coming into the three main political parties and their voices were being heard, but also that 'the public in general also appear to want change, without being too clear on the nature of the change required'.[8]

Kelly had not only highlighted the frustration and dashed hopes of its opponents, but also Fianna Fáil's enduring ability to confound its critics by continually mobilising its well-organised volunteers. As seen earlier, the party did not tolerate any 'slipshod' canvassing; it cultivated youth conferences, had very strict rules governing selection conventions and properly constituted *cumainn* and had 'any amount of recruitment posters and recruitment handouts available'.[9] It also had the advantage of a very successful history, and for those who had inherited Fianna Fáil loyalties, the party was a 'strong motivating force' in their life.[10]

In all of this, there was little room, it seemed, for ideological debate. Fianna Fáil excelled at organisation and winning power rather than policy debate, but it had other factors working to its advantage and the cult of the leader was one. The appeal of the exceptionally popular Jack Lynch was significant in this regard (see pages 79–83), as was a genetic antipathy to Fine Gael, regardless of the prevailing social and economic conditions. But as Kelly had recognised, there was no doubt that Fianna Fáil's ruthless pragmatism left Fine Gael struggling to carve its own political niche.

In 1972, a memorandum Kelly sent to his colleagues suggested that 'a very large unanimity exists in this country as to the proper objects and pace of social reform, a unanimity which though inarticulate makes a political polarity along "left-right", "conservative-Progressive lines unnecessary". The dilemma for Fine Gael, as Kelly saw it, was that Fianna Fáil 'has managed to claim a virtual monopoly of national spirit'.[11] He did not see any need to 'court' the Labour Party as it 'will have no option but to co-operate actively or passively in providing an alternative government'. But one of the answers for Kelly seemed to be about the potential for Fine Gael to be a catch-all party and thus to present itself as 'the farmer's party, the working man's party and the business man's party'.[12] Everyone was aware, he suggested, that 'since about 1960, the top men in Fianna Fáil have been heavily absorbed with their own personality cults and the party itself has been identified with the growth of a few large personal fortunes and ostentatious living'. He made much of the fact that, in the summer of 1969, Lynch had warned of the dangers of an 'alien philosophy' – a reference to socialism and the left-wing movements protesting about housing. In response, Kelly suggested that 'the Taca philosophy is, or should be, every bit as alien in a small and not very wealthy republic'.[13]

When draft answers were being prepared by Liam Cosgrave's private secretary, in response to a questionnaire sent by editor of the *Irish Press*, Tim Pat Coogan, in July 1973 (there was a determination that Cosgrave would give only 'short answers' and 'little information'), his take on the difference between Fianna Fáil and Fine Gael was as follows:

> Fine Gael represents the more straightforward, commonsense part of the Sinn Féin tradition to do one's best for Ireland in the conditions of today, rather than neglect the people's real problems for the sake of pursuing visions of doubtful practicality or value ... the other party is hamstrung by having built myths into its very foundations, which are now an embarrassment to its latter day members and which necessarily result in a certain amount of hollow pretence.[14]

Cosgrave came to power in 1973 after considerable criticism of his performance as leader of a lacklustre Fine Gael in the early 1970s; out of power since 1957, and facing renewed questions about what it was the party stood for: 'Too often, especially on really important issues like the EEC and the North, Fine Gael appears only to rubber stamp what is, in effect the government line.' Was it merely waiting to take advantage of the blunders of others rather than the achievements of itself? And was it still a party that was pledged to the achievement of a 'Just Society'?[15] What would this mean when the party was in power? Towards the end of his period as Taoiseach, Cosgrave, in a newspaper interview, suggested 'we are not particularly interested in the meaning of "isms". We are determined not to let any preconceived notions dictate our action. Our approach is truly pragmatic and flexible.' In response to the question 'There is little theoretical or ideological debate in this country?' Cosgrave answered, 'No, hardly any,' with apparent satisfaction.[16] Given that he had presided over a coalition involving the Labour Party – to which he was generous – he did not need to ponder the 'Just Society' notion for Fine Gael, as it was essentially the Labour Party's responsibility; in any case Cosgrave was admired for his conservatism and perceived steadiness (see below).

But even when the noticeably more liberal minded Garret FitzGerald took over the leadership of the party in 1977, he too sought to be careful about covering his bases: 'We are not conservatives and we are not socialists ... we are formulating policies within these parameters – within those limits – in accordance with the basic ideals of Christianity.'[17] During the late 1970s, the type of speeches made by FitzGerald prompted the assessment that he was 'an adventurous intellect' with a 'cautious instinct'.[18] Political correspondent Joseph O'Malley suggested in 1979 that despite the organisational revitalisation of the party, its policies were still too ambiguous, particularly regarding taxation and farmers, capital taxation and contraception.[19]

With regard to the 'new look' Fine Gael under FitzGerald, there were still party TDs who could not be considered anything other than mortifying by the leadership regime; Hugh Byrne, for example, the Dublin North West TD first elected in 1969, was characterised as 'a sore embarrassment to the Fine Gael party. He is racist, sexist and otherwise deeply reactionary. He was expelled from the Fine Gael party in 1978 for voting against the party whip and for abusive behaviour to nurses who were lobbying the Dáil.'[20] In relation to Fine Gael's Young Turks there was a determination that the party's youth group would operate independently of the senior party.[21] An estimated one thousand delegates attended the youth conference of the Fine Gael Ard Fheis in 1978, which suggested that 'organisationally, the party is on the verge of matching Fianna Fáil'.[22]

In an address at University College Cork in October 1978, John Kelly suggested that when the political history of the contemporary era was written, what would appear one of its strongest features was the large number of topics, 'not essentially connected, on which a person thought to stand left or right is expected to have fixed and predictable attitudes'. He regarded this stereotyping over a large range of issues harmful 'because it reduces the combinations of policy which can be put before the electors and may rule out the very mix of policies – some radical, some conservative – which the special conditions of Ireland call for'.[23]

The seemingly constant search for the middle ground was an inevitable part of Irish politics, given that neither of the largest parties operated along identifiable ideological lines. A reasonable question was posed by *Magill* magazine in May 1978 as to the logic of Fine Gael, insisting it was going to change its practice of the late 1960s and keep its more electorally appealing policies under wraps until an election campaign 'on the pragmatic grounds that if released beforehand Fianna Fáil would steal the more popular ones. The implications of this decision are considerable. It is a recognition that there is no intrinsic divergence of policy between Fianna Fáil and Fine Gael, for if there were there would be no question of Fianna Fáil stealing policies.'[24] Nonetheless, there was a commitment from Michael Keating in Fine Gael, the front bench spokesman on human rights and law reform, to a wide range of 'quite radical' reforms, including an independent complaints procedure into allegations of Garda brutality, a police authority and a Freedom of Information Act.[25]

Those regarded as radical in Irish politics were still lazily labelled communists. The genuine communists were on show at the start of a May

Day rally in 1970 organised by the Labour movement, which led to scuffles when a rival parade of Maoists, amounting to twenty people, chanted anti-fascist slogans and created confusion among some of the main body of the parade. The main marchers, including Young Socialists, called for the abolition of anti-union laws: 'a watching worker – a taxi driver – was not impressed and he called out: "Get your hair cut!"'[26]

In March 1977, Labour Party minister Conor Cruise O'Brien was incensed that, under parliamentary privilege, Fianna Fáil TD Flor Crowley referred to him as 'a former member of the Communist Party', which he regarded as 'extremely defamatory'. A resident of Achill, in a letter to Jack Lynch, took this further and suggested not only had Cruise O'Brien been a member of the Communist Party, but that he had 'been responsible for the infiltration of people with similar views into the various departments of RTÉ. This is evident not alone in the strong leftist bias in news reports but also in the number of short features imported from communist sources.'[27] There were also frequent assertions about communist complicity in the shipping of arms to Northern Ireland, and allegations that Russia had '800 IRA agents'. Bernadette Devlin, the young radical socialist-Republican MP for Derry, was singled out for opprobrium in the context of Red scares, as 'she has since affirmed that she is even left of the communists'.[28]

At least the Irish Communist Party could boast something after the 1973 general election that no other party could: it was the party that had the highest increase in its poll since the 1969 election. Michael O'Riordan's vote of 466 in the constituency of Dublin Central represented an increase of 92.6 per cent over Sam Nolan's 224 votes polled in 1969.[29] O'Riordan, with an IRA background, had joined the party in 1935, fought in the Spanish Civil War on the Republican side, and was active in various other Irish Marxist organisations including the Irish Workers League (1948–62) and the Irish Workers Party (1962–70) over five decades. Given the historical continuity among these organisations, 'as the vehicles of orthodox, Moscow-orientated communism in Ireland, O'Riordan may thus be described as the longest serving leader of a political party in the history of the Irish state'. He was also a frequent target of church denunciation.[30]

When Taoiseach Jack Lynch was interviewed by RTÉ journalist Mike Burns in January 1978, in response to the question as to whether there was a widening gulf between rich and poor, he responded: 'I think, even though we have not a great degree of affluence, there is less and less have nots in our country.' As well as promising that if there were 100,000 unemployed by the end of his term in office the electorate would be right to put him out of office, he asserted that the Irish electorate was 'much more volatile than we ever had before' and that the landslide victory for Fianna Fáil in 1977 could be explained because 'there was a volatile electorate who were no longer hung up on the old slogans and the old commitments and the old loyalties'. Given that, with 50.6 per cent of the vote, he had come close to securing the sort of vote achieved by Eamon de Valera in the 1938 general election (51.9 per cent; its best ever result), this was a bizarre assertion. He also made the false, if not farcical assertion that 'there is no question of arrogance creeping in anymore in Irish politics'.[31]

For all the talk of a new volatility or new approaches to politics, much satisfaction was still derived from the stoking of old enmities and divisions. For all his thoughtful reflections in private, as an orator of considerable prowess, John Kelly perfected the art of castigating Fianna Fáil at a host of party gatherings. He did not decry political partisanship, believing it was a 'good thing' for democracy; 'that there should be, on each side, a hard core of people committed with their hearts rather than with their heads'.[32] He suggested for Fianna Fáil, 'their gigantic edifice of jobbery, back-slapping and publicity-touting engages three-quarters of their attention'.[33] Kelly did himself no favours, however, with his hubris; by 1976 the government of which he was a part was being criticised for its intolerance of any kind of dissent and Kelly embodied this in referring to a plethora of protest groups who 'would be better off down on their knees'.[34] Tim Pat Coogan regarded the 1973–7 coalition as 'containing more liberals to the square inch than any of its successors' but it turned out to be, in his view, 'one of the most repressive administrations of the century',[35] an indication of the degree to which the Troubles infected the politics of the Irish Republic.

Not everyone was convinced of the depth of Kelly's political intellect, which is no surprise given his sometimes simplistic vituperation. As a member of the coalition government in 1975 he was portrayed as honest and intelligent, but he was also described as 'not an intellectual. His positive convictions and the trenchant expression of them spring from a mind that is untroubled by intellectual exploration, at least in the political area.'[36] Such a description may have been generated by the extent to which he was one of the chief denunciators of Fianna Fáil, often in a biting, sarcastic and humorous way, but his private papers also belie the above description afforded by *Hibernia*. There was depth to his feelings and thoughts about politics, and although these were not always of the utmost sophistication, by the standards of his time, he was advancing a critique that was often far-sighted and essentially accurate. Kelly was in effect suffering from a simple ailment; he was an intellectual in Irish politics and thus a rare breed. Michael D. Higgins was also to discover this; he once suggested being an intellectual in Irish politics was a greater disability than being sexually perverse.[37]

Bertie Ahern and others represented something different and were nakedly hostile to the idea of the intellectual in politics; Ahern thought Labour Party intellectuals like Conor Cruise O'Brien and David Thornley, a historian and broadcaster elected for the Labour Party in 1969 and 1973, would 'ruin the country ... I kept my appeal very simple ... I would turn up at Supermarkets, to flirt with the housewives and joke about football with the husbands'. For him, the oldest rule in politics was that 'the other lot are the opposition but you actually find your enemies on your own side ... from the moment I won in 1977 the only plotting I was doing was about how to hold on to the seat at the next election.'[38] On such sophisticated foundations was built the career of a three-time prime minister (1997–2008), the most electorally successful in modern Irish history after Eamon de Valera.

Charles Haughey, a prominent Fianna Fáil minister from the 1960s who was dismissed from the cabinet in 1970 as a result of the Arms Trial controversy and who plotted a comeback that succeeded gloriously (see pages 84–8), actively encouraged this anti-intellectual and anti-policy approach in order for the backbenchers to remain his fodder; he told Ahern 'don't worry about the old bullshit going on in Leinster House ... just concentrate on your constituency'.[39] Even those appointed to ministries were not encouraged to be adventurous; David Andrews recalls that when he took up the role of junior minister at the Department of Foreign Affairs in 1977 'I was given very little to do and my role was rather a vague one ... I was busy but not engaged.'[40]

The Labour Party was also struggling with internal tensions in the early 1970s, along with being determined that opposition 'will not put us in solitary confinement in the North Atlantic'. Newer TDs like Dr John O'Connell, a medical doctor first elected to the Dáil in 1965 for a Dublin constituency, were optimistic about its prospects on the cusp of the 1970s, despite the failure to win the hoped for number of seats in 1969 (Labour won only eighteen seats compared to twenty-three in 1965). O'Connell believed after 1969, 'now we had the energy and intellect at our disposal, now we should be able to make the Labour Party into a force in the political life of Ireland'. But factionalism very soon came to dominate, and party leader Brendan Corish was 'desperately trying to keep the party together'. There were tensions between urban and rural representatives, divisions over what line to take on the Northern Ireland question, on European integration and the issue of possible future coalition government.

While Labour 'ditched its go-it-alone strategy' in December 1970, neither it nor Fine Gael seemed greatly enthused: 'The two parties had looked like two giant pandas, snoozing in their respective bamboo patches, oblivious to each other's charms, while the political analysts waited impatiently for them to mate.'[41] The caution and coyness, however, were gradually overcome due to the desire to end Fianna Fáil's domination.

In relation to ongoing divisions in the Labour Party, Corish admitted frankly in 1972 that 'as leader I did my utmost to minimise personal differences and to remove tensions but it was obvious that I was not as successful as I had hoped to be'. He added the ominous warning: 'I am not prepared to lean over backwards in the future.'[42] He was also under pressure from the Socialist Labour Action Group, who insisted that, rather than working with the established parties, what was needed was 'a structure of socialist action groups preparing for people's power. No coalition with Tories North or South.'[43]

The annual report of the party for 1972–3 highlighted the need to deal with 'breaches of discipline' and 'the deterioration of the party's public image'. There were censures, for example, for Barry Desmond for 'publicly questioning party policy ... attacking David Thornley, a party colleague in public ... adversely affecting the party's fraternal relationship with the SDLP'. David Thornley was also censured for 'attacking Barry Desmond, a parliamentary colleague in public' and for 'making the question of party leadership a matter of public controversy'.[44] Was the party too centralised or too precious about internal debate? John O'Connell, regarded as something of a maverick, was moved to assert in May 1972, in a letter to John de Courcy Ireland, a leading maritime historian, founder member of CND in Ireland and secretary of the central branch of the Labour Party: 'I have found that the truth hurts, particularly when certain members of the Labour Party choose to regard my remarks as a personal indictment on them.'[45] In a letter the following year he told de Courcy Ireland: 'I mentioned to Brendan Corish the fact that your very valuable services were not availed of by the party. As you know, this is the great weakness of our party – that we have so many able and talented men, but the party does not seem to be able to avail of this expertise.'[46]

By the time the party was in coalition there were numerous resolutions at the annual conference about a new dilemma; the need to assert a separate identity within the coalition, with a suggestion from the mid Cork branch that the party 'has failed completely in its obligation to present its policy clearly'.[47] The following year there were more strident assertions about the party's identity being swallowed, this time from the Dublin Finglas Constituency Council, which insisted the party should withdraw from the coalition because it was 'not getting anywhere' with regard to health, education, mining prices, industrial democracy, capital gains tax, housing and Northern policy.[48] It was quite a roll call of failure.

Internally, the spleen continued to be vented in a personalised way; in October 1974, for example, de Courcy Ireland castigated party general secretary Brendan Halligan regarding a Labour Party conference in Galway, for the 'outrageous display of bad manners and ignorant contempt displayed by the party secretary, chairman and leader by 1. Their absence from the education debate and 2. Their failure to acknowledge the Portuguese victory over fascism'.[49] Clearly, tending to domestic socialist duties while also displaying international solidarity was an exhausting and fraught pursuit. Halligan replied the following month to suggest 'people who are asked to sit on a platform for 7 hours continually do require the shortest of breaks from time to time'. There were further tetchy exchanges which Halligan eventually sought to bring to an end; yet again in the Labour Party, it had got personal: 'I see no point in continuing correspondence in what has obviously become an issue of personality.'[50]

The attitude of the Liaison Committee of the Left in the Labour Party was also scathing about what it regarded as the abandonment of core socialist principles; lamenting the electoral mantra and promise of 1969 – 'the seventies will be socialist' – by 1974 it noted mournfully: 'so much for the socialist seventies'. It decried the 'purges' that had taken place in the party and various resignations, particularly in Dublin; in relation to Dublin South East constituency, for example, it observed that 'approximately 90 per cent of those who participated in the 1969 campaign had either resigned or had been expelled by 1973. Amongst those effectively purged was the outgoing deputy Dr Noel Browne ... previous purges have been disastrous. Will the leadership never learn?' It reserved criticism also for 'the Sellotape socialists who believe that society can be reformed through piece-meal reform in the capitalist system'.[51]

James Connolly, the labour movement leader executed for his part in the 1916 Rising, remained an iconic figure for many on the left, but just what did his legacy mean in practical terms by the 1970s? This was an issue debated between de Courcy Ireland and David Thornley in 1973. Thornley had called for a discussion on what was meant by 'the principles of James Connolly', a phrase that was, according to de Courcy Ireland, 'perpetually mouthed in and around the Labour movement ... Connolly was such a big figure and ... traditionally in Ireland we tend to worship big figures and expect them, alive or dead, to solve our problems for us'. In his view this was too uncritical an approach; it was necessary to subject Connolly to a more critical examination, which would include 'learning from any errors he made'.[52]

De Courcy Ireland's main concern was the danger of 'an unthinking chauvinism' and the historic concentration of labour action into military activity, which 'left behind the contest between heroic shooters and shoddy politicians that much of the country still believes in'. Neither did he believe there were suitable forums available in which to debate these issues: 'What I find irritating is that we have no labour journal in which such matters of theoretical importance with practical implications can be argued out. As it is one can only use the *Irish Times* and provide the spectacle of the "left" hopelessly sinking into civil war when it ought to be united'.[53] (Two years later, *Saothar*, the journal of the Irish Labour History society, was established.)

Some supporters of Fine Gael had queried whether a government with itself and the Labour Party would work and expressed doubts about the durability of a coalition between a party 'which retains some remnants of liberalism and another which is socialist in name'.[54] FitzGerald, however, was more than comfortable with the idea and felt moved to respond to one writer who marvelled at his transformation from a politician who was considered conservative: 'I have moved a good deal to the left since the days when you knew me.'[55]

Dissent within the Labour movement remained; David Thornley, for example, crossed swords with the party hierarchy over his Republican stance on the Northern Ireland question (see Part II); after he lost the party whip he demanded it back in a letter to Séamus Scally, the general secretary of the party, insisting that he had 'no regrets over what I did ...

my actions were dictated by emotional sincerity, whether right or wrong'. If the whip was not restored, he threatened to stand in the next election as an independent candidate in order to be elected 'or ensure that no Labour deputy is elected at all ... this is not an attempt at blackmail. It is simply the impression of a professional political scientist.'[56] Dissent about policy in other areas ultimately manifested itself in the emergence of a new Socialist Labour Party (SLP) in 1977, led by veteran radical Noel Browne, who had achieved fame and notoriety as a young health minister with the short-lived Clann na Poblachta Party in the coalition government of 1948–51, which he resigned from after medical, church and political opposition to his proposals for greater state involvement in the health of mothers and children. He held office in four political parties, was elected twice as an independent TD and senator over thirty-five years of political activism. He inspired great loyalty, but also had an exceptional capacity to alienate, and found great satisfaction 'in identifying and denouncing enemies, even if this obstructed his journey towards a desired objective'.[57]

Some optimistic commentators suggested the new SLP had the 'potential to spawn a dynamic left-wing force'. Journalist Gene Kerrigan observed that the various convulsions on the left were indicative of the idea that, throughout the decade so far, the left 'has had to run very fast just to stand still'. Despite the persistence of unemployment, reduction in (some) living standards and 'a wave of political repression' which should have offered the left opportunities for mobilisation, 'it didn't bring in the recruits'.[58] By the spring of 1978 the new socialist party was estimated to have 500 members, one-third of which were ex Labour Party members; but it was questioned whether it would offer a choice to what was referred to as 'that exploding youth'. This was delightful exaggeration, given that it was estimated that Fianna Fáil had captured a massive 62 per cent share of the youth vote in 1977.[59] One journalist suggested that, with Browne, 'the personal arrogance is countered by an organisational weakness'.[60] Journalist Vincent Browne suggested his namesake had probably 'damaged the cause of progressive politics in Ireland by his failure/refusal to work within a party structure' but that in spite of this 'it must be acknowledged that almost alone among Dáil members over three decades he has spoken out on behalf of the poor and deprived in Irish society. He has been virtually the only voice of radical dissent in Irish politics.'[61]

Noel Browne had found plenty of opportunities to decry the Labour Party once they were in coalition; one of his respondents was David

Thornley ('more in sorrow than anger that I engage in another polemic with Noel Browne' he commented ruefully in 1975). He claimed Browne had 'begged' him to help him get a Senate seat in 1973 and charged him with frequently spoiling his arguments through his reliance on personal abuse. He proceeded to demolish Browne over his impressive personal catalogue of political somersaults (Browne was, after all, the same man who had described Seán Lemass as the greatest socialist since James Connolly) but he agreed with him on one issue, regarding the Labour Party's role in government: 'of course Labour took the wrong ministers: a Marxist to control prices and an ex-trade union official to tell the unions where to get off' (Justin Keating as Minister for Industry and Commerce and Michael O'Leary as Minister for Labour).[62]

Michael O'Leary, who served as Minister for Labour from 1973–7 was a charismatic Cork man who had become liaison officer between the ITGWU and the Labour Party and won a seat for the party in Dublin North Central in 1965. A powerful speaker, unafraid to proclaim his socialism in the early days, he was one of the party's first graduate TDs, seen as 'the young dauphin of the party' and representative of the new breed of Labour representatives.[63] Like others, he reversed his initial anti-coalition stance, but allegedly commented, in reference to the party's 1969 slogan, 'the seventies will be socialist', that by the time there was a Labour-dominated government 'the socialists will be seventy'. Seen as ambitious but somewhat undisciplined and unreliable, 'his bonhomie coexisted with a strong desire for privacy. He was a light drinker, disliked gambling and spoke with contempt of "lounge-bar society"; this fostered a certain distance between him and the party's more clubbable members. More ominously he was also seen as mercurial and had a low boredom threshold.'[64] As Minister for Labour he also had responsibility for women's affairs and was associated with significant legislation on employment conditions and rights, though most of these were required by EEC directives. In 1976 he negotiated the National Wage Agreement with unions and employers.

Regarding the socialism or otherwise of the Labour Party, Frank Cluskey, junior minister with responsibility for social welfare in the coalition government, was depicted as someone who was the closest the party had to a 'genuine urban working class representative' as most Irish Labour Party deputies 'could scarcely be described as horny-handed sons of toil'.[65] Fianna Fáil TD David Andrews enthused that 'probably no one who ever became a TD had as much compassion for the less well off as Frank

Cluskey'.[66] First elected to the Dáil in 1965, Cluskey was gruff, witty and direct in his colourful speech and had an electoral base in Dublin's south inner city; he had been active in local politics in the 1960s in relation to the housing crisis and had served briefly as the city's Lord Mayor.

Cluskey's achievements highlighted the degree to which some of the socialist criticism of Labour in government was unfair; he implemented significant reforms in social benefit, even though this often involved facing a hostile cabinet. He introduced allowances for deserted wives, unmarried mothers, prisoners' wives, and single women caring for aged relatives and introduced payment of the children's allowance directly to mothers, which was regarded as radical for this era, and extended the allowance to age eighteen for children not employed. He also eased means tests, reduced the qualifying age for the old-age pension by four years to sixty-six, established the Combat Poverty Agency, and introduced Pay Related Social Insurance (PRSI).[67]

James Tully, the Labour Minister for Local Government, hardly endeared himself to the wealthy when in a radio interview in 1974 he said 'to hell with the rich'. Tully first came to prominence in the late 1940s as an organiser of rural workers and was regarded by *Hibernia* magazine as a complex and ambivalent character and it was suggested he was a 'tough, down-to-earth man of the people whose periodic abrasiveness is tempered by a deep layer of sound commonsense'. By the time of his death in 1992 'no other minister for local government had exceeded his house-building record of 25,000 a year for the four years of his tenure (1973–7). Moreover, the quality of local-authority housing was greatly improved during his term of office.'[68] But it was also pointed out that he was a supporter of mining speculators and 'ranchers' in County Meath and his son was secretary of the Tara Mines company (see Part VI).[69]

John Horgan, who represented South County Dublin from 1977 to 1981, had only joined the Labour Party in 1975 but was regarded 'as perhaps the only ideologue in the Labour parliamentary party from 1977 to 1981, arguing persuasively for a redistribution of wealth without this redistribution being contingent on future economic growth'.[70] On the same subject, young Dublin Labour Party TD Ruairí Quinn in a debate on the 1978 budget, was regarded as conservative in asserting, 'I accept that the primary task confronting this community is the creation of wealth. I reject rather traditionalist attitudes which would suggest that the redistribution of existing wealth would satisfy the aspirations of even 30 per cent or 40 per cent of the population, let alone the majority of the population. The wealth is not there.'[71]

As party leader, the unassuming Brendan Corish was regarded as so quiet in government, even after a few years, that 'he appears to have lost interest'. A contributor to *Hibernia* suggested 'only the most determined of political masochists would willingly devote fourteen years of his life to directing that motley company of clowns and prima donnas known as the Irish labour party', but credited him with transforming a group of essentially independent TDs into a modern party.[72] He had been in the Dáil since 1945 and leader of the party since 1960 and had served as a parliamentary secretary in coalition governments of the 1940s and 1950s but had taken an anti-coalition stance in the 1960s, and during the 1969 election had ambitiously and imaginatively positioned Labour as sponsors of a 'New Republic' in the 1970s, though, as seen earlier, the election result was disappointing. For his critics, Corish in his capacity as leader was 'too weak-kneed and weak-minded to administer captaincy and discipline',[73] but it has been pointed out that for much of the period 1973–7 he was 'indisposed' and 'was unable to make any significant impact'.[74]

– SIX –

LEADERS AND ASPIRANTS

There was also interest in the leadership qualities and personalities of the two men who held the office of Taoiseach in the 1970s, Jack Lynch and Liam Cosgrave. Civil servant Richard Stokes, in the Department of the Taoiseach, regarded them both as 'lovely' and 'wonderful to work for'.[1] Neither employed an ebullient or forthcoming communication style. Considerable preparation was done by civil servants like Stokes to ready them for media engagements. In May 1977, shortly before he left office, an introduction to an interview with Cosgrave in *Le Monde* newspaper observed: 'With his trim figure, his close-cropped moustache and eyebrows and ruddy complexion Cosgrave ... has kept the appearance of that officer he was and the horseman he still is. But it would be hard to imagine a country where there is less of a personality cult. Mr Cosgrave leads a team and he always speaks in the name of that team.'[2]

A qualified barrister and a TD since 1943, when he was elected at the age of twenty-three, he had served as Minister for External Affairs in the coalition government of 1954–7 (during his time as minister Ireland joined the United Nations) and he had taken over the leadership of the party in 1965. It was accurate to portray him as a chairman and team leader; he was also someone whose father, William T. Cosgrave, had held the title President of the Executive Council (in effect, prime minister) in the 1920s as leader of the first government of the Free State and this was a factor that was central, not only to Liam Cosgrave's appeal but also to his political identity, and it was recognised as such by many. When he was elected, the editor of the *Evening Herald* newspaper, Brian Quinn, wrote to congratulate him on his 'tryst with destiny' and gushed: 'I am delighted that a Cosgrave is, once again, in charge of Ireland. I was in Fine Gael headquarters in Parnell Square in 1932 with your esteemed father and my own father.'[3] In that context, comments on Cosgrave centred around the idea that because he was the son of William T. he would have a 'dogged devotion to the preservation of the institutions of the state'.[4] He was also dogged about the coalition sticking together. He was quiet, concerned for those he worked with and believed in preserving his privacy and 'a man of such few words that his opponents in the Dáil often found it difficult to get to grips with him'.[5]

He was also widely perceived as a delegator,[6] which suited individual ministers like Garret FitzGerald, who were able to control significant aspects of policy without interference. Fianna Fáil found 'the freedom that Liam Cosgrave apparently gave his ministers difficult to comprehend. Any minister could talk on any subject and frequently did.'[7] He was encouraged when dealing with certain media questions to give them short shrift; *Irish Times* journalist Geraldine Kennedy was regarded as encroaching on his privacy when she sent in her proposed questions: 'Under the question "home help" perhaps you could outline the type of help in employment e.g.: children's nanny, au pair, 2 maids and so on ... I would also appreciate if the value of [your] house could be mentioned.' Cosgrave was having none of it and refused to furnish such details.[8]

Cosgrave was not without humour, but it was often a hidden humour; after a profile of him by journalist Cathal O'Shannon on the RTÉ programme *The Tuesday Report* was broadcast, a member of the public wrote to him to wish him luck in the forthcoming election and commented that a number of people had said to her, 'Well, I never knew Liam Cosgrave was so witty.' Conor Cruise O'Brien also noted that Cosgrave had 'a curious explosive laugh, seldom heard'; and those who met him in old age (he was ninety-two in 2012) remarked on his 'totally different private persona; he has a wonderful sense of humour and loves a good story or amusing tale'.[9] For others, he was unimpressive and dull, if not dim: 'a trim little man with a toothbrush moustache and a toothbrush mind was no new broom', according to Tim Pat Coogan, who wondered if it was true that he had once suggested 'the Jews and the Muslims should settle their differences in a Christian manner'.[10]

For others, there were simply two things that summed up Cosgrave: 'fortitude and taciturnity'.[11] He was also deeply committed to his religious beliefs. In 1974, he made the notorious decision to vote against his own government's legislation on the limited legalisation of contraception, which was not, according to Conor Cruise O'Brien, really the political bombshell it is sometimes presented as; he had 'not let anyone down or failed to honour any commitment. He had insisted on a free vote and then made use of the freedom on which he had insisted'. According to a cleaner in Leinster House, 'what else would you expect him to do? Sure wasn't he an altar boy until he was 24?'[12] David Thornley castigated him for the decision, believing he had behaved 'like an idiot'.[13]

In contrast to the portrait of the government he led as lacking cohesion, Conor Cruise O'Brien suggested Cosgrave and Brendan Corish, the leader of the Labour Party, worked well together, as both 'were politically cautious, temperamentally equable and personally considerate'. As president in 1973, Eamon de Valera invited the new government to dinner and gave them advice, suggesting that coalition government could only work if members were guided by a feeling of 'personal loyalty to their Taoiseach'.[14] This may have been sound advice, but seems ironic coming from someone who spoke out against coalition as a government option throughout his career, as resting on 'rickety foundations', and he had never presided over one.[15]

Cosgrave's personal papers and correspondence in the National Archives of Ireland mostly contain incoming letters, but they provide clues as to his priorities and traits and the ministers who corresponded most frequently with him, including the prolific Conor Cruise O'Brien, underlining the extent to which he had a good relationship with his Labour Party colleagues. O'Brien wrote to him after the general election defeat of 1977 suggesting they had been members of a government 'which will, I believe be acknowledged in the perspective of history to have served this country well'.[16] It was a government which had made its case for re-election on the basis that 100,000 new houses had been built under its watch from 1973 to 1977 ('that is one in every eight houses in the country'), and that it had increased the money available for social welfare from £151 million to £520 million, and had increased expenditure on defence with more than 52,500 joint Gardaí/army checkpoints in its four years in power.[17] Cosgrave had to commiserate with his Minister for Justice Patrick Cooney, however, when he lost his seat: 'unfortunate that the reward is not commensurate with your personal efforts and achievements'.[18]

As revealed in his voting against his own government's contraceptive legislation, Cosgrave was rigid in sticking to his beliefs, despite Conor Cruise O'Brien's appeal to him that 'the spectacle of government ministers going into different lobbies on this question may present an image of our government as divided and ineffective – an impression which might long outlast the particular instance in which it arose ... we are at the moment giving the impression of irresolution and division'.[19] The same month, government press secretary Muiris Mac Conghail – who was impressed with Cosgrave's 'common sense approach to problems' – had to apply some pressure to him through Cruise O'Brien, as political correspondents believed the government was performing badly: 'I personally feel that I have come to a difficult point in the information area where I have to go on the defensive in relation to government policy in certain areas.'[20] Conor Cruise O'Brien was often trying to put words into his mouth, with mixed results.[21] But the softer side and kindness of Cosgrave was evident in his correspondence with the troublesome Labour TD David Thornley, who shared internal Labour Party correspondence with him. Although at odds over contraception, Thornley praised him privately as 'a gentleman' and for the courtesy he had shown him; Cosgrave agreed to act as a referee for him when he moved to a new flat.[22]

Cosgrave also received regular personal letters and health updates from his Minister for Defence, who sometimes wrote to him from his bed.[23] Cosgrave expressed a preference for short letters and in relation to a detailed memorandum on Northern Ireland after he had left office, he expressed the view that it was 'too long and deals with too many matters. It contains far too many statistics.'[24]

In the context of planning for the 1977 general election, Alexis FitzGerald, a prominent solicitor who had been elected to the Senate in 1969, advised a succession of senior Fine Gael figures and was married to John A. Costello's daughter, had suggested a theme of 'Support the pilots who weathered the storm' and insisted that 'throughout 1977 everyone must be in line and everything done to avoid deviance which can start to run again after we have won the election'.[25] Following the general election defeat in June 1977, Oliver J. Flanagan, veteran Fine Gael TD who had served as Minister for Defence from 1976–7, was furious and wrote to Cosgrave, adamant that 'this country does not deserve a man of your sincerity and integrity. There appears to be no place in Irish politics for honesty. I am sorry to have to say this. Those of us in public life often neglect our homes and children when we should be with them instead of rendering service to an ungrateful people.'[26] Historian Maurice O'Connell also wrote to him after the defeat: 'It was discouraging to see so many people lacking the discrimination to realise that the high prices and inflation were international and that a change of government is not the answer.'[27]

Cosgrave was also admired for his 'non-triumphalism' while in government and for having 'genuine religious convictions'. Cosgrave resigned the leadership after the election loss to be succeeded by Garret FitzGerald; Cosgrave shared the regret of one correspondent, Judge Frank Roe, who was sorry 'Peter Barry did not go on with his challenge for the leadership and get it'; Roe also criticised the Fine Gael members of the legal profession who lost their seats 'and walked away'.[28] These were not new complaints about the party; similar comments had been made in 1951 and 1957 after Fine Gael suffered defeat coming out of coalition government.

If there was an underlying political philosophy that motivated Cosgrave it was not something that he was going to wax lyrical about, or indeed wax about at all; in 1979 he came as close as he ever got to elaborating, by simply stating in a private letter that 'there have been key significant changes in our time – not all for the better, but we have to accommodate ourselves to them'.[29] He left politics in 1981, widely regarded as a decent, honest, steadying, if conservative influence; on his retirement, one supporter insisted 'the number of men of integrity and of your calibre in the Dáil are as scarce as roses in December and a lot of them would be rogues if the country was rich'.[30] There was something prescient in that observation.

Because of his earlier career as a diplomat and UN representative in Katanga, Conor Cruise O'Brien was someone with an international profile and this was something also quickly developed by another academic in politics, Garret FitzGerald, helped by his role as Minister for Foreign Affairs from 1973–7 and subsequently his leadership of Fine Gael after Cosgrave stepped down in the aftermath of the Fianna Fáil victory in 1977. Cosgrave was praised for his 'dignified and generous' retirement and his endorsement of FitzGerald, someone he had not had a close or warm relationship with, because the endorsement was offered 'in a surprisingly forthcoming manner'.[31]

FitzGerald had served many different constituencies from the late 1940s in his roles as freelance journalist, manager at the state airline Aer Lingus, economics lecturer at UCD, Fine Gael senator and TD. His background (his father Desmond had been prominent in Sinn Féin during the

War of Independence and served as Minister for External Affairs in the 1920s, and his mother was from a Northern Protestant background) left him with a commitment to reconciliation and tolerance, reflected in his 1972 book *Towards a New Ireland*, in which he argued that 'the concept of a mono-cultural state simply does not fit the Irish case'. He further maintained an 'authoritarian Southern Catholic State' was an obstacle to be overcome if Ireland was to be united to embrace Northern Protestants.[32] The initiatives he took in this regard over the course of his career suggested, according to historian Roy Foster, that the 'future was with him'.[33] FitzGerald also had a penchant for occasionally radical rhetoric about social justice and redistribution.

Given his profession as a university economics lecturer and his contribution to economic debate as opposition finance spokesman, it had been widely expected that FitzGerald would be Cosgrave's Minister for Finance in 1973. One of his academic colleagues in UCD mentioned: 'I am one of the many thousands who has "appointed you" Minister for Finance'. But given his father's service, his role as Minister for Foreign Affairs gave him particular pleasure. After accepting the post he wrote to Ernest Blythe, another minister in the 1920s: 'You, more than most, will appreciate what it means to me to find myself in the same position as my father half a century ago. I have his photograph, as Minister for External Affairs, on my desk.'[34]

Early in 1978, a French MP visiting Ireland went as far as to describe FitzGerald as 'the most formidable public figure in Europe'. The difficulty, as journalist Vincent Browne saw it in 1978, was that despite such kudos, and his considerable talents, whether 'Fine Gael can be rescued in the foreseeable future from protracted oblivion is very much open to doubt ... there must be doubt about his ability to retain the traditional Fine Gael support.'[35]

But there was great confidence within the party about his communications skills. From the middle of the 1960s and into the early 1970s, FitzGerald made much of his television appearances and was admired publicly and privately for them; letters praising his 'superb' performances were frequently sent to him.[36] As opposition spokesman on finance, he was regarded as having wiped the floor with Fianna Fáil's Minister for Finance George Colley during the 1973 general election campaign in a decisive television debate.

The importance of the personality cult in Irish politics was reflected in the popularity of Jack Lynch, even though to his contemporary critics, especially in *Hibernia* magazine, it appeared he had few political achievements to his credit and spent most of the early 1970s reeling from the convulsions within his own party. Lynch, a renowned hurler for his native Cork in his younger years and thus an icon of the Gaelic Athletic Association (GAA – see Part III), had left a civil service job in 1946 and was elected to the Dáil in 1948. Highly regarded by Seán Lemass, he served as a government minister in the 1950s and 1960s in the portfolios of Education, Industry and Commerce, and Finance, before succeeding Lemass as leader of Fianna Fáil in 1966, a job he was not keen to take, but did so at the behest of Lemass to prevent a divisive contest between Charles Haughey and George Colley, the Dublin TD who had been an impressive Minister for Education in the 1960s. He defeated Colley easily in the party vote after Haughey withdrew, but without a significant power base in the party and because he was not from a traditional Fianna Fáil background or dynasty like some of his colleagues, he was vulnerable to resentful rivals' machinations.

In August 1972 it was suggested that 'the achievements of Mr Lynch's premiership can almost all be counted in terms of his own political survival'.[37] The following year, questions were still being raised about just what he represented politically. Survival in office during a tumultuous few years may have been regarded as no mean personal feat, but 'where are the marks of his leadership? By what contribution will he be remembered? What positive and significant intervention has he made to date in the whole crisis? He has talked continuously of a New Ireland, but where is his blueprint?'[38]

After defeat in the 1973 election, Fianna Fáil seemed to believe it 'was not required to do very much in opposition' and Lynch had a hands-off approach which, to his critics, was born of an 'intellectual laziness' that 'got him into trouble'. He rarely initiated and was prone to allow matters 'to progress a certain distance without troubling himself to look into them', but he also had 'cuteness'. Others depicted this as 'the steel behind the friendly manner', or a combination of 'skill and steeliness'.[39] On the basis of letters sent to him by members of the public, he was widely regarded as a gentleman and a reassuring and impressive presence; the words 'firm', 'calm' and 'dignified' were frequently used.[40]

According to Albert Reynolds, first elected a TD for the party in Longford in 1977 and a future party leader, Lynch had told him after his election, 'Don't give any commitments in this business.'[41] Vincent Browne, one of the founders of the current affairs magazine *Magill*, the first issue of which appeared in October 1977, referred to the 'artful ambiguities' of Lynch, suggesting that 'Lynch speak' was 'a most subtle and baffling political language'.[42] But there were generous tributes to Lynch also; a sense that he had acted with decisiveness from 1977 to 1979, and credit offered for the idea that 'he gave a sense of serenity to Southern Ireland in the midst of bloodshed and violence in Northern Ireland and perhaps it is for this he will be best remembered'.[43] As his biographer Dermot Keogh saw it, he was difficult to unravel because of his 'self-contained' world, but Keogh maintained that his political pluralism was a strength that enabled him to 'stand out against the forces of atavism that risked returning the country to a state of war' and that he had an abundance of integrity and probity.[44] Likewise, Roy Foster heaps praise (perhaps too much – see Part II) on Lynch, in the context of his 'sane and careful' response to the Northern crisis, which stood in contrast to the machinations of Haughey and Blaney (see Part II) and 'time warped Irish-Americans'.[45]

But Tim Pat Coogan regarded Lynch, as 'a diffident Cork man with all the charm, politeness, shyness and slyness of his native county'. He was in a lot of pain with his Achilles heel 'which he tended to dull with the aid of Paddy Whiskey'. When in the mood to imbibe, he was fond of saying 'let's see if we can get below Thurles', a reference to the map of Ireland on the bottle.[46] Well known writer, historian and commentator Ulick O'Connor recorded that in relation to the sacking of the RTÉ Authority in 1972 over its broadcasting of the opinions of the IRA, when chided about the implications it had regarding his commitment to free speech, Lynch 'looks at me with a grin: "Fuck them", he says', an anecdote that suggests the description of him as a 'man without malice' may be overly kind.[47] Lynch was wry about the impression he created on television: 'I don't think the TV cameras flatter me unduly but I don't feel as badly as they make me look.' He also asserted that 'there are easier ways of making a living than in politics'.[48]

Others were contemptuous of the fact that Lynch had come into politics as a result of his popularity as a GAA player. Journalist John Waters recalled how his father 'did not regard Lynch as a proper politician. My father called him "baby face"'.[49] According to the party's press secretary Frank Dunlop, within the febrile atmosphere of the party, his critics even reduced themselves to privately using his childlessness as a stick with which to beat him.[50]

Lynch could bristle at directives; his response to clerical pressure was a case in point. Allegedly, when Cardinal Conway told a colleague to tell Lynch 'to keep his hands off our schools', he responded by making funds available for the Dalkey School Project, a multi-denominational educational initiative, and 'he never seemed to pay much attention to the Bishop's statements'.[51] But in relation to his own party, he was less effective; he did nothing to 'harness or direct the energies of his expanded parliamentary party' after the 1977 general election. Séamus Brennan's notes on how this election might be won included an emphasis on youth ('youth and Fianna Fáil – a great future together').[52] But Lynch did not engage with the new young backbenchers, Bertie Ahern recalling that 'a lot of us felt he didn't even know which constituency we were in'.[53] As the leadership began to slip away from him in 1979 he also castigated the political journalists who covered his American trip and 'virtually accused them of treasonous behaviour'.[54] But in contrast to the satirical pillorying of the coalition government, *Hall's Pictorial Weekly*'s portrayal of Lynch did him no harm; indeed, the opposite: he was presented as 'a benign, pipe-smoking homely character who used to indulge in fireside chats with his wife Maureen'.[55]

Lynch's personal papers in the National Archives of Ireland amplify some of these aspects of his character and leadership and the affection in which he was held. After he lost the general election of 1973 he received a huge volume of correspondence, some of which praised the 'courteous and dignified manner in which you acted when faced with the prospect of defeat' and emphasised the regret that he was out of office even on the part of those 'who rarely speak of politics'. Another view was that he was 'far too much of a gentleman to be in politics'.[56] T. K. Whitaker, the senior public servant, now governor of the Central Bank and one of his trusted confidants, sent him a personal note as 'I have always had a special admiration and affection for you as a most likeable person with a gentle and reasonable nature, a warm heart, real patriotism and a quiet strength of purpose. You can look back on your seven years as Taoiseach as a period not only of great material and social progress but also of rational evolution of Irish activities, particularly towards the problem of Northern Ireland. Your part in all this was outstanding and will be remembered ... you gave all to duty ... rebuild your reserves of energy.'[57] Whitaker had played a key role in explicitly advising him on Northern Ireland in the late 1960s and early 1970s, drafting speeches and memoranda and position papers.[58]

There was a general consensus that Lynch had earned a rest with his wife Maureen, who saw her role simply to make things 'reasonably comfortable for Jack'; she was a shy woman who hated cameras. She maintained she did not have time to read books and when asked to contribute to a book of recipes refused as 'she has no particular interest in cooking' and as 'she lives in a small suburban house in Rathgar it is not conducive to public viewing'.[59] One woman wrote to Lynch in 1972 wishing 'sometimes you would bring her more into the picture, as [US president] Nixon does with Pat, but there's our Irishmen'.[60] Maureen would not discuss current affairs as she 'is not herself in public life except in her role as wife of the Taoiseach which is most demanding and exacting'.[61] Notwithstanding, she was praised by T. K. Whitaker in 1979 for a letter 'carving up' John Healy,[62] the author of the political column in the *Irish Times* that frequently championed Charles Haughey and undermined Lynch.

The Lynches had a modest lifestyle, though Lynch treated himself to a yacht after the general election defeat of 1973, which he bought for £700, after a discount of 10 per cent. He estimated his house in 1973 to be worth 'at least £10,000' and in correspondence with insurers mentioned: 'I have some particular items, mainly silver, which are reasonably valuable', which presumably included the silverware his sporting prowess had brought in his younger days.[63]

His papers also highlight, however, his weaknesses and apathies as a political leader, underlined in the draft of an interview he did with communications consultant Tom Savage: 'I don't push myself. I don't know whether it's a good trait or a bad. I try to engage and involve all the people around me. I'm not a hard task master [because] I know myself my own limitations.'[64] Arguably, this was a good summary of his career; he was personally decent but lazy and not nearly as assertive or energised enough to be considered a good leader. His endorsement of the 1977 giveaway general election manifesto promising abolition of rates, motor taxation and wealth tax and provision of lump-sum subsidies for first time house buyers, was unwise, as its lavishness created public expectations not conducive to wage restraint and continued a situation where 'the Irish continued to insist on paying themselves far more than they were earning'.[65] Lynch noted with smugness at a FF National Executive meeting in May 1977 the favourable public response to the manifesto and 'the seemingly panic reaction of the coalition to same', but at what cost?[66]

There were those who were eyeing up the leadership of Fianna Fáil with considerable hunger, none more so than Charles Haughey, who had been brought back on to the front bench by Lynch in 1975 and became Minister for Health and Social Welfare when Fianna Fáil returned to power, a ministry which political insiders suggested bored him, but he was in any case 'biding his time'.[67] The convulsions of the Arms Trial had defined the public perception of Haughey for both good and ill; or as John Waters wrote in relation to his father, 'the Arms Trial both queered the pitch and galvanised his feelings for Haughey'.[68] Haughey's maiden Dáil speech in 1957 had focused on wealth creation and social justice, and during the 1960s he remained interested in these, providing free travel for pensioners against the wishes of T. K. Whitaker, the secretary of the Department of Finance. As Minister for Justice, he was also associated with the Succession Act (which had been pioneered by Brian Lenihan), safeguarding widows at a time when there was a 50 per cent intestacy rate; he left an admirable legislative record behind him in this ministry and was also regarded as an impressive Minister for Finance until his sacking in 1970.

Tim Pat Coogan recalls that, when he first met Haughey, 'I was both impressed and repelled by him.'[69] While he did acknowledge that there was some speculation as to his level of ability, Labour activist and journalist Proinsias Mac Aonghusa suggested in 1970, 'Haughey has a good second rate mind and is overall, a good second rater. But brains being in such short supply in the 17th and 18th Dálaí, many believed him to be a bit of a genius.'[70]

He was also keen to embrace any opportunity for exposure as long as he could control the presentation; before an appearance on the RTÉ programme *Seven Days* his aide wanted assurance that RTÉ 'would treat the boss fairly'. Following the programme, the same person complained about the lighting in the studio because 'it made Charlie's eyes look hooded'; the editor, Sheamus Smith, pointed out that 'Charlie's eyes *were* hooded'.[71] It was observed early in 1979 that he was 'the only member of the government to twice break the unofficial ministerial boycott of RTÉ television's *Frontline* programme'.[72] It was also noted that he had employed the services of a professional writer 'to enhance the impact and quotability of his speeches'.[73] For some contemporary journalists, Haughey's appeal lay in an 'inexplicable charisma'.[74]

Rumours about the shadowy sources of his personal wealth and ostentation had been apparent since the 1960s and the accountancy practice he was involved in had provided tax avoidance advice to the wealthy, 'but his way of life soon outpaced even that of the richest of his clients' as he amassed a property portfolio including a Georgian house in 1969 on twenty-five acres that was re-zoned while he was Minister for Finance and sold at a massive profit after he had, as minister, protected such profits from windfall tax. He went on to amass even more and had an overdraft of £244,000 in 1971. He simply ignored bank pleas for payment plans and by the end of 1979 his overdraft topped £1 million; he simply 'never lost his sense of entitlement' and his 'model of grandeur was an odd combination of Napoleonic enigma, Ascendancy hauteur, Gaelic chieftain and Tammany boss.'[75] In 2006, a tribunal report concluded that he took payments approximating to more than 11 million euros between 1979 and 1996; in the words of the report, the very incidence and scale of payments to Haughey, 'particularly during difficult economic times nationally, can only be said to have devalued the quality of a national democracy'.[76] His return to prominence in Fianna Fáil in the mid 1970s gave him full rein to indulge in the 'manipulation of power'.[77]

It helped Haughey that mid way through the coalition's term of office, Lynch was being referred to by *Hibernia* magazine as the 'limping leader of a lame opposition',[78] and this was reflected in some caustic observations from his own party members in Meath, for example, who insisted early in 1977 that 'Fianna Fáil are the inheritors of a radical tradition ... we must convince people to put us back in government not for the good of any one section but for the good of the whole community'.[79] The National Executive of the party also received resolutions decrying the 'unsatisfactory performance of FF as an opposition' in the Senate.[80] The party was also characterised as 'very disorganised in Drogheda' and in 1978 Séamus Brennan was reminded, again, 'the grassroots are just as important as the top'.[81] A party member in Tipperary South insisted that 'a party we selflessly built up under great sacrifice [is now a] shambles'.[82] It was those grassroots that Haughey had assiduously charmed and courted while in the wilderness.

After the general election of 1977, Haughey was sitting comfortably and contemplating covetously; in retrospect he was regarded as the 'real winner' of that election rather than Lynch. He had 'openly derided' Fianna Fáil's giveaway manifesto, which calls into question the assertion of Conor Cruise O'Brien that the manifesto 'bore all the marks of the mind of C. J. Haughey'[83] – O'Brien was probably blinded by his personal hatred of Haughey. In the election's aftermath, Haughey 'surprised questioners by gleefully welcoming the advent of the party's flood of new backbenchers: "They're all mine!"'[84] He was, according to Frank Dunlop, busy 'manipulating the vanity of those on the lower rungs of the party'.[85] There were stirrings within Fianna Fáil in the aftermath of the European elections in June 1979; the party's share of the vote had dropped from 50.6 per cent in the 1977 general election to 34.7 per cent in the European elections. Those who met in Leinster House in July 1979 were characterised as embarking on an act of 'semi-rebellion' and it marked the beginning of the end for Jack Lynch.[86]

One of his possible successors, Limerick TD Des O'Malley, who had been appointed Minister for Justice in 1970 and who served as Minister for Industry and Commerce in the late 1970s, seems to have been viewed in the mid 1970s as a peculiar kind of beast within Fianna Fáil. He was elected to the Dáil in 1968 after the sudden death of his uncle, Donogh O'Malley, famed as the Minister for Education who introduced free secondary education in 1967. Highly regarded and trusted by Jack Lynch, Des was not one to back slap or court popularity; he was regarded as having had the 'intelligence, the ambition and the stamina to make the national scene'. But, it was contended in *Hibernia* magazine, 'he has yet to prove that he can deliver the home pitch. Only when he has demonstrated that particular ability will the professionals in Fianna Fáil consider him seriously as possible future leader of the party.'[87] O'Malley supported George Colley over Haughey in 1979; Colley, seen by others as 'an honest but dull prospect',[88] had 'wanted to stay at one remove from everybody so that if successful he would be in a totally independent position when it came to appointing a cabinet. Lofty and laudable perhaps, but no contest for the opposition, who had no such scruples.'[89] Lynch's admirers saw him as standing in contrast to that culture, as someone who 'seemed the classical Fine Gael barrister who had strayed into Fianna Fáil and deserved to be forgiven for doing so'. In relation to himself and his wife Maureen, 'in the party and in government, they owed nobody any favours and asked for none for themselves. Those traits ran counter to the naked power ambitions of the party.'[90]

Such power ambitions were regarded by some as unworthy of the civil-war generation that was now almost completely departed from the political scene, including de Valera, who died in 1975 at the age of ninety-two. An estimated 200,000 people lined the streets of Dublin to pay their respects.[91] As journalist Frank Kahn recalled, 'those of us assigned to cover the obsequies witnessed a great outpouring of dignified grief by men and women, most of whom would never have had a personal attachment or link to "Dev". But they knew he had played no small part in all their lives and their country – and it was the end of an era.'[92] A special meeting of the National Executive of Fianna Fáil was convened to pay tribute; it stood 'in silent prayer' after Jack Lynch told the assembly that 'history will put Dev among the greatest Irishmen of all times'.[93] Three years later it was reported to the same Executive that a subcommittee that had been established to consider the erection of a de Valera memorial was 'now very depleted due to deaths'.[94]

But had the passing of the old guard also meant a change in culture in Fianna Fáil? Later in his career Garret FitzGerald, who had referred, controversially, to Haughey's 'flawed pedigree' after Haughey was elected leader of the party, was adamant that

> in the 1970s the surviving Fianna Fáil ex ministers were horrified at the prospect of the emergence of a very different kind of Fianna Fáil. It was only with great difficulty that Frank Aiken, [the veteran minister and member of the party's executive at its foundation] because of his concerns for the party and the country was prepared to stand for election in 1973. Later, President de Valera confided his deep fears for the country to a minister in whose integrity he had confidence. And when he was dying, Seán Mac Entee [a party stalwart from its foundation in 1926 to his retirement in 1969] asked to see me to confide his deep concern for the future of the state because of what had happened to his party, Fianna Fáil. The truth is that because of the widespread lack of a tradition of civic responsibility or a sense of civic morality, for which I fear the Catholic Church must bear some of the blame, the disappearance of the revolutionary generation from government in the 1960s removed the only barrier to the spread to politics of the socially inadequate value system that we, as a people, had inherited from our colonial past. Unhappily, that value system undervalued integrity in public life.[95]

The evidence from Jack Lynch's archive suggests he was thinking along the same lines; he made a speech marking the planned retirement of Frank Aiken at the end of May 1971 in which he pointedly said that 'as long as the party continues to attract to it young people – men of the same calibre as the founders of Fianna Fáil – we need have no fear for the future'.[96] Lynch's personal papers contain ledgers outlining constituency issues and requests – 'home assistance', 'military service pension', 'suitable employment', 'planning permission' – but he was also careful to point out in relation to requests for assistance with employment that 'as these appointments are made on a competitive basis there is nothing he can do to help. The family's political views would not, of course, be taken into consideration in a matter like this.'[97]

In 1976 he received an extraordinary letter from hotelier Dermot Ryan encouraging him to fight off challenges internally within Fianna Fáil ('ego is not always a bad thing. You never had enough ego') and offering him £5,000 'utterly without obligation or expectation of any sort' towards any campaign to maintain his leadership. Lynch was furious: 'I do not accept your assertion that I am at a crossroads. There is no personal struggle within my heart and soul affecting my position in politics ... if retaining the leadership depended on financial support rather than on the loyal support of the vast majority of members of the party and the organisation, then I would not be leader.'[98]

In relation to the succession, it was Haughey who prevailed. In December 1979 Lynch responded to his victory at a meeting of the parliamentary party: 'If the Taoiseach designate required it, he would be available to advise in the light of his thirteen years experience as party leader.'[99] It was unlikely Haughey would look for any such advice from Lynch.

– SEVEN –

SHUFFLING THE TRADITIONAL RANKS

Nuala Fennell's first foray into electoral politics came in 1977, when she declared as an independent candidate for Dublin County South just two weeks before polling day. Born Nuala Campbell, the daughter of a Garda, she described her childhood home in Portlaoise as 'an academy of duty, decency and self-sufficiency, of standards upheld and religion respected and well practised', with a 'most undomesticated' unfulfilled mother who found isolated provincial life frustrating and dull. In Dublin as a wife and mother herself, Fennell found she was facing her own mother's dilemma, invisible as 'one of the foot soldiers in the vast army of suburban housewives' in the late 1960s, and began writing articles for the women's pages of magazines and newspapers, receiving significant feedback from her frustrated peers. Journalism also provided an introduction to some of the leading figures of the emerging Irish Women's Liberation Movement (IWLM – see Part VIII), but she tended to regard herself as a social reformer who wanted to target political institutions rather than wave placards. Although she was not elected in 1977, she performed very well, securing 3,828 first preference votes (roughly 10 per cent of the poll; the candidate who won the last seat in that constituency received just over 4,600 first preference votes). In the aftermath of that election, Fennell criticised the assertion of the new leader of Fine Gael, Garret FitzGerald, that 'Women's rights are the wrong reason to want to get into government. It may be a worthy motivation but it is not an acceptable one.' Ironically, in joining Fine Gael the following year and eventually getting elected to the Dáil in 1981, she proved FitzGerald wrong, with his direct assistance through his co-option of her as a candidate.[1]

It was also believed in Fianna Fáil in 1974 that the emergence of women's political organisations was a move 'which does not do any damage to our party as such'.[2] But persuading men at local level that they needed to incorporate women into the political machinery was not always easy. A woman in Scarriff in Clare wrote to Séamus Brennan in 1978 emphasising the need for women at *cumann* level but she discovered 'in Clare traditions die hard; women do not shuffle the highly male traditional ranks of the organisation and get away with it!' a reference to the fun being poked at the chairman of the local *cumann* for granting the woman permission to organise cake sales for the party. Headquarters, she suggested, needed to do more to 'highly commend' older males in the party who were prepared to encourage women's involvement.[3]

In the few years after the establishment of the IWLM radical feminist groups emerged in the 1970s, including Irish Women United in 1975, demanding women's centres and self-determined sexuality, but it fell apart at the beginning of 1977. At a seminar to discuss the general election of that year, tensions came to a head 'with socialist women arguing that working-class men were more oppressed than middle-class women'.[4] Roy Foster points out that in the same year, the Women's Political Association (WPA) – which evolved from the Women's Representative Association – sent a questionnaire on women's issues to serving TDs. The reply of Fianna Fáil TD Tim O'Connor encapsulated the hostility that existed to women participating in politics: 'In my own county the women are doing a great job of work in keeping their homes going and bringing up their families. This I think is just what Almighty God intended them to do.'[5]

In the general election of that year the WPA produced campaign literature with the slogan 'Why not a Woman?' It did not result in more women being elected because the political parties failed to nominate more female candidates, but of the 376 candidates, 25 were women and, countrywide, first preference votes for women doubled from 42,268 to 81,967.[6] It was a turning point, in that women TDs were elected, but progress in its wake was slow and there were only thirteen women in the Dáil at the end of the 1980s. Following the 1977 election, Taoiseach Jack Lynch included three women among his eleven nominees to the Senate, 'a gesture that remained unmatched until ... 1997'.[7] The WPA had also circulated a questionnaire to serving politicians on their attitudes to women's rights; more than half of the TDs replied; all Labour Party TDs supported the introduction of a comprehensive family planning service, but only 31 per cent of the Fine Gael respondents and a mere 12 per cent of the Fianna Fáil respondents did.[8]

In reflecting on the position of women in politics at the end of the decade, R. K. Carty pointed out that 'young Irish Catholics with a religious vocation find it a distinctly earthly advantage to be male. Much the same appears to be true of those called to a political life'. But this was not just an Irish phenomenon; he cited an EEC survey which suggested almost a third of the Community electorate (of both sexes) agreed with the statement 'politics should be left to the men'. While there had been major advances for women in politics in some of the Scandinavian countries in the 1970s, and national legislative bodies in Finland and Denmark had female representation of 22 per cent and 17 per cent respectively, the figures in Ireland (the percentage of women in the Dáil in 1973 was 2.8 per cent and in 1977, 4 per cent) were similar to those in the UK (4 per cent in 1975) and the US (3 per cent in 1975), while in New Zealand, the first country to enfranchise women, the figure was just 3.5 per cent.[9] Family political dynasties, reflecting the excessive parochialism of Irish politics (political scientist Brian Farrell pointed out in 1973 that one-third of TDs had close family relations who were former members of parliament) was also of relevance to the six female TDs elected in 1977. They included three widows, a daughter and a granddaughter of former TDs. Kit Ahern was also elected a TD for Fianna Fáil in 1977, having failed to win a seat in three previous elections; numerous attempts in her case were required, perhaps, because she had no such dynasty to give her added advantage.

While 1977 could be seen as a time of breakthrough, building on the increased profile given to women during the local elections of 1974 and resulting in the election of Gemma Hussey as an independent senator on a specifically feminist ticket, only 10 per cent of voters had believed women's rights would be an important issue in the election and more Fianna Fáil voters than Labour Party voters were likely to see it as a significant issue.[10] Carty suggested that political parties were undoubtedly making a greater effort to promote women in politics and that it was the voters who might 'constitute a greater obstacle to the advancement of women into parliament than the politicians'. But this assertion should be qualified; as pointed out by some political scientists, the internal party selection processes for candidates remained a barrier to women's participation, as they were not altered enough to rectify gender imbalance. Politicians of the 1970s were not that energetically responsive to the feminist cause, which was precisely why the representation of women's rights 'fell to the emerging feminist movement, a reform minded judiciary and the European Commission'.[11] In relation to the historic representation of women in politics, historian Leland Lyons made the curious assertion in his influential book *Ireland Since the Famine* (1971) that Constance Markievicz, the Irish Republican who had the distinction of being the first woman elected to the UK parliament in 1918, 'played a man's part in and after 1916'.[12]

Mary Robinson, a future president of Ireland, also generated much interest during the late 1970s. It was asserted that she was 'the best known woman politician in the country' by 1973, having been elected to the Senate in 1969 on the panel of Trinity College Dublin, an institution 'which had previously confined its women members to widows and daughters'. Three years later she had made the decision to leave 'the backwater of academic politics for the shark-infested ponds' of the Labour Party. Her decision was regarded as one that suited not only the party in its quest to appeal to middle-class voters in Dublin, but her too, because it would increase her profile; it was therefore 'a marriage of mutual convenience' albeit 'one of little passion or warmth'.[13] But the electorate of the Dublin constituency where she ran for the Dáil showed little passion, warmth or even interest in Robinson, and the Senate rather than the Dáil remained her forum for the time being.

The 1970s saw her develop a formidable reputation as a champion of greater individual rights; a two-pronged battle in parliament and court; in her own words she had an image of one who was 'po-faced [and] hard working ... cold and hard' and attached to the idea that 'peaceful protest is part of the lifeblood of democracy'. She would not break the law, but she would defend those who would; 'she believed in the slow, sure processes of the law'. She was also courageous, driving to Dundalk, for example, to meet Cardinal William Conway, the Catholic Primate of All Ireland, to discuss her proposals regarding contraception in order to try to establish 'an atmosphere of mutual intellectual respect', but 'he took me to a room and tried to bully me'. Her campaigns also caused considerable distress to her parents.[14]

Mairín de Burca, who was active in Official Sinn Féin in the Republic until 1977, was associated with numerous causes, including the Dublin

Housing Action Group, established in the 1960s. A prolific letter writer and strong orator, she 'consistently emphasised working-class unification and broad-based left-wing action' with 'high visibility' and cultivated international links as a vocal critic of US foreign policy. Her ideological leanings also underlined the potential for conflict between women's liberation and Republican politics and she had a battle on her hands to persuade Official Sinn Féin to be more engaged with the feminist agenda, but also to negotiate the concerns of the feminists who did not want the Troubles to intrude. As Ailbhe Smyth, another active feminist, noted, republicanism was 'always present but rarely allowed to surface directly and explicitly'.[15] As a result of her activism, de Burca found that she was 'almost as unemployable in Ireland at the time as any suspected communist whose name was on the blacklist in 1950s America', even though she was 'clearly capable, and quite often over qualified, for the (clerical) jobs for which she was applying'. She subsequently moved into journalism.[16] As another housing campaigner, Hilary Boyle, saw there was a 'deeply entrenched notion among almost all men and a great many women too that any woman who fights for human rights promptly ceases to be a Helen and becomes a Harpy'.[17]

The appointment of Fianna Fáil TD for Galway, Máire Geoghegan-Quinn, as Minister for the Gaeltacht in 1979, the first woman to be appointed to the cabinet since Constance Markievicz in 1919, and Mella Carroll's appointment as a High Court judge in 1980, 'can be seen as symbols of the achievement of Irish women' in the 1970s.[18] But in terms of women being represented at political level and promoted to senior professional positions, there remained a mountain to climb. Journalist Pat Brennan provided some illuminating statistics about women's involvement in politics and the higher professions in 1979: in the civil service and local authorities, where there was a high concentration of women workers, only 7 per cent of senior positions were held by women. Only two out of forty-three district justices were women; there were no female judges in the High Court or the Supreme Court, only one woman in cabinet, only five women out of 148 TDs, and of 795 members of county councils and county borough councils, only thirty-two were women.[19]

The issue of political engagement was a troubling one for Ireland's largest women's organisation, the Irish Countrywomen's Association (ICA), throughout the 1960s and 1970s. Originally established in 1910, it evolved into an organisation intent on dealing with issues of social isolation, rural infrastructure, education, self-help and personal development. But at a time when women were beginning to mobilise and demand change under the auspices of the Irish Women's Liberation Movement, there were some caustic debates within the ICA about how they should approach politics. In 1969, its president, Peggy Farrell, precipitated a constitutional crisis for the ICA when, having been nominated to the Senate by Fianna Fáil, she resigned her ICA position, only to withdraw this resignation when it was accepted. The issue was then sent to the ICA guilds for voting. After advice from lawyers the executive decided that as a result of her actions she was ineligible for the position of vice-president.

The following year Farrell wrote a highly charged letter to an ICA member who criticised the stance she had taken in voting against an amendment allowing married women to become officers of the eight new regional health boards. Farrell was emphatic that she was not answerable to the ICA for her stance in the Senate, adding, 'Do you not think our association should put its own house in order by not discriminating against the members who are in public life before trying to straighten out the national scene?'[20]

A similar complaint was made by Bea Trench, who served as ICA president from 1974–6, and who lamented the fact that the association did not give enough support to women in public life and it was argued that the association's activities could only be taken seriously at the parish level as long as it remained non-political.[21]

In the context of younger people's engagement with politics in the 1970s, at the beginning of the decade, *Hibernia* magazine suggested that the Maoists had just '20 adherents in TCD',[22] so revolution in the short term was highly unlikely. When the Taoiseach Liam Cosgrave was asked in 1977 about the impression that Irish students were 'rather quiet' in comparison to their European counterparts (at that time, Ireland had the highest percentage of young people under the age of fifteen in Europe) he responded bluntly: 'Yes, our society is stable, the people want to work.'[23] But third-level students were vocal during the decade about fees and grants; thousands of them marched in a nationwide day of protest against the higher education grants scheme and alleged discrimination against technological education in October 1972. Two years later, 5,000 students took to the streets of Dublin demanding more government spending on higher education.

The question of the qualifying age for electors also generated much tension. In March 1970 a Private Member's Bill tabled by all seventeen members of the parliamentary Labour Party called for the voting age to be lowered from twenty-one to eighteen. The proposal was approved in a referendum in December 1972 but in February 1973, given the imminence of a general election, the National Youth Council, representing twenty-four affiliated organisations and with a membership of over 150,000, expressed concern that the youth would be disenfranchised despite the referendum result. Jack Lynch's limp reply was that 'it would not have been practicable to postpone the general election until after 15 April when the new voters register would be in force'.[24]

David Giles, president of the Students Representative Council in Trinity College Dublin, castigated Lynch for agreeing to hold the election '5 weeks before the date on which 140,000 18–21-year-olds would have been entitled to vote' and suggested it was within the domain of the Minister for Local Government (whose department had responsibility for elections) to request a High Court Order making the draft register valid. In February 1973, veteran Irish Republican and barrister Seán Mac Bride represented a twenty-year-old Dublin student, David Reynolds, in a High Court case in which he claimed that he was constitutionally entitled to vote. He lost the case, it being decided there was no legal authority for the draft register, but Reynolds was awarded costs as the question was deemed to be of 'considerable public importance'.[25] A student in Cork suggested that 140,000 young people and their rights were being 'sacrificed for the eternal good of Fianna Fáil',[26] but given its defeat in the 1973 general election it clearly did the party no good at all.

Hot Press magazine, newly launched in June 1977, was primarily concerned with creating a forum for the discussion and analysis of music and youth culture, but a number of its contributors, including editor Niall Stokes and Bill Graham, were apt to express their frustration with the political system and its irrelevance in the eyes of younger people. The general election campaign of 1977 was characterised by Stokes as an event dominated by 'the same boring old faces that have been popping up on posters since any of us can remember'. More telling and accurate was his 'creeping suspicion that voting patterns among the new voters will correspond exactly with those of the previous generation'. Following the result, Graham asked simply: 'Does it all matter? 7 per cent swings and party roundabouts and the same red-faced, shawled tinkers begging at O'Connell Bridge, year in, year out. Does Irish politics have anything to do with power or do we just swap systems of patronage?'[27]

To some young eyes, Irish politicians that were seen intermittently on television in the 1970s were 'grey and flavourless men, who appeared to run the country out of a sense of duty rather than with any real enthusiasm', though when Brian Lenihan, a Fianna Fáil minister, appeared in Castlerea in County Roscommon during the 1973 general election he wore 'a shiny blue suit, the likes of which nobody in the town had laid eyes on before ... so transfixed was the crowd with the minister's suit that nobody seemed to notice the swelling rhythms of the speech'.[28] His sartorial brashness, however, was not enough to see him elected and he was one of his party's high-profile casualties in that election. Lenihan in the 1960s had been part of the 'mohair-suit brigade' of brash, energetic young ministers promoted by Seán Lemass, and had served as Minister for Lands and subsequently Education, then becoming a reforming Minister for Justice before what was regarded as a demotion to Transport and Power. Shrewd, inquisitive and well read, he also cultivated a public image as an amiable bluffer and devoted party Loyalist. Another with an eye-catching suit who appeared after the 1977 general election was Pádraig Flynn, the new Fianna Fáil TD from Castlebar in Mayo; his appearance in a white suit with polka dot shirt prompted puzzlement: 'Who, in the name of God, is that?' wondered a bewildered Jack Lynch.[29] Charles Haughey was somewhat cruder, if funnier in his response: 'Would someone tell that fucking clown he's in the Dáil, not the circus,' he was overheard saying.[30]

The new arrivals were an indication of the generational change in Irish politics; another aspect of this was that not all came from the usual political stables. One of the interesting aspects of politics in the 1970s was the fate of those who came to the Dáil on the back of a prominence in academia and broadcasting rather than local politics, including historian and RTÉ broadcaster David Thornley and Conor Cruise O'Brien, both first elected for the Labour Party in Dublin constituencies in 1969 and re-elected in 1973. In different ways, they were both to discover the limitations and frustrations inherent in the system they became a part of.

As seen earlier, resentment against intellectuals in politics was not the preserve of any one party; in a Dáil debate on budgetary issues in 1978, new Dublin Labour Party TD Ruairí Quinn made a cutting remark about new Fianna Fáil TD Martin O'Donoghue, who was Fianna Fáil's main economic adviser and an academic economist: 'academics in government are not a great recipe for success'.[31] He might well have been talking about some in his own party in preceding years. Thornley, for example, died tragically young in July 1978, his life cut short by depression, diabetes and alcoholism; he had served as a TD for the Labour Party in Dublin North West from 1969–77. In trying in politics to maintain the independence he had as an academic historian and media commentator, he found that party discipline inhibited him; he delegated constituency work and despised the 'parish pump' mentality. He had little time for the notion of party discipline and used rhetoric 'more characteristic of a university debater than a parliamentarian chafing under the diurnal drudgery of practical politics'.

There was a widespread sense, at the time of his death, that he never got the opportunity to apply his talents effectively enough; one observer suggested that on a personal level, Thornley's own assessment of the founder of the late nineteenth-century Irish Home Rule movement, Isaac Butt, who was the subject of his impressive history PhD, could also have applied to himself, combining 'a love of country with a susceptible emotional nature'.[32] Thornley was open about his drink problem, telling *Irish Times* journalist Dick Walsh, 'When I get very depressed I drink too much. When I voted for the Criminal Law (Jurisdiction) Bill I went on a batter for a fortnight.' He derided the 'Gestapo tactics' being used by Labour ministers to get him to keep in line.[33] In contrast, Frank Cluskey, also a problem drinker, 'remained entirely off the booze' during the coalition government.[34] Nonetheless, a drink-sodden macho culture was still the hallmark of too much of Irish political endeavour. Patrick Donegan's comments that led to the resignation of President Cearbhall Ó Dálaigh in 1976 (see pages 112–14) were widely regarded as drink-fuelled, as it seemed to oil his predilection for blunt speech;[35] his denial of this was hardly convincing but has been supported by a contemporary witness.[36] David Andrews recalled that 'one deputy forgot himself sufficiently to attempt to light a cigarette in the [Dáil] chamber until promptly jumped on by one of the ushers'.[37] But those who did not drink were deemed to have the upper hand in 1979 when plotting for the leadership of Fianna Fáil, a contest between George Colley and Charles Haughey to succeed Lynch, reached its height; three of Haughey's key supporters were non drinkers – Albert Reynolds, Ray MacSharry and Pádraig Flynn – while supporters of Colley were more inclined to strategise over drinks and were therefore less focused and less effective.[38]

In the Labour Party, Justin Keating was regarded as another 'of the basket of eggheads' which general secretary of the party Brendan Halligan had brought 'to boil'; he was said to be 'scornful of the party hack' and 'contemptuous of the ward heeler'.[39] Keating, the son of renowned painter Seán, was a lecturer in veterinary medicine who had become well known as the presenter of a television farming programme, and along with his socialist principles was an environmentalist before it was fashionable, as well as a committed supporter of European integration (he was elected an MEP in 1979) and a humanist.

Conor Cruise O'Brien, who, like Thornley, was defeated in the 1977 general election as outgoing Minister for Posts and Telegraphs, and subsequently took up the prestigious £25,000-a-year job editing the *Observer* newspaper, was surprised by his seat loss; he 'assumed I'd hold it easily'.[40] Widely heralded when he died in 2008 as 'Ireland's foremost intellectual of the past half century' because of his ideas about Ireland and violence and 'the dangerous dynamic between thought and deed', he eventually became a committed Unionist. He was also characterised in a manner that suggested rather than being a mere iconoclast, he had a fundamental respect for the mainstream tradition of Irish politics and the office of Taoiseach; a curious mixture of respect for hierarchy and an almost anarchical independence.[41] He was the author of the influential book *States of Ireland* in 1972, seen as both an indictment of the assault on democracy that he thought militant Irish republicanism represented and also an invitation to 'internalize both the fears and aspirations of the Unionist community'.[42]

Historian, journalist, UN diplomat and politician, he was a clever, passionate and arrogant observer of Irish politics, but he succumbed too frequently to a self-regard that sometimes clouded his judgement. (In May 1973 he wrote to Garret FitzGerald, 'Perhaps I am getting very touchy and pompous but it does seem to me that for an airline to search members of the government is something of an affront.'[43]) For his critics, the longer he was in office, the 'steadily more authoritarian and reminiscent of the Blueshirt era' (the 1930s) he and Cosgrave and Patrick Cooney, Minister for Justice, became.[44] Given his frequent and often thunderous pronouncements on Northern Ireland, it was easy to forget that he was Minister for Posts and Telegraphs. As pointed out by one of his critics, former Labour Party TD Stevie Coughlan, it seemed that he 'did everyone's job but his own. While we were crying out for an up-to-date posts and telegraphic service he was going round the country creating strife between different sections of this island.'[45]

This was a selective take on his contribution; it was his views on respecting the Irish Unionist tradition that marked his significant intellectual and political contribution. For his defenders, none more trenchant than his wife, the well-known poet Máire Mhac an tSaoi, he was an unappreciated visionary. She was unabashed in her conclusions about the achievement of her husband: 'What Conor maintained today, the rank and file would espouse tomorrow; the trouble was that his reasoning always ran those 24 hours ahead of the consensus.'[46] There was truth in that, but the manner in which he espoused his views and castigated those who differed in their assessment sometimes bordered on the destructively and vindictively hysterical.

– EIGHT –

STATUS, PERCEPTION AND THE PRESS

How were politicians viewed more generally in the 1970s and how did the profession regard itself? In 1972, *Hibernia* magazine pointed out that the 'vast majority of TDs do not live on their parliamentary salary alone'.[1] In 1977, *The Economist* magazine compared the salaries received by MPs in various countries (the amounts were cited in dollars) and Irish TDs, paid $11,605, straddled the bottom of the league alongside British MPs ($11,599). West German MPs topped the league at $63,872 (for a parliament that sat on 110 days compared to 94 days for the Dáil); French parliamentarians were paid $25,990, Dutch $33,000 and Swedish $19,058.[2]

These figures did not take account of expenses, but even allowing for that, the *Irish Press* was prompted to suggest in the same year that 'the affluent, under-worked Dáil deputy lampooned by comedians, columnists and members of the general public for many years in this country is a myth. In the present inflationary situation, few deputies could afford to live on their salary and allowances. In fact, less than 6 per cent of the present 128 or so backbenchers attempt this Spartan exercise.' TDs were involved in various professions; included in their ranks were shopkeepers, publicans, farmers, lawyers and company directors. But the caveat was added that TDs 'do not do too badly … our TDs get five times the average income per head of population … compared with Swedish deputies who get 3 times the average'.[3] Figures discussed internally in Fianna Fáil early in 1976 listed a TD's salary in Irish pounds (punts) as £5,403; a senator earned £3,087, while £2,300 in expenses were paid to each TD and senator. The Taoiseach's salary was £14,952; senior ministers received £11,784 and junior ministers £8,696.[4]

After the general election of 1977, Lynch received a letter from Eugene Timmins, who had failed to win a Dáil seat, requesting a nomination to the Senate: 'I know that it is time for the older generation to make way for the upcoming generation but I am sure you will agree, especially in these days of inflation, that the pension earnings of a TD with no other source of income are a poor reward for a lifetime of work in the public interest.'[5]

In contrast, ex Taoisigh, by virtue of a decision in 1966 when Seán Lemass was retiring, and was a non-driver in ill health, were entitled to the privilege of a Garda-driven limousine for life. It was brought to Jack Lynch's attention that the wording of the decision in 1966 would perhaps unnecessarily and unjustifiably accord the privilege to every outgoing Taoiseach and could be changed, but according to Richard Stokes, the civil servant who highlighted this, 'I regret to say on that occasion his [Lynch's] feet of clay were in evidence. I felt that he was piggybacking on the sympathy for Lemass' and the wording remained unchanged.[6]

But what were the politicians being paid to do? Was it a full-time job and did it matter if they were suited to it? Political scientist John Whyte suggested in the early 1970s that 'the average TD has many admirable qualities such as approachability, common sense and lack of pomposity' but that 'the calibre of deputies seems in several ways less satisfactory than it might be'. As he saw it, not enough would make good leaders and not enough were interested in policy in relation to economic development or external affairs. Perhaps the more salient point was that 'the electorate does not seem greatly to care about such qualities in its representatives'.[7]

There were some who were sensitive to how they and their interventions were portrayed. Fine Gael's John Kelly, for example, frequently took issue with newspapers and their editors. In 1970 he had suggested that 'a weakness in the party's present arrangement' was that it was simply not organised enough to 'comment quickly and effectively from day to day on public issues which develop quickly in the Press'.[8] Over the next few years he sought to make good that deficiency and penned a lot of letters concerning Backbencher, the supposedly anonymous political column in the *Irish Times* newspaper written by John Healy, which he accused of spending years targeting and belittling politicians.[9] Healy's column had first appeared in 1963 and, with the benefit of informants from within politics including Brian Lenihan and Haughey, and Donogh O'Malley, the Fianna Fáil Minister for Education who died prematurely in 1968, was provocative and well informed and stood in stark contrast to the respectful traditions of Irish journalism. Healy was also a well-known television performer and dubbed Charles Haughey 'the golden boy', but the issues that engaged him were those of the marginalised, and he caustically lamented that 'the age of honest indignation is dead in Ireland. We're sophisticated now. We have learned to order the right bottle of wine and we take our salads in a side order and we have learned too, that it's not good breeding to lose your temper ... Holy economic writ is all.'[10]

Aside from the targeting of individual politicians by newspapers, John Kelly also took issue with their other agendas and their editorialising about political policy. As the foremost academic expert on the Irish constitution, for example, he rubbished the insistence of the *Irish Times* that a new constitution was necessary and went on to assert: 'It used to be said 20 years ago that every politician was terrified of getting a belt from a crozier, but his fear nowadays is more of a couple of swipes from an editor or from a political correspondent or columnist.'[11]

Michael Mills, political correspondent of the *Irish Press* at this time, suggested in his memoir that the rules of engagement between politicians and political correspondents had 'not been formalised' in the early 1970s.[12] But there is little doubt that politicians frequently leaked information to them; in 1971 Lynch got frustrated with leaks from the proceedings of parliamentary party meetings: 'the sneaking of information from party meetings had been going on for a long time and the position would soon be reached when ministers and members would be afraid to speak their minds at party meetings. Members who tried to buy popularity from political correspondents in this manner only earned the contempt of these correspondents.'[13] Three years later, reference at a party meeting was made to 'continued leakage of confidential decisions to press', while five years on Lynch referred to 'further breaches of confidentiality' of party meetings.[14]

Journalistic commentary on politicians was undoubtedly becoming more caustic (and perhaps in mitigation, they had considerable ground to make up for an unjustified deference in the past). Vincent Browne in particular excelled at this, as his comments in relation to Ben Briscoe, the Dublin South Central TD for Fianna Fáil, indicated. Briscoe had first been elected in 1965: 'winner of the British and Irish universities and Hospitals Boxing Championship (lightweight) in 1952. He is also a lightweight in politics.'[15] Some politicians were quick to react when they felt journalists had overstepped the line, with serious consequences for the newspapers. Minister for Justice Patrick Cooney, for example, successfully sued the *Sunday World* newspaper 'when the paper published an article insinuating a likeness between him and Richard Nixon and the possibility of "show trials" involving him at some future stage'.[16]

Michael Mills was showered with praise by *Hibernia* magazine in 1973, with the assertion 'there is no more honest or better informed journalist in the country'.[17] Mills had been a witness to the tumultuous Arms Trial events (see Part II) and was someone who had travelled regularly to Belfast, where requests for guns 'were made to almost every journalist from Dublin visiting Belfast at that time'. Mills also encouraged Jack Lynch to give his version of the battle within Fianna Fáil at this time but little was forthcoming, except to the extent that 'Lynch told me shortly afterwards that he lost all trust in people after the event'.[18] Mills observed the extent of patronage in operation in relation to public appointments and concluded that 'nobody gives £100 to sit down to a Fianna Fáil dinner unless they expect to get £200 in return'. He also saw Haughey as 'the most talented politician of his time' but one with a 'childish interest in style and pomp', and thought Cosgrave was particularly considerate with journalists.[19]

Very quickly after the new coalition government took office in March 1973 it circulated a cabinet memorandum on relations with the media. Authored by Conor Cruise O'Brien, it suggested 'we do need to rethink at this point any relations we have previously had with the media ... the government's collective image depends ultimately on its character and achievement. Public relations gimmickry is undesirable in itself and tends to be counterproductive.' The need was to 'set a style of accessibility and responsible democracy, different from the "we know what is best for you all approach from FF"'. What was recommended was a 'low key' approach to the media and 'holding a middle way between extremes of aloofness and inapproachability on the one hand and over exposure on the other'.

Ministers were encouraged to avoid participation in panel discussions and leave comment 'on the work, plans and prospects' of the government to the Taoiseach and Tánaiste (deputy prime minister), Brendan Corish. When reviewing all this subsequently in October 1973 O'Brien dissected the views of newspapers – the *Irish Independent* was regarded as having taken a 'favourable line' in relation to government policy; the *Irish*

Press 'predictably has continued its republican line'; the *Cork Examiner* has carried 'a fairly extensive anti-government business lobby' while RTÉ 'apart from its bias in Northern coverage has been fairly satisfactory'. Generally with the media, it was concluded 'a good image prevails' but nonetheless 'the 100 days grace is over', with mounting criticism that ministerial speeches 'contain not a single fundamental thought of any worth'.[20] When Cosgrave was preparing for an interview with current affairs anchor and political scientist at UCD Brian Farrell, on RTÉ's *Seven Days* in June 1973, one of the proposed questions was 'Communication: the National Coalition government is more open – is this deliberate policy and will it continue?'[21]

In his memoir, Tim Pat Coogan, who was editor of the *Irish Press* at this time, recalled that he 'simply refused to take calls from TDs, senators or ministers'. But Coogan was entirely inconsistent in his attitude, recording a few pages later that he was keen to meet with Charles Haughey and George Colley: 'acting on the general principle that I should be prepared to chat with anyone, I cheerfully went to meet him [Haughey] in his home'.[22] He was, however, like many journalists, horrified at the coalition's crackdown on media freedom in tandem with worsening violence North and South, and its determination to 'hound the media with prosecutions'. He met with Conor Cruise O'Brien in September 1976; O'Brien showed him clippings he had kept from the Letters to the Editor section of the *Irish Press*, which he regarded as seditious. Coogan bravely responded by reprinting a full page of the letters in the newspaper. When Coogan was interviewed on RTÉ, Brian Farrell, regarding proposed legislation affecting press censorship, said simply: 'The legislation is aimed at you, isn't it?' Fortunately, Coogan records, 'the publicity deflected the aim' and the proposal to extend sanctions to the newspapers was dropped.[23]

Liam Cosgrave also intervened regarding an 'attack on him' in the *Sunday Independent* in October 1976, which Brian Quinn and Aidan Pender, respectively editors of the Independent group's *Evening Herald* and *Irish Independent*, assured him was not 'the result of concerted action or a single view by Independent newspapers'. The managing director had deplored the *Sunday Independent* article and that sentiment had 'been conveyed to the Sunday Independent people'.[24]

RTÉ was well served by the calibre of its current affairs broadcasters, notably Brian Farrell, the principal presenter of the 1973 general election programme, with assistance from Basil Chubb and Ted Nealon. As editor of *Seven Days*, Sheamus Smith recalled that, with the exception of Haughey, he did not get much interference from politicians.[25] T. P. Hardiman, who had been appointed the third director general (DG) of the RTÉ television service in 1968, protected RTÉ's independence by insisting that any exercise of the government's reserved powers to intervene should be done in public.

As with other broadcasters, RTÉ recruited its share of politically motivated broadcasters. The award-winning and gifted producer Eoghan Harris, a trade union activist who had previously been influential in Official Sinn Féin and later developed a severe critique of the provisional Republican movement, was 'manifestly breaking the rules' in engaging with politics. He was to become the leading intellectual light in the Workers Party, which set up a secret branch in RTÉ with a militant anti-Nationalist agenda. Harris joined RTÉ in 1966 at a time when former leading republicans such as Pearse Kelly and Jim McGuinness were in senior positions in the newsroom and it has been maintained that 'RTÉ provided an ideologically congenial bolthole for various Trotskyist groups' in the 1970s who were sympathetic to republicanism as divisions emerged over section 31 of the Broadcasting Act (see Part II).[26] By the mid 1970s, Oliver Maloney, appointed director general in 1975, believed that too many producers lacked accountability and that 'small groups of strategically placed staff exercised inordinate influence', meaning he thought that the accusation by politicians that RTÉ broadcasters were biased was not without foundation. When Mary McAleese, a native of Belfast and legal academic at Trinity College, joined the station in 1979 she claimed 'there was a definite and tangible anti-Nationalist, anti-Catholic and anti-intellectual atmosphere', but the Workers Party by no means had a monopoly on antipathy towards the Provisional IRA's campaign.[27]

Frank Dunlop suggested that after losing the 1973 election, Fianna Fáil became 'useless at communicating with the media'. While Muiris Mac Conghail, the new government press secretary was briefing journalists twice weekly after cabinet meetings, 'FF found it difficult to come to terms with his organized professional communications strategy'. Dunlop, who was appointed the party's press officer in 1974 ('What is it exactly you'll be doing for us?' one veteran asked him) was vain, self-serving and delusional, referring to 'the sacrifices I had made in his and the party's interests' over the period 1975–9, in relation to his job as press secretary, having been appointed head of Government Information Services with the rank of assistant secretary at the Department of the Taoiseach. He expressed himself shocked 'at the antipathy towards journalists'.[28]

But were political journalists objective on the great political divides of the day in the Republic? Private correspondence suggests some had their own preferences and they were not shy in expressing them; for all his self-proclaimed independence, Tim Pat Coogan as editor of the *Irish Press*, a newspaper that had been established in 1931 for the express purpose of promoting Fianna Fáil, but had evolved into a much more rounded paper, still wrote Jack Lynch in February 1973 'a brief note to wish you every success in the election and to offer you any assistance I can give, either with the paper or personally, with the pen or any other way'.[29] In June 1977 Bruce Arnold, political correspondent with the *Irish Independent*, after the landslide Fianna Fáil victory in the general election, sent Lynch a private note of congratulations: 'It was enormously deserved.'[30] Arnold had been highly critical of the coalition of 1973–7.[31]

Another aspect of politics that was in its infancy but was assuming greater significance was opinion polls. Gallup had conducted the first independent opinion poll in Irish politics in 1969 after the Labour Party had commissioned it, but it was not followed by any commensurate poll for several years.[32] Political journalist Joseph O'Malley observed in 1979 that individual politicians like Cosgrave had been 'deeply sceptical' as to their merits or accuracy, but that with their more frequent use and greater professionalism and precision, 'Irish political life will never be the same again'.[33] Two years earlier, before the 1977 general election, the *Irish Times* commissioned its own poll, which showed Fianna Fáil would receive 52 per cent of the vote in a general election; the editor Fergus Pyle suppressed the story 'not because of political prejudice but because he too disbelieved the poll findings'.[34]

Closely linked to this issue of gauging public support was that of public relations; the manner in which politicians interacted with the public and the impression they created on television. In 1979, one of the more prickly of Irish politicians, Fianna Fáil's Des O'Malley, made an unusually frank admission: 'I accept that I have not concerned myself unduly with the public relations side of being a politician and that given my personality I have often gratuitously insulted and been rude to people. I regret the latter for it is obviously indefensible to be needlessly hurtful. But I do find the self-projection of politics somewhat repellent and I find myself quite incapable of dealing with it.'[35] Chain-smoking and often perceived as didactic and bossy, O'Malley had a particular ability to unnerve people.[36]

In terms of the perception of politicians, the rural/urban divide was still of significance and created some friction; it was notable, for example, and understandable, given the location of his home, that when he was elected a senator in 1969, congratulatory messages for John Kelly from the fashionable and salubrious district of Dublin 4 abounded, and the Benedictines running one of the country's most renowned private schools celebrated ('Glenstal rejoices – Abbot and Community').[37] But the following year he reacted angrily to the suggestion that Dublin politicians in visiting the West of Ireland were 'on safari to the natives of the west'. His response was, 'My own people are mostly from the West, but even if I were Dublin bred for ten generations I would still resent your words.'[38] Likewise, Garret FitzGerald brought considerable energy and vigour to the leadership of Fine Gael, but his status as a Dublin academic was not without its difficulties. There were numerous journalistic references in the late 1970s to internal tensions within the party, specifically the idea of a 'Garret cabal' – liberal, urban and organisationally quite ruthless – with a 'still powerful reactionary hard core'.[39]

Growing up in Roscommon, John Waters suggested that by the early 1970s, 'unlike previous generations we absorbed little of the language of the countryside ... plugged as we were to the universal city, the country represented backwardness, thick accents and the past ... our ideas of betterment were vaguely tied in with the glamorous world of the city, with showbiz, soccer and stardom. Such imagery was all around us and seemed to fit in with the political rhetoric of the time.'[40]

By the time of the 1977 general election, Fianna Fáil had unmasked a new approach to elections. The adored, affable and safe Lynch was perfect fodder for the introduction to Ireland of US-style presidential campaigns, but the credit should go to the party's general secretary, Séamus Brennan, who had been in the US to observe the 1976 presidential race. In 1977, Brennan persuaded the party to have a campaign record, the abysmal 'Your Kind of Country' sung by Colm T. Wilkinson, and T-shirts emblazoned with the slogan 'Bring Back Jack', glitzy campaign rallies and careful stage management. The US election also gave Brennan the idea of head-to-head TV debates between the leaders. He knew Lynch, in his understated way, was an accomplished performer, but Liam Cosgrave refused the invitation, handing Fianna Fáil a walkover. Significantly, the party's election strategy committee when formed in 1976 had no politicians as members, except for Senator Eoin Ryan, who was not a Dáil candidate. The coalition appeared to be 'in shock'. As Michael Mills was to recall, 'It's all over. It's a landslide. How did this happen?'[41]

Fianna Fáil itself had hardly been that confident, given that private correspondence to Eoin Ryan suggested 'enough members of the public don't believe that we have as much talent as the coalition therefore we need "impact" to be our guide in selecting candidates'.[42] But the simple answer to their success could be found in Fianna Fáil's giveaway election manifesto, entitled 'Action Plan for National Reconstruction' and which ran for forty-seven pages; given the extravagant promises in it, which are widely believed to have been economically grossly irresponsible, it is ironic that it contained the line 'the real threat to the future of our country lies in the economy'.[43]

Lynch's success created certain headaches, not least the voluminous correspondence from those seeking nominations to the Senate; he was, in his own words, 'inundated with suggestions' for these nominations and complained of 'literally hundreds of representations'.[44] There was no shortage of congratulatory messages, it being suggested that 'de Valera's opinions on coalition government in Ireland have again proven to be true', while the president of the Gaelic Athletic Association, of which he had been such a distinguished star performer in his earlier years, trumpeted: 'You have had many great achievements in many fields during your long and distinguished career but no doubt this achievement will go down in history as your greatest.'[45]

– NINE –

A TEDIOUS HONOUR?

Another political institution that achieved prominence in the 1970s was the office of the president. Largely ceremonial, though with the power to refer legislative bills to the Supreme Court to determine their constitutionality, the office had not been designed to be a centre of political energy; in journalist James Downey's phrase it was a position 'as full of tedium as of honour'.[1] There was, however, something quasi regal about it, as reflected in the notes on the inauguration of President Cearbhall Ó Dálaigh in 1974, for example: 'The escort of honour will render honours to the president ... on arrival at the state apartments some minutes before noon, the presidential party will be conducted to the Throne room.'[2] Or as was observed by the American ambassador to Ireland John D. Moore in a letter to Garret FitzGerald about the funeral of President Erskine Childers in 1974: 'the exquisite grace with which every aspect was carried out seemed to me to be extraordinary. There was a special perfection to the entire occasion.'[3]

Childers had died suddenly after only eighteen months in office; his predecessor Eamon de Valera, as an elder statesman, was seen as an appropriate person to have in the position in 1966 at the time of the fiftieth anniversary of the 1916 Rising of which he was the sole surviving commandant. But as his second term ended in 1973, there was a determination by some to create more of an interest in the office beyond the cut and thrust of a hotly contested election (de Valera had won by only 10,000 votes in 1966).

Proponents of a new style of presidency sought to find an effective way of banishing the 'sleepy president' stereotype. If successful, they could perhaps make the Irish people more interested in the presidency and the person who held it, a logic that set the tone for the successful election campaign of Fianna Fáil's Childers in 1973. An English-educated Protestant and son of a Republican executed during the Irish civil war, Childers, first elected to the Dáil in 1938, was regarded as a maverick in his own party. He maintained a sort of 'detachment from the factional side of politics' and was exceptionally long-winded but dignified. Because of his father's experience, he had devoted himself to the theme of reconciliation as well as serving in a variety of ministries from the 1950s to the 1970s; by 1969 he was the senior Fianna Fáil cabinet figure, where he served as Tánaiste and Minister for Health. He fought an energetic presidential campaign in 1973, travelling the length and breadth of the country, insisting that he had only agreed to run on the basis that he could 'expand' the role of president and play the role of 'composer and conductor of the National Orchestra'.[4]

He promoted the idea of 'think tanks' to discuss the country's future, but Liam Cosgrave would not allow this and though he may have had notions of being a 'super-peacemaker president', this faded as he became a prisoner of protocol. He did, however, invite people from Belfast to the presidential residence in the Phoenix Park in Dublin, and took on a huge variety of engagements before his active presidency was brought to an abrupt and premature end when he died suddenly in office in 1974.

During the election campaign there had been some mutterings about his background and religion; interestingly, Fine Gael members canvassing for his opponent Tom O'Higgins (who won 48 per cent of the vote, against Childers's 52 per cent) were told during the campaign not to criticise de Valera or promote the idea that Childers was an 'outsider' or mention his Protestantism.[5] During the election the Labour Party was concerned 'about getting the Labour vote in Dublin out for Tom O'Higgins ... not altogether easy'.[6] After the election, Conor Cruise O'Brien complained that Childers was rude to him at a function in Dublin; Haughey was also there and 'in private conversation, asked me why the government did not provide the president with someone to write his speeches, so that we should not be subjected to such a boring address as we had here this afternoon'.[7]

But Cosgrave had little intention of doing anything for Childers. Behind the scenes, in terms of the day-to-day workings of the presidency, there were considerable tensions and disagreements between president and government. The phrase 'guardian of the constitution', as often cited in relation to the president, has been dismissed by some. John Kelly's seminal work on the Irish constitution noted, 'It scarcely needs to be said that this flattering title sometimes bestowed on the Presidency ... is pure journalistic hyperbole. The Constitution nowhere describes the presidency in such terms and is extremely sparing in its attribution of any independent functions of the office at all.'[8] It was also an office with few financial resources; by 1977, the president was paid a salary (fixed at 10 per cent higher than that of the Chief Justice) of £18,000 per year but received just £15,000 a year 'to cover expenses in connection with the domestic establishment and the cost of official engagements', including wages of domestic staff.

The style rather than the substance of the office, however, was inevitably affected by personality; the campaign of Childers in 1973 for a new style of presidency was regarded as somewhat risky, if not downright unrealistic, and he irritated the government by his remarks on American television about the situation in Northern Ireland.[9] The files of the Department of the Taoiseach give a good overview of the restrictions placed on what Childers could say publicly; he was subjected to a systematic censorship, sometimes informed by the civil servants' own prejudices. It was regarded as positive and praiseworthy, for example, that he warned of the 'growth of a faceless, anonymous society of people'. In the view of Richard Stokes, this was 'the type of speech which should be made by the president – words of caution on the "progress" of society'[10] (see Part VII). But when he addressed a student society in UCD, the department insisted that he amend the line 'living was excessively frugal for a section of the population'. At a speech in Clare the following month, the department ordered the deletion of a clause that read 'in spite of all the known social and economic problems that still existed'. A speech shortly afterwards in Wexford fell foul of the censors because of the sentence 'There are strong reservations about community councils and their functions in local and central government.'

His references to church and Christian practices in the modern era at a function in St Patrick's College, Maynooth were also rejected as 'out of place in a speech by the president', while at the Law Society in UCC his proposed text on 'The Student Elector in the Modern World', with its warning of 'the evils of the capitalist system', was regarded as 'skating on thin ice in promising to give advice to young electors'. Other, more discursive proposed texts also elicited a negative: 'a most rambling speech with occasional lapses'.[11] As was well known, Childers was unconventional in some ways and was seen by many as someone to be controlled. He was very keen to be involved in a proposed television documentary about himself, but as recalled by RTÉ producer Sheamus Smith, RTÉ's assistant controller of programmes, Jack White, turned the proposed programme down, saying 'we must protect that man from himself'. The film-makers got independent finance and made it anyway – *A President for all the People*. Ironically, RTÉ was glad of it as it was able to broadcast it when he died suddenly, but had to pay £20,000 for the film.[12]

But it was the resignation of his successor, Cearbhall Ó Dálaigh, a former Chief Justice of Ireland and judge of the Court of Justice of the European Communities, who was nominated with cross-party support without an election, that caused something of a sensation in 1976. He resigned after he was castigated and insulted as a 'thundering disgrace' by the Minister for Defence Patrick Donegan for referring the Emergency Powers Bill (to give more extensive powers to the Gardaí in dealing with those suspected of subversive crime; a bill that created worries about civil liberties) to the Supreme Court for a judgement as to its constitutionality. A close supporter of Cosgrave, Donegan, first elected to the Dáil in 1957 and unsympathetic to the 'Just Society' wing of the party, had supported him when Cosgrave's leadership of the party was threatened during the crisis within Fine Gael over the Fianna Fáil government's Offences Against the State (Amendment) Bill of 1972, heavily criticised as a threat to civil liberties. Donegan was the only member of the parliamentary party backing Cosgrave, who in supporting the legislation was prepared to vote against his party but, as the Dáil debated, two Loyalist bombs exploded in Dublin city centre, killing two people and injuring 127; in the altered environment Fine Gael TDs dropped their opposition to the bill. According to reporter Don Lavery, who was present at the function in 1976 where Donegan made the remarks, he was being deliberately provocative – 'I'll give you some news' – and the fact that he was opening a new canteen in an army barracks added to the impact, given the president's constitutional position as titular head of the armed forces.[13]

Donegan and Cosgrave behaved disgracefully throughout the Ó Dálaigh controversy and there was a striking immaturity and partisanship about the way they handled it. Donegan issued a statement of 'regret' for his words, 'which arose out of my deep feelings for the security of our citizens. I intend to offer my apologies to the president as soon as possible.' But Donegan, though being advised by Attorney General Declan Costello,[14] did not really apologise at all, writing to Ó Dálaigh, 'It is now apparent that my words are open to misinterpretation and that they have in fact been subject to interpretations which certainly I did not intend.'[15] How exactly the words 'thundering disgrace' could be open to misinterpretation is a mystery; but Donegan sought to blame others: 'facile references by journalists, which can become emotive, are difficult to contend with' – an ironic assertion in the extreme.[16]

Ó Dálaigh was scathing in response, calling his behaviour 'outrageous' and asking pointedly and pertinently: 'Have you any conception of your responsibility as a minister of state and in particular as Minister for Defence?' The *Irish Times* called on Donegan to resign, suggesting that because of his 'enormous popularity among his subordinates' he had been indulged for inappropriate comments in the past, but that his latest lapse was far removed from the 'kick up the transom category'. This was a reference to the publicity coup he enjoyed shortly after taking office in March 1973 when the Irish naval service, with the assistance of British intelligence, intercepted an arms-running vessel, the *Claudia*, in Irish territorial waters off County Waterford, seizing rifles, grenades and gelignite supplied by Libya's Muammar Gaddafi, and arrested six people, including IRA chief-of-staff Joe Cahill.

Donegan had closely monitored the combined land-and-sea operation from a base in Cork and was triumphalist and boastful at a press conference the following day; outlining the decision not to press charges against the *Claudia*'s German captain and crew. He said they had been given 'a boot up the transom' and ordered to leave Irish waters. In 1975 questions about his judgement were also raised when he talked of asking the army to 'perform things they will not like' but which they would do anyway because of 'their tremendous loyalty'.[17]

Ó Dálaigh refused to receive Donegan, an 'ill-bred, moronic Minister' according to one observer, and also a drunk, or as the *Irish Independent* put it 'over-emotional', though Don Lavery maintained he was sober at the time (which is not the same as maintaining he had not drunk alcohol). Some, though, praised him for speaking what they regarded as the truth.[18] The *Irish Times* also expressed incredulity that Cosgrave would not act, 'in view of his own strict loyalty to the state's institutions'. There were even ironic mutterings from Fianna Fáil about Fine Gael being 'a slightly constitutional party'.[19] John Kelly, the foremost expert on the Irish constitution wrote to Cosgrave encouraging him to instigate a confidence motion in Donegan quickly and put 'the whole thing behind us'.[20]

In a letter to Garret FitzGerald, Conor Cruise O'Brien disputed the idea that the controversy amounted to 'a constitutional crisis'; he dismissed the 'cry of the FF pack' and suggested 'one indiscreet remark' by Donegan should not cancel out his years of service'.[21] The 'cry of the FF pack', as recalled by David Andrews, was genuinely an angry one, with Andrews 'even going so far as to refer to a "fascist" element emerging in the government'.[22]

Ó Dálaigh resigned on 22 October. When the Taoiseach was preparing to respond to the motion of no confidence in Donegan he turned his attention to the Arms Trial (see Part II) and those prepared to 'misappropriate funds voted by this house for a purpose ... which time has now shown has contributed to unparalleled carnage'. This line, which revealed a Cosgrave hopelessly at sea, was, in the event, not used.[23] *The Economist* suggested Cosgrave 'has ignored the Gaelic proverb which gives warning that a good retreat is better than a bad stand'.[24]

There was a broader context to the controversy than the insult from Donegan; there were other tensions and Ó Dálaigh had felt ignored and sidelined by the coalition government and by Cosgrave in particular. Ó Dálaigh had made it known that he was unhappy that letters for him received in the Department of the Taoiseach were being 'delayed for the purpose of preparing a substantive reply', while in relation to some of his proposed official travels, Bertie O'Dowd in the Department of the Taoiseach questioned 'whether a presidential state visit should be used by officials of government departments to promote trade'.[25]

Ó Dálaigh's own papers shed further light on the controversy that prematurely ended his presidential career, as well as an insight into what was undoubtedly a learned, but also a highly unusual and occasionally messianic mind. James Downey in his memoirs suggested Ó Dálaigh 'was at once pedantic and imaginative' and 'erudite but much too fond of displaying his erudition'.[26] A year before the Donegan diatribe he had drafted a letter to Cosgrave at the time of the kidnapping of Dr Tiede Herrema, a Dutch industrialist, by renegade Irish Republicans (see Part II), offering himself as a substitute hostage. He seemed to be afflicted by a Patrick Pearse type willingness to die for his country: 'It now seems to me that the only way to save Dr Herrema's life is to offer a substitute hostage who might succeed in persuading the kidnappers to reason. I accept the government cannot and should not yield to the kidnappers' demands. I am willing to offer myself as a substitute for Dr Herrema in the firm knowledge there can be no government compromise with blackmail. I believe I could bring the kidnappers to reason. If I fail, I do not mind dying – my death will vindicate Ireland's honour before the world.'[27]

In the run-up to the Donegan controversy, Ó Dálaigh received many letters encouraging him to refer the contested bill to the Supreme Court. For some it was necessary to challenge 'the aura of fascism pervading the land', while another supporter suggested 'you are a great international lawyer and also a man of immense intellectual ability. You can tear this bill into shreds.' Another correspondent suggested in relation to the power of referral he had that, 'those who don't appreciate such safeguards perhaps do not understand what democracy is all about'.[28] Likewise, there was no shortage of letters expressing disgust at Donegan – 'power must have gone to his head' – or decrying 'the appallingly intemperate utterances of a notorious boor who should never have been given government rank'. There was considerable warmth shown towards Ó Dálaigh and his integrity.[29]

Ó Dálaigh's rough notes written during the controversy made much of the fact that he was 'president by invitation ... I felt the invitation was no longer valid, moreover for the office of president to be of any value then there must be a minimum of acceptance. Clearly such acceptance was no longer forthcoming. I therefore concluded I could best serve my country, conscience and the office of president itself by resigning.'[30] Ó Dálaigh, the High King, also rambled: 'Irish historians speak of high kings with opposition. The contrast is with High Kings who enter an office without opposition in accordance with agreed procedure. It was a civilised equity.' He was, it seemed, particularly preoccupied with the fact that he had not been elected, and it bothered him: 'I accept I was a substitute for an elected president ... I didn't seek this office. I shall retain it only so long as I can do so with dignity.'[31]

But he was also bristling about the contemptuous manner in which he had been treated by Cosgrave, whose 'only contacts with the president were by telephone' during the controversy. Cosgrave, he recorded, had telephoned him three times, but at no time did he request to see the president, even though 'the president was at all times ready and willing to see the Taoiseach' and there was no apology, 'orally or in writing', from the Taoiseach in respect of the minister's speech. A second letter had arrived from Donegan after the president 'had left for last time'.[32] Ó Dálaigh had left express instructions that 'the president is not available to see anyone except the Taoiseach'.[33] By that stage, it seemed, Ó Dálaigh was already planning for life outside the Aras, with personal notes including descriptions of 'gas stoves', 'new home de luxe' and '26 inch colour'.[34]

Ó Dálaigh also made notes after the Supreme Court decision that the Emergency Powers Bill was constitutional, revealing he had considered resigning 'without signing the Emergency Powers Bill'. He went as far as to contend that 'today's decision of the Supreme Court so narrows the role of the president as Guardian [he had included the word 'protector', but crossed it out] of the Constitution (John Kelly had pounced on an editorial in the *Irish Times* suggesting the president was guardian of the constitution by pointing out that the Supreme Court was guardian of the constitution[35]) as to empty that office of any significant importance in the field of constitutional law'. His thinking at this stage was that 'I do not think it appropriate that I should close my career by presiding over the demise of the constitution' as a document 'for the protection of human rights and fundamental freedoms'.[36]

He had also drafted a letter to Ted Heath, the former British prime minister, castigating him for apparently saying in the US that Ó Dálaigh was 'a menace to civilisation' because of his opposition to the Bill. But there was another problem in relation to the Taoiseach and president and the issue that prompted the Bill: 'I had heard nothing from you – as I might have expected to have heard about the existence of a national emergency ... I have been conscious since I came here that for whatever reason I have never been furnished by you with information.'[37]

These were significant and frank musings, and they would suggest that Ó Dálaigh was of a mind to resign, independently of Donegan's intervention, which may indeed, have suited his purpose. His resignation was about more than a boorish, ignorant minister who had insulted him. His papers leave no doubt as to his perception of the seriousness of Cosgrave's shunning of him; he referred to Cosgrave's silence as 'a grave constitutional default'.

In a draft letter to Cosgrave, he suggested that on the surface, their relations may have been 'cordial' but 'I would however be failing in my duty if I did not record here – for history – that since I entered on the presidency ... that on none of the occasions of your infrequent visits ... did you, in your conversations with me, say anything to me that could be construed even remotely to amount to keeping the president generally informed on matters of domestic and international policy – a mandatory requirement of your office … never were the words national emergency uttered by you to me on any of these occasions.'[38] Not only was Ó Dálaigh keen for posterity to vindicate his stance, but he also seemed to hope a book would come of it, even going so far as to suggest a title: 'The Wrong man: Last days of a presidency.'[39]

For many, Ó Dálaigh was the right man, and was held in high esteem, partly because he was wonderfully original, and culturally sophisticated, or as journalist Liam Hourican put it in the *New York Times*: 'the president visited remote west coast islands and exchanged snatches of bardic verse with veteran Gaelic speakers as readily as he donned a white tie for the ballet or the Abbey Theatre'. As historian and Provost of Trinity College Leland Lyons put it, 'We, like many citizens felt proud to have as our head of state a man of scholarship and culture with a knowledge of the wider world which is too often lacking in our society.'[40] He received a large volume of letters after his resignation, many of which depicted him as dignified – 'when all about us are distressed by the confusion and weak-mindedness of our leaders, there was principle found in one man' – with the suggestion that his resignation was 'of heroic quality and one that will always shine out as the personification of integrity'.[41] Some saw his appointment as transformative as it was about the role of learning and culture being finally reflected in high public office, but, 'the tone of public life which had already seemed to me to be in some respects deplorably low now sinks lower still – the future is dark indeed'.[42]

His resignation was regarded in some quarters as 'symbolising a major victory for culture and integrity over that alien and despicable current trend which the last president, Childers, described as the "Anglo-American sub culture"'.[43] Honour and integrity were the most frequently used words in this correspondence. Many recognised that it was the politicians who had treated Ó Dálaigh with contempt, including all those who backed Donegan, especially Cosgrave, who had damaged public life. As well-known agricultural economist Raymond Crotty put it, 'Resignation is the ultimate sanction available to every public person to manifest his disapproval of the conduct of public affairs. It is one of Ireland's tragedies that few persons in public office have seen fit to use this sanction, but have instead compromised themselves and their principles by continuing to associate publicly with what they know to be indefensible.'[44]

Ó Dálaigh was undoubtedly much valued by the Arts community because of his own interest in that world. In a prologue to his poem 'A Resigned President', John Montague wrote: 'Cearbhall Ó Dálaigh's smile reinstated words like goodness, gentleness, generosity, words that had lost their meaning, crudely devalued ... Such qualities attract hatred from the unbelieving, the cynical.'[45] Ó Dálaigh's successor, Patrick Hillery, was determined to restore calm to the office and a dignified, low-key stability with a lack of self-projection that would inspire respect, but not poetry.

PART II

THE IMPACT OF THE TROUBLES ON THE REPUBLIC

'Make us pure, Lord, but not quite yet'

The Department of External Affairs in the Republic was simply not ready for the outbreak of the Troubles in Northern Ireland in 1969. Its officials have been characterised as 'poorly prepared' with 'little understanding' and there had not been much appetite for fact-finding missions over the border since the 1950s. While the political initiatives of the 1960s had involved a thaw between the governments and prime ministers and an attempt to persuade the Nationalist Party led by Eddie McAteer to support the reforms of Terence O'Neill's Unionist government, the response of a plea by Hugh McCann, the secretary of the Department of External Affairs at the outbreak of the Troubles, to twenty of his top diplomats asking their views on what the Republic's Northern Irish policy should be, revealed a mixture of shock, bewilderment and confusion.[1] *Most foresaw Irish unity, but there was also acknowledgement of ignorance about northern Unionists, doubts about the wisdom of using the United Nations as a forum to highlight the growing crisis, and a recognition that the Republic would have to change its self-perception. In the words of Eamonn Kennedy, the ambassador to West Germany, 'It is time we started thinking about these basic issues' as well as challenging 'outmoded attitudes inherited from the past'. In the words of Paul Keating, a future secretary of the department, 'we must change our conception of Ireland'.*[2]

The collective responses encapsulated the difficulties, ambiguities and occasional hypocrisies involved in the reaction of the Republic to the Troubles that remained relevant throughout the decade, matched by a sometimes similar confusion on the British side. Clearly, the diplomats were faced 'with a steep learning curve' from 1969, but one of the most significant developments was the formation of a dedicated Anglo-Irish section within the Department of External Affairs which came to play a crucial role for the next three decades.[3] *State papers reveal that, over the course of the decade, despite a traditional attachment to the notion of the state of Northern Ireland as some kind of temporary expedient, there was a parallel stream of more realistic analysis from busy, informative and frank diplomats. Eamonn Gallagher, for example, the senior Irish government official working in liaison with Northern Nationalist politicians, became a close confidant of John Hume of the Social Democratic and Labour Party (SDLP) – in July 1971 Gallagher noted that the Irish government recognised John Hume as 'the real leader of the non-unionists in the North',*[4] *even though he did not become leader of the party until 1978 – and was able to provide considerable insight into Nationalist thinking in Derry.*

In November 1969 a memorandum from the Department of the Taoiseach, reflecting on the outbreak of the Troubles, had referred to southern Irish perceptions of the civil rights disturbances of the previous year. It was a time of heightened interest and awareness of the emergency in the North, but there was a suggestion that there could now be a return to the lack of interest that had characterised southern attitudes to the North for decades. This was a position that had led to caustic remarks that the media and general public had only 'discovered' the North on 5 October 1968, when police had violently broken up a civil rights demonstration in Derry.[5] *It was an observation that underlined ambivalence; Northern Ireland disturbances forced people in the Republic to think seriously about the border for the first time in decades, but there was no guarantee that such an interest would be maintained. Other events over the next few years – most notoriously Bloody Sunday in Derry in January 1972 – again acutely focused southern attention on Northern Ireland, but what also became clear as the decade progressed was that despite the anger of the south in relation to the Troubles, there was also a concerted political determination to ensure that the Troubles were contained in Northern Ireland and would not spill over the border.*

This ensured that any heightened sense of all-Ireland Nationalist sentiment and anger was relatively quickly qualified. On the occasion of the fortieth anniversary of Bloody Sunday in 2012, Eamonn McCann, one of the original organisers of the Northern Ireland Civil Rights Association (NICRA) and a participant in the disturbances in Derry in the early 1970s, reflected on the degree to which it was an event that ultimately helped to reconcile the Republic to partition. The immediate aftermath of the killings witnessed mass protests, and never before or since has there been 'a sense in the south of oneness with the North'. But there was also, at the political and military level, nervousness about the course this sentiment might take. Within days, the insistence on preserving the institutions of the state, bolstering its policing and security and stamping out the menace of 'anarchists' characterised the political rhetoric. In the words of journalist John Healy, who wrote on politics for the Irish Times, *senior Fianna Fáil politicians' rhetoric created 'the feeling that the North is nothing more than a functional historical claim: a thing so long reduced to standard clichés like our fourth green field that it isn't real any more'. As observed by Eamonn McCann, there was a clear emotional and intellectual disengagement from the North.*[6]

This mixture of temporary anger, empathy, engagement but also impatience, paranoia, hostility and resoluteness about the security of the Republic marked the state's attitude to the Troubles of the 1970s. As Minister for Justice at the time, Des O'Malley, was later to characterise it, in relation to the burning of the British Embassy in Dublin after Bloody Sunday, 'the emotions of the times spent themselves in the flames of that building', the clear implication of his words being that there was, after this reaction, a return to rationality. O'Malley, appointed minister in 1970, characterised his three years in the Department of Justice as being like a 'chief fire officer; putting out fires all the time ... you couldn't concentrate on anything else because you were always waiting for a phone call with news of the latest atrocity'.[7] *The other reason for a return to political vigilance was to recover from the convulsions within Fianna Fáil over the Arms Trial of 1970 when two Ministers, Neil Blaney and Charles Haughey were sacked, and Haughey was charged with importation of arms for use by Northern Nationalists, which caused a sensation. Haughey was acquitted, but the issue poisoned the politics of the period.*

Early in the decade, questions lingered that resurfaced at various stages – just what was the real attitude to possible unity? Was it necessary to change articles of the Irish constitution that offended Unionist sensibilities, including the territorial claim over Northern Ireland? Was the issue of the Troubles an Irish question or a British question? In an address delivered to a Welsh audience in 1976, political scientist Brian Farrell, who was one of Irish television's current affairs presenters, was adamant that it was the latter; that the essential parameter was the will of the British government. But he insisted that for the Republic, that question also meant the need to confront its own ambiguities 'which remained, ambiguities in what I would have called constitutional republicanism – we have been very self-centred, we have very largely said "please God it will go away". We have almost prayed that the British would stay because the longer you stay, the further away is the point in time when we might have to accept some form of responsibility.'[8]

Accepting that kind of responsibility continued to be a struggle, reflected not just in tentative steps towards negotiating some kind of middle ground with the British government and Northern constitutional politicians, but also periods of confusion, drift and uncertainty about how the Republic might have to change to accommodate a more pluralist identity. Discomfort with some of these aspects also led to a reliance on the safer ground of protecting the security of the state, concentrating on damage limitation and putting energy into discouraging the romantic nationalism of Irish America, evident in abundance in the National Archives through the deluge of letters that came from all corners of the US. Nor was there any shortage of letters from the Irish public, emotive and accusatory, depending on the latest atrocity, though it was clear that the gulf between what many of those correspondents wanted to see – the British army gone, a united Ireland and the release of Republican prisoners – and the reality of what was politically feasible in the 1970s was wide indeed.

One of the main diplomatic missions of the 1970s became the undermining of support for the IRA from Irish America. Given the relative lack of power of Ireland internationally, this took time and effort in terms of getting access to the White House, particularly to move leading US politicians from the stance articulated by Secretary of State William Rogers early in 1972. While he said the American political establishment was sympathetic, he also asserted that the US could not 'judge, condemn, advocate any particular solution or intervene in this tragic and complex situation'.[9] *Diplomatic persistence paid off, however, and the undermining of IRA support groups by US politicians followed later in the decade.*

Some politicians, including Garret FitzGerald and Conor Cruise O'Brien, were honest about the scale of the ignorance that existed in the south about the North and its people, and according to historian John A. Murphy, a unified Nationalist Ireland was not a practical priority for most in the Republic. As he saw it in 1977, when there were some suggestions of a Nationalist resurgence or revival, such a notion was exaggerated: 'the economy still continues to be the overriding concern of politicians and people alike'. As with other assessments, it was a sense of ambivalence that formed the centre of his analysis: 'There is vague popular approval for the kind of Nationalist attitudes typified by Fianna Fáil. These, let it be said, are as nebulous and ambivalent as they ever were. We in the Republic are heirs, not of an authentic Republican ideal to which we have never paid more than lip service, but of the gut nationalism of a homogenous Catholic people.'[10] *Such 'gut nationalism' was complicated when the Troubles did emerge over the border, most distressingly with the Dublin and Monaghan bombs of 1974 orchestrated by the Ulster Volunteer Force, which killed thirty-three people.*

How to report on, mediate and present the Troubles was also problematic, reflected in ugly disputes over section 31 of the Broadcasting Act, prohibiting interviews with those perceived to be supportive of paramilitaries. For some, this was essential to prevent terrorists using the airwaves to promote and justify their aims, but for others was an instrument of state censorship that simplified the conflict and compounded further ignorance. One journalist with the Irish Times, *James Downey, suggested the coalition of 1973–7 'positively gloated over the harshness of the measures introduced' to combat subversion, an indication of the growing distrust between the media and politicians.*[11] *Certainly, the correspondence of Conor Cruise O'Brien, the Minister for Posts and Telegraphs in that government, suggests an obsession with this issue on his part, but given the frequency with which he was singled out as an extremist, the extent of his influence as chief philosopher of Armageddon should not be exaggerated.*

Although those in government in the Republic were anxious to maintain dialogue with Northern Nationalists, most notably with the SDLP established in 1970, there were fraught relations at times between them and within the SDLP. Some of these Nationalists were sceptical about the commitment to them that existed in the Republic. As recalled by one of the SDLP's leading members, Austin Currie, most southern politicians 'including Jack Lynch, had shown little interest in the North'. The failure of the power-sharing assembly initiative encapsulated in the Sunningdale Agreement of 1973, due to Unionist and Loyalist opposition, exposed fault lines in the Irish government's approach. In the view of Garret FitzGerald, Minister for Foreign Affairs at the time, 'I pushed too far for too much' in relation to a Council of Ireland, while in the view of Taoiseach Liam Cosgrave, the fault was with Britain as prime minister Harold Wilson did not have the bottle to stand up to the 'mobs' that brought down the power-sharing assembly, which he believed a Conservative government would have.[12] *Given the despair that existed in its aftermath, there was a psychological as well as political importance for the SDLP in being, in Currie's words 'wined and dined' in Dublin when party members were under 'considerable political and personal stress.'*[13] *Conor Cruise O'Brien, however, became uncomfortable about the relationship with the SDLP as in his view it 'came to complicate the development of Northern Ireland policy.'*[14]

On the British side, as recalled by Merlyn Rees, who served as Northern Ireland Secretary of State from 1974 to 1976, 'I had much to learn about the south ... the first time that I became really aware of the political problems of the province was in 1969.' With Harold Wilson, then leader of the opposition, he met IRA leaders in Dublin in March 1972, highlighting another ambivalence: for all the tough public rhetoric from the British side, there were attempts at private dialogue and these had the potential to create tension not just in London, but also in Dublin. As suggested by James Downey in relation to the negotiation of a possible ceasefire between the IRA and the British army, Jack Lynch was outraged: 'The British who had warned him – the elected leader – against meddling in the affairs of Northern Ireland were talking to people who threatened Irish democracy, who made his own position unstable.'[15]

The British also continued to insist that Dublin was not doing enough to prevent violence – 'the Dublin government surely knew that weapons and ammunition [were] being routed to the North by these paramilitaries' – but there was, it seemed, a recognition that neither was this straightforward. As Rees recalled in relation to one of the most spectacular killings of the decade in the Republic – the assassination of the British ambassador in Dublin Christopher Ewart-Biggs by the IRA in 1979: 'We could have been far more publicly critical of the Irish government for their lack of security control in Dublin, particularly given their own public criticism of us in South Armagh. I sympathised, however, with their difficulties.'[16]

What they could not agree on were issues like internment without trial, introduced in Northern Ireland in August 1971. Hugh McCann was trying to stress the politics of this issue and the degree to which it added to support for the IRA, and there was anger at what was regarded as a 'blank refusal' of Britain to listen to Irish politicians' 'sincerely offered advice'. But what became a recurrent theme was the degree to which the British were loathe to share the 'firm and unshakeable' conviction of Irish governments that 'if they were to call the extreme unionists' bluff they will crumble.'[17] *Unionists, as reflected in the memoirs of Brian Faulkner, the last prime minister of Northern Ireland before the abolition of its domestic government in 1972, were deeply distrustful of politicians from the Republic – Lynch he characterised with disdain as a 'wily Irishman' – and the ideas they might 'plant' in the British mind.*[18]

One of the things they wanted to plant was the notion that there had to be an 'Irish dimension' to any political solution to the Troubles, but what that should be, and how deep it should go, was not only contentious but also ambiguous; the notion of such a dimension was acknowledged in a British government position paper in late 1972. Britain was also likely to consider any solution that brought stability, including Irish unity.[19] *But, interestingly, the Irish governments also devoted attention, through the discussions of an inter-departmental unit on the implications of Irish unity under the chair of assistant cabinet secretary Dermot Nally, to the nature of its own state and the degree of sectarianism in its constitution of 1937. The clause that recognised the 'special position' of the Catholic Church was removed after a referendum in 1972, but such a development would not really answer the issue of the understanding of Unionist aspirations, or the culture of Protestantism.*

The combination of these various difficulties meant that by the middle of the decade, Garret FitzGerald and others felt a 'virtual impotence' and what seemed an even more frightening scenario in that context was that a British withdrawal might result in a full-scale civil war. The biggest issue, as it had been historically, even in the age of de Valera, was not the possibility of a solution that would create Irish unity – wedded in theory to this though the politicians were – but the vulnerability of the Republic to the collapse of Northern Ireland into anarchy. By the end of the decade, as identified by an independent senator, Trevor West, 'the mistake that has been made by southern politicians is that they have never followed up the logical consequences of their calls for Irish unity'. Or as Hugh Logue of the SDLP put it, 'spell out exactly what it does mean ... would Loyalists have the same access to parade O'Connell Street in Dublin on 12 July as they now have to parade on Royal Avenue?'[20] *How to handle such 'logical consequences' was one of the tasks facing Charles Haughey at the dawn of a new decade, after he had recovered spectacularly from the Arms Trial to take over the leadership of Fianna Fáil in 1979.*

– TEN –

A POST-1916 MOOD

In May 1971, speaking in Belfast, Fine Gael senator John Kelly suggested 'The Irishman from the South usually feels, and I think wisely, that the best contribution he can make to peace is to keep his mouth shut.'[1] In August the same year it was asserted in a contribution to *Hibernia* magazine that 'an outside observer would be excused from assuming that the south just couldn't care less about what happens North of the border'.[2] Six months later, in the aftermath of Bloody Sunday in Derry, when British paratroopers killed thirteen unarmed men following a march in Derry, the same magazine suggested that after this atrocity, all had 'changed utterly'. It maintained that 'the reunification of Ireland has emerged indisputably as the central issue at stake. That, above all, is what the conflict is now all about. The intensity of the reaction and the counter-reaction has swept away all lesser considerations. The polarisation is now complete ... after two and a half years of apathetic detachment the emotions of the south have at last spilt over.'[3]

Was this exaggerated wishful thinking, or a genuine turning point? Did citizens of the Republic remain partitionist in their thinking about the Troubles, which began in 1969 after decades of discrimination against the Catholic and Nationalist minority in the North, and involved armed campaigns by Irish Republican and Ulster Loyalist paramilitary groups and the deployment of British army troops? There is no doubt that Bloody Sunday was a seminal moment, but just how ingrained was the lack of concern identified by *Hibernia* in the summer of 1971 and would that sense of detachment return? And to what extent was the advice of John Kelly followed?

In the aftermath of Bloody Sunday, the historian Leland Lyons wrote to Garret FitzGerald, in relation to a paper he was preparing on conflict studies. Lyons was a native of Derry who was educated at Trinity College Dublin, where he subsequently lectured, after which he held the Chair of Modern History at the University of Kent in Canterbury (before returning to Trinity as Provost in 1974). Entirely comfortable in both countries, he was an acclaimed historian of the Home Rule era of the late nineteenth and early twentieth century, before producing *Ireland Since the Famine*. Given the gravity of what had happened on Bloody Sunday and the reaction to it, Lyons was struggling for perspective: 'A historian trying to manipulate a crystal ball is bound to end up making even more of a fool of himself than usual: I certainly got the impression after the Derry shootings of something approaching a post-1916 mood, but I can't tell whether or not it has begun to subside.'[4] The historian in Lyons was right to be wary of drawing definitive conclusions less than three weeks after the tragedy, and he had also identified that sense that feelings could and in all likelihood would, subside. As he saw it, he found himself 'with a terrifying assignment for a historian – to talk about the present and the future'.[5]

On Bloody Sunday, one man who corresponded with Garret FitzGerald was certainly approaching a 'post-1916 mood', writing, 'If the IRA are monsters they had two great tutors. In the first instance the British gave them quite a few lessons in 800 years. In the second place your lousy crowd used British guns against them ... TV news flash at this moment – 12 dead. The British are murderous bastards. I pray God the IRA will do their duty.'[6] Conor Cruise O'Brien also felt momentarily that 'the scenario seemed to have slipped back to 1921 or even earlier ... for a few days people talked and wrote of a national change of mood like that which had set in after the executions of 1916'. He suggested the burning of the British Embassy in Dublin in the aftermath of Bloody Sunday, following street protests and marches, changed this sentiment, as people then grew aware of the consequences of lawlessness and violence 'coming down here'.[7]

The day after the embassy burning, the *Irish Times* referred to it as 'the biggest demonstration the Republic has seen in a generation', amidst driving rain and bitter winds.[8] Lynch insisted in a speech in the Dáil that a small minority had 'infiltrated' the protestors and that 'the nation gains no credit from such an action' but that 'I think it is true to say that grief and sympathy were hardly ever more sincerely felt nor more widespread in this country, certainly not in my lifetime.'[9] There was also a national day of mourning for the victims of Bloody Sunday. A note from the Minister for Foreign Affairs, Patrick Hillery, about a discussion he had conducted with the British ambassador revealed the ambassador had referred to those responsible for the burning of his embassy as 'hooligans ... he said that London had put at his disposal a large aircraft to evacuate women and children and non essential personnel of his mission if he considered it necessary'.[10]

There was also much correspondence sent to the Irish government from outraged British television viewers because the 'Irish police stood and watched' as the embassy was burned. But there was also, from some who had been on the march, a refutation that the burning was the work of hooligans: 'I thought about my actions beforehand', wrote one such participant, 'and I considered it necessary to burn the Embassy as a gesture ... I am quite prepared to pay for the damage to the building by way of taxes.'[11] Solicitors acting for the tenants of the embassy's neighbours in Merrion Square (Irish Auctioneers and Valuers) looked for compensation of £75,000 as 'the government have already announced that they accepted responsibility for the damage to the British Embassy'; they were told the Office of Public Works would repair the damage.[12]

Fears about emotions running high also had to be addressed at the highest level of Anglo-Irish politics and state files released by the National Archives of Ireland in 2003 give a sense of the difficult atmosphere that Bloody Sunday created. On the evening of the slaughter in Derry, a distraught Taoiseach, Jack Lynch, rang his British counterpart, Edward Heath, Conservative prime minister since 1970. Lynch began by apologising for ringing at a late hour, 'but you will probably have heard the unfortunate news about Derry this afternoon'. Heath replied, 'It is very bad news, yes.' That was about all they agreed on.

The conversation was tense as an emotional Lynch grappled with the enormity of what had happened and the potential fallout. He told Heath that 'from reactions received around the country it looks as if a very serious point has now been reached and the situation could escalate beyond what any of us would anticipate at this stage. I am told that, according to reports I received and checked on the spot, the British troops reacted rather beyond what a disciplined force might be expected to, and, as you know, there were 13 killed and as many again injured.'

Heath was terse and defensive in reply: 'Well, now, as far as any accusations are concerned I obviously cannot accept that ... I must also point out that this arose out of a march which was against the law. Now the people therefore who deliberately organised this march in circumstances which we all know in which the IRA were bound to intervene, carry a heavy responsibility for any damage which ensued.' He pointed out that Lynch had asked him to ban marches the previous summer; Lynch accepted this, but replied, 'There is no indication at all that the IRA intervened before shots were fired from the British side.' Heath replied, 'I am not going to prejudge that.' Another part of the conversation witnessed Lynch asserting that 'the whole thing arises as a result of the Stormont regime', to which Heath responded, 'It arises as a result of the IRA trying to take over the country.'[13]

It was a difficult conversation, and an indication that Anglo-Irish relations were close to breaking point at the beginning of what was to be a bloody awful year, during which 470 people died, 323 of them civilians. Both men had addressed the essential points that would bedevil not just the Bloody Sunday controversy, but various aspects of assigning blame for the scale of the Troubles for nearly forty years: How and why did the British troops react the way they did? Were the marchers to blame? To what extent had the IRA intervened? What would the fallout be? Another crucial factor was that of propaganda. Heath may have insisted that he was not going to prejudge the situation, but, according to a document discovered in the Public Record Office in London in 1995, at a meeting he had two days after Bloody Sunday with Lord Chief Justice Widgery, who was appointed to chair a tribunal of inquiry into the event to commence the following day, and the Lord Chancellor Lord Hailsham, a key figure in Conservative politics whose father had been a staunchly pro-Unionist Lord Chancellor in the 1930s, Widgery was told, 'it had to be remembered that we were in Northern Ireland, fighting not just a military war, but a propaganda war'.[14]

In a draft letter to the London *Times* in the immediate aftermath of Bloody Sunday, John Kelly wrote in an impassioned and prescient way as someone who had in the past praised liberal British opinion. He reckoned that the tragedy had left the position of moderates in politics in the Republic 'nearly impossible, as there is less and less for us to say that seems relevant ... If there is one way in which the situation can be made even worse it will be to allow the truth about Sunday to be suppressed, the guilty to go unpunished and the innocent victims still alive to go uncompensated, and if experience of British handling of the situation up to this is a guide, this is exactly what will happen.'[15] It was precisely what did happen, as the Widgery Report duly ignored the people of Derry – the witnesses, the families of the victims and the survivors – in producing a scandalous and discredited 39-page report, symbolically torn in pieces in the Guildhall Square in Derry in June 2010 when the Saville Report finally vindicating the innocence of those shot was published.[16] More than 500 eyewitness accounts had been collected by the Northern Ireland Civil Rights Association and the National Council for Civil Liberties in the aftermath of Bloody Sunday. Taking on board their accounts would have diluted the potency of British propaganda. As a result, they were shut out, until they emerged vindicated in Saville's report. The report also addressed the essential questions that arose in the conversation between Lynch and Heath on the night of Bloody Sunday.

A week after Bloody Sunday, Garret FitzGerald wrote to Lord Moyne, a member of the Guinness family and prominent in the British Conservative Monday Club: 'The British government must act quickly if it is to avoid a civil war in Ireland. The atmosphere here last week was highly dangerous. It was, I think, defused somewhat as a result of the Dáil debate in which Neil Blaney misjudged the situation and made a warmongering speech, which provoked a prompt and vigorous reaction from all three parties.'[17]

This letter was a reminder of the other contexts; the political reaction on the British and Irish sides at both the public and private level. As leader of the Conservative Party and prime minister, Heath was not keen on an 'Irish dimension' to any proposals for a political solution in Northern Ireland. Other state files released in 2003 reveal that there was an obvious tension between Lynch and Heath; the British ambassador in Dublin, John Peck, described one of their meetings as a 'dialogue of the deaf'.[18]

Although Heath and his successors were gradually persuaded of the merits of a power-sharing solution to the Northern Ireland problem and, eventually, of the importance of an 'Irish dimension', all of these developments in Anglo-Irish relations were painstaking, slow and fractured, amidst the ability of tragic events to prompt different kinds of languages and often a perceived need to cool the political temperature. In early September 1972 Heath and Lynch had their first talks in almost a year, and they went on 'much longer than intended'. It seemed to be a better meeting than the previous one at Chequers, an encounter, suggested journalist Michael Mills, which had been dogged by the sense that Heath 'was very often unable to understand Lynch's arguments because of the British premier's failure to grasp the complexities of the Northern problem'.[19] John Whale, an influential journalist with the *Sunday Times* and regarded as having the ear of Heath, informed an official in the Irish Embassy in London in December 1972 that the British government 'want a united Ireland if only to get the problem off their hands'.[20]

Nothing encapsulates the sense of fear better than the continual use of the phrase 'civil war' in the context of what was possible in the early 1970s. It appears in many letters and speeches of this era and it was a genuine concern. Fianna Fáil's Minister for Justice Desmond O'Malley wrote to Jack Lynch from Hong Kong at the end of October 1972: 'There is now obviously a strong possibility of civil war coupled with a blood bath in Ireland.'[21] In March 1973, new Labour Party minister Conor Cruise O'Brien was also warning of the possibility of 'full scale civil war'. He wrote to FitzGerald, who was a good point of contact between the Labour and Fine Gael parties in coalition, to explain that he had just sent a memorandum to Cosgrave regarding Northern Ireland: 'You may find it alarmist and you may be right, but [I wrote it] to express a sense of alarm which I do actually feel and I hope you will agree that it is legitimate to communicate this sense to the Taoiseach and colleagues in this way.'[22] 'Holocaust' was another word employed; when Lady Wicklow (Eleanor Butler, a former Labour Party senator) called to the Department of the Taoiseach in early 1973 she 'said that isolated Catholics were lacking in essentials such as enough petrol to take them to the border on the day of the Holocaust'.[23]

In the midst of such stark warnings, some academics saw a role for themselves in attempting to cool the temperature and facilitate dialogue, although there was uncertainty as to the merits of their endeavours. Their efforts were characterised as involving 'those strange conferences by which our English friends set such store' by Leland Lyons.[24] One initiative resulted in the creation of the British Irish Association (BIA) in November 1972 to promote the development of academic, cultural and social relations between the two countries. Founder members included a good share of historians, including chairman Leland Lyons, Robert Kee, a journalist and award-winning broadcaster who later wrote and presented *Ireland: A Television History*, Cecil Woodham Smith whose published work included a powerful account of the Irish famine of the mid nineteenth century in which he indicted the British administration for its failures, and Desmond Williams, the cosmopolitan and media savvy Professor of Modern History in UCD, who was friendly with many prominent in British journalistic and academic life. It was contended that, despite extensive links in trade and tourism between the two countries, 'there is still widespread ignorance of the social and political realities of the "other country" on both sides of the Irish Sea'. Jack Lynch could not attend the inaugural conference in 1973 but encouraged his Minister for Health Erskine Childers to attend.[25]

But even at the early stages, the Irish ambassador in London was expressing concern that its proceedings, far from being confined to cultural aspects of Anglo-Irish relations, 'amount to a heavy incursion into the field of politics. This is a matter about which I am not at all happy.' These concerns were shared by Desmond Williams who in 1973 expressed 'grave disquiet' at the 'political tone' the association was beginning to develop.[26] By 1978 the association was walking something of a tightrope; its chairman, the British author and economist Lord Vaizey, wrote to Lynch after he had been in touch with Patrick Hillery expressing the hope that the government would understand that none of its members had been invited to its annual gathering because if any Fianna Fáil ministers were there, no Unionists would attend. (Garret FitzGerald and Cruise O'Brien were among the politicians who were invited.) Vaizey suggested the group comprised 'largely academics and people interested in cultural affairs. Occasionally we put our feet in it.' The *Belfast Telegraph* reported on the withdrawal of the SDLP's John Hume and Austin Currie, representing the dominant constitutional Nationalists in the North who opposed the IRA's campaign (and whose party had been formed in August 1970), from the meeting in Belfast because there were no Irish government representatives attending. FitzGerald also opted out, and Patrick Lynch, a UCD political economist, former chairman of the state airline Aer Lingus and senior civil servant as well as a founder member of the BIA, also expressed his annoyance, considering the decision to exclude government representatives to be 'a wrong one [that] may well defeat the very purpose for which the association was founded'. Seán Donlon, a diplomat and future general secretary of the Department of Foreign Affairs, disputed the association's contention that it had no financial support from official sources, pointing out that the government had in the past sent delegates to its conferences and financed receptions for it. In any case, Jack Lynch cared little; in a rare expression of personal opinion on matters of this sort, a handwritten note of his revealed that he believed 'This crowd, both the British Irish Association and the Ewart-Biggs Foundation seem to be naïve in the extreme.'[27]

Americans were also fond of conferences addressing Irish issues; at one such gathering of the American Committee for Irish Studies in Missouri in April 1976, Cork historian John A. Murphy referred to Bloody Sunday and was adamant that the Anglophobia which was apparent after the shootings 'was notably short-lived once its material repercussions became clear. Today it is remarkable that there is at least as much concern in the Republic about the sufferings of English victims of IRA terrorism as at the continuing tragedy in the North.' He suggested that by 1976, the IRA campaign 'further numbed' the 'so-called aspiration to a united Ireland' and that the impact of the Troubles on the Republic had been reactionary: 'There is evidence of a backlash against radical change of whatever nature and the religious and cultural homogeneity of the South has been underlined.'[28]

– ELEVEN –

STUDIED INDIFFERENCE OR GENEROUS TOLERANCE?

Murphy had underlined the multidimensional impact the Troubles had on the Republic and the transitory and sometimes simplistic and self-satisfied nature of emotive outrage. Aodhan Madden went to a Dublin pub as a young journalist with his colleagues after the burning of the British Embassy in 1972, for example, 'elated because we had done our bit for Ireland'.[1] There was also much ignorance about Northern Ireland, at both the political and personal level, even in the midst of worldwide media attention being given to the problem in the context of unprecedented bloodshed. Pamphlets issued by some left-wing movements were critical of careless and cheap talk – 'the pub republicans of southern Ireland do not have to suffer the consequences of the politics they propound. The Northern Catholic community does.'[2] In October 1972 Brian Walker of the New Unionist Movement in Belfast, wrote to Garret FitzGerald (who had established numerous contacts with Unionists) in strong terms about a recent visit to Belfast by Fine Gael's Liam Cosgrave and Richie Ryan: 'We were appalled at their incredible ignorance of the Northern situation and at Mr Cosgrave's apparent inability to understand what we were trying to say or to argue the case from his point of view.'[3]

FitzGerald was candid with his Northern contacts about the extent of this ignorance, writing to one of them in September 1972: 'I have had further occasions to test opinions in political circles here and have to say that the sense of involvement and concern for Northern Ireland is even less than I conveyed to the meeting. If only all our politicians were forced to spend some time in the North.'[4] That ignorance was also replicated at the more general public level. It was, in some senses, a wilful ignorance in the sense of simply not getting exercised about Northern Ireland and a maybe unspoken sense that partition 'had worked and continued to work … the reality was that throughout the entire decade of the 1970s more people in the Republic marched against the prevailing evils of taxation than ever did for Northern Ireland.'[5]

There were plenty who were busy 'furiously mouthing the anti-English lyrics of the Wolfe Tones [a popular Republican folk band] in grubby ballad bars',[6] but precious few of them had actually ever been in Northern Ireland, despite its physical proximity, and they had no intention of going near it. Words, slogans and lyrics were easy in this context, but how much empathy born of knowledge or experience was actually evident? Musician Christy Moore was unusual in seeking to understand the people and their living situations behind the slogans. Acknowledging that before 1976 he had 'little or no knowledge of the Ulster State', he began after that to visit Belfast and Derry, stayed in homes there, met families affected by the Troubles and 'started to understand what it was like to live in the Bogside or Ardoyne'.[7]

Paddy Harte as Fine Gael TD for Donegal North East and a committed ecumenist, was also active in establishing contacts. As far as he was concerned in the early 1970s in Fine Gael 'there was no-one with an informed opinion on Northern Ireland'. After Bloody Sunday, he became 'obsessed' with fear of retaliation and fear of reprisals but recognised that it was necessary to talk directly to those engaged in violence to encourage solutions and Jack Lynch was supportive of this. He even went as far as to bring an Ulster Defence Association member to Dublin and entertain him in the Dáil restaurant. And why not, given that Protestant Church leaders also met the army council of the IRA in Feakle in County Clare in December 1974? Harte, who valued his independence and his interviews with Jeremy Paxman on *Spotlight* on BBC Northern Ireland, recalled that, even through very tense times, 'it was still possible to make connections and establish dialogue, sometimes with the most unlikely people'.[8] But many more adopted a stance that amounted to a deliberate distancing; in Declan Kiberd's words: 'the general attitude to the North in the Republic was not unlike the approach to the Irish language: make us pure, Lord, but not quite yet (and certainly not if such purity entails financial or intellectual sacrifice)'.[9]

The Irish government, army and volunteers did involve themselves, however, in catering for refugees from Northern Ireland; in 1970 there were 1,588 such individuals and the army authorities arranged for them to be housed and fed. In early July 1971, refugees once again began to arrive over the border, this time 'in somewhat ominous numbers'. Those numbers peaked at 5,308 on 15 and 16 July 1971, with the numbers not dipping below 2,000 until the beginning of August. In effect this was a charitable endeavour to give holidays to children affected by the Troubles and in relation to their status as refuges, all 'are accepted as such at their word'.

It was a process regarded as having been accomplished with considerable smoothness and while a government memorandum reviewing the issue in February 1973 appreciated the distress of the majority of those involved, it was suggested some were also taking advantage of such charity:

> In 1972, however, the pattern was somewhat different. The refugees on this occasion had obviously made preparations in advance for a holiday in the South. Most of them had suitcases and numbers of the children carried swimming gear, tennis racquets, fishing rods etc. ... refugees are not always just frightened people who are thankful for the assistance being given them. Some of them can be very demanding and ungrateful, even obstreperous and fractious – as well as, particularly in the case of teenage boys, destructive. Although those who came south in 1972 were not driven from their homes and were largely holidaymakers, it was appreciated in civil defence headquarters that they were justifiably in need of a few weeks of peace and quietness away from the atmosphere of bombings and shootings in which they normally lived. Irrespective of their attitudes and behaviour and their motivation coming South, government policy has been interpreted – and continues to be interpreted – as requiring that they should all be accepted without question and treated to the best of our ability as groups of Irish people in need of help at a very difficult time.[10]

For some of those enduring the daily stress of the Troubles, the Republic seemed somewhat idyllic; in March 1978 a resident of Derry, with an unemployed husband and young children, wrote of occasional day trips in the summer across the border: 'Once I get over that border checkpoint I feel free as a bird. No soldiers or searches or bombed empty spaces where once shops and homes, dances and cinemas used to be. It's lovely.'[11]

For others, including Neil Blaney, carnage in Northern Ireland seemed to offer an opportunity for pious and patently false assertions about the tolerance of the Republic. Blaney had first been elected a TD for east Donegal in 1948, inheriting the seat from his Republican father; he became a legendary organiser and electoral strategist and first served as Minister for Posts and Telegraphs and subsequently Local Government before becoming Minister for Agriculture and Fisheries in 1966. In representing a county affected by partition and given his background (he was born at a time when his father was under sentence of death during the civil war in 1922 for fighting on the side of anti-Treaty Republicans) he was well placed to present himself as a traditionalist and the Republican conscience of his party in relation to the aspiration towards Irish unity. Blaney insisted in January 1972 on a BBC programme that since Ireland had been partitioned in 1920, 'there had never been any discrimination against Protestants'. G. B. McConnell, the outgoing chairman of the Dublin Council of Churches, dismissed this claim as 'nonsense' and pointed out that, while 'by and large' Protestants in the Republic had been encouraged to play a full part in the affairs of the state, in the recent past a Church of Ireland rectory had been bombed within a short distance from Blaney's own home in Donegal.[12] Only 4 per cent of the population of the Republic in 1971 was Protestant, amounting to 119,000 people, down from 9.9 per cent, or 311,000 people sixty years previously.

The *Church of Ireland Gazette* maintained that on the part of a certain section of older Catholics, there was still 'a deep-seated distrust and suspicion of those who are regarded as the remnant of the Ascendancy'. There was, according to the *Irish Times*, 'widespread rumour that Protestant families in the South and West Cork have been threatened during recent weeks'.[13] This was also an issue on which Taoiseach Jack Lynch corresponded with Revd William Wynne, from the Church of Ireland rectory in Monkstown in Dublin. Lynch agreed there was a need for more to be done 'to make known to the world at large that the Protestant community here plays such an important part at all levels of society', but he managed to wriggle out of having to say anything in public: 'I always feel that public statements to this effect are more likely to gain acceptance if they are made by members of that community'. If that could be done, he and his colleagues in politics would 'very much appreciate' it.[14]

There is little doubt that Protestants in certain parts of the Republic were feeling intimidated in the early 1970s; a scribbled note in the

Department of the Taoiseach read: 'Senator McGlinchey phoned. Protestants in St Johnstone [in Donegal] terrified that they will be burnt out tonight', a reference to Orange Lodge members returning to their hall after a march.[15] In February 1972 there was also intimidation of members of the Protestant community in Sligo, including the breaking of shop windows belonging to them. These were condemned by the Countess Markievicz Fianna Fáil *cumann* in Sligo, which also castigated reputed remarks made by Sligo Fianna Fáil TD Ray MacSharry: 'His [alleged] remarks, stating that Protestants should be bombed out if necessary, can only further sectarianism in our town.'[16]

Revealingly, another note prepared in the Department of the Taoiseach referred to 'Protestants in the Garda Síochána: 2 superintendents, 16 Gardaí. Total: 18 out of 7,261.'[17] When he met the West German Chancellor, Willy Brandt, in September 1972, Lynch was defensive about any charge of sectarianism in the Republic, insisting that 'there was no sectarian problem in the South and in some ways, e.g. School grants, Protestants were treated better. They had more than their proportionate share of representation on the judiciary and in professions and businesses.'[18]

But attacks on a number of prominent Protestants in the early part of 1974 led to the suggestion that Protestants in Dublin might set up their own vigilante group to protect themselves. Edmond O'Connor, from Raheny in Dublin rang the Department of the Taoiseach in June 1974 to say that he and several of his co-religionists were deeply concerned about recent attacks on Protestants in the south, most notably on Billy Fox, a Protestant Fine Gael senator killed by the IRA in Monaghan earlier that year, and the Earl and Countess of Donoughmore. O'Connor, who was one of five Protestant families living side-by-side in Raheny, said that he felt additional security should be provided for the minority Protestant community in the south. He also maintained that he had called the Department of Justice, but they had been unhelpful and, in consequence, a vigilante group might be set up.

Officials in the Department of the Taoiseach contacted Raheny Gardaí, who reported that O'Connor was 'a bit of a crank, but not an extreme one'. They also commented that O'Connor had previously been a Catholic but had 'changed', even though he had recently married a Catholic widow. In sum, the Raheny Gardaí viewed him as 'a nice enough fellow to talk to'. The Department of the Taoiseach brought the matter to the attention of the Taoiseach, Liam Cosgrave, who agreed that a substantive response should be sent to O'Connor. That letter, signed by Cosgrave's private secretary, Frank Murray, another influential civil servant of this era, noted 'interference with Protestants in the state has been a very rare occurrence and has, apparently, in many instances been motivated by reasons other than religious affiliation.' It concluded by stating that the Gardaí were 'fully trained and equipped to carry out these duties and can call on the Army for assistance if necessary. In these circumstances, the development of privately organised security groups would be a highly undesirable development.'[19]

In a speech to his own party members in May 1976, Garret FitzGerald was adamant that 'although religious bigotry in the Republic is minimal, and is a pale reflection of what prevails in the North, we cannot deny that it exists here.'[20] But in an indication that opinion in the Republic's Protestant community was not unanimous on the issue of sectarianism, writer Hubert Butler expressed himself troubled in 1975 by some of his fellow Protestants stressing the toleration of the Republic, suggesting they were 'meekly subservient to authority'.[21] One historical survey of southern Protestants has noted that in the 1970s, many younger members of the Protestant community made far more contact with 'the other side' than their parents would have done, partly due to diminishing religious commitment. By 1974, 14 per cent of pupils in Protestant schools were Catholic, which had increased to 19 per cent in 1978. In the new comprehensive schools (see Part VIII), the Catholic proportion rose from 3 per cent in 1971 to 33 per cent in 1974.[22]

But there were still tensions around the issue of mixed marriages where ecumenism was not yet a reality as a Catholic partner had to promise 'to do all in his power to have all children baptized and brought up in the Catholic Church'. Certain stereotypes also continued to endure; the view that all Protestants were rich, for example, drew an exasperated response from the Bishop of Cork, R. G. Perdue, in 1975, as seen in the pages of the *Church of Ireland Gazette*: 'Our fellow citizens know surprisingly little about us, about our difficulties and frustrations, economic, social and religious ... if we were to disclose the figures of income ... people would be amazed at the high proportion of our people who live on very low incomes ... the minority gets so accustomed to its handicaps and weaknesses that it ceases to expect, or struggle for, justice and equality of opportunity with others. We have seen examples in the field of education and of marriage.'[23]

– TWELVE –

LOST REPUTATIONS AND SUPPRESSED TRUTH

In the fervid atmosphere of 1971 and 1972 there were some calls for the formation of a national government, in order to give an appearance of 'national solidarity'. Jack Lynch agreed that such a government might have 'a certain superficial attraction', but insisted that it was unnecessary, given that 'all 3 main parties are agreed on basic policy in relation to Northern Ireland'.[1] That he would make this assertion in February 1972 suggested he was hoping to draw a line under the convulsions in his own party after the Arms Trial events of 1970. The actions of some of his party members in 1969–70 that led to the crisis, notably those of Charles Haughey and Neil Blaney, were driven, it seems, 'by a mixture of genuine ideological commitment and concern for the position of northern Nationalists, desire to assert control over the increasingly volatile forces of northern nationalism (including in this support for the northern-based nucleus of what became the Provisional IRA against the Marxist-oriented Official IRA leadership who were seen as threatening the Republic), personal contempt for Lynch' and a wish to assert claims to the succession of the leadership of Fianna Fáil.[2]

Blaney had advocated the sending of Irish troops into Northern Ireland to bring about United Nations intervention in 1969 and dismissed the view that unity could only come through consent, maintaining the use of force should not be ruled out. With Haughey, he secured the establishment of a cabinet subcommittee, which deliberately kept other cabinet members in the dark.

Most controversially, the two became involved in schemes to supply arms to Catholic self-defence groups in the North (largely fronts for the Provisional IRA) in association with the military intelligence officer Captain James Kelly. He had been visiting Belfast at the time of the outbreak of the Troubles and was deeply affected by what he witnessed and always maintained he acted with the knowledge of his superiors, including the defence minister James Gibbons, a TD since 1957 who was appointed minister in 1969. Kelly sincerely believed himself to be acting with proper authority.[3] As was later reported by the Committee of Public Accounts in August 1972, more than £76,000 of a £100,000 grant-in-aid voted in 1969 by the government for the relief of distress in Northern Ireland had not been accounted for; James Kelly admitted that £32,000 had been spent on the purchase of arms in Germany. According to John Kelly, a Belfast Republican who was one of the Arms Trial defendants, Blaney was the 'engine room' of the scheme and Haughey's role was relatively marginal. Blaney vetoed a proposal to import arms from traditional IRA suppliers in America, preferring European arms dealers to make it easier to ensure the arms would remain under the control of the government forces involved. At the end of 1969 Peter Berry, secretary of the Department of Justice, became aware of these developments and blocked the final attempt to import arms through Dublin airport in April 1970. The consignment consisted of 400 pistols, 400 sub-machine guns, twenty-five heavy machine guns and ammunition.

Lynch announced the resignation of his Justice Minister Micheál Ó Móráin (which Lynch had requested) on 5 May (he was replaced by Des O'Malley), and was then approached by Liam Cosgrave, who had received a tip-off about ministers' involvements in plots to import arms by a source within the Gardaí, apparently having failed to get the *Sunday Independent* interested in publishing the story due to difficulties in confirming the information.[4] Blaney and Haughey were then dismissed from cabinet on 6 May 1970, as Jack Lynch sought to impose discipline and unity.[5] It was sensational news and came at two o'clock in the morning; a copy boy was sent to *Irish Independent* political correspondent Arthur Noonan's house as he couldn't be contacted by phone and was told 'if necessary break a window to wake him up and we'll pay for the window later; but I urgently need him to ring in'.[6]

Lynch appeared to act late in the day, which may have been partly to do with the failure to give officials in any government department responsibility for framing an assessment of what was happening in Northern

Ireland. Following his appointment, the Minister for External Affairs, Patrick Hillery, had asked 'Where's the Northern Ireland desk?' at the end of his introductory tour of Iveagh House, the headquarters of his new department. An Anglo–Irish division in what became the Department of Foreign Affairs was not established until 1971.[7] The drafting of Lynch's famous television broadcast at the outset of the Troubles – the Republic 'can no longer stand by and see innocent people injured and perhaps worse' speech in August 1969 – had, as a result, been a confused and a collective cabinet effort. Lynch, of course, was under pressure to do more and deliver on his words but justified a balanced 'do nothing' policy on the basis that to do anything would lead to even more instability.[8]

He did, however, rely on T. K. Whitaker to advise him and by September 1969 he was emphasising that any pursuit of unity had to be through peaceful means and with the consent of the majority, and therein lay the problem as his more hawkish colleagues saw it in late 1969 and into early 1970. Lynch's mistake, however was that his 'do nothing' approach also involved ignoring the blatant breaking of ranks by Neil Blaney and Kevin Boland, Minister for Local Government, a former Minister for Defence and another hawk in cabinet. Boland's father Gerald had been a founder member of Fianna Fáil and Boland was contemptuous of those he considered lacking in Republican pedigree. Lynch got the better of Blaney and Boland at the Fianna Fáil Ard Fheis (party conference) in January 1970, after he had asked his former classmate and literary editor of the *Irish Press*, David Marcus, to draft a speech for him (as Lynch was feeling 'fatigued and unable to concentrate'). He faced down Kevin Boland's fiery diatribe about the primacy of unity and, in a forceful and direct way, dismissed the idea of coercion.[9] He was backed robustly by Patrick Hillery, who made an impassioned intervention and asserted the primacy of the party over Boland's faction, underlining his importance as an ally of Lynch. Hillery was an understated but steely politician, who before achieving an international profile as Minister for External Affairs at the outset of the Troubles had served as Minister for Education and also as Minister for Industry and Commerce.

But the events of May 1970, as they became public, made it clear Lynch had won only a temporary reprieve. When it emerged that Lynch had dismissed Blaney and Haughey from cabinet because 'they do not fully subscribe to government policy' on Northern Ireland (that same day at a meeting of the parliamentary party, he praised the dismissed ministers' 'outstanding service'[10]), Kevin Boland resigned from the government in protest and Lynch appointed Bobby Molloy as his replacement. On 28 May, Blaney and Haughey were arrested on charges of conspiring to import arms and ammunition. Blaney was discharged on 2 July, and in October, after two jury trials, Haughey was acquitted. Blaney had the charges dismissed on the grounds that there was no direct evidence of his involvement. The trials of the other defendants (a first trial, beginning 22 September, collapsed on 29 September when the judge withdrew from the case after one of the defence counsel accused him of bias; the retrial took place 6–23 October) witnessed clashes between James Kelly's claim that he had kept Gibbons informed of his activities, and a denial by Gibbons that he had authorised the importation.

Kelly's version of events was supported by Colonel Michael Hefferon, the former director of military intelligence, who was called as a prosecution witness in the first trial but not at the retrial; notwithstanding, the judge summoned him on his own initiative. Blaney's role in the arms plot was thus not fully explored at the Arms Trial, though Garret FitzGerald commented: 'When one reads this trial carefully, Deputy Blaney crops up time and time again and disappears again into the mist.'[11] The situation in Donegal had become more politically and emotionally charged for Fianna Fáil after the trials; posters of Lynch were torn down and party general secretary Séamus Brennan concluded that the only solution was for Fianna Fáil in Blaney's constituency of Donegal North East to 'be rid of Mr Blaney' and have him expelled as soon as possible to 'clear the decks'.[12] He was not expelled from the party until June 1972.

State papers released under the thirty-year rule in 2001 revealed that a copy of Colonel Hefferon's evidence had been altered to remove statements to the effect that Gibbons had been aware of Kelly's actions. In this context, some lawyers expressed the view that if these omissions had not been made the Arms Trial would never have taken place, but two subsequent official inquiries concluded that the changes were made in order to comply with the evidentiary rule against hearsay and did not materially affect the substance of the document.[13]

As Minister for Defence, Gibbons had been appointed to the cabinet subcommittee on Northern Ireland, but it met only once, and its existence had clearly been used as a front so that its leading members, Blaney and Haughey, could plot the importation of arms for possible supply to paramilitary organisations in Northern Ireland, at a time when the cabinet was simply not adequately discussing Northern Ireland policy. Gibbons may have been 'operating at cross-purposes to Haughey and Blaney, seeing himself as preparing contingency plans for a doomsday situation rather than immediate intervention.'[14] (He was acutely aware that the Irish army was under-strength and severely under-equipped; he submitted a report on this to the cabinet in August 1969.) He claimed at the Arms Trial that he had been unaware of the attempt to import arms and acted to prevent it when he became aware. But James Kelly insisted he had kept Gibbons informed of his actions and intentions at all times and had received at least tacit authorisation. He admitted Kelly had told him of the shipments but that he had not responded; Kelly's legal representatives said he interpreted the latter's non-response as tacit approval. In private, 'Lynch told the British ambassador of his anger at Gibbons's inept performance; some commentators have suggested that it indicates that he was attempting to tell the truth as he saw it or as he had persuaded himself he saw it.'[15] Colonel Michael Hefferon also testified that Kelly had kept both him and Gibbons informed of his activities. According to historian Patrick Maume, 'It is arguable, however, that Kelly's fierce commitment to the northern Nationalist cause led him to overestimate the extent of Gibbons's agreement with him; and most commentators agree that a policy of arming paramilitaries with the aim of destabilising Northern Ireland and causing a British withdrawal could only have led to bloodshed, economic disaster, and political destabilisation of the whole island to a much greater extent than actually took place.'[16]

Kelly undoubtedly sincerely believed himself to be acting with proper authority, though his trenchant Republican views and commitment to the northern Nationalists made him predisposed to believe this and perhaps to overlook danger signals. Kelly insisted that he had kept Gibbons fully informed, describing Gibbons's statement as 'a tissue of lies ... The man is an unmitigated scoundrel and I say this not under privilege of Dáil Éireann.'[17] After the Arms Trial, he found himself unemployable and endured a tough time; many believed he had been made a scapegoat for government ineptitude. Justice Minister Micheál Ó Móráin claimed he had passed on Garda intelligence reports about the involvement of cabinet ministers with the IRA to Lynch before the arms were seized at Dublin airport, which Lynch denied, but Ó Móráin's evidence at the trial was erratic.

Haughey claimed that although he had arranged customs clearance for an imported shipment through Dublin airport, he had not known that they were weapons. But both Gibbons and Berry, as secretary of the Department of Justice, claimed he was aware of the contents of the shipment. At the conclusion of the Arms Trial the judge stated that there was a direct conflict of evidence between Haughey and Gibbons, and that one or the other must be guilty of perjury. Kevin Boland suggested they both perjured themselves and insisted privately that Haughey had personally told him of the arms shipment and publicly declared that, while Haughey was not directly involved in the arms importation, he knew arms were being imported. Haughey had no intention, it seemed, of risking his career, underlining his lack of conviction on the Northern question. Instead, as observed by historian Paul Bew, 'he preferred to perjure himself ... It was an important moment; if Haughey had had the courage of his apparent convictions he might well have unleashed "a tidal wave" of naked nationalism by proclaiming that he had acted in the best interests of Ireland. His discretion was a key moment in the unfolding hypocrisy and realism of the Irish political class on the North.'[18] There was more hypocrisy on display outside the court when Haughey addressed his 'fellow patriots', these words coming from someone who insisted he knew nothing about arms importation.[19] Having issued a challenge to Lynch that was drowned out by a Fianna Fáil show of solidarity with Lynch, Haughey later 'swallowed his pride and marched through the lobbies to vote confidence in a Taoiseach he despised'.[20]

Peter Berry endured a horrendous time as a result of the Arms Trial. As secretary of the Department of Justice he had also been appointed to the committee on Northern Ireland; he believed it inappropriate, in the context of civil service protocol, to approach Lynch directly unless requested; instead, he reported to his minister, Ó Móráin. But he did not know how much of his material had been forwarded to the government and, like others, was unclear of the exact nature of government policy. He was very ill between 1969 and 1970 but remained centrally involved by receiving visitors to his sick bed, including Ó Móráin and senior members of Garda special branch.

According to his later account he informed Lynch in autumn 1969 that Captain James Kelly had promised money to the IRA for the purchase of arms. Lynch later claimed he had heard of this only in April 1970, suggesting that Berry (who was heavily medicated) might have retrospectively become confused about what he meant to say and what he actually said. Berry dismissed this. In April 1970 Berry told Lynch of the suspected involvement of Haughey and Blaney and did not think Lynch acted with sufficient urgency. Meanwhile, Berry received word from official sources that a cargo of arms was to be flown into Dublin airport on 21 April; he ordered members of special branch to surround the airport terminal with 'a ring of steel' and seize the weapons if they arrived.[21] He had a phone conversation with Haughey, who asked whether the cargo would be allowed through if it were sent directly to the North. After Berry refused, the shipment was cancelled. Berry deduced from this conversation that only individual cabinet ministers were involved, rather than the government as a whole. In another extraordinary twist he contacted President Eamon de Valera (Berry's son was married to the daughter of de Valera's secretary), who suggested further dialogue with Lynch. According to Berry, Lynch vacillated, hoping he could get ministers back into line and Berry did not believe the Arms Trial defendants were prosecuted with sufficient vigour in order to prevent the exposure of government mishandling of the events. In the aftermath of the trial, he and his relatives were intimidated by Republicans; the family were afforded armed protection and he and his wife suffered grave ill health. He retired in January 1971 and later claimed he had received assurances that the government would make up the £10,000 he would forfeit by premature retirement, but the government denied this and he received no compensation.

In March 1973 he wrote to O'Malley (the letter is in Jack Lynch's personal papers) insisting 'my family's financial loss, ill health, sufferings and public humiliations were caused by my fulfilment of my duty to the Taoiseach and the institution of government and the preservation of the rule of law', but Lynch refused to proceed with a motion in the Dáil that would have allowed him compensation. O'Malley disputed Berry's insistence that there was a 'moral obligation' on the government to compensate him, suggesting moral obligation 'means different things to different people and which in the present context I would see only as a source of possible argument and controversy'.[22] In 1980, *Magill* magazine sensationally published extensive extracts from Berry's memoir focused on the arms crisis; it was put together in the mid 1970s by Berry on the basis of contemporary notes, the extent of which are not clear. Those sympathetic to Lynch – including historian Dermot Keogh, who has written the most substantial biography of him to date – insist Berry 'was substantially to blame for the breakdown in communications that created so much unnecessary suspicion and mistrust between different strands of government, the Gardaí and military intelligence',[23] a verdict that seems excessively and conveniently harsh. For Captain James Kelly, the controversy was also devastating; when he died in 2003, Tim Pat Coogan gave his graveside oration and described him as 'the Irish Dreyfus'.[24] Hefferon too was 'treated abominably' for telling the truth.[25]

Des O'Malley's interpretation of Lynch's actions was understandably sympathetic:

> There has always been a long tradition in Ireland of ... subversion from outside. What made 1969–70 different was that for the first time ever you had subversion from inside. And that was the huge challenge that Lynch had to confront and he did it successfully ... He did it very calmly and he avoided the kind of violent reaction that some others who came after him would have created in the way that they might have handled it. To some extent he was minimalist in his approach but there are times in which a minimalist approach can be the most effective ... Blaney and Boland and Haughey could have been fired in a way that could have given them an excuse almost to foment a civil war but that didn't happen.[26]

But there were all sorts of questions left unanswered. Vincent Browne, the editor of *Magill*, called to see Lynch in May 1980 in advance of the publication of Berry's diaries. Lynch told Browne he 'had been approached to write my autobiography' and 'may or may not' answer Browne's questions, and if he did not, Browne 'was not to attribute any particular motive to it'. It is unlikely Lynch had any intention of writing that biography. Browne confirmed he was trying to write a biography of Haughey and told Lynch 'he had difficulty with some people; that they were unwilling or unable or afraid to talk to him because of the fear of some reprisals. I asked him from what source could the reprisals come and he replied in a rather vague way to me'. Lynch admitted that when he spoke to Berry 'he did mention that there were, from time to time, a number of attempts to import arms with some success' but reiterated that Ó Móráin had never told him of the plot and if Browne published that he had done so, then 'I would take my own remedy no matter what that might be.'[27]

Haughey was also reading the realities of sentiment; Irish opinion on this point may have included 'a significant sneaking admiration for those prepared to take risks for Northern Nationalists, but the predominant sentiment saw the stability of the Irish state as a greater value'.[28] The crisis raised a number of issues about collective cabinet responsibility, judicial processes and the independence of the civil service. Some concluded that 1970 'was the most extraordinary year since 1920' (during the War of Independence), while in the Dáil, Conor Cruise O'Brien suggested it had made the public 'shock-weary'.[29] On 7 May 1970 the *Financial Times* posed the question 'Is the gun coming back into Irish politics?'[30]

In May 1970 *Hibernia* magazine editorialised in relation to the crisis:

> After all the muck-raking, the half truths, the hypocrisy and the cover up of the past critical week, there still seems more reason to relish than regret the recent happenings ... the insufferable arrogance of selfish men too long in power has reaped its own reward. Our institutions have demonstrated that, not only are they capable of withstanding a most serious threat to stability, but that the balance is still not too lopsided. Reputations have been lost, the truth has been suppressed, justice has not been done and the whole story is far from revealed. But overall, the forces of democracy have enjoyed a rare and refreshing victory.[31]

This was the verdict that many passed in relation to Lynch, including Garret FitzGerald; seemingly he had steadied the ship of state and confronted and sacked the hawks.[32]

But throughout these episodes, Lynch was also subjected to much justifiable criticism on the grounds of weakness, incompetence and ambiguity. (It was, according to James Downey, 'impossible to believe' that he and Gibbons were completely ignorant of what was going on; it also seems likely that he was forced to act in May because Cosgrave had the information leaked to him.[33]) Privately, Fine Gael senator John Kelly wrote to Liam Cosgrave in August 1971 suggesting Lynch's talk of a political campaign to end Stormont (the discredited Unionist controlled parliament in Northern Ireland) was 'the greatest eye wash ... if you think he is simply trying to keep ahead of Haughey and Blaney, I think you should tell him that any policy so based will certainly end in disaster'.[34]

Downey suggested that Lynch had little interest in the North and was also apt to affect not to know what was going on around him: 'One morning the Taoiseach on his way into his office, was greeted by an official who mentioned the latest speech by the Minister for Agriculture [Blaney]. He took his pipe out of his mouth and replied: Oh! Has he said something?' For Downey the issue about Lynch crystallised into this: 'Either Gibbons passed on the contents of his intelligence briefings to the Taoiseach or he did not. If he did, Lynch's inaction was breathtaking. But even if he did not, Lynch's negligence was outrageous.'[35]

As Patrick Hillery saw it in relation to the arms crisis, 'there was a government within the government', during which 'Jack had a kind of innocence about him', but Hillery himself had to ask the *Irish Times* journalist Denis Kennedy, 'What's Blaney up to?'[36] Lynch had suggested privately and in a state of agitation that 'the only one I can trust is [Erskine] Childers and he is too naïve to be any good to me'. Lynch was clearly struggling to find anyone to trust.[37] One Fine Gael TD's notes on the debate drew a simple and stark conclusion in relation to Lynch: 'either he did not know what his colleagues were up to or did know and did nothing'; he also wondered 'what kind of debate would it have been if the leader of the opposition had come straight into the Dáil with his story instead of going with a great sense of national responsibility to the Taoiseach first'.[38]

At the conclusion of the Arms Trial debate in the Dáil, J. W. Sanfey, the general secretary of Fine Gael, wrote to TDs saying the Fine Gael senators had asked him to congratulate them for their performances and their 'remarkable achievement throughout the debate' and to invite them to partake of 'refreshments' in the party room.[39] It was clear that some were relishing the whole crisis and its aftermath; it was suggested in *Hibernia* in November 1971 after a motion of no confidence in James Gibbons was defeated (Lynch had allowed him to remain in cabinet) that there was 'something obscene' about a champagne party in the parliamentary secretary's restaurant at Leinster House: 'It was full of loud laughter and backslapping and apparent bonhomie – and when it finished after midnight, fourteen empty champagne bottles topped the debris.'[40]

John Kelly found himself speculating whether the controversy might mean an end to party politics as it was then known; 'we may find ourselves casting around oblivious of party distinctions, for some common ground on which all people who believe in parliamentary democracy and the rule of law can defend them together ... if the responsible and decent elements in FF can get no good out of their leaders, I am sure that our party – the other wing of the old Sinn Féin – will accommodate them with generosity and without triumphalism in a new and united national and democratic movement'. But, never one for understatement, he was chief denouncer of what might prevent that: 'the animal solidarity of Fianna Fáil'; the party was 'a tribe of cats'; 'this political dodo of boastful intransigence', 'a parcel of pygmy republicans afraid of their own shadow', 'latter day "republicans"' with their 'mohair suits and mutton chop whiskers'.[41]

The tensions in the aftermath of the crisis were apparent in the meetings of the Fianna Fáil National Executive and the parliamentary party meetings. The number of resolutions being sent by *cumainn* to the executive (such as 'that Fianna Fáil stand behind its original policy: a 32 county sovereign state') was regarded as 'getting out of hand' in October 1970, the same month that there was a roll call vote on confidence in Lynch.[42] In March 1972, Lynch 'was not yet able to clarify the proper channel for the disposal of funds towards Northern relief' while in relation to electing a constituency delegate from Donegal North East, headquarters staff 'compared the signatures and handwriting on the ballots and registration forms and many irregularities were evident'. The party also declined to send a speaker to the University of Ulster to debate the motion 'that the solution of Ulster's problems does not lie at Westminster'.[43]

Lynch may have been consistent in rejecting force as a way to bring about a united Ireland and occasionally talked of the need for conciliation with Unionists, but the reality was that he had simultaneously adopted a traditional Republican position on Northern Ireland by putting unification at the centre of government policy and he 'unsuccessfully attempted to undermine claims of legitimacy by the IRA by seeking to secure a declaration from the British government of its interest in unity'. He was also damaged by the scandal caused by the activities of the Littlejohn brothers, Kevin and Keith, in 1973, another case of Lynch struggling with the issues of when he knew what and who told him. The Littlejohns had received hefty sentences from the Special Criminal Court for their part in a Dublin bank robbery. They had fled back to the UK only to be extradited; they claimed they were acting on behalf of the British Ministry of Defence as spies and were seeking to discredit the IRA. British intelligence admitted they were agents but denied they were authorised to carry out illegal activities.

In August 1973 it emerged that in January of that year, before they were returned to Dublin, British government involvement had been revealed to Lynch, who said he had forgotten about the report.[44] It exposed serious breaches of trust between the British and Irish governments and it could have led to the resignation of Lynch as he was very 'shaken', but Garret FitzGerald acted decently and humanely to help Lynch 'find a way out of a dilemma that might have resulted in his premature resignation' by asking the secretary of the Department of Foreign Affairs, Hugh McCann, to remind Lynch of his lapse and of the contents of a document that he had originally received of which he was now denying knowledge. He then held a press conference to apologise. FitzGerald accepted that Lynch really had forgotten due to foreign travel and a general election campaign and this seems to have genuinely been the case.[45]

But the question remains as to why the Irish government had not made more of the breach of trust exposed by the Littlejohn affair. Liam Cosgrave's papers contain an account of a conversation Minister for Finance Richie Ryan had with the British ambassador in August 1973, in which he said London was 'very upset by the statement from the Irish government that it did not accept the British assurances on the Littlejohn affair'. Ryan doubted 'whether there was any such statement' and suggested the Irish government 'might be disposed' to accept the British version, but 'public opinion was quite another thing' and that the Irish government's ability to influence public opinion had been 'hampered by the indiscretions of the Littlejohn type',[46] suggesting this was by no means a one off.

Historian Catherine O'Donnell has suggested Lynch had 'a particularly poor understanding of Unionism' and that 'by demanding that which he could never achieve, Lynch failed in his quest to undermine support for the IRA'. By the end of the decade the inability to convince the British government that the Republic had a right to be involved in the search for a political rather than a military solution to the Troubles 'also contributed to the end of his leadership' with challenges from Síle de Valera (a new Dublin Fianna Fáil TD and granddaughter of the party's founder Eamon) and others to 'demonstrate his republicanism'. Lynch may not have been strong enough to exert leadership in terms of 'a stronger emphasis on the need for reconciliation', and was pragmatic enough to know that interim measures would be necessary before any unification, but he was also faced with 'the unwillingness on the part of the wider party to engage with his attempts to challenge their traditional views on partition and persistent IRA violence'.[47]

– THIRTEEN –

GREEN AMERICA AND BLUE BRITAIN

Governments of the 1970s were also sensitive to and made well aware of Irish-American attitudes to the Troubles, particularly in the context of support for the IRA at both a senior political and more populist level. When IRA leaders Ruairí O Brádaigh and Joe Cahill were arrested in Dublin in June 1972 letters poured in to the Department of the Taoiseach from California, New Jersey, Illinois, New York, Philadelphia and Ohio, one correspondent insisting that if the men were not released 'I shall cancel all plans to spend our vacations in Ireland'.[1] In April 1973, Conor Cruise O'Brien wrote to Garret FitzGerald stressing the necessity of meeting with US Democratic Party senator Ted Kennedy 'to try gently to influence the senator away from the pro-IRA mafia with which he has shown signs of going along'.[2] O'Brien also set his sights on the Irish Northern Aid Committee (NORAID), a fundraising group established in the spring of 1970 after the outbreak of the Troubles, and Irish-Americans 'who contribute the dollars out of vague sentiment and lack of knowledge of the realities of the situation … we ought to be making much more of an effort to stop this funding'.[3]

NORAID became the best known and most significant of the Irish-American Republican support groups and in 1970–71, 'more or less openly canvassed for funds for arms'. Historian Brian Hanley has observed, that although NORAID's propaganda differed little from the Provisional IRA's in Ireland, it was subject to different political and cultural pressures.

In its first year it had functioning units in most areas of New York and then spread to Boston, Chicago, San Francisco and New Jersey. In its early years it was almost exclusively made up of Irish-born Republicans, and support for it ebbed and flowed depending on the level of violence and the extent of IRA atrocities. It frequently faced a hostile climate and from 1972 was forced to register as an agent of a foreign organisation by the US State Department and was subject to wire tapping, infiltration and raids on its offices. It also employed a class argument, denouncing 'respectable' Anglophile Irish-Americans who refused to support the IRA.[4]

Michael Lillis, a diplomat in the Department of Foreign Affairs who was the department's information officer in the US, wrote a revealing memorandum on the whole subject of this Irish-American dimension in April 1975. He suggested that some members of NORAID had emigrated after the Irish civil war and had a hostility to the Irish government, but that there were also significant class tensions within Irish America. The Irish-born working-class emigrants felt that Irish state and semi-state attitudes in the US 'are geared only to the White Collar middle class Irish from whom they feel deeply separated and this carries over in their attitudes to visiting ministers'. Northern Ireland, he suggested, provided 'a heady focus' for many issues, including Irish failures, forced emigration and the idea that 'we owe you nothing; you could not even provide us with a job'.[5]

How to deal with the Irish-American lobby was a recurring problem. Many refused to distinguish between the IRA of the War of Independence period and the Provisional IRA of the 1970s, and the delusional simplicity of the sentiments and solutions was striking: 'Do not let history record that you failed the Irish race, Mr Lynch, when victory was within sight and grasp!'[6] Many veteran Irish-Americans, who had emigrated from Ireland in previous decades, had an acute misty-eyed exile syndrome that was exacerbated by the Troubles. They also had an emotional investment, or as John McGowan, president of the Irish Republican Army Veterans in New York City, put it in a letter to Lynch in December 1972, 'as men and women who have had a stake in Ireland and its freedom for more than 50 years we are appalled by the events of the past few weeks in Dublin'.[7]

They could also be assertive and possessive of their sense of destiny and history: an Irish-Canadian wrote to Lynch: 'I, Sir, claim the right as a son of a republican ... north east Area command 1916 and 1921 to write to you direct'. A tetchy reply on Lynch's behalf suggested 'the Taoiseach needs no reminding of the heroic sacrifice made for their country's freedom by the gallant men of 50 years ago'.[8] This was an example of the tone civil servants adopted in relation to letters that were regarded as discourteous; Lynch's secretary Frank Murray suggested to him in relation to another aggressive diatribe of a letter in February 1972, 'perhaps you would agree to a mere acknowledgement with a sting to it'.[9] Civil servants in the Department of the Taoiseach went to considerable trouble to draft replies to various letters from the public, although those with an abusive tone – or what Frank Murray termed those letters of 'the poison pen variety' – were deemed unworthy of 'reply or acknowledgement of any kind', including one that told Lynch to 'shove your Irish republic up your rectum'.[10] When it was suggested to Murray in February 1978 that a three-page reply to an Antrim Protestant who had written to explain how 'the southern people appear to us' was excessive and should be shortened, he disagreed. The letter writer, Murray maintained, had gone to a great degree of trouble to express his views and 'we should do all we can, however little that may be, to ease his worries'.[11]

Not all of the Republican diaspora was naïve in their approach. Cormac O'Malley, a lawyer based in New York and son of renowned Irish War of Independence Republican Ernie O'Malley, wrote to an Irish-American who had expressed concern in a letter to Lynch that all that was being reported in America was the violence rather than its causes. O'Malley pointed out that he was doing his best to educate Americans on the problem by stressing that Irish unification may be desirable, 'but neighbours must be made to live with their neighbours'. Another correspondent from Pennsylvania suggested that if the conflict was reported in the US 'in a true light' it could 'cut off most of the stateside aid that the IRA receives from deluded sympathisers'.[12] Lynch also received entreaties from such groups as the American Congress of Irish Freedom, which wanted UN involvement.[13] But there was an ongoing avalanche of bilge. Lynch had to reassure a US resident that 'at no time has the Taoiseach said he proposed to turn to Communist countries for aid.'[14] A resident of Rhode Island wondered plaintively, 'Why can't England be England and Ireland be Ireland?'[15] Lynch and many others would have smiled and nodded sagely.

In the immediate post-Bloody Sunday environment there was much praise for Lynch's dignity and patience – including from Risteard Mulcahy, a cardiologist and son of Richard Mulcahy who commanded the IRA during the War of Independence and was a former leader of Fine Gael.[16] But this cut little ice with many impatient Americans, who, with the benefit of distance (in more ways than physical), harangued him for doing no more than 'throwing lettuce leaves' at Prime Minister Heath: 'You are obviously a nice man Mr Lynch, a good natured family man and just possibly too nice in the present situation. You are up against hardened professional liars and deceivers.' Another suggested that the solution was for the Republic to 'take in' one Northern county per year from 1972 to 1977 'thus easing all tensions – it's as simple as that – no problem at all!'[17] A letter from New York maintained that, of IRA members imprisoned by the British at Long Kesh, 'their only crime [was] loving old Ireland'.[18]

The number of Irish-Americans was variously cited at between 15 and 20 million; there was even an 'Ireland, 51st American State Foundation', which did not think its proposal far fetched 'when compared with statehood for distant Hawaii or Alaska and the largely Spanish-speaking territories of the South West the US obtained from Mexico'.[19]

For other American letter writers, Lynch was simply 'Union Jack', another traitor 'with the proviso that he was more dupe than scoundrel', but there was anger expressed by other Irish-Americans at the discourtesy shown to Lynch when he travelled to America in 1973 and faced an onslaught from a small crowd of egg throwers in the context of his assertion that British troops needed to stay in Northern Ireland for the time being. The *Chicago Tribune* suggested in relation to this visit and the activities of NORAID, that 'guns bought with American money and eggs thrown at the leader of the Irish people would seem the worst possible contribution the citizens of this country might make at this time'.[20] In October 1976, when Garret FitzGerald was returning from a seminar at Harvard in Cambridge, Mass., Patrick Curry, the regional vice-chairman of the Boston chapter of NORAID, was also booked on the flight; he normally got VIP treatment at Logan Airport because Aer Lingus found him 'useful as a moderating influence in relation to some of the more aggressive NORAID members'. FitzGerald expressed 'strong disapproval' of this concession.[21]

A statement from the US president Jimmy Carter in August 1977 was regarded by some as an initiative that 'fell flat' in Ireland, although it 'broke a half century of silence' by the White House on Northern Ireland. It committed the US to supporting power sharing and averred that the US had an interest in a settlement. It demonstrated the Irish had leverage due to the influence of senator Ted Kennedy and Congress Speaker T. P. ('Tip') O'Neill. Garret FitzGerald was said to be Kissinger's 'favourite foreign minister' and got the Irish National Caucus, widely regarded as a Provo umbrella group, sidelined, but John Hume of the SDLP was disappointed with the response in Dublin to Carter's intervention.[22] When FitzGerald had visited Washington in March 1977 and spoken with the US Secretary of State Cyrus Vance, FitzGerald 'said he believed that as much as 60 per cent of the guns and ammunition getting in to Northern Ireland came from the US'.[23] The joint statement on St Patrick's Day that year from Kennedy, O'Neill, New York governor Hugh Carey and New York senator Patrick Moynihan (after which they were nicknamed the Four Horsemen by NORAID) called on Irish-Americans to refuse to contribute to NORAID and has been characterised by Brian Hanley as 'a watershed in terms of mainstream Irish-American politics'.[24] By the early 1980s they had broadened their ranks to include other Irish-American legislators.[25]

There were many difficulties on the British side in coming to any understanding of the nature of the Troubles. When Patrick Cosgrave, the Anglophile Irish historian, journalist and supporter and adviser to the British Conservative Party was reflecting on his career while in Corfu in 1997, he suggested if he was writing his memoirs he would be tempted to include a chapter with the title 'What the Average British Politician Knows about Northern Ireland' and have it consisting 'entirely of blank pages'. He ruminated: 'I could have designed just such a chapter at almost any time over the last 30 years of conflict in Ulster', though he made an exception in relation to Roy Mason, Secretary of State for Northern Ireland in the late 1970s.[26] The degree of ignorance was first revealed to him in the summer of 1970 when he was working in the Conservative Research Department and new Home Secretary, Reginald Maulding, wanted to see him. The two were left alone: '"Patrick", he said, "I'm told you were brought up a Catholic in Southern Ireland." I affirmed that this was so. "Then, for God's sake, will you please tell me why those buggers go around killing one another because of religion?"'[27]

Lord Hailsham, in a letter to Cearbhall Ó Dálaigh, while the latter was still a Supreme Court Judge, expressed regret that he could not travel to London for the opening of the legal year due to the situation in Ireland: 'But do the clouds ever lift over Ireland? Will they ever lift until men of distinction on both sides can meet and talk openly as friends and Christians without fear of misrepresentation ... both sides not giving in to the congenital idiots.'[28]

There were also complications in terms of the journalistic coverage of the Troubles (see pages 162–7); in November 1971 it was reported in the *Irish Times* that Jonathan Dimbleby of BBC's *World at One* complained that he was being 'repressed' in reporting the realities of Northern Ireland, and was not being allowed to report accurately what was going on. Jack Lynch was also frequently told by correspondents in London 'how little the British really know or understand about the Republic of Ireland'.[29]

Conor Cruise O'Brien was frequently accused of manufacturing propaganda that Britain would have been very happy with.[30] In January 1974, O'Brien complained to John Freeman of London Weekend Television about an interview with IRA leader Dáithí Ó Conaill by journalist Mary Holland (who had been the first British-based journalist to write in detail of the crisis in Northern Ireland) which had been broadcast on UTV: 'I have myself in the past inclined to the view that it is healthy to broadcast interviews with IRA leaders provided these leaders are exposed to cross-examination and counter-argument', but in the present climate he believed 'there is much more involved than rational argument. Elemental passions are involved. Fear, rage and hate and the retaliation it can provoke.'[31]

The *Irish Independent* wrote in 1972 of a plan to 'counter British propaganda on Northern Ireland', while Lynch corresponded with a senior lawyer, Dermot Kinlen, who had offered his services as a speaker for free as 'there is a need to get our case across to the educated, influential but not alas fully informed sections of British opinion'. Erskine Childers also complained to Lynch about a report on Ulster in *The Economist* which was 'full of inaccuracies', particularly about the government's attitude to violence: 'I mention this because the Minister for Education at the last government meeting said that when he went to a wedding in England there were a number of people there who thought the official IRA were the Irish army.'[32]

The Taoiseach and the Minister for Finance joined a group of sixteen journalists from the Westminster Lobby correspondents in September 1971 and the Taoiseach engaged in 'informal off the record discussions' with them. They returned in 1972 and obviously had another highly sociable encounter, given that thanks was expressed in the aftermath for the 'fringe activities – from which we are only just recovering'. They may have been united in their embracing of a binge in Dublin, but they were not regarded as a group singing in unison in relation to their coverage of the Troubles. Fourteen of them returned in September 1973 and the notes prepared on them for the Department of the Taoiseach suggested some were 'balanced and well informed' while others were 'not that well informed on the Northern Ireland question'. One was liable to 'ask one or two silly or stupid questions' (Jim Campbell of the *Daily Record*), while another was 'not particularly important from our point of view' (Alan Wood of the *Times*).[33]

FitzGerald was in demand to speak on the BBC; in 1974 it was 'particularly anxious' to interview him, but the fast-talking cerebral FitzGerald was warned in relation to an interview with Robin Day: 'You will appreciate that things have necessarily to be simplistic for a British audience.'[34] According to minutes of a meeting cited by *Magill* magazine, in October 1978, Dick Francis, director of news and current affairs at the BBC, had been happy to note that 'Northern Ireland matters, which had for so long dominated the thoughts of the meeting, could now have suitably been placed as the last item on the agenda. He hoped they would remain there.'[35]

There was also concern about the trade and commercial implications of misinformation. Paddy Lalor, Minister for Industry and Commerce, expressed concern to Lynch in 1972 that 'adverse publicity abroad arising from the situation in Northern Ireland' was 'seriously hampering' the efforts of the Industrial Development Authority (IDA) to attract new industry to Ireland. There was discussion on the potential cost of a government-funded 'intensive' publicity campaign across Europe and America to counteract this negativity, but Lynch insisted in November 1972 that 'it is not the time' for such a campaign to be mounted.[36] A 'buy-Irish campaign' had originally been launched in 1964 after the imposition of a British 15 per cent import surcharge, but by February 1972 the Department of Industry and Commerce was worried about a boycott of British goods, while Donal O'Sullivan, the Irish ambassador in London, wrote to Frank Murray in the Department of the Taoiseach suggesting there was some resistance to Irish foodstuffs in England and that he was aware of 'a notice recently circulated in Scotland calling for a boycott of Irish goods'.[37] Lynch, however, was also on the receiving end of many sympathetic letters from London, including some from those who characterised themselves as English 'haters of oppression'.[38]

When Lynch met the West German chancellor Willy Brandt in September 1972, while attending the Olympic games in Munich, he was at pains to correct what he saw as misleading claims in the British press that not enough was being done to crack down on IRA violence. He was also 'hoping with the British not to bring the problem into Europe' (and made the rather bizarre claim that the referendum on EEC membership was a success not only in terms of Ireland's membership, 'but also in support of his policy on the North'). But his main preoccupation seemed to remain what was being in his view erroneously reported in Britain: 'The British press must not propagate that he was soft on the IRA. The contrary was true. He had gone through the traumatic experience of dismissal and resignation of cabinet ministers on the issue.'[39]

As Taoiseach, Liam Cosgrave also robustly defended the record of Irish governments in this regard, highlighting in March 1974 for example, that in the previous year, 208 people had been brought to trial by the Special Criminal Court in relation to terrorist activities; he also pointed out that the strength of the Gardaí had been increased by 500 'and is now at its highest since the foundation of the state'. In 1973, 6,500 border controls and '16,500 joint Garda/army road check points were set up'.[40] After the Balcombe Street siege, a week long stand-off between the metropolitan police and IRA members holding hostages in London, the Department of the Taoiseach was unhappy with a report in the London *Times* which referred to this event as 'a serious blow to the morale of the IRA High Command in Dublin'.[41]

In the same year, Cosgrave and his ministers were more specific in relation to the question of violence being directed from the Republic. In response to accusations that not enough was being done by the Irish government, it was insisted by Cosgrave (through letters composed in the Department of the Taoiseach) that 'by far the greatest proportion of violence in Northern Ireland is indigenous. In fact, of all incidents of violence there, only 2 per cent have any connection with the border. May I add that it is notable that in NI where the security forces are more numerous than in the Republic and are patrolling an area one-third its size it has been found difficult to contain the violence occurring there. This is not said in any spirit of triumphalism.'[42]

A concurrent memorandum from Garret FitzGerald suggested that of all the violent incidents in Northern Ireland in the first eleven months of 1976, 'a maximum of 2.49 per cent are alleged by the British to have any border element or connection with the Republic, on our reckoning, the figure is about 2 per cent'. But it was also observed that 'according to British figures, 83 per cent of finds in the North of illegal commercial explosives have gone illegally from the South'.[43] In March 1978 Hugh Swift, a young first secretary in the Department of Foreign Affairs, pointed out that the British authorities were still furnishing on a weekly basis a list of terrorist incidents which they allege 'have their origin in or a connection with the Republic'. In 1977, twenty-eight such incidents were alleged: 'This is 1.06 per cent of the total number of terrorist-type incidents in NI during 1977, as published by the British authorities.'[44]

There is no doubt, however, that the British perception of Ireland was blackened by the Troubles; at a St Patrick's Night dinner at the Irish University Club in London in 1974, Fine Gael's John Kelly titled his speech: 'Ireland's Image: From Pig in the Parlour to Bomb in the Boot'.[45] Atrocities like the Birmingham pub bombs exacerbated this; these IRA bombs killed 19 people and injured 182 in November 1974 (six men subsequently convicted of the killings were innocent). Garret FitzGerald discussed with the ambassador Donal O'Sullivan the possibility of 'whether a minister should represent us at the funerals in Birmingham. He advised against, feeling that it might only provide a focus for resentment in a situation which is evolving fairly favourably.'[46]

– FOURTEEN –

REPORTING AND BROADCASTING THE CONFLICT

Governments were also concerned with domestic media perspectives. At the end of 1971, then in opposition, FitzGerald was less than complimentary about Irish newspaper coverage of the Troubles; as he saw it, 'The *Irish Press* has gone very Provisional, The *Irish Independent* is bitty and the *Irish Times*, while the best of them, has been pushing excessively the "unification line" ... *Hibernia* ... is rather republican in sympathy, but is, nevertheless, quite good.'[1] Cruise O'Brien was less sympathetic to *Hibernia* (which had coined the term 'Meglobrienia' in relation to him). He accused it of sympathy with the IRA and characterised it as 'a curious Dublin periodical which hovers somewhere between the objectives of Sinn Féin/IRA and those of the wine and food society'.[2]

Some journalists got close to the IRA. As recalled by *Magill*'s editor Vincent Browne, 'It was part of my job. I needed to know from them what was going on, why they were doing what they were doing. I got to like and respect several of them.' He thought many of them 'incorruptible' if chilling, but they were afflicted 'with a kind of fundamentalism which is uncontainable in a normal democratic society'. As he saw it, they were killers, but not mindless.[3]

In Conor O'Clery, the editor of the *Irish Times*, Douglas Gageby, had discovered what he wanted in 1972: 'A Catholic from the North who had some experience in student journalism and who might help redress the balance in the traditionally Protestant paper'. O' Clery was appointed

Northern editor in 1973 and told by his editor 'to be prepared to stay up late drinking with the likes of Paddy Devlin [a founder of the SDLP] and Bill Craig [leader of the Ulster Vanguard movement]'.[4] Despite the collapse of the Sunningdale power-sharing agreement (see pages 170–9), Gageby was reluctant to see the *Irish Times* abandon its support of power-sharing politicians and a headline 'Executive Show United Front' appeared even though the executive had resigned. This reflected Gageby's practice, under pressure from John Hume, of continuing to 'take the line Hume wanted ... but in the end it would lead him to unwise paths'.[5] Gageby was accurate, however, in insisting that 'what Northern Nationalists are aware of and what Unionists are smugly aware of is that in too many cases the words of Leinster House [the location of the Irish parliament] mark an ignorance of and an indifference to, the soil itself of the North and the people too'.[6]

The editor of the *Irish Press*, Tim Pat Coogan, liked the sense of himself as a player ('I had written part of Jack Lynch's speech') and his role as tormentor of what he labelled 'the anti-Republican Dublin elite'. He was keen to use the newspaper 'to highlight the difficulties of ordinary life for Catholics in Northern Ireland' and he despised the British Irish Association ('rightly described as Toffs against Terrorism') who could not accept the possibility of links between the North's police force, the Royal Ulster Constabulary, and Loyalist terrorists. According to Coogan, Jack Lynch chided journalists for their less than critical coverage of the IRA.

Coogan was also scathing about Cruise O'Brien, who later, as editor of the *Observer* newspaper, removed Mary Holland as Northern Ireland correspondent, suggesting she was naïve and a poor judge of Irish Catholics. Cruise O'Brien maintained 'that gifted and talkative community includes some of the most expert conmen and conwomen in the world and I believe you have been conned'.[7] Coogan was full of his own contradictions too; he insisted 'it is better for writers to keep clear of politics', but was also boastful about 'my self-appointed role as a conduit between the physical force movements and constitutional Ireland'.[8] Politicians went to great lengths to intimidate and censor the newspapers; at an informal off-the-record meeting with editors, for example, Minister for Justice Des O'Malley informed them that under the Offences Against the State Act, they were prohibited 'from using the letters IRA to describe contemporary activities by militant republicans'.[9]

From the perspective of RTÉ's masters, the interview with the chiefs of staff of both wings of the IRA on 28 September 1971 saw the station cross a line and punishment followed three days later in the form of a directive from Minister for Posts and Telegraphs Gerry Collins under section 31 of the Broadcasting Act: an instruction that RTÉ was not permitted to broadcast interviews that 'promoted the aims or activities' of illegal organisations. But 'despite the best efforts of RTÉ the government refused to clarify the ambiguities in the order'.[10] The following year RTÉ radio broadcast an account of an interview with Seán Mac Stiofáin, leader of the Provisional IRA; it did not use his voice, but the RTÉ Authority was sacked, 'an awesome moment in broadcasting's history'. The timing 'must have seemed singularly fortuitous' for Jack Lynch as he had agreed before this to meet the British prime minister Ted Heath for lunch and was able to impress him with his government's resoluteness on this issue.[11]

But what it meant in practice was that the 'silencing project' had commenced. As Kevin Myers, who was then reporting from Belfast for RTÉ, saw it, the directive would erode RTÉ's credibility: 'We feel we have been journalistically compromised.'[12] The new government in 1973 made it clear that there would be a ban on interviews with any 'spokesmen' for the IRA, but in practice the ban incorporated other areas if Sinn Féin activists were included. Section 31, it has been argued, was about 'amplifying one definition of a situation' in order to counteract 'a leaky national consensus', with those who questioned it accused of 'not being committed to the democratic state', but the result was 'zero public pressure on the Southern body politic to actively engage with what was happening north of the Border' along with 'insipid responses to injustices'.[13]

Overall, various censorship controls arguably left 'viewers in Ireland and Britain bereft of the means to understand the underlying causes of the conflict'. Regarding regular accusations of bias in the media, there was also occasionally a belief in London and Dublin that 'as long as both sides are complaining we must be doing something right'. Inevitably, given the duration of the Troubles, the news value dimmed over time, as did the interest. If it was true that quality coverage in the first few years was driven by curiosity and a desire to explain along with indignation, by 1974, boredom and a belief that the problem was insoluble created a perception that it had become 'predictable, regular and despairingly intractable', like the Middle East.[14]

Throughout this period, Cruise O'Brien, the chief media watchdog as Minister for Posts and Telegraphs, also regularly corresponded with Garret FitzGerald about the Troubles. His targets remained constant; after a visit to Clones in November 1973 he had a 'strong impression that the local people and the Gardaí were turning a blind eye to the Provisionals, provided that their activities were confined to the other side of the border and that the Provisionals found it convenient to abide by this provision.'[15]

In September 1973, on the subject of a bipartisan approach to the North, about which Cosgrave was meeting with Lynch, Cruise O'Brien wrote to Cosgrave urging him not to 'push courtesy to the point of extravagance' and suggested that, in relation to Lynch and Fianna Fáil, 'without him Fianna Fáil would become a rip roaring provisional institution'. Ever the self-appointed Messiah, he regarded FitzGerald's support for a bipartisan approach as a 'quixotic notion' and observed that FitzGerald 'is a much nicer man than I am and therefore more out of touch with public opinion'.[16] O'Brien gave the impression of always knowing what was best for all, and this created much linguistic conflict. But there were positive perceptions of his contribution from some quarters; as articulated by Magheramorne Presbyterians in July 1973, for example, when they told him 'your humanity and fair mindedness give us hope for the future'.[17] In an interview in 1978, after he had lost his Dáil seat but was holding on to his Trinity Senate seat to make his views on Northern Ireland known, he continued to dispute accounts of British army brutality, adding sarcastically and defiantly, 'we're not going to squeak every time Fr Dinny Faul squeaks'.[18] This was a reference to Fr Denis Faul, a critic of human rights abuses in Northern Ireland and also a trenchant critic of the IRA.

As far as Cruise O'Brien was concerned after he took office in 1973, he had to remain vigilant about the way in which RTÉ reported on the Troubles, or, as he put it in July 1973 in a private letter, 'the extremely peculiar concept of balance which seems to prevail in the RTÉ newsroom'. As noted by one of his biographers, he approached politics with the aim of 'expunging threats'[19]; he had long come to accept partition and his socialist views had been modified since the late 1960s. He was convinced that the notion of a class war had been replaced by a nakedly sectarian one in Northern Ireland and he had an inclination to apocalyptic vision and was consumed with the theme of siege, in this case in relation to Northern Protestant aspirations which he saw as legitimate and shamefully ignored by Irish nationalism.

There were also personal reasons for his profound pessimism that are apparent in *States of Ireland*; born in the civil war era, he was fearful of a recurrence of the sort of political divisions that had affected his own family and was very much preoccupied with religion.[20] Never one to opt for understatement, and with a fondness for the use of words such as 'distorted' and 'twisted', O'Brien was visceral in his lambasting of RTÉ's approach, which to him seemed to involve trying to achieve balance in its coverage by including those who condemned violence, but also those who thought 'after all, it was war'. This, he regarded as a 'twisted balance', believing that among the Catholic community 'the effect is to suggest that "Dublin" – of course envisaged monolithically – is at best equivocal in its condemnation of IRA activities'. Reporting of this kind he regarded as helping to 'fan the flames of sectarian civil war ... distorted reporting making a bad situation worse than it need be'.

O'Brien was not interested in dialogue in this regard, or discussion of guidelines ('not much use in a situation like this'); instead he wanted a controller of news who would not allow 'a spurious concept of journalistic ethics to be used to inject propaganda in favour of violence into the coverage of the news'.[21] O'Brien also wrote to Dónall Ó Móráin, chairman of the RTÉ Authority, in June 1973 to express 'disquiet' about the decision of RTÉ to lead off TV bulletins 'last Sunday week with the Provisional ceremony at Bodenstown'.[22] As someone publicly identified with trenchant denunciations of the IRA, O'Brien was also the subject of an anonymous call to Liam Cosgrave's office in September 1974. The caller 'respectfully suggested that the Taoiseach should consider trebling the bodyguard on Dr C. C. O'Brien, remembering what happened to two judges in Northern Ireland recently'.[23]

Earlier that year, O'Brien had informed Cosgrave that he was trying to avoid conflict with the RTÉ Authority or RTÉ staff as it would 'play into the hands of the IRA by enabling them to enlist liberal opinion on their side', but he suggested the head of news, Jim McGuinness, should be shifted to a 'less sensitive area' but 'to bring about those necessary changes without provoking confrontation, requires a certain amount of patience'.[24] This was the same year that the Broadcasting Review Committee had been established to evaluate RTÉ's performance and it was highly critical of its coverage of the early stages of the Troubles (see also Part I). McGuinness had anticipated this criticism and circulated a 'robust defence' to his staff against the charge of bias, as it implied the staff had 'for a protracted and vital period, acted in a professionally reprehensible manner'. McGuinness was also aware of criticisms of RTÉ from Northern Nationalists. RTÉ, he insisted, could not be allies of any side, but just report 'accurately and truthfully all that happened.'[25] For his part, Cruise O'Brien saw RTÉ as 'such a whispering gallery'.[26]

Many complications arose in relation to the BBC's coverage of the Troubles also. In December 1971 it successfully resisted pressure from the government not to broadcast a televised debate on Ulster, which included participants from the Republic, enraging Unionists.[27] FitzGerald suggested in June 1972 that he was 'the only person whose appearance on a TV programme in Britain has been banned because of criticism I made of the British army'. He maintained the British media had failed lamentably 'to give a true picture of what is happening'.[28] There were numerous limitations and intimidations with regard to how the conflict could be reported, it being suggested that important questions about why some Catholics supported the IRA 'cannot be asked by BBC employees'. Yet it is also the case that the BBC did make programmes reflecting Republican opinion, including a *Tonight* programme in 1977 investigating degrading treatment of Republican prisoners by the RUC. In the same year Thames TV broadcast an account of conditions in the Maze prison at Long Kesh, near Lisburn, where most IRA prisoners convicted in the North were interred. Nevertheless, there were many other programmes that were cut, cancelled or postponed.[29]

But just how much notice was taken by the British public? What level of interest was there on the mainland? Before discussions between Jack Lynch and British prime minister James Callaghan in London in September 1977, those preparing briefing material for the Irish side noted, 'We have been told on previous occasions that the British tolerate the casualties which they suffer in Northern Ireland more or less because the vast majority of the British public do not care much what happens in the North. They regard it as peripheral.'[30]

– FIFTEEN –

POSSIBILITIES, ENCOUNTERS AND INSTITUTIONS TO TRUST

Irish governments had to consider various strategies in relation to Northern Ireland policy during the decade, including possible military intervention by the Republic or internationalising the situation with a foreign military or peacekeeping presence. The possibility of an imminent withdrawal from Northern Ireland by Britain prompted the government to consider what the implications of such a dramatic move might be. The Irish government's Inter-Departmental Unit on Northern Ireland teased out various potential scenarios and was clearly worried about the possibility of an escalation of violence; the words 'civil war' were repeatedly used, particularly in relation to 'a united Ireland' type solution being imposed. A memorandum composed by the unit in 1974 noted: 'Even the mere prospect of an early British withdrawal would lead to an immediate and ruthless "consolidation of positions" on each side which would probably degenerate quickly into civil war.' Attorney General Declan Costello took the issue of possible UN intervention very seriously; in 1974 he mused over this and whether the North could be administered under the provisions of a UN charter for a limited period in the case of British withdrawal.

He pointed out that Britain had no 'strategic, economic or political reason for remaining in NI. Its continued presence arises from its appreciation of the consequences of withdrawal', but that there were precedents in the case of Israel and India for withdrawal despite the possibility of widespread bloodshed. The UN, he suggested, had succeeded 'in stopping bloodshed in Cyprus' and UN input would be necessary because 'the Irish army is incapable of assisting the Catholic community'. Regarding a UN role, he argued 'it would be undesirable to refer to the possibility in public. It leaves the impression that there is, perhaps, an easy solution through the UN which is, in fact, not available.'[1]

It is interesting that the Inter-Departmental Unit on Northern Ireland speculated on the possibility

> that the British government may try to do a deal with violent extremists on both sides. The most cogent argument against this is that it is simply not possible in a situation such as Northern Ireland to do a deal which will end violence by simultaneously satisfying two opposing factions. Nevertheless, wholeheartedly as we condemn violence, we must see that in their own view of the situation, the Provo theorists (if there are any) calculate that they cannot finally lose. Success in 'guerrilla' situations is not measured by conventional military standards but by the extent to which the constant attrition saps the domestic political will of the metropolitan power to continue its involvement.

The unit was uncertain as to the plans of the British army. In June 1974, it was noted that 'the role of the British army appears to be changing', and that 'a British withdrawal or at least a withdrawal of troops was a real possibility. It was probable that withdrawal of British troops would result in de facto repartition of the country'. In this scenario, the unit was concerned about refugees coming over the border, and the extent to which the Irish army could get involved in military action in the North:

> Plans are made to deal with refugees and our resources are sufficient to cope with an initial influx of 5,000–9,000 persons on six hours' notice. However, the final total could be as high as 50,000, and extra staff and accommodation would be needed to handle this number. This might require legislation to enable the government to acquire premises and requisition resources compulsorily ... the scope for military intervention would be narrowly restricted due to lack of resources. The present effective front-line strength of the army is about 5,500 men. They are presently engaged in border security and protection of vital installations, with a small reserve. To build up the army to the point where effective intervention would be possible would require 1–2 years ...

> to control the North with the majority population in revolt against Southern (or British) authority would require an army of the order of 100,000 (including about 60/70,000 front-line troops).

But it was ultimately concluded that in the event of British withdrawal, it was not envisaged that either the UN or EEC would get involved, 'as the NI situation did not hold the danger of a Great Power conflict'. There was some discussion of the 'supplies' that might be necessary for Northern Nationalists if the government broke down but a recognition that 'any supplies that might be made available from here to alleviate distress would almost certainly come under IRA control'. In the event of 50,000 refugees it was estimated 'the total cost of bedding' could be 'up to £600,000' while 50,000 meals of soup, stew and potato flake would be £8,300. Given a belief that 'the number of refugees could be up to 100,000', it was estimated that the cost of providing health services to them 'pro rata to the cost of providing these services for our existing population could be approximately £6 millions'.[2]

Regarding the more general economic implications of a change in the status of Northern Ireland, Brendan Dowling of the Economic and Social Research Institute concluded that it would be 'extremely difficult, if not impossible, for the Republic of Ireland to bear the present cost of UK transfers to Northern Ireland'. The cost of re-partitioning Northern Ireland ('a disastrous course' according to John Hume[3]) dividing the six counties into two parts, one of which would be integrated into the Republic, if Britain funded up to 56 per cent, was estimated at 'anywhere between £110 million and £352 million'. This would have left Northern Ireland with a residual population of 1.05 million, of which 25 per cent would be Catholic, after the Republic had taken a minimum of 308,000 and maximum of 470,000 people, of which 60 per cent would be Catholic. A possible resettlement allowance of £1,000 per family was also suggested. In 1973/4 UK exchequer payments to Northern Ireland amounted to £313 million.[4] Even on paper, it looked like a complicated and costly mess.

The tone emanating from a memorandum on the implications of a breakdown in the Sunningdale power-sharing arrangement remained bleak; a fear that a period of unrest and uncertainty might make the security forces irrelevant in controlling 'elemental mass reactions which could be spontaneous or more likely fomented and directed by subversives'; that if there was to be an influx of transferred population, they might be 'restless and demanding, even hostile after the traumatic events of the past five years, mistrustful of all government'.[5] Journalist Andy Pollak suggested the security problems facing the Republic in the event of a sudden emergency on the border were those of a 'small and scattered army' which had no troop-carrying aircraft; of the 18,500 members of the FCA (the army reserve), 'perhaps 5,000 could be usefully mobilised as a second-line reserve, but there is no highly-trained group of reservists ready to be mobilised at 24 hours' notice'.[6]

In May 1974, Cosgrave directed an inter-departmental committee to consider the implications of substantially increasing the size of the defence forces. The strength of the permanent defence forces in April 1974 was 11,333 and it was estimated that to increase that number to 25,000 would cost £27.5 million per annum ('it is recognised that women could discharge administrative, catering and other back up tasks in the forces'). Lieutenant Colonel Kevin O'Brien of the Irish army was adamant: 'It is our view that public opinion in the Republic will demand the intervention by the defence forces if the minority population comes under Loyalist attack. Failure to respond would have the most serious effects on the status and morale of the Defence Forces. It is also our belief that the government must have the option of military intervention and that the military capability to do so must be seen to exist.'[7]

The committee heard that 'to intervene in Derry, Strabane and Newry, about 5,000 troops would probably suffice. On the other hand, to intervene in the Glens of Antrim, many times that number would be required.' The committee's initial conclusions were that it was 'conceivable' though 'unlikely' that there would be full-scale civil war requiring intervention but that in the event, intervention 'to protect beleaguered minority communities' would not make matters worse as 'they would already be as bad as they could possibly be'. One apparently unviable option was compulsory military service. Although it was noted that conscription had been considered in 1944, thirty years on, the Minister for Defence Patrick Donegan insisted in the Dáil it was 'not in our tradition. I have no plans to change that situation.'[8]

What exactly would be involved in a political solution was another ongoing focus. Some on the left derided the notion of seeking political salvation in unity; if Great Britain was to leave Northern Ireland, 'do you believe that a trade union militia could then successfully stand between the Nationalists and Paisleyites?' asked maritime historian and senior

Irish Labour Party activist John de Courcy Ireland of David Thornley in 1973. As de Courcey Ireland saw it, demanding immediate national unity was of the utmost naivety; a 'decisive movement' towards socialism in Ireland could not happen 'without the support of a reasonable proportion of NI Prods and I think the greatest weakness of Irish republicanism has been the general feebleness if not lack of effort to try and win converts there – long ago, when in the North, I nearly broke my neck trying to get something done on those lines, in the end vainly'.[9]

The Irish Congress of Trade Unions left Northern affairs to its Northern Committee and was regarded as treading 'gingerly on any subject that could raise the tempers of its touchy members in Belfast'.[10] Alongside that were 'the diverse and disparate political fragments of the Provisional Republican movement', who resisted a class analysis. According to journalist Brian Trench, 'Sinn Féin must be the only party in Western Europe which claims to be socialist and which does not see this claim as being necessarily linked to the organised working class movement.'[11] Sinn Féin, in parallel with the IRA, had split at the end of 1969 between the 'Provisionals', nominally intent on a socialist republic but with the aim of first militarily defeating the UK's presence in Northern Ireland, and the 'Officials', who rejected the traditional Sinn Féin policy of abstentionism from parliament in the Republic and, in theory, urged a Marxist approach to creating a class politics aligning Protestants and Catholics in the quest to defeat British imperialism and create a unified socialist republic. Each wing rejected the other's legitimacy and both, in the 1970s, were lethal. Some of those involved in Official Sinn Féin, which evolved into Sinn Féin the Workers Party by early 1977, may have wanted to devote more attention to policy, but such debates were often 'inaudible due to the sound of gunfire'. By 1974 the Official IRA had been responsible for fifty deaths (compared to 600 caused by the Provisional IRA, 350 by Loyalists and 190 by state forces).

There was much infighting, personality clashes and an occasionally esoteric mix of 'republicanism, Christianity and Marxism', within the Officials, with individuals like Eoghan Harris capable of inspiring some to debate and discussion; others to trenchant denunciation of him. By 1973, arguments over the direction of the movement were fierce among the 300 members in Dublin 'and conducted in the language of the Communist purges of the 1930s'. The Resources Protection Campaign, launched in late 1973, became a 'key area of [Official] Sinn Féin agitation demanding the nationalisation of mining and energy rights'.[12] But as with its Provisional counterparts, its military wing continued to maim, murder, rob and seek revenge. By 1976 '[Official] Sinn Féin dominated the leadership of the 55,000-member Union of Students of Ireland, Eamon Gilmore and Johnny Curran having been elected president and education officer, respectively, in January.'[13] By the time of the 'Sinn Féin the Workers Party' departure its industrial department was exhibiting what many regarded as an obsession with secrecy, although it was also seen as bringing a fresh intellectual rigour to trade unionism.[14]

There were many aborted attempts to grapple with the dimensions of possible political compromise between Britain and the Republic in creating a solution in the early 1970s and up to the Sunningdale Agreement of 1973. In June 1972, Donal O'Sullivan, the Irish ambassador in London, wrote a confidential memorandum on his recent discussions with British politicians: 'It is clear, they contend, that reunification is a long way off.' The British Labour Party, then in opposition, was sending conflicting signals; a contention by Roy Hattersley, deputy foreign affairs spokesman for the party, that the majority in Northern Ireland might be 'engineered' into a united Ireland had caused resentment within the party. O'Sullivan suggested the Irish government could not rely on the Labour Party: 'There are, in fact, rumours that Harold Wilson himself has become a good deal less interested in the Northern problem ... according to Rees [Merlyn Rees, the front bench opposition spokesman on Northern Ireland] the Labour Party would not wish to see the North become an election issue. They would greatly hope to have it out of the way before the election comes.'[15]

In January 1973, O'Sullivan wrote of his encounter with Lord Windlesham, a liberal Catholic Tory and Minister of State at the Northern Ireland Office. He told him of the Irish government's disappointment 'at the negative attitude we encountered on the Council of Ireland idea', a proposed all-Ireland body to be operated alongside a proposed power-sharing assembly whose responsibilities were as yet undefined. The fear the British government seemed to have was of provoking the ire of the hardliners: 'I repeated several times to Lord Windlesham that it would be a ghastly mistake on their part to come forward with a half-hearted solution because of fear of a reaction from the hard-line Protestant element ... it would he said, probably be a great help to the future of politics in Northern Ireland if Austin Currie and John Hume could be persuaded to opt out of the SDLP and to join the Alliance Party' (formed in 1970 in an attempt to break the mould of sectarian politics by trying to draw support from both communities).[16]

This perhaps naïve hope that there was a middle way was also emanating from the Northern Ireland Office, but what it amounted to was a fudge, or as Philip Woodfield, the deputy head of the Northern Ireland Office, expressed it in a meeting in January 1973, the aim was 'not to put obstacles in the way of Irish unity, but equally, not to take positive steps in its direction'. What the Irish side were pushing for was a Council of Ireland 'with teeth' and a 'recognition of the Irish dimension was the important thing'. Sir Stewart Crawford, Deputy Under-secretary of State at the Foreign and Commonwealth Office, suggested to C. V. Whelan of the Irish Embassy that the Loyalist paramilitary group the Ulster Defence Association (UDA) 'contains moderates as well as tiresome people. What we have to do is separate them.'[17] William Craig's call for an 'Ulster Dominion' was dismissed by Conor Cruise O'Brien, but the SDLP's John Hume was more positive in his reaction.[18] The following month, the Conservative British government published its proposals under the title *Northern Ireland: Constitutional Proposals*, involving the establishment of a seventy-eight-member power-sharing executive and a Council of Ireland (still ill defined). Its proposals were supported by the SDLP, the Ulster Unionist Party (UUP), the Alliance Party and the Irish government, and opposed by Ian Paisley's Democratic Unionist Party (the DUP, more stridently Unionist than the UUP and with a strong appeal to working-class Unionists) and William Craig's Ulster Vanguard movement, which had links with the UDA.

The newly installed Taoiseach, Liam Cosgrave, suggested in June 1973 that what was needed was 'a willingness to accept and work forward from existing realities, rather than a concern with abstract legalistic or constitutional definitions'.[19] When he met the British prime minister the following month, Ambassador Donal O'Sullivan wrote to Garret FitzGerald, anxious to convey the message that the meeting 'should be played down with the Press'. Just before the meeting, FitzGerald suggested Cosgrave press 'very hard' the issue of police and civil service reform, 'even to the point of indicating that we should have difficulty about accepting the Northern Irish institutions if this is not carried through. We have earned and built up considerable goodwill in the last 3 months and should, I believe cash some of it in now in this way.' The government also received a briefing from its contacts in Belfast to the effect that their informants 'were certain that the majority of the people in the Catholic ghetto areas in Belfast were sick to death of IRA activity'.

The two prime ministers met in the 'blazing sunshine' of the garden of 10 Downing Street and discussed how 'to help discreetly' in bringing more Catholics into senior positions in the civil service, and a Council of Ireland which would be 'open ended' but would 'avoid giving the impression of collusion'. Heath wanted more from the Irish government on extradition from the Republic of those suspected of terrorism, but Cosgrave insisted the Irish government could not interfere with the courts in this regard.[20] Elections for the Northern Ireland Assembly held at the end of June gave the Unionist Party 24 seats, SDLP 19, with non-aligned Unionists, the Alliance Party and the DUP winning 8 each and the Ulster Vanguard 7.

The two leaders met again in September 1973 at Baldonnel, a military airport south-west of Dublin, when Heath created history by being the first prime minister to visit the Republic on official business since independence and he generated controversy by remarks about the 'integration' of Northern Ireland with Britain. Before the meeting, Sir Arthur Galsworthy, the British ambassador in Ireland, complained that there was too much publicity on the Irish side about the meeting through 'deliberate leaks' and that the talks were 'being built up too much'. Some got carried away with the notion of the visit as being particularly historic; Desmond Leslie of Castle Leslie in County Monaghan, for example, was positively poetic, if not borderline hysterical: 'Ireland's prayers will literally envelop you in a veritable powerhouse of spirit – nothing pietistic or imaginary, but a real and most potent force to guide you through the trickier moments.' In truth, the 'real and most potent' guiding force was Conor Cruise O'Brien, who gave Cosgrave a list of 'the more ticklish questions' to expect.[21]

Muiris Mac Conghail, the head of the Government Information Services, was adamant that 'there should be no difference between the amount and quality of coverage given to either leader. If Mr Heath makes himself more available than the Taoiseach the appearance of a Heath dominated conference could well develop. This would not be good for the government.'[22] Aside from the political optics, meetings of this kind also raised 'housekeeping' issues for the organisers; the inter-departmental committee preparing for the visit was not impressed with the scruffiness of Baldonnel ('would bring great discredit on us'). After the visit, a memorandum from the Department of the Taoiseach complained about the lunch which was 'rather cold and I gathered from Colonel Swan that there had been a dispute between the catering corps and the local chef regarding the use of hot plates. The meal generally was not, in my opinion, particularly outstanding'. The cold buffet provided later that evening, however, received the thumbs up ('it was a superb buffet with champagne') and the journalists, as usual, 'were amply refreshed and given good facilities'. The visit cost £3,118. After the telephone bill, the biggest cost was for journalists at the Shelbourne Hotel, where they waited; the bill there was for £862; clearly, these were by no means dry assignments. The Department of Finance wanted the Department of Foreign Affairs to pay the full cost but it would only agree to meet half the cost.[23]

Cosgrave was keen to reassure Unionists that the Council of Ireland was 'no trick to win a united Ireland'. Dermot Nally and Seán Donlon, who was working as a counsellor in the Anglo-Irish division of the Department of Foreign Affairs with responsibility for relations with Northern Ireland, and was a future secretary general of that department, met Ulster Unionist Party leader Brian Faulkner at his house at the end of October regarding the plans for the Council. Faulkner 'strongly emphasised the need for absolute secrecy. He would not be telling any member of his party about the meeting and there were obviously precautions in operation to see that no-one saw us with him.'[24] At the end of October the Ulster Unionist Party narrowly decided to take part in the proposed power-sharing executive; Faulkner was installed as Chief Executive and SDLP leader Gerry Fitt as deputy. The breakthrough was hailed in the Republic by Cosgrave and Lynch as 'momentous' and 'historic'.[25] Paisley and Craig's Unionists rejected it.

Discussions at Sunningdale, in Berkshire, took place between 6 and 9 December 1973 for those involved in the new arrangements. The clear need as expressed by Cosgrave was for institutions that would be trusted, would last and would be defended 'by all of us'. He prayed that the next generation and the one after that 'will have cause to thank us all for what we will do at this conference'. The following week, Brian Faulkner made it clear to Brendan Corish that while Corish had expressed a desire 'to see a sense of urgency in following up our broad discussion of principles' in relation to Council of Ireland functions, he would 'attach at least equal importance to taking urgent action in the field of law enforcement and counter terrorism'.[26]

What was agreed was the creation of a Council of Ireland containing ministers from the Dáil and the Northern Executive, a secretariat and consultative assembly with a membership from both those bodies. It would deal with policing ('as soon as the security problems were resolved') and cross-border co-operation on economic and infrastructural issues. There was also agreement that the Irish government accepted there could be no change to the status of Northern Ireland without the consent of the majority in the North. For all the optimism that was expressed, the reality was that 'the Unionists had to say that the Council of Ireland had scuppered Irish unity, the SDLP that it advanced it'.[27] A liberal Unionist at Sunningdale, Basil McIvor, recorded his despair at the Irish government's inability to move on terrorist extradition to balance the concession of a Council of Ireland: 'It was at this point that the Unionists could see the futility of it all.'[28]

Private uncertainty about how to present the Sunningdale Agreement was apparent by the manner in which civil servants were cautious in monitoring the drafts of Cosgrave's speeches in relation to it. The draft text of his message to the new executive had included the words 'your task is not an easy one, but let me assure you that my government will do all in its power to help you'. This, it was suggested by one civil servant, 'may be too patronising', while the phrase 'we look forward to co-operating with the representatives of the people of Northern Ireland, through their executive and assembly' was regarded as troubling as it amounted to 'recognition'.[29] There was also the issue of what the attitude of Fianna Fáil would be to the Sunningdale developments. In January 1974, an urgent note by Muiris Mac Conghail, who had been speaking to some of the political correspondents (in an interesting example of their influence and their urgings), 'wondered if the Taoiseach was aware of the extremely precarious position [of] Mr Lynch' in this regard.

In the Senate, former Fianna Fáil minister Brian Lenihan had been very critical of the Sunningdale communiqué and 'the pol corrs [political correspondents] stated that many of the Dáil members of Fianna Fáil are going around the country describing Sunningdale as a sell out ... the pol corrs suggested that the Taoiseach was not giving as much help to Mr Lynch as the situation required and that the best way of doing this was for the Taoiseach to take Mr Lynch into his confidence. They feel that the Taoiseach may not be aware of Mr Lynch's precarious position (their phrase) and that there are many in FF who will use the Sunningdale communiqué as a stick to beat Mr Lynch, since they seem determined to prove that Lynch has lost his grip on the party and on party affairs. Michael Mills, whom I regard as being extremely well informed was most emphatic on this point and I regard his judgement as being good.'[30]

Cosgrave was facing ominous warnings on all fronts. On the same day, a note from Dermot Nally, assistant secretary to the government, relayed a message from Faulkner about how important it was not to 'push our fences' regarding a Council of Ireland and that the Irish government should be content with 'small beginnings' or he and Gerry Fitt would find it difficult to maintain public support and the whole edifice 'might not be sustained'. From other Unionists ('West, Taylor and Co'.) there was 'contemptuous laughter' in relation to the Council of Ireland.[31] Seán Donlon also supplied reports of his visit to Belfast on 9 January and relayed internal tensions, with Currie and Devlin worried that Fitt was getting too close to Faulkner; they had adjoining suites at Stormont and 'according to Devlin since Fitt has no executive responsibilities ... he has plenty of time to develop a relationship with Faulkner which will work mainly to Faulkner's advantage'.[32]

The Sunningdale balancing act was further complicated and compromised when former Fianna Fáil minister Kevin Boland took a legal challenge to the agreement on the grounds that the Irish government's support of it amounted to a recognition of Northern Ireland that violated the Irish constitution. This was rejected by the High Court but the government's defence 'amounted to a declaration that its territorial claim to Northern Ireland was still in force', which enraged Faulkner as it 'robbed him of all credibility on the question of status'. This was later acknowledged by Garret FitzGerald, who conceded to a Unionist that 'our legal defence involved demolishing the entire political position which we had built up for you'.[33]

A UK general election the following month 'facilitated a concentrated expression of unionist discontent' and brought Harold Wilson to power; he believed the power-sharing experiment was doomed and indeed it was. In May the Loyalist Ulster Workers Council called for work stoppages and created mayhem, while in the midst of this the Dublin and Monaghan bombs killed thirty-three people (see pages 198–201). Promises to 'phase in' the Council of Ireland were not enough; the strike continued 'and the performance of the state and army in resisting it was hardly impressive'. Power sharing had collapsed by the end of the month.[34]

Fr Raymond Murray, from the Parochial House in Armagh, articulated the sense of anger on the part of Nationalists in the North after the collapse of Sunningdale. It was, he insisted, a betrayal of 'the minority here in giving in to the Loyalist thugs, but why make our case worse by allowing Conor Cruise O'Brien to speak about civil war ... would you please tell him to stop such inflammable language'.[35] According to the Alliance Party, which met the Irish government's All Party Committee on Irish Relations in May 1974, in relation to the Council of Ireland idea, 'as long as it was nebulous it was hard to sell it'.[36] In the aftermath of these upheavals, notes were prepared by the Department of the Taoiseach for briefings which included the suggestion 'there should not be too much identification with former SDLP ministers ... I think the main fault of the SDLP is that they misjudged the strengthening of Protestant feeling.'[37]

The collapse of Sunningdale had effectively left the Irish government without a strategy and it seemed to fold its tent. When a British parliamentary group visited Dublin at the end of February 1976, Cosgrave admitted to them that 'excessive emphasis on the Irish dimension' had destroyed Sunningdale and that as a result 'the Irish government had deliberately adopted a low profile for the past 2 years – without, apparently, contributing to any solution in Northern Ireland. They could possibly say that things would have been a good deal worse if the attitude of the government here had been different.'[38] In an honest and different take on the subject a few weeks previously, Fine Gael TD Paddy Harte, who privately asked for patience in his personal talks with Loyalists, when making a speech at UCD, maintained: 'In the South, instead of helpfully concerning ourselves we have again developed a dangerous capacity of thought which enables us to disown the North if called on to contribute and to claim it as our own when the occasions suits.'[39]

– SIXTEEN –

VISITORS FROM THE NORTH

Lynch and Cosgrave were regularly accused by Northern Nationalists and Republicans of 'blind support' for British policy, which 'amaze[s] the bulk of six county Catholics'. Such sentiments were often accompanied by files outlining in great detail the terror of British army harassment, 'less spectacular' than sectarian assassinations, 'but more constant and widespread is the day to day harassment of the whole Catholic population'.[1] Cosgrave received a letter from a widow in Omagh, looking for an answer to her question: 'Why were so many Catholic men and women savagely beaten, mutilated and shot and in the case of my own husband, RIP, his body strewn with petrol and set alight, a boy of 19 years beaten, hanged and thrown in the river, the autopsy reported, before life had gone out of his body?'[2]

Irish civil servants retained close contacts with Northern Nationalists involved in the relief of such distress. Seán Donlon, for example, met Fr Pádraig Murphy, the parish priest of St John's on the Falls Road in Belfast in February 1974. He reported that 'as usual, Canon Murphy is in financial difficulties ... the innocent dependants fund of which he is chairman is £18,668 in debt and interest is accumulating on it at 14 per cent. The fund was used to make payments to internees' families until February 1973. About £200,000 was paid out altogether in 1971–3 and an estimated £45,000 of this came from the Irish Red Cross. The balance was raised by Murphy from private sources in the US, Britain and Dublin.' One of the difficulties he had encountered was the drying up of various private sources of income 'largely because people had become so suspicious of any fundraising for NI causes'.

The co-ordinators for the centre of relief in Belfast had assisted moving up to 700 families since January 1973. Rather than having the government involved with non-official groups it was preferred to let the Irish Red Cross handle the matter. There was also an insistence that meetings with Northern Irish priests should be co-ordinated through the Department of Foreign Affairs and not the Department of Defence as 'it would be particularly objectionable if the news should leak out that priests from the six county area were in direct consultation with the Minister for Defence and chief of staff of the Army'.[3] In September 1973 a group of Belfast priests, including Fr Denis Faul, wanted a meeting with Cosgrave before he met Ted Heath; Seán Donlon 'would not be inclined to give their request too high a priority'.[4]

Individual politicians sometimes had their own intimate contacts with sections of the Republican movement. In January 1975, for example, Cruise O'Brien wrote to Garret FitzGerald with an account of his encounter with Labour TD Dr John O'Connell, who had told O'Brien about 'the Provisional leadership, with which he was in constant touch'. The conversation was in relation to the progress of ceasefire negotiations. He suggested the need to be helpful to the more 'reasonable' elements in the IRA and avoid 'the possible death of hunger strikers'. O'Brien 'gave him no quarter' and refused O'Connell's request to keep their conversation between themselves: 'I explained, as a member of the government, I did not have the right to accept confidential communications on political matters.' He accepted that O'Connell had expressed no sympathy for the Provisionals' ideology, but 'I had the impression that he enjoys his present rather ambiguous intermediary role and would dislike having to bring that to an end.'[5]

Contacts between Northern Irish politicians and Irish governments were also ongoing throughout the decade and often very discreet, but were mostly from the Nationalist minority side in Northern Ireland. It was noted by Lynch at a meeting of Fianna Fáil in September 1971 that '17 of the 19 representatives of the Northern Minority had visited him and met representatives of the government in Dublin'; at the same meeting it was resolved that 'the unionist grip on power must be broken'.[6] The SDLP MPs were the most frequent visitors; the decade for them involved being a 'party in waiting', 'years of hope' alternating with years of despair. Ultimately their journey was 'a story of persistence' and it involved a 'critical need' to develop a good working relationship with the Republic.[7]

The party was rarely united, partly as a result of the different backgrounds of its leading lights. In 1966 Gerry Fitt had won the West Belfast parliamentary seat from the Ulster Unionist Party, three years after he had formed the Republican Labour Party with Harry Diamond and was involved in giving a high profile to the nascent civil rights campaign in Northern Ireland. In August 1970 he became the founding leader of the SDLP; he had insisted on 'Labour' being included in the party's title, but he had a dislike for the middle-class, university-educated party activists from outside Belfast, whom he saw as more committed Nationalists than social democrats. He found some of the focus on strategy, party organisation and position papers irksome and condescending and tended to leave this work to other members, notably John Hume from Derry, who had a background in the credit union movement and was an Independent Nationalist before his involvement in the SDLP. Fitt's extensive Westminster contacts were useful for the party but there were was an abundance of personality clashes, including between himself and Paddy Devlin, another committed Labour man, and differences of opinion over many issues, including boycotting the Stormont parliament.

In April 1972 the Alliance Party privately approached the Department of the Taoiseach about the possibility of a private dinner at a hotel in Dublin to give its representatives 'an opportunity to speak about the party's outlook to influential people in the 26 counties'. The Taoiseach did not object.[8] It was a timely approach, given that a few weeks earlier Garret FitzGerald had suggested privately that 'the Alliance Party has not been taken sufficiently seriously down here'.[9] But Fianna Fáil National Executive minutes reveal that six years later there was little enthusiasm for the Alliance Party – the FF member who had been present at the Alliance Party's annual convention gave a verbal report: 'He did not consider the conference useful and had strong reservations about the Alliance Party in general.'[10]

In July 1973 Paddy Devlin of the SDLP had complained bitterly to Garret FitzGerald that discussions between the two of them had been leaked to the press and 'carried and dutifully elaborated on by Conor Cruise O'Brien's lap dog in the *Irish Times* and in a way that indicated preliminary briefing by someone with an iron in the fire'. He then moved into threatening mode: 'to quibble over leaks is a most unworthy exercise. Nevertheless, I would not like to give anyone the impression that we would spurn the use of it as a ploy if we are to be messed about anymore.'[11] Tensions between the SDLP and Cruise O'Brien endured; he saw it as intensely irritating that it was mandatory to say 'me too' to whatever John Hume said. He attacked the notion propounded by the SDLP of joint administration of Northern Ireland by the British and Irish governments and 'immediately fastened my political seatbelt'. For his part, Hume regarded O'Brien's book *States of Ireland* as 'the best statement of the Ulster Unionist case ever written'.[12] He clashed with him on RTÉ's *The Late Late Show*, challenging O'Brien's assertion that 'even mentioning Irish unity was to risk civil war'.[13]

Early in November 1973 a delegation from the SDLP – 'The Dublin social scene was beloved most of all by the SDLP,' according to journalist James Downey[14] – arrived to meet the Irish government, including the Taoiseach, to discuss issues of policing and security, and the party suggested lines of communication between it and the government 'had very much improved'. At dinner following the meeting, the party expressed itself 'completely satisfied' with the government's stance on policing: 'They had come prepared for battle and had been so glad that the battle was unnecessary that they forgot to show their appreciation,' though Cruise O'Brien expressed scepticism about the SDLP's demand for tripartite talks in the absence of an executive. He 'made it plain to the SDLP that the tactics suited to a political party are not necessarily those available to a government.'

Early the following year an account by Seán Donlon of a visit to Belfast made it plain that the SDLP was far from a happy or united family, and it was clear at a subsequent meeting between Gerry Fitt and Paddy Devlin at Iveagh House in Dublin that 'in a number of respects they held opposed opinions and in general it was clear that they had not settled on any joint line of approach for the meeting'.[15] But Donlon acknowledged in his reports of the situation in Belfast in the spring of 1974 that his information was 'based exclusively' on conversations with the SDLP and he stayed with John Hume, where he witnessed 'depression, frustration and despair' and 'much bickering between the leaders' within the party. The context here was the Ulster Workers Council controlling the situation and collapsing power sharing and the reality that 'any part of normal life which is continuing is doing so only by licence from the UWC ... There was also a swing away from them towards the IRA ... Devlin and Fitt said they had no support in Belfast' and Hume and Currie 'seem to feel that the SDLP is finished as a political force'. Hume was stark in his assessment: 'Any hope of Irish unity has gone forever.'

In all his discussions, 'the scenario of civil war and re-partition emerged with depressing frequency ... Hume and others are even talking of leaving politics and Hume is, for financial reasons, immediately looking for a job ... On the recriminations side, it may be worth recording that I saw no general criticisms of our recent policies and tactics ... they expect Faulkner to go to the House of Lords and be the first to write a book about power sharing in due course.'[16] It amounted to one of Donlon's bleakest memoranda, and another factor was the tension within the party over its relationship with Dublin. Devlin hated the impression that the SDLP was 'subservient to directions from the Republic'.[17]

The SDLP was back in Dublin in August 1974 and a measure of the significance attached to its visit was that six Irish government ministers were in attendance at the meeting to hear Gerry Fitt ironically note: 'It was a very sorry thing for him to have to say but he must say it – that the worst thing that had happened for the North in recent years had been the defeat of the Tory government. Labour policy in the North has been absolutely disastrous.' But Austin Currie, Nationalist MP for East Tyrone, who had been one of the SDLP negotiators involved in devising the Sunningdale Agreement, added that all ranks of the SDLP felt 'they had been let down by the Dublin government ... in his view there was an air almost of inevitability about the development of a doomsday situation. Despite anything that might be said here, the South would be embroiled in this.' It was clear they felt it necessary for the government in Dublin to take up the challenge of continued stalemate and the account of the meeting in the Department of the Taoiseach noted ominously 'there could well be a holocaust'.[18]

The frequency with which this word was used in the early 1970s gives some indication of the gravity with which the situation was viewed at that stage, the sense of despair and in particular the idea of very limited options. There was also concern at Cruise O'Brien seeming to imply in a briefing 'that the SDLP were coming to Dublin too often and thus frightening Loyalists'.[19]

The dynamics of these engagements were inevitably fraught during 1974; by November, for example, the SDLP had reached the stage of 'noting the number of times for which they have asked for a meeting and been out off' and they threatened to go ahead with a meeting with the opposition (Fianna Fáil) instead. When he visited Belfast at the end of October 1974, Seán Donlon observed a widespread feeling 'that the British are intent on a complete withdrawal from NI' and Hume saw a move towards independence for Northern Ireland 'as almost inevitable'. Once again, concern was expressed within the SDLP that the Dublin government was 'undermining' them: 'They regret as much as anyone the return to tribal patterns in NI but say that once this has happened there is nothing for Dublin to do but to join its tribe.'[20]

When the SDLP eventually secured a meeting with the government at the end of November 1974, Hume expressed the view that the IRA was deliberately trying to provoke civil war; he wanted to know how far Dublin was willing to go and what risks were worth taking.[21] There was no easy answer to that, it seemed, and the SDLP continued to fumble in the dark, while the IRA signalled its willingness to call a temporary ceasefire in December 1974 that lasted until the middle of January as British government officials talked to them about 'structures of disengagement from Ireland'. The announcement of an indefinite ceasefire by the IRA followed in February, allowing it to establish 'monitor centres' to bed down its hegemony in Nationalist areas. But there was no ultimate clarity as to what form British 'disengagement' might take (one British interpretation was that they were stringing the IRA along 'to the point where their military capacity went soggy'; another that they were looking at a means of getting rid of internment). The Irish government was wary of any such British disengagement and Unionists vacillated about the merits of pursuing some form of coalition with the SDLP.[22]

The ceasefire broke in September 1975 and a commitment to a 'long war' followed.

In early March 1976 FitzGerald did not want to meet the SDLP, as 'discussions on the eve of the London talks with Mr [Harold] Wilson could well be counter-productive'.[23] The two sides met instead later that month with Hume and Currie, Cosgrave and FitzGerald and Seán Donlon and Dermot Nally in attendance. Cosgrave informed them he had stressed to Wilson the importance of 'keeping the politicians in business in NI' and that having talks with representatives of illegal organisations was not helpful in this regard: 'The British ministers had drawn a distinction between talks and negotiations. They had said they would not negotiate with such persons but had said frankly that they would not cease talks which were useful to them.'

The SDLP made it clear it wanted to increase the profile of its meetings with the Irish government and desired 'a lot of publicity'. The view was also articulated that the IRA was under serious pressure and the SDLP wanted to take advantage of this to push for a new political initiative. (There were also 'expenses owed' to the SDLP for travelling to the meetings.[24]) But by the autumn of 1976 despondency had once again permeated the SDLP ranks, with their internal party discussions dominated by the theme 'The British must govern or go' and that Loyalists 'will come to their senses' if Britain left.[25]

There was much talk of ambivalence, drift, and the dilution of the 'Irish dimension'; Wilson was also regarded as having embodied some of this ambivalence when in power, whispering to Harry West, the anti-Sunningdale leader of the Ulster Unionist Party who had taken over from Brian Faulkner, that 'certain things which had been said did not in fact mean what they seemed to mean'.[26] Gerry Fitt was particularly forthright and pessimistic and also vaguely threatening in terms of the implications of drift for the Republic:

> Some members of the SDLP were beginning to think in Provo terms. It was no use waiting for another two years. By that time the SDLP would no longer be in existence. One could not expect men to continue to bear the burdens involved in a situation where there was no light at the end of the tunnel. Where were SDLP supporters to go if the party disintegrated? Some might go to the Alliance Party, which was basically a Unionist party. Others might turn to support the Provisional Sinn Féin and IRA and this was bound to lead, in the end, to an overspill of violence throughout the whole island.[27]

This was around the same time as the Peace Movement set up by Betty Williams and Máiréad Corrigan (subsequently Nobel Peace Prize winners), which had led to large rallies in the North and the Republic in an attempt to highlight civilian casualties and apply pressure on the paramilitaries; the SDLP had 'an ambivalent' attitude, suspecting it of having political ambitions 'and offering a distraction from the key issues that had to be addressed'.[28] In 1976, 308 people were killed as a result of the violence, an increase of 41 over the previous year.

One of the concerns expressed by Garret FitzGerald in January 1977 was uncertainty over the future of the SDLP and the need for the British government to react to the party as 'the influence of the Provisional IRA on SDLP thinking is now a major one'.[29] Later that year, following the SDLP's annual conference an attendee wrote to Jack Lynch: 'The rank and file members of the SDLP left me in no doubt that they were delighted with the result of the general election here and the change of government. They are convinced that we now have a government that cares about the North and that is working towards a solution to its problems without any surrender of principle.'[30] Lynch made it clear that he would prefer to deal with Hume and Currie 'if feasible'. This was a reference to a meeting request from Hugh Logue, the economic spokesperson for the SDLP, who, it was believed, wanted a meeting 'for reasons of his own which are directly related to internal SDLP politics'. Seán Donlon also told Richard Stokes in the Department of the Taoiseach that the SDLP had 'some reservations' about the extent of the access Donlon 'enjoyed to their thinking'.[31]

In interviews, Fitt was anxious to point out that the SDLP were 'not the Northern branch of Fianna Fáil' but there was anxiety in government about SDLP public relations exercises in meeting the government that could create the impression the government 'were acting in part as their standard bearer'. At the end of October, Lynch got his wish and met Hume and Currie in private in a meeting 'regarded as secret'.[32] In his meeting with British prime minister James Callaghan in September 1977, Lynch made the dubious assertion that the results of the June general election that had returned him to office 'perhaps indicated in some respects the feelings of Irish people about the problems of Northern Ireland. The impression had perhaps grown that the previous government had moved away from the aspiration of ultimate unity.'[33] The SDLP conference of November 1978 made it clear that it was difficult for the party to perform anything more 'than a holding operation'; what this amounted to in the view of Ian McAllister, writing in *Hibernia*, was that 'in terms of policy the SDLP is a shell'. In Dublin for a meeting with the government at the end of that month, Hume said 'essentially what they were seeking was another Sunningdale'.[34] They would have to wait another twenty years for a more advanced version of it to materialise.

– SEVENTEEN –

A MORE TOLERANT REPUBLIC?

Another interesting aspect of Irish governmental response to the early years of the Troubles was the extent to which it considered the changes that might be necessary to the Irish constitution to make the Republic more attractive or more acceptable to Protestants. In retrospect this seems fanciful and somewhat naïve given the scale and nature of the conflict, the forces that propelled it and the decades of failure to engage with unionism that preceded it, but it generated a degree of reflection at various stages during the decade, even if the omens were not remotely positive.

In November 1971, Dublin Labour Party TD Michael O'Leary – a future leader of the party, who along with colleagues Conor Cruise O'Brien and Frank Cluskey was an advocate of a Northern Ireland policy that focused not on partition but on the idea that the Republic should remove sectarianism from its state and constitution – called for the setting up of an Inter-Departmental Committee on the Implications of Irish Unity. His logic was that if Irish politicians were serious about unity there was an onus on them 'to outline the founding principles of the united state we envisage'.[1] Lynch did not envisage that such a committee would concern itself with economic matters; Labour Party leader Brendan Corish wanted ad hoc contact with 'Northern Irish opposition representatives' (the SDLP made it clear that it wanted to be involved). Liam Cosgrave expressed a preference for each individual party to have their own meetings with Lynch but when he did meet him, he was not keen on looking at the constitution 'on the terms indicated' and expressed disillusionment that the recommendations of the informal inter-party committee on the constitution that had been set up by the late Seán Lemass had been ignored. That committee had been chaired from 1966–7 by Minister for Education George Colley, and its report proposed removing the clause recognising the special position of the Catholic Church, relaxing the ban on divorce, and affirming that Northern Ireland could only be reintegrated by consent. Colley's suggestion that divorce might be permitted for non-Catholics resulted in strong episcopal criticism.

Notwithstanding the reservations he expressed to Lynch, Cosgrave agreed to take part in the proposed new initiative and it was decided no statements would be made to the media about the committee's deliberations, but when the Catholic Bishop of Clonfert, Thomas Ryan, got wind of it he suggested its mission would be to take the constitution, 'water it down and make it the constitution of a pagan country'. Another privately expressed view suggested it would offer a chance for those politicians who wanted contraception and divorce: 'If we have to lean so much over backwards to bring in the North, they were well left there. There should be a bishop on the committee ... if the committee consults, the bishop's advice would be wise and final.'[2]

In June 1972 Joseph Holloway, a counsellor at the Irish Embassy in London, had suggested to Richard Stokes in the Department of the Taoiseach that if a document was to be produced that would persuade Northerners to embrace unity, it would have to be one that would 'enable them to revert to their original position after a period of years if they are not satisfied with the way things have gone'. Stokes, however, felt 'this would give an incentive to perpetuate discontent'.[3] Four meetings of the committee in 1972 were adjourned due to the absence of a quorum.

Some of the issues the committee considered included whether there should be a reference to the Deity in any new constitution, provisions for proportional representation, the flag ('a relatively unimportant matter and negotiable') provision for an enlarged Senate (a suggestion that churches should be specifically represented was not favoured) and divorce ('Northern Unionists already know we would remove this provision for the sake of unity and it has, therefore, no bargaining strength'), articles 1–3 of the constitution (the territorial claim to Northern Ireland) and the differences in the education system (compulsory full-time schooling was from ages 5–15 in Northern Ireland and 6–14 in the Republic) as well as

Garret FitzGerald's writings on the economy. The committee began its proceedings in May and by November had contacted all parties in the North, except the DUP and Sinn Féin, to submit its views. The meeting convenors continued to struggle to assemble a quorum.

When Jack Lynch was interviewed by the BBC in December 1972 he said that if there was to be a united Ireland 'we really need a new constitution'.[4] Garret FitzGerald, a member of the committee, had written privately to Conservative Party MP William Whitelaw, who was about to become Secretary of State for Northern Ireland, in March 1972:

> There is a unanimous view amongst everyone I have talked to (other than British politicians!) that there should be no fiddling about with the boundary [border]; bad though it is, it has the virtue of having been there a long time and any change would carry incalculable dangers ... finally, even a hint that Britain would be happy to see, or would view with favour, a united Ireland, achieved with the consent and only with the consent of a majority in Northern Ireland, could mean a lot to the minority, without, I believe, exciting the majority too much.[5]

In July 1972 draft answers to the expected charge from the British side that the Irish government was 'doing nothing to promote a resolution to the Northern Ireland problem – by making constitutional changes etc.' included: 'The problem here is essentially a British one – they made the mess in 1920 and have no right to expect that the Dublin government will settle it for them ... We feel that if the British made a declaration of intent to leave the problem to be solved by the Irish the Northern Unionists, now sulking behind their guarantees, will be impelled to talk.'[6]

A letter to the Taoiseach Jack Lynch in 1972 from a Young Unionist Association alluded to the reforms that were needed to make the Republic's constitution and laws less sectarian, but insisted that even if these laws were changed Unionists would still resist reunification.[7] Nonetheless, it is striking to note the amount of attention governments and inter-departmental committees devoted to the consequences of eventual reunification in this regard. Given the sense of turmoil and uncertainty of the early 1970s and occasional talk of possible British withdrawal, it was seen as a serious and legitimate political endeavour to look at the social, political and economic consequences of unification, even if this was done in a relatively superficial way and was seen more in propaganda than substantive terms.

From an early stage in the Troubles Garret FitzGerald was active in travelling to Northern Ireland and exploring Protestant attitudes to 'the idea of some gradual move to bring the two parts of Ireland together politically', if the more contentious and sectarian elements of Irish law were tackled. He had suggested to Conor Cruise O'Brien in 1971 that 'it would be worth bringing our new Archbishop [of Dublin] Dermot Ryan [successor to John Charles McQuaid], in on this',[8] but he also chided a Northern religious minister that 'there is a reluctance in the churches to bear witness to Christian truth where this may be unpopular with the Flock'.[9] He maintained throughout 1972 and 1973 that there was 'a general consensus' that articles 2 and 3 of the Irish constitution, containing the Republic's territorial claim to Northern Ireland, should be deleted as they were of 'no practical value' and were standing in the way of Irish unity.[10]

He was also critical of the lack of engagement by southerners in the North: 'I have had further occasions to test opinions in political circles here and I have to say that the sense of involvement and concern for NI is even less than I conveyed.[11] He acknowledged that he got 'a fair amount of criticism' for this, but, in the face of such criticism, he was a robust and frank correspondent. The same was true of Cruise O'Brien, and FitzGerald saw himself as being in 'very close sympathy' with him on the subject of Northern Ireland, but he rejected O'Brien's two nations theory, insisting there were not two nations, but two cultures within a single historical national tradition.[12]

For the Fianna Fáil government, a memorandum was prepared in 1972 which argued that any proposed changes in laws or constitutions could be characterised as the type of reforms that might be needed for 'a new settlement in Ireland', necessary because of the 'disabilities that might be suffered by the minority here as a result of the present laws here', but they were also seen as exaggerated obstacles. While such disabilities were regarded 'as pin pricks compared to the massive disabilities and deprivations endured by the Northern minority, it must be recognised that the news media have made central issues out of what are, in their consequences, marginal issues'. The media, it was suggested, was manned by 'a liberal and even free-thinking elite ... these matters are made into issues as weighty as, and are used as counters to, such practices as gerrymandering and discriminatory housing and employment practices'.[13]

Areas of concern in this regard included the laws relating to adoption and contraception; in the Republic, the 1935 Criminal law Amendment

Act outlawing the sale and importation of contraception was still in operation, and adoption by parents of religiously mixed marriages was prohibited. There was recognition that changing these laws might achieve 'nothing with hard-line Unionists' but it was reckoned that 'there is some middle ground opinion in the North and especially in England where action on legislative reform under these two headings would have a tremendous propaganda value' even if 'we may regard it as a peripheral area'. The civil servant who drafted this memorandum pointed to the less than 'edifying' way in which a Private Member's Bill on contraception had been handled as it did not reach the printing stage, so that those most opposed to unity 'will get most mileage out of it' and those better disposed 'will see in it the confirmation of all they have read and heard of this state's alleged subservience to the church'.

Perhaps the difficulty with such detailed memoranda was that they still framed discussion of these topics in the context of 'public morality' and the need to safeguard it, while suggesting the possibility of being open to drafting something that might provoke a positive response from Protestants.[14] It was a cautious, narrow and unconvincing approach because the authors of such memoranda were not convinced of the merits of an agenda that was propelled by a 'free thinking elite' and rubbished by conservative Unionists. John Whale, an influential journalist with the *Sunday Times*, was met by an Irish official in the London Embassy in December 1972. Whale had been on a three-week tour of Ireland and his impression was that 'the general mood of the people was lagging behind the politicians at the moment in that the average man in the street in Ireland is not really interested in paying the price [of reunification] in terms of legislation on divorce, contraception and adoption etc., which would be necessary if a united Ireland is to become a reality'.[15]

The following year, representatives of the Church of Ireland and Presbyterians sent submissions to the Inter-Departmental Committee on the Implications of Irish Unity, supporting contraception and in the case of the Presbyterians, suggesting the removal of the constitutional prohibition on divorce.[16] Liam Cosgrave, known for his strongly held views on moral issues – he was a Knight of Grand Cross Pius XI – had a well-rehearsed answer in relation to legal change in the context of reunification. While he maintained he had an 'open mind' in this regard 'I think this cannot be pursued, even for the sake of Northern relations, whenever it does real violence to generally held convictions in the Republic, and I doubt if the

Northern people would in any case be impressed by our abandoning our convictions on topics like marriage or abortion.'[17] Yet when he was in opposition in 1971, Cosgrave had been quoted at a function to mark the fiftieth anniversary of the signing of the Anglo-Irish Treaty as saying the constitution was sectarian and a barrier to unity.[18]

Jack Lynch referred ambiguously to the need for 'a new more comprehensive identity', while others like Mary Robinson were more explicit in calling for a new non-denominational constitution. John Hume expressed concern about 'injudicious remarks' by Paddy Devlin in 1972 concerning the need for a new constitution, with Hume stressing that the SDLP was not pressing for any such change.[19] By July 1974, both the Department of Justice and the Attorney General Declan Costello were of the view that it would be 'unwise' to begin to draft a new constitution or initiate a referendum on articles 2 and 3, while Cosgrave was of the view that if there was to be a new constitution it should be 'an entirely new constitution rather than piecemeal amendment of the existing constitution'.[20] The Alliance Party made it clear that it 'did not consider that changes in say our adoption laws would have any significant effect on Northern opinion. Possibly the best contribution that could be made by the Republic would be to change articles 2 and 3.'[21]

When Garret FitzGerald met Archbishop Casaroli, who was effectively the Vatican foreign minister, at the Vatican in March 1977, he was frank in suggesting the question of Catholic laws in a possible reunified Ireland was 'an underlying problem which we are all ambivalent about in Ireland in a sense ... he himself thought that divorce should best be taken out of the constitution'. Casaroli said 'they in the Vatican saw reunification as the better solution for the future but they fully understood the reasons which led the government of Ireland not to speak of it for the time being'. FitzGerald also criticised the Bishop of Down and Connor, William Joseph Philbin (an outspoken critic of the IRA and Loyalist paramilitaries), for refusing to confirm Catholics attending state schools and not Catholic schools in Northern Ireland, which was 'a source of scandal to many Catholics. Indeed he himself speaking as a Catholic and not as a minister had found it a source of scandal that a sacrament could be used as a weapon of that kind.'[22]

Just how those in Northern Ireland viewed politicians from the Republic was also an interesting dimension to all the talk of a more pluralist state. In an interview with the *Belfast Telegraph* newspaper in June

1974, Cosgrave seemed somewhat uneasy in relation to questions about the perception of him in Northern Ireland:

> 'You seem a remote person to the Protestants of the North. Are you as remote as you seem?'
>
> 'I hope not. I don't know how you judge these things.'
>
> 'How do you get your point across to the Protestant in East Belfast or Sandy Row?'
>
> 'That's difficult enough to answer. How do you get it across except by what you do?'
>
> 'Have you met the Protestant "man in the street" from the North?'
>
> 'Oh, no. I have been to Belfast a number of times, but these people have become prominent lately.'[23]

Others praised him for being 'the first southern politician to have the integrity to state publicly what most of us have known for years, namely that reunification in the present climate is just not on'.[24] Some of the highly charged correspondence sent to Irish governments in the 1970s suggested a complete lack of understanding and empathy with the other 'side'. Although some of it was predictably vitriolic and dictated by the latest atrocity, there were other perspectives offered that suggested a perception by Ulster Protestants of a complete unwillingness on the part of both British and Irish governments to understand the mindset of Protestants in Northern Ireland.

They too, however, had their own prejudices and revealed their own inadequate understandings, particularly in the way they characterised the Republic. A letter addressed to Cosgrave in March 1974 from a resident of County Down was revealing in that regard; he articulated an intense hatred towards the Sunningdale Agreement and the Council of Ireland: 'I am a typical Ulster Protestant, I hope ... I do my daily work as best I can, I pay my debts and keep the laws of the land and I go to church when I feel like it ... I know nothing of Southern Ireland, how you live etc. I only know you are practically all Roman Catholics ... you see, we simply do not understand you.'[25] That same year, at a speech made in Cork, Justice Minister Patrick Cooney suggested 'we in the Republic should stand back and try and look at ourselves through the eyes of the Northern Protestant' and he criticised 'failure on the part of our people to give all possible help in rooting out subversive elements'.[26]

At a private dinner held in Down in May 1978, which included the Minister for Foreign Affairs Michael O'Kennedy, the editor of the *Irish News* quoted a woman on staunchly Loyalist Sandy Row as saying that what she feared most about a United Ireland was that Dublin would 'have us practising celibacy on the streets'.[27] A more visceral hatred of the Republic on the part of Northerners was evident that year in reports of the international soccer match between them at Lansdowne Road, which led to a baton charge by Gardaí at half-time. Journalist Gene Kerrigan reported for *Magill* magazine on the train journey from Belfast to Dublin: 'A mad cacophony of slogans erupts as if they all must be ejaculated before the train moves off. 1690, No Surrender, Pope John is dead and gone. John Paul has no balls. The Pope is not a virgin. Ulster, Ulster, U-U-UVF. UDA all the way, fuck the Pope and the IRA.' One traveller, however, stayed away from the chanters: 'He was surprised that Dublin was little more than two hours from Belfast. This was his first time to make the journey in his 28 years.'[28]

But did citizens of the Republic have any understanding of those from the North, whether Unionist or Nationalist, or did a partitionist mindset remain stubbornly in place? Journalist Nuala O'Faoláin was hardly alone in knowing 'nothing about Northern Ireland: I had been in Derry once, for one day, when I was twelve'.[29] Poet John Montague, who studied at UCD, suggested that 'the North of Ireland from which I emerged was barely comprehensible to my Southern contemporaries'.[30] Derry socialist and feminist Nell McCafferty surmised that 'Northerners were not always welcome in Southern society. Our accent alone marked us out, and our rapid-fire way of talking was associated with war'. She was clearly different from her southern counterparts and described herself as giving off the whiff of 'whiskey and petrol fumes' in contrast to *Irish Press* journalist Mary Kenny, who smelled of 'champagne and perfume'.[31]

Susan McKay, who grew up as a Protestant in Derry and came to Trinity College Dublin in 1975, referred to the 'strange silences' on the part of those who had lived through the early years of the Troubles and then moved to Dublin. When she came to Trinity, 'I met and became friends with Gerard McGurk. We were part of a circle that spent a lot of time in pubs, holding forth about Keats, angst, the price of a pint and the North. It was just four years since Gerard had lost his mother, his sister, his uncle, his friend and his neighbours in a horrific sectarian massacre. But we never spoke about it.' She also felt that 'many in the Republic were oblivious'.[32]

UCD's Literary and Historical Debating Society fielded many motions in relation to the Troubles during the 1970s (tomatoes were flung at Liam Cosgrave at one debate, leading to calls for the society to be disciplined), including the following selection: 'A United Ireland is impossible in our lifetime'; 'That there is now a final answer to the Irish question'; 'That the governments of the Republic have failed the politicians of the North'; 'That Britain's hands are bloody'. But these did not necessarily lead to mature or provocative debate. Kevin Cross, who served as the society's auditor from 1973–4, suggested 'the effect of the Northern violence was ultimately to de-radicalise the student body ... belief in the power of rational argument to influence other rational minds ... was in decline'.[33]

– EIGHTEEN –

TROUBLE SPILLS OVER THE BORDER

The potential for the Troubles to spill over the border remained an anxious preoccupation throughout the decade. From the end of 1972, the Department of the Taoiseach received correspondence from the Ulster Vanguard Alliance, which claimed it had also corresponded with 'selected TDs' and journalists. It threatened to carry out a bombing campaign in Dublin if the IRA violence continued in Northern Ireland: 'to prevent civilian casualties we will inform the staff of the Dublin newspapers in good time. The responsibility will rest with you. There will be a few hoax calls. To ignore any of them will be the height of criminal folly.'[1] The same group suggested that the cause of the turmoil was 'not eight hundred years, four hundred years or even fifty years of misrule. Instead, there is strong evidence to support the claim that the disease is due to sexual frustration of those in Holy Orders'.

In December 1972, correspondence was also generated on the sale of 'bomb Dublin' stickers in Belfast.[2] That month, bombs detonated by Loyalists killed two people and injured many more in Dublin; they had exploded after a two-minute warning. In January 1973 another bomb at the same location killed another person: 'The bombers were now beginning to thumb their noses at the security forces in the Republic by choosing to bomb the same location twice within seven weeks.'[3]

The December 1972 bombs exploded at a time when there was serious disunity in Fine Gael; Liam Cosgrave had become increasingly unpopular and isolated as leader, but the bombs, in the words of his biographer Stephen Collins 'saved Cosgrave's political life'. Earlier that year at his party's annual gathering in Cork, with a few whiskeys on board, he had castigated his enemies in the party as 'mongrel foxes'; he promised to 'dig them out and the pack will chop them when they get them'. Later that year, with IRA leader Seán Mac Stiofáin on hunger strike in Dublin and the sacking of the RTÉ Authority over the broadcast of the content of an interview with Mac Stiofáin, Minister for Justice Des O'Malley proposed the Offences Against the State Bill which would abolish jury trials for terrorist offences and provided that a person could be convicted of IRA membership on the word of a Garda superintendent.

The Labour Party and civil libertarians were opposed and many in Fine Gael wanted to oppose it in order to defeat the government; Cosgrave's instinct was to support the legislation but he may have vacillated and the issue threatened to exacerbate Fine Gael divisions. In the event, the bombs ensured that he and his party supported the vote on the Act and he was able to present himself as in the right; FitzGerald (of whom, according to Paddy Harte, Cosgrave 'could not conceal his dislike') admitted that in retrospect Cosgrave was proved correct and it bolstered his law and order credentials.[4]

But there was much worse to come with the Dublin and Monaghan bombings of May 1974. In Dublin, three car bombs exploded in ninety seconds and less than an hour and a half later a car bomb exploded outside a bar in Monaghan. In all, the UVF bombs killed thirty-three people. In their wake, a government statement praised the response of the Gardaí, army, ambulance and fire services, doctors and nurses and the 'hundreds of ordinary men and women who responded so readily and magnificently to donate their blood … it will also help to bring home to us here in this part of our island what the people in Northern Ireland have been suffering for five long years'.[5] A hurried note in the Department of the Taoiseach witnessed Cosgrave agreeing that in relation to a planned religious service for the victims in the Catholic Pro cathedral in Dublin, 'in the circumstances there would be no point in approaching the Church of Ireland Archbishop. It is probable, in any case, that all the victims were Catholics.' It was later noted that one victim was a Jewish French woman 'on a short visit to Ireland'.[6] Another victim was an Italian whose brother owned a fish-and-chip shop in Dublin.[7] Journalist Robert Fisk observed that 'one newspaper photographer was sick when he saw a gutter literally running with blood. A few feet away was a human leg and next to it a head.'[8]

A report in the *Evening Herald* that there would be no official day of mourning for the victims prompted a response from the Department of the Taoiseach suggesting 'some token gesture – such as the lowering of the flag tomorrow morning until after the mass in the Pro Cathedral might be desirable'.[9] The well-publicised withdrawal of 340 Irish soldiers from peacekeeping duties in the Middle East to bolster army strength after these bombings was 'a move which some army officers privately admitted was nothing more than a gesture'.[10] The bombs also led to demands for the initiation of legislation to ban the parking of unattended cars in the city. History was invoked by the parish priest of Castlemaine in County Kerry in a letter to Cosgrave regarding his dignified response to the killings: 'Never was I more proud of you than tonight ... a worthy son of WT ... your father faced an even greater crisis and dealt with it.'[11]

Another journalist, Vincent Browne, who was in Dublin at the time of the bombings with his brother Malachy, also recalled the devastating scenes:

> I was in the offices of Independent Newspapers on Middle Abbey Street when I heard the first bomb go off ... By the time I met Malachy at the door of Independent Newspapers another bomb had gone off, this time nearer to us. We walked out to O'Connell Street and saw people running into that street from Talbot Street. We began walking down Talbot Street, observing damage done to buildings by the explosion, a scene familiar to me from the years I had spent as a reporter in the North. As we approached the junction with Gardiner Street, and almost in slow motion, we focused on the real horror. There were bodies and bits of bodies amid the rubble and, in the silence, sounds of quiet moaning. There was a fine strapping man, I would have thought in his late 20s or early 30s, lying outside O'Neill's shoe shop. He had a big piece of metal from a car stuck into his right side. We went back out and lifted a woman, also outside O'Neill's. She was still alive and was moaning. As we lifted her, her body simply disintegrated in our arms. We placed her down again ... We brought others into Moran's Hotel, again down the stairs. The room downstairs was now in bedlam, people screaming, crying, moaning, others attending to them ... Malachy and I then went out to Daly's pub on the quays. There were

> only a few people in the pub. I recall us simply staring ahead towards the glasses on the mirror-backed shelves. And for the first time the emotion of it all was overwhelming. I was crying and I think so too was Malachy. We drove to my home, then in Churchtown, past the old blood bank, which was then at the top of Lower Leeson Street. There was a queue of people lined up to give blood. We watched Liam Cosgrave on television that night speak with sadness, firmness and dignity. I remember feeling proud of him and a confidence that his commitment to bring the perpetrators to justice would be realised.[12]

In 1993 an ITV documentary uncovered the extent of the incompetence of the handling of the investigation of the crime – taken together, the bombs and the victim count made it the worst atrocity of the Troubles – which created more questions for survivors and the families of victims. Joe Tiernan has suggested a 'fumbling' Garda investigation uncovered the plot and the names of the perpetrators, 'but little effort was made to bring them to justice'. Ineptitude and 'arrogance' in the Garda technical bureau were features of the investigation, but so too was the possible blocked extradition of a suspect ('this is the bastard we are looking for and we have enough evidence on him to stick him away' were the words attributed to one senior detective) and the bombers' links with British army intelligence officers who allegedly assisted them. Conor Cruise O'Brien lambasted 'monstrous, utterly unfounded innuendo' which argued that the government did not act on Garda information, but his castigation was not remotely convincing.[13]

Three decades on, Vincent Browne reflected on the Barron Report, the fruits of a private inquiry established by the Irish government in 1999, which revealed, in Browne's view, just how misplaced his confidence in Cosgrave had been in 1974. There was a 'shameful failure' to track down the perpetrators of the bombings:

> What of the evidence in the Barron report that some Gardaí were wittingly or unwittingly working for the British? Why have those who did so knowingly never been brought to justice, having betrayed the interests of the state? There seems to be an attempt to suggest that, by citing state security, it is possible to detract from the failure to protect the citizens of the Republic. With this in mind, the inaction of the Cosgrave government, when the British authorities gave names of

> suspect bombers to it, looks all the more sinister. To this must be added the loss of important forensic evidence, the slow motion conduct of the investigation and, finally, the disappearance of files from the Department of Justice. Cosgrave's government displayed such little concern for the lives of Irish people that it emboldened the British in the view that the North was essentially their internal problem. This simply served to prolong the conflict and cost more lives. It is to their shame.[14]

These were sentiments justifiably echoed by the families of the victims, who were not afforded enough dignity, respect or basic information about the status and progress of investigations into the bombings.

Just a week after the Dublin and Monaghan bombs, Minister for Finance Richie Ryan wrote to Cosgrave to stress the economic consequences of the carnage: 'We have just learnt that a US lender of $25,000,000 who was just about to sign the loan papers has decided to defer the matter in view of the occurrences in Dublin on 17 May. It doesn't make life any easier.'[15] Arising out of the bombs, an Inter-Departmental National Security Group stressed the need for civilians to 'watch for the parking of vehicles' and the establishment of a local security force was mooted but the Gardaí thought it might be 'counterproductive' if it led to more administration for them. Cosgrave announced it anyway in June 1974 in the context of desiring to promote 'a general sense of vigilance'. It was hoped to get 10,000 volunteers, but the view was also expressed that additional Garda manpower would be needed to make it work. There were cantankerous Dáil debates in January 1975 about the way in which this proposal was shelved; by the end of 1976, Cosgrave admitted it was an idea going nowhere; there was cynicism in the media and an apathetic response from the public.

Richard Stokes compiled a memorandum for the government on the issue in October 1974 suggesting it would be better for any local security force to be attached to the army, but that such a development could provoke a 'militant reaction' from Loyalists who 'would only be waiting for such an opportunity'. He also expressed strong reservations about the proposal as it stood: 'Given the Irish "informer" syndrome, I think it is unwise to attach this force to the local Garda station. In historical, emotional terms it will be too redolent of the RIC [the Royal Irish Constabulary, the pre-independence police force] and its function as "the eyes and ears of the government". There is a danger that many will regard the proposed service as some form of "stool pigeon" network and will have nothing to do with it.'[16]

The murder of Fine Gael senator and former TD Billy Fox also generated revulsion; he was the only member of the Oireachtas to be killed during the Troubles. A Church of Ireland farmer from Monaghan, he was on the liberal wing of Fine Gael and Republican in his views, making his killing by the IRA even more extraordinary. He insisted religion was an irrelevance in political terms, but had been subjected to taunts by Fianna Fáil ministers Brian Lenihan and Kevin Boland in 1970 that he was a B-Special, [a reserve police force in Northern Ireland from 1920 which was almost exclusively Protestant, widely distrusted by Catholics and disbanded in 1970], which they had to apologise for, though the slur continued to be used by those who successfully sought to prevent him keeping his Dáil seat in 1973.[17] Fox attracted attention by criticising the British army over its use of plastic bullets; in December 1971 he displayed two such bullets which he claimed had been fired across the border by British forces and was forcibly removed from the Dáil chamber, attracting national publicity.

On 11 March 1974 Fox was killed by a thirteen-member IRA gang who were raiding the home of his fiancée, Marjorie Coulson, near Clones; he arrived in the midst of the raid. Before Fox's arrival one of the raiders had burned the Coulson family Bible, a traditional anti-Protestant sectarian gesture; some analysts believed Fox was deliberately targeted. Five Provisional IRA members were convicted of his murder on 6 June, and sentenced to life imprisonment. The death of a member of the Oireachtas in a blatantly sectarian killing caused outrage. It was, said Cosgrave, 'unusually foul' for a man to be murdered who was 'selected by the people to represent them'.[18] The IRA attempted to defuse the fallout by claiming the Ulster Freedom Fighters were responsible, releasing a statement condemning the murder, and referring to Fox as 'someone who was known personally to a number of the leadership of the republican movement'.[19]

At the same time, local IRA supporters engaged in a whispering campaign, claiming – outrageously – that Fox had been involved in UVF activities and alleging that the Monaghan town bombing on 17 May 1974 had been a revenge attack for his death carried out by named Monaghan Protestants. (It later became known to have been perpetrated by Loyalists from Portadown, Co. Armagh.) According to historian Patrick Maume,

'Fox's career reflected both the increasing political integration of a new generation of border Protestants within the Republic's political system and the persistence of sectarian divisions and whispered hatreds along the border.'[20] The following year, members of the popular Miami Showband were travelling home to Dublin from a performance in County Down when they were stopped at what appeared to be a British army checkpoint near Newry, unaware that the soldiers were UVF members in disguise. Two of the UVF members attempted to plant a bomb in the back of the van (they seemed to want to create the impression the band was carrying explosives for the IRA) but it exploded, killing them, after which their accomplices opened fire on the band, killing three of them. Thirty-five years later, evidence of official collusion between the killers and members of the Ulster Defence Regiment, a regiment of the British army, was presented publicly.[21]

The kidnapping of Dr Tiede Herrema in Limerick in 1975, orchestrated by Eddie Gallagher, was another sensational development that created international attention. Gallagher, with a team that included his future wife Rose Dugdale – 'one of the most exotic recruits ever to the cause of Irish republicanism', the daughter of a millionaire underwriter at Lloyd's of London and graduate of Oxford – had carried out the 1974 robbery of Russborough House in Wicklow. It contained an acclaimed and hugely valuable private art collection with the total value of the stolen material estimated at up to £8 million. Dugdale was captured and sentenced to nine years in prison but Gallagher evaded arrest; he was subsequently imprisoned in Portlaoise Prison but was there only one day before being one of nineteen prisoners who dramatically escaped.[22] Gallagher – acting independently of the IRA – was determined to secure the release of Dugdale and had teamed up with Derry IRA member Marian Coyle and two others to organise the kidnapping of Herrema, the managing director of Ferenka manufacturing plant, one of the city's biggest employers. After his kidnap he was moved to a house in Kildare. Phil Flynn, a Sinn Féin activist and trade union official who acted as an unapproved intermediary, met Gallagher, who changed tack; it was not now apparently just about the release of Dugdale; he also demanded £2.5 million and a flight to Tanzania.

The house was subsequently raided; Gallagher fired indiscriminately and a siege began which lasted seventeen days before the kidnappers surrendered. That it had ended without bloodshed was seen as a 'triumph' for the government 'and there was international praise for the way the kidnap had been handled'. Herrema also suggested subsequently that a deal had been struck with the kidnappers concerning the length of their sentences to get them to surrender.[23] Herrema, a tough 'but fair' businessman who was sent to Ferenka to try and end its industrial disputes (and who was still running 6km every day and celebrating his ninetieth birthday in his native Holland in 2011) was helped in enduring the siege by his physical fitness and mental strength and 'his coolness and composure at the end of his 36 day ordeal during which he was bound and blindfolded and deprived of food, was astonishing'. He calmly stepped out of the Kildare house at the centre of the siege 'into the glare of the world's media and a war zone of armoured cars, uniformed snipers, barricades of bullet-proof glass and sandbags'. He believed his training as a psychologist helped; 'I said to myself, "All right, I'm lying here in this bedroom, but as long as I am not shot let me be happy in my own mind."'[24]

The decision to allow Dugdale and Gallagher to marry in prison three years later was also controversial; officially, the permission was granted because they had a three-year-old son. It was the first time two prisoners under sentence had been allowed to marry. The prison chaplain James O'Connell was reported as saying the couple, who had not met for almost four years, 'should have been allowed parole so that the wedding could be consummated'. The British Press referred to it in the context of the perceived indication from Jack Lynch the previous month of a possible amnesty for IRA prisoners.[25]

The Troubles and the response of those imprisoned in the Republic as a result had in fact created successive dilemmas for Irish governments. In September 1973, twelve prisoners in Mountjoy Jail in Dublin stopped taking meals and demanded political status, which the government refused. A memorandum from the Department of Justice noted that there were sixty Provisional IRA prisoners in Mountjoy. The prisoners who acted as spokesmen, according to the department 'would not elaborate on what they meant by their demand for recognition as "political prisoners" ... whether it meant that the title should be used when referring to them or that some special concessions should be accorded to them, or both'. Concessions had been made regarding cigarettes and food parcels, but it was maintained that any concession 'just becomes the signal for fresh demands'. The department was insistent about the merits of the 'direct effect of a strong statement from government standing firm'.[26]

The government was challenged by a member of Sinn Féin from Portadown, who suggested it was in a discredited league of its own: 'Even the Brits (and it galls us to say it) had the decency to acknowledge the importance of outside contact with the prisoners who at all times are allowed to correspond with their loved ones ... why then are the Republican prisoners in Mountjoy denied this?'[27] The Minister for Justice, Patrick Cooney, had also expressed concern about the picketing of the house of Fine Gael TD Paddy Harte 'by a group of some 50 persons', insisting that 'large-scale' arrests could ensue if it was continued.

John Hume was particularly worried about these protests and hunger strikes of IRA prisoners in Mountjoy in 1973 and offered to intervene (he suggested such intervention 'might get the government off the hook by appearing to yield from an offer of help by the SDLP', as had happened previously in the North) as he felt a death in Mountjoy would cause great anger and 'there would be a feeling among members of the minority that the word of the Dublin government would not be accepted in future'.[28] In the event this was not required; the strike ended on 3 October and the prisoners agreed to carry out certain prison work. Given the role they had played in Irish Republican history, and indeed the hard-line reaction to them in southern Ireland after independence, including during the civil war and Second World War, hunger strikes were particularly potent and emotive, not just in terms of the actions of prisoners but in the reaction they provoked. The state archives include a large volume of correspondence to government both from those who supported and those who condemned their actions. One telegram to Cosgrave in October 1973 demanded that he give them political status: 'Your father and his comrades got it from the British after the 1916 Rising, you fool.'[29]

It remained an issue throughout the decade and was complicated by the intervention of Catholic priests and bishops. Given the frequency with which a sectarian framework was employed to explain the Troubles, it was inevitable that questions and tensions would arise over the role of Catholic clergy and bishops as the conflict endured. In February 1971, the Association of Irish Priests declared support for a new all-Ireland constitution embodying the principle of religious freedom and affording no special position to the Catholic Church, but others, including Fr Denis Faul, opposed this.[30]

Dr Edward Daly, who had been active in the civil rights movement and was at the centre of an iconic image of the Troubles when photographed waving a bloodstained handkerchief in Derry on Bloody Sunday while helping to escort a wounded victim to safety, wrote to Conor Cruise O'Brien in 1976. He suggested that since he had become Bishop of Derry in 1974, 'I have had an opportunity to experience some similar pressures to that of a cabinet minister, especially in the circumstances prevailing here. You have my sympathy.'[31] But the following year in a letter to FitzGerald, Cosgrave expressed concern about comments of Daly in relation to prison conditions. There was a suggestion that the Vatican should be contacted through the Holy See to express the government view. Reference was also made to a successor to Cardinal Conway and whether 'our views on this matter could be made known', though after a phone call from Cosgrave it was decided this was 'not to be proceeded with'.[32]

The issue of prison conditions was one that caused strain between the government and the Vatican owing to the practice of Republican prisoners and their representatives petitioning Rome to intervene in relation to conditions and hunger strikes. While on a trip to Iceland in 1973, Garret FitzGerald composed notes from his hotel room in Reykjavik suggesting the Irish government was particularly disturbed that the 'Holy See should seem to accept propaganda statements of convicted criminals', particularly in light of his recent visit to the Vatican which he hoped 'would have dispelled any misunderstanding.'[33]

As expressed in a formal memorandum in May 1973, the Holy See 'has an importance to us in relation to Northern Ireland', but it was more important that government's freedom of action 'should not be inhibited by the danger of adverse reactions by the Holy See to any action we feel it is necessary to take'. In his discussions with Archbishop Casaroli, FitzGerald explained 'our problems' in relation to the sectarian elements of the Irish constitution and 'received a sympathetic hearing'. He also outlined his concerns about interventions by Irish bishops: 'He will do what he can vis-à-vis the Hierarchy here, although the Nuncio has since suggested that Vatican's influence on the Hierarchy here is very limited.'[34]

In January 1975 Cosgrave had a 'delightful dinner' with the Apostolic Nuncio, Archbishop Gaetano Alibrandi, at a time of more tension over hunger strikes and accusations that the government was permitting unchristian practices at the jail. Minister for Justice Patrick Cooney insisted explosives were being brought into Portlaoise Prison in contraceptives and heels of shoes and the government was unequivocal in rejecting the demands of hunger strikers; there was strong opposition to strip searching and little fear, it seemed, of taking on the Catholic Church. Cooney emphatically rejected representations made by Bishop of Kildare and Leighlin Patrick Lennon about the need for more religious services for prisoners and 'inhuman conditions for family visits in Portlaoise'. Lennon subsequently qualified this – 'perhaps "inhuman" was a bit too strong' – while Cooney maintained that 'the prisoners abused your generosity in visiting them by asking you to intervene in these areas'. Lennon took exception to this, but Cooney was adamant that church authorities were being duped by propaganda and allowing themselves to be used to 'involve themselves in matters the full implications of which they do not understand'.[35]

In September 1976, Bishop Edward Daly expressed fury at not being allowed to visit Portlaoise Prison: 'I was very angry about it ... visiting a prisoner does not imply support for what he has done ... to condone violence of the state and to condemn the violence of the paramilitary organisations is to my mind tantamount to hypocrisy.' Cosgrave, however, fully supported Cooney in not allowing the bishops to visit the prison, while the general secretary of Fine Gael urged all Fine Gael members not to support motions or questions regarding prison conditions.[36]

There was a suggestion that the prison in Portlaoise should be used for IRA prisoners only; in February 1977 the government rejected all and every accusation of ill treatment of prisoners there, and it was noted that 'one of the more surprising complaints is that no oratory or chapel is available for private meditation'.[37] At a cabinet meeting in April 1977, at a time of more hunger strikes in the Republic, Conor Cruise O'Brien reported on attacks by 'apparent Provo supporters' on Labour TD Frank Cluskey's residence and an attack on Deputy Brendan Halligan, 'who did not wish to give it any publicity because of the nervous state of his wife'. He referred to an initiative by Labour TD John O'Connell and Belfast priest and campaigner Fr Des Wilson to settle the hunger strike 'by promising to use an electronic device as they do in NI rather than strip searching'. (O'Brien had refused to keep their approach confidential and, like FitzGerald, was hostile to dialogue with the IRA; when Harold Wilson as Britain's opposition leader met IRA leaders at John O'Connell's house in Dublin FitzGerald labelled the encounter, in a view undoubtedly shared by Cruise O'Brien, 'an appalling act of treachery to another democratic state'.[38])

A number of other ministers and the Taoiseach 'reported tentative approaches by Bishops about the hunger strikes', but it was recorded at cabinet in 1977 that 'a visit by Dr John O'Connell to [IRA leader] Dáithí Ó Conaill was not allowed … Ó Conaill appears to think that negotiations are still possible with government'.[39] The previous month, the Grand Knight of Columbanus (a Catholic organisation regarded as secretive, elitist and conservative) was approached by a serving officer in the Irish army about 'conditions, ill treatment and abuse being meted out to the IRA prisoners in Portlaoise jail' and suggested the Supreme Knight could intervene by approaching a member of the Knights – 'the Minister for Defence, Brother Oliver J. Flanagan'.[40] Despite repeated calls for intervention on Christian and other grounds to end the 'defilement' of strip searches of those in solitary confinement ('The prisoners in Portlaoise and the Curragh may be bastards, Taoiseach, but they are, after all, our bastards … deep down you, a deeply religious man, must hear your conscience telling you to act.'[41]) Cosgrave remained steadfast, even when the Apostolic Nuncio was disposed 'in a secret and completely confidential way to go and request the prisoners involved for God's sake to bring their foolish action to an end'.[42]

The issue of hunger strikes continued to cause tension with the Vatican in 1977. A communication from Gerard Woods, the ambassador to the Holy See, to Seán Donlon in May 1977 regarding hunger strikes in the Curragh military prison and Portlaoise Prison, informed him that the tactic was 'to block Fenelli [the Vatican's Sostituto, or Deputy Secretary of State] from getting into the position of being able to say that he had lodged with the Irish government a note of such tone and content'. The concern was that the Holy See used language 'that seemed to accept propaganda statements of convicted criminals'. An account of a very tense meeting between the ambassador and the Sostituto witnessed Fenelli become 'rather nervous and he then, I thought changed his tactics – he said he wasn't sending the message; it was just for the embassy'.[43] It was suggested in *Magill* magazine in October 1977 that while strip searches in Portlaoise jail continued to be excessive, 'there has been a perceptible change in the atmosphere of the prison since the change of government, but only slight improvement in conditions'.[44]

By the end of the decade, southern audiences were offered occasionally graphic depictions of hunger strikers and their 'dirty protests', including an account by journalist Ed Moloney in *Magill* magazine in December 1979. He had initially wondered, when he visited one of the Maze's H

Blocks, 'what do you say to a man who has spent the last 8 months dressed only in an old British Army blanket and confined virtually 24 hours a day in a cell plastered with his own excreta and swimming in urine? "How are You?" seems a somewhat inadequate greeting … he hasn't washed since March and teeth were completely yellow. His skin was a cadaverous shade of white and stretched tightly across his cheekbones. His eyes were sunk deep into dark rimmed sockets and throughout the visit never ceased from wandering.'[45] In the same year, singer Christy Moore produced the album *H Block*, 'which was an attempt to focus attention on the situation in the prison, for it seemed that there was a silence verging on total apathy with regard to the dreadful conditions in Long Kesh'. The launch of the album in Dublin was raided by the Garda special branch.[46]

In December 1978 questions were being asked by Irish politicians about whether the British were making representations to prevent a history professor at Maynooth College, Dr Tomás Ó Fiaich, being appointed a cardinal. O'Fiach, a native of Armagh, was on record as favouring a British withdrawal; he had also visited Long Kesh and compared conditions there to 'the slums of Calcutta', although he was also accused by the Provisional IRA of being treacherous in criticising them. He had impressed representatives from the Church of Ireland when he spoke at a private meeting of the Irish Association in Belfast in 1978.

The *Guardian* suggested he was a 'shrewd political animal' but the Unionist perspective on him was that 'you can take the man out of Crossmaglen (a Republican area of south Armagh) but you cannot take Crossmaglen out of the man'.[47] When it became clear that his appointment was imminent a draft memorandum from the Department of the Taoiseach wondered if an 'official ceremonial at Dublin Airport on the Cardinal's return and unofficial seeing off ceremony are appropriate taking into account the Northern question', to which a more senior civil servant had responded 'NO!' There was an insistence that a military ceremony was inappropriate, lest the accusation of 'favouring one Christian church more than another' would be levelled 'and the likely effect of that on our Northern relations'.[48]

But the perspective from the Department of Foreign Affairs was somewhat different, with a suggestion that 'the level of government involvement should not be less than on previous occasions', and a military guard of honour was duly given.[49] There was some controversy over the absence of an Irish government minister from the consistory. The response of the Department of the Taoiseach was that Jack Lynch would have attended had he been asked, but 'he believed the government was represented by the ambassador to the Holy See'. Ó Fiaich had told Lynch he did not expect him to attend.

Heightened tension also exacerbated concerns about the safety and security of politicians. Cosgrave made an unusual request of Minister for Justice Patrick Cooney in May 1977, pointing out that he had a new escort car assigned to him, 'a Vauxhall Victor as usual'. He had no complaints about the 'first class' car but he wanted to 'question the wisdom' whereby this model of car 'are almost invariably used by the Special Defence Unit for escort duty. Surely there should be a greater variety of cars used for this function in the interest of general security. I feel that the Vauxhall is too easily recognisable by that element of the general public from whom we would prefer to keep our movements as secret as possible.' There was little comfort for him in Cooney's reply, which insisted other models would make no practical difference: 'As far as we know from seized documents, subversive elements take note of the registered numbers both of ministerial cars and of the police cars and there is no practical way in which that kind of information can be kept secret.'[50]

Such preoccupations had been strengthened by a number of high-profile controversies that embroiled the government as more consequences of the Troubles began to reverberate in the Republic (the Gardaí closed down Sinn Féin's headquarters in Kevin Street, Dublin, in October 1972 under the Offences Against the State Act). The hunger strike and death of Frank Stagg had created a dilemma; on 12 December 1975, as an IRA prisoner, he had begun his fourth hunger strike in two years. His wife Bridie sent a telegram to Cosgrave on New Year's Day 1976: 'I beg you please don't let my husband die'. Garret FitzGerald insisted on 20 January he would not intervene and on 10 February in a letter to a resident of Massachusetts, explained that as Irish governments had never made concessions to hunger strikers, 'it would be hypocritical for a representative of the Irish government to approach the British government to ask them to make concessions under pressure of a hunger strike which no Irish government would be prepared to make in this country'.[51] Stagg died in Wakefield prison on 12 February 1976 after sixty-two days without food. A Coroner's jury ruled that Stagg had killed himself, but those who sympathised with his actions claimed ill treatment had driven him to death and that the British government was guilty of murder. In the words of

Clonard Republican prisoners in Long Kesh he had 'borne the brunt of every sadistic and degrading torture technique'.[52] The *Irish Times* insisted that responsibility for his death lay with the IRA. His death provoked rioting and bomb scares in Belfast and Derry.

At a protest rally in his memory, leading Republican Marie Drumm claimed that Stagg had followed the example of 'great Christ, Who died for us on Calvary', and advised her listeners not to take matters into their own hands: 'Frank Stagg's death will be revenged ... by the soldiers of Óglaigh na hÉireann [the IRA].'[53] Stagg had requested that his body be handed over to a Sinn Féin organiser in England to ensure he would be buried in the Republican plot at Leigue cemetery, Ballina. The Irish government believed that the body and the journey from Dublin to Ballina would be used for propaganda purposes and when his body was released for return to Ireland, airport cargo handlers, members of the trade union to which Stagg had belonged for eighteen years, refused to handle it. The flight carrying the body was diverted from Dublin airport to Shannon with the consent of Stagg's widow (and legal next of kin), who held the IRA responsible for his fate. The Stagg family (he was one of thirteen children) was bitterly divided on the issue; some supported the measures taken by the government and received death threats; Stagg's mother and other siblings favoured a Republican funeral in accordance with his wishes.

A government helicopter took the body on from Shannon to Ballina on 21 February, where it was buried under eighteen inches of concrete some distance from the Republican section, though by the end of 1977 his body was clandestinely reburied in the Republican plot. Ruairí O Brádaigh of Sinn Féin referred to the diversion to Shannon as 'a clear case of body-snatching – in the best tradition of Britain', while the wife of well-known broadcaster Brian Farrell insisted that landing him at Dublin would be 'a threat to all law abiding citizens'. Her husband's colleague in UCD, Maurice Manning, also supported and congratulated the government.[54]

The sentencing to death of Noel and Marie Murray –'the closest thing Ireland had to Germany's Baader-Meinhof movement or America's Weathermen' – by the Special Criminal Court in June 1976 created another high-profile quandary. They had met as members of Official Sinn Féin but were regarded by some as more anarchist than Republican and had been part of a four-person armed gang involved in a Dublin bank robbery after which Garda Michael Reynolds had been shot dead in pursuit of them; the pair were found guilty of capital murder.[55] There were numerous requests for the death sentences to be commuted ('please do not let a woman be hanged in Eire'[56]) along with letters urging them to be carried out ('I see in today's *Belfast Telegraph* that you have no hangman to hang those sentenced. I wish to apply for the post'[57]). The issue of clemency was discussed at cabinet and the Minister for Justice 'asked ministers to be careful not to indicate to anyone outside the council chamber what their views are on the death sentence on the Murrays'.

British Labour MP Douglas Hoyle appealed to President Ó Dálaigh to make sure they were not hanged ('it could well make them martyrs and cause more misguided people to follow the example they have set'; preventing their deaths was also imperative 'in view of the reputation that the Republic has had for social and penal reform').[58] The Pope, through the Apostolic Nuncio, also appealed for clemency in a letter delivered on behalf of President Ó Dálaigh to Cosgrave by hand.[59] The Murrays' conviction for capital murder was subsequently quashed by the Supreme Court on the grounds that Garda Reynolds had not been in uniform so they could not have known he was a Garda.

The assassination of the British ambassador to Ireland, Christopher Ewart-Biggs on 21 July 1976 also caused shock and controversy. A landmine had been placed outside his official residence in Sandyford, County Dublin. Cosgrave cited this killing, as well as an attempted escape by five prisoners from the Special Criminal Court a week previously, as 'motivating his government to declare a state of emergency'.[60] Nine days before he died, Ewart-Biggs in his journal had expressed concern after meeting Gardaí about personal security: 'They are not very reassuring. They do not seem to have given much thought to the scenario of attack.' The bomb also killed Judith Cook, the secretary of Brian Cubbon, under-secretary at the Northern Ireland Office, who was badly injured, as was the ambassador's driver Brian O'Driscoll.[61]

At the Department of the Taoiseach, Richard Stokes underlined the importance of Ewart-Biggs's body lying in state in St Patrick's Cathedral 'in bringing home to television viewers in Britain that the state here and the general public should not be confused with the perpetrators of the outrage'.[62] There was also an urgency behind the scenes to ensure that a revenue official, who happened to have been at the scene of the murder and had seen and described the three men apparently responsible, and whose name had been mentioned on an RTÉ news bulletin as an eyewitness, would not be mentioned in any further media coverage, as he 'feared for his safety'. Ted Nealon, the head of the Government Information Services, told all media outlets not to use his name in subsequent updates.

There was much comment internationally about the ease with which the killers had got so close to the embassy.[63] When Garret FitzGerald addressed the memorial service in St Patrick's a week later, he insisted that 'Ireland, shamed by the deeds of men with minds twisted by the myths that for too many in this country have displaced history, will not forget this moment', though some criticised the absence of Liam Cosgrave from the service.[64] Brian Cubbon wrote to FitzGerald in August from St Vincent's Nursing Home in Dublin, expressing gratitude that he had been looked after brilliantly and praising FitzGerald's words on Ewart-Biggs as having 'caught our feelings exactly'. While acknowledging some differences between the Irish and British governments over 'presentational and local problems', he insisted both had 'our ruthless common enemy; the men of violence'.[65] The government subsequently paid Cubbon £10,000 to cover medical expenses, clothing, valuables 'and in respect of pain and grief suffered'. In response, Cubbon noted 'both the Northern Ireland Office and I will continue to regard this as a personal and confidential matter to which no public reference will be made'.

Ewart-Biggs's widow, Jane, also acknowledged a cheque for £27,000 'to pay the school fees of Henrietta, Robin and Kate over the coming years'.[66] There was some suggestion that Jane might be his successor as ambassador; in the event this did not materialise, but there was a determination to inaugurate some initiative that would commemorate Ewart-Biggs. By March 1977, £30,000 of a memorial fund had been raised, including £50 contributed by Garret FitzGerald. There was subsequently a letter-bomb scare at a bank in Dublin 'as a result of having been named in the newspapers as the address for contributors to the memorial fund'. In October 1976, the Irish ambassador in London met Lord Greenhill, formerly permanent secretary at the Foreign Office, at a private party. He was 'not enthusiastic' about the fund and 'would like to see the fund not exceeding 10k', thus enabling an annual prize for a publication advancing greater understanding between Britain and Ireland of '[£]1k over a period of ten years, at which stage the whole operation would end. He regards Jane as a rather tough operator who wants to get as much limelight as possible. According to Lord Greenhill she is unlikely to accept the temporary job offered by the FO. She has a much more attractive alternative in mind.'[67] In contrast, as far as author Thomas Pakenham was concerned, 'she is a tower of strength'.[68]

In pursuit of the perpetrators of such killings, the Emergency Powers Act of 1976 was regarded as a bill with 'a substantial anti-IRA context' holding out the prospect of a 'change of IRA tactics in the event of heavier penalties' by extending the power to detain a person arrested under section 30 of the original 1939 Act so as to permit their detention for a period of seven days after arrest.[69] The Attorney General Declan Costello suggested 'it is likely, in my opinion, to be declared unconstitutional'. When President Ó Dálaigh, after a four-hour Council of State meeting, referred it to the Supreme Court it was agreed at a cabinet meeting that the Attorney General 'should make an informal approach to the Chief Justice with a view to having a hearing arranged for the earliest possible date'.[70] There was also a suggestion that Cosgrave and his colleagues would be 'embarrassed and worried about this development'.[71] It was found not to be repugnant in any way to the constitution, though the saga ultimately led to the resignation of the president (see Part I).

Another high-profile assassination was that of seventy-nine-year-old Lord Louis Mountbatten, former viceroy of India and uncle of Queen Elizabeth II's husband, Prince Philip, in 1979. During the decade he had holidayed annually at Mullaghmore in County Sligo and it was maintained that 'he and the Gardaí were well aware of the risks', given his relationship with the British Royal family, but 'he adopted a fairly cavalier approach' to his own personal security.[72] A bomb on his boat was detonated by remote control; his grandson Nicholas Knatchbull and a local boy who had been working on the boat, Paul Maxwell, were also killed, along with the mother of Mountbatten's daughter-in-law. The reaction of Jack Lynch was to praise him as a man 'of great courage' with a 'remarkable record of service to mankind', while the perpetrators he described as 'relentlessly and invidiously proving to be the real enemies of Ireland'. The British demanded increased security concessions by the Irish government; it was an event that created a wave of disgust and anger.[73]

– NINETEEN –

A PASSION FOR UNITY?

Just how much did the Troubles of the 1970s cost the Republic? According to notes prepared for a meeting between the new Fianna Fáil government and British prime minister James Callaghan in London in September 1977, 'Northern violence' was estimated to have cost the Irish exchequer £175 million since 1969, including an estimate of approximately £50 million as the cost of extra Gardaí – one-eighth of the total strength of the force was committed to border areas – administrators, army personnel and compensation: 'the figures do not include any estimate of the economic cost of lost investments, tourism etc.'[1] Towards the end of 1978, that figure had been revised upwards to £200 million, with an estimated Troubles death toll in Northern Ireland of 1,900 killed and 20,000 injured.[2]

Bord Fáilte, the body responsible for promoting tourism in the Republic, did not favour an all-Ireland approach to tourism because of the Troubles and was keen to stress to prospective tourists that the Troubles applied to Northern Ireland only, 'and not the country as a whole'. Donegal was regarded as particularly badly affected by reason of its isolation, 'both physical and perceived from the administrative capital of Dublin and by being deprived of ready access to the regional centre of Derry'.[3]

In some ways, however, there was a quietly effective way of enhancing cross-border cultural co-operation. There were joint meetings of the two arts councils, including programmes of readings, recitals and exhibition exchanges, though it was suggested by the administrative officer of the Republic's arts council that 'infuriating delays in connection with transfer of exhibitions' would have to be rectified 'if our plan for gradually integrating our respective activities is to be achieved'. Patrick Grant in Newry, chairman of the Amateur Drama Council of Ireland, pointed out that north–south co-operation in amateur drama 'has been in existence for many years'.[4] RTÉ television penetration into Northern Ireland was poor, with an estimation in 1976 that it was reaching only 14 per cent of the population.

There were also meetings between Louth County Council and Newry and Mourne District Council over cross-border affairs. Reports on economic co-operation in June 1978 suggested there was a 'very wide range of contacts' between Customs and Excise and Revenue commissioners, agricultural activity, fisheries, drainage, water supply and conservation and wildlife but 'little contact at official level on mainstream educational matters'.[5]

A *Magill* national poll in 1977 suggested 63 per cent of those in the Republic were in favour of a united Ireland, but perhaps that was merely in theory. Five years earlier Sir John Peck, the British ambassador in Dublin, reported on a conversation with Jack Lynch after he had asked him how serious an issue reunification was in the context of a recent by-election, and how much it mattered to Irish people as a whole: 'His answer amounted to saying that they could not care less.'[6] An Economic and Social Research Institute survey the following year found that 60 per cent of respondents opposed IRA activity, 21 per cent supported it and 19 per cent were neutral; in contrast, 42 per cent supported the motives of the IRA, 33 per cent were opposed and 25 per cent were neutral. 72 per cent were anti-partition and 13 per cent pro. For those who supported section 31 of the Broadcasting Act this reflected 'the shaky climate of public opinion that republican spokespeople could supposedly manipulate to win support'.[7]

Labour Party TD David Thornley ran foul of his party and others when he defied a government ban by appearing on a platform at an illegal demonstration organised by Provisional Sinn Féin in 1976; he was critical that his party had turned its back on the Marxist republicanism espoused by James Connolly and insisted he was defending free speech. He lost the party whip (restored the following year) and was fined by the courts. Thornley's passion for empathising with the Northern Republicans, however, was somewhat abstract, and sometimes juvenile, in that he never actually visited Northern Ireland. He also seemed to have a 'psychological obsession with firearms'. Conor Cruise O'Brien insisted that Sinn Féin flattered Thornley while 'laughing at him behind his back', but arguably he also exposed some of the ambiguities of the political establishment's reaction to Republican violence and pointed to the hypocrisy of the constitutional territorial claim to Northern Ireland when it was accompanied by no plan to deliver on it.[8]

There was much reaction to Jack Lynch's perceived change of tone and stance early in 1978 regarding a united Ireland and his call for a British intent of withdrawal, or a commitment to implement an ordered withdrawal (which Gallup polls suggested an average of 57 per cent of the British public were in favour of[9]), during an RTÉ interview on the *This Week* programme. In typical Lynch fashion he maintained afterwards, 'I do not know what all the fuss was about' (it has been reckoned that after the 1977 general election, Lynch's 'private objectives on the North were rather limited'[10]). In a telegram, Eddie McAteer, a former Nationalist MP who had been eclipsed by John Hume and was now with the newly formed Irish Independence Party, suggested, 'Your voice is the true voice of Ireland ... one more heave and we can all get some real peace.'[11] The Irish ambassador in London reported, regarding the interview, that British officials did not want 'to make heavy weather of the question but they felt his remarks were a little out of key with the excellent working arrangements that had been established ... Judd [Frank Judd, the senior foreign office minister] was warm and friendly and really did not show much indignation though he put on an act of being more in sorrow than anger.'[12]

Lynch was informed by one correspondent that the perception of his speech 'in all the Protestant working class areas of Belfast [is] that you had given the green light to the Provos'. Fr Patrick Scott of the Clonard Monastery in Belfast wrote of a feeling that Fianna Fáil's victory in 1977 had buoyed some Northern Republicans who believed the election was won 'on the republican issue'. The local secretary of Sinn Féin 'quoted your call for a declaration of intent to withdraw as showing the will of the Irish people'.[13]

Perhaps it was indicative of a certain discomfort or annoyance that at the end of March that year, a government memorandum was entitled 'Anti-Irish government references by the NI secretary of state, Mr Mason' and it was suggested that Prime Minister Callaghan was only prepared to meet Lynch for fifteen minutes on the sidelines of a European Council meeting in Copenhagen. There was a concomitant 'irritation in Dublin at the way Mr Mason handled affairs … Mason had indicated an interest in talking about security but not about anything else.' Paul Keating, the Irish ambassador in London, suggested to Seán Donlon that there was a 'failure to recognise … our legitimate interest in what was happening in Northern Ireland'.[14]

In the event, the two leaders met for an hour and a half. Lynch acknowledged that 'in the recent past relations have been a bit ruffled' but he was adamant that 'there was no passive support for the IRA in the Republic' and that the government was 'on top of the IRA in the State … we were on their heels everywhere'. Callaghan disapproved of the statement prepared by the Irish side to be issued after the meeting, as in the view of the British, the meeting 'was a private matter. He wanted to make it clear that they did not wish to give the Republic any particular status.' A furious Lynch suggested 'a repetition of this attitude could be most dangerous'.[15] The two leaders had an informal phone chat the following month which was less tense. By the end of the year Lynch expressed concern about the situation in Long Kesh prison, suggesting 'it should be possible to take some measures to improve the situation without any concession on the principle of special category status'.[16]

In a report on the visit by the Minister of Foreign Affairs, Michael O'Kennedy, to Belfast in May 1978, Seán Donlon wrote of a dinner in County Down attended by members of the SDLP, academics and representatives of the Protestant churches. The general feeling was that north–south relations had suffered in recent months because of 'the unfortunate coincidence' of the Taoiseach's *This Week* interview, Archbishop Ó Fiaich's controversial comments about the need for a British statement of intent to withdraw from Northern Ireland, and the La Mon massacre (an IRA bomb had ignited the La Mon House hotel in County Down and twelve people, all Protestants, burned to death). John Hume, always keen to preserve the special status of the SDLP in its talks and relations with the Dublin government, 'strenuously objected' to a demand by Fergus McAteer, son of Eddie, of the Irish Independence Party (his party held thirteen district council seats and had succeeded in attracting some support from disaffected SDLP people) to meet the Taoiseach on the same basis as the SDLP.[17]

The autumn of 1979 witnessed many tensions within Fianna Fáil over Northern Ireland policy as Charles Haughey sought to play a greener card to undermine Lynch from within with the help of others. It was a development that greatly worried T. K. Whitaker, who was quite possessive about policy on the North and his influence over Lynch. He wrote privately to Lynch in September of that year, 'I am troubled by the apparent hardening of the FF line ... I would rather not hear again any calls for declaration of British intent to withdraw,' which he saw as too close to 'Brits Out', a popular IRA slogan. He elaborated on his plans for a Northern Ireland Assembly and 'no insistence on a formal Council of Ireland'. A weary Lynch responded, agreeing with most of what he had suggested, but took issue 'as to the possibility of their practical implementation'.[18]

Lynch had other things on his mind over the next two months; the resurrection of the idea that those identified with the Arms Trial episode were those whose 'hearts were in the right place' was destabilising for the party and his leadership and in the aftermath of the Mountbatten killing he was 'deeply embarrassed' and had agreed to British helicopters crossing the border, a permission refused by the previous government. (His party also lost two by-elections in his native Cork.) On a trip to Washington he had let the new security concession slip, 'relaxed after a couple of glasses of wine with his lunch'. He attacked *Irish Press* journalist Michael Mills at a press conference in Washington – 'You, Michael started all this with your ten mile air corridor', a reference to a story Mills had filed back to Dublin.[19] Haughey continued with the pressure, suggesting, in the context of the centenary of the birth of 1916 Republican martyr Patrick Pearse, that partition would have been 'totally inconceivable' to Pearse, to which Lynch responded 'the paradox of Pearse's message for the Irish nation today is that we must work and live for Ireland, not die, and most certainly not kill for it'.[20]

A few weeks before he resigned on 5 December, Lynch attended a briefing on security preparations for a meeting of the European Council in Dublin on 29 and 30 November and he explained the circumstances 'in which he had become aware of suggestions of a possible attempt to make an attack on the British prime minister Mrs Thatcher when she visited Dublin', possibly through the use of an aircraft 'operated by remote control and packed with explosives'. The source of the threat was not trusted but could not be ignored. While Gardaí 'assessed the possibility as very low' and the army estimation of the likely success of such an attack was 'of the order of one in ten', a decision was still taken to authorise training 'in the use of the guided missiles'.[21]

The following month saw Charles Haughey win the leadership of

Fianna Fáil and he took over as Taoiseach from Jack Lynch. Prior to this, Seán Donlon, who had been appointed Irish ambassador to the US in July 1978, had been given instructions to 'do everything possible' to reduce Americans' support for the IRA. At the time of Haughey's elevation, Independent Fianna Fáil TD Neil Blaney happened to be in the US as a guest of the Irish National Caucus (INC), which had been named by Irish governments as a group supporting the IRA. Blaney issued a statement stating that, with the formation of a new government under Haughey, 'It is the wish of all the friends of Ireland that the government will work with the INC in the important task it has undertaken ... it is doing the job that our embassy in Washington should be doing but is not doing.' The INC also looked for Donlon's removal as ambassador and the appointment of an ambassador that would reflect Haughey's supposedly more Republican view. 'Tip' O'Neill, Ted Kennedy, and other politicians in the US supportive of John Hume and the Irish government's anti-IRA stance were anxious, but Haughey was quick to telephone Donlon to insist 'he did not know the INC, had never met them and had nothing to do with them'. Later in December, he insisted that 'any claim by anyone else to speak for the government should not be taken seriously'. But Haughey was still determined to remove Donlon from Washington, prompting the intervention of Kennedy, O'Neill, and John Hume and forcing him to relent.[22]

Haughey may have been less concerned than Lynch to appear conciliatory towards Unionists, but he also knew, in practical terms, that he had to work closely with the British government and to come up with an answer to Hume, who took over the leadership of the SDLP from Gerry Fitt in November 1979 and was intent on stimulating discussion among political parties in the Republic. Hume had asked the basic question: what would be the implications of a British withdrawal from Northern Ireland?[23] Despite the upheavals, controversies and vacillations in Dublin throughout the 1970s in relation to the Troubles, and the change of leadership in Fianna Fáil, Hume was in for the long haul and would continue to insist that Dublin play its role and apply its pressure under his persistent guidance.

PART III

COMMEMORATION, MEMORY, CULTURAL LIFE AND ENTERTAINMENT

'Done with the innocent shit?'

When reflecting on change in Ireland from the 1970s to the early twenty-first century, historian Roy Foster highlighted many achievements in literature, poetry, theatre and film that suggested a 'dramatic development in confidence and innovation', with artists who transcended previous literary inhibitions while also revealing 'the power and suggestiveness of historical themes in the creative literature'. In tandem, he lamented the casual attitude to architectural and archaeological heritage that remained a 'fascinating and often depressing barometer of Irish attitudes to the past'.[1] *As in other areas of Irish life, it seemed that in relation to culture and memory there were contradictory impulses at work in the Republic in the 1970s.*

When he first published his seminal Ireland: A Social and Cultural History *in 1981, literary historian and critic Terence Brown, based in Trinity College Dublin, ended his narrative with a chapter covering the 1960s and 1970s under the headings 'Economic Revival', 'Decades of Debate' and 'Culture and a Changing Society'. He observed that it was widely sensed in these decades that the country was altering in radical ways. Seminars, articles, conferences, journals, magazines and newspapers debated by how much and in what manner, and 'the question as to how much Ireland's traditional identity could be retained in the new circumstances was a major preoccupation of social commentators'. The relationship of writers and artists with Irish society also underwent 'striking alteration' as, rather than focusing on the notion of 'indigenous' Irish life, they grappled with a new Irish reality that* was 'ambiguous, transitional, increasingly urban or suburban, disturbingly at variance with the cultural aspirations of the revolutionaries who had given birth to the state'.[2]

The impact of the Troubles on the Republic exacerbated this and prompted a reassessment by some of the way that particular revolutionary generation had managed its War of Independence. Sometimes, traditional and new interpretations sat uneasily alongside each other. In 1970, for example, The Capuchin Annual, an avowedly Nationalist and Catholic publication since its foundation in 1930, but also one which prized high culture and self-questioning, devoted much attention to a fiftieth-anniversary celebration of the heroism of the IRA during the War of Independence. It was billed as a 'tribute of honour to the integrity, courage, high idealism of the Irish men and women who in 1920 broke the despotism of Britain's overlords ... their total victory came from weapons more powerful than guns; their cause was just, they had the support of all the people, they had high ideals and an endurance which was ready to suffer everything in the cause of Ireland's freedom'.[3]

Yet alongside such pious and dubious simplicities, on the very next page, was an article by a talented young historian, Michael Laffan, on Sinn Féin from 1916–19. He maintained that throughout these years, the battle cry 'the Republic ... was used as a slogan and a symbol rather than a specific goal ... most of those who used the word gave it little thought'.[4] In subsequent years, Laffan went on to establish himself as one of a group of historians labelled 'revisionist' who used archival research and the backdrop of the Troubles to debunk some of the myths of modern Irish nationalism. Decades later, this was characterised as involving a 'green scare' which 'maimed' objective accounts of the past by ensuring those writing history would select only evidence supporting their preferred cause.[5] This itself was a selective view, however, and exaggerates the degree to which this was the dominant issue of the history profession in the 1970s, or the extent to which they operated as a group. Of note in this regard was what Terence Brown described as the 'patient, sane balance'[6] that characterised the evolution of historical research and writing at this time, reflected in seminal works like F. S. L. Lyons's Ireland Since the Famine (1971) and Louis Cullen's An Economic History of Ireland Since 1660 (1972). Much analytic excellence went into other individual and collaborative efforts, including the New History of Ireland series and new approaches to the writing of the history of the War of Independence, most notably David Fitzpatrick's Politics and Irish Life, 1913–21: Provincial Experience of War and Revolution (1977), the first study to examine the political experience of *'ordinary people', the social context in which the revolution was formed and the supremacy of local over national interests. It suggested 'The Irish Revolution was guided from below and few revolutionaries have been so conservative in their response to social and political cataclysm as those who gave their guidance during the Irish troubles.'*[7]

Other scholars, through some of the leading intellectual journals of the day, including the Crane Bag, *founded in 1977 by UCD philosopher Richard Kearney and Benedictine priest and educationalist Mark Patrick Hederman, sought to stake a claim for a more pluralist politics and recasting of old problems in order to tackle the issue of just what Irish identity meant in the modern era. Such issues were also debated in another journal, the* Irish University Review. *As one of its contributors put it in 1979, 'what is an Irishman? The question, though put in a variety of different ways has never been entirely satisfactorily answered and that may be because there is no entirely satisfactory answer to such a question.'*[8] *The notion of an Irish identity that equated to Republican in politics, Catholic in religion, Gaelic in language, peasant in social origin and culturally isolationist was being challenged. Attitudes to these categories were 'no longer so rigidly doctrinaire', but that did not mean that traditional aspects of identity had to be 'dumped overboard'. While acknowledging the influence of history, it was necessary to 'move with the current of his times'.*

The extent of the balance to be struck between these different currents and influences went to the heart of the cultural challenges and opportunities of this decade; it was time, it seemed, to let go of an older Ireland, but not quite yet and not quite fully. In the Crane Bag *in 1977, writer Francis Stuart maintained it was still the case that 'there is, on the politicians' part, suspicion, sometimes amounting to hatred, of the artist as disseminator of doubt and disloyalty',*[9] *but it was also the case that more attention was given to the Arts Council and arts funding.*

Charles Acton, music critic with the Irish Times, *had maintained in 1968 that the Arts Council, originally established in 1951, 'does not seem to have worked out any policy' after two decades. While it made possible certain events, 'nearly all of them have been of a hand-to-mouth, cheque writing nature without policy or permanence'. It was also notable that at that stage there was only one practising artist on the Council (composer Brian Boydell), no women, and no funding for ballet, festivals or design.*[10] *A new Arts Bill in 1973 created a new Arts Council which could appoint a full-time director, ushering in a period of greater vigour and expansion. The new council included women and professional artists, there was more contact with the media and a new director, Colm O Briain, who was 'controversial, dominant and not a civil servant but a TV producer and director'. More emphasis was placed on training, exhibition, performance and regionalisation and the council began to take over responsibility from the Department of Finance for the Abbey and the Gate Theatres. Government funding of the arts increased substantially, new festivals emerged and more political pressure was exerted, most obviously in the assertion of Arts Council chairman Patrick Rock that the government could not be considered to be proactive enough in driving arts policy. In relation to figures which showed that government support for the arts amounted to 50p per head of population compared to 78p in Northern Ireland and 89p in England, he insisted that 'the state as a patron of the arts reflects the general indifference of the people to the arts in general'.*[11]

Defenders of the central importance of the Irish language battled a government decision to make a pass in Irish no longer compulsory to succeed at state examinations, but it was still a subject that had to be studied. A government report from 1975 provided evidence of the new pragmatism in relation to the language. In theory, there was a commitment to cherishing tradition and a distinct linguistic culture, but in practice there was no desire to take responsibility for ensuring its survival. The average individual, the report noted, 'feels rather strongly that the Irish language is necessary to our ethnic and cultural integrity and supports the efforts to ensure the transmission of the language. At the same time, under present policies and progress, he is not really convinced that we can ensure its transmission.'[12]

Undoubtedly, some Irish artists sought to look outward; as recalled by Derek Mahon, one of a long line of poets whose careers involved literary journalism, one of the aims was 'to see Ireland in an international perspective, to lift its drowsy eyelid and disturb it into a sense of relationship and awareness'. For him and other writers, the question of Irishness did not require an answer; he suggested in 1974 that 'the time is coming fast, if it isn't already here, when the question "Is so and so really an Irish writer?" will clear a room in seconds. The question is semantic and not important except in so far as the writer himself makes it so.'[13] *But it was a question that remained because of the Troubles; poet Seamus Heaney noted, for example, that when he returned from a sabbatical in Berkeley, California to Northern Ireland, internment had just begun, there was an influx of journalists 'and we were all being interviewed about identity ... poetry had then moved from being a sensuous transport to being an intellectual crisis, it involved some sort of stress about politics and content and so on'.*[14]

He devoted much attention to inheritance, tradition and 'memory incubating the spilled blood'. This impetus was shared by other writers who focused on marginalisation; it was at the centre of the writing of William Trevor, for example, who reacted to the extent to which the Troubles meant 'compassion is thrown to the winds, distortion rules' in work such as Angels at the Ritz (1975). Jennifer Johnston also dealt with Irish individuals who felt they were outsiders in How Many Miles to Babylon (1974). Playwright Brian Friel was preoccupied with 'defining' rather than 'pursuing' Irishness and questioned the rural idyll and other myths on which independence had been built in The Mundy Scheme (1969) and The Gentle Island (1971). He depicted a depopulated island seething with anger and violence and a strident sexuality, while lambasting the materialism of Irish political culture and its Americanisation.[15] Novelist John McGahern focused on religion, family, death and sex, while John Banville's work was rooted in both Irish and international traditions, but he would not describe himself as an Irish writer ('to think of yourself as part of a movement would be fatal'). Instead, he liked to think of himself as a kind of 'internal exile', but Birchwood (1973) was, in his words 'my book about Ireland'.[16] Female writers and poets, including Eavan Boland, vigorously interrogated the relationship between women and Irish nationality. Given the iconic status of the state-funded Abbey Theatre – the first theatre in the world to receive such status in the 1920s – there was inevitably much debate, and bile, about the extent to which it was adequately addressing these contemporary dilemmas or was too reliant on past glories.

In the same way, there was a questioning of rural Ireland as 'the imagination's proper territory', as so many of those born in the countryside now lived in urban areas and Irish urban reality could serve as 'a matter for an art attentive to the demands of contemporary individual experience'.[17] What did this modernity in the Republic mean? For Richard Kearney, this was the dilemma; a problematic relationship between tradition and modernity, or as summarised by poet Seamus Heaney, a 'search for symbols and images adequate to our predicament'. Kearney quotes a diary entry for Brian Friel when he was working on his play Translations in June 1979, dealing with the loss of the Irish language in an increasingly anglicised Ireland, and which, it seemed, reverberated with Ireland in the 1970s: 'The cultural climate is a dying climate – no longer quickened by its past, about to be plunged overnight into an alien future. The victims in this situation are the transitional generation. The old can retreat into and find immunity in the past. The young require some facility with the new cultural implements. The in-between ages become lost, wandering around in a strange land. Strays.'[18]

There was no shortage of criticisms of the failures of the Republic in the work of contemporary writers, but the break with the past was by no means clear-cut. Dermot Foley, who had worked as a county librarian in Clare, observed in 1974 the new prosperity and demographic and educational change, but 'doubts come creeping into my mind'. He recalled the persecution of novelist John McGahern the pervious decade after his novel The Dark was banned and he was sacked from his teaching post, the dismissal of the RTÉ Authority 'by a bullying minister', the determination to destroy family planning clinics, Georgian architecture 'being ravished by speculators' and the spectre of the abuse of power in new disguises: '... one cannot but wonder if the malice and fanaticism that choked us for so long are not lying there just under the surface, waiting for a shaft of lightning before erupting'.[19] More pleasingly, he identified idealism in young people: 'Maybe the new education, new libraries, the churches stripped of a stale authoritarianism will do better for the generation taking over from mine. We made a shocking mess of it.'[20]

Those with a concern for the institutional preservation of Irish culture were appalled at the cavalier attitude to Irish heritage, most publicly manifest in the outraged response to the development of the Viking Wood Quay site in Dublin in 1978 in order to build a new office block, but also in the neglect of cultural institutions such as the National Library of Ireland and National Museum. As Galway historian G. A. Hayes McCoy noted in 1971, 'Ireland may be one of the poorest countries in the world ... in the number of its museums.'[21]

In terms of misused power in new guises, there was a determination by journalists to ask and broadcast new questions, and people became more dependent on the media for their information. In 1968 journalist John Mulcahy acquired the monthly magazine Hibernia, which had existed since 1937 and was aimed at the Catholic middle class, and transformed it into an extraordinarily eclectic and vigorous mix. It became a publication that was 'lively, irreverent and often well-informed' and included political analysis, book, theatre and art reviews, gossip, impressive financial and business journalism and a tone that was 'crusading and investigative' as it sought to engage with the heightened volatility in Irish life and increasingly educated young readers.[22] In many respects, Hibernia represented what was best about the Republic in the 1970s, asking new and difficult questions, providing a platform for talented journalists and critics, interrogating culture and tradition. But its strident tone also included a firm commitment to republicanism and the aspiration towards Irish unity. It lasted until 1980.

One of the most dynamic, original and polarising figures of modern Irish journalism, Limerick-born Vincent Browne, also came to national prominence in the late 1970s, charting new ground in investigative journalism with Magill, a monthly current-affairs magazine established by Browne, Noel Pearson and Mary Holland. The first edition appeared in October 1977, and included contributions from Holland, Conor Cruise O'Brien, Ulick O'Connor, Paul Foot and Bruce Arnold. The magazine sold well, being challenging, provocative and frequently revealing, shedding light on many of the dark corners of Irish society. Its success was never guaranteed, and the editorial process rarely uncomplicated, but it did succeed in providing an outlet for many talented young journalists who dominated investigative reporting into the 1980s and 1990s.

Irish television, which had first begun broadcasting at the very end of 1961, also settled into its niche. As seen earlier, Oliver Maloney, appointed director general in 1975, believed too many producers lacked accountability and that 'small groups of strategically placed staff exercised inordinate influence'.[23] But the template for public service broadcasting established in the 1960s included much that was strong; an idea of current affairs as the 'thumping heartbeat of the station'. Creative forces were strong overall, and the soap operas The Riordans and Bracken tackled taboo subjects and generated passion. Wesley Burrows from the drama department complained of the tendency to denigrate the serials by 'quasi-literary column-writing smart ass pub-poets',[24] but they were hugely popular with audiences. The station had endured a fractious period of soul searching and bickering in the late 1960s, and there were further crises. The blatant attempt to circumvent section 31 of the Broadcasting Act by journalist Kevin O'Kelly's broadcast of the opinions of the Provisional IRA's Seán Mac Stiofáin in November 1972 led to the 'awesome moment' of the sacking of the RTÉ Authority and censorship continued to create casualties. As actor and comedian Niall Tóibín discovered in RTÉ, when working on the irreverent series The Cap and Time Now, Mr T, 'your very own comedy show could mean a poisoned chalice clamped to your gob' due to the influence of the 'letters of the affronted ... one crusader had gone to the trouble of enclosing a sample of excrement in a plastic satchel ... RTÉ was out from now on, it seemed to me, so increasingly I turned to British television ... for 20 years I have been semi-detached, a foot on either side of the British sea.'[25]

Some younger musicians provocatively threw caution to the wind. Bob Geldof, lead singer in the late 1970s with the influential band the Boomtown Rats, who were intent on success at home and abroad, was interviewed on RTÉ's influential Saturday night programme The Late Late Show *and 'the venom and frustration which had been welling inside me for more than a decade spilled out' as he decried the suffocating clericalism and authoritarianism of Irish society.*[26] *But this was not necessarily the dominant narrative for those musically driven in the 1970s; one of the most striking successes of the decade was the ongoing rejuvenation of Irish music as new interpretations of traditional material produced impressive results in an illustration of cultural survival and robustness.*

In sporting terms, the uniqueness of the Gaelic Athletic Association (GAA), devoted to the promotion of Gaelic football and hurling since the late nineteenth century, continued to matter. It had many reasons to be fearful as television and new leisure possibilities extended their reach, but it responded robustly and brought a focus to leadership while developing the social role of the association. Eventually, after much soul searching and acrimonious exchanges, the ban on members playing foreign games was rescinded in 1971. But what was revealing in terms of the wider sports question was how low its promotion seemed to lie on government's lists of priorities. Creating a national sports infrastructure was often spoken of, but not delivered as voluntary effort continued to suit those in power.

– TWENTY –

REMEMBERING THE FIGHT FOR FREEDOM

The politics of memory and remembrance and the degree to which those involved in violent Irish republicanism in the past could be celebrated were contentious and emotive in the 1970s. This was perhaps inevitable given the determination of those waging war in the 1970s to stress their continuity with earlier battles. In order to try and stress the manner in which opponents of the Anglo-Irish Treaty in 1921 who fought on the Republican side in the civil war from 1922–3 had moved away from the tradition of violent republicanism by establishing Fianna Fáil in 1926, opportunities were taken in the early 1970s to emphasise that the party was the inheritor of Theobald Wolfe Tone, the eighteenth-century radical regarded as the father of modern Irish republicanism on account of his association with the 1798 insurrection and the Society of United Irishmen, committed to a union of Irishmen of all denominations.

But in the aftermath of the arms crisis this was complicated, as witnessed in June 1970 when there were rival Fianna Fáil camps at the annual Wolfe Tone commemoration. Jack Lynch, 'looking pale and drawn', was received with applause by the majority, but 'about ten yards from the graveside a man gave a loud "boo" and soon he was joined by others. One dark-haired woman in a white dress followed the Taoiseach hissing "Judas" and "Judas Lynch". People standing near Mr Blaney's group shouted "remember you are an Irishman" and "remember the Falls".'[1]

One phrase that was being employed in the early 1970s in the

Department of Defence was 'divisive implications'. This was its response to requests, for example, to commemorate the fiftieth anniversary of the taking over of Dublin Castle from the British administration in 1922 and the fiftieth anniversary of the occupation of the Four Courts in Dublin by the anti-Treaty IRA; their removal had begun the civil war. Such calls were refused on the grounds that 'it would not be appropriate to have any state commemoration of any of the events which were part of the aftermath of the Treaty up to and including the civil war'.[2]

There was also some concern about the Garden of Remembrance in Dublin, which had been opened in 1966, and confusion over whether it was for 'all those who died for Ireland' or 'all those who gave their lives in the cause of Irish freedom'. It was believed in any case that it was not 'practicable to try and put across the distinction to the public and we will be lucky if we get a Supra-1916 appreciation of the garden'. A substantial £500 prize was awarded to the author of the winning poem, 'Rinneadh Aisling Dúinn', (We Saw a Vision), to be inscribed on the curved wall in the garden in 1971. The prize went to Liam Mac Uistin, who worked in the Department of Education. An assistant secretary to that department thought the winning entry was 'sententious', which was explained by a memorandum in the Department of the Taoiseach as meaning 'unduly optimistic, affectedly or pompously formal'. But it was decided, rather sententiously, that 'rejection is not warranted, however, on the basis of subjective assessment of the literary merit of the proposed inscription' which was odd, seeing as this was a poetry competition. The third verse of the awful poem was translated as 'In the winter of bondage we saw a vision/ we melted the numbing snow/ and the river of resurrection flowed from it.'[3]

In relation to commemorating the civil war, Jack Lynch had suggested in 1968 that he would facilitate an all-party committee to see how this could best be done, but there was no indication in 1971 that there was any unanimity. In relation to a possible commemorative postage stamp, Lynch, who, to his credit, had insisted on the need to commemorate all those who 'fell' in the civil war, was criticised for including as a 'civil war figure' Arthur Griffith – the original founder of Sinn Féin and one of the chief negotiators of the Anglo-Irish Treaty, who died of natural causes at the outset of the civil war. Lynch was accused by Cork Fine Gael TD Liam Burke of carrying 'these regrettable bitternesses into the new generation'. Lynch responded that he would 'equally refer to Seán Lemass and

Eamon de Valera as civil war figures'. In December 1971, the celebrations of the fiftieth anniversary of the Treaty were regarded as a Fine Gael commemoration, though Cosgrave suggested 'it would be far better if they were organised by the state'. The Taoiseach's failure to mark the occasion was referred to as 'pygmy-minded pettiness' by Fine Gael's Richie Ryan: 'Is it expecting too much to hope that when the Taoiseach as head of the government was feted in London today, the honoured guest of the parliamentary correspondents in Westminster, he might have spared a thought for the sincere and responsible and anxious men who fifty years ago this night in London, had to make their lonely, critical but courageous decision to sign the Treaty?'[4]

The commemoration of the life and death of Michael Collins, killed during the civil war in August 1922 while commander-in-chief of the Free State army, also presented difficulties. This had traditionally been a Fine Gael controlled event, but in May 1972 it was agreed that the defence forces would be represented at the fiftieth anniversary commemoration. When the Welsh film-maker Kenneth Griffith sought to get Liam Cosgrave to intervene in July 1973 after his film on Michael Collins, *Hang Out Your Brightest Colours*, made to mark the fiftieth anniversary of his death, was suppressed by Sir Lew Grade's Associated Television, he was advised by a civil servant in the Department of Foreign Affairs not to get involved, even though the department had assisted Griffith with film locations. It had been screened privately at the Irish Embassy in London, 'who reported in regard to it that because of the way in which the life and death of Michael Collins was related to developments in the North of Ireland, the refusal of ATV to screen the film could perhaps be understood'.[5]

The same year, Noel Browne suggested there was a clear need for 'one agreed annual simple dignified civilian memorial gesture'. Likewise, Conor Cruise O'Brien in a letter to Cosgrave identified the need for a single day of commemoration due to 'the general weariness of so many people North and South with all these commemorations'.[6] A proposal to set aside St Patrick's Day as a day of reconciliation received a cool response in 1973; it was regarded as something that might offend Jews. In relation to how it should be marked, O'Brien made it clear in a letter to Minister for Defence Patrick Donegan, that he was 'frankly uneasy about the idea if a parade of unarmed soldiers ... might help lead credence to the idea that the IRA are the real armed forces of the state'.[7]

But it was decided that from 1974, St Patrick's Day would be set aside as a day of national commemoration for all those who had 'died for Ireland and victims of civil strife'. An eighty-year-old IRA veteran from Waterford, who wanted 24 April, the day the 1916 Easter Rising commenced, to be declared a public holiday to commemorate the Rising, was incensed with this. He informed Cosgrave that 'St Patrick had no hand in the fight for freedom. He came to convert our people and you should leave that day to the Church and children. Surely you do not think that the circus parade in Dublin was a fitting commemoration to our brave dead. Why do the Irish government try to outcast these men of 1916 to 1921 and the brave before them?' He included among those brave men, 'your father'.[8]

The ghost of Roger Casement, the Dublin-born British diplomat and Irish Nationalist who was executed for treason after the 1916 Rising, also proved troublesome, particularly regarding the planned erection of a commemorative statue by Oisín Kelly in Glasnevin cemetery. A committee had originally been appointed in 1966 by the Fianna Fáil government to advise the sculptor following Casement's re-interment the previous year after the British government agreed to return his remains to Ireland. But the question being asked in 1972 was whether an unveiling ceremony could be 'considered opportune in present circumstances'.[9] This issue was left in abeyance, though by March 1973, Richard Stokes in the Department of the Taoiseach believed it would be 'particularly fitting' if the present president, Eamon de Valera, could perform the function, but the Department of Finance, which controlled the Office of Public Works (OPW), continued to ignore the issue despite 'repeated reminders' from the Department of the Taoiseach. Eventually, an answer was dragged out of Finance to the effect that 'the statue should be put in position quietly and without attendant ceremony'. Stokes found this attitude troubling: 'The state should not be seen to do anything which would lend support to the allegations against Casement's personal reputation [his homosexuality and the controversy over his Black Diaries] and should, rather, be seen to honour his patriotism irrespective of that.' He pointed out that other executed leaders of 1916 had memorials dedicated to them and that 'Casement has not been a politically controversial figure in Irish terms such as, for example, Collins, [Cathal] Brugha etc. and other civil war figures. Failure to do appropriate honour now might encourage the Opposition to make him a figure of controversy by possibly holding a memorial or dedication service at the grave side ... whatever is done, there can be no avoiding the criticism that it has taken almost 9 years to provide and erect a simple statue – a statue which, apparently, has been in the OPW store for the last two years.'[10]

Hibernia magazine put this point more polemically: 'the statue languishes in some forlorn corner of bureaucratic neglect. Is this because Roger Casement is unfashionable with the coalition or is there some other reason?'[11] Minister for Finance Richie Ryan had no enthusiasm for this project, wanting it to be 'low profile' with no presidential involvement, but he acknowledged in a letter to Cosgrave that inaction 'could stimulate protest'.[12] Over three years later, there had still been no decision; it was suggested to Stokes that the new Fianna Fáil government could now get involved and that as the 'return of Casement's remains represented a considerable improvement in Anglo-Irish relations, this particular aspect is perhaps the one on which stress could be laid'.[13]

Stokes, always *au fait* with the latest literature in relation to Ireland's controversial icons, acknowledged that Brian Inglis's 1973 book *Roger Casement* gave credence to Casement's homosexuality but that the response to the book would suggest the public did not regard his 'perversion' as negating his idealism and patriotism. Stokes suggested that since 1973 there had developed 'a less jingoistic attitude to Irish nationalism ... but there has grown too a feeling that the pendulum has swung too far on this and that we have reached the stage of almost apologising for the deeds of our patriot dead'. Allowing the statue to remain in the store room was, he felt, 'particularly shabby'.[14] The legacy of Casement was also vigorously debated in the letters page of the *Irish Times* in 1973. A new irreverence was apparent and there no longer seemed a need 'to maintain a sober patriotic attitude to Casement', one writer declaring, 'I am quite certain that the younger generation of Irish don't give one damn if the supposed diaries were black, red, pink or blue.'[15]

Decisions were also required regarding what to do with the *Asgard*, the yacht which had transported the arms involved in the Howth gun running in 1914 that had armed the Irish Volunteer movement. It had been bought by the Irish government in 1961 at a cost of £4,325, and was now rotting in a Malahide shipyard in County Dublin. Richie Ryan was not remotely nostalgic about it – 'his prime interest is to see Asgard suitably disposed of at minimum cost' – but there was a belief that the public would not accept the idea of scuttling it, or as it was described more formally, 'burying Asgard at sea with appropriate honours', which the Minister for Defence also wanted and which Stokes thought was 'hare brained'.

It was decided instead in 1976 to give it to the Kilmainham Jail museum for display on an indefinite loan, which it was estimated would involve expenditure of about £6,000. This did not happen until June 1978.[16]

When a researcher in 1977 sought correspondence from renowned Nobel Prize-winning playwright and political activist George Bernard Shaw, Stokes, who had been one of the key proponents of archives legislation to facilitate research, was keen for her to be granted access because he was enthusiastic about a general reappraisal of Shaw, indicating his 'very strong Irishness and his nationalism as well as his munificence towards Ireland. This is an aspect which has been glossed over in Britain.'[17] He was less enthusiastic about the proposal for an Ernie O'Malley museum of art in Castlebar, following an initiative of the sculptor Helen Hooker O'Malley Roelofs (who had married O'Malley in 1935, though they subsequently divorced) to donate a collection worth £160,000. O'Malley had been an IRA commander during the War of Independence and an officer in the anti-Treaty IRA during the civil war. It was estimated that the capital requirements would be far too costly, as would the 'very stringent requirements' which the donor had set out regarding capital expenditure of £500,000 and £100,000 per annum ongoing costs ('a hopelessly bad bargain'). Not only were 'less dictatorial terms' desired; Stokes did not want preconditions or any memorial which 'might be exploited. A writer in today's *Irish Times* commenting on Ernie O'Malley's book *The Singing Flame* suggests that O'Malley would have approved of the present protest in Block H at Long Kesh.'[18]

The bi-centenary of the birth of Daniel O'Connell, an iconic nineteenth-century Irish politician who had led the successful campaign for Catholic emancipation and the less successful drive for repeal of the union between Britain and Ireland, was celebrated in 1975. Some of the newspaper coverage sought to do 'justice to a Giant'.[19] Earlier in the twentieth century the focus and commemorative emphasis had been on the securing of Catholic emancipation, but the emphasis in 1975 was on the idea of a European liberal and British parliamentarian who was also vulgar, preoccupied with the privileges of his own class and their preservation, and who was, in historian John A. Murphy's phrase, 'more than a bit of a rogue'.[20]

But a speech written by civil servants for Liam Cosgrave deliberately emphasised O'Connell's legacy in the context of the need for rehabilitation, as historians and politicians 'had allowed or even pursued a policy of denigration and unconsciously or otherwise, of misrepresentation of

O'Connell's life and work'.[21] Niall Montgomery, an architect, poet, literary critic and member of the Cultural Relations Committee of the Department of Foreign Affairs, wrote a trenchant letter to Cosgrave suggesting that commemoration of O'Connell needed to be placed outside of what he regarded as 'the ruinously romantic and ultimately cruel notions about nationality taught in certain schools'. This did not take account of the fact that a new history curriculum had been introduced a few years previously, part of an international reassessment of traditional approaches to the teaching of that subject. Murphy asserted in 1973 that the allegations of 'polluted' or 'contaminated' history teaching were 'woolly in the extreme'. While 'brutally simplified' versions of Anglo-Irish history had been taught in the past, a new curriculum and better text books meant there had been a move away from 'the drum and trumpets' approach.[22]

As Montgomery saw it, O'Connell was 'first in a line of men of peace running through Parnell [Charles Stewart, iconic constitutional Nationalist leader of the late nineteenth century] and Davitt [Michael, radical Nationalist and one of the founders of the National Land League in 1879] to Griffith [Arthur, founder of the original Sinn Féin movement in 1905]. Unfortunately, against that, you have the vastly more influential and disastrous line of the men of blood, from Tone through the men of '48 and '67 [the 1848 'Young Ireland' rebellion and the Fenian Rising of 1867] to the Irish Alfred Rosenburg [the Nazi philosopher], P. H. Pearse, and his disciple Mr de Valera.' Richard Stokes took issue with this, insisting, 'This is unfair – Pearse was trying to awaken a nation, not annihilate a race.' Cosgrave's reply, however, did not take Montgomery to task; he wrote that he shared his views on O'Connell but that 'it is difficult, however, for the government or any of its agencies to generate a movement at the popular level to secure a better place for O'Connell's memory'.[23]

In the same year, Oliver Plunkett, the Catholic Archbishop of Armagh executed for high treason in London on the basis of perjured evidence in 1681, was canonised in Rome, having been beatified in 1920 (see also Part VIII). This occasion was presented as an opportunity to underline his relevance to the modern era by Cardinal William Conway, Archbishop of Armagh and Primate of All Ireland, who wrote to Cosgrave: 'Blessed Oliver, as you know, was essentially a man of peace and worked heroically during his life to bring reconciliation and a cessation of violence in very turbulent times ... Oliver's outstanding role as a peace maker in his time gives the occasion a special relevance to our own day.'[24] But there was also criticism of the canonisation as sectarian and potentially divisive (because of the historical context of the religious conflicts of the seventeenth century). The Irish ambassador to the Holy See, Gerard Woods, pointed out to Paul Keating, secretary of the Department of Foreign Affairs, that Mgr Benelli, part of the Roman Curia as deputy to the Secretariat of State, had assured the British government that 'there were no ulterior motives and no mean or base prerogatives about the canonisation which have nothing to do with timing or relevance'.[25]

The centenary of the birth of 1916 Rising leader Patrick Pearse in 1979 also raised sensitivities. At the end of 1977, all government departments were asked to submit proposals as to how the centenary could be marked. The view was expressed that 'in the prevailing Northern Ireland situation such commemoration could raise delicate issues affecting relations between the communities in the North and possibly extending to Anglo-Irish relations', but that a decision not to mark the occasion 'could be open to misinterpretation and might leave the field to subversive elements who might seek to capitalise on the situation for their own ends'.[26]

There was a feeling that commemoration should concentrate on 'Pearse's contribution in the literary, cultural and educational fields ... Pearse's English associates could be given some prominence. A cousin of Pearse named Patrick Shovelton is deputy secretary of the UK Department of trade.' There were other proposals for musicals and pageants, and from the Department of Labour, a suggestion that commemoration could hinge on developing 'responsible attitudes to work'. Civil servants in the Department of Defence pointed out that there had been no formal centenaries of the births of three of the seven 1916 Proclamation signatories, Thomas Clarke (1958), James Connolly (1968) and Thomas MacDonagh (1976). The Department of Agriculture was perhaps relieved that 'we have been unable to trace any significant links between Pearse and the agricultural industry', while the Department of Foreign Affairs expressed the view that it would be 'inappropriate to commemorate the occasion very extensively'. It was also suggested the 'joyful theme of rebirth' should permeate the commemoration.[27]

But the Pearse centenary cabinet subcommittee, while being aware of the 'strong Provoish element who will be emphasising the physical force aspect of Pearse and 1916', also agreed 'to restore the memory of Pearse to a place of honour in Irish society and to counter the denigratory effects of certain commentators in recent years'. Singled out in this regard was an article published in the Jesuit publication *Studies* in 1972 by Fr Francis Shaw SJ, who had studied at UCD under Eoin MacNeill, an Early Irish History scholar who as Chief of Staff of the Irish Volunteers had tried to prevent the Rising of 1916. Shaw's article had been intended for publication in 1966 but because of its perceived attack on the legacy of 1916 was delayed. Entitled 'The Canon of Irish History: A Challenge', it maintained that 'Pearse, one feels, would not have been satisfied to attain independence by peaceful means'. It criticised the way Pearse 'consistently and deliberately and without reservation' equated 'the patriot and the patriot people with Christ' which Shaw argued was 'in conflict with Christian tradition'.[28]

In 1978, it was suggested in *Magill* magazine that it had become clear in 1976 that the coalition government had intended to mark the sixtieth anniversary of the Rising 'with the minimum of ceremony and the maximum denigration of its leaders'. It was also reported that Roddy Connolly, son of James Connolly, the labour leader executed in 1916, 'supported the ban on commemorating the sixtieth anniversary of the Rising', but his sister Nora took part. She was highly critical of Conor Cruise O'Brien's description of 1916 as 'a bourgeois affair', disputing this assessment of the signatories of the 1916 Proclamation.[29]

By 1977, historian Joe Lee, Professor of Modern History at University College Cork, who in 1973 had published a seminal study, *The Modernisation of Irish Society 1848–1918*, had concluded that due to the Troubles in Northern Ireland Pearse 'was in danger of falling victim to mindless condemnation having long been the victim of mindless adulation'.[30] This was the same year that Ruth Dudley Edwards's probing biography of him was published ('the book was not an assault on Pearse but was read as such'; she had simply underlined both his virtues and his flaws[31]). Dudley Edwards was the daughter of Robert, the Professor of Modern Irish History at UCD, and had completed her postgraduate studies at Cambridge before establishing herself as a freelance writer. Perhaps it was inevitable during this confused and uncertain era that Pearse would be knocked from the pedestal he had been placed on by his 'disciples'; but there was also a danger of forgetting 'the human being in Pearse', as Dudley Edwards put it.[32] When John A. Murphy asked secondary-school history students to write about Pearse for five minutes, some of the results he got included: 'He was a priest who helped the IRA against the English. He was a very good leader. He did not like the English. In the end they burned him alive. And in another boy's mind he was Padre Pio with bloody stigmata.'[33]

In January 1979, Lynch met with those who had formed the Pearse Commemoration Committee, but he 'expressed disquiet at the Provisional leanings of Eamon de Barra's committee … it made it difficult for the government to be seen to be involved in any way with such people or their proposals'. De Barra was keen to tell them that sculptor Gary Trimble had been approached to work on a Pearse statue and 'he praised the fact that it was taking the form of Pearse the teacher surrounded by a group of children. This he felt, was an indication that the committee was not as represented [i.e. as Provo]; if it were, it would, he said, be intent on a representation of Pearse the soldier giving the oration over O'Donovan Rossa's grave.'[34] (Pearse had given an impassioned eulogy at the funeral of this veteran Fenian in Dublin 1915 that finished with the warning 'Ireland unfree shall never be at peace'.)

The civil servants on the government-established committee to oversee the commemorations (there was a budget of £30,000, plans for 5,000 copies of Pearse's literary writings to be sent to schools and a film to be commissioned) focused on the 'need to concentrate on Pearse the educationalist and writer'. There was a desire for secrecy in the planning of the commemoration but also a contention that such clandestine planning was inappropriate: 'There is the possibility that we could adopt a subterfuge of providing, for example, for the film in the vote for Foreign Affairs where it could be "lost" in the general expenses on film publicity. This, I think, is unworthy and should not be done. It would suggest that we are trying to hide the expenditure on the commemoration.'[35]

Well-known writer and biographer Ulick O'Connor proposed that he be commissioned to write a one-man show on Pearse, for which he (extravagantly) sought £2,000; the committee was open to the idea but wanted to discuss the fee. As Richard Stokes saw it, £1,000 was as much as could be given to O'Connor, but there was another sting in the tail of his assessment of the possible enterprise: 'I would be reasonably happy that Ulick O'Connor would produce a sympathetic and entertaining show. Going on his performance of the [Brendan] Behan one-man show he is clearly no actor and I would be much happier if he allowed someone of greater ability and distinction to play the part.'[36]

While there was interest expressed in the commissioning of orchestral work, a museum at St Enda's, where Pearse had established his school, and the issuing of commemorative stamps, it was desired to 'hold off' on the idea of a statue. De Barra then threatened that if the government did not give support to his group he would not give memorabilia in his possession to the museum. As Stokes saw it, a proposal for a £75,000, thirty-five-foot high statue in O'Connell Street was outlandish and foolhardy: 'The scope of the project is considerably greater than the profile which prudence would suggest for a Pearse commemoration, given the implications in regard to the North etc. ... would be a major target for vandalism and for bomb attacks from certain quarters ... political correspondents and other commentators with their readiness to apply facile labels are likely to describe it as a victory of Hawks over Doves.'[37]

Jack Lynch was prepared to take it on if the government could finance and control this project but the Pearse Committee wanted to control it and Stokes wanted the government to withdraw and concentrate on St Enda's and a bust commissioned from Dublin sculptor John Behan. Pearse had established St Enda's in 1908 in Dublin and it was ahead of his time in its child-centred approach to education, concern for student welfare and dislike of corporal punishment. The school prized Irish language and culture with an emphasis on heroic inspiration from Irish history in order to inculcate idealism. President Patrick Hillery was not keen on performing the opening of the Pearse museum at St Enda's, but in the absence of the Taoiseach, who was in the US, was persuaded to do it. In his speech he focused on the idea that Pearse was remembered as a soldier, but 'we remember him too as a visionary who translated his vision into beautiful prose and poetry',[38] a highly dubious assertion, at least with regard to the poetry.

One conclusion to be drawn about the centenary commemoration was that, rather than clearing up confusion about Pearse, it added to it and provoked not just indifference but hostility; yet there was at least a greater sense of grappling with a more complex personality, 'awash with internal conflict'.[39] Conor Cruise O'Brien was trenchant and predictably hostile, describing Pearse as 'a manic, mystic nationalist with a cult of blood sacrifice and a strong personal motivation towards death. A nation which pretends to take a personality of that type as its mentor, without really meaning it, is already involved in a disaster, a disaster of intellectual dishonesty and moral obliquity.' But others challenged this interpretation, including Fine Gael's Alexis FitzGerald, who slugged it out with him at a debate in Trinity College. Newspapers also reported the Jack Lynch/Charles Haughey disagreement over his legacy. Quite clearly, Pearse's centenary was being used for internal jockeying for the leadership of Fianna Fáil (see Part II).[40]

In contrast, award-winning film-maker Louis Marcus presented him, in *Revival: Pearses's Concept of Ireland*, as a 'liberal intellectual of an intensity that I don't think this country is yet mature enough to take on'. Kerry writer Bryan MacMahon's *A Pageant of Pearse* opened to terrible reviews and indifference; it was three hours long and a cast of over a hundred on opening night was said to have 'outnumbered the audience'. There were also objections to artist Robert Ballagh's stamp design with an unclothed Statue of Liberty. What the centenary amounted to was 'a noble attempt to inspire public intellectual analysis which fell on deaf ears'.[41]

– TWENTY-ONE –

HISTORY WARS

Clearly, some were happy to bury the past with relish. John A Murphy suggested in 1976 that 'the state has emerged as a sophisticated polity, no longer troubled even in recession by doubts about the worthwhileness of its existence (as it was in the 1950s) and at the same time having outgrown emotional manifestations of nationalism'.[1] In contrast, in a presentation about the implications for Ireland of EEC membership in 1972, Terence Ó Raifeartaigh, chairman of the Higher Education Authority, argued passionately that 'our national morale is sick' and referred to 'the lack of charity, utter cynicism and extravagant denunciation in relation to patriotic or other ideals which are such a feature of the correspondence columns of our evening and sometimes our daily newspapers ... our intellectual and cultural resources have not proved sufficiently strong to offer the hope of their survival as distinctly Irish assets ... we do not think it odd that the national adjective should be on occasion a term of contempt (Oh, come now! That's a bit Irish!).'[2]

Others, including Fine Gael's John Kelly, became dismissive of what he described in a speech in Dublin in October 1977 as 'one particularly Irish characteristic ... a morbid preoccupation with the question of our own identity ... We alone among the peoples of Europe seem to be caught in recurrent dreary absorption with the problem of who we are.'[3] But others still took a vicarious pleasure in maintaining old enmities sparked by the divisions of the early twentieth century and delighted in the passing of those deemed guilty of treasonous manoeuvres in times past. As recalled by Eibhear Walshe in his memoir of a childhood in Waterford in the 1960s and 1970s, his grandmother and her friends'

> party-making abilities extended to the deaths of hated public figures. When Eamon de Valera died [in 1975], Cissie had all the girls over to Belgrave [her house] for a celebration on the night of his funeral, good Redmondite Ballybricken women as they were. I think it was the first time I saw Cissie drunk, a rare occurrence. As good loyal daughters and wives of pig dealers, members of the Fine Gael party and lifelong opponents of Fianna Fáil, they waked the former president by confident assertions that he was illegitimate, though this was not the term that they used, and that his name came from a New York Coffee brand ... as Cissie and the others got more excited, Dev's private life and morals, in actuality beyond reproach, all came into discussion and Cissie told us how her distant cousin, who was a bishop, had phoned her up to offer to drive her to Dev's funeral, simply for the pleasure of hearing the violence of her response and the unchristian nature of her language.[4]

De Valera had remained a divisive figure to the end. A few years before his death, Tom Barry, one of the country's best known War of Independence IRA veterans, who was involved in an RTÉ programme to commemorate the fiftieth anniversary of the 1920 Kilmichael ambush, in which fifteen British auxiliaries had been killed, was anything but reverential when he emerged from the television studio: 'Why don't the three of us go up to the park and shoot that bastard de Valera?' he (perhaps) jocularly remarked.[5] In contrast, in his notebooks containing notes for his speeches, President Ó Dálaigh suggested after de Valera's death: 'To the end, he bore himself as a scholar, a statesman and a soldier ... throughout the world and in particular among peoples striving to be free, his name has been a synonym for the struggle for Irish independence.'[6]

The 1970s witnessed the death of a number of others of that revolutionary generation, including in December 1971 Richard Mulcahy, the IRA leader during the War of Independence and subsequently leader of Fine Gael, who died at the age of eighty-five, just a week after the fiftieth anniversary of the signing of the Anglo-Irish Treaty. Fine Gael's John A. Costello, who served as Taoiseach from 1948–51 and 1954–7, died at the age of eighty-four in January 1976. He was referred to by Cosgrave as 'in the fullest sense a true Christian gentleman' and by James Dillon, Cosgrave's predecessor as leader of Fine Gael, in a nod to contemporary events, as one whose main aim was to take the gun out of Irish politics, and who 'made the pendulum of democratic life swing in this country in a healthy way'. His family (his son Declan was the Attorney General at the time of his death) refused the offer of a public funeral.[7]

Who owned the legacy of that battle for independence was something that inevitably surfaced in the 1970s, complicated by the ongoing Troubles in Northern Ireland. In 1971 John Kelly strongly disputed the idea that Cosgrave, 'because of past history', was disqualified from using Tone's phrase about 'the common name of Irishmen'. He pointed out that the first government of the state, led by Liam's father William T. Cosgrave, 'leaned over backward to conciliate the Protestant and ex unionist minority', while the 1922 constitution 'contained none of the sectarian bones that are now said to stick in the Northern Protestant throat'. He dismissed the 'Trendy Tones, lay and clerical who are great at telling us how we must restructure our stuffy old society but not so great at recognising savagery when they see it and denouncing it for what it is.'[8]

Historians, too, began to grapple in the 1970s with the 'antithesis between history and memory'. In 1973, Leland Lyons addressed the dilemma of the contemporary historian. He was wary of the contention, sometimes heard on BBC television, that the Irish 'are so imprisoned in their history that it is hard to see how they can find a way out of their present predicament'. The question for Lyons was 'Can contemporary history be history?' He argued that it suffered from certain 'fundamental disabilities which place it firmly and irredeemably outside the cognisance of the historical profession'. With television and modern media, what was being seen were only 'fragments' and it was difficult to recognise what was of permanent importance. He also suggested the Irish were afflicted with 'the chronic disease of islanders – which is to say, insularity. It comes very easily to us to regard Irish conditions, Irish dilemmas as palpitatingly unique.'

He was also wary of the cult of violence and the idea that it was key to Irish historical development, pointing out just how little had changed post 1922 with the effort 'to preserve not only the illusion, but in many instances the reality of continuity with the pre-revolutionary era'. What he was warning against, in short, was a theory of history which depended for its validity on the inevitability of violence, but he also acknowledged that if contemporary history was abandoned by the historians it would be left to propagandists and 'pseudo historians'. There was also a danger of over-emphasising constitutional history just to express revulsion at contemporary violence.[9]

Lyons's observations were searching, honest and perhaps even contradictory and underlined difficulties in the profession in dealing with the Troubles. There was much qualification and, it seemed, prevarication in this regard. It was reported for example that Lyons 'tends to agree, but with much qualification and misgiving that O'Brien's "Two Nations" thesis may have to be swallowed for a long time to come to see if it will staunch the bloodshed'.[10] Significantly, the 'mild, generous, confident nationalism' of Lyons's *Ireland Since the Famine* was overtaken by a much bleaker tone by the end of the decade in *Culture and Anarchy in Ireland*.[11]

An address to the Trinity College History Society in 1977 by T. W. Moody, titled 'Irish History and Irish Mythology', made a distinction between mythology – consciousness of the past as derived from 'popular traditions' – and knowledge acquired by the historian through 'the application of scientific methods to his evidence'. Educated at Queen's University Belfast and subsequently in London, where he was a contemporary of Robert Dudley Edwards, Moody had lectured in Trinity since 1939, the year after he had launched the journal *Irish Historical Studies* with Dudley Edwards, the beginnings of a project to professionalise and impose high standards in the pursuit of a national historiography. Leland Lyons also warned of the need to separate 'the realities of what have happened on this island' from 'the myths we have chosen to weave around certain symbolic events'.[12] What this seemed to amount to was, as was happening in Britain and France, the historian's duty to 'address the causes of communal division' which was disturbed by the prominence of the gun in Irish politics.

Interestingly, President Erskine Childers had also addressed this in a private letter to Cosgrave in May 1974:

> We do not do half enough to commemorate the lives of those who worked for Ireland in the social, political and cultural fields in the nineteenth and twentieth century to arouse the self-confidence of Irish people. When I opened the swimming pool in Tipperary I found a museum commemorating the life of Seán Treacy [one of the leaders of the IRA in Tipperary during the War of Independence]. The museum contained nothing but guns. I nearly called you up and asked that I

be allowed to alter the sentence which spoke of St Patrick's Day commemorating those who died for Ireland to read 'those who worked for and died for Ireland'.[13]

Moody saw myth-making as 'an ancient Irish industry' and highlighted the 'predestinate nation' myth that presented the achievement of Irish independence in 1922 as partial fulfilment of a destiny that required British withdrawal from Northern Ireland to complete itself. The truth, he asserted, was that revolutionary nationalism 'never comprehended by more than a small minority of Ireland's population', had no social programme and mainstream Irish nationalism in the nineteenth century had been moderate and did not envisage war with Britain, while the gulfs between Orangeism 'as viewed by a historian and as presented by Orange spokesmen are both obvious and profound and are of the essence of the Ulster predicament'.[14] Some saw in this approach to history a very concerted effort 'for avoiding commitment', a judgement also delivered in a review of Robert Dudley Edwards's *A New History of Ireland* in August 1972.[15]

Literary historian and critic Terence Brown has suggested that much of the revisionism propounded by Conor Cruise O'Brien in this decade was 'intellectually depressing' because it was 'unhistorical' speculation and an assumption that Irish independence would have occurred without the 1916 Rising.[16] Robert Dudley Edwards went beyond some of the more parochial issues in 1978 in looking at the task facing Irish historians and suggested there was a need to interpret Irish history in its European context.[17] UCD historian Mary Daly was later to suggest that the debate about revising historical interpretations during this era prompted a degree of 'armchair history'; prolonged and tendentious discussions about 1916 and its legacy were 'conducted without the benefit of any new research' and 'became a comfortable alternative to long hours spent in the archives'.[18]

On the left, Labour activist John de Courcy Ireland was more trenchant in reassessing Irish history: 'There is probably no country in the world that has had its history so distorted into myth as ours ... the now traditional myth of course, is that the Irish people are in no sense as other men are, but a mighty company of slumbering saints, pure Gaels by blood and temperament, awaiting the leadership of a heaven-sent elite to a pinnacle of political or ideological greatness (in some versions both) which will astonish the world.' As far as he was concerned the ultimate logic of this myth was sectarian warfare.[19]

Others, often privately, continued to resent the great silence about Irish soldiers who had served with the British army. Journalist Aodhan Madden's father had served in the Dublin Fusiliers, who suffered great casualties at the Somme, and 'often got angry at how the Irish state had ignored their sacrifice'.[20] More than 200,000 Irishmen fought in the First World War and all were volunteers. The Irish also made a significant contribution to the British army during the Second World War; at least 60,000 southern Irish citizens served and men of Irish origin won eight Victoria Crosses during that war. Joining the British army was a family tradition for many, and was not seen by most of them as either pro-British or anti-Irish. But this became an inconvenient truth. Because of the events of the War of Independence, the phrase 'Crown Forces' came to represent something abhorrent in the Republican narrative.

In relation to researching history, considerable concern was expressed in the 1970s about the state's archives. Robert Dudley Edwards was a pivotal figure in this regard, as 'unlike many historians, his understanding of [archives] was not limited to their functional value as primary sources'. He cared greatly about 'the need for their independent administration and for their professional preservation'. His efforts led to the establishment of the Irish Society for Archives, the UCD Archives Department and the Diploma in Archival Studies.[21] In March 1970, a deputation from the Irish Manuscripts Commission (IMC), originally established in 1928 to promote the preservation and promotion of historical documents, met the Minister for Education, Pádraig Faulkner, to press for the introduction of archives legislation that one of his predecessors, Donogh O'Malley, had promised in 1967 but to no avail. Dudley Edwards and his colleagues faced 'persistent official apathy towards archival preservation, access and administration'.[22]

A 1970 lecture given by Dudley Edwards was entitled 'Rescue the Records'; during it he praised the example of the Public Record Office of Northern Ireland. In a letter to the *Irish Times* in November 1970 he announced the foundation of the Irish Society for Archives with an open invitation to librarians, administrators, archivists, historians and academics to support the new society. Dudley Edwards enjoyed access to the corridors of power but sometimes exaggerated his influence; the Taoiseach's secretary in May 1972 informed Lynch that Edwards 'makes frequent reference to the fact that he can have access to you whenever he likes and that he uses this when he is displeased with the delay in achieving his requests'.[23]

It had also been pointed out when Lynch was Taoiseach in 1971, 'contrary to what appears to be a widely held belief that there is a fifty year rule here governing access to departmental records, there is, in fact, no rule', and it was further pointed out in 1971 that despite an announcement in 1967 that papers relating to the Anglo-Irish Treaty would be made available to 'bona fide' historians, 'not a single application has been received for access to the Treaty papers'.[24]

But there was criticism that nothing was available beyond 1922; Garret FitzGerald suggested in 1971 that the country was now mature enough 'to absorb whatever there is to absorb in an adult manner ... this country will look very odd indeed in international eyes if Britain continues to release information about Irish matters before we do – as has already happened. We will have to stop being afraid of our own history'. Meanwhile, Lynch informed Cosgrave that he was examining the option of a thirty-year rule governing access to state papers.[25] The Public Record Office (PRO) contained government records, while the State Paper Office (SPO) held the vital Chief Secretary's Office Papers, the most important archive relating to nineteenth-century Ireland, and also housed other official records such as court records and parish registers. The State Paper Office was an ill-equipped chaotic outfit with 'shelves upon shelves of untidy brown paper parcels', finding aids that were 'shameful', with no guide to the SPO and no deputy keeper's report since 1961 and 'the accumulated arrears of the last 50 years'. It also housed Dublin Corporation archives given in 1959 but not yet processed.

In August 1972 Brendan Mac Giolla Choile, Keeper of the State Papers, travelled to archives in Denmark and Germany 'to add a European dimension to our knowledge of modern archival practices' and to enjoy 'all the appointments, glasses and indeed food ... of first quality'. What was required in Ireland, he concluded in his commendably detailed report running to sixty-eight pages, was sufficient staff to create a 'modern archive' as the current situation was 'ad hoc'. There were only two archivists in the PRO and just one in the SPO; what was needed, at a minimum, was seven.[26]

Most disturbing was the attitude to preservation on the part of some state bodies. In November 1972 Mac Giolla Choile was approached by *Irish Independent* journalist Aengus Fanning, 'who told him that the Land Registry were in the process of destroying official documents' including instruments relating to wills, deeds and titles, with the sanction of the

Minister for Justice, Des O'Malley. The minister subsequently ordered that the PRO allow no future destruction of documents without evaluation, 'although a clearing out may have to take place from time to time'. Garret FitzGerald wondered if the minister was 'satisfied that historians would have the same definition of relevancy as the staff of the Land Registry?'[27] There was nothing new in this, nor did it mark an end to it. Irish historian Louis Cullen pointed out in 2011 that in 1970 Lynch had issued a circular to government departments calling for a halt to the destruction of records but 'it was not observed'. The destruction of 30,000 pre-1960 files of inmates of care institutions occurred 'at a date which the Department of Education has conceded could be as late as 1976'. A senior officer in the Department of Justice destroyed the files of the Waterford Courthouse ('an old and valuable collection') in 1979, 'and the department fought tooth and nail for years though in the end without success – to conceal the circumstances ... these simply happen to be the documented incidents'.[28]

Despite having the ear of Lynch, Dudley Edwards had to wait until the change of government in 1973, when Cosgrave met an IMC deputation (which again included Dudley Edwards and reiterated its grave concerns) and promised immediate action. New archival posts and support staff were 'provided speedily' and the first release of post-independence official archives followed in 1976. Cosgrave announced in the Dáil in December 1975 that he had decided to make available for access the government and cabinet minutes down to June 1944 (with it being noted in the Department of the Taoiseach that the texts would first have to be read individually 'to ensure that no seriously embarrassing material was released').

In September 1977 Dan O'Sullivan, secretary of the Department of the Taoiseach, was appalled at the conditions in which materials were being held at the SPO: 'I would describe the situation in relation to the custody of files, books and index records as chaotic and wonder how the system survives or how the staff can find anything.' He pointed out that three years had passed since an inter-departmental committee on the archives had reported to the Minister for the Public Service on a general scheme of legislation to enact a thirty-year rule, but it had still not been submitted to the government; there were predictions that it would be passed in 1981.[29] (No bill was actually enacted until May 1986.) In his private correspondence with Garret FitzGerald, when he was urging him to leave his papers in the archives at UCD, Dudley Edwards offered him 'grateful thanks for your government's helpful attitude to Irish archival problems generally'.[30]

There were also problems at the National Library, with a National Library of Ireland Society established in October 1969 to focus attention on 'the deplorable condition of the library'.[31]

These debates about the documentary heritage of the state, confined within the rarefied atmosphere of academia, the civil service or Leinster House, did not have the same impact as the very public and often emotive controversy over the destruction of Dublin's archaeological and architectural heritage in the 1970s. At the beginning of the decade, architectural students occupied Hume Street in order to prevent demolition by the Green Property Company of 'what is the last remaining example in Dublin of a small Georgian Street'. It was suggested in *Hibernia* in January 1970 that the Irish Georgian Society 'seems to have lost heart completely'.[32] In June of that year demolition workers stripped the roofs from these houses after students and other conservationists were removed from them in the middle of the night. Three years later, four-storeyed Georgian houses were demolished on Dublin's Lower Baggot Street as the Bank of Ireland planned to redevelop the site.

But a much more high-profile dispute emerged later in the decade. In 1976, UCD medieval historian F. X. Martin, an Augustinian friar, was elected chairman of the Friends of Medieval Dublin, and became one of the best-known public faces of the campaign to 'Save Wood Quay'. This was the proposed location for the erection of civic offices by Dublin Corporation. There were compelling reasons for new civic offices, as the staff of the corporation was based in '25 different offices over the city in a situation, which cannot but adversely affect the efficiency of services',[33] but Wood Quay was an important archaeological site for the exploration of Viking settlements in Dublin.

F. X. Martin led this campaign with aplomb, 'averaged only 2 hours sleep per night ... revelling in both the conflict and the publicity surrounding it ... allowing him to demonstrate the full range of his exceptional talents as historian, advocate, organiser, tactician, and popular leader. Nothing else engaged his multifaceted personality to quite the same extent.'[34] Ultimately the campaign did not prevent the erection of the civic offices, despite court action and a concerted effort to influence public opinion, but the campaigners did gain a stay of execution, which allowed excavations on the site to be concluded. The Irish Association of Professional Archaeologists also expressed its disgust, suggesting the government's attitude would result in the owners of other less well-known but equally important sites being 'untroubled about their preservation', while An Taisce (the Irish word for Treasury – a national trust for Ireland established in 1948 as a non-governmental body to promote the preservation of Irish heritage) decried the 'alarming precedent' the government was setting. Letters of protests were also sent to Jack Lynch late in 1978 by the mayor of Boston and the cultural attaché of the Federal Republic of Germany, while the dean of Christ Church Cathedral, Revd T. Salmon, urged Lynch to appreciate the wider significance: 'Wood Quay has become what might be described as a European question. History will remember.' In similar terms, Anngret Simms, the honorary secretary of Friends of Medieval Dublin, suggested 'our image in Europe may well be judged, at the cultural level, on this issue'.

Institutions in Denmark, Sweden and Finland also made representations, suggesting that 'the records of the Irish government in matters of archaeology has been most enlightened and generous and the scope of the excavations in the centre of Dublin has been the envy of many archaeologists all over Europe working in similar circumstances. It would be most sad if now this reputation should be vanished by allowing this ill-timed development to go ahead.'[35]

There was also potential embarrassment in April 1978 when Queen Margrethe of Denmark was visiting; not only was she a forebear of the original settlers in Wood Quay, but a professional archaeologist. She was taken to see a site in Meath rather than Wood Quay.[36] Richard Stokes in the Department of the Taoiseach had made it clear that it was imperative to avoid bringing her to Wood Quay, even though the Queen had an interest in archaeology, as 'this site and what we are proposing to do with it are not such as to invite international attention and certainly not in such a prestigious visit'.[37]

In the High Court in June 1978, Justice Liam Hamilton ruled that the site was a national monument, but stressed that he was not expressing a view 'one way or the other on whether other interests, commercial or economic may not require this site ... it is not a matter for the court to express any view.' This was deemed to be the prerogative of the Office of Public Works, which by August 1978 wanted to give the museum authorities six more weeks to continue excavations and if no more major archaeological finds transpired, Dublin Corporation would be allowed to go ahead with its building plans and would be asked to 'have a model of the excavations made for display in a suitable area in the new complex'. Some thought it incredible that it could be decided that 'a model will suffice'.[38] The general secretary of Fianna Fáil, Séamus Brennan, informed Kerry TD Kit Ahern, when she looked for guidance on whether she had permission to sign a petition in relation to Wood Quay, 'use your own judgement ... does not strike me as being a political issue'.[39]

By the spring of 1979 Noel Carroll, the public relations officer of Dublin Corporation, was dismissive of the protests. In a letter to Lynch's secretary, he asked him to inform Lynch that

> the total number of phone calls from the public to my office on the Wood Quay issue was 3. One of these would not leave a name, the other was a lady who expressed a genuine concern and a third sounded more of a crank than anything else. I visited the site on three occasions during the day and aside from the few archaeological workers who mounted an official picket, I didn't see a single member of the public near the place – not even a curious onlooker. I think this confirms my feelings, derived from playing a front line role in the saga, that there is very little concern and interest among the general public in the issue. The media treatment of the story is the worst example of slanted reporting I have seen in my fifteen years working with the Press.[40]

This was remarkably disingenuous. In 1978 John Doyle, the editor of *In Dublin* magazine, had informed Lynch that 12,000 people had signed a petition expressing alarm at the proposed development.[41] Thousands of people marched in Dublin 'in some of the largest protests the capital had ever witnessed'. In September 1978, for example, an estimated 20,000 participated in a march that culminated at the site. Senator Mary Robinson characterised it as a valuable lesson about democracy, warning 'there must be constant vigilance'. The protestors also symbolically 'seized' the site 'taking 20 voluntary hostages including writer Mary Lavin, poet Eavan Boland, former president's wife Rita Childers, architect Michael Scott and the lord mayor of Dublin'.[42]

There was also a large volume of protest letters from the public sent to the Department of the Taoiseach which castigated, among other things, 'this barbarism being perpetrated in our name' and the fear that the Irish would look like 'philistines in the eyes of the world'. It was also contended that 'there would have been an enormous outcry from Irish Nationalists had the British decided to destroy an Irish national monument 50 years ago'. The particularly salient point was also made that the government, for reasons of pragmatism, was making this decision without considering the wider message it was sending out about preserving historical heritage, given that 'there are many farmers who would be delighted to knock down the ruins of a Celtic Christian Church, a round tower or a High Cross or remove a Dolmen because the monument impedes the easy passage of a tractor on their land'.[43] The more cynical view, as articulated in music magazine *Hot Press*, was that Fianna Fáil's backers in the construction industry were required to be placated as many of them stood to lose fortunes if the development did not go ahead.[44] Construction work on the site followed.

– TWENTY-TWO –

IRISH IDENTITY ON STAGE

Despite the depredations at Wood Quay, the decade also witnessed many people finding heart culturally, even if their plans were sometimes frustrated. In this sense, the assertion of Declan Kiberd about a people 'still despondent about its capacity to shape its cultural future' is debatable.[1] In contrast, Terence Brown has highlighted a 'babble of voices to discuss Irish identity in the 1970s'.[2] There were numerous calls for greater state intervention to stimulate cultural endeavours, including a ministry for the arts, a state subsidised academy of dramatic arts (the Brendan Smith Theatre Academy, which Smith, the founder director of the Dublin Theatre Festival in 1957, had established in 1943, and the Abbey Theatre School were not deemed to be sufficient), national scholarships in music and a National Concert Hall. Inevitably, there was tension about what the relationship between the state and artists should be. At the end of 1973, poet Eavan Boland suggested ruefully that 'no two establishments in this community regard one another with more suspicion than those of the Arts and the State'.[3]

Artistic output and contribution were often linked to the wider theme of a crisis of, and challenge to, authority and certain fault lines rooted in class differences opened as a result. It has been suggested, for example, that 'the crisis of authority in the Irish state system paralleled, even if it did not cause, the crisis of authority in literary and cultural criticism'. This incorporated a preoccupation with and a searching criticism regarding identity and a corresponding rhetoric of blame on the part of a 'new class' of professional intellectuals, including economists, journalists, media commentators, administrators and academics, who in initiating projects like the *Crane Bag* journal with its interdisciplinary emphasis, were 'bold and new'.[4]

This thoughtful searching was relevant to theatre, language, music, sport, film, art and identity and provoked divided responses. It was sometimes accompanied by negative conclusions about the country's lack of confidence, encapsulated in the assertion of John Kelly in 1975 that the country was weakening as a nation as it had become 'so culturally porous, so pregnable, so vulnerable, so lacking in self-confidence and belief in itself'.[5] Five years previously, playwright Brian Friel, a native of Tyrone who had been a teacher in Derry before he became a full-time writer and achieved international fame with *Philadelphia Here I Come!* (1964), suggested Ireland had become 'a tenth rate image of America – a disaster for any country ... There is the Dublin society in the Dublin environs and then there is the rest ... a much closer link with rural roots is necessary'. Nevertheless, he acknowledged that Irish audiences were much more 'receptive to intellectual concepts' than they had been in previous decades.[6]

In another interview two years later, he was dismissive of those who wanted Irish playwrights to dispense with the past, for a more relevant contemporary drama:

> Show us the vodka and tonic society. Show us permissive Dublin. Forget about thatched cottages and soggy fields and emigration. We want the new Ireland. The demand is interesting. Leaving aside the confusion between the art of the writer and the craft of the commentator, it is interesting because it is not a genuine demand for the revelation of a new 'truth' about the country but for the confirmation of a false assumption. The assumption is that Dublin is a miniature New York, London, Paris, Tokyo and that it shares with these capitals identical social, economic, moral and cultural problems. And the postulate implies that if the artists could only concoct plays about drug addiction and high rise apartments and urban aggression and gay power then Dublin's place among the global capitals could be miraculously and publicly assured. The dramatists laugh at this because they see how spurious it is.[7]

Dublin, as he saw it, was schizophrenic because it was there that both urban and rural mingled; and such confluence gave the city its character (see also Part VII).

In March 1971, two plays opened on the same night in Dublin, which the historian of Irish theatre Christopher Morash suggested 'crystallised the spiralling sense of things falling apart': Tom Murphy's *The Morning After Optimism* at the Abbey and Hugh Leonard's *The Patrick Pearse Motel* at the Gaiety. Characters were scrambling around with no sense of right or wrong to guide them; as the pimp James in *The Morning After Optimism* exclaims, by 1971 Ireland was 'done with the innocent shit'.[8]

But there was also the assertion that Irish theatre remained out of date and was in the early 1970s reflective of a culture 'scrambling to chart the trajectory of its own tailspin', with a reliance on the revival of classics and no funding for younger alternative theatre companies. There were new political plays like Friel's *The Freedom of the City*, which opened at the Abbey in February 1973 to a muted critical response, but there was also a reliance on the revival of Seán O'Casey, the renowned playwright who had written the three Dublin plays, *The Shadow of a Gunman*, *Juno and the Paycock* and *The Plough and the Stars* between 1922 and 1926. He 'became the most frequently produced playwright in the Irish professional theatre during the 1970s, with the Abbey and the Lyric staging 18 of his plays in that decade'.[9]

Friel remained busy in the 1970s, producing *The Gentle Island* ('a terrifying play ... what is so disturbing about it is the notion of the violence inside you') and *Aristocrats* in 1979. Actor John Kavanagh, who played the role of Casimir, suggested acting in a Friel play 'was just glorious because the thing was so phrased that the actor was being instructed without being tyrannized over or dominated'.[10] Friel also completed *Translations* in 1979, keeping a sporadic diary during the writing of it. He reflected in the summer of 1979: 'One aspect that keeps eluding me; the wholeness, the integrity of that Gaelic past. Maybe because I don't believe in it.' He was also worried it was getting too political (some were to see it as a metaphor for the continuing trauma in the North): 'The play must concern itself with the exploration of the dark and private places of individual souls.'[11]

What he wanted to avoid, in his own words, was 'the threadbare device of realism' and such avoidance was managed through the self-conscious exploration of the state and the negotiation of space between the characters; the spatial question of off stage and on stage and their dynamics.[12] Friel did, in his own words, inflict tiny bruises on the historical realities which are apparent in *Translations*: 'Where there was tension between historical fact and the imperative of fiction,' he asserted, 'I'm glad to say I kept faith with the narrative.' But he was admirable in not seeking neat closure. The history that *Translations* represented continued to unfold as it was being written; with Friel there was no linear, one-way trajectory of history that proceeded from past to present, which is precisely why memory and history are such central features of his plays. In his words 'what memories are lodged in the storehouse of the mind' was pivotal in propelling his creativity.[13]

Tom Murphy was another busy playwright in the 1970s, creating plays that were 'extraordinarily word conscious'. His first successful play, *A Whistle in the Dark*, which brought a searing realism to the experiences of some Irish emigrants, had been performed in London in 1961, having been rejected by the Abbey Theatre. He had moved back from London in 1970 and wrote *The Morning After Optimism* (1971) and *Conversations on a Homecoming* in 1972 – 'the fact was, you felt that he didn't know the next sentence; that it was all being invented on the hoof. They often say about a work of art that it's inchoate, meaning that it's unfinished'[14] – and *The Sanctuary Lamp* in 1975. He was suspicious of nostalgia and instead exposed dystopia with humour and great force. He was lambasted for the supposed blasphemy of *The Sanctuary Lamp* when it was produced at the Abbey Theatre. The original version included a Mass with a satirical sermon by a guitar-wielding 'trendy' priest, making jokes about the Holy Spirit. A later, revised version removed this scene mocking Vatican II populism and left the church as essentially an abandoned space. Perhaps one of the most valuable contributions he made was to depict socially subordinate figures, thereby brushing Irish history 'against the grain by representing those discourses, which the Nationalist metanarrative has consigned to the margins of history'.

For Murphy's 'heroes', social exclusion created radical experiences of despair, which enabled his outsiders to 'let go of all preconceptions and invent their own destinies'; he created climates of anxiety for raising fundamental philosophical questions.[15] Friel felt that Murphy was 'the most destructive, the most restless, the most obsessive imagination at work in the Irish theatre today'.[16]

Some critics still felt Irish theatre was selling itself substantially short by indulging in lazy stereotyping. In 1970 Harold Hobson, the influential

English drama critic, expressed his desire to see Irish theatre generate plays 'that show the spirit of enterprise and modernity ... I have found precious little drama that is possessed of a vision of what Ireland now has to give to humanity.'[17] Two years later, Terence O'Raifeartaigh, chairman of the Higher Education Authority, observed that 'rarely is there depicted on our stage any of the decent, honest Irishmen or Irishwomen we all know. Nearly always there is somewhere a hint of either the "wag" or the rogue or even the buffoon.'[18] Friel himself was occasionally withering about the shallowness of what was on offer in Dublin's theatres, which he suggested provided a stark contrast to the situation in England, where Edward Bond was writing about violent self-destruction, or Germany, where Rolf Hochhuth was writing surrealistic documentaries, while in America Edward Albee was reflecting the impossibility of human communication.[19]

But individuals promoting Irish theatre heritage and innovative productions often found themselves pushed to the wire in the effort to secure funding, notwithstanding the fact that theatres received more funding in the 1970s than they had ever done before, and in 1974 the Arts Council established a state-funded touring group, the Irish Theatre Company. In the late 1960s Brendan Smith, director of the Dublin Theatre Festival, was proud to refer to it as one that had taken its place 'among the great international festivals, enjoying the distinction of being the world's largest drama festival with the smallest budget'. But by the early 1970s, he was referring to the hope of once again achieving 'the annual miracle' of balancing the expensive festival programme on a net budget of £19,000. Smith was widely admired and in February 1971 Jack Lynch agreed to open the festival, despite a civil servant drafting a letter indicating he wouldn't. (Lynch wrote 'I think I'll accept this year. He has had a bad time (ill health) lately and I'd like to help him.')[20]

But the following year the festival was indefinitely suspended after Bord Fáilte declined to sponsor the event. Seat occupancy had fallen to 55 per cent from a norm of 85–90 per cent due to 'the disturbed state of the country'. Despite Smith's appeals to Lynch in July 1972 that the suspension of the festival 'at this point in our history would be a most retrograde step', Lynch replied that there was little he could do as the Arts Council was autonomous in the disposal of its annual income. But there was better news for Smith when the Department of Finance intervened and agreed to finance it.[21] In October 1973 the festival's average seat occupancy was 87 per cent. Things then stabilised, with the Department of Finance giving it funding of £35,000 in 1975 and Smith, by 1977, was once again speaking of his wider mission, writing to Lynch about 'all we are doing in presenting the more civilised face of Ireland to the world'.

But in truth, the Arts Council, which in 1977 increased its contribution from £5,000 to £11,500, was not impressed by the festival and 'not very enthusiastic about the cultural merit' of it. There was a strong feeling in the Arts Council and 'in theatre circles generally that there are better ways of subventing the theatre in Dublin and in Ireland generally'. The standards of the festival were regarded as 'at much less than professional level ... there is also perhaps, a harsh reality to be faced in regard to theatre capacity in Dublin: while there is great lamentation at the possible closure of a theatre, the fact is that the total of attendances throughout the year in Dublin does not seem to be sufficient to support two large private theatres like the Gaiety and the Olympia as well as the state-subsidised Gate and Abbey and the small private theatres such as the Eblana and the Oscar'.[22] Nonetheless, Smith's perseverance paid off; funding was substantially increased in 1978.

The following year, 1979, there was some panic when the British National Theatre threatened to withdraw its planned production from the festival (which starred Michael Redgrave) 'as a protest against recent events in Mullaghmore [where Lord Mountbatten had been killed by the IRA] and Warrenpoint [where, on the same day Mountbatten was killed, two IRA bombs killed eighteen British soldiers]'. Dáithí Kelly, press officer at the Irish Embassy in London, and the festival director Michael Colgan engaged in shuttle diplomacy to prevent this happening, ultimately successfully. Redgrave performed as 'the silent epicentre' of Simon Gray's *Close of Play*; he only had to utter ten words of dialogue. The festival had no shortage of critics, including writer and poet Anthony Cronin, who in 1979 castigated it as a 'cultural non-event' and singled out Hugh Leonard's *A Life* as something that 'goes about as deep into our common human nature as a five minute talk by an enthusiastic clergymen of indeterminate denomination on late-night television'.[23]

The Abbey Theatre, which employed thirty-six players, had a seat occupancy that averaged only 65 per cent in the late 1970s, covering only a quarter of its yearly expenditure.[24] Assessments of the Abbey's role and output generated much bitchiness and emotive comment throughout the 1970s. Criticism of its priorities had emerged in 1971 when the centenary of the birth of J. M. Synge, whose hero-cult satire *Playboy of the*

Western World had caused a storm when staged at the Abbey in 1907, was being marked: 'At the moment, Dublin is a small body of land entirely surrounded by Synge. We are, as usual, engaged in our favourite occupation – commemoration or worship of the dead.'[25] Theatre director Tyrone Guthrie, who had made an impact in London but had become much more involved in Irish artistic life from the 1950s, writing in *Hibernia* in 1971, a few months before his sudden death, suggested any visitor to Ireland would encounter many people with gifts for song, story, gossip and repartee, but 'The Abbey now basks in past glories … of present glory there is no sign.' Its focus, he suggested, was far too parochial and its reluctance to embrace international plays regrettable. Tomás Mac Anna, who was to serve as artistic director of the theatre from 1973 to 1978, trenchantly rejected this. What eluded Guthrie, he suggested, was 'the fact that the Abbey's reason for being is not, and never has been, solely theatrical, it is essentially national'.[26]

Lelia Doolan, Mac Anna's predecessor as artistic director, had been a producer and director at RTÉ before resigning due to disagreement about the artistic and commercial priorities of the station. Regarding her time in the Abbey, she complained of the 'contradictions and limitations imposed on her' in her attempt to implement a new and socially relevant role for the theatre.[27] There is little doubt the Abbey often felt itself in a no-win situation regardless of the choices that were made. As observed by theatre critic Gerry Colgan, for example, 'the Abbey tends to get battered when the set is bad and abused for extravagance when it is good'.[28]

The Gate Theatre's Micheál MacLiammóir, a renowned actor, playwright and designer born in London who reinvented himself as an Irishman and had founded the Gate in 1928 with his life-long partner Hilton Edwards, had entered the twilight of his career. His one-man show on Oscar Wilde, *The Importance of Being Oscar*, had brought him to the West End and Broadway and to more than a hundred cities worldwide between 1961 and 1975. He was still writing plays in the 1970s, including *Prelude in Kasbek Street*, produced at the Gate in 1973. He and Hilton Edwards were jointly created Freemen of the City of Dublin in 1973, the first theatrical practitioners to receive this honour. He was full of pomp, grandeur, fierce intelligence and self-regard. After meeting him for lunch early in 1970, Ulick O'Connor recorded that such an encounter 'gives one an idea of what an hour with Oscar Wilde might have been like. His long rolling sentences mount like waves to a shore and just when you wonder where they are going, come to a calm and completely satisfactory conclusion.'[29]

MacLiammóir regarded the newly announced annual subsidy to the Gate of £30,000 from 1971 as 'the answer to an ageing maiden's prayer'; the Gate was now, finally, officially recognised, though ironically at a time when the founders were elderly 'and, by their own admission, out of touch with recent trends in international theatre', which meant many of the productions were revivals. This led to some criticism, but the plays by Shaw, Wilde and Shakespeare drew crowds and relied on the talents of a new generation of actors such as Jeananne Crowley, Pat Leavy and Gerard McSorley, marking something of a 'Gate Renaissance' for the theatre in the 1970s.[30] MacLiammóir died in 1978; Gabriel Byrne recalled: 'People cried when he died. Cried for what he had been, for the joy he had brought into their lives. The door of magic and wonder he opened. They were sorry they would never see his like again. They said he could have gone to Hollywood, but chose instead to remain in Dublin.'[31]

Those involved in the formation of the Druid Theatre Company in 1975, the first official theatre outside Dublin, embarked on what was a courageous initiative in Galway, given their lack of professional experience. In 1976 Garry Hynes, its co-founder and artistic director, suggested it was approached from two different viewpoints, seen as either 'a suicidal attempt by a group of jumped up amateurs to work in theatre or an alternative regional theatre enterprise of some value'.[32] The latter perspective was undoubtedly vindicated, despite or maybe because of the identified 'hegemony of the Pale in Irish life'.[33]

At the Project Arts Centre in Dublin, brothers Peter and Jim Sheridan ('Jim ... proved to be a strongly innovative and original whirlwind that swept through the mediocrity of Dublin theatrical life'), were producing challenging plays dealing with social issues like the penal system and those struggling at the margins. Gabriel Byrne, a young aspirant actor, later to achieve considerable fame nationally and internationally, joined the theatre, and future well-known actors and writers such as Neil Jordan, Mannix Flynn, Colm Meaney, Maureen Toal, Susan Slott, Liam Neeson and Gerard McSorley were also involved; a groundbreaking production of *The Liberty Suit – The Prison Life of Mannix Flynn* was transferred to the Olympia in October 1977, and with it, 'the Project had arrived. It was in a way the beginning of an artistic explosion.'[34]

Before his foray into the Project, Byrne had met Deirdre O'Connell, who in the early 1970s ran the Focus Theatre ('a tiny garage off the Pembroke Road') and who ended up teaching him everything he knew about acting:

> She was a well-known figure about the streets of the city, dressing in customary suits of solemn black as she rushed about putting up posters for plays, or begging money from the Arts Council to keep her tiny theatre alive. Initially, I fell in love with her selfless devotion, her integrity and single-minded pursuit of excellence. She was a brilliant actress steeped in the Stanislavski method and had taught some of the country's best actors like Tom Hickey and Johnny Murphy and Tim McDonnell. Her gentle demeanour belied her extraordinary energy and her commitment to giving Dublin alternative classical theatre.[35]

Byrne's first ever role was at the Focus, as Dr Kroll in Ibsen's *Rosmersholm* in 1976. After joining the Project Arts Centre ('the most exciting venue of the arts to emerge from Dublin since the days of the Pike') he left his teaching job 'all for the sake of a play at the Project in which I speak 12 lines', living on fruit and fish fingers and grilled tomatoes. There was nothing glamorous about the early days, including some poor productions at the National Stadium: 'The show is not good, technically or otherwise. Attendances fall off rapidly. Free tickets are distributed to ungrateful audiences who eat crisps and shout abuse at us. One day as we bow I hear a man in the front row proclaim: "Give it up for Jaysus sake, Yiz are useless."'[36] Many amateur companies around the country continued valiantly to produce challenging plays; Eibhear Walshe recalls that in the Waterford of his youth there was 'a season of European drama embarked on by the local dramatic society much to the detriment of their box-office takings'.[37]

Within 'conventional dramatic norms' Hugh Leonard's three major plays of this decade, *Da* (1973), for which he won a Tony award for the American production in 1978, *Time Was* (1976) and *A Life* (1979) were both entertaining and successful, depicting an Ireland of the urban middle class: 'In these suburban settings, Leonard charts a culture that is tearing away from its past, alternatively seduced by and fearful of the pleasures of nostalgia.'[38] In an interview in 1978, Brian Friel could not explain why young Irish writers did not seem to be attracted to Irish theatre: 'Artists in this country always seem to have found the novel and the poetry and the short story more satisfying forms.' He also referred to 'the blurring of the distinction between professional and amateur theatre, a confusion that tends to diminish both the seriousness of professional theatre and the parish values of the amateur theatre'.[39]

But John Devitt, who had been attending Irish theatre since the 1940s, detected a shift in the 1970s, as a society traditionally underpinned by religious consensus underwent a process of dissolution, giving theatre a new edge. There was a sense that 'some things are fading and other things replacing them, but the things that are fading are still vestigial presences'. Thomas Kilroy's play *Talbot's Box* (Kilroy was also a highly regarded novelist and academic) was performed at the Peacock in 1977; this Devitt saw as providing evidence of his assertion. (Matt Talbot had been a pietist in the early twentieth century, a working-class labourer from Dublin who had abandoned a dissolute alcoholic existence for a life of excessive prayer, abstention and self-sacrifice. Following his death he became a model for alcoholics in recovery and was declared venerable in 1975.)

Kilroy's approach seemed to be not to make the play particularly religious but to bring a certain coldness and rigour to it:

> This, I think is what interested Kilroy; his [Talbot's] whole life is an exercise in extremism of a kind only provoked by somebody who is so animated by faith, or that lively duet, faith and doubt. And what comes out in the play is that the livelier twin is doubt. The play seemed to treat Matt Talbot's life as an astonishing experiment the result of which is uncertain, whereas ten years earlier, it would have been difficult to have conceived of Matt Talbot's life other than as an extraordinary vindication of a spiritual commitment at enormous cost and with great pain.[40]

Friel's *Faith Healer* (1979) was also regarded as a play that was 'reconfiguring Catholic faith outside of the limits of institutionalised religion' and the collapse of the sanction of a central authority was a theme common to this and others.[41]

In relation to the administration of the arts, the new Arts Council created after legislation in 1973, with sixteen members appointed by the Taoiseach, representing all arts sectors, was undoubtedly seen as a welcome initiative. Richard Stokes, principal officer in the Department of the Taoiseach, had been instrumental in persuading the government to frame a new Arts Act and Dermot Nally, as assistant secretary of the department, subsequently suggested to Liam Cosgrave that Stokes would also be a very worthy member of the new council, which was agreed. There were fears that its structure was too hierarchical, but its more representative membership included, alongside Stokes, three women – novelist Eilís Dillon, archaeologist Máire de Paor and Kathleen Barrington, the Abbey Theatre's first education officer – as well as other professional artists and writers, including Seamus Heaney, John B. Keane and James White. Its full-time director Colm O Briain, a television producer and director, 'shook it out of its complacency' and gave it a new image, and there was a strong emphasis on training, exhibition and performance.[42] Significantly, it took over responsibility for funding theatre from the Department of Finance and supported new arts centres and festivals. It received a grant of £1.2 million in 1977, of which over £820,000 was expended on aid to the Abbey Theatre, Gate Theatre, the Irish Theatre Company, the Irish Ballet Company and the Dublin Theatre Festival. That year its report referred to the 'slow pace of regional development' and, despite the reforms, concerns remained about the straitened finances of the arts.

In the summer of 1978 the establishment of an inter-departmental study group on aid to the Arts had been prompted by the avalanche of requests for funding that came through the Department of the Taoiseach, including appeals from the Wexford Opera Festival, the Royal Hibernian Academy and Cork Opera House among others. The transfer of grants from the Department of Finance to the Arts Council seemed to backfire as 'disappointed applicants will regard the Taoiseach as an avenue of appeal when they are turned down by the Arts Council'.

The survey that was conducted by the review group concluded that subsidies to the theatre and other cultural groups were justified on economic grounds, 'although no particular amount of subsidy can be identified as an optimum'. This assertion was regarded in the Department of the Taoiseach as 'so vague as to be almost entirely useless'. What was concluded was that additional finance should be arranged through the Arts Council 'by way of a supplementary estimate', but that there were still 'fundamental questions in relation to the role of the state vis-à-vis that of the Arts Council'. The 'enhanced status' of the arts, it was argued, was reflected in the increased grants to the Arts Council, amounting to £1.75 million in 1979.[43]

– TWENTY-THREE –

MUSIC AND LANGUAGE: REDEPLOYING TRADITION

The Arts Council's report for 1977 had also referred to 'the low standard of living for creative artists', which was undoubtedly the case. When the widow of composer Seán Ó Riada died in 1977, a cheque for $100 was sent to Jack Lynch as a contribution to the Ó Riada foundation. The donor referred to the couple's seven children: 'Please do all you can for Seán and Ruth's children as I don't think they thought much of money and how their care would need it.'[1]

Ó Riada had died prematurely in 1971. An exceptional talent, though wilful and difficult, he had 'explored virtually every medium of musical life in Ireland', working as a broadcaster of traditional music, writing music for television and film documentaries, and receiving commissions for orchestral and chamber compositions as well as composing liturgical settings. From the mid 1950s to the mid 1960s, in the words of historian of Irish music Harry White,

> he entered a decisive claim for the significance of an emancipated art music in modern Ireland unrelated to the traditional repertory which he was subsequently to espouse so completely. He later abandoned this claim in a crisis that was both artistic and personal, with the result that formal composition became for him a marginal activity. In his symphonic essays and his music for film, and in his cultivation of an original ensemble of instruments dedicated to Irish traditional music,

he meditated on the question of voice and style in Irish music to such an extent that each overlapping phase of his compositional career tended to undermine its predecessor.

The notion of combining European and Irish traditions remained fraught for Ó Riada:

> It is fair to say that the success which he enjoyed as a national figure was intimately tied to his brilliant redeployment of traditional Irish melodies as an orchestrator, and more notably still as a performer and arranger, with Ceoltóirí Cualann [a band revitalising traditional Irish music]. Although his legacy in these respects is a distinguished one (not least with regard to successful traditional music ensemble formed in 1963, The Chieftains), the crisis of modernism in Irish music which he so compellingly identified has yet to be resolved.[2]

Composers who followed him, like Mícheál Ó Súilleabháin, Shaun Davey and Bill Whelan, sustained the intensity of Ó Riada's preoccupation with the traditional air 'either as a means of narrative or as a means of cross-fertilized variation'. Other composers in the 1970s, including Gerald Barry and Raymond Deane (who had made his debut as a composer at the Dublin Festival of Twentieth Century Music in 1969), found refuge in Cologne, Vienna and Berlin, 'encountering the European aesthetic at first hand', and young Dublin pianist John O'Connor made his mark in winning the Beethoven competition in Vienna in June 1973. For Aloys Fleischmann, Professor of Music at University College Cork, who in 1954 had co-founded the Cork International Choral and Folk Dance Festival, the determination was 'to infiltrate the school system with teachers who would remedy the dearth of music education' and he made a monumental contribution to the recording of sources of Irish traditional music while continuing to compose and write 'in a modern style that was intrinsically Irish. His compositions reflected the duality of his Irish/German upbringing and education'. His contribution to the cultural life of Cork was recognised in 1978 when he was made a Freeman of the City.[3]

Others promoting traditional Irish music were adamant that television needed to play its part in promoting such music. Comhaltas Ceoltóirí Éireann (the Society of Irish musicians), for example, campaigned to have regular TV programmes of that nature, disputing RTÉ's contention that

'Irish traditional entertainment is not "good television" and if used at all would have to be diluted or modernised'.[4] Brendán Breathnach, who did extraordinary work of preservation as a traditional music collector, also criticised RTÉ for how traditional music was 'dumped in the rag bag of popular entertainment'.[5]

But it continued to thrive, as did folk music, and the combination of both. By the mid 1970s, some thought the resurgence in traditional music had been 'the most enriching factor in Irish cultural identity over the last 15 years'.[6] Ciarán Mac Mathúna, another well-known broadcaster and music collector, referred to traditional music taking over the sanctuary of the pub and the widening interest in folk music reflected in the popularity of 'sessions' in O'Donoghue's pub on Merrion Row in Dublin and the popularity of Fleadhanna Cheoil (music festivals) as a 'cultural revolution'.[7] As the perceptive music journalist with *Hot Press*, Bill Graham, saw it in 1977, the folk movement of the 1970s was larger and more significant than the 1960s revival: 'The music is of a higher quality than before and the audiences more knowledgeable – as a result of which bands can no longer get away with coarsely cranking out belligerent ballads or churning out grandstanding sets of jigs and reels. Bands like the Chieftains and the Bothy Band are now competing in sales terms with Big Tom [McBride] and the Stones.'[8]

Christy Moore returned to Ireland in 1971 to record the album *Prosperous*, which led to the formation of his band Planxty; they stayed together until 1974, when Moore left to pursue a solo career that was initially something of a struggle. As he recalled, before he moved on to the concert stage, 'I performed in over a thousand kips that had the sale of liquor as the primary object and the stage was often situated in the least likely place. These kips are the places I love dearly for it's there I learned my craft and discovered the love of an audience and how to deal with any situation that might arise.' Planxty, consisting of Donal Lunny, Liam O'Flynn, Andy Ervine and Moore, recorded six albums, and performed in a variety of festivals drowned in alcohol, including the Claremorris Ham Festival in 1972 in Andy Creighton's Lounge; the festival consisted of 'a smoked leg of ham in Andy's window and eight late night bar extensions'.[9]

The Meeting Place pub in Dorset Street in Dublin was one of the venues where Moore was joined by a backing band ('a very trad and folk and hash-cake ensemble'); a folk festival was run there in 1975 which evolved into the Dublin Folk Festival, and included such talent as Clannad and

De Dannan and the Bothy Band. These were the wild years for Moore ('many of these gigs were followed by fierce sessions that often went on into the next day ... one night I was on stage 8 hours after dropping half a tab of very pure acid'). The Sherkin Island Festival in 1978 lasted for seven days and seven nights 'and it was only a one day festival'.[10]

Festivals became increasingly popular during the decade, incorporating all sorts and bound together with plenty of drink; they included such favourites as the Listowel Writers Week, the Cork International Film Festival and the Ballybunion Bachelor Festival. The Galway Races and the Dublin Horse Show were also big crowd pullers, while the robust appeal of traditional music was reflected in the popularity of the Lisdoonvarna Festival. In 1979, its contributors included the Chieftains and De Dannan, who made an original and invigorating sound through a synthesis of Kerry, Donegal and Galway music, with banjo, bouzouki, bodhrán, fiddle and mandolin. But as stipulated by traditional fiddler Frankie Gavin, they had an unusual attitude in not wanting to 'overplay oneself. Playing too often or listening too often, you get pissed off. We only want to do the odd gig here and there.'[11]

The audience of 20,000 at the Lisdoonvarna Festival was an eclectic mix also, as described by journalist Julian Vignoles in August 1979: 'There were tall, lean Europeans, blond and affluent, with children, camping gear, cameras and some with tape recorders, and of course the familiar gangs of lads in tatty denims, with sleeping bags in one hand, six pack in the other.'[12] A song about Lisdoonvarna by Christy Moore became one of his most popular and, much later, was listed in *The Penguin Book of Irish Poetry*.[13]

Like many others, Moore was enthralled by the unique talent of Luke Kelly 'who could fill a concert hall or silence a bar room' with the passion of his singing. Like Moore, he had been influenced by the revival singers in Britain and their repertoire: 'He incorporated that into the Dublin ballad singing style that he had created and introduced us to a form of singing that is heard today all over the world.'[14] Phil Coulter, who wrote some of the songs Kelly performed, saw him as someone who had a quality 'impossible to define and certainly impossible to learn'.[15] A committed socialist, Kelly railed against inhumanity and injustice. He was a member of the Dubliners, who by 1979 had spent eighteen years performing, and for some critics had become too packaged and predictable, but their impact in the early 1970s cannot be underestimated; they were all individualists bound together by 'artistic honesty'. They were also affected by the Troubles – leading member Ronnie Drew stopped singing 'rebel songs' in the 1970s, the climate deeming their Irish ballads politically incorrect. By the mid 1970s they were performing less often in Ireland and more in continental Europe 'where they could convey a clear musical expression of Ireland at a time when the country was more and more torn internally'.[16]

It was also the decade of Horslips, an Irish band whose first album enjoyed strong sales in the Irish market; they were also a huge draw as live performers. It was a 'delicate' topic as to whether the music they performed – and performed so well live – was folk or rock. As band member Barry Devlin pointed out in January 1979, this question created 'misunderstandings of our central objective and people couldn't cope with that so it was either seen as rock at a remove or folk at a remove when it was an attempt to create something indigenous and new – but essentially indigenous'.[17] They were praised as 'the only premier Irish act who live here and base their operations from Ireland'.[18]

There was little doubt, however, about the status of Rory Gallagher in the world of rock. The influential British music paper *Melody Maker* named Gallagher, a native of Donegal, the best guitarist in the world in the early 1970s.[19] As well as his Irish fan base, he had a keen following on the British and European circuits, and managed to make an impact in the US. A purist, 'unmoved by changing musical fashions', he was 'a folk type person in a rock world ... with Gallagher the music is everything. He plays rather than acts. Nor is he the slightest bit concerned with projecting an image.'[20] He excelled as an energetic live performer and live recordings of his shows, rather than studio albums, were where he made an impact commercially; notable recordings included *Rory Gallagher Irish Tour 1974* and *Stage Struck*, made during his 1979 world tour.

Talented songwriter and singer Paul Brady also made an impact with *Welcome Here Kind Stranger* appearing in 1978, while the difficult genius Van Morrison, a native of Belfast acclaimed for his albums *Astral Weeks* in 1968 and *Moondance* (1970), seemed determined to thwart the very few media people he spoke to. Donal Corvin attempted to interview him at his home in California in October 1978. He had enforced a self-imposed exile from 1974–8, then went back on the road in the US, but packed up the tour half-way through a concert in New York. Corvin asked him what his songs were about: 'It's the unknown to me,' he answered, 'I really haven't got a clue what I'm doing at all. It's completely unemotional ...

to me it's still a mystery'; he added intriguingly that he was 'interested in breaking down commercialism and brainwashing'.[21] As another music journalist had concluded in relation to Morrison's supposed promotional interviews for the *A Period of Transition* LP, 'to describe some of those as embattled is to put it mildly'.[22]

Pop music performers in Ireland in the late 1970s included: Chris de Burgh (who made quite an impact in South America and Canada because his music had 'an emotional Big Ballad South American feel'; a track from his first album became a hit in Brazil and sold 300,000 copies[23]); Dana, who won the Eurovision Song Contest in 1970; and Gilbert O'Sullivan, who by the end of the decade became the biggest-selling Irish artist of the 1970s in the UK thanks to songs including 'Clair' and 'Nothing Rhymed' – 'a highly gifted composer/lyricist ... both the musical talent and the originality of gimmick [with] his James Joyce (or Bisto Kid) image'.[24]

By 1978, 'Dublin Disco fever' had spread over Dublin along the Grand Canal 'from Leeson Street to that hallowed 1916 venue, Mount Street Bridge'; or as it was put more unkindly, 1977 was the year of 'Euro disco as the Common Market caused a musical free trade assault'.[25] The disco craze witnessed night become 'nite' accompanied by 'mirror balls, soggy chips at 2 a.m. and soggy wine'.[26] The mix of country and Irish music was also popular. Journalist Gene Kerrigan painted a memorable portrait of 'Saturday Night Fever in Drumshambo' in July 1978 as Big Tom McBride took to the stage: 'While the rest of the world was rolling with the Stones, creaming with Clapton, crooning with James Taylor or pogoing with the punks, thousands of Irish fans continued listening to Big Tom eulogising his mother [with the songs] "Gentle Mother", "Flowers for Mama", "Mama's Roses"'.[27]

Given that, by 1977, the Irish population was exceptionally young by international standards, with 50 per cent of the population under the age of twenty-six, and 41 per cent under the age of nineteen, a new initiative in the form of *Hot Press* music magazine was timely. With energy and eclecticism it oversaw the significant musical talent emerging in Ireland, and its proponents who were intent on overseas impact, included the Boomtown Rats headed by Dubliner Bob Geldof. The band was on tour in Britain in 1977 and Geldof, with deceptive false modesty, insisted 'we don't want to hype ourselves. In England it's catharsis; it's almost like starting afresh. Nobody knows who the fuck we are.' That situation was to alter dramatically as Geldof thrived, not just on the band's original sound but on his ability 'to mix it mouth-wise with the brashest of the London rock jungle'.[28] Rory Gallagher acknowledged that Geldof was 'the best PR man around', but someone who would need to match his 'supercharged energy' with 'a bit of substance'.[29] Geldof also made an impact due to his searing criticism of the oppressiveness of the clerical and political culture of the Dublin he grew up in; 'the only way for me to get noticed was by mouthing off and launching a hype thing, the like of which had never been witnessed here before'.[30]

Hot Press recorded in July 1977 that 10,000 people had attended the Macroom Mountain Dew Festival concert headed by Rory Gallagher, 'a resounding affirmation of the development of youth culture'.[31] Thin Lizzy, with their extraordinary front man Phil Lynott, who had a unique ability to communicate lyrically, developed iconic status; much of the band's first album reflected his knowledge and feeling for Dublin. He also developed a 'distinctive use of quasi-Gaelic melody lines' as seen in 'Whiskey in the Jar' (1972).[32] Together with Brush Shiels, he was the motivating force behind Skid Row, the band credited with 'kicking Irish rock music into the 1970s'.[33]

In April 1978 Bill Graham was perceptive about the potential impact of a young new band, U2, who generated attention when they won an *Evening Press* Harp Lager talent competition. Although they were still at school and their first demo session was somewhat rushed, 'U2 talk like they intend to be professionals, a primary asset in the battle for recognition ... they have the attitude to grow and evolve fast'. Four months later, Graham concluded that 'U2 are ready to pass everyone out'.[34] Some categorised U2's music as 'new wave' pop but ultimately they were to evolve into a serious rock band. By the end of 1979 they were seen as coming of age and 'boys in control' on the verge of international breakthrough, but there was no consensus as to how they should be labelled: 'They are not punk. They are not pop. They are not Glam. They are not "metal" let alone Heavy.'[35] This was a reminder that one of the interesting developments of the 1970s was what Paul Brady – another singer variously described as a folk or rock singer, or both – observed as the degree to which 'categories became blurred', as good a summation of music in 1970s Ireland as any other.[36]

But the music-buying Irish population, while embracing to a degree the new Irish sounds, also kept their attachments to the international and mainstream pop sounds; the top twenty singles sold in Ireland at the end of 1977, for example, included records by the Boomtown Rats and Joe Dolan, but they were in a minority; singles by David Soul, Rod Stewart and ABBA were selling more. In terms of albums, Fleetwood Mac, Diana Ross and Cliff Richard came before the Boomtown Rats, Brendan Shine and Thin Lizzy. In the spring of 1979, the Irish singles chart was topped by Art Garfunkel ('Bright Eyes'), Gloria Gaynor ('I Will Survive') and the Village People ('In the Navy'); Boney M were constantly in the Irish charts, while the lyrical and wholesome Dana continued to keep the Irish flag flying ('Something's Cooking in the Kitchen'). At the end of summer 1979, the Boomtown Rats song 'I Don't Like Mondays' topped the charts, with the Furey Brothers and Davey Arthur's 'The Green Fields of France' at number two.[37]

The exam hall in Trinity College Dublin was another venue for musicians, including in 1978 the Cimarons Reggae, five Jamaican-born London musicians whose set was received with a 'tumultuous response from the nearest Dublin could produce to a multiracial audience'.[38] Dublin pubs like Toners, The Baggot Inn, Morans and McGonagles were noted music venues for smaller gigs, though they had mixed success. At the end of 1978, it was suggested in *Hot Press* that the Irish scene 'isn't heartening' and that 'venues form the crux of the issue'. Punk music had taken on certain violent connotations which made publicans wary ('alcohol and punk don't mix'). Morans closed and then reopened 'timidly but now stands bereft of rock ... McGonagles has been a more than worthwhile addition fulfilling a long required need for late night rock revelry but local bands haven't thrived there.'[39]

Nonetheless, the classified advertisements section of *Hot Press* gave a good indication of the thirst for new bands and the embracing of the rock band dream and ambition. Typical examples in the summer of 1978 included: 'Any musicians interested in forming tight, funky band?'; 'Drummer and vocalist (no bores) wanted to join guitars and bass in forming energetic band into rocking and rolling'; 'Young new wave/pop group seek new drummer aged 17 or under.'[40] Bands from Northern Ireland also made an impression with 'an impressive excess of rock spirit', notably Stiff Little Fingers and the Undertones; it was suggested 'Northern rock isolation ends ... the last Derry singing star was Dana. There is no comparison.' This was regarded as something of a Northern renaissance in contrast to a previous silence enforced by violence and the 'lack of all but the most harmless night life'.[41]

The modernisation of audio equipment and recording technology also meant that there was a growing interest in high-quality sound reproduction. New BASF recording cassettes were notable in this regard, while a Hi Fi supplement in *Hot Press* in 1979 noted that 'in general equipment is expensive given our standard of living', VAT and import taxes being the main culprits.[42] More portable transistor radios began to appear, but some were still relying on cheap record players, like the one described by Pat Boran in an account of his childhood in Portlaoise in the early 1970s: 'a mono, suitcase-sized chipboard job covered with vinyl and held in place by fake gold studs'.[43]

In relation to other musical concerns, music critic Charles Acton – who from the middle of the 1950s to the 1980s reviewed over 6,000 concerts for the *Irish Times* – was a gifted polemicist. He 'campaigned unceasingly for a national concert hall and adequate Arts Council funding' (in 1974 it was announced that the Great Hall of University College Dublin at Earslfort Terrace was to become a 900-seat concert hall and the home of the RTÉ symphony orchestra at a cost of £700,000). He also continuously criticised RTÉ for what he considered to be 'a shirking of its national and institutional responsibilities to Irish artists, composers, concert-goers, and radio and television audiences'. He also greatly influenced concert-going conventions in Ireland.[44]

In his private correspondence with Garret FitzGerald, Acton mused over various matters musical, commenting in 1976 that Irish tenor Frank Patterson, 'who is pulling the divil by the tail financially', could not be blamed for 'exploiting a lode of more "popular" ore' and is 'thoroughly justified in [the] sort of records he makes'. He also singled out Bernadette Greevy ('a Brahms and Mahler singer second to none in the world'), soprano Suzanne Murphy, pianist John O'Conor ('as an interpreter of Beethoven on the one hand and of all the Northern European Classics on the other seems to me a world-class artist … he should become our first world pianist since John Field') and Mícheál O'Rourke, a Dublin pianist who moved to Paris and made his reputation performing the music of Field, as 'world class artists'.[45] He was later to suggest that by the end of the 1970s Ireland, with a multitude of choirs, festivals and concerts, was 'in a musical ferment and virtually every form and aspect of music that we have inherited, apart from those bronze-age horns and trumpets, is an ingredient in the vat.'[46]

Greevy made a big impact on audiences at home and abroad; she suggested that Irish singers were well capable of excelling in the European classical mainstream but that young Irish singers had little opportunity to gain experience because there was 'too much importation of singers for opera in particular'.[47] At the start of the decade it had been noted approvingly that the Dublin Grand Opera Society had staged five operas for its spring session and that 'the season was a boom one', with attendance averaging 84 per cent. The following year Harold Rosenthal, editor of *Opera*, expressed puzzlement at the continued success of the Wexford Opera Festival: 'I fail to discern any real shape or artistic purpose in the way the festival is planned. But then, perhaps that is the peculiar charm of Wexford, which appeals to so many of its regular visitors and which I find so baffling.' Fanny Feehan, a music critic with *Hibernia* magazine, also disputed its cultural impact, suggesting it would remain minimal in terms of lasting effect unless more was done to foster Irish opera talents.[48]

Charles Acton's survey of Irish music and musicians, published in 1978, was very positive about the 'remarkable range of international musicians' who were Irish, including flautist James Galway, violinist Geraldine O'Grady, organist Gerard Gillen and composers Brian Boydell and Seóirse Bodley ('it is characteristic that he extends the technique of a modern Irish harp by writing serious, almost avant-garde music for it'). He also suggested the real success of Irish music during this decade was evident at local level when Ireland was compared to other countries: 'Though demand and supply is as yet inchoate, the inherited musicality of the nation is such that recitals and concerts are enthusiastically supported even in small towns of between 5,000 and 15,000 which in France or Germany or Italy would be musical deserts.'[49] In this sense, perhaps the seventies had succeeded where the sixties had failed; as Fanny Feehan had suggested in *Hibernia* magazine in 1970, 'as far as music in this country is concerned the sixties were notable more for what did not happen as for what did happen'.[50]

But some events received more publicity and a higher profile than others. Feehan had identified a particularly endemic Irish disease by the early 1970s which she labelled 'Festivilitia' – but that the Festival of Modern Music, in its third year by 1971, had not succumbed. It had not had much of an impact on the public but was of a high quality: 'I regard it as a very healthy sign also that none of the phoney socialising and overdressed tomfoolery which are a feature of other cultural activities are necessary to this excellent stimulating event.'[51] This was perhaps not an assessment that could be applied to the Eurovision Song Contest, which, after Dana's victory with 'All Kinds of Everything' in 1970, presented RTÉ with something of a headache as the estimated cost of hosting it the following year, as was the winning country's duty, was between £35,000 and £50,000. For some it also prompted the rush to colour television.[52]

However vibrant Irish music was, Irish language activists were under considerable pressure in the 1970s, particularly when the decision was taken in 1973 to drop the necessity for school pupils to pass Irish in order to gain the state Leaving, Group and Intermediate Certificates. It was a move that has been characterised as representing an end to 'the most repugnant element of the revival campaign and the most damaging to the perception and status of Irish'.[53] The decision to abolish knowledge of the language as a prerequisite for entry into the civil service was also a milestone; as far as Minister for Finance Richie Ryan was concerned, 'the civil service was such a large organisation that there was room for persons with or without Irish'. But members of Conradh na Gaeilge [the Gaelic League, originally formed in 1893 to promote the spread of the language] expressed concern about the status of the language. One correspondent referred to the absurdity and 'futility' of the government's paltry lip service approach to the language in official correspondence, involving 'commencing in the Irish language, changing to the English language at a mid way stage and then reverting to the Irish language ... it makes a mockery of both the languages in question'.[54]

In 1972, an Irish language Gaeltacht radio service had been initiated, but the year after its establishment, a critic observed that 'Radio na Gaeltachta is broadcasting for an elite, for a mini elite within an elite. What service does the station provide for teenagers who want to hear pop music, housewives or local farmers or fishermen? Who is the station broadcasting for? Irish language aficionados?'[55] The Gaelic League complained in August 1974 about RTÉ's commitment to programming in the Irish language: 'Nach ligean ach 2.2 per cent de am na teilifíse le cláracha Gaeilge'[56] (Only 2.2 per cent of total television time is devoted to programmes in Irish). Between October 1975 and September 1976 Irish language television programming amounted to only 10 per cent of total home production.

There was certainly evidence of revived discourse on the position of the Irish language in Irish culture and also fresh constituencies of Irish speakers in some of the new city suburbs, but the demands for more Irish language broadcasting created tensions and a growing sense that this was a 'minority rights' issue. Those who launched a campaign for an Irish language television service in 1975 also framed their demands in the context of cultural nationalism, which created more tension and protests including the withholding of licence fees.

The notion of tokenism and an almost schizophrenic attitude to the Irish language was something that was satirised by historian John A. Murphy in his address to an American audience in 1976. He pointed out that 'the present generation speaks conventional and idiomless English – the result of the culturally levelling influence of the media and more so, perhaps, of second-level schooling'. He also took a swipe at 'the pathetic yearning for an unmistakable cultural distinctiveness' which was attested by the fact that 'Irish people abroad not infrequently speak Irish among themselves – perhaps the only time they do so – to establish the fact that they are not English'. He suggested there was widespread dissatisfaction with language teaching but that most favoured a bilingual policy: 'The brutal message would appear to be that 80 per cent of the people are benevolently willing that 4 per cent should go on speaking Irish.'[57]

Official statistics, as measured by census returns, revealed a somewhat different picture. According to the 1971 census, 789,000 people claimed a knowledge of Irish, greater than any time since 1891, and it was estimated that '30 per cent of the population have at least a moderate conversational ability in Irish'.[58] But this did not mean that they were speaking it with any degree of regularity.

The Gaelic League had developed a more urban focus in the 1960s and it had a militant element, but it was suggested that the working class still saw the organisation as 'a middle-class body and the Irish language as the language of the civil service'.[59] There was controversy and confrontation in Kerry in 1970 over the closure of an Irish language school in the heart of the Gaeltacht (Irish speaking district) at Dunquin, in West Kerry, the plan being to merge it with a school in nearby Ballyferriter, with one report suggesting the children were 'packed into buses and sent to nearby Dingle to speak English'.[60] The closure of the school generated a long-running, emotive campaign, which included in April 1971 a march from Dunquin to Dublin to protest about the government's neglect of the Gaeltacht. The Dunquin school was eventually reopened in 1973, representing a victory over the Department of Education.

In 1972 a young journalist, Charlie Bird, raised questions about a project on attitudes to the Irish language that was backed by a government grant of £90,000. There was much secrecy, it seemed, surrounding it and grievances and divisions among those involved.[61] The resultant report suggested that roughly three-quarters of the people still believed the language was essential to Irish identity 'but less than one-quarter' thought it would thrive into the twenty-first century.[62] Declan Kiberd has argued that during this period 'Irish continued to enjoy a privileged but strangely precarious position in national life. A book of poems published in the language was likely to have as many intelligent readers as a comparable volume in English, yet Irish was by common consent still in danger of disappearing as a community language within a generation.'[63]

In 1975 poet Michael Hartnett, who had extensive experience in translating and reworking poetry in Irish, as reflected in *Anatomy of a Cliché* (1968), expressed concern about the precarious position of the language: 'For Gaelic is our final sign that/ We are human, therefore not a herd'[64] – and announced that henceforth he would write only in Irish (he resumed publishing in English ten years later).

Breandán Ó hEithir, with a reputation as a sharp and witty journalist, in 1976 produced his extraordinary first novel, *Lig Sinn i gCathú*, which was unusual in being the only 'novel in Irish ever to reach the top of the national bestselling lists'. This happened partly because of the hype, his profile as a public personality and partly due 'to the rollicking narrative, which included all the ingredients of a good read – sex, politics, booze and the adventures of a loveable rogue' who in 1949 threw off the shackles of religious oppression.[65]

– TWENTY-FOUR –

ARTISTIC CREATIVITY AND CHALLENGES

New directions in art were also apparent, especially in the work of Robert Ballagh, a Dublin-born artist who had trained as an architectural draughtsman and also became involved in theatre-set design. Exhibiting in David Hendrick's Gallery in Dublin, by 1977 he was credited with a 'stunning tour de force of brash realism'. Ballagh had for some years been a trenchant critic of the private gallery system, which he maintained was 'exploitative of the artist' with an ensuing damaging impact on art itself. A dealer, he claimed, could get between half and one-third of the value of sales and the system forced the artist to 'bind himself to an elite'.[1] Some other young artists were making an impact in spite of the lack of autonomy and funding of the National College of Art, which art critic Dorothy Walker highlighted, suggesting the attitude to it was akin to treating it like a primary rather than tertiary institution.[2]

It was observed in 1975 that while Michael Farrell's 'In Memoriam' exhibition for the victims of the Dublin bombings in 1974 was powerful, 'there has been little overt reaction in the work of Irish artists to the Northern Troubles'.[3] This was an exaggeration, given the range of protest art as represented by Les Levine, Brian O'Doherty and, 'most viscerally', Robert Ballagh. A flourishing of the visual arts that had begun in the 1960s continued into the 1970s when 'relative boom time fuelled both corporate and public art programmes'. Due to the lack of a national venue for modern art, ROSC (an Irish word meaning poetry of vision), a major exhibition of international contemporary art, had been instigated in 1967; its internationally juried selections began to include Irish artists in 1977. The Douglas Hyde Gallery, to exhibit contemporary art with public funding, and named after Ireland's first president, was established in Trinity College Dublin in 1978, while international artists like Joseph Beuys, who came to Ireland for his exhibition 'A Secret Block for a Secret Person in Ireland' at the municipal gallery, sought to offer 'through his countrywide lectures and drawings a form of Utopian hope in the midst of the Troubles'. London-based Michael Craig Martin showed his conceptual sculptural works, including 'An Oak Tree' (which was actually a glass of water) at the Oliver Dowling Gallery in Dublin in the late 1970s and Barry Flanagan's conceptual sculptures were also beginning to appear; he was regarded as a significant post-modernist, as was artist Seán Scully.[4]

Sculptor Edward Delaney was also busy constructing memorials; his output was remarkable, given that he did much of the casting work himself. His son Eamon recalled of the 1970s that 'the visual arts scene and the broader arts world provided a ready made social life and the mantelpiece filled up with white card invites to galleries in the city'.[5] Painters and sculptors were interested in the style and artistic direction of their peers and bought each other's work, while the Delaneys turned making jewellery into 'a sideline cottage industry'. As viewed by art critic Aidan Dunne, Delaney had the age-old mystique of the medieval master craftsman and the sensibility of a European modernist: 'Add to this mix a concern with Irish national identity and romanticised Celtic imagery and you have something of the distinctive flavour of his rugged, Celtic, ancient-modern figures.' His well-known sculpture of Wolfe Tone, situated near Dublin city centre, was bombed in April 1971. Tone did not lose his head, however, and the event was 'treated with a curious mixture of shock-horror drama and Ealing comedy'.[6] Delaney was forthright about what he regarded as the laziness of some of his peers: 'Irish artists don't work hard enough. On the continent a 14-hour day is not abnormal for creative artists. Here too many are content with little industry and a lot of talk about problems. I make about 20 bronzes a year myself.'[7]

The contributions to *Magill* magazine by critic Bruce Arnold, who expressed himself vigorously, left little doubt as to the shortcomings of the Irish art scene, which were all too obvious, if not embarrassing. In October 1977, for example, he pointed out that

> at present, the country's only modern art gallery, the municipal gallery in Parnell Square, has no budget at all for mounting exhibitions and nobody on its staff capable of mounting them. It has no programme of exhibitions, either of foreign work or of Irish art. Virtually everything that happens within the municipal gallery has to be initiated outside it and this makes it eminently available for exercises such as ROSC. Virtually any organisation with a respectable committee and an acceptable exhibition can get hold of municipal gallery space. In Ireland, being 'respectable' and 'acceptable' has a special meaning.[8]

The following year, he railed against the 'tyranny of convention' represented by the Royal Hibernian Academy exhibition, which he depicted as 'narrow, insular and introverted'.[9] In 1979 he profiled James White, who had directed the National Gallery from 1964 to 1979, and whom Arnold characterised as 'enthusiastic, energetic, vulgar, not very knowledgeable about art, [but] he has always had his heart in the right place and backs his instinct with action'. Over the course of his stewardship, attendances at the gallery rose from 50,000 to 325,000; in the early 1970s he had maintained that the place of the gallery in national life had been curiously underwhelming and that his mission was to make it act as a 'front line in the effort to raise the quality of life'.[10]

Irish authors and fiction writers also held places in that cultural 'front line', though there was an acknowledgement that some had not always received the praise they deserved. Mary Lavin, for example, whose first collection of stories had been published in 1942 and who excelled at depicting difficult relationships, human endurance and stoicism, was profiled as a gifted, sensitive, natural writer ('a magical touch that time has not impaired' creating lives where the characters only half emerged from their backgrounds) who perhaps had not received enough critical attention because 'we dislike so much of what we see in the mirror held up to us' by her.[11]

There were also spats through the literary pages of *Hibernia* magazine on the merits of the writing of Edna O'Brien, who had left Ireland for London in 1959 and was author of, among others, the controversial *The Country Girls* (1960) and *A Pagan Place* (1970). Responding to the suggestion that 'dirty knickers writing is no substitute for genuine talent', poet Eavan Boland insisted that childhood and not sex was O'Brien's dominant theme.[12] There was fulsome praise too for other female writers including Jennifer Johnston, whose second novel *The Gates* was published in 1973; for novelist John Broderick, hers was a stunning achievement, 'compassionate, acute, full of sad beauty and sudden gay insights, with a troubling undercurrent of desperate, half-revealed violence, it is the Ireland of today'.[13] Mary Robinson was high in her praise in 1973 for Julia O'Faoláin's novel *Not in God's Image.*[14]

Others wanted to see a more robust engagement of Irish writers with contemporary controversy. In 1971 John Jordan, Irish poet and renowned literary critic, lamented the lack of a Seán O'Faoláin type cultural figure in Ireland at that time. O'Faoláin, father of Julia and a crusader for moral and intellectual freedom in previous decades and who had persistently decried the misuse of censorship, was content, it seemed, in the 1970s. He presented 'We the Irish' programmes in 1971 and 'he wrestled less with Irish conditions' that he had devoted so much to critiquing, but Catholicism continued to fascinate him; for him 'the very fact of its survival suggested worthwhile qualities'.[15]

Jordan suggested 'with two possible exceptions, the voice of the writer on public affairs is unheard in the Republic'. One of the exceptions he identified was Francis Stuart, who was sixty-nine that year and had published the autobiographical *Black List, Section H*. The previous year, the Abbey Theatre had rejected his play *Who Dares to Speak*, about the Irish War of Independence martyr Terence MacSwiney. His two Northern Ireland novels were also published in this decade, *Memorial* (1973) and *A Hole in the Head* (1977), though arguably his wartime experiences in Germany and apparent support for the Nazis remained more controversial than his literary output. The other artist singled out by Jordan was poet Austin Clark, seventy-five that year; in reaction to Ireland joining the EEC, Clarke had satirised 'Seánín Ó Loinsigh [Jack Lynch] waiting in the capitals of Europe, cap crumpled, to beg and whine for us'.[16]

John McGahern, whose novel *The Dark* (1965) had been banned and resulted in him losing him his teaching job and who subsequently moved to London, returned to live in Leitrim in 1974, on a farm near to his birthplace. He was still drawn to what he knew best; to walking up 'the narrow lane my mother loved ... the people and the language and the landscape where I had grown up were like my breathing; it would take years to gain that knowledge in a new place ... to make a living from my work turned out to be easier than I had imagined, and we didn't have to disappear into England or America, other than by choice, and we were never away very long'.[17]

It was this mastery of his home hinterland that propelled him to literary greatness. He produced *Nightlines* in 1970, *The Leavetaking* in 1975 and *The Pornographer* in 1979. As well as Leitrim, Dublin and London also featured in his writing, hinterlands that Denis Donoghue suggests were 'less suited to his gifts'.[18] But there was a sense that his writing, along with others like Benedict Kiely and Edna O'Brien, was also speaking to a younger audience about domestic matters like masturbation and exams, the death of parents and young girls determined to discover themselves and their sexuality.[19] McGahern also seemed to be adamant that his work be true to the pressures of life as they were lived; Derek Hand highlights his use of the line 'It happened this way and no other way' in *The Leavetaking*.[20]

McGahern had no interest in dealing with the Troubles in his fiction – 'seems strange and foreign to me; it doesn't engage me personally' – but other authors confronted the conflict directly and indirectly, including J. G. Farrell in *Troubles* (1970), set in 1920 and featuring the events of the War of Independence period but also mixing them with the present, as in the author's words 'exactly the same things were happening again, sometimes even in the same streets in Belfast'. At the end of the decade, in Julia O'Faoláin's *No Country for Young Men* (1979) there was further emphasis on traumatic experiences and a sense of history repeating itself. The central character, Judith Clancy, is seventy-five years old in 1979, but fixated on her experiences of 1922, 'attached' to a past event, as it interweaves with the present. In the late 1970s, Jennifer Johnston wanted to write about the Troubles but 'couldn't face them head on. So I started to write about World War I … in a way it was a metaphor of the Troubles, of how people try to keep their lives normal, their feet on the ground even though terrible things are going on around them.'[21] The narrative of Eilís Dillon's *Blood Relations* (1977) also had an explicitly historical nature while doing much, like Julia O'Faoláin, to highlight the world of women.[22]

John Banville, at the age of only twenty-seven, already had three impressive novels to his name in the early 1970s. *Birchwood* (1973), beginning with the line 'I am therefore I think', delves deep into family secrets, isolation and memory, as the character Gabriel Godkin returns to the family's dilapidated estate. Control and authority, both communal and individual, are central to this novel; 'that they are absent says much about the sense of catastrophe in the Ireland of the 1970s'.[23] Banville's *Doctor Copernicus* (1976) was regarded as a robust critique of academic claims to truth. In an interview after the book was published, he insisted 'the past doesn't exist in terms of fact; it only exists in terms of the way we look at it'.[24] There was no point, he maintained, in searching for the truth; with this book, Copernicus was seen by critics as a template for Ireland's uncomfortable position between tradition and modernity with the book demonstrating Banville's method of 'masking disorder in his aesthetic pursuit of the well made sentence' which 'becomes the keynote gesture of his art'.[25]

The censoring of Lee Dunne's *Paddy Maguire is Dead* in 1973, which was labelled obscene, even though it was more about alcoholism than sex, was regarded by fellow novelist John Broderick as an 'obscurantic and imbecilic' decision. Broderick wondered if the decision was influenced in reality by the fact that it was a cheap paperback written in the language of Dublin slums: 'What is safe for a man with money is dangerous for those who have to count their pennies.'[26] For aspiring writers, the much praised new Irish writing initiative in the *Irish Press* newspaper was regarded by its instigator David Marcus 'as a spur to scores of young writers who would otherwise have fallen silent'; in the five years to 1973 it had published 200 stories including those of Maeve Kelly and Desmond Hogan.[27] But while the revamped Arts Council provided bursaries for writers for the first time in 1975, of the overall budget for the arts in 1978 of £1.5 million, only £43,853 was spent on literature.[28]

There was also poetic talent in abundance, and one of the notable emergences was that of female poets, including Nuala Ní Dhomhnaill and Eavan Boland who were, in Declan Kiberd's view, repossessing 'energies which had informed the Irish renaissance only to be denied in the new state, energies which some connected back to Celtic ideas of womanhood'.[29] It was also a crucial decade for Seamus Heaney, the Derry-born poet who had joined the staff of Queen's University Belfast in 1966 and whose reaction to the Troubles was reflected in the collection *Wintering Out* published in 1972. John Boland, reviewing it in *Hibernia,* looked forward impatiently to his next volume 'when, instead of wintering out in the present ghastliness of the North, he may be summering in with a new renewed mastery and passion'.[30] In 1970, Ulick O'Connor had asked Heaney if the teaching career he had embarked upon would harm his poetry: 'When I teach,' he replied, 'I give away only my soft side. I keep the dangerous side for writing.'[31]

Michael Longley paints an intimate portrait of himself and Heaney around 1977 having a pint and reciting their poems to each other: 'We said these poems by heart to each other – one is looking for approval, which is a kind of stimulus, and a certain amount of jousting goes on; the subtext is "Cap that if you can!"'[32] But behind that image was a background of some tension. Heaney maintained that his generation of writers felt it was not necessary to deal directly with political issues because 'the subtleties and tolerances of their art were precisely what they had to contribute to the coarseness and intolerances of public life'. But it was not quite as straightforward as that with the Ulster poets, including Heaney, Longley, Derek Mahon and James Simmons, who had come to prominence in the 1960s. While initially, the outbreak of the Troubles may have united them in their assertions that poetry need not 'serve social commitments' and should approach violence indirectly through analogy and metaphor, the ongoing Northern crisis, and their own rivalries, made it difficult for them to maintain close relationships: 'The old sense of coherence and camaraderie would never again match the height of the Ulster Renaissance' of the 1960s. Shedding the 'Belfast group identity' was a necessary step towards autonomy.[33]

For Heaney, this involved a move to Wicklow in 1972. He felt he had passed probation and was now entering vocation as a poet. Clive James, writing in the *Observer* early in 1973, was in no doubt in relation to Heaney that 'soon people are going to start comparing him with Yeats; the packed forms, the understandable combination of clarity with argumentative density – it's all there, robust and abundant'.[34]

John Montague was another distinguished Northern poet who contributed to the contemporary debate, delivering a bleak prognosis for the future of the North ('a river of blood') in contrast to the more 'diplomatic' Heaney, 'trying to smooth ruffled feathers'. Montague found the arts scene in Cork stimulating, with young talented poets such as Michael Davitt, Nuala Ní Dhomhnaill and Theo Dorgan, 'who had a flair for aesthetic theory as well as poetry'.[35] The work of another young poet, Paul Durcan, began to appear in various publications. He highlighted the clash of generations and customs, humanised history and reflected on public life and scandal as well as ordinary people, often with a biting satire. He produced one of the most memorable poems of the decade to encapsulate tensions between a traditional and more impatient Ireland, 'Making Love Outside Áras an Uachtaráin'. It contains these concluding lines concerning an imagined confrontation between young lovers and old President de Valera:

I see him now in the heat-haze of the day
Blindly stalking us down;
And, levelling an ancient rifle, he says, 'Stop
Making love outside Aras an Uachtaráin.'[36]

Thomas Kinsella as a poet was brooding in the 1970s, but also 'loaded with wit'; a touching chronicler of domestic life and love though 'the ferocity of his invective, outrage, even hate, can be startling also' (*Butcher's Dozen* in 1972, written in response to Bloody Sunday, begins 'I went with anger at my heel'). A genuine dissident and stubbornly independent, as the 1970s progressed he grew more preoccupied with 'origin and myth'.[37] As a teenager, Colm Tóibín, later a renowned novelist, struggled with Kinsella's collection *Notes from the Land of the Dead* (1972): 'They were filled with mystery, magic, strangeness and obscurity. There was in them a sour music that pushed through the apparent towards some shimmering and unearthly clarity.' As Kinsella had seen it in the late 1960s, there was no virtue in the 'simple continuity' of a tradition; he felt compelled to 'grasp at identity for himself'.[38]

To what extent did writers in the Republic create a sense of an artistic community? Literary gatherings at the house of Monk Gibbons in Sandycove involved writers, composers and painters as he extolled the evocative prose of Brian Moore: 'Now, who today evokes a scene like Moore does?'[39] As a writer and poet the Oxford-educated Gibbon, who had served with the British army during the First World War, was prolific, and his subject matter recognised few boundaries: his output included autobiography, memoirs, biographies, travel books, and film and ballet criticism.

Heaney was often in the company of people involved in the traditional music scene, while in Donegal by the mid 1970s, with Heaney, Friel, Seamus Deane, another native of Derry and a leading academic and critic, and John Hume, there was a summer-school atmosphere. All were conscious of the Troubles over the border and there was much poetry, music and, in Heaney's words, 'the raking over of all matters of current concern, literary and political'. For others, like Nuala O'Faoláin, festivals like the Merriman Summer School provided 'a crash course in roots' and a 'visionary Ireland' that would force people to forge new links and break others while dressed in 'cheesecloth smocks', 'Long Indian skirts' and surrounded by a 'lavish amount of personality'.[40] The home of the head of Claddagh Records, Garech Browne, at Luggala in County Wicklow was also the scene of art parties with 'musicians, writers and revellers of all sorts' including artist Louis le Brocquy, sculptor Eddie Delaney and musician Paddy Maloney of the Chieftains.[41]

Heaney moved to Dublin in 1976 and he toyed with the idea of having a 'kind of literary open house one evening per week – for my own sake really, just to keep the young poet in me alive ... [Mine was a] dilemma that many people in the North were then experiencing very actively, stretched as they often were between the impulse to maintain political solidarity and their experience of a spiritual condition of complete solitude.'[42]

The question of 'grasping' for identity that preoccupied Kinsella was a troublesome one for many. Seamus Deane suggested in 1979 that 'there is no emergent, systematic and organic reformulation, whether of Irish tradition, Irish dilemmas or Irish problems' which Terence Brown has argued was an underestimation of 'the significance of much activity in various humanistic fields of study in the 1960s and 1970s'.[43] What exactly constituted 'Irish Studies' was also contested. Also in 1979, Declan Kiberd, who began lecturing in UCD that year, lamented that academic English departments were not embracing Gaelic experts, while Irish language departments continued to frown on literary criticism; he saw the need to 'take both Anglo-Irish and Gaelic literature out of quarantine and reassess each writer in the context of the culture of our whole island, its politics and history; its folklore and geography'.[44] John Banville maintained that 'we are inevitably an adjunct of English literature'.[45]

A lively forum was provided for exchange of views in this regard and others in the journal the *Crane Bag*. Much physical and mental effort went into the writing and publication of this and other periodicals, from people such as philosopher Richard Kearney, who studied under the direction of French philosopher Paul Ricoeur, and Mark Hederman, the Benedictine monk, writer and philosopher of education. Both discovered that puncturing the myths about Irish identity, or trying to occupy a critical position between the demands of politics and art, could be an exhaustive endeavour. The extent of a distinctive Irish soul, mind and race was one of their concerns, and one anchored to conceptions of national identity debated and challenged by Irish intellectuals since the early twentieth century, but in the late 1970s it was still a courageous debate, if at the same time elitist and incestuous.

Ultimately, it was about making an important public intervention in the politics of the Northern conflict and in attempting to decide whether it was better, to paraphrase Brecht as Seamus Deane did in taking issue with other contributors, to build on the good old days or the bad new ones.[46]

Meanwhile, interventions in the politics of the arts and its role for a new generation were encouraged by Colm O Briain, as director of the Arts Council. The council's report on the place of the arts in Irish education, written by its education officer Ciarán Benson, was published in 1979. It was acclaimed by many. Benson's report argued that there was a responsibility to plan seriously 'for a greater understanding and development of Ireland's artistic heritage ... The neglect of the arts in Irish education has meant that whole generations have lost the opportunity both of learning about their own artistic history and of acquiring the skills necessary for building upon it.'[47] The report was castigated, however, by Bruce Arnold as 'superficial, imprecise and filled from end to end with clichés'.[48] None of its recommendations were implemented.

– TWENTY-FIVE –

EXPANDING THE BROADCASTING HORIZONS

Broadcasting underwent significant expansion during the decade and had to endure considerable controversy. In 1971, RTÉ television coverage, in existence since 1961, still only extended to 88 per cent of urban areas and just 62 per cent of rural areas. By 1979 it was estimated that 90 per cent of all Irish homes had televisions.[1] Censorship was an issue that took on a meaning beyond the traditional confines of sexual morality due to the Troubles – film-maker Bob Quinn referred to section 31 as 'the single most destructive imposition on RTÉ in its history'.[2]

Coverage of the Troubles (see Part II) was not only contentious, but very costly. It was pointed out by the RTÉ Authority early in 1970 that its financial position had worsened owing to the cost of 'the exceptional coverage which has had to be given to events in the six counties' and there had been no television licence fee increases between 1963 and 1968. RTÉ found itself making the case for a licence fee increase and insisted that, as it stood, the fee was 'virtually the lowest in Western Europe', but that there was also a need for 'a major drive against defaulters'. As the Minister for Posts and Telegraphs, Gerry Collins, observed, 'If RTÉ is even to try and compete with the wealthy British services it is unrealistic to oppose reasonable increases in licence fees,' which were duly granted. Licences were available free to 'certain categories' of the elderly and 'veterans of the War of Independence'.[3]

In August 1973 it was pointed out that new RTÉ services, including Radio na Gaeltachta, had been undertaken with only marginal staff additions and it was contended that 'colour television sets may be considered at present a luxury item and those who can afford a colour set should also be able to pay a substantially higher licence fee for it'. Although £18 was desired, £15 was agreed.[4] RTÉ's finances were a constant headache; in 1974 it estimated a deficit of £2,355,000 over the two-year period March 1974 to March 1976 (55 per cent of expenditure went on salaries); an increase in the licence fee was regarded as urgent due to a financial situation that was 'deteriorating rapidly'.[5]

Early in the decade the Fianna Fáil government had a somewhat fraught relationship with RTÉ. Gerry Collins wrote to Lynch in May 1971 that the RTÉ Authority chairman, Dónall Ó Móráin 'finds my attitude illiberal',[6] while Erskine Childers wrote to Lynch in March 1970: 'Todd Andrews [a War of Independence veteran and senior public servant who had been appointed chairman of the RTÉ Authority in 1966] tells me he is getting the current affairs programme under control ... the recent programmes I have seen are more constructive or balanced. We have not arranged for monitoring for a month ... the controversial programmes, including the balanced programmes, occupy 130 minutes or so a week.'[7] That Childers was Minister for Health when he wrote this gives some idea of the sense of ownership the government had. In June 1971 Gerry Collins complained to Jack Lynch that Conor Cruise O'Brien, as a serving politician, was appearing in a history series with writer Seán O'Faoláin and historian Owen Dudley Edwards; Lynch agreed this was 'inappropriate'.[8]

In August 1972, Labour Party senator Michael D. Higgins had charged that Fianna Fáil 'have succeeded with continuing insidious pressure in making a shambles of our national television'.[9] When Jack White, the assistant controller of programmes, proposed a new politics programme to begin in 1973, which would involve a live studio audience asking questions of the panel, Lynch informed David Andrews, the chief whip of Fianna Fáil, that, while he had no objection to the proposed format, 'I feel that steps should be taken to ensure that neither the questions submitted to the panel nor the political composition of the studio audiences are loaded against the government'.[10] After the coalition government took up office in 1973 it wanted to avoid 'participation in panel discussions' but by October 1973 felt that RTÉ 'apart from bias in Northern coverage has been fairly satisfactory'.[11] By the end of the coalition's term of office, however, it was claimed in *Magill* magazine that RTÉ management had been 'intellectually overawed by Conor Cruise O'Brien'.[12]

Throughout the decade there were frequent references to the political climate in RTÉ; its personnel issues and accusations that it isolated individuals of independent mind. It was believed that in a more favourable political climate Muiris Mac Conghail, a current affairs producer and editor who moved to the Government Information Service before returning to RTÉ, would have reached the top position in RTÉ instead of being, in the opinion of many, 'the best Director General RTÉ never had'.[13] It was contended in 1976 that the level of political control over RTÉ was 'far more pervasive today than at any time since the station was established'.[14] In 1977 Neil Jordan, writer and future film director, maintained in relation to Conor Cruise O'Brien: 'RTÉ has been even more completely muzzled than ever before under a man, who, while he might be a lousy playwright, seemed once to be a logical thinker and was an excellent historian. It is not amusing to have to turn to ITV's News at 10 to find out what's happening in Ireland.'[15] Journalist Conor Brady was employed by RTÉ in 1975 and he found it 'a slow-moving organisation ... the grip of government was tight and executives were cautious. They had to be.'[16]

A sense of the politicians reasserting control over television had been apparent in the aftermath of a programme on illegal moneylending by the *Seven Days* current affairs programme. Broadcast in November 1969, it led to a tribunal of inquiry that generated a conflict of evidence between Gardaí and RTÉ, and Janet Moody of the programme's research team refused to reveal the sources of her information. The report was delivered in August 1970 and contained a damning indictment: 'Proper care was not taken in the planning, preparation, arrangement, production and presentation of the programme to provide viewers with an authentic and objective picture. It appears that the *Seven Days* team through hearsay evidence got a very colourful impression of the scale of illegal moneylending and of the supposed violent means associated with it. The studio commentary was biased towards the sensational.' The tribunal estimated the number of moneylenders at less than one hundred; the Gardaí estimated there were thirty and the programme maintained there were five hundred. The tribunal cost an estimated £31,000, according to a memorandum from the Department of Posts and Telegraphs. But the *Irish Press* suggested the true cost when all factors were taken into account – two High Court judges and the president of the District Court, sitting for fifty-one days, hearing a total of 141 witnesses, eight of them in camera – was £200,000. This was regarded by a contributor to the *Irish Times* as 'a blind shot in the dark' in terms of estimation[17] – though subsequent estimations went beyond that, citing a figure of £250,000.[18]

The tribunal had a significant impact on many, and on the careers of several individuals, including Bill O'Herlihy. He had worked on *Seven Days* and gave evidence at the tribunal for five days as, in his description, a 'pawn' in a political game. His career in current affairs was swiftly ended, before he became a much admired sports programme anchor.[19] The tribunal fitted into a wider climate of confusion, fear, clash of generations and occasional hysteria that was encapsulated in a letter Fianna Fáil TD Ben Briscoe sent to Lynch at the end of August 1970. Having read the report, he believed the *Seven Days* team 'have abused the responsibility entrusted them'. Not only that, but 'I feel democracy as we know it, is being threatened on all sides today and is endangered particularly when a centre for the dissemination of mass information is handed over to a group of young people who have no regard for that trust. I take this view particularly because of the defiant manner in which the RTÉ reply was made to the Tribunal's findings.'[20]

As recalled by Sheamus Smith, who worked on the *Seven Days* programme: 'Media coverage of the money lending tribunal frequently referred to the notorious illegal money lender "Golly" Green and the name captured the public's imagination. It was not long before a horse named Golly Green was running on Irish racecourses.' The real disappointment from the perspective of those who worked on the programme was that the tribunal report did not refer to the social evils of money lending. Smith also maintained that the programme in its techniques was ahead of its time: 'the hidden camera techniques instigated ... for the programme are commonplace in modern investigative journalism'.[21] Maurice Gorham, the former director of Radio Éireann, wrote privately to John Irvine, one of the key architects of the Irish television service, about what he regarded as a ridiculous spectacle: 'A whole pack of Senior Counsel, with the benevolent encouragement of the chairman, harrying reporters and producers day after day, labouring the ethics of hidden microphones and naming names, without any regard to the terms of reference, which heaven knows were searching enough; and all for no reason of public interest, as everybody knows.'[22]

Hibernia magazine depicted the tribunal as an expensive, wasteful and cumbersome method of public inquiry and suggested that it would have been a lot more helpful to direct the resources of the state against moneylending 'rather than against the fallible method of the exposé itself'.[23] Other critics of shows the *Seven Days* team produced, including an item on contraceptives – the profile of Dr Patrick Leahy, from the Ballyfermot Health Clinic, was greatly enhanced by his appearances on the programme – referred to 'alleged left-wing intellectuals propagating Greenwich Village morality'.[24]

Gay Byrne's Saturday night television show, *The Late Late Show*, which had begun in 1962, remained hugely popular, though some critics felt that after some of the controversial programmes of the 1960s tackling previously taboo subjects, by the end of the 1970s 'the banal dominates the controversial ... mostly it doodles along'. In the words of Adrian Cronin, RTÉ's head of light entertainment, there was 'very little new ground to break'. As Gene Kerrigan characterised it, the show was 'interesting, amusing, boring and insipid and still drawing the crowds', with Gay Byrne having started as 'the ringmaster', now 'the main event, the GB phenomenon, a mixture of reputation, ego and talent', not to mention conservativeness and 'anti republican, anti-trade union, conservative on law and order'. He won his ninth Jacobs Award in 1978 and responded: 'I think we've reached a plateau and the show just rolls along.'[25]

Another popular weekly show was *The Riordans*, set in the fictional Leestown (it ran from 1965 to 1979). It also established a precedent, subsequently mirrored internationally, of filming on location, using a real church, pub and farm. In 1975 one plot involved a main character falling off a ladder and being badly injured: 'Thousands of cards and 150 lots of flowers were sent to a Dublin hospital, who asked RTÉ to announce on a news bulletin that there was no such person as Mr Riordan as their switchboard was jammed with calls.'[26] It dealt with 'countless taboo subjects, helping to reshape Irish attitudes' and its appeal was copperfastened by the 'warmly humorous' writing of Wesley Burrowes.[27] But there was also criticism of the 'paucity of drama' on RTÉ, and sometimes the sloppiness of the drama that was aired.

Notwithstanding the quality of its current affairs coverage – 'in the circumstances our broadcasters are wonderfully good' and programmes like *Seven Days* benefited from the likes of Muiris Mac Conghail who was 'a good combination; he was a genuine intellectual with great ideas and incisive editorial skills'[28] – there were acerbic remarks about the overall standard of RTÉ's television output from Hugh Leonard when he was television critic of *Hibernia* in the early 1970s: 'If RTÉ were to be metamorphisised [sic] into a single human shape, that person would be a slouching corner boy who now and again makes a literate remark out of the corner of his poor mouth. Money may provide the wretch with clothes, but it will not, of itself, cure either his laziness or his ignorance ... It is ironic that the nature of a changing Ireland can be glimpsed in most TV commercials but hardly at all in the programmes they interrupt.'[29] This may have been reflected in the viewing preferences for those who were watching in multichannel houses on weekdays between 6 p.m. and 11.15 p.m. In May 1970, 65 per cent watched RTÉ in such houses at those times; by May 1972 the figure had dropped to 48 per cent.[30] By the autumn of 1973, Hugh Leonard had had enough of watching television and finished his two-year stint reviewing it for *Hibernia*: 'All-in-all the effect of watching RTÉ for nearly two years has been to cure me, not just of writing about television, but of writing for it.'[31]

What was on offer for viewers as part of a typical schedule? At the end of the night there was 'a predominantly Catholic five minute up lift chat' called *Outlook*, usually by a middle-aged rural priest, with the set comprising a chair and a table. There was no script: 'Christ's servants do not need notes and can improvise at will'. That description formed part of the assessment of a wry contributor to the *Crane Bag*, Bruce Merry, who gave his judgement of typical television fare on a night in November 1976: 'After the news comes a ten second weather flash: the whole map of Ireland was presented with the words RAINY and DRIZZLE in bold capital letters placed across an upper and lower level of the country.' There were advertisements for toothpaste, crackers, Maltesers, Bovril and Odlum Oats, Sanatogen vitamin tablets, Polaroid instant cameras, Calvita cheese, club ginger ale and Aspro for headache relief, Birds Trifle, Old Spice and Timex watches.

The advertisements made it clear that 'the bath, basin and bedroom are essentially female territory', with the products 'aimed at the middle-class fertile Irish family ... if you marry, then you will always be 34, you will always have two or three adorable cuddly little children who will always hunger for fresh rustic foods, hot soup, nourishing cheese and be clad in warm Irish knitwear (Tivoli, Aran, Glen Abbey etc.)'. But there were also advertisements on national television that were particularly localised:

> Next we are informed that Des Johnson is manager of Phibsboro First National at 357 North Circular Road. A card is shown of the

> bank's name with a mug shot of the manager himself at the left hand corner in miniature. This is a type of commercial in which Irish TV leads the world. Nor was it the first such gem of information from the world of Irish high finance with which the viewer was regaled on this Saturday evening. Earlier, we had been told the name of Terenure's First National manager in Terenure's Road South. He was a contented looking gentleman in a red shirt. Later on, we were to learn that Harry Barry was manager of Thurles First National. In the similar 'name and pedigree' manner, another advert would tell us that Margaret Quinn, 'teacher of domestic science' is very concerned about her own children's diet. Naturally she chooses Blue Band margarine – It's made with natural oils.[32]

But this critic also had a serious point to address; the lack of a tradition in Ireland of informed television criticism and the newspaper coverage of programmes and weekly summaries that were 'totally lacking in speculative self-analysis' and 'far too often the latest comment on a book or an economic measure or a political decision is handed over to the Dublin university lecturer whose office is two miles north or one mile south of RTÉ's studios in Donnybrook'.[33]

But the template for public service broadcasting that had been established in the 1960s endured and was often impressive. Undue attention on what was censored prevents enough focus on what was created, and creative forces were strong overall. *Féach* (Look) a provocative current affairs programme, was refreshing and courageous in its irreverence and challenging of sacred cows and brought to the fore, among others, Eoghan Harris and Proinsias Mac Aonghusa early in the decade. At a later stage, Muiris Mac Conghail as controller of programmes did not want the moral purists and censors to win; there was, he believed 'a high anti-porn and slightly hysterical note' in the public controversy over *The Spike*, a series set in working-class Dublin, which was axed in 1978.[34]

A survey conducted by Irish TAM Ltd in November 1978 showed that 715,000 private householders in the state (87 per cent) had TV sets, compared to 685,000 (85 per cent) in November 1977, and there had been an increase from 142,000 to 188,000 colour licences. The average adult watched RTÉ for two hours during the main evening period, with viewing of RTÉ accounting for 73 per cent of all TV watched during this period. The growing news demands of radio and television witnessed two senior executives assigned to these areas while advertising for the year 'remained buoyant' and 'the biggest TV undertaking of RTÉ Sport was the presentation of the world soccer cup from Argentina'. (RTÉ went on to excel in its sports coverage.) Home produced television programming had increased significantly; it stood at 44 per cent of total broadcast hours at the end of 1978.[35]

Reservations had been expressed in the early 1970s about the demands of a pressure group from Cork city in 1972 heading a campaign for multichannel television. It 'led the charge for total access to British channels' and wanted the same access to channels as Dublin viewers.[36] In responding to this group, Gerry Collins suggested that aside from the cost of such ventures, it was questionable whether it was 'in the national interest to pick up and rebroadcast to the whole country the programmes of another country with different background, different interests and very different cultural values in many respects'.[37] The tensions in this regard endured throughout the decade. A survey commissioned by RTÉ and the Department of Posts and Telegraphs in 1975 indicated that 62 per cent of respondents wanted to see a second RTÉ channel, but many others wanted 'open broadcasting' which would give BBC to single-channel areas. The view was also expressed that in single-channel areas, programmes were 'too Dublin orientated' and not 'racy of the soil'.[38]

During 1977 and 1978, Jack Lynch received numerous pleas from Cork to make BBC available, as promised in Fianna Fáil's election manifesto in 1977: 'Well, Jack boy, if you are the Cork man you profess to be you will do right by us and give us the same as Dublin.' Others saw it as necessary to affirm their patriotic credentials before demanding that they be in a position to embrace two cultures: 'I love Irish music and Irish culture. I attend Irish classes. But my wife and myself like English plays and thrillers and English musical shows on TV. We are sincere when we ask for permission to get BBC. That's not much to ask.'[39] By 1978, the need for a new second national television and radio channel was recognised and its delivery was the responsibility of the new director general, George Waters. He concluded that it was not British television that most people wanted, what they required 'was choice'.

The second station was duly launched as RTÉ 2 in November 1978. Jack White felt the challenge facing those promoting the new station was 'to create a new channel out of a production plant already designed to deliver at top pressure to meet the needs of RTÉ 1'. It revived 'worries about cultural domination' and was a reminder of 'unsolved problems on our plate – among them our service to Irish speakers, our service to education and our service to minorities overall'. Settling the relationship between the two channels involved much experimentation, audience research and rebranding.[40]

Terry Wogan was a guest at the launch of RTÉ 2. One of Britain's best-known broadcasters whose career took off in the 1970s, he was a native of Limerick and in the early part of the decade had been working in Irish radio and commuting to the BBC. This could be difficult, given the political climate: 'The seventies in particular were not a great time to have an Irish accent in Britain ... at times, atrocities perpetrated in Britain in the name of my country made it very difficult to open the microphone and address the British public in a cheery Irish voice.' But it did not remotely affect his popularity – as well as his radio show's success on BBC Radio 2, the star attraction of BBC TV's Christmas 1979 was *Blankety Blank* and it topped the season's ratings for that year. Wogan was even approached by a fan to 'thank you for what you have done for the Irish in Britain during the Troubles'. What was the essence of his success? According to one wry press comment: 'He is not good looking, but he looks as if he hopes to be one day, and it is this ability to keep it going in the face of almost continuous small failure, which helps him to flourish.'[41]

By 1978, 779,000 houses (95 per cent) had at least one radio of which 205,000 (26 per cent) had more than one, and 176,000 (23 per cent) had car radios. There was also considerable emphasis placed on programmes from regional centres. It had been suggested in 1973 that the dilemma for Irish radio was the difficulty of striking a balance; it was too small a country to ignore provincial issues but too large to devote too much time to it.[42] There was a strong demand by the end of the 1970s for local radio services with promises of an independent local radio authority to grant licences and John E. Nolan, the founding director of Eire Broadcasting Corporation, bombarded politicians with publications on the case for local radio.[43] National radio hours ran from 7.30 a.m. to 11.45 p.m. before being extended in 1978, as were the Cork and Shannon services: 'The average adult listened to RTÉ radio for two hours a day. 63 per cent of adults listened to RTÉ radio at some time each day.' By 1978, *The Gay Byrne Hour* on RTÉ radio had a listenership of 600,000.

The dilemmas about radio broadcasting were also generational. As was noted by the Department of Posts and Telegraphs in May 1978, RTÉ had informed it that 'there is a large and increasing group of younger people whose tastes in radio programming cannot be fully met in a single channel service'. This was deemed to be a particular problem given that 'some 50 per cent of the population is now under the age of 25'. There was, perhaps inevitably as a result, a threat to RTÉ's advertisement income by pirate radio stations, particularly in Dublin. In relation to the control of pirate stations, the Attorney General had advised that it would be 'imprudent' to bring in prosecution provisions alone by legislation 'because a prosecution brought under such provisions would inevitably lead to a challenge to the constitutionality of the RTÉ monopoly situation and such a challenge would be likely to be successful since it would be well nigh impossible to show that public order or morality and the authority if the state requires monopoly rather than any other form of regulation or control'.

There was considerable disagreement between the Department of the Taoiseach and the Department of Posts and Telegraphs on this issue. As far as Richard Stokes in the Department of the Taoiseach was concerned, a second RTÉ channel for pop music was not needed as it should be left to the local stations to provide such fare and they were already self-financing: 'There is no reason whatsoever why the taxpayer should be burdened with the costs of providing pop music for the general public – especially when there is an alternative, such as exists at present which is entirely self-financing.' He also felt Posts and Telegraphs was being 'too emotive' about what competition might do, but it got its way with the authorisation for a second station.[44]

In *Magill* in February 1978, Gene Kerrigan argued that with the exception of Pat Kenny's *Nightbus* on RTÉ radio, RTÉ was 'bereft' of programmes presented 'by the young, for the young'. Kenny, 'a graduate engineer' with a 'disciplined mind' went on to have further success with another show, *Day by Day*, which foreshadowed a confessional approach that would continue to have an impact in subsequent decades. It was a programme whose basic format was 'to take almost any subject of interest to listeners and throw some light into its darker corners. The mailbag is heavy – over 200 letters in the first five weeks alone – and includes some fairly poignant letters. One of them followed the abortion programme and came from a woman who had an abortion 30 years ago and never, until the programme, told a soul.'[45]

But the failure to cater more broadly for a younger audience explained the popularity of Dublin's pirate stations; the founders of one such station, Radio Melinda, were in Court in February 1973 for running a radio station from a cellar in Dublin's north inner city and were fined £2, hardly a deterrent.[46] Radio Dublin, led by Eamon Cooke and broadcast from a house in Inchicore, claimed to have 30 per cent of the radio audience in the Dublin area. It was raided by the Department of Posts and Telegraphs in January 1978, when it had an estimated listenership of 100,000.[47]

Young working-class Dublin was particularly keen; Cooke's 'technical prowess' had resulted in 80 per cent of regular listeners being in the 16–30 age group and he gave them exactly what they wanted: 'These were interested solely in music and requests. They were not interested in discussions, news or current affairs ... nearly every factory with female workers in Dublin piped in Radio Dublin on a daily basis.' Following the P&T raid, 10,000 people protested at a rally on O'Connell Street; most of Cooke's staff went to a new pirate station, Big D.[48] More worryingly, there were allegations that Cooke had molested children at his home; it was deemed puzzling how Cooke 'could have enjoyed the privacy in his tiny home, thronged with Radio Dublin employees and fans throughout the day and most of the night to engage in such activities', but that's precisely what he was doing. In 2003 he was convicted on thirty-three counts of sexual assault on four girls on dates between May 1974 and January 1989 at the Central Criminal Court and jailed for ten years All of the girls were under fifteen years of age at the time and some were as young as six years old when the abuse began.[49]

RTÉ Radio 2 began broadcasting in May 1979. In the run-up to its launch, an *Irish Times* journalist suggested that 'there may be exciting times ahead. On the other hand, there may be, once the first novelty has worn thin, merely twice as much boredom'.[50] Despite this new initiative, there were still numerous pirate stations operating in Dublin alone; as media historian Chris Morash has pointed out, a succession of them were small concerns, sending out signals from back bedrooms, but many 'faded like so many fireworks'.[51] *Hot Press* was withering in its sarcasm about the patronising attitude of some who entered the debate about a second station; as Niall Stokes saw it, RTÉ had no policy in relation to rock music ('they've paid sweet damn all attention to the needs of the rock audience'). *Hot Press* readers, it was maintained, did not want to hear bad popular radio but alternatives: 'Speaking on RTÉ radio, Professor John A Murphy [historian and independent senator] allowed that he ... had danced the hokey pokey in his youth – a clumsy effort at identifying with the mass radio-listening public.'[52]

The status of women in broadcasting and journalism was also a vexed one, and undergoing some serious change. In the early 1970s, female broadcasters continued to be confined mainly to features, drama, news reading and presentation. The first woman journalist to cover 'hard' news was Olivia O'Leary, who was appointed to RTÉ radio's news features in 1972: 'They were not often heard in areas where decisions affecting people's lives were being made: politics, current affairs, and the world of work, nor in areas where the decision-makers were spending a good deal of their leisure time: the world of sport.' Indeed, as late as 1979, when Caroline Murphy was appointed as RTÉ radio's first sports reporter, a journalist in the *RTÉ Guide* remarked that it would take some time before people could get used to the idea of a female voice in sports programmes.[53]

But current affairs broadcasting, coming out of the radio programmes division, which was a separate entity from the news division, began to use more women presenters in the early 1970s, including Doireann Ní Bhríain, who presented a weekly current affairs programme in Irish in the mid 1970s. *The Gay Byrne Show*, which began in 1973, also began to cover a lot of topics relevant to women, and it had a large female listenership: 'It could be said that the ground was being prepared for the advent of the more brash, self-confident and sometimes openly proselytising *Women Today* programme' which began broadcasting in 1979. This represented the culmination of various attempts, including programmes to mark International Women's Year in 1975, 'to examine assumptions about women's role in society in a thoughtful and provocative way'.

Producers Clare Duignan and Betty Purcell, reporter, Hilary Orpen, researcher Patrick Farrelly and presenter Marian Finucane were the pioneering team who launched *Women Today*:

> Here at last was the reflection on radio of the clamour for change being heard all over Ireland, and elsewhere ... It took on, head first, some of the basic women's rights issues of the day ... Politics, education, social justice, employment and unemployment, health, sexuality, sport, the arts – they were all on the agenda, and all examined from a woman's perspective. To some listeners, the very idea of discussing anything to do with sex on the radio was anathema, and they made their voices heard. To others, those who wanted and needed to hear sexual matters

> talked about, and in many cases, explained, it was a liberation and an education, not to mention a solace. *Women Today* encouraged women to talk, and they did.[54]

In 1979, the RTÉ Authority established a working party on women in broadcasting which revealed that only 9 per cent of its radio producers, 16 per cent of its television producers and 15 per cent of its journalists were women. It noted 'a lone Martian orbiting the earth, who happened to tune in to Irish radio or television, might well conclude that humankind is divided into two sexes in a proportion of six to one'.[55]

– TWENTY-SIX –

SCREENING AND REPORTING IRELAND

The Irish remained keen cinemagoers; there were just over 200 cinemas in the twenty-six counties and their gross receipts were in excess of £7 million a year by 1973.[1] But the quest to develop an indigenous film industry had become a long and frustrating saga. In August 1969 the government had approved the general scheme of a bill to implement the recommendations contained in a report of a committee on the film industry. It recommended the establishment of a film board that could make or guarantee a loan up to a maximum value of £10,000 to cover pre-production costs of an Irish film feature, or £50,000 towards the full cost of such a film. It was estimated by the spring of 1970 that as several new film production companies had been set up in recent years and 'because of the steady market available in RTÉ, a sound basis for expansion of a native film industry has already been laid'.

In October 1970, when opening the new Adelphi cinema at Middle Abbey Street in Dublin city, Jack Lynch suggested 'there has been a more broad minded approach to the type of adult film on view'. He contended the aims of the new Film Industry Bill were 'not extravagant' but would provide 'limited resources' to 'mainly provide for encouragement, advice and financial assistance to those interested in promoting the industry here', a sector that should provide for 'the projection abroad of a true image of Ireland and the Irish way of life and traditions'.[2] That same year, film-maker Louis Marcus warned that, before the big films, it would be necessary to have 'a regular foundation of regular short film production'. He and others protested in the summer of 1972 at the action of the Industrial Development Authority 'in importing a British company and a New York director to make a promotional film of a kind that we have been making successfully for many years'.[3] Marcus excelled at making documentary films; evidenced by the success of his film *Páistí ag Obair* (children at work), filmed in three Dublin Montessori schools, which was nominated for an Academy Award in 1974, and *Conquest of Light*, a film on the making of Waterford Glass, nominated for an Oscar in 1976.

In June 1972, in relation to the Film Industry Bill, Noel Coade complained about a lack of movement and the fact that the bill, mooted in 1969, 'has been on the stocks for some considerable time now. During the last 12 months I could have arranged at least three films for shooting in Ireland and indeed I am currently involved in preparing two for shooting in the coming months, but almost all foreign producers are asking continuously about our proposed legislation.'[4] They remained asking: ten years after the bill was first conceived, Ireland, in the sole European company of Luxembourg, still did not have a national feature film industry and was the only European country without a national film archive.

Draft legislation proposed by the Department of Industry and Commerce in 1979 'completely ignored' a submission made by the Arts Council, even though an act of 1973 had added film to the list of specified fine arts in which the council would have a function. As pointed out by Richard Stokes, the council had also introduced a film script award, which had led to the production of two 'much acclaimed' short films, *Poitín* by Bob Quinn and *Exposure* by Kieran Hickey, one of the few film-makers of his era to formally study film. Quinn, regarded by some as 'a self-styled maverick',[5] had worked in RTÉ and in 1969 had challenged the station, or the 'Factory' as he termed it, which had become a 'bloated and swelling corpse' feeding 'an increasing number of parasites'. Quinn's insults were compounded by criticisms from the head of light entertainment at RTÉ, Lelia Doolan, about RTÉ management's 'hypocrisy, lack of candour, lack of trust'. Both resigned, along with producer Jack Dowling; the three then published *Sit Down and Be Counted*, a critique of the excessive influence of commercial criteria and ratings in influencing television programme content.[6] Quinn and Doolan went on to have distinguished careers as impressive independent film producers.

Sheamus Smith had been appointed managing director of Ardmore

Studios – which had been originally opened as Ireland's first film studio in 1958 and was acquired by the state in 1973 – by Justin Keating, Minister for Industry and Commerce. He sent proposals to the government in 1976 having travelled to Australia, Sweden and Denmark to learn about tax incentives in film production, but the proposals were not implemented until twenty years later. He also went on a promotional trip to Hollywood, but the government did not provide capital. When *The Last Remake of Beau Geste* was filmed with Peter Ustinov and Marty Feldman, Keating hosted a private dinner in Sachs Hotel; Smith recalled that 'a few days later I received a telephone call from the minister's private secretary. He told me the bill for dinner had exceeded the minister's budget and asked for our help in paying it.'[7]

A proposal to film *Equus*, which was eventually made in Canada and was a huge success with three Oscar nominations, was cancelled after the killing of Britain's ambassador to Ireland Christopher Ewart-Biggs. In 1976 the film *Un Taxi Mauve* (lambasted by Keating as 'a bad film') was made at the studios and Jack Lynch visited the set and chatted with Peter Ustinov. (He cancelled his planned meetings in Leinster House later that day due to whiskey consumption.) The studio lost money on the film (a gala world premiere at the Metropole cinema included a feast of Dublin Bay prawns, suckling pig, roast pheasant, French wines and brandies), but it was a success in France and regarded as good for tourism.[8]

But there was still a need for a film board and a national film studio. The Department of Industry and Commerce, Richard Stokes suggested in 1979, 'appear to go along with the popular misconception that, with the purchase of Ardmore, the state had taken a big step towards creating an Irish film industry. Since acquisition of studios in 1973, £2 million has been invested, but it's losing money.' He elaborated on the 'pointlessness of diverting state aid to the maintenance of studio facilities which belonged to the Hollywood era'. His overall assessment was scathing about the degree to which the problems identified had been

> compounded by the public relations strategy of Ardmore who have glamorised their loss making activities by parading a few film stars in press and television to give the impression of a thriving industry. The recent case of *Taxi Mauve* illustrates this: the status of this film – Peter Ustinov, Charlotte Rampling and others were used by the studios in a major PR job on *The Late Late Show* and elsewhere – but

> there was no assessment of the losses to the studios including probably the £250,000 that they invested in the film itself as an added inducement to have their studios used. In addition, the production company have, apparently, left a trail of debts to Irish workers and suppliers ... more important than this, perhaps, is the fact that these film producers leave little behind in the way of accumulated expertise that might go towards the making of a native industry. The Irish employees in such films tend to be given the more menial jobs while more skilled posts of camera men, assistant directors, lighting directors, sound technicians are filled by imported personnel. A considerable amount of the £2.1 million invested by the state so far has been spent in unjustifiable capital development – the creation of luxury dressing rooms, over equipping the studios, refurbishing Ardmore House at a cost of £100,000 to provide offices which have not so far been needed.

It was quite clear, he concluded, that there was no national film industry; what was available in Ireland was literary and visual creativity but no institutional framework. Too many 'half hearted' efforts had been made in this regard and 'the gestation period has been long and painful'. It was not enough 'to tout for international film business for a white elephant studio'.[9]

That same year, film-maker John Boorman, who had settled in Wicklow, and chaired the National Film Studios of Ireland, was also trenchant, pointing out that a production fund had been promised that would finance low-budget Irish films, as had incentives that would attract foreign producers. In 1977 *The Great Train Robbery* had been made on location in Ardmore, creating a loss of £470,556. Two years later,

> Regretfully, indeed tragically, the legislation necessary to set up this production has still not been presented to the Dáil ... the studio and its equipment represents a valuable base for such an industry but unless we are making films it becomes merely a factory without a product. During these last years we have watched Australia, Canada and Israel burst onto the international scene with films that result from the kind of scheme we have proposed ... since the company has never been properly capitalised by the government and was set up on bank borrowings, it carries a crippling burden of interest payments. In last year's report I sounded a similar dire warning and a year later noted that

'time is running out'. During this last year, I am very much afraid that it has run out.[10]

On that note, a frustrating decade for Irish film ended.

Similar frustrations were experienced in relation to preserving historical film. In 1971, George Morrison, the acclaimed director of Irish history film documentaries, made an impassioned appeal for a national film archive; he insisted 'the authority of RTÉ has been guilty of a grave dereliction of duty in permitting the destruction of essential records'. Backing his stance, another contributor to this debate, Liam O'Laoghaire, argued that as there was no machinery to preserve valuable historic films, and that if such films were discovered 'the obvious solution would be to present them to the British National Archive in the hope that they would regard them as worth taking care of. Is this a solution we can with any pride maintain? The need for a national film archive is urgent.'[11]

Morrison was also vocal about the absence of a native film industry, suggesting film making in Ireland had been retarded due to Ireland's colonial position: 'It is significant that the most noteworthy Irish efforts towards native production, in the early years, were made at the very time, 1915–20, when a vigorous movement towards independence was afoot.'[12]

One development that had caused particular consternation was the erasing of an RTÉ video tape of musician Seán Ó Riada. Interestingly, Jack Lynch, not someone who usually intervened in an adamant fashion, wrote a strongly worded letter to Gerry Collins on this issue, referring to it as 'a tragedy ... Seán Ó Riada was one of the greatest musicians Ireland has produced for a long time and his successor probably has not been born yet ... It is a tragedy that any of his work which was on record should now no longer be available.' He demanded that Collins find out what happened; Collins duly replied that 'RTÉ slipped' but he was satisfied 'the general arrangements in RTÉ for maintenance of recordings of works of permanent importance are satisfactory'.[13]

Journalists were also receiving more official attention in the 1970s, reflected, for example, in a state reception in their honour at the annual delegate conference of the National Union of Journalists in Dublin in 1974 at the Talbot Hotel in Dublin. There were also journalists from overseas branches treated to free drink. The Department of the Taoiseach subsequently questioned the budgeting of £2 per head per drink, which was a lot considering that a pint of larger was 24p and Irish whiskey, gin and

Vodka measures were 28p each. Dressed ox tongue, Slaney salmon mayonnaise and Irish tipsy cake were also on offer: 'This department intends to raise a number of queries in connection with the invoice so that the final cost may be lower.'[14]

Although some reflections on journalism in the early twenty-first century depicted a backward priest-ridden provincial ethos in the 1970s, suffocating talent and radicalism, these were wide of the mark. Emmanuel Kehoe recalled in contrast: 'Strangely, my recollection of the decade, when I was in my 20s was that it was an exhilarating and liberating time to be alive and in journalism, even, God help us, mainstream journalism.'[15]

Newspapers were experiencing shifting fortunes; the weekly *Catholic Standard*'s circulation, for example, was down to 12,000 from a high of 72,000 in the 1950s.[16] By 1971, daily papers imported into the Republic accounted for 18 per cent of total circulation, compared to only 10 per cent a decade previously.[17] Of the main dailies, by the end of 1978, the *Irish Independent* had a circulation of 174,000, the *Irish Press* 86,000, the *Cork Examiner* 66,000 and the *Irish Times* 66,000, while on Sundays, the *Sunday World*, established in 1973, raced ahead with a circulation of 320,000, meaning it had passed the *Sunday Independent* (276,000) and was not too far behind the *Sunday Press* (384,000).

There were two evening papers in Dublin, the *Evening Press*, whose circulation rose from 146,000 to 161,000 between 1970 and 1978, while circulation of the *Evening Herald* fell from 140,000 to 117,000 during the same period. The circulation battle between these two titles was regarded as somewhat detrimental to tone, as pointed out in *Hibernia* in May 1970: 'There's a battle of words on the front pages of the evening papers. Every verb is explosive. Ministers rap, Priests slam, Bishops slate, the Pope lashes, nearly every one hits out or steps in, crises proliferate, councils clash, drama is everything, and that's before you get to what happens on the streets.'[18]

Significantly, 61 per cent of the population read a provincial paper along with the national dailies and 49 per cent of the population read two provincial papers per week, while 88 per cent of the population read a Sunday newspaper.[19] Provincial newspapers were regarded as having considerable editorial strength, if conservative, due to intensive readership and 'the intensely local ambience of their work'.[20] Strong examples included the *Longford Leader* (in Longford there was also the maverick *Longford News*, published by Vincent Gill, who would occasionally inform his readers 'No news this week') and the *Carlow Nationalist*. From Sinn Féin there were two offerings: *An Phoblacht* in Dublin and *Republican News* in Belfast. Chris Morash in his history of the Irish media has suggested that, far from being off limits, *An Phoblacht* was 'avidly read by politicians, senior public servants and administrators in Dublin' because it reported on events which 'media lack of interest in' or censorship had kept below the political horizon.[21]

The *Sunday World* was valued at £2 million by the end of the decade, and its success was helped by TV stars and well-known personalities such as Gay Byrne, sports commentator Jimmy McGee, self-appointed chaplain to the showbiz set Fr Brian D'Arcy and Frank Hall of *Hall's Pictorial Weekly* fame contributing columns. A great deal of market research had been done before the *Sunday World*'s launch; it covered 'dolly birds and shock horror but also original news material such as exposés on the house building methods of large construction firms'. Vincent Browne estimated that the former major shareholder in the newspaper, Hugh McLaughlin 'has made almost £1 million on the paper in 5½ years following an initial investment of about £30,000'.[22]

The *Irish Times* was edited by Douglas Gageby from 1969–74 and he came back to rescue the paper after an unsuccessful stint by Fergus Pyle from 1974–7; Pyle was picked, according to James Downey, 'essentially because he was a Protestant', but represented 'a fatal mix of tyranny and uncertainty ... one of the worst editors ever to preside over any considerable newspaper'.[23] Gageby was a Belfast-reared Protestant who believed in Irish unity and had a passionate interest in Northern Ireland as well as being overly sensitive about criticism of the army (he had served in the Irish army during the Second World War) and Gardaí. He also wanted a full-time correspondent in Brussels, a suggestion seen as indicating he was 'ahead of his time', but he was not interested in economics.

The newspaper was also, under his control, 'a safe haven for liberals' but journalist Kevin Myers saw him as a 'crook'. The creation of the Irish Times Trust, he suggested, had meant Gageby 'enriched himself to the tune of £325,000' in 1974. The creation of the trust was announced on the paper's front page in April 1974, suggesting it would maintain it as a 'serious and independent newspaper', and it was seen as something that confirmed the paper's autonomy. But in relation to the technicalities of the arrangement, as one journalist put it, 'nobody understood it'.[24] A more negative reaction developed when it was realised that a small minority of contributors had made a lot of money out of it due to a tax-free dividend.

Gageby oversaw a hefty increase in sales from a low of roughly 30,000 up to a high of roughly 80,000 and was assisted by the remarkable news editor Donal Foley, who was 'a central figure in the success story'. Gageby was regarded as someone who 'feminised and softened' the face of Irish journalism, 'but it could be argued that a far more vigorous friend to Irish women journalists was Tim Pat Coogan', editor of the *Irish Press*.[25] The *Irish Times* also launched the country's first education journal, *Education Times*, in 1973 (see Part VIII), and was notable for developing features at a time when the country was coming out of recession, under the clever slogan 'Keep up with the Changing Times'.[26]

Tim Pat Coogan was also surrounded by considerable talent, including writer John Banville ('one of the best craftsmen ever to grace the sub editor's desk') and Mary Kenny; one of the 'wild, wild women', a description offered by Vivion de Valera, son of Eamon. As controlling director of the *Irish Press*, Vivion had 'absolute control' of the company according to the articles of association. The shares and control structures of his company were referred to in 1978 as 'the most brazen concentration of power in the hands of one individual known to the newspaper industry anywhere in the western world. For although the de Valera family owns only a minority of the shareholding in the company, the articles of association make it absolutely impossible for any outside individual or group of individuals to wrest any measure of control from it.'[27]

In 1976 *In Dublin* magazine was launched as a fortnightly guide to entertainment and pursuits in the capital, while the launch of the current affairs magazine *Magill* in 1977 was ambitious and provocative and was to provide invaluable experience for a generation of investigative journalists and columnists. Vincent Browne had established it, in the words of John Waters, 'more or less as a weapon for hitting politicians across the head ... for the first time it seemed, here was someone who was not taking sides, who had the same exceedingly dim view of all politicians ... everyone wanted to work for him but dozens failed in the attempt, unable to stand his moods and his extraordinary capacity for aggravation ... Magill was an extension of his personality.' Perhaps his saving grace was that 'his destructiveness was just about outweighed by his charisma'.[28] *Magill* was now a rival for the well-established *Hibernia*, whose editors 'had a particularly intense fascination with the Irish media itself and its ability or inability, to analyse a confluence of political, cultural and economic circumstances that often seemed to elide understanding in the daily rounds of news reporting'; more evidence perhaps, of a significant counter culture, as was the readiness with which the phrase 'Banana Republic' was being used.[29]

There were many fine journalists in Ireland, including Michael Mills ('no more honest or better informed journalist in the country'), Con Houlihan, who made marvellous contributions to *The Kerryman*, and in the *Irish Times* Maeve Binchy, later to become an extraordinarily successful novelist, who was regarded as creating a new field for Irish journalism in London. Her editor Douglas Gageby had told her when she was going to London to 'try to make the English sound like people when you get there, not the enemy'.[30] She caused quite a stir in 1973 with her irreverent reporting and colour pieces from London on the wedding of Princess Anne: 'The bride looked as edgy as if it were the Badminton Horse Trials and she was waiting for the bell to gallop off ... Princess Margaret looked like a lighting devil with a cross face and an extraordinary hideous coat, which may have been some multicoloured fur, but then was there ever an animal or even a selection of animals which would have been given such a coat by Nature.'[31]

Other female journalists, including powerful writers such as Nell McCafferty and Mary Holland, also influenced the way society looked at issues that affected women, including the manner in which the law and the legal system treated them. In 2004, Trinity legal academic Ivana Bacik recalled,

> My first introduction to Nell McCafferty was through her radical writing. In 1985, Trinity College law lecturer (later president) Mary McAleese told her first year class to read *In the Eyes of the Law*, a collection of McCafferty's [1970s] columns in *The Irish Times* observing proceedings in the Dublin District Courts over previous years. These insightful, often poignant descriptions of the humdrum reality of law in action had a huge effect on us teenaged school-leavers – and remain relevant today. The book is still on the first year criminal law reading list in Trinity.[32]

The female journalists often broke new ground and continued to ask difficult questions. The editor of the *Irish Times*, Geraldine Kennedy, when she spoke at Mary Holland's funeral in 2004, summed this up by saying of Holland that 'she interfered with our comfort zones and challenged all of us'.[33]

Journalist Joe MacAnthony published his 8,000-word exposé of the corruption of the Irish sweepstakes under the title 'Where the Sweep Millions Go', in 1973 (see also Part VII). The Sweep, as it was known, had come into being in 1930 at the request of Dublin hospitals, who saw it as the only way to raise funds. Run on major English horse races, it had raised staggering sums over the decades, much of it by illegal sales in the US and Britain. It was a private company that ultimately became embarrassing to the state, whose legislation facilitated a lax attitude to accounting and massive profits to the organisers.[34] MacAnthony's story was particularly courageous because, as pointed out by historian and broadcaster John Bowman writing in *Hibernia*, 'the exposé is not a common journalistic exercise in Ireland. Irish society is too small and too personal and relations between the establishment too intimate to allow such treatment from the national papers.' In that sense MacAnthony's story was a significant breakthrough, even if 'it told relatively little that was new to informed people'.[35] Bowman's observations highlighted the problem of getting to the bottom of arrangements that were patently corrupt in a closed, class-conscious society where powerful alliances closed ranks and sometimes blatantly abused their power in a vindictive way.

According to Tim Pat Coogan, after the story was published, Tommy Murphy, who controlled Independent newspapers, sought to shake Patrick McGrath's hand at the Leopardstown races and McGrath 'publicly abused the older man calling him amongst other things a fucking traitor'.[36] The McGrath family had been one of the main organisers and therefore one of the main beneficiaries of the Sweep. What happened to MacAnthony afterwards was even more instructive of the toll investigative journalism could exact; quite simply, the promoters survived, but MacAnthony had to move to Canada.[37]

In terms of less sensational but vital communications, the Irish telephone network became something of a national joke in the 1970s and it was not just domestic users, or those hoping to be users, who found it frustrating. In March 1973 it was pointed out that the 'existing switchboards are obsolete and subject to recurring faults'. The previous summer, in relation to the Taoiseach Jack Lynch, it was noted, 'There is at present no way of knowing when the Taoiseach is engaged on the telephone in his room other than by listening at the door. This is not an attractive way of finding out and the Taoiseach suggests that a little warning light be fitted above the door in the [private secretary's] room, which will be operated by a switch in his room. This will indicate to us when he is engaged and does not want to be disturbed.'[38] At least eavesdropping civil servants had the chance to get snippets of what might have been some interesting, if tense, conversations, given the political climate in 1972.

In April 1973 Garret FitzGerald expressed his frustration to Conor Cruise O'Brien, the minister whose department, Posts and Telegraphs, had responsibility for the telephone network: 'I have never understood why delays should occur in relation to the telephone service which is a commercially viable enterprise and which should be capable of both planning ahead – as I am sure it is – and able to raise the money necessary to implement their plans – which I understand it hasn't been!' The following month, Cruise O'Brien referred to the 'pressure on the switchboards at Iveagh House' (where the Department of Foreign Affairs was located). FitzGerald returned to the issue soon after, pointing out that the chairman of the Fine Gael national council, Peter Prendergast, from Dundrum in South Dublin, 'has been looking for a telephone for a number of years. The department installs them in his house at election times, but takes them away next morning which suggests that there cannot be much of a problem in his area.'[39] In August of that year, O'Brien referred to a 'huge increase in demand' for telephones and noted 'there are shortages of subscribers' equipment in most of the main 25 exchanges in Dublin'.[40] Later in the year the government obtained a £7.5 million loan from the European Investment Bank to help finance the expansion of the Irish telephone service and in 1974 a major new automatic telephone exchange came into operation in Ballsbridge, Dublin.

But at the end of 1977, writing in *Magill* magazine, journalist Liam O'Toole maintained 'our telephone service is a national sick joke', and also referred to 'Victorian attitudes to staff relations' in the telephone exchanges, pointing out that staff at the exchange in St Andrew's Street in Dublin had staged a walkout one night in June 1974 claiming 'oppressive supervision' and alleging that 'visits to the toilet were subject to the permission of the night supervisor who insisted that each man sign a special form'.[41] Writer Ulick O'Connor claimed that the Department of Posts and Telegraphs cut off his telephone in 1977 when he complained to the operator that the Irish telephone system was appalling: 'A High Court judge ordered his phones put back. Knowing Dublin and officialdom his honour explained that while it was an easy matter to disconnect a Dublin phone it was a hard thing to get it back to work. The inspectors in the Department, the judge explained are "a mysterious triumvirate with tremendous powers". The three persons who could exercise these powers were not anywhere to be found, his honour went on and no one could indicate when they might be available.'[42]

– TWENTY-SEVEN –

THE SPORTING IRISH

Some traditional modes of entertainment and what were dubiously labelled 'sport' came under scrutiny as being indefensible in the 1970s, including activities that were targeted by the Irish Council Against Blood Sports. At the end of 1969, it wrote to Jack Lynch, who had been invited to present the Texaco Sportsmen of the Year awards, urging him to boycott the event. Hare coursing was included in the awards category and the council noted it was a pursuit opposed by 'all the Christian churches'. A draft reply from the Department of Justice justified coursing on the grounds that it was actively accepted and defended by a large number of people and had considerable economic value.[1]

In 1973, the Council sought to take advantage of Conservation Year to get its message across about conserving wildlife; harrowing accounts of the torture and distress of the animals that were killed during coursing were also sent to government. One account of a coursing meeting at Millstreet in County Cork in January 1974 reported on eighty-eight courses resulting in twenty kills: 'I saw the two greyhounds sink their teeth into the hare and twice it wriggled free only to be snapped up again. It would cry out for several minutes until the men reached the dogs. Their main concern would be recapturing the greyhound, then finally they would turn to the still living hare and give it a few belts over the head before handing it to a boy of about 13 who would again hit it since it was still flinching.'[2]

It was obvious that an Irish coursing club regulation that hares could not be coursed more than once on the same day was being blatantly broken. Liam Cosgrave made no observations on these disclosures and just passed them on to the ministers for Justice and Lands, which was hardly surprising given his own leisure pursuits. As was suggested to him the previous year regarding the delay in the introduction of a long-promised wildlife bill 'one impediment to such a Bill is a Taoiseach who actually partakes in the perverted pastime of fox hunting'.[3]

In relation to sports policy, some proposed Fine Gael election manifestos suggested in 1970 were perhaps premature in arguing that the aim should be to 'initiate a campaign to succeed at Munich Olympics and present Irish application as venue for 1976 games'.[4] It was revealing that government files in relation to sports came under the heading 'revival of athletics'. In the early 1970s, Noel Carroll – a kind, eccentric and forthright character (and later public relations officer for Dublin Corporation, as seen earlier in relation to Wood Quay) who dominated Irish 400 and 800 metre running at his peak, winning fourteen national titles in total, and held national record times in those events as well as being involved in the establishment of the Dublin City Marathon in 1980 – advocated a special government department to look after sport and recreation.[5] There was clearly much ground to make up in Ireland regarding the underdevelopment of sports infrastructure.

Sports policy at that stage was the responsibility of the Department of Education. In 1970 Michael O'Kennedy, the junior minister in that department, wanted to set up a National Council for Sport and a scheme of assistance for youth sport activity; such a council was regarded as 'one of the most pressing requirements in Irish sport today'. The council was announced in January 1971 as COSAC, the National Council for Sport and Physical Recreation, an advisory body with twenty-one members. It was introduced on the basis that: 'Life in the 70s is changing our living habits drastically. An increased standard of living, the breakdown of social barriers, extra leisure time, greater mobility and increased living pressures are some of the obvious factors involved.'[6]

An article in the *Sunday Press*, however, did not gloss over the realities of the infighting that was an intrinsic part of the Irish sporting infrastructure, suggesting the day after O'Kennedy's announcement that 'in the turbulent arena of Irish sport there are jealousies both petty and monumental. Ecumenism is often considered a dirty religious word and in-fighting is part of the scene even in the non-physical contact sports.'[7]

(When President Ó Dálaigh was asked to officially open the Rás Tailteann – an international cycling stage race inaugurated in the 1950s – in 1975, an official in the Department of the Taoiseach was worried about it in the context of 'the subversive reputation of some cycling organisations', an intriguing assertion and interesting choice of language. A request to light the games torch of the national community games in the Aras was also ruled out as not 'in keeping with the dignity of the Aras'. There was clearly a worry that the president playing a role in launching sports events was somewhat beneath the dignity of the office.[8])

Such infighting had already begun in relation to membership of the sports council; to his credit, Lynch rejected opposition within his own party to the appointment of Joe Connolly, a former national boxing champion and a Labour Party councillor, on the grounds that this was about sport rather than politics.[9] In a press release issued in February 1972, O'Kennedy pointed out that '85 per cent, or five out of every six people in this country do not take part in any form of sport or physical activity', though it was suggested 'this ... is not peculiar to Ireland alone'. The following year, the BLE, the body overseeing Irish athletics, complained about a lack of proper athletic facilities and a growing demand for their provision, both indoors and out.

Speaking at the Texaco Sports Awards in 1975, Cosgrave referred to the fact that 'many of our young people fail to develop a lasting interest in sport ... could the reason for this lie in the limited range of sports offered in schools?'[10] Government policy on sport was frequently referred to in the context of health; frightening statistics indicating an increase of 34.4 per cent in deaths from heart attacks among men aged forty-five to fifty-four between 1951 and 1970, justified such alarm (see Part VII) and the necessity of a 'Sport for all' programme. But the money being spent on sports promotion and support was paltry; in 1974, for example, only £115,000 was given in grants by the Department of Education to the governing bodies of sport.

Another problem was the absence of a centralised policy, with government departments operating independently of each other. As was observed in June 1974, 'there is no means of formulating any overall national strategy for sport and physical recreation'. During the term of the coalition government, Fine Gael TD John Bruton had responsibility for youth and sport as parliamentary secretary to the Minister for Education (this responsibility had been delineated first in 1969) and often found the delay in the response to his requests to the Department of the Taoiseach frustrating. An indication of civil service bureaucracy, and of the lack of priority given to promotion of sports as a function of government, was that Bruton's reminder of a need for a reply to his proposals a month after he had sent them to the department was regarded as 'unwarranted'.[11]

In 1975, the government committed £622,000 to youth and sport but Bruton's attempts to formulate a more coherent policy were dismissed by Stokes in the Department of the Taoiseach, who suggested his proposals demonstrated 'confused thinking in relation to policy on youth, in sport, on recreation and on culture and how these should be linked'.[12] COSAC, as pointed out by Bruton, had lapsed in 1974 because of its 'inadequate structure' and 'absence of clear objectives'. What he wanted was a sports council with the object of promoting sport for all to improve the standard in Ireland's international performances and to capitalise on 'the upward trend in national interest in outdoor pursuits in recent years'. The sports sector, he mused, could deliver the greatest benefits 'with the least expenditure'. He was insightful in this regard, but the possible cost (estimated by the Department of the Taoiseach at possibly up to £2 million) prompted a negative reaction from the Department of Finance in 1976, as 'such expenditure must rank low in comparison with many tax, employment and welfare proposals at present suspended for lack of cash'.[13]

There was a determination, it seemed, to suck the life and cost out of Bruton's blueprint, by suggesting it should be published as a discussion document with a particular emphasis on (conveniently) 'the primacy of voluntary organisations'.[14] Bruton disputed the costs estimated by Finance, emphasising in April 1977 that he was only looking for £175,000 for the following year, 'a very modest financial requirement'.[15] It was clear, however, that what was needed was more than modest investment, given the observation in the summer of 1977 that 'less than 10 per cent of our schools outside the cities have any sort of gymnasium' and 'only about 25 per cent of our schools have any sort of an area for a field game'.[16]

Bruton also thought a sports policy for youth could be a potential vote-getter; he wrote to Cosgrave in January 1977, 'as there will be five years of new voters on the electoral register for 1977 there are obvious advantages in any policy which will appeal to young people. I think the document prepared should be looked at in this light.'[17] In contradiction of some earlier contentions, it was maintained that, 'while Ireland has not had conspicuous international success' in sport, 'it is probable that a larger number of ordinary people take part in sport here than in many countries. This is due almost entirely to the successful work of voluntary organisations.'[18]

The GAA was instrumental in this regard. Originally established in 1884 to promote Irish football and hurling, it had undergone a series of modernisation processes, including dropping its ban on its members playing so-called 'foreign' sports such as soccer, cricket and rugby. Jack Lynch had been an advocate of the removal of the GAA ban ('I have been convinced for many years that it has no protective value'); his views on this were particularly significant because of his own sporting and GAA pedigree. In the 1940s he had played on the teams that won four successive All-Ireland Hurling Championships in 1941, 1942, 1943 and 1944, and in 1945 he played on the Cork side that won the All-Ireland Football Championship. He was also on the winning Cork hurling team of 1946, becoming the only player to play in six successive winning senior All-Ireland teams, and in 1947 he became the only player to play in seven consecutive All-Ireland finals.

The 1960s was a decade in which the GAA could have gone into terminal decline. It faced many pressures; the continuing decline of rural Ireland and its population, the growing emphasis on urban living, the increase in the popularity of soccer and the emergence of Irish television, which many believed would fatally damage attendances at Gaelic games.

It thus had many reasons to be fearful, but responded robustly. Despite many tetchy encounters with RTÉ, by the end of the decade the relationship between the two organisations was harmonious, and both realised they could benefit from each other. The GAA also embarked on a hugely ambitious and successful building programme after establishing a grounds board, Bord na bPáirc, to administer ground development throughout the country (this committee is regarded by some within the GAA as the most important in its history). It brought a focus to club leadership in urban and rural areas and into the universities, while developing the social role of the association.

Eventually, after much soul searching and acrimonious exchanges, the ban on foreign games was rescinded in 1971 (although the ban on British armed forces playing was maintained) owing largely to the courage of Tom Woulfe, chairman of the Civil Service Football Club, who almost single-handedly forced a national debate on the issue. The association had gone to great lengths to prevent discussion on changing their rules, often by a farcical censorship. One historian of the GAA, Emmet Vaughan, highlighted how they prevented debate about objections to the rule, sometimes on the basis that written notification to bring the issue to discussion at congress level was not on Irish watermarked paper. In some cases, objections that were otherwise in order were deemed inadmissible because they were not enclosed in an envelope bearing an Irish watermark.[19]

Even if it was still on the occasional receiving end of criticism due to its perceived 'autocracy, chauvinism, insularity and xenophobia', it showed a 'shrewd awareness' of engagement with the mass media and was socially stabilising in many respects. As writer Breandán Ó hEithir recorded, 'The GAA will have to contain the Provo, the Garda Síochána who plays on the same team, but who may have to arrest him, the bank clerk who thinks all politics are boring, the Northern nationalist who wants more attention focused on British army harassment, the Munster anti-nationalist who believes all such stories are Provo propaganda ... it will have to contain them all and many more diverse elements and trim all their views so as to keep the ship on an even keel in rough seas.'[20] Nonetheless, harmony was not always maintained; in April 1973 there was a pitched battle between supporters at Croke Park after a GAA National League football match between Kerry and Derry.

The organisation also introduced All Star awards with the winners taken to North America to bring the games to the Irish Diaspora.[21] Another milestone of the decade was the first ever inter-county ladies Gaelic football match in County Offaly in July 1973; a newspaper noted that 'perfume took over from embrocation as the prevailing odour in the dressing rooms when Offaly hosted Kerry'. The following year the Ladies Gaelic Football Association was established.[22]

It also received a new lease of life due to the great Dublin/Kerry Gaelic football duels of the 1970s.[23] The rivalry between the two teams became something of an epic; between them, by the end of the 1970s, 'they had reinvented the sport and changed the way we look at the GAA', in the words of sports writer Tom Humphries. By the early 1970s, the Dublin county football team was a relative nonentity, 'defiantly stagnant and ramshackle.' In a new urban culture the GAA did not receive the devotion and loyalty 'which had kept it more vibrant in more frugal times'. The population of Dublin was 984,000 by 1979 compared to 693,000 in 1951, so the GAA appointed a commission on how to adapt.

All-Ireland success for Dublin footballers in 1974, 1976 and 1977 followed, and 'brought the city of Dublin alive again.'[24] The energetic and focused management of Kevin Heffernan, who could pick his own selectors, had changed the team's fortunes. There was a new discipline, and 'surveillance operations' to keep the most talented players out of pubs was effective. A new urban audience and interest among school children was timely; in Heffernan's words 'I said to myself, it's great to be coming now. The economy has slumped. There was no soccer team going well. The rugby team were struggling. We were arriving. There was a space for us to make a difference.'[25] The new style of play involved the abandonment of the 'catch and kick' practice and the imposition of more rigorous training. Mick O'Dwyer, the Kerry team manager, prioritised 'flat-out sprints', while in the winter he had the players 'running the roads and the beaches and the hills'. For players under O'Dwyer's management, 'being in the circle of his enthusiasm was addictive' as he kept his players 'fresh and interested for so long'.[26]

Hurling also continued to generate huge interest; the rivalry between individual counties noted for hurling prowess was influential in this regard. In September 1971, Tipperary beat Kilkenny in the All-Ireland hurling final to win a record twenty-second title, while in 1973, Limerick hurlers won their first All-Ireland title since 1940 ('to say that grown men wept is an understatement ... celebrations continued for weeks'[27]). Christy Ring, regarded as the greatest ever hurler, who had won a record eight All-Ireland medals with Cork, died suddenly in March 1979. His funeral was one of the biggest ever seen in Cork, with up to 60,000 people lining the streets of the city, a reflection of his iconic status and indeed the status of the unique hurling game.[28] Jack Lynch, who had been his sporting contemporary, gave an emotional oration, but he was also unprepared; a letter in his personal papers a few years later to a publisher who wanted to include his speech in a book saw him lament: 'I am afraid it is very badly written. I wrote it in the car on my knee as I was proceeding towards the cemetery.'[29]

It was contended that psychological factors as well as lack of physical facilities were an impediment to the promotion of sports at a more general level because of an Irish shyness 'about being seen togging out'. A civil servant in the Department of the Taoiseach, however, was not so sure about the merits of an Irish fitness revolution: 'Not everyone is fit for active sport and it could be as easily proved, if research was undertaken, that many would be healthier on the sideline.'[30] But criticisms about lack of investment in sport continued in the late 1970s. In 1977, Noel Carroll suggested 'we must have the most neglected youth in the world. It is a shocking waste of our sporting potential.' As Eamon Dunphy, who by 1977 had returned from his football career in England to play soccer with Shamrock Rovers, saw it, government was not an initiator of sport with a central role for the simple reason that 'there are no votes in sport'.[31]

But there was optimism about some aspects of Irish soccer development, at home and abroad. John Giles, the thirty-seven-year-old manager of League of Ireland club Shamrock Rovers, who had also returned to Ireland after a distinguished career in English soccer as a midfielder with Leeds United, had set himself the hugely ambitious but ultimately unrealisable task of winning the European Cup ('it isn't all that outrageous an ambition' he maintained), having not just brought back Dunphy from England, but also Eoin Hand and Ray Tracey.[32] But Irish soccer fans were still more likely to support English soccer clubs, where the Irish presence was significant.

Liam Brady continued to make waves with Arsenal FC in the late 1970s. He was regarded as one of the most talented players in the world ('that left foot of his – he could open a can of peas with it if he wanted to' was the verdict of David O'Leary, his Irish colleague at Highbury) with suggestions that he would end up in Europe; this he eventually did, with Juventus. At the end of the 1970s, as a twenty-three-year-old, earning £300 a week, he seemed remarkably frank, honest and modest when interviewed by Vincent Browne.[33]

Also interviewed by Browne was John Giles, when he was appointed player/manager of the Irish international team: 'The only reason I agreed was because if I did not do it, it might go to someone I did not rate that much.'[34] He believed in a less hectic and more disciplined and purist style of play than was the case earlier, when in Giles's words, 'we were a bit of a joke at international level'. The Irish team could justifiably regard itself as having made significant headway with a draw against England in 1978, given that the English manager and his six assistants were full time, in contrast to the Irish situation, where there was only a part-time manager and a part-time assistant. The following year the Irish team beat Denmark, creating considerable expectations about its prospects for the 1980s.[35] Giles was dignified and strong on tactical awareness, poor at public relations ('his own worst enemy') but successful to the extent that he established an expectancy that the Republic could qualify for major finals[36] (first achieved in 1988). Steve Heighway, another squad member of the Republic's soccer team, a world-class left-winger at Liverpool, 'had a perfectly good goal disallowed against Bulgaria in Sofia in 1977. Had it stood, Ireland would have gone to the 1978 World Cup finals in Argentina.'[37]

Athletics also achieved a higher profile through the exploits of Mary Peters of Belfast, who won the women's pentathlon in the Olympic Games at Munich in September 1972, setting a new world record, and Eamon Coughlan, who won a silver medal at the European Championships at Prague in 1978, coming second to Steve Ovett in what was one of the most 'formidable line ups for a 1500 metres race that had ever been assembled'.[38] His duels with Brian Walker in New Zealand and Australia were also great crowd pleasers, as were the victories of John Treacy. Though struggling sometimes to make an impact on the track, Treacy won the World Cross-Country Championships in Glasgow in 1978 and Limerick in 1979, carrying 'the aspirations of the whole nation starved of major international sporting success'.[39]

Thousands developed their own aspirations towards the end of the decade in relation to the most gruelling race of all; it was announced in *Magill* magazine in October 1978 that 'huge numbers of adults of all shapes and sizes are to be seen doing it in public, with no trace of embarrassment, confident that they are part of one of the great mass movements of the 70s. The phenomenon of jogging is upon us.'[40] Rather than the sole creation of Noel Carroll, the first Dublin City Marathon in 1980 was essentially 'a promotional vehicle' for the new pop radio station RTÉ Radio 2, which sponsored it. Louis Hogan, an RTÉ radio producer, was charged with the task of generating a public profile for the station and, having seen the New York race in 1978, suggested to Carroll, in his capacity as public relations officer of Dublin Corporation, that Dublin should have its own marathon which would be open to everyone and 'not under the control of the athletics establishment'. Carroll was keen and it had the corporation's support.[41]

Cricket was a niche sport – including those at school there were roughly 15,000 participants – with Irish players 'members of a tightly knit family who may, in Dublin, play each other's teams ten times a season'. But the standard was regarded as high, given the small numbers involved, the shoestring budget and relative public indifference. When Ireland played Denmark in the summer of 1978, 'the players outnumbered the spectators

... It's conceivable that the match was one of the most anonymous international sporting events ever to have taken place in Ireland.'[42]

There were rugby players of tremendous ability, like Mike Gibson, who retired at the end of 1979, Tom Kiernan, who won his fiftieth cap for Ireland and led the rugby team to a victory against England at Twickenham in February 1972, the popular Willie John McBride, and Moss Keane, 'a true icon of Irish rugby'. Capped fifty-one times for Ireland, Keane played his part in the Munster team's famous victory over the All Blacks in Limerick in 1978. He had made an extraordinary transition from a Gaelic footballer to an Irish international and British Lions rugby player and was described by commentator Bill McLaren as 'eighteen and a half stone of prime Irish beef on the hoof'.[43]

The defeat of the All Blacks was a sensation that generated the headline 'All Blacks are tamed for the first time on Irish soil'. Twelve thousand spectators were in attendance to witness a score line of 12–0. Many had to pinch themselves: 'For the better part of this century successive generations of Irish rugby men have had unsatisfied longings of seeing an All Blacks side beaten on Irish soil. All those privileged to have seen it will talk with pride of this victory to the end of their days.'[44] The match, for Munster players and fans, was 'the day a legend was born'; it was immortalised and took on mythical status and 'up to 100,000 jubilant fans claim to have turned up'.[45]

But there was much critical comment about the organisation of international rugby; it was regarded, at a time when other sports were becoming better organised, as 'in a state of chaos and indiscipline with inevitable consequences in international championships'. For some, the problem lay with administration at the top of the Irish Rugby Football Union, responsible for the 'bizarre choice' of selectors and coach.[46] Wales and Scotland did not travel to Dublin for the Five Nations Championship in 1972 because of the Troubles; Ireland won the championship two years later.

Golf was also growing in popularity and price and some clubs were rampant in their showcasing of the snobberies and prejudices of wealthy professionals. At Portmarnock Golf Club in County Dublin, women were excluded from membership and could not enter the bar. In 1978 there was a membership fee of £200 per annum: 'A prospective member has his application placed on the notice board and any individual member with a special prejudice can blackball the applicant merely by tearing down the notice in the view of three other members. Such arcane, quasi-Masonic rites are common enough.'[47] Popular Irish golfer Christy O'Connor Jr won the first Carroll's Irish Open in August 1975 and the following year Eamon Darcy won the Under-25 World Golf Championship in Evian, France.

Irish jockeys continued to excel; in March 1970, L'Escargot, ridden by Tommy Carberry and trained at the Curragh in Kildare by Dan Moore, won the Cheltenham Gold Cup, while the following month the Irish-bred Gay Trip, ridden by Pat Taaffe, won the Aintree Grand National. In 1975 Pat Eddery won the Epsom Derby; the same year Vincent O'Brien from Tipperary equalled Sir Cecil Boyd Rochfort's post-war record of training six winners at Royal Ascot. In April 1977 Tommy Stack rode Red Rum to victory in the Grand National; along with Ron Barry and Pat Eddery he was making an impact on British racing. In Ireland there were an estimated 3,200 owners of bloodstock 'producing nearly half the output of foals in the British Isles', though most owners had no more than three mares. At the other end of the scale 'the top ten stallions are owned by only a handful of studs, increasingly backed by syndicates and involved in a multi-million pound business'. Taoiseach Liam Cosgrave opened Goffs bloodstock sales complex in County Kildare in September 1975.

Every aspect of Irish racing was seen to be booming; race attendances in 1977 were estimated at 1.1 million people 'who bet £39.73 million with the bookmakers and the Tote'. One in five of the top 148 horses trained in Europe in 1977 was Irish bred (horses with plenty of bone and structure bred on unploughed grass lands). Success at the Cheltenham National Hunt Festival, including ten Gold Cup wins between the mid 1960s and the late 1970s, was said to vindicate Ireland's reputation 'as the home of the best steeplechasers in the world'.[48] In the late 1970s Eddie Macken, with a natural riding ability and 'meticulous technique', was one of the most outstanding show jumpers; he came second twice in the Show Jumping World Championships, missing gold by fractions of time faults.[49] Show jumping was one of the biggest spectator sports of the decade, with large television audiences for the annual Aga Khan Trophy grand prix as part of the Dublin Horse Show: 'Such was the prestige of the competition that in 1975, the British team pulled out of the European championships in Germany just to have a crack at the Aga Khan, which they duly won'; though a hat-trick of Aga Khan victories for Ireland was to follow with Macken at the helm.[50] The horse-riding Irish polished off a decade that, in sporting terms, generated many positive narratives.

PART IV

RIGHTS, RESPONSIBILITIES AND JUSTICE

'One gets the feeling that justice as such has taken a back seat'

In 1973 Conor Brady, a young Irish Times *journalist, took over the editorship of the* Garda Review, *a monthly publication designed to provide a forum to publicise the Irish police force's priorities, grievances and achievements. The publication was timely, as its predecessor version had collapsed and there was a perceived need to highlight the particular challenges for the force. It was a time when the Troubles in Northern Ireland were creating new policing dilemmas and many of the tensions within the force over status, promotion and overtime came to the boil. By the end of the 1960s, Garda dissatisfaction with pay and conditions had reached crisis point and a commission chaired by Judge John Charles Conroy was established to update antiquated terms of police service and issued its report in January 1970. It recommended reform of every aspect of police life, including training, the work environment, industrial relations, promotion, and pay.*

The Garda Commissioner appointed in 1968, Michael Wymes, faced not only the implications of the Conroy Report but also tensions generated by the introduction of Garda overtime and government resistance to it, the border security problem, increased urban crime, and various civil rights and protest movements. The arms crisis of 1970 exacerbated the sense of volatility, as did the shooting dead of Garda Richard Fallon in April 1970, the first of several Garda murders as a result of the Troubles.

One of the force's grievances in the early 1970s was centred on the belief that it was isolated, in contrast to the attention devoted to the Irish army. As was asserted in the Garda Review *in October 1973, 'too often in the past five years Gardaí on the job have had to sit back in embarrassment while army back-up services tend to the needs of the military personnel'. As a result of the Troubles, the defence forces were expanded to an unprecedented level of peace-time strength, barracks were built and improved, with increases in army pay and allowances for those engaged in border duties. In this context, The* Garda Review*'s mission was unequivocal and reflected the mood of militancy and demand for respect that had emerged in the 1960s. It was there to demand 'better conditions, higher standards and a more clearly defined, purposeful role in the community ... There is little doubt at present that the Garda is looked upon as the poor relation by many if not all of the agencies concerned with the administration of justice and social help.'*[1]

Most dramatically, it was asserted that the Gardaí were facing their biggest test since the 1930s, a time when the new police force faced the challenge, as an unarmed force, of creating cross-community allegiance in the shadow of civil war in a society that was not yet fully demilitarised and the legitimacy of the state, and by extension the police force, was contested by various subversives, including those in the IRA. What was also clear was that the force in the 1970s became exceptionally sensitive to media criticism about the administration of justice. One of the interesting developments of the decade was that in parallel with increased pressures on the force and demands for it to be respected, journalists and human rights campaigners also sought to make it more accountable and highlight some of its excesses. This attention exposed one of the dilemmas with regard to the administration of justice during the 1970s; while there was a focus on modernisation, law reform and expanding the definition of justice, the backdrop of the Troubles, a political determination to play the law and order card, and preoccupation with threats to the state meant that the decade witnessed a harshness that undermined justice. The Garda Review *also complained that politicians did not take the force seriously enough; they 'had no concept of the Gardaí as a group with a changing role in a society whose horizons change and merge and resettle themselves again'.*[2]

There is little doubt that individual Gardaí took the law into their own hands during this decade, under the cloak of fighting subversion, and politicians also played their part in turning blind eyes. Journalists Gene Kerrigan and Derek Dunne, for example, in looking at the handling of Nicky Kelly and other socialist Republicans charged with a train robbery in 1976, concluded 'there is a substantial body of evidence that a number of Gardaí committed crimes of assault during the investigation of the train robbery and that a number of Gardaí perjured themselves during the subsequent trial ... this body of evidence has been ignored by the authorities and the Gardaí over whom this shadow hangs have been promoted. Whether or not that evidence would stand up in an independent inquiry is not the point – the point is the fact that the authorities by not initiating an inquiry wilfully covered up substantial evidence of a possible crime.'[3]

It was surely significant that when addressing Gardaí at their training centre in Templemore in Tipperary in early 1977, the Garda Commissioner Edmund Garvey, who was subsequently dismissed under controversial circumstances at a time when there was criticism of a 'heavy gang' operating in the force, had to remind Gardaí to 'stay within the law'.[4] *The mistake those representing the Gardaí made was to blame both the media for creating 'public confusion' and criminal law procedures which were outdated – to which their response was 'over to the legislators'*[5] *– rather than errant Gardaí, a very convenient washing of police hands. This, of course, was not the only narrative relevant to the Gardaí in the 1970s. Many were involved in community work in their own time and, while they may not have had the technological and operational efficiency of other forces, they did have, overall, good relations with the community that other forces struggled to achieve. But in the context of the security threat, they were under political and often personal pressure and took considerable risks that undermined justice.*

In 1974, when assistant Garda Commissioner Patrick McLaughlin spoke at Trinity College Dublin, he worryingly quoted the late FBI director J. Edgar Hoover: 'If crime is to be contained, the criminal must know that his arrest will be swift, his prosecution prompt and his sentence substantial.'[6] *The subtext to this was clear; the burden of proof needed to be eased as far as the law enforcers were concerned and they accompanied these assertions with an insistence that for the first time in the state's history, organised professional crime was a serious issue, along with what was termed a 'crime explosion'. It was maintained in 1976 that due to budgetary constraints, policing was 'so reduced throughout the country as to give virtually free rein to the criminal'.*[7] *Sociologists and criminologists devoted attention to the increase in crime, particularly the substantial increase in assaults and the transformation 'in the extent and nature of officially recorded crime that in the US and in much of Europe was accompanied by gradual accretion [but] was in Ireland crowded into little more than a decade. It was a transformation not by stages but by one rapid step', and the bulk of crime involved the illegal acquisition of property.*[8]

In responding to a 32 per cent increase in indictable offences from 1965–71, and an increase in the same period of 55 per cent in offences by the 17–21 age group, a sociologist with the Economic and Social Research Institute engaged in Irish crime research, placed the rise in social context: 'the rise in Irish crimes represents the fact that neither philosophy, the modern socialist one or the more ancient religious one, can cope with the strains of rapid urbanisation',[9] a fascinatingly narrow framework for Irish modernisation to be viewed through.

Inevitably, given such an increase, there was also new pressure and focus on prisons, but the official reports of visiting committees seemed to belie the new strains, in contrast to the assessment of Conor Brady who, along with other journalists at the behest of Minister for Justice Patrick Cooney in 1974, conducted a week-long tour of Irish prisons. Acknowledging that 'creature comforts are good', he nonetheless wrote starkly of the 'monotonous and demoralising inactivity ... they were walking around but many of them did not seem to be living.'[10] The tension between diagnosing the problem or the reform impulse, and the desire to contain the subversive threat within the prison service was a characteristic of the 1970s, an issue relevant not just in Ireland, but also in relation to Irish prisoners in Britain. One of their champions, Sr Sarah Clarke, an Irish nun who gave up teaching to do full-time pastoral work with prisoners and their families, frequently clashed with the Home Office. She maintained that her motives were 'humanitarian and religious – not political' and highlighted the viciousness of forced feeding and strip searches, but she 'met opposition when I might have expected co-operation among middle class Irish people in Britain and apathy from the Irish government'. One Irish government minister 'took me out to the courtyard in case he would be heard speaking about Irish prisoners in English gaols.'[11]

There was also a growing recognition that prison after care in the Republic was lamentable and not fit for purpose due to recidivism. Of the 1,579 prisoners in custody in 1969, 70 per cent had previously served prison sentences[12] and there was no statutory provision for the prisoner's welfare on release. Those demanding reform insisted penal issues should not be viewed in isolation but needed to be assessed in the context of education, rehabilitation and societal attitudes. One of the main problems – and this remained an issue across many areas in the 1970s – was lack of information as, 'prisons are surrounded by a closed system of administration' which gave rise to 'a kind of siege mentality.'[13]

The sense of emergency created by the Troubles and the degree to which it would be enshrined in law and reflected in the administration of justice, was accompanied by a parallel stream of engagement with the notion of law reform and the creation of the Law Reform Commission (LRC). The Act that created it conferred a wide-ranging law reform function on the LRC to 'keep the law under review and ... undertake examinations and conduct research with a view to reforming the law and formulate proposals for law reform' as well as the removal of obsolete laws. Its statutory mandate involved a combination of developing, codifying, simplifying and modernising the law. The concerns, opportunities and complaints of the legal profession were reflected in the pages of Irish Jurist*, where it was noted in 1971 that 'it has become popular to criticize the legal profession as being conservative, unprogressive, over privileged and overpaid', charges that were rejected. It was insisted, for example, that solicitors' costs were not a significant contributor to inflation and there was a stout insistence on the legal profession's need to regulate its own affairs.*[14]

In 1976, the editor of Irish Jurist*, Nial Osborough, a member of the Faculty of Law in University College Dublin, noted that while progress had been made in relation to academic legal publications despite legal academics being subject to 'the distractions of popularization, pressure group agitation, committee meetings and general educational flapdoodle' (proving, as usual, that the legal profession was in a league of its own when it came to the use of arcane language), there were still a host of areas of modern Irish law which 'have hitherto still escaped that detailed description and analysis which is their due ... The insights of sociology too, have been almost totally ignored ... Elementary critical data on the workings of the criminal justice system is almost completely lacking.'*[15] *Initiatives like the LRC were welcomed as a code of law was deemed necessary 'for the needs of modern Ireland. But modern Ireland is part of the new age of international co-operation and interdependence and her legal system must be redesigned to reflect that position. Now, with the establishment of a permanent LRC, perhaps a real beginning will be made on the task of providing the state with a truly modern legal system based on the rational foundation of an exclusive code.'*[16]

There was much legal focus on aspects of that 'modern Ireland', including how to define family in the modern era, custody disputes, the impact of EEC Treaty Rules, legal protection and marital violence, recognition of foreign divorce law and private law aspects of the Irish constitution. It was suggested in 1978 that 'the process of alienation between law and social practice which has already begun ... will continue.'[17] *There was also a recognition that violence in marriage 'happens on a sizeable scale', it being noted in 1976 that*

'190 women last year faced violence bad enough to seek refuge' in Dublin.[18] *The rights of the child were also of relevance here; by 1970, in light of the Kennedy Report into residential institutions which had recommended children no longer be housed in industrial schools, there was a recognition about the need 'to combat the ethos of the institutions themselves' and that 'child psychology not to mention common humanity suggests that radical change is the children's due'.*[19] *At the end of the decade, a social worker suggested there was too much confusion between a child's need for care and treatment and a child's commission of an offence: 'greater, longer and more damaging intervention is taking place than would be permissible if these two issues were treated separately'. There was a 'widespread reluctance' to acknowledge the deficiencies in the juvenile justice system.*[20]

But this was another area where reform was mooted, sometimes promised but not sufficiently delivered on. In relation to sexual abuse, in particular child abuse by priests, as was revealed by an inquiry published in 2009 into such abuse from the middle of the 1970s onwards, successive archbishops of the Dublin Catholic archdiocese handled allegations of child sexual abuse badly, with 'denial, arrogance and cover-up', and did not report their knowledge of abuse to the Irish police over a period of three decades. The structures and rules of the Catholic Church facilitated the cover-up of abuse. Auxiliary bishops of Dublin were also aware of complaints of child sex abuse, yet assignments of priests to parishes were often made without any reference to such issues. Senior members of the Gardaí regarded the actions of priests as being outside their remit, and some of them reported complaints to the archdiocese instead of investigating them. While some priests did bring allegations of abuse to their superiors, there was, it was found, a 'don't ask, don't tell' policy.[21] *While the 1970s can be seen as a decade where those who were, both historically and in contemporary terms, victims of neglect, abuse or violence had some champions, who took issue with the notion of a Republic that was progressive, at ease with itself and sufficiently wise, outward looking, capable of self-criticism and learning from mistakes, traditional deference and power alliances continued to damage the welfare of the vulnerable.*

– TWENTY-EIGHT –

TROUBLING TIMES FOR THE GUARDIANS OF THE PEACE

Prior to the 1970s, Ireland was by no means a violent country, and the Gardaí had been an unarmed force since its foundation in 1922 (though there were specialist armed units within the force). The total indictable number of crimes reported to the Gardaí from September 1968 to September 1969 was, however, at 25,972 (15,270 in the Dublin metropolitan area and 10,702 in the rest of the country) the highest on record, up from 23,104 in 1968 and 19,029 in 1966. Two-thirds of the indictable crimes in 1969 were offences against property without violence (simple larcenies). The rise was officially said to 'reflect a pattern also evident in other countries' and the detection rate of 55 per cent was regarded as 'high by comparison with other countries'.[1] The increase was seen in the early 1970s to be a product, similar to other countries, of 'urban growth … industrial expansion and an increasingly affluent society' which 'provided greater opportunities for theft. Motor transport became available to criminals in growing numbers.'[2] A substantial rise in indictable crimes was evident in the crime report for the year ended 30 September 1971 at 37,781, compared to 30,756 in 1970, a rise of 23 per cent. But while the number of offences against property with violence had more than trebled since 1961 'offences against the person have not varied much in recent years'. The overall detection rate at 46 per cent was precisely the same as England and Wales, but what was notable was the diversion of Garda manpower due to the Troubles.[3]

A notable increase in tension was evident in the early 1970s regarding how crime was defined and dealt with. The Irish Association of Civil Liberty, for example, opposed the Prohibition of Forcible Entry Bill, one clause of which provided that one who 'encourages or advocates' committing an offence under the Bill would themselves be guilty of an offence, 'but that even to be a member of a group on whose behalf a statement encouraging or advocating such an offence is issued is to be an offence'. The National Union of Journalists was also worried about the implications for press freedom because of provision for penalties for those found guilty of charges relating to the investigation, reporting and photographing of particular activities. Some trade unionists also linked the Prohibition of Forcible Entry Bill to protests against internment in Northern Ireland, writing of 'a trend of repressive legislation in both the 6 and the 26 counties'.[4]

Attacks on unarmed Gardaí, however, caused greater alarm, and the murder of Garda Richard Fallon in April 1970 not only prompted public consternation ('on the day he was buried Dublin came to a standstill') but also some reflection in a memorandum for the government on whether the Gardaí should be armed, even though the Gardaí and their representative bodies 'have not even asked that this be considered and they would probably be the first to oppose it. Arming Gardaí does not necessarily give them more protection – it could well make them more liable to be shot themselves.'[5]

Fallon was the first member of the police force to be killed on duty since 1942. He was shot dead during a raid on a bank in Dublin by an IRA splinter group, Saor Eire (Free Ireland) and no one was ever convicted of the crime: 'In the days following Garda Fallon's funeral there was outrage among the Gardaí when stories of indiscriminate ministerial contacts with subversives, including Saor Eire, gained wide currency,' a reference, in particular to Neil Blaney.[6] The position of the Minister for Justice Micheál Ó Móráin was also problematic in this regard as he 'appeared to be losing his grip on reality'.[7] For the first time in the history of the force a Scott Medal (awarded for bravery and named after Walter Scott, the former honorary commissioner of New York City Police; ninety-two Scott Medals were awarded from 1923–1972) was awarded posthumously, to Deirdre Fallon, widow of the murdered Garda. Despite this, his son Richard, one of his five children, later recalled the lack of support given to the family: 'My mother paid for my father's funeral herself ... the first thing my mother was given was sedatives. She was on them for 3 years. She always felt she had been "handled". It was a complete circus around the funeral and then nothing, no backup, absolutely nothing.' The family many years later were still looking for the file relating to their father's killing to be reopened and critical of the 'muddle' in the handling of its investigation.[8]

Five years later Garda Michael Reynolds was killed after another Dublin bank robbery by Republican subversives. Off duty, he had pursued them on foot and was shot in the head. Noel and Marie Murray were subsequently convicted of capital murder (see Part II). The following year Garda Michael Clerkin was killed in Laois after the IRA detonated a bomb, having lured five Gardaí to the site through an anonymous phone call. His body 'had to be identified by reference to his signet ring'. Thousands attended his funeral in Monaghan. The IRA had not targeted Gardaí in this way before as 'its standing orders expressly barred them' from doing so. The killing created friction within the IRA about the legitimacy of such an action, and was also seen as reflecting heightened tensions between the Gardaí and Republican prisoners in Portlaoise Prison, and bringing into question the force's interrogation techniques. As in the Fallon case, the Clerkin family were not happy with the investigation into this crime – 'all we got was hearsay' – while the Garda Representative Association (GRA) suggested the death penalty needed to be imposed on those convicted of capital offences.[9] (The last execution of an Irish prisoner had been carried out in 1954. While the death penalty was retained on the statute books until 1990, in practice, those convicted of capital offences, including the murder of an on-duty Garda, had their sentences commuted to forty years in prison.)

In 1972 the Garda Síochána celebrated its golden jubilee, and the degree to which the attendant commemorations were dominated by religious services is striking. A Mass was co-celebrated by fifty priests who were sons of members and ex-members of the force, while serving and retired Gardaí assisted on the altar. But there was also a service at St Patrick's Cathedral during which the congregation heard a homily from the Church of Ireland Archbishop of Dublin Alan Buchanan that was like nothing they would have heard from a Catholic Bishop: 'The more I reflect on today, the more I see the resemblance between your job and mine. We both wear uniform; we are both marked men. People expect a high standard from both clergy and Guards, forgetting sometimes that they are all men of flesh and blood. Both of us have to place our public service before our private life. Both need to take positions that are frequently unpopular. Both can be lonely and both can be disappointed; both of us have to deal with much that is sordid and seamy.'[10]

Minister for Justice Des O'Malley took the opportunity during the jubilee to heap praise on himself for introducing a new disciplinary code for the force, 'a code which is acknowledged to be a liberal one, not just by comparison with what it replaced but also with what applies in other police forces,'[11] an assertion that may be looked on as somewhat ironic as the 1970s progressed. But amidst the celebrations, difficult issues remained to be resolved. While the Conroy Commission had made recommendations on the remuneration and conditions of service for Gardaí, it was also very critical of the administration and internal operations of the force. The commission's report had urged the government to carry out a complete reorganisation, especially in respect of the relationship between the Garda and the Department of Justice, suggesting the commissioner of the Gardaí should be answerable to an authority other than the Minister for Justice. According to the *Irish Times*, 'the real pity is that the senior officers of the force have not fought against the steady erosion of their powers and responsibilities by the Department of Justice and the Gardaí'.

It was also maintained that, at between 7,000 and 8,000, the number of serving Gardaí was inadequate, though 'of late the poor conditions, severe discipline and low pay of the Gardaí which caused the Conroy Commission to be set up have been somewhat alleviated'.[12] Nonetheless, as the decade progressed it became obvious that 'the negotiating machinery available to Gardaí for sorting out difficulties and grievances with their senior officers was ineffective and outdated'. By 1978, there were four representative associations for the force; improvements in pay and welfare and the introduction of overtime and payment for unsociable hours brought their own problems and led to 'wide disparities in earnings between members of the same rank'; procedures for promotion were found to be unfair.[13]

In the midst of this, there seemed to be mixed messages from the crime figures. In 1973 the overall crime figures were down 3.1 per cent on 1972 but offences against the person were up 25 per cent. There were twenty-one cases of murder, 123 armed robberies and two cases of infanticide ('the dead body of a female infant found in a river; drowned. A woman, 39 years charged. Fined £25').[14] The following year there was an increase of 5.5 per cent in indictable offences, to 40,096; notable in that year was the highest number of murders yet recorded at fifty-one, 'this figure includes 33 victims of car bomb blasts in Dublin (26) and Monaghan (7) on 17 May 1974'. The value of property stolen amounted to £7,335,656, of which property to the value £5,428,666 was recovered. As commented by the Garda Commissioner, 'the overall increase in crime figures over the previous year is not great, but the general level of serious crime and vandalism in the community is a cause of concern. I should like to see more attention given to aspects of policing which relate to the prevention of crime and offences. This is difficult to achieve in prevailing conditions when so many members of the force have to be employed on duties of a security nature, the necessity for which is likely to continue for some considerable time.'[15] In July 1975 the Department of Justice stressed the need to cut overtime for Gardaí by a third as it was costing £6½ million a year, but the issue was withdrawn from the cabinet agenda.[16]

At the end of 1976, when Minister for Justice Patrick Cooney was planning on increasing Garda strength from 8,500 to 9,000, there were said to be six applicants for every post available and the desire to change the system of entry – under new proposals those with the Leaving Certificate would no longer be exempt from the entrance exam – met strong resistance. The *Irish Independent* suggested 'we are still awaiting a modern and comprehensive recruitment policy for the force'. One question that was being asked was why the force could not attract graduates who had emerged from the third-level institutions 'since the boom in higher education during the sixties'.[17]

There were serious tensions between the Department of Justice under Patrick Cooney and the Department of Finance under Richie Ryan, who accused Justice of not bringing the proposal to increase the numbers of Gardaí to cabinet in the proper way and not making a convincing case for extra recruitment. Cooney responded to the criticisms with vigour:

> The Finance memorandum is an extraordinary document, both in tone and content. Its tone is offensive. Its content is an amalgam of a lecture to the Department of Justice and a line of argument so tendentious as to be unworthy of a government department. It is as if the people responsible for its compilation feel themselves under such pressure to suggest savings in public expenditure that they resort to any kind of argument in order to show that they are doing something and that the blame lies elsewhere. Substantial savings cannot be made

in police expenditure except by cutting the level of service but Finance try to brush facts aside and look for scapegoats in the Department of Justice.[18]

Ryan's reply to Cooney was hilariously bitchy as the festive holiday began:

> I have now read the diatribe attached to the memorandum ... if the time wasted by the authors, stenographers, typists and copiers had been put to proper use you might have been able to comply with cabinet procedures. As the conscientious officers of both my departments have useful work to do, I have directed them not to dissipate their time and talents in replying to your department's logorrhoea. I will deal with it at cabinet level. Meanwhile, it is well to recall that the government decision of 18 June last was the result of an oral statement by you that an article in the Garda Review could cause embarrassment were you not in a position to announce an increase in Garda strength. Small wonder public expenditure gets out of control when millions are spent on such flimsy grounds. A happy Christmas to you.[19]

Cooney, of course, had no intention of leaving it at that and returned to the fray with his wounded pride after Christmas, accusing Ryan of effectively telling him 'you have been seriously falling down on the job for the last so many years. Diatribe is defined in my dictionary as bitter criticism. All in all, I think if there was a scale with which to measure bitterness of criticism [your memorandum] would rank higher than the reply to it ... A dog that is kicked is apt to bite and this dog was being kicked very seriously.' He expressed his wish to reduce the temperature of the exchanges between them and then, dripping with sarcasm, took the opportunity 'to wish you in return an outstandingly prosperous new year'.[20] Ryan may have got the better of Cooney in terms of the potency of his poisonous pen, but as usual, he lost the battle at cabinet and the increase in Garda numbers was sanctioned.

– TWENTY-NINE –

A DISCREDITED FORCE?

Various claims and counterclaims as to the effectiveness and discipline of the Gardaí were made throughout the decade. In November 1971, Jack Lynch was contacted by an anonymous 'old guard' who decried a new generation of Gardaí with no concept of loyalty or respect for the institutions of democratic government: 'The present situation of the Garda Síochána is due to the laxity in enforcing the regulations plus the widespread activities of those members who are engaged in business. Their police duties are secondary from dance hall bouncers, taxi drivers to assisting in operating "businesses" usually under their wives names.'[1]

By the middle of the 1970s it was becoming apparent that some official response to complaints against Gardaí was required. In February 1974 the cabinet had agreed that it would be necessary to 'initiate a complaints procedure for alleged offences committed by police on an all-Ireland basis and that this should be taken up with the British government'. The following summer, a solicitor in Dublin complained that denials of Gardaí misbehaviour were being issued without any proper investigation.[2] The Gardaí were also accused throughout the decade of demonstrating no willingness to co-operate with the media; *Hibernia* complained in 1971 that 'the silence from Garda headquarters is always deafening. There is hardly a newsman in Dublin who can recall ever getting a satisfactory reply there to even the most innocuous query.'[3] In 1976, journalist Vincent Browne, then with the *Sunday Independent*, was said to have drawn 'from a semantically-minded member of the Dublin interrogation squad the explanation that their treatment of prisoners could not be described as torture because "we do not use instruments"'.[4]

The *Irish Times* caused a stir in February 1977 with its exposé of Garda brutality under the headline 'Gardaí Using North-style Brutality in Interrogation Techniques' and alleged that 'the "heavy gang" as the group has been nicknamed within the force, physically assaults and applies severe psychological pressure on suspects. The pressure includes threats, lies and psychological tricks and is intensified by depriving suspects of sleep, food and water over long periods ... there are also suggestions that the "heavy gang" are forcing people to stand spread-eagled against a wall for lengthy periods.' The articles also included extensive interviews with victims of Garda misconduct. The newspaper insisted that it had not been seduced by Republican propaganda but rather the articles were 'the product of many weeks' diligent research and investigation by skilled journalists'.[5]

The report of an Amnesty International Mission to the Republic in June 1977 examined twenty-eight cases relating to the period April 1976 to May 1977 and referred to interrogation and maltreatment by plain-clothes detectives: 'Allegations common to every case examined are that the victims were at various times beaten and punched' and deprived of food, drink and sleep and there was a consistency in the nature of allegations from 'persons arrested at different times and in different parts of the country'. Lawyers could not get access to their clients and this was 'exacerbated by a common practice of moving an arrested person to several different police stations in the course of one day or night'.

It concluded that the Special Criminal Court (see page 362) 'decided that the consistency in police testimony was a mark of the truth of police testimony and attributed consistency in the defendant's testimony to a "criminal conspiracy" on the part of the accused to defame the police'. The report claimed that the government was doing nothing in this regard and this was highlighted as particularly troubling in light of the fact that the government had made a 'significant contribution' towards securing the adoption by the UN General Assembly in December 1975 of the declaration on the protection of all persons from being subjected to torture or other cruel and inhuman or degrading treatment or punishment and which specifically recommended impartial investigation of such allegations.

As Minister for Foreign Affairs, Garret FitzGerald had conducted extensive correspondence with Amnesty in the previous few years. Kevin White of Amnesty International praised FitzGerald in 1975 for 'the active concern which you personally and the Irish government shows in human rights and continues to press in UN'.[6] A year earlier, however, one of the civil servants in FitzGerald's department had suggested in relation to a UN resolution on torture that 'our approach to the conference is generally to support proposals on humanitarian grounds where they do not create serious problems or are not impracticable',[7] hardly a ringing endorsement of the Irish state's championing of human rights. Three years later FitzGerald decided not to allow his name to be included in an Amnesty poster campaign in connection with 'Prisoner of Conscience' year.[8] When he corresponded with Cooney over the allegations of Garda brutality, however, he felt 'we need to give the Amnesty letter serious and urgent consideration in view of the gravity of the allegations and the accepted reputation of Amnesty International'.

The coalition refused to co-operate and later in 1977 there was pressure on the new Fianna Fáil government to do something about it. The report was given to the Garda Commissioner Edmund Garvey with request for a response within fourteen days.[9] As one respondent put it to Jack Lynch, 'I don't believe we can be two faced about this – seeking enquiries abroad [the Irish government had taken a case against the British government to the European Court of Human Rights in Strasbourg regarding the ill treatment of those interned in Northern Ireland in 1971] and not conceding them at home,' while the Irish Association of Civil Liberty insisted that an independent police tribunal was needed, although, somewhat naively, it was far from convinced of the veracity of most claims: 'It is likely that most of these charges are baseless and are brought to cover up the misdeeds of the accused. Such charges must, nevertheless, have some effect not only on the morale of our admirable police forces but on public opinion.'[10]

Frank Murray in the Department of the Taoiseach felt the Amnesty report made for disturbing reading and that, if published, 'it would, to say the least, take greatly from the likely outcome in the Strasbourg case' (which concluded in 1978 that the use of interrogation techniques in Northern Ireland had constituted 'inhuman and degrading treatment'). He felt 'either a formal or informal inquiry' which would not be published was necessary, as was an independent complaints board; while another view was that a report by a 'foreign body' should not be allowed to influence the government to take any action 'which would have the effect of undermining the effectiveness of the Gardaí dealing with crime'.[11] The advice from the Attorney General Tony Hederman was that there was nothing to indicate that a pubic inquiry into alleged torture could vindicate the rights of citizens 'in a more efficacious way than the normal procedures at present available under our constitution and the courts'.[12]

The atmosphere in relation to policing had become so poisoned by 1978 that there was said to have been secret Garda surveillance placed on the Director of Public Prosecutions Eamon Barnes, and an atmosphere of 'distrust and suspicion' as a legacy of the coalition's security policy and the tenure as Commissioner of the force of Edmund Garvey (who had been appointed in 1975 by the coalition government). A deeply religious teetotaller who had no interest in activities outside of work, he announced at the commencement of his commissionership that he would keep in touch with the grassroots of the then 8,500-strong force and improve morale. His term, however, was dogged by bitter controversy, rancorous relations with his own force, and party-political feuds. His appointment, over the heads of three more likely candidates, had been largely as a result of his impressive performance in the anti-subversive section C3 of the Gardaí at a time when security against paramilitaries was one of the state's paramount concerns. The Minister for Justice Patrick Cooney acknowledged that he had appointed him because he was considered a 'tough cop', which in itself placed Garvey under unprecedented political pressure to produce results.

At this time the Gardaí and their representative body were at loggerheads with the Department of Justice over pay and conditions, and morale and disciplinary problems were matters of concern. Garvey's almost ruthless approach to discipline merely exacerbated tensions, as did his farcical off-the-record demand that each Garda should issue 200 summonses per year for traffic and other minor offences (which, if put into practice, would have involved the summonsing of 1.5 million people per year). Garvey's excessive paranoia resulted in his attempting to persuade Eamon Barnes to prosecute the editors of the *Garda Review* in the Special Criminal Court over an editorial written in June 1976, which was critical of his leadership. He argued that the editors were illegally usurping the functions of the government, but the bemused DPP refused to proceed.

As well as facing accusations that the editors of the *Garda Review* were being placed under Garda surveillance and that members of the force were being penalised for minor breaches of regulations, Garvey was also beset by disagreements over transfers and promotions. At the same time he was under pressure to achieve results in detecting subversive crime, and he presided over a regime which spawned the above-mentioned notorious 'heavy gang' who took violent shortcuts in the process of law enforcement, badly tarnishing the reputation of the force. One of the successes of his tenure was the rescue in 1975 of the kidnapped Dutch industrialist Tiede Herrema (see Part II) for which he was decorated as a member of the Orange Order by the Dutch government, though retrospective controversy was attached to his signature on the document that effectively ended the kidnap siege.

Just how had the special branch found Herrema? According to Conor Cruise O'Brien, one of the detectives told him that 'one of the gang had been arrested and we felt sure he knew where Herrema was. So this man was transferred under Branch escort from a prison in the country to a prison in Dublin and on the way the car stopped. Then the escort started asking him questions and when at first he refused to answer, they beat the shit out of him. Then he told them where Herrema was. I refrained from telling this story to Garret [FitzGerald] or Justin [Keating] because I thought it would worry them, it didn't worry me.'[13] There was a hypocrisy to all this, given O'Brien's pious assertions that he could not keep the conversations he had with John O'Connell about IRA contacts secret as it was a matter of state security (see Part II).

Garvey's fate was sealed following controversy over the investigation of the IRA assassination of the British ambassador to Ireland, Christopher Ewart-Biggs, in July 1976. The mistaken identification of a fingerprint at the scene of the crime led to concern over the reliability and integrity of the fingerprint section of the force. Four members of the section were dismissed in 1977 without reference to the Minister for Justice, Gerry Collins. Not only that, but the detectives who had exposed the mistaken identification were victimised. Two of the Gardaí who had been dismissed began legal proceedings, and the minister also accused Garvey of failing to inform the government that the assassination suspect had been wrongly identified. In May 1978, Collins confirmed in the Dáil that Garda experts had made wrong fingerprint identifications in four murder cases during the previous eight years but the DPP had decided not to take criminal proceedings against the Garda officers responsible.

Although he was dealing with both a hostile force and a hostile government, Garvey resisted the representations made to him to resign. It was also clear that many Gardaí had made representations to Fianna Fáil during the general election campaign of 1977, urging politicians to replace Garvey if the party was elected, which was precisely what happened. Fianna Fáil TD Máire Geoghegan-Quinn, elected in a by-election in Galway in 1975 and who in 1979 became the first female cabinet minister since Constance Markievicz in 1919, was reputed to have told Fianna Fáil's press officer Frank Dunlop, that TDs 'were fed up with the Gardaí in their constituencies coming into their clinics every weekend complaining about Garvey and his *modus operandi* and asking the government to do something about him. Enough Gardaí managed to harass enough ministers.' Garvey was 'known to have Fine Gael sympathies', and Dunlop is also likely to have been involved in trying to influence the newspapers to create the publicity necessary for the dismissal of Garvey.[14]

On 19 January 1978 Garvey was dismissed after refusing to resign, with the government giving no reason for the decision, except that it had no confidence in him. It was the first dismissal of a commissioner since fascist sympathiser Eoin O'Duffy was dismissed by the new Fianna Fáil government in 1933. Despite rumours that the government was considering appointing a civil servant as commissioner, the deputy commissioner, Patrick McLaughlin, to the satisfaction of the Garda representative body, replaced Garvey. The government's incompetent handling of the dismissal prompted Garvey to sue them, and a High Court judgment, confirmed by the Supreme Court, maintained that the dismissal was null and void, and the state was forced to pay him £13,000 compensation.[15]

In the same month as Garvey's dismissal, it was maintained in *Magill* in January 1978 that Minister Gerry Collins was now providing 'the face of liberal and humane administration of justice. The image has been maintained by simple measures which put no strain on the state's security, such as allowing the Gallagher–Dugdale wedding'[16] (see Part II). But Collins was also criticised for promoting Gardaí against whom allegations had been made in relation to brutality: 'Of the approximately 40 Irish Republican Socialist Party [IRSP, an organisation that had split from Official Sinn Féin and had engaged with a bloody feud with it and whose founder Séamus Costello was shot dead in Dublin in 1977] members who were arrested on 5 April 1976, nine subsequently alleged that they had been beaten by plain-clothes Gardaí,'[17] including those arrested for the Sallins train robbery in 1976 when £150,000 in used banknotes and postal orders was stolen.

Four IRSP members were charged with the Sallins robbery at the Special Criminal Court in 1978; in all, over the course of the investigation of the robbery, fifteen IRSP men 'reported being beaten and nine of them alleged grievous assault'. But this was only the beginning of what became a saga. The court found 'as a fact' that a judge who had clearly been asleep during the trial had been awake; the Supreme Court agreed but the death of the judge in question mid-trial, 'ended that judicial charade'. A new trial began and three accused, Nicky Kelly, Osgur Breathnach and Brian McNally (charges against a fourth were dropped) were convicted on the basis of false confessions beaten out of them. Justice Liam Hamilton ruled that the injuries on the accused 'were either self-inflicted or inflicted with collaboration with others, but were not caused by members of the Gardaí'. The counsel defending the accused, Patrick MacEntee, wondered: 'Must we wait for a corpse before reasonable doubt emerges?' The convicted men received sentences ranging from nine to twelve years but Kelly had jumped bail and fled to the US.

He returned in 1980 after the convictions of his co-accused were overturned on appeal and the IRA admitted it had carried out the robbery, but the courts rejected Kelly's appeal. He endured four years in prison and a thirty-eight-day hunger strike before being released on 'humanitarian grounds' in 1984; it took another eight years before he was pardoned and compensated. The Catholic Church played a vital role in the campaign to free Kelly but 'it has never been explained or inquired into how he confessed to a crime he did not commit; how the courts accepted that "confession" as evidence, despite details presented of its circumstances'.[18] In the same year as the Sallins train robbery trial, the government was clearly not keen on many of the recommendations made in the April 1978 report of a committee chaired by Justice Barra Ó Briain into additional safeguards necessary for the protection against ill treatment of people in Garda custody and protection of Gardaí against unfounded allegations of brutality; the committee had proposed a complaints tribunal.[19]

The Troubles also provided the backdrop to the controversial Emergency Powers Act of 1976. The proposal was to extend the power to detain a person arrested under section 30 of the original 1939 Act so as to permit their detention for a period of seven days after the arrest, instead of the existing forty-eight hours, but one for which the government sought immunity from challenge by declaring a state of emergency, an issue that was causing 'obvious distress' to Cosgrave, while Attorney General Declan

Costello thought it 'likely' that it would be declared unconstitutional.[20] It was regarded as an Act with 'a substantial anti-IRA content' that could create the possibility of 'a change of IRA tactics'.[21]

Some lawyers were arguing that the Northern Ireland conflict was not a state of war. The motion, however, was carried in the Dáil after heated debate on 2 September 1976 and the Attorney General's Office sought to draft a letter of derogation from obligations imposed by the European Council's Convention for the Protection of Human Rights in light of the bill which would be delivered to the secretary general of the Council of Europe as soon as the bill was signed by the president. On 20 September, President Ó Dálaigh consulted his Council of State (the body provided for by the constitution to advise, but not direct, a president on the exercise of his or her discretionary powers) for four hours, a measure of the complexity of the constitutional issues and perhaps also 'the depth of division in the counselling of Ó Dálaigh'.[22] When the cabinet was informed that Ó Dálaigh was sending the bill to the Supreme Court it was decided 'that the AG should make an informal approach to the Chief Justice with a view to having the hearing arranged for the earliest possible date'. On 15 October the court decided it was 'not repugnant in any way' to the constitution.[23] But, as was seen in Part I, the whole episode was in many ways repugnant to decency in politics.

The Troubles also led to an increase in the profile and professionalism of the Irish army. As was maintained by journalists Don Lavery and Brian Trench in 1979, the 15,000 strong force had become 'the only European defence force geared primarily for counter-subversive operations; the new Irish army has become modern, professional and commonplace in Irish life ... In the last ten years the Irish defence forces have doubled the numbers of their permanent membership and now cost the state nearly £120 million a year.' In contrast to the undermanned naval service and air corps, this was a modern, well-regarded army, which had a significant reputation for UN service since 1960. In October 1973 the Dáil approved the dispatch of a contingent of 240 Irish troops to serve with the UN peacekeeping force in the Middle East, though reports from the Lebanon later that decade indicated that many of the soldiers were not 'altogether comfortable in the largely passive role which is assigned to them ... More importantly, it is the only European army conceived above all for anti-guerrilla activities and internal security.' There were thirty daily army patrols on the Irish border by the end of the decade.[24] In 1977, five soldiers were killed by shrapnel on the army's artillery range in County Wicklow in the worst military accident since the 1940s. The army was also called on to assist in civilian affairs, which was apparent in 1978 when troops 'were alerted to deal with a possible road blockage arising from trade union anti-unemployment demonstration in Waterford'. Problems of discipline, drunkenness and assault and the large proportion of soldiers living at home were also cited.[25]

– THIRTY –

THE TERROR OF URBAN DECAY?

Crimes of a subversive nature were not the only law and order issues to contend with in the 1970s. There were frequent assertions of concern about urban crime or, as was discussed at Dublin City Council in 1976, 'the general disquiet and fear among our citizens arising from the unprecedented and increasing incidence of robberies with violence (and vandalism) in our city'.[1] It was not just elected representatives who pushed a hard law and order line; in July 1976, Dr John Nash from Limerick, a member of the Medico-Social Research Board, maintained 'it is a reasonably just society in this country' but that 'the present comparatively mild punishments meted out encourage an ambivalent attitude in many people, particularly those who have emotional feelings about political problems'. He suggested that there was a need to reconsider capital punishment and firmer government, concluding 'there exists in the media and in some of the less reliable psychiatrists, a very sympathetic and quite unreliable view of psychopathic people'.[2] Members of the cabinet at various stages in the 1970s examined their options in terms of combating crime; in November 1976 the Minister for Justice Patrick Cooney mooted a possible referendum on the right to restrict bail, while the lack of Gardaí at night in large urban centres like Ballyfermot and Limerick was criticised. Conor Cruise O'Brien mentioned 'the deterioration in Garda attitudes caused by their excessive overtime earnings a few years ago', while Cooney was concerned that 'one of the biggest difficulties, particularly in Dublin, was the lack of a custodial institution for hard core young criminals'. He was also conscious in 1977 of 'recent agitation in press etc. re: failure of Gardaí to combat criminal activities, vandalism etc.'. Dublin City Council had also notched up the rhetoric by referring in 1977 to 'the terror which afflicts us today' in Dublin city.[3]

Fine Gael TD John Kelly also sought to make political capital out of the crime issue, referring in November 1977 to an 'incredible and sudden rise in the number of armed robberies and attempted armed robberies … unequalled since the civil war'.[4] In August 1977 new measures to combat crime, including new mobile units in the main cities and Garda overtime, were announced. Later that year one correspondent came up with a novel solution when she asked of Lynch: 'Do you think that instead of putting violent people into prison they could be put onto one of the islands off the coast?'[5]

Others preferred the more drastic option of the reintroduction of the death penalty; in contrast, in 1976 the Labour Party's Ruairí Quinn sought to introduce a Private Member's Bill to abolish capital punishment.[6] While overall indictable offences had increased from 40,096 to 54,382 between 1974 and 1976, the detection rate had also dropped significantly, from 48.1 per cent to 41.3 per cent in the same period. Taking a longer view, from 1966 to 1976 'serious crime has gone up 165 per cent and the detection rate has fallen by one-third'. More than 30,000 crimes involving violence against the person were recorded in 1976.[7]

There were also suggestions that the right to silence should be modified; rigorous interrogation was what was needed, the argument went, rather than more sophisticated forensics, and therein lies some of the explanation as to why the tactics of some members of the force became disreputable and tarnished during this decade: 'The police service in the North has access to what are probably the most advanced forensic techniques in the world; they are highly computerised, they have almost unlimited cash, but, despite these advantages, they find it essential to use what they regard as tried and trusted police methods.'[8]

In 1976, the Department of Justice was keen, even though it suspected it might be regarded as unconstitutional, to amend prison rules to exclude legal advisers or impose conditions on their visits to prisoners in light of a Supreme Court decision that 'a prisoner on remand or awaiting trial has the right to visits from his solicitor out of the hearing of a prison officer'. The Irish Association of Civil Liberty regarded a change in this status as not only a grave violation of civil rights but also an interference with the rights of the legal profession.[9]

Reflecting on the crime figures for 1975, with 48,387 indictable offences, an increase of 20.7 per cent over the previous year, Edmund Garvey suggested the overall crime picture 'can only be described as disturbing ... criminals are becoming more vicious and mean. Attacks on old and disabled people in their homes, a type of crime practically unknown in this country some years ago, are now on the increase. The use of firearms and other offensive weapons in robberies is becoming more widespread and menacing.' He also maintained that 'violent criminal activity designed to intimidate for political purposes in the border areas has undoubtedly influenced crime trends throughout the whole country'.[10]

The year 1975 also saw an increased number of persons charged with drug offences. By means of courses with the drug unit at Dublin Castle, 'more of our members are receiving specialised instruction on dealing with these types of offences'. The Drugs Squad had begun operations in 1968, when only four arrests were made (all for possession of marijuana); that figure had jumped to 184 by 1973.[11] Overall, 293 people were charged with drug offences that year; 'cannabis continues to be the most widely used drug' (resulting in 117 charges) but only one person was charged in relation to heroin.[12] A new drug law in 1977 – the Misuse of Drugs Act – distinguished between marijuana and other kinds of illegal drugs and extended search rights. The chief of the Garda Drugs Squad, Denis Mullins, maintained that '90 per cent of all drug users are experimenters ... The majority of young experimenters will manage to hold down jobs and even succeed in business.' The Drugs Squad was regarded as well organised, but senior detectives 'say that the problem is sufficiently small and they are more concerned with the number of people drinking cheap wine and cider'.[13] Much more potent was poitín; in 1977, seventy-two people were convicted on charges arising from distillation or possession of poitín out of 138 prosecutions.[14]

In 1977 there was a further 15.7 per cent increase in indictable crime and the detection rate was 38.8 per cent, down from 43.4 per cent in 1975. There were 2,767 Gardaí in Dublin (35 per cent of the total) and 5,211 in the rest of the country, which meant that 35 per cent of the force had to deal with 57 per cent of the crimes taking place in the state; this was seen as an obvious indication of the need to increase the size of the force in Dublin. In August 1978 reference was made in the *Irish Press* to the notion of Gerry Collins considering the arming of Gardaí. It editorialised that 'we cannot tolerate a situation whereby Gardaí are being pushed around by youngsters with guns'.[15]

The youngsters supposedly 'pushing around' Gardaí generated considerable correspondence and resolutions, and the provision of more detention homes for young offenders was considered urgent. A memorandum in March 1977 referred to 'government anxiety to have custodial accommodation for young offenders provided without delay'. At a cabinet meeting two months later the Minister for Labour, Michael O'Leary, mentioned 'Garda difficulties in bringing kids before court as it is necessary to satisfy the court that parents have been interviewed. Daingean [a former Industrial School in County Offaly] was mentioned as a possible temporary place of detention.'[16] The same month, priests of the parish of Seán McDermott Street in Dublin's inner city, including the Jesuit Fr Peter McVerry, who was subsequently to open a hostel for the homeless and became one of their leading champions, wrote to Cosgrave about 'the breakdown of law and order in this area in relation to young offenders under 16 years of age'; small gangs who robbed, terrorised and destroyed property. The priests also referred to the lack of custodial care for such lawbreakers: 'we understand Ireland is the only country in the EEC in this unique position'. What they were demanding was 'enlightened' custodial care. But just who was responsible at government level? This was a core issue; as recognised by the priests concerned: 'We could address this open letter to the Minister for Justice, but he would probably refer us to the Minister for Education who, in turn, would advise us to consult the Minister for Health ... The ultimate sanction for their contempt of the law at present is a lecture from a district justice.'

The Minister for Education Richard Burke rejected the notion of a 'juvenile crime wave', suggesting 'the extent of the problem tends to be exaggerated by those who are the victims of the delinquents in question'. It was, he maintained, the 'hardcore which is quite small in numbers which needs to be tackled ... In many cases secure arrangements will serve only to contain, without succeeding in reforming, the delinquents in question.'[17] In 1977 Gene Kerrigan, writing in *Magill* magazine, suggested, after a district justice had announced he was scared to walk through the streets of Dublin, that 'there are very good reasons why a District Justice should be scared to walk through the centre of Dublin', but that 'somehow the problem wasn't so pressing before it spilled into O'Connell Street'. Teenagers and youth workers insisted that police beating of wayward kids was 'common'. Many reports by youth workers were predicting the consequences of neglect (in Ballyfermot, for example, there were an estimated 10,000 teenagers with only 4 per cent catered for by youth clubs), while the *Sunday World* asked if the birch was the answer. Kerrigan pointed out that 'in all of Dublin there are only 4 full-time youth workers face to face with the kids. In the much feared, much criticised North City Centre area, there is only one full-time youth worker in the field.'[18]

By the end of 1978 it was being asserted that 'robbery is becoming a way of life in Ireland with over £8 million stolen last year and the armed robbery proceeds showing a major boost this year'. There were 817 armed robberies in 1977 and reference was made to a '16-fold increase in turnover in a decade', helped by the Gardaí's 'archaic structures and equipment', while Garda beatings were creating 'ferocious bad feeling' in the underworld.[19] The rise in armed robberies was one factor that contributed to the increase in private security, which by 1978 was believed to be one of Ireland's leading growth industries. It was estimated that year that there were 110 security firms in the Republic, up from fifty in 1974 and employing 7,000 people. It was also maintained, ironically, that 'the business is riddled with crooks and criminals'.[20]

But statistics could be used in a variety of ways. A memorandum from the Department of Justice in June 1978 made the point that, 'Despite our reputation, we are, apparently, not a nation greatly given to crime. The number of indictable offences here, in 1977, was approximately 21 per 1,000 of the population. In the UK in 1976 [it was] 44 per 1,000 ... Neither are we policed particularly heavily. We have now over 10,000 Gardaí or approximately 3.3 per 1,000 of the population' (the equivalent figure in the UK was 2.2).[21]

Some of the pious assertions about a decline in values and contempt for law and order were hypocritical. There seemed to be much mental compartmentalisation on the part of people as to what constituted crime, given the attitudes that existed, for example, towards tax evasion. Many people were greatly given to such evasion, a matter that became clear in the context of the move to computerise motor vehicle registration. This was believed necessary as, according to a memorandum in October 1976, some 400,000 inquiries were made by the Gardaí each year at local taxation offices in connection with ownership, accidents, parking offences and tax: 'Queries in relation to ownership are at present processed manually at considerable expense. For example, a vehicle which is first registered in Dublin may subsequently be registered in Cork and then say in Monaghan. The Gardaí have to go around the three before locating the necessary information. In the case of parking fines the time wasted in this exercise may mean that the offences are statute barred.' But it was also believed that 'centralisation of ownership records would be of considerable help to local taxation offices in their efforts to deal with tax evasion problems ... evasion of payment of road tax is a source of serious concern ... On certain assumptions, the annual tax loss in the Dublin area was £1 million approximately ... Given the same pattern of evasion, the loss for the whole country would be £3 million.'[22]

VAT rates also exacerbated the smuggling problem. It was suggested in 1978 that 20 per cent of the luxury electrical goods market was taken over by smuggled goods, largely due to a VAT rate of 8 per cent in Northern Ireland compared to 40 per cent in the Republic. Cars were being smuggled but so were pigs, to the extent that 'in the period between early spring 1976 and the autumn of the same year, pigs were being wheeled round and round the border until they were dizzy. There was an EEC subsidy to be gained from exporting pigs north. The loophole was that this subsidy was available every time the pigs went north. Consequently, the pigs were going north, collecting the subsidy, being smuggled south and then being sent back north to collect the subsidy once again.'[23]

In tandem with the focus on crime, human and civil rights groups became more vocal in highlighting what were perceived as frequent abuses of power. The Irish Association of Civil Liberty was active in this regard; originally formed in 1948 to draw particular attention to the odious impact of censorship, its champions had included Owen Sheehy Skeffington and writer Seán O'Faoláin, and it had been labelled communist by its right-wing detractors. It was said to have 'worked on relatively thankless tasks' in the early 1970s, 'such as investigating conditions in convent laundries, mental homes, national schools, borstal institutions, the Bridewell [a Garda station in Dublin city] and nursing homes'.[24] A new organisation, the Irish Council of Civil Liberties, (ICCL) emerged in June 1976. Its executive committee included Kader Asmal, Mary Robinson and Mairín de Burca and it identified a number of issues of 'immediate concern', including the need for an independent Garda complaints procedure, a proper system of legal aid in civil and criminal cases, equality for women, a campaign for children's rights, and an end to capital punishment. In response to its formation, an *Irish Times* editorial observed: 'The new body has already been attacked in some quarters as "conservative" and "middle class"; it is likely to incur equal criticism from those who consider its bias too radical. Between those two poles, it may well strike the correct balance.'[25] Asmal (who had also assisted in the establishment of the Free Legal Aid Centres) asserted that the ICCL opposed 'extremism from the State and individuals'. He insisted there was no need to apologise for the promotion of civil liberties and that the exercise of state power needed continuous supervision. The same year as it was inaugurated, it was maintained in *Hibernia* that social workers and free legal-aid workers were listening to 'dozens of cases of police brutality' and complaining of the excesses of the Garda special branch.[26]

Minister for Justice Patrick Cooney, however, made it clear that he would view things from an alternative perspective: 'Police chiefs here are coming around to the view that a lack of discipline on the part of society is responsible for this increase in crime. They see the world riding a materialistic whirlwind with people not being prepared to work anymore to earn the money they want in order to buy material goods. Not being prepared to work and wanting everything at once, more and more they steal it.'[27] In truth this was the sort of defence and state of mind that was used by the state in order to afford no tolerance to protest of any kind; John Kelly, for example, referred to a plethora of protest groups in 1976 who would be 'better off down on their knees'.[28]

Certain individuals were singled out for vindictive harassment. In 1978, Marie McMahon, a member of Irishwomen United, formed in 1975 by women with a background in radical and socialist politics and which advocated free contraception, self-determined sexuality, equal pay and the establishment of women's centres, was prosecuted for putting up posters for a demonstration against censorship after the feminist publication *Spare Rib* was banned for carrying information on contraception. She was initially held under the Emergency Powers Act and was interrogated about the women's movement. She was eventually charged with loitering and prostitution and bail of £1,000 was demanded; at the time of her arrest she had been chatting with a woman who had been involved in an RTÉ programme on prostitution, which had become the subject of a legal dispute between RTÉ and the Gardaí.

After her final court hearing in August 1978 she refused to be bound to the peace and was given a suspended sentence; both she and members of her family 'were harassed by the police during the 3 years of her suspended sentence'. The feminist protests relating to this case were significant as they demonstrated the emergence of more co-ordinated and effective lobbying and much more public discourse about violence against women, and 'key issues in this case were censorship, contraception, prostitution, women's freedom of movement in the public sphere on the city streets, activism and the freedom to protest'.[29]

Domestic crime was also put under the spotlight in new ways. Wife-beating was something that received unprecedented publicity in the late 1970s. In 1975 *Hibernia* magazine highlighted, through feminist Nuala Fennell and solicitor and family law expert Alan Shatter, the case of a woman who was forced into hospital against her will with the connivance of a local doctor and the parish priest after she had tried to flee a bad marriage. She had suffered from depression and endured beatings at the hands of her husband and had sought to make a new life with her children; her 'crime' it was concluded 'is an Irish one'.[30]

Journalist Janet Martin referred to wife-beating in 1978 as 'a frequent feature of Irish family life'. Between 1976 and 1977, the Dublin Women's Aid organisation provided 19,000 bed nights for over 210 families and the issue of 'sexual assaults' was also raised. In Martin's coverage, it was recorded 'one woman says her husband intersperses the beatings by dousing her with holy water'. One former Garda Commissioner maintained the Garda were reluctant to become involved 'in domestic squabbles' and a 'flair for understatement seems to carry over into the courts. A judge expresses regret that law makes no provision that would enable courts to give husbands, barred from their homes, visiting rights to their children'. As Nuala Fennell saw it, 'there is a simplistic belief that you can separate the husband who is a bastard to his wife from the man who is father to the children'. It was also found that 'solicitors for their part are notoriously unwilling to take on family casework. For one thing, it doesn't pay. Indeed, a measure of their unwillingness is the fact that the free legal advice centres (FLAC) which are operated by law students in Dublin, reckon to have dealt with 6,000 family law cases in 8 years of operation.'[31]

Journalist Nell McCafferty encountered a woman whose children were in care; she had met her future husband through a lonely-hearts column in the Catholic family magazine *Ireland's Own*:

He was a minor civil servant. On the first afternoon they met they

> had sexual intercourse and she became pregnant. The child died in the womb and she became pregnant again. They married immediately. The ceremony was attended by neither kith nor kin on either side. He soon broke her jaw. Then he broke her arm. After a few years she fled their council house. Though the Catholic Church annulled their marriage, Mary could not claim the welfare benefits to which a single mother was entitled because she was still a wife in the eyes of the state and she could not get the benefits to which a deserted wife was entitled because she was deemed to have deserted her husband.[32]

Nuala Fennell, in particular, made an exceptional contribution to increasing awareness about domestic violence and providing shelter to its victims[33] (see Part VIII). Women's Aid opened its first home for battered wives in 1974, and within its first year of existence sheltered 117 women and children in a four-bedroomed house.[34] Chiswick Women's Aid had opened in London in 1971 and contact with Chiswick had established that 'substantial numbers of Irish women and children were making their way there in the absence of a refuge service in Ireland'.[35] Irish feminists did much to shatter 'the traditional view of the idyllic Irish family, by exposing that the family can also be a dangerous place to be'.[36]

In March 1979, an exploration of the lifestyle of Dublin's prostitutes in *Magill* magazine revealed grimness in spite of the earning capacity enjoyed by some of them. In 1977 there were 475 charges and 415 convictions for prostitution in Dublin city, an average of eight a week, representing a sharp rise from just 69 in 1975 and 250 in 1976, but 'proceedings and convictions against men accused of receiving immoral earnings have remained static at 5 per year in the years 1976 and 1977' and 'it's almost impossible to meet a prostitute who hasn't a story of being beaten up by the Gardaí'.[37]

The Council for the Status of Women, concerned about sexually violent crimes against women, made a submission to the Department of Justice on the issue of rape in 1978.[38] Another group that emerged was the Committee Against Rape (CAR) and one of its first political actions was to object to the exclusion of women from the jury that was to try a man for the rape and murder of a young Mayo woman. It had been argued that the facts in the case were too emotionally disturbing for women and might result in a bias against the defendant.[39]

In October 1978, thousands of women attended an anti-rape protest in Dublin city, marching under the banner 'Women against violence against women', which led ultimately to the establishment of the Dublin Rape Crisis Centre (DRCC) in 1979. The march occurred after eight young men had raped a sixteen-year-old girl and left her badly injured in a basement in inner-city Dublin. Journalist Pat Brennan later referred to the march as the last unified act of the radical women's movement of the 1970s. There was a furore over Nell McCafferty's reported comments when speaking at the march: 'The streets are ours. We are not looking for jail for men; we are not looking for castration for men. We are not looking for men at all.' Other accounts suggest that McCafferty also said 'there were no men on this march tonight and that is why nobody was raped', which led to accusations of extremism.[40] Those advocating change suggested facilities for rape victims be available in every hospital, half the jurors in rape trials should be women and that the offence should be brought to trial within three months of being committed. When independent senator Gemma Hussey demanded in the Senate that the law on rape be radically changed, one senator said that many women 'upset the biological balance of a man and then claim they were raped'. The DRCC demanded law reform, proper services for victims and treatment programmes to stop rapists re-offending. Anne O'Donnell suggested the centre 'broke the taboo on talking about rape and incest'. Campaigners, however, had to wait until 1990 before marital rape was criminalised and many victims remained hidden, but discussion of sexual violence as a social and legal problem was also helped by the publication in the early 1970s of influential US studies of rape.[41]

– THIRTY-ONE –

CONTROVERSIAL CUSTODIES AND CONTEMPTUOUS JUDGES

Throughout the decade there were detailed reports available on the state of Irish prisons and a number of particular themes began to assume significance. In terms of penal policy, it was a decade characterised by crisis management due to the increase in the number of paramilitary prisoners (in 1972, the daily prison population breached 1,000 for the first time since the civil war) but also by a more rehabilitationist approach to imprisonment. The Prison Act of 1970 was the first legislative act involving the prison system and was notable for its statement that rehabilitation was one of its aims, but the foundation of this notion 'did not get solidified'. Patrick Cooney in 1974, for example, asserted that 'no prison, no institution and no system can rehabilitate anybody'.[1] A Prisons Bill of 1972 allowed the legal transfer of civilian prisoners to military custody. The use of the Curragh military prison, which had previously been used during the civil war, the Second World War and at the time of the IRA's border campaign in the 1950s, was also contentious (a hunger strike at the Curragh lasted thirty-three days in the summer of 1972) and it was observed that paramilitary prisoners 'present an array of daunting problems: difficult to house, awkward to handle, not simple to occupy, not cheap to guard'. There were also numerous controversies over strip-searching, denial of visits, lack of free association and escapes, and in 1973 a Prisoners Rights Organisation was established.[2]

The annual report for prisons in 1970 recorded an increase from 656 to

749 'in the daily average of persons in custody', which reflected 'the upward trend in crime over the last few years'. A total number of 3,221 were committed to prison that year, rising to 3,966 in 1971, while the daily average in custody in St Patrick's Institution for Younger Offenders was 211; only 50 per cent of them were 'able to read and write well'. In Mountjoy Jail in Dublin in 1971 the conduct and industry of the prisoners was regarded as 'on the whole ... very good' with 'food of good quality, well cooked and served'. Alcoholic prisoners were manifold and it was believed a unit for alcoholics was needed ('it is a very sad feature to see many middle-aged men drifting between the various city hostels and the prison month in month out').

The prison inspectors also complained about negative stories 'in the mass media which were either inaccurate or untrue'. Significantly, all the reports from the various prisons were upbeat and quite positive. What seemed to exercise the visiting committee of Mountjoy most was not what was going on internally, but the parking of cars on the avenue leading to the prison: 'This problem at the moment to say the least, is almost chaotic and is getting worse as time goes by.'[3]

Some of the reports stand in stark contrast to the memoir of Philip Bray, who started out as a prison officer in Limerick in 1977: 'Looking at the building which hadn't changed since 1821 except for a couple of hanging light bulbs and the odd lick of paint ... it smelled exactly like the lion house in Dublin Zoo, that acrid, sharp smell of urine that caught in your throat.' But for prison officers there was also the attraction of good money: 'You had 19-year-olds getting over £300 a week which was big money back then ... we felt we were being hired by the state to fight the IRA.'[4]

The report on Mountjoy for 1976 referred to seven prisoners attempting suicide and in Portlaoise, the state's highest security prison, 'the conduct of the main body of prisoners during the year was poor' as ninety-nine prisoners had attempted to burn down the prison and 'for security reasons no formal education programmes were available during the year'. In relation to Mountjoy, the inspectors seemed dismissive of agitation: 'Most of the complaints, on investigation, are found to be frivolous and bordering on the ridiculous; one prisoner, for example, said, "I am a vegetarian and I am not getting enough salads."' Regarding Portlaoise, 'contrary to allegations persistently made through the news media as to the inhuman treatment of prisoners at Portlaoise, we found no evidence whatever of brutality or violence meted out by prison staff to prisoners'.[5]

By the end of the decade the Department of Justice was concerned about the 1978 report of the visiting committee of Mountjoy Jail and the manner in which it was written, even though 'members visited without prior notice on 26 occasions and everything was as ship-shape then as on the usual monthly inspections', although there were 'a couple of serious assaults' committed by prisoners. The committee was impressed with the new courses being offered: thirty men took a cookery course and 'emerged at the end competent and cocky in the culinary art'. During the year there were 3,634 male and 209 female prisoners, a daily average of 438 men compared with 371 in 1977, while the daily average number of female prisoners was just 13.

While there was harsh comment in 1976 on the lack of remedial teaching at St Patrick's, the closure of the school unit and 'the constant neglect of the education of the young people in our charge', the members of the visiting committee were also adamant that 'the efforts made by those in the media to discredit us in the eyes of the public have been calculated and vicious in the extreme. We have in reality discharged our duties impartially and conscientiously.'[6] In 1978, 1,406 were accommodated during the year at St Patrick's; there was 'a big increase in the number of assaults on staff' and it was found that 'unquestionably the greatest obstacle to successful rehabilitation is the failure of an inmate to secure early employment'.[7] It was noted in January 1979 that only one of the fifteen boys in Loughan House [near Cavan] in Christmas 1978 'does not come from Dublin's decaying city centre'.[8] The Loughan House project had been controversial because of the extent of the opposition to the provision of a detention facility for 12–16-year-olds staffed by prison officers. Mary Robinson characterised it as 'a place where prison officers will control children in need of special care and support'; numerous organisations described it as 'the first children's prison in Europe'.[9]

There were parallel and wholly contrasting assessments of what was going on in Irish prisons. Complaints from Amnesty International gathered pace in the late 1970s and highlighted grievances of prisoners and the concerns of prisoners' welfare action groups, who demanded, among other things, an independent public inquiry into conditions in Portlaoise Prison: 'One visit was stopped because the mother spoke in Irish. Other visits have been stopped; for example, one woman said to her husband "You look pale. Are you getting any exercise?" and the warder said they were talking about conditions; another man told his wife that he had been beaten and the visit was stopped.'[10]

A memorandum from the Department of Justice in April 1977

referred to twenty-five prisoners who were then in military custody and the need to extend the power of the Minister for Justice to transfer persons in custody from the prisons to military custody, an issue which had first arisen after a riot in Mountjoy Jail in May 1972, after which 180 prisoners had to be transferred out of the prison and the Curragh had had to take 40 IRA prisoners. It was recalled that 'prisoner union' activity had caused a total breakdown of control in Portlaoise and Mountjoy prisons during 1973. There were now, in 1977, 127 subversive prisoners in Portlaoise (19 IRA prisoners had escaped from Portlaoise by blasting open a gate in August 1974 prompting an unprecedented and largely unsuccessful manhunt; later that year 27 prison officers were overpowered and held captive after a riot at the prison) and 20 IRA hunger strikers in the Curragh Hospital. The Minister for Defence noted that at the Curragh detention barracks, the military personnel 'are not prison officers and find the work distasteful and arduous'; there was insufficient space for outdoor recreation and no provision for workshops.[11]

Tim Pat Coogan maintained that 'the Portlaoise pressure cooker would have exploded as did that in Long Kesh had not the coalition government gone out of office in 1977'. He suggested that, in practice, Fianna Fáil granted the IRA prisoners status as prisoners of war and the government allowed the editors of national newspapers to see how things had improved. They were still Victorian prisons but 'every effort was made to render the running of the jails as humane as possible'. Apart from the normal contingent of prison officers 'there were 16 uniformed Gardaí on duty on one floor of the republican section of the jail'.[12]

The possibility of an amnesty for certain prisoners was raised in the context of the visit to Ireland of Pope John Paul II in September 1979 (see Part VIII), but in the event, caution was apparent. Seventy-six prisoners – 'non subversive' and 'non-disruptive' – were released to mark the visit but 'it is considered that it would be unwise to take the risk of releasing a large number of offenders during the first day of the visit when Dublin's dwelling houses would be virtually empty'. One senior civil servant in the Department of the Taoiseach was adamantly and piously opposed to any releases: 'I would recommend against an amnesty because of public reaction. We have a serious level of crime. A very poor rate of detection, complaints regarding the ineffectiveness of pre-trial procedures and a serious problem of recidivism ... The Pope's visit should be a time of prayerful remembrance of the victims of crime in our society.'[13]

Other interesting developments of the decade included a much-increased focus on the administration of justice, the status of the legal profession and the operations of the court system, particularly regarding subversive crime and in relation to those who were vulnerable. In 1972 there was concern that the Special Criminal Court, originally established in 1939 to counteract the IRA threat during the Second World War and now reincarnated to deal with the modern subversive threat, consisted of only three judges, which had resulted in 'an unduly heavy burden' on them, and it was decided to increase membership of the court to seven.[14] In December 1974 Mary Robinson was critical of abuses by the Special Criminal Court. It was clear that certain people with no association with unlawful organisations were being tried there with no jury; the case of a dance-hall proprietor charged with hiring a man to blow up a rival dance hall was cited as an example.[15] Two years later, in the wake of an article criticising the Special Criminal Court, quoting the Association of Legal Justice, the *Irish Times* was summonsed by the High Court to answer a charge of contempt but escaped sanction.[16] Over the course of the decade a significant disparity developed between the numbers charged and arrested under the Offences Against the State Act. In 1973, 271 were arrested and 181 charged, in 1975, 607 were arrested and 116 charged, while in 1977 1,144 were arrested but only 169 charged, which would suggest a siege mentality and 'the abuse of the section towards those who attended meetings and protests that the state viewed as undesirable'.[17]

Legal aid was also a contentious issue throughout the decade. In 1970 barristers complained about the low level of fees paid in legal-aid cases (only £18,000 was spent on legal aid in 1969[18]) and the Minister for Justice Mícheál Ó Móráin discussed it with Jack Lynch. There had been no review since 1965, when state legal aid was introduced, and the fee for a legal-aid case was about £10, 'while counsel for the prosecution were paid fees which could be several times bigger'. Barristers were pulling out of the scheme in protest.[19] Ó Móráin wrote to Lynch to explain that he had proposed a 25 per cent increase in the fee; the initial proposal had been to increase it by 45 per cent, which the Department of Finance rejected. Barristers themselves were demanding a 200 per cent increase.

Ó Móráin was furious with the Attorney General Colm Condon for what he saw as his deliberate delaying tactics in drafting the necessary paperwork: 'This matter has been allowed to drag on all this time because the AG was dissatisfied with the new fees being provided and intended to take the matter up with you and the Minister for Finance. I think this is an outrageous attitude on the part of the AG and an unwarranted interference on his part in a matter of policy with which he is not concerned.' He referred to it as the AG's 'unwarranted interference as an influence peddler for his colleagues in the Law Library'.[20]

The civil servants also slogged it out, with Peter Berry, the secretary of the Department of Justice, writing to Charles Murray, secretary of the Department of Finance, blaming Finance for the problem and threatening that Ó Móráin, who at the time was in hospital, would 'publicly disclaim all responsibility for the unfortunate situation in which the work of the criminal courts in indictable cases is being brought virtually to a halt. I feel that there is no point whatsoever in my carrying on further official correspondence with your people who seem to have no understanding of our difficulties and have no object but the saving of money at all costs.'[21] By the mid-1970s, the country's first full-time community law centre had opened in Coolock, Dublin, run by the Free Legal Advice Centre (FLAC), a voluntary organisation of law students.

Given the separation of state and judiciary, it is difficult to gauge the reaction of the legal profession to some developments regarding their status, though the papers of Cearbhall Ó Dálaigh do reveal Judge Brian Walsh's attitude to the 1969 review of the public service, the Devlin Report, and its recommendations regarding salaries. He was resentful that judges had not been consulted and 'I think we have done very badly by comparison with government department secretaries etc.'[22] Walsh had been appointed to the Supreme Court in 1961 at the age of forty-three, its youngest ever member, and had been active in interpreting the meaning of unspecified 'fundamental rights' in the Irish constitution.

In 1972 Ó Dálaigh was appointed a member of the European Court in Luxembourg and he wrote to Walsh to explain the implications, as this appointment would involve him leaving the Supreme Court. It was a decision that

> I think is the right one. I have been a member of the court for too long ... special skill and leadership are called for if the court is to be held to the lines, which, in recent years, have earned it the respect and trust of ordinary people. This is a task which I could not hope to fulfil at my age and with my temperament. For the task, great patience is needed, backed by erudition and it is therefore better, I think, that I should go

> and that you should remain. In a few years the position will be sufficiently consolidated to leave you free to follow into Europe.[23]

Walsh's reply was equally complimentary:

> It was always quite clear that you were the only person the government could ask if they wanted to indicate clearly what importance our country attaches to our entry into the communities. It was also the result I had hoped for, though I did not of course venture to discuss it with you. In this I can claim I was putting the country before self because I had always looked forward to sitting beside you in the Supreme Court for at least the next ten or eleven years secure in the knowledge that the court would be led with the integrity, regard for principle and courtesy which made the first decade of your tenure as Chief Justice so outstanding and which earned the court the high respect which I believe it now enjoys ... I cannot at all agree with your reference to your age and temperament and patience ... I also have the suspicion that the administration may also avail of the opportunity so to adjust the leadership and the personnel of the court to reduce the risk of a continuation of the court's initiatives of the past decade ... there is also something I find it easier to write than to speak. That is to thank you for the great pleasure and happiness I have derived from 30 years of your friendship ... I hope you are escaping for a few weekends of pâté and wine on the Loire ... I would recommend the Pouilly Fumé or Muscadet. The Loire wines go very well with fish ... please send me your address in case I have to tell you that the Four Courts has fallen.[24]

Few of those who populated the columns of Nell McCafferty when she wrote about court proceedings would get to savour such fine vintages. The very act of a journalist attending court hearings and reporting verbatim what she saw and heard was radical and unsettling and shed light on a corner that had not been explored. It also succeeded, at least partially, in exposing some judges who were arrogant, snobbish, contemptuous, pompous, alcoholic, hungover and utterly removed from the sort of life experiences born of poverty on which they were sitting in judgment. As recalled by McCafferty in relation to her column 'In the Eyes of the Law', which ran from 1972 to 1974 in the *Irish Times*, 'I just let them open their mouths and put their feet in ... the column's strength was that I reported verbatim the remarks of the judiciary. The judges often showed themselves to be a vain, abusive lot, lording it over the poor who came before them'. But with time she felt the column 'became predictable',[25] an indication that her reports were not enough to alter judges' behaviour.

There were others who expressed their concerns about the Children's Courts to senior members of government in private. In January 1974, Brian Quinn, the editor of the *Evening Herald*, wrote a powerful letter to Liam Cosgrave on this subject:

> The Children's Court is a sad affair – mumbled evidence, poor representation and every sign of conveyor belt justice. I have been there and really it does little to even grapple with the clear result of every case – that the defendant will be back again. The court of criminal appeal is positively seedy. Dreadful surroundings, evidence cannot be heard, poor lighting. I heard 15 cases there recently. Three cases should never have got past the district court. The unfortunates involved were clearly retarded. Six cases had an element of doubt – poorly presented evidence. Six cases should have had the sentences confirmed or increased. There was a grim affair of a fellow with a knife who was almost patted on the back. Once again I believe all 15 will be back before the courts again. It sounds bad, looks bad and is bad. The waiting rooms are grim, the halls packed with people struggling to find out what is going on. One gets the feeling that justice as such has taken a back seat. A clean up operation with a pot of paint would be a start. A more humane approach, plus rehabilitation is needed in the Children's Court. A more refined and sharper attitude plus decent facilities is badly required in the court of criminal appeal. I had a feeling that the free legal aid in the Children's Court was of poor quality.[26]

That same year, Mairín de Burca, the social, feminist and Republican activist who was also involved in advocating prisoners' rights and penal reform (and successfully challenged the constitutionality of the Juries Act, under which women were not automatically called to jury service), wrote a candid letter to Garret FitzGerald about other aspects of this problem (some of the issues would have been imparted to her by sympathetic lawyers). She explained her letter by reminding him, 'you did say once that you would not mind me writing on matters of social concern'. Her primary concern was district justices and the treatment of people by the courts (de

Búrca used the judges' full names, which have been abbreviated to initials here):

> I am not betraying confidences when I say that both DJ B and DJ Ó are alcoholics. DJ G is crippled from a stroke and DJ Ó has high blood pressure. This is common knowledge amongst the legal profession in Dublin; it is spoken about quite openly. These are human misfortunes which might happen to anyone. The problem is that they are likely to and do impair tempers and also judgement. You must agree that to sit for hours in a district court facing a long succession of offenders, many of them coming up time and again would be enough to try anyone's patience. How much more likely to try the patience of men under stress of one kind or another. However, looking at it from the point of view of the plaintiffs it comes down literally to what kind of mood the justice is in whether or not their freedom is taken away for months or maybe even years. Nell McCafferty's articles shocked a lot of people. They did not shock me. I had been aware of the scandal for years before the Irish Times decided to take it up. There is no independent tribunal to which one can bring complaints, the relevant minister refuses to believe it is happening. What in God's name do you do then? ... the shouting bantering manner of the justices and the lengthy rambling sermons, offensive remarks to which no reply can be made – it all makes for what must be the most haphazard attempt to impose law and justice in any civilised country.

FitzGerald wrote a note beside the letter: 'replied to it by telephone. Copy to AG please.'[27]

Attorney General Declan Costello was an important conduit between the government and judges and was also adamant that he 'should not engage in private practice' while serving as AG: 'Any fees which I may obtain in my official capacity should be paid into the exchequer.'[28] He also took their side over pay and conditions. In March 1974 he informed Cosgrave that he had talked 'in confidence' with Judge Brian Walsh about a judges' dispute and threatened industrial action by the Bar, suggesting 'it would be a mistake to feel that the government is being blackmailed ... For years the judges' requests for meaningful talks have just been ignored.'[29] But it was an issue that festered: in April 1975, Costello again corresponded with Liam Cosgrave about 'a potentially dangerous situation ... because of the action threatened by the Bar'.[30]

– THIRTY-TWO –

REFORMING THE LAW

Costello was a busy Attorney General between 1973 and 1977 (before being appointed a High Court judge) and regardless of his ability to bring reprobate judges into line he was a significant figure in the context of legal reform during his time in office. Son of John A. Costello, Fine Gael Taoiseach 1948–51 and 1954–7, he had withdrawn from politics in 1969, after a decade in which the 'Just Society' idea he promoted within Fine Gael had met with a decidedly mixed response. His decision to retire temporarily was lamented by Labour TD Michael O'Leary as involving the departure of a 'young man of great courage and idealism'. But senior members of Fine Gael may not have been so saddened, given that Cosgrave was perceived as having 'left Costello on the fringe of things. Declan Costello deserved better: he did not get it,' was the view of journalist John Healy.[1]

But he returned to politics and was elected to the Dáil in 1973 for Dublin South West, and was appointed Attorney General; he subsequently established the Law Reform Commission to codify, rationalise and prepare legislation and separated the offices of Attorney General and Director of Public Prosecutions, creating a new role independent of the Executive. He also played a significant role in the Sunningdale conference on Northern Ireland, and he prosecuted the Irish case relating to the ill treatment of internees before the European Commission of Human Rights.

When Costello died in June 2011, Liam Cosgrave singled out for mention his 'great social concern for the underprivileged and those who suffered from ill health. He understood and appreciated with genuine sympathy the sufferings and problems of people so affected. In his career in politics this was his abiding interest which he strove to alleviate or improve by clear sighted recommendations in his speeches.' In reference to the 1970s, Cosgrave maintained:

> The creation of the position of director of public prosecutions was a progressive and independent approach established under the Prosecution of Offenders Act 1974. The office created has on the whole worked well. No human institutions are ever perfect. Costello's foresight established the Law Reform Commission under the 1975 Act. This body has done valuable work in recommending changes in the law which the commission thought desirable. Such changes had of course, to be approved by the government and the Oireachtas. As a constitutional lawyer he was outstanding, clear and distinctive in his opinions whether given instantly or after some extra consideration. He was never wrong, a truly extraordinary achievement – in particular in regard to the Emergency Powers Act 1976 which the Supreme Court upheld after a reference under article 26 of the Constitution [a convenient dig at Cearbhall Ó Dálaigh].[2]

The memorandum circulated by Costello early in 1974 on the creation of the office of DPP (prior to which only the AG could discharge and perform functions relating to criminal proceedings; there had been a DPP in England since 1879 and Northern Ireland since 1972), underlined the forceful and convincing manner he had of expressing his ideas and justifications for them. It mentioned that it was a necessity in light of 'current public attitudes to the administration of criminal justice ... it is considered highly desirable to establish a system for the direction of prosecutions that is not only free from political influence but is manifestly so'. It would also enable the AG to concentrate solely on legal advice to the government, though the AG would retain the power to initiate, intervene and conduct criminal prosecutions, a retention opposed by the Minister for Justice. Costello referred explicitly to the 'widespread belief in this country that political influence can be brought to bear successfully in the administration of the criminal law'. In response, the Minister for Justice insisted political influence in this regard needed to become a criminal offence itself: 'It is inevitable that, at least for some time ahead, people (including public representatives) will persist in believing that a letter or telephone call to the director (or to the AG or even to a minister) will achieve results.'[3]

Reforming the law inevitably created tensions. In 1974, it was argued in the Department of Public Service that to give the AG further responsibilities through a law reform commission 'could be wasteful and could lead to time-consuming tensions'. The kind of language Costello was using, however, was far removed from such civil-service speak propelled by conservatism (though he was a conservative in relation to his Catholic faith). His case, as articulated in a memorandum for government in March 1974, was that the development and implementation of law reform programmes 'should play an important role in the work of any progressive government. Law reform in this country has been extremely limited. It is unnecessary to apportion blame for this unfortunate fact but it is helpful to identify the reasons for it. Basically there are two: 1. Failure to establish a suitable institutional framework in which law reform can take place and 2. An inadequate number of qualified personnel available to engage in the research and study necessary to effect reforms.' He also suggested the need to adapt the procedure for law reform adopted in England and Scotland which 'has been extremely successful'. On the question as to whether the commission should be answerable to the Department of Justice or the Attorney General, he maintained that it should be the AG, as he advised all government departments. Costello had to remind Cosgrave of this memorandum nearly two weeks later as he had not responded and Costello felt 'for a variety of reasons the matter is an urgent one'. He was keen for Cosgrave rather than the Minister for Justice to circulate it as a discussion document as it was a memorandum 'which contains my views. They may well not be the Department of Justice views.'[4]

Most departments responded positively; there were a few reservations that the proposed commission could be 'swamped giving expert advice on EEC matters' to the detriment of the reform programme, while the Department of Labour was anxious that the setting up of the commission would not 'inhibit any department from pressing ahead with reform in its own area of legislation'.[5]

Another preoccupation throughout the decade was the issue of family law reform. In January 1973, at a meeting of Action Information

Motivation (AIM), the pressure group concerned with family, maintenance and justice founded by Nuala Fennell to provide legal advice for women, John Kelly suggested family law needed urgent study and that 'if state commissions can find time to deal with monopolies in the scrap trade, or with the greyhound industry, surely it is not too much to ask for a commission on the law surrounding what the constitution ponderously calls "the natural primary and fundamental unit group of society" – the family'.[6] Costello saw nullity of marriage as an area where there was 'a real and pressing need for reform'; the fact was that the constitution prohibited the enactment of a law providing for the grant of a dissolution of marriage but there was no constitutional prohibition on the power of courts to grant a decree of nullity.

Cosgrave thought this was something that should be considered by the Law Reform Commission instead of announcing that the government had made any kind of a decision. In a Dáil debate on the LRC in February 1975 John Kelly insisted 'the civil matrimonial law of the state is unbelievably antique; it has been far overtaken in liberality and sophistication by the Canon law of the Catholic Church ... It seems to be a ridiculous anomaly that the Church should be more liberal and sophisticated than the state in its interpretation of the rules regarding nullity whether consent is defective and so on.' When it was put to Patrick Cooney that in relation to an increase in the amount of annulments being granted by the Catholic Church, 'most people understand that church law is state law', Cooney responded that 'the government could not be put in the position of having to recognise annulment granted by a specific church. The government is the government for all the people, of all religions.' Significantly, the following year, Cosgrave, in correspondence with Declan Costello, observed that 'you have already had informal discussions with 3 of the main religious denominations in the country' and suggested that this was a better course of action than publishing a draft bill as a discussion paper.

In September 1974 Costello met, at his request, Cardinal William Conway, Archbishop of Armagh, to be told that the Standing Committee of the Catholic Hierarchy – the Irish bishops – wanted the civil law relating to nullity amended to bring it into line with ecclesiastical law. Costello noted that 'my personal view was in favour of the suggested reforms. I did not think it would be wise for the Hierarchy to make a formal approach to the government on this matter but that the legislation should be drafted with the Hierarchy's approval,'[7] which suggested that church–state relations at this stage had changed only in so far as the public optics; legislation would be drafted to be in line with church views, but there would be no 'formal' and public dictation of terms.

In August 1976, however, the government authorised the publication of the AG's memorandum as a discussion document; when it was discussed at cabinet it was noted 'there was a possibility that the discussion would make it clear that the constitution and the law would make it impossible to legislate a new nullity code as liberal as that at present operated by the Catholic Church. It was recognised that the response of non-Catholics here and in the North would probably be that divorce was what was required and that Catholic nullity law was no substitute.' Significantly, within these discussions, as well as individual demands from some members of the public about the need for divorce legislation and an exaggerated report in the *Daily Telegraph* that there was a 'limited divorce plan for Irish couples',[8] the foundations for what would become the first Irish divorce referendum ten years later in 1986 were being tentatively laid.

By 1978, there were 5,010 women receiving deserted wives payments, introduced in 1974, but that only represented a fraction of those deserted; one estimate in the 1970s put the number of deserted wives 'at between five and eight thousand, with a minimum annual increase of about 500'.[9] At the end of 1977, 1,386 petitions for church nullity were being processed (between 1976 and 1977, 109 decrees of nullity were granted) and 'unless a couple can agree on the terms of separation, there is no appropriate legal remedy to regularise all the aspects of a legal separation'. It was prohibitively costly to get a judicial separation (which did not leave a couple free to remarry) through High Court proceedings. Between 1970 and 1976 there were 237 such cases. Desertion, it was clear, was more 'crude but effective' and it was evident that this – dubbed 'divorce Irish style' – was still 'one of the commonest ways to escape marriage. Typically, it is a male working class way out; relatively few women desert their families.' *Hibernia* magazine highlighted the case of an Irish-style 'divorce' in 1973; a deserted wife due to a husband who had 'disappeared' and 'at 28 Mary has 4 sons under the age of 8, a 2 bed roomed flat in Ballymun and £11.50 to get her through each week'.[10]

Family law evolved to raise the minimum legal age of marriage to sixteen for girls and boys (prior to 1975, a valid marriage could be contracted in the case of a boy when he reached the age of fourteen and in the case of a girl when she reached twelve), while the Maintenance Orders

Act of 1974 allowed for the reciprocal enforcement of maintenance orders between the Republic and the UK and a Family Law Act of 1976 provided for periodic payments by one spouse to the other in cases of failure to provide reasonable maintenance, with deductions of earnings at source and barring orders. The Family Home Protection Act protected the family home and required prior written consent of both spouses for sale of the home. Women could now claim children's allowance in their own name and could apply to be taxed separately, with working wives receiving the same personal allowances as their husbands.[11] But few lawyers specialised in family law as cases were regarded as time consuming and financially unrewarding.[12]

The emergence of the LRC increased the focus on the potential for tensions between reform impulses and government reluctance. There was a certain scepticism about the effectiveness of the LRC. One civil servant in 1979 suggested Jack Lynch should 'prompt the AG to enquire further about progress, which to date has not been spectacular – the commission was established in October 1975 and has already cost over £¼ million without any recommendations being available'. Lynch informed the AG Tony Hederman that he was 'particularly concerned to know what progress is being made in relation to family law and nullity'.[13]

The president of the LRC, Judge Brian Walsh, replied to the AG by pointing out that the LRC had already published six papers, four of which dealt with aspects of family law. What Walsh's response also revealed was a lawyer's frustration with the advocates of reform who did not seem to appreciate the complexities involved in the recognition of foreign divorces and legal separations and that there could be no question, for example, of introducing a law which could in effect permit a dissolution of marriage by calling it 'nullity' without infringing the constitution: 'This point does not seem to be fully appreciated by some who are active in urging nullity of marriage as a substitute, more or less, for dissolution of marriage.'[14] He also elaborated at length on the dangers of the tendency to treat certain family law issues in isolation from each other: 'This is a matter which frequently seems to escape the attention of those who are urging one particular reform or another.' He also wondered if there was a genuine appetite for dealing with the complexities of family law change or was there more interest 'in questions than answers'.

He gave the example of the LRC paper on criminal conversation (under this law, which was not abolished until 1981, a man had the right to take legal action against another man for having sex with his wife on the grounds that she was her husband's 'chattel'), which was published in December 1978. This dealt with a subject

> which for years has been the cause of agitation, has so far prompted no comment whatsoever from anybody ... There has not even been a letter in the correspondence columns of any newspapers on this subject which hitherto appeared to cause so much concern to various groups ... You might be interested to know that among all our publications, and notwithstanding the concern which is always expressed to exist in relation to family law, the only one of our publications which was completely sold out and had to be reprinted was the working paper dealing with builder's liability and the second most sought after was the one dealing with the liability for animals. The working paper dealing with the age of majority and the age for marriage etc. and which had been the result of a great deal of detailed research and work did not attract many buyers and brought in virtually no comment.[15]

Later that year, however, the Department of the Taoiseach was still concerned about the government being under pressure regarding family law: 'The recent ESRI survey indicated that 46 per cent of the respondents in the Republic felt that the government should take the steps necessary to make divorce legal. Even allowing for exaggeration and the possible changing climate since the Papal visit, the reality is that this represents increasing pressure on the government in relation to nullity.' In the Department of the Taoiseach, Dermot Nally maintained in correspondence with Richard Stokes, that 'the commission has been set up nearly four years and there is not yet a line on the statute books ... It seems to me that there is a preoccupation in the commission with legal precision rather than workable results ... although this may not be the place to raise it, there does seem to be a need for more administrative drive in the commission ... If I thought I could help to get some real work done down there I would not be averse to a suitable secondment arrangement.'[16]

– THIRTY-THREE –

INALIENABLE RIGHTS OF THE CHILD?

How societal attitudes were evolving and the law was operating in relation to vulnerable children were also questions being tentatively examined. In 1971 Erskine Childers as Minister for Health had drawn attention to 'the very limited number of social workers engaged in statutory services' in contrast to the United Kingdom and Northern Ireland. He also suggested that in considering the future of community services 'one was sometimes taken aback by the range and variety of services which had to be provided'.[1] That year, it was maintained in *Hibernia* magazine that Childers was very highly regarded by health professionals as he was making the child health services 'his own' and was 'a damned good listener and a damned fast learner'.[2]

At the end of the previous year, journalist and former Labour Party activist, Proinsias Mac Aonghusa, then writing for *Hibernia*, drew attention to a horrific and barbaric case of the abuse of 'a 16 year old boy from an industrial school' who was working in a bar in Murrisk, County Mayo: 'He was brutally attacked by 4 local youths. They beat him very badly. They then castrated him. They tied him to a car and dragged him about a mile along the road thereby tearing his backside off him, rupturing his spine and damaging his liver. They left him for dead in the middle of the road. They boy lived. He was first in Castlebar Hospital and is now in Merlin Park in Galway. The criminals are free. The boy is afraid to name them. The guards know who they are but cannot prove it. The locals are silent. Will anyone do anything for this boy?'[3]

The Health Act of 1970 envisaged social-work teams working with the community care services, and soothing noises were being made in the early 1970s about the extent to which 'the key to the well-being of the community lies significantly in the extent of its concern for the welfare and young children', as articulated by an inter-departmental committee report on mentally ill and maladjusted people. This had been set up by the Minister for Justice in 1972 and looked at the need for secure centres for 'juvenile socio-paths' and residential schools.[4] But the over-reliance on institutions and lack of social and child-care workers was still apparent. The Campaign for the Care of Deprived Children (CARE) had been set up as a lobby group in the aftermath of the Kennedy Report of 1970, which was highly critical of the state's reliance on residential institutions and industrial schools and made it clear that it was 'imperative that the whole concept of child care be examined afresh'.

CARE produced a memorandum on the rights of deprived children in 1972; other organisations that assumed significance in this regard included Children First and the Irish Association of Social Workers, but the transfer of all statutory child welfare duties to one central government department did not happen, and a 'radical overhaul' promised by a task force on child care in 1975 did not materialise.[5] The coalition government was praised by Charles Mollan of Children First for 'the efforts of your government to improve social welfare and family law legislation and to protect the interests of those most in need',[6] but in 1974 there were only 235 social workers employed nationally; they were distributed between health boards, local authorities and voluntary agencies.[7] From the mid 1970s, social-work practice in Britain was an influence on Irish thinking, and this was also true in relation to community care services, but 'what appears to have happened was as community care social work developed in Ireland it became preoccupied with child welfare and protection almost to the total exclusion of the needs of other groups, such as the adult mentally ill'.[8]

In the mid 1970s there were thirty residential centres throughout the state catering for up to 2,000 children. In 1975 the Association of Workers for Children in Care (AWCC) wrote of the 'critical situation' confronting those administering and working in these homes and centres and the refusal of the state to provide a salary scale or career structure for child-care workers. It was estimated there were '200 or so' residential child-care workers. In October 1974 the Minister for Health had established a working party to look at the improvement of services for deprived children at risk but it did not address the question of administrative restructuring in the area of child care. The crucial complication in all this was that responsibility for children's services was diffused between three government departments and that presented 'serious obstacles to reform'.

In 1976 the AWCC complained that the Minister for Education Richard Burke had declined to meet its representatives; they insisted there was 'widespread confusion in regard to which department of state is in fact responsible for these homes'.[9] John Bruton, the parliamentary secretary to the Minister for Education, pointed out in 1976 that the rate of grant per child per week was £15 but the AWCC wanted to get rid of capitation grants and finance the homes on the basis of the budgets submitted and approved, as recommended by the Kennedy Report. In a letter to Cosgrave, Bruton noted 'the decline in vocations for religious orders has resulted in a preponderance of lay staff in homes; these will not be satisfied with the conditions of service (including the absence of salary scale) under which the religious have worked'.[10]

But Burke made it clear that the state, conveniently, had no intention of sponsoring or initiating reform in this area of child care, at a time when 30 per cent of the homes' income came from the Department of Education, 22 per cent from the local authorities and 48 per cent from the health boards: 'This department is of the view that nothing should be done which would detract from the voluntary character of all these homes. Whether they are financially supported by this department or the Department of Health or a mixture of the two – and that the state should not interfere in this sensitive area any more than is necessary.' The salaries, it was maintained, should be paid by voluntary bodies.[11]

In August 1976 Bruton authorised an increase in the grants payable to the homes from £15 to £18 per child per week; according to the Department of Education there were 1,100 children in twenty-five homes conducted by religious orders under the control of the Department of Education. Bruton was in favour of the capitation system and the AWCC was unhappy with its meeting with him in September 1976 because of this and the emphasis on keeping the homes voluntary. The Sisters of Mercy intervened to insist that, 'since the children's welfare depends on the care staff and since it is impossible to employ competent staff unless a just salary scale is given, the fundamental rights of the children are being denied them'.[12]

The Department of Finance also had its say; unsurprisingly it was firmly of the view that greater rationalisation and fewer homes were needed to reflect the fact that the number of children in care had dropped from 2,900 in 1965 to 1,200 in 1976. Early in 1977, Fr Brendan Comiskey of the Conference of the Major Religious Superiors of Ireland threatened the Minister for Education Peter Barry, the Cork Fine Gael TD who had succeeded Richard Burke after the latter was appointed Ireland's new EEC Commissioner, that unless more funding was provided they were giving six months' notice of the closure of eight residential centres. The following month the government agreed to raise the capitation grant to £22 per child while Minister for Health Brendan Corish announced government action on child care including new homes, buildings, day service centres and neighbourhood youth projects.[13]

Other vulnerable children were living the nomadic, traveller life, one that was frequently cut short. In 1977 Mairín de Burca reported for *Magill* magazine that an 'Irish itinerant baby' born in 1977 'can expect to grow up illiterate, to go to prison for begging, to become an alcoholic and to die before his 40th birthday'. In 1976, there were still 862 traveller families living on roadsides, many making their living from scrap metal. In Dublin, sixty families had been housed by 1976 and 135 were on service sites, though the settling of travellers was provoking public antagonism.[14]

In February 1976 a memorandum for the government was prepared in relation to 'battered babies', or more formally, 'non-accidental injury' to children (a committee had been established in May 1975 after it was agreed 'that there was a significant problem of non-accidental injury to children') The need for staff training, legislation to give powers to staff engaged in management and prevention of such abuse and community care services were highlighted, while a central registry of cases was regarded as vital. Brendan Corish wanted the report published as 'there is widespread public interest in this highly emotional subject' and it was agreed it would be published without commitment to its recommendations.[15]

Revealingly, the following month, Dr Brendan O'Donnell, the chief medical officer of the Eastern Health Board, suggested that when the report became available 'the Health Board would have to consider the problem and whether it was a medical or social problem ... this is early days yet'.[16] But there was another impulse at work in relation to the publication of the report, which was explained in a memorandum from the Department of Health:

> Considerable publicity was given by the media to an earlier report on the subject which was prepared by a committee comprising members from the Irish Society for the Prevention of Cruelty to Children and the North Dublin social workers. This earlier report was released to the press on 12 December 1975. It caused great public disquiet by a reference in the report to an estimate that as many as a hundred children a year may die in Ireland as a result of non-accidental injury by their parents. The publication of the report now under submission will help to allay the disquiet caused by this estimate which, from the information available to the Department of Health, is regarded as being grossly inflated.[17]

In relation to sexual abuse of children, one of the first graduates of a new child-care worker's course established in Kilkenny in 1971, David Murray, secured employment in St Joseph's Industrial School (these institutions were now smaller with child-centred units). In 1997 Murray was sentenced to ten years in prison for gross sexual abuse at the school, a part of a complex of buildings housing Kilkenny Social Services, and regarded as 'the most progressive such venture in the country'. Sexual abuse continued throughout the 1970s, with four staff members abusing. As early as 1975, complaints were made about sexual abuse at Trudder House in Wicklow, which accommodated traveller children.[18]

The Ferns Report of 2005, which although specific to the incidence of abuse by priests in one diocese (in Wexford) also looks at the history of public and state consciousness of child sexual abuse, asserts that in the decade 1965–75, 'the extent of sexual abuse of children both within and outside families was recognised as a world-wide problem', but does not elaborate on by whom or where this recognition was held. It also asserts that the Department of Health's 1976 report and memorandum on non-accidental injury to children made no reference to sexual abuse, but as noted by archivist and critic Catríona Crowe, the report 'does not reveal why Irish state agencies which employed professionals in the field of child protection took so long to deal with an issue "recognised as a world-wide problem" since 1975 at the latest'. From the late 1970s, priests with behavioural problems, including child sexual abuse, 'were being sent for assessment and treatment to reputable psychologists and psychiatrists in Ireland and to a treatment centre in Stroud in England'. It was known to various authorities with direct responsibility for Fr Seán Fortune, a serial and vicious abuser, that he had perpetrated abuse as a seminarian in St Peter's College and several complaints had been made between 1976 and 1979, but he was still ordained in 1979.[19]

The other landmark reports of the early twenty-first century that revealed the extent of child sexual abuse within and outside of institutions were the Ryan Report of 2009, which looked at sexual abuse in residential institutions from the 1930s to the 1990s, and the Murphy Report the same year, which looked at the issue of how child sexual abuse allegations were handled in the Catholic diocese of Dublin from 1975. It had its origins in the 2002 broadcast by RTÉ television of a series produced by the acclaimed Irish documentary maker Mary Raftery, *Cardinal Secrets*. The report detailed cases involving forty-six priests and more than 320 children, most of them boys. The report highlighted a litany of failures by senior Catholic Church figures and the Gardaí, and a 'don't ask, don't tell' policy.

That phrase is pertinent also to many of the issues addressed in the Ryan Report, which had its origins in the response by government to exposure in the late 1990s of the extent of residential abuse; investigations by Mary Raftery had also been central to these revelations. In providing such an overwhelming body of evidence about an 'obsessive concern with secrecy and the avoidance of scandal [with] little or no concern for the welfare of the abused child', the reports provided a corrective to the atmosphere of secrecy and shame that surrounded these experiences for so many years. The Murphy Report's use of the phrase 'avoidance of public scandal' was revealing and underlined the determination to hide and deny rather than confront. The great irony is that the obsession with avoidance of scandal facilitated ever-greater scandal. Another tragic irony is that the unvarnished detail of the abuse experienced by children contained in the reports underlines that some of those most associated with urging others to avoid 'occasions of sin' were perhaps the greatest sinners of all.[20]

During the 1970s, some attempts were made to highlight what had happened to vulnerable children in institutions. In November 1972 A. J. Wallace, a twenty-four-year-old former inmate of Artane Industrial School, who moved to London after his release, wrote a letter to the Taoiseach Jack Lynch:

> It is now eight years since I left the Republic a free individual. Unfortunately for me, I can never forget one day of my 16 years in your

> country ... Your governments have also made miserable the lives of thousands of unwanted babies within the Republic. I was admitted to an orphanage at the age of two years; at the age of ten I was transferred to Artane [Industrial] school where I was to stay another six years. I do not intend to put in writing at this very moment the treatment to which helpless children are subject to while in the care of the Irish Catholic authorities. I do not know if it could be possible, but I sure wish I had the opportunity to speak with you personally.

Wallace wrote two follow-up letters in which he pointed out that he had been subjected to 'a life of fear and hatred ... in the claws of the Irish Christian Brothers' and was 'still suffering from the terrifying effects of my upbringing in Irish government care'. He also referred to 'great psychological damage' that had been done to 'literally thousands of young people'. He finished by insisting, 'I do believe that if I had a chance to tell my story to members of your government a great deal of good could be done ... I must be permitted to speak to people who should be concerned with this situation ... the Irish people must know the psychological damage they had subjected these children to.'[21]

Rarely were platforms provided for the public articulation of such truths; Frank Crummey was exceptional in his campaigning, having appeared on RTÉ's *The Late Late Show* in 1967, when he looked into the camera at the end of the show and announced: 'As I sit here tonight, the Irish Christian Brothers are abusing our children.' In the 1970s he went further, 'marching' into schools to confront principals and teachers who were beating children (and he later took up the causes of prostitutes beaten by their pimps). Ultimately, his years as a social worker led to a nervous breakdown and he became a legal executive facilitating access to justice for the needy.[22] As Nell McCafferty recalled, in the 1970s Crummey told her of incest, overcrowded slums, sexual abuse by priests, and, she regretted, 'Even I assumed he was exaggerating.'[23] In 1971 Fr Raymond Freld, the chaplain appointed to St Patrick's Institute for young offenders by the Archbishop of Dublin John Charles McQuaid, referred critically to food deprivation and solitary confinement at the institution and had to apologise to McQuaid for a letter he sent to the *Irish Times* on the subject. McQuaid told him to 'just keep quiet', an indication that, whatever his private concerns, he did not want publicity given to the allegations.[24]

The 'natural and imprescriptible' rights of the child are expressly mentioned in article 42 of the Irish constitution, but the hollowness of these words was underlined in an account of the life of a fifty-two-year-old woman born outside marriage in the mid 1920s, which was brought to the attention of Jack Lynch in 1978. The woman

> spent the first 16 years of my life in various institutions (religious) 36 years ago. Aged 16 I left, since then I am still a loner … all these institutions are run by vested interests, the more unfortunates they get in the more money they get in. When I wrote back to them asking them to help me to trace my next of kin all I got from them was evasive answers and holy pictures and [requests] to pray for them … I witnessed with my own eyes 2 nuns batter a woman who tried to take her 7 year old son from a dining hall … these institutions are worse than jails … I have spent my life hiding from my illegitimacy.

(Bernadette Devlin, interviewed about her premarital pregnancy in 1971, snapped that 'there are no illegitimate children, only illegitimate parents, if the term is to be used at all'.[25]) It was also pointed out that 'many TDs, senators … have horrific accounts of other so-called homes, including Presbyterian'.[26] Writer Ulick O'Connor recorded in his diary in October 1977 that Mannix Flynn 'is a celebrity with his play The Liberty Suit about a Reform School [Flynn had been incarcerated in Letterfrack Industrial School as a child] produced and directed by Jim and Peter Sheridan in the Olympia and which is a runaway success'.[27]

The adoption of children also raised legal and social concerns during the decade. A Private Member's Bill proposing to extend the Adoption Acts of 1952 and 1964 was presented to the Oireachtas in 1971. Mary Robinson sought a reading of the bill in the Senate that summer, her impatience unappreciated by scourge of the liberals, Tomás O'Maoláin, who suggested 'before we start the round-the-houses debate again on this, as is usual with Senator Robinson in any manner of this nature … she also knows very well that this threatening attitude is not going to get anywhere'.[28] The Bill sought to ensure that the welfare of the child would be paramount in relation to any applications or procedures around making an adoption order. Certain sectors were critical of adoption by religiously mixed parents; the Department of Justice wanted a change on this regard, as did the Church of Ireland.[29] The Adoption Act of 1976 allowed for adoptions in which the natural and the adoptive parents of children were not of the same religion. There was considerable upset that year about the invalidation of adoption orders as a result of a Supreme Court decision. A referendum was held and approved in 1979 to ensure that adoption orders that had not been court approved would not be deemed unconstitutional.

The previous year, Minister for Justice Gerry Collins had informed the AG that he 'wanted to avoid a referendum if that were possible' but he did not see any other way if reassurance was to be provided for 'the thousands of people affected' (24,000 adoption orders had been made since 1952 and *Hibernia* magazine suggested that approximately 1,400 of the 1,600 children born outside marriage in 1970 were adopted).[30] But Collins did not accept that 'a case has been made for inserting a "children's charter" into the constitution and he considers that any attempt to do so could have unforeseen consequences'. These were not elaborated on but were interpreted in *Magill* magazine in July 1979 as meaning that Collins was against any statement in the constitution that the welfare of the child is the 'first and paramount consideration' on the grounds that it would represent 'a potential threat to the well being of families'.[31]

The government's original decision to hold a referendum to deal with the new interpretation was widely praised, by, among others, the Children First organisation. Its spokesman, Charles Mollan, insisted that child-centred child-care laws were needed and made the accurate observation that while article 41 of the constitution referred to the inalienable and imprescriptible rights of the family, 'the problem is that the interpretation of this clause seems to have placed the family above the interest of its members'.[32] The Irish Council of Civil Liberties, chaired by Kader Asmal, published a report in 1977 on children's rights under the constitution which called for a 'new balance' between parental and children's rights and argued that children should be mentioned specifically in article 41.4.[33]

When deciding on how to mark the International Year of the Child in 1979, as designated by a UN resolution, a memorandum from the government suggested the Department of Health should take the lead and form a national committee; (the department hoped its most significant contribution to the initiative would be 'if at all possible the introduction of a new Children's Bill during 1979'). Such a committee was designed to continue to peddle an illusion; it would apparently 'serve to confirm this country's commitment, as expressed in the constitution, to the place of the family unit, including children, in our society'.[34]

Heaping irony upon irony, the Department of the Taoiseach was concerned that some of the groups it was suggested should be consulted about participation, such as CARE, the Dublin Itinerant Settlement Committee, the Irish Society for the Prevention of Cruelty to Children, the National Youth Council of Ireland and Unicef (Irish branch), 'have a general negative flair about them. While I am not suggesting that the Arts Council should be given a place it occurred to me that to mark the occasion the council might perhaps consider holding some artistic competitions.'[35] The Minister for Justice agreed to nominate an officer from his department to the committee, but 'only on the understanding that it is made clear to the committee from the outset that any efforts by a member thereof (from the CARE organisation or otherwise) to use the committee as a platform for attacking his policies in regard to juvenile crime and in particular, the decision on Loughan House will result in the minister's representative being withdrawn from the committee'.[36] Later that year Charles Haughey advised Lynch to decline an invitation to open an international conference being organised by the Association of Workers in Child Care in July 1979, 'given the association's relatively minor status when compared to other organisations in this country'.[37]

Other children whose case for justice received attention in the 1970s were those who had been born with physical deformities due to the use of the German manufactured drug Thalidomide, which was licensed for sale in Ireland in 1959 and approved by the state as a 'wonder drug' that was taken to prevent morning sickness and nausea. Many mothers taking the drug suffered miscarriages, while babies that did survive suffered varying degrees of deformity, including shortened or absent limbs and stunted internal organs. Safety concerns meant the drug was not allowed to be marketed in the US in the 1960s but it continued to be sold elsewhere; in Ireland, an estimated 51,000 packets were sold or given away as free samples to 'grateful mothers' and it was available in Ireland seven months after its manufacturer withdrew it.[38]

Pressure grew in the early 1970s from parents and their supporters in the medical profession for compensation and Ralph Nader, the American consumer advocate, met parents of the victims in Dublin to discuss ways of maximising compensation. Minister for Health Brendan Corish authorised the payment of a small lump sum to parents along with a monthly disability payment, but these modest amounts did not take into account how long the children might live. Nor were any apologies offered. As a twenty-three-year-old reporter for RTÉ, Olivia O'Leary worked on the story in the early 1970s. As she recalled, 'there was an atmosphere in Ireland at the time about any handicap to accept it as the will of God ... Back then, the notion that you would stand up for your rights was embarrassing.'

When reporting, she had asked Minister for Health Erskine Childers why no public warnings had been issued about the drug in the early 1960s when its side effects were discovered and he replied that a decision had been taken not to issue a public warning in Ireland 'because it could have frightened pregnant women into miscarriages', a disingenuous way of saying it was worried that women affected might seek abortion abroad. One of the victims' great champions was Labour TD and future Minister for Health Dr John O'Connell, whose agitation helped secure the 1970s compensation, but there was no legal process to establish the state's responsibility towards them and the compensation paid was only a fraction of that paid to UK survivors.

A memorandum for the cabinet in 1974 recorded that 'the Attorney General made it clear that the government was under no legal obligation or moral obligation arising from neglect on its own part'. It also suggested that topping up payments made by the drug's manufacturer might dispose of the problem, but that if this was done 'the state will be paying considerable sums to children who may be maintained in an institution, free of charge, for the rest of their lives'. When the government decision was made to augment the payments, each child was to be given a lump sum – of between £6,000 and £20,000 – and a small monthly payment – of between £50 and £150 – costing 'about £24,000 annually, diminishing eventually as the beneficiaries died'. The average lump-sum payment in the UK was £55,000.[39] The exact number of Thalidomide victims in Ireland is unknown, though tentative estimates published in the early 1970s varied from fifty to a hundred.[40] What is certain is that, by 2011, there were thirty-two Irish survivors of the scandal and they were still campaigning for proper compensation, having rejected a small increase in the monthly payment and a derisory lump sum payment of just under £60,000 in 2010.

PART V

FOREIGN AFFAIRS

'Some of their foremost preoccupations have tended perhaps to lack the breadth of outward vision'

When he published his seminal account of modern Ireland in 1971 under the title Ireland Since the Famine, *distinguished historian Leland Lyons, who also served as provost of Trinity College Dublin in the 1970s, characterised the Emergency in Ireland during the Second World War, when Ireland remained neutral, as a time when the country retreated into a 'Plato's Cave', conspiring to insist that the rest of the world did not exist.*[1] *At the time Lyons wrote his account, priorities were different, and he addressed them in a lecture to the Historical Society, also broadcast on RTÉ, that same year on 'The Meaning of Independence'. He asserted: 'In the present situation, with the dire past still overhanging the dire present, the need to go back to fundamentals and consider once more the meaning of independence, asserts itself with almost intolerable urgency. The theories of revolution, the theories of history, which have brought Ireland to its present pass, cry out for re-examination and the time is ripe to try to break the great enchantment which has for too long made myth so much more congenial than reality.'*[2]

This was his response to the outbreak of the Troubles, but in terms of getting back to 'fundamentals' and 'the meaning of independence', his words were also of direct relevance to the 1970s reassessment of Ireland's interaction with the rest of the world. This was an issue that took on an added momentum with Ireland's successful application to join the EEC, culminating in membership at the same time as Denmark and Britain in January 1973. For some, this was not in any sense about undermining Irish sovereignty, but quite the opposite. Garret FitzGerald, who served as Minister for Foreign Affairs between 1973 and 1977, was a Europhile. His father Desmond, one of the War of Independence generation who served in government in the 1920s in the same position (it was then titled External Affairs) had been a Francophile and, as political scientist Tom Garvin saw it, Garret's emergence from the 1950s as an economist 'with a pronouncedly Europhile outlook, presaged Ireland's future growing awareness of the importance of a new European trading bloc'.

In 1962, a year after Ireland's first unsuccessful application for membership, FitzGerald insisted that joining the EEC would not in any sense be a betrayal of those who had died to achieve Irish independence:

> *Our independence was won for us just in time to enable most of Ireland to enter the European Community as one of Europe's ancient nations, rejoining once again the Europe from which for so many centuries she was cut off by the imposition of British rule. We shall negotiate our entry as a sovereign state ... the voice of Ireland will be heard in Europe in the decades ahead. But for the sacrifices of those who won our freedom, none of this could have been. We have the right to believe that they will feel as they view this prospect that their sacrifices were not after all in vain.*[3]

It would lead, he hoped, to a final discarding of economic dependence on Britain, for which some diminution of sovereignty was a price worth paying. But that same year T. K. Whitaker, in correspondence with veteran Fianna Fáil minister James Ryan, also pointedly referred to the need for a realistic acceptance of Ireland's status: 'Nobody so loves us as to want us in the EEC on our own terms'.[4]

There was a broad political consensus (though this was challenged by the Labour Party, the trade union movement and others on the left) about the desirability of Ireland joining the EEC in January 1973, but not necessarily for the reasons advocated by FitzGerald. Embracing the concept of European integration was not about a devotion to a long-submerged Europhilia, but partly a result of Britain's decision to enter. As Ireland's closest and most important trading partner, it seemed essential that Ireland also apply for membership. It was also presented as something that would lead to a substantial economic dividend in terms of common agricultural policy and social and regional policies. But it undoubtedly also facilitated a reorientation of Ireland's foreign policy, away from a strictly Anglo-Irish perspective.

As it emerged in the 1970s, scholarly writing on foreign policy in relation to the formative decades of independence presented it largely in the context of the British commonwealth (which Ireland left in 1949); the era of contested statehood, neutrality and diplomacy on a small scale. What had been central to that era was the capacity to implement an independent foreign policy and maximise sovereignty. But in the words of historian Desmond Williams, by the 1970s, 'two principal points arise for a small state; policy cannot be a single grand design and freedom of action is limited'.[5] *In the 1960s, Seán Lemass had demonstrated a pragmatic realism in this regard in pursuing entry to the EEC, a pro-US stance and détente with Northern Ireland. He grew 'impatient with the pieties of neutrality', insisting as early as 1962 that Ireland would be prepared to yield 'even the technical label of neutrality ... we are prepared to go into this integrated Europe without any reservation as to how far this will take us in the field of foreign policy and defence'. This was essentially about a process, also evident in the 1970s, of becoming wedded 'to the realism of interdependence'.*[6] *As was stated quite explicitly by the Department of Foreign Affairs in 1972, the Republic was 'a small country with little capacity at present to influence events abroad that affect our interests'.*[7]

Economically, the benefits of membership were trumpeted, with some justification, as it turned out. In 1973, Ireland's GDP per capita was 58 per cent of the European average. It is estimated that the Common Agricultural Policy (CAP) resulted in increased output and incomes for one-third of Irish farms. It also gave some breathing space for those farms that were struggling to survive. Membership of the EEC was not going to halt the decline of the importance of agriculture to the Irish economy, but it certainly softened the blow. While membership could not and did not prevent recession, without membership, the 1970s would have been a lot worse in the absence of the boost to agriculture, transfers from the Regional Fund and free access to wealthy European markets. By 1978 real per capita farming incomes were more than double their level in 1970. In addition, between its initial payout from the Regional Fund in 1975 and 1981, Ireland received £159 million from the fund to aid the growth of infrastructure, and Irish receipts from the European Social Fund rose from £4.1 million in 1973 to £53.5 million in 1980.

Socially, it has been argued that membership for Ireland involved all gains and no losses, particularly in the areas of social freedoms and social policies. Much of the Republic's consumer, environmental and equality legislation also had its origins in Europe. It also enhanced the skills and experience of the personnel of the Department of Foreign Affairs. But there was also the question of at what cost it came. There are those who believe that it increased rather than decreased a sense of 'peripherality'; with the Republic now a minor member of a European state system dominated by powerful nation states. The shifting of the axis of economic dependency away from Britain towards mainland Europe and the US also increased vulnerability and compromised independence. Staying aloof from the EU, the argument goes, might have forced Irish governments to scrutinise more closely their historic failures. The historian Joe Lee has argued that membership continued the tradition of regarding poor Irish performances as a result of external factors rather than examining domestic causes.[8]

But the question of entry was not necessarily accompanied by quality public and inclusive debate, partly because there was little tradition of public engagement with foreign policy, though committed activists on both sides devoted much attention and energy to the referendum debate in 1973. For most, the overriding issue was the potential for tangible economic gains. It is interesting to see how politicians and civil servants reacted to the question of EEC entry and sovereignty in this context. Based on the archival evidence, political scientist Gary Murphy has suggested the 'debate of 1970 shows that it was simply economic necessity that was the main rationale for entry'. In March 1970, when Minister for External Affairs Patrick Hillery sought the views of Irish ambassadors abroad on this issue, it was clear that sovereignty had different connotations than it had in previous decades. Seán Kennan, Irish ambassador to the EEC, was optimistic that 'membership would obviously contribute significantly towards the ending of partition',[9] *but the overriding logic was simple; retention of economic sovereignty by staying outside the EEC did not make sense unless it was to Ireland's economic advantage, which it clearly was not. Refusing to join would involve such economic disadvantages that 'the very existence of the state and therefore of its sovereignty, could be threatened'.*[10]

The challenge in seeking to join, as later explained by Patrick Hillery, was that 'we had to prove that we were fit, but also we needed to show that we needed a lot of help from the other countries' and civil servants rose to this challenge very successfully.[11] *Hillery, as Minister for Foreign Affairs, was the key negotiator on Ireland's behalf, and was very enthusiastic about the application; he subsequently became Ireland's first EEC commissioner in 1973. Even the renaming of the department from External to Foreign Affairs in 1971 was presented by Hillery as embracing a new identity; he suggested the title 'external affairs' was of British Commonwealth origin and that a distancing from British influences was timely and would create greater international respect.*[12] *In 1970 he and the Department of Foreign Affairs secretary Hugh McCann visited the EEC capitals and Hillery insisted that all negotiations with applicant states had to proceed on the same basis. He confronted the thorny issues of fisheries, transitional arrangements for industry and the preservation of the Anglo-Irish Free Trade Agreement, which dated from 1965 and allowed goods tariff-free access to each country, reflecting the progress made in Anglo-Irish relations but also the continued dominance of Britain in Irish trade patterns. He also pushed for commitments in relation to regional policy and a protocol to protect industrial incentives, all of which gave 'considerable leverage' to successive governments.*[13]

For the public, political ideas about integration were a side issue. The early Eurobarometers, taken twice a year to monitor feelings about the Community in the member states, suggested that it was economics rather than politics that was foremost in the mind of the Irish. The second Eurobarometer taken in autumn 1974, for example, found that 82 per cent of Irish people polled considered the most important aspect of the Community was economic. It is perhaps unsurprising that the image of Ireland in Europe was one of being mostly concerned with the begging bowl, or as historian Joe Lee mischievously put it, 'Paddy the amiable pick-pocket'.[14] *But as National Archives documents reveal, those working in the civil service were realistic in their approach and the approaches and stances to be taken at various negotiations were carefully weighed up and debated as a balance was sought between self-interest and self-definition.*

The 1970s also raised questions about the extent to which foreign policy horizons could be broadened beyond policy relating to the EEC, something strongly desired by Garret FitzGerald after his appointment as minister in 1973. The public had showed little interest in foreign policy prior to the 1960s, except when it came, in the words of Fianna Fáil minister and Irish president, Seán T. O'Kelly, to 'whipping John Bull'.[15] *The Department of Foreign Affairs had also historically been quite secretive, but after United Nations entry in 1955, and the participation of the Irish army in peacekeeping duties, notably from 1960–64 in the Congo, where twenty-six Irish soldiers died, and also in Cyprus and, later in the 1970s, in South Lebanon, there was more of a public awareness of the idea that Ireland had developed a role for itself internationally.*

This was sometimes presented as being appropriate due to Irish empathy for the underdog, a desire to promote peace, and sensitivity to exploitation born of the historical experience of colonisation, but it was also about capitalising on the development of regional and political alliances.[16] *In tandem, there was little appetite to challenge US foreign policy and some of the earlier independence demonstrated at the UN was diluted. There is no doubt there was a heightened interest in Africa owing to the history of Irish missionaries abroad and the extraordinary Irish response to the Biafran humanitarian crisis of 1967–70 – 'a significant benchmark in Irish involvement with the developing world' – which changed the environment in which official development assistance policy was made by encouraging a structured programme.*[17] *The late 1960s also witnessed the emergence of a strong and enduring Irish Anti-Apartheid Movement (IAAM), helped by the presence in Ireland of Kadar Asmal, a native of South Africa who worked in Trinity College Dublin and became the organisation's chair.*

Did an expanded foreign policy allow governments to change their definition of Irish nation-statehood? In one sense, EEC membership amounted to a 'second declaration of independence'. But this should not distract from what was also a degree of ambivalence. There may have been the insistence in official discourse that a European identity incorporated rather than replaced national identity, but such an assumption rested on a 'substantial ambiguity' as to the relationship between 'national' and 'European'. Garret FitzGerald, in this regard, preferred to develop the notion of 'unity in diversity' by suggesting: 'In Europe, as in Ireland, we need and are actively seeking the many benefits of unity while doggedly preserving our heritage of cultural and social diversity.'[18] *This was a grandiose claim that did not mean very much in practice in the 1970s; what was being actively sought for much of the decade was as much funding as possible.*

– THIRTY-FOUR –

TAKING THE EUROPEAN PLUNGE

A summary of the implications of Ireland joining the EEC was laid before the Houses of the Oireachtas in March 1970, following on from the reactivation of Ireland's application for membership in July 1967 (the first application had been made in July 1961 because it was regarded as imperative to join, given Britain's application; the subsequent veto of Britain's application also collapsed the Irish application). While this 1970 summary acknowledged the difficulty of precisely defining the political consequences, as there was no agreement among the six member states as to what these might involve, there was an invitation to bear in mind 'that all international co-operation involves some limitation on sovereignty' and 'a range of limitations on the freedom of actions of its members'. There was also an explicit acknowledgement that 'as the communities evolve towards their political objectives, those participating in the new Europe thereby created must be prepared to assist, if necessary, in its defence'.[1]

Two years later, the Minister for Foreign Affairs Patrick Hillery advised the Taoiseach Jack Lynch to decline an invitation to become a member of the honorary committee for the commemoration of the fiftieth anniversary of the Pan European Union. Instead, Lynch sent a message of congratulations: 'Ireland, mindful of its historic associations with the European mainland, looks forward to a full participation in the movement towards a greater unity in Europe.'[2] Was this an accurate summation of feelings about Ireland's relationship with Europe and its impending membership of the EEC? It did not seem to be much debated; nor did the idea of a European identity within Ireland generate much public discourse or even consciousness; after all, in a refreshingly honest speech to EEC heads of governments in 1972, Lynch acknowledged, 'It may be said with some justification that Irishmen have been somewhat sensitive to the burdens of their history and that some of their foremost preoccupations have tended perhaps to lack the breadth of outward vision.'[3]

In June 1970, Aidan Pender, the editor of the *Irish Independent*, conscious of a lack of concrete information on the significance and consequences of Irish membership, wrote to Fine Gael senator John Kelly seeking his willingness to contribute articles on the implications of Ireland joining. Pender felt the public was

> very much in the dark ... one reader has asked if, under EEC, a French man or some other continental will have the right to attend a public auction here in Ireland and purchase land by outbidding the poorer native neighbours. He asks if, because of superior skill in some technical matters, foreigners will be able to get jobs here, which Irish people would normally fill. He also wonders if collective farming can be imposed on Irish small farmers and managed by technocrats from the Continent ... is there a danger of importation of foreign ideologies? Can the church survive this situation? Could obligatory military service be introduced? Will our population rise to 10 million people in 15 years' time?[4]

Kelly agreed to write some explanatory articles. He first sent them to Denis Corboy of the EEC Information Centre (Corboy was a barrister who had been one of the founders of the Irish Council of the European Movement in 1955 – see pages 395–6), who was clearly unimpressed and felt Kelly had little grasp of the issues: 'I do not agree with the approach of the article nor the conclusions you reach ... the decision process is not as you describe it ... there is no question of people being forced off the land ... you cannot separate economic from political integration ... I am enclosing a recent fact sheet.'[5] The tone of the correspondence from Corboy seemed to suggest that perhaps Kelly was not that much better informed on the issues than the readers he was being asked to enlighten.

The editorial line in 1972 from *Hibernia* magazine regarding EEC membership was that Ireland should stay out. It suggested that Fianna

Fáil's 'simple, strongest argument for leading the country into the EEC has been that there is no realistic alternative', given that the per capita income of the Irish population was half that of the western European average. But the real problem, it argued, was that EEC membership 'will provide an excuse for Irish politicians to pass the buck indefinitely'. Opting out, the logic went, might drive Ireland to true independence, and it lamented later that year that, 'if even a fraction of the national leadership energy that has been devoted to EEC entry over the past decade had been directed towards reaching an understanding with the North', the country would be in a much stronger position.[6] In January 1972 a White Paper titled 'The Accession to the European Communities' was published by the government, containing predictions that the first five years of membership would witness a net increase of 50,000 jobs, an additional rise in the cost of living of no more than 1 per cent and yearly savings to the exchequer of £30 million.

An Irish Council for the European Movement (ICEM) had originally been established in 1955 and in the early 1970s its officers included senior Fine Gael politician and judge T. F. O'Higgins, a former minister and presidential candidate, Fianna Fáil senator Eoin Ryan, Garret FitzGerald, and Fianna Fáil's Michael O'Kennedy, the party's spokesman on foreign affairs. In relation to negotiations on Ireland's application for membership in 1970 and 1971, one report on a discussion between the European Commission and the ICEM referred to the possibility of an 'indirect method' of funding the ICEM and a desire for no publicity regarding 'communications in both directions'. A memorandum sent to Denis Maher in the Department of Finance in February 1971 was upbeat: the ICEM 'was left in no doubt that Ireland has now acquired a special position at the Commission; the good will for us is phenomenal. They support our policy and have come to appreciate particularly the way in which official relations have been handled. They made no secret of the fact that this has been in marked contrast to Denmark and other countries.'[7]

That, of course, was only part of the challenge for the ICEM and its director from July 1971, Michael Sweetman, a businessman, industrialist and adviser to Fine Gael who had 'long been fascinated by the new thinking coming from mainland Europe' and who had authored the seminal *Challenge: Industry and Free Trade* in 1968.[8] The other was to make Irish people interested and there was much focus on the idea of market research in order to ascertain attitudes. One EEC questionnaire sent to the 194 individuals on the mailing list of the Marketing Society (mostly senior business executives) in January 1972 revealed that 95 per cent were in favour of membership: 'Attitudes to EEC entry overall are overwhelmingly favourable and very few respondents can envisage any realistic alternative ... the optimism of the respondents about the consequences for their own firms in the short term is on the whole greater than their optimism about the consequences for industry generally.'[9]

There was also a report on the attitudes in individual companies. Those in control of Jacob's biscuit factory, for example – an iconic Irish business in a country that was one of the highest consumers of biscuits per capita in Europe – were in favour but felt it would bring problems, suggesting the advantages gained by the reduction of tariffs would be largely offset by an increase in the price of home-grown raw materials and the imposition of taxes on raw materials from countries outside the EEC because of the Common Agricultural Policy and common external tariff. The report also referred to trade unions and the work force: 'In Jacob's case the majority of the employees follow the unions and are quite adamant about it. The management believes this to be largely due to the large amount of female labour. It appears that the majority of the female staff have no opinion on Ireland's entry but will follow the union's directives, because they have been told.'[10]

Another public relations company suggested targeting housewives on the grounds that 'it is safe to assume that the cost of living is an important issue for women', but also warned of the 'danger of talking down to those women who are reasonably aware of the broad economic implications'. In relation to students, it was advised that 'the area of student interest is a delicate one and in approaching it, care must be taken to avoid accusations of manipulation ... Having said this however, it is plain that students will be associated with the anti-common market campaign and the field should not be left to the opposition.' Another public relations company thought it would be wiser to concentrate on a direct communication campaign to the employees of the top fifty companies in Ireland, amounting to approximately 100,000 people, with the main argument that 'entry will secure the future of their livelihoods'.

It suggested presentations which would match questions and answers with slides: The question 'What about our neutrality?' would be answered as follows: 'Joining does not involve us in any defence commitment', accompanied by a slide that would depict 'Ireland surrounded by a heart or other symbol of love'. The question 'What about Northern Ireland?'

would be answered 'With the common market the North and South will have to solve all their problems and share responsibilities', with a slide depicting a 'Map of Europe all green'.[11]

There were accusations towards the end of 1971 that not enough information was being presented to the electorate on the Common Market question. In response to this, Patrick Hillery disagreed and declared the opposite was the case: 'He thought they were getting too much information. The people did not require the detailed knowledge being fed to them by economists. He thought that people would make their decision on entry or not to the EEC on a political basis.'[12] It may have suited Hillery to maintain that stance, if he felt that there were too many messages emerging about possible negative economic effects, but it was a dubious assertion. This was an issue that was going to be decided overwhelmingly by one central issue: how much monetary gain would ensue from membership? The overwhelming majority of the press cuttings kept by the ICEM in relation to this period make it clear that the main concerns were food prices and jobs. As seen earlier, Hillery had played a crucial role in managing Ireland's entry along with Hugh McCann, the secretary of the Department of Foreign Affairs, underlining the significant role civil servants would play in the new foreign policy mission. The same month that Lynch sent his message to the Pan European Union, February 1972, the government set up a committee of civil servants to ensure ministers were fully briefed on the implications of EEC membership and that they were provided with speaking notes. On issues like equal pay it was deemed necessary to point out that it 'will fall to be dealt with regardless of our entry in the EEC'. It was also suggested 'it is necessary to clear up some misunderstandings and misrepresentations about the effects of EEC membership on consumer prices'. Whatever Lynch's message regarding 'historic associations' with the European mainland, the reality was that the European question was framed in the context of commerce. It was seen as 'very irresponsible and misleading' to select prices of particular products 'and say that the Irish prices for the same goods will be similar'. It was also asserted that 'there is no question of any farmer, large or small, part-time or full-time, being forced off his land as a result of membership of the EEC'. Rather, 'with the increased prosperity that membership of the EEC will bring we shall be able to devote more money to social services – the social services gap between North and South will thus be reduced and eventually closed ... if we were to stay out of the enlarged community then the border would become further entrenched. We would, in effect, be conferring on the border the status of a frontier between ourselves and the Common Market countries.'[13]

It was clear from these musings what the broad parameters of the government's pro-EEC campaign were going to be – refuting perceived scaremongering, presenting it as a golden economic opportunity and suggesting it could ultimately enhance Irish unity. The Labour Party, in opposing membership, insisted that an underdeveloped economy would not be able to prosper in free-trade conditions in the EEC. Its leader, Brendan Corish, in his address to the party's annual conference in Wexford in 1972, suggested that 'nothing could more vindicate our stand than the fact that we are being opposed by both Fine Gael and Fianna Fáil'. He refused to accept the notion that opposition to the EEC would 'put us in solitary confinement in the North Atlantic'.[14]

The Labour Party had to alter its stance relatively soon after membership (see pages 399–406), and there is no doubt that its posturing in 1972 caused tension on the left in Irish politics. A few weeks earlier, Andrée Sheehy Skeffington, well-known feminist and widow of radical senator Owen Sheehy Skeffington, wrote to John de Courcy Ireland about the Common Market Defence Committee (CMDC), which had been established to oppose entry. Though prone to exaggeration and occasionally dramatic in her predictions, there was no doubting the depth of her frustration:

> I'm prepared to believe that the CMDC have no evil intentions! But they must be rather stupid not to see the consequences of their decisions – they give a cloak of respectability to the most rabid anti-British nationalism and in fact place the anti-EEC campaign in the hands of the militant wing of Sinn Féin ... I'm most depressed these days. The clock has been put back 55 years ... the splintering of the Left is disastrous and those who want to show they are the best patriots are the worst ... If it is intended to use EEC entry as a spring board for a new War of Independence, I opt out. There is, I'm afraid, great confusion in all ranks – a propitious time for those who favour force.[15]

In reaction to the CMDC, the *Farmers Journal* was withering: 'Most of the voices on the radio and TV against entry you'll notice, have Dublin accents. One thing though stands out very strongly ... one and all are devoted disciples of Karl Marx. Do you find any one among them who earns his living the hard way? Instead, you'll find ESB officials, Gardiner Street Sinn Féin, teachers in vocational schools, Kevin Street Sinn Féin, university lecturers, Parlour Pinks and, over all, a motley collection of £3,000 plus a year white collar-type Dublin trade union officials.'[16] Another vocal opponent of membership was economist Raymond Crotty, who criticised the ICEM as 'an organisation which has been subvented both by Irish tax-payers money and by the Brussels Commission to produce EEC propaganda in favour of EEC membership'.[17] Crotty was joint secretary of the Common Market Defence Campaign in the run-up to the 1972 referendum on joining the EEC, which, he insisted, would provoke a dramatic increase in unemployment and result in the failure of Irish agriculture to modernise.

On the other side, Garret FitzGerald consistently made the argument that EEC membership would liberate Ireland from its over-dependence on the UK and 'at a psychological level, the more involved Irish people, both North and South, became in a wider community, the less significant will appear their own internal differences, economic or political'.[18] The pro-EEC campaign, backed by the two largest parties, the Confederation of Irish Industry, the ICEM and the National Farmers Association, was obviously much better funded. Opponents of entry were energetic and prolific – *Irish Times* journalist Denis Kennedy noted 'the nineteenth century art of pamphleteering, an indigenous art, has been revived up and down the country' – including Sinn Féin, the Labour Party and the ITGWU, who attempted in vain to create a framework of resistance around the ideas of lost sovereignty, the submerging of Irish culture and identity, higher prices for food (a message deliberately targeted at housewives) and the elitism of a club for the rich: 'there is nothing idealistic about being bound to an association of enormous wealth, striving to become even wealthier at the expense of the still undeveloped'.[19]

In a move excoriated by Conor Cruise O'Brien, the CMDC also sent leaflets to convents and monasteries, warning that if Ireland joined the EEC, 'the same forces which have done so much to weaken Christianity on the continent would be given full-play here, with undoubtedly the same consequence'.[20] *Irish Times* journalist Donal Foley, in an article entitled 'The Church Goes to Market', satirised the notion of an impending dilution of Catholic Ireland: 'Massive redundancies will take place in the Roman Catholic Church when Ireland enters the European community in January ... according to plans prepared by the most Reverend

Dr Mansholt, Bishop of Brussels at the request of the Irish Management Institute.'[21]

Fianna Fáil's referendum campaign was initially regarded as lacklustre; Erskine Childers went as far as to suggest that 'the present organisation of Fianna Fáil headquarters is totally incapable of running a referendum'.[22] Lynch kept his energy for the final stages of the campaign in the guise of an effective 'whistle stop tour' and his party began to denounce opponents of entry as deceitful extremists. The referendum vote, on 10 May 1972, was a resounding victory for the Yes side, with a clear majority in all forty-two constituencies in favour of joining, amounting to 83 per cent of the votes cast on a 71 per cent turnout. It was a result which, according to Joe Lee, indicated that 'the dangers appeared distant, vague and abstract, while the gains appeared immediate, precise and concrete'.[23]

But was the EEC, as Lynch seemed to imply, going to provide a forum for active intervention in the problem of Northern Ireland? When Lynch met West German Chancellor Willy Brandt in Munich in September 1972 (to coincide with the Olympic Games) Lynch was adamant that 'he was hoping with the British not to bring the problem into Europe', but rather more far fetched was his assertion that the EEC referendum was a success 'not only on the EEC but also in support of his policy on the North'.[24] This seemed a curious claim to make and Lynch was inconsistent on the question of framing the Northern Ireland problem in a European context. A month after his meeting with Brandt there was a meeting of EEC heads of government in Paris and he addressed a lunch gathering organised by the Anglo-American Press Association. He was asked to speak on 'the whole Irish problem' and insisted it was a problem which would become 'in a certain sense, a European problem as well as an Anglo-Irish one'. This was a false optimism, if it was genuine at all; by the time of a summit conference in Dublin in 1975 it was asserted in *Hibernia* that 'anything will be discussed by the EEC prime ministers in Dublin next week, but not the one thing which one might expect an EEC summit conference in Dublin to discuss – the Northern Irish question'.[25]

While the vote in favour of Ireland's accession was emphatic, little thought was given to how or if this development should be officially marked or celebrated. Towards the end of May 1972, Lynch received an urgent message by hand, requesting information for use in responding to a Dáil question from Fine Gael as to whether 'it is intended to hold any public ceremony to mark the entry of this country into the EEC'. It was observed that 'the British are not planning a public ceremony' but that the British government was intending to provide £250,000 for a ten-day 'fanfare of Europe' festival. Some suggestions for Ireland included the idea of a stamp or a function at Dublin Castle 'to which dignitaries of church and state' would be invited.

Rather naively, Kenneth Thom from the British Embassy contacted Bobby MacDonagh, the young third secretary in the political division of the Department of Foreign Affairs, informing him it had been agreed that 'the armed forces of the other eight EEC countries shall be invited to assist in providing a party to line the foyer of the Royal Opera house ... for a performance to be attended by the Queen' as part of the fanfare for Europe. He extended a formal invitation for the Irish government to send ranks from its armed forces. Lynch's response was that 'it would be inappropriate in present circumstances, for any personnel to participate'.[26]

Lynch also rejected the idea of a Dublin Castle event as being 'too restrictive' and 'unrepresentative' and instead wanted 'countrywide symbolic tree planting ceremonies' and a concert of European music by the RTÉ orchestra. Noel Mulcahy of the Irish Management Institute wrote to Patrick Hillery after a brainstorming session to come up with other ideas. Suggestions included a new national anthem, a 'beauty competition' and a 'European Folk dancing festival' or 'some attempt to show that the 6 counties and the 26 are entering the EEC at the same time. Would it be possible to negotiate for a demonstration of solidarity for the 32 counties entering the EEC?' Judge Cearbhall Ó Dálaigh suggested to Patrick Hillery that 'Kildare Street [the location of the Irish parliament] might be named 'Rue de L'Europe', which Hillery thought was 'extremely interesting'.[27] But he was not interested enough, it seemed, to do anything about it, and the *Irish Times* announced on 1 January 1973 that 'Ireland enters EEC without any fanfares ... ceremony or flourish'.[28]

The safer option of tree planting was preferred, though it was noted in the *Irish Press* in January 1973 that two of the nine trees planted by Tralee Urban District Council in Tralee Town Park had been 'pulled up and replaced by black flags'. A decision had also been agreed to provide special medallions for babies born on New Year's Day 1973, the date of official accession.[29] This was something overseen by the ICEM and would also include births on 1 January in Northern Ireland. One hundred and sixty such medallions were commissioned, but by February 1973, the Fianna Fáil senator Neville Keery, who had replaced Michael Sweetman as director of the ICEM – Sweetman, along with eleven other Irish businessmen, was killed in the Staines air crash in June 1972; they were on their way to Brussels to arrange the establishment of an Irish business bureau – conceded that 'our estimated number of children born January 1st 1973 (100 approximately) has far exceeded our expectations. We have to date received over 180 applications and are receiving applications daily'.[30] A press release in May 1973 announced that Ireland's 'Euro babies' had received their medals, which were 'dye stamped from bronze and dipped in silver'. Keery felt sure that 'each of the medallions will be of considerable historic interest in the years ahead'.[31] A skilled communicator who had worked as a research officer for Fianna Fáil, a journalist and university administrator as well as with the IPA, Keery had played a prominent part in the referendum campaign.

– THIRTY-FIVE –

BRITTANY REUNIONS, PUBLIC APATHY AND THINKING EUROPEAN

In April 1973, when civil servants and their ministers were discussing proposals for a national day of reconciliation, it was doubted in the Department of the Taoiseach if a day of prayer 'would catch on ... The attempted celebration of EEC entry is perhaps a precedent. Very few were interested.'[1] This was also something that was commented on by the ICEM; indeed much of its correspondence in the early 1970s revealed a frustration with public apathy, not helped by the fact that in seeking meetings with the government to discuss the processing of 'various matters arising from Irish membership of the EEC' it did not intend 'that the meeting should be given any publicity'.[2]

Neville Keery also informed journalist Denis Kennedy that he was planning a programme of monthly European discussions to keep people informed about a range of European developments 'and that they should stimulate a continuing interest in European affairs'.[3] If the desire was to generate popular as opposed to professional engagement, this proved wishful thinking. Most of those getting receipts for group membership of the ICEM were wealthy and established business interests as well as the Irish Farmers Association. In 1971 the ICEM's membership included 380 individuals and 42 groups. An executive committee of 31 included George Colley, Richie Ryan, Mary Robinson and John Hume. By 1973 there were 705 individual memberships and 45 group memberships. Only 25 parliamentarians (19 TDs and 6 senators) were members, which did not suggest a ringing endorsement of its significance.

Reference was made at its AGM in 1973 to the 'massive support from private subscriptions' during the referendum campaign, a reminder of the degree to which it represented wealthy vested interests. Farcically, executive members who were members of the Labour Party had to withdraw from the council during the referendum period due to the party's opposition to EEC membership,[4] a reminder that the party's stance would have proved embarrassing to some committed Europhiles within it. Its position had not involved a 'blanket refusal' to countenance an Irish relationship with the EEC; instead, it advocated a 'wait and see' approach. Its official line in 1972 was that the Republic was not yet ready for full membership and associate membership would be needed for a period for the country to adapt. In the aftermath of the referendum, its change of stance was 'clear and quick'. Party leader Brendan Corish immediately accepted the vote in favour and described Labour's task as 'to minimise the disadvantages of membership and to transform the common market, if possible, into a more democratic and humane organisation'. The party's first ever international secretary was appointed in 1974 and it established a European Affairs Committee in 1978. There were in the party a number of pro-European voices who had undoubtedly been dismayed by its opposition in 1972 and would have been pleased at the repositioning, but pragmatism was also at play here; had Labour not changed its position on EEC membership it would have risked an ongoing marginalisation.[5]

But the ICEM had to contend with an ongoing apathy; it was noted in May 1973, for example, that Europe Day, on 5 May, 'has passed by here without any celebration of note' and that there was a need for 'a national committee for Europe Day'.[6] Nonetheless, it did generate jollity for some: in June 1973 Keery was anxious to hold a 'Brittany reunion' for those – 'a group of various Irish interests' – who had been led by Justin Keating as guests of the French government in co-operation with the ICEM. Although those who could afford it were asked to pay all or part of the costs, 'by agreement there was very little publicity associated with the visit itself'.[7]

Keery, however, was almost constantly engaged in correspondence as leader of a lost cause, even having to remind John Hume to renew his annual subscription and lament that the Irish selection committee for the College of Europe Scholarships in Bruges was 'disappointed by the small number of applicants and their calibre'; successful applicants were told to 'improve your French'.[8] A letter to the ICEM of January 1976 suggested 80 per cent of Irish businessmen dealing with the EEC 'have not mastered another language of the community'.[9]

Sometimes it appeared that the ICEM, which Keery described as 'largely a lobby organisation', felt it had to act like an underground secret society; when inviting the editor of the *Irish Times*, Douglas Gageby, to an ICEM seminar, Keery noted that 'because of its anxiety that the seminar should provide an opportunity for members of the government, senior civil servants and others to discuss together in an informal way it feels that coverage of the seminar by press, radio and television may create unusual difficulties'.[10] Neither were its communications skills exemplary and its part-time directors were often on the defensive due to complaints about lack of acknowledgement of correspondence. Trevor Salmon, a lecturer in politics at the National Institute of Higher Education in Limerick, complained in January 1975 to the director that 'we seem to have heard nothing from you for several months as to any activities or speeches etc.', which prompted an acknowledgement that there was 'a distinct Dublin bias' to its activities.[11]

By 1975 it was branding itself as reorganised and redeveloped with its first full-time director, Rory Dunne, who was a graduate in Agricultural Economics from Trinity College Dublin and had spent time working with the Economic and Social Research Institute. Following his appointment, there was more of an edge to his correspondence and letters to the press in an effort to make its presence felt. But some of those in senior officer positions, including the titular president of the ICEM, Jack Lynch, had little interest; Lynch thanked Dunne on his re-election as president in 1976, 'which is most undeserved and therefore all the more appreciated'.[12] Dunne also revealed that the ICEM in June 1976 was 'still losing around £3,000 per year'.[13]

The movement was also chastised for avoiding some difficult issues; in October 1976, for example, UCC economist David O'Mahony, who felt there was no need for an Irish army ('no one is likely to attack us and we don't want to attack anyone'), insisted that the EEC needed a 'Swiss type army' and 'we should be part of it'. He argued 'it is deplorable that the subject of defence is not discussed openly. I would urge very strongly that the ICEM should face up fairly and squarely to this issue and see to it that it is put before the public.'[14] Putting information before the public was hampered at times by lack of information coming from Brussels.

Miriam Hederman O'Brien, who in 1977 was researching her book on Irish attitudes to European integration, informed Denis Corboy that she was 'having great difficulty in getting information from Brussels'.[15] But there was also a problem in getting information closer to home; Hederman O'Brien's book was published in 1983 and underlined that, while eventually she received help from the College of Europe in Bruges and the Council of Europe in Strasbourg, it was actually the Department of Foreign Affairs that was 'courteous but unrewarding' in relation to files documenting its involvement with the Council of Europe and the OEEC, and the ICEM papers she sought were 'not available'.[16]

By 1977 Dunne had resigned; in the same year, Mary Robinson informed the chairman Barry Desmond, a Dublin Labour Party TD, that as she had joined the Labour Party she would not be seeking re-election as vice-chairman: 'I am conscious that ICEM tries to maintain a political balance in the officers and since I joined the Labour Party this has meant that both the chairman and vice-chairman have been members of the Labour parliamentary party.'[17] This can be seen as an ironic dominance, given the Labour Party's opposition to EEC entry four years earlier, but Mary Robinson's involvement was an indication that some of those involved in feminist causes were likely to be keen advocates of Ireland in the EEC, and they had every reason to be, given the improvement in the status of women as a result of EEC directives (see Part VIII). Towards the end of 1977, probably in a response to a questionnaire from the Women's Political Association, it was pointed out that 'eight members of the executive committee, including the chairman, are women. They are also active in women's organisations.'[18]

But overall, there were contradictory messages in 1977, it seemed, about Irish citizens' attitudes to the EEC. Joe Hayes, the Irish ambassador in Bonn, wrote to the secretary of the Department of Foreign Affairs in January of that year regarding a film report on Irish, Italian and Greek attitudes towards the EEC which had been shown on German television. Hayes's perception was that it portrayed 'a rather gloomy picture of Irish attitudes towards the EEC'. Yet later that year, attention was drawn to a recent Eurobarometer – designed to survey attitudes to the EEC in its member states – which had found that 57 per cent of the Irish population thought that the community was 'a good thing' compared to 35 per cent in the UK and 30 per cent in Denmark.[19] The bottom line was that people's attitudes depended on how they believed membership would affect them financially. In a contribution to the Senate in March 1977, Mary Robinson suggested 'much of the debate in Ireland on further extension of the EEC seems to be coloured by our increasing tendency to regard the European Community as a benevolent fund and ourselves as deserving recipients'.[20] Rarely were truer words spoken, and behind the scenes, it seemed there was little apology made for that approach and mindset, albeit with the occasional nod to political correctness.

Terence O'Raifeartaigh of the Higher Education Authority suggested in February 1972 in a lecture to the ICEM that the cultural implications of joining had not been sufficiently considered, even though 'if we fail to join the EEC we face eventual cultural annihilation'. Provincialism, as he saw it, was 'a disease of the Irish' and he dismissed those who suggested 'most of those who are interested in the Arts are opposed to Irish entry into EEC'.[21] As part of the same series of lectures, historian John A. Murphy, regarding the European influence on Irish nationalism, suggested that in view of its past experiences, Ireland should not be naively enthusiastic about Europe: 'We might do well to remember the words of John Mitchell in 1848 when the second French Republic turned a politely deaf ear to Irish nationalist entreaties: "We are well pleased that M. Lamartine has let us know distinctly we must rely on ourselves."'[22] Four years later, in a lecture delivered in Missouri in April 1976 Murphy elaborated further in relation to the EEC: 'Membership has not really affected our distinctiveness or identity one way or the other. The path from Dublin to Brussels and Luxembourg is indeed well trodden but only by politicians, diplomats and the bosses in industry and agriculture. Irish people go to Europe mainly on holidays ... but there is little feeling of being European.' He observed there was a 'constant propaganda campaign' to make people 'think' European but the response was one of apathy 'if not incipient hostility'. Despite the increased profits for many farmers, the EEC was also associated in the public mind with increased consumer prices and limits on fishing rights. As for its cultural influence, he singled out the Eurovision Song Contest 'rightly described by the late Seán Ó Riada as a farrago of feeble-mindedness'.[23]

Declan Kiberd suggests there was also a fear that EEC membership would foster the spreading of a 'dole mentality', long perceived as being associated with the west of Ireland, to the whole island, as leaders and civil servants became 'expert in the small print of European handouts'. Some of that money may have promoted enterprise, but it could also retard it and with the dying out of small farms, the future of certain rural areas seemed to lie only in tourism, reflected in the satire of Brian Friel in his play *The Mundy Scheme* 'devoted to the idea of Ireland as a gigantic theme park, retirement commune and cemetery for European industrialists'.[24] In 1976 it was suggested in the Department of Foreign Affairs that 'Ireland's commitment to European integration springs from a combination of idealism and enlightened self-interest,'[25] a conveniently self-serving and disingenuous definition.

– THIRTY-SIX –

NEGOTIATING THE BENEFITS AND THE DILEMMAS

As Minister for Foreign Affairs from 1973, Garret FitzGerald was in a pivotal position to increase Irish influence at the EEC; he was involved in many formal and informal meetings of foreign ministers in Europe and frequently at these meetings was able to produce detailed notes of previous meetings to correct people.[1] But it had also become apparent that Irish representatives at the EEC would have to fight to be heard and to push the notion of investment in undeveloped regions due to its comparative poverty compared to some of the bigger and richer member states, and to get adequate information on time. The EEC Committee of Irish Civil Servants included Paul Keating, appointed secretary of the Department of Foreign Affairs in April 1974, who questioned the value of EEC summit meetings that produced nothing concrete from an Irish point of view. As he put it in October 1974 'if we were to get anything on regional policy we could go along', while a counsellor from the Department of Foreign Affairs 'said the small countries were irrelevant to the last summit and would be irrelevant to the next one … Mr Keating said the only thing we could get out of it was regional policy.'[2]

Denis Maher, an assistant secretary in the Department of Finance, was equally gloomy and 'said we would be dependent on the secondary spillover from anything the larger member states would get … we could provide technical assistance, but there was no money in that'.[3] The following month, FitzGerald was disappointed that in relation to the Regional

Fund, there had been 'no adequate budge' at a meeting in Brussels, while there were complaints from the Department of the Taoiseach that in relation to a meeting of EEC heads of government in Paris in December 1974, 'briefings for meetings of this level have tended to be too long and too late'.[4] Two years later, ahead of a summit meeting in Luxembourg in relation to an examination of monetary questions, FitzGerald wrote that 'experience is that Commission papers on this subject arrive well after the 11th hour' while the following year he suggested in relation to a Commission communication to the European Council on the economic situation: 'While parts of it are somewhat waffly, it is reasonably good on the whole.'[5]

The visit of Jacques Chirac, the French prime minister, to Dublin earlier in 1974 had provided an opportunity to press for the Regional Fund but it was not until the conference of heads of government in Paris in December 1974 that it was agreed a Regional Fund would be put into operation with effect from January 1975. The fund was not actually established until March 1975 but over the course of the next few years began to bear fruit. From the fund, in 1975, the commitment to Ireland was £8.3 million and increased thereafter in 1976 (£14.4 million), 1977 (£12.6 million), 1978 (£23.6 million) and up to the summer of 1979 (£31.9 million). In 1979 it was observed that the EEC had also approved the commitment of Regional Fund assistance of £4.09 million for twenty Irish infrastructural projects, nearly all for new telephone exchange buildings.

The first Irish presidency of the EEC occurred in 1975 and there was a concern about the need to be seen 'as an efficient, businesslike administration and country' and a self-warning that 'any obvious attempt by the Chair to pursue national objectives is likely to be counter productive'. But it was seen as imperative that Ireland would seek to influence regional and social policy and there was a decidedly selfish and partisan mindset about the enlargement of the EEC: 'Our national interests might dictate a less than enthusiastic approach to progress on the negotiations with Portugal and Spain but, in view of the established schedule of meetings, it is unlikely that effective action is possible in this area.'

There were other priorities; the Commission's attitude on the 'accumulation of regional and other state aids could present a problem for Ireland' and indications of 'an initiative to the effect that Ireland should be treated as a community pilot project in the fight against unemployment'. It was also maintained that 'during the Irish presidency, the Irish line should continue to be that no basic revision of the Common Agricultural Policy

(CAP), nor any review on which it could be based, is justified'. There were also concerns about relations with a proposed directly elected European Parliament: 'Ireland already enjoys a store of goodwill in the parliament as we have generally supported parliament exercising to the full its influence in its present areas of competence and also have an open mind on the broadening of that influence.'

While it held the presidency, Ireland developed a reputation for being more keen on open government than some of its European partners: 'Nothing so assisted the public image of the presidency than the willingness of Irish ministers to tell the press just what was going on behind closed doors of council and summit meetings, even to the point of identifying the less salubrious manoeuvres of the larger member states.' In this context, FitzGerald's control of the European brief was of vital importance in terms of his stature both at home and away. He established himself as someone with 'an aptitude for the Union's style of policy making' and his role was regarded abroad as a major success. In the view of Roy Jenkins, later president of the European Commission, 'As Foreign Minister he made Ireland not merely an official but an integral part of the European Community, an honorary member of the somewhat exclusive club of the original six ... This was not his motive, but FitzGerald succeeded in making London look peripheral to Europe, while Dublin was metropolitan.'[6] It was noted by those monitoring foreign press coverage of Ireland in 1975 that the coverage of the Irish presidency of the EEC and the meeting of nine heads of government in Dublin in March of that year

> enhanced the image of Ireland as a country capable of hosting a meeting on such a scale and of 'steering' it to concrete results. This positive and widespread publicity was a welcome counter to the almost daily diet of agency-based factual reports of violence in Northern Ireland ... many reporters, mainly British, who had previously expressed doubts regarding the ability of the Irish to mount a summit and had particular suspicions of the efficiency of the Irish telephone system were magnanimous [enough] to eat their words publicly ... many journalists from Europe commented on the irony of the fact that a conclusion to British re-negotiation was being sought not alone in Dublin but in Dublin Castle! [The seat of British power in Ireland before independence.][7]

There was serious praise internationally for FitzGerald, who was perceived as 'cheerful, relaxed, his jacket hung over the chair and braces down off his shoulders', and a belief he had managed to extend the role of chairman. A Canadian newspaper went so far as to contend that the Irish inferiority complex was now gone and was 'finally broken' in the first six months of 1975 due to the EEC presidency and had become 'unshackled from British domination'.[8] In that context, in May 1975, British leader of the opposition Ted Heath visited Dublin and Cosgrave entertained him for lunch, but did not attend the business lunch at which Heath was guest speaker on the subject of continued UK membership of the EEC. He was advised by civil servants that he should not go 'as an ordinary guest to listen to another speaker unless he is of really outstanding importance. This feeling is reinforced now by the impression I have that his attendance could add to the public feeling that the British may be telling us what to do.'[9]

But there was still uncertainty as to the strategy the Irish government should deploy in relation to contentious EEC issues. Secretary of the Department of Foreign Affairs Paul Keating, in his capacity as chair of the European Communities Committee, warned in January 1976 of the danger of being too defensive and parochial: 'One could on the one hand remain reticent on particular issues and work towards a global solution [but] a defensive posture in which we concentrated on these matters to which we objected could be considered a rather negative strategy.' Concern was also expressed – and this was something repeatedly aired from an early stage – about a 'two tier' Europe and a feeling, as Keating concluded, that 'we would not get something for nothing'.[10]

The government was particularly happy that the report on European Union by the Belgian prime minister Leo Tindemans in 1976 suggested regional policy should be concentrated in regions 'where economic development has been most retarded. Funds should be allocated on the basis of objective criteria applicable throughout the community, without national quotas.'[11] Two months later, Walter Kirwan in the Department of the Taoiseach elaborated on some of the issues that had arisen in relation to the Tindemans Report, pointing out that the Irish approach to European Monetary Union was to stress the need for massive community assistance to 'get us up to the starting line'. But he suggested a new realism was necessary as 'the better off countries will not be prepared to make the massive transfers of resources required for a full economic and monetary union without being in a position to influence in some significant way the economic policies of the recipient countries which they see as out of tune with the aim which resources transfers would be designed to achieve, i.e. self-sustaining growth soundly based on an expansion of productive investment'.

The next stage in the development of the community would be, it was surmised, a 'considerable surrender of national sovereignty' by member states. It was argued that Ireland should be in favour of extending the powers of the parliament into legislative fields ('without such powers the process of direct elections may fail to evoke an appropriate interest amongst the peoples of the community'), but there was broad Irish welcome for Tindemans's support for 'the supra-national character of the institutions' and the idea of one European foreign policy, while again 'we reject any proposal tending towards a two-tier community'. In relation to a common defence policy, there was no mention in the briefing memoranda on the possible impact on Irish neutrality. The Irish position would be 'to avoid if possible a commitment to co-operation in arms production and to be hesitant about regular exchanges of views on defence/security matters advocating that any discussions to be held should be confined to security rather than on defence issues'.[12]

In 1977 a cabinet subcommittee on the EEC Regional Development Fund sought assistance for ten industrial projects (four large and six small) and twenty-four infrastructural projects (fourteen local telecommunications and ten water and sewerage schemes), but Mark Clinton, as Minister for Agriculture and Fisheries, suggested in a letter to Richie Ryan that this list 'does not constitute a particularly attractive package and hardly makes the best use of our opportunities for using European Regional Development Funds for the benefit of the economy'. The Department of Finance not only wanted a major increase in the size of the Regional Fund but wanted to press 'for a higher percentage share for Ireland ... our present effective share is 6.05 per cent ... We have no particular interest in widening the variety of measures that the fund may assist, apart from achieving a less restrictive attitude to the question of the types of infrastructure which may qualify for fund aid.'[13]

There was also a concern that in selecting projects for Regional Fund assistance a good geographic spread should be achieved, as some 'have fared much better than others', but overall it was suggested the fund had had a 'minute impact' on regional problems. Garret FitzGerald elaborated on this when the recently appointed Commissioner for Regional Policy, Italy's Antonio Giolitti, arrived in Dublin for a visit in March 1977:

> The small amount of the fund had led to great disillusion in Ireland. This was one of the 3 great disappointments the Irish had with the EEC – the others [were] the lack of help during the cattle crisis of 1974 [cattle numbers had increased in anticipation of new markets, but a shortage of feed forced farmers to try and sell quickly with the result that the market became choked and prices temporarily tumbled] and the present fishing controversy. He doubted whether 83 per cent of the electorate would be in favour of the EEC today. He termed the fund a flea bite as far as our needs were concerned. It amounted to only 2 per cent of our capital investment expenditure and while every 2 per cent was helpful, it was marginal. The contradiction whereby money for regions went instead to states has not helped the community to produce a policy to cope with the Regional Fund.

But maybe it was also the case that FitzGerald was contradicting the contradiction in this regard, by suggesting in relation to regional interest groups that 'he had no ideological opposition to such bodies playing a part in forming and implementing regional policy but he felt they would complicate life. In this country, for example, there was very strong local feeling in all areas.' Finally, he criticised the 'complete arbitrariness' of the quota system because 'regions the average income of which was just below the community average were treated in the same way as the poorest regions in Italy and Ireland'.[14] The following year Jack Lynch received the deputy prime minister of New Zealand in Dublin and when they discussed the EEC, the Taoiseach said that 'he had felt a certain disappointment about its progress. He felt that many countries were reverting to strongly nationalistic stances on many issues. We, of course, were not immune from this. Fisheries might be cited, for or against us, in this respect.'[15]

– THIRTY-SEVEN –

FEAR OF ENLARGEMENT AND STRIVING FOR SEX APPEAL AFTER THE HONEYMOON ENDS

The Common Agricultural Policy (CAP) was also a recurring preoccupation. By 1979, Ireland had received £1 billion in CAP payments since 1973, in comparison with £179 million from the other main sources of direct community funding, while higher market prices had meant that agricultural export earnings had risen 450 per cent since 1970. In relation to the visit of Roy Jenkins to Dublin in 1977, in his role as president of the European Commission, the most important thing was to 'discover if his heart is in the right place' regarding CAP.[1]

The subtext of these concerns for the next two years was that while Ireland would express itself in favour of EEC enlargement, this was conditional on such enlargement being accompanied by sufficient additional resources to protect the Irish share. There was a perceived need to stress the urgency of increasing own resources by highlighting the effect of enlargement on the redistributive capacity of the EEC budget, but it was believed it would be difficult to push that line politically.[2] In 1977, civil servants, including Walter Kirwan and Dermot Nally, reflected on the conclusions of an inter-departmental working group in the Department of Foreign Affairs on the enlargement of the EEC, to the effect that such an expansion 'would be directly detrimental to the economic and financial interest of Ireland' and that the Irish needed to make a case for a 'substantially larger Regional Fund'. Regarding the strengthening of community institutions and the European Commission, Kirwan suggested this was 'a matter which in my view has not received adequate consideration at government level'. If there were to be new members Ireland should argue to 'phase them in over a fairly long period', and not just the five years suggested by Garret FitzGerald.[3]

At a meeting of the EEC Committee in May 1977, the assistant secretary of the Department of Foreign Affairs noted that Ireland 'had entered reservations on the Greek application' regarding transfer of resources and improved decision-making. But there were also inconsistencies identified by the Department of Foreign Affairs regarding Irish attitudes to enlargement of the EEC. One memorandum contained a paragraph which 'describes our support for enlargement as being conditional and paragraph 14 refers to areas in which we would not be prepared to make concessions under any circumstances while paragraph 13 states that we could not realistically oppose enlargement openly unless a majority of other member states were of the same view',[4] a product perhaps of a nervy and somewhat sloppy and self-interested but ultimately confusing stance. When the committee met in Iveagh House in March and May 1977 it was stressed that 'we cannot underestimate the effect which accession by even one country would have on the transfer of community resources'. Maurice Doyle of the Department of Finance maintained 'there were arguments on philosophical grounds for enlargement and on economic grounds against'.[5]

In June and September 1977 there were further very lengthy committee meetings. The report of the minutes ran to twenty-eight pages and Noel Dorr from the Department of Foreign Affairs was a key and substantial contributor. Maurice Doyle made it clear that the general approach of the Irish should be one of the poor mouth: 'Our fundamental approach in Brussels should be that we are the poorest country in the EEC and that we cannot be expected to subscribe to subventions for countries and regions which will subsequently compete with us ... Mr Nally suggested that we might be better off, like Norway, outside the community, with perhaps special arrangements for agriculture and fisheries.'

Joe Holloway, the secretary of the Department of Industry and Commerce, was not exactly overcome with a profound sense of European identity in his contribution, which again underlined the profound parochialism and self-interest of the Irish approach to the EEC and the mindset that accompanied it: he 'expressed regret that many of our people going to Brussels seemed to have the idea that they ought not to be too dogged about things and that it should be impressed upon them that they should look after the national interest'. There was some toying with the idea of opposing the Spanish application but a realisation that it would not be realistic to do so as 'political factors would be the decisive ones'. For all the talking done at this committee, Minister for Finance George Colley in a letter to Minister for Foreign Affairs Michael O'Kennedy suggested the government needed more direct assistance from the committee and that it needed to meet more regularly to give 'recommendations for strategic options'.[6]

The first democratically elected Spanish prime minister, Adolfo Suárez, visited Dublin in October 1977 in the context of its application for membership of the EEC. Richard Stokes noted in relation to catering that 'we have been slated by Finance for the excessive cost of dinners recently done by the Hibernian [Hotel] ... the menu was not distinguished – "rasher of veal and peas" was one DFA [Department of Foreign Affairs] comment'. As for the drink – 'a small point perhaps, but it might be a nice gesture if the wine for this occasion were Spanish rather than French as approved'.[7] The briefing notes for this visit made clear that the main concern was the European Social Fund, where the outlook was despondent: 'Clearly the bigger Spain's hypothetical share the more difficult it would be for us to get a substantial share ... there is no evidence that the richer member states of the community would be prepared to countenance a massive increase in the size of the fund in the foreseeable future.' There was a caution with regard to the issue of enlargement; recognition that Ireland could not be seen to reject it publicly and that 'from a political point of view' there would be an Irish welcome, but it was also maintained that 'the community has not yet fully adjusted to the effects of the 1973 enlargement'. There was also a stated need for improvements in the decision-making processes and more money.

When chatting with Suárez, Lynch suggested 'for us, agriculture had been the primary attraction in gaining access ... prices to farmers had been good and other agricultural policies had been well worth while'. He also stressed the importance of opportunities for young people and added that 'the ultimate alternative might be danger to democratic structures themselves – as they grew tired of the system. This was not a problem at the moment but it was something which must be kept firmly in mind'. Suárez was more whimsical, suggesting 'it was an open question whether Spain loved Ireland more than Ireland loved Spain'. (It was noted that Aer Lingus, the state airline, was the only foreign owned company that had been granted access to an official low-interest Spanish government loan in the tourist sector.) Affection between the two was also certainly reflected in the lavishness of the dinner, the bill for which came to a costly £1,264 – more than double the usual amount – which included £563 on alcohol as well as fifty cigars and 180 cigarettes. It was no wonder the Department of Finance was unimpressed. Stokes explained that 'the cost of the dinner exceeded that allowed under the limit for such functions by £716.67p. This excess arose due to general increases in the cost of catering and the selection of a menu which was in keeping with the usual standards for such occasions hosted by the Taoiseach.'[8] There was no mention of the booze, of course.

The continuing difficulty about enlargement, as was recognised into 1978, was that, while it was easy to identify the requirements which would allay fears about expansion, 'it is somewhat more difficult to translate these general requirements into politically realisable objectives ... it would be very difficult to slow up or veto the enlargement process if we were to overtly phrase our demands solely in terms of our own self-interest. Indeed, even if a nakedly self-interested approach were successful in enabling us to achieve our objectives in the short term there is the risk that our longer-term interests would suffer as a consequence of our having incurred both the wrath of some of the larger existing member states and the hostility of the applicants.'[9]

There was an even more frank if gloriously pompous assessment from Kevin Jordan in the Department of Industry and Commerce, who clearly enjoyed composing the following, in the context of whether or not Ireland should demand a fund for the new enlargement:

> Free money under any name, of course, presupposes a benefactor; in current circumstances this can be only the Federal Republic of Germany. Before we don our rags and assume the role of mendicants we should be reasonably convinced that we can collect. If we play our little trump and lose (we cannot hold out alone against Greece) we would have cast ourselves down grovelling to our wealthier partners only to find ourselves left there – effectively relegated to a lower tier in the company of Greece, Spain and Portugal – they with community aid and goodwill and we with none. We might even suffer the indignity of references to our recent and current unhappy strike record – Ferenka, Asahi, telecommunications etc. and told that our inferior economic position was largely of our own making and that we should

put our house in order before looking for charity from others. Essentially then, in our view, whether or not we engage in the kind of brinkmanship which is contemplated depends on a very fine judgement of the odds. We are not in a position to make such a judgement.[10]

Whatever about enlargement, there were other problems encountered for Ireland as a smaller country within the EEC. In 1978 there was concern expressed about monetary affairs within the Union; not only that policies for growth and employment would aggravate inflation and the permanence of exchange rates in a community where rates of inflation differed dramatically in different states, but also 'our concern in regard to not being kept informed about the development of the monetary stability proposals, as apparently, other smaller EC countries had'. As Dermot Nally pointed out to Lynch, with considerable annoyance: 'It would be no harm, if a suitable opportunity arises, to bring out once more again the fact that we are <u>not</u> an appendage of the British in the European communities.'[11]

When Roy Jenkins visited Dublin in his capacity as president of the European Commission in September 1978, Lynch asserted that with the end of the transitional period 'the honeymoon, with us, was over'. There were now a number of different policy areas and individual policies which were potentially harmful to Ireland including proposals to restrict investments in refineries, worries about export tax reliefs and the need for community aid in relation to youth unemployment, which was a bigger problem in Ireland than elsewhere because the Irish population was a young one. Yet again, the Regional Fund was in the frame: 'A marked characteristic of the community was the insufficiency or the total absence of regional policy as such.'

The dissatisfaction expressed in February 1978 with the way in which the commission was dealing with Irish affairs seems to have paid off, as in the following six months it had shown itself 'considerably more sympathetic to Ireland's interests and special problems' with aid for drainage, fisheries and resources from the Social Fund. Jenkins was duly rewarded with a dinner at the Royal Hibernian Hotel for himself and fifteen others which cost £400 and included seventeen bottles of wine, brandies, sherries, Scotch whisky and pints, with eighty cigarettes and eleven cigars thrown in for good measure, the only problem being, as usual, an overspend of almost 100 per cent ('the cost of the dinner exceeded that allowed under the limit for such functions by £197.76').

Issues remained, including resource transfers and the fear that the planned European Monetary System (EMS) could slow down Irish economic growth. During discussions with Jenkins, Lynch insisted that if the British left the EEC Ireland would stay in (just under 50 per cent of Ireland's total exports went to the UK market in 1978) but that the development of a two-tier Europe was 'another bogey man which this country had always feared'. In relation to the EMS, Jenkins suggested 'the French and Germans will go ahead with this system anyway'.[12] Ireland joining the EMS in 1979 was, in the event, regarded by some as the 'breaking a long link with sterling and escaping from economic and psychological dependency on the UK' (see Part VI).[13]

When he addressed the Dáil before it adjourned for the summer in 1979, Lynch was upbeat about Ireland's economic prospects, but officials were less than enthused by a draft speech by the European Council Secretariat to form the basis of Lynch's address to the inaugural meeting of the European Parliament. It was observed by one civil servant: 'Given the extensive media coverage which the Taoiseach's speech will probably receive, the draft needs to be worked over by someone with the gift of phrase. In addition to lacking "sex appeal" the speech as drafted by the Council Secretariat understandably lacks an adequate Irish dimension.'[14]

In relation to the European Parliament, advice was sought from the Attorney General in 1977 as to whether membership of the European Parliament should debar MEPs from being members of the Dáil and Senate. He advised that such dual membership 'must be allowed and cannot be abolished under EEC rules', although those elected MEPs could opt to resign their national parliament seats.[15] Those who were MEPs and TDs or senators and operating the dual mandate from 1973 expressed frustration at their plight in correspondence with Liam Cosgrave in September 1973. Charlie McDonald, also a Fine Gael TD for Laois, and Brian Lenihan, who had lost his Dáil seat in the 1973 general election and was now Fianna Fáil leader in the Senate and led the Fianna Fáil delegation in the European Parliament, where he was active in forging alliances with the French Gaullists, complained: 'We have now been in Europe for 9 months and our dual mandate is proving to be a heavy burden with a constant conflict of loyalties.' They also insisted on the need for parliamentary assistants and a senior official to be shared by all Irish MEPs: 'We need at least brief factual memoranda and some speeches to be prepared if possible.' Earlier that year, McDonald had emphasised to Garret FitzGerald that they also required help 'in projecting the Irish point of view on every occasion possible'. But it was the physical exertion and possible long-term political implications that was taking its toll: 'since 15th January last – a period of 46 days, I have spent 24 days out of the country and missed 7 days meetings because of the general election ... There is a growing clash of priorities, of loyalties to country, to constituents, to EEC, not to mention family.'[16]

Walter Kirwan in the Department of the Taoiseach felt that the Irish government was a trail blazer in relation to its preparation for direct elections and lamented that it did not receive enough publicity for its efforts. He suggested that the Department of Foreign Affairs should have been doing more in this regard: 'I have noted in the past that Irish developments in relation to the communities get a poor community press by which I mean reporting in leading papers in other member states ... So far as I am aware, no other member state has yet introduced its national legislation to govern the holding of direct elections.'[17]

In relation to representation in the proposed parliament, Kirwan expressed pessimism about Ireland's chances of getting its desired representation: 'We have no hope now of securing acceptance of our proposal giving 18 seats out of 384 and that to maintain our position was not even a worthwhile bargaining position.' He suggested looking for thirteen seats, three more than current representation.[18] The number eventually agreed was fifteen. A Dáil debate in 1977 focused on the possible annual salaries of MEPs – one of the figures being mooted was £30,000 – and Michael O'Kennedy suggested that the issue of the European Commission is 'frankly too remote a problem' for the public. It was much more interested, he suggested, in the proposed MEP salaries. Dublin Labour Party TD Ruairí Quinn noted that 'a salary which would be considered normal for a TD in Germany or France is perceived to be enormously bountiful in Ireland or in Southern Italy'. Donegal TD for Fine Gael, James White, a farmer as well as being a supermarket and hotel director, argued that 'as parliamentarians we have been too apologetic to the Irish people in the past in regard to our salary which is in the region of £5,000. Many salesmen earn more than £5,000 per annum and there is not a word about it.' Michael Woods, a new Fianna Fáil TD in Dublin, felt there was nothing extravagant about £30,000 for an onerous task, adding very conveniently, 'If we are to be Europeans we must make up our minds that we will be Europeans in the full sense.'[19]

The Labour Party's David Thornley, who represented Ireland in the European Assembly before direct elections, talked of his pained attempts 'to dispel the myth that being a deputy to the European Parliament is a well paid "cushy number"'. On the contrary he maintained the life was 'physically exhausting, intellectually sterile and possibly electorally suicidal'. Whether the last of those was correct, he suggested, 'I shall shortly find out'.[20] Thornley did indeed lose his seat in the Dáil in 1977, but its fair to observe that membership of the European Parliament was only one item on his rather extended political suicide note. It has also been observed that there is little evidence that he took his role as an MEP all that seriously. In 1975, he earned one of the quotes of the year from the *Irish Times* when he observed: 'When I attend a session of the European Parliament, I don't know what I'm talking about half the time.'[21] But the figures being bandied about in relation to the salaries of directly elected MEPs fuelled the perception that in Irish terms, this was going to make the successful Irish candidates fantastically rich. *Business and Finance* magazine repeated in May 1978 the '£30,000 figure already operating in Dublin gossip circles'.

Information from Eurobarometers and market research conducted prior to the direct European elections in 1979, as recorded by the ICEM, suggested Irish attitudes to the EEC varied according to socio-economic background and education. Farmers and those in managerial or professional roles were positive: 'farmers felt that they themselves had benefited and look upon such developments as a reaping of just rewards'. In contrast to that assertion, Dan McCarthy, president of the National Land League, maintained in 1979 that 'the EEC has been a Utopia for 20 per cent of Irish farmers, while the remaining 80 per cent have hung on by the skin of their teeth'.[22]

Working-class men and housewives were deemed to be more hostile; along with having 'no feelings of personal contact with the EEC' they blamed the community for food inflation and the fact that young people's expectations were not delivered ('Weren't we told that cars would be the same price as they are in England?'). Those with a negative view of the EEC, it was found, had a low level of knowledge of the structures and operations of the community itself, but were also fatalistic in believing it was simply not realistic for Ireland to exit the EEC. In relation specifically to the direct elections: 'It was evident that many respondents distrusted the suitability of Irish politicians to "jobs in Europe". Such attitudes would appear to be part of a developing antipathy towards the body politic and many respondents seemed to agree "there's only a very few good politicians in this country".'

Notwithstanding, the Eurobarometers consistently found that Irish attitudes were more positive than in other member states; as to whether membership was a good thing, in Autumn 1978, 63 per cent of Irish respondents replied positively when the EEC average was 60 per cent (and as low as 36 per cent in Denmark and 39 per cent in the UK).[23] The language barrier, however, remained and there seemed a reluctance to embrace it, though there were exceptions. Regarding the upcoming direct elections, in April 1979 Tom Crotty, the county registrar for County Kilkenny, wrote to Denis Corboy on behalf of returning officers: 'a suggestion has been made by some of the media people that it would be desirable that the results of the Assembly [European Parliament] elections should be announced in one of the other community languages as well as in English. This does not appeal very much to some of my colleagues, but I would be prepared to chance my slightly fractured French, if I could be sure I had the terminology reasonably correct.'[24] He gave the impression he actually relished the challenge.

In March 1979 the Catholic Hierarchy released a statement in relation to Europe, warning of the danger of the exploitation of immigrant labour but which also foreshadowed some of the divisive debates and social, cultural and moral paranoia that manifest themselves in such an emotive and hate-fuelled way in the 1980s, suggesting 'our part in Europe's history has been played more on a spiritual and cultural rather than in a political or economic level'. It stressed the need for diversity within the unity of Europe and that 'reprehensible behaviour may be the statistical norm ... in an age when statistical evidence is highly regarded. Abortion has been made legal in many European countries ... any interpretation of European unity which would do violence to the Christian conscience is unacceptable.'

Nevertheless, the bishops' statement embraced the notion of direct European elections: 'Our forefathers did not hesitate to step into the unknown when they sailed for Europe as missionaries or teachers or students.'[25] The assertion that 'the renewed link with continental Europe resonated with Catholic Ireland'[26] seems almost amusing in its delusional piety. The ICEM was against the dual mandate and in September 1979 referred to the indignity of the procedural wrangling on the opening day of the European Parliament: 'It could be that the tantrums of some of our representatives and the publicity seeking of many is a true reflection of the European political scene.'[27] Fianna Fáil performed poorly in the elections, winning 35 per cent of the vote. Lynch treated the elections 'with a casualness so curious for so sensitive an electoral tactician that it becomes explicable only on the assumption that he had already decided definitely to retire in the near future and saw no reason to inflict one more gruelling campaign on himself'.[28]

In the same year, 1979, Ireland's six-month presidency of the EEC Council of Ministers commenced in July and there was a sense that it would be difficult to match the performance of Garret FitzGerald – the man dubbed 'Mr Europe' – when Ireland had previously held the presidency in 1975. By 1979, there were 'a bewildering number of problems awaiting agreement' and it was 'little wonder that the minister and his officials refuse to spell out precise political objectives for the presidency'.[29]

This stood in contrast to the experiences of Patrick Hillery. As Ireland's first EEC commissioner, being at the heart of European endeavour enhanced his reputation and status. He held the Social Affairs brief, and according to Mary Kenny at the end of 1973, after she had spent a year travelling around the EEC for London's *Evening Standard* newspaper: 'Though able, he often struck observers as a narrow, rather inarticulate man when he was in party politics in Ireland. It is strange to see him emerge in Brussels now as the great and wise humanitarian, a left winger by anyone's measure, full of concern for the workers, for immigrants, for *women* for heaven's sake ... the last time I saw him in Brussels he enquired after [Irish novelist] Edna O'Brien. He was worried he said, that she might feel alienated from her roots, that she might feel Ireland had treated her badly' (some of her work had been censored).[30] Hillery, a very effective negotiator, was instrumental as commissioner in successfully pushing for a European social policy, despite the unfavourable economic backdrop.[31]

There were other dimensions to this mind broadening. As suggested by economist John FitzGerald, membership of the EEC represented a 'tremendous cultural change' in that for the previous fifty years, for most civil servants

> the economic relations with the outside world meant a trip to London to find out how they did things there. [This was an exaggeration, given that there had been economic aspects to Irish relations with the League of Nations and the UN.] From 1 January 1973, all

> the files dealing with bilateral relations with London were sent to the basement and never again opened. Instead, many young civil servants found themselves at meetings in Brussels with equal rights and status to their opposite numbers, generally much older, from all over the rest of the EU. It is not surprising therefore, that for the administration, EU membership represented the culmination of Ireland's journey to independence.[32]

Political scientist Tom Garvin has also alluded to this; in political terms, he suggested, EEC membership offered a reality 'which had always been fantasised about; a powerful entity that was perceived as benign, was not English and was not controlled by England'.[33] In the case of the Fianna Fáil government that was elected in 1977, Jack Lynch and thirteen of his ministers made 154 trips abroad; two-thirds of these were on EEC business, but fewer than twenty were to Britain.[34] As president of Ireland on a trip to France in 1975, Cearbhall Ó Dálaigh wanted to speak the language of the host country not just to demonstrate his linguistic skills, or because 'Ireland and France have never been enemies', but also 'to underline, a point still sometimes overlooked in Continental Europe, that Ireland is no longer England'.[35]

There were occasional references to enhanced religious and cultural bonds due to the EEC, but they appeared somewhat lacklustre. In 1974 Bobby McDonagh, Irish ambassador to West Germany, corresponded with Noel Dorr in the Department of Foreign Affairs about the prospect of a cultural agreement with the country which had been 'vaguely in the air for some years. So far as I know we have cultural agreements only with France and Norway, the French one being quite active and the Norwegian rather dormant' (only 554 Irish pupils took German in the Leaving Certificate examinations in 1972).[36] But others disputed the notion that there was much appreciation in France for Irish culture. In 1973 Garret FitzGerald and Minister for Labour Michael O'Leary were informed that 'the French people, even well-informed, seem to have no real idea of what, if anything, is happening in Ireland in the cultural field ... It is really a shame that the French are almost totally unaware of our existence except in connection with the "civil war" raging in the North.'[37] At a gathering of heads of government in Dublin in 1975 there was an informal meeting of foreign ministers at Farmleigh at which, regarding problems with Portugal, FitzGerald suggested that 'Ireland and Spain had always had quite warm relations because of the religious link and it was possible that we might have some useful part to play there.'[38]

EEC membership may also have encouraged a more European-style 'consensus approach' to economic and social issues, reflected, for example, in the establishment of the National Economic and Social Council (NESC) in 1973,[39] though this should not be exaggerated. As was recognised by Peter Brennan, an Irish civil servant who spent two tours of duty as Ireland's permanent representative to the EEC from 1973–5, one of the main themes stressed by Irish negotiators in Europe was the 'unique character of the Irish problem'. What did become 'one of Ireland's hallmarks' of EEC membership was the speed 'in getting projects to Brussels' when allocation of funding was announced.[40] In this and other ways, it has been maintained that EEC membership 'somehow enhanced Irish capabilities'.[41]

– THIRTY-EIGHT –

GARRET'S WIDER MISSION

In 1973 Garret FitzGerald had arrived into Iveagh House as Minister for Foreign Affairs as a man on a mission to shake up foreign policy. He was determined to ensure that a new generation of civil servants were placed in positions where they – 'the band of brothers' as one of those civil servants later labelled them[1] – would be able to bring credibility, professionalism and dynamism to his review and expansion of Irish foreign policy. With this in mind, FitzGerald had intensive discussions with Department of Foreign Affairs staff in April 1973, the same year that Ireland's first woman ambassador (to Sweden and Finland), Mary Catherine Tinney, was appointed. FitzGerald also came to office in the same year that Patrick Keatinge's book *The Formulation of Irish Foreign Policy*, on the formulation of foreign policy in the modern era, the first of its kind, was published. Keatinge, a political scientist in Trinity College Dublin who had studied international relations at the London School of Economics, made the observation that 'since the inception of the Irish state, foreign policy has remained something of a mystery to the general public and informed observers alike', but acknowledged the recent 'increased tempo' as a result of EEC membership.[2]

A measure of FitzGerald's determination to increase this tempo was a 35-page memorandum for the government on foreign policy in early May 1973, which was sent to government ministers the day before the cabinet meeting was due to take place. There was undoubtedly little precedent for this kind of urgent dynamic in foreign policy as FitzGerald made clear what his priorities were going to be. He identified a 'new openness in British thinking' to facilitate a rapprochement between the north and south of Ireland, which might enable Britain to 'phase out' of Ireland and also called for a more 'coherent policy' regarding the EEC in order not to be reacting to proposals in 'a fragmented way'. He also devoted attention to eastern Europe: 'The fact that Poland courageously voted for our application for UN membership, when Russia sought to impose a pattern of negative votes on her satellites is worth recalling. Czech cultural circles have a special interest in relations with this country.'[3] FitzGerald was unequivocal in his view that Ireland needed to open diplomatic ties with Russia (TASS, the Soviet news agency, had opened its first office in Ireland in August 1970) and in November 1973 announced in New York, with his Soviet counterpart, Andrei Gromyko, that their countries were to exchange diplomatic missions. In March 1974 Dr Edward Brennan was appointed as the first Irish ambassador to the Soviet Union; a few months later, Anatoli Kaplin presented his letter of credence as the Soviet Union's first ambassador to Ireland.

FitzGerald also sought to dispel what he regarded as the 'illusion ... that pro-Irish sentiment is an important factor in US policy. The State Department has never shown such sentiment; the White House is not disposed to treat this country with any preference, as may be seen from the Dublin landing rights issue and such ethnic lobby as now exists in the USA seems more concerned with financing and arming the IRA than with helping Ireland in its relations with the US. The contrast with the effectiveness of the Jewish lobby in the US is startling.'[4] (The landing rights issue had caused disagreement for almost twenty years between Aer Lingus and US company Pan Am over entitlement by the US airline to land in Dublin. In order to protect its business, Aer Lingus sought to prevent this happening and compromise was eventually reached later in the decade with Aer Lingus agreeing to act as Pan Am's sales agent in the Republic.)

Correspondence early in his tenure as Minister for Foreign Affairs witnessed FitzGerald argue that foreign policy discussions needed to be bolstered by 'well informed public opinion' at home. (This was also a point made by Mary Robinson that year when she suggested there was 'far too little discussion' and 'no real public awareness' in relation to foreign policy.)[5] He believed that non-government organisations concerned with international relations 'should receive a measure of government support', but it is doubtful if anything like the level of public participation he desired materialised, given that he was writing about small, elite and in some cases relatively moribund groups. There was little interest in such organisations as the Irish Institute for International Affairs, the Irish United Nations Association (hardly a group that was of any interest to most) and the ICEM.[6]

The Irish public were more galvanised by issues such as apartheid in South Africa (see pages 445–8), rather than concerning themselves with lower-profile and technical issues. What was achievable, however, was an improvement in the staffing and infrastructure of Irish foreign policy endeavours. In January 1974 the government authorised the strengthening of the information services of the Department of Foreign Affairs, which included the appointment of full-time press and information officers to missions abroad in London, Paris, Bonn, Rome and Washington. Cosgrave was probably happy to let Garret globetrot as minister (relations between them were cool) although he may have wondered whether FitzGerald was overloading the new government. FitzGerald wrote to him on 2 January 1974, probably when Cosgrave was still on holiday: 'As you know there are five foreign affairs papers before the government – it was not possible to reach them at a meeting some weeks ago when we had hoped to deal with them.'[7]

There was also some concern expressed by a civil servant in the Department of the Taoiseach about information services at the foreign ministry and FitzGerald's proposals for change because they had not been consulted: 'I am surprised that this department with its particular function in relation to all information services and its experience of DFA ineptitude in this matter since August 1969 was not, apparently, consulted ... The present proposals may be good but DFA alone are not, I would suggest, capable of the necessary objectivity. Some of the methods tried in the past failed because DFA refused to co-operate.'[8]

Africa was also singled out for special mention, FitzGerald articulating a view that Ireland's historic position as an ex colony that had suffered 'from various forms of discrimination' and which now had a 'commitment to human rights and the dignity of the individual', enabled Ireland to understand Africa better: 'While we should not delude ourselves that this gives us a particularly important role, it does suggest that we may be able at times to help to create a more equal relationship between Europe and these countries and we should strive to do so.' (In private, Conor Cruise

O'Brien warned against giving blanket support to 'liberation movements' because the 'concept of the liberation movement is vague and ramshackle in the extreme' in Africa).[9] There was also a need, he argued, to make overseas aid, 'comprehensive and coherent' as a programme.[10]

Charitable organisations focusing on Third World aid came to prominence during this decade. Africa Concern had been established in 1968 and there had been an enormous response to the Biafra famine appeal. There was undoubtedly a determination to maintain that momentum in relation to other problems in Africa, but also many internal tensions associated with the aid sector. In early 1970, those involved were effectively told by an Irish bishop to stay away from Nigeria and 'find some less politically involved babies to feed' and in the early 1970s Africa Concern faced 'a very tough reassessment of the way it was run and what it should be doing'.[11] It was renamed Concern in 1973. In May 1974, regarding a proposed Africa Centre in Dublin, Alan Matthews, who had been involved in a Third World group in Trinity College Dublin, and had spent time working in Zambia, made the point that such a centre 'would set new ground' in that it would be the first agency 'to emphasise the need to develop trading links as well as aid if a lasting impact is to be made'. There was also a need for a business approach to the venture in order to 'project an image of the continent which would change people's attitudes towards it'.[12]

Crises in Bangladesh and Ethiopia in 1975 were further challenges and there was a perceived need to reconstitute Concern as a 'secular' organisation with a conflict between 'the inspired enthusiast and the cool professional' with the dilemma of long-term development projects and an insistence that volunteers 'sleep on their own pillows' due to stories of 'intimate liaisons' with native Africans. Between 1974 and 1975 it raised over £500,000 and had thirteen full-time paid staff. The emergence of another aid charity, Trocaire (the Irish word for compassion), in 1973 also provided a challenge to its fundraising and Concern was in debt by 1976. There were numerous personality divergences and rows regarding the balance of power between head office and field directors.[13]

In relation to aid commitment targets for developing countries, in 1974 FitzGerald had expressed his fear that 'the failure on our part to bring our development aid programme up to at least half the required level for other member states would be likely to have adverse effects on the attitude of other member countries to Ireland as a net recipient of EEC funds'.[14] In 1976, two Irish aid charities, Gorta (the Irish word for famine) and Concern were looking to the government to commit itself to a target of 1 per cent of GNP. In 1975 it was just over 0.09 per cent, which they regarded as 'grossly inadequate'. In response, an unusually ebullient Cosgrave replied that in 1976 aid would reach a figure of £5.7 million, up from £3 million in 1975, or 0.14 per cent of GNP, which he insisted was seven times larger than when the government had taken up office.

FitzGerald continued to stress the importance of an 'active public opinion' in relation to Ireland's role in world development but Trocaire was adamant in 1976 that 'verbal commitments by the Irish government to a more just international economic order and a fair deal for the developing world are yet unmatched by anything like an adequate level of resources for development co-operation'.[15]

In July 1975 Ken Whitaker, chairman of the Agency for Personal Service Overseas (APSO, which had its origins in a seminar on justice and peace through world development organised by the Catholic Church's Commission for Justice and Peace in Dublin in October 1974), pointed out that aid targets were modest – to add as little as 0.05 per cent of GNP from 1974–8 to its official development aid input – but that 'I am thankful that we live in a country where our aid programme does not have to be and is not very strongly tinged with self-interest'. He expressed his gratitude to FitzGerald in January 1976 for continued support and a £175,000 grant as 'our expectations had been so dimmed by all the dark budgetary clouds'.[16]

In March 1976, however, George W. P. Dawson, a geneticist at Trinity College Dublin and a philanthropist with an interest in developing countries, who in 1977 became the second chairman of APSO, raised questions about the aid sector, NGOs, government involvement and funding structures 'which do not alienate the groups, whose experience etc. the structures are intended to harness. This is not going to be easy'. He suggested that many voluntary agencies were alienated from government, and that while they 'have the ear of the public', their contributions were seldom central to Third World development problems in a way government backed schemes such as APSO were.[17]

By the end of 1977, Jerome Connolly of the Irish Commission for Justice and Peace suggested that 'on the basis of the Fianna Fáil position as expressed since 1975, the official development assistance allocation for the coming year, 1978, ought to be approximately £17 million', but what the government was then promising was £9.638 million, which was 0.15 per cent of GNP. Most involved in the aid sector sought to be diplomatic, in contrast to the Catholic Bishop of Galway Eamon Casey, seen by some on the left as 'a huge breath of fresh air in terms of his espousal of social justice, not just in Ireland but in the third world as well [who] supported the third world issue through Trocaire in some cases, but also off his own bat right throughout his career ... Casey combined the qualities of a Prince of the church with the broth of a boy. He liked the authority that he held and he thought it was very important, but he also liked to enjoy himself.'[18]

In February 1978, Alex Tarbett, the executive director of Concern, wrote to Jack Lynch to express himself very happy with the co-operation of the DFA, so he was 'rather surprised ... to hear of Bishop Eamon Casey's rather intemperate attack on your government ... I presume that you do know that Bishop Casey's political feelings would not be disposed towards FF.' Lynch replied that 'I too was rather surprised at them'.[19]

President Idi Amin of Uganda's aviation adventures and intentions caused something of a stir in Ireland in the summer of 1977 when troops and sightseers stood by at Dublin airport 'as an unidentified aircraft circled overhead'. The Minister for Justice, after consultation with the Minister for Foreign Affairs, made an exclusion order against Amin, who would only be permitted to land for emergency refuelling, 'in which case the pilot would be ordered to taxi to a remote part of the airport and be informed that the government would not allow anyone to leave or join the plane and that an adequate army presence should be provided at the airport to enforce this decision if necessary'. The *Irish Independent* subsequently reported that it was a hoax, and that the unidentified aircraft was an Aer Lingus training plane. Journalists enjoyed writing humorously about the prospect of Amin seeking to 'gatecrash the [British Queen's silver] jubilee celebrations in Britain and get in to the Commonwealth conference by the back door' but it was taken seriously by the cabinet.[20]

In relation to foreign policy and the Middle East, given the extent of the oil crisis and its ramifications in the early 1970s, it was believed to be important to agree to the request of Lebanon to the accreditation of its ambassador in London to Ireland, but also for the non-resident ambassadors of Egypt and Israel. It was deemed imperative that because of the existence of an Irish contingent in the UN emergency force 'we avoid accusations of partiality by any of the combatant states'.[21] In December 1975 a memorandum was presented to the government on diplomatic relations with Egypt, Iran and the OECD. It explained that in January 1974 the government had decided to exchange diplomatic representatives with

Egypt on a non-resident basis but FitzGerald was convinced there was a need to have a resident embassy in Cairo, a diplomatic representative in Tehran and 'an additional counsellor post at the embassy in Paris to deal with OECD work', all of which were agreed to by the government. (This was usual with FitzGerald's proposals as he made compelling cases.)[22] Evidence of a growing interest in the region had also been reflected in the activities of campaigners like John de Courcy Ireland, who opened an exhibition on Palestine's heritage in February 1973 at the Arab Information Centre in Dublin's Grafton Street. He also frequently spoke on war in the Middle East and Algeria; the following year a lecture was hosted at the Arab Irish Society entitled 'Who Are the Arabs?'. In its annual report for 1973–4 the Society expressed pleasure that during that year it had 'achieved a degree of influence and consequent publicity that we scarcely conceived of as being possible'.[23] The same year, Ireland voted in favour of the Palestinian Liberation Organisation participating in UN plenary meetings, which 'greatly disappointed Israel' and indicated that Ireland was quickly emerging as a leading supporter of the Palestinian cause in the newly enlarged EEC.[24]

Ireland's role at the UN had developed a higher profile in the 1960s due to the efforts of Fianna Fáil's Frank Aiken as Minister for External Affairs, though 'Ireland's United Nations policy on Cold War issues during the mid to late 1960s was typically formulated within a United States oriented pro-Western context'.[25] (Aiken, for example, was mute on the Vietnam war.) His crowning achievement was the nuclear non-proliferation treaty which he had championed and which was signed in Moscow in 1968. A reflection of his dedication in that regard was that he was invited to be its first signatory; 'That treaty is Frank Aiken's monument,' observed Conor Cruise O'Brien, a vocal member of the Irish delegation during his early years at the UN.[26] But Aiken was no radical; unlike FitzGerald, he had been opposed to expenditure on new embassies and saw the UN as an alternative to working with the permanent representatives of the countries where Ireland had no diplomatic missions.

Given its status as a neutral country, Ireland had some opportunities to push some 'soft power' as a country involved in peacekeeping and regarded as relatively impartial.[27] In March 1977 the chief of staff of the Irish defence forces wanted to make a contingent of the army available for a UN peacekeeping force in Cyprus. At that point there were 15,503 members of the permanent defence forces with 1,900 of them deployed in the Irish border area. The Minister for Defence was anxious that 'such a move might be interpreted (wrongly) as weakening the available resources for security at home', but in truth it was believed 'it would not create any problems' and was given the go ahead.[28]

As recalled by Irish diplomat Noel Dorr, who worked on preparations for an 'enormous number of resolutions' presented at the UN in the 1970s, including many on disarmament, 'the number of resolutions [was] inversely proportional to the level of success they achieved'. After joining the EEC, however, 'as most other UN members saw it there was a new seriousness to Ireland's voting position since we were now an active member of the most important group economically and politically in the General Assembly'.[29] The assembly also approved the appointment of Seán Mac Bride, a former IRA leader in the 1930s and minister in the first coalition government from 1948–51, who had carved out a role for himself as a human rights activist, and a leading voice of Amnesty International, as commissioner of Namibia in December 1973. The following year, he shared the Nobel peace prize with the former Japanese prime minister Eisaku Sato, and was the first Irishman to achieve the honour.

In the early 1970s, Irish representatives at the United Nations also found themselves pondering taking a stance on recognition of Taiwan. A policy review of Ireland's attitude to China, contained in a memorandum by Seán Ronan, an assistant secretary in the Department of Foreign Affairs, suggested the Irish position regarding the recognition of the governments at Peking and Taipei 'has not been altogether coherent'. It was regarded as inconsistent to maintain Ireland always recognised the state of China 'and then going on to say that we recognize de facto two governments of that state'. The new position was not to recognise Taiwan's self-determination but to assert 'the future status of Taiwan remains to be determined'. The *Irish Press* was justifiably scathing in its critique of a lack of forthrightness in foreign policy in September 1971: 'For a country which braved American and clerical displeasure to pioneer discussion of the China question back in the 'fifties, Ireland in recent years has played a disappointingly negative role, with the result that we are now scrambling to trim our sails to the prevailing wind when we could have least had the merit of pursuing a more independent and consistent role in the matter.'[30]

A week later, the view from the DFA was that 'in our voting at the UN this session, nothing should be done which would have the effect of keeping Peking out of the China seat'. That same month, perhaps giving an indication of the significance of Catholic missionaries, the Apostolic Nuncio sought a meeting with Jack Lynch and informed Lynch's private secretary, in confidence, that 'he had received instructions from the Holy See to seek the support of the Irish government for the retention of Taiwan in the United Nations'.[31] There was also the issue of the public reaction to a vote to admit China and expel Taiwan; Senator 'Tip' O'Neill, the majority whip in the US house of representatives, suggested it would be 'a great act of iniquity to expel Taiwan' and its population of 14 million.

The following month, in private, Lynch wrote that while 'there was much pressure exercised on behalf of Taiwan, I am afraid it would have been completely unrealistic to do other than what we did at the UN',[32] hardly the confident assertion of an independent foreign policy. In September 1976 FitzGerald was unequivocal in his call for full diplomatic relations with China, pointing out that the two countries had had some trade contacts since 1973. The Minister for Defence was opposed 'on security grounds', but FitzGerald was of the view that 'there is little evidence of espionage activity by Chinese embassies in Western Europe'. Irish exports to China in 1975 were valued at only £60,000 while imports were valued at £1.2 million.

It was not until September 1978, when it was made clear that the Chinese believed business relations 'would not be fruitful' in the absence of mutual diplomatic accreditation, that a cabinet decision authorised FitzGerald to indicate that the government was in favour of diplomatic relations between the two countries, 'but our difficulties arising from limited resources and absence of any substantial knowledge of Chinese needed to be recognised'.[33]

The FitzGerald expansionism was not without its tensions due to budgetary constraints. In June 1976, for example, Cosgrave informed FitzGerald that it was not affordable to open a mission in East Africa and suggested that some of the DFA staff needed rationalisation. FitzGerald insisted he could not cut back and that the level of expenditure incurred by his department was less than £10 million out of a total public expenditure of over £1,500 million. He also insisted Ireland needed to meet its development aid targets, which Cosgrave insisted could not be met.[34]

– THIRTY-NINE –

LEVERAGE WITH WASHINGTON

When Ronald Reagan, the governor of California, arrived in Ireland in 1972 as part of a European tour designed by President Richard Nixon to emphasise the importance the US attached to its ties with Europe, he was treated to a private dinner at Iveagh House of Dublin Bay prawns and fillet of Irish beef. He was not an official guest of the government during his visit, but it was regarded as an opportunity to increase leverage with Washington to reconsider the question of landing rights in Dublin and a permit for Aer Lingus in New York. DFA secretary Hugh McCann, in a letter to the Department of the Taoiseach, surmised that 'in view of the vague nature of the purpose of Governor Reagan's visit, it would seem not unlikely that President Nixon is seeking to build up his stature as a possible candidate for the Vice-Presidency or for some other high office such as that of Secretary of State'. Despite this, he reckoned that 'it would scarcely be appropriate to refuse to receive him ... If he should be earmarked for high office it would be just as well to retain his goodwill.'[1]

Nixon himself had travelled to Ireland in October 1970. His top-level American advance contingent met representatives of various Irish government departments to remind them of the need for communications efficiency as Nixon 'must be in constant touch with the outside world at all times'. There were various leaks about the travel plans; Irish ambassador to the US William Warnock suggested these resulted in the White House being 'in a terrible flap', but the Irish government had received only short notice of the visit, which was largely a private one but did include a state lunch. Local passions ran high regarding where the president might appear. Tipperary Town Council was anxious for him to stop there, even though he was only planning to pass through, and resorted to threatening 'that they could prevent his car getting through ... and if the Americans didn't agree there would be no flags or decorations'. In the event the motorcade bypassed the town altogether.[2] Nixon's security chiefs wanted to ensure that if crowds assembled in Dublin there would be the 'elimination of obscene or profane placards', while Nixon was anxious 'not to be buttonholed or monopolised by people'.[3] The Taoiseach Jack Lynch had been thinking about raising the issue of Vietnam, but was told by Hugh McCann that the Americans saw it as a US problem 'and I gather are not encouraging us to raise it'. In the event, Lynch did raise the issue by saying 'we sympathise with the US involvement'.[4]

In June 1973 John D. Moore, The US ambassador in Ireland, wrote to FitzGerald about civil aviation matters, expressing great satisfaction at 'the impressive and logical manner in which you dealt with this matter', which he described as 'prompt and businesslike'. But a few days later, a report in the *Irish Times* referred to collusion by US lobby groups on the landing rights issue in which the US was deemed to have 'blackmailed' the Irish government into allowing landing rights in Dublin airport to a US Embassy. The collusion, it alleged, was between 'American big business, the American ambassador to Ireland and US business in this country', with a concomitant threat to ban Aer Lingus in New York if they did not get their way. Reference was made to Nixon's connection to Pan American Airways and Moore, who had been 'for years directly linked' to that airline. FitzGerald responded the following day in an emotive letter to Moore (but which did not address the issue directly nor refute the allegations): 'I was shocked by the reference to you in yesterday's Irish Times. I hope that it has not distressed you too much. All of us in public life – ambassadors as well as politicians – have to put up with a good deal of abuse whose unfairness is often very hard to take. I very much resent it on your behalf . . .'[5]

Hugh McCann's successor, Paul Keating, corresponded with FitzGerald in 1974 about the US ambassador's desire to meet the Taoiseach as 'his government was concerned lest the Russian Embassy here should provide a base for spying on American installations in Great Britain and Western Europe'. Keating felt such fears were wholly exaggerated:

> We have to consider to what extent we must protect ourselves from undue American influence as much as we have to protect ourselves from Russian or Communist influence ... I think we should just listen to them and make no commitment about feeding them with information ... we also have to consider the extent to which a request of the ambassador to be received by the Taoiseach should be granted in view of the difficulties the ambassador in Washington has in being received at any kind of high level by the American authorities and the continued failure of Dr Kissinger to see you.[6]

But a few years later there was great warmth in the letter that Walter Curley, the American ambassador to Ireland, sent to FitzGerald as he was preparing to depart; he referred to 'the co-operation, courtesy and genuine friendship'. The practical issue of an understanding on air passenger charter services was also mentioned.[7]

Visits to the United States by senior Irish politicians on St Patrick's Day were high-priority diplomatic occasions, including Cosgrave's trip in March 1976, which it was suggested in January of that year could incorporate New York, Washington, Philadelphia, Chicago and 'possibly Boston though he is not enthusiastic about Boston'. The major themes of the visit would be American investment in Ireland and a discouragement of funding for the IRA, while the Americans 'do not wish to stress the direct link with the Bicentennial'.[8] Keating, as secretary of the DFA, corresponded with Dermot Nally in February in relation to the states with the heaviest concentration of Irish-Americans: 'In spite of over 50 years of independence, it is very difficult to impress on some of the more hard-shelled members of their communities the fact of the legitimacy of the Irish government and the Taoiseach's reception by people such as the president and the governors and mayors of various states and cities will do very much to lend weight to his words when he speaks about the national situation.' There was a need, he felt, to 'press' for an address to the joint houses of Congress, but the main disadvantage in the programme as then conceived was that 'it does not do as much as, perhaps, was the original intention, for economic development'.

Visiting an Irish exhibition in Altman's department store was regarded as 'perhaps a bit below the dignity of a Taoiseach', while the chief executive of Aer Lingus was keen to highlight that it was launching a major marketing programme in North America with a strong emphasis on the eastern seaboard and in the Chicago area. By the end of February, Irish diplomats had secured an invitation to address both of the houses of Congress. Dermot Nally told Cosgrave that Democratic senator Ted Kennedy 'has been largely responsible in getting this concession which is regarded as a great honour'.[9] Waterford Crystal ashtrays at a cost of £6 each were all the rage for presents for federal officials; others were given Waterford Crystal bowls while Mayor Richard Daley of Chicago, who had been regarded as very helpful in diverting elsewhere funds that might have gone to the IRA, was given six Irish silver engraved goblets in Celtic design at a cost of £161. Aer Lingus was unwilling to give the Taoiseach's son, Liam Jr, a first-class seat 'in return for the economy fare, so an economy seat has been reserved'.[10]

In April, after the trip, Ambassador Moore – who, as a rule, only seemed to write in superlatives – wrote to FitzGerald referring to the 'splendid success' of Cosgrave's visit and his 'courage and candour' in dealing with the sensitive issue of fundraising: 'It was superb in every way, from start to finish and I think it has accomplished great things in educating the government and people of the US regarding the facts and the stature of the modern Ireland which you have done so much to create.'[11]

A few months later, it was the turn of the Irish to be hosts of US governors, an initiative that had originated in a proposal of January 1976 to invite the thirteen governors from the original founding states of the Union, which the DFA reckoned would cost in the region of £2,000. The draft invitation invoked 'the part played by Irishmen in the American struggle for independence ... We gladly acknowledge the welcome, the freedom and the opportunity which the US have given to millions of Irish emigrants down through the years.' There was a very enthusiastic response, though there was a suggestion that extending invitations to deputy governors where the governors could not attend 'debases the invitations'.[12]

But there were other, more significant tensions. It was regarded within the Department of the Taoiseach as 'altogether inappropriate' that the programme for the visit was essentially drawn up by a committee completely dominated by state sponsored bodies.[13] There was also a parallel committee in New York, which it was felt was taking liberties. Regarding the president posing for a separate photograph with each governor, for example, it was stressed, 'the president may well agree to do this, but I consider it a gross impertinence on the part of the New York committee to say that the group may expect him to do so'. One and a half hours at the president's residence, Áras an Uachtaráin, was regarded as 'over-generous'. The party was greeted at Dublin airport by Cosgrave, FitzGerald and the US ambassador, which was regarded by Frank Murray, Cosgrave's private secretary, as 'excessive and [I] am not at all satisfied that the status of the visiting party warrants the attendance at the airport of the head of the government, who will honour the group sufficiently, in my view, by hosting a function for them'. Richard Stokes disagreed.[14]

In March the following year, FitzGerald travelled to Washington and had discussions with the US Secretary of State Cyrus Vance and FitzGerald said 'he would have the temerity to comment that recent signs of some shifts in US foreign policy were satisfying and were appreciated in Europe'.[15] But there were others who felt no such appreciation. In 2008 journalist Paddy Woodworth reflected on how events in Latin America influenced young Irish leftists in the 1970s, including people like him who had been 'seduced by [Irish artist] Jim Fitzpatrick's poster of Che' (Guevara; the famous two-tone poster was created in 1968 based on a photograph by Alberto Korda). With regard to Cuba, it was believed that it 'blended tough anti-imperialism with good schools and a great health service and still managed to be laid back, sexy and young. It seemed a fine model for Latin America and possibly for Ireland as well.'[16]

In June 1979 a Boeing 707 was hijacked by the Serbian revolutionary Nikola Kavaja on a flight from New York to Chicago and was en route to Shannon but he surrendered. Apparently his lawyer had advised him that 'since there was no formal extradition treaty between Ireland and the US, he could not be extradited to the US'. But the fact was that as both Ireland and the US were signatories of The Hague and Montreal conventions on the prevention of air piracy, he could be either tried in Ireland or returned to the US to face charges. He surrendered in Ireland and was returned to the US.[17]

Irish links with Australia were also taken seriously. It was regarded as essential in 1974, for example, that the prime minister of Australia, Gough Whitlam, be facilitated and welcomed warmly as the Australians 'have been very helpful to the Department of Foreign Affairs on various occasions in the past'. In 1970, Jack Lynch had received a letter from an Irish-Australian who lamented the difficulty of trying to keep the next generation in Australia interested in Ireland: 'For many years I have noticed how children of migrant families quickly lose their Irish identity. The gap widens with each succeeding generation. Frequently this reflects

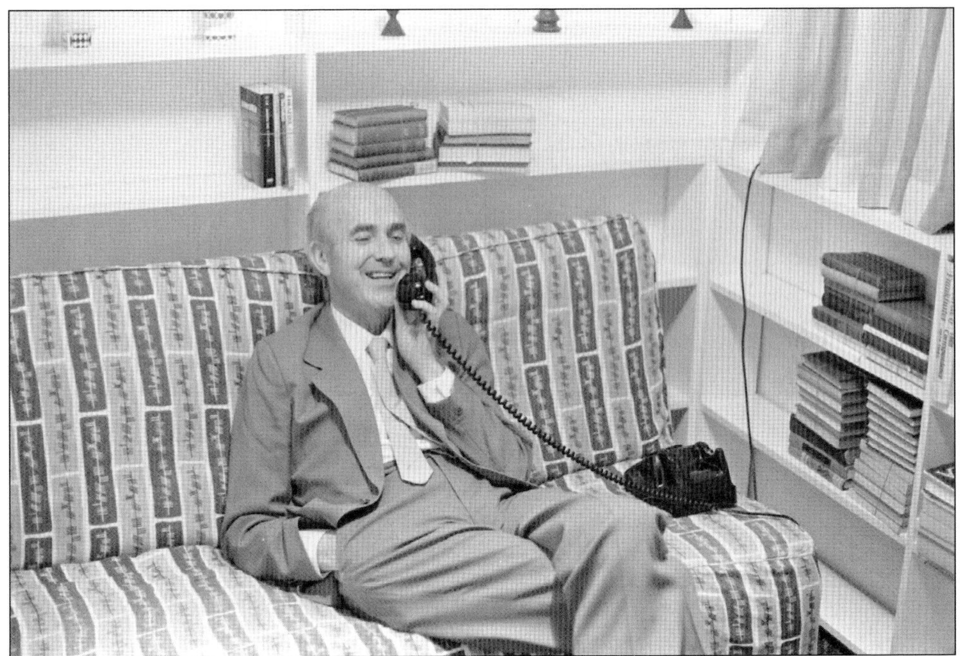

1. Nominated unopposed to the office of President of Ireland in 1974, following the sudden death of Erskine Childers, Cearbhall Ó Dálaigh sensationally resigned the office two years later after he was described by Minister for Defence Patrick Donegan as a 'thundering disgrace'.

2. As assistant secretary in the Department of Taoiseach and one of a number of influential civil servants that included Richard Stokes and T. K. Whitaker, Dermot Nally was involved in a wide range of activities including reform of the civil service, negotiations regarding National Wage Agreements, the enlargement of the EEC and the implications of potential Irish unity.

3. John Kelly was a UCD law professor before he was elected a Senator for Fine Gael in 1969. He subsequently served as a TD in the Dáil between 1973 and 1989. He was appointed parliamentary secretary to Liam Cosgrave in 1973 and served briefly as Attorney General in 1977. His book *The Irish Constitution*, first published in 1980, remains the most authoritative work on the subject.

4. Thousands in Dublin attended the state funeral of former Taoiseach and President Eamon de Valera on 2 September 1975. His coffin, carried by members of the Irish army to its final resting place at Glasnevin Cemetery, marked his interment in a space that is sacred to Irish nationalists. He was the most dominant and polarising politician of his generation.

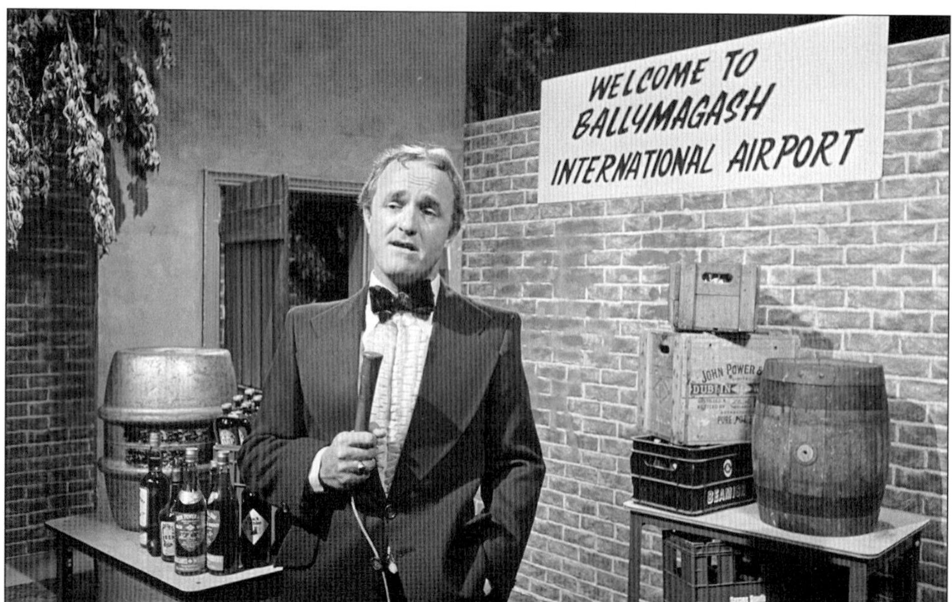

5. Irish actor Frank Kelly is seen here at Ballymagash Airport in a scene from *Hall's Pictorial Weekly,* which was broadcast on RTÉ throughout the 1970s. This satirical look at Irish political life lampooned its parochialism, eventually described as 'Ballymagash-style politics'. The programme also provided a sharp learning curve for Irish politicians who were only coming to grips with the power of television during the 1970s.

6. Irish Labour Party TD, historian and writer Conor Cruise O'Brien being interviewed by broadcaster and political scientist Brian Farrell on the set of RTÉ's current affairs programme *7 Days* in 1973. O'Brien was Minister for Posts and Telegraphs from 1973–7 and an unrelenting critic of the IRA and its supporters.

7. David Thornely: historian, broadcaster and Labour party TD from 1969 to 1977. He was at odds with members of his party throughout the 1970s. In 1976 he lost the party whip after disagreement with the leadership over his Republican stance on Northern Ireland. This was symptomatic of the problems within the Labour Party throughout the 1970s.

8. Mary Robinson: feminist, lawyer, Senator, and future Irish President, she believed the Irish Parliament in the 1970s remained a 'nineteenth century debating parlour'. A leading advocate of law reform, in 1971 she introduced an unsuccessful 'Family Planning Bill', which sought to legalise contraception. Minister for Health Charles Haughey eventually passed a limited family planning bill in 1979.

9. Leader of the British Labour Party Harold Wilson with Irish Tánaiste and Labour Party leader Brendan Corish in 1971. They met occasionally during the 1970s to discuss the situation in Northern Ireland.

10. The burning of the British Embassy on Merrion Square in central Dublin in February 1972 came after 'the biggest demonstration the Republic had seen in a generation'. The protests occurred in response to the events of Bloody Sunday during which thirteen people were killed by British soldiers in Derry a few days earlier. 'The emotions of the times spent themselves in the flames of that building', according to Des O'Malley, the Minister for Justice.

11. In August 1979 the IRA murdered former Viceroy to India Lord Louis Mounbatten; a remote-controlled bomb aboard his boat was detonated as he sailed out from Mullaghmore in County Sligo where he holidayed every year. Three more people, including a local Sligo teenager, were also killed. Here, his body is being removed from Sligo General Hospital.

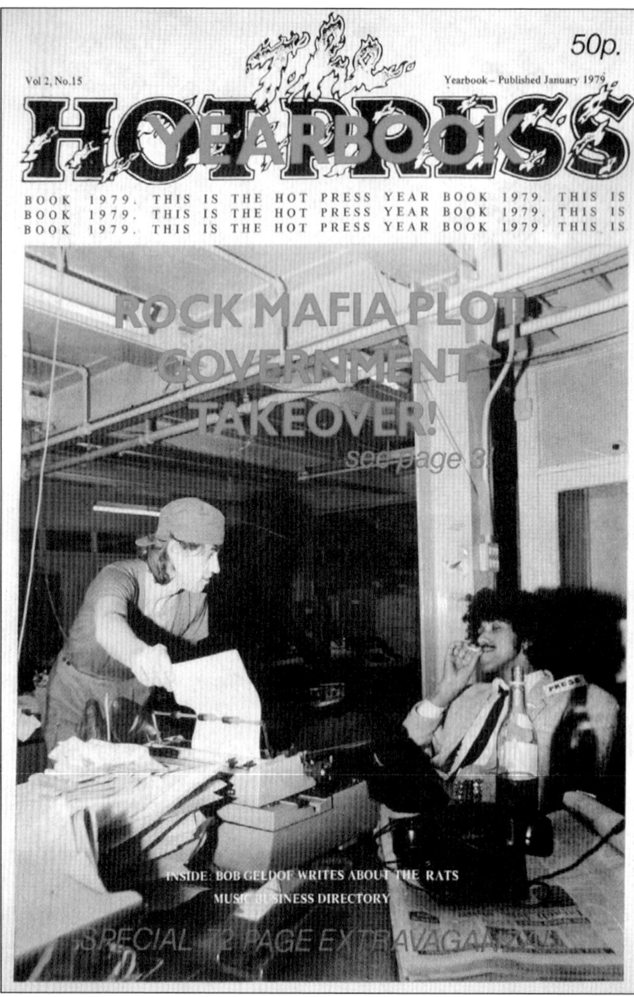

12. *Hot Press* music magazine, reflecting Ireland's burgeoning youth culture, was first published in 1977. It was particularly timely given that fifty per cent of the population were under twenty-six. On this 1979 cover two of the most prominent members of the Irish music scene, Bob Geldof (of the Boomtown Rats) and Phil Lynott (of Thin Lizzy), are 'plotting government takeover'.

13. Folk singer Christy Moore was part of the 'Anti-Nuclear Road Show' that took to the stage at Carnsore in August 1978 to protest about plans to build a nuclear energy plant on the site. The proposed plant never went ahead, but the debate surrounding Ireland's natural resources and its energy dependence remains a live one today.

hibernia
FORTNIGHTLY REVIEW
September 10th, 1976
Price 22p (inc. 2p VAT)
'EMERGENCY' SPECIAL
THE IRISH PRESS
THE CENSOR COMETH

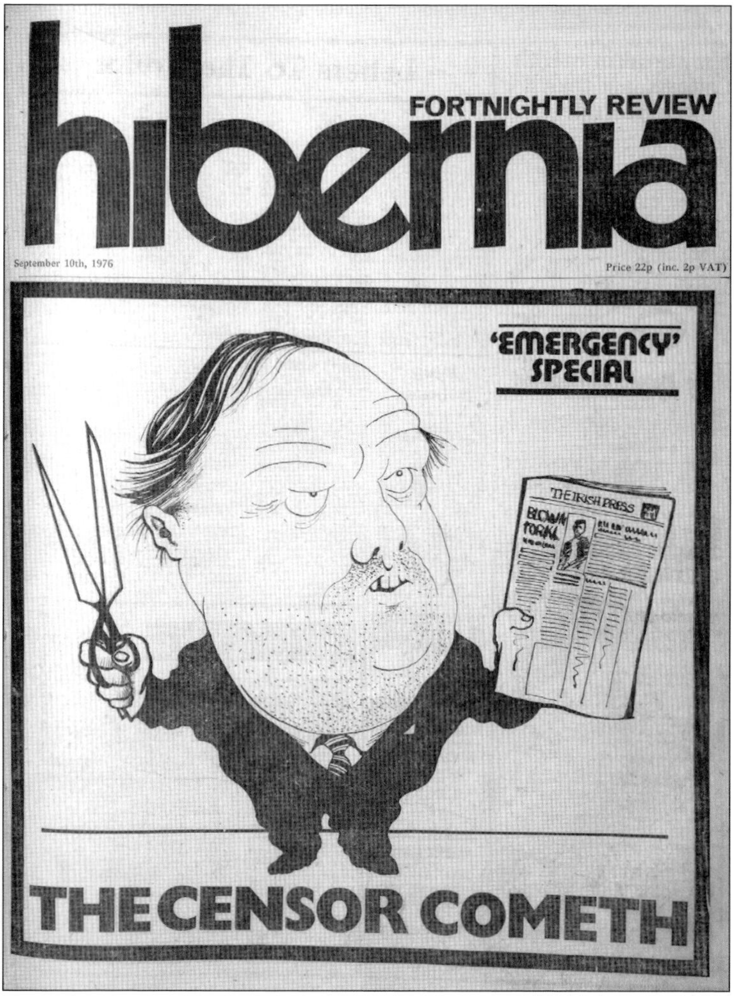

14. As Minister for Posts and Telegraphs, Conor Cruise O'Brien was part of a coalition government that clamped down on freedom of the press and broadcasters. Despite Irish society opening up since the 1950s through investment in education and the arrival of television, worsening violence in Northern Ireland and attempts to highlight breaches of civil liberties meant that censorship became an issue for journalists and broadcasters.

SAVE WOOD
NERO FIDDLED THE CORPO MUDDLES!

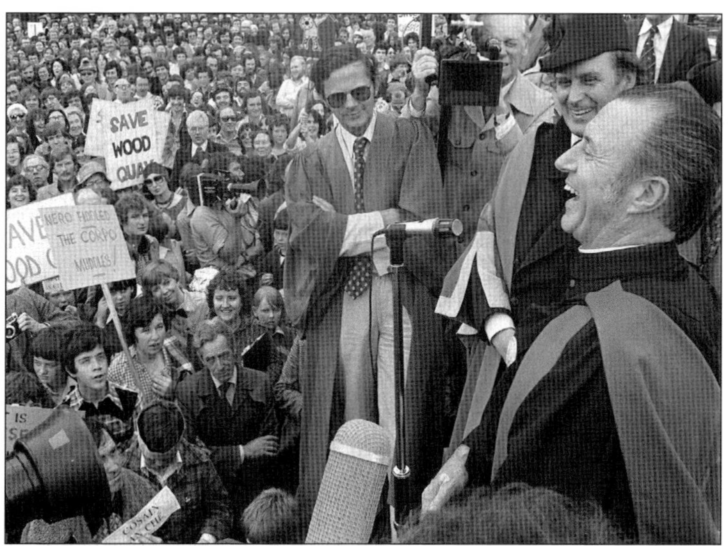

15. This protest in 1978 at the site of the Wood Quay archaeological dig along the River Liffey arose because of plans to build the civic offices of Dublin Corporation on top of this Viking settlement. The medieval historian F. X. Martin who worked at UCD became a leader in the unsuccessful movement to 'Save Wood Quay'.

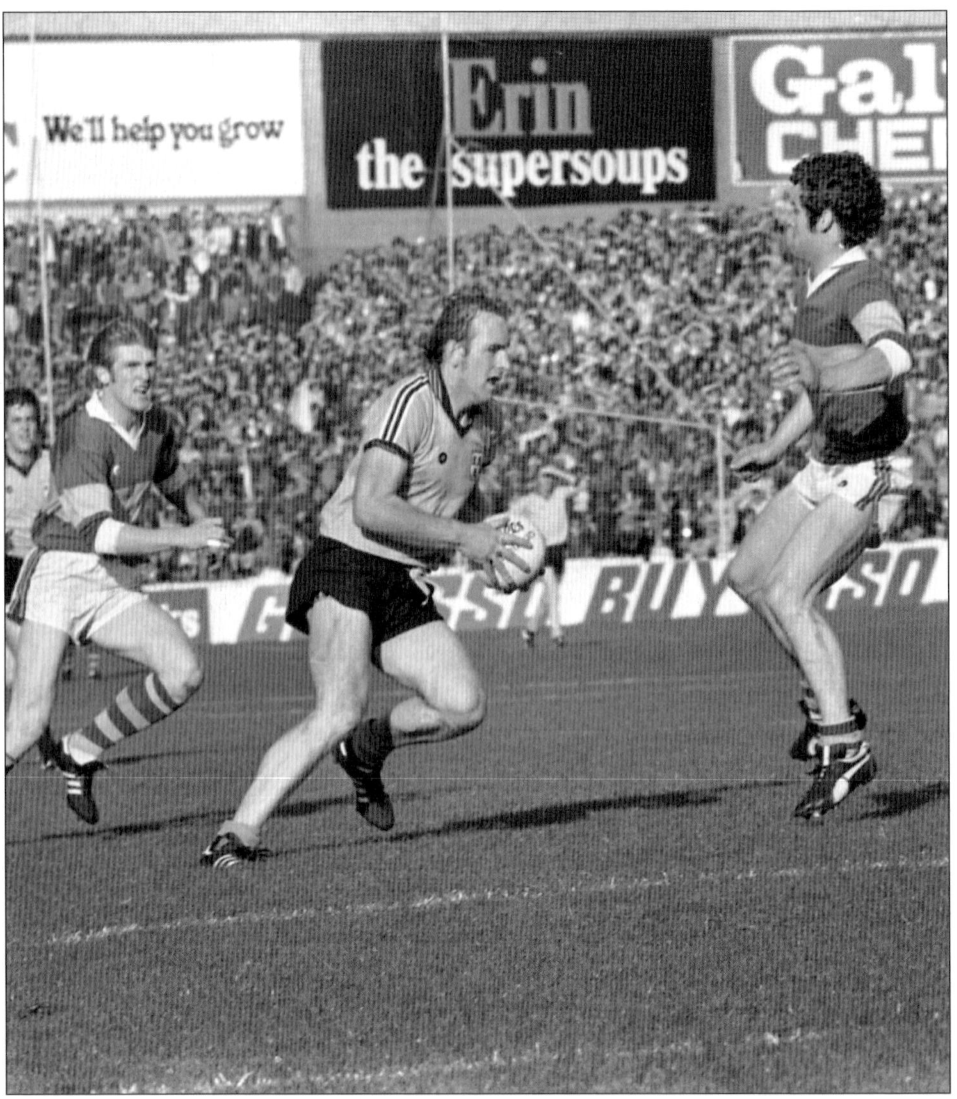

16. Confrontations between Dublin and Kerry in Gaelic football became emblematic of the confidence and profile that the GAA had in the 1970s, in both urban and rural areas. This image shows Dublin's Brian Mullins facing the Kerry defence in the 1978 All-Ireland Final.

17. Edmund Garvey, appointed Garda Commissioner in 1975, was a controversial figure. One of the more successful operations overseen by his force was the rescue of kidnapped Dutch industrialist Tiede Herrema in 1975 but his fraught relationship with the government and the Gardaí themselves, both of whom were under pressure because of the worsening security situation, led to his eventual dismissal in 1978.

FORTNIGHTLY REVIEW
hibernia
May 7th, 1976
Price 22p (inc. 2p VAT)
GARDA SIOCHANA
"ALL YOU NEED IS LAW..."

18. Edmund Garvey reminded Gardaí graduates at Templemore in 1976 to remember to 'stay within the law'. There were problems with both Garda behaviour and policy during the 1970s but also problematic were laws and a legal system deemed by many to be outdated.

19. Refugees from Northern Ireland came into the Republic of Ireland throughout the 1970s, but others came much greater distances. This image shows some of the fifty-eight Vietnamese refugees who arrived in 1979. Their arrival generated some resentment, testing the notion of Ireland as the land of a thousand welcomes.

20. The Irish Anti-Apartheid Movement was created in Dublin in the 1960s and headed during the 1970s by South African and Trinity College Law Professor, Kadar Asmal. The movement protested throughout the 1970s, particularly when the Irish rugby team played the All-White Springboks.

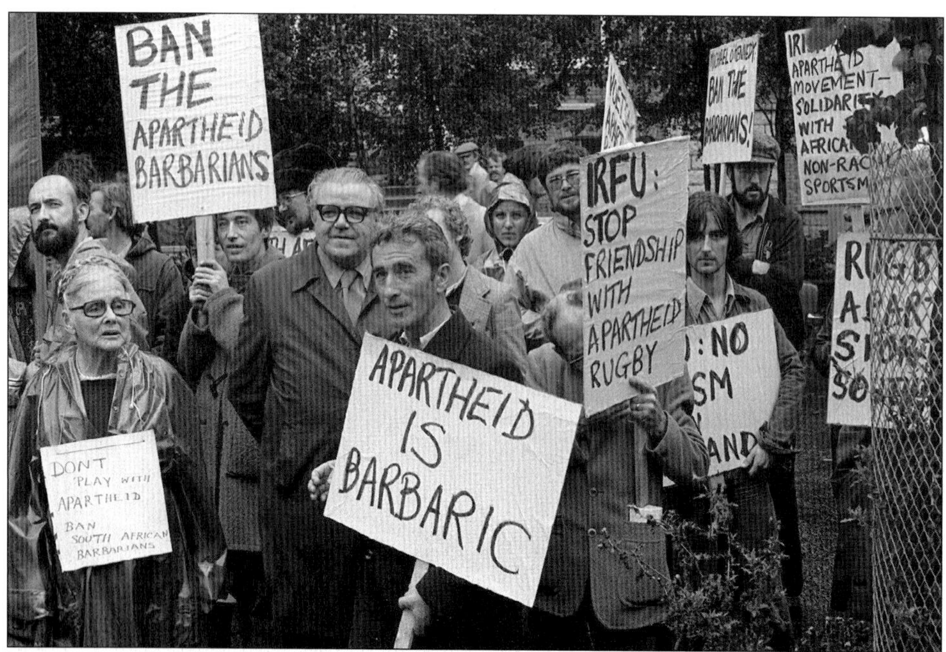

21. Margaret Thatcher's first visit to the Republic of Ireland as UK Prime Minister took place in November 1979 during an EEC Summit held at Dublin Castle, the former seat of British power in Ireland.

22. This protest in March 1979 outside the GPO on O'Connell Street in Dublin was one of many such protests throughout the late 1970s. By 1975 PAYE workers were contributing 71.4 per cent of the income tax taken by the government and were insisting on a more equitable tax system.

23. Conservative estimates suggest that up to one quarter of the population were living in poverty during the early 1970s. Here, children are seen playing on a derelict site in Dublin; there was much poverty experienced by children, especially those from large families.

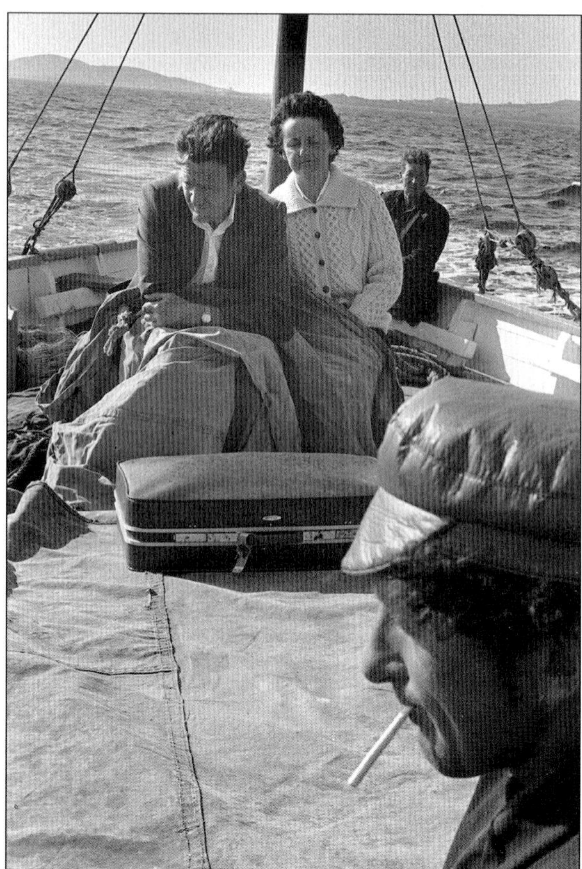

24. On the boat to Inisbofin, which was one of the inhabited islands off the west coast. During this period some islanders had been re-settled on the mainland at considerable cost to the government. Island life was supported by reliance on fishing, welfare and charitable efforts, but was sometimes beset by hardship and tragedy.

25. The advent of 'Discomania' in Dublin in the late 1970s was evidence of a new and more international youth culture influencing the Irish social scene, but many continued to listen to the showbands of an earlier era that included performers like Big Tom and the Mainliners.

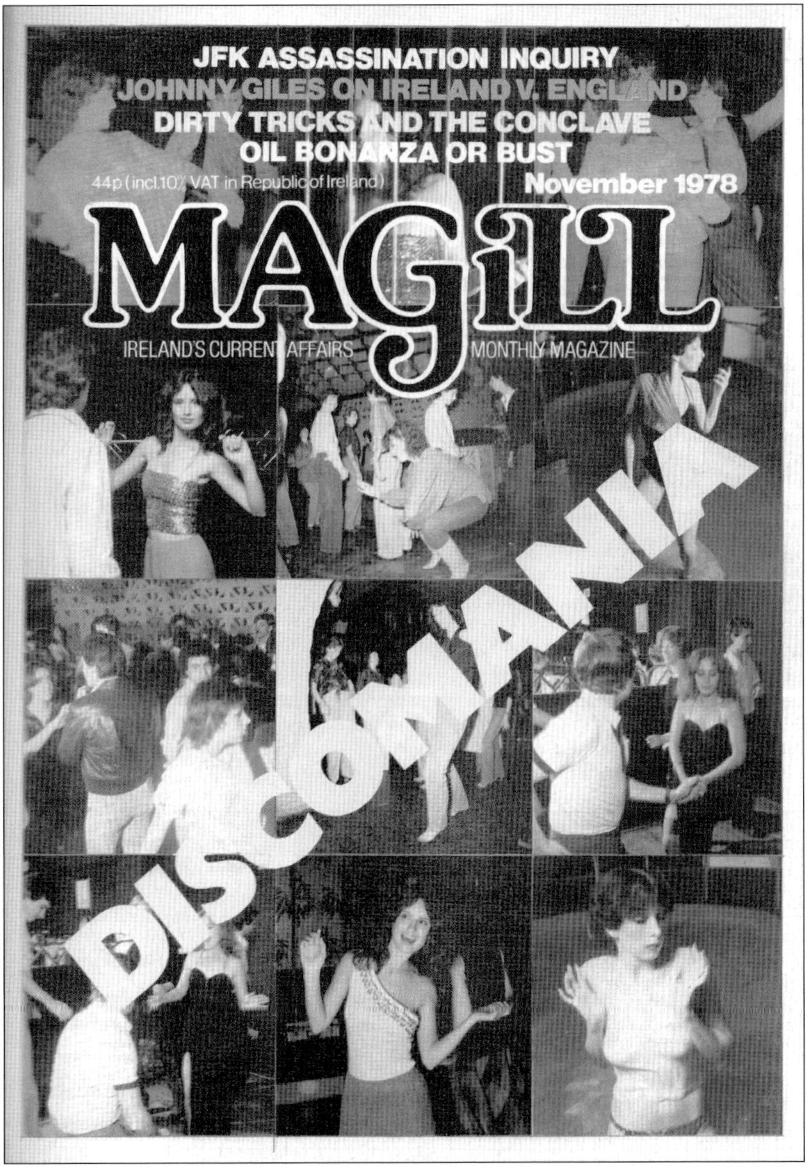

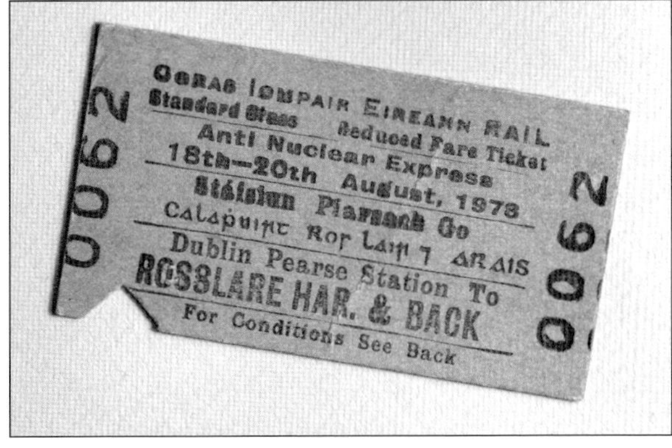

26. 'The Anti-Nuclear Express' carried journalists, photographers (including Derek Speirs who kept this ticket), protestors and musicians down to Rosslare Harbour to attend the protests at Carnsore Point in 1978.

27. During his 1979 visit to Ireland, Pope John Paul II said masses in Galway, Drogheda and Dublin. Here he greets crowds on 29 September in Drogheda atop his 'Pope Mobile' accompanied by Gardaí and members of the Special Branch.

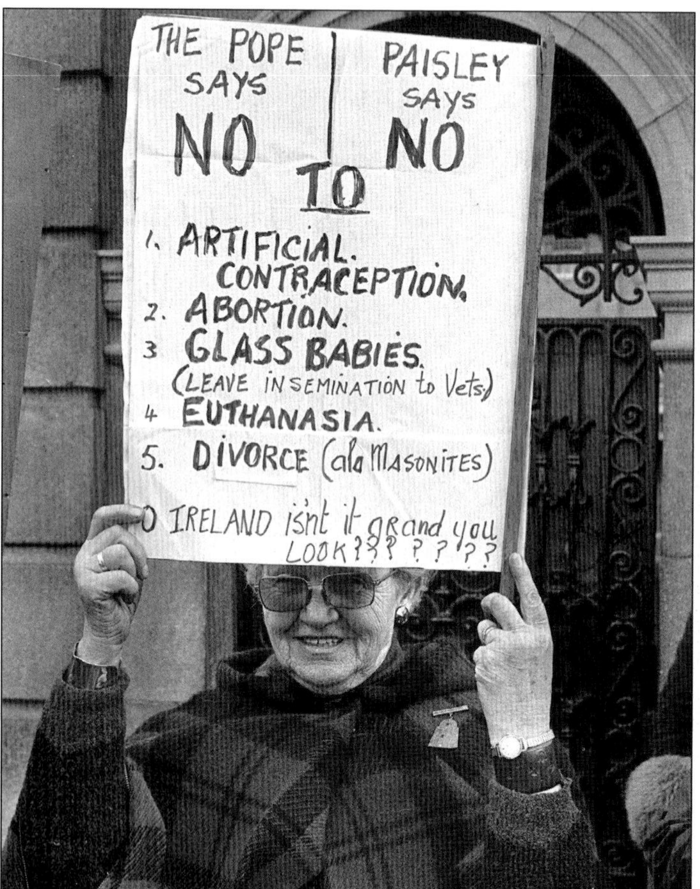

THE POPE SAYS NO
PAISLEY SAYS NO
TO
1. ARTIFICIAL. CONTRACEPTION.
2. ABORTION.
3 GLASS BABIES.
(LEAVE INSEMINATION to Vets.)
4 EUTHANASIA.
5. DIVORCE (ala MASONITES)
O IRELAND isn't it grand you LOOK??? ????

28. Traditional Catholic beliefs and practices were being challenged by social, medical and cultural developments, and membership of the EEC prompted debate about how or whether controversial issues, including abortion, contraception, euthanasia and in-vitro fertilisation (IVF), would be dealt with. This lady holds a placard outside the Houses of Parliament at Leinster House in Dublin on 28 February 1979.

29. A march held in October 1978 by 'Women against violence against Women' that led to the establishment of the Dublin Rape Crisis Centre. Crimes and violence against women were being discussed more openly in Irish society but change was slow to happen in some areas, including criminalisation of marital rape, which did not happen until 1990.

30. The visit of the 'Up with the People' group to St Patrick's College, Maynooth in October 1978 included (from left to right) Eamon Casey (Bishop of Galway), Jeremiah Newman (Bishop of Limerick), Tomás Ó Fiaich (Archbishop of Armagh) and Edward Daly (Bishop of Derry). The Catholic Church remained powerful during this decade but its dominance was critically questioned and it faced more challenges than previously.

31. The women's movement in Ireland included outspoken historian and Dominican nun Margaret Mac Curtain who taught at UCD and was one of the pioneers of the womens' history movement in Ireland as well as being an informed critic of conservative male-dominated Catholicism.

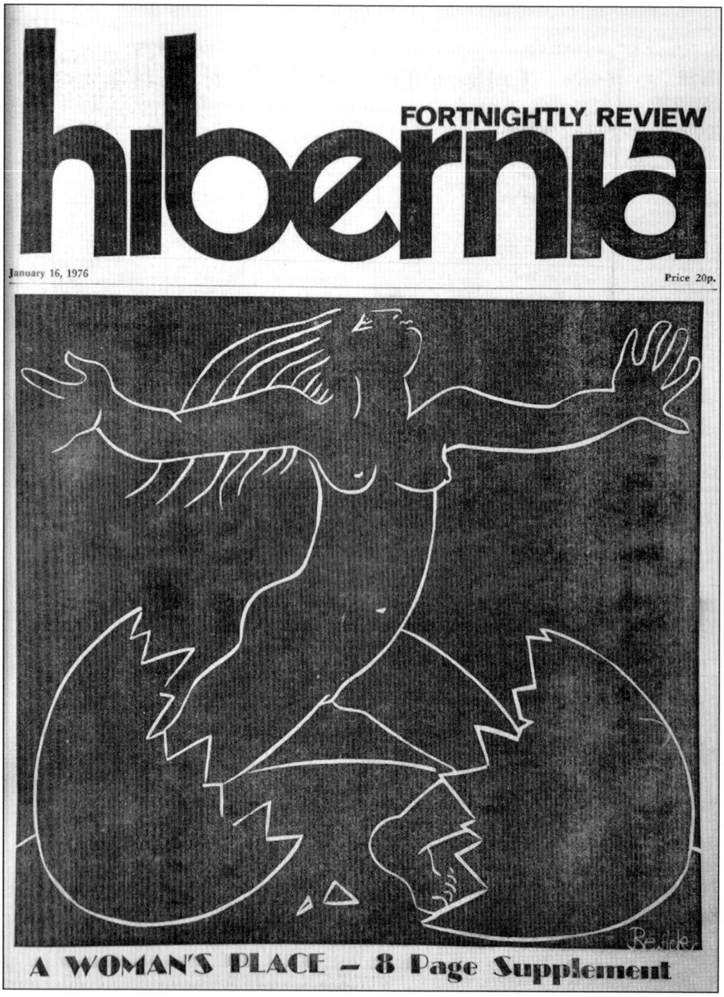

hibernia

FORTNIGHTLY REVIEW

January 16, 1976

Price 20p.

A WOMAN'S PLACE – 8 Page Supplement

32. The Commission on the Status of Women was established in 1970 and reported in 1972; it created a momentum that led to the creation of the Council for the Status of Women in 1973, an umbrella group for womens' organisations led by a voluntary committee and funded on a subscription basis. It was a significant development in the evolution of women's rights in Ireland.

to the discredit of our national image abroad and indeed is very noticeable here in Australia.'[18]

Whitlam's speech during his 1974 visit focused on the role in Australia of immigrants from Ireland, 'a country so close in history and spirit to my own, and whose valiant and poignant story has so stirred the imagination of the Australian people ... we remain in many ways the most Irish country outside Ireland', although not, it seemed, to the extent that the Australians would visit or invest in Ireland on a large scale. There was only a single Australian company established in Ireland, employing ten people, and for Ireland, Australia represented only 1.24 per cent of total tourism revenue which, it was believed, needed to be expanded. The value of exports to Australia in 1973 was £6 million and the value of imports from Australia £4.5 million.[19]

Whitlam acknowledged that diplomatic contacts between the two countries had not always been active or comprehensive but he was able to announce that his government was assisting University College Dublin in establishing a Chair of Australian History. In his private meeting with Cosgrave and FitzGerald, Whitlam noted that 'some years ago approximately one-quarter of the population of Australia could claim Irish blood. This proportion now was probably of the order of one-fifth.' He also said that 'Australians had been highly impressed in the past with the way in which Ireland had voted on issues coming before the UN'.[20] Earlier that year, the Attorney General, Declan Costello, had travelled to Australia and met the prime minister and also suggested there was a lot of goodwill towards Ireland, and 'virtually no support for the IRA amongst the Australian Irish'. He maintained that 'it has been difficult to develop in practical ways the links between the two countries but it seems to me desirable and in the interests of this country that they should be strengthened'.[21]

– FORTY –

IRELAND OF THE WELCOMES?

Some of FitzGerald's claims in 1973 about an empathetic Irish commitment to human rights and the dignity of the individual born of historical experience were put to the test early the following year when the government discussed the possibility of Ireland accepting refugees from Chile (an Irish Committee for the Restoration of Democracy in Chile was also active in 1974). At that point all members of the EEC with the exception of Ireland and Luxembourg had agreed to accept refugees. The issue at stake was not temporary asylum, as had been the case with Hungarian refugees in 1956, many of whom had a sour experience in Ireland due to the conditions in which they were held and restrictions on their movement (most of them left Ireland), but permanent resettlement. The government decided that the maximum number of Chilean families it could accept was just twelve due to 'the absence of full employment and of Spanish speaking communities into which refugees could readily integrate'.

Even accepting twelve families would, it was maintained, entail 'serious problems of a personal, social and administrative nature'. The Department of Justice had serious reservations due to its belief that 'our society is less cosmopolitan than that of Western European countries generally and in consequence, the absorption of even a limited number of foreigners of this kind could prove extremely difficult'. It recalled, in a self-serving piece of historical revisionism, that the 1956 Hungarians in Ireland 'failed to settle down and caused trouble and we had to make an "ad misericordiam" plea to Britain and the US authorities to agree to take them off our hands'. But the real fear was communism; it was maintained that all or many of the Chilean refugees

> are refugees because they are Marxists and probably communists and it is to be assumed that a significant proportion of their numbers are activists and that they are likely sooner or later to engage in political agitation here. There would be no effective sanction against such a person – deportation would not be possible ... extreme left-wing or other political activists or agitators would be likely to present a far greater problem for this country than for other Western European countries as there is in existence here a relatively large and well organised subversive group towards whom such persons could be expected to gravitate ... the question whether an effective 'screening' of refugees before admission is possible in such circumstances would need to be considered.

The government authorised the Minister for Justice Patrick Cooney to consider applications but the DFA objected to this and insisted it was the Minister for Foreign Affairs who should be so authorised,[1] an interesting indication of conflicting interpretations as to whether this was a security or foreign policy issue. There was certainly no mention of it being a humanitarian issue.

Britain was also cautious in accepting just 23 of these families, while France took 600, Italy 200 and Belgium 125. The small Chilean community faced many problems in Ireland, highlighted in the correspondence of Garret FitzGerald in 1976. All the Chilean refugees in Galway remained unemployed and they had no insurance stamps. One family with five children was trying to live on £27 a week; though they praised the Chilean solidarity groups, a letter from the refugees, which makes a mockery of the supposedly renowned Irish welcome, noted that 'in the past we refugees were informed by Mr Desmond McGreevy, chairman of the committee for Chilean refugees, of the existence of a climate of objection to the granting of help to the Chilean community. On account of this the committee kept absolute reserve as regards the presence of the Chilean refugees in Ireland.' There were also references to workers in industry meeting to express 'strong opposition to the employment of foreigners'.[2] Two Chilean brothers who arrived aged eight and twelve in 1974 recalled that the language difficulties were paramount, 'but we found a common language, which was football. Things improved a lot after that ... we didn't know anything about the country, except what we had seen on the news about the Troubles ... Ireland was poor in the 1970s and our dad was forced to emigrate for a while to England to find work.'[3]

In 1974, during a South American tour, the Republic of Ireland soccer team became the first international team to play Chile in Santiago's Estadio Nacional where Pinochet's forces had tortured and murdered. Eamon Dunphy, a member of the Irish team, was later to recall 'when we went out to inspect the pitch, armed guards ordered us back to the dressing rooms. It was a sobering experience; we knew we were being used,'[4] which raised questions as to why they and the Football Association of Ireland agreed to play.

The issue of asylum also arose in 1979, this time in relation to Indo-China refugees. In January 1979 there was a reference in the Department of the Taoiseach to the need for the hundred refugees to be tested 'for VD etc.'. There was also some racist correspondence to the department that railed against the idea of an intake of foreigners or the prospect of a multiracial society. One Irish woman, ironically living in London, concluded that the necessity was to keep 'Ireland for the Irish, every time'. In contrast, another correspondent insisted that if the refugees were not accepted, 'I don't think this country is fit to be called a Catholic country'.[5] The Irish Red Cross and the Legion of Mary among others, joined a working group to facilitate the admittance of 'about 100' with a pledge to accept a further hundred. An Irish teacher in Tokyo suggested thousands rather than hundreds should be admitted as 'these people are suffering now what we Irish suffered in previous centuries'.[6]

As seen earlier, whatever the fears about communism, FitzGerald was determined to extend Irish diplomatic ties with Eastern bloc countries as evidenced by the exchange of ambassadors between Ireland and Czechoslovakia on a non-residential basis in 1975. It was also suggested in the *Irish Times* that FitzGerald's plans to expand the country's diplomatic contacts were being curtailed by 'economic restraints'. The Department of the Taoiseach regarded these newspaper reports as having 'clearly come from an official source'.[7] Sensitivities remained; in May 1975, Paul Keating at the DFA, expressed concern about the tendency of President Ó Dálaigh 'to accept invitations without seeking advice and without adverting to the possible implications of his presence at a particular function. Mr Keating mentioned, as an example, the president's acceptance of an invitation to attend a concert at the Gaiety Theatre presented by a group from Lithuania. This could have had embarrassing consequences as we have not given recognition to the incorporation of Lithuania in the USSR.'[8] (Another issue that arose regarding the presidency and Irish foreign policy was in relation to trade. Bertie O'Dowd in the Department of the Taoiseach suggested in a letter to John Burke of the DFA that it was 'questionable ... whether a presidential state visit should be used by officials of government departments' to promote trade.)[9]

Apartheid in South Africa also created tensions about the government's stance on international controversies and the question of sanctions. High-profile disputes about the Springboks, the all-white South African rugby team, visiting Ireland increased the profile of the apartheid question in 1965 and 1970, though not all were engaged. In January 1970 journalist Bernard Share recalled that after protesting against the Springboks' presence in Ireland he went to a pub where 'an entire lounge bar [was] glued to the television commentary'.[10] Nonetheless in the region of 8,000 protested against the visit in 1970, including Conor Cruise O'Brien, socialist-Republican MP Bernadette Devlin and trade unionist Denis Larkin. The objectors were led by Kader Asmal of the Irish Anti-Apartheid Movement. As far back as the 1950s a nascent anti-apartheid movement was apparent when groups of African students took to the streets of Dublin to raise awareness of the issue and there were calls for the boycott of South African goods. At the UN in the 1960s the Irish, while explicit in their denunciation of racial segregation and being to the forefront in getting the UN Assembly to condemn apartheid, initially vacillated about sanctions, suggesting they could be counterproductive.

The IAAM was formed in Dublin in 1964 and by the early 1970s it had branches in almost all parts of Ireland.[11] Its first chairman was Dublin barrister Ernest Wood, the honorary secretary was trade unionist and future Labour TD Barry Desmond, and its vice-chairman was Asmal, who had also been a founder member of the Anti-Apartheid Movement in London and had joined the staff of the Faculty of Law at Trinity College Dublin in 1963 (he remained there for twenty-seven years, before returning to his native South Africa to become a minister in the country's first democratically elected government in 1994). Conferences, lobbying, publications and education quickly followed with support from many high-profile artists and politicians from all parties; Conor Cruise O'Brien and Noel Browne were particularly visible and its campaign against the Springboks in 1965 was regarded as a success, but the 1970 demonstrations were much larger and the campaign was spread out over six months, with the support of the Irish Congress of Trade Unions (ICTU).

There were clashes with Gardaí and condemnation of a Fine Gael TD's invitation to the Springboks to visit Leinster House, home of the Dáil.[12] The Springboks received a warmer reception in Limerick, a city unique in Ireland in relation to rugby because it cut across all social barriers. Significantly, after the protests in 1970, George Colley as Minister for Industry and Commerce cancelled a planned trade mission to South Africa and declared that there would be no more promotions of Irish goods in South Africa.[13]

Asmal, who became chairman of the IAAM in 1972 (his wife Louise Parkinson was the highly effective secretary of the group), remarked in October 1973 on the significance of Garret FitzGerald as minister opening the AGM of the IAAM, as such a senior political endorsement was unprecedented internationally. The same year a Rhodesian team took part in the World Ploughing Championships in Wexford. Due to a UN resolution, the Irish government 'had been bound by international law' not to sanction Irish involvement, but the Rhodesian team had come into the country on British passports.[14] In 1974 *Hibernia* referred to 'overt discrimination in denying posts to coloured doctors in Ireland', and it maintained that in 1969 'only 2 per cent of the landladies on lists of the UCD chaplaincy were prepared to admit black students'.[15] In 1975 Asmal (who lamented the 'lack of books on international law and practice in Ireland') drew attention to advertisements appearing in the *Irish Independent* for nurses in Johannesburg which referred to 'white patients only', which, he suggested, 'brings apartheid right on to our doorsteps'.[16]

In 1975 and 1976 Asmal wrote to FitzGerald reminding him of the need for ratification by the Irish government of the 1966 international convention on the elimination of all forms of racial discrimination. Its failure to ratify it was, according to Asmal, 'a source of embarrassment at international gatherings'. *Hibernia* also referred to the seventeen Nigerians who were refused entry to Ireland in 1976; refusal was at the discretion of immigration officers.[17] The previous year, FitzGerald's rather tetchy correspondence with Minister for Justice Patrick Cooney on this issue revealed that the Department of Justice was not 'able to give this a high priority'. FitzGerald was also frustrated a few years later that he was 'under constant pressure' from Amnesty International about civil rights covenants and 'I'm getting very little from your department despite several reminders'.[18]

The same year Asmal informed FitzGerald that 'the majority in South Africa do not rule out force as a means of change and we should show a greater understanding and sensitivity towards their views'. He added, 'I know you personally feel very deeply' on the issue of apartheid. He also referred to the inappropriateness of tug-of-war and hockey teams from South Africa travelling to Ireland, to which FitzGerald's response was that these were private organisations.[19] Of particular relevance here was the world tug-of-war competition in Dundalk. The Minister for Education, Richard Burke, refused a grant for this after consultation with FitzGerald 'because it appeared to us likely that the South African team which proposed to take part would not be selected on a genuinely multi-racial basis'. The previous year the general assembly of the UN had adopted a declaration to bring about the cessation of sporting contacts with any country practising apartheid and called on countries to deny entry to teams concerned: 'Ireland abstained but we indicated our intention to implement the declaration as far as possible.'

But were the Irish government's contradictory stances sustainable? When the new Minister for Foreign Affairs, Michael O'Kennedy was quizzed in the Dáil about the government's view of the South African team participating in the world golf championships in Ireland (at Waterville in County Kerry) in 1978, he said he was 'reluctant to consider direct intervention by the government in this field'. But privately, reference was made to the significance of 'the zeal of the Irish anti-apartheid movement' and while it was acknowledged that the South African team could not be prevented from entering the country, 'it also seems inappropriate to take a completely neutral stance on the issue'.[20]

In April 1978 one of the organisers of the golf tournament wrote to Lynch urgently requesting a statement from him ('which we discussed briefly at our meeting in Cork') as Dáil answers on the issues did not 'clarify the situation without ambiguity'. The international golf association was seeking such clarification and sponsors contacted the tourist board, Bord Fáilte, threatening to pull out if no statement was made. Lynch suggested it was for the golf authorities to assert and publicise 'the non-discriminatory selection of the South African representatives'.[21] Bord Fáilte informed the Department of Transport and Tourism that the world cup organisers were cancelling the tournament as 'it appears that all of the organisers had got letters from the anti-apartheid group in Ireland and they were now convinced that there would be trouble here if they proceeded with the event'. Well-known industrialist, businessman, lifelong Fianna Fáil supporter and friend of US president Richard Nixon, John Mulcahy, was one of the organisers, and subsequently wrote to the International Golf Association asking it to consider his Waterville Course for the following year instead: 'says he will have got full government support and that the anti-apartheid will fade away after 1978'. In May 1978 the cabinet agreed that if Mulcahy could satisfy the government that qualifying rounds for the 1979 tournament were not racist the government would not object to Waterville being used but, 'this does not imply of course that the anti-apartheid movement would be less active in their opposition to the holding of the world cup in Ireland next year [than] they were this year'.[22]

Some racist correspondence was sent to the Department of the Taoiseach, including assertions that Asmal was 'a propagandist'. For his part, O'Kennedy in April 1978, in a reply to a request for a meeting from Asmal to mark International Anti-Apartheid Year, ruled out such a meeting 'for the next few months'. Lynch maintained that while the Irish government wanted to see an end to apartheid he did not feel 'I could endorse by way of formal statement the full programme of activities planned by the movement'.[23] The government faced the issue of acceding to Asmal's request for the IAAM to be designated the 'national committee' for Anti-Apartheid Year; this was, according to O'Kennedy 'something of a dilemma'. It had prominent supporters but could the government endorse protests? 'I have myself – as I am sure you have – a certain general sympathy for the broad aims of the movement.'[24]

O'Kennedy also visited Tanzania and was received by President Julius Nyerere, who stressed the important contribution of Irish missionaries to his country's development and spoke out against racist minority regimes discriminating against the majority, arguing that 'only armed struggle could secure them their rights'. In reply, O'Kennedy emphasised that Ireland had first-hand experience of foreign rule and economic deprivation 'indeed over a longer period than most. This gave our people a particular appreciation of the problems faced by the countries of Africa.' Rather than endorsing armed resistance, O'Kennedy mentioned the need to resolve these issues 'by negotiation'.[25]

– FORTY-ONE –

MARKETING IRELAND

Visits abroad by Irish ministers were mentioned in a very casual way by Jack Lynch in 1978 in the context of St Patrick's Day. He asked colleagues to let him know 'if any of them were going abroad – particularly to US around the St Patrick's Day holiday. Generally, it would be better if no more than a very few were abroad together.' That year, Lynch was advised to turn down a request from the St Patrick's Day Parade Committee of Washington for him to view the parade in that city in 1978; Seán Donlon informed Dermot Nally that 'the committee is not a very significant one in Irish-American affairs and as you are aware, Washington DC is not a major centre of Irish-American activity, even in March.'[1] No one seemed to be offering to go to the state of Bahrain, even though His Highness Sheikh Isa bin Salman Al-Khalifa Amir had sent a goodwill message to the government on St Patrick's Day in 1977.

In relation to ministerial travel the issue of an executive jet for this purpose arose at various stages during the 1970s, including in 1972 when the government approved a proposal by the Minister for Finance for the purchase of an executive jet for ministers and officials travelling to the Continent. This decision was rescinded by the coalition government in March 1973. The following year the commissioner of the Gardaí, Edmund Garvey, was in favour of the acquisition of a government jet on security grounds after a security incident during the president's visit to Belgium 'when an unauthorised person attempted to board the plane at Brussels'.

It seems at that stage, however, that it was regarded as an unaffordable extravagance. The issue arose again in the summer of 1977 when the Minister for Foreign Affairs mentioned delays in scheduled air services between Dublin and Brussels and urged the government to reconsider but at the end of that year the Department of Finance was dismissive, pointing out that in the previous three years the average annual air travel cost of ministerial visits to Europe was £30,000, 'including air fares of accompanying officials'. A jet would cost in the region of £2 million or a turbo propeller £0.82 million: 'such an acquisition would probably give rise to controversy. However a good case can be made for sharing the use of an executive type plane,' and in January 1978 the cabinet decided to lease a second Air Corps plane.[2]

The potential for tourism and the international perception of Ireland were growing challenges in the 1970s that were inevitably influenced by the Troubles. By the end of the 1960s, some were turning their attention to how best to market Ireland as a tourist destination. The Irish Overseas Agency Trust, based in Bray, for example, conducted research in the US to establish who had an interest in or connection with Ireland and 'who wish to be assisted in their enquiries, or in transactions in Ireland'.[3] But there was also much displeasure with some of the projections and representations of Ireland, including a BBC 1 documentary called *The Land of Ireland* which was broadcast in November 1969 and was regarded by a resident of Bedfordshire, who wrote to the Taoiseach, as reprehensible as it 'showed the Irish people as a lot of clowns living in filth and conditions that I know is not true of the West of Ireland ... The British people who saw this programme will never go to Ireland on holiday or otherwise.'

He wondered why there was no depiction of modernisation and industry and transformation: 'the success as well as the poverty'. Bertie O'Dowd, private secretary to the Taoiseach, replied that 'reaction here from viewers who did see it was not dissimilar to your own. The Taoiseach regrets that an outside film unit should present, and not for the first time, such a slanted and distorted picture of Irish life.'[4] Foreign newspapers also lapped up stage-Irish yarns and the quaintness of the survival of traditions of old, although sometimes with an edge that caused disquiet. A Sydney newspaper in 1971 reported on the annual Lisdoonvarna matchmaking festival in County Clare, with attendant 'haggling over dowries' in the back of pubs, suggesting that 'the very minimum dowry these days is £400 but can go up to £4,000'. A 'girl' would need £3,000, it was suggested, to marry into 'a 50 cow farm', but the dowry was also being replaced by educational qualifications: 'a girl with a domestic science diploma or a nursing certificate is a desirable property – no matter what she looks like' while 'the prestige of having a priest in the family is reckoned to add £100 to a dowry'.

The article quoted Irish poet Brendan Kennelly, who attacked the dowry as 'a slur on emotional integrity ... it is a begrudging gift from the ignorant to the greedy in order to perpetuate the mindless ... I've often heard a farmer say of his son "I had him well backed" meaning he had brought in a large dowry. He may have been talking of greyhounds or racehorses.' The journalist also asserted 'all over Ireland there are hundreds of eminently respectable wives who earned their marriage money on Liverpool's dockland streets or in North London brothels'.[5]

The following month, Lynch received a bitter complaint about the David Lean film *Ryan's Daughter* (filmed in West Kerry and centred on the affair of an Irish woman with a British officer during the First World War) from an Irish woman in Pennsylvania: 'This time they've reached the sewer. This is art?' The Irish-Americans, she maintained, 'are sickened by this loathsome display labelled Irish. Why are our men portrayed as forever drunken and our women abused. Always, always, the same.'[6] At the end of 1971 the Department of the Taoiseach decided to engage an international public relations organisation to develop abroad a better understanding of Irish affairs 'particularly in an extended EEC'. A note for the Taoiseach observed that the PR consultant employed 'says he would be very embarrassed if the fee paid to him were publicised, because, he says, the fee is a very low one'.[7]

But there were also reasons for optimism about tourist potential at the outset of the decade. Something of a coup was achieved with a supplement in the *New York Times* in November 1970 on contemporary Ireland and 'the excitement of change' which emphasised the Shannon Free Airport Development Company and the Shannon Free Trade Industrial Zone, incorporating forty-four companies, 5,500 workers, accounting for 24 per cent of Ireland's total export of manufactured goods and home to the world's first duty-free store. It was noted that sixty-three US companies had manufacturing plants in Ireland, availing of 'complete tax exemption on all total exports until 1990'. Even more pleasingly from a tourist perspective, it complimented the soulfulness and creativity of the Irish who could boast of both Yeats and machines and 'insist on the human touch ... The fact that Dublin has more daily newspapers than New York City, with over 12 times the population, is an indication that there is more to Ireland than meets the eye ... The gross national humanity seems to rate at least as high as the gross national product.'[8]

Efforts were also made to develop national parks. In June 1970, 300 acres of land at Derrynane, County Kerry were handed over to the Office of Public Works to be developed into Ireland's first seashore national park, and the following year Coole Park, near Gort, County Galway, once the home of Lady Gregory, a key individual in the Irish cultural revival of the late nineteenth and early twentieth centuries, was opened as a national park. The Booterstown Marsh in Dublin was also acquired by the state as a bird sanctuary. In 1975 the Furry Glen nature park was opened in Dublin's Phoenix Park and the University College Cork acquired Fota Park Island in Cork, a 780-acre estate with a world-famous collection of rare trees and shrubs.

There were 27,900 registered guest bedrooms in Ireland by 1970 (up from 16,527 in 1955 at a time when tourist income stood at £31.8 million) and expenditure by visitors to the country had increased from £75.7 million to £97.2 million between 1968 and 1969. Bord Fáilte had been hoping tourist revenue would reach the 'magical figure of £100 million' but it fell just short, and it was reported that in Donegal 'the trouble in Northern Ireland brought the season to a quick end'. There was a 25 per cent increase in the numbers flying direct to Ireland, mostly from North America, but Bord Fáilte was worried about 'confusion in the minds of potential visitors as to the location and extent of unrest'.

The buoyancy of car traffic was also noted. During 1969, British registered cars brought into the Republic rose by 19,000 compared to the previous year, to 103,500, while 19,000 students had been brought to Ireland. Ireland's tourist infrastructure was less than impressive, however: 'Once again there were frequent complaints from visitors about the lack of public toilets and the poor standard of existing ones' and the number of complaints about accommodation had risen from 1,200 in 1968 to 1,600 in 1969: 'The main theme of complaints by overseas visitors concerned the physical standard of hotels and guesthouses – uncomfortable beds, small rooms, inferior furnishing, inadequate heating and hot water.'[9] But perhaps there was also relative good value to be found. It was reported in the *Irish Independent* in January 1970, for example, that travel writer Beth Bryant had returned to the country to revise, pricewise, her book *Ireland on Five Dollars a Day* which had originally been written in 1966, 'and the remarkable thing about it is that she has found no need for revision'.[10] Car ferry services and visitors from Scandinavia and Holland and Belgium were also increasing.

But complaints persisted that there was no effective central body to embrace all aspects of tourism and Fine Gael insisted on the need for a Minister for Tourism. The Troubles also continued to cast a costly cloud, and there were numerous references in the early 1970s to the 'crisis which has hit the tourist trade'.[11] While Bord Fáilte's review of 1970 revealed that total tourist revenue had reached £101 million and the total number of visitors staying over twenty-four hours was 2 million (125,000 were continental European tourists, 240,000 from the US and Canada and 1,175,000 were British), there was a decline of 7.1 per cent in the number from Northern Ireland visiting the Republic. The main areas of complaint in 1970 were 'high prices generally and inadequate standards of hygiene', but despite the generally upbeat nature of Bord Fáilte's reports, it was accused by some of being 'a hidebound bureaucracy accountable to no-one'.[12] In 1972 the *Irish Press* reported that the tourist and travel industries had been 'undergoing some traumatic self-examination of late' with a suggestion that 'there is a deep and serious dissent among the various agencies involved in tourism on even the most fundamental principles of the industry'.[13]

William Kelly of the Strand Hotel in Rosslare insisted in 1974 that 'everything in the hotel business is going from bad to worse despite what Bord Fáilte keep putting out', and the National Tourism Council was 'gravely concerned about the lack of development of Irish tourism'. It insisted responsibility for tourism needed to be taken from the Department of Transport and Power and required a designated junior minister. Minister for Finance Richie Ryan rejected the idea of a concession on tourist petrol, as it would be abused due to 'the large ethnic content of Irish tourism'.[14]

But for all the negative comment, there were also numerous letters of praise generated by positive tourist experiences (who could make curious analogies). One visitor from London took the trouble to write to Lynch in September 1971 to commend Ireland as 'the Switzerland of the Western world'.[15] On a similar note, the Italian newspaper *Il Giornale* praised the IDA and Córas Tráchtála (the Irish Export Board) in 1975 and suggested that 'if things continued as at present Ireland will be the Switzerland of

North West Europe'.[16] Lynch had to stress to potential British visitors that 'there is absolutely no cause for fear or apprehension because of the GB plate on your car' but he was urged to do more to reassure would-be British visitors who had concerns about travelling to Ireland.[17] Bertie O'Dowd also had to reply to many of these types of queries, including one from a potential tourist worried about whether 'a party of English people (Protestant) could be certain of a trouble free holiday'. O'Dowd suggested 'it is regrettable that many good people permit themselves to be misled by the anti-Irish propaganda which unfortunately finds a place in certain sections of the British press', though another English visitor during her visit was 'amazed that a nation who have been so badly oppressed over the centuries should have retained such a wealth of fondness and humour'.[18]

In May 1976, journalist Ian Nairn in the *Sunday Times* insisted in relation to Irish tourism, 'the bewildering thing about Ireland is that the tourist clichés are all true ... and there is no resentment. I cannot say it loud enough and often enough that the British are welcome.'[19] In 1977, Aer Lingus, Bord Fáilte and the two main Irish banks initiated a visit to Ireland by some British lord mayors which the Department of the Taoiseach felt 'could be valuable particularly in view of recent reports in the press of a considerable drop in the number of visitors coming here from Britain'[20] (reports which were not actually borne out by the figures presented by Bord Fáilte).

Anomalies in the licensing laws regarding intoxicating liquor caused irritation and embarrassment and were regarded as damaging to tourism. Many restaurants were permitted to serve wine with meals but were forbidden from serving beer; the reasons for this distinction, it was maintained 'are long since dead'.[21] In March 1977 Lord Killanin, president of the International Olympic Committee, on behalf of the Galway Race Committee, Jonathan Irwin, the managing director of Goffs Bloodstock Sales and James Meenan of the Royal Dublin Society, which hosted the annual Dublin Horse Show, wrote to Liam Cosgrave. They insisted that a recent High Court ruling that upheld the decision of a district justice not to grant a licence for more than three days to the races, and that the previous practice of granting an occasional licence for the additional two days of the five-day event could not continue, was, given that the Galway Races had been built up from two to five days, likely 'to make both ourselves and the country a laughing stock among overseas visitors'. The government duly amended the relevant legislation and extended the licensing limit to six days and did it with great speed (two weeks), to the delight of Lord Killanin: 'Certainly you moved very rapidly.'[22]

Towards the end of the decade Bord Fáilte maintained it had much reason to be positive. In reviewing the year 1978, for example, it indicated that '1978 was our best ever year for tourism. A contributory factor was the 23 per cent increase recorded in the number of British tourists visiting Ireland as against an 8 per cent increase in 1977. The number of tourists to Ireland from all markets rose by 15 per cent to 2.257 million, surpassing the 1977 record-breaking figure of 1.963 million. Total revenue from all out-of-state visitors including day excursionists amounted to £278.7 million, an increase of 17 per cent.' By the end of that year, 68 per cent of all hotel bedrooms had a private bath or shower and the target was to have all bedrooms with such facilities by 1985.[23]

In 1978 at a seminar on tourism in Killarney, Fine Gael TD John Kelly posed an interesting question about the improvement of the environment in this context: 'The commonest reason given for improvement of our urban surrounding is its supposed beneficial effect on tourism – as though it was indifferent to us for our own sakes if we lived in ill-planned dilapidated towns.'[24]

PART VI

THE ECONOMY

'Effective management of our financial affairs seemed to be slipping out of our hands'

In 1970, economist James Meenan published his account of the performance of the Irish economy since the foundation of the state under the title The Irish Economy Since 1922. *Meenan held the Chair of National Economics and Political Economy in UCD, was a veteran of government commissions and actively engaged in business, cultural and charitable endeavours. In his approach to economic analysis he was humane and suffused his work with a strong sense of historical perspective. As he saw it, people worked not to restore the balance of payments, but to increase their chance of a better life, and he concluded that at that point in the state's existence there was much hope for optimism in this regard. The country had undergone more rapid social and economic change in the previous decade than in the preceding sixty years, he noted. Prior to that, efforts to invigorate the economy had floundered due to a nationalism that was 'arid, introspective and unsure of itself', while emigration had stymied initiative. Now, industry had grown more rapidly than agriculture, but the importance of the export capacity of agriculture had increased.*[1]

Meenan, of course, had no crystal ball in relation to the fuel and inflation crises of the 1970s and his optimism was, at the end of the 1960s, well grounded. The reversal of the nationalistic, protective approach to the economy in the late 1950s and the creation of an open economy had undoubtedly generated more optimism and produced tangible results for a country in which one in three people under the age of thirty in 1946 had left by 1971.

The scale of the exodus had dropped dramatically, but the economy was also vulnerable to the external threats of inflation and fuel crises and internal mismanagement, which centred on wage and price supervision, handling of industrial difficulties and control of borrowing. There was much talk of a new affluence but also many warnings about spending beyond means.

There was also a belief and a desire that EEC membership would yield substantial economic dividends. In delivering the Seán Lemass Memorial Lecture in Exeter in 1974, to commemorate the late Taoiseach with whom he had worked in the late 1950s and early 1960s to reorient economic policy towards free trade, T. K. Whitaker insisted that although Lemass did not live to see Ireland join the EEC, he would have been happy to see tariffs 'razed to the ground in return for the benefits to Ireland of membership of the Community'. The narrative here was one of clear progress; a journey from economic darkness to light: 'We can salute Seán Lemass for having so effectively pursued policies which have taken Ireland from the embattled and impoverished protectionism of the 1930s into the more exposed but also better off 1970s.'[2]

But the economic narrative of the 1970s proved to be more mixed, hazardous and sometimes confused. In 1976, Fr John Brady, a Jesuit who lectured at the College of Industrial Relations in Dublin, wrote trenchantly about 'The Economics of Survival'. At the close of 1975, the Irish economy, he noted, was

> *in a very sorry state indeed. All trace of growth and dynamism has vanished; unemployment has never been higher since the end of World War II; inflation has reached a record rate well in excess of 20 per cent; the government deficit on current account has turned out to be an unprecedented £259 million. The deficit on current account of the Balance of Payments is expected to be £30 million. Emigration, that traditional Irish socio-economic safety valve, has been closed off by the world recession. The almost total inability of the economy to cope with the swelling numbers about to emerge from a greatly expanded educational system is truly frightening ... How did we get into this mess? How did it come about that the brave new world of economic and social development, so confidently heralded in the early 1960s, turned out to be such a hollow promise?*

As he saw it, in the previous decade, economic decision-making had been concerned with maximising benefits for those already secure in jobs and there had not been the right balance struck between raising personal income and expanding employment. It was about 'the misuse of power by those who had found a secure place in the economy' and, he concluded, 'for the next five years we have to think out and implement the economics of survival. If we do not, we will all go down with the ship.'[3]

In relation to his question 'How did we get into this mess?' T. K. Whitaker noted that the net increase in gross national product (GNP) from 1969–76 was approximately 25 per cent. Consumer prices doubled in the same period; agricultural incomes were estimated to have increased by 175 per cent and non-agricultural incomes by just over 200 per cent. Government expenditure rose as a percentage of GNP from 38 per cent to 49 per cent, and outstanding foreign debt accounted for just £55 million in 1969 but had risen to £1,000 million by the end of 1976.[4] *These figures encapsulate the reasons for both optimism and pessimism in the 1970s. People had more to spend, but they were spending too much borrowed money, and the more prices increased, the more they needed. While the population was expanding, and many were leaving agriculture, the labour market could not keep up and the decision in 1972 to resort to borrowing for current budgetary purposes had been a major policy mistake by George Colley, Fianna Fáil's Minister for Finance.*

Throughout the decade, economists, increasingly professionalised, found more outlets for their research findings. The first issue of the journal Economic and Social Review, *for example, appeared in 1970. There were symposia on inflation and a growing awareness of international developments in economic theory and a variety of papers on social issues and demographic forecasting. But it also became clear that there were widely differing views on the true structure of the economy.*[5] *There was a considerable growth in central bank activities, with formal liquidity requirements for the banking system announced in 1973, but its caution was not usually matched by politicians. Whitaker, who served as governor of the central bank until 1976, saw much to criticise in relation to public expenditure, taxation and borrowing. What he wanted to see was a moderate rate of growth of money incomes in order not to destroy competitiveness. Collective bargaining had to be realistic and 'the price of job preservation is income restraint'.*[6] *Marvellously understated, as befitting his standing as a senior civil servant, in looking back at this decade, Whitaker concluded in relation to his time as governor 'as to how far advice was listened to, appearances might incline one to take a pessimistic view ... The temptations to stray from financial orthodoxy were stronger and not always resisted.'*[7]

This was where the difference between being an economist and a politician came to the fore; the temptation to stray was also driven by the desire to stay in government or be elected, and crucial mistakes were made in this regard in the 1970s. Credit is due to Minister for Finance from 1973–7, Richie Ryan, for his attempts to rein in colleagues he regarded as spendthrift, his introduction of a wealth tax and capital gains and acquisitions taxes to 'get at the speculators'.[8] But Ryan's caution about spending was not shared widely; politics and the reality of coalition dictated that salary and substantial welfare increases were delivered in the 1970s. Despite worries about the overall public expenditure, balance of payments figures and threats to long-term solvency, ordinary people wanted to be able to borrow and spend after the historical experience of relative austerity and they embraced a 'giveaway' election manifesto by Fianna Fáil in 1977 which the country could ill afford.

The wisdom of the introduction of a Department of Economic Planning and Development after the 1977 general election was questioned, notably by Whitaker, whom Jack Lynch had nominated to the Senate. Whitaker was critical of the establishment of this ministry as a distinct entity from the Department of Finance. As he saw it, it was Finance which should have been 'confirmed and strengthened in its planning responsibilities' rather than its 'development consciousness' diminished without a transfer of its powers.[9] It was a decision that has also been criticised by historian Joe Lee: 'If strategic thinking is to be given administrative weight, it must be undertaken under the aegis of Finance ... a dose of Finance scepticism would, for once, have done no harm in the euphoria of 1977.' The new minister in that department, Martin O'Donoghue, may have been correct in believing that cyclical recovery from the mid-1970s slump would not be enough to create full employment, but his solution 'proved sadly misguided'.[10] His expansionist urge, reversing Ryan's attempt to reduce deficit financing and based on the hope that a consumer boom would lift the private sector, was a gamble that backfired, exacerbated by a new oil crisis in 1979. A temporary decrease in unemployment was not sustained as wage increases and inflation proved a major ingredient in a deadly cocktail. If the Irish economy had endured a troubled 1970s, it was set to experience a traumatic 1980s. The 'irrational optimism' that underlay the resumption of economic planning in 1977 led to an accumulation of debt which was financing current expenditure rather than national development.[11]

The notion of restraint simply did not hold enough sway in the 1970s, and the trade unions played their role in creating unrealistic expectations. Irish trade unionism had evolved 'outwards and upwards' to the extent that even some sympathetic to its cause wondered in the 1970s if it would be strong enough 'to bind so many disparate and sometimes conflicting interests into a workable unity' and create greater willingness to submit to discipline. Sectionalism and elitism were being created by 'the question of the preservation of differentials'.[12] On the basis of the percentage of workers organised, the Republic on the cusp of the 1970s had 'one of the strongest trade union movements outside the communist world' with about 56 per cent of workers organised (compared to 49 per cent in Britain and 23 per cent in France). Affiliated membership of ICTU was 551,000, but the trade union movement was 'unsatisfactory structurally' with too many unions and too much overlapping. There were eighty-seven unions in Congress 'and one often finds two or three unions organising the same type of worker'.[13]

The value of wage agreements was questioned and the number of industrial disputes soared. In 1970 trade unionist Charles McCarthy sought to identify the essence of the dilemma, under the title 'Workers' participation in management'. He diagnosed 'a marked sense of alienation, of non-belonging which expresses itself in a desire on the one hand for greater participation and on the other in industrial unrest'. Leadership was needed in management, trade unions and government, 'and this is why the way ahead is so dark, because for some reason which I confess quite escapes me, I see very little of that leadership in our community at present'.[14] It was not a dilemma that was realistically confronted during this decade. As McCarthy characterised the situation a few years later in relation to the negotiation of National Wage Agreements, 'Society itself, with its affluence and its obsessive concern with higher and higher consumption, makes men profoundly ill at ease. In industrial bargaining itself, the position in this regard is alarming; each settlement is higher than the last, each period of agreement is shorter than the last, prices are rising, expectations are rising and there is a sense of acceleration.'[15]

In relation to industrial expansion and progress, Joe Lee and others have suggested that the Industrial Development Authority (IDA) exaggerated its success. In their 1975 publication The Irish Economy, sponsored by the European Commission, economists Kieran Kennedy and Richard Bruton noted that half the output in recent years had come from IDA-assisted foreign firms but their impact on employment had not been substantial.[16] This question of industrial progress and its limitations was eventually addressed in the Telesis Report, published in 1982, but which had much relevance to the 1970s as it represented the first substantial debate on industrial policy in twenty years and involved identifying some of the mistakes made in those twenty years. In 1973 Noel Whelan, a young civil servant, had co-authored a report *which was dubious about the long-term benefits of an over-reliance on foreign investment as native industry was not growing to the extent it needed to. In 1980, after Whelan had moved to the Department of the Taoiseach, the Telesis Report was commissioned and came to similar conclusions. It advocated greater commitment towards developing an indigenous industrial base and challenged the IDA's self-congratulations. The foreign industry that did exist was not feeding back into the rest of the economy, with little of their research and development function being carried out in Ireland. More needed to be done to help native firms with potential and build them up as international competitors with funds for export-oriented companies.*[17]

In 1970 Bertram Hutchinson also highlighted 'non-economic' factors hampering Irish economic development, which he identified as the historic emphasis placed on conformity and traditionalism rather than innovation. Admiration, he suggested, had been reserved, not for those who by their own efforts 'emerged above the ruck of his fellows' but for those who conformed to the narrow limits 'laid down by the community for the material prosperity of its members'. Systems of reciprocal aid and strong family loyalty had also played their part.[18]

The decade was also notable for more meaningful and empirical attempts to define poverty, which were hampered by a frequently acknowledged lack of concrete information about personal distribution of income. Inequality in Ireland was regarded as greater than that in the UK and distribution of income in rural areas was more unequal than in urban areas.[19] *Research also confirmed that children from large families and lower socio-economic groups remained at a disadvantage despite the rise in living standards and that 'the pressures of living in present-day society bear hardest on those least able to withstand them'.*[20] *In the Jesuit journal* Studies, *which for fifty years had addressed economic, political, social and philosophical issues, Séamus Ó Cinnéide a research officer at the IPA, confronted 'the illusion, widely held, that ours is an egalitarian and just society, or becoming one'. This was being dispelled, he suggested, by research that highlighted the need to institutionalise the recognition of human rights instead of seeing the poor as a separate group, 'out there'. He cited the minimum wage of an agricultural labourer in 1971 as £16 a week (£800 per annum), an average male industrial worker wage of £30 a week (£1,560 per annum) and the chief executive of a large company earning £10–12,000 per year. The standard used as a poverty line required a man, wife and five children to have, at the bare minimum, £1,000 a year in 1971. Ó Cinnéide concluded that at least one-fifth of the population could be classed as poor, and that the most necessary thing was public education about social problems.*[21]

In November 1971 a three-day conference at Kilkenny, organised by the Council for Social Welfare, a committee of the Catholic Hierarchy, also sought to dispute the notion that poverty was no longer a pressing issue. Garret FitzGerald spoke and suggested the challenge was to excite the social conscience of what he termed 'the new privileged class', while two bishops dismissed the notion of the 'dignity' of poverty as belonging 'in the sphere of romantic mythology'. This conference was informed that between a fifth and a quarter of the population could be classified as poor.[22]

Overall, the pace of economic development was unevenly distributed nationally in relation to incomes, employment opportunities and emigration, and there was fury on the part of the public sectors that farmers, after entry to the EEC, seemed to be getting a bigger slice of the economic cake without paying their due tax. The economic climate for the employment of women changed, especially married women after the abolition of the marriage bar in the public service, but the question of equal pay, which became urgent after an EEC directive, revealed contrasting attitudes as to its supposed appropriateness and feasibility in Ireland.

Some of those writing about economics suggested that the problem of the Irish economy was not a shortage of analysis – the combined research of economists generated a relative consensus that what was necessary was fostering of enterprise, recovery of profit levels, lowering of inflation, income and price restraint to recover competitiveness and public works to raise demand in the economy – but that their advice was being ignored.[23] *Economic policy was another area in the 1970s when suggested reforms and reorientations were shirked, with serious long-term consequences.*

– FORTY-TWO –

THE IRISH ECONOMIC DILEMMA

In September 1974, T. K. Whitaker, as governor of the central bank, wrote a strongly worded letter to the Minister for Finance, Richie Ryan, about the state of the national finances:

> I had been hoping for some good result to the efforts you have been making over recent months to pull back public expenditure from its present disaster course but I am appalled by the information given in confidence to me by Mr Murray [secretary of the Department of Finance]. I find it hard to credit that the government could be seriously contemplating budgetary dispositions involving such enormous (and even impossible) increases not only in taxation but also in foreign borrowing in order to finance additional current expenditure. I make the envisaged increase in current public expenditure in 1975 about 25 per cent. I wrote in dismay last March to Mr Murray that effective management of our financial affairs seemed to be slipping out of our hands. As a public servant who has had reason to believe in the predominant influence on our economic development of a general public confidence founded on evidence of good management of the national economy, I am most disheartened by the prospect ahead.[1]

Of all the bleak predictions and warnings about the Irish economy in the troubled mid 1970s, Whitaker's carried considerable weight, not only because of his position as central bank governor, but because of his contribution to the reorientation and recovery of the Irish economy in the late 1950s and 1960s after the publication of his Programme for Economic Recovery in 1958, when he was secretary of the Department of Finance. For all the radicalism implied by a shift in economic orthodoxy that his 1958 plan represented, however, he was ultimately cautious and a believer in prudent management and the prime necessity of the country living within its means. Establishing what those means were was often a tortuous process during the 1970s, particularly given the impact of external events, including the oil crises prompted by instability in the Middle East at the end of 1973 (and again in 1979), which 'merely exacerbated, however abruptly, the underlying inflationary trend'. The reaction was 'to respond as if the crisis was of a once-for-all nature, whose consequences would soon vanish as a new surge of economic growth resolved the resultant problems'.[2] Advanced inflation, industrial disputes, the cost of security and rows about taxation were other considerations. In view of all these factors, Whitaker was decrying the practice, adopted by Ryan's predecessor George Colley, of deliberately incurring deficits on the current account of the budget, and was urging instead that what was important for the prospects of expanding the economy was to keep the total borrowing requirement to realistic and manageable levels and avoid aggravating inflation.

As Whitaker saw it, it was vital to contain public expenditure while also reducing the rate of growth of money incomes and avoid excessive pay settlements in what was now a small, open economy and therefore particularly vulnerable to external economic instability: 'As a community we are at present living vastly beyond our means [this exact phrase was later used by Charles Haughey in 1980 in his infamous address to the nation after he took over the leadership of Fianna Fáil], running an external deficit of around £250 million per annum or even more, but getting little value for this, and the associated foreign borrowing, in terms of real economic growth ... Profligate small countries can expect only short shrift from foreign lenders.'

Expansionary policies, he argued, directed towards economic growth, high employment and social advance, depended on a more moderate increase in money incomes: 'There is simply no room for any expansionary leverage, given existing price and external deficit conditions, if money incomes rise in future at the rate your department apprehends. It is only by trying in good time to propagate a general understanding of this truth that there is any chance of establishing reasonable expectations and attitudes.' As was often the case, Whitaker viewed economic policy through a social and human as well as an economic lens and his observations also touched on something that was of profound relevance in the 1970s – rising expectations and, alongside them, rising demand for a more equitable distribution of wealth, a scramble for pay increases and a fairer system of taxation.

The periods of the decade that were expansionist inevitably created more expectations. Many farmers did well out of EEC membership, for example, but this raised the issue of the balance to be struck between the agricultural and non-agricultural sectors of the economy. Whitaker's warning implied that for all the new opportunities, ill judged and reckless policies could lead to a return to the dark days that had propelled his original foray into Irish economic policy formulation. His letter also highlights the difficult balancing act that had to be performed in the 1970s by Richie Ryan and others charged with management of the economy, given the mix of good and bad news. There was great optimism in 1978, for example, about the speed with which the economy had expanded in the previous year, with an increase of 17,000 in non-agricultural employment and a rise in farm incomes of 20 per cent. It led to a boom in house prices 'which, by mid-year, had risen by more than 30 per cent over a year earlier' and consumer spending rose by 9 per cent, while at 7.6 per cent, the inflation rate was the lowest it had been since 1969. From August 1977 to August 1978, 'personal borrowings from the banks increased by an extra 45 per cent. It was the year of the big spenders.'[3] But such consumerism and buoyancy were short-lived as a result of the international oil dilemma and the scale of Irish borrowing.

Looking at the decade as a whole, the economy continued to grow at 4 per cent a year, similar to the 1960s, and the free trade involved in EEC membership proved beneficial overall. Irish industrial wages rose to almost equal UK levels by the end of the decade. But Irish consumer prices rose by 13.8 per cent a year from 1970 to 1977, 4 per cent above the EEC average.[4] There was alarm at the rise in budget deficits, leading to a severe budget in 1976, which Fianna Fáil promised to reverse in 1977 based on the notion that increased borrowing would lift the economy. But despite an annual increase of over 1 per cent at work, an expanding labour force meant that unemployment also rose from 5.5 per cent to more than 7 per cent. Whatever plans existed were rendered unworkable by the second oil crisis in 1979; in any case 'it seems unlikely that the plan would ever have worked as intended'. By the end of the decade national debt was in the region of 90 per cent of GDP 'so there was no scope to temper the loss of income with more borrowing'.[5] But it was borrowed anyway. As Joe Lee has characterised it, 'Ireland chose to treat itself as a closed economy for standard of living purposes, behaving as if no change had occurred in the world outside, insisting on borrowing to sustain increases in living standards that it could not earn for itself.'[6]

Or as economist Peter Neary saw it, behind the approach to planning economic expansion in the 1970s 'lurked dangers: the danger that we would neglect the external constraints facing our small open economy, the danger that we would not be flexible enough to respond to changes in these constraints and the danger that we would build up expectations of continued growth which could not be realised. All these dangers became real.' The reliance on foreign borrowing, the use of government spending to raise employment 'without attention to efficiency of that spending' and attempts to build up confidence in the private sector were paramount, and by the end of the decade these initiatives were brought together and carried further than they had been previously. Neary told an anecdote about a friend of his who remonstrated with him: '"Why are all you economists so pessimistic? Everywhere you look people are prosperous; they are buying new cars, buying new houses, taking foreign holidays." I had to point out to him that it was precisely that apparent prosperity, or rather that boom in consumption, which was the problem. For, whether the individuals could afford it or not, the country as a whole could not, and as a result we were building up foreign debt at an unsustainable rate.'[7]

It is interesting to see how some of these economic issues and dilemmas in the 1970s were dealt with, or avoided, at government level, the many battles they inspired and the attempts by the coalition government in particular to deal with national and international economic pressures. Richie Ryan, first elected to the Dáil for Fine Gael in 1959, as a 'brash young Dublin TD', had studied economics in UCD before qualifying as a solicitor and he remained an active partner in a solicitor's practice until his appointment as Minister for Finance in 1973. In opposition, he had been spokesperson on health and social welfare in the late 1960s, before taking responsibility for foreign affairs and Northern Ireland. His appointment to Finance was a surprise for many who expected it to be given to

FitzGerald (see Part I), but Ryan was intensely loyal to Cosgrave and 'resented FitzGerald as a presumptuous newcomer who wanted to take over the party' and as a 'peppery and combative operator', Ryan 'did not shirk conflict [with] FitzGerald and the liberal faction'.[8] Given the task facing Ryan as minister, his combativeness would be put to full use.

In 1975, the year after Whitaker's grave letter to Ryan about borrowing, Richard Stokes in the Department of the Taoiseach prepared notes for Liam Cosgrave to be used by him in interviews, and they outlined the nature of the mid-decade Irish economic problems:

> It is often difficult for strangers to understand the extent to which the Irish economy is open to influences from outside. This is illustrated by the fact that our imports represent more than 40 per cent of gross domestic product and exports more than 35 per cent. These figures compare with those for the US where, for example, exports are approximately 6 per cent of GDP and imports about 5 per cent; or with those of the UK where the corresponding figures are 22 per cent and 22 per cent respectively. The openness of our economy has left us particularly subject to the economic blizzard which has swept the world and was aggravated by the quintupling of oil prices. The greatest problems facing the economy are unemployment which, at more than 100,000 now represents more than 11 per cent of the workforce and inflation which at an average annual rate, estimated at 24 per cent, is putting employment and investment prospects in danger.[9]

Worries about inflation had been apparent for some time. At the end of the 1960s, Erskine Childers, for example, had written to Jack Lynch in his usual frank manner:

> the members of the government may feel that because we have failed to arrest inflation in the past no purpose is served by giving warnings. In my view we have a responsibility to tell the truth, even if our advice is not taken ... In previous propaganda exercises we have never compared profit increases with remuneration increases ... has the proportion that profits represents to prices ever been used as a counter-argument to all those people who constantly claim that they are not going to show any restraint unless everybody else does?

A fed-up Lynch replied dismissively that he and the Minister for Finance had indeed been issuing warnings of the difficult situation. The major concern here was pay agreements and the need to place a ceiling on them.[10] In its economic outlook for 1970, the Department of Finance pointed out that national income was estimated to have increased by 10.5 per cent in 1969 compared with 11 per cent in 1968. The main strategies to achieve full employment were based on making the country 'more competitive in freer international trading conditions in the 1970s' but the preliminary figures forecast for 1970 'represent a threat to this fundamental objective'.[11]

Some estimates put the inflation rate at 8.6 per cent between November 1970 and November 1971 while money earnings rose by 12.9 per cent in the same period. The average annual rate of inflation expected over the five years 1974–8 was 16 per cent.[12] It was recognised within Fianna Fáil during the 1973 election campaign that 'we will get knocked on prices and too long in office'.[13] Richie Ryan in 1973, only weeks into the job as Minister for Finance, found himself and his officials composing memoranda on inflation and the rate of increase in food prices in particular, at a time when it was clear that Irish Congress of Trade Unions (ICTU) workers' real incomes were effectively being eroded by price increases. The Irish Housewives Association, a champion of consumers' interests since its formation during the Second World War, was calling for a boycott of cheese following the latest price increase. ICTU estimated the rise of food prices at 16 per cent in the previous year at a time when there was a 4 per cent growth in the economy. Ryan's own figures suggested that consumer prices rose 11.5 per cent in 1973 and by May 1974 had increased to 16.5 per cent and could rise to 17 per cent in 1975.

At a meeting between representatives of ICTU and the government in April 1973, a member of ICTU's executive council referred to the 'poverty trap' that resulted, which was exacerbated by many people spending 30–40 per cent of their total income on housing at a time of high mortgage rates. Denis Larkin 'referred again to the question of interest rates and urged the provision of 100 per cent loans for the purchase of houses' and the exemption of food from VAT 'as an indication at least of the government's good faith'. Richie Ryan sought to emphasise the positives in the economy, specifically the 'great buoyancy in external trade'.[14] This is a reminder that contradictory assessments abounded during these years regarding the health of the economy and its various components, hampered by the volatility of international affairs and disagreements as to who was bearing the burden of the domestic response.

In terms of distribution of income, for example, there was perhaps little genuine desire to challenge the wealthy elites. In 1972 it was reported that Fine Gael was suggesting 'a mutinous spirit' could arise against efforts to bring about an incomes policy 'unless the few who made millions by speculation are at least subject to tax'. Fine Gael TD Paddy Donegan reassured those perturbed that 'Fine Gael did not wish in any way to interfere with our free enterprise system, however hotch potch it was'.[15] When it was in power, Fine Gael's middle-class supporters became nervous about the possibility of a wealth tax. In May 1974 John Kelly wrote to Cosgrave suggesting there was a strong feeling against it, amounting in some cases to 'outright declarations by deputies that they would vote against such legislation ... it will have to be pruned so radically as to be unrecognisable ... There is some feeling to the effect that the Minister for Finance does not appreciate how serious the position is politically or is now so temperamentally committed to the proposal that he finds it hard to concede anything.' Cosgrave responded, 'I fully understand the extent of the concern.'[16]

Many of Cosgrave's own well-heeled Dublin constituents were horrified at the government's talk of introducing wealth or capital gains tax. According to files from the Department of the Taoiseach, Fianna Fáil had considered this issue in 1970, when the Minister for Finance accepted that 'a case exists in principle for the taxation of wealth' in order to 'secure a more acceptable relationship between different categories of income'. But it was subsequently withdrawn from the cabinet agenda. In 1974 Richie Ryan returned to the issue in the context of the publication of a White Paper on capital taxation. The considerable unease on the part of Fine Gael supporters about this question was reflected in a letter to Cosgrave in February 1974 from Dr Edward Moore, Church of Ireland Bishop of Kilmore, Elphin and Ardagh, in which he warned the Taoiseach to tread carefully and not adopt the 'doctrinaire' approach of the Labour Party to such issues (which was ironic, given that the originator of the idea was Garret FitzGerald, who had been trying to get it accepted by Fine Gael as far back as the mid 1960s). Fine Gael senator Alexis Fitzgerald, a prominent solicitor, was more blunt in appealing to Cosgrave 'not to sell out to Labour', and warned that accountants and bankers would advise clients to look abroad for investment opportunities in the event of a capital gains tax.

Cosgrave's constituents in the Stillorgan and Blackrock areas of south County Dublin felt likewise, as did Redmond Gallagher, a hugely successful businessman in both industry and agriculture, who in the 1960s moved into stud farming and acquired the Ballygoran Stud in County Kildare. He pleaded with Cosgrave not to allow the tax 'as you are personally so interested in the blood-stock industry'. John Bruton, who was parliamentary secretary to the Minister for Education, was on the receiving end of protests from wealthy farmers in his Meath constituency, and alerted Cosgrave to the feeling that the tax idea had 'fundamentally shaken the confidence of our supporters', and that it would damage his electoral prospects due to his strong family connections with the Irish Farmers Association, who 'played no small part in my election to the Dáil'.

Another letter, representative of the views of many, was sent to Cosgrave by John and Ned McGuire:

> Since we sold Brown Thomas [the fashionable Dublin city-centre department store] both he and I have been living on capital, because as the law stood up to now as regards death duties, under the best legal advisers we both had created trusts for our families in a perfectly legal and accepted manner. Not only the McGuire family but many people like us and people who trusted in Fine Gael as a solid and reliable party for people who had created property by hard work and service to the community are shocked ... We have been responsible for the employment of thousands and thousands of Irish people ... There is alarm and consternation among decent people who expected better from a Fine Gael government that so many of us looked forward to and worked for so long to put in power. I am well aware that nowadays one must accept the fact that people of property, even moderate property, are living with ever creeping socialism which aims at the destruction and confiscation by taxation and other means, of their effects and privacy, but the present White Paper proposals, at least as far as I am concerned, are instant social infringement and confiscation of property.

The government's standard response to such correspondence was that a system of capital taxation to replace estate duties (as outlined in the White Paper) was in response to demands for a system which would enable people to pay capital tax by instalments over a lifetime, instead of obliging their next-of-kin 'to surrender a substantial slice of the family estate once or twice in a generation'. In his correspondence with Cosgrave in April, Richie Ryan was unapologetic, arguing that there was considerable avoidance and evasion of death duties, and that the state needed to recoup the loss of £13 million annually as a result of this. He also derided the 'highly emotional reaction' to one proposal for a wealth tax on property valued in excess of £50,000 at rates of from 1.5 to 2.5 per cent:

> For instance, some commentators have estimated that [the proposed tax] would yield £100 million annually. If this estimate is a correct one it means that there must be £4,000 million of wealth in private hands in this country conferring no benefit on the community and unknown to the Revenue Commissioners ... of course there is nothing radical or 'out left' in our proposals. As the White Paper indicates, all other progressive democracies have patterns of taxation of wealth on lines similar to those proposed by us.

The tax was introduced in 1975, levied at 1 per cent of the value of assets in excess of £100,000. The family home was exempt, as were bloodstock, livestock and pension rights.[17]

By the beginning of 1977, Richie Ryan found the pressures to exclude working capital from the tax a step too far; as he saw it, it was already so diluted that he could not offer any more exemptions. Dermot Nally in the Department of the Taoiseach also had representations made to him about Doyle Hotel Group's owner P. V. Doyle, who had maintained that 'effort, risk and investment becomes senseless' due to the wealth tax. In 1978 Feargal Quinn, founder of the Superquinn supermarket company, pointed out to George Colley, who had taken back his post as Minister for Finance from Ryan following Fianna Fáil's election victory, that there was also the anomaly of an Irish family owned company having to pay an additional dividend each year to its shareholders so that the wealth tax could be paid by these shareholders while non-national shareholders did not have to. In February 1978 George Colley announced its abolition. Quinn responded, 'you will not find us wanting in responding to your initiative'.[18]

– FORTY-THREE –

THE COST OF LIVING, POVERTY AND GIVING UP MEAT

At the other end of the social and economic spectrum, in 1971, there were 717,000 people, including 213,000 children, dependent wholly or in part on social security payments of some kind. There were 15,000 local authority housing applicants and an estimated 160,000 small farmers and dependants living on non-viable holdings. In some deprived areas of the inner city, conditions still seemed Dickensian. The Pearse Street branch of a group called People before Profit, for example, conducted a survey: 'of all respondents 78 per cent had no baths, but worse still, 71 per cent had no hot water'.[1]

The challenge early in the decade, according to an editorial in *Hibernia* in 1971 was 'the eradication of that extreme degree of poverty which still persists in patches'. The same year Garret FitzGerald reiterated his concerns about 'the alienation of the Dublin working class from the mainstream' of Irish life, drawing attention to a 1969 survey that revealed that only 6.5 per cent of Dublin-born residents of Dublin held professional, higher administrative, managerial or executive positions, but 30 per cent of immigrants to Dublin from other large cities held such posts.[2]

These concerns were exacerbated by the shortcomings of the Third Programme for Economic Expansion, covering the years 1969–72 (which projected an annual growth rate of 1.75 per cent and was entitled Economic and Social Development). George Colley admitted in February 1971 that 'it has not been as successful as the others'.[3] In the words of historian Joe Lee it was 'quietly shelved',[4] and by the end of that year the number of unemployed in Ireland at 69,000 was the highest in two decades. Much was made of this by Fine Gael, which rounded on the government for the 'disaster stage' that had been reached in the underdeveloped areas of Ireland due to decreases in population and the 'fall in the number of young people of marriageable age'. Garret FitzGerald decried 'the flagrant dropping of output targets for agricultural products from this programme, which makes it impossible to assess just where things have been going wrong in agriculture'. He also referred to 'the unhappy combination of shortfalls in output and unplanned excess of expenditure especially in the public sector, which were a feature of the second programme [and] have continued since that programme was abandoned and replaced by the third programme. Little or nothing seems to have been learnt from the experience of the second programme.'[5]

John F. O'Carroll of the ITGWU, in a letter to Jack Lynch in October 1972, asserted that 70 per cent of the wealth of the country was in the hands of 5 per cent of the population. The following month he wrote again: 'I am quite sure you accept that there's far too much brash display of wealth by those who seem to come about it very easily'. He argued that the current system of economic and social development was 'ad hoc' and that the power vested in semi-state companies meant that 'a whole set of new empires is being set up.'[6]

Given the prevalence of poverty, it was little wonder that some were forced to resort to moneylenders. The controversial programme broadcast by RTÉ's *Seven Days* team on moneylending in November 1969 had sparked serious controversy and led to a Tribunal of Inquiry in 1970 (see Part III). Evidence given at the tribunal recounted the experiences of some of those at the mercy of moneylenders:

'When she was first going to work she needed a smock or something of that sort ... it cost £2 and she hadn't it so she borrowed it from Mrs Ahern. She agreed to repay the £2 at the rate of 10 shillings in the £. She obviously didn't make much money in the job because she could never pay off the principal. Her mother found out she was in the hands of a moneylender but by this time the girl had paid £28.'[7]

Others involved were aware of 'violence and strong-arm tactics'. There was a conflict of evidence between Gardaí and RTÉ; Jack Lynch suggested 'the important thing here is to ensure that the extent of this social evil as it has been described will be identified, will be pursued and the Gardaí can come to grips with those responsible for the evil'.[8] Despite the tribunal report's conclusion that proper care was not taken in the planning, production and presentation of the programme, it was acknowledged that 'the Tribunal noted that before the programme the Gardaí had not considered that illegal money lending was a great problem; their investigations occasioned by the programme disclosed to them that money lending was so prevalent in the city as to constitute a minor problem and that a number of unlicensed money lenders carried on business in other areas. To this extent and because the public had been made aware of the problem, the result of the programme had been beneficial.'[9]

The tribunal did find that children's allowance books were commonly taken as security for loans and 'repayments are secured by taking advantage of the fear of borrowers'. The RTÉ Authority was quite defiant, insisting that 'the programme was authentic in respect of the existence of moneylending. Many social workers, clergy, medical officers and others gave evidence that illegal moneylending was widespread and that it was fundamentally a social problem surrounded by an extreme secrecy that tended to prevent its being brought to the knowledge of the Gardaí.'[10]

There was no consensus, however, on how to measure poverty and its alleviation. In 1972, Trinity College Dublin economist Patrick Lyons estimated that slightly less than 5 per cent of the adult population in Northern Ireland owned 47 per cent of the total personal wealth whereas in the Republic 'slightly over 5 per cent of the adult population own as much as 72 per cent of total personal wealth', while 65 per cent in the Republic and 60 per cent in the North possessed no personal wealth at all, though the welfare state in the North was a lot more developed than in the Republic.[11]

But the following year social policy academic Anthony Coughlan maintained that in real terms, children's allowances were as good 'if not better' in the Republic than in Northern Ireland and that this represented 'a remarkable achievement for a country with one third of its population dependent children and with an income per head just two thirds of the UK level'.[12] Overall, public expenditure per head of the population on social services (education, health and social welfare) in 1971/2 had been 91 per cent higher in Northern Ireland than the Republic; by 1973 it was 60 per cent.[13] But at the end of 1974 a report published by the European Commission revealed that the Republic had the lowest expenditure on social services in relation to the GNP of all the members of the EEC at 15.3 per cent, compared to Holland's 26.3 per cent, for example. It was suggested in 1979 that in the Republic, 'after several years of debate' economists had come to accept figures that indicated 'that about 5 per cent of the people own 70 per cent of the personal wealth', 20 per cent were living in poverty and that the whole tax system needed to be radically overhauled.[14]

In March of that year writer Anthony Cronin, a frequent contributor to *Magill* magazine, suggested that if there was a boom in Ireland, it was for an elite: there was no shortage of phrases being uttered about prosperity – 'there's plenty of money in the country' or 'there's still lots of money about' or 'there's plenty of money stirring' – but it was confined to those at the top and it represented a polarisation between town and country and between 'those classes and sections of classes which are ahead of the inflationary game and those which aren't'.[15] In the same vein, it had been maintained earlier in the decade that autonomous regional development was not happening and that there was a growing economic imbalance between the western and eastern halves of the country; Labour politician and sociologist Michael D. Higgins was vocal as western Ireland was 'in revolt' with protest meetings at the end of 1971 and denunciations of politicians; it was maintained that Leinster had 62.9 per cent of the jobs of the country and Connacht only 5 per cent.[16] In October 1973 a report commissioned by the Labour Party entitled 'Poverty in Ireland' underlined what it termed 'the statistics of shame'. It estimated that 40 per cent of all full-time farmers in the western counties earned gross margins of £400 or less per year, while in relation to housing, another report contended that 'we delude ourselves if we think we can equalise the social distribution of life chances by expanding educational opportunities while so many children live in slums without baths, decent lavatories, leisure facilities, room to explore and the space to dream'.[17]

But there was also vagueness about some of the assertions of poverty, which was acknowledged; quantification of the extent of poverty was hampered by lack of basic research, information, definition and methodology. Séamus Ó Cinnéide of the Economic and Social Research Institute (ESRI), which had been established in 1960 to conduct empirical research on economic and social change to inform public policy-making and analyse Irish economic data in an international context, estimated the numbers in poverty in five major categories: those aged sixty-five and older, widows and wives with absent husbands, farmers, especially small farmers, other self-employed persons and low-income employees: 'the total figure arrived at was 664,000, or 24 per cent of the entire population, and including no less than 21 per cent of all children under 14 years of age'.[18]

In 1974 journalist Brian Trench interviewed Sr Stanislaus Kennedy, director of the Kilkenny Social Services Centre and chairperson of the committee to advise the government on combating poverty (the idea of launching such a programme within the EEC was proposed by the Irish government in 1973). She had noted a change – 'it's fashionable to be concerned about poverty' – but she suggested that family poverty was still 'a difficult concept for many people to understand' with the survival of an idea that it was a consequence of personal inadequacy. Given that an estimated one in six children was brought up in poverty, she suggested there was a need to look at the social structure and more research to be conducted into that.[19]

In tandem, there was proposed reform of the social assistance services. Those availing of these assistances in the early 1970s included those receiving old-age and blind pensions (113,000 recipients), widows and orphans pensions (17,000), deserted wives allowances (1,400), unemployment assistance (43,000), disabled persons' maintenance allowance (23,000) and home assistance (16,000).[20] A memorandum on social welfare in January 1973 suggested re-examination of these assistances was a matter of 'extreme urgency' and that, unlike in other European countries, in Ireland it was 'difficult to identify a clear cut philosophy underlying the schemes'.

In Ireland, for example, 98 per cent of the total child population benefited from child allowance in contrast to France (80 per cent), Belgium (73 per cent), Italy (45 per cent) and Germany (28.4 per cent). The first child was excluded in many countries. If the first child was excluded in Ireland it was reckoned the dependent figure could be reduced to 65 per cent. But the rates for the 1,006,000 children were regarded by the department as 'derisory': a family with one child receiving 12p a week, with three children, 33p a week for each child and with seven children 44p a week for each child. These payments compared 'very unfavourably' with other countries (an assertion that contradicted Anthony Coughlan's research): in Britain and Northern Ireland the rate was 90p a week for the second child and £1 a week for each subsequent child. In Ireland 'because the present coverage of the allowance is so wide any general increase in rates is very costly'. There was also the issue in any proposed reform of the difficulty of means testing 353,000 families; it was preferred to look at excluding families with one child and increase the rates for those with two or more to the UK levels. A Fianna Fáil policy in 1973 on social and economic issues aimed by 1980 to 'drastically reduce and in many cases abolish the differences which exist between the two parts of our own country in these areas'.[21]

In relation to old-age pensions, Liam Cosgrave received a succession of letters in 1973 stressing it was time to deliver on the election promise to reduce the qualifying age and increase the amount. It was estimated that the cost to the exchequer of reducing the qualifying age to sixty-six from seventy would be £13.5 million in a single year.[22] The commitment was honoured, and in November 1974, a draft White Paper on the economic situation, provisionally entitled 'A National Partnership', emphasised the need for equity and social justice, arguing that the budgets of 1973 and 1974 had been 'expansionary and socially progressive'.[23] Is this a verdict that withstands scrutiny? Undoubtedly, there were important strides made in relation to social welfare. Frank Cluskey, who as parliamentary secretary to the Minister for Health and Social Welfare was delegated full authority over the social welfare budget, introduced biannual rather than yearly increases in payment levels. He also oversaw a threefold increase to £274 million in exchequer allocation for social welfare during the coalition's lifetime, and an increase of 125 per cent in benefits, considerably ahead of wages and prices.

As recorded by Stephen Collins,

> Welfare expenditure as a percentage of GNP rose from 6.5 to 10.5 per cent during the lifetime of the coalition ... The qualifying age for the old-age pension was brought down from seventy to sixty-six and groups like unmarried mothers and prisoners' wives received allowances for the first time. Cosgrave went on record after the start of the oil crisis to say that the poor were not going to bear the brunt of the problem and he was true to his word. The political return to the coalition for all its concern for social welfare was absolutely zero. Richie Ryan recalls the tempestuous arguments he used to have with the late Frank Cluskey around the cabinet table over the scale of the welfare increases being sought by Labour. He chuckles at the memory of meeting Cluskey for the first time after the 1977 election debacle: 'Jayzus Richie, you were right. You always said we'd get no fucking thanks for all the welfare increases' was the Labour man's blunt assessment.[24]

Other achievements highlighted by the Department of Social Welfare reports from 1972–5 included the extension of social insurance protection to non-manual workers, social assistance allowances for single women aged fifty-eight and over, and substantial relaxation of the means test for non-contributory pensions and allowances as well as the national committee on pilot schemes to combat poverty as part of the social action programme of the EEC.[25]

But inflation (which an EEC report estimated at 18.9 per cent in November 1976, the highest in the Community) continued to cause concern as the decade drew to a close. The increase in the rate of inflation, as disclosed by the consumer price index, was from 12.4 per cent in the year to mid May 1979, to 13.6 per cent in the year to mid August 1979, with Des O'Malley, the Minister for Industry and Commerce, as a result insisting on the need to minimise price increases.[26] Throughout the decade, at the household level, the shifting fortunes in the health of the Irish economy were felt most obviously in the cost of necessities, including fuel. Between 1960 and 1972, the year before VAT came in to force in Ireland, there was a 129.5 per cent increase in the price of coal, for example, and the price of gas rose by 76.5 per cent in the same period.[27] (The implementation of VAT was a product of EEC harmonisation, but the rates of VAT were not harmonised.)

Concern about fuel supply and prices had remained constant during the decade. In 1974 Dublin Fianna Fáil TD Seán Moore suggested the shortage of fuel was less of a problem than the equitable distribution of it: 'There are areas of the greater Dublin conurbation where one can have all the fuel one wants, the ability to pay being the only test.'[28] The oil crises exacerbated the situation and it was suggested at government level that such crises could be offset by 'prospects for discovering offshore oil' (see pages 525–30).[29]

By the end of the decade, concern was being expressed about the sale of cheap turf briquettes. Their maximum retail prices were fixed by order and it was suggested in the Department of the Taoiseach that 'turf products are cheap compared to most other fuels. This under pricing of turf must encourage extravagance in the use of a wasting asset and is undesirable since, with the exhaustion of turf supplies the Board [Bord na Mona; the Irish Peat Board] will have to change its function completely.' The fuel crisis had reached the point by August 1979 where, given the oil requirements of educational institutions of 5.5 million gallons for national schools, the Minister for Education was considering a possible solution involving 'operating a 4 day week during the heating season and a 6 day week at other periods of the school year'. Des O'Malley ruled out at that stage the introduction of fuel rationing, but if the uncertainty continued, rationing 'may be the only possible alternative'.[30]

Ireland had a 75 per cent dependence on oil for its energy needs, a reliance that became all the more troublesome with the petrol shortage in 1979. Car sales had boomed in 1978 when an estimated 100,000 new cars came on the road. It was predicted in *Magill* in July 1979 that more petrol queues were likely, but also that 'the ESB has warned of power cuts, Bord na Mona says turf briquette supplies will be short and the oil companies predict they will not be able to meet demand for home heating oil. Des O'Malley's stand [to get prices moderated] as David against the Goliath of the oil companies failed. Now, the air is thick with suggestions for ways of getting around the oil companies, diversifying our energy sources or cutting back on oil consumption. But the conservation efforts being boosted by a publicity drive this month may be too little, too late.'[31]

Household budget surveys in the 1970s revealed much about consumption and the prioritisation of domestic income. One large-scale survey conducted by the Central Statistics Office during 1973 covered a random sample of 7,748 urban and rural private households nationwide, the first time rural as well as urban households had been included in such surveys. Total average weekly expenditure was £41.03: £45.04 for urban households and £35.81 for rural dwellers. In absolute terms, the urban figure was 112 per cent higher than in 1966, and even 'allowing for price increases during the intervening 7 year period, the volume of expenditure per household rose by more than one quarter (28 per cent) for urban households'. The average household consisted of 4.01 persons; in it, food was the main expense and constituted 32 per cent of total expenditure.[32]

There was also a particular focus on the compilation of household budget reviews. Such surveys were initiated in April 1974, when fieldwork on the 1973 survey terminated. The results of the 1977 annual urban inquiry, covering 1,893 households, revealed that the average weekly expenditure in urban households was £45 in 1973, £75 in 1976 and £87 in 1977, and with an overall increase in value terms of 16.4 per cent between 1976 and 1977 and 92.2 per cent between 1973 and 1977: 'The survey shows that over the 4 years 1973–7, the average household expenditure increased in the fuel and light group by 121 per cent and on consumer durables such as furniture, carpets, electrical appliances etc. by 109 per cent while expenditure on food increased by only 84 per cent in the same period. Expenditure on clothing and footwear, on tobacco and on miscellaneous goods increased by 59 per cent, 54 per cent and 117 per cent respectively in the four year period.'[33] In the Dublin and Dun Laoghaire region, in relation to average household expenditure, the food categories on which most money was spent were white bread, meat (mostly beef and veal), sweets, chocolate and ice-cream and fresh milk, butter, potatoes, pork and rashers and sugar, while there was a low expenditure on fish, vegetables and fresh fruit. The average total food expenditure was £25.40 while average expenditure on alcohol and tobacco was £8.95.[34]

The results of the household budget survey for 1976 also revealed that the main outlay was food, amounting to approximately 29 per cent of total household expenditure, while 'expenditure on alcoholic drink [at 5.5 per cent] was considerably understated ... this phenomenon is, on international experience, a normal feature of household expenditure surveys'. The figure for tobacco was 3.9 per cent, clothing 8.6 per cent, fuel and light 5.2 per cent and transport 11.1 per cent.[35] It was maintained in *Hibernia* in 1974 that there was little evidence that the National Prices Commission was effective in actually holding down prices, pointing to inflation that witnessed the consumer price index over the twelve months to mid February 1974 increasing by 134.5 per cent with individual prices of detergents up 26 per cent, TV rentals up 22 per cent, cornflakes up 29 per cent and margarine up 30 per cent.[36] But the commission continued to issue monthly reports, and a memorandum from the Department of Industry and Commerce in March 1978 referred to arrangements it had made with RTÉ to broadcast weekly retail prices of fruit and vegetables for the Dublin area which had been collected by prices inspectors, with a monthly broadcast of meat prices also initiated.

A survey conducted in November and December 1977 to compare grocery prices in Dublin, Belfast and Liverpool on 224 common items revealed that the total cost of the items in Dublin and Belfast was practically the same, while Dublin was 7 to 8 per cent higher in cost than Liverpool. The Prices Commission also did work on 'least cost diets' and found that consumption of chicken in the Republic had risen from 19.7 million birds in 1974 to an estimated 22.7 million in 1977, of which imports were 1.6 million (from Northern Ireland); supermarkets sold 25 per cent of them, small and medium retail outlets 20 per cent and catering and institutions 55 per cent. Ireland was regarded as a country which was 'relatively well fed'; at 1975 prices it was 'theoretically possible' to feed a family of two adults and two children at a nutritionally adequate level for only £4.55 per week. The 'grave disadvantage is the monotony of this diet which includes only five items' – chips, custard (as a basis for milk consumption), brown bread, liver and carrots'. Obviously, such diets 'are not intended for practical use'.

Taking a lead from American research, more detailed consumption surveys were undertaken by the nutrition and dietetics department of the Kevin Street College of Technology in Dublin. In 1975 it was found to be possible to feed two adults and two children for a week at a cost of £5.97 with eleven food items: oatmeal, cornflakes, milk, white sugar, white bread, brown bread, margarine, calf liver, onions, potatoes and custard. As was acknowledged, 'despite the dullness and apparently fattening character of the week's food, it in fact conforms with all the recommended daily allowances of the main nutrients, supplying adequate Vitamin C, iron, calcium etc., more than enough Vitamin A and only just reaching the recommended allowances for carbohydrates and calories'.[37] Research on low-cost but nutritious diets carried out by Trinity College Dublin students and student dietitians in Kevin Street involved devising a menu to feed a family in 1977 at a cost of £17.43. The six families who tried it made clear their preference for butter over margarine ('this appeared to be disliked on social grounds – they would not want to offer it to guests'), their view it contained insufficient meat ('unsuitability of sausages as a main meat dish') and there was 'non acceptance of porridge'. The menu involved had included porridge, plain biscuits, bread, margarine, liver, custard, chicken, potatoes, bananas, beans, cabbage, peaches and stewing beef.[38]

Continued uncertainty about the cost of living and inflation prompted resentment against the coalition government. In March 1977, a resident of Dublin 4 wrote to Cosgrave: 'We are literally impoverished since the coalition took over, and it continues to go from bad to worse. Is it any wonder that Frank Hall on RTÉ calls one of the ministers the Minister for Hardships? As I see it, I would call it the government for hardships ... I have £7 per week and I don't smoke. I can't afford to. Of course, we had to give up meat long ago.'[39] Nor, it seemed, was the Minister for Finance immune from distaste about the consequences of his own government's policies: *Hibernia* gleefully reported in February 1976 that 'the most unpopular man in cabinet, Richie Ryan, is feeling the pinch these days. Recently, he and his good wife went into a well-known hardware and ironmongers store in Dublin to buy some bathroom fittings for his house – staggered by the total price asked for of £700, Richie refused to buy when he heard that the unexpectedly high sum was due to VAT.'[40]

But there had also been, by 1976, a 'spectacular rise in personal saving', which increased from £384 million in 1974 to £597 million in 1975.[41] In March 1973, Allied Irish Banks had spent £4.3 million on a site in Merrion Row, Dublin, for its new headquarters. There was an increase in bank lending in 1978 as land and house prices soared (see Part VII) and there was also much evidence of a proliferation of modern household items such as new washing machines and televisions, and by 1979, the arrival of the home video cassette machine that cost over £700. Journalist Paul Tansey, educated at Trinity College Dublin and the London School of Economics, suggested 'It was President Hoover's dream come through. A car in every garage and a chicken in every pot. In the year to mid August 1978 alone, personal lending increased by 45 per cent,' but by 1979, excessive credit growth was being frowned upon as a new 'get tough' policy witnessed a restrictive stance on credit policy.[42]

In relation to the haves and the have nots and those somewhere in between, there was a colourful description early in 1978 of the enthusiasm of shoppers who were bargain hunting in the January sales: 'Packed shops, St John's ambulance in attendance, tough faced women with scarves and tartan shopping bags jostling and clawing, long rails of off colour dresses with huge "sale" labels on them, harassed shop attendants and a general air of hyperactivity as housewives and some househusbands search for that elusive deal – the bargain.'[43] The grocery market in Ireland was estimated to be worth £250 million by 1977, and in that year British Home Stores opened on a prime site in O'Connell Street ('more than a touch of irony in the fact that the new branch is to be situated beside the GPO'). Woolworth's also had two branches in Dublin city, alongside Irish stores including Arnotts, Roches, Penneys, Dunnes, Switzers and Brown Thomas. It was suggested in *Magill* magazine in October 1977 that 'despite the so-called recession – or perhaps because of it – people have money in their pockets and are prepared to spend it'.[44]

Consumers were also offered a heightened awareness of their rights. In early 1978, a Consumer Information Act was passed – in effect, 'truth-in-advertising legislation' – which made it an offence for a seller to give a misleading description of goods or services and created a Consumer

Affairs Office. But the Dáil had still not appointed a director seven months after passing the new law and there was criticism that the prospective holder of the position would be a civil servant.[45] In October 1978, *Magill* was moved to establish what it rather grandiosely termed 'a new consumer affairs department' which insisted that supermarkets were not the answer to everything, drawing attention to a Prices Commission report that accused the supermarkets of making excessive profits on fruit and vegetables. *Magill* suggested better value for these products was to be found in the greengrocers'.[46] There was also comment and analysis in 1979 about the fate of Austin Kennan, a civil servant who had been appointed examiner of restrictive practices six years previously and who had begun a public inquiry in 1977, only to be sacked by Des O'Malley, supposedly because he was 'impolitic and indiscreet to make public his thinking', in the words of Judge Séamus Henchy of the Supreme Court. As others saw it, he 'took on the big guns of the cinema business, travel agents, the petrol businesses and the grocery trade. They wanted him out; he got the boot.'[47]

– FORTY-FOUR –

LOCAL FINANCE, ECONOMIC PATRIOTISM, COMPETITIVENESS AND EMPLOYMENT

Another issue that received much attention throughout the decade was the issue of local finance generally and rate payments in particular. The paying of rates was undoubtedly unpopular and frequently resented, but it did give local government some autonomy and control. A White Paper on local finance and taxation in 1971 as well as an inter-departmental committee on the rating system provided an opportunity to reflect on issues that historically had caused much tension, in terms not just of demands for initiating a better system of local finance but also of delineating areas of responsibility between central and local government. There was even a suggestion that local authorities should be 'empowered to operate lotteries for the purpose of relieving rates'.[1]

For some, the paying of rates was also a moral issue. A Church of Ireland Bishop, Edward Moore, for example, suggested in a letter to Jack Lynch in January 1970 that the relief of rates was necessary on dwelling houses: 'In a Christian country the people ought to be encouraged to own and live in better houses, not be heavily taxed for doing so.' At the root of the problem, he saw a strong urban bias and a fundamental discrimination against landowners: 'I believe that your rate policy is a contributory factor to the massive decline in the rural population.' ACTRA, the central body for residents associations, also decried the imposition of rates as a policy that was 'out-moded and out-dated and bears heavily on those who have to pay without any question of ability to pay'. The same year a seventy-five-year-old man from Scarriff in County Clare wrote to the president to explain that he could not afford his rates: 'I am 75 years old having been in the First World War, the War of Independence and the civil war. My income is £6.6.0 per week .... my rates have been increased from £6.5.0 to £13.0.0. I am living in a labourer's cottage.' The following year, Jack Lynch was informed of 'a very worried and harassed widow whose rates last year were the unbearable burden of £151.20'. She was told she was not eligible for a waiver as her income after payment of rates was £9 per week whereas the Corporation's limit for a rates waiver was £7 per week.[2]

There were also complaints from the commercial sector. As the minister responsible for local government, Fianna Fáil's Bobby Molloy received representations in 1970 from small businesses in Roscommon that were closing due to the rates burden. It was pointed out in reply that state grants as a proportion of local authority income were higher in the western counties – 74 per cent from state grants as against 20.5 per cent from rates, whereas in Dublin the state grant provided 34.3 per cent and the rates 42 per cent.[3]

In 1971, Lynch gave a speech to the Wexford Chamber of Commerce and referred to the difficulties of local finance and the failure of Wexford Corporation to strike a rate. He suggested an alternative tax system to the rates 'would imply a further reduction in the degree of financial autonomy which local authorities have at present ... the overall burden would still have to be carried by the community', indicating that Fianna Fáil was not yet ready to commit itself to rate abolition; its later conversion to abolition proved popular in its manifesto for the general election of 1977 that led to a landslide victory.

In the early 1970s Bobby Molloy pointed out that the health levy (imposed by the regional health boards) usually accounted for the greater part of county council rate increases and it was the health levy that was the core of the dilemma. Exhibiting his customary directness and often urgency, in July 1971 Molloy sent his observations on the White Paper on local finance to other members of the cabinet and summed up the impact that the health levy issue was having on the robustness of local finance, but also underlined that the government was not going to contemplate the abolition of rates at this stage:

> The real issue in local finance, is not, of course, the abolition of the rating system for we simply cannot afford to do away with a tax which

> yields over £60 million. But we must reform the rating system; otherwise public opinion may force us to scrap it altogether and secondly, we must ensure that the system is not made to carry burdens which it is obviously unable to bear. The problem at the moment is, simply, that the demands on the rating system are increasing very rapidly (the biggest single factor being the cost of the health services) and that these demands are already entirely disproportionate to the capacity of the system. The result is that very serious hardship is being caused for many ratepayers ... the White Paper comes down in favour of reducing the demands on local authorities as the obvious means of relieving the strain on existing local resources. What is involved here is the gradual termination of levies on local authorities (the principal levy, of course, being the demand from the health boards) and the gradual transfer or termination of certain services not appropriate to local authorities ... The key to the whole problem of local finance is the stabilisation of the cost to local authorities of the health services. These services are no longer directly administered by local authorities and yet they absorb about 50 per cent of the amount actually raised in rates. This whole question of the burden of the health services on the rates is urgent because it is certain to become a major issue in the next 2–3 months when local authorities, for the first time, will come up against the reality of having to strike a rate to finance substantially increased demands from the regional health boards. If we do not take action, I am certain that we will be faced with a rates crisis much worse than anything we have had to face before.[4]

Fianna Fáil was warned on numerous occasions that the rates issue would cost it votes. In February 1973, Lynch received a letter from a committed FF voter ('as long as I live') who had received a rates arrears bill for £25: 'I used to save the rates but this year I could not, the weather was so cold ... I don't want anyone to know only yourself. I would sooner die than ask anyone for anything.'[5] In seeking office, Fine Gael and Labour had promised rates would be reduced by transferring health charges and housing subsidies to central taxation and at the end of March 1973 the Department of Local Government reduced rates by 25 per cent, but they remained contentious.

As Minister for Finance from 1973–7, Richie Ryan was not convinced that the system of local finance was working. He gave a speech to the Institute of Certified Public Accountants in November 1976 in which he identified the need to re-examine local authority spending, as well as free school transport, disability benefits, children's allowances and farmers exemption from rates, as possible ways to cut public expenditure. He maintained that this was not 'budget thinking' but merely to open a debate on how expenditure might be cut. Charles Haughey described his suggestions as 'mind boggling' and promised that FF would 'go down fighting' to resist them.

But he also faced incredulity from his own cabinet. The Minister for Local Government James Tully rounded on him, demanding to know why he had spoken like that about local finance, arguing that the government needed a strong hand on the rates issue: 'The effect must be, I think, to further weaken the government's position on rates and on local government finance generally – something that could cost the exchequer the whole amount (£107 million in 1976) collected annually in rates.' Tully also suggested that the idea of a parliamentary committee to control current expenditure in the context of local finance would amount to centralised control which would 'cut right across the concept of local democracy the government is committed to fostering'.[6] But electoral considerations ultimately won out the following year, when Fianna Fáil committed itself to abolishing rates on private dwellings and the coalition made 'broadly similar' proposals.[7]

One of the historians of local government in Ireland, Mary Daly, has suggested that a healthy revenue from rates or some alternative local tax was a prerequisite for devolved government, but 'continued pressure for a reduction or removal of rates from farmers and urban householders alike and the electoral imperatives of party politics as seen in both the 1973 and 1977 general elections destroyed the prospect of greater devolution of local government'.[8]

In terms of supporting local produce, a 'buy Irish' campaign, originally launched in 1964, was deemed, by 1972, to be less than effective. The ITGWU suggested it was too 'ad hoc' and needed to be more systematic. Minister for Finance George Colley had informed Lynch in 1970 that 'the larger manufacturers do not appear to be interested'. In January 1972 the *Sunday Independent* newspaper reported on a brief 'buy Irish' campaign conducted before Christmas (a more concerted campaign was conducted from 1975). This was part of a 'war on prices' sponsored by the Irish Housewives Association in which leading women's organisations, including the

Irish Countrywomen's Association, took part: 'Several women reported buying goods – shirts in this case – which were stamped "Made in Ireland" on the package and "Made in Britain" on the garment itself.' Well over a hundred women 'reported that when they went to buy the Irish goods they required, the shops didn't have them in stock'.[9]

In the summer of 1972 Fintan Coogan, a Galway TD, caused some mirth within the fruit and vegetable trade when he fulminated about the sale of 'Dutch cabbage' on the street market in Galway: 'It is absolutely ridiculous that Dutch cabbage is being sold in shops in Galway. I can't see that this country needs to import cabbages and other vegetables – it's like bringing coal to Newcastle.' As was pointed out, 'Nobody imports cabbage to Ireland from Holland; Dutch cabbage is in fact a variety of cabbage grown here just like other varieties with names such as Copenhagen cabbage and Spring cabbage.'[10]

Irish industry was put under scrutiny by a Committee on Industrial Progress (which had been established in 1968) and which in April 1973 in a memorandum for the government, stressed the importance of the state taking responsibility for creating a climate where 'job changing' would be accepted. It also drew attention to manufacturing industry and the 'widespread weaknesses in the marketing and product policy functions'. The increase in Irish unit wage costs since 1966, which was well above the average of other countries, meant 'the competitiveness of Irish goods has been diminished'. Workers and managers had been conditioned, it was suggested, to work in a protected home market and needed to adapt and change: 'There has been a tendency to blame factory closures on free trade even where it was not a factor.' One example given was that of the furniture industry. The majority of the 150 firms in this sector employed fewer than twenty people each; the value of gross output in 1972 was estimated at £10.5 million and less than 8 per cent of that output was exported. Between 1964 and 1972 the share of the home market taken by imports increased from 10 per cent to 25 per cent and employment fell by nearly 300 people to 3,500.[11]

Some native firms expressed fears about the competition they would face with Ireland joining the EEC, particularly in certain parts of the country where the welfare of whole towns depended on one factory. One example given in 1971 was the jute industry (processing natural fibres to make mostly traditional types of jute products like sacks and bags). There was just one firm involved in this with factories in Clara in Offaly and Waterford; it employed 600 in Clara and 400 in Waterford. It was pointed out that in Clara it was 'the only source of industrial employment in the area ... the town of Clara has a population of something less than 3,000 and the welfare of its inhabitants and, to some extent, of the surrounding area is almost entirely dependent on the fortunes of this one industry'; there were obvious fears about the bigger jute producers in the enlarged European community.[12]

But there were also jobs that could not be filled. The Department of Tourism and Transport reported in May 1978 the concerns of Bord Fáilte, that there was a 'severe shortage' of hotel staff throughout the country. The new Berkley Court Hotel, offering 'excellent pay and conditions', was unable to obtain the staff it needed ('the industry itself has not a very good image as a work provider and that may account for the present difficulty'). Because of this, it was worried about a request from the West German Labour Market Institute to embark on a recruitment campaign to get Irish workers to fill vacancies in the hotel and catering trade in Germany and 'would prefer that the emigration of catering staff should not be facilitated'.[13]

External trade figures received much attention during these years. Total exports to EEC countries in the year ended September 1971 amounted to £51.4 million; to Britain £278.8 million, Northern Ireland £64.1 million and the USA and Canada £66.7 million.[14] The Shannon Free Airport Development Company had, since 1968, been concerned with the promotion of industry in the Clare, Limerick and Tipperary region (the mid west) as well as its work at Shannon airport involving industrial, tourism and airport promotion. In the year to March 1974, twelve new firms had either commenced or announced their intention to establish in the region outside Shannon while seven new firms had commenced operation at Shannon Industrial Estate: 'Of the total national exports of manufactured goods in 1973, 10.9 per cent came from Shannon.'[15] In 1975 exports of manufactured goods to markets outside the UK represented 50 per cent of total Irish exports for the first time. Ireland exported goods to the value of almost £4 million to the United Arab Emirates in 1976. The following year Michael Begley, the parliamentary secretary to the Minister for Local Government, reported to Garret FitzGerald on the sale of eleven sika deer from the Killarney National Park to His Highness Sheikh Mohammed Rashid Almaktoum of Dubai; they were flown out from Cork airport on the Sheikh's private plane.[16]

In 1975 it was decided that special measures were necessary to combat adverse balance of payments and it was clear that certain sectors of the manufacturing industry were struggling, with the footwear industry 'the most seriously affected as regards unemployment' with a belief that there was a need to regulate imports. Given that the overall number of unemployed had exceeded 100,000, the ITGWU expressed grave concerns about 'the defects within the EEC structure' but the Minister for Agriculture and Fisheries, Mark Clinton, insisted that protecting home industries against imports was not the answer; curtailing steep wages was.[17]

The first results of the Labour Force survey in 1977 suggested that at the end of April 1977, 'of the usually resident population aged 15 years and over, 1,043,000 were at work, some 86,000 declared themselves to be unemployed and about 15,000 were seeking regular work for the first time'. In terms of sectoral estimates of those employed, 218,000 were engaged in agriculture, forestry and fishing; 228,000 in the manufacturing industry and 181,000 in commerce, insurance and finance.[18] Other estimates suggested in the early 1970s that there were 1,821 full-time fishermen and 3,816 part time, but in 1974 it was claimed that the fishing industry supported 7,000 fishermen and an estimated 20,000 people engaged in shore-based back-up activities who were 'under threat of extinction' unless there was an extension of EEC member states' exclusive limits.[19]

This remained a sore point throughout the decade. In May 1975 six major Irish ports were blocked by trawlermen who demanded government action on a fuel subsidy, fishery limits and a plan for the development of the country's fishery resources. The following year the European Commission limited the national fishing zone to twelve miles. Pierre Lardinois, the EEC commissioner, made it clear to the Irish Fishermen's Organisation in 1976 that it had no hope of obtaining an exclusive fifty-mile fishing limit. The same year it was estimated that since 1967, the contribution of fishing to the economy increased from £4.5 million to £16.5 million and (highlighting the disparity between the various estimates offered), the total number of jobs in the industry rose from 6,300 to 11,500, but it was still regarded as 'hopelessly underdeveloped' with only two Irish ships over 110 feet. In 1973 Ireland had no boats over fifty tons while England and Wales had 348. But there was also an obvious over-exploitation of the sea; from 1973–4 the Irish herring catch was 11,000 tons; by 1975–6 that had dropped to 6,500 tons.

In 1977 the government announced the setting up of a separate

Department of Fisheries with Patrick Donegan as minister. He announced that certain specified larger boats would not be allowed to fish within fifty miles of the Irish coast and the government subsequently imposed unilateral fishery conservation measures. In April of that year ten Dutch trawlers were arrested off Cork and formally charged with illegally fishing within the new fifty-mile limit. The case was subsequently referred to the European Court of Justice, which suggested that the government's fishery measures discriminated against the fleets of other EEC member states and ordered the Irish government to suspend its unilateral measures. By 1978 there was further analysis of under-capitalisation and non-management of fish resources amidst Ireland's continued claim for a national fifty-mile fishing limit (corresponding roughly to the continental shelf off Ireland): 'In 1922 the amount of fish consumed annually per head of population was 10lbs. In 1977 this figure had only risen to 12lbs per year. Therefore, fish were not presented as a sound investment'; 83 per cent of the fish caught were exported.

Charles Haughey posed an interesting question in the Dáil in 1978: 'Why should Irish fisheries, this one natural resource that our under-developed economy has at its disposal to develop, be thrown into a community pool for the benefit of all the member states of the community when German steel, British Oil, Dutch Gas – none of these are thrown into a community pool?'[20]

Long-time maritime and labour activist John de Courcy Ireland was adamant that 'the potential of the sea around us has never been exploited. The wealth of the sea has not figured in any programme for economic development as a natural resource which could provide substantial employment or contribute to the income of the nation'. He cited the example of what had been done in Norway and bemoaned the failure to provide a separate government department to deal with maritime affairs. He also suggested the Irish were prisoners of their history and stuck in a neocolonialist relationship: 'No country in Europe with a coastline pays tribute to foreigners on such a huge percentage of its trade.'[21]

– FORTY-FIVE –

SPENDING, PLANNING AND PLEADING

The economic fluctuations of the decade made for a cautious approach to estimates, predictions and projections about spending and employment figures, especially for the coalition government. In January 1975 it was maintained that for the first time since 1942, unemployment in Ireland exceeded 100,000. But just how reliable were the unemployment figures in the 1970s? Writing in *Magill* in June 1978, Brendan Dowling suggested they were anything but, while it was also maintained that economic forecasting was crude and underdeveloped, and akin to 'backing horses at Leopardstown' (a racecourse in Dublin). It was impossible to rely on the projections about economic growth as statistical information was 'poor and is slow in coming' and the quality and availability of data much inferior to that of other EEC countries.[1] Another contributor to *Magill*, Brian Trench, noted laconically in 1979 that 'Don't you ever get tired of being wrong' was the title given to a critical review of economic forecasting presented to the staff of the ESRI 'by two of the country's leading analysts some years ago.'[2]

These uncertainties were apparent at government level throughout the decade. In March 1974, for example, it was decided to postpone the publication of a programme for economic expansion for six months, even though the Minister for Social Welfare thought this a step too far; 'while in present conditions of uncertainty planning may be more than usually difficult, this is not a reason to down-grade it sharply'. Officials from the Department of the Taoiseach suggested there was much to be said 'for avoiding a commitment in public' regarding economic projections because of the pessimism that existed.[3] Richie Ryan appeared to agree, maintaining in his 1975 budget speech that 'of all the tasks which could engage my attention, the least realistic would be the publication of a medium or long-term economic plan based on irrelevancies in the past, hunches as to the present and clairvoyance as to the future'.[4]

A cabinet economic subcommittee meeting in the spring of 1975 was faced with a litany of public spending dilemmas. There was pressure, for example, from the religious orders and the Catholic Archbishop of Dublin, Dermot Ryan, regarding the funding of secondary schools, which had been getting 70 per cent grants for capital expenditure: 'The existing system of capital financing of voluntary secondary schools is on the verge of general collapse and has already reached the stage where the majority of the religious orders are no longer in a position to undertake the financial burden related to the provision of new schools or major improvements to existing premises.'[5]

A memorandum from the Department of the Taoiseach in April 1975 in relation to public expenditure pointed out that 'the government is now spending £1 out of every £2 of the total earnings of the entire community', and in relation to the balance of payment deficit, 'In 1974, out of every £100 we spent, almost £14 was provided by foreign creditors. This is a result 3 times worse than that of the UK.' The really urgent problem identified was the rise in inflation and how to reduce it, with the answer deemed to be by shifting some of the burden of taxation from indirect to direct taxes.[6] By the end of the summer in 1975 the preoccupation was once again with the control of public expenditure. As was put in a memorandum from the Department of Finance: 'No provision to be made for new services or for the improvement or expansion of existing services ... Charges for services to be introduced or increased wherever possible ... The level of all services being provided to be reduced wherever possible.'[7]

As Minister for Finance, Ryan frequently found himself at loggerheads with cabinet colleagues who were not willing to share his caution and obey calls to rein in spending. He revealed his frustration in a handwritten note to Cosgrave in May 1975 regarding school grants: 'Once again, government has made a decision on a presentation which was not put before the department of finance for their observations. The result = a wrong decision ... I asked for time to sort all this out but no; time was of the essence because of pressure groups. This, if I may say with respect, in my view, is bad government.'[8]

Ryan was engaged in constant battles over the rate of growth in public expenditure and had to struggle to instil a sense of collective cabinet discipline in this regard; and perhaps the label attached to him as 'Richie Ruin' was somewhat unfair, given the stubbornness of his colleagues. He sent constant pleas to his ministers to restrain spending. He corresponded with James Tully, the Minister for Local Government, in August 1975, for example: 'Yet again I feel compelled to write to you about the observance of budgetary allocations.' Unhappy with the lack of response from Tully he appealed to Cosgrave: 'The Department of Local Government, of all departments, seems to believe that it can go its own merry way in expenditure. They have chosen to ignore completely the several pleas from this department and indeed, the decisions of the government regarding expenditure.' He was also under pressure from Garret FitzGerald as Minister for Foreign Affairs, who was looking for more money or 'his department will not be able to continue operating effectively, fulfilling its responsibilities'. By the end of 1975, a battle-weary Ryan could only conclude that his biggest problem was 'the refusal of ministers and of the government collectively to operate the existing systems properly'.[9]

When the cabinet economic subcommittee met in September 1975, Ryan pointed out 'that the gap between departmental demands and resources was a staggering £794 million, or 30 per cent of the total budget. The additional borrowing or taxation which such a gap would require would be economically ruinous even if it were feasible, which it wasn't.' It was predicted that unemployment could rise to 120,000 the following winter. The simple message was that it was essential to restore cost competitiveness. FitzGerald, who took a very hands-on approach to these matters, insisted that priority had to be given to the preparation of a national plan. At a subsequent meeting of the committee in January 1976 the Minister for Industry and Commerce Justin Keating suggested a short-term plan was required but also 'a change in the state's economic policies as fundamental as that in the mid 1950s'.[10] That month, Ryan presented one of the toughest budgets ever, imposing an extra £107 million in taxes, increasing the price of petrol by 10p a gallon and raising VAT to 10 per cent on a wide range of goods and services. Later that year, Ryan was again angered by the Department of Health's demands for an increase in its budget, as the Minister for Health, Brendan Corish, 'did not take steps to bring about even the minimum policy changes required to keep within his approved allocation'. Corish defended himself by complaining that he was on the receiving end of huge pressure from the health boards 'and the Dáil'.[11]

Ryan also fulminated about the actions of the Minister for Labour, Michael O'Leary, who in February 1977 announced a new public holiday for the last Monday in October which would bring the number of public holidays to eight. (There had been seven since 1974, when the minister had declared 1 January a public holiday.) Before the 1977 announcement, of the EEC countries, Ireland and the Netherlands had the lowest number of public holidays. The UK had eight, Denmark ten, Italy sixteen, France ten and Germany between ten and thirteen. At the cabinet meeting a few days later, Ryan complained that 'the present times were hardly suitable for the announcement of a further holiday with pay – which could cost the public service and other employees a fair sum of money'. Irish employers' representatives also complained that the announcement was 'at variance with everything the Minister for Finance has been saying in recent months'.

Ryan lamented that O'Leary had made his decision and announcement 'without consulting the government'. The broader context here was the ratification of the new National Wage Agreement on 23 February; Ryan suggested the new public holiday announcement was 'entirely unacceptable' and that 'the concession is the equivalent of 0.5 per cent of an increase in wages'. He pointed out that at the end of 1978 employers would be required under an EEC recommendation to increase basic holiday entitlement generally to four weeks. He thought it 'absurd' that the public holiday was allowed and rubbished the suggestion that 'the incidence of strikes between summer and Christmas is attributable in some significant degree to the lack of holiday breaks in that period'.[12]

A memorandum from the Department of the Taoiseach suggested it should support Ryan in his opposition as the new public holiday was 'not sought by anybody' and 'the point that we have less public holidays in this country than elsewhere, taken by itself, just is not an argument. It does not take into account the longer working hours generally obtaining in most of the countries in the EEC and it certainly does not take into account the higher productivity in those countries – due in fact to better industrial relations, better equipment and the longer hours.'[13] It was another battle that Ryan lost and an indication, not only perhaps of the sway that Labour ministers held in government, but of the determination of Cosgrave not to antagonise them. O'Leary signed the regulation giving effect to the new holiday in June 1977.

Concerns about the cost of the public service continued to be aired and there were suggestions, which were not acted on, that a separate Minister for Public Service was necessary as Ryan, in his dual capacity as Minister for Finance and Minister for Public Service, doubted if existing ministerial portfolios 'have the correct functions, balance of duties or responsibilities'. But there was also a worry that any proposals for change should be kept strictly confidential as they could require additional staff, which was contrary to a government decision on limiting civil service numbers.[14]

The complaint expressed in the Department of the Taoiseach was that the public service was still 'vastly' expanding 'irrespective of its utility', while Ryan stressed: 'as you know only too well, public expenditure and its growth is now probably the most serious problem facing the government with increases in debt service and public service pay alone estimated to absorb some 94 per cent of the increase in tax revenue in 1976'. The health authorities 'now employ more than one in ten of the total population ... Public service employment in central departments alone has risen from some 82,000 in 1970 to an estimated 103,000 in 1975, including teachers, army and Gardaí.'[15]

Observations made the following year indicated that while in 1966 total public expenditure was 35 per cent of GNP, by 1976 this had increased to 55 per cent, or put more starkly, 'We have now reached the stage at which the public sector accounts for more than one half of national resources.' Rates of direct taxation were consequently very high: 'In the case of a married man (no children) the point at which taxation absorbs 50 per cent of earnings is £13,300; this threshold is by far the lowest figure in the EEC and compares with £100,000 in Italy. Our top marginal rate [77 per cent] is the second highest in the community and applies at a point far lower than elsewhere in the community.'[16]

In September 1976 John Bruton, the parliamentary secretary to the Minister for Industry and Commerce, wrote to Cosgrave suggesting that Fine Gael would be punished at the next general election on the growth of public expenditure and 'the consequential level of direct taxation'. His solution to this impending threat was to set up a commission to review all public spending which would, in effect, divorce public spending from the political process, as politicians could gain nothing politically 'by making specific suggestions of public spending cuts'. Walter Kirwan in the Department of the Taoiseach rejected such an approach, surmising that it would be presented as if 'the government were seeking to shirk' one of their primary responsibilities 'and/or giving to a non-elected body a function properly appropriate to the elected legislative'.[17] There was also a cool response to a tentative suggestion by Richie Ryan in 1976 that an all-party Dáil committee could be created which would have the responsibility of controlling current expenditure.[18]

The coalition government had hoped for better economic news in 1977 to enhance its prospects of re-election, but the budgetary outlook for 1977 revealed a current deficit of £218 million: 'The potential total addition to the 1977 budget deficit – and to the exchequer borrowing requirement – arising from the decisions, contingencies, "threats" and revisions could be of the order of £130 million. For all the Minister for Finance knows, there may indeed be other ideas which have not yet been flushed out and which could add to this wholly staggering total.'

It was also pointed out that the budget target level of government borrowing at 11 per cent of GNP was by far the highest of any EEC country; additional expenditure already approved by the government brought it to 11.5 per cent, which was the same as 1976. When Ireland had received a loan from the EEC in 1976 the agreement was that the borrowing requirement in 1976 should not exceed that of 1975 and should be reduced in subsequent years, so Ireland was already non-compliant: 'The minister would remind the government that there was extensive community condemnation of Italy when they failed to comply with their loan conditions and much more severe conditions were imposed for later borrowing.'[19]

With the change of government in 1977, largely as a result of Fianna Fáil's generous campaign promises – 'the electorate were offered a fairly simple solution to a complex problem. Vote to abolish rates, motor taxes and reduce income tax and there will be a fall in unemployment of over 25,000 per annum during the next three years'[20] – Lynch was moved to comment in a speech in Cork in October that 'in many respects the economic scene is bright at the present time'. Although over 100,000 were out of work, the increase in consumer prices was slowing and there was cause for optimism due to 'exporters boosting their sales so remarkably'.

As inflation was down, interest rates were dropping and unemployment had begun to fall, it seemed that the task Martin O'Donoghue had as Minister in the new Department of Economic Planning and

Development was more manageable. But much of this reflected external factors and the stimulus of more public sector jobs, and there was a fear that 'we could have a bloated public sector requiring higher taxations or borrowings or both to Finance. These are the nightmare scenarios.' The emergence of O'Donoghue in this new ministry was a significant development. He was a member of Trinity College Dublin's Economics Department and Lynch had appointed him as his first non-civil service adviser in 1970. O'Donoghue's influence was particularly significant because of Lynch's lack of interest in policy detail, and he was essentially given responsibility for implementing the economic promises in the election manifesto by being appointed as minister on his first day as a TD. His appointment had been criticised by T. K. Whitaker, who insisted that tension between George Colley and his officials in the Department of Finance and O'Donoghue's new department were inevitable (on which point Whitaker was vindicated). Compounding the problems was that Lynch had no stomach for difficult budgetary decisions and, as Joe Lee eloquently put it, O'Donoghue 'reposed an enormous burden of hope on very fragile foundations'.[21]

Garret FitzGerald suggested Fianna Fáil's 'manifesto crisis' would emerge within eighteen months, as the party would inevitably be confronted with the reality that it had sacrificed medium-term national economic gains for short-term party advantage.[22]

FitzGerald was correct: private notes for the Taoiseach on tax, pay and inflation made it clear that the election manifesto had promised things that would not or could not be delivered. He was advised 'to avoid being drawn into interpretations of the manifesto commitment; he could say in general terms, that we are on course'. In an indication that the government also had to be mindful of the attitude of American investment in the Irish economy, Richard Stokes also wrote to Lynch to inform him that Jack Molloy, the Irish ambassador to the US, had contacted him about the closure of the SPS steel factory in Galway, to relay the message that Tom Hallowell of SPS identified the problem as wages and costs: 'the products of the Galway factory were exported to the US and had for some time been unable to compete with Japanese imports. He suggested that it was essential for the government here to take a strong stance against inflation.'[23]

In relation to plans at the end of 1978 for the control of public expenditure in 1979, reference was made to the 'enormous and unprecedented borrowing' of £800 million in 1978 and a warning given that 'the significant public sector stimulus to growth in output and employment in the period of end 1978 must be followed by a policy of containing expenditure'. A secret memorandum in September referred to a draft memorandum circulated by the Department of Finance reviewing the operation of certain public expenditure programmes and proposed savings, but 'the response to date of these memoranda has been most disappointing and has been characterised in the main by a lack of urgency or a reluctance to face squarely up to budgetary realities by the departments concerned'.[24] Four years on, and with a new government, it seemed T. K. Whitaker's warnings had yet to be accepted.

What did politicians really know about economics in any case? With few exceptions, precious little, it seemed. Garret FitzGerald stood out precisely because he was an economist and as opposition spokesman on finance for Fine Gael in 1972, his mastery was on display in the Dáil. Even if he was seen not to have offered enough alternatives regarding spending, and although he felt that more should have been done in the budget to aid redistribution, he hesitated at the point of commitment. Nonetheless, it was observed, 'It is not often that any deputy devotes himself seriously to the subject of finance in Dáil Éireann, so when one deputy mounts a tour de force extending to almost six hours and including approximately 60,000 words, his effort is worthy of special attention.'[25] But, as seen earlier, when in government the following year it was to the Foreign Affairs portfolio rather than Finance that he was posted.

And what of the economist as minister? Martin O'Donoghue announced at the end of the decade that 'we are well on the way to ... the attainment of full employment by 1983'. But by 1980, 'in a more sober frame of mind can be found issuing warnings for his successors after Haughey dropped him'.[26] Academic accomplishments in economics were no guarantee, it seemed, of successful economic policies once in government.

– FORTY-SIX –

TAXING, DODGING, NEGOTIATING AND PROTESTING

Was there consistency with regard to budgetary policy throughout this decade and was there enough debate about the balances that were involved in taxing and spending? Ministers for Finance were hardly inspirational in this regard; there was regular critical comment of the superficiality of the annual budget exercise, and the lack of long-term thinking. One observation was that 'the telescope of public attention is focused on the top mast of the budgetary ship to see what kind of flag is flying [tax] with the result that the hull glides by almost unnoticed'.[1]

Should the emphasis of taxation have been shifted from earning to spending as recommended by *Hibernia*'s financial editor? It was a magazine that gave serious, analytical and in-depth coverage to business, banking and economic policy and suggested that the budget needed 'a more imaginative exercise than the simple book-keeping of raising some new revenue to meet estimated increases in expenditure?'[2] Fianna Fáil insisted in 1972 that there was no realistic alternative to EEC membership as the annual per capita income of the Irish people was half the western European average, but in economic terms, sceptics of such embracing of the European project suggested it 'will provide an excuse for Irish politicians to pass the buck indefinitely'.[3]

George Colley came in for criticism in this regard. He had practised as a solicitor before entering politics, and was the son of Harry Colley, a veteran of the War of Independence and Fianna Fáil TD. First elected to the Dáil in 1961, George despised his constituency colleague Charles Haughey, and ran unsuccessfully for the leadership of the party in 1966. He was widely regarded as a politician of integrity, and keen to preserve Fianna Fáil's traditional image as a 'national movement', being critical of the priorities of some of his brasher and more materialistic contemporaries, whose ambitions he saw as more personal than in the interests of party or country, most obviously Haughey. Before becoming Minister for Finance he served as Minister for Education and subsequently took the Industry and Commerce portfolio. He had overseen preparations for the introduction of the decimal currency in 1971 and participated in the negotiations surrounding Ireland's entry into the EEC. The budget he unveiled in 1972 effectively abandoned the principle of balancing current as opposed to capital expenditure; this has been seen as a move that set a precedent for some of the fiscal irresponsibility of the 1970s. In 1973 Colley was Fianna Fáil's director of elections for the general election and performed poorly in a televised debate with Garret FitzGerald, finance spokesman for Fine Gael, and was then blamed for panic-stricken 'auction politics' on the abolition of rates.[4]

His 'double-entry book keeping' approach to budgets when he was Minister for Finance from 1970 to 1972 had been criticised, but what was really needed, maintained *Hibernia* in 1972, was a fundamental analysis of the tax structure: 'What we now operate is a ramshackle hotch potch of tax systems inherited from various periods of the past' and the budget of 1973 was deemed to be one that once again 'spread the largesse widely instead of concentrating it specifically'.[5] Those who avoided paying tax had little to fear, it seemed. There were lucrative loopholes in the tax laws and 'the really big tax dodgers are encouraged in this country by the certain knowledge that, if all comes to all, the revenue authorities will settle on a compromise. If one or two of that fraternity spent a few months behind bars, many others might think twice before taking the risk.'[6] *Hibernia* had a particular preoccupation with capital enjoying such exemption from tax that was not permitted in other countries and welcomed the introduction of capital gains, acquisition and wealth taxes, though somewhat cautiously: 'In the past the state has taxed the working man as it has the manufacturer, but it has turned a blind eye on the speculator, the stock manipulator, the land grabber and the property tycoon. In theory it now appears to have plugged these gaps. The practice remains to be seen.'[7] In 1974 it maintained: 'Ask any accountant or solicitor in Dublin today and he will confirm that large sums of money are being transferred out of the country to avoid the forthcoming wealth tax.'[8]

One issue that caused considerable controversy in the 1970s was the taxation of farmers, of whom there were 180,000 in the country according to the census of 1971. Deciding a fair way of addressing this question created tension and resentment and pressure was applied by the National Income Tax Reform Organisation. The response of one farmers' representative was that 'certain elements in the country are always looking to grab more from the farmer'. It was estimated that as a result of the 1974 budget 'only 5 per cent of the total number of farmers were brought into the tax net'.[9] In March 1976 there was a budget proposal to remove the tax exemption from agricultural co-operatives and in May of that year farmers from south Leinster sent a rather optimistic telegram to Liam Cosgrave demanding 'that you remove Richie Ryan from position of Minister for Finance immediately'. Meanwhile George Jeffrey of the East Cork Region of the Irish Farmer's Association (IFA), expressed 'shock and amazement' that Paddy Hegarty TD had said in the Dáil 'I can tell the house that farming was never better. We never had it better and farmers must face up to this tax.'[10]

Concern was expressed about land evaluations being uneven in their effects; that farms in the south and west of the country tended to have substantially better incomes per pound valuation than those in the midlands. But what was regarded as the government's strongest defence of new tax proposals was that in 1975 farmers paid an average of 4.3 per cent of farm income on rates and income tax, compared to 23.2 per cent of income by other business and self-employed people. A memorandum from the Department of the Taoiseach in January 1976 suggested the government could not insist on farming accounts being intrinsic to the issue of farmer taxation because it would not only create a paper mountain but would also give a chance to uncooperative farmers to 'evade and delay'. Instead, the preference was to use a multiplier system: 'If a farmer feels aggrieved by his assessment, let him employ accountants and carry on an argument with the Revenue. If he proves he is over assessed – then more power to him. But do not let farmers and the rest of the community get into a sterile battle on accounts which helps nobody except the accountancy industry and keeps farmers from doing their paperwork.'

John Bruton made representations to the Taoiseach on behalf of midland farmers, pointing out that farming organisations were looking for exemption from rates on their land: 'It would be hard to justify going this far on the basis of equity,' he suggested, 'but we need compromise and they are all complaining about paying tax on a notional basis.'[11] In 1977 a memorandum for Cosgrave on pay talks and personal taxation highlighted the percentage of GNP paid in Ireland in taxation, including social security contributions, suggesting it was 'not high' at 37 per cent, compared to 40.1 per cent in Belgium, 51.4 per cent in Denmark, 42.2 per cent in West Germany and 37.7 per cent in the UK. But it was acknowledged that 'the effect of this low average payment is eroded completely by the totally disproportionate share of taxation borne by certain sections of the community ... At one end of the scale are the farmers who, in 1976, paid £3 million in income tax – and a negligible figure in rates. If farmers had paid the same proportion of their income in taxation as the rest of the population they would have been liable for approximately £90 million in 1976. This is a measure of what they are escaping now.'[12] When Richie Ryan widened the tax net in 1977 it was maintained that 'the countryside turned against the coalition' and that 'a further sign of the coalition's incompetence [was] that they were unable to signal to their traditional supporters just how light was the imposition they were being asked to bear'. The threshold at which farmers became liable for tax was now £60 rateable valuation of land, which meant that 22,500 farmers out of a total of 170,000 were in the tax net.[13] The budgetary outlook for 1977 revealed that a revenue estimate included an additional £35 million for receipts from taxation of farming profits, but that 'only £11 million can now be expected from this quarter in 1977, leaving a shortfall of £24 million on the budget estimate'.[14]

Writing in *Magill* in March 1978, economics journalist Alan Matthews suggested that only one in eight farmers were liable for tax and that if Irish farmers paid taxes on the British basis they would be paying at least three times more than they did. He estimated that the notional system of tax paying underestimated farmers' income by 12 per cent. The same year, George Colley maintained that farm incomes had more than doubled between 1974 and 1978. Given that taxation of farmers was a notional system, in January 1979, Minister for Agriculture James Gibbons addressed the issue of raising additional tax revenues from them. There were various proposals for charges and levies on farm produce but he urged caution:

> I do not subscribe to the wild statements by some farmer's leaders

> about taxation, or their perpetual 'poor mouth' attitude. Indeed, many of the more far-sighted larger farmers fully appreciate the situation and are quite prepared to pay their share of direct taxation. However, I think we must grasp the nettle and come up with a proper taxation system that, on the one hand, will be equitable to farmers and will encourage continued development of agriculture and, on the other hand, will be regarded as reasonable by the rest of the taxpaying community. An agricultural produce levy which hits all farmers big and small would not meet these criteria and could not be regarded as a satisfactory long-term solution.[15]

In the estimates for 1979, £160 million was provided in state aid for agriculture, while there was £385 million from the EEC Agricultural Fund for Irish farmers. The 1977 farm management survey of an Foras Talúntais (the Agricultural Institute) had drawn attention to 'the standard of living enjoyed by a sizeable proportion of our farmers' which 'must have improved out of all recognition', estimating that 'modernised farming is very prosperous, with many farmers having assets, investment levels and incomes formerly associated with the world of commerce only'. As far as Gibbons was concerned in 1979, there was an onus on farmers to pay more tax and the figures produced made it clear that his argument was irrefutable:

> Farmers will pay about £16 million in income tax in 1979 and about £36 million in rates on land. This total of £52 million represents a contribution of 5.5 per cent of farm income. Last year the contribution was £38 million or 4.5 per cent of farm income. Making due allowance for investment needs in agriculture, the farmer's contribution falls far short of the share of income contributed in taxation by the rest of the community, as is clear from the fact that employees paid about £526 million in income tax in 1978, representing about 16 per cent of their earnings.[16]

Jack Lynch insisted that the introduction of a 2 per cent levy on sales of farm produce, announced by George Colley (who had been reappointed Minister for Finance in 1977) in February 1979, was necessary as part of a fairer system of taxation. Farmers, of course, had their own interpretation of such figures. At a four-hour meeting in February 1979 with representatives of the government, they bemoaned the media impression that 'farmers were fiddling', insisting they had to invest to protect their positions and that 'a PAYE taxpayer does not invest in the same way to preserve his job'. It was suggested the levy could be dropped if a new tax system could be agreed. Trade union leaders reacted angrily to this, maintaining the government was capitulating to farmers.[17] The government agreed a deal with the farmers that would see the levy dropped with an understanding there would be an income tax yield from farmers in future 'in line with other sectors in the community'. There was an 'outraged response' from PAYE workers.[18]

Undoubtedly, many farmers prospered as a result of EEC membership and were 'peasants no more'.[19] A *Magill* report on the lifestyle of three representative Irish farmers in 1979 revealed much in that regard. It featured one family farming sixty-five acres in Galway that had seen its annual gross income increase from £3,000 to £12,000 between 1973 and 1978 as an EEC farm modernisation scheme had given them capital to invest in more productive methods. The EEC had classed 80 per cent of Irish farms as 'transitional' (unable to earn the equivalent of an industrial wage) and the initiatives that resulted, including milking machines and a switch to dairy herds as the price of milk went up, meant that much of the new-found prosperity was evident in house extensions and central heating.

For those with more substantial acreage, the rewards were even greater. The journalist Inga Saffron interviewed a family farming 225 acres in Carrigaline in Cork: '"Before Ireland became part of the EEC, farmers were the dregs of society," according to Mary Lynch presiding over the interview. "Now", she added with a pleased smile, surveying the splendid living room furnished with heavy wood pieces, over stuffed chairs, exotic vases, large plants, an ivory chess set laid out on a low table and brass fire implements, "we are socially acceptable", a nice euphemism for wealthy.' Such 'social acceptability' meant the family were able to indulge in an indoor swimming pool and employ two full-time farm hands on a farm that now had an estimated turnover of £125,000 a year.[20]

By the end of the 1970s it was clear that there was a growing militancy in the public sector on the distribution of the tax burden but also in relation to the disparity between public and private pay rates. Brian Trench observed in *Magill* in January 1979, 'The year 1978 will be remembered as one in which public service workers sought to close the growing gap between them and workers in the private sector,' with nurses, teachers and Gardaí displaying more militancy in this regard. Martin O'Donoghue, when Minister for Economic Planning and Development, told the ICTU economic conference in December 1978 'there is no problem with pay policy in the public sector except that private employers are paying too much'. It was also suggested that the strike monitoring unit originally set up by Michael O'Leary in the Department of Labour in 1976 to provide warning and prevent looming strikes 'has had no tangible effect other than to provide the more detailed break-down of strike statistics which has revealed the scale of the public sector problem'.[21]

At the core of the public sector disillusionment was the degree to which PAYE contributions to the total income tax revenue had increased dramatically throughout the 1970s. In 1975, PAYE workers paid 71.4 per cent of all income tax revenue; by 1978, the total was 86.5 per cent. But the broader picture was more complex. A summary of the situation by 1979 read as follows:

> In the period 1974–8 PAYE workers paid £1800 million in income tax, self-employed people paid £320 million and farmers paid £20 million. The average industrial worker pays 25.2 per cent of his income if single, 20.6 per cent if married and 12.7 per cent if married with two children. The maximum rate of income tax is lower in Ireland (60 per cent) than in any other EEC country except West Germany and Luxembourg. Households whose heads are self-employed pay an average of 16 per cent of their income on all taxes. Householders of employees pay 26 per cent of their income in tax. Urban households pay 25 per cent of their income in tax, rural households pay 13 per cent.

PAYE workers expressed their grievances in marches and demonstrations. In March 1979 workers again mobilised; an estimated 50,000 in Dublin at a rally organised by the ITGWU on 11 March, while on 20 March 'upwards of 150,000 PAYE workers took to the streets of Dublin to demand tax reform in the largest demonstration in the history of the state'. The protests were carried out 'peacefully and with little rancour', according to Jack Lynch. The turnout was extraordinary, especially given that ICTU 'had opposed the idea of a work stoppage and had asked the Dublin Council of Trade Unions to postpone the strike.[22] It was argued by Brian Trench that the marches in a sense were actually undermining the power of the trade union establishment as a pre-budget march organised by the Dublin Council of Trade Unions had been poorly attended. But George Colley's announcement that he was modifying the farm sales levy (farmer organisations had threatened commodity strikes when the sales levy was introduced and there was then an offer to exempt pigs and sheep) had obviously infuriated many; as Alo Brady, president of the Irish Conference of Professional and Service Associations, put it: 'It is a truly Glibertian situation: the PAYE sector is paying for the running of a country in which farmers dictate to the government on budgetary taxation matters,' although economists pointed out that even if farmers were paying a lot more tax it would not substantially relieve the burden on PAYE workers.

But it was also argued that the ICTU executive was not keen on work stoppages and trade unions were divided. The PAYE protest movement was 'fragmented', which, according to Trench,

> makes its size and duration all the more remarkable. It has lacked any clear demands but has expressed more of a gut feeling. It has brought on to the streets and into protest action for the first time large numbers of white-collar workers. It has given many trade unionists a new experience in democracy and has shown the ICTU leaders to be either unwilling or unable to use the massive potential of organised workers to make political and economic gains. It may not represent much of a threat to the government, but it could do damage to the authority of the trade union leadership.[23]

The debate over taxation of farmers and the PAYE sector was also occurring in the midst of concern about National Wage Agreements. Mixed views on the merits of such agreements had been apparent at regular intervals. Dermot Nally in the Department of the Taoiseach was wary, arguing in December 1974, regarding the difficulty in reaching agreement: 'I think it would be important that the government should not get itself into the position of being blindly in favour of National Wage Agreements. The advantages of this type of agreement to the economy generally, have, in the past been arguable. They tend to give the vast bulk of workers wage settlements higher than they would otherwise have obtained, basically because they can ride on the backs of the more militant and powerful unions.'[24] Historian Roy Foster has pointed out that (given the preoccupation with social partnership as a factor in economic recovery in the late

1980s and 1990s), the National Wage Agreements of the 1970s are often ignored, partly because 'both parties to the agreements often ignored them themselves'.[25]

There was some attempt at a structured approach to pay regulation, in line with what was happening elsewhere in Europe, and between 1970 and 1978 there were seven National Wage Agreements, 'but everything was conditional on pay policy, itself conditioned by the threat of an oil crisis and the ever present terror of inflation, the spectre that stalked the newspaper columns of the age'.[26] The agreements of 1970, 1972, 1974 and 1975 had been negotiated under the aegis of the employer-worker conference, but the summer of 1976 was one of 'breakdown' between the FUE (Federated Union of Employers) and ICTU over a new wage agreement. The Department of Finance was now arguing that it needed more of a say and a pay pause. There was an 'urgent need for restraint', given that it was necessary that year to borrow 'the record figure of £679 million, 32 per cent of the total budget'. But there were always mixed signals; indeed, such signals seemed to dominate these tortuous negotiations, Cosgrave at the same time insisting 'the government are concerned to cushion the effect of the economic recession on the weaker members of the community'. But it was acknowledged that a pay pause and increased taxes would be necessary, while the FUE insisted 'wasteful expenditure' in the public service needed to be addressed while reducing the burden of taxation and tackling abuses of the social welfare system.[27]

The same month, an editorial in *Hibernia* argued that economic debate was once again 'bogged down in wage-round negotiations, as if wages alone were the answer to our fundamental difficulties'.[28] The pre-budget talks between Cosgrave, ministers and ICTU in 1977 discussed 'elements of recovery' that were apparent in the economic situation, with ICTU's Harold O'Sullivan castigating the 'total failure' of EEC economic planning and regional economic provision, and lamenting 'a continuing rash of calumny and backbiting in respect of the role played within congress by the public service unions'. Senator Fintan Kennedy, president of the ITGWU, also made a contribution which can be seen as an indication of why the coalition was not going to fare well in the forthcoming general election: 'hitherto, their members had not held the government primarily responsible for the economic blows they had suffered'.

Two days later, Minister for Labour Michael O'Leary believed 'the sides are now very close ... there is an impression that certain remaining points of difference have an emotional or psychological element'. A deal was done, yet a few months later ICTU complained to Cosgrave that rising prices were eroding workers' living standards. The national agreement of 1977 had settled on an 8 per cent increase in pay, but prices had increased, it maintained, by 12 per cent, 'notwithstanding the decision of the government – which we welcome – to increase the food subsidies'.

Dermot Nally advised Cosgrave: 'I don't see much point in a meeting now, 3 months after the national agreement to last for 14 months was ratified. Wages have risen out of all proportion to production in recent years'.[29] That was hardly a message that the electorate bought. Another difficulty, as revealed in notes prepared for Jack Lynch in January 1978 (who was told the talks of the National Wage Agreement for 1978 'now appear to be at or close to a point of breakdown') was the strong feeling in ICTU that 'they are gradually losing control at local level'.[30]

In 1979 Vincent Browne, editor of *Magill*, maintained that the big cost of the failure of national partnership was that wages and inflation soared as trade unions sought compensation for what was 'an externally caused price rise – oil', and that in 1979 industrialised countries going into recession would deflate the Irish economy at the very time that the Irish government would be forced to do much the same. The problem was that the impact of the oil price rise on living standards and employment gave the government few options 'using traditional tools'.[31] The National Understanding of 1979 was 'intended to be the most ambitious attempt at an integrated policy yet'.[32] But what was clear from the National Wage Agreement era was that, far from eliminating workplace bargaining, the agreements 'merely changed its focus and productivity became a means for work groups to gain pay agreements above stated maxima'.[33]

– FORTY-SEVEN –

STRIKES RAGING, BABIES HOWLING

Industrial disputes plagued the decade and caused many headaches for workers, employers, government and consumers. A measure of the discontent that existed was that the first official strike in the 215 year history of Guinness's brewery took place in Dublin in 1974 when 1,200 general workers served strike notice. Pat Boran, in his memoir of his Laois childhood in the 1970s, recalled wryly:

> When Irish people remember the 1970s, nationwide strikes are among the first things to come to mind; postal disputes, railway blockades, stoppages by teachers, nurses, bus drivers, farmers and on an on ... in fact, when almost 30,000 man days were lost in the printing sector alone in 1976, there was a real possibility that it might not be possible to print sufficient posters and placards for all the other industrial disputes that were gong on ... the sight of my father hauling in a gas canister or of my mother rooting in presses and drawers for misshapen candles was the first sign that the adventure was about to commence.[1]

At a more academic level it has been asserted that the 1970s witnessed 'limited policy' and 'class differentiation' among the political parties and 'a relatively weak and fragmented labour movement provided less coherence to efforts aimed at developing a national pay and wage policy'.[2] The 1960s had seen a steady growth in union membership including in the areas of insurance and finance, which had slowed by the early 1970s only to increase again due to the expansion of the public sector towards the end of the decade. The growth of multinationals and plant-level bargaining also complicated industrial relations (the foreign industry sector grew at an average rate of 21.4 per cent per year in the period 1960–74 compared to a rate of 5.6 per cent for all industry). So called 'sweetheart deals' with individual unions were a feature of industrial relations and the industrial relations framework represented a new experience for the multinationals.[3]

After a decade of strikes, in April 1979 a government memorandum on the industrial relations situation left little room for ambiguity, referring to the plague of inter-union rivalry, the growth of militancy and

> a state of more or less perpetual leap-frogging within the public sector, with groups in the ESB and Aer Lingus setting a headline, usually by use of industrial muscle. This headline is followed by other groups in the post office, local authorities, civil service etc. Often the process begins again before the previous 'round' is completed ... productivity has become a term largely devoid of credibility in the sense that the productivity clause has been used to circumvent the limits of the agreement and to enable increases to be paid which, whatever their justification on relativity grounds, has little basis in genuine productivity. The consequence has been that to a large extent flexibility in working operations, even in the clerical/executive sphere where it used to be taken for granted, has been rendered unavailable.

It was also made clear that George Colley was open to amending the Trade Disputes Act, 1906 to remove the protection of the act from unofficial strikers 'and from picketing of private residences'. He was also in favour of 'legislative provisions requiring the observance by trade unions and employers of certain minimum standards of procedure, including the holding of ballots, before the service of official strike notice'.[4] These observations came during the worst year for industrial disputes in the history of the state, a year that witnessed a national bus strike, the first national post strike in more than fifty years and a refuse-collection strike.

There were frequent complaints to government throughout the decade about the public being 'used unwillingly' by strikers. The cement industry and bank disputes in 1970 generated controversy and anger. A former employee of the National Bank's head office suggested 'Bank directors are natural born bullies of their staffs ... They bullied the striking go slow staff recently by cutting their salaries 25 per cent which put lower paid junior staff and married staff in great hardship ... The way to bully those bullies is to nationalize the Irish banks ... Even the threat of nationalization will bring the bank gombeen men to their senses.'[5] The bank strike lasted for almost six months ('the level of fraud afterwards was reported to have soared ... as 750 cases were investigated'). As journalist Donal Buckley recalled,

> the abiding memory of the event is how people survived. Businesses and organisations had to divert staff around to shops and churches looking for cash to pay wages. As the strike continued, traders found themselves with increasing amounts of cheques ... one publican in Dublin's Liberties stored a heap of them up the chimney in the summer and didn't tell his wife. She lit the fire on the first cold September evening and when he realised his cheques had gone up in smoke he had a severe heart attack ... Ernie McElroy, a former bank official who was involved in processing the cheques after the strike, recalls seeing cheques made out on the backs of cigarette boxes and even on toilet paper.

Many property dealings were blocked, not just because of the difficulty of transferring funds but because documents such as property deeds were held by banks.[6]

A standard response to those insisting the government should intervene in such strikes was to point to the existence of the Labour Court and to maintain that it would be 'neither prudent nor desirable' for governments to 'side step this machinery' by taking direct action. In the Dáil, George Colley simply said, 'We have a system of free collective bargaining and that this means if there are strikes, people are inconvenienced.'[7] There were reasons for believing the Labour Court was doing an effective job; its annual report for 1970 revealed that the court and its conciliation service dealt with 569 disputes during 1970, compared with 443 in 1969:

> Conciliation conferences were held in 564 cases and produced settlements in 451 cases (80 per cent). The court issued 80 recommendations on disputes of which the employers accepted 79 and the workers 59 ... the number of man-days lost through strikes during 1970 was 1,007,714 compared with 935,900 during 1969. The man-days lost

> in 1970 were mainly attributable to two major disputes. The banks dispute involving about 6,500 officials occasioned the loss of 786,500 man days and the dispute in the cement industry involving about 700 general workers occasioned a loss of 88,128 man days.[8]

In 1970, the loss of wages and salaries through disputes was £6 million, with 28,752 people involved in those disputes. In any case, according to international comparisons, Ireland was not faring too badly in this regard. Days lost through industrial disputes in 1971 per 1,000 people employed were 660, compared to 720 in Belgium, 430 in France, 1,060 in Italy, 10 in Norway, 240 in Sweden, 1,130 in the UK 3,320 in Finland and 1,610 in the US. In 1972, 206,955 man-days were lost with 22,274 work people involved.[9]

In 1970 Lynch was being warned of the reputational damage strikes were doing in terms of possible external investment in Ireland: it took some time for an agreement to be reached between unions and the contractors for the Pfizer Chemical Corporation project at Ringaskiddy in Cork, a significant development as it represented a switch to capital-intensive labour projects. Lynch was informed through an intermediary in the Industrial Development Authority that Barney Quinn, executive vice-president of Pfizer, wanted to take the third phase of the project to Holland: 'He said he regretted having to make the statement in view of his Irish background, but nonetheless, he thought it was foolish for Pfizer to plan any further expansions in Ireland until such time as legislation is adopted which would prevent labour from resorting to blackmail tactics.'

Joseph Brennan from the Office of the Minister for Labour was given the task of drafting a reply, and the one he penned was quite defensive, insisting that most industrialists in Ireland had no problem with their staff, though he acknowledged 'I cannot claim to be happy about our industrial relations affairs'.[10] (The formal opening of Pfizer's operation at Ringaskiddy took place in May 1972.) The report of a meeting between Lynch and Maurice Stans, the US Secretary of Commerce, in April 1971 included Lynch's response to Stans's question: 'What can I say to American industrialists about the state of industrial relations?' Lynch 'pointed out to him the absence of real authority in Congress [ICTU] over individual trade unions. I also said that I wanted to be quite frank about the lack of effective control that trade union executives had over their members.'[11]

In 1977 Lynch was still being warned about reputational damage in the light of employer/union confrontations at the Ferenka steel plant at Limerick, 'which began when a production worker ... refused to clear a blocked toilet on a day when cleaning workers were not available'.[12] Within two months the factory was closed for good, with 1,400 jobs lost, making it 'the biggest factory closure in Irish labour history'. It was estimated that the steel plant – born of high investment grants, relatively cheap labour and access to Limerick's port – required an £11 million modernisation injection. It had failed to reach optimum capacity and was run on what was described as a rigidly authoritarian regime, with posters in the plant announcing 'Miss a day, your mates will Pay'. A worker who was five minutes late lost fifteen minutes of pay and it was regarded as a factory 'ridden with petty rules and penalties'.[13]

Inter-union rivalry and harsh working conditions had combined to create an industrial relations crisis. A Cork businessman wrote to Lynch that 'during our marketing trips to America over the last few years I know that many top American executives are more worried about the unions and potential problems in this country than any other single item'.[14]

Secondary school teachers went on strike in 1971; the Minister for Education rejected their claim for a pay increase, insisting that salaries were 'considerably in excess of those being paid to similar teachers in Great Britain'. Once again there were calls for Lynch to intervene and a query from one member of the public: 'I can't honestly understand why you have a national schoolteacher as minister for education – how can he be impartial?'[15] The mood at the Association of Secondary Teachers of Ireland convention in 1970 had been 'one of anger – a deep, cold anger'. ASTI's case was that graduate secondary teachers should be better paid than non-graduate primary teachers (see Part VIII) and there were divisions and generational conflict within the union about its industrial relations strategy. There was an influx of younger teachers and ASTI members were drawn to meetings 'in unprecedented numbers'. There was acceptance of agreement on posts of responsibility in 1972.[16]

In the same year there was an Electricity Supply Board (ESB) dispute. Under a Fuels Act, the Minister for Transport and Power was entitled to take control of supply and distribution of electricity due to the 'exigencies of the common good'. The issue was seemingly resolved in April 1971 only to re-emerge later that year, at which point Lynch was informed by T. J. Maher, the National Farmers Association president: 'you must regard this as a national crisis', or, as it was put by a disgruntled Kilkenny farmer in a telegram to Lynch 'harvest in jeopardy. No electricity for corn dryers. ESB on strike. Wheat intake stopped dead. Cut off. No notice. Unless restored immediately may result in loss of £250,000 to farmers in this area. Who is running this country?'[17]

In April 1972 there was further trouble when ESB shift workers unofficially went on strike looking for a salary structure instead of a weekly wage ('600 or so men who keep the power stations going'), in defiance of the official unions and had 'taken the country to the brink of total shut down' even though it was claimed in a government memorandum that in comparison with other workers in Ireland and abroad 'they are the best paid and have the best hours, allowances and conditions of employment'.

There were numerous denunciations from a disgruntled public – 'a pack of unofficial strike ruffians ... we are unfortunately witnessing a slide down the precarious and slippery slope of anarchy'. There were also reminders that 'they would not be tolerated in the USA ... They had a post office strike and President Nixon sent in the army.'[18]

There is no doubt these strikes and power cuts caused considerable distress. In November 1973 a resident of Dalkey in Dublin wrote to Liam Cosgrave about yet more power cuts: 'As I write, my seven month old baby is howling in his frigid room and despite the pile of rugs I have on him, his bronchitis is – understandably – worsening. Yours in desperation and darkness'.[19] There were also disputes that year in the ranks of the medical profession. In October 1973 Dr Philip Cawley, an executive member of the Irish Medical Association, wrote to Cosgrave about this, pointing to the 'uneasy partnership' between the Medical Union and the IMA, with a suggestion that 'the union delegates are treated in a fraternising manner particularly by [parliamentary secretary to the Minister for Health and Social Welfare] Mr Cluskey [and] that the IMA delegates are practically ignored ... Please destroy my letter.'[20]

The number of man-days lost due to industrial disputes in the period January to June 1973 was 80,953. The following year in May there was a dispute over the possibility of introducing a five-day week for Dublin busmen. Discussions on this had been ongoing since 1964. Three of the unions involved objected to the five-day week and the schedules involved; 'There was a government decision taken to introduce army lorries. That decision was negated by the events of that very tragic weekend.'[21] Those devastating Dublin and Monaghan bombs of May 1974 (see Part II) inaugurated a bleak summer; there was further uncertainty for commuters with the commencement of a bus strike that lasted for nine weeks. The Department of the Taoiseach was on the receiving end of a large volume of correspondence from the inconvenienced public, but also the business community who were still trying to deal with the fallout from the bombings.

Cosgrave was asked to mediate personally, but instead, along with Minister for Labour Michael O'Leary and Minister for Industry and Commerce Justin Keating, met representatives of Dublin city traders. They informed him, 'Fashion goods industries such as clothing and footwear were very worried as they were producing seasonal items which were not being sold. These stocks would have to be let go at a loss. There had been a 30–50 per cent drop in the sale of fashion goods for the first six weeks of the strike.' Cosgrave acknowledged the gravity of a situation that was exacerbated by the understandable fear people had about travelling into the city centre. He commented that 'there could be no diminution of the security precautions at present in force and indeed they were hardly vigorous enough'.

Significantly, the business representatives insisted 'the bombings had little or no effect on the situation. If the buses were back, confidence in the city would be restored. The Dublin bombings of 1972 caused a fall off in trade for about eight days but after that everything was back to normal.' They also pointed out that a survey of Dublin shoppers had shown that '80 per cent of them travelled to the city centre by bus'. Liam Cassidy of the O'Connell Street Business Association suggested that 'the time had come for a hard look at the system of public transport in Dublin. The city had a recurring transport problem and the government should set up an inquiry into the whole question.'

The Dublin Chamber of Commerce was more direct, bemoaning the fact that 'there is no opportunity for competition to aid customers', but Cosgrave regarded the idea of licensing private contractors as counterproductive, as it would only extend the strike. O'Leary wrote to Cosgrave: 'In the present state of "leap frogging" in industrial relations, it is possible to foresee even graver implications for the economy arising from shorter hours in CIÉ than arise even from the present dispute.' O'Leary was reluctant for the government to intervene, suggesting 'there is no substitute in our situation for good open communication between employer and employee representatives'. The nine-week strike was estimated to have cost businesses £9 million in lost trade by the time it ended in August.

By September, busmen were threatening more strikes over new rotas. The Dublin Chamber of Commerce voiced the opinion that there were simply too many trade unions in Ireland.[22]

Unfair dismissals were also regarded as a provocation that led to strike action. A draft memorandum from the Minister for Labour in 1974 indicated he was determined to legislate for an Unfair Dismissals Act (introduced in 1977 and which excluded civil servants from its scope as they could not be dismissed) in accordance with the government's commitment to transforming the country 'into a modern progressive society based on social justice'. In June 1975 it was maintained that 'there are serious obstacles in the way of an employee seeking legal redress for what he may consider to be his unfair dismissal leading to disproportionate industrial conflict'.[23]

The year 1975 witnessed unofficial strike action from a breakaway post office officials association as well as a telephone dispute, and at the end of it RTÉ television programmes were off the air because of an overtime ban by technical staff. There were elements of both farce and vindictiveness to some disputes. In January 1976, 1,100 members of the Department of Posts and Telegraphs engineering staff in Dublin went on strike after the suspension of forty of their colleagues, the majority of whom had 'refused to park their vehicles in an official parking place and instead parked them on a clearway at Harold's Cross'. There were no telephone repairs as a result, and delays for applications. Conor Cruise O'Brien rejected demands for an 'objective enquiry' into the running of the post office. The disruption of phone services also caused chaos in the business community; it escalated into an official national strike of 6,000 post office engineering workers over grading and reorganisation. In February 1976 the post office officials wrote to Cruise O'Brien about 'the time-wasting petty bureaucracy which we had hoped your presence in the GPO might have changed. We are chipping away at it from our side; what we need to hear are sounds of chipping from the minister's side.'[24]

A memorandum from the Department of Posts and Telegraphs in July 1976 referred to professional engineers in the post office engaged in a 'go slow' campaign since the beginning of June: 'Industrial action by a managerial group is a most serious matter and concessions could not be made to them without risk of far reaching consequences. The Minister for Posts and Telegraphs does not propose to make any concessions even if the industrial action has a serious effect on the telecommunications service.'[25]

As seen earlier, *Magill* magazine's Liam O'Toole had referred to the telephone service as 'a national sick joke' and pointed to 'Victorian attitudes to staff relations', reflected in the fact that 'telephonists in St Andrew's Dublin, staged a walkout one night in June 1974 claiming "oppressive supervision" and alleging that visits to the toilet were subject to the permission of the night supervisor who insisted that each man sign a special form'.[26]

There was also the question of how these issues were disseminated through the media. In November 1977 in *Magill*, Gene Kerrigan, writing about the Ferenka strikers, criticised the media for its 'habitual use of loaded headlines' and a style of reporting on industrial problems that 'concedes the right to strike, but makes explicit propaganda against the exercising of the right'.[27]

The following year, there was a threatened strike by psychiatric workers looking for a 5 per cent salary increase that other workers in the public sector had obtained. There were, at that stage, 13,000 psychiatric patients in twenty district mental hospitals and it was 'not anticipated that more than 3,000–4,000 of them could be discharged in the event of the strike'. The total number of psychiatric nurses involved was almost 6,000. The Psychiatric Nurses Association, which had broken away from the ITGWU in the late 1960s, was regarded as 'militant and intransigent'. Walter Kirwan in the Department of the Taoiseach insisted it would be better in this case 'to settle as quickly and as quietly as possible, and, so far as possible on a basis that it is so differentiated as to minimize the danger of the settlement being used as a headline'. However, George Colley insisted they be resisted as the Labour Court had rejected their claim and to give in would involve 'undermining of the whole of the government's pay policy'. It was agreed not to grant them the increase.[28]

In the same year, a strike in the milk production sector was also regarded as something of an emergency. It led to a telegram from independent feminist senator Gemma Hussey to Lynch: 'Please take action immediately in the milk strike for the sake of mothers, young children and infants.'[29] A draft speech of Lynch's the following month referred to community concern about the level of strikes; he pointed out that there had been a reduction of the number of man days lost through strikes in 1977 but that the 1978 figure might show 'a reversal of what we had hoped would be a downward trend'.

The establishment of a proposed commission on industrial relations was delayed but in May 1978 the Minister for Labour, Gene Fitzgerald, a former company director and future finance minister, announced a commission of inquiry on industrial relations. The same month, Lynch was in receipt of a number of letters from America including one from the Milton Bradley Company in Massachusetts: 'I, like many chief executive officers of multinational companies who have operations in Ireland are becoming increasingly nervous over the prospect of labor unrest in your beautiful country.'[30] The government's general policy of non-intervention was justified on the grounds that 'experience has shown that ... industrial peace is best promoted if ministers refrain from personal intervention',[31] which seemed just a little self-serving. There was more trouble that autumn, when bin men went on strike; in October it was pointed out to Lynch: 'It is now four weeks since the dustmen's work to rule and bins of all shapes and sizes and contents litter the roadways, side by side with slogans telling us to "Keep Dublin Tidy".'[32]

A few months later, Lynch gave a speech to the Chamber of Commerce in Cork in which he asserted 'there are ways of resolving industrial disputes without irreparable destruction. If these are inadequate, the government are only too willing to improve them,'[33] which seemed rather late in the day. But by April 1979, it was asserted that the problem was a handful of unions that were negotiating wage increases with no reference to the terms of the National Wage Agreements.

The new National Understanding for economic and social development agreed between the government, employer and industrial organisations and ICTU in 1979 represented, announced Lynch, 'a whole new approach' as he promised that the taxation system would be revised to distribute the tax burden more equitably and would create 'a new unity, a new stability and a new attitude'.[34] There was little evidence of that the same month however, when the ITGWU placed a picket outside a McDonald's restaurant in the city centre. Pat Rabbitte, an ITGWU official, complained of the heavy handed approach taken: 'Since when is it normal practice to have a full time Garda escort on a picket?'[35]

That year's biggest dispute was a national postal strike that lasted from February to June and involved over 13,000 employees, but the Post Office Workers Union was faced down in its quest for pay increases of up to 37 per cent. It was understood the 'highest claim' the government was prepared to concede was 9 per cent. Crippling the country's postal collection and deliveries, and operator assisted phone calls, it was described by the Fine Gael spokesperson on labour, Jim Mitchell, as 'the most malevolent strike the country has ever known' and included violence between Gardaí and strikers on picket lines. It finally ended with acceptance of a 15 per cent pay increase for postmen and telephonists and 12 per cent for clerks and was thought to have prompted second thoughts about public sector militancy.[36]

By May 1979, Rory O'Hanlon, chairman of the Civil Service Arbitration Board, had adjudicated on '3 dozen separate claims' for increases in pay in the civil service and had '3 dozen more' awaiting his consideration. Reference was made to a 'queue of claims' some of them looking for up to 50 per cent increases in pay, though it was suggested that nurses contemplating industrial action had been 'chastised by the government's rigorous handling of the 3 month postal strike'. Reliance on overtime was a big issue but it was observed that 'some of the steam has gone out of the public service revolt'. Trade unionist and writer Charles McCarthy, a firm believer in resolving these disputes through negotiation, and who was respected by both union and management alike, remarked to the Confederation of Irish Industry that government policy appeared to be guided by an ambition 'to create at all times a vast interrelated scheme of wages and salaries, all locking in to one another ... This process becomes the overwhelming preoccupation of the system, which develops more as a control system than an administrative one.'[37]

In June 1979 it was reported that ICTU were to reject the proposed National Understanding owing to internal divisions. The Executive was struggling, it seemed, to deliver the ITGWU and 'the balance of general, craft and public service unions within Congress requires some alliance of all three elements, with their various aspirations, to defeat a proposal of that kind'. In Longford the previous month, Fianna Fáil's Brian Lenihan had offered the government's help to the unions 'in dealing with the Reds' and he went on to attack 'the attempted importation of alien ideologies'.[38] Eventually, the National Understanding was approved by the ICTU in July and it was observed that 'cabinet wrangles, conflict between unions and within unions and nearly a year of jockeying and manoeuvring lie behind the acceptance'.[39]

When speaking on the adjournment of the Dáil in July 1979, Jack Lynch was upbeat about the economy, suggesting 'Ireland did well in 1978', with economic growth, total employment increased by 17,000 (which he said 'was the best performance since the foundation of the state') and inflation falling to 7.5 per cent for the year as a whole. He also forecast that the inflow of young people into the workforce would be 'very much higher than elsewhere in the EEC', which was 'an obligation and an opportunity unique in our history' and would require the creation of 'jobs at an unprecedented rate ... This in turn calls for fresh approaches and a radical break with our past.' What needed to be tackled, he said, was an 'Irish disease' which he defined as 'the frequency and duration of disputes in basic public services, most often but not always in the public sector'. He observed that 1.3 million man days had been lost as a result of industrial disputes in the previous six months alone.[40]

The need to tackle these issues was also brought more sharply into focus by Ireland's entry into the European Monetary System (EMS) in 1979, which has been 'instanced as one of the preconditioning factors' behind the desire for social partnership. It also involved breaking the link between the punt (the Irish pound) and sterling – for the first time since 1826 – which it was hoped would lead to an appreciation of the punt against sterling. (It didn't.)[41] In Joe Lee's words, the decision to enter the EMS was 'impelled by the search for cheap money and cheap discipline' with loans and interest subsidies 'to cushion the Irish economy against the shock of exposure to a hard money area. It was the hard money that was expected to provide the chief discipline' with a belief that the association with such hard currency instead of the 'soft' currency of sterling would reduce inflation. But such hard discipline required 'discipline on incomes that the government felt was needed but did not have the courage to impose directly'.[42]

Within six months, however, the shakiness of any National Understanding became apparent when the new Taoiseach Charles Haughey made a televised address in January 1980:

> I wish to talk to you this evening about the state of the nation's affairs and the picture I have to paint is not, unfortunately, a very cheerful one. The figures which are now just becoming available to us show one thing very clearly. As a community we are living way beyond our means. I do not mean that everyone in the community is living too well. Clearly many are not and have barely enough to get by. But taking us all together, we have been living at a rate which is simply not justified by the amount of goods and services we are producing. To make up the difference, we have been borrowing enormous amounts of money, borrowing at a rate which just cannot continue. As few simple figures will

make this very clear. At home, the government's current income from taxes and all other sources in 1979 fell short of what was needed to pay the running costs of the state by about £520 million. To meet this and our capital programme, we had to borrow in 1979 over £1000 million. That amount equals to one-seventh of our entire national output ... There is one thing above all else which we can do to help get the situation right and which is entirely within our control. I refer to industrial relations. Any further serious interruption in production, or in the provision of essential services, in 1980 would be a major disaster. I believe that everyone listening to me tonight shares my anxiety about our situation in that respect. Strikes, go-slows, work-to-rule, stoppages in key industries and essential services, were too often a feature of life in 1979. They caused suffering and hardship; at times it looked as if we were becoming one of those countries where basic services could not be relied upon to operate as part of normal life. Immediately following my election as Taoiseach, I received countless messages from all over the country from people in every walk of life, appealing to me to do something about this situation. Let us clearly understand, however, that this is not a one-sided affair. Managements that do not give first-class attention to their firm's industrial relations, who ignore situations and let them drift into confrontation, are just as blameworthy as the handful of wild men who slap an unofficial picket and stop thousands of workers from earning their living. Apportioning blame, however, is not going to get us anywhere. What we need is a new way forward and that is my primary purpose, as head of government, in talking to you tonight.[43]

– FORTY-EIGHT –

HOPING TO STRIKE IT RICH

The issue of natural resources was also something that surfaced in this decade, particularly in the context of oil, nuclear energy, gas, mining and planning. Resolutions at annual Labour Party conferences in the early 1970s emphasised 'the scandal of the exploitation of the country's mineral, gas and oil reserves'.[1] Just what natural resources did Ireland have? Who actually owned them? And how would they be explored and managed or sold? Perhaps it was the muddied answers to these questions that created lost economic opportunities in the 1970s and well beyond.

Given the international oil crises, reducing Irish dependence on oil was deemed imperative – in December 1974 petrol prices rose by 30 per cent from 50p to 65p a gallon – but the question of alternative sources of energy was not straightforward. A memorandum from the Department of Transport and Power in November 1973 noted that the ESB were 'satisfied that they must lessen their dependence on imported oil as a source of primary energy, having regard to growing uncertainty about oil price levels and continued availability of oil supplies and have recommended the provision of a nuclear power station'. It was suggested it would require a down payment of £4 million in 1975, that it was 'the only feasible alternative to continued dependence on imported oil' and that the Northern Ireland electrical authorities were 'in full agreement with the project'.[2]

Earlier that year the Dublin city manager, Matthew Macken, rejected a planning application for a £40 million oil refinery in Dublin Bay. The prospects of such a development, as well as proposals from the Dublin Ports and Docks Board, had mobilised environmentalists who feared a polluted bay, and in particular, brought to prominence activist Seán Loftus, who changed his name by deed poll to Seán Dublin Bay Loftus. Oil spillages in Bantry Bay, including the leaking of 115,000 gallons of heavy fuel oil by the tanker *Afran Zodiac* in January 1975, exacerbated concerns. The following year, Minister for Local Government James Tully rejected the appeal of Aquarius Securities Ltd to build an oil refinery in Dublin Bay after consideration of the evidence given at a public hearing that lasted for sixteen days.

But oil and natural gas exploration in the sea within the territorial waters of Ireland and mineral exploration on its land were too often shrouded in ambiguity. In September 1972 journalist Chris Glennon, writing in the *Irish Independent*, referred to a tax and royalty 'honeymoon' enjoyed for years by the mining companies, involving exemptions for up to twenty years, and suggested the whole issue was being re-examined. Glennon's point was that 'the deposits of minerals, gas and oil [nature] left on or around the island should see the exchequer benefit to the tune of tens of millions of pounds'. A policy for the future, according to Paddy Lalor, the Minister for Industry and Commerce, 'should give the state an equitable share of increasing profits while, at the same time, being sufficiently attractive to the mining companies to ensure the continued development of the country's mineral resources in an orderly and efficient manner ... There is a quite high degree of state control over the development of mineral resources. All reserves of gold, silver and petroleum and more than 60 per cent of all other mineral rights are state owned. The minister can attach to leases any conditions that he sees fit.'[3]

Jack Lynch was informed in November 1972 that a consortium of North American corporations, mainly Canadian-based, had been formed to finance the exploration of oil and gas in the Irish continental shelf. Risk capital of £4 million was committed and a company, Irish Offshore Oil, which included Senator Eoin Ryan of Fianna Fáil, a lawyer and businessman whose father had been a minister from the 1930s to the 1960s, Lord Killanin, film producer and president of the International Olympic Committee, and John Guinness, future chairman of British Nuclear Fuels, on its board, was established as the Irish partner in this consortium. It had raised £400,000 from private investors, with 10 per cent set aside for the ESB if it wished to participate. Frank Lemass, former general manager of state transport company CIÉ and brother of former Taoiseach Seán Lemass, requested a meeting between the government and the consortium, though there is no record of such a meeting taking place.[4]

In May 1973, after the change of government, solicitor Donough O'Connor contacted Liam Cosgrave, stressing that once oil leases were given and exploration rights exercised it was difficult to change the rules of the game when and if there were significant finds, and suggested there was a need for independent legal advice: 'I note there is growing concern over the oil and gas exploration rights and potential profits. This is a very sensitive subject and I know that the government is examining it in great detail. The fact that the problem has not arisen before in any great measure on this side of the Atlantic has meant that governments dealing with oil and gas rights have very little experience to guide them.'[5]

O'Connor had touched among many things here that were vital, but there is no record of either Lynch or Cosgrave acting on these suggestions for meetings. Back in 1959, Marathon Oil had been given an exclusive licence to explore for oil and gas off the south and south-east coasts; it was suggested in 1973 that 'there are about 40 other oil companies with non-exclusive licences. There is a very big interest among these other companies in obtaining exclusive rights of the sort which Marathon possesses.'[6]

In March 1974 it was reported that Marathon had discovered reserves of 1.4 million cubic feet of natural gas off the coast of Kinsale in Cork; not a big find, but one which could 'supply about 12 per cent of Ireland's overall energy requirements'. The company signed an agreement with Bord Gáis (the Irish Gas Board) to supply a portion of gas daily for a twenty-year period starting in 1979. The *Irish Independent* insisted the following month that the government should have gone for 50:50 arrangements instead of giving away 'the whole of its ... valuable off shore rights'. The concessions given to Marathon Oil were constantly referred to in the trade and scientific magazines as 'amusing' and 'exceptional' and the writer elaborated: 'It is maddening to see Britain selling off oil blocks for exploration at figures over £250,000, while one oil company held more than a hundred such blocks belonging to the Republic', with oil companies allowed free use of an oil terminal in Bantry Bay for storage. An academic in Edinburgh suggested oil production 'would have a much greater effect on individual wealth in Ireland than in Britain because of the differences in population and industrial usage'.[7]

In the summer of 1974, US oil barons including Lord Granard of

Texaco, informed Cosgrave, who was a friend of Granard, that they could come to Ireland to meet him at short notice. Justin Keating, the Minister for Industry and Commerce, advised him against meeting them as the procedure was for him to invite tenders in the public interest and for him to decide the conditions, but he offered to meet them if it would be 'helpful ... In the circumstances, I do not think that a "presentation" of the kind mentioned by Lord Granard would be called for in connection with the important decisions which we are to make in this area. However, if you feel that you would like to make some gesture towards Lord Granard I would be willing to receive him and his friends at some stage in Dublin for the purposes of a short discussion.'[8]

At the end of October 1974, Keating agreed that, as he would be out of the country, his officials would hear a 'short presentation' from Texaco (in reality it was a lengthy presentation with five government officials and Texaco senior executives in attendance) while Cosgrave brought the Texaco representatives, including Granard, for lunch in the Gresham Hotel (where he chose the most expensive menu of Galway Oysters and beef fillet accompanied by Nuits-Saint-Georges wine). Government officials did a lot of preparation for this lunch; civil servants in the Department of Industry and Commerce stressed that they wanted industrial employment in return. It seems no commitment was given and, a week after the meetings, Keating issued a statement insisting 'the right of state participation will be an essential feature of each petroleum licence', to which the Irish Petroleum group reacted with hostility on the grounds that they, not government, were the risk takers.[9]

There was much ambiguity around this. As was pointed out in *Hibernia* magazine in February 1974, there was simply not enough information on the operation of the oil companies. The companies were accused of using Peter Barry, Minister for Transport and Power, as 'a mouthpiece, feeding him inadequate information'.[10] The following year Keating, described by Joe Lee as being 'anxious to ensure the safeguarding of the national interest', with the assistance of civil servant J. C. Holloway, devised licensing terms announced in 1975 'that would secure 50 per cent as the state's share and oblige companies to use an Irish base of operations', production royalties of between 8 and 16 per cent and production bonuses on significant finds, while the standard corporation tax of 50 per cent would also apply.[11] Keating, who was critical of the terms originally agreed by Fianna Fáil with Marathon for the development of the Kinsale gas fields, was influenced by the manner in which the Norwegian government had sought to develop its indigenous oil and gas resources 'in the face of stiff opposition from the oil majors'.[12]

In 1973 Fergus Cahill, who was head of communications at the Institute of Industrial Research and Standards, had proposed that the government set up a study group to examine offshore development. Norway's tough bargaining position with the oil companies was clearly an influence as at a conference in Dublin in December 1973 on the issue, Norway sent representation. Keating was similarly influenced by the Norwegian situation, prompting his insistence on a 50 per cent 'state take', as he termed it, and surprising the oil companies by his resolute stance.

Keating's terms were designed to require companies to drill at least one exploratory well within three years and 'surrender 50 per cent of the original licensed area they were granted within four'. Under the terms, the state would take a share of the project after a discovery, thereby not having to bear the costs of exploration: 'It was clear from the 1975 terms that the minister envisaged the formation of a state oil company similar to the Norwegian state company, Statoil, if significant finds of oil or gas were made.' The Norwegian government offered assistance, 'partly in exchange for fishing rights in Irish waters', to set up such a state oil company and 'offered them a direct involvement in the commercial development of North Sea fields as a means of gaining the necessary experience and financial ability to properly develop the potentially rich Irish offshore resources',[13] though this never happened. In establishing the state-owned Irish National Petroleum Company (INPC) to control Ireland's petroleum reserves, Keating recalled that he 'wanted this company for more reasons than just money ... We had to understand the industry from end to end.'[14]

Keating was still criticised by his successor Des O'Malley of Fianna Fáil, who was not keen on the INPC. He accepted it grudgingly, due to the 1979 international oil crisis, but it was not given 'adequate finance or powers to realise its potential and was actually prohibited in its memos and articles of association from drilling for oil and gas'. Over the course of the next two decades, in the absence of significant finds, pressure grew to dilute the terms Keating had established in 1975, and such dilution 'weighed heavily in favour of the oil and gas companies', including exemption of oil and gas production from royalty payments and the abolition of all state participation and the reduction of corporation tax they were obliged to pay.[15] Instead of securing state involvement in the drilling or development of resources through the INPC, O'Malley hired oil and gas consultants whom he refused to identify in the Dáil in view of what he called 'the national interest', a practice continued by his successors.[16]

In January 1979 disaster struck Whiddy Island oil terminal in Cork when an explosion occurred while a French tanker was unloading its cargo; all forty-three crew members were killed as well as seven workers on the Gulf Oil terminal. A subsequent inquiry held two transnational oil companies, Gulf and Total, responsible for the disaster. Total, owners of the tanker, had knowingly not kept the vessel properly maintained while Gulf Oil was criticised for not taking adequate measures to ensure the safety of the men on Whiddy. It has also been suggested that the Whiddy disaster 'may have played its part in reducing the government's enthusiasm for building a nuclear power station'. Only twenty-seven of the fifty bodies were recovered; the *Irish Independent* headline referred to it as a 'Holocaust'. Whiddy Island inhabitants, numbering just forty 'fled in a flotilla of small boats', while those who fought the flames were commended for their bravery. Survivors accused Gulf of 'closing ranks when investigations began'. The terminal was never fully repaired.[17]

The reference to a nuclear power station came at the end of a decade that had witnessed dissension and protest over the appropriateness or feasibility of such a development in the Republic. In November 1973 the government approved in principle an ESB proposal to construct a nuclear power station because of the level of dependence on oil, which had sharply risen due to the demand for electricity. The growth rate in this regard was one of the highest in Europe 'averaging about 10 per cent per annum over the past 10 years or so'; in 1961 oil-fired units accounted for 20 per cent of the ESB's generating capacity; the figure by 1973 was 64 per cent.[18] A number of proposed sites were mentioned for a possible nuclear station, including Kilrush in County Clare, Sallenstown in County Louth, Easkey in County Sligo, Whiting Bay in County Waterford and Carnsore in County Wexford. The Minister for Transport and Power, Peter Barry, was conscious that the EEC was in favour of the speedy development of nuclear energy and 'confident that it should be possible to protect the environment fully. Nuclear plants are in operation in many countries without serious deleterious effects.'[19]

The ESB favoured the Carnsore location but was slow to respond to government requests. In October 1977 a bleak note from Richard Stokes to Jack Lynch summed up the urgency: 'our oil imports went up from just over £60 million in 1973 to a current level of about £300 million as a result of the oil crisis. We are among the countries in the EEC which are most dependent on external sources for our energy. This makes us extremely vulnerable to another oil crisis. The 50 per cent increase in prices mentioned [in the international media] could well wreck any hope of economic progress here.' There were projections that oil supplies would be exhausted in thirty years based on present usage.

On this basis, he felt it imperative that the nuclear option was explored and suggested objections to it were exaggerated and that, in any case, it would probably take ten years from the date of the initial decision to the date of the final commissioning of any nuclear plant.[20] In the spring of 1978, John Kelly referred in one speech to his misgivings about the safety of a nuclear station and was critical of Des O'Malley's 'sarcastic references in the Dáil to the Friends of the Earth and the recent distinguished winner of the Lenin Peace Prize [Seán Mac Bride] ... then there is Mr O'Malley's petulant behaviour towards the people who are specifically concerned about the proposed location ... To tell them, as he did at his party's Ard Fheis, that if Wexford did not want the station there were other places that did, is to treat them as though they were children refusing to eat rice pudding.'[21] O'Malley refused to countenance a public inquiry and scorned opponents of the project, but protestors and the Nuclear Safety Association managed to mobilise a significant opposition and it was regarded as a campaign that stirred 'the notoriously apathetic youth of the country'.[22]

A festival was organised in August 1978 featuring prominent musicians, including Christy Moore, who then took their 'anti-nuclear road show' on tour. The success of the protest and the awareness it generated led to the proposal being discreetly dropped in the late 1970s. As well as involving 'cultural mobilisation', these protests were partly an Irish manifestation of international resistance to nuclear power encouraged by the anti-war movements in the US, Germany and France in the late 1960s and early 1970s and partly 'an attempt to resist aspects of modernisation by a sceptical community'. They were also bolstered by concern over the plans of British Nuclear Fuels Limited (BNFL) to expand the Windscale plant's reprocessing capacity. John Carroll, president of the ITGWU, was a vocal opponent of Carnsore and edited a book with Petra Kelly, active in the German Green movement and 'doyen of the European environmentalists', entitled *A Nuclear Ireland?* (1978) in which Kelly invoked 'a familiar rallying call for the Irish audience, that of dependency on a foreign source' (for nuclear expertise and supplies). The Three Mile Island reactor meltdown in the US in 1979 also bolstered the campaign.[23]

There were disturbing developments in relation to mining in the 1970s. When huge deposits of lead and zinc were discovered outside Navan in 1970 by Canadian company Tara Exploration and Development, the owner of some of land on which the proposed mine was located, Patrick Wright, ended up negotiating not just with Tara, but unbeknownst to it, with Michael Wymes, the solicitor who was advising him and who bought the land for himself, his father-in-law Thomas Roche, head of Cement Roadstone Holdings and his son, also Thomas. Wright signed a contract with them in 1971 to sell the lands and also become a shareholder in the company of four, named Bula. Minister for Industry and Commerce Paddy Lalor failed to get the land back under a compulsory acquisition order, after the High Court found in favour of Bula, which had challenged Lalor's order, though this court decision was made for technical rather than constitutional reasons. In 1974 it was commented in *Hibernia* magazine: 'not for one moment must it be forgotten that the minerals belong not to any company or group of individuals but to the Irish people. On the other hand, Tara mining and exploration [sic] have every right to expect priority in concluding a reasonable and fair contract with the government'.

Later that year it queried why Lalor's successor, Justin Keating, had become so mute on the Bula issue: 'He has been saying very little and initiating very little ... Is it because he considers it essential for the state to have a stake but not the controlling stake?'[24] The reaction of the Liaison Committee of the Left in the Labour Party to Justin Keating's performance in government from the outset had been hostile, summed up in the withering put-down 'so much for the socialist seventies'. It referred to 'the great mine robbery' and called for a resources protection campaign to 'fight the sell out of Irish minerals'.[25] Another reference was made to legislation enacted in the 1960s that meant a mining company got 91 per cent of the minerals (the state getting the remaining 9 per cent) together with a twenty-year exemption from tax; these were regarded as 'suicidal concessions'. Keating abolished tax exemptions for the mining industry but was still condemned – notably by those in the Resources Protection Campaign – for not nationalising the mines, a criticism also levelled by ICTU and his own Labour Party.[26]

As the earlier part of the Tara story was relayed by the Liaison Committee of the Left, in October 1970 James Tully, Labour TD for Meath (who was hostile to the socialist trend that developed in the Labour Party prior to the 1969 general election. At the annual conference of the party in 1970 he referred to some fellow-members as being 'commies' and 'smart-alecs … with sweat dripping on to their schoolbooks who talk about the workers of this country'[27]) was holding a clinic in Navan when a local farmer mentioned that he had dug up rock that contained a mineral. 'Tully immediately passed on the information to his son, the secretary of Tara Exploration. Later that week quarry workers in the area blew up some rock and discovered a copper seam. When the other mining companies learned of the discovery there was a rush for prospecting licences – but too late. Three days earlier Tara had acquired a licence for the area. Thanks to Mr Tully they had acquired the largest lead/zinc mine in the world, current worth some £2,000 million.'[28] (There is no indication how this figure was arrived at.) *Hibernia* also thought it odd that Tully – 'the most complex and ambivalent figure in the coalition … whose periodic abrasiveness is tempered by a deep layer of common sense' and who uttered 'to hell with the rich' in an RTÉ interview – also supported mining speculators and ranchers in County Meath and also mentioned that his son was secretary of Tara mines.[29]

In 1975 Keating agreed the terms of a state mining lease with Tara mines which would see Tara give the government a 25 per cent share in the company and a flat 4.5 per cent royalty on profits as well as the usual 50 per cent corporation tax. But much more controversially, rather than amending legislation to enable an acquisition order to withstand a legal challenge, Keating struck an extraordinary deal which left Bula in possession of the minerals and lead with a 25 per cent shareholding given to the government and 24 per cent share sold to the state at a price of £9.54 million, which was given to the four men tax free rather than being invested in the development of the mine. As Judge Kevin Lynch subsequently put it (in 1997), Keating 'invested in the pockets of the private shareholders'. Keating defended his action on the grounds that the state got a 49 per cent share, which gave it leverage with Tara and enabled him to get 25 per cent of the company's Irish operation for the state also, an inadequate and unconvincing defence given what he could have done as minister if he had desired, most obviously compulsory acquisition of the Bula lands and minerals since, in the 1974 case referred to above, the High Court and Supreme Court confirmed that such compulsory acquisition was not unconstitutional.[30] (Judge Lynch's decision was delivered in the High Court in 1997, the culmination of a court case which began in 1989, one of a number of legal actions in relation to Bula. The directors of Bula, Patrick Wymes and Richard Wood, sued Tara mines, the state and Outukumpu, the Finnish company which had acquired Tara mines, for economic loss, breach of contract and breach of constitutional duty, and claimed compensation of over £300 million. Negotiations between Tara and Bula on the mining of the Navan site had broken down on several occasions over the years and Bula had claimed that an agreement in 1975 to exploit the mine expeditiously had been breached and that the government had failed to force Tara to comply with its obligations under its lease. The High Court rejected Bula's claims. Keating was never on trial; it should be pointed out that in 1985 he was awarded £65,000 after a successful legal action against the publishers of the *Sunday Tribune* newspaper and its editor Vincent Browne for an article on the Tara/Bula affair which had claimed 'Keating gave £10 million of state money to four people tax free for effectively nothing'. The jury did not accept he was personally dishonest in his handling of the affair.)

In relation to the acquisition of shares in the Bula mine in 1977, a memorandum from the Department of Industry and Commerce noted that a valuation of £39.75 million had been placed on the mine and that the government would be taking shares 'not exceeding £9.78 million'. Reference was also made regarding the 'apparent ambiguity about the manner in which the Board had incorporated their valuation of the mine in the balance sheet of the company' but it was decided that no publicity would be given to the issue on the grounds that 'in the case of agreements with petroleum exploration companies providing for state participation in the development of oil or gas discoveries, it is the invariable practice of governments not to make the terms of such agreements public'.[31] In February 1977 Keating met Cosgrave to discuss the valuation which had been put on the mine. The owners claimed they did not have to pay tax and it was suggested 'we don't know yet [whether this is true] but the people involved were very clever'. But Cosgrave insisted it was essential to ensure that 'innocent transactions were not also hit' regarding liability for tax.

In a Department of Taoiseach memorandum it was observed that 'it could be that the present agitation will blow over. Inequitable amendments in the tax code to deal with a company crisis will be forgotten but the effects of an unjust tax law will not.' However, it was agreed that 'in no circumstances should the possibility of an amendment to the tax laws be mentioned' in the Dáil. Dermot Nally, however, was more critical of advancing the company over £9 million of public money: 'It is not hard to understand the unease so emphatically expressed at the non-publication of a document which deals with such large amounts of exchequer finance.'

The valuation put on the mine was 'a major source of controversy', given the lack of information about the price of lead and zinc in the future, what it contains and the cost of developing it: 'Every one of these items can be questioned ... nobody can even be 50 per cent certain of what will happen. There are too many imponderables.'[32] But the following week Cosgrave reminded ministers that 'the contents of this agreement which had been circulated to ministers under "secret" cover – are to be treated in the same manner as budget secrets. It was essential to ensure that no leak of information – if such were to occur – would be traced to the cabinet.'[33] It was a shameful development reflecting poorly on all those involved and all those who refused to speak up. In January 1978, Fine Gael's John Kelly referred to the publication of the Bula agreement by the Fianna Fáil government as something that caused 'damage to our international reputation', alleging that it was done for political point scoring and involved the breaking of confidentiality and was an 'exercise in reckless spite'.[34] This seemed contradictory; why had the coalition of which Kelly was a member agreed to something which was so damaging of Ireland's reputation internationally in the first place?

As was argued at a later stage in relation to Keating, 'For a man who had once denounced the "leopards of capitalism" he now found himself involved in one of the most dramatic and legally convoluted sagas in modern Irish business history ... The money was paid free of all income tax, capital gains tax and a wealth tax. Not only did he lose a lot of support from within the Labour Party but in the Dáil he was reduced to silence by the then Fianna Fáil spokesman Dessie O'Malley, who accused him of making a series of "misleading statements" on the issue.'[35] In the event, the Bula company failed. A High Court judgment in February 1997 concluded that Tara had been 'gazumped' and 'cheated' and that Bula had breached planning laws and had deprived Tara of the fruits of its drilling programme on which in the region of £300,000 had been spent.

In April 1979 John Kelly again had Des O'Malley in his sights, referring to the 'publication of the Bula agreement minus the accounts' and a reported 'top level secret deal with Russia for unlimited oil supplies ... A day has gone by without denial.'[36] The following month he referred to the Minister for Foreign Affairs, Michael O'Kennedy, apparently in negotiations 'with the Finnish national oil corporation for a supply of oil from Finland'. He was scathing about the government's energy conservation policy, or lack thereof: 'The total amount spent on promotional advertising for [energy] conservation in the first four months of 1979 was £150 – less than the cost of a return ticket from Dublin to Brussels, whereas the last government spent £70,000 on this in 1976.'[37]

The Fianna Fáil government's Green Paper on energy policy – 'not that it's actually coloured green ... it's more the colour of diluted bullshit'[38] – which underlined that 75 per cent of Ireland's total energy requirements were reliant on imported oil and dismissed fears about nuclear energy – was described by one critic in September 1978 as representing thinking that 'is ten years out of date' due to its concentration on how the country was to supply energy 'but places much less emphasis on how people may be encouraged to use less'.[39]

Another issue that emerged in the late 1970s in the context of potential fuel supplies was the appropriateness of doing financial business with certain regimes that presided over human rights abuses. A confidential note in the papers of Garret FitzGerald refers to Noel Browne ringing him in December 1974 to discuss Libya's desire to have diplomatic contacts with Ireland in return for oil and financial investment 'and would reconsider their "Provo" line on Northern Ireland'. The government, he said, could contact Libya at "PO Box 888, Tripoli"',[40] a message that was hardly taken seriously on the basis of that address. But a few months later FitzGerald wrote to John Bruton about a possible visit to Libya by a parliamentary delegation: 'I do have a slight worry that the visit will attract disproportionate attention and I would ask you, for that reason, to keep a low profile.'[41]

Objectionable regimes were also a matter that was exercising the mind of Desmond O'Malley in September 1978 when he wrote to Jack Lynch:

> I received some time ago an invitation from the oil minister of Iraq to pay an official visit there. They have an interest in possibly building an oil refinery here and supplying us with Crude. Because of the nature of the Iraq regime I was loath to accept it but on the advice of Michael

> O'Kennedy [Minister for Foreign Affairs] a month or so ago I did accept although no date has yet been fixed. Since then, as you know, eleven Iraqi diplomats have been expelled from London and there is a strong suggestion that the regime is officially involved in the murder of a former Iraqi prime minister. For these reasons I am again rather loath to go and would propose to consult Michael O'Kennedy again when he returns from Africa.[42]

Lynch offered no response, but in terms of Irish foreign trade, Iraq's human rights record was not going to be an obstacle to doing business in the future.

PART VII

SOCIAL CHANGE

'New expectations have been generated – expectations that have risen faster than the capacity to fulfil them'

There was no shortage of barometers of social change in the 1970s and no dearth of comment on their significance and whether or not they reflected a society progressing or were signals of crisis. Some observers were equivocal about how to measure progress, reflected in an anecdote told by writer and librarian Dermot Foley in 1974. The previous year he had met a woman in Clare: '"Are they still making that lovely butter round here?" I asked her. "By my soul, they're not," she replied. "The big North Clare Creamery at Ennistynom has the three tits of every cow in this parish nowadays"'. Foley observed laconically, 'Money in the bank, the craft gone and the hind tit left. It is, I suppose, a sort of prosperity.'[1]

At what price came progress and modernisation was an inevitable question and there were various answers that focused as much on what was being lost as on what was being gained. In 1978 Jesuit writer Fr John Brady, in a contribution to Studies *under the title 'Ireland in Transition', highlighted the focus during the decade on the notion of pluralism and the redefining of values in relation to the law, public policy, religion and education. One of his colleagues, Timothy Hamilton, suggested people were beginning to see 'that it is possible for the Irish to create a community which is not a sell out to permissiveness, nor to modernism, nor to secularism but which is yet something new and modern in Irish relationships'. The logic was that there could be due regard for what was best about 'traditional values' but also a new premium placed on freedom and reconciliation.*[2] *This suggested that Ireland was experiencing a decade later some of the debates that had raged elsewhere during the 1960s, but it was also somewhat contrived and amounted to wishful thinking; there was to be no such smoothness or careful balancing, as the preponderance of the word 'crisis' in relation to so many areas indicated. As well-known* Irish Press *journalist T. P. O'Mahony saw it, Ireland in 1976 encapsulated both pain and paradox:*

> *That Irish society has changed is uncontestable. The very style of life today shows this – it is more brash, strident, garish and vulgar, for one thing. It is also more affluent. But whether the quality has improved is altogether another matter ... the refinements of language and taste have been blurred. Self-reflection, the spirit of creativity, the life of the imagination and social grace have all fallen victim to our obsessive preoccupation with economic progress, material benefits and unadulterated hedonism. We are lured increasingly by affluence. Progress is one of the most chameleon and pernicious concepts in our present-day vocabulary.*

O'Mahony acknowledged that progress had been made in lessening the extent of poverty, but insisted the ideals of the revolutionary generation of the early twentieth century had been abandoned. There existed a 'plastic environment' of office blocks, supermarkets and urban estates, a superficial and selective sense of social justice, a lack of humanity in religion and politics and little understanding of pluralism. It all amounted to 'a crisis of identity' which left 'little ground for optimism'.[3] *He was being unduly harsh, however, and his very expression of such trenchant views and prognosis in a sense undermined his conclusion, for the articulation of such dissatisfaction was one of the achievements of the 1970s as he and a succession of others challenged authority, demanded reform, and developed a discourse of criticism in the midst of social upheaval.*

Such social change was reflected in a variety of ways, as revealed, for example, in census data. Births began to increase in the decade, the population grew at a rate of 1.55 per cent per annum, over four times the EEC average, and the marriage rate rose steadily in the late 1960s and early 1970s. Migration turned from outward to inward – reversing one of the great failures of the independent state – with the result that the population grew by 465,000 between 1971 and 1981. Of the 160 rural districts in the state, 80 per cent recorded population increases in the 1970s. In 1946, less than one-third of households had more than four rooms; by 1971 this had increased to 46.3 per cent. The school-leaving age was raised from fourteen to fifteen in 1972 and the number of full-time students over the age of fifteen increased from 137,000 in 1971 to 200,000 in 1981. Labour-force participation for married women increased from 8 per cent in 1971 to 17.4 per cent in 1981.[4] *Changes in farm technology, in the household economy and in transport and communications were striking, though remnants of all sorts of traditional patterns and 'all sorts of intermediate stages' were also apparent.*[5]

These changes, and increasing urbanisation, raised the issue of what constituted the notion of community in the 1970s and sociologists identified much ambiguity in this regard. There were contests over space, wealth and power, with cities and rural areas being studied closely in relation to social, housing and class relations and uneven economic development, as was the issue of whether rural values still dominated the urban areas.[6] *One of the issues addressed by the sociology journal* Social Studies *in 1974 was the question 'Is community dead?' to which the answer was no, but community identity was being expressed in new and different kinds of social forms, with a growing sense that people needed to speak for themselves.*[7]

The development of sociology and the desire by some scholars to depict traditional societies and communities in transition or in danger of demise led to some fascinating studies, including Hugh Brody's Inishkillane *(1973), which depicted a small farm community under pressure, with children still seen as a hedge against old age. It seemed to suggest that a harmonious self-sufficient system of the past was disintegrating, though its historic robustness was probably exaggerated anyway. Nancy Scheper-Hughes's* Saints, Scholars and Schizophrenics *(1979) also presented a very pessimistic portrait of Irish child rearing and consequent high rates of mental illness. Conflicts abounded it seemed, about nurturance, physicality and sexuality, which Scheper-Hughes concluded were the product of the 'ascetic Jansenist tradition of Irish Catholicism' with a focus on discipline to combat weakness and sin; silence and passivity, it seemed, were the most admired qualities in young children.*[8]

The legacy of emigration was still paramount in some communities, and despite economic development, for some from traditionally poorer districts it was still the only viable option. From a compilation of estate duties it was maintained in 1975 that 1 per cent of the population owned around 33 per cent of personal wealth and 5 per cent owned 60–63 per cent, while 25 per cent of the population could be considered poor.[9] *The extent to which contemporary governments needed to take responsibility for emigrant welfare seemed to raise uncomfortable questions for them. Others in traditionally neglected districts, including the inner city of Dublin, began to form robust community organisations that politicised the issues affecting their quality of life and demanded a say in decisions affecting their welfare and the physical infrastructure of their hinterlands.*

There was still a tendency to romanticise the west of Ireland. Leon Uris's Ireland: A Terrible Beauty *(1976) suggested 'The Irish will join a sort of European uni-sex and become not so different and apart from other people ... in truth, the west is the Irish conscience, when it goes, so much of what is great about being Irish will go with it.'*[10] *This assessment was in stark contrast to that offered by Hugh Brody, who seemed to suggest that the people of Inishkillane did not see themselves as being in any way in a socially or morally advantageous position in their own society, but marginalised.*[11]

The health of the Irish also came under the microscope and between 1967–8 and 1973–4 there was a 30 per cent increase in expenditure on health services, which grew faster than any other component of government expenditure during those years.[12] *Historically, reform in this area had been bedevilled by the stubbornness of vested interests, most obviously the Catholic Church and the medical profession, both of which had resisted greater state encroachment, but by the 1970s only some elements of the medical profession remained uneasy about greater state funding and the church's misgivings having been mollified owing to its greater preoccupation with social justice and more frequent criticism of poverty. The decision of Dr John O'Connell, who went on to become a Labour Party TD and later Minister for Health, to establish the* Irish Medical Times *in 1967 was audacious because of its determination, with the assistance of talented doctors like Robert Towers, a campaigner for legalised contraception, Risteard Mulcahy, a heart disease expert, and psychiatrist Anthony Clare, to be a campaigning newspaper. It consulted doctors nationwide, gave an insight into the problems they faced and provided them with a platform for their grievances.*

The involvement of doctors in public discussion – without fear of censorship – was timely. The Health Act of 1970 inaugurated administrative reforms in a profession split between the Irish Medial Association, which traditionally had a much closer relationship with the state, and the more anti-establishment Irish Medical Union, established in 1963. The tone established by the newspaper anticipated a decade of debate and discord: 'It seems likely that we shall be in opposition no matter what political party is in power.' But there were also tensions about the questioning of the profession, demands for accountability, and what some journalists considered was 'an obsession with secrecy on the part of the medical profession'. It has been suggested prior to the 1960s that the medical profession had lived 'in a warm wash of deference'.[13]

There was also perceived underfunding of general practice, and for some overworked doctors a rationale that 'by working until near exhaustion you learned more quickly'. The big issues of the decade were access and eligibility; the determination to kill off the poor law system and dispensary service, conceived in the nineteenth century for the poorest, witnessed the introduction of a choice-of-doctor scheme in 1972. This new scheme was a 'boom period' for some GPs who succeeded in getting a basic fee per item. Medical cards covered just under one-third of the population in 1972. Upheaval in the medico-political arena did not stop there; consultants distrusted Brendan Corish as Minister for Health, who in 1974 persisted with the doomed 'pipe dream' of a medical scheme that would cover all the population. As things stood, there was a three-tier system in relation to hospital care – state-funded eligibility for the poorest, none for the wealthiest and part-eligibility for the middle classes. Consultants – still wanting and often getting the 'warm wash of deference' – conveniently depicted Corish and the 'doctrinaire socialists in his team' as delusional, and the consultants won, without the need for their erstwhile allies in the Catholic Church.[14]

There were also significant developments in relation to private health care and private health coverage. Voluntary Health Insurance (VHI) membership increased from 321,777 in 1968 to 645,165 in 1978. But health proposals necessarily continued to embrace both political and health considerations. The Hospital Development Plan (1975), for example, suggested there was a need for twice as many hospitals as had been recommended by a report in 1967. Nobody, it suggested, should be more than thirty miles away from a hospital; whereas the recommended limit in 1967 was sixty miles.[15] *One thing was clear in the 1970s, despite or because of the reform urge: vested interests with a financial stake in the status quo – whether in relation to consultants or tobacco – still had inordinate clout, though contraception for married couples was finally legalised, only with a prescription, by the end of the decade.*

What was also striking was how the issue of defining health care moved beyond traditionally narrow confines to embrace the ideas of community care and lifestyle as government, through the creation of the Health Education Bureau, and non-government agencies, highlighted fatal Irish lifestyles and the dangers of excess in food, alcohol and smoking. Consumption, nutrition and fitness were much more closely observed and dissected. There was an interesting focus on Ireland's place in the international league table of drink consumption; average consumption was not high by international standards but there were clearly problems with overindulgence and the corresponding health issues.[16] *The extent to which personal indulgence had increased was perhaps reflected in the Boomtown Rats' hit song, 'Looking after Number One', which singer Bob Geldof saw as 'a quintessential seventies song for the "me" decade'; it was penned in response to the 'pervasive selfishness' of the time.*[17]

– FORTY-NINE –

THE URBAN/RURAL DIVIDE

In relation to how lives were lived and ended there was interesting debate in the 1970s about the impact of modernisation and new standards of living, but it was also clear that there would be a stubborn continuity in certain areas. Historian John A. Murphy maintained in 1976, for example, that 'the traditional air of leisureliness shows no sign of diminishing', but he also asserted that the Troubles in Northern Ireland and the way they impacted on the Republic had meant the drive towards social progress was halted. There was evidence, he maintained, of a 'backlash against radical change of whatever nature and the religious and cultural homogeneity of the South has been underlined'. The notion of a 'chosen people', it seemed, was no longer part of the Irish consciousness: 'we no longer have immortal longings in us. Nor the arrogance to think we can be, in Pearse's phrase "the saviours of idealism"'.[1]

But, as Murphy's reflections suggested, more engaged debate was apparent about the kind of society the Republic was and could become and there was no shortage of warnings about the growth of materialism and individualism that could threaten a (sometimes mythical) sense of Irish community and traditional social and cultural priorities. As seen in Part I, such misgivings were underlined in a speech given by President Erskine Childers when addressing the Irish chapter of the Junior Chambers of Commerce International in October 1973. He warned against 'the growth of a faceless anonymous society of people with no immediate responsibility except the preservation and advancement of their own personal incomes'. Like all presidential speeches, this was passed on to the government for vetting before delivery; and it was viewed by Richard Stokes 'as the type of speech which should be made by the president – words of caution on the "progress" of society'.[2]

It was a revealing observation, not only in demonstrating the view that the president, with little power and no input into policy, should be the transmitter of appropriate messages about the nature of society, but also in the scepticism about what constituted societal progress in Ireland at that time. The following month, also as seen in Part I, equally revealing was the desire of a civil servant for Childers to remove a line from a speech he was delivering to a student society in UCD: 'living was excessively frugal for a section of the population'.[3] The objection to expressing such an obvious and blatant truth underlined that, whatever private misgivings there were regarding societal problems, challenges and inequality, there was no desire to see the nation's dirty linen aired in public. This in many respects represented a continuity in the official approach to these issues.

There were many throughout the 1970s who felt that this persistent refusal to confront such realities rendered the public assertions of progress somewhat hollow. The accuracy of Labour TD Justin Keating's assertion in June 1971 that 'we are in a decade when democracy means that people who participate in something must run it'[4] was debatable, but one of the notable developments of the decade was a growth in community organisation and structures as activists sought to empower grassroots members to demand control over or participation in the key decisions and policies that affected the quality of their lives, albeit with mixed results.

For some, the quality of life in the Republic was 'oddly ambiguous' by the end of the 1970s. Journalist James Downey suggested that the transition to affluence was 'speedy and disruptive' with less social conscience apparent, albeit in a society that was 'alive, vivid and thrusting'.[5] Nuala O'Faoláin, a Dublin-born television and radio producer and journalist who worked in the BBC before returning to Dublin in 1977, identified contradictory impulses in feeling an 'exhilaration' at returning from England to Ireland and being 'free of its rigid class structure. It was wonderful to be with people who were what they were, not cowed and classified from birth'; and yet at the same time it was manifestly clear that in Ireland there was in essence another hierarchy; insiders and those perceived to be important, and a periphery of those deemed to be less important; a 'pecking order which was a matter of difficulty, and often, hurt'.[6]

The Irish environment was still in many respects monocultural. Eibhear Walshe was certainly not alone in growing up in an area where everyone on his street 'had a mother and a father married to each other; everyone was Irish, white and Catholic'.[7] Although demographic change could be measured by the fact that by the end of the 1970s only one-fifth of people depended directly on agriculture for their livelihoods, a rural background, according to Liam de Paor 'continues for the moment to dominate many aspects of Irish culture', including the problems of breakdown, displacement and emigration. As seen earlier, there was a sense in Hugh Brody's book *Inishkillane*, for example, that the 'traditional' life of rural Ireland had come to an end, something also made clear in political journalist John Healy's books *Death of an Irish Town* (1968) and *Nineteen Acres* (1978), which addressed rural depopulation and decline central to the experiences of his native County Mayo. Healy championed the need for more investment in schools, industry, and infrastructure in the west of Ireland and described himself as representing the views of those from the 'snipegrass country'. De Paor also described the consequences of migration to urban centres: 'In Dublin the pubs are full every weekday evening of young people, refugees from the appallingly overcrowded and squalid rack-rented lodgings to which they are condemned. In the national capital the atmosphere is reproduced which is familiar to those who in recent decades have visited the Irish retreats in Birmingham or Kilburn or Paddington and the sense of alienation in exile.'[8]

As seen in Part III, in the view of playwright Brian Friel, Ireland by 1970 had become 'a tenth-rate image of America – a disaster for any country ... our country should be as distinctive and individualistic as Belgium and Holland – I'm talking of small countries. Instead of that we've become more and more Madison Avenueish in a very shabby sort of way ... there are 2 societies. There is the Dublin society in the Dublin environs and then there is the rest.' In his view they did not complement each other. What there was in Dublin, he maintained, was a 'deep schizophrenia ... because it is there and only there that the urban man and the rural man meet and attempt to mingle. It is this confluence that gives the city its distinctive flavour.' This, as he saw it, was about the coexistence of 'land speculation with rosary crusades, of Torremolinos package holidays with dole queues, of the necessary intimacy of slum dwelling with the intense intimacy of slum dwelling with intense privacy of the countryman. There is no victory for either side because neither side can retain its purity.'[9]

The traditional complaint about neglect of the west of Ireland continued and requests that governments formulate clear policies 'as regards keeping rural Ireland alive' were frequent. In late 1969 the National Farmers Association, originally established in 1956, and which had campaigned militantly in the 1960s for increased prices for agricultural produce, claimed that government-backed industrial development in the west 'would indicate sincere patriotism and is a matter signifying true justice based on human rights'.[10] A memorandum for the government in March 1971 dealt with the possible publication of a report on the planning of the Connemara Gaeltacht by Dáithí Hanley, in place of an associated survey by the social science research centre of University College Galway (UCG) which had its origins in a 1967 government-commissioned study. Hanley, a distinguished architect and designer who had been involved in the design of the Dublin airport building in the 1930s, produced a report that was much more positive than UCG's preliminary survey, which was regarded as 'heavily marred by unscientific and emotional criticism of government policies and actions as well as containing some proposals that were absurd, e.g.: a new railway line between Galway and Rossaveal and a tidal power station', and the government decided not to publish it.[11]

The UCG report certainly did not seek to be neutral in the expression of views and the apportioning of blame, as this extract reveals:

> The choice before the Irish people is a simple one. Either it continues along the road to a new form of banana republicanism, or it shows in a practical and urgent way that it is tired of the lip service of hypocrites who cannot see beyond narrow party advantage and that it is prepared to make a fresh start. A relatively small investment of sincerity, thought and money could rehabilitate the Galway Gaeltacht and enable it to stand on its own feet again ... a wall of distrust, born of despair, separates the Gaeltacht people from central government and a fog of apathy hangs over them. This atmosphere of decay and death will not be dispelled by the sight of outsiders building large hotels nor of foreign industrialists erecting factories. It is sad to reflect that many non-Christian states show a greater awareness of the demands of social justice in terms of fair regional distribution of wealth than does this country.[12]

The Sligo/Leitrim Development Organisation also complained of 'the marked economic imbalance which affects this region of Ireland ... The problem in Leitrim is so bad that apart altogether from emigration the number of deaths exceeded births at the 1971 census.' In relation to farms in Leitrim, it estimated that 10.7 per cent were viable, 56.4 per cent problematic and 32.9 per cent non-viable.[13] The low farm income problem was looked at by an inter-departmental committee and there were county development teams established in thirteen western counties and proposed leasing of land to younger farmers, but the real hope lay in EEC membership to 'substantially improve' the income of small farms.[14] In 1972, youth clubs in North Leitrim came together for a meeting and emphasised the need for self-help: 'We should seek what good can be achieved rather than pity ... Leitrim land is bad but not useless.'[15]

Land, its ownership and acquisition generated much heat; there was stinging criticism of the Irish Land Commission for its habit of compulsorily acquiring land and then paying for it in land bonds (a practice begun in 1923), which could not only depreciate in value but were not accepted by some banks at par in settlement of a debt. In a memorandum for the government in 1974, the Minister for Lands, Cavan Fine Gael TD Tom Fitzpatrick, insisted it was necessary to move away from the bonds system as owners wanted cash: 'For many years now there has been a chorus of protest inside and outside the Dáil from landowners, solicitors, auctioneers etc. about what has been called the noxious and villainous system of land bonds ... It is irksome, wearisome and image-wrecking to have to try to do business with a blemished paying medium. Expropriation of land in this country for land structural reform is contentious enough without having a tarnished payment medium.' The Minister for Finance Richie Ryan believed the Land Commission should cease purchasing land – the traditional work of the commission was to increase the size of holdings by adding land to a farmer's existing holding – as the EEC was promoting a scheme for retiring farmers which would see them transfer land to younger farmers who needed extra land for farm modernisation, with the retired farmer getting an annuity and cash.[16]

The National Land League was also vocal in its castigation of the Land Commission and proclaimed 'a crisis of confidence affecting Ireland's family farmers' due to poor prices for young cattle and a 'collapse' in the pig industry. It contended that farmers' indebtedness to the banks and Agricultural Credit Corporation had almost doubled between 1972 and 1974 from £123 million to £205 million, while costs of fertiliser and fuel had soared: 'It has been hitherto universally accepted that however poor conditions on family farms might have been, small farmers were the backbone of the country. The farm modernisation scheme, which the state is now pressing on the farming community, is based on an entirely contrary philosophy. It seeks to pressure those farmers who have not and are unlikely to obtain what is regarded as an acceptable income level to leave farming while it simultaneously prevents others from replacing them.'[17]

By the mid 1970s, research by economist Alan Matthews revealed that less than 5 per cent of farm output was consumed on the farm, compared to 40 per cent in the 1940s. One-quarter of the population worked in agriculture (producing 15 per cent of GNP), but between 1960 and 1976 the number of people working on farms dropped from 382,000 to 236,000. The average age of farmers was fifty-six compared with thirty-nine for other workers and 20 per cent of all farmers were over sixty-five. Owners of small farms tended to obtain off-farm employment; 80 per cent of all land was transferred within the family while 5 per cent was acquired through the Land Commission and 15 per cent was sold on the open market.[18] In 1979, the year of the centenary of the foundation of the Irish Land League, which had been reformed in 1965 and had a membership of about 7,000 small farmers, the League criticised government for a failure to instigate a proper programme of land reform and the practice of multinationals buying land, suggesting the EEC 'has been a utopia for 20 per cent of Irish farmers, while the remaining 80 per cent have hung on by the skin of their teeth'.[19]

The linkages between rural communities and urban centres had also become apparent, but land was still seen in Ireland very much as an important end in itself and part of the family heritage (unlike in other countries, where it was seen more as a marketable commodity). Although this attachment was weakening and the traditional neighbourhood co-operative network was also under some pressure, in South Leinster and East Munster the strength of rural organisations such as the GAA, NFA and Muintir na Tíre (People of the Land), originally established in the 1930s, were to the fore in helping communities to adapt to change and also in promoting continuity in what was healthy and distinctive about Irish rural life.[20] There was also a generational tension here, however, as recalled by John Waters, who grew up in Roscommon: 'Unlike previous generations we absorbed little of the language of the countryside – the names of plants and birds for example, or the strange and wondrous working of nature's casual cycle. Many of us grew up to have almost a contempt for what was at best the womanly wonder of nature. We could not reconcile it with the bright lights of the town.'[21]

– FIFTY –

TAKING RESPONSIBILITY FOR THE IRISH ABROAD?

One of the more obvious demographic developments involved migration from the provinces to Dublin and other urban centres, and the 1979 census was noteworthy because the annual average in relation to migration figures was calculated as a net inflow of 13,350, representing a reversal of a long-standing pattern of net emigration, but a move abroad was still common for those from economically disadvantaged areas. The issues of who had responsibility for the welfare of the Irish diaspora, the options available to them, and the possibility of their return to a more prosperous Ireland emerged frequently in the 1970s. There were regular Dáil questions about emigration in the early 1970s in the context of continuing population decline along the western seaboard. One response given in November 1970 was that in the preceding twelve months 'the net outward passenger movement by sea and air was 7,696 compared to 13,410 for the twelve months ended November 1969'. But these figures were regarded as 'unreliable as a measure of net emigration. From 1966 to 1971 net emigration was estimated to be 88,207. In relation to County Mayo, it was reported that there was 'no marriage in the Kiltimagh area in 1970; the age structure of the framing community in one area showed that 60 per cent are over 50 years'. Fine Gael TD Gerry L'Estrange insisted that 'the west is dying'.[1]

An Irish Emigrants Rights Association was vocal in calling for the government to assist Irish people abroad who were anxious to return, promising to make it 'a major political issue' if it was ignored. It also wanted postal votes for emigrants and insisted 'the Irish government has completely disowned its emigrants'. Its chairman Brendan Hickey met Jack Lynch briefly in July 1970 and complained of the Taoiseach's 'negative approach'. Lynch characterised his interpretation of their meeting as 'distorted', pointing out that the government already contributed to voluntary organisations advising emigrants and that to issue threats would be counterproductive.[2] In 1973 one Irish emigrant in London complained to Liam Cosgrave that the coalition government's election manifesto did not contain any plans 'for attracting the many emigrants who would wish to return home'.[3] Between 1951 and 1971, four out of every five Irish emigrants had gone to Britain, and there were 957,000 Irish-born people living in Britain in 1971.[4]

When the Australian government was seeking to incentivise emigrants, the Irish ambassador in Canberra told the Australian Minister for Immigration Al Grassby, 'We are opposed to the promotion within Ireland of emigration.'[5] When Garret FitzGerald was asked to intervene to assist the American-Irish National Immigration Committee regarding legislation there, he declined on the grounds that the issue was 'an internal American one' and maintained it would not be appropriate for the government to intervene, which was rejected by the chairman of the committee who insisted previous ministers had intervened.[6]

Niall O'Dowd, later to become one of the most prominent Irish-American journalists of his generation, arrived in California in 1978 as a twenty-five-year-old: 'San Francisco seemed an antidote to life in narrow, constricted Ireland.' But grand dreams gave way to a 'scary reality'. Perhaps it was ironic that those seeking anonymity first needed to tap into intense localism; a barman from Mayo told him, 'If you can play Gaelic football you'll get along fine,' as it could give you a start and a first job in construction; and at the parish hall, 'once inside I discovered I could have been back in any parish hall in Ireland'.

But it was different in the 1970s for emigrants compared to their 1950s counterparts: 'We were some of the lucky ones, the first generation really, that would never be more than a plane flight away from home.' There was also tension between the different generations of emigrants; an older emigrant who provided O'Dowd with construction work 'had it in for me from day one because I was educated I guess ... These immigrant men like [him] had never got anything easy, were used to living by the sweat of their brow and suspicious of those who got the education they never had.' Some things, however, remained constant: 'Nights alone at the bar drinking alone only added to the sense of displacement', while 'many of the Irish I drank with were unfinished souls'. He was struck by 'just how deprived we were of basic news from Ireland' which prompted him to start an Irish newspaper.[7]

Throughout the decade, emigrant centres in Britain sought financial assistance from Irish governments, partly due to the sharp increase in emigration in the fifteen to twenty-four age group: in 1975 and 1976, 7,000 of this cohort emigrated. The overall figures for emigration were estimated at 10,300 in 1975, 2,200 in 1976, 7,600 in 1977 and 11,000 in 1978. In February 1974, Garret FitzGerald and Liam Cosgrave met with a deputation of Irish Catholic bishops in Cosgrave's office to discuss the Irish Episcopal Commission's work in Britain. Historically, the Catholic Church had been to the forefront in promoting Irish emigrant welfare, particularly in the 1950s, when in the region of half a million people left the country. At the end of 1974, FitzGerald informed Cosgrave that the Department of Finance was opposed to any financial assistance 'for reasons of financial stringency', but he wanted that decision reassessed in January 1975 in view of the 'fairly discouraging picture' presented by the Episcopal Commission.

In 1975, 2,356 people were assisted by the Welfare Department and the hostel attached to the Irish Centre in London (Camden), where there was deemed to be a need for a specialised service for 'homeless, rootless and problem type Irish youths'. The Episcopal Commission was looking for £270,000 for hostels and social workers in London and Birmingham, whereas a committee set up by the Department of Labour to advise on emigrant welfare favoured loans, because grants 'could result in a slackening of voluntary fund raising efforts by the Irish in Britain'. It was also regarded as 'unsound in principle. Public funds should be spent at home on pressing problems here requiring remedial action.' It was pointed out that Irish people had voluntarily contributed over a quarter of a million pounds for emigrant welfare in response to an appeal by the Irish Catholic bishops in March 1971, but it was wondered 'whether the Irish community in general in Britain, many of whom are well off, is doing sufficient to help the small proportion of the less fortunate immigrants'. The possibility that, as welfare work was 'mainly a Catholic Church effort', public funding could be unconstitutional was also mooted, as an article of the

Irish constitution stipulated that 'the state guarantees not to endow any religion'.[8]

On balance, it was decided state funding was not justified, notwithstanding the advisory committee on emigrant services' warning that there was evidence of 'growing problems amongst the aged single Irish persons living alone in the bigger cities' and a 'big increase in the number of psychiatric cases'. The government accepted it had 'some responsibility' for emigrant welfare but would not finance welfare services in Britain 'for which it could be said that a similar demand exists in Ireland but which has not so far been provided from government's resources here'. Cosgrave, who took a more direct interest than usual in this matter, suggested to FitzGerald that, if granted, there was a 'near certainty that assistance could not be confined to London' or to the amounts mentioned.[9]

Attorney General Declan Costello then intervened; having talked to Bishop of Galway Eamon Casey, he wondered 'Would it be possible to make even a small financial contribution?'[10] But Cosgrave was not going to give in to the bishops. His own feeling was against funding and there was much foot dragging; by the end of 1975 there was still no decision.[11] FitzGerald was also opposed and Joseph Cunnane, Archbishop of Tuam, did not hide his displeasure: 'We felt that an approach at top level would be best ... after a long and friendly discussion we felt that you had accepted our propositions as reasonable.' Costello, also demonstrating a persistent interest in this, and clearly more anxious than some of his colleagues to satisfy the bishops, sought a compromise, or a delay, by suggesting the government could look at the possibility of funding social workers.[12] Bishop Eamon Casey was excoriating: 'We are genuinely bewildered.' He complained that the government 'have not taken the trouble to explain' why funding had been refused and, significantly, insisted that it had been Costello who 'invited, unprompted by us', the Episcopal Commission to a meeting.[13] Clearly, Costello's manoeuvre, which was arguably inappropriate in any case, had backfired.

Later that year the Irish Centre in London sought a grant of £426,000. The Irish ambassador to the UK, Donal O'Sullivan, insisted there was 'no justification for entertaining the application' in its entirety, even if the money was freely available. The Irish Centre's memorandum suggested most Irish immigrants were now from the city and referred to the

> continuous arrival of destitute people of all ages; over 2,500 people

> were visiting the Irish centre each week and despite some bordering on destitution they still seemed unwilling to accept what they considered underpaid jobs ... Sometimes the mentality prevails that money spent on tax, good accommodation or food and clothes is wasted ... Their outward appearance does not enhance their marriage prospects and for some, this realisation comes too late ... Young people coming from an insecure background often confronted with an identity crisis and sometimes confronted with conflicting religious and moral values, are constantly at risk in being caught up in the maelstrom and anonymity of London society.

But there was much praise for the British attitude, which 'sees integration into the civic life of the country as a responsibility'.[14]

The position of single mothers was also a problem and the report of the Irish Centre was unambiguous on this point: 'The relentless war continues to rage between family decency as assessed by the neighbours and Christianity, and when Christianity blushes and recedes in the face of public opinion its authenticity is questionable. The position of the pregnant girl who decides to take flight to London rather than incur the wrath of her parents is becoming critical.' In 1976 Fr Oliver McTernan, a priest working with a voluntary housing group in Islington in London, insisted in a letter to FitzGerald that there was a 'moral obligation' on the part of the Irish government to reimburse English local authorities for costs incurred in housing newly arrived destitute Irish families. He maintained that the Irish Embassy in London was 'ignorant' of many of these problems and 'totally irrelevant' to those trying to address them. He cited the example of a mother and three children who arrived homeless and had to be put into emergency bed and breakfast accommodation and then sent home at the English local authority's expense: 'During their short stay in London this family cost the ratepayers of the London Borough of Camden a total of £256.05.' Legally the Boroughs were obliged to assist, but 'what is acceptable in judicial terms may be morally unacceptable'.[15]

The following year FitzGerald argued that such funding as requested by the Irish Centre was not possible and was critical about 'lack of direction of Irish societies in Britain'.[16] In early 1978 it was suggested that perhaps an interest-free loan of £250,000 could be provided but the Minister for Finance George Colley was opposed. As he saw it, the welfare of the emigrants was the responsibility of the host country and it was better for

Irish emigrants to integrate 'rather than to isolate themselves, thereby accepting the ghetto mentality'.[17] Between 1971 and 1976, 37,000 people aged twenty to twenty-nine had emigrated but the net outflow had 'virtually ceased' for those aged between fifteen and nineteen. The London Irish Centre's annual welfare report for 1977 referred to a majority of new emigrants having secondary education and 'their expectations and aspirations are high' but there were also 'deprived urban emigrants' who did not relate to traditional supports of home and parish in a way rural emigrants had in the past. Overall, however, as pointed out by the sociologist Liam Ryan 'the Irish in Britain are a very flexible group in that the speed of their total assimilation into British society is probably the fastest that occurs among any emigrants anywhere in the world'.[18]

In December 1978, an inter-departmental committee reported on the issue of possible financial assistance for welfare services for the Irish community in Britain as Irish centres were once again reporting an increase in welfare problems. It was agreed that there was a case to be made for providing such assistance but that there could be the disadvantage of 'escalation of requests for aid not necessarily confined to welfare' and voluntary effort 'might decline'. In March 1979 it was decided not to offer a grant for the London Irish Centre as it was deemed a commercial project and there were concerns of 'the precedent which would be created in the case of similar centres in other locations not only in the UK'.[19]

The government was more comfortable with a proposed grant of £18,000 towards the employment of six social workers in Irish centres in Britain. The annual welfare report for the London centre in 1978 pointed out that Spain paid the salaries of twelve social workers in London and that the Bonn government paid all the administrative expenses of the German Welfare Council. Forty-three single mothers had approached the Irish Centre in 1978; thirty-seven had arrived pregnant from Ireland; they had also had seventy-three cases of people with psychiatric issues: 'People who have difficulty in coping with Irish society stand little chance of making progress in London's complex world, yet because of these very problems they are often determined to emigrate.' The reports also offered interesting insights into changed attitudes:

> The single characteristic which is most noticeable about the new arrivals of the late 1970s is the change in attitude towards themselves that has taken place over the years. Few, with the exception of some

> coming here with acute social and other difficulties see themselves as the traditional emigrants forced to abandon their native shores. The majority suffer no severe emotional trauma on leaving Ireland and although sometimes ill equipped they are confident and looking forward to their time abroad. It is difficult to apply the term 'emigrant' emotionally loaded as it historically has been, to them, yet it is the most accurate definition we have to describe those who go abroad to search for work.[20]

But there were still those with strong feelings of displacement; singer Christy Moore recalled, 'There is an edge to my Irishness when I'm in the ghetto ... I wear it like a badge of exile – It was macho and violent and sexist and racist and wild and drunk and stoned and kinky and loud and underneath it all lay tenderness but no words to describe it and from that to show tenderness or affection could be misconstrued as weakness so fuck them all just in case.'[21] By the end of 1979, the Irish Centre was once again seeking funds from the Irish government as a matter of the 'greatest urgency ... this is surely our great hour of need', but their pleading did not have the desired effect.[22]

Some older emigrants who had returned to Ireland found the transition difficult to cope with. An anthropological study by California-educated George Gmelch, in the summers of 1977 and 1978, focused on some of the difficulties faced by return migrants to Ireland. His team interviewed 606 migrants in eight counties along the western seaboard and it was clear readjustment was difficult for many. During their first year back in Ireland, 51 per cent were 'dissatisfied' with life and would have been happier if they had not returned, and at the end of the second year 21 per cent 'still regretted the decision to return ... they often expect Ireland to be the Ireland of their holidays, when people make time to greet you, a fuss is made and everyone is pleased to see you. Often emigrants don't take into account that vast changes have taken place in their absence; they all too often expect a return to the traditional close-knit folk society of memory.'[23]

– FIFTY-ONE –

LIVING ON THE EDGE

Other marginalised communities closer to home were also receiving attention, with mixed results. The plight of islands off the coast of Ireland continued to generate considerable emotion, with pleas to devise special policies to assist them, including cost-of-living subsidies and telecommunications, while others sought assistance to enable island residents who so desired to transfer to the mainland. In 1971 there were eighty inhabited islands off the coast, with a population of 11,537, which dropped slightly to 10,828 in 1979[1] (130 years previously there had been 211 inhabited islands with a population of just over 38,000; the Blasket Islands, off the coast of Kerry, which had achieved renown due to the writing of their inhabitants, including Peig Sayers, and their interest for visiting scholars, had been evacuated in 1953). Air travel to the well-known Aran Islands off the coast of Galway began in 1970 and transformed the lives of the communities there: 'Electricity, post-primary education and industry all came to the islands as a result of the flights, along with hundreds of thousands of tourists. One hundred in 1969 became 14,000 in 1976.' Before such flights, any of the 1,000 residents of these islands who required hospital treatment faced a thirty-mile journey to Galway via lifeboat, 'through crashing black waves and wailing winds', and it could take three hours to reach the mainland by ferry.[2]

Other islands did not fare so well. Six of the seven families on Inishturk (population 37) off the coast of Mayo, for example, wanted to move to the mainland, as did twelve of the sixteen families on Turbot (population 66).[3] The combined cost to the Land Commission of their resettlement was estimated at £80,000. (The Department of Finance, unusually, was supportive.) The islands were 'small, low-lying, bleak' and the residents were living in primitive conditions:

> There is no priest; doctor or nurse on the islands and mass is said on each island only on one Sunday per month. There is no electricity; some islanders use bottled gas for lighting and cooking. Contact with the mainland is by radio-telephone. All the men on both islands over eighteen and under pension age are reported to be getting social welfare assistance. These are not Irish speaking communities. The islanders, who own lands ranging from three acres to eighteen acres plus a share of commonage, cannot be described as farmers in the true sense. The Turk islanders are in the main fishermen.

It was reported that those who wished to stay on Turbot 'comprise 3 elderly bachelors and an elderly couple whose family have emigrated'.[4] In 1974, Fr Pádraig Staunton, based on Inisheer, lamented the death of that island but realised that the limitations of island living were becoming hazardous: 'There was a time when the last thing I would do would be advise someone to leave the islands. I'm not so sure now.' There were twenty-seven unmarried men and two women between the ages of fourteen and thirty, living on the dole. While he wondered why there was not more effective co-ordination of the efforts of various government departments, he did not see it as just an issue of government neglect: 'What are the churches or the clergy doing? Are they too comfortable to care? Are they waiting to muzzle anything in a dog collar that pisses on the sacred cows of church or state?'[5]

The secretary of the Department of the Gaeltacht in 1975, Liam Tobin, thought it was 'wrong to have wholesale evacuation of islands': he did not want to see any part of the national territory becoming 'a deserted black spot'.[6] Minister for Transport and Power, Fine Gael's Peter Barry, informed Cosgrave in May 1975 that it would be too expensive and simply not feasible to provide electricity on Clare and Inishturk, off the coast of Mayo, and Inishturbot residents were reported to want to move to the mainland at Clifden in Galway 'before next winter'.

What had remained consistent over the course of the life of the state was confusion about just who was responsible for island life and communities when it came to policy. The islanders' welfare essentially fell between the stools of different government departments. There was also an enduring tendency to depict them as almost alien and deliberately lazy. A memorandum regarding the evacuation of seven families from Turbot in 1975 recorded: 'The people are poor and uneducated, without resources and completely lacking in initiative; their income is derived from fishing on a very small scale, social welfare payments and – in some cases – contributions from the St Vincent de Paul Society [a Catholic Church charity] ... morale on the island is reported to be very low as a result of the drowning of 3 islanders while returning from the mainland last September' (they had been socialising and watching the all-Ireland hurling final on the mainland). The cost of the resettlement was estimated at £250,000 over three years. Richie Ryan was opposed to central government financing this, insisting it was a housing issue for the local authority. The Minister for Lands insisted his department had no funds available and the Minister for Local Government 'strongly disagrees with the suggestion that the islanders should be forced by government policy to leave their island homes for the wholly unsuitable environment of a semi-urban housing scheme'. It was ultimately decided that it should be the responsibility of the Land Commission.[7]

Marie Mannion, the island teacher, said that because they were not told about their options 'there wasn't one person on the island who realised that it was possible for them to live in their homes with the same facilities as on the mainland'. Journalist Brian Wilson concluded that 'islands and islanders seem to be regarded as irritants rather than assets in present-day Ireland'. Eighty-four-year-old islander Michael Ward described the move as going 'from heaven to hell', but another life-long resident thought that due to the 'living conditions and associated hardships, women and children deserve the chance of something better'.[8]

As to complaints that the non-Gaeltacht (English-speaking) islands were being discriminated against, Fianna Fáil's Bobby Molloy, representing the constituency of Galway West, wrote to Cosgrave in 1975: 'Your recent voyage around our coast must have sharply demonstrated that the hardship of island life is not determined by the language spoken, but bears heavily on all.'[9] In 1977 the government announced a £750,000 grant for the Gaeltacht islands; residents of English-speaking Clare Island had complained of discrimination against the non-Gaeltacht islands which, in addition to Clare (population 150), included Inishbofin (population 250) and Inishturk (population 67), whose islanders maintained all requests for assistance had been refused. In September 1977 the Minister for the Gaeltacht visited these islands and promised them equal status with the Gaeltacht islands.[10] The following year a telegram from Tory, off the coast of Donegal, contained a desperate plea: 'Short of food. Please arrange helicopter express delivery'.[11] A memorandum for the government in late 1978 reported on the condition on inhabited non-Gaeltacht islands as compiled for a 1976 report. The total population of those islands off the west coast in 1975 was approximately 1,100; they needed electricity and 'female-employing projects' to prevent women of marriageable age leaving. There were disagreements as to whether these were social or financial problems; George Colley did not accept 'without qualification that the same services as on the mainland must be available to islanders'. There were reports of 'intentions to desert Tory island' and the vacation of Inishturbot; it was felt in the Department of the Taoiseach that 'in view of the trend for the populations of islands to fall and eventually disappear ... the question of capital investment should be approached with great caution'. There were only thirty-one residents on Long Island off West Cork: 'It is proposed to canvass the population to ascertain if they want electricity.'[12]

Over many decades, drownings had afflicted those living and working on or near the islands and the sea. Four young men drowned when a trawler sank six miles from Skerries harbour in Dublin in October 1973. Eleven trawlermen died in two separate tragedies twenty-three months apart in 1975 and 1976. Rescuers were not contacted in time to save the lives or recover four of the six bodies lost on the trawler *Evelyn Marie* off the coast of Donegal in January 1975. The family of one of the victims, Hughie Gallagher, living on the island of Arranmore in Donegal, picked up news of the disaster on CB radios, as it struck rocks off Rathlin O'Birne island and 'vanished without trace'. This family, and others, spent years unsuccessfully searching for answers about the inadequacies of the response to the tragedy, the failure to send a helicopter to attempt a rescue and the lack of transparency around the official government inquiry into the event. Almost two years later, in November 1976 a second trawler, the *Carrig Una*, went down at the same spot with the loss of five lives.[13] Stormy weather conditions continued to bring great grief, as was evident during the Fastnet sailing tragedy in 1979 that left fifteen dead after storm force 10 gales along the south coast.[14]

– FIFTY-TWO –

THE BROADER SOCIAL OUTLOOK

The total population of the Republic in 1971 was 2,978,248, which rose to 3,364,881 by 1979, a 13 per cent increase, representing a considerable rate of population growth compared to recent intercensal periods and a restoration of the figure 'to about the average level which pertained during the 1891–1901 intercensal period'. It was decided not to conduct a census in 1976 because it was considered that the 1975 Labour Force survey (with a sample of 33,000 households) contained sufficient data to provide estimates of the total population. It was estimated that it would save £1.75 million. (The UK also cancelled its 1976 census as an economy measure.) All the Irish local authorities were opposed to this, as were some geographers and planners. A geographer at UCD wrote to James Tully, the minister responsible, to inform him that the contention the postponement would save £1.75 million was 'specious. Incalculable costs may be incurred as a result of decisions based on 5 to 10 year old data which are no longer accurate.'[1]

According to the census of 1979, the population increase was highest in Leinster at 16.3 per cent, while the population of Dublin city and county increased from 852,219 to 982,587. One-third of the population now resided in the greater Dublin area. Counties adjacent to Dublin experienced substantial increases in population between 1971 and 1979; Kildare up 34.9 per cent, Meath up 26.6 per cent and Wicklow up 26.4 per cent: 'It is likely that these increases are in part due to the increasing tendency for these counties to serve as dormitory areas for Dublin.'[2] Very high levels of net inward migration were shown for the counties adjacent to Dublin. For Cavan, Donegal, Longford, Mayo, Roscommon and Sligo the population increases recorded were the first since the census of 1841. The census results prompted one description of the Republic as 'a fast-growing industrializing frontier on the edge of industrial Europe'.[3]

In February 1977 the government received a report from the National Economic and Social Council (which had been established in 1973 to advise the Taoiseach on strategy relating to social and economic development). It was called 'Towards a Social Report' and it aimed to chart social change in Ireland over previous decades and to improve policy-making by highlighting social problems and 'providing insight into how different measures of national well-being' could be addressed. It pointed out that the country had no comprehensive set of social statistics.[4] It was regarded as the first time 'an attempt has been made to prepare a social report in this country'. It indicated that by 1975 average earnings in agriculture had 'almost caught up' with average industrial earnings for adult men and women but did not hold out a favourable prospect for farmers' incomes from 1976 onwards. The section on social welfare services concluded that 'while publicly funded income maintenance services have developed rapidly in the last decade, both in the scope of the services provided and in the level of benefits, reflected in the substantial real increase in the level of expenditure and the proportion of national output they absorb, the level of many benefits remains low in absolute terms and in comparison with the incomes of the working population'.

Richie Ryan felt a major defect of the report was 'its failure to outline the public expenditure implications of the social developments recounted'. The report referred to dissatisfaction with many social services, including health, housing and education, by '"consumers"', with this word being placed in inverted commas, as if the authors were not sure that this was an accurate or appropriate description of the service users, or an indication that the idea of people as consumers of services was still in its infancy. But the report was unequivocal in its assertion that 'new expectations have been generated – expectations that have risen faster than the capacity to fulfil them'.

Factors that contributed to such sentiment and a change in social outlook included a consistent fall in the age at which people married, with the average age of a bride at twenty five years and ten months in 1957, the first year such statistics were collected, falling to twenty-three years and four months in 1974. The equivalent figures for men were twenty-nine years and five months falling to twenty-five years and four months (while the marriage rate per 1,000 had increased from 5.4 in 1961 to 7.5 in 1973, reflecting rising income and prospects for professionals in particular). There had been a decrease in the rural population and a decreasing birth rate, which, during the course of the decade, reduced the average number of children in each family from about four to about three. Overall, fertility in marriage fell 31 per cent between 1961 and 1981, with the most rapid decline from 1966–79. There was also a substantial increase in conceptions and births outside marriage. Economic historian Brendan Walsh has observed that

> throughout the first half of the twentieth century about 2% of all births registered in Ireland were classified as illegitimate but by 1983 this proportion had risen to 6.8%. At the same time there seems to have been a marked increase in the incidence of pre-nuptial conceptions. The evidence for this is indirect, being based on the proportion of marriages in a calendar year to which a birth is registered in the same year. This proportion rose from 7% in 1961 to 15.5% in 1979. If this is taken as a rough estimate of the number of pre-nuptial conceptions, then illegitimate births plus pre-nuptial conceptions amounted to almost 9% of all births in 1979 compared with about 4% in 1961.

But what marked Ireland as distinctive in comparison with the rest of Europe was the small proportion of marriages that ended in divorce, the small numbers living in 'consensual unions', and the still large size of families.[5] Infant and general mortality rates had dropped significantly; infant mortality (death aged less than one year) per 1,000 live births had fallen from 30.5 in 1961 to 17.8 in 1974.

There had also been continued growth in the service sector and in the number of full-time pupils and students at all levels; 642,000, or 22.4 per cent of the total population in 1963–4 compared to 816,000 or 26.4 per cent of the population in 1973–4. At secondary level, the numbers had doubled between 1963–4 and 1974–5 from 129,365 to 256,751. The average weekly earnings in industry in December 1975 were £58.94 for men and £30.85 for women. There had been improvements in the rates of benefit, and weekly income maintenance payments were being paid to 948,907 people in 1975 compared to 536,711 in 1966.[6]

Life expectancy had increased; male life expectancy had been sixty years and five months in the late 1940s and was sixty-eight years and six months in the late 1960s, while the corresponding figures for women were sixty-two years, four months and sixty-nine years, six months. Those who reached the age of one hundred were entitled to a centenary bounty from the president. As if it was not even deemed worth pretending that the state was a secular republic, such bounties were transmitted through the local clergyman. Requests by government ministers in the early 1970s to present them were rejected in favour of sticking with the system of using the parish priest. There were three requirements for receipt of the bounty; a baptismal certificate, a birth certificate and a letter from the local clergyman, a reminder of the degree to which they were still seen as the most significant individual in the parish; the cheques were actually issued to them.[7] One centenarian in Tubber, County Clare, was deemed to be 'in fairly good health but believes she is about 70 years of age and she does not realise her true age. The relatives have requested that the pensioner's age should not be disclosed to her as they fear that this disclosure would have a detrimental effect on her health'. The daughter of a Limerick centenarian had to refuse her mother's bounty: her mother insisted she was ninety-three: 'I know her to be more but as she is happy thinking she is only this age her happiness does mean a lot to me.'[8] There were twenty-six centenarian bounty applications in 1974; most of them had no knowledge about the Irish language and typical comments about them included 'in good health but a bit senile'; 'blind and confined to bed, otherwise he is in fairly good health for his age'; 'as good as can be expected at her age' and 'full faculties and active mind and takes a great interest in current affairs'.[9]

One case provided a reminder of the tumultuous and divisive events these people had lived through: the woman in question, 'because of her strongly held political views would not accept the bounty if it was given by the president and after consultation with the president the bounty was issued from the Department of Social Welfare'.[10] Referring to those applicants who just missed out by dying before they reached the landmark, in June 1978 Richard Stokes in the Department of the Taoiseach had to remind officials in the Department of Social Welfare that 'it would be ludicrous to pay a bounty to the deceased', even if applications were approved while they were alive.[11]

Liam Cosgrave was contacted in 1977 about the problem of elderly people living in unsuitable accommodation. It was pointed out that the grants for housing the elderly were much more generous in the UK. The government was keen to use non-profit voluntary housing groups that had been providing about a hundred dwellings a year and the government agreed to increase the grants available from £300 to £1,000. Dermot Nally insisted the voluntary groups needed to be encouraged: 'There is well documented evidence to the effect that old people looking after their own housing live a more active life but may well die sooner than those cared for in institutions. Persons in this latter category tend to become "vegetables". Social policy generally favours the course of encouraging people, as far as possible to look after themselves ... There are not that many concerns or organisations interested in providing housing for old people that we should be exercising our brains in devising restrictions.'[12]

Other vulnerable and neglected communities also came under the microscope. In relation to tenancy, there were tensions nationally about low-cost accommodation, along with sub-standard conditions and widespread exploitation. A row at a housing estate in Athlone in late 1971, for example, witnessed soldiers assisting the Gardaí to keep order as a result of tensions over housing travellers and resistance to evictions.[13] At Clondalkin in Dublin in 1973 there were 139 families living in caravans on a council estate; some of the privately owned sites were earning £4,000 a year for their landlords, even though there was a lack of water, sewerage and electricity.[14] The tenants of Benburb Street and other ghetto areas, housed in a building erected in 1888, were described as living in conditions of 'wretchedness' with toilet and water facilities in a corridor and large families in one room. The Togher Tenant's Association in Cork decried the poor planning of rushed estates that were blighting their lives and organised rent strikes.[15]

By 1972 it was suggested that community associations were 'a familiar feature of most local authority housing estates, evidence of tenants' determination to rectify the environmental inadequacies resulting from inept and unimaginative housing policies and bureaucratic indifference to social needs'. It was estimated, for example, that the Ballyfermot Community Association was catering for 40,000 people with its own community centre and newspaper; it also wanted greater autonomy for its area.[16]

Another concern was the drive to move inner-city dwellers to new suburban developments, which were not adequately equipped or serviced to create thriving communities. Great optimism, for example, had existed about the original development of high-rise apartment blocks in the Ballymun area of Dublin in the mid 1960s before its 'decline into a notorious ghetto' that came to represent 'Ireland's vision of Apartheid', a description coined by future assistant Dublin city manager Ciarán Murray. In retrospect, it seems blindingly obvious why the original project was doomed. Creating large-scale housing schemes that were physically and socially excluded from normal city economic and social activity was a recipe for malaise. Social policy expert Anne Power, who included Ballymun as a case study in her 1993 book *Estates on the Edge: The Social Consequences of Mass Housing in Northern Europe Since 1850*, and who first visited Ballymun in 1968, observed that 'people were being plucked out of established communities into isolated, separate and dislocated boxes, with few social networks'. She returned in 1980 to scenes of 'horror' and 'an impossible social, physical and organisational cocktail'. But she also made the point that this disaster was by no means unique; in Europe in the 1980s, some 17 million homes in post-war modern estates were experiencing similar problems. But there was also a long and turbulent history of the admirable community groups and individuals who stood up and voiced the concerns of residents against the backdrop of systemic neglect.[17]

The status and welfare of inner-city Dublin communities and their social problems were highlighted by a report of the inner-city development advisory committee of the Dublin Chamber of Commerce. It referred to a 'rapidly deteriorating social fabric', while 'the situation is not yet as desperate as is to be found in some other countries' (it was suggested things were worse in the United States and Britain) partly because of the 'heroic efforts being made by numerous bodies to improve the inner city'.

Priorities identified included housing, regulating land use, special education needs and an inner-city redevelopment company, with a suggestion that the private sector needed to provide the bulk of the funding. In July 1978 in the Department of the Taoiseach, Dermot Nally noted that the existence of a government inter-departmental group looking at the problems of the inner city was 'being kept quiet since if it were known publicly it would be subjected to innumerable representations and pressures'. An unusually direct instruction from Jack Lynch was that 'no time should be lost by this group in completing their examination of this problem. I will expect the confidentiality of their deliberations to be maintained.'[18]

The population decline in the area of Dublin between the canals in previous decades had been dramatic – falling from 266,000 in 1936 to just 132,000 in 1971. The 'symptoms of the decay' that were noted included too much corporation housing, road congestion in the heart of the city and lack of amenities and tax incentives. In certain city-centre wards unemployment rates had reached 20 per cent in 1971 when the national average was 5.8 per cent: 'A survey by Fr Mícheál Mac Gréil, a prominent Jesuit sociologist and social activist, in 1972–3, showed that 74 per cent of the respondents in the inner city had received only primary education compared with 51 per cent in County Dublin and 24 per cent in Killiney. A survey made in May 1978 by the Prisoners Rights Organisation, of fifty children aged between twelve and sixteen from the Summerhill/ Seán McDermott Street area recorded a total of 2,600 court appearances by them on criminal charges.'

The report of the inter-departmental committee recommended an inner-city agency, industry in the port area, penal taxation on derelict property, public agencies to employ inner-city residents, education initiatives, mixed housing and relief of traffic congestion. In relation to community development it was stated that 'the target communities in the inner city are probably amongst the least interested or able to form community associations',[19] which was nonsense and contrasts strongly with the assertions of the organisers of the Liberties Festival in Dublin the previous summer. The vice-president of the festival, Matt Larkin, pointed to its existence as demonstrating an era 'that has seen the emergence of the voluntary organisation at local and national level, an age of "get up and do" to replace the age of "sit down and ask others to do"'. There were various representative groups within the Liberties, including the National Association of Tenants Organisations.[20] Community festivals had also brought together a nucleus of people who formed the North Central Community Council in 1975, with Tony Gregory as secretary; their priorities were local consultation and accountability. They also wanted to tackle the 'vandals in pinstripe suits' whose demolition plans (there were 311 derelict sites in the city in 1978) highlighted the need for a community-based strategy to focus on the human consequences of the physical decline of the inner city and the lack of consultation about its future.

In *Magill* magazine in 1979 it was claimed that there were still twenty-six tenements in Dublin city, housing 120 families without baths or toilets. There was a fear that the city council's redevelopment plan, by scooping out a section of the north inner city to make it available for offices, would destroy communities, along with concerns about job losses (sewing factories had been hit hard during the 1973–6 recession). The layout of the tenements was regarded as facilitating the type of crime common to the area, including car theft and handbag snatches, while the activities of the so-called 'Bugsy Malone' gang of young criminals caused media overdrive. Fr Peter McVerry, another socially active priest in the inner city, claimed Dublin Corporation was 'trying to solve a social problem with a housing policy' but that people scattered throughout the corporation housing estates would not have their problems addressed. Activists on the North Central Community Council championed the long-term residents who were determined to stay.[21]

Those protesting against the worsening condition of flats in north inner-city Dublin blocked traffic at the junction of Gardiner Street and Summerhill in 1979, insisting that the 'detenanting' of the tenements in Gardiner Street and Summerhill 'have left old people alone on top floors with only the rats for company'. The behaviour of the organisers of the protests, including Mick Rafferty and Tony Gregory, was described by District Justice Kelly as 'downright blackguardism'.[22] The protests resulted in the imprisonment of social worker Fergus McCabe, while a local priest insisted the city-centre community was 'slowly strangling to death'.[23] But this assessment needs to be qualified with recognition of the significance of the community organisations and networks they created by focusing on educational initiatives for young inner-city children. Locals liaised with psychiatrist Ivor Browne, who had established a community development division in the UCD Psychology Department, which led to the Irish Foundation for Human Development. Browne believed that the mental health of Dublin's north inner-city community was 'inextricably bound up with the social conditions of that community' and had experience of similar initiatives in Derry and Ballyfermot.[24]

Tony Gregory was elected to Dublin City Council in 1979 and was able to confront directly the officials endorsing the plans affecting his electorate. The previous year a picket designed to provoke Dublin's assistant city manager, Davy Byrne, had included a poster 'Davy fiddles, while the inner city burns'. Gregory and his community activists were now in a position more directly to challenge council officials; he subsequently took his causes to the national parliament in 1982.

– FIFTY-THREE –

EATING AND DRINKING THROUGH THE SEVENTIES

The heightened awareness of the social and economic status of various communities also generated a preoccupation with consumption and changing culinary habits. The National Prices Committee's monthly reports (which began in 1971) gave a good overview of what people were consuming and how prices varied depending on location. Along with the staples, popular brands included Findus beef burgers, Birds Eye potato chips, Galtee rashers, Little Chip marmalade, HB Vanilla ice-cream, Aero, Rolo, Toffo, Crosse & Blackwell Salad Cream, Goodall's YR sauce, Goldenvale Cheese, Cookeen cooking fat, Yoplait yoghurts, Jacob's biscuits, Gateaux Swiss roll, Campbell's soup, Shamrock Almonds and walnuts, Lyons tea bags, Kellogg's cereals, Uncle Ben's boil in the bag rice, Maxwell House coffee granules, Liga baby food and SMA powder. Popular confectionery launched in the 1970s included the Curly Wurly bar, 'one of the relatively few British confections on sale' in the Republic. The market was still dominated by native confectionery such as Twirl and Catch chocolate bars and the Wibbly Wobbly Wonder ice lolly: 'But for Irish kids exposed to British TV, the real objects of desire were the sweets beamed into Irish living rooms every night in adverts that got brighter, catchier and more glamorous with the coming of colour TV at the start of the seventies. Spangles, Skybars, Swizzels, Double Dips, Texan Bars, Treets, Revels and a host of other sweets flashed before young eyes, but for a while it was a case of you can look but you cannot touch.'[1]

The main supermarkets included Dunnes Stores, Five Star, Liptons, Quinnsworth, Superquinn, H. Williams and Besco and the appearance of 'own brand' products was also noted, as were regional disparities: 'The overall difference between Tralee and Carlow of roughly £2 in a shopping basket of £38 (or 5.5 per cent) masks considerably greater variations for individual categories. Thus, for example, for bread and biscuits and cakes, Bray is 21 per cent cheaper than Ennis.'[2] What was also notable was the amount of tinned meats, fish, vegetables, fruit and puddings consumed and it was noted that 'the prepacked trade is primarily based around Dublin, where it is estimated that some 60 per cent of fresh fruit and vegetables sold are prepacked'. John Quinn, the managing director of H. Williams and Company, wrote to Liam Cosgrave in 1976 emphatically rejecting the idea that the onus for the classification, description and responsibility for these prepacked goods should be on the retailer. It was 'impractical, inoperable and unacceptable and will not be tolerated ... We have no intention of paying people to do the work which should be done by the Department of Agriculture inspectors ... This country is not in a position at the moment to supply goods according to EEC regulations to retail outlets.' He threatened that H. Williams might have to resort to canned, packaged and frozen foods.[3] There were also campaigns in the late 1970s to get the Irish to eat more cheese to help reduce the EEC cheese mountain ('we are low consumers of this exotic dairy product') and there was no shortage of culinary crimes inflicted on the Irish, including in 1970, new Knorr mashed potato, 'delicious, smooth, fluffy mashed potatoes in seconds ... just add water to the granule'.[4]

Some of the old-style shops survived, selling a bit of everything: 'Washing detergents and breakfast cereals, tins of black or brown or oxblood polish, boxes of matches, ham off the slicer, corned beef, loose tea, 3 or 4 fresh vegetables, blackjacks and jellies and, for my father, boiled sweets either by the packet or the pound ... and the broken biscuit box where surprise and chance and luck were everything ... bourbon creams, fig rolls and the bristling with sugar Nice biscuits.'[5]

As for eating out, the decade saw the beginnings of a more expansive restaurant trade, but there were numerous food critics to decry its lack of sophistication. Writing in *Hibernia* in 1970, food critic Alec Reid yearned for the days when the restaurant was an extension of the home, as 'now it has become part of one's image – you eat the scampi, the steak or whatever is the appropriate executive food in the appropriate pseudo-intimate, half-lit sham panelled utterly unreal surroundings'.[6] In the same vein, Theodora Fitzgibbon found herself looking around 'the average over-priced Dublin restaurant and see people eating poorly cooked food with apparent relish'.[7] Fitzgibbon was well placed to make such judgements; she had built up an international reputation as a cookery writer, and from 1968 to 1984 was cookery correspondent for the *Irish Times* and author of thirty-one cookery books, including the renowned 'Taste of' series covering Britain and Ireland, and *Food of the Western World* (1976). She embellished her recipes with historical and literary references to food.[8]

Behind Mount Street in Dublin, John O'Byrne opened Dobbin's Bistro, a favourite haunt of politicians, businessmen and show business stars. The highly rated King Sitric fish restaurant opened in Howth, as did the Mirabeau in Dun Laoghaire ('never out of the headlines ... owned by chef/patron Seán Kinsella, a brilliant self-publicist ... only the host got the menu with the prices on it'). There was also 'a trend towards opening restaurants in the increasingly affluent suburbs'.[9] Writer Ulick O'Connor, reviewing the restaurant scene for *Magill* in 1977, mentioned Bernardos, Dublin's oldest Italian restaurant ('Mamo, the owner will always be there for consultation at lunch or dinner'), while Jammets, 'with its world reputation as a restaurant' and which had closed in 1967, 'became a self-service joint'. The oldest restaurant in Cork, the Oyster Tavern, was praised by O'Connor for its 'splendid chops ... nerve enough to serve Irish food without smothering it in continental sauces'.[10]

Ulick O'Connor was scathing about the dearth of quality food in some establishments; chicken dishes were mocked witheringly as 'the frozen leather served up in many Dublin restaurants today', while the Trocadero, where the 'actors hang out', was regarded 'from the point of view of value ... the best in the city. A sirloin steak costs £2.50 and you can get out under £3.50 for yourself with wine, which is cheap, God help us, in this costly kip that masquerades as a capital city.'[11]

Cork was singled out as home of one of the best restaurants in 'the British Isles' by the *Egon Ronay Guide* (not a single restaurant in Dublin had a star in the guide), Arbutus Lodge in Cork, run by the Ryan brothers, Declan and Michael, which got two stars. It was concluded that 'there has been, it would seem, a gentle revolution in eating habits around the country. The Ronay organisation says that the influx of foreign owned and run restaurants may account for the new interest natives are acquiring in the business. The Ryans have ferreted out old Irish country recipes for their menu, Declan lamenting that in bygone years Ireland had its own cheese-making tradition rivalling that of France.'[12] In 1975 the *Ronay Guide* had also, for the first time, given its Gold Plate award to an Irish hotel, Ashford Castle in Cong, County Mayo, which it described as 'the most luxurious hotel in the British Isles'. There was also a newly expanded market of 'expense account executives' hungry for posh restaurants: 'Moneyed members of what [journalist] John Healy insists on calling the Wicklow set.' One of their favoured haunts was rising chef Paulo Tulio's Armstrong's Barn in Annamoe, County Wicklow, where the delicacies included squid provençale, lamb's kidneys with mustard sauce, leek tart, Chinese beef, venison with juniper berries and vegetables from his own garden.[13]

In London in 1976 'an Irish hell raiser', from County Clare, Peter Langan, joined forces with actor Michael Caine to create a landmark in the history of London's restaurants, Langan's in Piccadilly, 'that ushered in the age of the celebrity chef'. Langan was 'driven by reckless hedonism', got away with 'drunkenly insulting everyone from Princess Margaret to Marlon Brando' and had a habit of crawling under tables to nuzzle the ankles of female diners. Langan was the son of Irish rugby international Dan Langan and had been educated in one of Ireland's most prestigious private schools, but his antics as a restaurateur did not impress Caine: 'Peter stumbles around in a cloud of his own vomit and is a complete social embarrassment. You would have a more interesting conversation with a cabbage.' In retaliation, Langan described Caine as a 'mediocrity with halitosis who has a council-house mind'.[14]

But Irish restaurant critics could be conservative too, with the establishments they reviewed likely to be praised for a 'limited, sensible menu' of prawn cocktail, corn on the cob, sirloin steak and apple pie, and service 'crisp and efficient, as it should be'.[15] As well as more convenience food (like Findus's frozen 'sliced roast beef in gravy'[16]), a gourmet food festival in Kinsale in 1978 was also heavily advertised. Delicatessen and specialist food shops were making their presence felt, which meant, according to women's rights campaigner Nuala Fennell, that it was now possible 'for mothers like me to have a cook-free day. You can buy cooked chickens, cold meats, salads, croissants, fish and even cakes.'[17] It was also a notable pattern that advertisements aimed at a middle-class audience came to be increasingly centred around dinner parties.

There were also a number of American-style hamburger joints 'from the fairly grotty to the slightly chic' that had sprung up in Dublin in the mid 1970s (with a hamburger and chips costing roughly 75p), including Captain America's in 1971, which became 'a melting pot in a city finding its feet', and Dublin was introduced to iceberg lettuce, 'deep dish apple pie, those sesame-sprinkled buns and ice-cream with chocolate sauce'. One of the founders recalled, 'several people told us we'd never get 38p for a bun burger', but the formula worked, and the staff recalled a Dublin 'full of youthful energy' who experienced 'friendships, relationships, broken hearts, riotous behaviour, the freedom and energy of being twenty something in Ireland ... everyone was on their way somewhere. The kitchen was stacked with economists ... Chris de Burgh strummed guitar in the corner for a fiver and a glass of wine.'[18] American import McDonald's was also 'opened with a flourish' by Minister for Labour Michael O'Leary in 1977.[19]

Middle-class women at home were urged to take charge of the poor diets of their fat, lazy husbands. This text appeared promoting Flora margarine under a photograph of a wife giving a cup of tea to her portly man slouched in a deckchair:

> Have you looked at your husband lately? Really looked at him? Does his waistband betray that he's desk bound too often? Do his fingertips tell you that he's smoking too much? Do his eyes give a clue as to his business lunches? Get back the husband you had. Plenty of exercise. Fewer cigarettes and at evenings and weekends something light to eat – with Flora ... Flora is higher in polyunsaturates than any other spread because it's made with pure sunflower oil and contains no animal fats at all ... so when he's home, look after him. Because he'll never look after himself.[20]

Consumers were also urged to think continental: 'The French have a way with food. More and more Irish people are now sharing this appreciation for the good things in life as French food and wine become available in ever-increasing variety throughout Ireland.'[21]

In terms of the alcohol trade, popular drinks included Guinness, Harp, Phoenix, Smithwicks and McCardles beers, Hennessy brandy, CDC gin, Power's whiskey, Huzzar vodka and Double Century sherry. Of the factors that were contributing to Irish ill health, alcohol remained a dominant factor and excessive drinking was, during this decade, framed more broadly as a health as well as a social problem. As far back as the late 1940s Fianna Fáil's Erskine Childers had presented himself as something of a temperance martyr in reminding the Pioneer Total Abstinence Association, one of the country's largest voluntary Catholic organisations whose members abstained completely from alcohol, that, though he was not a teetotaller, he had 'courted unpopularity by saying publicly many times that four glasses of stout instead of five would hurt no-one, and this during the general election'. Twenty-five year later, as president of Ireland, he returned to the subject, informing young members of the Pioneer Association of his personal experience and confessing that 'until he was Minister for Health he used to drink four or five spirit drinks ... at cocktail parties, and without any effect, luckily for himself. He had then decided to take only two drinks and drink soft drinks subsequently and he had never noticed the slightest effect on his capacity for enjoyment, for drawing out people's ideas and interests and he experienced no sense of fatigue.' The association also sought to enlist the GAA to promote a 'No Rounds' car sticker, to highlight the custom of each individual buying drink for a group, a practice that contributed to excessive consumption.[22]

Such civilised suggestions by Childers about promoting a modicum of temperance came at a time when alcohol was increasingly seen as contributing to misspent youth, with wider access to cheaper alcohol. The owner of an off-licence in Dorset Street, in Dublin, for example, Patrick McDonnell, who was chairman of the National Off Licence Traders Association in 1970, wrote to the government to complain that the Minister for Justice Des O'Malley 'is not taking any notice of the serious problem of teenagers consuming alcoholic drinks. The situation is ready to erupt into a national scandal and will, if not erased now, have disastrous effects on the physical, mental and moral conditions of the children of Ireland.'

He maintained that the licensing laws were out of date (the last Intoxicating Liquor Act had been in 1962) and that 'it has become the in-thing with over 14-year-olds to get half stoned before they attend the "baby dances" on Friday and Saturday nights' and that cider was being sold by those with 'sweet licences' that allowed shopkeepers to sell wine of Irish manufacture. What was needed, he argued, was 'maturity regarding their drinking as the European children have'.[23] Jack Lynch expressed his regret that McDonnell's letter 'should be couched in rather intemperate terms'. There were only 256 off-licence holders (spirit grocers) in the Republic but there were 11,000 publicans.

W. Herlihy, a Garda inspector, was asked to investigate McDonnell's claims that well-known Dublin pubs like Bartley Dunnes, the Bailey and

Davy Byrnes were serving teenagers alcohol, and while he accepted that McDonnell was genuinely concerned about teenage drinking, he also saw him as championing his own trade 'and that of the other spirit grocers who he feels are being squeezed out of business by the larger combines'. O'Malley refused to meet McDonnell and told Lynch he was not representative, and O'Malley did not accept that cider was being sold in shops with sweet licences. He found the tone of some of McDonnell's statements 'grossly offensive'. He was also 'far from satisfied that the problem of drinking by young persons, in so far as it exists, can be materially reduced by any practicable change in the law or by increased Garda action'.[24] When asked in the Dáil that month by Dublin Fine Gael TD Hugh Byrne, a district medical officer, if he would consider raising the legal drinking age from eighteen to twenty-one on the grounds that 'nowadays a 14 year old can pass for a person of 18 years', O'Malley was dismissive: 'Surely a 20 year old can pass even more easily for a 22 year old. I consider Deputy Byrne's suggestion ridiculous.' Byrne also suggested that 'in a certain area of Dublin firelighters, which contain a high content of methylated spirits, are being mixed with cider and cheap wine'.[25] Concerns about young people 'physically maturing at an earlier age' continued to be raised in the late 1970s, to which the response from the Department of Justice was that it was the job of parents and not the state to police under-age drinking.

Those involved in the licensed trade remained concerned about the burden of taxation their products had to bear, the Licensed Vintners Association informing Richie Ryan in 1973 that it was 'excessive and out of scale'. Wages had gone up 82 per cent in four years in the Dublin area, they maintained, and profit margins were 30–50 per cent higher in Britain and other European countries: 'We have the highest taxed pint of beer in Europe.' Revealingly, the number of special exemption orders granted by the courts – to allow drink to be served outside normal licensing hours – increased from 6,342 in 1967 to 14,814 in 1972, rising to 34,300 in 1978.[26]

Although there were calls for it to be made more difficult to get these exemptions or attach more conditions, such as the inclusion of a 'substantial meal', Vivian Mulcahy, an assistant principal officer in the Department of the Taoiseach, was unimpressed: 'Most people who go dancing after normal pub closing time probably do not want a substantial meal and I see no reason why they should be asked to pay for it ... Attempts to restrict drinking by prohibition or by measures such as the proposed order [requiring substantial meals] have little chance of success. The best we can hope to do in the short term is to limit the consequences of such drinking (rigorous enforcement re drink driving) and hope that more sensible attitudes will be generated by the education system in the longer term.'[27]

As seen earlier, those involved in promoting tourism were more concerned that the licensing system was placing Irish restaurants at a disadvantage compared to other European countries, arguing that they needed full licences rather than just wine licences. Gerry Collins as Minister for Justice in 1979 suggested there was 'more pressing work' to deal with than intoxicating liquor legislation which would be 'highly controversial'. An unusually highly charged memorandum from the Department of the Taoiseach was adamant that Irish licensing laws were anachronistic. There was, it was maintained, 'a crying need for the liberalization of the licensing laws ... in other words we should no longer tolerate the ridiculous situation that a person seeking a drink of beer brewed in Ireland and made almost exclusively of Irish products – is denied the privilege, while at the same time, he can imbibe as much as he wishes of wine made abroad from products which have little or no Irish connection. This is a totally ludicrous situation.'[28]

When it launched in October 1977, *Magill* magazine made much of its guide to social life in Dublin and its pub listings at a time when a pint of stout was 43p and vodka and gin measures roughly 38p. Writer Anthony Cronin praised the style and continuity of Davy Byrnes pub, which accommodated 'swingers and intellectuals', while O'Brien's in Leeson Street was 'the young swingers bar in Dublin ... convivial and unpretentious'. Sachs in Morehampton Road was 'the most fashionable bar in town ... the clientele are very much of the "beautiful people" variety with a few chancers and lots of ladies on the make thrown in'. Ryan's in Parkgate Street had a 'reputation for excellent pints of stout ... very discreet snugs, which can be opened only from inside the bar', while Sinnotts was 'the best of the Grafton Street area bars, coming down with lefties, actors, economists and other drop outs including the entire cast of the Riordans'. Mulligan's in Poolbeg Street, according to Gene Kerrigan, was 'a natural for those who are into basic living', though 'on a crowded night you're likely to wind up next to a Trinity student brandishing his cut price copy of the Irish Times, dipping his scarf into your drink and emoting about Annie Hall in a voice that sounds like all his teeth are loose'.

Another special Dublin pub was O'Donoghue's in Merrion Row, where 'every Irish traditional musician with any self-respect and many more with none, have featured ... in the last 15 years.'[29] Meanwhile, 'In Barbarella's in Fitzwilliam Lane are the most naked girls you can see in Dublin' with only tiny pieces of silk covering them up.[30]

It was asserted in *Magill* in December 1977 that 'the country has been on a massive drinking rampage'. Sales of alcohol had 'rocketed by 15 per cent' in the three months June to September 1977 compared to the same period in 1976. In 1968, 58 per cent of the adult population were estimated to have drunk alcohol; by 1975 this figure had increased to 65 per cent and it was maintained that by the end of 1977 this had risen further to 70 per cent with women and younger people accounting for most of the increase. But Irish consumption figures were not high by international standards; in the late 1970s the per capita consumption expressed in litres of 100 per cent alcohol for France was 16.5, West Germany 12.5, Denmark 9.2, UK 8.4 and Ireland 8.7. What did mark Ireland out as different was that 75 per cent of all drinking was done in pubs or clubs, and while Ireland spent more of its consumed expenditure on alcohol than other EEC countries (12 per cent), 'This anomaly is explained by the very high duties on drink in Ireland and the relatively low income per capita.'

There had also been a doubling of the consumption of spirits in a decade (there were a lot of advertisements for Huzzar vodka and Black and White Scotch): 'Every Saturday night in the 26 counties ... 195,000 vodka drinks are consumed by women under 30 years of age and these same women drink 4,500 cases of vodka a week. The social consequences of these consumption patterns bear investigation.'[31] Black Tower wine was presented for a country relatively new to wine in terms of popular consumption as an exotic, historic sophistication: 'Today the soft, light refreshing wine is bottled in a replica of the stone crock of Roman times and can be enjoyed as an aperitif or with good food.' Another popular sweet German wine was Blue Nun ('a reflection of good taste', according to the advertisements); the joke peddled at a much later stage about the 1970s was: 'You wanted a choice of wine? Well, you had little or Nun',[32] which is an interesting piece of revisionism as in the mid 1970s Mitchell and Sons wine merchants actually stocked fifty-six different German wines, with prices starting at £1.80, along with just four Australian and two Chilean labels. A bottle of 1970 Dom Pérignon champagne could be bought in Shrimps Wine Bar in Dublin in 1978 for £16.[33] McGowan's of Blackrock in County Dublin, which billed itself as Ireland's 'leading off licence' celebrated its twenty-fifth anniversary in 1977, boasting of a stock of one thousand wines, including Blanc de Blancs at £1 and Château Mouton Rothschild 1970 at £12.45 for those with deeper pockets and more expensive palates.[34]

The country's first international wine fair took place at the Mansion House in Dublin (residence of the city's lord mayor) in October 1978 'in celebration of a new Irish drinking record – 8 million bottles of wine a year at a cost of £13 million'.[35] For those who preferred to stick to lager, they were urged to have a 'wonderful time' with 'Harp and lime' while the promoters of Guinness were more elaborately lyrical in describing what was not just an alcoholic, but a spiritual experience: 'When you get really close to your Guinness, close enough that it's almost touching your lips, pause briefly, look at that tender creamy head poised delicately at the rim of the glass. Then close your eyes and swallow. There's a feast for the eyes too in Guinness.'[36]

The Health Education Bureau was active in the late 1970s, running radio and television ads warning young people of the dangers of excessive drinking: 'If you drink, don't die' was one of the messages using footage of a number of well-known rock stars,[37] which was perhaps somewhat ironic given that Harp lager was one of the sponsors of a musical talent competition that first brought U2 to notice.[38] Drink continued to be pervasive in artistic, journalistic and political circles. Actor and comedian Niall Tóibín, a marvellous mimic, who with talented writers like Eoghan Harris and Wesley Burrows, had 'ploughed a furrow into the virgin earth of Irish satire' on RTÉ television, and who in 1970 garnered plaudits for his performance in the Tony Award-winning production of Brendan Behan's *Borstal Boy* on Broadway, fell out of the Belfast to Dublin train in Connolly Station Dublin uproariously drunk one day in March 1974. He spent the following week drying out in a Dublin hospital. It was his last act as a drinker; his doctor calmly explained: 'You can continue to drink like this, or you can continue to work like this, but you cannot do both.'[39]

The film critic for the *Irish Press* was nearly sacked after the opening of a new cinema in Dublin: 'Adrian proceeded to urinate on Jack Lynch's shoes. There was uproar and Adrian was ejected from the premises. Meanwhile, the phone rang on the editor's bedside locker: "Your fucking film critic" an irate cinema manager roared "is down here pissing all over the Fucking Taoiseach!"'[40] Michael Mills, political correspondent with the *Irish Press*, recalled an annual dinner of the Leinster House Press Gallery for which expensive wine had to be bought specifically for Charles

Haughey, which witnessed Haughey scarpering without thanks after a drunken row between two of the journalists about civil war allegiances.[41] Nor was the drinking journalistic culture a male preserve; in 1970 Nell McCafferty and Mary Cummins from the *Irish Times* would sit in a pub and 'drink from left to right off the shelves, working our way through the rows of bottles'.[42]

Aodhan Madden, a journalist with the *Irish Press* in the 1970s, may have viewed drink as the 'great liberation from a 1950s Irish childhood' but he came to realise its horrendous grip. He was also struggling with his (hidden) homosexuality. Whatever the degree of social liberalisation there was in some areas, there was nothing approximating free love and tolerance of sexual diversity, but instead the persistence of a homophobia that was 'tangible and frightening'. When Madden appealed in a newspaper article for a more compassionate attitude to gay people, a priest from his parish called to the house to tell him he was 'most concerned' about the views he had expressed.[43]

Eibhear Walshe, growing up gay in Waterford, found in the gentlemen's outfitters 'the sole sexually attractive image from my entire teenage years. It was a large coloured ad of a handsome young man in white vest and underpants, staring at the camera with his arms folded.' Most difficult, however, was that 'at the core of my understanding of sex and romance was the absolute certainty that I would always be outside it'.[44] Around the time of the foundation of the Irish Gay Rights Movement in 1974, one of its founders, Edmund Lynch, was aware that at meetings of the sexual liberation movement in Trinity College Dublin 'we could wax lyrical' about patriarchy and contraception 'but the reality of our own lives was so much more pressing, so much more urgent. The reality was that we were still facing a possible prison sentence'. In 1973 and 1974, forty-three men were sentenced in the district court for acts of 'gross indecency' under 1885 legislation.[45]

RTÉ took up the issue with a documentary in July 1977 by the multi-talented Cathal O'Shannon, who had worked in BBC current affairs in the 1960s before returning to RTÉ. His documentary included footage of a gay disco in Parnell Square while an *Insights* documentary by Ruth Dudley Edwards, shown on RTÉ in November 1979, concluded that Patrick Pearse was a latent homosexual. But there was a mountain to climb to make homosexuality acceptable. Councillor Frank Sherwin, in a letter to the *Evening Press* in February 1977, defended Dublin Corporation's decision not to fund the Project Arts Centre: 'If people want to indulge in homosexuality then they should keep quiet about it. In my opinion these people are not only weak but also sick and they should not be permitted to contaminate others, especially the young.' The Irish Censorship Board banned the *English Gay News* in April 1976 and by the end of the decade, David Norris, a Joycean scholar and Trinity College Dublin academic, who became the Republic's best known gay rights activist, put in motion a constitutional challenge against the laws making male homosexuality illegal.[46]

– FIFTY-FOUR –

A NEW AFFLUENCE

Just what was ranked high in terms of personal financial priorities? Aside from food and drink, what were those with money to spare consuming and desiring during this decade? Ulick O'Connor was undoubtedly in a minority in seeking out 'a perky little tailor in Abbey Street, one of the very few in the city who knows how to cut an Edwardian suit. No shoulder padding, four buttons, lapels on the waistcoats and flaps on the lower pockets of it.'[1] Eibhear Walshe recalled of the young people working in shops, factories and glass factories, 'the older brothers had the kinds of noisy cheap car that adults disapproved of on principle', while girls working in the shops were 'jingling with golden chains and bangles'.[2] Elephant flares, platform-heeled boots and floral shirts were in vogue, and some students opted for 'Indian shirt, Moroccan beads, Jesus sandals'.[3] The first punks began to appear on Dublin streets by the mid 1970s and, as journalist Aodhan Madden recalled, in the balmy summer of 1976 'for weeks the sun burned relentlessly and Dublin began to look like a dusty southern European city ... Girls strolled down Grafton Street in the skimpiest of skirts ... the bishops objected but the harm had gone out of their clout.'[4]

Italian boots, regarded as 'very dressy', were advertised in *Magill* for £40; a cheaper option in 1977 were 'Beige leather rodeo boots' for £20. For the younger market, advertisements appeared in *Hot Press* for Wrangler cord jeans in 1978 for £10.50. Other fashion staples of the decade included cheesecloth, Afghan furs, satin hot pants, bell bottoms, tank tops and 'four-inch platforms gave disco divas a whole new stature and with the advent of central heating, people peeled off and dispensed with sturdy tweeds in favour of new man-made fabrics like Courtelle, polyester and Trevira'.

The boutique concept began to flourish and clothes were 'very, very short, or very, very long' as a number of designers came to prominence including Paul Costelloe, Peter FitzSimons, Brian Tucker, Carolyn Donnelly and Liz Spillane, while model Jean O'Reilly became the face of a new fashion magazine, *Image*, which was launched in October 1975. Geraldine Brand opened a new model agency and Jackie Purcell became one of the country's best-known models, 'advertising everything from Guinness and Harp to car dealerships' as well as announcing the launch in 1973 of the new *Sunday World* newspaper under the provocative banner: 'Are You getting it every Sunday?'[5] Muriel Kerr opened the first Irish fashion chain, Mirror Mirror, in 1974 and hairdressers were besieged with requests for 'gypsy cuts' and 'layered shags', while some Irish men began to use aftershave. Old Spice was advertised as 'The Mark of a Man' while Tabac 'came as a shaving cream and aftershave and had the manly smell of tobacco'.[6]

Travel agents were busy advertising – 'more for your pound with Sunbound'[7] – and a holiday in Lanzarote with Bray Travel in the autumn of 1978 was advertised at an all-in cost of £180.[8] In 1979, two-week holidays in Europe were being advertised for approximately £350. Spain was popular with younger people and it was noted in 1979 that 'Irish holiday makers discovered Greece relatively late but are making up for lost time. Last year, 16,000 Irish went there, a 60 per cent increase over 1977.'[9] Joe Walsh Tours (JWT) became one of the most successful travel businesses, having started with pilgrimages to Rome and Lourdes, but by the mid 1970s Walsh had set his sights on Spain. Families were implored to 'Join the JWT set', while a rival, Budget Travel, was established by Gillian Bowler in 1975. Many were applying for passports for the first time and 'there were still some moral strictures, of course. Even in the 70s, some Irish travel agents refused to take bookings from couples unless they were respectably married.'[10] As recalled by Pat Boran, whose father ran a travel agency, 'the better off families were already beginning to take occasional breaks in Spain and on their walls or mantelpiece might be castanets, earthenware jars garishly painted, tea towels that said Benidorm or Torremolinos'.[11] Home holidays were also being promoted, including cruises on the Shannon, visits to stately homes, camping and caravans, while the 'joys of youth hostelling' were savoured by others and bicycles were seen as an ideal way to absorb the countryside.[12]

A new £7 million terminal at Dublin airport had come into partial service in May 1972 and two years later Trans World Airlines opened its new Atlantic service to Dublin, nearly thirty years after it had first sought permission to gain landing rights there. There was no shortage of complaints about the prices Aer Lingus was charging for its London to Dublin route, which at £56 for a return trip at Christmas 1976 was regarded by one complainant as 'exorbitant ... we are being held to ransom'.[13] In 1979 an alleged cartel arrangement between Aer Lingus and British Airways leading to a cost of £72 for a return ticket was also criticised and regarded as inimical to tourist growth. Later that year it was reported that 'middle-class rage is mounting over the continued fare increases' by Aer Lingus and British Airways on the Dublin–London run, with the return fare rising to £83, which seemed to be massively subsidising the operations of the rest of the airline.[14]

Aer Lingus was inevitably affected by the Troubles, which increased its 'war risk' insurance, and it recorded a loss of £2.3 million for 1971–2, but 'one answer to the airline's problems was to diversify'. It invested in hotels in London and Spain, and moved into the financial services and computing sectors which paid dividends and 'would lead to Aer Lingus having one of the earliest computerised booking and seat allocation systems in the aviation industry'. By 1978 it employed over 6,000 people 'and was the state's largest exporting company, earning £120 million overseas' as well as providing the livelihoods of many connected to the tourism business at home. In 1977 the Employment Equality Agency had criticised the airline for running advertisements for stewardesses and excluding men, and in 1978 it employed its first male member of cabin crew.[15] The following year the airline's first female pilot, Gráinne Cronin from Dublin, flew on her first scheduled flight. (Dublin city's first female bus-conductors also took up their posts that year.)

Advertisements that appeared in *Hibernia* magazine in 1970 saw banks offering 8¾ per cent interest on deposit accounts, paid without deduction of tax, while in 1971 the Bank of Ireland loudly trumpeted its new status as the 'first Irish bank ever to open a representative office in the United States'.[16] Spiralling interest rates also increased bank profits; to the spring of 1974, Bank of Ireland and Allied Irish Banks had accrued profits of £27.3 million between them, representing a 43 per cent increase for BoI and a 17 per cent increase for AIB, while the minimum lending rate had increased 'to an unheard of rate of 13 per cent'.[17] But in tandem with this, it seemed like a good time to save for those who could afford to; there was a 'spectacular rise in personal saving', which increased from £384 million in 1974 to £597 million in 1975.[18] Nonetheless, tetchy encounters with bank managers were also a part of this new dispensation; Eibhear Walshe recalled that his grandmother Cissie, in relation to her abattoir business, conducted a long session with her bank manager in Waterford, subsequently emerging to ask, 'Did you ever see such a look of pure evil on a human face?'[19]

Another manifestation of a new affluence was the number of people driving cars. New car sales over the five years 1970–74 witnessed an average 3 per cent annual growth, though the figure in 1974 was 19 per cent down on the previous year before trade picked up again in the late 1970s.[20] Irish road fatalities were alarmingly high throughout the 1970s. In February 1972 Bobby Molloy, the Minister for Local Government, whose department had responsibility for roads, wrote an extraordinarily heartfelt letter to Jack Lynch about this issue; he was concerned that an additional 800 Gardaí were being recruited but none were going to be assigned solely to traffic duty:

> The road deaths figures issued by the Gardaí for January show another shocking increase to 62 deaths – 22 more than in January 1971. It looks as if we must expect 700 road deaths this year and at least 25,000 people injured unless we can take some drastic action to prevent it ... the big gap I see in the whole organisational approach is the low level of traffic supervision and enforcement of statutory requirements by the Gardaí. It is commonly accepted that speed limits and road signs can virtually be ignored, as long as one gets away with it. There is a plethora of 'bangers' on the road with bald tyres, defective steering and little or no brakes. Cars are more frequently not taxed or insured. Above all, there is frightening (though confidential) evidence of the level of alcohol in the bodies of accident victims, while drivers under the influence are a common sight after closing hours ... I don't think we can be morally justified in not assigning men and equipment to the protection of road users ... in most countries the correctness of devoting police resources to road accident prevention is accepted as a proper and necessary part of upholding a code of civic behaviour. The

> establishment of a special traffic corps within the force has been talked about for years and seems as far away as ever ... Drunk driving and excessive speed should be eliminated or reduced to a 'tolerable level'.

He finished by writing of the 'despair which I feel. I even thought of asking for a day of national mourning for the 600 dead last year and making it an annual event.'[21]

But a new device – the breathalyser – was also making its mark. In 1974, 4,217 samples were received for analysis to detect drink driving; there was over 200 milligrams per hundred millilitres in 50 per cent of them; the legal limit for driving was 125 milligrams.[22] Anthony Cronin suggested in September 1978 that the summer just gone was 'undoubtedly the summer of the breathalyser. It may just be that without the breathalyser the Irish people en fête would have been drunker than they were.'[23]

The National Road Safety Association's main activities during 1976 and 1977, with a staff of fourteen and a budget of £234,000, centred on a new edition of the rules of the road, a campaign to get cyclists to use reflective arm bands, drivers to wear seat belts and a 'special TV publicity campaign over the Christmas period against drunken driving' as well as the Clontarf 'traffic school for children'.[24] The fitting of seat belts in new cars had not been obligatory until 1971, but using them remained voluntary and in April 1978 it was proposed that it should be made compulsory. A memorandum of that month revealed the following figures for yearly road deaths: 1973 (592), 1974 (594), 1975 (586), 1976 (525) and 1977 (576) with over 8,000 injured in most of those years. A 1969 report had found that, where fitted, the seat-belt usage rate for drivers and front-seat passengers was only 5 per cent and it was suggested in 1978 that this figure 'has not significantly improved in the interval'.

As another report of 1976 had suggested, 'the percentage of car drivers wearing seat belts involved in fatal or injury accidents had not exceeded 10 per cent'. Although efforts to make seat belts compulsory in Italy and the UK were reckoned to have failed 'through lack of interest', in other EEC countries, such mandatory wearing suggested the numbers killed in Ireland from 1974–6 'could have been reduced by 44 per cent if all car drivers wore seat belts at the time of accident'. It was acknowledged that with the new legislation 'visiting motorists would be exempted from the proposed requirement' and children would not be allowed to travel in the front.[25] The April 1978 proposals were quickly accepted and from February 1979 the wearing of seat belts by drivers and front seat passengers became a legal requirement.

There were also serious deficiencies in the quality of roads, it being pointed out in 1973 that, while in 1972 Northern Ireland had '57 miles of motorway in operation, we have none. In fact, we are unique in the EEC in not having any motorways'. There was inadequate spending on national primary routes that could not cope with the new volume of traffic; 327,000 motor vehicles had been registered in the Republic in 1961; by 1971 the number had risen to 573,000 and was expected to reach 773,000 by 1976; 96 per cent of passenger traffic was carried by road.[26] At the end of 1978 there were 214,000 registered motor vehicles in Dublin city and county. There were 78,888 driving tests taken in 1976, the highest ever figure since passing a test became a requirement in 1964, and the pass rate was 48.4 per cent; 68,375 new cars were registered in 1976 and £24.698 million was spent on roads in that year.[27]

But they were a mess by the end of the 1970s. Journalist Kevin Myers reflected on Dublin's traffic chaos in 1978, suggesting it had reached 'crisis point'. There was then a car for every five people living in the greater Dublin metropolitan area, almost 300 one-way streets in Dublin and 'one of every 3 cars parked in Dublin is parked illegally but the penalty for illegal parking is derisory: £2 on an ordinary street, £3 on a clearway. The average stay in a car park in most European city centres costs more than that.' A Living City group had proposed car-free areas, bus ways and pedestrianisation and intensive public transport, to which one councillor responded that they were 'plaguing the unfortunate motorist'.[28] Another article on traffic congestion in Dublin highlighted 'notorious bottlenecks' with about, for example, 19,000 cars passing through the village of Shankill in south County Dublin every day; the article faced an advertisement for a new front-wheel drive Renault 18 on the opposite page.[29]

By the end of the 1970s the dilemma seemed to be about the degree to which the level of attention devoted to secondary roads could be maintained, county roads comprising 80 per cent of the total public road network. In the early 1970s, 35 per cent of the national primary routes and 24 per cent of the national secondary routes 'were assessed as being inadequate' and now, many urban roads 'are seized up with traffic flows far above their capacity'. In 1978 it was estimated that there would be a 100 per cent increase in traffic by 1990.[30]

In 1974 a decision had been taken by government to develop Dublin rail commuter services with an electrified rapid rail transit system; (what became the Dublin Area Rapid Transit or DART) at an estimated cost (on 1977 figures) of £198 million to be completed by 1991. The priority identified in 1977 and 1978 was the electrification of the Howth to Bray railway line. Since the late 1960s passenger demand on Dublin's suburban rail services had risen sharply, the numbers carried rising from 4.3 million in 1970 to 8.1 million in 1977, an increase of 88 per cent: 'The daily carryings increased from 16,300 to 30,000 in the same period while daily carryings on the Howth/Bray section increased from 11,000 to 25,000, an increase of 125 per cent.' The locomotives then in use had been purchased in the 1950s. Dermot Nally in the Department of the Taoiseach was not convinced that CIÉ should automatically entrust the state Electricity Supply Board (ESB) with the work and argued it should be awarded on the basis of competitive tender. He wanted to discourage 'this sort of incestuous relationship between semi-state organisations. If the ESB can win the contract by competitive tender, then they should get it. If not, they should not be allowed to use their status and their relationship with another semi-state organisation to featherbed inefficiency.'[31]

In May 1979 the Minister for Economic Planning and Development, Martin O'Donoghue, opposed the DART initiative (his opposition was leaked by 'an official source') as there was not significant off-peak demand for suburban rail services. He wanted 'replacement of worn out stock with new diesel-engined stock'. The Minister for Transport, Pádraig Faulkner, demolished this argument: 'The suggestion that travellers are prepared to accept appreciably larger periods of sitting in stationary buses or cars rather than take the trouble to change to a speedy and attractive rail system is scarcely credible.'

The message from the Department of the Taoiseach was that a new system, using diesel only 'would be regarded as a joke ... the cost of the new system over 5 years is roughly equivalent to what CIÉ is now losing in a single year'. The civil servant went on to castigate CIÉ's 'stranglehold on public transport in Dublin: many people believe that a better system would be provided if CIÉ simply closed down and let others operate. Belfast has what is probably a better system – because the buses have been largely bombed out and the private market has taken over. The black taxis get people where they want to go quickly and cheaply'. The Minister for Transport won the argument and the government approved the DART at a cost of £42.2 million at September 1978 prices; it was estimated it would take 2½–3½ years to complete (an optimistic prediction as it turned out because the service was not ready until 1984 and was operated by CIÉ).[32]

For taxi drivers in the Republic, the 1970s was a decade of fear and loathing. It had been suggested in 1975 that a Taxi Board was necessary to oversee the service; taxi drivers complained loudly and regularly that there were too many taxis. Cork and Dublin drivers organised in the Irish Taxi Federation were pressing for aspects of competition in the trade to be regulated as people with other jobs were engaging in it on a part-time basis and

> operate during the most remunerative times of the day and that such persons, because they are not dependent on the trade for a livelihood are less responsible and are the cause of public complaint about the trade. On the other hand, there has recently been a growing body of complaint about the standard of vehicles, the inadequacy of the service and the abuses within the trade such as over-charging, refusals of short distance journeys etc. The Dublin Regional Tourism organisation has described the current position as the 'worst ever' experienced. It has proved impossible to obtain precise particulars of taxi men's incomes, to assess the effort which must be made to earn a given income or to form a basis on which corrective measures might be considered. In this connection it is worth noting that operators are traditionally highly individualistic.[33]

As the Minister for Justice Patrick Cooney saw it, creating a monopoly through a reduction in licences 'can lead to the creation of interests which, in turn, can become an impediment to change and rationalisation'.[34]

In September 1978, journalist Inga Saffron wrote a revealing account of the 'sub-culture' of the Dublin taxi world. In the early morning hours the taxi drivers claimed that 'most of their passengers then are either drunk, crazy or prostitutes. This sameness is the basic theme of their anecdotes.'[35] There were estimated to be 1,800 taxi men in Dublin (1,400 working full time) and some were working eighty hours a week to bring home just £40. Although the Irish Taxi Federation had united drivers, there was still no Taxi Board, no standard taxi, no social welfare available to them and, according to the drivers, 'no decent standard of living possible within a 40 hour week'. Environment Minister Sylvester Barrett's proposal in August 1978 to issue 300 licences prompted a strike; he promised to set up a taxi advisory council instead.[36]

The cost of housing was another major preoccupation of the 1970s, to the extent that in 1972, the Taoiseach was asked if he would consider appointing a Minister for Housing, which he would not countenance.[37] The Irish preoccupation with property ownership seemed as strong as ever and the extent of house building over six decades was reflected in figures that revealed, by 1981, that less than one-quarter of Irish houses dated from before 1919.[38] Passions continued to run high regarding entitlement and occupancy, an emotive issue in Irish society historically. *Hibernia* reported in 1972 a case in which a widow from Oughterard in Galway, whose family had lived in a house she was occupying for three generations but could not demonstrate title. When she was given six months by a court to make arrangements to vacate the house, 'the plaintiff, Commander Burgess, was chased through the Galway streets and he eventually took refuge in the local Garda station'.[39]

In 1970, a three-bedroomed pre-war house in the south Dublin suburb of Sandymount was on sale for £6,100 while a three-storey semi-detached house in Rathmines was £12,000. At the end of 1973, the Sisters of Charity order of nuns reputedly received £1.5 million from the sale of St Vincent's Hospital on St Stephen's Green, reckoned to be 'the biggest single property transaction ever to take place in the state'. This land was not used for charitable purposes and journalist Brian Trench asserted that 'the records of land disposal by church bodies shows little regard for social responsibilities'.[40] The same year, a new record for a Dublin property was established at auction, when nine-tenths of an acre of land in south Dublin sold for £115,000. In 1976 a semi-detached pre-war four-bedroom house in Terenure was on sale for £27,000.[41] From the end of 1976 'a backlog of demand for housing from the stagnated 1973–6 years has driven up the price of land for residential development by 120 per cent, not including inflation'. With the economic recovery in 1976 came rock-bottom interest rates and looser credit. In 1978 it was reported, 'The Fianna Fáil government has made good on their election promises, introducing £1,000 grants to house buyers and raising the SDA [small dwellings acquisition] loan limits. Demand for houses has soared. People owning homes have seen their value jump 24 per cent [in real terms] despite a 6.2 per cent inflation rate.'[42] By 1979, it was observed that flats in Dublin 2 and 4 that sold in 1972 for £10,000 were now being resold for £25,000, while for those renting, a one-bed flat costing £55 a month in 1973 now cost £86. As a result of EEC membership, the price of agricultural land soared 150 per cent between 1973 and 1978.

In 1978 the *Irish Independent* reported that half of all new houses in Dublin were detached houses, built 'for the upper end of the market'.[43] The new affluence was reflected in the contemporary advertisements for such housing, like the Woodburn Development in Rathfarnham, close to the Grange Golf Course: 'The sitting room is large and well-proportioned with a featured brick fireplace. A spacious dining room looks out over the ample gardens. The fully fitted kitchen is a housewife's dream and comes complete with a cooker, refrigerator and an automatic washing machine. Upstairs, four family-sized bedrooms. Master bedroom en suite. Second bedroom with fitted wardrobes.'[44]

Domestic comforts were in demand. Youghal Carpets employed more than 600 people in Cork, while shag rugs were also popular and central heating became much more common. Lava lamps, bean bags, colour televisions were other creature comforts, while 'Mrs Nineteen-seventies would have been hugely proud of her new set of non-stick pots and frying pans and on her kitchen counter there would probably have been a Soda Stream, the clever CO_2 device that produced endless litres of fizzy drinks ... Toasted sandwich makers ... also made their debut ... as did the electric carving knife.'[45] Some were intent on indulging in the luxury of second or holiday homes, which caused some negative comment about the damage holiday-home developments might do to the 3,498 miles of coastline in the Republic: 'Unique in western Europe with a small population and as yet limited industrial growth, Ireland enjoys the great advantage of being able to plan its coastline development with thought and care.'[46]

But the boom of the late 1970s in relation to private dwellings was not the only housing narrative of the decade. By the mid 1970s there were 775,000 houses in the state; approximately 110,000 were rented local authority houses. The average rent per local authority house in 1973–4 was £1.57 a week and the average expended on maintenance per house was £1.50 a week. In 1975, James Tully 'mentioned that there were about 700 families squatting in Corporation houses in Dublin – without paying the normal rent',[47] while the following year, *Hibernia* magazine reported that Dublin Corporation had records of 870 squatters.[48]

In the context of periods of economic uncertainty, James Tully expressed concern about the prospects of those in the house-building industry, which employed 82,000 people and which was very dependent on public capital. Twenty-five thousand houses (public and private) had been completed in 1973–4 but in 1975, 'prospects in the private housing sector are particularly grim, present indications are that building societies will be able to provide mortgage loans for only 3,500 new houses in 1975' and that employment in house building would drop by 10,000. The Department of the Taoiseach produced a memorandum which insisted more private housing was needed, as 'no matter what happens, the housing programme simply cannot be sustained if money is not induced to flow to the building societies'. It maintained that the government's housing programme, with a plan of 25,000 new houses a year was not sustainable, but the Department of Local Government received an extra £3 million in the 1975 capital budget allocation for local authority housing (an estimated 100,000 local authority houses were built between 1973 and 1977).[49]

Further gloom was apparent in January 1976 when the outlook for the construction industry was assessed. It was predicted that employment levels would 'fall drastically' unless there was an increase in the overall capital allocation in real terms. The Construction Industry Federation maintained that '8,433 building workers are unemployed who were working this time last year and the total number employed in the industry is 20,274. The present government cannot be blamed for the world-wide economic decline, but it can be blamed for ignoring the pleas and warnings previously given by us.'[50] Later that year the Department of the Taoiseach pointed out that the cost of maintaining local authority housing had risen from approximately £5 million in 1973–4 to £8.6 million in 1975. As seen by the Department of the Taoiseach, the bottom line was that an exchequer subsidy met the deficit on current expenditure on local authority housing accounts. There was not enough of a balance between cost and rent received and local authorities were passing their entire bills to the exchequer:

> What does matter and seriously is that the gap between the rent which a new tenant pays and the economic cost of the house is now immense ... people will always queue up for accommodation which is being offered to them at this sort of give-away price. In housing, as in everything else, demand is in proportion to cost. This may well account for the fact that no matter how many houses Dublin Corporation, for example, build, or how large their programme may be, they have always a need for 20,000 houses – and have had the same sort of need since the Second World War.[51]

Payment of ground rents was also a contentious issue. ACTRA, the central body for residential tenants, launched a campaign in April 1977 to wipe out ground rents on 500,000 Irish homes 'once and for all', which Patrick Cooney found 'rather extreme' as what they were looking for in effect was 'confiscation in whole or in part of the landlord's interest'. The intended effect of the proposed Landlord and Tenant Law Bill in 1977 was prohibition of the creation of ground rent.[52]

Escalating house and land prices inevitably generated a blame game. It was suggested in 1973 in *Hibernia* that the big issue in housing was 'the tax free speculative profit which separates the cost of normal land from the inflated prices now demanded and received for development land'. As seen earlier, questions were being raised about the practice of councillors' voting for the re-zoning of land and the conflicts of interests involved. The Workers Union of Ireland pointed to the irony of a bill to prohibit squatting being introduced by a government 'which has failed so dismally to prevent the exploitation of land by speculators'.[53] In 1971 Minister for Local Government Bobby Molloy commissioned a report on the cost of building land from a committee chaired by John Joseph Kenny, a High Court judge subsequently promoted to the Supreme Court. The Kenny Report, published in January 1974, recommended that development land should be compulsorily acquired by local authorities at a 25 per cent premium above its existing use value, and that a register of property sale prices be established. Its recommendations were essentially ignored (probably because restrictions on land speculation threatened powerful pressure groups and vested interests), something that 'always rankled' with its author.[54]

Kenny's report, which ran to 195 pages, was frequently invoked in the decades after its publication when scandals relating to land re-zoning and attendant corrupt practices came to light, it being pointed out that such practices had their origins in the housing shortages, land prices and re-zoning practices of the 1960s and early 1970s. One of Kenny's conclusions was that the demand for housing would continue to grow, and that if nothing was done to restrict them, prices would rise 'at an even more rapid rate than previously'. But as was observed twenty-five years later, 'one administration after another failed to meet the challenges of profiteering and corruption'.[55]

– FIFTY-FIVE –

FATAL LIFESTYLES AND THE HEALTH SYSTEM CHALLENGE

Given some of the excesses highlighted in relation to consumption, it is unsurprising there was no shortage of reminders that the Irish needed to become healthier, a nagging that became more pronounced by the end of the decade, when average life expectancy was sixty-seven years and seven months for males and seventy-three years and five months for women (compared with fifty-seven years four months and fifty-seven years nine months fifty years previously). In June 1978 John Feeney exclaimed in *Magill* magazine that 'the Irish lifestyle is fatal ... We have adopted the behaviour patterns of affluent consumerism and it is slowly but inexorably killing us' due to poor food, excessive drinking and lack of exercise. In 1976 heart attacks killed 1,985 Irish people under the age of sixty-five, 2,644 between the ages of sixty-five and seventy-five and another 3,997 over seventy-five. According to a World Health Organisation Report that year, Dublin had the third highest incidence of heart attacks among young males, exceeded only by two cities in Scandinavia.[1] A diet rich in animal fats was partly to blame. There were contradictory messages, it seemed, for those seeking a healthier diet. The foods 'traditionally associated with ease and pleasure' such as cream, butter and eggs and fatty meat (Ireland's main food exports) were being frowned upon, but at the same time 'we now have the ludicrous sight of one government agency, the Health Education Bureau, hitting at fat eating and another, the Department of Agriculture, pushing it. No wonder we're paranoid.'[2] A health questionnaire from 1978 suggested a generous definition of moderate drinking – 'up to two large whiskies a day, a half litre of wine or 2 pints of beer'.[3] The appearance of numerous health clubs in Dublin city in the early 1970s was characterised as indicating a 'leisure boom' with 'fitted carpets and piped music' alongside yoga sessions and saunas and the idea of 'natural food products' began to be aired for the middle classes.[4] Much more attention was given to the promotion of healthier living and lifestyles with an emphasis on the idea that care of health needed to be a part of educating the young (slogans stamped on envelopes in the early 1970s read 'teach your children to clean their teeth'[5]).

Mental health was also highlighted. There were 16,500 hospitalised schizophrenics – 'a uniquely high number' – and 'one Irish male in nine is hospitalised at some stage in his adult life suffering from alcoholic psychosis, a staggering figure, and if you survive to the age of seventy no matter what sex you are, you have one chance in five of being hospitalised in a mental hospital. The total number of patients attending outpatient clinics in psychiatric hospitals alone in 1974 was 28,900.'[6] Psychiatric institutions generated fear – 'the belief that once people went into a place like that, they never came out' – and historically that had indeed been the case for many. Inmates at St Patrick's Hospital in Dublin, which specialised in treating mental illness, saw St Brendan's Hospital in Grangegorman, the largest psychiatric hospital serving the greater Dublin area 'as being for the no-hopers'.[7] Nuala O'Faoláin recalled that in the late 1970s 'the damaged underclass I was part of in the afternoon pubs was as much a part of Ireland as its beauty' and it drove her into a psychiatric hospital.[8]

In 1978 there were 13,000 psychiatric patients in Ireland's twenty district mental hospitals.[9] Throughout the decade, Dublin Health Authority's chief psychiatrist Ivor Browne was a proponent of community psychiatric development, which was slow to develop in Ireland, coming ten years after its establishment in Britain, France, the US and elsewhere. In attempting reform, Browne and others like him were faced with 'processes continually at work within society that mitigate against the acceptance back into normal life of those who have already been rejected by the community'.[10] One of the main problems was that financial investment was geared towards 'shoring up' the mental hospitals, instead of using the money to create alternative community facilities. There was much publicity in the late 1970s given to the exposure by junior doctors of the appalling conditions in Grangegorman and its dilapidated rat-infested wards. Staff had no control over admissions as patients were admitted directly to wards whether they needed in-patient treatment or not; there was no assessment unit established until 1979. For the ten years prior to that the admission rate had been 2,000 patients a year, which had also involved an 'influx of inappropriate groups of patients into the ordinary admission wards'.[11]

J. P. Moore, the Master of St Patrick's Hospital in Dublin, opened a new research unit in 1975 and insisted 'it is more important than ever that illnesses should be diagnosed early and more people treated in their own houses. In psychiatry, too, we are all agreed that the principles of community-based medicine should be put into practice ... Stays in hospital should be as brief as is consistent with the relief of the symptoms and the rehabilitation of the patient.'[12] Delivering on such sentiments and rhetoric, however, was a tortuous process, given the abundance of historic neglect and prejudice to be overcome, much of which still lingered. Documentary maker Mary Raftery later exposed the use and abuse of power in relation to psychiatric institutions, 'the forbidding custodial approach' and the longevity of risky and dangerous treatments such as lobotomy and insulin-induced coma therapy.[13]

At the end of the decade, Minister for Health Charles Haughey was asked in the Dáil when the Inspector of Mental Hospitals had last submitted an annual report, a statutory requirement since 1945. His response revealed there had been none for the previous thirteen years; the stark conclusion was that 'nobody noticed'. Haughey suggested they were not needed any more as 'the mental hospitals were no longer closed institutions', a self-serving lie that 'would have surprised anyone who had ever tried to get into one of these institutions ... most of the wards in all the mental hospitals were locked'. But 'the minister was not the only one to confuse the razing of perimeter walls with the opening up of institutions'. Helen Connolly in *Magill* magazine in 1980 exposed the disgraceful state of the hospitals but publication of annual inspector's reports did not resume until 1988.[14]

In 1976, James McCormick, Dean of the Faculty of Medicine at Trinity College Dublin, suggested in a public lecture that despite the positives of the advances of modern surgery, Irish society had an over-dependence on 'hypnotics, tranquillisers and anti-depressants' and a an enthusiasm 'for pills as the solution to life's problems'. The relationship between society and doctors, he argued 'is possibly less happy now than at any previous time' with a 'growing disparity between society's expectations of its doctors and doctors' conception of their role', with a complaint that 'doctors guard knowledge too closely'. Alongside 'ostrich like' responses to illness by those who would not go to a doctor, sick notes were also becoming a way of life, along with recurrent prescriptions being sought by those not seeking a cure: 'sick-role behaviour is underpinned by a culture which regards sickness as being induced by external agencies and in no sense the result of personal shortcomings or failures'. But he also suggested the medical profession needed to be more 'self-appraising and self-critical'.[15]

Wealth and class were clear determining factors regarding access to medicine, and begging letters were still being sent to government seeking medical cards. One asthmatic woman from Finglas with four children and a husband on a salary of £27 a week, facing the cost of inhalers and tablets amounting to £4 a week, was at her wits' end in 1973: 'Does one have to try to take one's life before the Eastern Health Board will help? ... I think I'd be better off dead, my 4 children would be looked after by the state.'[16]

Administratively, one of the major developments of the decade was the establishment of eight area health boards under the Health Act of 1970 to take over local authority functions in health matters, a reminder that much of the governmental preoccupation with health reform was going to lie in the realm of structural change. The new health boards were packed with local councillors. A health levy was imposed on middle and upper-middle income groups in 1971 but the health charge on rates was so unpopular it was phased out by the coalition government in 1973, which left health boards with power without responsibility, or 'local control without local taxation', meaning 'it was always easier to vote for more services than to take hard decisions about their optimal location'.[17]

Health services were deemed in need of improvement due to both public demand for choice of doctor and improvement of hospital services. Getting former dispensary patients and private patients into the same doctor's waiting rooms was 'regarded as an advance' but most patients, even those on low incomes, still had to pay. Only those unable to arrange GP care 'without undue hardship' would be eligible for free care. Doctors had reluctantly accepted the fee-for-services basis and by early 1973 Erskine Childers as Minister for Health was referring to the 'impasse' that had been reached over the choice of doctor scheme (to replace the dispensary service). He suggested that only a small number of doctors were earning 'very high incomes' from the scheme and though some doctors 'with relatively small incomes may be claiming excessive amounts in relation to the numbers on their lists', for most participating, 'there does not seem to be evidence of abuse'.[18] It was maintained that the new system gave doctors the incentive to keep patients at home whereas 'the dispensary system encouraged hospitalisation'.

Powerful Dublin voluntary hospitals were permitted to retain control of consultant appointments and consultants in the health board hospitals were given greater opportunity for private practice. There were also disputes over junior hospital doctors and tensions between the Irish Medical Union and the Irish Medical Association. Dr Philip Cawley, an executive member of the IMA wrote to Cosgrave in confidence in October 1973: 'There has been an uneasy partnership between the Medical Union and the Irish Medical Association. FF ministers have been most careful to treat both organisations equally. Now, my friends tell me that the Union delegates are treated in a fraternising manner particularly by Mr Cluskey – that the IMA delegates are practically ignored ... please destroy my letter.'[19] The same year, Cosgrave was accused of deploring the setting up of the health boards while in opposition, but when in office avoiding the challenge of how to 'unscramble the egg' in the face of accusations of extravagance and over staffing of the new system.[20]

The Labour Party at the end of the 1960s had committed itself to eliminating the two-tier system of health care and, in 1973, new Labour Health Minister Brendan Corish sought to extend free health care to the entire population, and announced (in a move supported by the Catholic Church) that by April 1974 hospital services would be available free to all, funded by a flat rate contributed by all employees. This was opposed by the Irish Medical Association and the Irish Medical Union, who threatened industrial action. They wanted fee-for-service, not salaried contracts and feared losing private practice income. Corish abandoned his plan: 'Representatives of the medical consultants opposed the introduction of my scheme until such time as they decided the population should have free hospital and medical services.' In any case, he had not suggested the abolition of private practice, but to give everyone the option of free treatment in a public ward.[21]

A memorandum for the government on health expenditure in 1976 made it clear there was a belief that there was 'a great deal of waste in the health services', a view 'widely accepted' and emphasised by Richie Ryan but rejected by Brendan Corish – in one of his rare interventions in government discussions – who was 'unable to accept this charge without evidence'. It was, he complained, 'facile' to conceive of rising health expenditure in terms of 'housekeeping economics'.[22] There were considerable tensions on this front. Ever direct, Ryan wrote to Corish to tell him he did not put his own children, who were students aged over sixteen, on the pubic health service as he was entitled to do under the Health Act Benefit: 'I have adopted this line as I consider it is wrong for me to impose the cost of my medical care on the public purse.' It was no wonder, he believed, given this act, that 'the cost of the health service is multiplying by leaps and bounds'.

He even enclosed a Voluntary Health Insurance claim in respect of one of his children to illustrate the point and also sent a copy of it to Cosgrave: 'Need I say any more?' Ryan was particularly exercised about this issue. He sent another letter to Corish to underline 'another indication of the wastefulness of including students over 16 years of age in the free health scheme' without a means test as to their parents' ability to pay. Some doctors, for example, were applying for medical cards in relation to their own children and then getting paid for attending them. The scheme, according to Ryan, was costing £800,000 to cover 40,000 students.[23]

What Ryan wanted to see was a flat-rate social insurance contribution changed to a pay-related contribution. Later in 1976 there was a suggested need for a parliamentary review about whether the health boards were a success, and further allegations of waste. TDs and the IMA were calling for an all-party committee in the Dáil on health service priorities, which was opposed by Ryan on the grounds that health services should be a function of government, but he was overruled.[24]

Eligibility for free primary care remained very limited and the issues of deficiencies on primary care and rationalisation of the local hospital network were not addressed. Fianna Fáil made an issue of local hospitals in the 1977 general election and was leaned on by the medical profession, resulting in the introduction of fee payment for GPs in the general medical system and greater opportunity for private practice for consultants in the health board hospitals. The same year, the president of the IMA, Dermot Gleeson, suggested state financing of the health system should be reduced and charges introduced for those who could afford to pay as free services were being abused: 'The end result of a completely free medical service would logically seem to be a complete erosion of any sense of self-reliance and that is an undesirable thing.'[25]

A cabinet minute in January 1978 recorded Haughey informing the government that discussions with consultants had broken down as they were insisting on a 'fee-per-item' basis and he was unwilling to concede this. He wanted them to accept a fixed salary plus additional remuneration for extra duties; his stance was informally approved by the government.[26] Throughout the decade the consultants sought to resist what they regarded as an unreasonable extension of their public remit, the government being informed in 1979 that they saw 'any material departure from the 85 per cent of the population which has traditionally been entitled to their services at public expense as a serious inroad into their field for private practice. At the present limit of £5,500 a year, it is estimated that about 83 per cent of the population are eligible and 17 per cent thus ineligible. At £7,000 a year, the latter figure is reduced by about half to 8 per cent.' At meetings, the consultants put their case 'forcibly' in rejecting a hospital service free to the entire community. Haughey referred to 'rates of remuneration so high' and was opposed to payment by way of schedule of fees as under this system of payment 'the consultant is projected as an entrepreneur, exercising and pricing his skills in detail'. It was pointed out that 'of about 38,000 people employed in the hospital service consultants number only about 1,000 and of the total expenditure of nearly £315 million on the hospital services consultants' pay amounts to about £12 million'.[27] Haughey extended access to free hospital care, making the entire population eligible, but the highest 17 per cent of earners were still obliged to pay consultant's fees. But the contract he negotiated with them 'gave them the best of both worlds' – state salaries and the right to unlimited private practice in or outside public hospitals. These developments 'turned heavily state subsidised private medicine into a growth industry, encouraged the development of private hospitals staffed by consultants on state salaries and consolidated the 2 tier system of preferential access for private patients in public hospitals'.[28]

By the end of the decade there had been a 'spectacular increase' in the number of people covered by medical cards, from 864,000 in 1972 to 1,227,000 in 1977, an increase of 42 per cent, meaning almost 40 per cent of the population qualified for free medical services. It was believed a 'more rigorous definition of eligibility' was needed to get that figure down to 900,000 and to introduce a modest charge for each item of service: 'There is no reason why those insured under VHI or paying their own fees in hospitals should be subsidised by the Exchequer.' At the end of 1978 there was a desire to reduce the exchequer subvention of the health services by £30 million.[29] The National Health Council Report (see pages 605–6) for 1978 also expressed concern that the general medical services scheme 'appeared to provide services virtually on demand by the patient. This has resulted in undue demands being made on the doctor's time. It has also led to insufficient control in relation to medication.' These abuses 'needed to be curbed', perhaps with some form of national prescription charge.[30]

In relation to the funding of hospitals through the sweepstakes under the Public Hospital Acts – a lottery initiated as a way to raise money for chronically underfunded Irish hospitals and which became internationally famous because of the scale of ticket sales outside of Ireland and the phenomenal prize money on offer – the blatant corruption of the Sweep process was brought to public prominence by the work of journalist Joe MacAnthony. He wrote an article dealing with the most important issue – 'Where the Sweep Millions Go' – which was bravely published by the *Sunday Independent* in January 1973 (see Part III). Blind eyes had been turned to its shortcomings and the extent to which it ultimately damaged the Irish health services by postponing necessary reforms. MacAnthony detailed the allegations of corruption and was branded as unpatriotic and forced to leave the country for Canada for asking difficult questions. The companies controlled by one of the families involved in the Sweep came looking for revenge. It had made the organisers rich, particularly the families of Joseph McGrath, a government minister in the 1920s, and businessmen Richard Duggan and Spencer Freeman and ensured a steady flow of money into the country, but not enough of it went to Irish health services. An excessive amount went into the organisers' hands as successive governments were relieved of responsibility for financing the state's hospital services from public funds.

It was suggested in the Dáil in 2000 that in the fifty-seven years of its existence the Irish state benefited to the tune of £170 million from the sweepstakes; as a result the voluntary hospitals were saved and most counties could boast a new hospital. But it was plagued by scandal, skulduggery, forgeries and gangsterism. Notwithstanding, it had an important impact on the development of Irish advertising and broadcasting, horse racing in Britain and Ireland, the development of indigenous Irish businesses and the commercial sponsorship of sport, not to mention Irish medical history, and it was also one of Ireland's largest employers, with a workforce of 4,000 women at the height of its success.[31]

The secrecy around it that continued to prevail was exceptional. In

May 1974 a memorandum from the Department of Justice informed the government that, despite its efforts, 'there is no indication of the true extent of the profits made by the Hospital Trusts Ltd with the exception of the organisation and management fees paid to them'. It was now being suggested that 30 per cent should go to the hospitals.[32] In October of that year Patrick McGrath, the son of Joseph, who had groomed him as his business heir, met Cosgrave and Minister for Justice Patrick Cooney, suggesting it was no longer economically feasible to run a sweep and that a domestic lottery was needed instead (which he also wanted to run, though he said he was 'aware of the possibility of an unfavourable public reaction').[33]

Increased spending on health in the 1970s was understandably presented as indicating significant progress in tackling the problems of the system and international catch-up, and improvements in some crucial areas were evident. In 1972–3, £105 million was spent on health, up from £56 million in 1969–70 (4.7 per cent of GNP was being spent on health care compared to 6.4 per cent in Sweden). In the early 1970s, Erskine Childers pointed to the vast improvements in infant mortality rates which in 1948 had been 50 per 1,000 live births but which in 1970 had 'for the first time ever in this country fallen below 20, and at 19 per 1,000 live births it now compared well with those of neighbouring countries'. But he also suggested that in the field of social services, more thought had been devoted to allowances and payments 'and rather less to the provision of social work services through trained social workers than had been the case in other countries' and there was a 'very limited number of social workers engaged in statutory services' unlike in the UK and Northern Ireland.[34]

National Health Council reports were also revealing about the way in which health priorities were identified at different stages. It was particularly preoccupied with smoking and the belief that cigarette packets needed to carry health warnings and advertising them on radio needed to be banned (see pages 607–11), while in relation to food hygiene it was suggested 'the public is not sufficiently hygiene conscious'. There was no mention of alcohol in its report for 1972. The following year the council drew attention to the Misuse of Drugs Bill, children's hospital services, the regional hospital boards and their relationship with the national secretariat and the home help service.[35]

The report for 1975 highlighted discussions that had centred on the relationship between expenditure on health services and the quality rather than the quantity of service given. The presence of lay people on the council ensured, it maintained, that it would be 'a form of consumer council for the health services' and would guarantee 'critical assessment of policies and planning'. The fear was that the administrative costs of the service were rising at a much faster rate than the degree of patient care but that there was also a need for more focus on preventive and outpatient services and the absence of a uniform costing system for all health boards, while public dental services were 'totally inadequate' and 'a major blot on the child health services in this country'.[36]

The 1976 report suggested that services on the whole had improved but patients were not benefiting enough from 'vast increase in expenditure' because, again, an undue proportion of resources were being devoted to administrative structure at the expense of patient care. Nutritional advice needed more publicity; many more public health nurses were required and the image of welfare homes needed to be improved 'and could be achieved by an appropriate change in title which would remove the "poor house" connotation often associated with the word "home" in the welfare area'. The council was also concerned about families that were unwilling to accept older people back into the home after hospital treatment, though families were not always to blame. There was a need for more medical social workers in Irish hospitals and the medical profession needed to play a greater role in the 'techniques of hospital administration'.[37]

Ireland also lagged behind in dental care; only one-third of the 600,000 eligible children estimated to need attention were examined under the public dental scheme, while only 50,000 of the 570,000 eligible adults covered by the scheme received treatment: 'In Ireland, dental consultancies were not yet recognised.' In relation to nutrition, 'the public in general were not well informed on proper diet and nutrition and did not appreciate its significant effects on general health. It was noted that incorrect diet was one of the major factors contributing to coronary heart disease and other serious illnesses.'[38]

In 1977 a National Economic and Social Council report dealt with some major issues in health policy; it was authored by commissioned consultants from the University of York. They identified a growing demand for 'universal services free at the point of use', a desire to experiment with new methods of financing the health services and paying doctors, and an increasing concern about the effectiveness of medical treatment as well as concern about the cost effectiveness of medical procedures: 'The study argues that, in essence, the rationing of scarce resources has been left to physicians who have no clear mandate from society as to how that rationing function should be discharged.' The study also revealed 'a high bed stock and low physician stock in comparison with the EEC' and that the coverage provided was less than that provided elsewhere in the Community. The criteria used to determine eligibility were complex and 'may consume considerable resources in their implementation'; there was 'confusion for many people' regarding their entitlement and a likelihood that rules were not being administered uniformly throughout the country.

The NESC stated that 'little research has been carried out to establish whether highly skilled and expensive medical manpower could be replaced by personnel with different skills but whose training was less costly – e.g., by social workers, public health nurses and clerical staff'.[39] The regularity with which these ideas were being expressed was striking and an indication that there was no shortage of diagnosis of the problems in the Irish health services. Once again, the importance of preventive health services were stressed as 'adults were increasingly beset by serious illnesses which were self-imposed. The means to prevent them were available and in the main simply involved the adoption of a more responsible life-style.'[40]

Smoking was obviously a consideration in this regard. Tobacco advertising was widespread and depicted smoking as a joyous, pleasurable indulgence: 'During 1969 the sales of Major Extra Size increased by a further 123,000,000 cigarettes, proof that more and more smokers are discovering that Major Extra Size gives Big Smoking enjoyment. The extra thickness gets the full tobacco flavour right through to give you a full free flowing smoke.'[41] Other popular cigarettes included Carrolls No. 1, Player's Medium Navy Cut and Silk Cut. In 1973 Players No. 6 'give you guaranteed quality' at 22p for twenty, while John Player King Size cigarettes cost 42p for twenty in 1978.

Noel Browne had first moved a Private Member's Bill in relation to the control of sale and advertising of tobacco in 1964 (having first asked a question about it in 1958) and justified its resurrection in February 1972, when he was a Labour Party TD and consultant psychiatrist to the Eastern Health Board, on the grounds that whatever doubts there may have been in 1964 regarding the dangers of the cigarette smoking habit from the scientific point of view, such doubts had by now been 'eliminated completely'. But he suggested that cigars and pipes 'so far as is known, are not dangerous' (something that would have pleased Jack Lynch, ever puffing on his pipe, even though it was the same habit that had hastened the demise of his predecessor Seán Lemass). Browne's initiative was not couched in the language of the zealot. Those who supported the bill, he suggested, had no intention 'of gaining satisfaction from depriving people of this simple pleasure and God knows there are few enough pleasures available to humanity', but 'these people need help'.

His case was bolstered by the research of cardiologist, health campaigner and anti-smoking advocate Dr Risteard Mulcahy (the son of Richard Mulcahy, War of Independence veteran and former leader of Fine Gael) in the Irish Medical Association's journal. Browne thought it ironic that there was 'near hysteria' involved in the anti-drugs campaign that focused on cannabis and LSD but no such crusade against cigarettes, though his own diagnosis of the smokers was somewhat crude: 'Most people smoke a cigarette when they are in a state of anxiety or emotional stress. They do so because of some defect in their personality for which they are not responsible.' The Minister for Health, Erskine Childers, agreed with Noel Browne's case. It was, he said, an 'excellent exposition of the dangers of cigarette smoking' but he did not believe that there was any point in directing a campaign at adult smokers ('I do not believe one can alter [their] habits'); any campaign should be aimed instead at the young. Browne was critical of the complacency of the Department of Health in view of figures that revealed the increase in the number of youngsters smoking between 1967 and 1970 was from 31.9 per cent to 35.2 per cent for boys and from 10.5 per cent to 18.4 per cent for girls: 'We know that children start smoking at the age of 7 years,' Browne declared. He also wanted health warnings in advertisements.[42] In his memoir of his childhood in Waterford in the 1970s, Eibhear Walshe recalled that 'children were accommodated in their wish to begin smoking early by the availability of a single cigarette and match for a penny in all good local sweet shops'.[43]

The Irish were relatively heavy smokers in comparison to some of their European counterparts; total tobacco consumption in kilograms per head in 1975 was 3.1 in Ireland compared to 2.7 for France, 2 for Italy and 2.8 for the UK, but was lower than Denmark (3.6) and the Netherlands (4.4).[44] In 1977, the IMA maintained that of the 8,000 deaths of people under sixty-five which occurred in Ireland in 1974, 2,500 could be directly attributed to cigarette smoking and there was also pressure building from the Irish Heart Foundation, the Irish Cancer Society and the Irish Association of Non-smokers. Advertisements for cigarettes on television had been banned since 1971; they were not banned from radio until December

1975, but the call in the late 1970s was for more widespread restrictions on advertising, and no-smoking hospital wards.[45]

It was left to Charles Haughey as Minister for Health to attempt to take on the tobacco companies regarding control, advertising and sponsorship of cigarettes. His proposals were radical for the era and he had mixed success. The government wanted to ensure that the operation of any regulation 'would not be to the disadvantage of the Irish cigarette manufacturer as against his foreign competitors', but meetings with the Chairmen of those Irish companies 'had concluded with an impasse' in April 1978, necessitating the intervention of Jack Lynch. In February 1978 Donal Carroll, chairman of P. J. Carroll and Company, which had control of 50 per cent of the Irish cigarette market at the start of the decade, had written to Lynch to suggest it was 'unreasonable that health issues are taken in disproportion to other important social and economic question ... It is not our policy to seek to encourage new young smokers, rather to persuade existing smokers to choose specific brands.' The meeting between Lynch and the chairmen of the tobacco companies in April 1978 saw the executives assert that they were unaware of 'any research which had demonstrated a close association between pipe smoking or smoking of cigars and serious or fatal diseases' and make the point that UK tobacco companies enjoyed a 'considerably greater measure of freedom' in relation to sponsorship of sports events. They 'did not see the tobacco business as being very important in 25 years' time and were endeavouring to diversify'. The Irish cigarette and tobacco industry employed 2,400 people at that stage and the excise duty it generated was £88 million. Carroll's employed 1,400 people and earned an after-tax profit of £3.7 million in 1976; the annual cost of treating smoking-related diseases was estimated at £15 million in 1977; in contrast, in *Magill* in 1978 this figure was put at between £20 and 30 million. The companies were utterly shameless in suggesting a reduction in smoking would lead to more violence, maintaining 'they saw the dangers that if employment was not provided for our growing young population, there could be a fusion between Marxism and the IRA with disastrous effects for our country.'[46]

Lynch asked Haughey to meet them again in May; as Dr Risteard Mulcahy saw it in a letter to Lynch, Haughey was being stymied by differences of opinion within and outside the government, but 'we have a refreshing opportunity of giving our neighbours the lead'. Lynch declined to meet him.[47] The chairman of the Medico-Social Research Board had written to Haughey that same month to congratulate him 'on the fine example you gave the nation' when he persuaded those on the platform at the FF Ard Fheis 'to refrain from smoking throughout the meeting'.[48] Haughey again met the companies over the following few months with drafts of legislation to which they suggested amendments and succeeded in getting the compromise that the operation of any new regulations would not be to the disadvantage of an Irish cigarette manufacturer vis-à-vis foreign competitors. They were worried about English publications that would not come under the new code. Haughey was unimpressed that this issue was not a priority for the EEC: 'I wish the EEC were as forward looking and progressive in this area as they are in many others. They simply are not. There are only faint stirrings at community level as yet about the problem of tobacco advertising and promotion.'[49]

But how would restrictions on advertising work? Frank Murray in the Department of the Taoiseach pointed out 'we do not want to have men or women standing at ports with scissors'. There was nothing to stop people subscribing to publications which advertised tobacco and there could be accusations of censorship, 'a notion we are getting away from in the proposed legislation on family planning'. It was also pointed out that there was an issue of 'individual liberty. To what extent has the state the right to go beyond certain simple measures so as to protect the individual from himself? The issue is one of burning importance to Protestant representatives in Northern Ireland. We should, on no account, get ourselves into another contraceptive-type row on this particular issue.'[50]

By August 1978 a series of concessions had been made to the industry, including a dropping of the restriction on colour advertising, but health warnings would be required. Manufacturers objected to the warning 'SMOKERS DIE YOUNGER' as it would affect sales and 'could leave them open to legal action for damages for selling such products'. Haughey decided on a choice of warnings that could be attributed to the Department of Health or Royal College of Physicians. By September 1979 cigarette manufacturers were still complaining of possible job losses and unfair discrimination against Irish companies, which saw Haughey consult with the Minister for Industry and Commerce, Des O'Malley. In the Department of the Taoiseach Dermot Nally argued that 'this is pre-eminently the sort of regulation or directive which should come from Brussels and apply equally throughout Europe. The attempt by a small country like this to go it alone in a matter which is, admittedly, serious, is likely to have disadvantages here altogether disproportionate to the benefits.'[51] Irish cigarette manufacturers continued to be granted concessions; although outdoor poster-site advertising was to be banned, in newspapers and magazines cigarettes could still be advertised but with just the box and name and no 'glamorous advertising depicting people, places and things'. Health warnings would now be more prominent and specific, while publications coming into Ireland would need to comply 'while not entirely at one with the provisions of the regulations'.[52]

– FIFTY-SIX –

PROTECTING THE PURITY OF THE REPUBLIC

Whatever the concerns about individual pollution, it was also recognised that the wider issue of the quality of the natural environment, threats to it, protection of it and the planning process needed attention in the 1970s, again with mixed results. In 1969, in a memorandum on the battle against asthma in the Republic, it was pointed out that 'pressure is mounting to prohibit the pollution of the air in Dublin that the people have to breathe'.[1] But the extent to which there was a serious political will to tackle pollution is doubtful. Writing in the *Education Times* in 1975, the Labour Party's Michael D. Higgins argued that, while 'it is clear there is a new interest in the environment', it 'springs less from any new feelings of responsibility for life in all its forms than from the simple realisation that contemporary vulgarisation can no longer be masked. The concern of those with economic power is how to acquire an environmentally aware image on the cheap – an ecologically acceptable face.'[2]

An Foras Forbartha (the Institute for Physical Planning) drew attention to Ireland's unique heritage in terms of historic sites which were 'being steadily whittled away by neglect, natural forces, human exploitation, pollution and other aspects of modern development' and that there was a need to 'keep pace with international effort in this field'. European conservation year in 1970 was seen as an opportunity 'to publicise the comparatively unspoiled nature of the Irish countryside and coasts',[3] but *Hibernia* was rather sceptical about the sorry looking Irish conservation year caravan, concluding that 'if the government is not interested, little can be done'.[4] The chairman of the Electricity Supply Board, Thomas Murray, believed a separate department was needed to frame and enforce regulations regarding pollution as its responsibility was spread over too many departments (principally local government) and bodies. He was far sighted, insightful and urgent: 'I think we are fortunate in this country that the alarm has been raised at a point in our development where it is still possible to reverse the dangerous processes which have led almost to crisis point in other countries. We are doubly fortunate in that the near drought conditions which prevailed in Ireland this year have suddenly brought home to all of us in a dramatic way the dangers that have been creeping up on us so stealthily.'[5]

It was also believed more inspection was needed, and Jack Lynch was regarded as too slow in reacting, while in 1971, Seán Flanagan, Minister for Lands, expressed his disquiet about 'the continued delay in the adoption of a coherent policy in regard to conservation, particularly conservation of the environment. At the present time responsibility is diversified among too many ministries.'[6] It was also believed in some quarters that a single unified authority was needed for use and management of the freshwater resources of the country, and feared that those waters 'are rapidly reaching the limits of exploitation'.[7] In 1974 the Dublin city manager suggested that the 'universal use of labour-saving devices' that were water consuming, such as washing machines, dishwashers and sink waste disposal units, along with 'the advent of cheap plastic hosepipes and sprinklers means that virtually every suburban house can use enormous quantities of water in dry summer weather', and there was a struggle to maintain supply, resulting in 'low pressure over wide areas of the city and ... reduced water quality'.[8]

Those polluting water were dealt with leniently. In 1976, thousands of fish were killed in the River Dodder in Dublin due to a waste disposal dump set up without planning permission; those responsible were fined just £50.[9] A National Environmental Council was not appointed until June 1978, with eighteen voluntary members. Its report of 1979 referred to the importance of public attitudes and the 'deep concern of the public on environmental matters and the growing demand for consultation on such issues' as there was a 'perceptible deterioration in the physical environment'. Investment in the environment, it concluded 'will be regarded by many as a luxury that the country cannot afford at present'. Even though

Ireland had been experiencing 'a minor industrial revolution' it still, with a population of only 3.2 million, had 'sizeable resources of pure air, clear waters, unspoilt landscapes and an extensive scenic coast line'. There were 4,500 acres of parks and open spaces in the Dublin Corporation area and the Forest and Wildlife Service was busy throughout the decade acquiring more space. In 1970 it planted 22,000 acres and the total area under woods and plantations in state forests at that stage was half a million acres. The policy of opening state forest areas for public recreation continued while the John F. Kennedy Park (Slieve Coillte) in Wexford (so named because, as US president, Kennedy had visited there in 1963) was a major tourist attraction.

But those who decried pollution, effluent discharge and the destruction of the landscape for the sake of commerce sometimes faced hostility as well as indifference. Cosgrave was informed in April 1976 that the Minister for Local Government, James Tully, had dismissed as 'cranks' and 'dishonest people' those who objected to a proposed pharmaceutical factory in Clonmel (Schering Plough, which later withdrew from this planned operation). One protestor alleged objectors had been subjected to 'pressures and threats' and damage to their property. He also objected to Justin Keating, Minister for Industry and Commerce, accusing objectors of 'hysterical working up of irate fears to save themselves from being disturbed'.[10]

Tully had been adamant in autumn 1973 that there was a need to 'determine a coherent national environmental policy' and an 'autonomous policy' because no single government department was taking responsibility. He was praised that year for showing 'great energy and determination in dealing with some of the existing sources of pollution and conservationists have welcomed his obvious commitment to putting right some of the damage being done to the environment'. But the problem was that in promoting new planning control legislation and by openly promising 'a liberal approach to individual cases he has invited the resubmission of thousands of applications previously turned down', and in doing so Tully had 'undermined the whole tradition of town and country planning and has weakened the community's control of private exploitation of property and amenity and in purporting to ease the burden on planning staff has made their job immeasurably more difficult'.

In the context of planning, many new developments were believed to be of poor quality and it was maintained that 'there is an inherent conflict between development and the environment'; urban planning, industrial location research and study were needed.[11] An Taisce (the National Trust) was satisfied planning refusals and appeals had contributed 'very little' to the development of the housing crisis. The real causes were the failure to provide adequate water and sewage facilities and adequate finance; it wondered would 'the public commitment to orderly planning' be lost.[12] Tully's memorandum on planning control problems at the end of 1973 noted that planning permission applications were up from 32,518 in 1971/2 to 38,778 in 1972/3 and that there were 1,669 appeals to him in the first six months of 1972/3 and 2,093 in the first six months of 1973/4. In 1975, the year the Irish Planning Institute was inaugurated, there were 3,692 appeals to Tully against decisions of the planning authorities: in 51.5 per cent of these cases the decision of the planning authority was reversed by the minister.[13] He insisted planning authorities needed to approach applications 'in a far less restrictive way'. Five years later, Labour Party TD Ruairí Quinn, an architect, who had in 1977 insisted on the need for a fully comprehensive Department of the Environment, was still wondering 'just who is responsible for the co-ordination of urban planning?'[14] Historian and conservation activist Kevin B. Nowlan had wondered earlier in the decade why developers who abused planning regulations were not treated like other law breakers and imprisoned.[15]

In the Dáil in 1977, in light of the report of an inter-departmental environmental committee on pollution that had recommended a single department to fulfil these duties, Jack Lynch again noted 'there has always been a degree of uncertainty as to which department or agency is responsible for environmental matters'. He believed responsibility should rest with the Department of Local Government and proposed to rename it the Department of the Environment. This duly happened, but there was still confusion over the transfer of roles. In a letter to the newly titled Minister for the Environment Sylvester Barrett, Lynch suggested 'probably the greatest single blot on the urban environment, certainly in Dublin and Cork, is not so much water or atmospheric pollution, serious as this may be in places, but the combination of derelict or semi-derelict buildings and sites and litter covered streets.'[16] In the Department of the Taoiseach, civil servants were divided as to the necessity of an Environment Council or a Water Pollution Advisory Council.[17]

Rectifying environmental problems, suggested Barrett, would require that 'ordinary people and young people especially, will become civic minded'. There was therefore a need to 'develop an environmental conscience at the primary and other educational levels'. Regarding a possible penal tax on those who were 'hoarding' property for future redevelopment, this possibility 'is further complicated now by the abolition of domestic rates'. It was also clear, he suggested, that 'urban renewal was not ranked highly in the financial priorities'. Creating a civic-minded Republic was a work in very slow progress.

PART VIII

NEW HORIZONS: EDUCATION, RELIGION AND THE STATUS OF WOMEN

'The Conservatives and the Progressives?'

In the realm of education, the Catholic Church had exercised and continued to exercise extraordinary control, but some of it was being challenged in the 1970s, as demonstrated by the creation of new community schools and the demand for lay involvement in management of education. In October 1970, sociologist Liam Ryan identified 'a new urgency, a new awakening in Irish education' in relation to investment, equality, personnel, resources and the environment in which children were being taught: 'In Ireland we are in the process of enlarging our schools physically, but there is also a need to enlarge them socially and psychologically.'[1] *There was also an urgency to negotiating the parameters of the church–state relationship in all this. The triumph of the denominational system supported and subsidised by both church and state had led to an absence of tension until the 1960s, a tension that would have been desirable, as it would have indicated more 'vitality', according to Margaret Mac Curtain. As she saw it, the question of education 'now lies within the domain of justice'.*[2]

A reflection of the new premium attached to education questions and the increase in the number of people affected was the appearance in April 1973 of a new publication, Education Times *(an Irish Times publication). Its inaugural edition covered such issues as the status of Gaeltacht schools, union representation for university staff (including a reference to 'the monolithic, administrator-dominated machinery which now controls UCD') the size of classes in primary schools and the lack of effective co-operation between primary and secondary schools.*[3] *Professional standards and teacher unity came under scrutiny, and there were frank rejections of the authoritarian approach to education in the past, as memorably recorded by Republican and feminist campaigner Mairín de Burca: 'I have nothing now left of my education, such as it was. This is a good thing. Every value that authority tried to inculcate into my person has been rejected.'*[4]

There were indicators of change and expansion, not just in the numbers accessing second- and third-level education, but also in services for those who were then termed the physically and mentally handicapped and a new primary school curriculum described as 'a momentous event' and 'progressive', as it encouraged the 'natural flowering' of the mind.[5] *In another indication of the growing visibility and influence of civil servants there was much mention of Seán O'Connor, the assistant secretary of the Department of Education, who in 1968 had given the first expression in public of an official change in state policy by emphasising the need for the church to be partners rather than masters in education. In the 1970s, O'Connor was a regular public speaker at education events and expressed himself unusually colourfully for a civil servant. In June 1973 he urged those involved in the sector to accept 'that laicization is going to happen ... go out and meet it and not back into forests, dungeons and enclaves'.*[6] *In 1974 he spoke 'as a participant', suggesting students in Ireland needed to study a year of philosophy, in the way other countries had military service ('one gets carried away. It is probably a crazy idea'), and emphasised that he preferred the community school model as it satisfied 'equality of opportunity and community involvement'.*[7]

Although teachers' unions clashed with governments and were voluble in their demands, by the middle of the decade, the editor of Education Times, *John Horgan, suggested the Irish National Teachers Organisation (INTO), representing primary school teachers, the largest of the unions, was 'in a curious state of disarray', appearing 'hesitant and unprepared on the issue of management'. It had, he suggested, devoted more attention to pay than to education, lulled into inaction by 'the now comparatively smooth-running salary and negotiating structure and only intermittently raising a sleepy eyelid to gaze at the world around it'.*[8] *The salary issue had caused much disruption; there had been separate conciliation and arbitration schemes for the different teaching groups, but in 1967 Minister for Education Donogh O'Malley established a tribunal on the issue which recommended a common basic salary, a development much desired by INTO. Secondary school teachers deemed it unacceptable and revised proposals were made which were unacceptable to INTO. There were a number of industrial disputes before new salary scales were devised and the principle of a common basic salary was established by early 1971; INTO had achieved 'its main objective'.*[9]

By the early 1970s, the career of one of the towering figures of twentieth-century Irish Catholicism, Dr John Charles McQuaid, Archbishop of Dublin since 1940, was coming to a close. The Vatican accepted his resignation in 1971 after three decades during which he had exercised extraordinary power over many areas, including health, education, industrial relations and social services. He had cast a cold eye on some of the international initiatives of the 1960s to update the church and emphasise it as an assembly of people, with a need for liturgical innovation and ecumenical advances, most notably the reforms agreed by the Vatican II Council, summoned by Pope John XXIII, which sat from 1962–5. McQuaid famously asserted the council's decrees and declarations would 'not disturb the tranquillity of your Christian lives'.[10] *There was stubbornness, denial and delusion at the heart of that assertion; in truth, Irish Catholicism could not and did not remain immune from international debates about the status of religion and growing secularisation.*

During the 1970s there were vigorous debates about the place of religion and numerous challenges to traditional religious priorities. A host of periodicals aimed at those in religious life and educated lay Catholics, including Doctrine and Life, Christus Rex *and* The Furrow, *turned their attention to what was often termed the 'crisis' of religious identity. They debated the relevance to Ireland of Pope Paul VI's warnings about 'the movement of corrosive criticism towards the institutional church spreading from not a few intellectual centres of the West'.*[11] *While attendance at Mass remained remarkably high by international standards, there were certain 'danger signs' in relation to the religious commitment of young single males in Dublin, counteracting the 'strength of the female subculture with regard to weekly Mass'.*[12] *The number returning 'no religion' or 'no statement' in census forms rose sharply from 0.2 per cent in 1961 to 1.9 per cent in 1971.*[13] *There were references to the questioning of authority and the 'collapse of the cherished beliefs and values of so many people' and a report by the Association of Irish Priests on the departure of priests from the active ministry. This, Enda McDonagh, Professor of Moral Theology at Maynooth, suggested, 'has been ... puzzling, painful and sometimes even shocking to Catholics, lay, clerical and religious'.*[14] *The first AGM of the National Conference of Priests of Ireland was held in November 1976, but 'the young clergy were conspicuous by their absence. There was only one priest under 30'; the issues that dominated were the need for ongoing 'formation' and in service (training in the spiritual, intellectual and pastoral areas of priestly life and ministry).*[15]

The undesirability of the priest having a life of religious involvement without a life of social involvement was emphasised; part of the 'priests' identity crisis' articulated in 1971. One contributor to this debate was moved to imagine a suburb in 2000 'where the number of Mass goers has dropped from 100 per cent to 25 per cent.'[16] *It was acknowledged that priests were struggling with 'the cult of the teenager', while questions were also raised about the function and profile of the more senior church figures. The notion of the bishop as 'a remote administrator' had to change, it was argued, it being suggested that hitherto, it had been unlikely that 'an Irish bishop ever lost a night's sleep over his image.'*[17] *Given the shallowness of religious education, there was a danger that the priest would 'bore a young person into atheism', a reaction to them being told 'until they must be heartily sick of it that Ireland is a uniquely Christian-Catholic country surrounded by a sea of modern paganism ... A little less emphasis on how Christian Ireland is and a realistic recognition of how far she is currently removed from qualifying for the title and we might have more deeply committed Christians and incidentally, a good deal less mediocrity.'*[18]

More of an emphasis on social justice was also apparent. In a revealing comment in November 1971 at a conference on poverty, Bishop of Kerry Eamon Casey suggested 'even a respectable church' needed to be prepared to speak out on social justice.[19] *The status of women within the church was also commented on by Dominican sister and historian Margaret Mac Curtain, who referred to the 13,065 professed women religious in Ireland as recorded by the 1971 census as, 'largely unemancipated.'*[20]

There was also a growing frustration that the much heralded reforms of Vatican II were slow to translate into action on the Irish ground. Fr Walter Forde, a priest in Wexford, had reflected in 1969 on the extent of the need for adaptation in church structures and techniques: 'What are the priorities for the church's action in Ireland today?'[21] *As historian John A. Murphy saw it the same year, anti-clericalism 'of the negative, secular type' had not put down significant roots in Ireland due to the history of a 'unique priests-people relationship', but the priest of the future 'may have to serve or to follow rather than expect to command.'*[22] *In light of Vatican II, priests were deemed to need further education in a society industrialising and urbanising: 'The Irish church, though slow moving, has a tradition of solid and serious approaches to pastoral problems. Nowhere is this more required than in the challenges of post Vatican II renewal.'*[23] *For all the enthusiasm about the visit to Ireland of Pope John Paul II in 1979, it was the very decline in religion's status in Ireland that prompted the invitation to him in the first place.*

Advances in the rights of women were apparent throughout the decade and the emergence of the Irish Women's Liberation Movement in 1970 was one of the most exciting and dynamic public developments of the decade. As journalist Mary Maher, one of its leading members, saw it, 'the radical granddaughters of the suffragette' generation were emerging to challenge stereotypes which 'are all right for stage plays, pageants ... processions with incense and organ music and cassocked attendants. Ceremony is one thing and life is another.'[24] *The Report of the Commission on the Status of Women (1972) examined issues such as the civil service marriage bar, maternity leave and equal pay and proved to be a watershed in Irish women's rights. It led to the formation of the Council for the Status of Women (eventually, two statutory bodies grew out of the council; the Women's Representative Committee in 1974 and the Employment Equality Agency in 1977). The report also expressed the aspiration that women would retrieve their own history and 'writing women into Irish history became a subversive activity for women historians in the 1970s'.*[25]

In 1975 there was much rhetoric about International Women's Year, during which Taoiseach Liam Cosgrave suggested the notion of women being pleased to accept 'a more lowly place in society' was an attitude that 'remains fairly widespread'. Minister for Labour Michael O'Leary presented his government as one committed to ending sexual discrimination: 'As I see it, the movement of women's rights in Ireland is a movement to restore a new order in human relations.'[26] *This assertion came on the back of what were notable developments in ending discrimination against women. In 1973, the Civil Service (Employment of Married Women) Act removed the barriers against employing and promoting married women, and in the McGee case, the Supreme Court established that marital privacy was protected under the constitution, and that the law prohibiting the importation of contraceptives even for private use by married persons infringed that privacy and was thus unconstitutional. An unmarried mother's allowance was introduced in 1973, and under the Social Welfare Act of 1974, payment of the Children's Allowance was transferred from fathers to mothers. The Maintenance Orders Act of 1974 and, subsequently, the Family Law Act of 1976 gave protective directives for non-maintained families. The Save the Equal Pay Act Committee was another feminist group that exerted considerable pressure, to persuade the government to enforce the Anti-Discrimination Pay Act of 1974, which came into operation at the end of 1975. This was a reminder that EEC directives were paramount in advancing equality, as was also reflected in the Employment Equality Act, which came into operation in 1977, prohibiting discrimination on grounds of sex or marital status.*

Many in the women's movement in the 1970s also focused on the issues of marital breakdown and separation, rape, and violence against women. The emergence of feminist action and organisation and the breaking of taboos did not occur without division and rancour, both within and outside the liberation movement. There was still much resistance to equality both in the 1970s and beyond. But two things are striking; the sense of optimism, subversion and concrete achievements recalled by some of the activists, and the proud claim that in the 1970s they had sowed the seeds for the destruction of the authority of the Catholic Church and a greater separation of church and state.[27] They could also justifiably claim to have ignited a movement that would ultimately transform Irish women's lives irrevocably.

– FIFTY-SEVEN –

DEMOCRATISING EDUCATION?

By the 1960s, *Studies*, an Irish quarterly journal that had been published by the Jesuits since 1912, was calling for a new openness to the disparate intellectual traditions that had shaped Irish society. Its demand implied that creating space for discussion of the connections between morality, politics, economics and society was not about a crudely drawn or simplistic conflict between conservatives and progressives, and that institutional Catholicism was by no means monolithic. Throughout the 1960s and into the 1970s it provided a forum for important debates about the development of third-level education, the expansion of education beyond clerical control, and a more complex understanding of Irish social inequalities, informed by looking abroad and relegating theology and church history to the book-review pages.

Christus Rex, a Catholic sociological journal first published in 1947, may have avoided most of the debates within the academic study of sociology until its last issue in 1970, after which it was replaced by the *Social Studies* periodical. But it had played an important role in pioneering empirical studies of Irish social issues, including emigration, rural decline, feminism, and early school leavers. It was this very frankness about social factors that made it stand out and it provided a forum for committed but critical Catholics like David Thornley to castigate what they regarded as the intellectual isolationism of Irish clerical sociology.[1] Many of the issues covered by these publications, and others in the 1960s, were brought even more sharply into focus in the 1970s, particularly as three issues – education, religion and feminism – assumed a new dominance in public and academic discourse.

A measure of the extent of the change in education and how it was perceived was apparent from a contribution to *Studies* in 1970, under the heading 'Ireland and the World Educational Crisis' in which it was stated 'the student flood has already hit Ireland at every level. Education is the most rapidly and inexorably expanding business in the country.'[2] Indicators of change but also criticisms abounded. A new primary school curriculum in 1971 was regarded as a 'radical contrast' to what went before. It was based on a more child-centred, discovery type approach to education and 'admitted in its introduction a dependence on educational thinking abroad'.[3] It gave teachers much more freedom and flexibility but the Department of Education was not considered to have communicated the essence of the changes very effectively, and its implementation was gradual.

There was a degree of centralisation in the reform of management of education, but also lost opportunities at a time when a much greater effort towards inclusion and far-reaching reform was necessary, given that in 1970 historian Joe Lee maintained that the Irish education system had prevented underprivileged young people of high ability from making any progress in their own country. He argued that the system 'achieved the intellectual isolation of Ireland much more effectively than protection achieved economic isolation'.[4] According to the 1971 census, 51 per cent of the population had left full-time education before the age of fifteen. But a measure of the new premium attached to education was reflected in higher investment. State funding of education as a percentage of GNP doubled from 3.05 per cent in 1960–1 to 6.29 per cent in 1973–4; it increased from £61 million in 1970 to £215 million in 1975 and by 1978 education was second only to health as the highest spending government department. By the end of the decade there were 894,000 children in full-time education, one-quarter of the total population.[5]

A Department of Education memorandum in January 1970 noted that there was a commitment in the Second Programme for Economic Expansion to raise the school-leaving age from fourteen to fifteen by 1970 and it observed that 'the greater interest being taken by parents generally in education has been to increase considerably the numbers staying on voluntarily at school for a longer period'. It was estimated that the cost of raising the school-leaving age would be £785,900, necessitating capital expenditure of £250,000 per year for four or five years. But the response of the Department of Finance was that this was 'completely out of the question' and it wanted the issue deferred due to costs; instead it was to take effect from 1 July 1972.[6] In terms of church control of schools, parents were also more vocal about a say in education. *Hibernia* reported in February 1970 on a public meeting organised by the Parent School Movement, which blamed school managers for 'their frequent hostility towards parents who tried to play their part in their children's education'.[7] One indicator of changes in the balance of power governing national school education was the reorganisation of the management of the schools with a new parental involvement which teachers tended to be wary of, but the process of change was given added momentum by Richard Burke, Minister for Education in the new coalition government (he was a former secondary school teacher who had first been elected to the Dáil in 1969 for a Dublin constituency) and Seán O'Connor of the Department of Education in 1973. Church, state, teachers and parents negotiated and a new structure for boards of management was agreed in October 1975. According to an INTO survey in 1976, 64.4 per cent of teachers believed these changes 'affected favourably' their job satisfaction.[8]

But there was still much complacency about other aspects of primary education, reflected in comments made by Minister for Education Pádraig Faulkner. A Fianna Fáil TD for Louth, who had been appointed in 1969 after serving as Minister for the Gaeltacht, Faulkner, as a former teacher, was 'elated with my new appointment'.[9] But in 1972, in relation to a long-promised planning document on education, he insisted 'there is nothing of such a complicated nature in our policy that would demand an elaborate White Paper to explain it'. As one historian of Irish education, John Coolahan, noted, this statement 'could be read in a number of ways, none of which reflect creditably on him'.[10] There was no such White Paper until 1980.

For years there had been a commitment to improve the teacher–pupil ratio at national schools, but by 1971, 35 per cent of students were still in classes of more than forty. There was an insistence in 1973 that enrolment in any class should not exceed forty-five pupils. At the INTO annual congress in Easter 1973 the results of a survey on the size of classes in Dublin city and county revealed that the average number of pupils per teacher was forty-one, and of the 3,087 classes in the 333 schools surveyed, only 552, or 18 per cent, had under thirty-five pupils per class while 1,021, or

33 per cent, had over forty-five. Of the 127,985 children attending the 333 schools, 111,833, or 86 per cent, were in classes of over thirty-five. The previous year an INTO representative had suggested that, in Cork city, '15 per cent of pupils were in classes of over fifty, 63 per cent in classes of over forty and 88 per cent in classes over 30'.[11] But overall, there was a reduction in large classes during the decade. The number of teachers employed to assist pupils with learning disabilities remained minimal, however, at only 342 in the school year 1977–8.[12] Also contentious in this sector was the closure of smaller schools, which had generated much anger since the 1960s when a seminal report on investment in education had questioned the wisdom and economics of having so many small schools scattered widely. There was a commitment to act on this, but insufficient communication with the local communities affected. Between 1966 and 1973 the number of one- and two-teacher schools was reduced by roughly 1,100, while early in the decade there was significant improvement in the design of school buildings.[13]

As with all other areas, primary education felt the bite of the mid-decade recession and by 1975 Richard Burke was worried that a ban on recruitment of new teachers could lead to industrial disputes and was angered that the Minister for Finance Richie Ryan sought to draw a distinction between new posts and additional posts, as extra teachers were clearly needed for remedial education and improving the teacher–pupil ratio in disadvantaged areas. He threatened, in order to get new teachers, to suspend the concession of allowing teachers to be retained after the age of sixty-five and require managers of schools to replace unqualified teachers with qualified teachers.[14] The following year his successor John Wilson made the controversial announcement that he was creating an extra 1,200 teaching jobs by recruiting university graduates as 'temporary whole-time teachers' in order to cut class sizes in primary and post-primary schools.

In relation to the disadvantaged areas highlighted by Burke, much attention was devoted to the Rutland Street experiment in early education for children aged three to eight living in a socially disadvantaged area in Dublin, which operated from 1969–74. The Department of Education wanted it continued because it was successful 'to the extent that they were educationally in a position of parity' with their peers by the age of six 'but had not maintained this progress at the age of 8'. More funding was needed to expand the scheme and research the implications of these limitations. The Department of Finance was opposed, as 'justification for continued special treatment for this area is not obvious'. Burke robustly defended it: 'The children living in this area are heirs to a tradition of hopelessness in their personal affairs and of opposition to all authority.' If they were not targeted, 'many of these children will succumb to their environment and will themselves become the parents of deprived children thus continuing the vicious cycle of failure, idleness and abnormal, anti-social and deviant behaviour'. It was also a project that had generated international interest ('a great degree of national prestige has been involved') and created a new community spirit. It was agreed to continue funding it at a cost of £60,000 per year.[15]

School transport was another emotive issue for many and generated a constant local lobbying of politicians: 'I want to ask you would you get the school bus for Waterville to come to my house for Mary and Bridie. I and Patrick are Fianna Fáil at all times.'[16] Children under the age of ten who resided at least two miles from their nearest national school were eligible for free transport but children over ten had to be at least three miles from the school in order to qualify. This was farcical, as it meant 'children who reside between 2 and 3 miles from their nearest school have free transport up to 10 years of age and then lose it for the balance of their primary school careers'.[17] One father had a long battle to prove that his family lived two miles from the local school and he rejected CIÉ's measurement: 'This has been measured 4 times. CIÉ measured it with a used car, which I would suggest is not a very accurate method.' Jim Tunney, the minister of state at the Department of Education, had it measured again and the distance 'has been confirmed at 1.9 miles'.[18] It was estimated that by the end of 1978, 164,000 primary and post-primary pupils would have free transport, which was not sustainable without a parental contribution.

In reviewing developments in education policy from 1973 to 1976, Burke pointed to increased expenditure, proposals for management boards for primary schools ('the first major change in the primary school system since its inception almost 150 years ago'; it was also believed INTO 'are very nervous about the idea of "parent-power"'[19]); teacher training extended to three years (see page 638) and 150 extra remedial teachers, but there were inevitably many other areas that were contentious, including the issue of religious education and statutory provision, which Burke called for a debate on. Parents in Rathfarnham, for example, were looking for a multi-denominational primary school, while Fine Gael's Oliver J. Flanagan, a proud and defiant conservative, suggested Burke 'had done more than any other man in the history of our country to prevent the establishment of a Godless society in our schools'. Flanagan lambasted the pressure groups trying to 'drive God out of education'.[20] The Dalkey School Project was opened in September 1978, the first multi-denominational national school 'to be recognized by the department of education since 1922, with the exception of those for some handicapped children'. For those involved, suggested *Magill* magazine, 'it represents a triumph over prejudice, intolerance and polite stone-walling on the part of the coalition government lasting 4 years'. Burke had reputedly refused to meet those involved, while an anonymous extremist Catholic pamphlet wondered, 'Are the snakes coming back?' Fianna Fáil was clearly more interested than Fine Gael and it was an initiative that in the words of its chairman 'unlocked the system'.[21] As Labour Party TD Barry Desmond saw it, 'Liam Cosgrave and several of his fellow Fine Gael ministers had hoped that the project would fade away.'[22]

But neither was funding of primary schools an area without problems and tensions, and for all his reputation as a conservative Catholic, Liam Cosgrave resisted church pressure when he felt it necessary. The Catholic Archbishop of Dublin Dermot Ryan (see pages 642–3) wrote to Cosgrave in April 1975 to inform him that 'in the context of diocesan debt [of £3 million], the cost of primary school sites has been the source of considerable anxiety to me', pointing out they would require £1.528 million over the next two years for this purpose. Discussions with ministers over the previous two years had found no solution (how times had changed regarding interaction of church and state). The population of the diocese had increased from 780,000 in 1956 to 935,000 in 1971 and from 114 parishes in 1967 to 153 in 1974, and between forty-five and fifty new schools were needed. Richie Ryan approached the central bank 'to improve their credit rating' but there was still a limit to what the diocese could borrow, and the government maintained there was little it could do. The archbishop said 'it was not his wish to have any open controversy on this matter'. Burke agreed that it was 'very desirable to avoid publicity on the matter'. Archbishop Ryan appealed to Cosgrave again in September. Richie Ryan pointed out in response that Dublin already enjoyed higher rates of grant assistance for new primary school buildings than anywhere else in the state at 92 per cent of building costs, and in May 1976 Cosgrave informed the archbishop there was nothing the government could do for him.[23]

There was also considerable debate about the 'dimensions and directions' of secondary education because of increased social and occupational mobility and 'a growing concern for the notion of equality and democracy and the spread of these' along with 'the search for a meaningful relationship between the school and the community it serves'. But there was much that was impractical, with little attempt to link school work to 'real and meaningful life situations' and concern about lack of representation of the teaching staff in management structures.[24] Concern about a lack of co-ordination and failure to plan an education programme in sequential stages prompted the appointment of a committee to review this issue in 1978.

The usefulness of the Intermediate Certificate examination was also placed under scrutiny; a report of 1974 suggested more school-based continuous assessment was needed. Its uniform targets were not suitable for many and 'of little practical use to the majority of successful candidates ... It samples a narrow range of skills [and] discourages innovation and curriculum development.'[25] But there was no fundamental change in this regard, despite a growth in private tuition.[26] Industrial disputes over pay (disputes that ultimately brought great satisfaction to INTO in relation to pay parity, as seen earlier) were another feature of the decade which also garnered younger recruits for the Association of Teachers of Ireland (ASTI) (see Part VI). By the end of the decade secondary teachers were making their way on to school boards and the ASTI was being increasingly consulted.[27]

There was also controversy in the early 1970s regarding what was referred to as 'the radical and in some ways provocative nature of the Department of Education's community school proposals'. As Pádraig Faulkner recalled, 'For historical reasons the emphasis in Ireland had always been on academic education. Vocational education was often bedevilled by the assumption that where it began, liberal education ended.' Following the introduction of free secondary school education in the late 1960s, many parents opted for secondary schools where pupils could study for Intermediate and Leaving Certificate courses, seen as gateways to third level. Only a two-year Group Certificate course was available to those in vocational schools. Faulkner characterised his aim as 'changing public perceptions about vocational education' and introduced the Leaving Certificate for these schools.[28]

But he also wanted larger schools to provide 'equal educational opportunities' and saw shared facilities as the way to achieve this. The response was negative, so he introduced a new type of community school which would have facilities catering for many different subjects. Vocational education authorities were concerned at what was regarded as an erosion of their traditional role providing non-denominational vocational schools to make way for the community schools. Faulkner sent his memorandum on this subject to the Catholic bishops 'as a preliminary to the discussion I intend having with interested parties'.[29] There was talk of a takeover of the religious orders and property, which Faulkner dismissed.

In May 1971 Jack Lynch too simplistically characterised those involved in debating these reforms as 'the conservatives and the progressives' and maintained that there were 'many wise people in each of these groups'. He justified the new community school proposals because 'in most European countries about 70 per cent of post-primary children are in vocational-type schools and the remaining 30 per cent follow a grammar-school type of education. The reverse is true here. This is a pattern which is hardly suited to the needs of all our children in second-level education or to their prospects of future employment.'[30]

But the notion of amalgamating existing Catholic schools with vocational schools, and in effect creating Catholic community schools, was criticised as sectarian, and some parent–teacher associations looked for church involvement as 'equal partners' in a community-based educational endeavour rather than controlling boards of management.[31] Faulkner was having no truck with such suggestions, writing to Lynch of 'a simple fact that where over 98 per cent of the pupils are Catholics and a similar proportion, if not all, of the teachers are Catholic, that the atmosphere and ethos of the school will be Catholic ... If the new school is to be truly a community school its composition and management must inevitably reflect the religious beliefs of almost 100 per cent of the pupils.'[32]

Lynch told a delegation of clergymen in January 1972 that he was too busy to meet them to discuss the issue of boards of management of these schools and the proposal that there be two members of religious orders, two parents and two representatives elected by the area's vocational education committee. There was correspondence lamenting the confusion all this was creating. Cardinal William Conway also criticised the 'gross misunderstanding' regarding the proposed schools and insisted 'a few politicians and publicists' were accusing him of wanting to take over vocational schools; why should these schools be 'neutral' when 93 per cent were Catholic, he wondered.[33] In the same year, *Hibernia* criticised Cardinal

Conway's approach to education 'debates' as 'he failed to distinguish between a religious society and a religion-controlled society'. Nuns – and this was not unusual – decried the notion of state schools with no religion and threatened revenge at the ballot box: 'You will lose the votes of all the sisters.' The Christian Brothers did likewise when Lynch seemed to be suggesting non-denominational education could be the way of the future: 'Down through the years the Christian Brothers have been 80–90 per cent FF, but I'm afraid that no longer holds.'[34] As usual, the ever ambiguous Lynch insisted he had been misquoted.

With a new minister, Burke, in office in 1973, the same year the first of the new community schools opened, the *Sunday Independent* suggested he would have to face down the church: 'They seem to think that because they built certain schools a century ago, control must still rest in their hands in the new order of things. The minister will need tact, firmness and endless patience here.'[35] As soon as Cosgrave was elected Taoiseach Cardinal Conway, clearly happier with Cosgrave than Lynch in office, invited him to dinner at the Archbishop of Dublin's house in Drumcondra as the Catholic Hierarchy and the religious orders 'have been devoting considerable thought to the subject of post-primary education in the Republic'.[36] Cosgrave, conscious of his need for independence, inquired of the Ministers for Finance and Education as to whether he should attend and then replied to Conway that, instead, the religious deputation should come to government buildings.

At the meeting it was pointed out that of the 591 post-primary schools in the Republic, only thirty-two were non-Catholic, and of the Catholic schools, all but forty-two were run by religious communities 'yet despite the extent of their interest the church was being left in the dark as to the policy of the department'. Burke suggested the proportion of religious to lay teachers would drop significantly within a few years to 'about 28 per cent' (it was estimated that in 1966 religious constituted 50 per cent of secondary teachers but that by 1973 it was 34 per cent and falling).[37] Conway said they did not like 'the present wearing down practices' and more consultation was needed, but Burke was adamant 'there were many other post-primary interests involved. These interests also must be safeguarded.'[38]

The government was clearly trying to keep control of the direction of this issue but by the end of 1973 Burke was suggesting that, because the religious authorities were 'hostile' to community schools, what could be offered instead was 'an association of schools physically linked by a single specialist block which would be common to the associated schools'. In his memoirs published in 2005, Pádraig Faulkner described the coalition government as one that 'misinterpreted the controversy' surrounding the community schools and 'took tentative steps to stop their development', but that they soon learned 'the reverse was the case ... Needless to say, I was pleased with the success of the project ... There are now 81 community schools in Ireland.'[39]

While Burke was attempting to placate opponents of the new schools, Cosgrave was praised by one religious brother for agreeing that 'effective statutory guarantees be given to the clerical managers of secondary schools' which had been ignored by the last three ministers for education.[40] The balance of power between lay and religious in the secondary schools, however, continued to be highlighted and contested. In 1976, for example, John Horgan, who wrote extensively about religion and education, pointed out that there was a growing controversy about demands by lay teachers in secondary schools for access to principalships. One religious in seven (including Brothers and Secular Clergy) in secondary schools was a principal. For lay teachers the ratio was roughly one principal for every 2,300: 'the odds are absurdly unfair'.[41]

There were also discussions about more overall co-ordination in state investment in tertiary education. From 1961 to 1971 there was an expansion of traditional university numbers from 9,000 to 20,000. By 1981, the number of students in higher education was 41,516; of these, 23,000 were in university, 13,000 in the technology colleges and 3,000 in teacher training. The period 1976–81 saw the number of third-level students rise by 15 per cent.[42] In March 1970 the Higher Education Authority (HEA), which had been established in 1968, wanted to be the sole body from which the allocation of education budgets would come. It also desired a greater say in rationalisation and co-ordination of higher education rather than to have a situation in 'respect of staffing, equipment and financing generally, a kingdom within a kingdom in the institutions in question'.[43] The Union of Students in Ireland (USI) expressed disappointment that in proposed legislation to establish the HEA on a statutory basis, which happened in 1971, there would be no effective student representation and that the bill would not oblige the HEA 'to promote the democratisation of higher education and the attainment of equal opportunity for all as part of its functions'.[44]

In December 1967, Fianna Fáil Minister for Education Donogh O'Malley had announced the creation of nine regional technical colleges, indicating a broadening of the Irish higher education system beyond a solely academic focus. Ed Walsh took up the job of director of Limerick's new Institute of Higher Education in January 1970 with 'no staff, no budget and no premises'. He had to deal with some civil servants who seemed more preoccupied with what they did not want than with what they did, meaning the new institute was in 'an ill-defined space', straddling the gap between the universities and the regional technical colleges. Walsh fitted out a temporary office in Limerick City; he moved in without lease or decoration and went into Woolworth's 'for one shilling and six pence worth of bell wire and some insulating tape. The phone was still working and with some crude cutting and splicing I extended the line, opened the window and dangled the phone downwards to the lower floor.'[45] He faced a mammoth bureaucratic struggle to get official sanction for the premises, which 'became a more arduous affair' than purchasing what eventually became the campus of the University of Limerick, a reminder that strong personalities were necessary to forge certain advances in educational provision at third level.

Other government proposals for the future of third-level education had been controversial in the late 1960s, not least because of a proposed merger of University College Dublin and Trinity College Dublin announced by O'Malley which had created opposition from both institutions as they feared absorption by the other. The idea lost steam after O'Malley's death in 1968, but it did create a focus on the possibility of co-operation and rationalisation between the two universities, so making it more difficult to sustain the ecclesiastical prohibition on Catholics attending Trinity (which ended in 1970). A file from 1967 in the archive of Archbishop of Dublin John Charles McQuaid was revealing in this regard. Addressing 'safeguards in respect of Trinity College' for those Catholics who received a dispensation to attend, it insisted on 'avoidance of all societies that may propagate ideas contrary to Catholic faith or morals' and Catholic students required 'habitually to consort with Catholic companions', but beside the instruction was a note: 'NB: now out of date.'[46]

What was examined instead of a merger in the early 1970s was the scope for the two universities to co-operate to achieve rationalisation and prevent duplication. As the HEA saw it in April 1970, the advantage of this approach was 'the fact that this solution has been worked out by the universities themselves (albeit under some pressure) and that it thus seems to offer an end to the "insidious partition" and "truceless cold war" which have heretofore been a blot on our higher education system, whereas the plan of 6 July 1968 would have to be imposed on an unwilling and possibly resistant UCD'.[47]

Two senior academics wrote to Jack Lynch that month to inform him that the universities were claiming victory by insisting that the merger had been scrapped. But they urged him to keep control of policy, as decisions about finance and access to third level were matters of social concern. They also maintained that 'university staffs have many sensitive, cautious people who abhor publicity and are not in the habit of initiating complaint. The arrangement in some institutions, where 'most of the staff are employed on a year-to-year basis' and the rationalisation of facilities did not, it was suggested, 'make for democratic participation especially when staff associations voted openly by raised hands. Many overwhelming votes by university staffs against changes in universities might not have had the same validity as a democratic secret ballot.'[48]

In truth, decisions were just being fudged. A deputation from TCD met Cosgrave and Burke in January 1974 but it was clear the universities could not agree on the distribution of faculties like medicine, law, pharmacy and engineering. Burke said he wanted to make decisions as early as possible while Cosgrave said the government 'were not in favour of piecemeal decisions'.[49] The following year, TCD provost Leland Lyons wrote to Cosgrave to express concern about the proposals to reorder third-level education. Even though he had talked to the Minister for Education, he was not reassured about, for example, the possible removal of business and veterinary studies from Trinity: 'TCD is more than a university of international repute; it belongs to that small group of universities which are known throughout the world.'[50] In UCD at the same time, greater security of tenure was given to junior lecturing staff and faculty membership was given to non-statutory staff, which shifted the balance of power within the university. The move to the Belfield campus in south Dublin in 1972 came at the beginning of a decade which witnessed UCD evolve 'from being primarily and simply a teaching institution' to a 'complex business organisation'.[51]

By the mid 1970s more than 80 per cent of the cost of universities was being met by the state but in reflecting on UCD, UCG and UCC's desire for a 25 per cent increase in fees for the year 1975–6, it was acknowledged that 'there are difficulties in measuring the "output" of universities and in defining "quality" or what is meant by "efficiency" in the case of universities'.[52] In 1978 a report on Irish education expenditure argued that scarce resources needed to be spent on aspects of education 'which benefit society at large as opposed to the individual learner ... and in particular for the less advantaged'. A study of the socio-economic background of all students in universities in 1977–8 revealed that there had been no significant change from the mid 1960s. For Dublin entrants in 1978–9, 72 per cent came from the highest socio-economic groups, even though these groups constituted less than 21 per cent of the population of the country.[53]

At the end of 1978 there was a proposed reduction in the exchequer subvention for third level on the grounds that 'the level of support enjoyed by third-level education in this country relative to the resources available for education generally is unduly generous ... In EEC countries as a whole the cost to the state of third-level education relative to primary education is about 3:1 whereas in this country the corresponding ratio is 6:1'. The cost per pupil from public funds in 1977 was £196 for primary schools, £359 for secondary schools and £1,200 for universities. It was also believed that a common assumption was that all those who qualified should go to university. This was not 'desirable' and there were too many 'proceeding to university without any definite purpose'. There was too much 'wasted attendance'. Maintenance grants were regarded as too generous for the rural community, 'most of the benefits from third-level education would appear to accrue to the students themselves rather than to society as a whole' and 'many Irish graduates emigrate'.[54] Minister for Education John Wilson announced in February 1979 that university fees for new students would rise by 25 per cent, but that grants would also rise.

The National Institute of Higher Education's (NIHE) first students in Dublin were admitted in 1972. Director Danny O'Hare suggested NIHE's significance was due to 'the relatively inadequate provision of technological student places nationally'. The Department of Education wanted it to be a third-level education institution offering degree, diploma and certificate courses.[55] The two colleges of technology at Kevin Street and Bolton Street had a combined enrolment of 7,000 in the early 1970s and the success of Bolton Street's School of Architecture was singled out for comment.[56] A new system of granting college places – through the Central Applications Office (CAO) – came into being at the end of 1975, which meant anyone could apply to any college: 'The rules were straightforward and could not be bent. The colleges had the relief that no-one could usefully lobby them.'[57]

Poet Seamus Heaney began working at the Catholic teacher-training college in Carysfort in 1976 and began to see a less regimented and more independent-minded student body evolving. The staff were also far from smothered by a rigid religious ethos. As he saw it, 'To my certain knowledge I was a hell of a lot more emancipated from Catholic practice at the time than many a star in the UCD firmament.'[58] The student body of St Patrick's College of Education, which trained primary school teachers, grew rapidly from 216 in 1964 to 600 in 1972–3 and the institution was substantially reoriented in the 1970s. No longer a male preserve and with a degree programme in teacher education by the middle of the decade, the traditional character of the college underwent a 'profound transformation'.

In contrast to previous decades, during which, in the words of one of its former students, novelist John McGahern, it had mirrored the 'official country', now it sought to prepare students for a more complex role than the word 'training' would imply. The students were more assertive, jostling the car of Minister for Education Pádraig Faulkner in 1971 and boycotting the graduation ceremony in protest at the lack of a degree programme for students, the same year the first women arrived at the college. Two years later the college president asserted that 'the conduct of the students is on the whole satisfactory. In spite of a complaint to the contrary we do not have a serious drink problem ... There are only a very small number of students drinking to excess ... The main criticism that can be made of students is that they do not work hard enough.'[59]

There was also adverse comment on the lack of political passion that third-level students demonstrated during this decade. The UCD students were referred to as 'extraordinarily quiet' in 1971 with an obvious lack of radicalism, 'and there is the curious fact that the only student orator of note at the present time – Adrian Hardiman – has views to the right of Cumann na nGaedheal [the governing party in the Free State in the 1920s]'.[60] Hardiman recalled the camaraderie and intense debating rivalry of the elite students who preened their feathers in UCD's legendary and testosterone-fuelled L&H debating society: 'Though nonchalance was the required demeanour, the main players worked harder than they'd ever admit on their speeches.' He lost the History Society auditorship to Frank Dunlop and was notoriously ungracious in defeat, his concession speech noting that 'the History Society has had its annual flirtation with democracy and like many such flirtations, it has produced a bastard'. His debating colleagues were future journalists, lawyers and writers, including Gerard Barry, Mary Finlay (the first female auditor), Gerry Danaher and Gerry Stembridge. The succession of illustrious guests included the leading politicians of the era, though Kevin Cross, who was auditor from 1973–4, suggested that 'the effect of the Northern violence was ultimately to de-radicalise the student body ... Belief in the power of rational argument to influence other rational minds ... was in decline.'[61]

James Ryan arrived in Trinity College Dublin as a student in October 1970, a month after the ban on Catholics enrolling in Trinity without the permission of the Catholic Hierarchy was removed. One-third of the TCD students were now Catholic. Ryan immediately encountered

> seated at a small fold-up table ... the Marxist Leninists, every bit as grim as the Maoists – or were they Stalinists ... I'd never seen a real life self-declared communist so I stared; a big mistake. I'd caught the attention of the fierce-faced, androgynous recruitment officer. Paralysed by first-day courtesy I became an unwitting victim of what felt like a show trial. Was I prepared to stand by while the proletariat remained enslaved and wantonly exploited by the capitalist machine? All at once, I was back in my primary school, my attention piously focused on Sister Xavier as she led us through prayers for the conversion of Russia.[62]

As he saw it, Trinity had its own brand of conservatism 'as many emerging agents of change discovered but crucially, that conservatism was, in the main, negotiable. Indeed, several of those who came to play significant roles in public life served their political apprenticeship challenging the guardians of college traditions.' The drive to 'catch-up' with the rest of the Western world was 'manifest' in Trinity in terms of moral attitudes to condoms, travel to the US on student visas, access to an ever expanding media 'and an all-out rejection of the still smouldering belief that suffering has its rewards'. Ryan was also close to UCD students, comfortable 'with that brand of rebellion, self-assured, dogmatic and fad-ish, particular to the sons and daughters of professional, Blueshirt (faded denim by then) families'. He also recalled the 'exceptionally caring relationship that existed between teaching staff and students'.[63]

Patricia Quinn arrived at Trinity in 1977 as a lapsed Catholic to find 'mostly Protestants with a sense of autonomy and personal responsibility, and a strongly defined, if somewhat diffidently expressed cultural identity'.[64] Trinity had its fair share of immature 'brawny male undergraduates' some of whom were 'hauled up in front of a Dublin magistrate for deliberately pouring Double Diamond beer from a balcony at Punchestown races onto the head of a plain-faced girl below; when asked if they had anything to say in their defence, one of them replied straight-faced that they'd merely been testing to see if Double Diamond really "worked wonders"'. As historian Roy Foster recalled, 'Sometimes I was reminded why I spent a lot of my TCD years socialising at UCD.' But what was not acknowledged adequately in some of the memoirs of TCD in the 1970s was the quality of the teaching.[65]

At University College Galway, historian Gearóid Ó Tuathaigh noted in 1976 'the postponement of a radical re-examination of the role and function of the college in national life'. He criticised the framework of statutes governing the NUI universities as 'basically undemocratic, seriously inefficient and in some cases, comically anachronistic', which also prevented the universities discharging their social functions through using resources for the benefit of the community.[66] Historian John A. Murphy referred to the 'stolid conservatism' of the students at University College Cork but observed that there was a decline in college authoritarianism and clerical influence, seen in the publication of *The Red Rag* in 1973, although the Dean of Arts refused to present a degree to its editor. The so-called 'Irish statute' was abolished in 1973, it had amounted to 'a cultural purity test which had required candidates for statutory posts in a number of departments to establish their competence in the Irish language', which was 'hypocritical to boot, since the Irish language was rarely used as a teaching medium in the stipulated departments'.[67]

At UCD, philosophy students were revolting, by organising counter-seminars to the official ones: 'They do not, they say, object to Thomist philosophy being taught. But they do object to its being made into the official philosophy of the department.' UCD chaplains also clashed with Catholic Archbishop of Dublin Dermot Ryan when seeking more autonomy. There was also a call by a senior professor at Maynooth, which housed the Catholic seminary, for a lessening of episcopal control at the university, while a rule that those who were laicised could not teach in a seminary or theological faculty was upheld by the High Court and Supreme Court as a right Maynooth College could legitimately assert.[68]

– FIFTY-EIGHT –

PRACTISING LAPSED CATHOLICS

Many developments in education during the seventies were obviously of central relevance to the influence and status of the Catholic Church in Ireland. In January 1971, Archbishop John Charles McQuaid, approaching the end of his thirty-year reign, had been informed that a group of activists in the Irish Women's Liberation Movement (IWLM) were planning to protest about contraception at the laying and blessing of the foundation stone for a new church in his diocese. 'Let them all come!' he wrote defiantly in the margin.[1] He may have been defiant, but the fact that the women were prepared to confront him publicly was yet another sign that his domination and unquestioned obedience to his church's teaching was coming to an end and the contraception debate was not one he could contain.

A keen educationalist, McQuaid had vastly expanded the size of his Dublin diocese and was active in promoting Catholic social welfare services among other things. He was also vigilant in identifying and removing perceived dissidents and liberals, but by the end of the 1960s, the climate of international Catholicism was at odds with his pre-Vatican II outlook. As he looked askance at growing ecumenical trends, criticism of his style of leadership became more vocal. McQuaid, though fearsome and demanding unquestioned obedience, had dispensed much charity; a lay member of his diocese contacted him a month before his departure: 'I am glad to see that there is no sign of you retiring yet. I hope you will stay where you are for a few years for the sake of the poor.'[2]

But he could no longer control and direct as he had done for so long. It was instructive, for example, that in responding to complaints in his last years about the increasing secularisation of society and perceived vulgarisation of public discourse, he was moved to assert that church teaching was not adaptable but 'it is now for the lay people to make themselves felt'.[3] He was also concerned about the number of priests who were opting out of marriage guidance 'on the plea of being too busy' and the preponderance of 'rather passive' local clergy.[4] Some of them, however, desired from him 'a word of authoritative praise' for their endeavours, suggesting he may have been out of touch with 'ordinary honest-to-God priests'.[5]

McQuaid left his post at the very end of 1971, somewhat shocked that his resignation had been accepted, to be succeeded by Dermot Ryan, a critic of McQuaid since their disagreement the previous decade over the status of theology as a subject in the universities. When McQuaid, speaking for the last time as archbishop, asked that the same loyalty afforded to him be given to Ryan to 'rule the see of Dublin', his language was regarded as out of date.[6] Ryan had been ordained a priest in 1950 and had a passion for scripture and Near Eastern languages. He was appointed Chair of Semitic Languages at UCD in 1970 and had also chaired the Dublin Diocesan Council of Priests, with whom he was popular. It was expected he would not be 'rigid or authoritarian' but neither would he be 'excessively permissive ... those who hasten to pin on his cassock the loose labels of "liberal" or "progressive" will have cause to eat their words'.[7] But historian Bridget Hourican has argued he took office 'with an undeserved reputation as a liberal, which he may have played on to gain support in the Dublin council of priests. On most matters he was a moderate conservative, as his tenure proved, though he was progressive and differed markedly from his predecessor in his ecumenism.'[8] Some of the more pressing issues throughout his tenure from 1972–84 were managing the debt he inherited from McQuaid (which Ryan didn't hesitate to publicise), the building of more churches and schools (seventy-four schools were built in his first ten years in office) and the creation of new parishes. This expansion was achieved by Ryan through an independent committee to oversee diocesan finances, the creation of a central fund and the subsidising of poorer parishes by those richer, though it was estimated that the debt accumulated as a result of these endeavours was in the region of £11 million.[9] Ryan had considerable organisational skills and also became well known internationally as the Irish hierarchy's representative at the World

Synod of Bishops in Rome, helped by his fluency in a number of languages. Though seemingly modest in his ambitions – he once declared that all he had ever wanted to be was a parish priest, although he never experienced such service – he was regarded by many as dignified and intellectual, but aloof. He was also criticised over his failure to act on claims of child abuse in his diocese in the Murphy Report of 2009, which investigated abuse by priests in the diocese from the 1970s onwards.[10]

Underlining his commitment to ecumenism, in November 1972 Ryan attended a service in Christchurch Cathedral in Dublin, the first time a Catholic Archbishop of Dublin had done so since the Reformation. The same year, article 44.2.1 of the Irish constitution, granting the Catholic religion a special status in the state, was deleted following a referendum, with little opposition from the church; 721,003 voted in favour and 133,430 against. The ban on priests and religious attending horse or greyhound meetings, or betting on the results, was also lifted that year, but bans remained in place that forbade them 'to continue playing cards after midnight or play for high stakes' or 'smoke publicly in the streets' and they were to 'use motor cars only in moderation and without the appearance of luxury'.[11] At the start of the decade the Catholic Hierarchy had announced that it was no longer obligatory to abstain from eating meat on Fridays.

But there was, it seemed, still precious little communication between Catholic shepherds and their flocks. In April 1971 *Hibernia* posed a stark question: 'Will some bishop actually dialogue with our people – ever?'[12] – this distance was regarded as all the more galling, given that new churches were built using 'the proceeds of hundreds of whist drives, parish raffles and talent shows'.[13] At a bishops' meeting in Mayo in 1974, the need for greater dialogue was recognised when it was stated that 'the main thrust of the Irish church over the next 5 years should be the implementation of the principle of the involvement of the laity in the spiritual mission of the church'. Eventually, at the end of the decade the creation of an Irish Commission for the Laity held out some promise in this regard, but it did not transpire to a significant degree.[14]

In the midst of debate on the need to amend the constitution to make it less sectarian, one woman who corresponded with Jack Lynch wondered 'how Catholic we Irish really are; we say prayers but do we really pray? We talk a lot but do we act on the principles of which we speak?' Lynch rejected the notion that the Republic was a church-controlled state: 'The Church, in fact, plays no part either in the making or the administration of the law of the land and, indeed, Protestant spokesmen have frequently and publicly referred to the fair treatment that people of their faith receive here.'[15] This was disputed by a Dublin Protestant who wrote to Lynch in 1978: 'After 56 years of home rule (as predicted) there is only one Protestant left in Dáil Éireann and in the last intake of Gardaí at Templemore there was only one Protestant out of 300 recruits.'[16] The Labour Party's Barry Desmond maintained that Fianna Fáil regarded Erskine Childers as 'a traditional decent Protestant prop – he was never an integral part of the inner party core'.[17] Political assemblies were still opened with a Catholic prayer. As seen earlier, in December 1978 Nell McCafferty observed the proceedings of Cork County Council: 'The Angelus was cited in full by the assembled councillors, the manager, the secretary and the pious press under the sorrowful gaze of a crucified Christ nailed to the wall above them.'[18]

John A. Murphy maintained there were in 1976 'very few southern Protestants who think of themselves as British and they are as mystified by and alienated from the Northern Protestant' as southern Catholics.[19] Writer Hubert Butler, who had frequently chided his own Protestant community on its lack of self-examination and assertion, was troubled by Protestants stressing the supposed toleration of the Republic and being 'meekly subservient to authority'. He argued there was an obligation on humanists to work towards separation of church and state and that it was incumbent on them

> to oppose all those religious manifestations which are bound to exasperate the Protestant North. For example, recently we read that the new church at Knock was to be the largest in the British Isles and attract as many pilgrims as Fatima. Elsewhere I read that Mayo County Council were to put up a very large sum of money in order to make roads to this gigantic place of pilgrimage. I don't know if there are Protestants on Mayo County Council but there are for sure among the ratepayers. Why should they be forced to subscribe to this thing?[20]

In contrast, Terence Brown suggested that, though the Protestant population had declined to about 4 per cent, there was an increase in Catholic applications to Protestant schools (the largest Protestant primary school in Ireland, with 310 pupils, opened in Dundrum in south Dublin in November 1970) and that social isolation of Protestants was giving way to 'co-operative activity in a wide variety of civil institutions', which had once been exclusively Catholic (see Part II).[21] In 1970 The Irish School of Ecumenics was inaugurated at Milltown Park in Dublin. George Otto Simms, the Church of Ireland Archbishop of Armagh appointed in 1969 (having been Archbishop of Dublin since 1956) was a courageous ecumenist, with a commitment to the Irish language; he also communicated effectively through his 'Thinking Aloud' column in the *Irish Times.* Conor Cruise O'Brien was the only confessed agnostic in the Dáil (and the only divorced member). In an interview with journalist Geraldine Kennedy in 1975 he commented, 'I think the authority of celibate male clergy in the field of educational and sexual morality is itself anomalous and I would say that its social consequences are bad both for the clergy themselves and for those who are affected by them.'[22]

In July 1972 Maurice Hayes, a native of County Down, an even-handed observer of the Troubles and future Ombudsman in the North, wrote to Garret FitzGerald about 'my own impression of the Catholic Church as a great incubus resisting change in defence of its own institutional interests. If they would even say that they only want a confessional state in the south it would be a help.'[23] FitzGerald's own views were perhaps less severe, but in 1972 he was reported as addressing the issue of class barriers between priests and their people when speaking to 'the left-wing association of Irish priests' at Maynooth, in which he questioned their 'less than total commitment' to the poor. This association of priests was referred to by one bishop as 'a bunch of dissidents'.[24] Fr Enda McDonagh, the Professor of Moral Theology at Maynooth, read a speech FitzGerald had drafted on church–state relations, and though he thought it excellent he felt he needed to avoid 'provocative language which could take away from the solidity and serenity of the overall work', suggesting he replace the phrase 'the depth of sectarian feeling' with 'of religious discussion'.[25]

The degree to which politicians still saw themselves as Catholics first and politicians second should not be exaggerated. While Liam Cosgrave famously voted against his own government's bill (along with Minister for Education Richard Burke) to legislate for the McGee decision in 1974 (see pages 673–78), the majority of Fine Gael and Labour Party deputies voted in favour. By the early 1970s 'there was a political constituency for changes in moral politics', which represented a new challenge for the church. Historian Brian Girvin has suggested this 'liberal constituency was predominantly urban and well educated. It was never a unified or cohesive force but was a shifting coalition that came together depending on the issue, but could divide on others. By the early 1970s it was a stronger presence than at any time since the establishment of the state.'[26]

In 1977 Jesuit sociologist Mícheál Mac Gréil's survey of Dublin opinion also revealed a shift in attitudes. The percentage of those attending church weekly or more had not declined, but attitudes towards church doctrine had, and 63 per cent disagreed with the view that the use of contraceptives was always wrong. Forty-three per cent agreed that laws against homosexual behaviour should be decriminalised; 46 per cent agreed that priests should be allowed to marry: 'opinion in Dublin in the early 1970s was now seriously divided on a wide range of issues on which there had been a consensus only a decade earlier'. Mac Gréil also identified the social basis for this new liberalism: it could be found 'among those under 35 (born after 1940), university educated males and those in executive or professional occupations'.[27] A survey published by the Catholic Bishops Research and Development Commission in 1978 showed a rise in the number of university students leaving the church.

John A. Murphy maintained in 1976 that, even if it was accepted that overall weekly attendance at Mass was still in the region of 90 per cent (as had been suggested by an MRBI survey in 1973, which also found that 25 per cent of single men and women in the 18–30 age group and 30 per cent of those aged twenty-one to twenty-five did not attend weekly[28]), it was 'merely evidence of the strength of ritual and custom in a strongly homogenous society. One suspects that a survey of confession-going habits would be much more interesting – and from the Church's standpoint far less reassuring: The Irish priest has lost his mystique.'[29] He was correct to suggest a more nuanced analysis, and there were many playwright Brian Friel spoke for when he was interviewed in 1970 and in response to a question about his faith he responded, 'From the religious point of view I'm a very confused man ... I suppose I'm a sort of practising lapsed Catholic ... and I don't see any great contradiction in this either.'[30]

There was also, arguably, a significant shift in tone from the church on some of the controversies of the era. Even though it reiterated its opposition to artificial contraception after the McGee case, it maintained, 'There are many things which the Catholic Church holds to be morally wrong and no one has ever suggested, least of all the Church itself, that they should be prohibited by the State.'[31] The following year, indicating another subtle shift, this time on the state's side, Richard Stokes in the

Department of the Taoiseach suggested that talk of positive Christianity in a speech by President Childers was not appropriate as 'it suggested that non-Christian forces in our society are not positive'. In relation to the consideration of a national day of reconciliation, Stokes expressed 'doubt' that a day of prayer 'would catch on' and felt that a day at Easter, given the religious ceremonies at that time of year and the dominance of Catholicism, would be inappropriate: 'all of these manifestations of the "special position" would have to be reviewed in the context of the [proposed] day of ecumenical non-sectarian reconciliation'.[32]

Clearly, the extent to which Ireland could be characterised as a Catholic Republic continued to generate sensitivities throughout the decade. When Oliver Plunkett was canonised in 1975, a cause that had been promoted for decades and backed by Eamon de Valera in the 1940s, Cardinal William Conway had invited Cosgrave to the canonisation service in Rome, but his attendance was regarded as diplomatically inappropriate, as such invitations were issued only following a request by the ambassador in Rome to the offices of the papal nuncio. Conway placed the government in 'a delicate and awkward' position, according to the Department of Foreign Affairs; he had also invited President Ó Dálaigh, 'which involves a much greater national and formal commitment to Catholic sympathies. I do not see how either can go in other than an official capacity'.[33]

Retired diplomat Con Cremin, who had a long and distinguished career representing Ireland on foreign missions and at the UN, and who in retirement continued to represent Ireland at international conferences, suggested that the issue should be dealt with through the nuncio in Dublin or the ambassador to the Holy See 'if we are to adhere to the principle of separation of church and state'. In the event it was Cosgrave who went. Although President Ó Dálaigh wanted to go he was sidelined when Cosgrave conveyed to him 'orally the government's view that it would be better if the president did not accept Cardinal Conway's invitation'.[34] Cosgrave extended the visit into a personal vacation; he wanted to stay with the Little Company of Mercy Nuns but was persuaded to use the embassy in Rome for diplomatic and security reasons.

There was some adverse comment that the canonisation was politically inappropriate since it could be regarded as sectarian and divisive in the context of the Northern troubles (see Part II), but this did not deter the partygoers in Rome. There was a dizzying round of dinners, cocktail receptions and lunches. Some events required that 'ladies would be excluded'. The Irish also got a rap on the knuckles for seeking too many private audiences with the Pope.[35] But there was little interest, it seemed in 1978, in commemorating the centenary of the death of Cardinal Paul Cullen, Ireland's first cardinal who was instrumental in the nineteenth century in laying the foundations for the transformation of Irish Catholicism into a more powerful force, loyal to Rome. Lynch informed Cullen's great-great-grandniece that the state had no proposals to mark the occasion.[36]

There were inevitable battles as a result of the new demands for more tolerance and less sectarianism. In November 1972 the *Irish Medical Times* accused Bishop Cornelius Lucey of Cork of 'a deplorable form of ecclesiastical blackmail' as a result of the closing down of the Cork Marriage Guidance centre.[37] As pointed out by Brian Girvin, there were different views and tensions within the Hierarchy and by 1977 the new Archbishop of Armagh, Dr Tomás Ó Fiaich, publicly supported the idea of separating church and state. In contrast, the Bishop of Limerick, Jeremiah Newman, appointed in 1974 and the most outspoken and controversial Catholic bishop of his era, slammed a new liberalism, insisting 'the Catholic people of our State have a right – a political right – to have the provision of the kind of social framework that supports them in the living out of their moral and religious principles'. Adamant that the need for reconciliation arising out of the Troubles did not require any relaxation in the Catholic ethos of the Republic and opposed to any legal change regarding divorce, contraception and abortion, Newman was also known for addressing the 'sociological implications of secularization' that came with increased urbanisation.[38]

He had been disturbed in Maynooth as Professor of Sociology in the early 1970s at student demands to contribute to their own theological formation: 'it seemed to some as if truth could be arrived at by a democratic process of uninformed debate'. This was an 'airy-fairy' approach which he denounced, while those religious who engaged in social work, and 'Third World relief and the like' took, in his view 'an over-secular approach to things'.[39] Aspects of Irish missionary endeavour during the Biafran war had been controversial: seventeen Irish missionaries were sentenced to imprisonment in Port Harcourt, Nigeria, in January 1970 for illegally entering the country during the war. Between 1965 and 1975 the number of Irish candidates entering missionary societies and congregations for men dropped by approximately half.[40]

The Catholic Church had much else to worry about during this decade. It was maintained in a church publication aimed at 'an invitation to priestly concern' that 'there are clear signs today that there are real reasons for concern about marriage ... more marriages do break down than say, a generation ago', particularly among those in urban areas marrying too young and because of 'a lessening of the fervour and the regularity of religious practice'. Problems were also attributed to change in the social status of women and too many whose relationship 'has at no stage advanced beyond the superficial level of a social round' or those who got married solely because of pregnancy.[41]

An analysis of the addresses and sermons of Archbishop Dermot Ryan from 1972–7 reveals a concern with poverty and deprivation. His installation address suggested that 'it is easy in these days of affluence to think that the poor are no longer with us and that all the causes of poverty have been quietly and efficiently disposed of'.[42] Other issues he addressed included a defence of learning by rote in religion classes, the 'hazardous process' of the 'exaggerated focusing' on sex education, abortion, sleep deprivation in children, road safety, uneven distribution of wealth, drug abuse, alcoholism and 'slot-machine spirituality ... One can easily assume that by performing the few spiritual exercises one automatically receives full forgiveness.'[43]

There were other indications of some slippage in the fortunes of the Catholic Church. The very fact that the church committed itself to 'religious renewal' was an indication of its concern about a decline in influence. By 1972 the total figure for the diocesan clergy (those ordained to work in a particular diocese or archdiocese under the control of a bishop) was 3,944 and priest religious (priests who were members of particular religious orders or institutions, only some of whom worked in parishes) 7,946; these figures appeared to have stabilised, 'but the future is none too bright' as ordination totals were down and departures up. There had been a decline of 58 per cent in the number of entries to convents since 1965. The decline in priestly vocations between 1966 and 1974 was also striking, from 1,409 to 547.[44] At Maynooth there were 280 seminarians for the academic year 1974–5: 42 left during the year (15 per cent) compared to 1962–3 when there were 546 seminarians and 50 left (9.5 per cent) and a brief rise in vocations after the papal visit in 1979 was not maintained.[45] The establishment of a National Council of Priests was approved by the Hierarchy in 1975 and priests were subjecting themselves to more 'critical analysis'.[46] By 1977 it was estimated that the circulation of the *Catholic Standard* newspaper had fallen to 12,000 per week, down from 72,000 in the 1950s.[47]

The degree to which the Catholic Church was fulfilling its welfare and social obligations was also questioned. In January 1973 Archbishop Dermot Ryan had consulted Bishop Eamon Casey to seek his advice on homelessness (Casey had particular experience on this, having been an emigrant chaplain in England and gained extensive experience in housing movements). An announcement was made of the formation of a foundation to build half-way houses for those on waiting lists on land donated from religious orders. But by 1978 there was no sign of the houses: 'First of all, none of the religious communities were at all forthcoming with donations for the project.'[48] Casey had plenty of other things on his mind. In April 1973 he had met Annie Murphy, with whom he subsequently fathered a son which he tried unsuccessfully to pressure her into giving up for adoption. She was also forced to spend time at the mother and baby home St Patrick's in Navan Road, a story that did not become public until 1992, though it was no secret that he was fond of the good life. *Hibernia* reported in 1974 that 'since being made Bishop of Kerry, Casey has built up a reputation for fast cars and frequent absences from his diocese: a child in Catechism class once said that the difference between God and Bishop Casey is that while God is everywhere, Bishop Casey is everywhere except in Kerry.'[49]

Religion was also being viewed as a business that had to adapt and the Catholic Communications Centre was applying its work to slick marketing and business techniques, a witness to 'clerical ambitions into secular territory'.[50] In the early 1970s a new episcopal conference had evolved and various commissions were established so that church personnel could become expert lobbyists, and there was recognition of the need for socio-religious research. A research and development unit was established as a branch of the Catholic Communications Institute and subsequently became the Council for Research and Development.[51] A Catholic Press and Information Office was also established. But probing questioners of the church and its institutions and personnel faced hostility. An official history of the Knights of Columbanus was published in 1979 by Sr Angela Bolster. It had first been commissioned in 1973, and in 1974, when she became the first woman to attend a Supreme Meeting, she explained to the Knights some of the difficulties she was facing with deficient records and members reluctant to give interviews.[52] Political scientist John H. Whyte, who produced his seminal *Church and State in Modern Ireland 1923–70* in 1971, had been told to cease his research while he was working in UCD in the mid 1960s because it was suspected the book would be subversive. He moved to Queen's University Belfast. Ironically, over time, the book came to be seen as 'a moderate defence of the Catholic stance and as a portrait which seriously understates the extent of clerical power'.[53]

Declan Kiberd suggested that the dilution of the Catholic Church's 'special position' in the 1970s meant that those who now went into religion would choose it 'in a most deliberate and conscientious way, rather than seeking social prestige or career opportunity' and that many spoke increasingly of their 'option for the poor' and took radical positions on travellers, unemployed and children's rights.[54]

Journalist Mary Kenny, in her survey of the difficulties facing the church in the late twentieth century, has also characterised the Catholic Church and its publications from the mid 1970s as 'drifting leftwards', with much praise for Don Helder Camara, a Latin left-wing pacifist, and Daniel Berrigan, an anti-Vietnam Jesuit protestor, while in 1972 the *Missionary Magazine* backed Salvador Allende, the Marxist candidate, to be Chilean leader. The word 'rights' now entered 'the lexicon of Catholic Ireland'.[55]

Fr Austin Flannery, a Dominican friar and regarded as one of the more liberal of the Irish Catholic clergy, had a significant profile. But there were suspicions too about this new-found focus on just causes. When Labour TD Barry Desmond attended a dinner in Dun Laoghaire and gave his version of grace before meals – 'Bless those who prepared it and give bread to those who have none' – one of the waitresses said to another, 'I told you he was a communist! Did ye hear what he said about God and the food?'[56]

Cardinal William Conway died in 1977 and was remembered as cautious, deferential to tradition and opposed to integrated education. Journalist T. P. O'Mahony suggested his 'reputation has always seemed higher outside of Ireland than in it'. In April 1977 it was mentioned by Garret FitzGerald that in going to Conway's funeral President Hillery 'was moving outside of the state ... His remark did not appear to be taken seriously by his colleagues and no question of formal or informal approval by the government was raised.'[57] Later that month the cabinet expressed its anger at the comments of Edward Daly the Bishop of Derry, about prison conditions (see Part II) and wanted make its views known to the church authorities. Reference was also made as to who might succeed Conway, 'and there was a brief discussion on the question whether there is any way in which our views on the matter could be made known'. What those views were was not recorded.[58] Gerard Woods, the Irish ambassador to the Holy See, wrote to the Department of Foreign Affairs to suggest that Archbishop

Benelli, deputy to the Secretariat of State, 'hardly knew any of our present bishops'. This, for Woods, 'raised in my mind doubts which I have long and privately held about the general acceptance in Ireland of the power of the Irish hierarchy in Rome'.

When appointed Archbishop of Armagh in August 1977 Tomás Ó Fiaich was the first holder of the see for 110 years who was not already a bishop on appointment.[59] He said one of his priorities would be 'to try and enable the church to face a more materialistic age and that his new position would not "muzzle" him and he would still speak out on matters of conscience'. It was regarded by some as significant that his doctorate was in history rather than theology, and while he would not challenge anti-democratic sentiment within the ruling structures of the church, 'he does not have the static pre-conciliar approach [opposition to the liberalising climate represented by Vatican II reforms in the 1960s] we are used to' and was 'more open and in touch with people'.[60]

In the autumn of 1979 the Literary and Historical Society in UCD ran as its debate the motion that 'the papal visit has reinforced our theocracy'.[61] A more considered historical verdict would make no such assertion about Pope John Paul II's visit to Ireland in September of that year (he had been elected to the papacy in October 1978), but perhaps even the opposite. Tom Garvin notes that the visit was 'a truly mythic event' with a brief upturn in Mass attendance and no shortage of babies born nine months after the visit that were christened John Paul, but it did not reverse trends in motion, such as birth rates moving towards the European average and the introduction of contraceptives: 'The Irish had tried the traditional religious life one last time and found they really didn't like it. The papal visit may actually have had the effect of destabilising an already fragile public-belief system.'[62] But there was no denying the fervour, occasional hysteria and national giddiness the visit created.

Speculation about a papal visit was apparent in February 1979, but Jack Lynch told a TD 'we have heard nothing from official sources'. In April, Minister for Posts and Telegraphs Pádraig Faulkner wrote to Lynch to tell him that Fr John Magee, the Newry-born cleric who served as one of the Pope's secretaries, and who was ill in hospital in Dublin, had spoken with Archbishop Ó Fiaich about a possible visit, but 'the fact is that the Archbishop does not know whether the Pope is coming or not. He has heard nothing in recent times.'[63] In May the Department of Foreign Affairs had no knowledge of any planned visit and by June the *Irish Press* was speculating that a visit was unlikely. Surprisingly, an official in the Department of Foreign Affairs wrote to Bertie O'Dowd in the Taoiseach's office in early May: 'There appear to be indications that elements in the Vatican may well be trying to engineer a situation which they would see as putting pressure on the Irish government to issue an official invitation to the Pope.'

In mid May the secretary of the Department of Foreign Affairs' embassy to the Holy See spoke to the rector of the Irish College in Rome, Monsignor Eamon Marron, suggesting the Pope had made it clear in speaking to him he wanted to go to Armagh, was aware of the political implications of such a visit and that, in the Pope's own words, 'there are certain people in the milieu who don't want me there'. Marron felt the government had not done enough work in preparing for a visit and that it was up to it to take the initiative. The visit was announced towards the end of July and it was made clear to the government that it needed to move quickly on what would be an extraordinary organisational challenge: a 'massive crowd control operation – all the state's resources will have to be mobilised'. But it was felt a state reception for the Pope 'might not be appropriate. I understand that the Pope does not smoke, drinks wine only occasionally and cares nothing for food, dress or social distinctions.' The main problem, it believed, was 'the Holy Father's lack of respect for timetables and deadlines'.[64]

An official in the Foreign Office in London insisted that if the Pope wished to visit Northern Ireland 'we will facilitate him graciously: How could we refuse?' but it was also suggested that the Vatican Secretariat was putting pressure on him to confine his visit to the Republic, and the Taoiseach suggested a peace and reconciliation theme for the visit. The SDLP's Gerry Fitt insisted he needed to come to the North or it would be seen as a victory for Ian Paisley, but Seán Ó hUiginn, a senior official in the Department of Foreign Affairs' Anglo-Irish section, felt 'the political risks are not great. Paisley has not many worlds left to conquer in terms of Northern Ireland Protestant extremists.' The government wanted the Pope to visit the North and conveyed this to Ó Fiaich, who was not enthusiastic.[65]

News of the impending visit generated interesting but also some trivial and some excessively demanding correspondence to the government and Cardinal Ó Fiaich, including a letter from Dermot Kinlen, a senior lawyer and future High Court judge, seeking to have the Pope say Mass to mark a new law term ('probably an outrageous brainstorm on my part'). He emphasised the huge enthusiasm for the idea among the legal profession: 'The Chief Justice, the Chairman of the Bar Council and the President of the Incorporated Law Society ... are all extremely enthusiastic about the idea ... The Holy Father might regard it as a suitable forum to speak of justice and human rights in the world.'[66]

Dreadful poetry was also flowing in to the government:

As his plane touches down in Dublin
From every Church and Cathedral grand
The bells will toll to welcome the Pope
To the emerald Isle of Ireland.

There was also a request to pass on a letter to the Pope from a Maltese Catholic priest looking for a hurried dispensation to get married.[67] In the wake of the visit there was much praise from the public for its smooth organisation and success (with close to one million people attending the papal Mass in the Phoenix Park in Dublin, it involved the biggest public transport operation in the history of the state), including emotional letters from Irish emigrants watching it on BBC. Unfortunately, the afterglow also generated yet more bad poetry:

His papal robes and smiling face stood out amid the throng
Cheered and feted by the people, he knelt and kissed the soil
As he held his hands on high the crowd broke into song
The first Pope to visit Ireland, this man who knew what toil
And sweat was all about; but unto his faith was loyal
While in a forced labour camp it had stood the test of time
Today love shone deep from his heart, the setting was sublime.[68]

Even the statues of Oliver Goldsmith and Edmund Burke in front of Trinity College had received a polish for the visit and the Office of Public Works planted 6,000 shrubs in several parks which were required for the 8,000 square feet of beds around the papal altar in the Phoenix Park.[69] One joke doing the rounds was that 'if only those who ran the Papal visit could be allowed to run the country we would be all right'.[70] A total of 980,000 tickets were issued for the Phoenix Park and 'one out of every 3 people in the country had come here'. Even some feminists cheered, including Nell McCafferty: 'I saw absolutely no contradiction in opposing his daft policies on birth control and cheering the great day for the Irish. It was a cheerful fingers up to Cromwell.'[71]

Those who devised the Pope's schedule demanded 'more of him in terms of physical stamina than the fittest of men 20 years his junior could have endured'. But he did not stop, as apparently planned, in a working-class area, and a meeting with representatives of other Christian churches was truncated. He referred in his homilies to ideologies and trends 'alien to Irish society' while his appeal in Drogheda for the IRA to abandon violence 'will be remembered and quoted for centuries ... The power of its appeal in its forgiving rather than condemnatory tone', though it was considered unlikely it would have 'any direct effect on those immediately engaged in violence'.[72] Not everyone shared the view of *Irish Times* editor Douglas Gageby, a Protestant, that the visit was 'a marvellous historic moment ... Our running joke was that he had overnight become the Paper's first Catholic editor.'[73]

For *Irish Press* editor Tim Pat Coogan, who turned down an invitation to attend a special papal audience for journalists, the visit was 'a Roman triumph, a crescendo of mind-bending triumphal display on the part of one of the most powerful and cynical geopolitical multinationals in the world'. The Pope declared, 'Young People of Ireland, I love you,' and 'he got a tumultuous response from his audience, a sizeable proportion of whom had spent the previous night in their sleeping bags energetically loving each other'.[74] Fr Michael Cleary, dubbed Ireland's 'singing priest' and a shameless self-publicist, who along with Bishop Eamon Casey played a prominent role in warming up the young audience before the Pope's arrival in Galway, was also the other type of father, a story which did not emerge until 1995, three years after Casey's fathering of a son generated a storm. RTÉ reporters at Knock were told not to refer to political or other demonstrations unless specific shots had been chosen by the director for fear that demonstrations might be given disproportionate publicity.[75]

But it had also been maintained – indicating that not everybody had been convinced that Irish Catholicism had developed enough of a social conscience – that the papal visit was about his mission 'to chastise the Irish bishops for failing to identify with the poor and repressed', which he apparently did at a private address to them on the eve of his departure. He reputedly criticised them for 'remaining passive in response to 30 letters and communications from Pope Paul VI (who was in office from 1963 to 1978) asking them to take an "oppositionist" position to the Irish establishment'. It was further maintained that 'while the Pope expects his influence will have a socially radicalising effect on the Irish church, it is by no means certain that this is what will happen. The implicitly triumphalist nature of much of the festivities inevitably fosters the reactionary elements in the Irish church, the concentration on Mariology which is implicitly antipathetic to women's rights and the assaults on materialism, also contribute to a strengthening of the conservative elements in Irish Catholicism.'[76]

– FIFTY-NINE –

BREAKING THE SHACKLES

What of the status of women? When addressing the American Committee for Irish Studies at Missouri in April 1976, John A. Murphy asserted 'The "will of God" concept as the resigned explanation of life's miseries has vanished among Irish womenfolk in this generation.'[1] But what constituted Irish 'womenfolk' in the 1970s? Had the sort of woman in Tom Murphy's play *A Crucial Week in the Life of a Grocer's Assistant*, set in the 1950s and first staged in 1969, where John Joe's mother is described as 'harsh in expression and bitter: a product of Irish history – poverty and ignorance', been consigned to history?[2]

Some were undoubtedly asserting their independence and defying convention. Eibhear Walshe recalled his grandmother in the 1970s: 'Proper grandmothers had white hair innocent of perming and wore huge shapeless floral dresses with tiny white collars. They certainly didn't … chain-smoke, drive a gold and black mini with an eight-track player or call everyone "boy" or "girl" regardless of their age.'[3] Advertisers certainly sought to appeal to women throughout the decade in a new way. In 1970 an advertisement for the *Irish Times* boasted that 'nearly 50 per cent of *Irish Times* readers are women – influential women. Elegant women. The *Irish Times* has a larger proportion of women using cosmetics than any other national daily.'[4]

But a variety of influential and elegant women also became political and social activists and demanded more respect. Singer Christy Moore, for example, remembered, 'I encountered women in the seventies who began to expose my chauvinism and slowly, wash it away.'[5] Those who became involved in the feminist 'battle' in the late 1960s and early 1970s have been identified as 'second wave' feminists. They were not united or coherent in their campaigning and the relatively speedy rise and demise of the Irish Women's Liberation Movement (IWLM) was partly because it developed, in sociologist Linda Connolly's words, in an 'erratic, disorganised and chaotic fashion in 1970–2'[6] but also because of the emergence of ideological debates and tensions within Irish feminism during the 1970s.[7] When reviewing Julia O'Faoláin's *Not in God's Image* in 1973 for *Hibernia*, Mary Robinson wrote that it was the first book 'which falls under the general umbrella of women's liberation that I have been able to read without suffering pangs of indigestion',[8] a reminder that interpreting and defining the liberation of women did not in any sense create unanimity.

Nell McCafferty recalled that fellow journalist Patsey Murphy sometimes pointed out that 'if any of us in the women's movement were unmarried mothers we'd have half a clue. She had a point; when we were compiling our information pamphlet *Chains or Change* [the IWLM's manifesto for change] the poet Eavan Boland, also a founder member of the movement, had rung Mary Robinson to ask if she could give us seven examples of legal discrimination against women and Robinson had asked "Why only seven?"'[9]

But collectively, the extent to which these women succeeded in bringing to the fore issues that had been considered private and taboo is striking, and they played a crucial role in informing and politicising a generation of women who achieved much in terms of changing attitudes and changing the law, though innovation came more slowly than they would have wished. Historians also played their part, including Mary Cullen and Dominican nun and UCD lecturer Margaret Mac Curtain, one of the editors of *Women in Irish Society: The Historical Dimension* (1977), which originated as a series of Thomas Davis lectures on RTÉ in 1975 to mark International Women's Year.

As enunciated by Mac Curtain in this important publication:

> The Irish woman presents one of the enigmas of twentieth century Ireland. Her public face is that of wife and mother, enshrined in the 1937 constitution as guardian of public morals and repository of the state's regard for family life. Her private face is that of one who has

> been awarded no place at the conference tables and who, increasingly, knows she has been hidden from history ... Many Irish women find it difficult to learn about their historical identity, or their role in the life of the country because they have neither the information readily available nor the skills of evaluation at their disposal.[10]

Twenty years later, Mac Curtain identified this book as the one she wanted to be remembered for, as its essays she regarded as 'an expression of the intellectual and creative energy of the 1970s'.[11] But the aspiration that women would retrieve their own history was complicated by the sense that 'the universities were not ready for an innovation, which, in the opinion of the historical establishment, possessed neither a sound methodology nor reliable sources'.[12]

Feminists also had to negotiate with those in power to begin the formal process of highlighting and then ending state-sponsored discrimination. It took over a year for the government to respond to demands for a Commission on the Status of Women (CSW), which had been presented by the organisations that came together to form an ad hoc committee to press for women's rights in 1968, ranging from the Association of Business and Professional Women to the National Association of Widows. In November 1969 Taoiseach Jack Lynch announced the establishment of the commission; its terms of reference were published in April 1970. It was required to 'Examine and report on the status of women in Irish society, to make recommendations on the steps necessary to ensure the participation of women on equal terms and conditions with men in the political, social and cultural and economic life of the country, and to indicate the implications generally – including the estimated cost – of such recommendations.' That year, a civil servant in the Department of the Taoiseach observed in relation to the Minister for Finance Charles Haughey, 'I think people are not generally aware that he is the minister responsible for setting up the Commission.'[13]

Haughey also, recalled Nell McCafferty, caused the CSW to be 'mortified' when he arrived at its headquarters 'to present them with a chain of office which he had personally commissioned; they wanted equal pay; he offered them chains'. McCafferty intervened and denounced him.[14] While the commission was still deliberating, trade unionist Ruairí Roberts suggested that Lynch was 'deflecting' questions on the issue of equal pay for equal work to the CSW,[15] which was what Haughey had intended.

The CSW was chaired by Thekla Beere, who had achieved the distinction in 1959 of becoming the first female secretary of an Irish government department. Although not 'an overt and certainly not an ideological feminist', she had made it to the top of the civil service and, now retired, was seen as an ideal candidate. She expressed herself reluctant (she had already spent three years working on the Devlin Report) but 'felt I had to do it'.

She was adamant that the commission would comprise an equal number of men and women 'reflecting her innate pragmatism', and securing an agreed report 'proved much easier than I had anticipated'. The commission met fortnightly for two years in all-day sessions. According to her biographer, she was 'more concerned with what the commission could achieve for marginalised women in Irish society – widows, unmarried mothers, prisoners' wives and deserted wives – rather than the advancement of career women'.[16] As an educated middle-class woman from a comfortable background, joined by those similarly situated, 'a lot of us were absolutely amazed at the things we found ... appalled because they didn't affect many people but they affected people who had really no means of communicating with the Press'.

In tandem with the commission's deliberations, the IWLM had begun informally in 1970 and included in its ranks journalists, Labour Party activists, teachers, broadcasters, writers and other professionals who would often meet at Gaj's restaurant in Baggot Street, owned by Margaret Gaj, a Scottish feminist who, as remembered by journalist Mary Maher, another founder of the IWLM, was 'absolutely fearless in taking on the establishment' (she went on to play an important role in the Prisoners Rights Organisation).[17] There was disagreement from the outset as to how liberation could or should be achieved by this combination of left-wing socialists and middle-class women, though they agreed an outline of their demands, published as a pamphlet, 'Chains or Change?' in 1971. They demanded these key changes: equal pay, equality before the law, equality in education, justice for deserted wives, unmarried mothers and widows, and one family, one house. According to Nell McCafferty, 'It is a measure of our utter innocence that we did not include divorce. It just did not occur to us that marriage could or should be legally terminated.'[18]

Mary Kenny, then women's editor of the *Irish Press*, sent 'Chains or Change?' to Jack Lynch on International Women's Day in March 1971: 'It is a model of serious documentation and facts and really quite removed from the hysteria that people have been persuaded to associate with women's lib elsewhere ... one doesn't have to wait for the commission's report to start removing some of the more glaring points of discrimination – starting, possibly, with the position of women in your very own civil service, would you believe?'[19] They highlighted the various legal inequities and concluded that 'an Irish woman enters into a state of civil death on marriage ... On the face of it, the single woman in Ireland is perhaps legally and economically the best off of Irish women ... if you live in sin you don't submit to the insult that society offers to women who marry – the status of property.'

'Chains or Change?' also pointed out that in 1966 Irish women accounted for one-third of all employees in the Republic and were earning 54.9 per cent of men's wages. The biggest category of employment for women was factory operatives; only 6 per cent of administrative, executive and managerial workers were women. Although there were 100,000 female trade unionists in 1970, it was estimated that only seven out of 230 trade union officials were women, while at school 'girls will learn needlework and domestic science – a boy taking domestic science was regarded as a sufficient oddity to warrant a radio interview in Britain recently'. At third level, 'the UCD appointments officer says that final year girls feel that the only career open to them is teaching. Business and industry are almost completely closed to women graduates, apart from a back door as "graduate secretaries".'[20]

It also highlighted discrimination against widows with many of them forced to work because a contributory pension was deemed to be payable to a widow only if her husband had fulfilled certain employment contributions. There were a whole host of discriminations against married women. The husband was the legal guardian of the children and 'a wife's domicile is wherever her husband chooses to be'. He legally received the children's allowance and 'if a wife pays tax on her own income, it is her husband who is entitled to any rebates ... She must have her husband's consent for a mortgage ... If she wants goods on hire purchase or approval most firms demand his signature ... If she decides to go out to work to supplement their income, she runs into equal pay, the marriage bar and penalising taxation.'[21]

In 1971 the IWLM was offered a platform on RTÉ's Friday night programme *The Late Late Show* to publicise its aims (historian Mary Cullen was introduced by Gay Byrne as 'the wife of a psychiatrist'[22]), though when the audience joined in, according to June Levine, another key activist, 'the whole strategy of the IWLM fell apart'. The intention had been to present themselves as a moderate group, with Mary Robinson addressing legal inequities in women's status, Mary Cullen making the case for working mothers and Lelia Doolan addressing social conditioning, the role of the media and education. Others addressed job discrimination, the status of unmarried mothers and widows, and the role of trade unions. But as the audience joined in, the anger mounted and the publicity garnered was massive. June Levine found herself roaring: 'You don't have to be black in Ireland, you only have to be a woman.' Politicians were accused of not giving a damn and an irate Garret FitzGerald left his home near the television studio and gatecrashed the programme to insist otherwise. The women were 'furious, feeling that such a takeover could only happen on a women's programme'. It was a show, in Levine's words, that was 'chaotic but riveting ... most of the women got carried away, forgetting about their planned display of moderacy'.[23]

In its aftermath, a number of events were then organised, including the picketing of the residence of the Archbishop of Dublin (McQuaid) in protest at the Catholic Church's continued opposition to contraception, and a public meeting at the Mansion House, which a thousand people attended. A trip to Belfast on World Communications Day in May 1971 to buy contraceptives in defiance of the Criminal Law Amendment Act prohibiting the sale and importation of contraceptives on what became known as the Condom Train, attracted considerable controversy and publicity, though as June Levine recalled, 'our day was to become an international media story, lauded far more elsewhere than it was at home'. In Belfast, Levine was showered with questions from her fellow felons-in-waiting about various contraceptive devices ('What do you do with this jelly stuff?' and 'Would I take the same size Dutch cap as you?') in an 'amazing display of ignorance of the facts of life ... now I saw them as their mother's daughters, women who knew little about their own bodies, who had never been free to feel responsible for their own fertility and felt awkward about it.'

No legal action was taken after they arrived back in Dublin with the contraceptives to a rousing reception organised by Mairín de Burca: 'On World Communications Day, we had certainly succeeded in communicating ... The question was, what would we do for an encore?'[24] According to Nell McCafferty, the IWLM was 'more interested in avoiding pregnancy than achieving orgasm'.[25] Mary Maher, an *Irish Times* journalist who had come from Chicago to Ireland and was an active IWLM member, underlined the determination they felt to have new choices: 'I think we automatically understood that we were not the previous generation ... We wanted to make a big splash.'[26]

A picket at the General Post Office over the paying of children's allowances to fathers was also organised, as was a picket of the Four Courts to protest against women not being included in juries, and a picket of Leinster House when Mary Robinson's Family Planning Bill failed to get a reading in the Senate in October 1971. Nell McCafferty recalled that at that time, outside the Senate, 'Senator Joe Lenehan [a Fianna Fáil representative] was telling the rest of us that we should be fucked on our hands and knees, like animals.'[27] McCafferty was keen to empower working-class women ('in 1970 in Ireland 96 per cent of married women worked, unpaid, within the home and their situation did not feature in any plans for the worker's revolution') and highlight that a husband in Ireland was not obliged to support his wife beyond what he considered she needed. Some judges also treated women with contempt. In one of her Eyes of the Law *Irish Times* columns in December 1972, McCafferty recounted this scene:

> There's no place like a courtroom to dismiss the nonsensical notion entertained by housewives that they are in any degree independent of their husbands. A woman appeared before District Justice Ó Donnchadha in Court 4 at 11.45 a.m. on Wednesday, 29 November, offering herself as bondswoman of her friend, who had been convicted for shoplifting.
>
> 'Do you do any work other than housework,' she was asked. No, she did not. 'Are you dependent on your husband for money?' 'Yes,' she said. 'I cannot accept you then,' said the justice. It was as short, simple and brutal as that; in the world where money matters, women matter not.[28]

But divisions were also apparent from the early stages of the IWLM due to disagreement as to what constituted issues that affected women. As Levine recalled, 'The Forcible Entry and Occupation Bill of 1971 distracted the attention of many of the women from purely feminist issues and emphasised the divergence between socialists and other members of the group. The socialists argued that women were the primary victims of the Bill, which was directed against the homeless.'[29] After the initial enthusiasm, these divisions ensured the movement became fractured. As pointed out by *Magill's* Pat Brennan, 'A mass movement cannot be built on euphoria and then restructured into a highly autocratic organisation.' Brennan depicted the movement as one that had been riven by conflict, with an inability to develop operational organisational structures.[30]

But neither had their efforts been in vain. One group that emerged from the IWLM was Action Information Motivation (AIM). Formed by Nuala Fennell and others, it was instrumental in achieving many of the legal reforms that affected women. The Save the Equal Pay Act Committee was another group that exerted considerable pressure, in order to persuade the government to enforce the Anti-Discrimination Pay Act of 1974 (see pages 668–71).

Fennell recalled finding herself in the late 1960s facing her mother's dilemma, invisible as 'one of the foot soldiers in the vast army of suburban housewives'. She began writing articles for the women's pages of magazines and newspapers and got significant feedback from her frustrated peers. Journalism also provided an introduction to some of the leading figures of the emerging IWLM and she was mesmerised by Mary Kenny in particular ('set out to shock and mostly she succeeded'). Fennell was more cautious. She disliked the anti-man rhetoric of some of her new-found mentors, regarded the Contraceptive Train stunt as histrionic and tended to view herself as a social reformer who wanted to target political institutions rather than wave placards. In October 1971 she left the movement, writing an extraordinary public resignation letter decrying 'the elitist and intolerant group that is using women's liberation as a pseudo-respectable front for their own various political ends, ranging from opposition to the Forcible Entry Bill to free sedatives for neurotic elephants'.[31] It made for great copy, but when writing her memoirs she was magnanimous enough to acknowledge that she was wrong in this assessment. The IWLM may have been chaotic, short-lived and riddled with class tensions, but an irreversible start had been made in making the status of women a political issue.

This development was given added momentum when the report of the Commission on the Status of Women was published in 1972. June Levine suggested 'its moderate tone made it widely acceptable'.[32] The following year in the Senate, Mary Robinson referred to it as 'the most important social document in recent Irish history'.[33] When the Irish Housewives

Association (IHA, established in 1942) attended the congress of the International Alliance of Women in India in November 1973, where there were 203 women from twenty-five countries, including Hilda Tweedy, the IHA founder, the Irish delegation expressed pride in being able to announce the publication of the report. The IHA referred to the previous three years as 'an exciting time for the women of Ireland', highlighting new approaches to single women, deserted wives and working women and referring to the commission's report as 'far reaching and imaginative' while acknowledging that there was a need for its recommendations to be 'accepted in spirit as well as law'.[34]

The report contained forty-nine recommendations, of which seventeen related to equal pay and women's working conditions. It outlined the need for training facilities, an end to sex discrimination in employment and the provision of twelve weeks' maternity leave. Inequities that existed for women under the social welfare system, the law, taxation and the educational system were also highlighted, while women in political life, their right to sit on juries and family planning were also covered. To oversee the report's findings, the Council for the Status of Women was established, and it became an umbrella group of over thirty organisations. Two statutory bodies grew out of the council; the Women's Representative Committee in 1974 and the Employment Equality Agency in 1977, chaired by Sylvia Meehan.

Thekla Beere estimated that by 1974, half of her recommendations had been implemented or were in the process of implementation, one-third had been accepted in principle and one-fifth had not yet been acted on. Personally, her main concern was that women rearing families in the home should have enough money. She desired to see a staged implementation of equal pay. The fact that she was not an outspoken feminist, suggests her biographer, gave her added stature and influence (and presumably acceptability). As she put it herself: 'My aim was to get a united report. I'm not a great liberationist.' In reality she was anything but, suggesting in 1973 that women had not been active enough in seizing opportunities available to them due to 'inertia' and that 'if women stopped being touchy about their sex and tried to behave as equals they would achieve more'.[35] By the end of 1976, the Women's Representative Committee, in assessing the degree to which the commission's recommendations were being implemented, noted the considerable advances in relation to social welfare, equal pay, family law reform and jury service. But it also highlighted 'other major areas of discrimination' including penal tax laws against married working women, no maternity protection legislation and no progress in relation to provision of child care facilities for working mothers.[36]

In 1973 the Civil Service (Employment of Married Women) Act removed the employment and promotion bar requiring women to give up their jobs after marrying (which in practice had been circumvented by women being retained after marriage on fixed contracts with payment on a daily fee basis, which led to 'unevenness in the treatment of individual members', according to the Civil Service Executive Association). Garret FitzGerald noted that there was an agreement in government to get rid of the marriage bar but he was worried about its implications in his own Department of Foreign Affairs, where women could be posted abroad, and the Minister for Finance Richie Ryan highlighted the case of tax inspectors, who could also be moved around; in his view 'if such officers cannot be accommodated within their own departments, the alternative will most likely be discharge'.[37]

There was opposition to the removal of the bar from various quarters. A resolution of Kilkenny Urban District Council encapsulated a common complaint that females in the public service should not be working after marriage 'to give opportunity to our young girls leaving school and to prevent massive female emigration'. But in truth, the number was not very large. Richie Ryan pointed out to Cosgrave in September 1975 that in June of that year there were 1,005 married women in the civil service as a consequence of the abolition of the marriage bar out of a total civil service of 46,970 (30,146 men and 16,824 women). By 1979 the Labour Force survey estimated there were 91,900 married women employed in Ireland (26,200 of whom were employed in the public service), representing 28.5 per cent of the total women employed.[38]

Nuala Fennell's memoir suggests Minister for Justice Patrick Cooney has not been given enough recognition for his role in introducing the sort of family law legislation that AIM campaigned for, including the Maintenance Orders Act of 1974. During the 1970s, Fennell made an exceptional contribution to increasing awareness about domestic violence and providing shelter to its victims through Women's Aid.[39]

As an activist with AIM, she also insisted that proper maintenance for Irish wives was necessary and that 'alcoholism, excessive gambling and irresponsibility in Irish husbands has led to the deplorable financial conditions of many wives'.[40] It questioned why the means test for a deserted wife was so 'deplorably low' which Minister for Justice Des O'Malley insisted was 'a social welfare matter rather than a justice matter'.[41] In January 1973 John Kelly rejected pronouncements from AIM that suggested he had ignored its lobbying; he insisted he personally had persuaded Fine Gael to introduce parliamentary bills regarding maintenance and that he had 'not sought any special publicity for any of this'.[42]

Two years later a deserted wife with two dependent children was entitled to £14.75 per week. In February 1975 a memorandum on proposed family law reform regarding desertion and maintenance made the observation that the proposals envisaged went beyond those of Northern Ireland regarding provisions relating to the ousting of a violent spouse from the family home and a provision that an application for maintenance could be made and enforced while the spouses were still cohabiting; by March the government was satisfied that it was meeting the 'short-term demands' made by the AIM group, a significant achievement for Fennell.[43]

Shortly before he left office in 1973, Jack Lynch had been defensive about his government's record on advancing equality. In responding to the women's editor of the *Irish Times* he suggested 'the government's policy in relation to the rights of wives has been one of consistent and considered advance even in the face of sustained criticism' and that it was 'regrettable' that in seeking to give a lead to public opinion the government 'do not always get support from the quarters from which support might be expected'. He deemed divorce to be inappropriate and a change in the Juries Act would have to take account of 'the special problems which compulsory jury service would pose for women with young children'.[44]

The Juries Act was deemed to be unconstitutional, however, after a legal challenge by Mairín de Burca and Mary Anderson. In the Supreme Court, Justice Séamus Henchy in his judgment surmised in relation to all-male juries: 'What is missing in decisions so made is not easy to define, but reason and experience show that such decisions are not calculated to lead to a sense of general acceptability, or to carry an acceptable degree of representativeness, or to have the necessary stamp of responsibility on the part of the community as a whole.'[45] Another judge concluded simply that all-male juries 'fall short of minimum constitutional standards'.[46] De Burca was by now an outspoken and experienced campaigner and attracted the ire of a monk who wrote to Fianna Fáil's Séamus Brennan in 1979: he thought 'she was certainly no credit to the "fair sex" and her caustic remarks gave rise to some very original epithets – even among the brothers'.[47] The same year Josey Airey, a legal-aid campaigner who had suffered domestic violence at the hands of her husband, reached the conclusion of her seven-year battle when the European Court of Human Rights decided Ireland had violated the European Convention on Human Rights by depriving her of effective access to the courts to seek a judicial separation by denying her legal aid. Her victory was essential in securing the introduction of a civil legal-aid scheme in Ireland. The judgment also represented the first time in the history of the state that Ireland 'was judged guilty before an international court of having violated the human rights of one of its citizens'.[48]

In March 1976 the European Commission made its directive on equal pay binding on the Irish government, which had requested to be exempt from its provisions. This is a reminder that Ireland's entry to the EEC in 1973 was of profound significance for the advancement of women, as it 'hastened the emergence of a different model of family life, one based on equality legislation and the participation of both partners in the workforce, so that dual-earner households increasingly became the norm. Membership of the EEC contributed to a series of significant changes in regulations governing the employment of women and the entitlement of married women to individual social welfare payments. These measures by and large strengthened women's economic independence outside marriage'.[49] The refusal of the EEC to grant derogations to Ireland gave 'a strong underpinning to the demands from women's organisations'. There were further directives in the late 1970s regarding equal treatment of women in relation to access to employment, vocational training, working conditions and the protection of self-employed women in relation to pregnancy.[50] Given this, it is perhaps not surprising that in 1977 the Irish Council for the European Movement was able to point out that '8 members of the executive committee including the chairman, are women. They are also active in women's organisations.'[51]

In February 1974 the Minister for Labour, Michael O'Leary, had circulated information on the Equal Pay Act and the costs of implementation in the public service by the end of 1975 which would amount to a total of £7.2 million over four years. He insisted, 'It is not a realistic political posture for us to maintain our reservations much longer. The directive will therefore be adopted,' noting that if the directive regarding implementation by 31 December 1975 was inevitable 'it would seem sensible for the government to ensure that it gets whatever political credit is available for it'.[52] He wanted to change the title of the bill from Equal Pay Bill to Anti-discrimination Bill. In the Dáil, Charles Haughey, then in opposition, wondered, 'Is it good or normal parliamentary practice to have a piece of legislation beginning with the word "anti"?' Jack Lynch echoed his concerns, adding, 'that legislation should now be introduced into this house under this title suggesting that this country is a repressive regime is a decadent step on the part of the government', to which O'Leary responded: 'I have never seen such annoyance on the faces of an opposition at seeing a government do its work.'[53]

There were numerous representations by organisations and individuals in relation to equal pay. In September 1974 clothing manufacturer H. L. Temple, one of the largest employers in Donegal, suggested 'wholesale closure of factories' was possible unless the introduction of equal pay was delayed: 'Ireland has been a male orientated society and we are now trying, in the space of 18 months, to reverse a decade of male dominance.' In July 1975 O'Leary told Cosgrave that he would give 'serious consideration' to any representations made to him by employers and trade unions regarding amendments to equal pay legislation if it would 'adversely affect the economic viability of the company and the level of employment'. An employer in the confectionery business insisted 'equal pay fully implemented at one stroke would increase our wage cost by about 10 per cent. Comment is superfluous.'[54]

The managing director of the H. Williams and Company supermarket chain pointed out that his firm agreed with equal pay in principle, but that it could not be phased in too quickly, noting that 78 per cent of the chain's labour force was female: 'We are being asked to follow, like sheep, legislation of other countries who were given ample opportunity to consider the effects and consequences of such legislation.'[55] Although some women's groups were generous in their praise of the coalition government's record to date on promoting different aspects of equality, the intention to postpone equal pay infuriated the Council for the Status of Women, as pointed out forcefully to Cosgrave by its chairperson, Hilda Tweedy. Cosgrave justified the seeking of a derogation from the obligation in a letter to Senator Evelyn Owens of the Labour Women's National Council (who was another pioneering woman in public life and the first female chairman of the Labour Court; she also served two terms as a Labour Party senator) on the grounds that its implementation 'would lead to further unemployment, especially among women workers'.[56]

But up to 35,000 people signed a petition protesting the government's derogation request. Women's groups mobilised to great effect. Roisín Conroy, who worked as an information officer in the research unit of the ITGWU, and was active in the Equal Pay ad hoc committee, which had organised a meeting attended by 1,000 people the previous month, wrote a damning letter to Cosgrave in February 1976: 'The government's image and reputation has deservedly taken a battering over the fiasco on equal pay ... It became apparent that your government had clearly not worked out its strategy as to the manner of postponement when we all heard the howls of outrage from nearly every section of the Labour Party and Labour movement.' Hilda Tweedy also wrote to the president of the European Commission and went to Strasbourg to protest directly at the European Parliament, while ICTU was also vocal and active.[57]

In contrast, Míne Bean Uí Chribín, a staunch Catholic traditionalist and scourge of Irish feminists, insisted it was unconstitutional to remove the marriage rate for men as it would, in violation of article 41 of the constitution, force married women 'out of her home to work due to economic necessity'. It was really about an attempt by 'women's libbers and fellow-travellers to trample on the most basic rights of thousands of wives and mothers in this country'.[58] The European Commission rejected the derogation and Patrick Hillery, the former Fianna Fáil minister and Ireland's first EEC commissioner with responsibility for Social Affairs, and thus this measure, which he had helped to draft, had no intention of playing local politics with it. He told Michael O'Leary that the derogation was being rejected 'for all practical purposes'.[59]

Garret FitzGerald was also dealing with correspondence on equal pay at this time. He received an urgent telegram from the Irish Embassy in Paris: 'Have heard that Commission are giving us nothing on equal pay ... essential that we submit alternative proposals for employment fund and loans at preferential rates immediately.' Brendan Dillon, the permanent Irish representative at the European Commission, stated baldly: 'In the commission itself there is now a total lack of sympathy with us.' FitzGerald saw this as a 'moral' issue and was dubious that 'people should be paid exactly the same for the same work regardless of their family responsibilities'.[60] Earlier that month a constituent of his had wondered: 'What has become of the Just Society? Gone with the wind, like equal pay for equal work', while another who described herself as a 'spinster public servant' suggested 'your volte face is on a par with de Valera's mental reservations of decades ago'[61] (about taking the oath of allegiance to the Crown under the terms of the Anglo-Irish Treaty).

Another issue the coalition government and the women's movement had to face was that of equality of treatment for men and women in social security. In April 1977 a memorandum from Brendan Corish, the Minister for Health and Social Welfare, highlighted the position regarding women receiving lesser benefits. The period during which unemployment benefit could be paid to married women was restricted to 156 days instead of 390 days for men and single women. The estimated cost of the payment to women of benefit in respect of dependants on the same conditions as men was £23 million; the principle was not disputed but the timescale for implementation was; it would cost £32 million to eliminate all these discriminations.

In the Department of the Taoiseach, Walter Kirwan corresponded with Dermot Nally suggesting this was essentially about the extension of social security involving a gradual move away from the concept of a single breadwinner, but he insisted the situation in Ireland differed from that pertaining in other EEC countries: 'The notion of a single breadwinner which permeates our social security schemes is still in line with the Irish reality. In the face of the long-term outlook for employment it might well be that a considered verdict by the majority of the population would favour the reintroduction of some of the former discrimination against married women.' But due to government policy there was no question of objecting to the principle of the proposed directive on the issue from the European Commission.[62]

In December 1977 a memorandum from the new Minister for Finance, George Colley, disputed the notion that the directive would generate employment and maintained it would instead increase the live unemployment register 'through facilitating access by married women to unemployment assistance ... This country's perception of the priority to be accorded to equal treatment should not be dictated by the attitude of the more advanced countries where, in particular, the employment position is very different.'[63]

In February 1978 the government approved the principle of equal treatment but wanted a delay in the timetable. Later that year the Department of Finance expressed annoyance with the Department of Social Welfare for refusing to instruct the Irish representative on the EEC social questions group to enter a general reservation on behalf of the government before the draft directive went to the Council of Ministers for consideration.

A memorandum the following month from Finance highlighted its main concern. It wanted a differentiation in social welfare entitlements as between heads of households and dependent spouses ('a differentiation which would not be based on sex even though it would inevitably affect married women mainly') and desired an amendment to that effect. Social Welfare angrily objected to this stance as it 'shows no appreciation of the realities underlying EEC legislation', pointing out that they had six years to change legislation. Although Finance won the argument within government, the EEC insisted funding was not possible for this decision.[64] Earlier that year George Colley had referred contemptuously to 'articulate well-heeled middle-class women' campaigning for improved income tax allowances.[65] The following year a married couple, Francis and Maura Murphy, claimed in the High Court that special provisions in the Income Tax Act relating to married persons were repugnant to the constitution and the court ruled in their favour, which meant that married couples now had the right to be assessed for tax separately.

Some of the radical women's groups that emerged in the 1970s fell apart towards the end of the decade. Nell McCafferty, who was a member of Irishwomen United, found it 'a relief to be in a group that did not fear discussion of the North' but she was also conscious of 'the hard-pressed working women of Ballyfermot [who] were simply not interested in the revolutionary tourists who had come to spout theory'. Article 3 of their charter – 'recognition of motherhood and parenthood as a social function' – she suggested was an indication that they had no clue about parenting and they were perhaps naïve in demanding '24 hour nurseries provided free of charge'. But many of the things they called for were eventually implemented, including state-funded birth-control clinics, women's studies programmes at third level, state-funded women's centres and divorce.[66] McCafferty's style was also novel; she had once grabbed Fianna Fáil's Patrick Hillery by the tie, backed him up against a wall 'and told him Irishwomen wanted contraception legalised – yesterday'.[67]

Pat Brennan, writing in *Magill*, described the women's movement by 1979 as 'riven with divisions and conflict'.[68] She also pointed to ongoing discrimination. Although between 1974 and 1977 women's hourly earnings in industry rose from 59 per cent of men's to 62 per cent, less than one-third of female workers were in trade unions. *Hot Press* reported in

June 1978 that the average male worker in the Republic earned £76.84 on average for 44.8 hours of work a week while women earned £40.87 for 38.2 hours.[69] While a married woman could file a separate tax return, her income was still regarded as that of her husband. Although 16 per cent more girls than boys reached Leaving Certificate stage, only 'just over one-third of those in third-level education are women'.[70] In 1976 *Hibernia* published an eight-page special supplement on 'A Woman's Place' (which included an account of the 'malevolent, malingering malefulness' of Irish politicians by Nell McCafferty). It highlighted that 'of the 455 new entrants to engineering schools in 1974, only 4 were women'.[71]

But the decline in marital fertility – in 1981, the average number of children per family was three compared to four in 1971 – was another signal of changed times for women and was facilitated by the McGee case of 1973, when the Supreme Court established that marital privacy was protected under the constitution, and that the law prohibiting the importation of contraceptives even for private use by married persons infringed that privacy and was thus unconstitutional. Mary McGee, a twenty-seven-year-old mother of four, had been told that another pregnancy could endanger her life and was issued with a prescription for spermicidal jelly. She ordered it from the UK and it was seized by customs officials as a shipment in violation of the 1935 Criminal Law Amendment Act preventing the importation and sale of contraceptives. The Irish Family Planning Association aided her in bringing the case to court. The Chief Justice William Fitzgerald dissented from the majority view in the Supreme Court, describing the risks to McGee's health as 'natural hazards which must be faced by married couples with such fortitude as they can summon to their assistance'.[72] Prior to that, the report of the Commission into the Status of Women had approached contraception in a veiled way, recommending that information and advice be provided to married couples and that their 'medical requirements' in relation to family planning should be met.[73] A National Health Council report for the year ended 1972 had pointed out that the first issue they had considered had been contraception, as 'there exists for certain married women in this country a need for contraception on health grounds'.

Proposed legislation to deal with the McGee decision, the doomed Control of Importation, Sale and Manufacture of Contraceptive Bill 1974 (after the debate on which Liam Cosgrave and Minister for Education Richard Burke voted against their own government), was the result.

The most interesting correspondence on this was between the Attorney General Declan Costello and the Department of Justice. According to a memorandum prepared for the government on the issue, Costello suggested 'the inclusion of a provision making it unlawful for any unmarried person, other than certain exempted persons, to be in possession of a contraceptive'. The response from the Department of Justice, headed by Patrick Cooney, was that 'such a provision would involve an excessive intrusion into privacy. It will not be an offence for an unmarried person to accept (otherwise than by purchase) a contraceptive. Under the existing law possession of a contraceptive is not an offence.'

Cooney presented another memorandum on the subject, suggesting the proposed legislation to 'allow certain categories of persons, namely pharmacists' to import contraceptives under licence, would enable married people to have 'reasonable availability of contraceptives'. But there would be no personal right to importation – his interpretation of the McGee judgment was that it did not cover individual importation. He also noted 'there will be no legal right of personal importation for tourists, travellers etc., from abroad. Assuming reasonable attempts will be made to enforce the proposed prohibition of general importation, embarrassment may arise in relation to visitors bringing in contraceptives in their personal luggage.' He also argued the proposed bill would please Northern Protestants, and would 'liberalise our laws sufficiently ... in relation to the laws to apply in a future united Ireland', but that 'it would clearly be impossible to secure any political support for a move to legalise abortion'.

The severity of the Attorney General's proposals for inclusion in the Bill were striking. He wanted, for example, the following to be inserted:

> A member of the Garda Síochána who has reasonable grounds for suspecting that a person who is in possession of a contraceptive has committed or is committing an offence under this Act, may require the person to state if he is married, and in case that he states that he is married, the place where and the date on which the marriage took place. A person ... who refuses to comply ... or who, in purported compliance with the requirements, gives any information which he knows to be false in a material particular shall be guilty of an offence and shall be liable on summary conviction to a fine.

The Minister for Justice was again unimpressed:

> The Minister is against the inclusion of such a provision. It is, of itself, insufficient to enable a charge to be proved as there would still be the need to prove purchase of the contraceptive and the Gardaí could very rarely do that. Moreover, the provision, as far as it goes, could perhaps be criticised as (a) an unjustified invasion of privacy and (b) an attempt to transfer the onus of proof, which appears to be prohibited by the European Convention on Human Rights, and also an attempt to make a person who has contraceptives incriminate himself, contrary to the UN Universal Declaration of Human Rights ... even if possession were to be made an offence, this would not significantly reduce the problem of proof, since a power of search would normally be necessary to enable the Gardaí to prove possession.[74]

Not too many men were aiding contraception. In 1975 it was suggested that vasectomy was 'not yet a subject for polite conversation' but *Hibernia* readers were reassured that 'it is not the same as, nor anything like, castration'.[75] The following year, the Supreme Court overruled the Censorship Board, declaring the Irish Family Planning Association's book *Family Planning* (1971) should not be banned because it was neither indecent nor obscene, the first such challenge brought under the censorship legislation in fifty years. Contraception remained a preoccupation throughout the decade as a social, moral, religious and health issue; after the failure of the coalition's attempt to legislate in 1974, in 1977 the Fianna Fáil manifesto stated as one of its health policy aims 'to ensure the widest possible acceptance of a positive policy for family planning and enact the necessary legislation'. But it was recognised that 'the practical enforcement of a restriction of contraceptives to married persons would be very difficult'. It was also suggested in 1978 that 'most doctors knew little about alternative methods of birth control' other than the pill.[76]

Catholic extremists were unashamedly applying pressure after the victory of the IFPA over censorship in 1976, and although many praised Cosgrave for his vote in 1974, they sought to use electoral blackmail with his successor. A correspondent from the Loreto Convent in North Great George's Street, for example, informed Lynch in June 1977 that 'all the nuns in the country would vote against Fianna Fáil at the next election' if it legislated for contraceptives 'and they constitute a formidable body – so be wary!'[77] They also continued to indulge in their conspiracy theories. Lynch was informed in June 1977, for example, that the McGee case was 'the invention of a minute minority of internationalists deliberately contrived to break down the constitution of the people'.[78] Lynch's replies were straightforward; legislation was necessary as a result of the McGee case, and 'some people that write to me seem to avoid the realities of it'.[79] He still made a point of visiting as many convents as he could during the 1977 general election.

A group called Mná na hÉireann (Women of Ireland) castigated the International Planned Parenthood Federation, of which the IFPA was the Irish affiliate, as a group 'teaching masturbation and perversion to babies of five years with the help of lurid sex film' while the Irish Family League maintained the decision on contraception was 'as critical for our people as was the decision on the Treaty of 1921 or on neutrality in 1939'.[80] The put down by Major Vivion de Valera (son of Eamon and a Fianna Fáil TD for the Dublin Cabra constituency) of a constituent who complained that the Fianna Fáil TD would not engage with her over the issue, as relayed to Lynch, was brilliantly cutting: 'I am being bombarded with all sorts of well meaning but ill-informed representations on contraceptives, very largely from virgins of both sexes, whether by design or default.'[81]

Over 150 medical missionaries of Mary signed a letter of complaint about the supposed instalment of a vending machine for contraceptives in UCD (condoms were also said to be on sale at the Dandelion Market off Stephen's Green), while the daughter of the man who had been the university's Professor of Chemistry in 1909 (and who had fathered twelve children) also complained to Lynch. The Irish Family League wrote to the Taoiseach's wife Maureen about the same issue, adding for good measure that 'communists have been allowed to insult the Pope on RTÉ'. A weary civil servant in the Department of the Taoiseach batted away another rant from a woman representing a group called Parent Concern: 'She has a bit of a thing about teenage magazines and her criticisms of the Bill are not worth taking seriously.'[82] John Cunningham, writing from the Presbytery in Rathdrum, County Wicklow, warned of Armageddon for the state's largest political party: 'Of course, at the age of 72, I cannot expect to live much longer, but it is possible that I may outlive the Fianna Fáil party which, if it passes this immoral act will sign its own death warrant.'[83] One woman wrote to Jack Lynch on New Year's Eve 1978 to inform him 'my heart is breaking too as the new year rings in and I pray God that the proposed family planning bill will never become a reality'.[84] Others vilified Mary Robinson, who had been active in the Senate since the start of the decade in attempting to legalise contraceptives – 'a descendant of the Protestant Landlord class'[85] – while others insisted Fianna Fáil TDs should have a free vote on the matter.

The two family planning clinics in Dublin saw 25,000 patients in 1978, the year before Minister for Health Charles Haughey's Family Planning Bill that made contraception available to married couples only, once they had a prescription from their doctor.[86] Interestingly, the DPP, Eamon Barnes, informed the AG Tony Hederman in February 1979 that those selling contraceptives were deliberately inviting prosecution, a 'very obvious and blatant attempt to force the constitutional issue in the courts in advance of the proposed legislation, in order, it would appear, to pre-empt the function of the Oireachtas in seeking to strike a legislative balance between the public interest and private rights. If this is so it would not alone be putting the judicial cart before the legislative horse, but would also be an abuse of the criminal process with which I would be very reluctant to co-operate.'[87]

Haughey pointed out in November 1978 that he had consulted widely throughout the year: 'The view generally expressed was that contraceptives should be available only to married couples. Those putting forward this view accepted the difficulty of enforcing a restriction of this nature' and that there would be provision in the legislation for a person with 'conscientious objections to opt out' without detriment to that person's participation otherwise in the health services. He proposed in the bill 'to give equal if not greater emphasis in the legislation to natural as opposed to artificial methods of family planning'.[88] His legislation was, in his own words, not designed to open the 'floodgates', but sought to 'provide an Irish solution to an Irish problem. I have not regarded it as necessary that we should conform to the position obtaining in any other country.'

While most of the attention in relation to contraception and reproductive rights focused on Dublin there were also battles being fought in other regions. Partisans on both sides mobilised in particular as a result of efforts to establish regional family planning services that opened in Cork (1975), Limerick (1976) and, 'after several setbacks', Galway in 1977.[89] Labour senator and UCG lecturer Michael D. Higgins had supported Mary Robinson's 1974 Family Planning Bill, which polarised Galway Corporation. At the end of the following year the Galway Family Planning Association was founded. Its first meeting attracted, according to one local newspaper, about a hundred 'youngish people' with men 'sporting fine beards' and 'ladies looking friendly and idealistic'. But it was difficult to find a premises for the association, so it opted for a stop-gap postal service in 1977 (the same year that Brendan Corish wrote to the chairman of Fine Gael to bemoan the failure to reach all-party consensus on the issue of legislating for contraception even though he believed 'the present law in relation to contraception is unsatisfactory and riddled with anomalies'[90]). The parents of one member of the Galway group were visited by a priest who advised them that their son 'was spreading VD all over Connacht'. Michael D. Higgins blamed his failure to be elected to the Dáil in 1977 on an anti-contraception group who, by subterfuge, acquired his canvassing schedule and sabotaged his campaign by distributing their message in estates and villages shortly before he was due to arrive.[91] London was also of relevance to the choices some women were making about pregnancy; a House of Commons written reply in November 1972, for example, disclosed that, in 1971, 577 women from the Republic had legal abortions in England and Wales, more than twice as many as in 1970.

Socially and culturally, blatant discriminations against women continued but were vociferously confronted by many of the activists who emerged in these years as the women's movement evolved into a broad-based social movement and by 1979 the first Irish Pregnancy Counselling Centre was in operation. But the movement also broached cultural issues, focusing on feminist fiction, poetry and music, and the abundance of feminist periodicals today are a permanent reminder of the level of activism. These also gave many women experience in community projects and the techniques involved in journalism and publication that led some into successful careers in the arts, publishing and broadcasting fields.[92]

Irish womanhood may have been celebrated in genteel and patronising terms at the annual Rose of Tralee Festival in County Kerry, but there was a parallel robustness in challenges to male preserves. The cover of *Banshee*, the journal of Irishwomen United, documented the invasion by women of the Forty Foot all-male bathing area in Sandycove in County Dublin in 1976, accompanied by a banner that exclaimed 'In Ireland private property means men's property'.[93] Nell McCafferty and others protested against the pubs that would still not serve women, including one that would, but not with pints of beer. She ordered thirty-one brandies and one pint for a group of women and then refused to pay when she was not served the pint.[94] The cover of *Wicca,* another Irish feminist publication, declared defiantly and confidently in 1978:

I swear it to you
I swear on my common woman's head
The common woman is as common
As a common loaf of bread . . .
And will rise.[95]

But in rising in the 1970s, Irish feminists were facing a 1980s that would, in many respects, seek to vehemently push them back down. The extent of that backlash, which included divisive referenda over abortion and divorce, rows over contraception and a determination to resist or delay further advances towards equality, is another reminder of the complexity of the 1970s legacy and the extent to which there was a significant ambiguity about change and its consequences. As has been highlighted, this was not just true in relation to the status of women; it was relevant to a whole host of social, economic, cultural and political themes.

At the time of writing, Ireland faces an unprecedented crisis after the collapse of its banking system, its need for international assistance to stave off national bankruptcy resulting in significant loss of sovereignty. Fianna Fáil's historic dominance has been brought to a crushing end following the general election of 2011. Questions are being raised about the betrayal of the ideals of the revolutionary War of Independence generation. Public confidence in the Catholic Church is at a low ebb as the extent of its failings regarding the protection of children are relentlessly exposed. Tribunal and Commission reports into political and religious culture have exposed corruption, venality and abuse of power that stretch back decades. A multitude of questions are being asked about governance, authority, morality and identity and the degree of complicity of Irish citizens in tolerating poor leadership and turning blind eyes. In early 2012, the letters page of the *Irish Times* was filled with indignation – much justified – about the failure to introduce promised reform in local government, the welfare of abused children, plans for a new children's hospital, secularism in schools, financial crisis, the power of unelected EU officials, treatment of mental illness, protection of the environment and unanswered questions about a murder in Northern Ireland.[96] What such observations highlight is that questions, or versions of them, that had first been aired in the 1970s cast a long shadow that the Irish Republic continues to live under.

BIBLIOGRAPHY

Archives

National Archives of Ireland (NAI)

Department of the Taoiseach

Papers of Liam Cosgrave

Papers of Jack Lynch

University College Dublin Archives, School of History and Archives (UCDA)

Papers of Garret FitzGerald

Papers of John Kelly

Papers of Cearbhall Ó Dálaigh

Papers of Patrick Cosgrave

Papers of the Irish Council of the European Movement

Papers of John de Courcy Ireland

Papers of the Fianna Fáil Party

Dublin Diocesan Archives (DDA)

Papers of Archbishop John Charles McQuaid

Official Publications

Annual Reports of the Department of Local Government

Annual Reports of the Garda Commissioner

Annual Reports on Prisons

The Ferns Report: Presented to the Minister for Health and Children (2005)

Official Reports of the Debates of Dáil Éireann, 1969–1981

Official Reports of the Debates of Seanad Éireann, 1969–1981

Reports of the Law Reform Commission

Report of the Commission to Inquire into Child Abuse (2009)

Newspapers

Belfast Telegraph
Cork Examiner
Daily Telegraph
Economist
Education Times
Evening Herald
Evening Press
Guardian
Irish Catholic
Irish Examiner
Irish Independent
Irish Press
Irish Times
New York Times
Sunday Business Post
Sunday Independent
Sunday Tribune
Sunday World
The Times (London)

Periodicals, Magazines and Academic Journals

Administration
Atlantis
Capuchin Annual
Christus Rex
Crane Bag
Doctrine and Life
Dublin Review
Economic and Social Review
Fortnight
Furrow
Garda Review
Hermathena
Hibernia
History Ireland
Hot Press
Irish Archives
Irish Historical Studies
Irish Jurist
Irish Studies in International Affairs
Irish Studies Review
Irish University Review
Journal of the Social and Statistical Inquiry Society of Ireland

Magill
Maynooth Review
Social Studies
Studies
Village

Television

Seven Ages: The Story of the Irish State: The 1970s: A Decade of Terror, Tension and Transformation, an Araby production for RTÉ in association with BBC Northern Ireland and directed by Seán O Mórdha, Dublin 2001

Books, Academic and Newspaper articles and Chapters

Acton, Charles, *Irish Music and Musicians* (Dublin, 1978)
Ahern, Bertie and Richard Aldous, *Bertie Ahern: The Autobiography* (London, 2009)
Andrews, David, *Kingstown Republican* (Dublin, 2007)
Andrews, Paul, 'Ireland and the World Educational Crisis', *Studies*, vol. 9, Winter 1970, pp. 381–4
Asmal, Kader, *Irish Opposition to Apartheid* (Dublin, 1971)
Bacik, Ivana, 'Tales of an Outspoken Woman', *Irish Times* 27 November 2004
Barrington, Thomas, 'Is There a Future for the District?', *Administration*, vol. 19, no. 4, Winter 1971, pp. 219–318
Barrington, Thomas, 'Organising for Development', *Administration*, vol. 21, no. 1, Spring 1973, pp. 3–15
Barrington, Thomas, *From Big Government to Local Government: The Road to Decentralisation* (Dublin, 1975)
Bax, Mart, *Harpstrings and Confessions: Machine-style Politics in the Irish Republic* (Assen, 1976)
Beausang, Ita, 'Aloys Fleischmann', in McGuire and Quinn, *DIB*, vol. 3, pp. 1012–14
Benson, Ciarán, *The Place of the Arts in Irish Education* (Dublin, Arts Council, 1979)
Bew, Paul, *Ireland: The Politics of Enmity, 1789–2006* (Oxford, 2007)
Blayney, R., 'Alcoholism in Ireland: Medical and Social Aspects', *Social and Statistical Inquiry Society of Ireland*, vol. 23, part 1, 1973–4, pp. 108–25
Boran, Pat, *The Invisible Prison* (Dublin, 2009)
Bowman, John, 'How Jack Lynch Helped Lay the Foundations for Powersharing in the North', *Irish Times*, 1 January 2003
Bowman, John, *Window and Mirror: RTÉ Television: 1961–2011* (Dublin, 2011)
Boyd, Brian, 'How Ballymagash Became Part of Folk Culture', *Irish Times*, 4 December 2004
Boyle, Denis, 'James Tully', in McGuire and Quinn, *DIB*, vol. 9, pp. 514–15
Boyne, Seán, *The Gunrunners* (Dublin, 2006)
Bradley, John, 'The Legacy of Economic Development: The Irish Economy, 1960–87', in John F. McCarthy (ed.), *Planning Ireland's Future: The Legacy of T. K. Whitaker* (Dublin, 1990), pp. 128–50
Brady, Conor, 'Inside Story', *Garda Review*, vol. 2, no. 1, January 1974, pp. 10–15

Brady, Conor, *Up with the Times* (Dublin, 2005)
Brady, John, 'The Economics of Survival', *Social Studies*, vol. 5, no. 1, Spring 1976, pp. 3–26
Brady, John, 'Ireland in Transition', *Studies*, vol. 67, Spring/Summer 1978, pp. 1–2
Bray, Philip, with Anthony Galvin: *Inside Man: Life as an Irish Prison Officer* (Dublin, 2008)
Brennan, Pat, 'The Women's Movement in Ireland', *Magill*, April 1979
Brennan, Peter, *Behind Closed Doors: The EU Negotiations that Shaped Modern Ireland* (Dublin, 2008)
Brody, Hugh, *Inishkillane: Change and Decline in the West of Ireland* (London, 1973)
Brown, Terence, 'Dublin in Twentieth Century Writing: Metaphor and Subject', *Irish University Review*, vol. 8, no. 1, Spring 1978, pp. 7–22
Brown, Terence, *Ireland: A Social and Cultural History, 1922–2002* (London, 2004; first published in 1981 as *Ireland: A Social and Cultural History, 1922–1979*)
Browne, Ivor, *Music and Madness* (Cork, 2008)
Browne, Maureen (ed.), *Irish Medical Times 1967–1992: 25 Years Ahead* (Dublin, 1992)
Browne, Vincent, 'The Artful Ambiguities of Jack Lynch', *Magill*, October 1977
Browne, Vincent, 'The Arms Trial', *Magill*, May 1980
Browne, Vincent (ed.), *The Magill Book of Irish Politics* (Dublin, 1981)
Bryson, Anna, *No Cowardly Soul: Thekla Beere – A Biography* (Dublin, 2009)
Burke, Helen and Olivia O'Leary, *Mary Robinson: The Authorised Biography* (London, 1998)
Butterfield, Peter, 'The Crisis of Authority Within the Church', *The Furrow*, vol. 22, no. 8, August 1971, pp. 466–71
Byrne, Gabriel, *Pictures in My Head* (Dublin, 1994)
Caldicott, C. E. J., 'Owen Sheehy Skeffington', in McGuire and Quinn, *DIB*, vol. 8, pp. 86–7.
Callanan, Frank (ed.), *The Literary and Historical Society, 1955–2005* (Dublin, 2005)
Carroll, John F. and Petra K. Kelly (eds), *A Nuclear Ireland?* (Dublin, 1978)
Carty, R. K., 'Women in Irish Politics', *Canadian Journal of Irish Studies*, vol. 6, 1980, pp. 90–104
Castle, Tony, 'The Priest in Youth Work', *The Furrow*, vol. 22, no. 2, February 1971, pp. 87–93
Chafe, William H. (ed.), *A History of Our Time: Readings on Postwar America* (Oxford, 1991)
Chubb, Basil, *The Government and Politics of Ireland* (Dublin, 1970)
Clancy, Patrick, Sheelagh Drudy, Kathleen Lynch and Liam O'Dowd (eds), *Ireland: A Sociological Profile* (Dublin, 1986)
Clark, Heather, *The Ulster Renaissance: Poetry in Belfast, 1962–1972* (Oxford, 2006)
Clarke, Aidan, 'Robert Walter Dudley Edwards and a Decade of Archival Achievements', *Irish Archives*, vol. 1, no. 1, 1989, pp. 5–15
Clarke, Peter, *Hope and Glory: Britain 1900–1990* (London, 1996)
Clarke, Sarah, *No Faith in the System* (Cork, 1995)

Clifford, Dermot, 'The Image of the Bishop', *The Furrow*, vol. 22, no. 8, August 1971, pp. 46–66
Clifford, Michael and Shane Coleman, *Bertie Ahern and the Drumcondra Mafia* (Dublin, 2009)
Clutterback, Catríona (ed.), 'Thomas Kinsella', *Irish University Review* Special Issue, vol. 31, no. 1, Spring/Summer 2001
Coleman, Marie, *The Irish Sweep: A History of the Irish Hospitals Sweepstake* (Dublin, 2009)
Collins, Stephen, *The Cosgrave Legacy* (Dublin, 1996)
Collins, Stephen, *The Power Game: Fianna Fáil Since Lemass* (Dublin, 2000)
Collins, Stephen, *The Power Game: Ireland under Fianna Fáil* (Dublin, 2001)
Connolly, Colm, *Siege! Monasterevin* (Dublin, 1976)
Connolly, Frank and Ronan Lynch, *The Great Corrib Gas Controversy* (Dublin, 2005)
Connolly, Linda, *The Irish Women's Movement: From Revolution to Devolution* (Dublin, 2003)
Connolly, Linda and Niamh Hourigan, *Social Movements and Ireland* (Manchester, 2006)
Connolly, Linda and Tina O'Toole, *Documenting Irish Feminisms: The Second Wave* (Dublin, 2005)
Coogan, Tim Pat, *A Memoir* (London, 2009)
Coolahan, John, *Irish Education: Its History and Structure* (Dublin, 1981)
Corcoran, Mary and Mark O'Brien (eds), *Political Censorship and the Democratic State: The Irish Broadcasting Ban* (Dublin, 2005)
Corish, Patrick. J., *Maynooth College, 1795–1995* (Dublin, 1994)
Cosgrove, Art, 'Francis Xavier Martin', in McGuire and Quinn, *DIB*, vol. 6, pp. 383–4
Cox, Gareth, 'Charles Acton', in McGuire and Quinn, *DIB*, vol. 1, pp. 14–15
Crawford, Heather, *Outside the Glow: Protestants and Irishness in Independent Ireland* (Dublin, 2010)
Cronin, Mike, *Doesn't Time Fly? Aer Lingus: Its History* (Cork, 2011)
Cronin, Mike, Mark Duncan and Paul Rouse (eds), *The GAA: A People's History* (Cork, 2009)
Cronin, Mike, William Murphy and Paul Rouse (eds), *The Gaelic Athletic Association, 1884–2009* (Dublin, 2009)
Cronin, Seán, *Washington's Irish Policy, 1916–1986* (Dublin, 1987)
Crotty, Patrick, *The Penguin Book of Irish Poetry* (London, 2010)
Crotty, Raymond, *Ireland and the Common Market* (Dublin, 1971)
Crotty, William and David E. Schmitt (eds), *Ireland on the World Stage* (London, 2002)
Crowe, Catríona, 'On the Ferns Report', *Dublin Review*, no. 22, Spring 2006, pp. 5–26
Cruise O'Brien, Conor, *States of Ireland* (London, 1972)
Cruise O'Brien, Conor, *Memoir: My Life and Themes* (Dublin, 2009)
Crummey, Frank, *Crummey v. Ireland* (Dublin, 2010)
Cullen, Louis, *An Economic History of Ireland Since 1660* (London, 1972)
Cunningham, John, *Unlikely Radicals: The Irish Post-Primary Teachers and the ASTI, 1909–2009* (Cork, 2009)

Cunningham, John, 'Spreading VD all over Connacht: Reproductive Rights and Wrongs in 1970s Galway', *History Ireland*, March/April 2011, pp. 44–7
Currie, Austin, *All Hell Will Break Loose* (Dublin, 2004)
Curtin, Chris, Hastings Donnan and Thomas M. Wilson (eds), *Irish Urban Cultures* (Belfast, 1993)
Daly, Mary, *The Buffer State: The Historical Roots of the Department of the Environment* (Dublin, 1997)
Daly, Mary, *The Spirit of Earnest Inquiry: The Statistical and Social Inquiry Society of Ireland* (Dublin, 1997)
de Courcy Ireland, John, *Ireland's European Traditions: The Historical Case Against the Common Market* (Dublin, 1970)
de Paor, Liam, 'The Ambiguity of the Republic', *Atlantis*, no. 3, November 1971
de Paor, Liam, 'Ireland's Identities', *Crane Bag*, vol. 3 no. 1, 1979, pp. 22–9
DeGroot, Gerard, *The Seventies Unplugged: A Kaleidoscopic Look at a Violent Decade* (London, 2010)
Delaney, Eamon, *Breaking the Mould: The Story of Art and Ireland* (Dublin, 2009)
Delaney, Enda, *Irish Emigration Since 1921* (Dublin, 2002)
Dempsey, Pauric, J. and Lawrence William White, 'Erskine Childers', in McGuire and Quinn, *DIB*, vol. 2, pp. 498–501
Department of Foreign Affairs, *Into Europe: Ireland and the EEC* (Dublin, 1972)
Desmond, Barry, 'The Houses of the Oireachtas: A Plea for Reform', *Administration*, vol. 23, no. 4, 1975, pp. 423–44
Desmond, Barry, *Finally and in Conclusion: A Political Memoir* (Dublin, 2000)
Devitt, John, *Shifting Scenes: Irish Theatre-going, 1955–1985* (Dublin, 2008)
Dixon, Paul, 'Northern Ireland and the International Dimension: The End of the Cold War, the USA and European Integration', *Irish Studies in International Affairs*, vol. 13, 2002, pp. 105–20
Donoghue, Denis, *Irish Essays* (Cambridge, 2011)
Dorr, Noel, *Ireland at the UN: Memories of the Early Years* (Dublin, 2010)
Downey, James, *Them and Us* (Dublin, 1983)
Downey, James, *In My Own Time: Inside Irish Politics and Society* (Dublin, 2009)
Dudley Edwards, Robert, 'An Agenda for Irish History, 1978–2018', *Irish Historical Studies*, vol. 21, no. 81, March 1978, pp. 3–20
Duncan, W. R., 'Supporting the Institution of Marriage in Ireland', *Irish Jurist*, vol. 13, 1978, pp. 215–32
Dunlop, Frank, *Yes Taoiseach: Irish Politics from Behind Closed Doors* (Dublin, 2004)
Dunne, Derek and Gene Kerrigan, *Round Up the Usual Suspects* (Dublin, 1984)
Durcan, Paul, *A Snail in My Prime: New and Selected Poems* (London, 1993)
English, Richard, *Armed Struggle: A History of the IRA* (London, 2003)
Fanning, Bryan, *The Quest for Modern Ireland: The Battle of Ideas, 1912–1986* (Dublin, 2008)
Fanning, Ronan, 'Jack Lynch', in McGuire and Quinn, *DIB*, vol. 5, pp. 630–41
Farmar, Tony, *Believing in Action* (Dublin, 2002)

Farrell, Brian, 'Dáil Deputies: The 1969 Generation', *Economic and Social Review*, vol. 2, 1970–71, pp. 309–27

Farrell, Brian, Robert Fisk and P. N. Ferns, *A One Day Symposium on 'The British Question' Erroneously Called 'The Irish Question', the Effect of Violence and Why Conservation Matters* (Pontypridd, 1978)

Farren, Seán, *The SDLP: The Struggle for Agreement in Northern Ireland 1970–2000* (Dublin, 2010)

Faulkner, Brian, *Memoirs of a Statesman* (London, 1978)

Faulkner, Pádraig, *As I Saw It* (Dublin, 2005)

Fennell, Nuala, *Political Woman: A Memoir* (Dublin, 2009)

Ferriter, Diarmaid, *Mothers, Maidens and Myths: A History of the ICA* (Dublin, 1995)

Ferriter, Diarmaid, *A Nation of Extremes: The Pioneers in Twentieth Century Ireland* (Dublin, 1999)

Ferriter, Diarmaid, *Lovers of Liberty? Local Government in Twentieth Century Ireland* (Dublin, 2001)

Ferriter, Diarmaid, *The Transformation of Ireland, 1900–2000* (2nd edn, London, 2005)

Ferriter, Diarmaid, 'Commemorating the Rising, 1922–65', in Mary Daly and Margaret O'Callaghan (eds), *1916 in 1966: Commemorating the Rising* (Dublin, 2007), pp. 198–218

Ferriter, Diarmaid, *Judging Dev: A Reassessment of the Life and Legacy of Eamon de Valera* (Dublin, 2007)

Ferriter, Diarmaid, *What If? Alternative Views of Twentieth Century Ireland* (Dublin, 2007)

Ferriter, Diarmaid, *Occasions of Sin: Sex and Society in Modern Ireland* (2nd edn, London, 2012)

Ferriter, Diarmaid and Patrick Maume, 'William Fox', in McGuire and Quinn, *DIB*, vol. 3, pp. 1086–7

Finnegan, Richard and James Wiles, *Women and Public Policy in Ireland: A Documentary History, 1922–1997* (Dublin, 2005)

FitzGerald, Garret, *Towards a New Ireland* (London, 1972)

FitzGerald, Garret, *All in a Life: An Autobiography* (Dublin, 1991)

FitzGerald, Garret, 'The Threat of a British Withdrawal from Northern Ireland in the mid 1970s', *Irish Studies in International Affairs*, vol. 17, 2006, pp. 141–50

Fitzpatrick, David, *Politics and Irish Life, 1913–21: Provincial Experience of War and Revolution* (Dublin, 1977)

Fitz-Simon, Christopher, *The Boys* (Dublin, 1994)

Foley, Dermot, 'A Minstrel Boy with a Satchel of Books', *Irish University Review*, vol. 4, no. 2, Autumn 1974, pp. 204–18

Forde, Walter, 'Religious and Social Change in Contemporary Ireland', *Christus Rex*, vol. 23, no. 1, January 1969, pp. 21–8

Foster, Roy, *Luck and the Irish: A Brief History of Change* (London, 2007)

Foster, Roy, 'Turbulent Times in Front Square', *Irish Times*, 19 November 2011

Fulbrook, Mary (ed.), *Twentieth Century Germany: Politics, Culture and Society* (London, 2001)

Fuller, Louise, *Irish Catholicism Since 1950: The Undoing of a Culture* (Dublin, 2002)
Gaffney, David, 'The Priest in the Year 2000', *Doctrine and Life*, vol. 21, no. 6, June 1971, pp. 308–16
Galligan, Yvonne, 'Women in Politics', in John Coakely and Michael Gallagher (eds), *Politics in the Republic of Ireland* (4 edn, Dublin, 2005), pp. 272–97
Gardiner, Frances, 'The Women's Movement and Politicians in the Republic, 1980–2000', in A. Bourke et al. (eds), *The Field Day Anthology of Irish Writing*, vol. 5, *Irish Women's Writing and Traditions* (Cork, 2002), pp. 228–37
Garratt, Robert, *Trauma and History in the Irish Novel* (London, 2011)
Garvin, Tom, 'The Strange Death of Clerical Politics at UCD', *Irish University Review*, vol. 28, no. 2, Autumn/Winter 1998, pp. 308–15
Garvin, Tom, *Preventing the Future: Why Was Ireland so Poor for so Long?* (Dublin, 2004)
Geldof, Bob, *Is That It?* (London, 1986)
Geraghty, Des, *Luke Kelly: A Memoir* (Dublin, 1994)
Gilfillan, Kathy (ed.), *Trinity Tales: Trinity College Dublin in the Seventies* (Dublin, 2011)
Gillespie, Gordon, *A Short History of the Troubles* (Dublin, 2010)
Gilligan, Robbie, *Tony Gregory* (Dublin, 2011)
Girvin, Brian, 'Church, State and Society in Ireland Since 1960', *Eire-Ireland*, vol. 43, nos 1&2, Spring/Summer 2008, pp. 74–99
Gogan, Brian, 'Continuing Education in a Changing World', *The Furrow*, vol. 26, no. 5, May 1975, pp. 270–83
Grene, Nicholas (ed.), *Talking about Tom Murphy* (Dublin, 2002)
Gunnigle, Patrick, Gerard McMahon and Joseph Wallace, *Industrial Relations in Ireland* (Dublin, 2004)
Hamilton, Timothy, 'The Upholding of Values in a Pluralist Society', *Studies*, vol. 67, Spring/Summer 1978, pp. 5–13
Hand, Derek, *A History of the Irish Novel* (Cambridge, 2011)
Hanley, Brian, 'The Politics of NORAID', *Irish Political Studies*, vol. 19, no. 1, Summer 2004, pp. 1–18
Hanley, Brian and Scott Millar, *The Lost Revolution: The Story of the Official IRA and the Workers Party* (Dublin, 2009)
Hannan, Damian, 'Kinship, Neighbourhood and Social Change in Irish Rural Communities', *Economic and Social Review*, vol. 3, 1971–2, pp. 163–88
Harmon, Maurice, *Seán O'Faoláin* (London, 1994)
Hart, Ian, 'The Rise in Irish Crime', *Garda Review*, vol. 2, no. 1, January 1974, pp. 10–13
Harte, Liam and Yvonne Whelan (eds), *Ireland Beyond Boundaries: Mapping Irish Studies in the Twenty First Century* (Dublin, 2007)
Harte, Paddy, *Young Tigers and Mongrel Foxes* (Dublin, 2005)
Hayes McCoy, G. A., 'Museums and Our National Heritage', *Capuchin Annual*, 1971, pp. 128–36
Hayward, Kathy, *Irish Nationalism and European Integration: The Official Redefinition of the Island of Ireland* (Manchester, 2009)

Healy, John, *Death of an Irish Town* (Cork, 1968)
Healy, John, *Nineteen Acres* (Mayo, 1978)
Hederman O'Brien, Miriam, *The Road to Europe: Irish Attitudes 1948–61* (Dublin, 1983)
Heffernan, Thomas, *Wood Quay: The Clash over Dublin's Viking Past* (Austin, 1988)
Hennessey, Thomas, *Northern Ireland: The Origins of the Troubles* (Dublin, 2005)
Hennessey, Thomas, *The Evolution of the Troubles 1970–72* (Dublin, 2007)
Higgins, Michael D., *Causes for Concern: Irish Politics, Culture and Society* (Dublin, 2006)
Higgins, Roisín and Regina Ui Chollatain, *The Life and After Life of P. H. Pearse* (Dublin, 2009)
Hill, Myrtle, *Women in Ireland: A Century of Change* (Belfast, 2003)
Hogan, Desmond, *The Edge of the City: A Scrapbook 1976–91* (Dublin, 1993)
Hogan, Edmund, *The Irish Missionary Movement: A Historical Survey, 1830–1980* (Dublin, 1990)
Hogan, Gerard, 'John Joseph Kenny', in McGuire and Quinn, *DIB*, vol. 5, pp. 131–3
Holland, Mary, 'Eye on the Twentieth Century: Ireland 1970–79', *Irish Times*, 9 November 1999
Holland, Mary, *How Far We Have Travelled: The Voice of Mary Holland* (Dublin, 2004)
Holmes, Michael, 'The Irish Labour Party: The Advantages, Disadvantages and Irrelevance of Europeanization?', *Irish Political Studies*, vol. 24, no. 4, December 2007, pp. 527–41
Horgan, John, *Noel Browne: Passionate Outsider* (Dublin, 1998)
Horgan, John, *The Irish Media: A Critical History Since 1922* (London, 2001)
Hourican, Bridget, 'Dermot Joseph Ryan', in McGuire and Quinn, *DIB*, vol. 8, pp. 680–83
Humphries, Tom, *Dublin Versus Kerry: The Story of the Epic Rivalry that Changed Irish Sport* (Dublin, 2006)
Hutchinson, Bertram, 'On the Study of Non-economic Factors in Irish Economic Development', *Economic and Social Review*, vol. 1, no. 1, 1969–70, pp. 509–28
Hyde, Douglas, 'Warts on the Face of Ireland', *Doctrine and Life*, vol. 21, no. 8, August 1971, pp. 429–38
Jackson, Alvin, *Ireland, 1798–1998* (Oxford, 1999)
Johnson, Paul (ed.): *Twentieth Century Britain: Economic, Social and Cultural Change* (London, 1994)
Judt, Tony, *Postwar: A History of Europe Since 1945* (London, 2005)
Kearney, Noreen and Caroline Skehill, *Social Work in Ireland: Historical Perspectives* (Dublin, 2005)
Kearney, Richard, *Navigations: Collected Irish Essays: 1976–2006* (Dublin, 2006)
Keatinge, Patrick, *The Formulation of Irish Foreign Policy* (Dublin, 1973)
Kelly, Adrian, *Compulsory Irish: Language and Education in Ireland, 1870s–1970s* (Dublin, 2002)
Kelly, Captain James, *Orders for the Captain* (Dublin, 1971)
Kelly, Captain James, *The Thimbleriggers* (Dublin, 1999)
Kelly, James (ed.), *St Patrick's College, Drumcondra: A History* (Dublin, 2006)

Kelly, John, *The Irish Constitution* (Dublin, 1980)

Kennedy, Brian P., *Dreams and Responsibilities: The State and the Arts in Independent Ireland* (Dublin, 1990)

Kennedy, Finola, *Cottage to Creche: Family Change in Ireland* (Dublin, 2001)

Kennedy, Kieran and Richard Bruton, *The Irish Economy* (Brussels, 1975)

Kennedy, Michael, *Division and Consensus: The Politics of Cross-Border Relations in Ireland, 1925–69* (Dublin, 2000)

Kennedy, Michael, '"This tragic and most intractable problem": The Reaction of the Department of External Affairs to the Outbreak of the Troubles in Northern Ireland', *Irish Studies in International Affairs*, vol. 12, 2001, pp. 87–97

Kennedy, Michael and Deirdre McMahon (eds), *Obligations and Responsibilities: Ireland and the UN, 1955–2005* (Dublin, 2005)

Kennedy, Michael and Joseph Morrison Skelly (eds), *Irish Foreign Policy 1919–66: From Independence to Internationalism* (Dublin, 2000)

Kenny, Colum, *Moments that Changed Us* (Dublin, 2005)

Kenny, Ivor, *Talking to Journalists: Conversations with Editors of the Irish News Media* (Galway, 1994)

Kenny, John, *John Banville* (Dublin, 2009)

Kenny, Mary, *Goodbye to Catholic Ireland* (Dublin, 2000)

Kent, M. P. and J. J. Sexton, 'The Influence of Certain Social Factors on the Physical Growth and Development of a Group of Dublin City Children', *Journal of the Social and Statistical Inquiry Society of Ireland*, vol. 22, part 5, 1972–3, pp. 188–206

Keogh, Dermot, *Jack Lynch: A Biography* (Dublin, 2008)

Kerrigan, Gene and Derek Dunne, *Round Up The Usual Suspects* (Dublin, 1984)

Kiberd, Declan, 'Writers in Quarantine? The Case for Irish Studies', *Crane Bag*, vol. 13, no. 1, 1979, pp. 17–21

Kiberd, Declan, *Inventing Ireland: The Literature of the Modern Nation* (London, 1995)

Kinsella, Patrick, 'War and Peace on the Screen: Television Representations of Conflict in Ireland', in John Horgan, Barbara O'Connor and Helen Sheehan (eds), *Mapping Irish Media: Critical Explorations* (Dublin, 2007), pp. 95–111.

Kinsella, R. P., 'The Health Sector and Resource Allocation', *Administration*, vol. 21, no. 4, 1973, pp. 150–60

Kinsella, Thomas, *Butcher's Dozen* (Dublin, 1972)

Laatikainen, Katie Verlin and Karen E. Smith, *The EU at the UN* (New York, 2006)

Laffan, Brigid and Jane O'Mahony, *Ireland and the European Union* (New York, 2008)

Laffan, Michael, 'The Sinn Féin Party', *Capuchin Annual*, 1970, pp. 227–35

Lavery, Don, 'A Thundering Disgrace', in 'Rolling Back the Years, 1975–1979', *Irish Independent* Supplement, 29 October 2011

Lee, Joe, *Reflections on Ireland in the EEC* (Dublin, 1984)

Lee, Joe, *Ireland: Politics and Society, 1912–1985* (Cambridge, 1989)

Leonard, Liam, *Green Nation: The Irish Environmental Movement from Carnsore Point to the Rossport 5* (Louth, 2006)

Levine, June, 'The Women's Movement in the Republic', in Angela Bourke et al. (eds), *The Field Day Anthology of Irish Writing*, vol. 5, *Irish Women's Writing and Traditions* (Cork, 2002)

Longley, Michael, *Tuppenny Stung: Autobiographical Chapters* (Belfast, 1994)

Lyons, F. S. L., *Ireland Since the Famine* (London, 1971)

Lyons, F. S. L., 'The Dilemma of the Irish Contemporary Historian', *Hermathena*, no. 115, Summer 1973, pp. 45–57

McAleese, Dermot, 'European Integration and the Irish Economy', in Cormac O'Gráda (ed.), *The Economic Development of Ireland Since 1870, Volume II* (Aldershot, 1994), pp. 76–96

MacAnthony, Joe, 'Where the Sweep Millions Go', *Sunday Independent*, 21 January 1973

Mac Bride, Ian (ed.), *History and Memory in Modern Ireland* (Cambridge, 2001)

McCafferty, Nell, *Nell* (Dublin, 2004)

McCann, Eamonn, 'Bloody Sunday Helped Reconcile Southern Nationalists to Partition', *Irish Times*, 28 January 2012

McCarthy, Charles, *The Distasteful Challenge* (Dublin, 1968)

McCarthy, Charles, 'Workers' Participation in Management', *Journal of the Social and Statistical Inquiry Society of Ireland*, vol. 22, part 2, 1970–71, pp. 2–38

McCarthy, Charles, 'The Function of National Pay Agreements', *Administration*, vol. 22, no. 1, 1974, pp. 60–72

McCarthy, Conor, *Irish Modernisation: Crisis and Culture in Ireland, 1969–1992* (Dublin, 2000)

McCartney, Donal, 'The Quest for Irish Political Identity: The Image and the Illusion', *Irish University Review*, vol. 9, no. 1, Spring 1979, pp. 13–21

McCartney, Donal, *UCD: A National Idea: The History of University College Dublin* (Dublin, 1999)

McCormick, James S, 'Medicine and Society', *Hermathena*, no. 122, Summer 1977, pp. 5–14

McCrann, Aibhlín, *Memories, Milestones and New Horizons: Reflections on the Regeneration of Ballymun* (Belfast, 2008)

Mac Curtain, Margaret (Sr Benvenuta), 'Education: A Church–State Problem in Twentieth Century Ireland', *The Furrow*, vol. 24, no. 1, January 1973, pp. 3–13

Mac Curtain, Margaret, 'Women: Irish Style', *Doctrine and Life*, vol. 24, no. 4, April 1974, pp. 182–98

Mac Curtain, Margaret, *Ariadne's Thread: Writing Women into Irish History* (Dublin, 2008)

Mac Curtain, Margaret and Donnchadh Ó Corráin (eds), *Women in Irish Society: The Historical Dimension* (Dublin, 1978)

McDaid, Shaun, 'The David Thornley Affair', in Caoimhe Nic Dháibhéid and Colin Reid (eds), *From Parnell to Paisley: Constitutional and Revolutionary Politics in Modern Ireland* (Dublin, 2010), pp. 182–200

McDiarmid, Lucy, 'The Posthumous Life of Roger Casement', in Maryann Valiulis and Anthony Bradley (eds), *Gender and Sexuality in Modern Ireland* (Amherst, 1997), pp. 127–59

McDonagh, Enda, 'Why Do They Leave?' *The Furrow*, vol. 26, no. 11, November 1975, pp. 652–68
McDonald, Henry and Jim Cusack, *UDA: Inside the Heart of Loyalist Terror* (London, 2004)
Mhac an tSaoi, Máire, *The Same Age as the State* (Dublin, 2003)
McGahern, John, *Memoir* (London, 2005)
McGarry, Patsy, *While Justice Slept: The True Story of Nicky Kelly and the Sallins Train Robbery* (Dublin, 2007)
McGowan, Brendan, *Taking the Boat: The Irish in Leeds, 1931–81* (Mayo, 2009)
Mac Gréil, Mícheál, *Prejudice and Tolerance in Ireland* (Dublin, 1977)
Mac Gréil, Mícheál and Micheál Ó Glasáin, 'Church Attendance and Religious Practice of Dublin Adults', *Social Studies*, vol. 3, no. 2, April 1974, pp. 163–213
McGuire, James and James Quinn (eds), *Dictionary of Irish Biography: From the Earliest Times to the Year 2002* (Cambridge, 2009)
MacIntyre, Tom, *Through the Bridewell Gate* (Dublin, 1971)
McKay, Susan, *Without Fear: 25 Years of the Dublin Rape Crisis Centre* (Dublin, 2005)
McKay, Susan, *Bear in Mind These Dead* (London, 2008)
McKittrick, David (ed.), *Lost Lives* (Edinburgh, 2001)
McLoughlin, Patrick, 'The Policeman, the Criminal and the Law', *Garda Review*, vol. 2, no. 6, June 1974, pp. 10–15
McMahon, Deirdre, 'Robert Dudley Edwards (1909–1988) and Irish Archives', *Irish Archives*, vol. 17, no. 21, 2010, pp. 1–14
McMillan, James F., *Twentieth Century France: Politics and Society 1898–1991* (London, 1992)
McNiffe, Liam, *A History of the Garda Síochána* (Dublin, 1997)
MacRéamoinn, Seán, *Towards a Church Re-attuned to Spirit: The Church in a New Ireland* (Dublin, 1996)
Madden, Aodhan, *Fear and Loathing in Dublin* (Dublin, 2009)
Maher, Mary, 'Women's Liberation', *Doctrine and Life*, vol. 21, no. 8, September 1971, pp. 457–65
Mahon, Derek, *Journalism: Selected Prose, 1970–1995* (Meath, 1996)
Mair, Peter, *The Changing Irish Party System* (London, 1987)
Malcolm, Elizabeth, *Swift's Hospital: A History of St Patrick's Hospital, Dublin, 1746–1989* (Dublin, 1989)
Matthews, Alan, 'The State of Irish Agriculture', *Magill*, May 1978
Maume, Patrick, 'Neil Blayney', in McGuire and Quinn, *DIB*, vol. 1, pp. 597–603
Maume, Patrick, 'George Colley', in McGuire and Quinn, *DIB*, vol. 2, p. 668
Maume, Patrick, 'James Gibbons', in McGuire and Quinn, *DIB*, vol. 4, pp. 61–3
Maume, Patrick, 'Michael O'Leary', in McGuire and Quinn, *DIB*, online entry added December 2011, www.dib.cambridge.org
Maume, Patrick, 'Frank Stagg', in McGuire and Quinn, *DIB*, vol. 8, pp. 1114–15
Meenan, James, *The Irish Economy Since 1922* (Liverpool, 1970)
Merry, Bruce, 'A Sense of Humour', *Crane Bag*, vol. 1, no. 1, Spring 1977, pp. 4–9
Miller, Rory, *Ireland and the Palestine Question, 1948–2004* (Dublin, 2005)

Mills, Michael, *Hurler on the Ditch: Memoir of a Journalist Who Became Ireland's First Ombudsman* (Dublin, 2005)

Minnis, Ivan, *The Troubles in Northern Ireland* (Oxford, 2001)

Moloney, Ed, 'Inside H Block', *Magill*, December 1979

Moloney, Ed, *A Secret History of the IRA* (London, 2002)

Montague, John, *The Pear is Ripe* (Dublin, 2007)

Moody, T. W., 'Irish History and Irish Mythology', *Hermathena*, no. 124, Summer 1978, pp. 7–25

Moore, Christy, *One Voice: My Life In Song* (London, 2003)

Morash, Christopher, *A History of Irish Theatre, 1601–2000* (Cambridge, 2002)

Morash, Christopher, *A History of the Media in Ireland* (Cambridge, 2010)

Moroney, Michael, *National Teachers' Salaries and Pensions, 1831–2000* (Dublin, 2007)

Mulcahy, D. G. and Denis O'Sullivan (eds), *Irish Educational Policy: Process and Substance* (Dublin, 1989)

Mullan, Don and John Scally, *Eyewitness Bloody Sunday* (Dublin, 2002)

Murphy, Edmund, 'The New Primary School Curriculum', *Studies*, vol. 61, Spring 1972, pp. 199–218

Murphy, Eoin, *Munster Rugby: The Phenomenon* (Meath, 2006)

Murphy, Gary, '"A Measurement of the Extent of Our Sovereignty at the Moment." Sovereignty and the Question of Irish Entry to the EEC: New Evidence from the Archives', *Irish Studies in International Affairs*, vol. 12, 2001, pp. 191–202

Murphy, Gary and Niamh Puirséil, 'Is It a New Alliance? Irish Entry to the EEC and Popular Opinion', *Irish Political Studies*, vol. 23, no. 4, December 2008, pp. 533–53

Murphy, John, 'The Irish Penal System', *Doctrine and Life*, vol. 24, no. 3, March 1974, pp. 144–59

Murphy, John A., 'Priests and People in Modern Irish History', *Christus Rex*, vol. 23, no. 4, October 1969, pp. 221–35

Murphy, John A., 'History in the Classroom', *Education Times*, 30 August 1973

Murphy, John A., *Ireland in the Twentieth Century* (Dublin, 1975)

Murphy, John A., 'Further Reflections on Irish Nationalism', *Crane Bag*, vol. 1, no. 2, 1977, pp. 156–62

Murphy, John A., *The College: A History of Queen's/University College Cork, 1845–1995* (Cork, 1995)

Murphy, William, 'Between Change and Tradition: The Politics and Writing of Garret FitzGerald', *Eire-Ireland*, vol. 43, nos 1&2, Spring/Summer 2008, pp. 154–79

Murray, Christopher, *Alive in Time: The Enduring Drama of Tom Murphy* (Dublin, 2010)

Murray, Christopher (ed.), *Brian Friel: Essays, Diaries and Interviews 1964–1999* (London, 1999)

Neary, Peter, 'The Failure of Economic Nationalism', in *Ireland: Dependence and Independence: The Crane Bag* (Dublin, 1984), pp. 68–77

Nevin, Donal (ed.), *Trade Union Century* (Dublin, 1994)

Newman, Jeremiah, *Balance in the Church* (Dublin, 1980)

Ní Bhrían, Doireann, 'Women and Social Change on Radio', unpublished Thomas Davis Lecture, broadcast on RTÉ Radio 1, May 2001

Nolan, Brian, 'The Personal Distribution of Income in the Republic of Ireland', *Journal of the Social and Statistical Inquiry Society of Ireland*, vol. 23, part 5, 1977–8, pp. 163–217

Nolan, Patrick, 'The Irish Trade Union Movement', *Christus Rex*, vol. 23, no. 1, January 1969, pp. 21–8

Nolan, William, *The GAA in Dublin, 1884–2000: Volume II* (Dublin, 2005)

O'Brien, Carl, *Protecting Civil Liberties: 30 Years of the ICCL* (Dublin, 2006)

O'Brien, Justin, *The Arms Trial* (Dublin, 2000)

O'Brien, Mark, *De Valera, Fianna Fáil and the Irish Press* (Dublin, 2001)

O'Brien, Mark, *The Irish Times: A History* (Dublin, 2008)

Ó Cinnéide, Séamus, 'Power and Its Victims in Ireland', *Studies*, vol. 62, Winter 1972, pp. 355–65

O'Connor, John, 'The Law Reform Commission and the Codification of Irish Law', *Irish Jurist*, vol. 9, 1974, pp. 14–41

O'Connor, Thomas P. and R. W. L. Wilding, 'The Civil Service in the Modern State', *Studies*, vol. 59, Summer 1970, pp. 164–79

O'Connor, Ulick, *The Ulick O'Connor Diaries, 1970–1981: A Cavalier Irishman* (London, 2001)

O'Daly, Niamh, 'Changing Attitudes to Children', *Social Studies*, vol. 27, no. 4, Winter 1979, pp. 475–94

O'Donnell, Catherine, *Fianna Fáil, Irish Republicanism and the Northern Ireland Troubles, 1968–2005* (Dublin, 2007)

O'Dowd, Niall, *An Irish Voice* (Dublin, 2010)

O'Driscoll, Dennis, *Stepping Stones: Interviews with Seamus Heaney* (London, 2008)

O'Faoláin, Nuala, *Are You Somebody?* (Dublin, 1996)

O'Flynn, John, *The Irishness of Irish Music* (Farnham, 2009)

O'Flynn, Mary, 'Prison After Care in the Irish Republic', *Irish Jurist*, vol. 6, 1971, pp. 1–17

Ó hEithir, Breandán, *The Begrudgers Guide to Irish Politics* (Dublin, 1986)

Ó hEithir, Breandán, *Over the Bar* (Dublin, 1991)

O'Leary, Michael, 'Gentle Revolution', *Administration*, vol. 23, no. 1, Spring 1975, pp. 4–7

O'Loughlin, Thomas, Interview with Margaret Mac Curtain, *History Ireland*, vol. 2, no. 1, Spring 1994, pp. 52–4

O'Mahony, T. P., 'Poverty in Ireland', *Doctrine and Life*, vol. 22, no. 1, January 1972, pp. 50–52

O'Mahony, T. P., 'Ireland in 1976: The Pain and the Paradox', *Doctrine and Life*, vol. 26, April 1976, pp. 240–47

O'Malley, Tom, 'Perceptions of Sexual Violence', in Anne Byrne, Jane Conroy and Seán Ryder (eds), *UCG Women's Studies Review*, vol. 2, 1993, pp. 131–47

Ó Móráin, Pádraig, *The Health of the Nation: The Irish Healthcare System, 1957–2007* (Dublin, 2007)

O'Neill, Kevin, 'The National Conference of Priests of Ireland', *The Furrow*, vol. 28, no. 1, January 1977, pp. 39–43

O'Nualláin, Colm, 'Public Service Reform', *Administration*, vol. 26, no. 3, Spring 1978, pp. 293–305

O'Súilleabháin, Séamas, 'Second Level Education: Dimensions and Directions', *Maynooth Review*, vol. 1, no. 1, June 1975, pp. 3–17

O'Sullivan, Kevin, 'Biafra to Lomé: The Evolution of Irish Government Policy on Official Development Assistance, 1969–75', *Irish Studies in International Affairs*, vol. 18, 2007, pp. 91–107

O'Toole, Fintan, *The Irish Times Book of the Century* (Dublin, 1999)

Osborough, Nial, 'Reformatory and Industrial Schools', *Irish Jurist*, vol. 5, 1970, pp. 294–6

Patterson, Henry, *Ireland Since 1939: The Persistence of Conflict* (London, 2006)

Peillon, Michael, 'A Case Study in Social Dynamics: The Irish Working Class', *Social Studies*, vol. 5, no. 1, Spring 1976, pp. 26–66

Plunkett, Eric A, 'Solicitors in the Republic', *Irish Jurist*, vol. 6, 1971, pp. 18–27

Plunkett, James, *The Boy on the Back Wall and Other Essays* (Dublin, 1987)

Pollak, Andy, 'Defence Forces: Waiting for Doomsday?', *Hibernia*, 7 June 1974

Power, Anne, *Estates on the Edge: The Social Consequences of Mass Housing in Northern Europe Since 1850* (London, 1993)

Puirséil, Niamh, *The Irish Labour Party 1922–73* (Dublin, 2007)

Pyne, Peter, 'The Irish Civil Service', *Administration*, vol. 22, no. 1, Spring 1974, pp. 26–60

Quinn, John, *My Education* (Dublin, 1997)

Quinn, Patricia, 'Working through the College', in Gilfillan, *Trinity Tales*, pp. 274–9

Quinn, Ruairí, *Straight Left: A Journey In Politics* (Dublin, 2005)

Raftery, Mary, 'Revealing the Horrific Past of Psychiatric Hospitals', *Irish Times*, 5 September 2011

Raftery, Mary and Eoin O' Sullivan, *Suffer the Little Children: The Inside Story of Ireland's Industrial Schools* (Dublin, 1999)

Redmond, Adrian (ed.), *That Was Then, This Is Now: Change in Ireland, 1949–1999* (Dublin, 2000)

Rees, Merlyn, *Northern Ireland: A Personal Perspective* (London, 1985)

Regan, John, 'Dr Jekyll and Mr Hyde: The Two Histories', *History Ireland*, vol. 20, no. 1, January/February 2012, pp. 10–14

Regan, Mary, *Prison Policy in Ireland: Politics, Penal-welfarism and Political Imprisonment* (New York, 2011)

Reynolds, Albert and Jill Arlon, *Albert Reynolds: My Autobiography* (Dublin, 2010)

Robinson, Mary, 'The Role of the Irish Parliament', *Administration*, vol. 22, no. 1, Spring 1974, pp. 3–26

Robinson, Mary, 'Women and the New Irish State', in Mac Curtain and Ó Corráin, *Women in Irish Society*, pp. 58–70

Roche, Anthony, *Brian Friel: Theatre and Politics* (London, 2011)

Roche, Richard, 'The Role of the Department of Public Service', *Administration*, vol. 27, no. 4, Winter 1979, pp. 408–15

Rottman, David B, 'The Changing Pattern of Crime in Ireland', *Journal of the Social and Statistical Inquiry Society of Ireland*, vol. 23, part V, 1977–8, pp. 163–217

Rouse, Paul, 'Rory Gallagher', in McGuire and Quinn, *DIB*, vol. 4, pp. 12–13

Ryan, Annie, *Walls of Silence* (Kilkenny, 1999)

Ryan, Dermot, *Marriage and Pastoral Care: An Invitation to Priestly Concern with Appropriate Directive* (Dublin, 1975)

Ryan, Dermot, *Dermot Ryan: 1972–77: The First Five Years* (Dublin, 1977)

Ryan, James, 'In Search of the Beautiful People', in Gilfillan, *Trinity Tales*, pp. 145–57

Ryan, Liam, 'Social Factors in Irish Education', *Christus Rex*, vol. 24, no. 4, October 1970, pp. 273–87

Ryan, Seán, *The Boys in Green: The FAI International Story* (Edinburgh, 1997)

Ryle Dwyer, T. *Nice Fellow: A Biography of Jack Lynch* (Cork, 2001)

Sacks, Paul Martin, *The Donegal Mafia: An Irish Political Machine* (London, 1976)

Scheper-Hughes, Nancy, *Saints, Scholars and Schizophrenics: Mental Illness in Rural Ireland* (Berkeley, 1979)

Sharp, Paul, *Irish Foreign Policy and the European Community* (Aldershot, 1990)

Shaw, Francis, 'The Canon of Irish History: A Challenge', *Studies*, vol. 61, Summer 1972, pp. 117–51

Siggins, Lorna, *Once Upon a Time in the West: The Corrib Gas Controversy* (London, 2010)

Skehill, Caroline, *History of the Present of Child Protection and Welfare Social Work in Ireland* (New York, 2004)

Skelly Joseph Morrison, *Irish Diplomacy at the United Nations, 1945–65* (Dublin, 1997)

Smith, Raymond, *Urbi et Orbi and All That* (Dublin, 1995)

Smith, Sheamus, *Off Screen: A Memoir* (Dublin, 2007)

Smyth, Jane, 'Violence in Marriage: Battered Brides', *Doctrine and Life*, vol. 26, no. 4, April 1976, pp. 223–32

Smyth, William J, 'Continuity and Change in the Territorial Organisation of Irish Rural Communities', *Maynooth Review*, vol. 1 no. 1, June 1975, pp. 52–74

Stopper, Anne, *Monday at Gaj's: The Story of the Irish Women's Liberation Movement* (Dublin, 2006)

Stuart, Francis, 'Literature and Politics', *Crane Bag*, vol. 1, no. 1, Spring 1977, pp. 72–7

Sweeney, Eamonn, *Down, Down, Deeper and Down: Ireland in the 70s and 80s* (Dublin, 2010)

Sweetman FitzGerald, Barbara (ed.), *The Widest Circle: Remembering Michael Sweetman* (Dublin, 2011)

Thomson, Tara Keenan, *Irish Women and Street Politics, 1956–1973* (Dublin, 2010)

Tiernan, Joe, *The Dublin and Monaghan Bombings* (Dublin, 2010)

Titley, Alan, 'The Novel in Irish', in John Wilson Foster (ed.), *The Cambridge Companion to the Irish Novel* (Cambridge, 2006), pp. 171–88

Tóibín, Colm, 'The Dark 16th Century', *Dublin Review*, no. 43, Summer 2011, pp. 31–55

Tóibín, Niall, *Smile and be a Villain* (Dublin, 1995)

Tora, Ben and Eilis Ward (eds), *Ireland in International Affairs: Interests, Institutions and Identities* (Dublin, 2002)

Trench, Brian, 'Power of the Pump', *Magill*, June 1979

Uris, Leon, *Ireland: A Terrible Beauty* (London, 1976)

Walsh, Brendan, 'Marriage in Ireland in the Twentieth Century', in Art Cosgrove (ed.), *Marriage in Ireland* (Dublin, 1985), pp. 132–50

Walsh, Brendan, 'Trends in the Religious Composition of the Population in the Republic of Ireland, 1946–1971', *Economic and Social Review*, vol. 6, 1974–5, pp. 543–55

Walsh, Ed, *Upstart: Friends, Foes and Founding a University* (Cork, 2011)

Walsh, John, *Patrick Hillery: The Official Biography* (Dublin, 2008)

Walsh, Liz, *The Final Beat: Gardaí Killed in the Line of Duty* (Dublin, 2001)

Walshe, Eibhear, *Cissie's Abattoir* (Cork, 2009)

Waters, John, *Jiving at the Crossroads* (Dublin, 1991)

Watts, William, *William Watts: Provost Trinity College Dublin: A Memoir* (Dublin, 2008)

Whelan, Diarmuid, *Conor Cruise O'Brien: Violent Notions* (Dublin, 2009)

Whelan, Mary, 'Reflections on a Community Survey', *Social Studies*, vol. 3, no. 1, February 1974, pp. 3–13

Whelan, Noel, 'Reform or Change in the Public Service', *Administration*, vol. 23, no. 1, Spring 1975, pp. 103–26

Whelan, Noel, 'The Irish Public Service: Its Reform', *Administration*, vol. 25, no. 1, Spring 1977, pp. 1–12

Whitaker, Andrew (ed.), *Bright, Brilliant Days: Douglas Gageby and the Irish Times* (Dublin, 2006)

Whitaker, T. K., 'From Protection to Free Trade – the Irish Experience', *Administration*, vol. 21, no. 4, 1974, pp. 405–24

Whitaker, T. K., *Interests* (Dublin, 1983)

White, Harry, *The Keeper's Recital: Music and Cultural History in Ireland, 1770–1970* (Cork, 1998)

White, Harry, *The Progress of Music in Ireland* (Dublin, 2005)

White, Lawrence William, 'Patrick Donegan', in McGuire and Quinn, *DIB*, vol. 3, pp. 379–80

White, Lawrence William, 'Michael O'Riordan', in McGuire and Quinn, *DIB*, vol. 7, pp. 879–81

White, Lawrence William, 'David Thornley', in McGuire and Quinn, *DIB*, vol. 9, pp. 335–6

Whyte, John H., *Church and State in Modern Ireland 1923–70* (Dublin, 1971)

Williamson, Daniel, 'Taking the Troubles across the Atlantic: Ireland's UN Initiatives and Irish-US Diplomatic Relations in the Early Years of the Conflict in Northern Ireland, 1969–72', *Irish Studies in International Affairs*, vol. 18, 2007, pp. 175–89

Wogan, Terry, *Is It Me? Terry Wogan: An Autobiography* (London, 2000)

Woodworth, Paddy, 'How Did Events in Latin America Influence Young Irish Leftists in the Early 1970s?', *History Ireland*, vol. 16, no. 4, July/August 2008, pp. 28–52

Wren, Maev Ann, *Unhealthy State: Anatomy of a Sick Society* (Dublin, 2003)
Wright, Julia M, *A Companion to Irish Literature: Volume Two* (London, 2010)
Young, John N., *Erskine H. Childers, President of Ireland: A Biography* (London, 1985)

NOTES

Introduction: Old Moulds Broken?

1. Liam de Paor, 'The Ambiguity of the Republic', *Atlantis*, no. 3, November 1971, p. 7.
2. Dennis O'Driscoll, *Stepping Stones: Interviews with Seamus Heaney* (London, 2008), p. 118.
3. Ibid.
4. John Montague, *The Pear is Ripe* (Dublin, 2007), pp. 226–8.
5. Gerard DeGroot, *The Seventies Unplugged: A Kaleidoscopic Look at a Violent Decade* (London, 2010), pp. xii–xv and chapter 3, 'Old Arguments: New Deaths: Belfast, Bloody Sunday', pp. 65–73.
6. Thomas Kinsella, *Butcher's Dozen* (Dublin, 1972) and Montague, *The Pear is Ripe*, pp. 226–8.
7. Mary Holland, 'Eye on the Twentieth Century: Ireland 1970–79', *Irish Times*, 9 November 1999.
8. Ibid.
9. DeGroot, *The Seventies Unplugged*, p. xi.
10. Tony Judt, *Postwar: A History of Europe Since 1945* (London, 2005), p. 459.
11. Ibid., pp. 477–80.
12. Mary Fulbrook (ed.), *Twentieth Century Germany: Politics, Culture and Society* (London, 2001), p. 192.
13. James F. McMillan, *Twentieth Century France: Politics and Society 1898–1991* (London, 1992), pp. 186–95.
14. William H. Chafe (ed.), *A History of Our Time: Readings on Postwar America* (Oxford, 1991), pp. 407–51.
15. Paul Johnson (ed.), *Twentieth Century Britain: Economic, Social and Cultural Change* (London, 1994), p. 300.
16. Peter Clarke, *Hope and Glory: Britain 1900–1990* (London, 1996), p. 335.

17. Martin Mansergh, 'Inside the civil service sanctum', *Irish Times* Weekend Review, 10 December 2011.
18. Eamon Sweeney, *Down, Down, Deeper and Down: Ireland in the 70s and 80s* (Dublin, 2010). Just a sample of Troubles books from the last ten years include David McKittrick (ed.), *Lost Lives* (Edinburgh, 2001), Thomas Hennessey, *Northern Ireland: The Origins of the Troubles* (Dublin, 2005), Gordon Gillespie: *A Short History of the Troubles* (Dublin, 2010), Ivan Minnis, *The Troubles in Northern Ireland* (Oxford, 2001), Richard English, *Armed Struggle: A History of the IRA* (London, 2003), Ed Moloney, *A Secret History of the IRA* (London, 2002), Henry McDonald and Jim Cusack, *UDA: Inside the Heart of Loyalist Terror* (London, 2004).
19. Conor Brady, review of Sweeney, *Down, Down*, *Irish Times* Weekend Review, 30 October 2010.

Part I Irish Political and Administrative Culture

1. Basil Chubb, *The Government and Politics of Ireland* (Dublin, 1970), p. 217.
2. Chris Curtin, Hastings Donnan and Thomas M. Wilson (eds), *Irish Urban Cultures* (Belfast, 1993), p. 82.
3. Ibid., pp. 79–99, Mart Bax, *Harpstrings and Confessions: Machine-style Politics in the Irish Republic* (Assen, 1976) and Paul Martin Sacks, *The Donegal Mafia: An Irish Political Machine* (London, 1976).
4. Brian Farrell, 'Dáil Deputies: The 1969 Generation', *Economic and Social Review*, vol. 2, 1970–71, pp. 309–27.
5. Breandán Ó hEithir, *The Begrudgers Guide to Irish Politics* (Dublin, 1986), pp. 67–8.
6. Peter Mair, *The Changing Irish Party System* (London, 1987), pp. 37–40.
7. Desmond Hogan, *The Edge of the City: A Scrapbook 1976–91* (Dublin, 1993), pp. 13–17.
8. Michael Peillon, 'A Case Study in Social Dynamics: The Irish Working Class', *Social Studies*, vol. 5, no. 1, Spring 1976, pp. 26–66.
9. John Quinn, *My Education* (Dublin, 1997), pp. 100–101.
10. James Plunkett, *The Boy on the Back Wall and Other Essays* (Dublin, 1987), p. 180.
11. Mary Robinson, 'The Role of the Irish Parliament', *Administration*, vol. 22, no. 1, Spring 1974, pp. 3–26.
12. *Seven Ages: The Story of the Irish State: The 1970s: A Decade of Terror, Tension and Transformation*, a documentary series produced and directed by Seán O Mórdha, Dublin, 2001.
13. Margaret Mac Curtain, 'Women: Irish Style', *Doctrine and Life*, vol. 24, no. 4, April 1974, pp. 182–98.
14. Tom Barrington, 'Is There a Future for the District?', *Administration*, vol. 19, no. 4, Winter 1971, pp. 219–38.
15. Tom Barrington, 'Organising for Development', *Administration*, vol. 21, no. 1, Spring 1973, pp. 3–15.
16. Peter Pyne, 'The Irish Civil Service', *Administration*, vol. 22, no. 1, Spring 1974, pp. 26–60.

17. Thomas P. O'Connor and R. W. L. Wilding, 'The Civil Service in the Modern State', *Studies*, vol. 59, Summer 1970, pp. 164–79.
18. Noel Whelan, 'Reform or Change in the Public Service', *Administration*, vol. 23, no. 1, Spring 1975, pp. 103–26 and *Irish Times*, 11 November 1975.
19. Noel Whelan, 'The Irish Public Service: Its Reform', *Administration*, vol. 25, no. 1, Spring 1977, pp. 1–12.
20. Colm O'Nualláin, 'Public Service Reform', *Administration*, vol. 26, no. 3, Spring 1978, pp. 293–305 and Richard Roche, 'The Role of the Department of Public Service', *Administration*, vol. 27, no. 4, Winter 1979, pp. 408–15.
21. Cited in Quinn, *My Education*, p. 17.

1 Ballymagash Style Politics

1. Brian Boyd, 'How Ballymagash Became Part of Folk Culture', *Irish Times*, 4 December 2004.
2. John Bowman, *Window and Mirror: RTE Television: 1961–2011* (Dublin, 2011), pp. 150–51.
3. Ibid.
4. *Irish Times*, 7 January 2011.
5. *Irish Times*, 27 January 2011.
6. Tom Garvin, *Preventing the Future: Why Was Ireland so Poor for so Long?* (Dublin, 2004), p. 213.
7. University College Dublin Archives (hereafter UCDA), Papers of Garret FitzGerald (hereafter FitzGerald Papers), P215/481, copy of paper by John A. Murphy, 'Identity in the Republic of Ireland Now', presented in Missouri, April 1976.
8. Thomas Barrington, *From Big Government to Local Government: The Road to Decentralisation* (Dublin, 1975).
9. Diarmaid Ferriter, *Lovers of Liberty? Local Government in Twentieth Century Ireland* (Dublin, 2001), p. 44.
10. Michael D. Higgins, *Causes for Concern: Irish Politics, Culture and Society* (Dublin, 2006), p. 69.
11. Ibid., p. 90.
12. Ibid., p. 91.
13. Barry Desmond, 'The Houses of the Oireachtas: A Plea for Reform', *Administration*, vol. 23, no. 4, 1975, p. 426.
14. UCDA, Papers of John Kelly (hereafter Kelly Papers), P147/16, 18 January 1971.
15. Vincent Browne (ed.), *The Magill Book of Irish Politics* (Dublin, 1981), p. 271.
16. UCDA, Papers of John de Courcy Ireland (hereafter de Courcy Ireland Papers), P29, 48, Barry Desmond to de Courcy, 14 August 1970.
17. Browne, *Magill Book of Irish Politics*, p. 214.
18. Michael Clifford and Shane Coleman, *Bertie Ahern and the Drumcondra Mafia* (Dublin, 2009), p. 38.
19. *Magill*, November 1978.
20. *Hibernia*, 17 December 1971.

21. Brian Trench, 'Power of the Pump', *Magill*, June 1979.
22. Ibid., p. 26.
23. *Magill*, December 1978.
24. UCDA, Kelly Papers, P147/8, c. July 1969.
25. Ibid., P147/31, 1977 General Election, List of Constituents to be Canvassed.
26. Ibid., P147/15, 2 August 1970.
27. Ibid., P147/17, c. January 1972.
28. Ibid., P147/55, election material, c. 1972, paper on Electoral Systems by John Whyte and responses.
29. Ibid., P147/61, Fine Gael magazine 1970.

2 How to Win the Next Election

1. National Archives of Ireland (hereafter, NAI), Private Accessions, Papers of Liam Cosgrave, (hereafter, Cosgrave Papers), 1194, 54–79, Ted Nealon to Cosgrave, 3 November 1976.
2. UCDA, Papers of the Fianna Fáil Party (hereafter Fianna Fáil Papers), P176, parliamentary party minutes, 11 November 1979.
3. Ibid., 7 May 1975 and 21 January 1976.
4. Ibid., P176/89, circular of 1 March 1972.
5. Ibid., P176/90, Séamus Brennan to Niall Maguire, 14 December 1976.
6. Ibid., P176/89, Patrick Smith to Eugene Boyle, 14 June 1973.
7. Ibid., P176/88, letter of Mary O'Rourke, 7 September 1971 and James Crehan to secretary, 28 October 1971.
8. Ibid., P176/89, Rathowen *cumann* to Jack Lynch, 28 August 1973.
9. Ibid., P176/96, Brennan to Br Robert Ruane, 1 March 1979.
10. Ibid., P176/98, T. Reynolds to Séamus Brennan, 25 November 1977.
11. Ibid., Darren Clarke to Brennan, 22 November 1973.
12. Ibid., P176/102, Desmond Power to Brennan, 5 April 1977.
13. Ibid., P176/88, Ramage and Britten Solicitors to Mullins, 15 May 1970.
14. Ibid., P176/344, notebook on organisational aspects of 1973 general election.
15. Ibid., P176/370, Organisation Committee minutes, 17 February 1970, and Erskine Childers to T. Mullins, 19 March 1970.
16. Ibid., 1 December 1975.
17. Ibid., P176/374, Organisational Review, April 1976.
18. Ibid., 20 September 1977.
19. Ibid., P176/448, parliamentary party minutes, 25 February 1970.
20. Ibid., P176/368, Finance Committee minutes, 8 November 1971, 12 November 1973, 13 December 1976, 18 April 1977, 23 October 1978, 12 November 1979 and 26 September 1977.
21. Ibid., P176/99, Michael Shorthall to Brennan, 25 May 1976.
22. Ibid., circular of 17 August 1973 and George Colley to Mullins, 13 August 1973.
23. Ibid., P176/90, Ciarán Murphy to Séamus Brennan, 5 January 1977.
24. Dermot Keogh, *Jack Lynch: A Biography* (Dublin, 2008), p. 126.

25. NAI, Private Accessions, Papers of Jack Lynch (hereafter Lynch Papers), 1195, 3/120/33, D. M. McGing, Kean and Company Accountants to Lynch, 16 March 1976.
26. Ibid., Patrick Meade to Lynch, 6 May 1977.
27. UCDA, Fianna Fáil Papers, P176/350, National Executive minutes, 25 May 1977.
28. Ibid., T. C. Kerr to Hon. Sec. Wicklow *cumann*, 10 July 1974.
29. Ibid., P176/90, Ruairí Brugha to Séamus Brennan, 12 February 1976.
30. Ibid., P176/448, parliamentary party minutes, 4 November 1970.
31. NAI, Lynch Papers, 1195/3/120/31, briefing session for European election candidates, 8 February 1979.
32. UCDA, FitzGerald Papers, P215/545, Maeve Binchy to Garret FitzGerald, 5 April 1973.
33. Ibid., Declan McDonnell to FitzGerald, 8 March 1973.
34. John Waters, *Jiving at the Crossroads* (Dublin, 1991), p. 72.
35. James Downey, *In My Own Time: Inside Irish Politics and Society* (Dublin, 2009), p. 156.
36. *Hibernia*, 16 March 1973.

3 Identifying the Problems

1. NAI, Files of the Department of the Taoiseach (hereafter DT), 2004/21/19, 31 March 1973.
2. Ibid., memorandum of 22 March 1973.
3. *Hibernia*, 16 November 1973.
4. Sweeney, *Down, Down*, p. 125.
5. NAI, DT 2004/21/19, Ministers, Parliamentary Secretaries and Ministers of State: Financial and Other Interests, FitzGerald to Cosgrave, 18 June 1973.
6. Ibid., John Temple Lang, McCann FitzGerald Solicitors, 9 August 1973 and Department of Taoiseach memorandum, 14 August 1973.
7. NAI, DT 2005/7/520, Members of Oireachtas and Members of Local Authorities: Financial and Other Releases, 18 October 1974.
8. Ibid.
9. *Irish Times*, 16 May 2001.
10. NAI, DT 2005/7/488, County Councils: Corruption and Conflict of Interest, and *Sunday Independent*, 23 June 1974.
11. NAI, DT 2006/133/348, December 1974 to June 1975, Allegations against the Minister for Local Government.
12. NAI, Lynch Papers, 3/120/30, Robert Molloy to Lynch, 3 July 1975.
13. *Hibernia*, 11 July 1975.
14. Browne, *Magill Book of Irish Politics*, p. 151.
15. *Hibernia*, 4 August 1972.
16. *Hibernia*, 8 September 1972.
17. *Hibernia*, 16 March 1973.
18. UCDA, FitzGerald Papers, P215/495, Tom FitzGerald to Garret FitzGerald, 22 March 1977 and reply of 5 April 1977.

19. Ibid., P215/584, Donegan to FitzGerald, 16 April 1975.
20. Ibid., P215/539, Cluskey to FitzGerald, 3 June 1977.
21. Ibid., P215/545, Brendan Joyce to FitzGerald, 23 March 1973.
22. *Irish Times*, 18 February 1999 and 7 December 2000.
23. NAI, DT 2004/21/341, Parliamentary Reform, 1972–1980, O'Malley to Lynch, 1 June 1972 and note of 2 May 1973 in relation to report submitted on 5 December 1972.
24. NAI, DT 2004/21/341, Declan Costello to Cosgrave, 5 June 1973.
25. NAI, Cosgrave Papers, 1194/25–38, Conor Cruise O'Brien to Cosgrave, 24 October 1973.
26. *Hibernia*, 5 March 1970.
27. UCDA, Kelly Papers, P147/8, Kelly to FG members, 12, 16 and 23 July 1969.
28. Ibid., T. D. Burke to Kelly, 27 July 1969.
29. *Hibernia*, 15 March 1974.
30. Conor Cruise O'Brien, *Memoir: My Life and Themes* (Dublin, 2009), p. 357.
31. *Hibernia*, 25 June 1970, C. E. J. Caldicott, 'Owen Sheehy Skeffington', in James McGuire and James Quinn (eds), *Dictionary of Irish Biography: From the Earliest Times to the Year 2002* (Cambridge, 2009) (hereafter, McGuire and Quinn, *DIB*), vol. 8, pp. 86–7.
32. NAI, DT 2005/151/251, 15 January 1970 and *Evening Press*, 19 January 1970 and Published Debates, Dáil Éireann (hereafter Dáil Debates), 23 July 1970.
33. NAI, DT 2007/116/241, 1 July 1976, An Irish Ombudsman.
34. Joe Lee, *Ireland: Politics and Society, 1912–1985* (Cambridge, 1989), pp. 552–3.
35. NAI, DT 2005/151/608, Dáil Debates, 2 May 1973, memorandum from the Office of Minister for Public Service, July 1975 and Richie Ryan to Liam Cosgrave, 13 October 1975.
36. Ronan Fanning, 'Jack Lynch', in McGuire and Quinn, *DIB*, vol. 5, pp. 630–41.

4 Servants of the Minister

1. Author interview with Richard Stokes, Dublin, 6 April 2012.
2. Ibid.
3. NAI, DT 2002/8/42, Civil Servants and Politics, April 1970.
4. Ibid., *Irish Independent*, 19 June 1971, *Irish Press*, 21 June 1971.
5. *Magill*, May 1978.
6. Browne, *Magill Book of Irish Politics*, p. 315.
7. *Hibernia*, 16 March 1973.
8. UCDA, FitzGerald Papers, P215/408, Gerard Sweeney to FitzGerald, 3 May 1978.
9. NAI, DT 2007/116/26, Private Secretaries, Richie Ryan to Conor Cruise O'Brien, 7 January 1974.
10. NAI, DT 2008/148/24, July 1978, memo from Department of Public Service, and note from Dowd to Stokes, 27 November 1978.
11. NAI, DT 2008/148/425, memo from Department of Public Service, January 1978.
12. Ibid., note of Stokes, 9 February 1978 and Dermot Nally to Taoiseach, 18 July 1978.
13. *Irish Times*, 17 April 2010.

14. Quinn, *My Education*, pp. 17–25.
15. NAI, DT 2009/135/74, Decentralisation of State and Semi-State Administrative Organisations, 13 July 1978.
16. NAI, DT 2008/148/572, Department of the Environment, Leak of Confidential Documents, 1978, 12 May 1978.
17. Ibid.

5 Political Soul-Searching

1. UCDA, Kelly Papers, P147/21, 3 September 1972.
2. Ibid., 15 September 1972.
3. Ibid., P147/44, Kelly to Alan Dukes, 27 February 1989.
4. Ibid., P147/8, Peter Barry to Kelly, 28 July 1969.
5. Ibid., Gerard Sweetman to Kelly, 30 July 1969.
6. Ibid.' P147/17, n.d., Kelly memo on dilemma facing FG.
7. Ibid.
8. NAI, DT 2000/6/314, *Nusight*, February 1969.
9. UCDA, Fianna Fáil Papers, P176/90, John Murphy to Séamus Brennan, 6 June 1974 and Séamus Brennan to Christina O'Brien, 14 June 1976.
10. Ibid., Bernard Keating to Brennan, 6 September 1977.
11. Ibid., P147/55, electoral material, 1970–73.
12. Ibid.
13. Ibid., P147/16, speech in Nenagh, 13 March 1970.
14. NAI, Cosgrave Papers, DT 2004/22/36, press, radio and television interviews.
15. *Hibernia*, 14 May 1971.
16. NAI, DT 2007/116/337, Interviews Given by the Taoiseach, 13 May 1977.
17. *Magill*, April 1978.
18. *Magill*, May 1978.
19. *Magill*, July 1979.
20. Browne, *Magill Book of Irish Politics*, p. 169.
21. Ibid.
22. *Magill*, June 1978.
23. UCDA, Kelly Papers, P147/47, speech at UCC, 19 October 1978.
24. *Magill*, May 1978.
25. Browne, *Magill Book of Irish Politics*, pp. 148–56.
26. NAI, DT 2008/148/101, Communism: General: Left Wing Movement and *Sunday Press*, 3 May 1970.
27. Ibid., c. March 1977 and Joseph O'Reilly to Jack Lynch, 20 March 1978.
28. Ibid., W. N. Powell to Lynch, 3 March 1972.
29. *Hibernia*, 16 March 1973.
30. Lawrence William White, 'Michael O'Riordan', in McGuire and Quinn, *DIB*, vol. 7, pp. 879–81.
31. NAI, DT 2008/148/280, Interviews Given by the Taoiseach, 8 January 1978.
32. Ibid., speech at Macroom, 29 June 1970.
33. Ibid., speech in Rathmines, 11 December 1970.

34. *Hibernia*, 22 October 1976.
35. Tim Pat Coogan, *A Memoir* (London, 2009), p. 199.
36. *Hibernia*, 14 November 1975.
37. *Irish Times*, 29 October 2011.
38. Bertie Ahern and Richard Aldous, *Bertie Ahern: The Autobiography* (London, 2009), pp. 23–34.
39. Ibid.
40. David Andrews, *Kingstown Republican* (Dublin, 2007), p. 70.
41. Niamh Puirséil, *The Irish Labour Party 1922–73* (Dublin, 2007), pp. 272–308.
42. UCDA, de Courcy Ireland Papers, P29/13, 26 February 1972.
43. Ibid., P29/14, draft memo of Socialist Labour Action Group, February 1972.
44. Ibid., P29/15, Annual Report of the Labour Party, 1972–3.
45. UCDA, de Courcy Ireland Papers, P29/40, John O'Connell to de Courcy, 4 April 1972.
46. Ibid., P29/41, John O'Connell to de Courcy, 2 May 1972.
47. UCDA, de Courcy Ireland Papers, P29/23, Annual Conference, Cork, 1973.
48. Ibid., P29/26, Annual Conference, Galway, 1974.
49. Ibid., P29/58, John de Courcy Ireland to Brendan Halligan, 21 October 1974.
50. Ibid. Halligan to de Courcy Ireland, 26 and 29 November 1974.
51. Ibid., P29/79, Liaison Committee of the Left, Newsletter, 1973–4.
52. Ibid., P29/63, de Courcy Ireland to David Thornley, n.d., c.1973.
53. Ibid.
54. UCDA, FitzGerald Papers, P215/545, G. A. Duncan to FitzGerald, 29 March 1973.
55. Ibid., FitzGerald to Mrs Redston, Oregon, c. March 1973.
56. NAI, Cosgrave Papers, 54–79, David Thornley to Seamus Scally, 19 October 1976.
57. John Horgan, *Noel Browne: Passionate Outsider* (Dublin, 1998), p. 79.
58. *Magill*, December 1977.
59. *Magill*, May 1978.
60. *Magill*, March 1978.
61. Browne, *Magill Book of Irish Politics*, p. 156.
62. *Hibernia*, 14 November 1975.
63. Ruairí Quinn, *Straight Left: A Journey In Politics* (Dublin, 2005), p. 109.
64. Patrick Maume, 'Michael O'Leary', in McGuire and Quinn, *DIB*, online entry added December 2011, www.dib.cambridge.org.
65. *Hibernia*, 14 December 1973.
66. Andrews, *Kingstown Republican*, p. 52.
67. Stephen Collins, *The Cosgrave Legacy* (Dublin, 1996), pp. 158–210.
68. Denis Boyle, 'James Tully', in McGuire and Quinn, *DIB*, vol. 9, pp. 514–15.
69. *Hibernia*, 27 September 1974.
70. Ibid.
71. Ibid.
72. *Hibernia*, 3 October 1976.
73. *Magill*, June 1979.
74. Browne, *Magill Book of Irish Politics*, p. 344.

6 Leaders and Aspirants

1. In a letter to the *Irish Times*, 21 February 2011.
2. NAI, DT 2007/116/337, Interviews Given by the Taoiseach, 12 June 1975 to 13 May 1977.
3. NAI, DT 2004/22/36, Brian Quinn to Liam Cosgrave, 3 March 1973.
4. *Hibernia*, 2 March 1973.
5. Ibid.
6. *Magill*, January 1978.
7. Frank Dunlop, *Yes Taoiseach: Irish Politics from Behind Closed Doors* (Dublin, 2004), pp. 3–9.
8. NAI, DT 2004/22/36, Geraldine Kennedy to Liam Cosgrave, 6 July 1973.
9. NAI, DT 2007/116/337, Interviews Given by the Taoiseach, Florence King to Cosgrave, 22 May 1977, Cruise O'Brien, *Memoir*, p. 343 and *Irish Times*, An Irishman's Diary, 25 July 2011.
10. Coogan, *A Memoir*, p. 193.
11. Downey, *In My Own Time*, p. 173.
12. Cruise O'Brien, *Memoir*, pp. 345–7.
13. Shaun McDaid, 'The David Thornley Affair', in Caoimhe Nic Dháibhéid and Colin Reid (eds), *From Parnell to Paisley: Constitutional and Revolutionary Politics in Modern Ireland* (Dublin, 2010), pp. 182–200.
14. Cruise O'Brien, *Memoir*, pp. 337–43.
15. Diarmaid Ferriter, *Judging Dev: A Reassessment of the Life and Legacy of Eamon de Valera* (Dublin, 2007), p. 107.
16. NAI, Cosgrave Papers, 1194/39–53, Conor Cruise O'Brien to Cosgrave, 28 June 1977.
17. Ibid., 1194/25–38, The National Coalition: Four Years at Work.
18. Ibid., Cosgrave to Patrick Cooney, 27 June 1977.
19. Ibid., 1194/39–53, Conor Cruise O'Brien to Cosgrave, 14 and 19 February 1974.
20. Ibid., Muiris Mac Conghail to Conor Cruise O'Brien, 11 February 1974 and to Cosgrave, 13 September 1975.
21. Ibid., Cruise O'Brien to Cosgrave, 17 May 1973.
22. Ibid., 1194/54/79, David Thornley to Cosgrave, 2 August 1974 and 4 November 1976.
23. Ibid., 194/39–53, Patrick Donegan to Cosgrave, 8 July 1974.
24. Ibid., 1194/80–83, comments by Cosgrave on memorandum regarding Northern Ireland, c. 1978.
25. Ibid., Alexis FitzGerald to Cosgrave, 13 January 1977.
26. Ibid., Oliver J. Flanagan to Cosgrave, 25 June 1977.
27. Ibid., 1194/80–83, Maurice O'Connell to Cosgrave, 21 July 1977.
28. Ibid., Michael Turner to Cosgrave, Frank Roe to Cosgrave and Cosgrave to Frank Roe, 18 July 1977.
29. Ibid., Cosgrave to Madeleine Dundon, 12 February 1979.
30. Ibid., 1194/84–7, Louie O'Connell to Cosgrave, 14 April 1981.
31. *Magill*, December 1977.

32. Garret FitzGerald, *Towards a New Ireland* (London, 1972), pp. 88–175.
33. Roy Foster, *Luck and the Irish: A Brief History of Change* (London, 2007), p. 52.
34. UCDA, FitzGerald Papers, P215/545, E. J. Clarke to FitzGerald, 15 March 1973 and FitzGerald to Ernest Blythe, 27 March 1973.
35. *Magill*, January 1978.
36. UCDA, FitzGerald Papers, P215/545, Donough O'Connor to FitzGerald, 18 March 1973.
37. *Hibernia*, 25 August 1972.
38. *Hibernia*, 3 January 1973.
39. Dunlop, *Yes Taoiseach*, pp. 9–16, Ahern, *Bertie Ahern*, p. 33, Andrews, *Kingstown Republican*, p. 49.
40. See for example, NAI, DT 2003/16/131.
41. Albert Reynolds and Jill Arlon, *Albert Reynolds: My Autobiography* (Dublin, 2010), p. 73.
42. Vincent Browne, 'The Artful Ambiguities of Jack Lynch', *Magill*, October 1977.
43. Browne, *Magill Book of Irish Politics*, p. 68.
44. Keogh, *Jack Lynch*, pp 470–83.
45. Foster, *Luck and the Irish*, pp. 108–21.
46. Coogan, *A Memoir*, p. 155, Dunlop, *Yes Taoiseach*, p. 111.
47. Ulick O'Connor, *The Ulick O'Connor Diaries, 1970–1981: A Cavalier Irishman* (London, 2001), entry for 24 November 1972, and Andrews, *Kingstown Republican*, p. 61.
48. NAI, Lynch Papers, 1195/3/120/27, Lynch to Alice Conway, 4 December 1972.
49. Waters, *Jiving at the Crossroads*, p. 72.
50. Dunlop, *Yes Taoiseach*, p. 39.
51. Ibid., p. 55.
52. UCDA, Fianna Fáil Papers, P176/103, Séamus Brennan, Winning the General Election, August 1976.
53. Dunlop, *Yes Taoiseach*, pp. 75–86, Ahern, *Bertie Ahern*, p. 42.
54. Dunlop, *Yes Taoiseach*, pp. 120–22.
55. Andrews, *Kingstown Republican*, p. 69.
56. NAI, Lynch Papers, 1195/3/120/27, John Jagoe to Lynch, 2 March 1977, Ann Martina to Lynch, 19 March 1977 and R. Warren to Lynch, 12 March 1977.
57. Ibid., T. K. Whitaker to Lynch, 14 March 1973.
58. Keogh, *Jack Lynch*, pp. 201–8, 303–4, 138–46.
59. NAI, Lynch Papers, 1195/3/120/30, Mrs Lynch's correspondence, Maureen Lynch to Nuala O'Farrell, 11 December 1980 and to Nicholas Tinne, 22 August 1972. *Irish Independent*, 23 February 1973 and *Irish Press*, 27 February 1973.
60. Ibid., 1195/3/120/27, Alice Conway to Lynch, 30 November 1972.
61. Ibid., letter of D. Manifold, 14 January 1972.
62. Ibid., Whitaker to Lynch, 5 September 1979.
63. Ibid., 1195/3/120/30, Lynch to Derek Martin, 9 March 1973 and to P. Lucey, 15 October 1973.
64. Ibid., draft of Lynch interview with Tom Savage, 28 January 1981.

65. Lee, *Ireland, 1912–1985*, p. 489.
66. UCDA, Fianna Fáil Papers, P176/350, National Executive meeting, 30 May 1977.
67. *Magill*, July 1978.
68. Waters, *Jiving at the Crossroads*, p. 73.
69. Coogan, *A Memoir*, p. 155.
70. *Hibernia*, 20 March 1970.
71. Sheamus Smith, *Off Screen: A Memoir* (Dublin, 2007), pp. 133–45.
72. *Magill*, January 1979.
73. *Magill*, April 1979.
74. *Hibernia*, 8 November 1974.
75. Foster, *Luck and the Irish*, pp. 75–7.
76. *Irish Times*, 20–22 December 2006.
77. Foster, *Luck and the Irish*, p. 80.
78. *Hibernia*, 3 October 1975.
79. UCDA, Fianna Fáil Papers, P176/97, letter from Athboy FF *cumann*, 8 February 1977.
80. Ibid., P176/350, National Executive minutes, 13 January 1975.
81. Ibid., P176/97, Hugh O'Flaherty to Brennan, 20 August 1977 and Seamus Flynn to Brennan, 6 February 1978.
82. Ibid., P176/103, Seamus Babbington to Séamus Brennan, 23 June 1976.
83. Cruise O'Brien, *Memoir*, p. 357.
84. Downey, *In My Own Time*, p. 173.
85. Dunlop, *Yes Taoiseach*, p. 38.
86. Browne, *Magill Book of Irish Politics*, p. 16.
87. *Hibernia*, 15 August 1975.
88. Barry Desmond, *Finally and in Conclusion: A Political Memoir* (Dublin, 2000), p. 88.
89. Andrews, *Kingstown Republican*, p. 77.
90. Desmond, *Finally and in Conclusion*, p. 88.
91. *Irish Independent*, 3 September 1975.
92. 'Rolling Back the Years, 1975–1979', *Irish Independent* Supplement, 29 October 2011.
93. UCDA, Fianna Fáil Papers, P176/350, National Executive minutes, 2 September 1975.
94. Ibid., 11 December 1978.
95. *Irish Times*, 16 October 2010.
96. NAI, Lynch Papers, 1195/3/120/27, speech of 28 May 1971.
97. Ibid., Ministers Office ledger and Lynch to Mary O'Regan, 6 December 1972.
98. Ibid., 1195/3/120/30, Dermot Ryan to Jack Lynch, 16 June 1976 and Lynch's reply, 25 June 1976.
99. UCDA, Fianna Fáil Papers, P176/448, parliamentary party minutes, 7 December 1979.

7 Shuffling the Traditional Ranks

1. Nuala Fennell, *Political Woman: A Memoir* (Dublin, 2009), pp. 95–107.
2. UCDA, Fianna Fáil Papers, P176/90, Nancy O'Neill to Séamus Brennan, 16 October 1974.
3. Ibid., P176/107, Mary McMahon to Brennan, 4 August 1978.
4. Pat Brennan, 'The Women's Movement in Ireland', *Magill*, April 1979.
5. Foster, *Luck and the Irish*, p. 41.
6. June Levine, 'The Women's Movement in the Republic', in Angela Bourke et al. (eds), *The Field Day Anthology of Irish Writing*, vol. 5, *Irish Women's Writing and Traditions* (Cork, 2002), p. 183.
7. Frances Gardiner, 'The Women's Movement and Politicians in the Republic, 1980–2000', in Bourke et al., vol. 5, pp. 228–37.
8. Sweeney, *Down, Down*, pp. 133–4.
9. R. K. Carty, 'Women in Irish Politics', *Canadian Journal of Irish Studies*, vol. 6, 1980, pp. 90–104.
10. Ibid.
11. Ibid., and Yvonne Galligan. 'Women in Politics', in John Coakely and Michael Gallagher (eds), *Politics in the Republic of Ireland* (4th edn., Dublin, 2005), pp. 272–97.
12. Carty, 'Women in Irish Politics' and F. S. L. Lyons, *Ireland Since the Famine*, (London, 1971), p. 286.
13. *Hibernia*, 22 October 1976.
14. Helen Burke and Olivia O'Leary, *Mary Robinson: The Authorised Biography* (London, 1998), pp. 43–73.
15. Tara Keenan Thomson, *Irish Women and Street Politics, 1956–1973* (Dublin, 2010), p. 183.
16. Anne Stopper, *Monday at Gaj's: The Story of the Irish Women's Liberation Movement* (Dublin, 2006), pp. 216–17.
17. Thomson, *Irish Women and Street Politics*, p. 185.
18. Levine, 'The Women's Movement in the Republic', p. 187.
19. Brennan, 'The Women's Movement in Ireland', p. 46.
20. Diarmaid Ferriter, *Mothers, Maidens and Myths: A History of the Irish Countrywomen's Association* (Dublin, 1995), pp. 52–78.
21. Ibid.
22. *Hibernia*, 20 March 1970.
23. NAI, DT 2007/116/337, Interviews Given by the Taoiseach, 13 May 1977.
24. NAI, DT 2004/21/420, Electors: Qualifying Age, William Haugh to Lynch, 5 February 1973.
25. Ibid., 15 February 1973.
26. Ibid., Dermot McInerney to Lynch, 16 February 1973.
27. *Hot Press*, 9 and 23 June 1977.
28. Waters, *Jiving at the Crossroads*, p. 56.
29. Dunlop, *Yes Taoiseach*, pp. 75–86.
30. Ahern, *Bertie Ahern*, p. 42.

31. *Magill*, April 1978.
32. *Magill*, July 1978, Lawrence William White, 'David Thornley', in McGuire and Quinn, *DIB*, vol. 9, pp. 335–6 and McDaid, 'The David Thornley Affair'.
33. *Irish Times*, 8 May 1976.
34. Desmond, *Finally and in Conclusion*, p. 198.
35. Lawrence William White, 'Patrick Donegan', in McGuire and Quinn, *DIB*, vol. 3, pp. 379–80.
36. Don Lavery, 'A Thundering Disgrace', in 'Rolling Back the Years, 1975–1979', *Irish Independent* Supplement, 29 October 2011.
37. Andrews, *Kingstown Republican*, p. 49.
38. Ibid., p. 73.
39. *Hibernia*, 3 February 1971.
40. Cruise O'Brien interview with Henry Kelly, *Magill*, March 1978.
41. Diarmuid Whelan, *Conor Cruise O'Brien: Violent Notions* (Dublin, 2009) p. xi.
42. Ibid., p. xvii.
43. UCDA, FitzGerald Papers, P215/566, Conor Cruise O'Brien to FitzGerald, 15 May 1973.
44. Browne, *Magill Book of Irish Politics*, p. 27.
45. *Magill*, June 1979.
46. Máire Mhac an tSaoi, *The Same Age as the State* (Dublin, 2003), pp. 306ff.

8 Status, Perception and the Press

1. *Hibernia*, 22 September 1972.
2. *The Economist*, 5 November 1977, UCDA, Papers of Irish Council of the European Movement (hereafter ICEM Papers) P204/110.
3. Ibid. and *Irish Press*, 14 November 1977.
4. UCDA, Fianna Fáil Papers, P176/106, figures listed in letter from John Reidy to Séamus Brennan, 12 February 1976.
5. NAI, Lynch Papers, 1195/3/120/34, Eugene Timmins to Lynch, 30 June 1977.
6. Richard Stokes, Letter to the *Irish Times*, 21 February 2011.
7. UCDA, Kelly Papers, P147/55, paper on Electoral Systems by John Whyte.
8. Ibid., electoral material, 1970–73, 11 June 1970.
9. Ibid., draft letter to the *Irish Times*, 16 December 1972.
10. *Irish Times*, Irishwomen's Diary, 4 January 2011.
11. UCDA, Kelly Papers, P147/16, speech in Dublin, 25 January 1972.
12. Michael Mills, *Hurler on the Ditch: Memoir of a Journalist Who Became Ireland's First Ombudsman* (Dublin, 2005), p. 110.
13. UCDA, Fianna Fáil Papers, P176/448, parliamentary party minutes, 28 April 1971.
14. Ibid., 10 July 1974 and 11 November 1979.
15. Browne, *Magill Book of Irish Politics*, p. 177.
16. Ibid., p. 266.
17. *Hibernia*, 19 January 1973.
18. Mills, *Hurler on the Ditch*, p. 62.
19. Ibid., pp. 91–103.

20. NAI, DT 2004/21/597, memoranda from Department of Posts and Telegraphs, 22 March 1973 and 15 October 1973.
21. NAI, Cosgrave Papers, DT 2004/22/36, press, radio and TV interviews, 22 June 1973.
22. Coogan, *A Memoir*, p. 152.
23. Ibid., pp. 207ff.
24. NAI, DT 2006/133/606, Brian Quinn to Cosgrave, 25 October 1976.
25. Smith, *Off Screen*, pp. 133–45.
26. *Sunday Independent*, 27 November 2011.
27. Bowman, *Window and Mirror*, p. 127.
28. Dunlop, *Yes Taoiseach*, p. 3.
29. NAI, Lynch Papers, 1195/3/120/33, Tim Pat Coogan to Lynch, 5 February 1973.
30. Ibid., 1195/3/120/127, Bruce Arnold to Lynch, 19 June 1977.
31. Collins, *Cosgrave Legacy*, p. 194.
32. Gary Murphy and Niamh Puirséil, 'Is It a New Alliance? Irish Entry to the EEC and Popular Opinion', *Irish Political Studies*, vol. 23, no. 4, December 2008, pp. 533–53.
33. *Magill*, August 1979.
34. Downey, *In My Own Time*, p. 173.
35. *Magill*, December 1979.
36. Dunlop, *Yes Taoiseach*, p. 59.
37. UCDA, Kelly Papers, P147/12, 16 August 1969.
38. Ibid., P147/15, Kelly to editor of *Roscommon Herald*, 2 August 1970.
39. *Magill*, March 1979.
40. Waters, *Jiving at the Crossroads*, p. 66.
41. Cited in Dunlop, *Yes Taoiseach*, p. 68.
42. NAI, Lynch Papers, 1195/3/120/134, Frank Ryan to Eoin Ryan, 7 April 1977.
43. Ibid., 1195/3/120/39, 1977 general election manifesto: 'Action Plan for National Reconstruction'.
44. Ibid., 1195/3/120/34, Jack Lynch to T. Fitzgerald, 22 August 1977 and to Vera Kinsella, 11 August 1977.
45. Ibid., 1195/3/120/28, Dermot Bradley to Lynch, 24 June 1977 and Conchúr O'Murchu to Lynch, 20 May 1977.

9 A Tedious Honour?

1. Downey, *In My Own Time*, pp. 170–73.
2. NAI, DT 2005/7/543, Inauguration of President, 1974, 19 December 1974.
3. UCDA, FitzGerald Papers, P215/387, John D. Moore to FitzGerald, 25 November 1974.
4. John N. Young, *Erskine H. Childers, President of Ireland: A Biography* (London, 1985), pp. 160–92.
5. Ibid., and NAI, Cosgrave Papers, 1194/25–38, Presidential Election Advice, 22 May 1973.

6. NAI, Cosgrave Papers, 1194/25–38, Conor Cruise O'Brien to Cosgrave, 20 April 1973.
7. Ibid., Conor Cruise O'Brien to Cosgrave, 16 July 1973.
8. John Kelly, *The Irish Constitution* (Dublin, 1980), pp. 79–87.
9. Pauric J. Dempsey and Lawrence William White, 'Erskine Childers', in McGuire and Quinn, *DIB*, vol. 2, pp. 498–501.
10. NAI, DT 2005/7/422, President of Ireland Speeches: Clearance, 1973.
11. Ibid., 6 October, 27 November and 9 December 1973, 8, 15, 16 and 22 January 1974.
12. Smith, *Off Screen*, p. 130.
13. 'Rolling Back the Years 1975–1979', *Irish Independent* Supplement, 29 October, 2011.
14. NAI, DT 2006/133/606, Declan Costello to Donegan, 21 October 1976.
15. Ibid., statement of Minister for Defence, 8 October 1976 and Donegan to Ó Dálaigh, 22 October 1976.
16. Ibid., Donegan draft letter, 21 October 1976.
17. Ibid. and *Irish Times*, 19 October 1976.
18. NAI, DT 2006/133/606, 25 October 1976.
19. Letter to Editor of *Irish Times* by Maureen Dunne, 21 October 1976, *Irish Independent*, 19 October 1976, and *Irish Times*, 20 and 22 October 1976.
20. NAI, DT 2006/133/606, John Kelly to Cosgrave, 23 October 1976.
21. UCDA, FitzGerald Papers, P215/568, Conor Cruise O'Brien to FitzGerald, n.d., c. 20 October 1976.
22. Andrews, *Kingstown Republican*, pp. 61ff.
23. NAI, DT 2006/133/606, 25 October 1976.
24. *The Economist*, 30 October 1976.
25. NAI, DT 2007/116/379, 12 January 1976 and H. J. O'Dowd to John Burke, Department of Foreign Affairs, 23 August 1977.
26. Downey, *In My Own Time*, p. 170.
27. UCDA, Papers of Cearbhall Ó Dálaigh (hereafter Ó Dálaigh Papers) P5/163, draft letter to Cosgrave, 22 October 1975.
28. Ibid., P51/206, letters of Gerard Byrne, Seosamh MacChoilte and Elizabeth Ryle, 21 and 24 September and 19 October 1976.
29. Ibid., P51/297, letters of Michael McCann, P. H. Gallagher and Maureen Dunne, 19 and 20 October 1976.
30. Ibid., P51/208(4), notes on the Emergency Powers Bill, October 1976.
31. Ibid., P51/209, notes made after the Supreme Court Decision, 15 October 1976 and P51/211, notes of 19 October 1976.
32. Ibid.
33. Ibid., P51/201, 18 October 1976.
34. Ibid.
35. Downey, *In My Own Time*, p. 170.
36. UCDA, Ó Dálaigh Papers, P51/209, 15 October 1976.
37. Ibid., P51/214.

38. Ibid., P151/215(33), folder of notes including a description of events leading to resignation.
39. Ibid., P51/217.
40. Ibid., P151/213, Liam Hourican in *New York Times*, 23 October 1976 and letter of Leland Lyons, 24 October 1976.
41. Ibid., letters from Marie Barrett, 3 November 1976 and from Church of Sacred Heart, Limerick, n.d.
42. Ibid., letter from Leland Lyons, 24 October 1976.
43. Ibid., letter from Francis J. Feeney.
44. Ibid., P51/213(F), letter from Raymond Crotty, 23 October 1976.
45. *Irish Times*, Irishman's Diary, 7 February 2011 and *Journal of the Bray Cualann Historical Society*, No. 6 (Dublin, 2011).

Part II The Impact of the Troubles on the Republic

1. Michael Kennedy, '"This tragic and most intractable problem": The Reaction of the Department of External Affairs to the Outbreak of the Troubles in Northern Ireland', *Irish Studies in International Affairs*, vol. 12, 2001, pp. 87–97.
2. Ibid.
3. Ibid.
4. Thomas Hennessey, *The Evolution of the Troubles 1970–72* (Dublin, 2007), p. 176.
5. Michael Kennedy, *Division and Consensus: The Politics of Cross-Border Relations in Ireland, 1925–69* (Dublin, 2000), pp. 332–68.
6. Eamonn McCann, 'Bloody Sunday Helped Reconcile Southern Nationalists to Partition', *Irish Times*, 28 January 2012.
7. *Seven Ages* documentary series.
8. Brian Farrell, Robert Fisk and P. N. Ferns, *A One Day Symposium on 'The British Question' Erroneously Called 'The Irish Question', the Effect of Violence and Why Conservation Matters* (Pontypridd, 1978).
9. Daniel Williamson, 'Taking the Troubles across the Atlantic: Ireland's UN Initiatives and Irish-US Diplomatic Relations in the Early Years of the Conflict in Northern Ireland, 1969–72', *Irish Studies in International Affairs*, vol. 18, 2007, pp. 175–89.
10. John A. Murphy, 'Further Reflections on Irish Nationalism', *Crane Bag*, vol. 1, no. 2, 1977, pp. 156–62.
11. James Downey, *Them and Us* (Dublin, 1983).
12. *Seven Ages* documentary series.
13. Austin Currie, *All Hell Will Break Loose* (Dublin, 2004), pp. 141–80.
14. Garret FitzGerald, 'The Threat of a British Withdrawal from Northern Ireland in the mid 1970s', *Irish Studies in International Affairs* vol. 17, 2006, pp. 141–50.
15. Downey, *Them and Us*, p. 114.
16. Merlyn Rees, *Northern Ireland: A Personal Perspective* (London, 1985), pp. 14–16, 301–14.
17. Hennessey, *The Evolution of the Troubles*, pp. 176–98.
18. Brian Faulkner, *Memoirs of a Statesman* (London, 1978), pp. 127–9.

19. Paul Dixon, 'Northern Ireland and the International Dimension: The End of the Cold War, the USA and European Integration', *Irish Studies in International Affairs*, vol. 13, 2002, pp. 105–20.
20. *Fortnight*, 3 March 1979.

10 A Post-1916 Mood

1. UCDA, Kelly Papers, P147/16, 24 May 1971.
2. *Hibernia*, 8 August 1971.
3. *Hibernia*, 4 February 1972.
4. UCDA, FitzGerald Papers, P215/4, Leland Lyons to FitzGerald, 17 February 1972.
5. Ibid., Lyons to FitzGerald, 6 February 1972.
6. Ibid., Florence O'Donoghue to FitzGerald, 30 January 1972.
7. O'Brien, *Memoir*, p. 337.
8. *Irish Times*, 3 February 1972.
9. NAI, DT 2003/16/189, Dáil Debates, 3 February 1972.
10. Ibid., note from Minister for Foreign Affairs, 4 February 1972.
11. Ibid., letter to Jack Lynch, author's identity censored, 9 February 1972.
12. Ibid., Roger Greene and Sons Solicitors to Lynch, 8 February 1972.
13. NAI, DT 2003/16/472–3, 30 January 1972.
14. Don Mullan and John Scally, *Eyewitness Bloody Sunday* (Dublin, 2002), pp. 26–30.
15. UCDA, Kelly Papers, P147/15, draft letter to *Sunday Times*, 2 February 1971.
16. *Irish Independent*, 19 June 2010.
17. UCDA, FitzGerald Papers, P215/4, FitzGerald to Lord Moyne, 7 February 1972.
18. John Bowman, 'How Jack Lynch Helped Lay the Foundations for Powersharing in the North', *Irish Times*, 1 January 2003.
19. *Irish Press*, 5 September 1972 and NAI, DT 2003/16/589.
20. NAI, DT 2004/21/465, Partition: Government Policy, memorandum of McColgan, London Embassy, 21 December 1972.
21. NAI, DT 2003/16/131, National Government, Proposed Formation, Des O'Malley to Lynch, 25 October 1972.
22. UCDA, FitzGerald Papers, P215/566, Cruise O'Brien to FitzGerald, 23 March 1973.
23. NAI, DT 2004/21/465, unsigned memo, c. January 1973.
24. Ibid., letter of Leland Lyons, 6 February 1972.
25. NAI, DT 2004/21/578, British Irish Association, 1 February 1973.
26. UCDA, FitzGerald Papers, P215/15, D. O'Sullivan to Keating, 17 January 1973.
27. NAI, DT 2008/148/716, British Irish Association meeting, 24 June 1978; Minister for Foreign Affairs cabinet minute, 8 May 1978; Lord Vaizey to Lynch, 25 May 1978; Patrick Lynch to Marigold Johnson, 23 June 1978; handwritten note of Jack Lynch, 20 July 1978.
28. UCDA, FitzGerald Papers, P215/481, American Committee for Irish Studies, April 1976.

11 Studied Indifference or Generous Tolerance?

1. Aodhan Madden, *Fear and Loathing in Dublin* (Dublin, 2009), pp. 7–13.

2. UCDA, de Courcy Ireland Papers, P29/27, Workers Association for the Democratic Settlement of the National Conflict, 18 October 1974.
3. UCDA, FitzGerald Papers, P215/4, Brian Walker to FitzGerald, 6 October 1972.
4. Ibid., FitzGerald to Henry Stevenson, 10 September 1972.
5. Coogan, *A Memoir*, p. 180.
6. Madden, *Fear and Loathing*, p. 17.
7. Christy Moore, *One Voice: My Life in Song* (London, 2003), p. 55.
8. Paddy Harte, *Young Tigers and Mongrel Foxes* (Dublin, 2005), pp. 112–64, 177–88.
9. Declan Kiberd, *Inventing Ireland: The Literature of the Modern Nation* (London, 1995), p. 575.
10. NAI, DT 2004/21/494, Charity to Give Holidays to Children from the Troubles, memorandum of 16 February 1973.
11. NAI, DT 2008/148/689, Partition, Marie Hetherington to Lynch, 11 March 1978.
12. NAI, DT 2003/16/76, Religious Tolerance in Ireland, 13 January 1972 and *Irish Press*, 13 January 1972.
13. Ibid., and *Irish Press* and *Irish Times*, 12 February 1972.
14. Ibid., Jack Lynch to William Wynne, 15 February 1972.
15. NAI, DT 2003/16/76, 14 July 1971.
16. *Irish Times*, 18 February 1972.
17. NAI, DT 2003/17/76, 16 October 1972.
18. NAI, DT 2003/16/589, Olympic Games, Munich 1972, account of meeting with Brandt, 8 September 1972.
19. NAI, DT 2005/151/711 and DT 2005/151/671, January 1974 to October 1975.
20. NAI, DT 2006/133/674, Movements for Peace in Ireland, 26 May 1976, speech by FitzGerald to Fine Gael Dublin South East Executive.
21. *Hibernia*, 25 July 1975.
22. Heather Crawford, *Outside the Glow: Protestants and Irishness in Independent Ireland* (Dublin, 2010), p. 37.
23. Ibid., pp. 95–116.

12 Lost Reputations and Suppressed Truth

1. NAI, DT 2003/17/76, National Government, Proposed Formation, Hugo Flinn to Lynch, 1 February 1972 and Liam O'Brien to Lynch, 15 February 1972 and Lynch reply, 17 February 1972.
2. Patrick Maume, 'Neil Blayney', in McGuire and Quinn, *DIB*, vol. 1, pp. 597–603.
3. Captain James Kelly, *Orders for the Captain* (Dublin 1971) and *The Thimbleriggers* (Dublin, 1999). See also Tom MacIntyre, *Through the Bridewell Gate* (Dublin, 1971) and Seán Boyne, *The Gunrunners* (Dublin, 2006).
4. Mills, *Hurler on the Ditch*, pp. 62–77 and Collins, *Cosgrave Legacy*, pp. 103–6.
5. Maume, 'Neil Blaney'.
6. 'Rolling Back the Years, 1970–1974', *Irish Independent* Supplement, 22 October 2011.
7. Fanning, 'Jack Lynch'.
8. T. Ryle Dwyer, *Nice Fellow: A Biography of Jack Lynch* (Cork, 2001), p. 178.

9. Keogh, *Jack Lynch*, pp. 225–31.
10. UCDA, Fianna Fáil Papers, P176/448, parliamentary party minutes, 6 May 1970.
11. Justin O'Brien, *The Arms Trial* (Dublin, 2000), p. 66.
12. UCDA, Fianna Fáil Papers, P176/89, Séamus Brennan to Mullins, 8 June 1972.
13. *Irish Times*, 16–21 July 2003.
14. Patrick Maume, 'James Gibbons', in McGuire and Quinn, *DIB*, vol. 4, pp. 61–3.
15. Ibid.
16. Ibid.
17. O'Brien, *Arms Trial*, pp. 135–6 and Vincent Browne, 'The Arms Trial', *Magill*, May 1980.
18. Paul Bew, *Ireland: The Politics of Enmity, 1789–2006* (Oxford, 2007), pp. 500–501.
19. Downey, *In My Own Time*, p. 124.
20. Stephen Collins, *The Power Game: Fianna Fáil Since Lemass* (Dublin, 2000), p. 84.
21. O'Brien, *Arms Trial*, p. 117.
22. NAI, Lynch Papers, 1195/3/120/27, Peter Berry to Des O'Malley, 6 March 1973 and reply, 13 March 1973.
23. Keogh, *Jack Lynch*, p. 257.
24. Coogan, *A Memoir*, p. 183.
25. Diarmaid Ferriter, *The Transformation of Ireland, 1900–2000* (2nd edn, London, 2005), pp. 688–90.
26. Fanning, 'Jack Lynch'.
27. NAI, Lynch Papers, 1195/3/120/37, undated account of meeting with Vincent Browne, c. 6 May 1980.
28. Bew, *Politics of Enmity*, pp. 489–501.
29. *Hibernia*, 8 January 1971.
30. *Financial Times*, 7 May 1970.
31. *Hibernia*, 15 May 1970.
32. O'Brien, *Arms Trial*, p. 222.
33. Downey, *In My Own Time*, p. 117 and Henry Patterson, *Ireland Since 1939: The Persistence of Conflict* (London, 2006), pp. 174–5.
34. UCDA, Kelly Papers, P147/14, Kelly to Cosgrave, 14 August 1971.
35. Downey, *In My Own Time*, pp. 121–6.
36. John Walsh, *Patrick Hillery: The Official Biography* (Dublin, 2008), p. 207.
37. Ibid., p. 210.
38. UCDA, Kelly Papers, P147/18, notes on arms crisis, May 1970 on Dáil Éireann notepaper. Author unclear.
39. Ibid., J. W. Sanfey to Fine Gael TDs, 11 May 1970.
40. *Hibernia*, 19 November 1971.
41. Ibid., P147/57, Fine Gael policy on Northern Ireland, 1970–71, Kelly's speech to Kildare Constituency Executive of Fine Gael, 17 January 1972 and speeches of 18 February 1972, 27 February 1976, and 25 February 1974.
42. UCDA, Fianna Fáil Papers, P176/448, parliamentary party minutes, 27 October 1970.

43. Ibid., P176/350, National Executive minutes, 26 January and 26 October 1970, 13 March and 23 October 1972.
44. *Irish Times*, 14 August 1973.
45. Keogh, *Jack Lynch*, pp. 380–87.
46. NAI, Cosgrave Papers, 1194, 35–59, Richie Ryan account of conversation with British ambassador, 11 August 1973.
47. Catherine O'Donnell, *Fianna Fáil, Irish Republicanism and the Northern Ireland Troubles, 1968–2005* (Dublin, 2007), pp. 21–45.

13 Green America and Blue Britain

1. NAI, DT 2003/16/241, IRA Activities: Representations from Organisations and Individuals, Patrick Fahy to Lynch, 6 June 1972.
2. UCDA, FitzGerald Papers, P215/566, Cruise O'Brien to FitzGerald, 9 April 1973.
3. Ibid., P215/567, Cruise O'Brien to FitzGerald, 30 April 1975.
4. Brian Hanley, 'The Politics of NORAID', *Irish Political Studies*, vol. 19, no. 1, Summer 2004, pp. 1–18.
5. NAI, DT 2003/16/241, memorandum from Michael Lillis on the Irish-Americans, 18 April 1975.
6. Ibid., Timothy Scannell to Lynch, 2 June 1972.
7. NAI, DT 2003/16/262, IRA: Activities in Ireland, 7 December 1972 to 31 March 1973, John McGowan to Lynch, 7 December 1972.
8. NAI, DT 2003/16/509, Patrick McGuinness to Lynch, 1 February 1972 and response, 10 February 1972.
9. NAI, DT 2005/151/307, Constitution 1937: Suggested Amendments, 11 February 1972.
10. NAI, DT 2007/116/732, William Green to Lynch, 24 October 1977 and F. Murray to Miss Murphy, 27 October 1977.
11. NAI, DT 2008/148/689, Partition, Robert Robinson to Lynch and McCarthy to F. Murray and reply, 22 February 1978.
12. NAI, DT 2003/16/283, Cormac O'Malley to Seán Cooney, 17 October 1971 and Seán Cooney to Lynch, 12 January 1972 and Fred Broughton to Lynch, 29 November 1972.
13. NAI, DT 2003/16/509, Partition: Miscellaneous Correspondence and Resolutions, James Heaney to Lynch, 3 February 1972.
14. Ibid., Lynch to C. L. O'Donnell, 11 February 1972.
15. Ibid., John McKenna to Lynch, 2 February 1972.
16. Ibid., Risteard Mulcahy to Lynch, 4 February 1972.
17. Ibid., E. Flood to Lynch, 7 February 1972, Pat Kilroy to Lynch, 3 February 1972, card from Wendy McKee, 11 February 1972 and letter of Gearóid Mac Nultaigh, 11 February 1972.
18. NAI, DT 2004/21/487, H. Quigley to Lynch, 14 December 1972.
19. NAI, DT 2008/148/755, Partition: Statements and Resolutions, Thomas O'Donnell to Lynch, 11 May 1978.

20. NAI, DT 2004/21/487, Partition: Miscellaneous Correspondence, Ronald Callon to Lynch, 19 January 1973 and Paul Meighan to Lynch, 9 January 1973 and *Chicago Tribune*, 12 January 1973.
21. UCDA, FitzGerald Papers, P215/495, Consulate General in Boston to Secretary, Department of Foreign Affairs, 12 October 1976.
22. *Irish Times*, 18 January 1978.
23. UCDA, FitzGerald Papers, P215/387, visit to Washington, 14–18 March 1977.
24. Hanley, 'The Politics of NORAID', pp. 16–18.
25. Seán Cronin, *Washington's Irish Policy, 1916–86* (Dublin, 1987), pp. 311–13.
26. UCDA, Papers of Patrick Cosgrave, P233/48, Corfu, July 1997.
27. Ibid.
28. UCDA, Ó Dálaigh Papers, P51/106(2), Hailsham to Ó Dálaigh, 30 June 1971.
29. NAI, DT 2003/16/283, Publicity on Ireland Abroad: General, 24 November 1971 and *Irish Times*, 24 November 1971 and J. E. Mattison to Lynch, 6 January 1972.
30. Dáil Debates, 19 January 1972.
31. UCDA, FitzGerald Papers, P215/567, Cruise O'Brien to John Freeman, LWT, 21 January 1974.
32. NAI, DT 2003/16/283, Lynch to Dermot Kinlen, 17 February 1972 and Erskine Childers to Lynch, 5 September 1972.
33. NAI, DT 2004/21/470, Westminster Lobby Correspondents: Visits to Ireland, 9 August 1971, 2 September 1971, W. E. Fairley to Lynch, 22 September 1972 and notes on journalists, 10–15 September 1973.
34. UCDA, FitzGerald Papers, P215/503, Colin Martin to Declan Kelly, Department of Foreign Affairs, and Colin Martin to FitzGerald, 6 November 1974.
35. *Magill*, August 1979.
36. NAI, DT 2003/16/344, Paddy Lalor to Lynch and reply, 6 November 1972.
37. Ibid., memorandum from Department of Industry and Commerce, 14 February 1972 and Donal O'Sullivan to Department of Taoiseach, 15 May 1972.
38. NAI, DT 2003/16/509, 10 February 1972.
39. NAI, DT 2003/16/589, Olympic Games, Munich 1972, 8 September 1972.
40. NAI, DT 2005/7/587, Cosgrave to Robin Glassock, 25 March 1973.
41. NAI, DT 2007/116/734, IRA activities in Great Britain, 10 February 1977.
42. NAI, DT 2007/116/742, IRA activities in Ireland, Cosgrave to D. L. Armstrong, 9 February 1977.
43. NAI, DT 2007/116/749, Partition: Government Policy, memorandum of 14 January 1977.
44. NAI, DT 2008/148/689, Partition, Hugh Swift to Frank Murray, 10 March 1978.
45. UCDA, Kelly Papers, P147/47, 17 March 1974.
46. UCDA, FitzGerald Papers, P215/497, 22 November 1974.

14 Reporting and Broadcasting the Conflict

1. UCDA, FitzGerald Papers, P215/497, 31 December 1971.
2. *Hibernia*, 25 May 1973.

3. Ivor Kenny, *Talking to Journalists: Conversations with Editors of the Irish News Media* (Galway, 1994), p. 112.
4. Andrew Whitaker (ed.), *Bright, Brilliant Days: Douglas Gageby and the Irish Times* (Dublin, 2006), p. 99.
5. Ibid., p. 104, and Downey, *In My Own Time*, p. 152.
6. Mark O'Brien, *The Irish Times: A History* (Dublin, 2008), p. 191.
7. Ibid., p. 211.
8. Ibid., pp. 212–17.
9. Ibid., p. 192.
10. Ibid.
11. Bowman, *Window and Mirror*, p. 125.
12. Mary Corcoran and Mark O'Brien (eds), *Political Censorship and the Democratic State: The Irish Broadcasting Ban* (Dublin, 2005), p. 48.
13. Ibid., p. 53.
14. Ibid.
15. UCDA, FitzGerald Papers, P215/566, correspondence with Cruise O'Brien, 12 November 1973.
16. Ibid., Cruise O'Brien to Cosgrave, 6 September 1973.
17. Ibid., P215/566, Magheramorne Presbyterian Church to Cruise O'Brien, 17 July 1973.
18. *Magill*, April 1978.
19. Whelan, *Conor Cruise O'Brien*, p. 7.
20. Ibid., pp. 155–74.
21. NAI, DT 2004/21/69, Radio and TV: Political Broadcasts, Cruise O'Brien to Dónall Ó Móráin, Gael Linn, 18 July 1973.
22. NAI, DT 2004/21/605, National Day of Reconciliation, Cruise O'Brien to Ó Móráin, 19 June 1973.
23. NAI, Cosgrave Papers, 1194/25–38, note of 26 September 1974.
24. Ibid., Conor Cruise O'Brien to Cosgrave, 21 March 1974.
25. Bowman, *Window and Mirror*, p. 125.
26. NAI, Cosgrave Papers, 1194, 25–38, Cruise O'Brien to Cosgrave, 21 January 1974.
27. Patrick Kinsella, 'War and Peace on the Screen: Television Representations of Conflict in Ireland', in John Horgan, Barbara O'Connor and Helen Sheehan (eds), *Mapping Irish Media: Critical Explorations* (Dublin, 2007), pp. 95–111.
28. UCDA, FitzGerald Papers, P215/4, FitzGerald to Mary Taafe, 7 June 1972 and to Peter Hoey, 24 May 1972.
29. Ibid.
30. NAI, DT 2007/116/749, Partition: Government Policy, 28 September 1977.

15 Possibilities, Encounters and Institutions to Trust

1. UCDA, FitzGerald Papers, P215/555, Costello to FitzGerald, 7 June 1974 and 23 October 1974.
2. NAI, DT 2005/7/666, Partition: Inter-Departmental Unit, June and November 1974.

3. *Irish Times*, 17 June 1974.
4. NAI, DT 2005/151/703 and DT 2005/7/666, Partition: Inter-Departmental Unit, 9 and 15 November 1974, and paper by Brendan Dowling: 'Some Economic Implications of a Federal Ireland' and 'Cost of Repartition', 26 November 1974.
5. NAI/DT 2005/7/484, Defence Forces: Increasing Numbers: Notes on Implications of the Breakdown in Power Sharing in Northern Ireland, June 1974.
6. Andy Pollak, 'Defence Forces: Waiting for Doomsday?', *Hibernia*, 7 June 1974.
7. Ibid., assessment of possibilities of military intervention, memorandum by Lt Col. Kevin O'Brien, 14 June 1974.
8. Ibid., 20 June 1974 and Dáil Debates, 10 July 1974.
9. UCDA, de Courcy Ireland Papers, P129/63, n.d., c. 1973.
10. *Hibernia*, 27 August 1971.
11. Bew, *Politics of Enmity*, p. 525, and Brian Trench in *Magill*, November 1978.
12. Brian Hanley and Scott Millar, *The Lost Revolution: The Story of the Official IRA and the Workers Party* (Dublin, 2009), p. 305.
13. Ibid., p. 326.
14. Ibid., pp. 220ff., chapters 6–8.
15. NAI, DT 2004/21/456, memorandum from Donal O'Sullivan, 14 June 1972.
16. NAI, DT 2004/21/465, Donal O'Sullivan to Hugh McCann, secretary of the Department of Foreign Affairs, 10 January 1973.
17. Ibid., memorandum on meeting in the Foreign and Commonwealth Office, 22 January 1973, *Irish Press*, 6 February 1973 and account of conversation between C. V. Whelan and Stewart Crawford, 2 February 1973.
18. Ibid., 14 February 1973.
19. NAI, DT 2004/21/441, Partition: Inter-Departmental Unit, 21 June 1973.
20. NAI, DT 2004/21/469, discussions between Taoiseach and British prime minister; Donal O'Sullivan to FitzGerald, 18 June 1973, FitzGerald to Cosgrave, 1 July 1973 and note of conversation with Tom Canaty and Pádraig Murphy, 28 June 1973 and account of meeting between prime minister and Taoiseach, 2 July 1973.
21. NAI, DT 2005/7/403, Conor Cruise O'Brien to Cosgrave, 13 September 1973, Desmond Leslie to Cosgrave, 14 September 1973 and note of discussion with British ambassador, 13 September 1973.
22. Ibid., Mr Heath, British Prime Minister, Visit to Ireland 1973, memorandum of Muiris Mac Conghail, 10 September 1973.
23. Ibid., summary of visit.
24. Ibid., account of meeting between Faulkner and Nally and Donlon, 26 October 1973.
25. Sweeney, *Down, Down*, pp. 28–9.
26. NAI, DT 2004/21/628, Proposals for a Northern Ireland Settlement, Discussions in Sunningdale, 6–9 December 1973 and Brian Faulkner to Brendan Corish, 17 December 1973.
27. Seán Farren, *The SDLP: The Struggle for Agreement in Northern Ireland, 1970–2000* (Dublin, 2010), pp. 17–35.
28. Bew, *Politics of Enmity*, pp. 509–10.

29. NAI, DT 2005/7/624, Proposals on Northern Ireland Settlement, 13 January 1974.
30. Ibid., note from Mac Conghail, 7 January 1974.
31. Ibid., note for Taoiseach from Dermot Nally, 7 January 1974 and note from Mac Conghail, 5 January 1974.
32. Ibid., Seán Donlon's account of visit to Belfast, 9 January 1974.
33. *Seven Ages* documentary series.
34. Bew, *Politics of Enmity*, pp. 513–15.
35. NAI, DT 2005/7/587, Fr Raymond Murray to Cosgrave, 23 May 1974.
36. NAI, DT 2005/7/622, All Party Committee on Irish Relations, meeting with Alliance Party, 1 May 1974.
37. NAI, DT 2004/22/36, notes on briefing by Taoiseach, June 1974.
38. NAI, DT 2006/133/691, visit by British Parliamentary group to Taoiseach, 23 February 1976.
39. NAI, DT 2006/133/696, Partition: Miscellaneous Correspondence, 23 January 1976.

16 Visitors from the North

1. NAI, DT 2004/21/79, Partition: Statements, Resolutions by Northern Irish Groups, Daniel Marron to Lynch, 1 January 1973 and letter of Br M. Brady, 9 February 1973.
2. NAI, DT 2005/7/587, Catherine McGerty to Cosgrave, 29 May 1974.
3. NAI, DT 2005/7/616, Northern Ireland: Financial Assistance, Peaceful Resistance and Relief of Distress, report of Seán Donlon, 8 February 1974.
4. NAI, DT 2005/7/403, visit to Ireland by Heath, 1973, note of Seán Donlon, 14 September 1973.
5. UCDA, FitzGerald Papers, P215/567, Cruise O'Brien to FitzGerald, 27 January 1975.
6. UCDA, Fianna Fáil Papers, P176/448, parliamentary party minutes, 22 September 1971.
7. Farren, *The SDLP*, pp. 17–35.
8. NAI, DT 2003/16/601, Social, Cultural and Economic Co-operation between 26 and 6 Counties, April 1972.
9. UCDA, FitzGerald Papers, P215/4, FitzGerald to Phelim O'Neill, 22 February 1972.
10. UCDA, Fianna Fáil Papers, P176/350, National Executive minutes, 24 April 1978.
11. Ibid., Paddy Devlin to FitzGerald, 23 July 1973.
12. Cruise O'Brien, *Memoir*, pp. 335–43.
13. Farren, *The SDLP*, p. 66.
14. Downey, *In My Own Time*, p. 176.
15. NAI, DT 2005/7/649, Northern Ireland: Relations with SDLP, January 1974 to August 1975, Seán Donlon to Dermot Nally, 6 November 1973, memorandum by Seán Donlon on visit to Belfast, 13–14 February 1976 and account of meeting at Iveagh House, 22 April 1974.

16. Ibid., report of Donlon for 21 May 1974 and report on visit of 31 May to 2 June 1974.
17. Farren, *The SDLP*, p. 50.
18. NAI, DT 2005/7/649, 21 August 1974.
19. Ibid.
20. Ibid., Department of Taoiseach note of 8 November 1974 and Seán Donlon's account of his visit to Belfast, 23–25 October 1974.
21. Ibid., SDLP and government meeting, 22 November 1974.
22. Bew, *Politics of Enmity*, pp. 522–3.
23. NAI, DT 2006/133/684, Northern Ireland: Relations with SDLP, 14 January 1976 to 29 September 1976.
24. Ibid., W. Kirwan to Donlon, 12 April 1976.
25. Ibid., letter of Seán Donlon, 15 September 1976.
26. Ibid., report of meeting with SDLP, 22 September 1976.
27. Ibid.
28. Farren, *The SDLP*, pp. 125–6.
29. NAI, DT 2007/116/749, Partition: Government Policy, 14 January 1977.
30. NAI, DT 2007/116/740, Farrell McElgunn to Lynch, 14 November 1977.
31. NAI, DT 2005/7/649, Northern Ireland: Relations with SDLP, 15 August 1977 and 23 August 1977 and F. Murray to Donlon, 25 August 1977.
32. Ibid., Murray to Nally, 14 November 1977.
33. NAI, DT 2007/116/750, account of meeting between Lynch and Callaghan, 28 September 1977.
34. NAI, DT 2008/148/716, Northern Ireland: Relations with SDLP, report by Donlon of visit of Minister for Foreign Affairs to Belfast and account of meeting with SDLP, 8 January 1978 and DT 2008/148/721, Northern Ireland: Implications of a British Withdrawal, 3 January 1978 to 19 December 1978.

17 A More Tolerant Republic?

1. NAI, DT 2003/16/533, Inter-Departmental Committee on the Implications of Irish Unity, Michael O'Leary to Lynch, 29 November 1971.
2. Ibid., account of meeting between Lynch and Corish, 21 December 1971 and meeting with Cosgrave, 6 January 1972 and note signed 'FF', author unclear.
3. Ibid., J. Holloway to Stokes, 2 June 1972 and marginal note of Stokes in response.
4. NAI, DT 2003/16/533, 6 December 1972.
5. UCDA, FitzGerald Papers, P215/8, FitzGerald to William Whitelaw, 4 March 1972.
6. NAI, DT 2004/21/456, 18 July 1972.
7. NAI, DT 2003/16/460, memorandum from Department of Taoiseach, 18 February 1972.
8. UCDA, FitzGerald Papers, P215/3, c. January 1971, FitzGerald to Cruise O'Brien.
9. Ibid., FitzGerald to Revd R. Adams, Lisburn, 20 October 1972.
10. UCDA, FitzGerald Papers, P215/4, letter to Manus O'Riordan, 23 October 1972 and letter to Michael O'Loinsigh, 21 February 1973.

11. Ibid., FitzGerald to Henry Stevenson, 10 September 1972.
12. Ibid., FitzGerald to Judy Hayes, 23 October 1972 and letter to Manus O'Riordan, 27 September 1972.
13. NAI, DT 2003/16/460, memorandum from Department of Taoiseach, 18 February 1972.
14. Ibid.
15. NAI, DT 2004/21/465, Partition: Government Policy, 1 December 1972 to 28 February 1973, memorandum of McColgan at London Embassy, 21 December 1972.
16. NAI, DT 2004/21/505, Inter-Departmental Committee on the Implications of Irish Unity, 17 January 1973 and 17 April 1973.
17. NAI, Cosgrave Papers, DT 2004/22/36, press, radio and TV interviews, 19 July 1973.
18. NAI, DT 2005/151/307, Constitution 1937, Suggested Amendments and *Irish Independent*, 6 June 1971.
19. Ibid., 30 August 1972.
20. Ibid., 18 July 1974 and 26 October 1974.
21. NAI, DT 2005/7/622, Inter-Departmental Committee on the Implications of Irish Unity, 1 May 1974.
22. NAI, DT 2007/116/749, Partition: Government Policy, notes on discussion between Minister for Foreign Affairs and Casaroli, 28 March 1977.
23. NAI, Cosgrave Papers, DT 2004/22/36, press, radio and television interviews, 21 June 1974.
24. NAI, DT 2005/7/587, Kevin Donaghy to Cosgrave, 14 June 1974.
25. Ibid., Partition: Statements and Resolutions, John Cleland to Cosgrave, 14 March 1974.
26. NAI, DT 2005/151/307, Constitution 1937: Suggested Amendments, 20 September 1974.
27. NAI, DT 2008/148/716, NI: Relations with SDLP, report by Seán Donlon of visit to Northern Ireland by Minister for Foreign Affairs, 17 and 18 May 1978.
28. *Magill*, October 1978.
29. Nuala O'Faoláin, *Are You Somebody?* (Dublin, 1996), p. 133.
30. Montague, *Pear is Ripe*, p. 127.
31. Nell McCafferty, *Nell* (Dublin, 2004), pp. 147–50.
32. Susan McKay, *Bear in Mind These Dead* (London, 2008), p. 3.
33. Frank Callanan (ed.), *The Literary and Historical Society, 1955–2005* (Dublin, 2005), pp. 165–74.

18 Trouble Spills Over the Border

1. NAI, DT 2004/21/252, IRA Activities in Ireland, 7 December 1972 to 31 January 1973.
2. NAI, DT 2004/21/487, Partition: Miscellaneous Correspondence, 12 December 1972.
3. Joe Tiernan, *The Dublin and Monaghan Bombings* (Dublin, 2010), p. 123.
4. Collins, *Cosgrave Legacy*, pp. 115–25, Harte, *Young Tigers*, p. 105.

5. NAI, DT 2005/7/660, 26 Counties: Explosions, May 1974.
6. Ibid., 17 May 1974.
7. Sweeney, *Down, Down*, p. 35.
8. Tiernan, *Dublin and Monaghan Bombings*, p. 7.
9. Ibid.
10. NAI, DT 2005/7/484, Defence Forces, Increasing Numbers, memo of June 1974 and *Hibernia*, 7 June 1974.
11. NAI, DT 2005/7/660, David Walsh to Cosgrave, 17 May 1974.
12. *Sunday Business Post*, 4 December 2003.
13. Tiernan, *Dublin and Monaghan Bombings*, pp. 7, 258–9.
14. *Irish Times*, 12 July 2006.
15. NAI, Cosgrave Papers, 1194/35–59, Richie Ryan to Cosgrave, 25 May 1974.
16. NAI, DT 2006/133/270, Local Security Force: Establishment 1974, meeting of Inter-Departmental National Security Group, 17 May 1974, announcement by Cosgrave, 26 June 1974 and memorandum by Richard Stokes, 17 October 1974.
17. Diarmaid Ferriter and Patrick Maume, 'William Fox', in McGuire and Quinn, *DIB*, vol. 3, pp. 1086–7.
18. *Hibernia*, 15 March 1974.
19. Ferriter and Maume, 'William Fox'.
20. Ibid.
21. *Sunday Business Post*, 18 December 2011.
22. Sweeney, *Down, Down*, pp. 43–4.
23. Ibid., p. 80.
24. *Irish Times*, Health Supplement, 4 October 2011 and Colm Connolly, *Siege! Monasterevin* (Dublin, 1976).
25. NAI, DT 2008/148/701, IRA activities in Ireland, *Irish Press*, 2 January 1978, *Irish Times*, 25 January 1978 and *Sunday Express*, 5 February 1978.
26. NAI, DT 2004/21/105, Hunger Strikes: memorandum from Department of Justice, 14 September 1973.
27. Ibid., letter of Julie Dongan, Sinn Féin, Portadown, 1 October 1973.
28. Ibid., note of conversation with John Hume, 3 October 1973.
29. Ibid., telegram to Cosgrave from Michael O'Flanagan, 3 October 1973.
30. NAI, DT 2005/151/307, Constitution 1937: Suggested Amendments, 4 February 1971 and 6 December 1971.
31. UCDA, FitzGerald Papers, P215/568, Edward Daly to Cruise O'Brien, 15 February 1976.
32. Ibid., P215/403, Cosgrave to FitzGerald, 27 April 1977.
33. Ibid., c. April 1973.
34. Ibid., P215/403 and 404, 4 May 1973 and undated notes.
35. NAI, DT 2007/116/794, Prison Conditions: Republic of Ireland, 30 January 1975 and 24 February 1975 and letter of David Green, 14 February 1977 and Mary Grant, 24 January 1977. Correspondence between Cooney and Bishop Patrick Lennon, 9 April, 20 June, 8 August and 23 September 1975.

36. Ibid., Edward Daly to Cooney, 16 September 1976 and 28 December 1976, Cosgrave to Daly, 30 March 1977 and J. W. Sanfey to Fine Gael members, 6 April 1977.
37. NAI, DT 2007/116/742, IRA Activities in Ireland, 2 February 1977.
38. Desmond, *Finally and in Conclusion*, p. 151.
39. NAI, DT 2007/116/729, cabinet meeting, 19 April 1977.
40. Ibid., Eugene Wynne to Supreme Knight, 13 April 1977.
41. Ibid., letter of Sighle Bean Ui Donnchadha, 14 April 1977, and letter of Joseph Clany, 18 April 1977.
42. Ibid., Apostolic Nuncio to Cosgrave, 20 April 1977.
43. NAI, DT 2007/116/750, ambassador at Holy See to Seán Donlon, 9 May 1977 and 6 May 1977.
44. *Magill*, October 1977.
45. Ed Moloney, 'Inside H Block', *Magill*, December 1979.
46. Moore, *One Voice*, pp. 55ff.
47. *Guardian*, 30 June 1979.
48. NAI, DT 2009/135/572, Dr Tomás Ó Fiaich, Appointment as Cardinal.
49. Ibid., 30 May 1979.
50. NAI, DT 2007/116/729, Cosgrave to Cooney, 6 May 1977 and reply, 11 May 1977.
51. NAI, DT 2006/133/707, Frank Stagg: Hunger Strike and Death, 2 January 1976 to 10 March 1976, and Garret FitzGerald to Patrick Cosgrave, 10 February 1976.
52. Ibid., 20 January 1976.
53. Patrick Maume, 'Frank Stagg', in McGuire and Quinn, *DIB*, vol. 8, pp. 1114–15.
54. Ibid., Mrs Brian Farrell to Cosgrave, 19 February 1976 and Maurice Manning to Cosgrave, 22 February 1976.
55. Sweeney, *Down, Down*, pp. 81–2.
56. NAI, DT 2003/133/700–704, Brian Ward to Cosgrave, 9 June 1976.
57. Ibid.
58. Ibid., cabinet discussion, 15 June 1976 and Douglas Hoyle to Ó Dálaigh, 13 June 1976.
59. Ibid., Ó Dálaigh to Cosgrave, 8 July 1976.
60. Sweeney, *Down, Down*, p. 85.
61. Ibid., p. 89.
62. NAI, DT 2006/133/708, British Ambassador to Ireland: Assassination, 1976, 21 July 1976.
63. Ibid., digest of foreign press coverage of Ireland, 23 July 1976.
64. Ibid., address by FitzGerald at memorial service, 28 July 1976 and Bernard McGinley to Cosgrave, 29 July 1976.
65. Ibid., Brian Gubbon to FitzGerald, 11 August 1976.
66. UCDA, FitzGerald Papers, P215/603, Brian Cubbon to FitzGerald and Mrs Ewart-Biggs to FitzGerald, 10 January 1977.
67. Ibid., Donal O'Sullivan to FitzGerald, 5 October 1976.
68. Ibid., Thomas Pakenham to FitzGerald, 30 September 1976.

69. NAI, DT 2006/133/580, Emergency Powers Act 1976, Department of Justice memorandum, 10 August 1976.
70. Ibid., memorandum of Declan Costello, 4 August 1976 and record of cabinet meeting, 24 September 1976.
71. Ibid., 25 September 1976.
72. Sweeney, *Down, Down*, pp. 184–6.
73. Ibid., pp. 184–5.

19 A Passion for Unity?

1. NAI, DT 2007/116/749, Partition: Government Policy, 28 September 1977.
2. NAI, DT 2008/148/708, Partition: Government Policy, 10 October 1978 to 21 December 1978, memorandum of W. Kirwan, 10 October 1978.
3. NAI, DT 2007/116/780, Cross Border Communications: Study for the Derry/Donegal area, 14 November 1977.
4. NAI, DT 2008/148/700, Social, Cultural and Economic Co-operation between 26 and 6 Counties, 24 May 1978 and Patrick Grant to Lynch, 27 November 1978.
5. Ibid., report on economic co-operation, June 1978.
6. *Magill*, October 1977 and Bew, *Politics of Enmity*, pp. 509–10.
7. Corcoran and O'Brien, *Political Censorship*, p. 49.
8. McDaid, 'The David Thornley Affair'.
9. NAI, DT 2008/148/721, Northern Ireland: Implications of a British Withdrawal, 24 August 1978.
10. Bew, *Politics of Enmity*, p. 525.
11. NAI, DT 2008/148/733, Partition: Miscellaneous Correspondence, Lynch to Tom O'Maoláin, 13 January 1978 and Eddie McAteer to Lynch, 9 January 1978.
12. NAI, DT 2008/148/280, Interviews Given by the Taoiseach, 9 January 1978 and message for London Embassy.
13. NAI, DT 2008/148/689, Partition, Fr Patrick Scott to Lynch, 25 February 1978.
14. NAI, DT 2008/148/709, discussions between British PM and Taoiseach regarding 6 counties and Paul Keating to Seán Donlon, 31 March 1978.
15. Ibid., 7 April 1978.
16. Ibid., 8 May 1978 and 27 November 1978.
17. NAI, DT 2008/148/716, Northern Ireland: Relations with SDLP, report by Donlon of visit of Minister for Foreign Affairs to Belfast and account of meeting with SDLP, 8 January 1978 and DT 2008/148/721, Northern Ireland: Implications of a British Withdrawal, 3 January 1978 to 19 December 1978.
18. NAI, Lynch Papers, 1195/3/120/37, Whitaker to Lynch, 5 September 1979 and reply, 17 September 1979.
19. Mills, *Hurler on the Ditch*, p. 128.
20. Keogh, *Jack Lynch*, pp. 430–34.
21. NAI, Lynch Papers, 1195/3/120/37, Secret: Security Preparations for Meeting of European Council, report of meeting on 19 November 1979.
22. *Irish Times*, 27 July 2009.
23. Farren, *The SDLP*, pp. 157–8.

Part III Commemoration, Memory, Cultural Life and Entertainment

1. Foster, *Luck and the Irish*, pp. 147–84.
2. Terence Brown, *Ireland: A Social and Cultural History, 1922–2002* (London, 2004; first published in 1981 as *Ireland: A Social and Cultural History, 1922–1979*), pp. 297–315.
3. 'The Irish Volunteers in 1920', *Capuchin Annual*, 1970, pp. 225–6.
4. Michael Laffan, 'The Sinn Féin Party', *Capuchin Annual*, 1970, pp. 227–35.
5. John Regan, 'Dr Jekyll and Mr Hyde: The Two Histories', *History Ireland*, vol. 20, no. 1, January/February 2012, pp. 10–14.
6. Brown, *Ireland*, pp. 278–81.
7. David Fitzpatrick, *Politics and Irish Life, 1913–21: Provincial Experience of War and Revolution* (Dublin, 1977), p. ix.
8. Donal McCartney, 'The Quest for Irish Political Identity: The Image and the Illusion', *Irish University Review*, vol. 9, no. 1, Spring 1979, pp. 13–21.
9. Francis Stuart, 'Literature and Politics', *Crane Bag*, vol. 1, no. 1, Spring 1977, pp. 72–7.
10. Brian P. Kennedy, *Dreams and Responsibilities: The State and the Arts in Independent Ireland* (Dublin, 1990), p. 157.
11. Ibid., p. 189.
12. Kiberd, *Inventing Ireland*, p. 569.
13. Derek Mahon, *Journalism: Selected Prose, 1970–1995* (Meath, 1996), p. 75.
14. Quinn, *My Education*, p. 177.
15. Julia M. Wright, *A Companion to Irish Literature: Volume Two* (London, 2010), pp. 196–208.
16. John Kenny, *John Banville* (Dublin, 2009), pp. 40–63.
17. Terence Brown, 'Dublin in Twentieth Century Writing: Metaphor and Subject', *Irish University Review*, vol. 8, no. 1, Spring 1978, pp. 7–22.
18. Richard Kearney, *Navigations: Collected Irish Essays: 1976–2006* (Dublin, 2006), p. xvii.
19. Dermot Foley, 'A Minstrel Boy with a Satchel of Books', *Irish University Review*, vol. 4, no. 2, Autumn 1974, pp. 204–18.
20. Ibid.
21. G. A. Hayes McCoy, 'Museums and Our National Heritage', *Capuchin Annual*, 1971, pp. 128–36.
22. John Horgan, *The Irish Media: A Critical History Since 1922* (London, 2001), p. 16.
23. Bowman, *Window and Mirror*, pp. 144–5.
24. Ibid., p. 160.
25. Niall Tóibín, *Smile and be a Villain* (Dublin, 1995), pp. 146–218.
26. Bob Geldof, *Is That It?* (London, 1986), p. 122.

20 Remembering the Fight for Freedom

1. NAI, DT 2000/6/53, Annual Commemorations of Wolfe Tone and *Irish Press*, 22 June 1970.

2. NAI, DT 2000/16/84, Garden of Remembrance, memorandum of Jerry Cronin, 24 February 1972.
3. Ibid., memorandum from Department of Taoiseach, 21 September 1971.
4. NAI, DT 2003/16/411, 6 December 1972, as reported in *Irish Independent*, 7 December 1972.
5. NAI, DT 2004/21/648, Michael Collins: Film on Life, Joe Hayes to secretary, Department of Foreign Affairs, 17 July 1973.
6. NAI, DT 2001/6/506, Civil War: Commemoration, *Irish Press* and *Irish Times*, 31 May 1971, Lynch in Dáil Debates, 9 December 1971 and Noel Browne to Lynch, 7 February 1973 and DT 2004/21/605, National Day of Reconciliation, Cruise O'Brien to Cosgrave, 14 June 1973.
7. NAI, DT 2004/21/605, National Day of Reconciliation, Cruise O'Brien to Paddy Donegan, 13 July 1973.
8. NAI, DT 2007/116/33, Bank and Public Holidays, Tomás O'Cleírigh to Cosgrave, 22 March 1974.
9. NAI, DT 2007/116/44, Roger Casement: Re-interment in Ireland, Department of Taoiseach memorandum, 31 August 1972.
10. Ibid., 7 November 1973.
11. *Hibernia*, 10 May 1974.
12. NAI, DT 2007/116/44, Richie Ryan to Cosgrave, 10 June 1974.
13. Ibid., S. C. O'Riordáin to Stokes, 6 December 1977.
14. Ibid., memorandum of Stokes, 20 December 1977.
15. Lucy McDiarmid, 'The Posthumous Life of Roger Casement', in Maryann Valiulis and Anthony Bradley (eds), *Gender and Sexuality in Modern Ireland* (Amherst, 1997), pp. 127–59.
16. NAI, DT 2008/148/105, Howth Gun Running 1914: Offer for Sale of Asgard, 29 October 1975 and 22 June 1978.
17. NAI, DT 2007/110/552, G. B. Shaw, Access to His Correspondence, 17 January 1977.
18. NAI, DT 2008/148/555, Ernie O'Malley: Museum of Art, Castlebar, 2 May 1978.
19. NAI, DT 2005/151/418, Daniel O'Connell: Bicentenary, *Irish Times*, 14 August 1975.
20. Ibid.
21. Ibid., speech of Liam Cosgrave, 15 August 1975.
22. John A. Murphy, 'History in the Classroom', *Education Times*, 30 August 1973.
23. NAI, DT 2005/151/418, Niall Montgomery to Cosgrave and Cosgrave's reply, 17 and 22 October 1975.
24. NAI, DT 2005/151/445, Oliver Plunkett: Canonisation 1975, Cardinal Conway to Cosgrave, 3 and 19 March 1975.
25. Ibid., Ambassador Woods to Paul Keating, 19 September 1975.
26. NAI, DT 2008/148/443, Pádraig Pearse: centenary of Birth, N. McMahon, Department of Tourism to Dan Ó Súilleabháin, assistant secretary of the Department of Taoiseach, 23 December 1977.

27. Ibid., 11 and 3 and 21 February 1978 and cabinet subcommittee meetings, 3 and 11 May 1978.
28. Francis Shaw, 'The Canon of Irish History: A Challenge', *Studies*, vol. 61, Summer 1972, pp. 117–51.
29. *Magill*, May 1978, Browne, *Magill Book of Irish Politics*, p. 266 and *Hibernia*, 19 November 1976.
30. Cited in Roisín Higgins and Regina Ui Chollatain, *The Life and After Life of P. H. Pearse* (Dublin, 2009), pp. 128ff.
31. *Irish Press*, 10 November 1979.
32. Ibid.
33. Ibid.
34. NAI, DT 2009/135/341, Pádraig Pearse, Centenary of Birth, 9 January 1979.
35. Ibid., 12 January 1979.
36. Ibid., 19 January 1979.
37. Ibid., 16 and 21 February 1979.
38. NAI, DT 2009/135/346, 24 October 1979.
39. Diarmaid Ferriter, 'Commemorating the Rising, 1922–65', in Mary Daly and Margaret O'Callaghan (eds), *1916 in 1966: Commemorating the Rising* (Dublin, 2007), pp. 198–218.
40. *Irish Times*, 12 and 15 November 1979.
41. Daly and O'Callaghan, *1916 in 1966*, p. 148.

21 History Wars

1. UCDA, FitzGerald Papers, P215/481, Murphy, 'Identity in the Republic of Ireland Now'.
2. UCDA, ICEM Papers, P204/99, address to ICEM symposium, 24 February 1972.
3. UCDA, Kelly Papers, P147/47, speech in Dublin, 10 October 1977.
4. Eibhear Walshe, *Cissie's Abattoir* (Cork, 2009), pp. 56–7.
5. Smith, *Off Screen*, p. 129.
6. UCDA, Ó Dálaigh Papers, P151/172, notebook on death of de Valera, 1975.
7. NAI, DT 2008/133/405, John A. Costello, Funeral, January 1976, *Irish Press*, 6 January 1976 and note on telephone conversation between Declan Costello and Cosgrave, 10 January 1976.
8. UCDA, Kelly Papers, P147/15, draft letters of 14 February 1971 and 30 January 1972.
9. F. S. L. Lyons, 'The Dilemma of the Irish Contemporary Historian', *Hermathena*, no. 115, Summer 1973, pp. 45–57.
10. *Hibernia*, 8 November 1974.
11. Alvin Jackson, *Ireland, 1798–1998* (Oxford, 1999), pp. 4–5.
12. Ian Mac Bride (ed.), *History and Memory in Modern Ireland* (Cambridge, 2001), p. 37.
13. NAI, DT 2005/7/605, Erskine Childers to Cosgrave, 13 May 1974.
14. T. W. Moody, 'Irish History and Irish Mythology', *Hermathena*, no. 124, Summer 1978, pp. 7–25.

15. *Hibernia*, 25 August 1972.
16. Brown, *Ireland*, p. 277.
17. Robert Dudley Edwards, 'An Agenda for Irish History, 1978–2018', *Irish Historical Studies*, vol. 21, no. 81, March 1978, pp. 3–20.
18. Liam Harte and Yvonne Whelan (eds), *Ireland Beyond Boundaries: Mapping Irish Studies in the Twenty First Century* (Dublin, 2007), p. 95.
19. UCDA, de Courcy Ireland Papers, P29/C/10, c. July 1974.
20. Madden, *Fear and Loathing*, p. 152.
21. Aidan Clarke, 'Robert Walter Dudley Edwards and a Decade of Archival Achievements', *Irish Archives*, vol. 1, no. 1, 1989, p. 5 and Deirdre McMahon, 'Robert Dudley Edwards (1909–1988) and Irish Archives', *Irish Archives*, vol. 17, no.21, 2010, pp. 1–14.
22. McMahon, 'Robert Dudley Edwards'.
23. NAI, DT 2003/16/51, State Paper Office: Proposals for Rationalisation, 24 May 1972.
24. NAI, DT 2006/133/520, State Paper Office: Transfer of Files to, Department of Taoiseach memorandum, 15 April 1976 and notes for the Taoiseach, 13 January 1971.
25. Ibid., *Irish Independent*, 28 January 1971 and Lynch to Cosgrave, 9 February 1971.
26. NAI, DT 2003/16/51, State Paper Office: Archives: Proposals for Rationalisation, Mac Giolla Choile, report of visit to archives in Denmark and Germany, 28 August to 5 September 1972 and memorandum by Mac Giolla Choile, 17 October 1972.
27. Ibid., Department of Taoiseach memorandum, 8 November 1972 and Dáil Debates, 16 November 1972.
28. L. M. Cullen to *Irish Times*, 12 January 2011.
29. NAI, DT 2008/148/356, State Paper Office: Transfer of Files To, Dan Ó Súilleabháin to S. C. O'Riordáin, 5 September 1977.
30. UCDA, FitzGerald Papers, P215/587, Dudley Edwards to FitzGerald, 20 June 1977.
31. *Hibernia*, 6 February 1970.
32. *Hibernia*, 9 January 1970.
33. NAI, DT 2007/116/167, Dublin Corporation: Excavation of Wood Quay, Department of Local Government memorandum, 6 May 1977.
34. Art Cosgrove, 'Francis Xavier Martin', in McGuire and Quinn, *DIB*, vol. 6, pp. 383–4 and NAI, DT 2007/116/167, *An Taisce, Ireland's Conservation Journal*, vol. 1, no. 5, December 1977.
35. NAI, DT 2009/135/533, Dublin Corporation: Office Accommodation and Excavations of Wood Quay, Chris Lynn's letter, 1 December 1977 and letter of Madeleine O'Rourke, 21 November 1978. Letters of Kevin H. Whyte, 30 October 1978, Karl Gustov Gerold, 27 November 1978 and Revd T. Salmon, 30 November 1978 and DT 2008/148/119, Anngret Simms to Lynch, 11 July 1978; letter from institutions in Denmark, Norway and Sweden, 10 June 1978.
36. NAI, DT 2008/148/119 and *Sunday Press*, 23 April 1978.
37. NAI, DT 2008/148/257, Queen Margrethe of Denmark, Visit to Ireland, April 1978, memorandum by Stokes, 26 January 1978.

38. NAI, DT 2008/148/119, 22 August 1978 and Brenda Moran to Lynch, 5 September 1978.
39. UCDA, Fianna Fáil Papers, P176/105, Séamus Brennan to Kit Ahern, 10 October 1978.
40. NAI, DT 2009/135/533, Noel Carroll to Brian McCarthy, 9 March 1979.
41. NAI, DT 2008/148/119, Dublin Corporation: Office Accommodation and Excavations at Wood Quay, 23 April 1978.
42. Thomas Heffernan, *Wood Quay: The Clash over Dublin's Viking Past* (Austin, 1988) and 'Rolling Back the Years, 1975–1979', *Irish Independent* Supplement, 29 October 2011.
43. NAI, DT 2008/148/120, Dublin Corporation: Excavations at Wood Quay, letters of E. Griffiths, 15 September 1978, Heather Dunwoody, 15 September 1978, Peter Reid, 13 September 1978 and Brian de Breffney, 13 September 1978.
44. *Hot Press*, 6 October 1978.

22 Irish Identity on Stage

1. Kiberd, *Inventing Ireland*, p. 568.
2. Brown, *Ireland*, p. 269.
3. *Hibernia*, 13 July and 16 November 1973.
4. Harte and Whelan, *Ireland beyond Boundaries*, p. 78.
5. *Hibernia*, 14 November 1975.
6. Christopher Murray (ed.), *Brian Friel: Essays, Diaries and Interviews 1964–1999* (London, 1999), pp. 25–34.
7. Ibid., p. 53.
8. Christopher Morash, *A History of Irish Theatre, 1601–2000* (Cambridge, 2002), p. 231.
9. Ibid., p. 243.
10. John Devitt, *Shifting Scenes: Irish Theatre-going, 1955–1985* (Dublin, 2008), pp. 85ff.
11. Murray, *Friel*, p. 74.
12. Anthony Roche, *Brian Friel: Theatre and Politics* (London, 2011), pp. 60–130.
13. Ibid.
14. Ibid.
15. Nicholas Grene (ed.), *Talking about Tom Murphy* (Dublin, 2002), p. 42.
16. Murray, *Friel*, pp. 74ff.
17. *Hibernia*, 26 June 1970.
18. UCDA, ICEM Papers, P204/99, ICEM symposium, 24 February 1972.
19. Murray, *Friel*, p. 53.
20. NAI, DT 2009/135/199, Dublin Theatre Festival, memorandum by Brendan Smith, October 1967; Brendan Smith to Lynch, 12 February 1971 and *Irish Press*, 18 February 1972.
21. Ibid., Smith to Lynch, 17 July 1972, and letter from Department of Finance, 22 July 1972.
22. Ibid., Department of Taoiseach note for Lynch, 30 August 1977.
23. *Magill*, November 1979.

24. *Magill*, July 1978.
25. *Hibernia*, 30 April 1971.
26. *Hibernia*, 22 January and 3 February 1971.
27. *Hibernia*, 30 November 1973.
28. *Hibernia*, 19 September 1975.
29. O'Connor, *Diaries*, 20 March 1970, p. 22.
30. Christopher Fitz-Simon, *The Boys* (Dublin, 1994), pp. 280–91.
31. Gabriel Byrne, *Pictures in My Head* (Dublin, 1994), pp. 82ff.
32. *Hibernia*, 16 July 1976.
33. Ibid.
34. Byrne, *Pictures in My Head*, pp. 77ff.
35. Ibid.
36. Ibid., pp. 82ff.
37. Walshe, *Cissie's Abattoir*, p. 81.
38. Morash, *History of Theatre*, pp. 248–9.
39. Murray, *Friel*, p. 71.
40. Devitt, *Shifting Scenes*, pp. 103–5.
41. Morash, *History of Theatre*, pp. 248–9.
42. Kennedy, *Dreams and Responsibilities*, p. 182.
43. NAI, DT 2009/135/431, Inter-Departmental Study Group on Aid to the Arts, 3 October 1978 and 24 October 1978.

23 Music and Language: Redeploying Tradition

1. NAI, DT 2007/116/279, Seán Ó Riada Foundation, Elizabeth Spillane to Lynch, 4 October 1977.
2. Harry White, *The Progress of Music in Ireland* (Dublin, 2005), pp. 17–36, and Harry White, *The Keeper's Recital: Music and Cultural History in Ireland, 1770–1970* (Cork, 1998), pp. 159ff.
3. White, *The Progress of Music*, p. 169 and Ita Beausang, 'Aloys Fleischmann', in McGuire and Quinn, *DIB*, vol. 3, pp. 1012–14.
4. NAI, DT 2003/16/187, Comhaltas Ceoltóirí Éireann to Gerry Collins, 12 May 1971.
5. *Hibernia*, 14 April 1972.
6. UCDA, FitzGerald Papers, P215/481, April 1976.
7. *Magill*, October 1977.
8. *Hot Press*, 21 July 1977.
9. Moore, *One Voice*, p. 16.
10. Ibid., p. 55.
11. *Hot Press*, 28 January 1978.
12. *Magill*, August 1979.
13. Patrick Crotty (ed.), *The Penguin Book of Irish Poetry* (London, 2010), pp. 982–5.
14. Ibid., p. 150.
15. Des Geraghty, *Luke Kelly: A Memoir* (Dublin, 1994), p. 138.
16. *Magill*, August 1979 and Geraghty, *Luke Kelly*, p. 125.
17. *Hot Press*, 25 January 1979.

18. *Hot Press*, 10 December 1977.
19. Paul Rouse, 'Rory Gallagher', in McGuire and Quinn, *DIB*, vol. 4, pp. 12–13.
20. *Hot Press*, 8 June 1978.
21. *Magill*, February 1979.
22. *Hot Press*, 27 July 1977.
23. *Hot Press*, 21 July 1977.
24. *Hibernia*, 17 November 1972.
25. *Magill*, September 1978, *Hot Press*, 14 January 1978.
26. 'Rolling Back the Years, 1975–1979', *Irish Independent* Supplement, 29 October 2011, p. 26.
27. *Magill*, July 1978.
28. *Hot Press*, 9 June and 19 August 1977.
29. *Hot Press*, 8 June 1978.
30. *Hot Press*, 23 June 1978.
31. *Hot Press*, 7 July 1977.
32. *Hot Press*, 19 August 1977.
33. *Hot Press*, 17 September 1977.
34. *Hot Press*, 28 April and 17 August 1978.
35. *Hot Press*, 12 October 1978.
36. *Hot Press*, 23 June 1978 and John O'Flynn, *The Irishness of Irish Music* (Farnham, 2009), p. 29.
37. *Hot Press*, 30 October 1977, 20 April and 31 August 1979.
38. *Hot Press*, 11 May 1978.
39. *Hot Press*, 30 November 1978.
40. *Hot Press*, 3 August 1978.
41. *Hot Press*, 21 August and 2 November 1978.
42. *Hot Press*, 28 September 1979.
43. Pat Boran, *The Invisible Prison* (Dublin, 2009), p. 172.
44. Gareth Cox, 'Charles Acton', in McGuire and Quinn, *DIB*, vol. 1, pp. 14–15.
45. UCDA, FitzGerald Papers, P215/477, Charles Acton to Garret FitzGerald, 26 November 1976, to Francis Gannon, 28 November 1976 and to FitzGerald, 29 February 1976.
46. Charles Acton, *Irish Music and Musicians* (Dublin, 1978).
47. *Magill*, March 1979.
48. *Hibernia*, 1 May 1970, 8 October 1971 and 17 October 1975.
49. Acton, *Irish Music*, p. 25.
50. *Hibernia*, 9 January 1970.
51. *Hibernia*, 8 January 1971.
52. *Hibernia*, 5 March 1971.
53. Adrian Kelly, *Compulsory Irish: Language and Education in Ireland, 1870s–1970s* (Dublin, 2002), p. 38.
54. *Irish Press*, 15 January 1975, NAI, DT 2009/135/6, Irish in the Civil Service, Cait ni Chuimin to Cosgrave, 4 December 1974 and Joseph Mangan to Lynch, 26 October 1977.

55. Linda Connolly and Niamh Hourigan, *Social Movements and Ireland* (Manchester, 2006), p. 133.
56. NAI, DT 2005/7/17, Broadcasting in Ireland, 21 August 1974.
57. UCDA, FitzGerald Papers, P125/481, Murphy, 'Identity in the Republic of Ireland Now'.
58. UCDA, ICEM Papers, P204/57, Cecily Golden to Rory Dunne, 6 January 1976.
59. *Magill*, April 1978.
60. *Hibernia*, 25 September 1970.
61. *Hibernia*, 1 December 1972.
62. Kiberd, *Inventing Ireland*, p. 568.
63. Ibid.
64. Brown, *Ireland*, p. 265.
65. Alan Titley, 'The Novel in Irish', in John Wilson Foster (ed.), *The Cambridge Companion to the Irish Novel* (Cambridge, 2006), pp. 171–88.

24 Artistic Creativity and Challenges

1. *Magill*, October 1977, *Hibernia*, 8 January 1971.
2. *Hibernia*, 30 April 1971.
3. *Hibernia*, 13 June 1975.
4. 'The Moderns: The Arts in Ireland from the 1900s to the 1970s', *Irish Times* Supplement, 20 October 2010.
5. Eamon Delaney, *Breaking the Mould: The Story of Art and Ireland* (Dublin, 2009), p. 67.
6. Ibid., p. 267.
7. Ibid., p. 211.
8. *Magill*, October 1977.
9. *Magill*, July 1978.
10. *Magill*, November 1979.
11. *Hibernia*, 15 May 1970 and 3 November 1972.
12. *Hibernia*, 5 March 1971.
13. *Hibernia*, 19 January 1973.
14. *Hibernia*, 13 April 1973.
15. Maurice Harmon, *Seán O'Faoláin* (London, 1994), pp. 247–64.
16. *Hibernia*, 19 February 1971.
17. John McGahern, *Memoir* (London, 2005), p. 260.
18. Denis Donoghue, *Irish Essays* (Cambridge, 2011), p. 234.
19. Murray, *Friel*, pp. 53ff.
20. Derek Hand, *A History of the Irish Novel* (Cambridge, 2011), p. 246.
21. Donoghue, *Irish Essays*, p. 234 and Robert Garratt, *Trauma and History in the Irish Novel* (London, 2011), pp. 4–20.
22. Hand, *Irish Novel*, p. 218.
23. Ibid., p. 238.
24. Kiberd, *Inventing Ireland*, pp. 634–5.
25. Hand, *Irish Novel*, pp. 238–46.

26. *Hibernia*, 11 May 1973.
27. *Hibernia*, 2 November 1973.
28. Brown, *Ireland*, p. 301.
29. Kiberd, *Inventing Ireland*, p. 601.
30. *Hibernia*, 1 December 1972.
31. O'Connor, *Diaries*, 3 September 1970, p. 48.
32. Michael Longley, *Tuppenny Stung: Autobiographical Chapters* (Belfast, 1994), p. 123.
33. Heather Clark, *The Ulster Renaissance: Poetry in Belfast, 1962–1972* (Oxford, 2006), pp. 174–82.
34. Quoted in *Hibernia*, 2 February 1973.
35. Montague, *Pear is Ripe*, pp. 160–228.
36. Paul Durcan, *A Snail in My Prime: New and Selected Poems* (London, 1993), p. 41.
37. Catríona Clutterback (ed.), 'Thomas Kinsella', *Irish University Review* Special Issue, vol. 31, no. 1, Spring/Summer 2001.
38. Colm Tóibín, 'The Dark 16th Century', *Dublin Review*, no. 43, Summer 2011, pp. 31–55.
39. O'Connor, *Diaries*, 2 March 1970, p. 19.
40. O'Faoláin, *Are You Somebody?*, p. 152.
41. O'Driscoll, *Stepping Stones*, pp. 123–77.
42. Ibid., pp. 210–15.
43. Brown, *Ireland*, p. 311.
44. Declan Kiberd, 'Writers in Quarantine? The Case for Irish Studies', *Crane Bag*, vol. 13, no. 1, 1979, pp. 17–21.
45. Ibid., p. 76.
46. Bryan Fanning, *The Quest for Modern Ireland: The Battle of Ideas, 1912–1986* (Dublin, 2008), pp. 10–41.
47. Ciarán Benson, *The Place of the Arts in Irish Education* (Dublin, Arts Council, 1979).
48. *Magill*, August 1979.

25 Expanding the Broadcasting Horizons

1. Chris Morash, *A History of the Media in Ireland* (Cambridge, 2010), p. 181.
2. Ibid., p. 192.
3. NAI, DT 2001/6/10, Broadcasting in Ireland, 1 July 1970.
4. NAI, DT 2004/21/14, Broadcasting in Ireland: Establishment and Organisation, memorandum from Posts and Telegraphs, 23 August 1973.
5. NAI, DT 2005/7/17, Broadcasting in Ireland, 27 August 1974.
6. NAI, DT 2003/16/187, Gerry Collins to Lynch, 12 May 1971.
7. NAI, DT 2001/6/140, Television: General File, 20 March 1970, Erskine Childers to Lynch, 20 March 1970.
8. Ibid., Gerry Collins to Lynch, 11 June 1971.
9. NAI, DT 2007/116/107, *Irish Press*, 21 August 1972.
10. NAI, DT 2004/21/69, Radio and TV: Political Broadcasts 1972, Lynch to Andrews, 3 January 1973.

11. NAI, DT 2004/21/597, Media: Relations With, 22 March 1973 and 15 October 1973.
12. *Magill*, December 1977.
13. Smith, *Off Screen*, p. 134.
14. *Hibernia*, 17 December 1976.
15. *Hot Press*, 9 June 1977.
16. Conor Brady, *Up with the Times* (Dublin, 2005), pp. 39–45.
17. NAI, DT 2001/6/400, RTE Telecast on Illegal Money Lending, 6 August 1970 and memorandum from Posts and Telegraphs, 4 August 1970; *Irish Press*, 19 August 1970 and *Irish Times*, 26 August 1970.
18. Bowman, *Window and Mirror*, p. 116.
19. Interview with Bill O'Herlihy, *Irish Times*, 1 October 2005.
20. NAI, DT 2001/6/400, Ben Briscoe to Lynch, 28 August 1970.
21. Smith, *Off Screen*, p. 133.
22. Bowman, *Window and Mirror*, p. 116.
23. *Hibernia*, 28 August 1970.
24. NAI, DT 2003/16/17, Broadcasting: Improvement of and Representations Re: Programmes, Rory Doyle to Lynch, 7 April 1971.
25. *Magill*, February 1979.
26. Morash, *History of Media*, p. 177, *Hibernia*, 13 June 1975.
27. Bowman, *Window and Mirror*, p. 159.
28. *Hibernia*, 19 January 1973 and Smith, *Off Screen*, p. 116.
29. *Hibernia*, 28 April 1972.
30. *Hibernia*, 14 July 1972.
31. *Hibernia*, 7 September 1973.
32. Bruce Merry, 'A Sense of Humour', *Crane Bag*, vol. 1, no. 1, Spring 1977. pp. 4–9.
33. Ibid.
34. Bowman, *Window and Mirror*, pp. 145–7.
35. NAI, DT 2009/135/144, RTE: Reports and Accounts, Annual Report 1978.
36. Bowman, *Window and Mirror*, pp. 151–2.
37. NAI, DT 2003/16/17, memorandum from Gerry Collins, 13 January 1972.
38. NAI, DT 2007/116/147, Television: General, memorandum of Micheál O'Cíosoig, 20 November 1977.
39. NAI, DT 2009/135/322, RTE: Second Channel, John A. Foley to Lynch, 29 January 1978 and John J. O'Reilly to Lynch, 28 November 1977.
40. Bowman, *Window and Mirror*, pp. 151–3.
41. Terry Wogan, *Is It Me? Terry Wogan: An Autobiography* (London, 2000), pp. 190–218.
42. *Hibernia*, 19 October 1973.
43. NAI, DT 2009/135/531, Local Radio Development, c. January 1978.
44. NAI, DT 2008/148/681, RTE Radio: Development of Service, memorandum of 4 May 1978 and response from Stokes, 23 May 1977 and 13 July 1978.
45. *Magill*, August 1978.
46. Morash, *History of Media*, p. 187.

47. *Magill*, February 1978.
48. *Magill*, May 1978.
49. Ibid. and *Irish Times*, 3 March 2003.
50. Morash, *History of Media*, p. 189.
51. Ibid., p. 187.
52. *Hot Press*, 23 June 1977 and 7 September 1978.
53. Doireann Ní Bhríain, 'Women and Social Change on Radio', unpublished Thomas Davis Lecture, broadcast on RTE Radio 1, May 2001.
54. Ibid.
55. 'Rolling Back the Years, 1975–1979', *Irish Independent* Supplement, 29 October 2011.

26 Screening and Reporting Ireland

1. *Hibernia*, 3 August 1973.
2. NAI, DT 2001/6/427, Film Industry Bill, 1969–70, memorandum from Posts and Telegraphs, May 1970; speech of Jack Lynch, 8 October 1970.
3. *Hibernia*, 7 April 1970 and 14 July 1972.
4. NAI, DT 2004/21/414, Film Industry Bill, 1969, Noel Coade to Lynch, 22 June 1972.
5. Morash, *History of Media*, p. 183.
6. Bowman, *Window and Mirrors*, pp. 113–14.
7. Smith, *Off Screen*, p. 151.
8. Ibid., p. 157.
9. NAI, DT 2009/135/68, Film Production in Ireland, memorandum by Richard Stokes, 7 March 1979.
10. NAI, DT 2009/135/308, National Film Studios of Ireland Reports, letter of John Boorman, 6 July 1979.
11. NAI, DT 2003/16/17, Broadcasting: Improvement of and Representations Re: Programmes, *Irish Times*, 18 October 1971.
12. *Hibernia*, 7 May 1976.
13. NAI, DT 2003/16/17, Lynch to Collins, 27 October 1971 and Collins to Lynch, 2 November 1971.
14. NAI, DT 2005/7/461, State Reception, NUJ, Department of Taoiseach memorandum, 9 May 1974.
15. *Sunday Business Post*, Agenda Magazine, 6 February 2011.
16. *Magill*, December 1977.
17. *Hibernia*, 19 March 1971.
18. *Hibernia*, 19 May 1970.
19. *Magill*, November 1978 and Morash, *History of Media*, p. 184.
20. *Hibernia*, 17 April 1970.
21. Morash, *History of Media*, p. 192.
22. *Magill*, March 1978 and November 1978.
23. Downey, *In My Own Time*, p. 160.
24. O'Brien, *Irish Times*, p. 200.

25. Whitaker, *Bright, Brilliant Days*, pp. 45–124.
26. Brady, *Up with the Times*, p. 45.
27. *Magill*, August 1978, and Mark O'Brien, *De Valera, Fianna Fáil and the Irish Press* (Dublin, 2001).
28. Waters, *Jiving at the Crossroads*, p. 112.
29. Morash, *History of Media*, p. 190.
30. Whitaker, *Bright Brilliant Days*, p. 19.
31. 'From the Archives', *Irish Times*, 29 April 2011; *Hibernia*, 18 January 1974.
32. Ivana Bacik, 'Tales of an Outspoken Woman', *Irish Times*, 27 November 2004.
33. Mary Holland, *How Far We Have Travelled: The Voice of Mary Holland* (Dublin, 2004) p. x.
34. Joe MacAnthony, 'Where the Sweep Millions Go', *Sunday Independent*, 21 January 1973; Marie Coleman, *The Irish Sweep: A History of the Irish Hospitals Sweepstake* (Dublin, 2009).
35. *Hibernia*, 2 February 1973.
36. Coogan, *A Memoir*, p. 166.
37. Coleman, *Irish Sweep*, pp. 180–84, 197–224.
38. NAI, DT 2004/21/14, Department of Taoiseach: Telephone, memoranda of 3 August 1972 and 15 March 1973.
39. UCDA, FitzGerald Papers, P215/566, FitzGerald to Cruise O'Brien, 18 April 1973; Cruise O'Brien to FitzGerald, 21 May 1973 and FitzGerald to Cruise O'Brien, 18 June 1977.
40. Ibid., Cruise O'Brien to FitzGerald, 27 August 1973.
41. *Magill*, December 1977.
42. O'Connor, *Diaries*, 28 January 1977, p. 209.

27 The Sporting Irish

1. NAI, DT 2005/7/327, Bloodsports, A. MacNeill to Lynch, 29 December 1969.
2. Ibid., Seán Allan to Cosgrave, 21 January 1974.
3. Ibid., Monica Alcock to Cosgrave, 29 May 1973.
4. UCDA, Kelly Papers, P147/60, Media Campaign for Next Election, 4 November 1970.
5. NAI, DT 2005/151/59, Revival of Athletics; *Irish Times*, 7 October 1970.
6. Ibid., DT 2005/151/59, Revival of Athletics, memoranda of Michael O'Kennedy, 12 October 1970 and 23 January 1971.
7. *Sunday Press*, 24 January 1971.
8. NAI, DT 2005/151/461, President of Ireland: Attendance at Functions, 24 March 1975 and 8 July 1975.
9. NAI, DT 2005/151/59, 10 May 1971.
10. Ibid., press release of 23 February 1975.
11. NAI, DT 2006/133/463, Youth and Sport, Government Policy, 14 August 1975.
12. Ibid., note of Richard Stokes, 16 September 1975.
13. Ibid., John Bruton to Cosgrave, 15 November 1976 and memorandum from Department of Taoiseach, 23 November 1976.

14. NAI, DT 2007/116/434, Department of Finance to Department of Education, 22 April 1977.
15. Ibid., Bruton to Cosgrave, 28 April 1977.
16. NAI, DT 2007/116/435, Youth and Sport: Government Policy, Mac Caffrai to Cosgrave, 6 June 1977.
17. NAI, DT 2007/116/434, Youth and Sport: Government Policy, Bruton to Cosgrave, 19 January 1977.
18. NAI, DT 2006/133/463, Youth and Sport: Government Policy, memorandum of 20 June 1974.
19. *Village*, 15 April 2005.
20. Breandán Ó hEithir, *Over the Bar* (Dublin, 1991), p. 210 and Mike Cronin, William Murphy and Paul Rouse (eds), *The Gaelic Athletic Association, 1884–2009* (Dublin, 2009), p. 242.
21. Cronin, Murphy and Rouse, *The Gaelic Athletic Association*, p. 242.
22. Mike Cronin, Mark Duncan and Paul Rouse (eds), *The GAA: A People's History* (Cork, 2009), p. 128.
23. *Magill*, December 1978.
24. William Nolan, *The GAA in Dublin, 1884–2000: Volume II*, (Dublin, 2005), pp. 637–9.
25. Tom Humphries, *Dublin versus Kerry: The Story of the Epic Rivalry that Changed Irish Sport* (Dublin, 2006), pp. 21–90.
26. Ibid., p. 156.
27. 'All Our Yesterdays, 1970–74', *Limerick Leader*, 31 March 2012.
28. *Irish Times*, 5 March 1979.
29. NAI, Lynch Papers, 1195/3/120/38, Lynch to Teddy O'Donavan, 12 March 1981.
30. NAI, DT 2006/133/463, note of D. O'Sullivan, 7 August 1975.
31. *Magill*, November 1977.
32. *Magill*, December 1977.
33. *Magill*, February 1979.
34. Seán Ryan, *The Boys in Green: The FAI International Story* (Edinburgh, 1997), p. 127.
35. *Magill*, November 1978 and May 1979.
36. Ryan, *The Boys in Green*, p. 139.
37. 'Rolling Back the Years, 1970–1974', *Irish Independent* Supplement, 22 October 2011.
38. *Magill*, September 1978.
39. *Magill*, May 1978.
40. *Magill*, October 1978.
41. Letter of Louis Hogan, *Irish Times*, 6 June 2011.
42. *Hibernia*, September 1978.
43. Obituary of Moss Keane, *Irish Times*, 9 October 2010.
44. *Irish Times*, 1 November 1978.
45. Eoin Murphy, *Munster Rugby: The Phenomenon* (Meath, 2006), p. 64.
46. *Magill*, October 1978.

47. *Magill*, January 1978.
48. *Magill*, November 1977, February and March 1978.
49. *Magill*, August 1979.
50. 'Rolling Back the Years, 1970–1974', *Irish Independent* Supplement, 22 October 2011.

Part IV Rights, Responsibilities and Justice

1. *Garda Review*, vol. 1, no. 1, October 1973.
2. *Garda Review*, vol. 1, no. 2, November 1973.
3. Derek Dunne and Gene Kerrigan, *Round Up the Usual Suspects* (Dublin, 1984), p. 13.
4. *Garda Review*, vol. 5, no. 2, February 1977.
5. Ibid.
6. Patrick McLaughlin, 'The Policeman, the Criminal and the Law', *Garda Review*, vol. 2, no. 6, June 1974. pp. 10–15.
7. *Garda Review*, vol. 1, no. 2, 1973 and vol. 4, no. 7, July 1976.
8. David B. Rottman, 'The Changing Pattern of Crime in Ireland', *Journal of the Social and Statistical Inquiry Society of Ireland*, vol. 23, part V, 1977–8, pp. 163–217.
9. Ian Hart, 'The Rise in Irish Crime', *Garda Review*, vol. 2, no. 1, January 1974, pp.10–13.
10. Conor Brady, 'Inside Story', *Garda Review*, vol. 2, no. 1, January 1974, pp. 10–15.
11. Sarah Clarke, *No Faith in the System* (Cork, 1995), pp. 68–107.
12. Mary C. O'Flynn, 'Prison After Care in the Irish Republic', *Irish Jurist*, vol. 6, 1971, pp. 1–17.
13. John Murphy, 'The Irish Penal System', *Doctrine and Life*, vol. 24, no. 3, March 1974, pp. 144–59.
14. Eric A. Plunkett, 'Solicitors in the Republic', *Irish Jurist*, vol. 6, 1971, pp. 18–27.
15. Nial Osborough, Editorial, *Irish Jurist*, vol. 11, 1976, pp. 1–2.
16. John O'Connor, 'The Law Reform Commission and the Codification of Irish Law', *Irish Jurist*, vol. 9, 1974, pp. 14–41.
17. W. R. Duncan, 'Supporting the Institution of Marriage in Ireland', *Irish Jurist*, vol. 13, 1978, pp. 215–32.
18. Jane Smyth, 'Violence in Marriage: Battered Brides', *Doctrine and Life*, vol. 26, no. 4, April 1976, pp. 223–32.
19. Nial Osborough, 'Reformatory and Industrial Schools', *Irish Jurist*, vol. 5, 1970, pp. 294–6.
20. Niamh O'Daly, 'Changing Attitudes to Children', *Social Studies*, vol. 27, no. 4, Winter 1979, pp. 475–94.
21. Diarmaid Ferriter, *Occasions of Sin: Sex and Society in Modern Ireland* (2nd edn., London, 2012), Foreword.

28 Troubling Times for the Guardians of the Peace

1. NAI, DT 2001/6/134, Report of the Garda Commissioner on Crime for Year Ended 30 September 1969.

2. NAI, DT 2005/7/141, Report of the Garda Commissioner on Crime for Year Ended 30 September 1973.
3. NAI, DT 2003/16/179, Report of the Garda Commissioner on Crime for Year Ended 30 September 1971.
4. NAI, DT 2005/151/285, Squattings, Sit Ins etc. in Relation to the Garda Síochána, 19 February 1971 and C. O'Neill, ITGWU, to Lynch, 12 August 1971.
5. NAI, DT 2001/6/64, Garda Síochána: Attacks On, 3 April 1970.
6. Stephen Collins, *The Power Game: Ireland under Fianna Fáil* (Dublin, 2001), p. 42.
7. Keogh, *Jack Lynch*, p. 240.
8. Liz Walsh, *The Final Beat: Gardaí Killed in the Line of Duty* (Dublin, 2001), p. 9.
9. Sweeney, *Down, Down*, pp. 97–8 and Walsh, *The Final Beat*, p. 74.
10. NAI, DT 2004/21/511, Garda Síochána: Golden Jubilee, 1922–1972.
11. Ibid., and *Irish Independent*, 14 June 1972.
12. *Irish Times* and *Irish Independent*, 14 June 1972.
13. Liam McNiffe, *A History of the Garda Síochána* (Dublin, 1997), p. 166.
14. NAI, DT 2005/7/141, Report of the Garda Commissioner on Crime for Year Ended 30 September 1973.
15. Ibid., Report of the Garda Commissioner on Crime for Year Ended 30 September 1974.
16. Ibid., 18 July 1975.
17. NAI, DT 2007/116/47, Garda Síochána and *Irish Independent*, 11 November 1976.
18. NAI, DT 2007/116/47, memorandum from Department of Justice, 20 December 1976.
19. Ibid., memorandum from Department of Justice, 20 December 1976 and Richie Ryan to Patrick Cooney, 23 December 1976.
20. Ibid., Cooney to Ryan, 4 January 1977.

29 A Discredited Force?

1. NAI, DT 2007/116/264, Garda Síochána: Pay and Conditions.
2. NAI, DT 2007/116/395, Complaints against the Gardaí, 22 February 1974 and 30 June 1975.
3. *Hibernia*, 6 August 1971.
4. *Hibernia*, 16 July 1976.
5. *Irish Times*, 14 February 1977 and O'Brien, *Irish Times*, p. 215.
6. NAI, DT 2007/116/395, letter of Kevin White, 16 February 1975.
7. Ibid., 12 March 1974.
8. UCDA, FitzGerald Papers, P215/484, 5 January 1977.
9. NAI, DT 2007/116/395, Complaints against the Gardaí, Report of Amnesty International Mission to the Republic of Ireland, June 1977 and note of 6 September 1977.
10. Ibid., Rory Barnes to Lynch, 7 September 1977 and Edgar Deale, Irish Association of Civil Liberty, to Lynch, 7 September 1977.
11. Ibid., F. Murray, Department of Taoiseach memorandum, 14 September 1977 and J. Walls to Gerry Collins, 29 September 1977.

12. NAI, DT 2008/148/308, Complaints against the Gardaí, Attorney General to Gerry Collins, 12 April 1978.
13. Cruise O'Brien, *Memoir*, p. 355.
14. Dunlop, *Yes Taoiseach*, pp. 86–94; Downey, *In My Own Time*, pp. 176ff.
15. *Garda Review*, September 1975; *Irish Times*, 13 September 1975; *Magill*, November 1977 and February 1978; *Irish Times*, 21, 22, 23 January 1978, 30 November 1989 and *Garda Review*, December 1989.
16. *Magill*, February 1978.
17. *Magill*, January 1979.
18. Patsy McGarry, *While Justice Slept: The True Story of Nicky Kelly and the Sallins Train Robbery* (Dublin, 2007) and Dunne and Kerrigan, *Round Up The Usual Suspects*.
19. NAI, DT 2009/135/251, Law Reform Commission, report of 13 April 1978.
20. NAI, DT 2006/133/580, Emergency Powers Act, 1976, 25 July 1976 and 4 August 1976.
21. Ibid.
22. *Irish Times*, 21 September 1976.
23. Ibid., 24 September 1976 and NAI, DT 2006/133/580, 15 October 1976.
24. *Magill*, May 1979.
25. Ibid.

30 The Terror of Urban Decay?

1. NAI, DT 2009/135/124, Crime, Measures to Combat Increase, 7 April 1976.
2. Ibid., letter of John Nash, 22 July 1976.
3. Ibid., 24 November 1976, 8 March 1977, 23 March 1977 and memorandum of 18 April 1978 on crime statistics.
4. UCDA, Kelly Papers, P147/53, statement of Kelly, 19 November 1977.
5. NAI, DT 2009/135/124, Crime: Measures to Combat Increase, Una Fallon to Lynch, 1 December 1977.
6. *Hibernia*, 5 November 1976.
7. NAI, DT 2009/135/124, Una Fallon to Jack Lynch, 1 December 1977 and letter of W. J. Callan, 13 March 1978.
8. Ibid., 18 April and 1 June 1978.
9. NAI, DT 2006/133/705, Prison Rules: Revision, 18 March 1976.
10. NAI, DT 2008/148/94, Report of the Garda Commissioner on Crime for Year Ended 30 September 1975.
11. *Magill*, August 1978.
12. NAI, DT 2005/7/141, Report of the Garda Commissioner on Crime for Year Ended 30 September 1973.
13. *Magill*, December 1978.
14. *Magill*, October 1979.
15. NAI, DT 2008/148/94, Report of the Garda Commissioner on Crime for Year Ended 30 September 1977, Department of Taoiseach memorandum, 26 May 1978 and *Irish Press*, 4 August 1978.

16. NAI, DT 2007/116/617, Detention Homes for Young Offenders, 19 March and 19 May 1977.
17. Ibid., 2 May 1977.
18. *Magill*, October 1977.
19. *Magill*, December 1978.
20. *Magill*, January 1978.
21. NAI, DT 2007/116/617, Department of Justice memorandum, 1 June 1978.
22. NAI, DT 2007/116/497, Motor Vehicle Registration: Computerisation, memoranda of October 1976 and 5 January 1977.
23. *Magill*, September 1978.
24. *Hibernia*, 17 April 1970.
25. Carl O'Brien, *Protecting Civil Liberties: 30 Years of the ICCL* (Dublin, 2006).
26. *Hibernia*, 27 February 1976.
27. *Hibernia*, 7 May 1976.
28. *Hibernia*, 22 October 1976.
29. Linda Connolly and Tina O'Toole, *Documenting Irish Feminisms: The Second Wave* (Dublin, 2005), pp. 38–41.
30. *Hibernia*, 4 April 1975.
31. *Magill*, January 1978.
32. McCafferty, *Nell*, pp. 300–320.
33. Fennell, *Political Woman*, pp. 42ff.
34. Susan McKay, *Without Fear: 25 Years of the Dublin Rape Crisis Centre* (Dublin, 2005).
35. Connolly and O'Toole, *Documenting Irish Feminisms*, p. 102.
36. Ibid., p. 98.
37. *Magill*, March 1979.
38. NAI, DT 2009/148/94, *Irish Times*, 13 October 1978, 9 October 1978 and 15 February 1979.
39. NAI, DT 2009/148/94.
40. McCafferty, *Nell*, p. 319.
41. Tom O'Malley, 'Perceptions of Sexual Violence', in Anne Byrne, Jane Conroy and Seán Ryder (eds), *UCG Women's Studies Review*, vol. 2, 1993, pp. 131–47.

31 Controversial Custodies and Contemptuous Judges

1. Mary Regan, *Prison Policy in Ireland: Politics, Penal-welfarism and Political Imprisonment* (New York, 2011), ch. 6.
2. Ibid.
3. NAI, DT 2003/16/317, Prisons: Annual Reports, 1971.
4. Philip Bray with Anthony Galvin: *Inside Man: Life as an Irish Prison Officer* (Dublin, 2008), pp. 9–21.
5. NAI, DT 2008/148/174, Prisons: Annual Reports, 1976.
6. Ibid.
7. NAI, DT 2009/135/148, Prisons: Annual Reports, 1977–9, 29 June 1979.
8. *Magill*, January 1979.

9. Sweeney, *Down, Down*, p. 145.
10. NAI, DT 2007/116/395, Complaints against the Gardaí, Cabinet Decision, 22 February 1974, Amnesty International complaint, 6 July 1976 and Prisoners Welfare Action Group, May 1977.
11. NAI, DT 2007/116/603, Prisons Act 1977, memorandum from Department of Justice, 21 April 1977.
12. Coogan, *A Memoir*, p. 207.
13. NAI, DT 2009/135/635, Visit to Ireland of Pope John Paul II: Amnesty for Prisoners, 20 and 27 September 1979 and Department of Taoiseach memorandum, 21 September 1979.
14. NAI, DT 2007/116/452, Special Criminal Court, 4 August 1972.
15. *Hibernia*, 6 December 1974.
16. O'Brien, *Irish Times*, pp. 212–13.
17. Corcoran and O'Brien, *Political Censorship*, p. 49.
18. *Hibernia*, 6 February 1970.
19. NAI, DT 2007/116/208, Legal Aid, Lynch to Colm Condon, AG, 12 February 1970 and *Irish Press*, 14 February 1970.
20. NAI, DT 2007/116/208, Micheál Ó Móráin to Lynch, 18 February 1970.
21. Ibid., Peter Berry to C. H. Murray, 18 February 1970.
22. UCDA, Ó Dálaigh Papers, P51/48(38), Brian Walsh to Ó Dálaigh, 14 September 1972.
23. Ibid., P51/123, Ó Dálaigh to Walsh, 16 August 1972.
24. Ibid., Walsh to Ó Dálaigh, 25 August 1972.
25. McCafferty, *Nell*, p. 288.
26. NAI, DT 2005/7/21, Trial of Children, Brian Quinn to Cosgrave, 24 January 1974.
27. UCDA, FitzGerald Papers, P215/555, Mairín de Burca to FitzGerald, 12 June 1973.
28. NAI, Cosgrave Papers, 1194, Costello to Cosgrave, 22 March 1973.
29. Ibid., Costello to Cosgrave, 16 March 1974.
30. Ibid., Costello to Cosgrave, 12 April 1975.

32 Reforming the Law

1. Obituary of Declan Costello, *Irish Times*, 7 June 2011.
2. Ibid.
3. NAI, DT 2005/7/430, Prosecution of Offences Act, 1974, 21 January 1974.
4. NAI, DT 2005/7/121, Law Reform, memorandum of Costello, 4 March 1974 and letter to Cosgrave, 15 March 1974.
5. Ibid., 26 April 1974.
6. UCDA, Kelly Papers, P147/16, 24 January 1973.
7. NAI, DT 2005/151/313, Family Maintenance Legislation, Costello to Cosgrave, 13 September 1974.
8. NAI, DT 2006/133/368, Nullity of Marriage, The Law of Nullity in Ireland, memorandum from AG's office, 25 August 1975; Dáil Debates, 4 February and 18 June 1975, and Cosgrave to Costello, 12 April 1976; *Daily Telegraph*, 3 May

1976; note on cabinet meeting, 18 May 1976 and James Kennedy to Cosgrave, 4 December 1976.

9. Myrtle Hill, *Women in Ireland: A Century of Change* (Belfast, 2003), p. 148.
10. *Hibernia*, 19 January 1973.
11. Connolly and O'Toole, *Documenting Irish Feminisms*, pp. 92–103.
12. *Magill*, August 1978.
13. NAI, DT 2009/135/251, Law Reform Commission, Lynch to A. J. Hederman, 20 February 1979.
14. Ibid., Brian Walsh to Hederman, 9 March 1979.
15. Ibid.
16. Ibid., note of Nally, 12 September 1979 and Nally to Stokes, 19 October 1979.

33 Inalienable Rights of the Child?

1. NAI, DT 2002/8/163, speech by Erskine Childers to Vincent de Paul Society, 11 September 1971.
2. *Hibernia*, 16 April 1970.
3. *Hibernia*, 4 December 1970.
4. NAI, DT 2005/151/563, Inter-Departmental Committee on Mentally Ill and Maladjusted Persons, 23 May 1975.
5. Ibid., pp. 67–96.
6. Ibid., Charles Mollan to John Bruton, 13 June 1976.
7. Caroline Skehill, *History of the Present of Child Protection and Welfare Social Work in Ireland* (New York, 2004), pp. 19–61.
8. Noreen Kearney and Caroline Skehill, *Social Work in Ireland: Historical Perspectives* (Dublin, 2005), p. 34.
9. NAI, DT 2007/116/98, Children: General: Kennedy Report and Care Proposals, 17 November 1975 and letter from AWCC, 21 January 1976.
10. Ibid., Bruton to Cosgrave, 10 February 1976.
11. Ibid., memorandum from Minister for Education, 10 May 1976.
12. Ibid., 23 September 1976 and Sister of Mercy memorandum, 11 October 1976.
13. Ibid., Department of Finance memorandum, 2 November 1976, Brendan Comiskey to Peter Barry, 12 February 1977, and *Irish Independent*, 29 March 1977.
14. *Magill*, December 1977.
15. NAI, DT 2006/133/455, Non-accidental Injury to Children, 20 February 1976.
16. Ibid., *Irish Independent*, 6 March 1976.
17. Ibid., memorandum from Department of Health, 20 February 1976.
18. Mary Raftery and Eoin O'Sullivan, *Suffer the Little Children: The Inside Story of Ireland's Industrial Schools* (Dublin, 1999), pp. 379–81.
19. Catríona Crowe, 'On the Ferns Report', *Dublin Review*, no. 22, Spring 2006, pp. 5–26.
20. Ferriter, *Occasions of Sin*, pp. 407ff.
21. NAI, DT 2003/16/453, Contraceptives: Resolutions and Miscellaneous, A. J. Wallace to Jack Lynch, 13 November 1972.
22. Frank Crummey, *Crummey v. Ireland* (Dublin, 2010).

23. McCafferty, *Nell*, p. 246.
24. Dublin Diocesan Archives (hereafter DDA), Papers of Archbishop John Charles McQuaid (hereafter McQuaid Papers), AB8/B, Government Box 3, Department of Justice, 2 August 1971.
25. McCafferty, *Nell*, pp. 231ff.
26. NAI, DT 2008/148/377, J. E. Algeo to Lynch, 20 October 1978.
27. O'Connor, *Diaries*, 15 October 1977, p. 230.
28. NAI, DT 2003/16/460, Adoption Bill, 1971, Seanad Debates, 22 July 1971.
29. Ibid., 16 June 1972.
30. *Hibernia*, 3 February 1971.
31. *Magill*, July 1978.
32. NAI, DT 2007/116/71, Adoption of Children, Unmarried Mothers and Illegitimate Children, letter of Charles Mollan, 2 July 1976.
33. Ibid., January 1977.
34. NAI, DT 2008/148/585, International Year of the Child, 13 April 1978.
35. Ibid., note from Department of Taoiseach, 22 May 1978.
36. Ibid., 2 June 1978.
37. Ibid., Haughey to Lynch, 20 October, 1978.
38. *Irish Times* Weekend Magazine, 29 October 2011.
39. NAI, DT 2005/7/382, memoranda of October and December 1974, and *Irish Times*, 5 April 2010.
40. *Irish Times*, 16 May 1973.

Part V Foreign Affairs

1. Lyons, *Ireland Since the Famine*, pp. 557–8.
2. Cited in Conor McCarthy, *Irish Modernisation: Crisis and Culture in Ireland, 1969–1992* (Dublin, 2000), p. 90.
3. Quoted in William Murphy, 'Between Change and Tradition: The Politics and Writing of Garret FitzGerald', *Eire-Ireland*, vol. 43, nos 1&2, Spring/Summer 2008, pp. 154–79.
4. Gary Murphy, '"A Measurement of the Extent of Our Sovereignty at the Moment." Sovereignty and the Question of Irish Entry to the EEC: New Evidence from the Archives', *Irish Studies in International Affairs*, vol. 12, 2001, pp. 191–202.
5. Michael Kennedy and Joseph Morrison Skelly (eds), *Irish Foreign Policy 1919–66: From Independence to Internationalism* (Dublin, 2000), p. 324.
6. Ibid.
7. Department of Foreign Affairs, *Into Europe: Ireland and the EEC* (Dublin, 1972).
8. Joe Lee, *Reflections on Ireland in the EEC* (Dublin, 1984).
9. Murphy, '"A Measurement of the Extent of Our Sovereignty"'.
10. Ibid.
11. *Seven Ages* documentary series.
12. Walsh, *Patrick Hillery*, p. 200.
13. Ibid., pp. 297–316.
14. Lee, *Reflections on Ireland in the EEC*, pp. 32–5.

15. Kennedy and Skelly, *Irish Foreign Policy*, p. 18.
16. William Crotty and David E. Schmitt (eds), *Ireland on the World Stage* (London, 2002), pp. 11–33.
17. Kevin O'Sullivan, 'Biafra to Lomé: The Evolution of Irish Government Policy on Official Development Assistance, 1969–75', *Irish Studies in International Affairs*, vol. 18, 2007, pp. 91–107.
18. Kathy Hayward, *Irish Nationalism and European Integration: The Official Redefinition of the Island of Ireland* (Manchester, 2009), pp. 107–45.

34 Taking the European Plunge

1. NAI, DT 2006/6/392, Draft: Membership of the European Communities: Implications for Ireland, March 1970.
2. NAI, DT 2003/16/248, Paneuropa: Union, 21 February 1972.
3. NAI, DT 2003/16/574, EEC: Meeting of Heads of Government, Paris 14–20 October 1972, speech of Lynch, 18 October 1972.
4. UCDA, Kelly Papers, P147/20, Aidan Pender to Kelly, 1 June 1970 and 9 June 1970.
5. Ibid., Denis Corboy to Kelly, 30 June 1970.
6. *Hibernia*, 21 January, 28 April and 12 May 1972.
7. UCDA, ICEM Papers, P204/96, EEC: Negotiations on Ireland's Application 1970–71, February 1971.
8. Barbara Sweetman FitzGerald (ed.), *The Widest Circle: Remembering Michael Sweetman* (Dublin, 2011).
9. UCDA, ICEM Papers, P204/97, Research and Marketing, Marketing Society EEC questionnaire, January 1972.
10. Ibid., Report on Company Attitudes by Peter Owens Ltd Advertising.
11. Ibid., Proposal from Norman Freeman PR, April 1972.
12. Ibid., P204/99, Press Cuttings, *Irish Times*, 19 November 1971.
13. NAI, DT 2003/16/527, 3rd Amendment of Constitution: Referendum Committee, 18 February and 27 April 1972.
14. UCDA, de Courcey Ireland Papers, P29/13, address by Brendan Corish at annual conference in Wexford, 26 February 1972.
15. Ibid., P29/12, Andrée Sheehy Skeffington to John de Courcy Ireland, 5 February 1972.
16. Quoted in Desmond, *Finally and in Conclusion*, p. 76.
17. Raymond Crotty, *Ireland and the Common Market* (Dublin, 1971), p. 19.
18. FitzGerald, *Towards a New Ireland*, p. 107.
19. John de Courcy Ireland, *Ireland's European Traditions: The Historical Case Against the Common Market* (Dublin, 1970), p. 3, *Irish Times*, 12 March 1971.
20. *Irish Times*, 8 and 9 May 1972.
21. Fintan O'Toole, *The Irish Times Book of the Century* (Dublin, 1999), p. 292.
22. NAI, DT 2004/22/10, Childers to Jack Lynch, 28 March 1972.
23. Lee, *Ireland, 1912–1985*, p. 465.
24. NAI, DT 2003/16/589, Olympic Games, Munich 1972, 8 September 1972.
25. *Hibernia*, 7 March 1975.

26. NAI, DT 2004/21/548, Ireland's Accession to the European Communities: Ceremonies to Mark, 22 May 1972 and Kenneth Thom to Bobby McDonagh, 28 November 1972.
27. UCDA, Ó Dálaigh Papers, P51/39(35), Hillery to Ó Dálaigh, 6 July 1972.
28. *Irish Times*, 1 January 1973.
29. NAI, DT 2004/21/548, Lynch memorandum, 4 December 1972, Noel Mulcahy to Patrick Hillery, 4 December 1972 and *Irish Press*, 3 January 1973.
30. UCDA, ICEM Papers, P204/52, Neville Keery to Sheila O'Doherty, 16 February 1973.
31. Ibid., May 1973 press release.

35 Brittany Reunions, Public Apathy and Thinking European

1. NAI, DT 2004/21/605, National Day of Reconciliation, 6 April 1973.
2. UCDA, ICEM Papers, P204/52, Neville Keery to Lynch, 16 January 1973.
3. Ibid., Keery to Denis Kennedy, 18 January 1973.
4. Ibid., 18 June 1973 and AGM, 30 April 1973.
5. Michael Holmes, 'The Irish Labour Party: The Advantages, Disadvantages and Irrelevance of Europeanization?', *Irish Political Studies*, vol. 24, no. 4, December 2007, pp. 527–41.
6. UCDA, P204/52, Keery to A. Laucher, Council of Europe, 15 May 1973.
7. Ibid., Keery to Katherine Meenan, 14 June 1973 and Keery to Justin Keating, 14 June 1973.
8. Ibid., Keery to L. Parklons, 27 July 1973, to Alison Kelly, 26 July 1973 and to John Hume, 5 October 1973.
9. Ibid., P204/57, Cecily Golden to Rory Dunne, 6 January 1976.
10. Ibid., Keery to Douglas Gageby, 5 October 1973 and to Gerry McCann, 13 November 1973.
11. Ibid., P204/56, Trevor Salmon to Rory Dunne, 28 January 1975 and reply, 5 February 1975.
12. Ibid., P204/57, Jack Lynch to Dunne, 14 May 1976.
13. Ibid., Dunne to Michael Killeen, 29 June 1976.
14. Ibid., David O'Mahony to Dunne, 22 October 1976.
15. Ibid., P204/58, Miriam Hederman O'Brien to Denis Corboy, 13 February 1977.
16. Miriam Hederman O'Brien, *The Road to Europe: Irish Attitudes 1948–61* (Dublin, 1983), p. vii.
17. UCDA, P204/58, Mary Robinson to Barry Desmond, 28 March 1977.
18. Ibid., questionnaire, c. October 1977.
19. Ibid. Joe Hayes to secretary Department of Foreign Affairs, 29 January 1977 and memorandum, July 1977.
20. Ibid., P204/99, Press Cuttings, *Irish Times*, 25 March 1977.
21. Ibid., Address of Terence O'Raifeartaigh on the cultural implications of joining the EEC.
22. UCDA, ICEM Papers, P204/99, address by John A. Murphy: 'Irish Nationalism: the European Influence', c. February 1972.

23. UCDA, FitzGerald Papers, P215/481, Murphy, 'Identity in the Republic of Ireland Now'.
24. Kiberd, *Inventing Ireland*, pp. 567.
25. NAI, DT 2006/133/328, EEC: European Union, 3 February 1976.

36 Negotiating the Benefits and the Dilemmas

1. UCDA, FitzGerald Papers, P215/378, Informal Meeting of Foreign Ministers, Luxembourg 14–15 May 1976.
2. Ibid., EEC Committee of Irish Civil Servants, 29 October 1974.
3. Ibid.
4. Ibid., Walter Kineen to P. Murphy, 29 November 1974.
5. NAI, DT 2007/116/421, Summit Meeting, Luxembourg, March 1976, 26 March 1976 and DT 2007/116/525, European Council Meeting, Brussels, 5/6 December 1977, 29 November 1977.
6. Murphy, 'Between Change and Tradition', pp. 170–72.
7. NAI, DT 2006/133/309, Foreign Press Coverage of Ireland, Monthly Digests, February and March 1975.
8. Ibid., September, October and November 1975.
9. NAI, DT 2005/151/523, Heath MP Visit to Ireland, May 1975, note of 5 April 1975.
10. NAI, DT 2006/133/328, EEC: European Union, 23 January 1976.
11. Ibid., 5 January 1976.
12. NAI, DT 2007/116/421, Summit Meeting, Luxembourg, March 1976, memoranda of 25 March 1976 and 16 February 1976.
13. Ibid., Mark Clinton to Richie Ryan, 13 December 1976 and Department of Finance memorandum, 24 February 1977.
14. NAI, DT 2007/116/295, 21 March 1977, account of meeting between Antonio Giolitti and FitzGerald.
15. NAI, DT 2007/116/568, Enlargement of the European Community, 13 July 1977.

37 Fear of Enlargement and Striving for Sex Appeal after the Honeymoon Ends

1. NAI, DT 2007/116/568, Enlargement of the European Community, 13 July 1977.
2. NAI, DT 2009/135/579, Cabinet Subcommittee to Co-ordinate Arrangements Concerning Irish Presidency of the European Community, April and 12 September 1979.
3. NAI, DT 2007/116/525, European Council Meeting, Brussels, 5/6 December 1977, Kirwan to Nally, 10 November 1977.
4. NAI, DT 2007/116/568, Enlargement of the European Community, D. McCutcheon to K. Heaslip, 6 October 1977.
5. NAI, DT 2008/148/243, European Communities: Committee, 11 March 1977 and 16 May 1977.
6. Ibid., 17 June 1977 and 26 September 1977 and George Colley to Michael O'Kennedy, 23 December 1977.
7. NAI, DT 2007/116/666, Spanish Prime Minister: Visit to Dublin October 1977, memorandum of Richard Stokes, 11 and 18 October 1977.

8. Ibid., account of conversation between Lynch and Suarez, 20 October 1977 and Stokes to Department of Finance, 12 December 1977.
9. NAI, DT 2008/148/401, Office of Minister for Economic Planning and Development to E. O'Conghaile, Department of Foreign Affairs, 23 February 1978.
10. Ibid., memo of Kevin F. Jordan, 24 February 1978.
11. NAI, DT 2008/148/549, European Council Meeting in Bremen, July 1978, Bonn ambassador to Secretary, Department of Foreign Affairs, 1 July 1978 and Dermot Nally to Lynch, 3 July 1978.
12. NAI, DT 2008/148/613, Jenkins: President of the European Commission: Visit to Ireland, February and September 1978, 23 February 1978, note of W. Kirwan, 6 September 1978 and account of meeting between Lynch and Jenkins, 4 September 1978.
13. Crotty and Schmitt, *Ireland on the World Stage*, p. 62.
14. NAI, DT 2009/135/586, Relations with the European Parliament, 13 July 1979.
15. NAI, DT 2007/116/403, European Parliament: Method of Election, 4 January 1977.
16. UCDA, FitzGerald Papers, P215/600, Charlie McDonald and Brian Lenihan to Cosgrave, 20 September 1973 and Charlie McDonald to FitzGerald, 2 April 1973.
17. NAI, DT 2007/116/403, 1 February 1977.
18. NAI, DT 2007/116/421, Summit Meeting, Luxembourg, March 1976, 26 March 1976.
19. NAI, DT 2007/116/525, European Council Meeting, Brussels, 5–6 December 1977 and Dáil Debates, 26 October 1977.
20. Ibid., *Irish Times*, 25 March 1977.
21. McDaid, 'The David Thornley Affair', pp. 182–200.
22. *Magill*, May 1979.
23. UCDA, ICEM Papers, P204/106, Eurobarometer and market research prior to direct elections c.1978 and Eurobarometer data from autumn 1978.
24. Ibid., P204/109, Returning Officers: Tom Crotty to Denis Corboy, 10 April 1979.
25. Ibid., P204/119, Bishops' Statement, 1 March 1979.
26. Crotty and Schmitt, *Ireland on the World Stage*, p. 85.
27. UCDA, ICEM Papers, P204/114, The Directly Elected European Parliament, September 1979.
28. Lee, *Ireland, 1912–1985*, p. 495.
29. *Hibernia*, July 1979.
30. *Hibernia*, 14 December 1973.
31. Walsh, *Patrick Hillery*, p. 374.
32. Crotty and Schmitt, *Ireland on the World Stage*, p. 73.
33. Cited ibid., pp. 85ff.
34. Paul Sharp, *Irish Foreign Policy and the European Community* (Aldershot, 1990), pp. 108–9.
35. UCDA, Ó Dálaigh Papers, P51/196, 7 March 1975.
36. UCDA, FitzGerald Papers, P215/401, Robert McDonagh to Noel Dorr, 16 October 1974.

37. Ibid., P215/479, Ann Cremin to FitzGerald and Michael O'Leary, 12 June 1973.
38. Ibid., P215/396 and 397, 11–12 March 1975.
39. Ben Tora and Eilis Ward (eds), *Ireland in International Affairs: Interests, Institutions and Identities* (Dublin, 2002), p. 164.
40. Peter Brennan, *Behind Closed Doors: The EU Negotiations that Shaped Modern Ireland* (Dublin, 2008), pp. 15–19.
41. Sharp, *Irish Foreign Policy*, pp. 100–107.

38 Garret's Wider Mission

1. Letter of Michael Lillis, *Irish Times*, 27 May 2011.
2. Patrick Keatinge, *The Formulation of Irish Foreign Policy* (Dublin, 1973), pp. 295–9.
3. NAI, DT 2005/7/185, Government Foreign Policy: General, memorandum on foreign policy, 7 May 1973.
4. Ibid.
5. *Hibernia*, 13 April 1973.
6. NAI, DT 2009/135/178, memorandum of 11 December 1973.
7. Ibid., FitzGerald to Cosgrave, 2 January 1974.
8. Ibid., note from Department of Taoiseach, n.d., c. January 1974.
9. UCDA, FitzGerald Papers, P215/566, Cruise O'Brien to FitzGerald, 4 July 1973.
10. NAI, DT 2005/7/185, 7 May 1973.
11. Tony Farmar, *Believing in Action* (Dublin, 2002), pp. 19–33.
12. UCDA, de Courcy Ireland Papers, P29/23, Alan Matthews to de Courcy Ireland, 11 May 1974.
13. Farmar, *Believing in Action*, pp. 55ff.
14. UCDA, FitzGerald Papers, P215/478, letter of FitzGerald, February 1974.
15. NAI, DT 2009/135/178, Aid for Developing Countries, 23 January and 11 February 1976.
16. Ibid., Whitaker to FitzGerald, 3 July 1975 and 2 January 1976.
17. Ibid. G. W. P. Dawson to FitzGerald, 11 March 1976.
18. Diarmaid Ferriter, *What If? Alternative Views of Twentieth Century Ireland* (Dublin, 2007), pp. 65–76.
19. NAI, DT 2009/135/178, Alex Tarbett to Lynch, 16 February 1978, and Lynch reply, 21 February 1978.
20. NAI, DT 2007/116/632, President Amin of Uganda: Entry into Ireland, 7 June 1977, *Irish Independent*, 8 June 1977 and *Irish Times*, 8 June 1977.
21. Ibid., 11 December 1973.
22. NAI, DT 2005/151/3, Irish Missions Abroad: General File, memorandum of 15 December 1975.
23. UCDA, de Courcy Ireland Papers, P29/31, Arab Information Centre, 20 November 1974, February 1973 and Irish Arab Society annual report, 1973–4.
24. Rory Miller, *Ireland and the Palestine Question, 1948–2004* (Dublin, 2005), p. 79.
25. Michael Kennedy and Deirdre McMahon (eds), *Obligations and Responsibilities: Ireland and the UN, 1955–2005* (Dublin, 2005), p. 252.

26. Joseph Morrison Skelly, *Irish Diplomacy at the United Nations, 1945–65* (Dublin, 1997), p. 264.
27. Katie Verlin Laatikainen and Karen E. Smith, *The EU at the UN* (New York, 2006), pp. 20–23.
28. NAI, DT 2007/116/183, Cyprus: Fight for Freedom, March 1977.
29. Noel Dorr, *Ireland at the UN: Memories of the Early Years* (Dublin, 2010), p. 11.
30. NAI, DT 2005/7/185, Government Foreign Policy: General, *Irish Press*, 21 September 1971.
31. Ibid., Department of Foreign Affairs to Department of Taoiseach, 30 September 1971 and note of private secretary to Lynch regarding Nuncio, 19 September 1971.
32. Ibid., Lynch to J. F. Dempsey, 25 November 1971.
33. NAI, DT 2008/148/379, China: Diplomatic Relations With, memoranda of 20 September 1976 and 26 September 1978.
34. UCDA, FitzGerald Papers, P215/410, Cosgrave to FitzGerald, 10 June 1976 and FitzGerald to Cosgrave, 2 June 1976.

39 Leverage with Washington

1. NAI, DT 2003/16/564, Governor Ronald Reagan California, Visit to Ireland, 1972, 22 May 1972.
2. NAI, DT 2001/6.490, visit of President Nixon to Ireland, 21 September 1970.
3. Ibid., 22 September 1970.
4. Ibid.
5. UCDA, FitzGerald Papers, P215/480, Moore to FitzGerald, 15 June 1973; FitzGerald to Moore, 20 June 1973 and *Irish Times*, 19 June 1973.
6. UCDA, FitzGerald, P215/406, Paul Keating to FitzGerald, 27 August 1974.
7. Ibid., P215/480, Walter Curley to FitzGerald, 30 April 1977.
8. NAI, DT 2006/133/433, Taoiseach to Mr Cosgrave: Visit to America, March 1976, memorandum of 22 January 1976.
9. Ibid., Keating to Nally, 10 February 1976, David Kennedy to D. O'Sullivan, 10 February 1976 and Nally to Cosgrave, 24 February 1976.
10. Ibid., note of V. Mulcahy, 13 February 1976.
11. UCDA, FitzGerald Papers, P215/480, John D. Moore to FitzGerald, 12 April 1976.
12. NAI, DT 2006/133/489, Visit of US Governors to Ireland, May 1976, 9 February 1976 and secretary, Department of Foreign Affairs to secretary, Department of Taoiseach, 24 March 1976 and 9 April 1976.
13. Ibid., memorandum of 8 April 1976.
14. Ibid., 26 April 1976.
15. UCDA, FitzGerald Papers, P215/387, Visit to Washington 14–18 March 1977.
16. Paddy Woodworth, 'How Did Events in Latin America Influence Young Irish Leftists in the Early 1970s?', *History Ireland*, vol. 16, no. 4, July/August 2008, pp. 28–52.
17. NAI, DT 2009/135/598, Hijack Incident, Shannon Airport, 21 June 1979.
18. NAI, DT 2003/16/283, Publicity on Ireland Abroad: General, Thomas Patrick Foley to Lynch, 30 September 1970.

19. NAI, DT 2005/151/247, Prime Minister of Australia: Visit to Ireland, December 1974, Department of Taoiseach notes, 18 October and 18 December 1974.
20. Ibid.
21. UCDA, FitzGerald Papers, P215/555, Report of Declan Costello's Visit to Australia, 21 March to 1 April 1974.

40 Ireland of the Welcomes?

1. NAI, DT 2005/7/445, Resettlement in Ireland of Refugees from Chile, memorandum for government, 12 February 1974.
2. UCDA, FitzGerald Papers, P215/530, 15 September 1976, Problems of the Chilean Community in Ireland.
3. *Irish Times* Magazine, 18 June 2011.
4. 'Postscript', *History Ireland*, vol. 16, no. 4, July/August 2008, pp. 46–7.
5. NAI, DT 2009/135/562, Indo-China refugees, 10 January 1979 and letters of 10, 15 and 25 January 1979.
6. Ibid., Ruth Sheehy to Lynch, 27 June 1979.
7. NAI, DT 2005/151/3, Irish Missions Abroad: General File, *Irish Times*, 29 December 1975 and Department of Taoiseach note, 30 December 1975.
8. NAI, DT 2005/151/461, President of Ireland: Attendance at Functions, 1 May 1975.
9. NAI, DT 2007/116/379, President of Ireland: Visit to India, H. J. O'Dowd to John Burke, Department of Foreign Affairs, 23 August 1977.
10. *Hibernia*, 23 January 1970.
11. Kader Asmal, *Irish Opposition to Apartheid* (Dublin, 1971).
12. *Irish Times*, 2 January 1970.
13. *Irish Times*, 21 February 1970.
14. UCDA, FitzGerald Papers, P215/398, 29 October 1973.
15. *Hibernia*, 11 October 1974.
16. UCDA, FitzGerald Papers, P215/487, Asmal to FitzGerald, 6 May and 13 December 1975.
17. *Hibernia*, 3 October 1976.
18. UCDA, FitzGerald Papers, P215/487, Asmal to FitzGerald, 20 May and 22 November 1976; P215/548, FitzGerald to Cooney, 2 February 1976 and 6 December 1974.
19. Ibid., P215/487, Asmal to FitzGerald, 16 September 1976.
20. NAI, DT 2008/148/691, South Africa Apartheid, 31 January 1978 and memorandum of 14 February 1978.
21. NAI, DT 2008/148/553, World Cup Golf Competition, 31 January 1978 and Paul Mulcahy to Lynch, 3 April 1978.
22. Ibid., 27 April and 16 May 1978.
23. Ibid., letter of C. A. McCarthy, 11 February 1978 and Michael O'Kennedy to Asmal, 27 April 1978.
24. Ibid., O'Kennedy to Lynch, 30 May 1978.
25. NAI, DT 2008/148/620, President of Tanzania, November 1978.

41 Marketing Ireland

1. NAI, DT 2008/148/769, St Patrick's Day, Seán Donlon to Dermot Nally, 8 December 1977 and note of Lynch's request, 17 January 1978.
2. NAI, DT 2008/148/421, Executive Jet, 17 June 1974, 19 July 1977, memorandum from Department of Finance, 9 December 1977 and cabinet decision, 17 January 1978.
3. NAI, DT 2000/6/306, Publicity on Ireland Abroad, 21 October 1969.
4. Ibid., David Coyle to Jack Lynch, 25 November 1969 and reply of O'Dowd, 1 December 1969.
5. NAI, DT 2003/16/283, Publicity on Ireland Abroad: General, 14 March 1971.
6. Ibid., Bridget O'Boyle to Lynch, 29 April 1971.
7. Ibid., note for Taoiseach, 14 December 1971.
8. NAI, DT 2003/16/283, Publicity on Ireland Abroad: General, *New York Times* Supplement: 'Today in Ireland: The Excitement of Change', 15 November 1970.
9. NAI, DT 2003/16/123, Tourist Development, Bord Fáilte Éireann: Review of 1969, 1 January 1970.
10. *Irish Independent*, 15 January 1970.
11. Ibid., 17 June 1970.
12. Bord Fáilte, Review of 1970, 1 January 1971, Dáil Debates, 25 October 1972.
13. *Irish Press*, 11 January 1972.
14. NAI, DT 2007/116/95, Tourist Development, William Kelly to Cosgrave, F. X. Burke to Cosgrave, 25 July 1974 and Richie Ryan to National Tourism Council, 26 March 1975.
15. Ibid., 11 September 1971.
16. NAI, DT 2006/133/309, Foreign Press Coverage of Ireland, May 1975.
17. NAI, DT 2003/16/123, Tourist Development, Lynch to Barbara Parkinson, 21 March 1972 and Walter Morgan to Lynch, 18 May 1972.
18. NAI, DT 2007/116/95, Tourist Development, O'Dowd to David Thomas, 13 February 1973, J. F. Fazackerly to Lynch, n.d., c. 1973.
19. NAI, DT 2006/133/309, Foreign Press Coverage of Ireland, monthly digests, May 1976.
20. NAI, DT 2007/116/591, British Lord Mayor and Mayors, Visit to Ireland, 1977.
21. NAI, DT 2007/116/589, Intoxicating Liquor Acts 1977, memorandum from Department of Taoiseach, 9 March 1977.
22. NAI, DT 2007/116/589, Intoxicating Liquor Act 1977, 9 March 1977; letter of Lord Killanin, 11 March 1977 and letter of Jonathan Irwin, 29 March 1977 and letter of James Meenan, 10 March 1977.
23. NAI, DT 2009/135/164, Bord Fáilte Éireann, report and accounts, 1977 and 1978.
24. UCDA, Kelly Papers, P147/47, Killarney Seminar on Tourism speech, 17 January 1978.

Part VI The Economy

1. James Meenan, *The Irish Economy Since 1922* (Liverpool, 1970).

2. T. K. Whitaker, 'From Protection to Free Trade – the Irish Experience', *Administration*, vol. 21, no. 4, 1974, pp. 405–24.
3. John Brady, 'The Economics of Survival', *Social Studies*, vol. 5, no. 1, Spring 1976, pp. 3–26.
4. T. K. Whitaker, *Interests* (Dublin, 1983), p. 177.
5. Mary Daly, *The Spirit of Earnest Inquiry: The Statistical and Social Inquiry Society of Ireland* (Dublin, 1997), p. 163.
6. Whitaker, *Interests*, p. 182.
7. Ibid., pp. 184–5.
8. Raymond Smith, *Urbi et Orbi and All That* (Dublin, 1995), p. 237.
9. Whitaker, *Interests*, p. 174.
10. Lee, *Ireland, 1912–1985*, pp. 487–90.
11. Whitaker, *Interests*, p. 3.
12. Plunkett, *Boy on the Back Wall*, p. 106.
13. Patrick Nolan, 'The Irish Trade Union Movement', *Christus Rex*, vol. 23, no. 1, January–March 1969, pp. 21–8.
14. Charles McCarthy, 'Workers' Participation in Management', *Journal of the Social and Statistical Inquiry Society of Ireland*, vol. 22, part 2, 1970–71, pp. 2–38.
15. Charles McCarthy, 'The Function of National Pay Agreements', *Administration*, vol. 22, no. 1, 1974, pp. 60–72.
16. Kieran Kennedy and Richard Bruton, *The Irish Economy* (Brussels, 1975).
17. Lee, *Ireland, 1912–1985*, pp. 531–7.
18. Bertram Hutchinson, 'On the Study of Non-economic Factors in Irish Economic Development', *Economic and Social Review*, vol. 1, no. 1, 1969–70, pp. 509–28.
19. Brian Nolan, 'The Personal Distribution of Income in the Republic of Ireland', *Journal of the Social and Statistical Inquiry Society of Ireland*, vol. 23, part 5, 1977–8, pp. 163–217.
20. M. P. Kent and J. J. Sexton, 'The Influence of Certain Social Factors on the Physical Growth and Development of a Group of Dublin City Children', *Journal of the Social and Statistical Inquiry Society of Ireland*, vol. 22, part 5, 1972–3, p. 188.
21. Séamus Ó Cinnéide, 'Power and Its Victims in Ireland', *Studies*, vol. 62, Winter 1972, p. 355.
22. T. P. O'Mahony, 'Poverty in Ireland', *Doctrine and Life*, vol. 22, no. 1, January 1972, p. 50.
23. John Brady, 'Ireland in Transition', *Studies*, vol. 67, Spring/Summer 1978, pp. 1–2.

42 The Irish Economic Dilemma

1. NAI, DT 2005/151/255, Control of Public Expenditure, T. K. Whitaker to Richie Ryan, 5 September 1974.
2. Lee, *Ireland, 1912–1985*, pp. 470–71.
3. Sweeney, *Down, Down*, pp. 140–41.
4. Dermot McAleese, 'European Integration and the Irish Economy', in Cormac O'Gráda (ed.), *The Economic Development of Ireland Since 1870, Volume II* (Aldershot, 1994), pp. 76–96.

5. 'Rolling Back the Years, 1975–1979', *Irish Independent* Supplement, 29 October 2011.
6. Lee, *Ireland, 1912–1985*, pp. 472–3.
7. Peter Neary, 'The Failure of Economic Nationalism', in *Ireland: Dependence and Independence: The Crane Bag* (Dublin, 1984), pp. 68–77.
8. Collins, *Cosgrave Legacy*, pp. 101–2.
9. NAI, DT 2007/116/337, Interviews Given by the Taoiseach: Background Notes, 12 June 1975.
10. NAI, DT 2000/6/364, Economic Situation, Erskine Childers to Lynch, 10 October 1969, Lynch reply, 13 October 1969.
11. NAI, DT 2001/6/348, Review of 1969 and Outlook for 1970, memorandum from Department of Finance, December 1969.
12. NAI, DT 2005/17/363, Fourth Programme for Economic and Social Development, October 1972.
13. UCDA, Fianna Fáil Papers, P176/344, notebook on organisational aspects of 1973 general election.
14. NAI, DT 2005/7/283, Economic Situation 1973–4, 21 March 1973.
15. Ibid., *Irish Press*, 27 October 1972.
16. UCDA, Kelly Papers, P147/44, Kelly to Cosgrave, 3 May 1974 and Cosgrove to Kelly, 7 May 1974.
17. NAI, DT 2005/7/292, Wealth Tax, 22 October 1970, 12 and 25 March 1974.
18. NAI, DT 2008/148/192, Wealth Tax, memorandum of Richie Ryan, 3 January 1977, note of Dermot Nally, 31 January 1977 and Feargal Quinn to Colley, 12 January and 1 February 1978.

43 The Cost of Living, Poverty and Giving Up Meat

1. *Hibernia*, 3 February 1971.
2. *Hibernia*, 3 February 1971 and 30 April 1971.
3. NAI, DT 2004/21/385, 9 February 1971.
4. Lee, *Ireland, 1912–1985*, p. 353.
5. Ibid. and *Irish Press*, 13 January and 6 May 1971.
6. NAI, DT 2005/7/363, Fourth Programme for Economic Expansion, John F. O'Carroll to Lynch, 5 October and 27 November 1972.
7. NAI, DT 2001/6/400, RTE Telecast on Illegal Money Lending, 24 January 1970.
8. Ibid., Dáil Debates, 16 December 1969.
9. Ibid., Report of Tribunal, delivered 6 August 1970.
10. Ibid., statement of RTE Authority, 20 October 1970.
11. *Hibernia*, 17 March 1972.
12. *Hibernia*, 8 June 1973.
13. Ibid.
14. *Magill*, March 1979.
15. *Magill*, July 1979.
16. *Hibernia*, 2 and 17 December 1971.
17. UCDA, de Courcy Ireland Papers, P29A/16, Poverty in Ireland, October 1973.

18. Ibid.
19. *Hibernia*, 26 April 1974.
20. NAI, DT 2003/16/325, Social Services: General, February 1972.
21. NAI, DT 2004/21/237, Social Welfare: Children's Allowances, memorandum of 25 January 1973.
22. NAI, DT 2006/133/54, Old Age Pensions, 14 December 1973.
23. Ibid., memoranda of Richie Ryan, 22 July and 14 November 1974.
24. Collins, *Cosgrave Legacy*, pp. 141–9, 158.
25. NAI, DT 2007/116/143, Department of Social Welfare Reports, 1972–5.
26. NAI, DT 2009/135/48, 10 September 1979.
27. NAI, DT 2003/16/102, Fuel: Supplies and Prices.
28. NAI, DT 2005/7/120, Fuel Situation, 11 October 1974.
29. NAI, DT 2005/7/363, memorandum for government on inflation, 22 March 1974.
30. NAI, DT 2009/135/614, Educational Institutions: Heating Of, 2 August 1979.
31. *Magill*, July 1979.
32. NAI, DT 2006/133/513, Household Budget Survey 1973, presented 6 May 1976.
33. NAI, DT 2009/135/329, Household Budget Survey, report presented 25 September 1979.
34. Ibid.
35. NAI, DT 2007/116/658, Household Budget Survey: Annual Urban Inquiry, 1974–6, results for 1976, 17 November 1977.
36. *Hibernia*, 26 April 1974.
37. NAI, DT 2008/148/528, National Prices Commission: Monthly Report, January 1978.
38. Ibid., Low Cost Diets, May 1977.
39. NAI, DT 2007/116/402, Cost of Living: Control of Prices, Betty McGarry to Cosgrave, 4 March 1977.
40. *Hibernia*, 13 February 1976.
41. *Hibernia*, 14 January 1976.
42. *Magill*, December 1979.
43. *Magill*, January 1978.
44. *Magill*, October 1977.
45. *Magill*, October 1978.
46. Ibid.
47. *Magill*, July 1979.

44 Local Finance, Economic Patriotism, Competitiveness and Employment

1. NAI, DT 2003/16/296, Local Government Policy, 6 July 1971.
2. Ibid., Jeremiah O'Brien to secretary to president, 4 December 1971 and Denis McDermott to Lynch, 17 April 1972.
3. NAI, DT 2004/21/305, Bishop Edward Moore to Lynch, 19 January 1970 and 27 February 1970 and Seán Brady to Hugh Gibbons, 24 April 1970.
4. Ibid., memorandum of Molloy, 23 July 1971.

5. Ibid., note on phone call from 'Mrs Dunlop from Rathfarnham' and Kathleen Dunne to Lynch, 22 February 1973.
6. NAI, DT 2006/133/191, Public Expenditure: Control Of, 1976–8, James Tully to Richie Ryan, 9 November 1976.
7. Sweeney, *Down, Down*, p. 121.
8. Mary Daly, *The Buffer State: The Historical Roots of the Department of the Environment* (Dublin, 1997), p. 513.
9. NAI, DT 2003/16/344, Buy Irish Campaign, 1964–72, George Colley to Lynch, 25 February 1970 and *Sunday Independent*, 9 January 1972.
10. NAI, DT 2005/7/168, Economic Relations with Foreign Countries and *Evening Herald*, 23 July 1972.
11. NAI, DT 2004/21/388, Free Trade: Preparation of Industry For, 2 April 1973.
12. UCDA, ICEM Papers, P204 /96, EEC: Negotiations on Ireland's Application, 1970–71.
13. NAI, DT 2008/148/611, West Germany: Recruitment of Irish Workers, 23 May 1978.
14. NAI, DT 2005/7/168, Economic Relations with Foreign Countries; Total Exports in the Year Ended September 1971.
15. NAI, DT 2005/7/224, Shannon Free Airport Development Company: Report and Accounts 1959–77, year end to March 1974.
16. UCDA, FitzGerald Papers, P215/496, Michael Begley to FitzGerald, 17 May 1977.
17. NAI, DT 2005/151/170, 31 July 1975.
18. NAI, DT 2008/148/682, Labour Force Survey 1977: First Results, 30 November 1978.
19. UCDA, ICEM Papers, P204/96, EEC: Negotiations on Ireland's Application, 1970–71 and FitzGerald Papers, P215/496, Joey Murrin to Michael Begley, 9 August 1974.
20. *Magill*, February 1978.
21. UCDA, de Courcy Ireland Papers, P29A/8, Labour: Maritime Policy, c. 1971.

45 Spending, Planning and Pleading

1. *Magill*, June 1978.
2. *Magill*, March 1979.
3. NAI, DT 2005/151/255, note of 27 November 1974.
4. Quoted in John Bradley, 'The Legacy of Economic Development: The Irish Economy, 1960–87', in John F. McCarthy (ed.), *Planning Ireland's Future: The Legacy of T. K. Whitaker* (Dublin, 1990), pp. 128–50.
5. NAI, DT 2006/133/317, Cabinet Economic Subcommittee, 7 March 1975.
6. NAI, DT 2006/133/317, Cabinet Economic Subcommittee, memorandum from Department of Taoiseach, 30 April 1975.
7. NAI, DT 2005/151/255, Control of Public Expenditure, 11 August 1975.
8. Ibid., 7 May 1975.
9. Ibid., Ryan to Cosgrave, 1 August 1975, 4 September 1975 and memorandum of Ryan, 7 November 1975.

10. NAI, DT 2006/133/317, Cabinet Economic Subcommittee, 19 September 1975 and 15 January 1976 and FitzGerald to Ryan, 29 March 1976.
11. NAI, DT 2006/133/191, Public Expenditure: Control of 1976–8, memorandum from Ryan, 25 October 1976 and Minister for Health's response, 27 October 1976.
12. NAI, DT 2007/116/33, Bank and Public Holidays, 18 and 22 February 1977 and memorandum from Minister for Public Service, 16 March 1977.
13. Ibid., Department of Taoiseach memorandum, 22 March 1977.
14. NAI, DT 2005/151/608, Functions of Government, 30 September 1974 and memorandum from Ryan, 13 October 1975.
15. Ibid., Ryan to Cosgrave, 13 July 1975.
16. NAI, DT 2006/133/191, Public Expenditure: Control Of, 1976–8, 6 February 1976.
17. Ibid., John Bruton to Cosgrave, 13 September 1976 and response of W. Kirwan, 15 September 1976.
18. *Irish Times*, 8 November 1976.
19. NAI, DT 2007/116/605, Budgetary Outlook 1977, Department of Taoiseach memorandum, 25 April 1977.
20. *Magill*, June 1978.
21. Lee, *Ireland, 1912–1985*, p. 490.
22. *Magill*, November 1977.
23. NAI, DT 2007/116/402, Cost of Living: Control of Prices, Stokes to Lynch, 15 December 1977.
24. NAI, DT 2008/148/194, Public Expenditure: Control Of, 1979, memoranda of 18 and 21 September 1978.
25. *Hibernia*, 26 May 1972.
26. Sweeney, *Down, Down*, pp. 140–41; Foster, *Luck and the Irish*, p. 194.

46 Taxing, Dodging, Negotiating and Protesting

1. *Hibernia*, 3 March 1971.
2. *Hibernia*, 16 April 1971.
3. *Hibernia*, 21 January 1972.
4. Patrick Maume, 'George Colley', in McGuire and Quinn, *DIB*, vol. 2, p. 668.
5. *Hibernia*, 14 April 1972 and 25 May 1973.
6. *Hibernia*, 2 April 1974.
7. *Hibernia*, 1 March 1974.
8. *Hibernia*, 16 May 1974.
9. Sweeney, *Down, Down*, p. 110.
10. NAI, DT 2007/116/539, Farmers: Taxation Of, 18 May 1976 and George Jeffrey to Paddy Hegarty, 27 May 1976.
11. Ibid., Department of Taoiseach memorandum, 11 January 1976 and John Bruton to Cosgrave, 18 March 1977.
12. NAI, DT 2007/116/436, National Wage Agreements, memorandum for Cosgrave, c. January 1977.
13. *Magill*, March 1978.
14. NAI, DT 2007/116/605, Budgetary Outlook 1977, 25 April 1977.

15. NAI, DT 2009/135/310, Taxation of Farmers, Jim Gibbons to Lynch, 30 January 1979.
16. Ibid.
17. Ibid., account of meeting with farmers, 28 February 1979 and *Irish Times*, 1 March 1979.
18. Sweeney, *Down, Down*, pp. 175–6.
19. *Magill*, April 1979.
20. Ibid.
21. *Magill*, January 1979.
22. Sweeney, *Down, Down*, pp. 176–7.
23. *Hibernia*, April 1979.
24. NAI, DT 2006/133/587, Public Sector Pay, Department of Taoiseach memorandum, 31 December 1974.
25. Foster, *Luck and the Irish*, pp. 16–17.
26. Ibid.
27. NAI, DT 2006/133/465, National Wage Agreement, 11 May 1976, 5 March 1976 and Arthur Shiel to Cosgrave, 9 April 1976.
28. *Hibernia*, 9 April 1976.
29. NAI, DT 2008/148/343, Nally to Cosgrave, 24 May 1977.
30. NAI, DT 2008/148/343, National Wage Agreement 1978, note for Taoiseach, January 1978.
31. *Magill*, July 1979.
32. Foster, *Luck and the Irish*, pp. 16–17; Donal Nevin (ed.), *Trade Union Century* (Dublin, 1994), p. 170.
33. Patrick Gunnigle, Gerard McMahon and Joseph Wallace, *Industrial Relations in Ireland* (Dublin, 2004), p. 131.

47 Strikes Raging, Babies Howling

1. Boran, *Invisible Prison*, p. 109.
2. Crotty and Schmitt, *Ireland on the World Stage*, p. 4.
3. Gunnigle, McMahon and Wallace, *Industrial Relations in Ireland*, pp. 131–2.
4. NAI, DT 2009/135/372, memorandum for government on the industrial relations situation, April 1979.
5. NAI, DT 2001/6/114, Bank Disputes, Mary Mulcahy to Jack Lynch, 1 May 1970.
6. 'Rolling Back the Years, 1970–1974', *Irish Independent* Supplement, 22 October 2011.
7. NAI, DT 2001/6/114, Lynch to Thomas Kirk, 22 June 1970 and Dáil Debates, 1 July 1970.
8. NAI, DT 2002/8/357, Labour Court: Reports 1965–73, 24th Annual Report, 1970.
9. NAI, DT 2005/7/275, Industrial Relations, Government Policy, 18 February 1974.
10. NAI, DT 2003/16/404, Pfizer, John A. Mulcahy to Lynch, 18 March 1970 and draft reply.
11. NAI, DT 2002/8/163, Report of Meeting Between Taoiseach and Maurice Stans, US Secretary of Commerce, 19 April 1971.

12. Sweeney, *Down, Down*, p. 130.
13. *Magill*, November and December 1977.
14. NAI, DT 2009/135/372, Robin Power to Lynch, 30 November 1977.
15. NAI, DT 2003/16/397, Secondary School Teachers Strike 1971, Minister for Education to Máire Mac Donagh, general secretary ASTI, 23 December 1970 and Florence Cooke to Lynch, 16 February 1972.
16. John Cunningham, *Unlikely Radicals: The Irish Post-Primary Teachers and the ASTI, 1909–2009* (Cork, 2009), p. 173.
17. NAI, DT 2003/16/298, ESB: Trade Disputes, John M. Murphy to Lynch, 10 October 1971.
18. Ibid., John Hogan to Lynch, 10 April 1972, J. J. O'Reilly to Lynch, 13 April 1972, G. McGahon to Lynch, 11 April 1972 and Catherine Hoban to Lynch, 14 April 1972.
19. NAI, DT 2004/21/243, Sheila Barrett to Cosgrave, 18 November 1973.
20. NAI, DT 2004/21/243, Irish Medical Association, Dr Philip Cawley to Cosgrave, 20 October 1973.
21. NAI, DT 2005/7/275, Industrial Relations: Government Policy, 16 May 1974.
22. NAI, DT 2005/7/237–8, September 1974.
23. NAI, DT 2005/151/363, Unfair Dismissals Act 1977, March 1974 and 4 June 1975.
24. NAI, DT 2006/133/297, Post Office Workers, 19 and 23 December 1975, 30 January and 13 February 1976.
25. Ibid., memorandum from Posts and Telegraphs, 2 July 1976.
26. *Magill*, December 1977.
27. *Magill*, November 1977.
28. NAI, DT 2008/148/384, Psychiatric Nurses: Strike, 16 and 19 January 1978.
29. NAI, DT 2009/135/56, Milk Supply, Maintenance during Emergency, Gemma Hussey to Lynch, 20 October 1978.
30. NAI, DT 2009/135/372, J. J. Shea to Lynch, 4 May 1978.
31. Ibid., letter to Ciaran O'Callaghan, 18 August 1978.
32. Ibid., G. Porter to Lynch, 13 October 1978.
33. Ibid., Lynch speech, Chamber of Commerce, Cork, 26 January 1979.
34. NAI, DT 2009/135/437, National Wage Agreement: National Understanding, May Clifford to Lynch, 20 March 1979 and statement of Lynch, 24 April 1979.
35. *Magill*, April 1979.
36. Sweeney, *Down, Down*, pp. 178–9.
37. *Magill*, May 1979.
38. *Magill*, June 1979.
39. *Magill*, August 1979.
40. NAI, DT 2009/135, 586, Lynch speech in Dáil on adjournment of Dáil for summer, 13 July 1979.
41. Foster, *Luck and the Irish*, pp. 34–5.
42. Lee, *Ireland, 1912–1985*, p. 492.
43. Sweeney, *Down, Down*, p. 184.

48 Hoping to Strike It Rich

1. UCDA, de Courcy Ireland Papers, P29/23, Labour Party Annual Conference 1973: Resolutions.
2. NAI, DT 2004/21/219, Nuclear Power Project, memorandum from Department of Transport and Power, 27 November 1973.
3. NAI, DT 2005/7/286, Oil and Natural Gas Exploration, 16 September 1972.
4. Ibid., Frank Lemass to Lynch, 13 November 1972.
5. Ibid., Donough O'Connor to Cosgrave, 7 May 1973.
6. Ibid., 4 September 1973.
7. Ibid., 12 March 1974 and *Irish Independent*, 19 April 1974.
8. Ibid., Justin Keating to Cosgrave, 15 July 1974.
9. Ibid., 4 November 1974.
10. *Hibernia*, 2 and 15 February 1974.
11. Lee, *Ireland, 1912–1985*, p. 473.
12. Frank Connolly and Ronan Lynch, *The Great Corrib Gas Controversy* (Dublin, 2005), p. 9.
13. Ibid.
14. Lorna Siggins, *Once Upon a Time in the West: The Corrib Gas Controversy* (London, 2010), pp. 10–13.
15. Connolly and Lynch, *Corrib Gas*, pp. 10–11.
16. Siggins, *Once Upon a Time*, p. 13.
17. Sweeney, *Down, Down*, pp. 208–9, *Irish Independent*, 8 and 9 January 1979 and 'Rolling Back the Years, 1975–1979', *Irish Independent* Supplement, 29 October 2011.
18. NAI, DT 2004/21/219, Nuclear Power Project: Carnsore Point, memorandum from Department of Transport and Power, 27 November 1973.
19. Ibid.
20. NAI, DT 2008/148/125, Nuclear Power Project: Carnsore Point, Richard Stokes to Lynch, 5 October 1977.
21. UCDA, Kelly Papers, P147/47, 13 March 1973.
22. Sweeney, *Down, Down*, pp. 144–5.
23. John F. Carroll and Petra K. Kelly (eds), *A Nuclear Ireland?* (Dublin, 1978); Liam Leonard, *Green Nation: The Irish Environmental Movement from Carnsore Point to the Rossport 5* (Louth, 2006), pp. 79–101.
24. *Hibernia*, 15 March, 21 June and 9 August 1974.
25. UCDA, de Courcy Ireland Papers, P29/A/79, Liaison Committee of the Left newsletter, c. 1974.
26. Sweeney, *Down, Down*, p. 64.
27. Boyle, 'James Tully'.
28. UCDA, de Courcy Ireland Papers, P29A/79, Liaison Committee of the Left newsletter, 23 January 1974.
29. *Hibernia*, 27 September 1974.
30. *Irish Times*, 19 February 1997.

31. NAI, DT 2007/116/536, Bula Ltd, Acquisition of Shares 1977, memorandum from Department of Industry and Commerce, 17 January 1977; meeting between Keating and Cosgrave, 8 February 1977 and Department of Taoiseach memorandum, 8 February 1977.
32. Ibid.
33. Ibid., 14 February 1977.
34. UCDA, Kelly Papers, P147/47, speech in Dublin, 9 January 1978.
35. *Irish Independent*, 3 January 2010.
36. Ibid., 16 April 1979.
37. Ibid., 17 May 1979.
38. *Hot Press*, 17 August 1978.
39. *Magill*, September 1978.
40. UCDA, FitzGerald Papers, P215/506, confidential note re Noel Browne phone call, 20 December 1974.
41. Ibid., P215/508, FitzGerald to Bruton, 21 February 1975.
42. NAI, DT 2008/148/165, Visits Abroad by Ministers, O'Malley to Lynch, 1 September 1978.

Part VII Social Change

1. Foley, 'A Minstrel Boy'.
2. Brady, 'Ireland in Transition', and Timothy Hamilton, 'The Upholding of Values in a Pluralist Society', *Studies*, vol. 67, Spring/Summer 1978, pp. 5–13.
3. T. P. O'Mahony, 'Ireland in 1976: The Pain and the Paradox', *Doctrine and Life*, vol. 26, April 1976, pp. 240–47.
4. Adrian Redmond (ed.), *That Was Then, This Is Now: Change in Ireland, 1949–1999* (Dublin, 2000), pp. 14–52 and Patrick Clancy, Sheelagh Drudy, Kathleen Lynch and Liam O'Dowd (eds), *Ireland: A Sociological Profile* (Dublin, 1986), pp. 26–49.
5. Damian Hannan, 'Kinship, Neighbourhood and Social Change in Irish Rural Communities', *Economic and Social Review*, vol. 3, 1971–2, pp. 163–88.
6. Curtin, Donnan and Wilson, *Irish Urban Cultures*, pp. 2–23.
7. Mary Whelan, 'Reflections on a Community Survey', *Social Studies*, vol. 3, no. 1, February 1974, pp. 3–13.
8. Nancy Scheper-Hughes, *Saints, Scholars and Schizophrenics: Mental Illness in Rural Ireland* (Berkeley, 1979), p. 133.
9. Clancy et al., *Ireland*, p. 98.
10. Leon Uris, *Ireland: A Terrible Beauty* (London, 1976).
11. Clancy et al., *Ireland*, p. 64.
12. R. P. Kinsella, 'The Health Sector and Resource Allocation', *Administration*, vol. 21, no. 4, 1973, pp. 150–60.
13. Maureen Browne (ed.), *Irish Medical Times 1967–1992: 25 Years Ahead* (Dublin, 1992), pp. 2–49.
14. Ibid., p. 45.
15. Pádraig Ó Móráin *The Health of the Nation: The Irish Healthcare System, 1957–2007* (Dublin, 2007), p. 29.

16. R. Blayney, 'Alcoholism in Ireland: Medical and Social Aspects', *Social and Statistical Inquiry Society of Ireland*, vol. 23, part 1, 1973–4, pp. 108–25.
17. Geldof, *Is That It?*, p. 116.

49 The Urban/Rural Divide

1. UCDA, FitzGerald Papers, P215/481, Murphy, 'Identity in the Republic of Ireland Now'.
2. NAI, DT 2005/7/422, President of Ireland Speeches: Clearance, 6 October 1973.
3. Ibid., 27 November 1973.
4. *Hibernia*, 29 June 1971.
5. Brown, *Ireland*, p. 252.
6. O'Faoláin, *Are You Somebody?*, pp. 158–9.
7. Walshe, *Cissie's Abattoir*, p. 84.
8. Liam de Paor, 'Ireland's Identities', *Crane Bag*, vol. 3, no. 1, 1979, pp. 22–9, p. 25.
9. Murray, *Friel*, p. 53.
10. NAI, DT 2000/6/143, Christy Loftus to Lynch, 27 November 1969 and NFA, Mayo Branch, to Lynch, 24 December 1969.
11. NAI, DT 2002/8/190, Connemara Development Board, memoranda of March 1971 and 2 April 1971.
12. Ibid.
13. NAI, DT 2005/7/303, Regional Development, Sligo/Leitrim Development Organisation, 31 July 1973.
14. NAI, DT 2003/16/288, Small Farms: Inter-Departmental Committee, 24 January 1972.
15. Ibid., Una Brennan to Lynch, 21 June 1972.
16. NAI, DT 2005/7/34, Land Division: Government Policy, memorandum from Minister for Lands, 29 April 1974.
17. Ibid., message from the National Land League and Family Farm Organisation, 19 July 1974.
18. Alan Matthews, 'The State of Irish Agriculture', *Magill*, May 1978.
19. *Magill*, May 1979.
20. William J. Smyth, 'Continuity and Change in the Territorial Organisation of Irish Rural Communities', *Maynooth Review*, vol. 1, no. 1, June 1975, pp. 52–74.
21. Waters, *Jiving at the Crossroads*, pp. 65–6.

50 Taking Responsibility for the Irish Abroad?

1. Dáil Debates, 12 November 1970, 24 June and 27 October 1971 and NAI, DT 2000/6/203, Emigration: Parliamentary Questions.
2. NAI, DT 2001/6/197, Irish Labour Emigration, Lynch to Brendan Hickey, 27 August 1970 and *Irish Press*, 23 July 1970.
3. NAI, DT 2004/21/188, Anthony Dillon to Cosgrave, 15 June 1973.
4. Enda Delaney, *Irish Emigration Since 1921* (Dublin, 2002), p. 39.
5. NAI, DT 2005/7/59, Australia: Assistance to Migrants, c. October 1974.

6. UCDA, FitzGerald Papers, P215/483, John Collins to FitzGerald, 27 June 1973 and FitzGerald to Collins, 10 October 1973.
7. Niall O'Dowd, *An Irish Voice* (Dublin, 2010), pp. 33–108.
8. NA, DT 2006/133/380, Emigrant Centres in Britain: Financial Assistance, FitzGerald to Cosgrave, 12 December 1974 and 11 February 1975.
9. Ibid., Cosgrave to FitzGerald, 20 March 1975.
10. Ibid., Costello to Cosgrave, 4 April 1975.
11. Ibid., Cosgrave to FitzGerald, 1 September 1975.
12. Ibid., Joseph Cunnane to Cosgrave, 4 December 1975 and Costello to FitzGerald, 8 December 1975.
13. Ibid., Statement of Eamon Casey, 2 April 1976.
14. NAI, DT 2007/116/412, Emigrant Centres in Britain: Financial Assistance, 23 December 1976.
15. UCDA, FitzGerald Papers, P215/486, Fr Olivier McTernan to FitzGerald, 9 February, 5 March, and 2 April 1976.
16. NAI, DT 2007/116/412, FitzGerald to Cosgrave, 17 January 1977.
17. NAI, DT 2008/148/319, Emigrant Centres in Britain: Financial Assistance, 13 February 1978.
18. Ibid., 28 July 1978 and 4 July 1978.
19. NAI, DT 2009/135/272, Emigrant Centres in Britain: Financial Assistance, report of inter-departmental committee, December 1978 and memorandum of 7 March 1979.
20. Ibid., London Irish Centre: Annual Welfare Report, 1978.
21. Moore, *One Voice*, p. 17.
22. NAI, DT 2009/135/272, Letter to Jack Lynch, 11 October 1979.
23. Cited in Brendan McGowan, *Taking the Boat: The Irish in Leeds, 1931–81* (Mayo, 2009), p. 148.

51 Living on the Edge

1. *Census of Ireland, 1979* (Dublin, 1980), Population Table 14: Population of Inhabited Islands off the Coast.
2. *Irish Times*, 31 July 2010.
3. NAI, DT 2004/21/280, Islands off the Coast of Ireland: Living conditions, 'Manifesto for the Islands' c. April 1973.
4. Ibid.
5. *Hibernia*, 12 April 1974.
6. NAI, DT 2005/151/193, Islands off the Coast of Ireland: Living Conditions, 29 April 1975.
7. Ibid., memorandum of 20 May 1975.
8. *Magill*, August 1979.
9. NAI, DT 2005/151/193, Peter Barry to Cosgrave, 21 May 1975 and Robert Molloy to Cosgrave, 28 May 1975.
10. NAI, DT 2009/135/127, Islands off the Coast of Ireland: Living Conditions, C. O'Grady to Cosgrave, 26 January 1977 and *Irish Press*, 23 September 1977.

11. Ibid., 22 March 1978.
12. Ibid., memoranda of 20 October and 1 November 1978 and Department of Taoiseach note of 1 November 1978.
13. *Sunday Independent*, 2 January 2011.
14. *Magill*, September 1979.

52 The Broader Social Outlook

1. NAI, DT 2007/116/381, Census of Population 1976, A. Horner to James Tully, 23 September 1975.
2. NAI, DT 2009/135/627, Census of Population 1979.
3. Brown, *Ireland*, p. 242.
4. NAI, DT 2007/116/574, National Economic and Social Report: 'Towards a Social Report', 1 February 1977.
5. Brendan Walsh, 'Marriage in Ireland in the Twentieth Century', in Art Cosgrove (ed.), *Marriage in Ireland* (Dublin, 1985), pp. 132–50.
6. NAI, DT 2007/116/574, National Economic and Social Report, pp. 8–126.
7. NAI, DT 2005/151/350, Centenarians: Bounties 1974 and Messages from the President, Department of Taoiseach memorandum, 14 May 1974.
8. NAI, DT 2008/148/461, Centenarians: Bounties 1978, letter of Mary Flood, 22 September 1978.
9. NAI, DT 2005/151/350, letters of 16 and 13 September, 6 August, 25 July and 20 November 1974.
10. NAI, DT 2008/148/461, Centenarians: Bounties 1978, note of B. O'Connell, 20 July 1978.
11. NAI, DT 2008/148/461, Centenarians: Bounties 1978, memorandum of Richard Stokes, 21 June 1978.
12. NAI, DT 2008/148/450, Grants for Housing of Elderly Persons, Department of Taoiseach memorandum, 30 March 1978.
13. *Hibernia*, 17 December 1971.
14. *Hibernia*, 19 January 1973.
15. *Hibernia*, 25 May and 5 October 1973.
16. *Hibernia*, 4 August 1972.
17. Anne Power, *Estates on the Edge: The Social Consequences of Mass Housing in Northern Europe Since 1850* (London, 1993); see also Aibhlín McCrann, *Memories, Milestones and New Horizons: Reflections on the Regeneration of Ballymun* (Belfast, 2008).
18. NAI, DT Inner City Development: Draft Report of the Inner City Development Advisory Committee; Dermot Nally to Liam Alyward, 24 July 1978 and Lynch to Sylvester Barrett, 25 July 1978.
19. Ibid., Report of Inter-Departmental Committee, n.d., c. July 1978.
20. NAI, DT 2007/116/633, The Liberties Festival, 13–23 May 1977.
21. *Magill*, January 1979.
22. *Magill*, June and July 1979.
23. *Magill*, December 1979.

24. Robbie Gilligan, *Tony Gregory* (Dublin, 2011), p. 41.

53 Eating and Drinking through the Seventies

1. 'Rolling Back the Years, 1970–1974', *Irish Independent* Supplement, 22 October 2011.
2. NAI, DT 2006/133/549, National Prices Committee: Monthly Report May 1976, 51st Monthly Report, p. 48.
3. NAI, DT 2006/133/549, John Quinn to Liam Cosgrave, 27 July 1976.
4. *Magill*, January 1978 and *Hibernia*, 22 January 1970.
5. Boran, *Invisible Prison*, pp. 87–108.
6. *Hibernia*, 22 January 1979.
7. *Hibernia*, 19 November 1971.
8. *Irish Times* and *Irish Independent*, 21 March 1991.
9. 'Rolling Back the Years, 1975–1979', *Irish Independent* Supplement, 29 October 2011.
10. *Magill*, October 1977.
11. *Magill*, February 1978.
12. *Magill*, October 1978 and March 1979.
13. *Magill*, May 1979.
14. *Sunday Independent*, *Life Magazine*, 6 February 2011.
15. *Magill*, September 1978.
16. *Hibernia*, 1 March 1974.
17. *Hibernia*, 16 November 1973.
18. *Irish Times* Magazine, 21 May 2011.
19. *Magill*, October 1977.
20. *Magill*, June 1977.
21. *Magill*, December 1978.
22. Diarmaid Ferriter, *A Nation of Extremes: The Pioneers in Twentieth Century Ireland* (Dublin, 1998), pp. 256–7.
23. NAI, DT 2009/135/117, Intoxicating Liquor Acts, Patrick McDonnell to Jack Lynch, 3 February 1970.
24. Ibid., letter of W. Herlihy, 24 July 1971 and Des O'Malley to Lynch, 13 August 1971.
25. Ibid., Dáil Debates, 5 August 1971.
26. NAI, DT 2009/135/117, memorandum submitted to Richie Ryan in May 1973 and Department of Justice memorandum, 30 September 1977 and memorandum on Special Exemptions, March 1979.
27. Ibid., memorandum of V. Mulcahy, Department of Taoiseach, 3 April 1979.
28. Ibid., Department of Taoiseach memorandum, 21 May 1979.
29. *Magill*, October 1977 and March and April 1978.
30. *Magill*, February 1978.
31. *Magill*, December 1977.
32. 'Rolling Back the Years, 1975–1979', *Irish Independent* Supplement, 29 October 2011.
33. *Magill*, February and October 1978.

34. *Magill*, October 1977.
35. *Magill*, October 1978.
36. *Magill*, December 1978, *Hibernia*, 4 February 1971.
37. *Hot Press*, 25 January 1979.
38. *Hot Press*, 28 April 1978.
39. *Irish Times*, Weekend Review, 12 December 2009.
40. Madden, *Fear and Loathing*, p. 147.
41. Mills, *Hurler on the Ditch*, p. 109.
42. McCafferty, *Nell*, p. 198.
43. Madden, *Fear and Loathing*, p. 27.
44. Walshe, *Cissie's Abattoir*, p. 117.
45. Connolly and Hourigan, *Social Movements and Ireland*, p. 89.
46. Ibid., p. 95.

54 A New Affluence

1. O'Connor, *Diaries*, 9 September 1973, p. 154.
2. Walshe, *Cissie's Abattoir*, pp. 86ff.
3. James Ryan, 'In Search of the Beautiful People', in Kathy Gilfillan (ed.), *Trinity Tales: Trinity College Dublin in the Seventies* (Dublin, 2011), pp. 145–57.
4. Madden, *Fear and Loathing*, pp. 18–27.
5. 'Rolling Back the Years, 1975–1979', *Irish Independent* Supplement, 29 October 2011, p. 20.
6. Ibid.
7. *Magill*, February 1978.
8. *Magill*, October 1978.
9. *Magill*, February 1979.
10. 'Rolling Back the Years, 1970–1974', *Irish Independent* Supplement, 22 October 2011.
11. Boran, *Invisible Prison*, p. 121.
12. Ibid., p. 158 and *Hibernia*, 23 April 1976.
13. NAI, DT 2006/133/380, Emigrant Centres in Britain: Financial Assistance, Bernard Devine to Cosgrave, 1 November 1976.
14. *Magill*, April 1979.
15. Mike Cronin, *Doesn't Time Fly? Aer Lingus: Its History* (Cork, 2011), pp. 52–125.
16. *Hibernia*, 5 March 1970 and 8 October 1971.
17. *Hibernia*, 7 June 1974.
18. *Hibernia*, 30 January 1976.
19. Walshe, *Cissie's Abattoir*, p. 44.
20. *Hibernia*, 2 May 1975.
21. NAI, DT 2003/16/142, Road Traffic: General and Legislation, Bobby Molloy to Lynch, 7 February 1972.
22. NAI, DT 2005/151/293, Medical Bureau of Road Safety, Report and Accounts, 1974.
23. *Magill*, September 1978.

24. NAI, DT 2008/148/416, National Road Safety Association Accounts, 23 May 1978.
25. NAI, DT 2008/148/602, Seat Belts: Compulsory Wearing Of, memorandum of April 1978.
26. NAI, DT 2004/21/98, Roads: Post War Development, memorandum of 31 October 1973.
27. NAI, DT 2007/116/86, Department of Local Government Report, 1976.
28. *Magill*, September 1978.
29. *Magill*, January 1979.
30. NAI, DT 2009/135/243, Road Development 1975–9, memorandum of 22 September 1978.
31. NAI, DT 2009/135/487, Dublin Suburban Rail Services: Electrification, memorandum of 17 April 1978 and Department of Taoiseach memorandum, 9 February 1979.
32. Ibid., 4, 21, 30 and 31 May 1979.
33. NAI, DT 2005/151/497, Organisation of Taxi Service, 6 March 1975.
34. Department of Justice memorandum, 3 October 1974.
35. *Magill*, September 1978.
36. Ibid.
37. NAI, DT 2001/6/104, Michael Begley to Jack Lynch, 15 November 1972.
38. Ferriter, *Lovers of Liberty?*, p. 76.
39. *Hibernia*, 14 July 1972.
40. *Hibernia*, 19 January, 11 May and 2 November 1973.
41. *Hibernia*, 24 September 1976.
42. *Magill*, September 1978.
43. Brown, *Ireland*, p. 248.
44. *Magill*, February 1979.
45. 'Rolling Back the Years, 1970–1974', *Irish Independent* Supplement, 22 October 2011.
46. *Hibernia*, 7 June 1974.
47. *Hibernia*, 17 January 1975.
48. *Hibernia*, 4 June 1976.
49. NA, DT 2005/151/427, Building Industry (Including Housing), 28 November 1974 and Department of Taoiseach memorandum, 2 January 1975.
50. NAI, DT 2006/133/281, Building Industry (Including Housing), 8 January 1976.
51. Ibid., Department of Taoiseach memorandum, 21 May 1976.
52. NAI, DT 2007, 116/240, Landlord and Tenant Law Bill 1977, Cooney to Cosgrave, 10 May 1977 and *Irish Times*, 27 April 1977.
53. NAI, DT 2005/151/285, 4 August 1971.
54. Lee, *Ireland, 1912–1985*, p. 486, Gerard Hogan, 'John Joseph Kenny', in McGuire and Quinn, *DIB*, vol. 5, pp. 131–3.
55. *Irish Times*, 6 February 1999.

55 Fatal Lifestyles and the Health System Challenge

1. *Magill*, June 1978.

2. *Magill*, September 1978.
3. *Magill*, July 1978.
4. *Hibernia*, 26 May 1972 and 18 June 1976.
5. NAI, DT 2003/16/325, Social Services: General, c. March 1973.
6. Ibid.
7. Madden, *Fear and Loathing*, pp. 58–97.
8. O'Faoláin, *Are You Somebody?* pp. 158–9.
9. NAI, DT 2008/148/384, Psychiatric Hospitals: Strike, 16 January 1978.
10. Ivor Browne, *Music and Madness* (Cork, 2008), pp. 133–46.
11. Ibid., pp. 147ff.
12. Elizabeth Malcolm, *Swift's Hospital: A History of St Patrick's Hospital, Dublin, 1746–1989* (Dublin, 1989), pp. 285–6.
13. Mary Raftery, 'Revealing the Horrific Past of Psychiatric Hospitals', *Irish Times*, 5 September 2011.
14. Cited in Annie Ryan, *Walls of Silence* (Kilkenny, 1999), p. 2.
15. James S. McCormick 'Medicine and Society', *Hermathena*, no. 122, Summer 1977, pp. 5–14.
16. NAI, DT 2004/21/106, Health Services: Reorganisation and Development, Mary O'Rourke to Cosgrave, 9 July 1973.
17. Maev Ann Wren, *Unhealthy State: Anatomy of a Sick Society* (Dublin, 2003), pp. 48–9.
18. NAI, DT 2004/21/106, memorandum by Childers: Health Services Reorganisation and Development, 1972–4.
19. NAI, DT 2004/21/243, Irish Medical Association, Dr Philip Cawley to Cosgrave, 20 October 1973.
20. NAI, DT 2004/21/106, Health Services: Reorganisation and Development, C. G. McGahon to Cosgrave, 22 August 1973.
21. Wren, *Unhealthy State*, p. 51.
22. NAI, DT 2006/133/56, Health Services: Memorandum for Government on Health Expenditure, 1 March 1976.
23. Ibid., Richie Ryan to Corish, 30 March 1976; and Ryan to Corish, 2 April 1976.
24. NAI, DT 2006/133/559, Health Services; Parliamentary Review, 10 June and 30 August 1976.
25. NAI, DT 2007/116/101, Health Services and *Irish Times*, 14 April 1977.
26. NAI, DT 2008/148/139, Irish Medical Association, and cabinet minute, 24 January 1978.
27. NAI, DT 2009/135/63, Health Services: Development and Organisation, memorandum for government, 29 June 1979.
28. Wren, *Unhealthy State*, p. 57.
29. NAI, DT 2008/148/69, Health Services, memoranda of 5 April and 24 October 1978.
30. NAI, DT 2008/148/129, National Health Council: Annual Reports for Year Ended 31 March 1978.
31. Coleman, *Irish Sweep*, pp. 197–224.

32. NAI, DT 2005/7/102, Sweepstakes under Public Hospital Acts, memorandum from Department of Justice, 17 May 1974.
33. Ibid., 17 October 1974.
34. NAI, DT 2002/8/163, speech by Erskine Childers, 11 September 1971.
35. NAI, DT 2003/16/224 and DT 2004/21/221, National Health Council: Reports for Years Ended 31 March 1972 and 31 March 1973.
36. NAI, DT 2006/133/108, National Health Council Report for Year Ended 31 March 1975.
37. Ibid., Report for Year Ended 31 March 1976.
38. Ibid.
39. NAI, DT 2007/116/631, National Economic and Social Council: Report on Some Major Issues in Health Policy, memorandum from Department of Finance, 3 May 1977.
40. NAI, DT 2008/148/129, National Health Council Report for Year Ended 31 March 1978.
41. *Hibernia*, 6 February 1970.
42. NAI, DT 2003/16/457, Tobacco Bill 1971: Private Member's Bill, 15 and 16 February 1972.
43. Walshe, *Cissie's Abattoir*, p. 86.
44. NAI, DT 2008/148/182, Cigarette Smoking, 13 April 1978.
45. NAI, DT 2007/116/229, Cigarette Smoking/Marketing, memorandum from Department of Health, 17 November 1977.
46. NAI, DT 2008/148/182, Cigarette Smoking; Cigarette Marketing, Don Carroll to Lynch, 27 February 1978; meeting between Lynch and chairmen of tobacco companies, 18 April 1978.
47. Ibid., Risteard Mulcahy to Lynch, 9 June 1978.
48. Ibid., M. J. Mac Cormac to Haughey, 24 February 1978; *Magill*, December 1978.
49. NAI, DT 2009/135/623, Tobacco Products: Regulation, 29 December, 18 April and 31 May 1978 and memorandum of 25 October 1978.
50. NAI, DT 208/148/182, Department of Taoiseach memorandum, 13 April 1978.
51. NAI, DT 2009/135/623, Department of Health memorandum, 30 August 1979, and Dermot Nally memorandum, 25 September 1979.
52. Ibid.

56 Protecting the Purity of the Republic

1. NAI, DT 2000/6/199, Health Services: Health Bill 1969, November 1969.
2. Higgins, *Causes for Concern*, p. 124.
3. NAI, DT 2000/6/219, memorandum for the government on European Conservation Year 1970, March–September 1969.
4. *Hibernia*, 5 March 1970.
5. NAI, DT 2000/6/219, Thomas Murray to Jack Lynch, 23 December 1969.
6. NAI, DT 2002/8/163, Nature Conservancy, Seán Flanagan to Lynch, 20 October 1971.

7. NAI, DT 2004/21/385, Third Programme for Economic Expansion: Freshwater Research, 16 April 1971.
8. NAI, DT 2004/21/103, Public Health Works; Water Supply, Report of Dublin City Manager, 12 March 1974.
9. *Hibernia*, 28 November 1976.
10. NAI, DT 2006/133/70, Nature Conservancy: Pollution, R. P. Finnegan to Cosgrave, 8 April and 11 May 1976.
11. NAI, DT 2009/135/595, National Environmental Council: Reports, April 1979; DT 2003/16/95, Reports of Minister for Lands on the Forest and Wildlife Service, 31 January 1971 and 31 March 1972.
12. NAI, DT 2008/148/472, The Environment, 21 September 1973, DT 2008/148/30, Town Planning: General File, 12 November 1973.
13. NAI, DT 2006/133/46, Department of Local Government Report, 1975.
14. Ibid., Dáil Debates, 31 January 1978.
15. *Hibernia*, 29 March 1974.
16. Ibid., 12 November 1973, and Dáil Debates, 31 January 1978 and DT 2007/148/472, The Environment; Dáil Debates, 5 July 1977 and Lynch to Barrett, 10 October 1977.
17. Ibid., Barrett to Lynch, 2 December 1977 and Department of Taoiseach memorandum, 16 December 1977.

Part VIII New Horizons: Education, Religion and the Status of Women

1. Liam Ryan, 'Social Factors in Irish Education', *Christus Rex*, vol. 24, no. 4, October 1970, pp. 273–87.
2. Margaret Mac Curtain (Sister Benvenuta), 'Education: A Church–State Problem in Twentieth Century Ireland', *The Furrow*, vol. 24, no. 1, January 1973, pp. 3–13.
3. *Education Times*, 26 April 1973.
4. *Education Times*, 17 May 1973.
5. Edmund Murphy, 'The New Primary School Curriculum', *Studies*, vol. 61, Spring 1972, pp. 199–218.
6. *Education Times*, 21 June 1973.
7. *Education Times*, 21 February 1974.
8. *Education Times*, 27 March 1975.
9. Michael Moroney, *National Teachers' Salaries and Pensions, 1831–2000* (Dublin, 2007), pp. 174–83.
10. Seán MacRéamoinn, *Towards a Church Re-attuned to Spirit: The Church in a New Ireland* (Dublin, 1996).
11. Peter Butterfield, 'The Crisis of Authority Within the Church', *The Furrow*, vol. 22, no. 8, August 1971, p. 466.
12. Mícheál Mac Gréil and Micheál Ó Glasáin, 'Church Attendance and Religious Practice of Dublin Adults', *Social Studies*, vol. 3, no. 2, April 1974, pp. 163–213.
13. Brendan Walsh, 'Trends in the Religious Composition of the Population in the Republic of Ireland, 1946–1971', *Economic and Social Review*, vol. 6, 1974–5, pp. 543–55.

14. Enda McDonagh, 'Why Do They Leave?' *The Furrow*, vol. 26, no. 11, November 1975, pp. 652–68.
15. Kevin O'Neill, 'The National Conference of Priests of Ireland', *The Furrow*, vol. 28, no. 1, January 1977, pp. 39–43.
16. David Gaffney, 'The Priest in the Year 2000', *Doctrine and Life*, vol. 21, no. 6, June 1971, pp. 308–16.
17. Tony Castle, 'The Priest in Youth Work', *The Furrow*, vol. 22, no. 2, February 1971, pp. 87–93; Dermot Clifford, 'The Image of the Bishop', *The Furrow*, vol. 22, no. 8, August 1971, pp. 46–66.
18. Douglas Hyde, 'Warts on the Face of Ireland', *Doctrine and Life*, vol. 21, no. 8, August 1971, pp. 429–38.
19. O'Mahony, 'Poverty in Ireland', p. 50.
20. Mac Curtain, 'Women: Irish Style'.
21. Walter Forde, 'Religious and Social Change in Contemporary Ireland', *Christus Rex*, vol. 23, no. 1, January 1969, pp. 21–8.
22. John A. Murphy, 'Priests and People in Modern Irish History', *Christus Rex*, vol. 23, no. 4, October 1969, pp. 221–35.
23. Brian Gogan, 'Continuing Education in a Changing World', *The Furrow*, vol. 26, no. 5, May 1975, pp. 270–83.
24. Mary Maher, 'Women's Liberation', *Doctrine and Life*, vol. 21, no. 8, September 1971, pp. 457–65.
25. Margaret, Mac Curtain, *Ariadne's Thread: Writing Women into Irish History* (Dublin, 2008), pp. 18ff.
26. Michael O'Leary, 'Gentle Revolution', *Administration*, vol. 23, no. 1, Spring 1975, pp. 4–7.
27. Foster, *Luck and the Irish*, p. 63.

57 Democratising Education?

1. Fanning, *Quest for Modern Ireland*, ch. 4.
2. Paul Andrews, 'Ireland and the World Educational Crisis', *Studies*, vol. 9, Winter 1970, pp. 381–4.
3. Brown, *Ireland*, p. 242; John Coolahan, *Irish Education: Its History and Structure* (Dublin, 1981), p. 135.
4. Garvin, *Preventing the Future*, p. 162.
5. Coolahan, *Irish Education*, pp. 137–50.
6. NAI, DT 2001/6/79, Education Developments: 1968 to July 1970, Department of Education memorandum, 13 January 1970.
7. *Hibernia*, 6 February 1970.
8. Brown, *Ireland*, p. 242.
9. Pádraig Faulkner, *As I Saw It* (Dublin, 2005), pp. 61–5.
10. Cited in D. G. Mulcahy and Denis O'Sullivan (eds), *Irish Educational Policy: Process and Substance* (Dublin, 1989), p. 29.
11. NAI, DT 2007/116/93, Education: Developments: 1973–1976.
12. Mulcahy and O'Sullivan, *Irish Educational Policy*, p. 37.

13. Ibid., p. 42.
14. *Hibernia*, 14 April 1972 and NAI, DT 2005/151/8, Primary Education: Proposals for Improvement, education memorandum, 13 February 1975.
15. NAI, DT 2006/133/515, Rutland Street: Educational Project: memorandum of 11 May 1976.
16. NAI, DT 2009/135/97, Transport for School Children, Ann Sheehan to Lynch, March 1978.
17. Ibid., Report of School Transport Committee, March 1978.
18. Ibid., Patrick Dervan to Lynch, 13 October 1978 and Jim Tunney to Patrick Dervan, 14 December 1978.
19. NAI, DT 2007/116/93, M. A. Jaycock to Cosgrave, 19 July 1976.
20. NAI, DT 2007/116/93, Education: Developments, Report of Minister, 12 May 1976, *Irish Times*, 20 and 26 June and 21 July 1976.
21. *Magill*, September 1978.
22. Desmond, *Finally and in Conclusion*, p. 178.
23. NAI, DT 2007/116/319, Primary Schools: Provision of Sites. Dermot Ryan to Cosgrave, 23 April 1974, account of meeting with Archbishop Ryan, 17 June 1975; Richie Ryan to Cosgrave, 4 September 1975 and 21 April 1976 and Cosgrave to Richie Ryan, May 1976.
24. Séamas O'Súilleabháin, 'Second Level Education: Dimensions and Directions', *Maynooth Review*, vol. 1, no. 1, June 1975, pp. 3–17.
25. NAI, DT 2005/151/265, Intermediate Certificate: The ICE Report, September 1974.
26. Coolahan, *Irish Education*, p. 137.
27. Cunningham, *Unlikely Radicals*, p. 193.
28. Faulkner, *As I Saw It*, pp. 73–6.
29. NAI, DT 2004/21/95, Education: Developments: August 1970, *Irish Times*, 13 November 1970 and Dáil Debates, 18 November 1970.
30. Ibid., speech of Lynch in Cork, 22 May 1971.
31. Ibid., Parent–Teacher Association in Tallaght to Lynch, 8 December 1971.
32. Ibid., Pádraig Faulkner to Lynch, 10 December 1971.
33. Ibid., Cardinal Conway to Lynch, 30 January 1972.
34. Ibid., Sr Mary Columba to Lynch, 8 February 1973 and Brother T. O hAnnaín to Lynch, 26 February 1973.
35. Ibid., *Sunday Independent*, 29 April 1973.
36. Ibid., Conway to Cosgrave, 19 April 1973.
37. *Hibernia*, 21 September 1973.
38. NAI, DT 2004/21/95 and DT 2005/7/82, account of meeting, 1 June 1973.
39. Faulkner, *As I Saw It*, p. 84.
40. NAI, DT 2005/7/82, Education: Developments, August 1970 ff., memorandum of 13 December 1973 and Brother E. Creed to Cosgrave, 25 February 1974.
41. *Hibernia*, 23 June 1972 and 23 April 1976.
42. *Irish Times*, 3 May 1982.

43. NAI, DT 2001/6/405, Proposals for Legislation for the Establishment on a Statutory Basis of the HEA, 4 March 1970.
44. Ibid., Richard O'Toole to Jack Lynch, 15 November 1970.
45. Ed Walsh, *Upstart: Friends, Foes and Founding a University* (Cork, 2011), pp. 17–57.
46. DDA, McQuaid Papers, AB8/B/xxxx, Diocesan Press Office, 1966–7, Trinity Ban, 1967.
47. NAI, DT 2005/7/323, Merger of UCD and TCD, HEA memorandum, April 1970.
48. Ibid., John McKenna and Michael O'Farrell to Lynch, 27 April 1970.
49. Ibid., Cosgrave to Dick Burke, 22 January 1974.
50. NAI, DT 2005/151/296, Higher Education: General, Leland Lyons to Cosgrave, 14 March 1975.
51. Donal McCartney, *UCD: A National Idea: The History of University College Dublin* (Dublin, 1999), p. 404.
52. NAI, DT 2005/151/589, Schools, Colleges and Universities: Control of Fees, 1975/6.
53. Coolahan, *Irish Education*, p. 148.
54. NAI, DT 2008/148/224, Higher Education: General, Department of Education memorandum, November 1978.
55. NAI, DT 2008/148/523, NIHE, Dublin, Danny O'Hare to Lynch, 3 May 1978.
56. *Hibernia*, 25 August 1972.
57. William Watts, *William Watts: Provost Trinity College Dublin: A Memoir* (Dublin, 2008), p. 89.
58. O'Driscoll, *Stepping Stones*, pp. 16–30.
59. James Kelly (ed.), *St Patrick's College, Drumcondra: A History* (Dublin, 2006), pp. 158–84, 235 and McGahern, *Memoir*, p. 211.
60. *Hibernia*, 5 March 1971.
61. Callanan, *Literary and Historical Society*, pp. 161–5.
62. Ryan, 'In Search of the Beautiful People'.
63. Ibid.
64. Patricia Quinn, 'Working through the College', in Gilfillan, *Trinity Tales*, pp. 274–9.
65. Roy Foster 'Turbulent Times in Front Square', *Irish Times*, 19 November 2011.
66. *Hibernia*, 17 July 1976.
67. John A. Murphy, *The College: A History of Queen's/University College Cork, 1845–1995* (Cork, 1995), pp. 311–31.
68. *Hibernia*, 20 March 1970, 25 September 1970 and 16 July 1976; Patrick J. Corish, *Maynooth College, 1795–1995* (Dublin, 1994), p. 382.

58 Practising Lapsed Catholics

1. DDA, McQuaid Papers, AB8/B/xxxxic, Dowling to McQuaid, Diocesan Press Office, 1971, 23 January 1971.
2. Ibid., AB8/B/xix, Catholic Social Welfare Bureau (CSWB) Box 6, Peter Byrne to McQuaid, 9 December 1971.

3. Ibid., AB8/B/xxxx, Communications: Television, 1970–71, McQuaid to Ms Callanan, 18 March 1971.
4. Ibid., CSWB Box 7, Marriage Counselling Service, 1966–71, Barrett to McQuaid, 16 March 1971.
5. Ibid., Communications: 1970–71, 'Group of Priests' to McQuaid, 22 January 1970.
6. Louise Fuller, *Irish Catholicism Since 1950: The Undoing of a Culture* (Dublin, 2002), p. 139.
7. *Hibernia*, 21 January 1972.
8. Bridget Hourican, 'Dermot Joseph Ryan', in McGuire and Quinn, *DIB*, vol. 8, pp. 680–83.
9. Ibid.
10. *Irish Times*, 12 December 2010.
11. *Hibernia*, 1 December 1972.
12. *Hibernia*, 2 April 1971.
13. Walshe, *Cissie's Abattoir*, p. 81.
14. Fuller, *Irish Catholicism*, p. 145.
15. NAI, DT 2005/151/307, Constitution 1937: Suggested Amendments, Maureen O'Riordan to Lynch, 12 June 1972 and Lynch to John P. Walters, 29 June 1972.
16. NAI, DT 2008/148/688, Religious Tolerance in Ireland, E. O'Connor to Lynch, 16 January 1978.
17. Desmond, *Finally and in Conclusion*, p. 189.
18. *Magill*, December 1978.
19. UCDA, FitzGerald Papers, P215/481, Murphy, 'Identity in the Republic of Ireland Now'.
20. UCDA, de Courcy Ireland Papers, P29G/76, Hubert Butler to de Courcy Ireland, 12 October 1974; *Hibernia*, 25 July 1975.
21. Brown, *Ireland*, p. 292.
22. NAI, DT 2005/151/307, Constitution 1937, *The Word*, November 1975.
23. UCDA, FitzGerald Papers, P215/4, Maurice Hayes to FitzGerald, 27 July 1972.
24. *Hibernia*, 4 January 1972.
25. UCDA, FitzGerald Papers, P215/534, Enda McDonagh to FitzGerald, 25 April 1976.
26. Brian Girvin, 'Church, State and Society in Ireland Since 1960', *Eire-Ireland*, vol. 43, nos 1&2, Spring/Summer 2008, pp. 74–99.
27. Mícheál Mac Gréil, *Prejudice and Tolerance in Ireland* (Dublin, 1977), pp. 411–21.
28. *Magill*, April 1979 and Brown, *Ireland*, p. 289.
29. UCDA, FitzGerald Papers, P215/481, Murphy, 'Identity in the Republic of Ireland Now'.
30. Murray, *Friel*, pp. 25–35.
31. *Irish Times*, 26 November 1973.
32. NAI, DT 2004/21/605, National Day of Reconciliation, Richard Stokes memorandum, 7 April 1973 and DT 2005/7/422, President of Ireland, Speeches, Clearance, 16 January 1974.

33. NAI, DT 2005/151/475, Oliver Plunkett: Canonisation, Department of Taoiseach note of 6 March 1975 and Department of Foreign Affairs to D. Ó Súilleabháin, Department of Taoiseach, 20 March 1975.
34. Ibid., 4 March and 15 September 1975.
35. Ibid., 17, 25 and 26 September 1975.
36. NAI, DT 2008/148/635, Cardinal Cullen, Lynch to Kathleen Cullen Buckley, 26 September 1978.
37. NAI, DT 2004/21/456, Visitors to Ireland 1971–3, 17 November 1972.
38. Girvin, 'Church, State and Society' and Brown, *Ireland*, p. 286.
39. Jeremiah Newman, *Balance in the Church* (Dublin, 1980), pp. 24–6.
40. Edmund Hogan, *The Irish Missionary Movement: A Historical Survey, 1830–1980* (Dublin, 1990), p. 187.
41. Dermot Ryan, *Marriage and Pastoral Care: An Invitation to Priestly Concern with Appropriate Directive* (Dublin, 1975), pp. 5–16.
42. *Dermot Ryan: 1972–77: The First Five Years* (Dublin, 1977).
43. Ibid.
44. *Hibernia*, 28 April 1972 and Brown, *Ireland*, p. 289.
45. Corish, *Maynooth College*, p. 382.
46. Fuller, *Irish Catholicism*, p. 148.
47. *Hibernia*, December 1977; Mary Kenny, *Goodbye to Catholic Ireland* (Dublin, 2000), p. 267.
48. *Magill*, January 1978.
49. *Hibernia*, 24 May 1974.
50. *Hibernia*, 25 September 1970.
51. Fuller, *Irish Catholicism*, p. 142.
52. *Magill*, September 1979.
53. Tom Garvin, 'The Strange Death of Clerical Politics at UCD', *Irish University Review*, vol. 28, no. 2, Autumn/Winter 1998, pp. 308–15.
54. Kiberd, *Inventing Ireland*, p. 571.
55. Kenny, *Goodbye to Catholic Ireland*, p. 267.
56. Desmond, *Finally and in Conclusion*, p. 45.
57. NAI, DT 2007/116/224, William Conway: Death, April 1977, *Irish Press*, 18 April 1977 and Department of Taoiseach note of 19 April 1977.
58. Ibid., 27 April 1977.
59. NAI, DT 2008/148/424, Tomás Ó Fiaich – Appointment as Archbishop of Armagh, Gerard Woods to secretary of Department of Foreign Affairs, 12 May 1977.
60. NAI, DT 2009/135/572, Dr Tomás Ó Fiaich: Appointment as Cardinal, 26 May 1979; *Magill*, July 1979.
61. Callanan, *Literary and Historical Society*, p. 199.
62. Garvin, *Preventing the Future*, pp. 206–13.
63. NAI, DT 2009/135/505, Pope John Paul II: Visit to Ireland, Lynch to J. Brennan TD, 19 February 1979 and Pádraig Faulkner to Lynch, 7 April 1979.

64. Ibid., Tim Corcoran to Bertie O'Dowd, 10 May 1979; Account of Meeting between Department of Foreign Affairs and Mgr Marron, Department of Taoiseach memorandum, 23 July 1979 and 10 August 1979.
65. Ibid., Department of Taoiseach memorandum, 23 July 1979; letter of Newington in British Foreign Office, 23 July 1979 and note of Ó hUiginn, 24 July 1979 and 10 August 1979.
66. NAI, DT 2009/135/618, Visit of Pope John Paul II: Miscellaneous Correspondence, 23 July 1979, Dermot Kinlen to Ó Fiaich, 23 July 1979.
67. Ibid., Peggy Perry to Lynch, 3 September 1979 and Joseph Mifsud to Lynch, 13 September 1979.
68. Ibid., A. E. Sperrin to Lynch, 4 October 1979.
69. *Magill*, October 1979.
70. Ibid.
71. McCafferty, *Nell*, pp. 320ff.
72. *Magill*, October 1979 and Colum Kenny, *Moments that Changed Us* (Dublin, 2005), p. 262.
73. Whitaker, *Bright Brilliant Days*, p. 43.
74. Coogan, *A Memoir*, p. 225.
75. Kenny, *Moments*, p. 262.
76. *Magill*, October 1979.

59 Breaking the Shackles

1. UCDA, FitzGerald Papers, P215/481, Murphy, 'Identity in the Republic of Ireland Now'.
2. Christopher Murray, *Alive in Time: The Enduring Drama of Tom Murphy* (Dublin, 2010), p. 240.
3. Walshe, *Cissie's Abattoir*, p. 5.
4. *Hibernia*, 9 January 1970.
5. Moore, *One Voice*, p. 94.
6. Linda Connolly, *The Irish Women's Movement: From Revolution to Devolution* (Dublin, 2003), p. 129.
7. McCafferty, *Nell*, pp. 147–50.
8. *Hibernia*, 13 April 1973.
9. McCafferty, *Nell*, p. 126.
10. Margaret Mac Curtain and Donnchadh Ó Corráin (eds), *Women in Irish Society: The Historical Dimension* (Dublin, 1978), Preface.
11. Thomas O'Loughlin, Interview with Margaret Mac Curtain, *History Ireland*, vol. 2, no. 1, Spring 1994, pp. 52–4.
12. Mac Curtain, *Ariadne's Thread*, pp. 41–59.
13. NAI, DT 2001/6/40, Status of Women: International Conventions: Equal Pay for Equal Work, 3 February 1970.
14. McCafferty, *Nell*, pp. 292ff.
15. NAI, DT 2001/6/40, Ruairí Roberts to Lynch, 15 January 1970.

16. Anna Bryson, *No Cowardly Soul: Thekla Beere – A Biography* (Dublin, 2009), pp. 140–44.
17. *Irish Times*, 27 June 2011 and Stopper, *Monday at Gaj's*, pp. 21–33.
18. McCafferty, *Nell*, p. 201.
19. NAI, DT 2002/8/60, Status of Women: Mary Kenny to Jack Lynch, 8 March 1971.
20. NAI, DT 2002/8/60, Status of Women: International Conventions and Equal Pay for Equal Work, The Civil Wrongs of Irish Women published by the IWLM.
21. Ibid.
22. McCafferty, *Nell*, p. 227.
23. Levine, 'The Women's Movement in the Republic', pp. 180–81.
24. Levine, *Sisters*, pp. 138–45.
25. Cited ibid., p. 235.
26. Thomson, *Irish Women and Street Politics*, p. 185.
27. McCafferty, *Nell*, p. 228.
28. Ibid., p. 201 and *Irish Times*, 5 December 1972.
29. Levine, 'The Women's Movement in the Republic', p. 282.
30. *Magill*, April 1979.
31. Fennell, *Political Woman*, pp. 64ff.
32. Levine, 'The Women's Movement in the Republic', p. 283.
33. NAI, DT 2004/21/241, Seanad Debates, 25 July 1973.
34. NAI, DT 2004/21/282, International Alliance of Women, report of the Irish Housewives Association, 7–14 November 1973.
35. Bryson, *No Cowardly Soul*, pp. 159–63.
36. Mac Curtain and Ó Corráin, *Women in Irish Society*, pp. 58–70.
37. NAI, DT 2004/21/241, Married Women: Employment in Civil Service, n.d., c. July 1973.
38. NAI, DT 2009/135/111, Employment of Married Women in the Civil Service, Kilkenny UDC Resolution, 16 September 1975, Richie Ryan to Cosgrave, 22 September 1975 and Dáil Debates, 3 November 1981.
39. Fennell, *Political Woman*, pp. 65–71.
40. NAI, DT 2005/151/313, Family Maintenance: Legislation, and Nuala Fennell quoted in *Irish Press*, 7 September 1972.
41. Ibid., 8 February 1973.
42. UCDA, Kelly Papers, P147/15, Kelly to Honorary Secretary of AIM, 20 January 1973.
43. NAI, DT 2005/151/313, memorandum for government, 25 February 1975 and note of 5 March 1975.
44. NAI, DT 2004/21/32, replies by Lynch to Women's Editor of the *Irish Times*, February 1973.
45. Mary Robinson, 'Women and the New Irish State', in Mac Curtain and Ó Corráin, *Women in Irish Society*, pp. 58–70.
46. Ferriter, *Occasions of Sin*, p. 442.
47. UCDA, Fianna Fáil Papers, P176, Br Robert Ruane to Séamus Brennan, 7 January 1979.

48. Sweeney, *Down, Down*, pp. 192–3.
49. Finola Kennedy, *Cottage to Creche: Family Change in Ireland* (Dublin, 2001), p. 114.
50. Brigid Laffan and Jane O'Mahony, *Ireland and the European Union* (New York, 2008), p. 39.
51. UCDA, ICEM Papers, P204/58, c. end of 1977.
52. NAI, DT 2005/7/388, Equal Pay Act 1974, 15 February 1974.
53. Ibid., Dáil Debates, 26 February 1974.
54. NAI, DT 2008/148/331, Equal Pay: Representations by Organisations and Individuals, H. L. Temple to O'Leary, 27 September 1974, O'Leary to Cosgrave, 2 July 1975, J. Marnane to O'Leary, 27 November 1975.
55. Ibid., John Quinn to O'Leary, 8 December 1975.
56. Ibid., Hilda Tweedy to Cosgrave, 6 January 1975 and Cosgrave to Evelyn Owens, 14 January 1976.
57. NAI, DT 2008/148/331, copy of Tweedy letter to European Commission, 6 January 1976.
58. Ibid., Roisín Conroy to Cosgrave, 9 February 1976 and Mina Bean Uí Chribín to Cosgrave, 5 March 1976.
59. NAI, DT 2006/133/396, 16 February 1976, note of meetings between Hillery and O'Leary.
60. UCDA, FitzGerald Papers, P125/594, FitzGerald to B. Neylon, 26 February 1976.
61. Ibid., Roisín Conroy to FitzGerald, 9 February 1976, and Eileen M. to FitzGerald, 27 January 1976 and Mary Gleeson to FitzGerald, 22 January 1976.
62. NAI, DT 2008/148/410, Social Security: Equality of Treatment for Men and Women, 10 January 1977 and Kirwan to Nally, 22 April 1977.
63. Ibid., memorandum of Department of Finance, December 1977.
64. Ibid., 23 October 1978, Department of Finance memorandum, 6 November 1978, Social Welfare memorandum, 9 November 1978 and *Irish Times*, 27 November 1978.
65. Maume, 'George Colley', p. 668.
66. McCafferty, *Nell*, p. 298.
67. Ibid., p. 300.
68. *Magill*, April 1979.
69. *Hot Press*, 23 June 1978.
70. *Magill*, April 1979.
71. *Hibernia*, 14 January 1976.
72. Sweeney, *Down, Down*, pp. 83–4.
73. Richard Finnegan and James Wiles, *Women and Public Policy in Ireland: A Documentary History, 1922–1997* (Dublin, 2005), p. 210.
74. Ferriter, *Occasions of Sin*, pp. 420–21.
75. *Hibernia*, 27 June 1975.
76. Ferriter, *Occasions of Sin*, pp. 420ff.
77. NAI, DT 2007/116/268, Contraceptives: Resolutions and Miscellaneous Correspondence, M. J. O'Brien to Lynch, 22 June 1977.
78. NAI, DT 2007/116/126, F. J. O'Meara to Lynch, 5 June 1977.

79. NAI, DT 2007/116/273, 8 August 1977.
80. NAI, DT 2008/148/219, Contraceptives: Resolutions and Miscellaneous Correspondence, 3 March 1978.
81. NAI, DT 2008/148/219, Major Vivion de Valera to Lynch, 19 April 1978.
82. Ibid., Mary Kennedy to Mrs Lynch, 29 January 1979; Department of Taoiseach note, 28 February 1979.
83. Ibid., John Cunningham to Lynch, 2 May 1979.
84. NAI, DT 2009/135/194, Contraceptives: Resolutions, Miscellaneous Correspondence, Bridie Kenny to Lynch, 31 December 1978.
85. Ibid., K. Langan to Lynch, 11 January 1979.
86. Foster, *Luck and the Irish*, p. 49.
87. Ibid., Eamon Barnes to Hederman, 2 February 1979.
88. NAI, DT 2008/148/217, Health (Family Planning) (Amendment) Bill, 7 November and 12 December 1978.
89. John Cunningham, 'Spreading VD all over Connacht: Reproductive Rights and Wrongs in 1970s Galway', *History Ireland*, March/April 2011, pp. 44–7.
90. NAI, Cosgrave Papers, 1194, 25–38, Corish to John L. Sullivan, 10 February 1977.
91. Cunningham, 'Spreading VD', p. 46.
92. Connolly and O'Toole, *Documenting Irish Feminisms*, p. 133.
93. Ibid., p 35.
94. McCafferty, *Nell*, pp. 300–304.
95. Connolly and O'Toole, *Documenting Irish Feminisms*, p. 132.
96. *Irish Times*, 21, 23 and 25 April 2012.

LIST OF ILLUSTRATIONS

1. Former President of Ireland Cearbhall Ó Dálaigh. Photo taken by Colman Doyle. © National Photographic Archive of Ireland.
2. Influential civil servant Dermot Nally. © Photo by Victor Patterson.
3. Former Attorney General John Kelly. © Photo by Derek Speirs.
4. The funeral of Eamon de Valera. © RTÉ Stills Library
5. Actor Frank Kelly. © RTÉ Stills Library
6. Historian and writer Conor Cruise O'Brien. © RTÉ Stills Library
7. Historian, broadcaster and Labour party TD David Thornely. © RTÉ Stills Library
8. Future Irish President, Mary Robinson. © Photo by Derek Speirs.
9. Harold Wilson with Brendan Corish. © Irish Photographic Archive.
10. British Embassy alight, February 1972. © Irish Photographic Archive
11. The body of Lord Mountbatten is removed from Sligo General Hospital. © Irish Independent Newspapers Ltd.
12. Cover of *Hot Press* Magazine. © Hot Press Limited.
13. Christy Moore. © Photo by Derek Speirs.
14. Caricature of Conor Cruise O'Brien in *Hibernia*. © Photo by Derek Speirs.
15. Protest at the site of the Wood Quay archaeological dig. © Photo by Derek Speirs.
16. Brian Mullins in the 1978 All-Ireland Final. © Independent Newspapers Ltd.
17. Edmund Garvey. © Independent Newspapers Ltd.
18. Edmund Garvey in *Hibernia* © Photo by Derek Speirs.
19. Vietnamese refugees to Ireland. © Photo by Derek Speirs.
20. Irish Anti-Apartheid protestors. © Photo by Derek Speirs.
21. Margaret Thatcher's first visit to the Republic of Ireland as UK Prime Minister. © Photo by Derek Speirs.
22. Protest on 20 March 1979 outside the GPO. © Photo by Derek Speirs.
23. Children playing on a derelict site in Dublin. © Photo by Derek Speirs.

24. The boat to Inisbofin, on the West Coast. ©Photo by Derek Speirs
25. 'Discomania' cover of *Magill*. © Photo by Derek Speirs.
26. Ticket for 'The Anti-Nuclear Express'. © Photo by Derek Speirs.
27. John Paul II greets crowds atop his 'Pope Mobile'. © Photo by Derek Speirs.
28. Protestor outside the Houses of Parliament, Dublin. ©Photo by Derek Speirs
29. Women against violence against Women demonstration. ©Photo by Derek Speirs
30. The visit of the 'Up with the People' group to St Patrick's College, Maynooth. © Independent Newspapers Ltd.
31. Margaret MacCurtain. © Photo by Derek Speirs.
32. *Hibernia* magazine front, 16 January 1976. © Photo by Derek Speirs.

INDEX

A
ABBA 273
Abbey Theatre, Dublin 117, 225, 226, 257, 258, 260–61, 265, 282
Abbey Theatre School 255
abortion 193, 298, 384, 423, 648, 649, 674, 678, 679
Action Information Motivation (AIM) 369–70, 664, 666–67
Acton, Charles 224, 274, 275
ACTRA (central body for residents' associations) 486
Adelphi cinema, Dublin 302
Administration (journal) 18
adoption 191, 192, 381–82
Adoption Acts
  1952 381
  1964 381
  1976 381–82
Aer Lingus 78, 133, 156, 417–18, 428, 432, 437, 438–39, 454, 513, 587
Afran Zodiac (tanker) 526
Africa 429–30
  see also individual countries
Africa Concern 430
Aga Khan Trophy grand prix 324
Agency for Personal Service Overseas (APSO) 431
Agricultural Credit Corporation 551–52
Ahern, Taoiseach Bertie
  attitude to the intellectual in politics 66
  'Drumcondra Mafia' 28
  a locally focused politician 28
  on Lynch 82
  successful prime minister 66
Ahern, Kit 91, 253
aid commitment targets 430–31
Aiken, Frank 87, 433
AIM *see* Action Information Motivation
Aintree Grand National 324
air piracy 440
air pollution 612
Airey, Josey 668
Albee, Edward 259
alcohol consumption 544–45, 577–83, 597
Alibrandi, Archbishop Gaetano, Apostolic Nuncio 206, 208, 212
All Blacks 322
All Party Committee on Irish Relations 179
All-Ireland Football Championship 318
All-Ireland Hurling Championship 318
Allende, Salvador 651
Alliance Party 173–74, 175, 179, 182, 186, 193
Allied Irish Bank (AIB) 45–46, 484, 587, 588
Almaktoum, His Highness Sheikh Mohammed Rashid 491
Altman's department store, New York: Irish exhibition 438
Amateur Drama Council of Ireland 216
American Committee for Irish Studies, Missouri 25, 134, 657
American Congress of Irish Freedom 155

American-Irish National Immigration Committee 555
Amin, Idi 432
Amnesty International 341, 360, 434, 447
  Mission to the Republic report (1977) 340
Anderson, Mary 667
Andrews, David 66, 71–72, 97, 114, 290
Andrews, Niall 43
Andrews, Todd 290
Anglo-American Press Association 400
Anglo-Irish Free Trade Agreement 390
Anglo-Irish Treaty (1921) 32, 193, 231, 232, 233, 244, 249, 671, 676
Anne, HRH The Princess Royal 310
Anti-Apartheid Year 448
Anti-Discrimination Pay Act (1974) 623, 664
anti-intellectualism 14, 25, 66, 96, 105
apartheid 429, 445, 447
Aquarius Securities Ltd 526
Arab Information Centre, Dublin 433
Arab Irish Society 433
Aran Islands, off the coast of Galway 561
Áras an Uachtaráin 440
Arbutus Lodge, Cork 575
Ardmore Studios 303–5
Ardoyne 136
Arms Trial (1970) 10, 33, 66, 84, 103, 114, 122, 126, 141–51, 219, 326
Armstrong's Barn, Annamoe, County Wicklow 576
Arnold, Bruce 106, 228, 280–81, 288
Arnotts store 484
Arranmore island, Donegal 564
Arsenal FC 321
art 279–81
Artane Industrial School 379
Arthur, Davey 273
Arts Bill/Act 224, 264
Arts Council 224–25, 259, 260, 263–66, 274, 284, 288, 303, 383
arts councils 215–16
arts funding 225
Ascendancy 85, 138
Asgard (yacht) 235–36
Ashford Castle, Cong, County Mayo 576
Asmal, Kader 353, 354, 382, 391, 445–48
Associated Television 233
Association of Business and Professional Women 659
Association of Irish Priests 205, 620
Association of Legal Justice 362
Association of Secondary Teachers of Ireland 516
Association of Workers for Children in Care (AWCC) 375, 376, 383
Astral Weeks (album) 270
athletics 322
Atlantis (literary and political magazine) 1, 3
Attorney General's office 54, 346
Australia 440–41

B

B-Specials 202
Baader-Meinhof movement 211
Baggot Inn, Dublin 273
Bailey pub, Dublin 578
balance of payments deficit 435, 492, 495
Balcombe Street siege 160
Baldonnel military airport 175–76
Ballagh, Robert 279
Ballsbridge, Dublin 312
Ballybunion Bachelor Festival 269
Ballyfermot 348, 352, 572, 672
  Community Association 569
  Health Clinic 293
Ballygoran Stud, County Kildare 472
'Ballymagash style politics' 23, 32
Ballymun area, Dublin 570
Bangladesh 430
Bank of Ireland (BoI) 251, 587
banking 9, 587–88
Banshee journal 678
Bantry Bay 526, 527
Banville, John 226, 287, 309
  Birchwood 226, 283
Barbarella's pub, Fitzwilliam Street, Dublin 581
Barnes, Eamon 342, 677
Barrett, Sylvester 592, 615–16
Barrington, Kathleen 265
Barrington, Tom 18, 21, 25, 55
Barron Report 200
Barry, Gerald 267, 639
Barry, Harry 295
Barry, Peter 59–60, 78, 377, 528, 530, 562
Barry, Ron 324
Barry, Tom 244
Bartley Dunnes pub, Dublin 578
'battered babies' 377
BBC 41, 43, 138, 158, 159, 167, 190, 245, 296, 297, 450, 548, 583, 654
  BBC Northern Ireland 136
  BBC Radio 2 297
  BBC1 450
Beere, Thekla 660, 665
Beethoven competition (Vienna, 1973) 267
Begley, Michael 491
Behan, Brendan 240
  Borstal Boy 582

Behan, John 241
Belfast 184, 662
  Cosgrave visits 194
  Donlon visits 178, 183, 185
  and the IRA 174–75
  priests in 180–81
  response to Stagg's death 211
Belfast Telegraph 133, 193, 212
Belfield campus, south Dublin 636
Benedictines 107
Benelli, Mgr 238, 651–52
Benson, Ciarán 288
Berkley Court Hotel, Dublin 491
Bernardos restaurant, Dublin 575
Berrigan, Daniel 651
Berry, Peter 142, 146–48, 363
Beuys, Joseph: 'A Secret Block for a Secret Person in Ireland' exhibition 280
Bew, Paul 146
Biafran humanitarian crisis (1967–70) 391, 430
Biafran war 648
Big D pirate radio station 299
Binchy, Maeve 38, 310
Bird, Charlie 277–78
Birmingham pub bombs (1974) 161
births
  birth rate 567
  illegitimate 567
Blackrock area, south County Dublin 472
Blaney, Neil 10, 81, 122, 131, 138, 141–45, 147, 148, 150, 220, 231, 334
Blankety Blank (game show) 297
Blasket Islands, off the coast of Kerry 561
BLE 316
Bloody Sunday (Derry, 30 January 1972) 2, 121, 122, 127–30, 134, 136, 206, 286
Blythe, Ernest 79
Bodenstown 166
Bodley, Seóirse 275
Bogside 136
Boland, Eavan 226, 253, 281, 284, 658
Boland, Gerald 143
Boland, John 44, 284
Boland, Kevin 41, 143, 144, 148, 178, 202
'Boland's gerrymander' 41
Bolster, Sr Angela 650
Bolton Street, Dublin: College of Technology 637
Bond, Edward 259
Boney M 273
Boomtown Rats 229, 271, 273, 545
Boorman, John 305–6
Booterstown Marsh, Dublin 452
Boran, Pat 274, 512, 586
Bord Fáilte (Irish Tourist Board) 215, 259, 447–48, 452, 453, 454, 491
Bord Gáis (Irish Gas Board) 527
Bord na bPáirc 318
Bord na Mona (Irish Peat Board) 480
Bothy Band 268, 269
Bowman, John 311
Boydell, Brian 224, 275
Boyle, Hilary 93
Bracken (soap opera) 228
Brady, Alo 509
Brady, Conor 326, 329
Brady, Fr John
  'The Economics of Survival' 459–60
  'Ireland in Transition' 540
Brady, Liam 321
Brady, Paul 270, 272
Brando, Marlo 576
Brandt, Willy 139, 159–60, 400
Bray, Philip 359
Bray Travel 586
breathalyser 589
Breathnach, Brendán 268
Breathnach, Osgur 345
Brendan Smith Theatre Academy 255
Brennan, Dr Edward 428
Brennan, Joseph 515
Brennan, Pat 93, 357, 664
Brennan, Peter 426
Brennan, Séamus 10, 34–35, 37, 82, 85, 90, 107, 144, 253, 667, 672
Bridewell, Dublin 353
Briscoe, Ben 102–3, 292
British Airways 587
British army
  ceasefire negotiations 125
  FitzGerald criticises 167
  Fox criticises 202
  joining 248
  O'Brien disputes British army brutality 165
British Commonwealth 388, 389, 432
British Embassy, Dublin 401
  burning of 122, 128–29, 135
British Home Stores 484
British intelligence 113
British Irish Association (BIA) 132, 133, 134, 163
British National Archive 306
British Nuclear Fuels Limited (BNFL) 526, 531
'Brittany reunion' 404
broadcasting 289–301
  advertising 294–95, 296, 298
  growing news demands 295
  multichannel 296
  new RTÉ services 289–90
  pirate radio stations 298, 299
  RTÉ 2 launched (1978) 296
  RTÉ television coverage 289

Seven Days issue 291–93
television survey (1978) 295–96
women in 300–301
and youth 297–300
see also media; Press, the
Broadcasting Act: section 31 105, 124, 164, 228
Broadcasting Review Committee 166
Broderick, John 282, 284
Brody, Hugh 543
Innishkillane 542, 549
Brown, Terence 247, 255, 287, 644–45
Brown Thomas department store, Dublin 472, 484
Browne, Garech 286
Browne, Ivor 572, 598
Browne, Malachy 199, 200
Browne, Dr Nöel 52, 68, 70–71, 233, 445–46, 536, 607, 608
Browne, Vincent 11, 70, 79, 80–81, 102, 148, 162, 199–201, 228, 308, 309, 321, 339–40, 511, 534
Brugha, Cathal 234
Bruton, Taoiseach John 472, 498, 536
and child care 376
and farmers 504–5
and reform of parliamentary institutions 27–28
and sports 316–18
Bruton, Richard 462
Bryant, Beth: *Ireland on Five Dollars a Day* 452–53
Buchanan, Archbishop of Dublin Alan 335–36
Buckley, Donal 514
budget deficit 499
'Bugsy Malone' gang 57
Bula mine 532–35
Burgess, Commander 593
Burke, Edmund 654
Burke, John 445
Burke, Liam 232
Burke, Ray 35, 42–43, 44
Burke, Richard 351, 376, 377, 447, 627–30, 633–34, 636, 645, 673
Burlington Hotel, Dublin 37
Burns, Mike 64
Burrows, Wesley 228, 293, 582
Business and Finance magazine 422
Butler, Anthony 48
Butler, Hubert 140, 644
Butt, Isaac 97
'buy-Irish campaign' 159, 489
Byrne, Davy 572
Byrne, Gabriel 262–63
Byrne, Gay 293, 308, 661
Byrne, Hugh 63, 579

C

Cahill, Fergus 529
Cahill, Joe 113, 153
Caine, Sir Michael 576
Callaghan, James 167, 187, 215, 217, 218
Camara, Don Helder 651
Camden, London 556, 558
Campaign for the Care of Deprived Children (CARE) 375, 383
Campbell, Jim 159
Cap, The (comedy show) 228
capital punishment 348, 353
Captain America's 577
Capuchin Annual, The 223
Carberry, Tommy 324
Cardinal Secrets (film) 379
Carey, Hugh 157
Carlow Nationalist 307
Carnsore, County Wexford 530, 531
Carr Communications 38
Carrig Una (trawler) 564
Carroll, Donal 609
Carroll, John 531
Carroll, John and Kelly, Petra, eds.: *A Nuclear Ireland?* 531–32
Carroll, Mella 93
Carroll, Noel 315, 321, 322
Carroll's Irish Open 324
cars
drink driving 588–89
registration 352–53
seat belts 589–90
taxis 591, 592
traffic volume 590
Carter, President Jimmy 7, 156, 157
Carty, R.K. 91
Carysfort Catholic teacher-training college 638
Casaroli, Archbishop 193
Casement, Roger 234–35
Black Diaries 234
Casey, Eamon, Catholic Bishop of Galway 432, 557, 621, 650, 655
Cassidy, Liam 518
Castle Leslie, County Monaghan 175
Castlebar Hospital 374
Castlemaine, County Kerry 199
Castlerea, County Roscommon 96
Catholic Bishops Research and Development Commission 646
Catholic Church 5, 87, 126, 140, 189, 205, 331, 345, 356, 370, 371, 399, 431, 543, 556, 601, 618, 623, 641, 645, 646, 648–49, 651, 662, 679
Catholic Communications Centre 650
Catholic emancipation 236
Catholic Hierarchy 370, 423, 464, 633, 639, 643, 648, 649
Catholic Press and Information Office 650
Catholic Standard newspaper 307, 649

Catholicism 14, 282, 542, 625, 641, 647, 648, 655, 656
statistics 5
Cavan 27, 566
Cawley, Dr Philip 517, 601
Cement Roadstone Holdings 532
censorship 6, 8, 111, 124, 164, 284, 289, 295, 319, 353, 355
Censorship Board 675
centenary bounties 568
Central Applications Office (CAO) 637
Central Bank 9, 82
Central Criminal Court 299
Central Statistics Office 481
centralisation 24, 25, 38, 54, 626
Ceoltóiri Cualann 267
Cheltenham Gold Cup 324
Cheltenham National Hunt Festival 324
Chequers 132
Chicago Tribune 156
Chief Secretary's Office Papers 249
Chieftains, The 267, 268, 269, 287
child rights 331
Childers, Erskine 35, 109–12, 133, 150, 158, 246–47, 290, 374, 384, 400, 469, 547–48, 600–601, 605, 608, 644, 647
Childers, Rita 253
children
rights of 353, 374–84, 651
status of 8
Children First 375, 382
children's allowance 72, 372, 476, 622
Children's Courts 365
Chilean refugees 442, 443–44
China 434–35
Chirac, Jacques 410
Chiswick Women's Aid 356
Christ Church Cathedral, Dublin 252, 643
Christian Brothers 380, 633
Christus Rex 620, 625
Chubb, Basil 24, 104
The Government and Politics of Ireland 14, 15
Church of Ireland 138, 192, 209, 381
Church of Ireland Gazette 138, 140
CIÉ (Córas Iompair Éireann) 51, 527, 591, 592, 629
cigarettes *see* smoking
Cimarons Reggae 273
Citizens Advice Bureau 48
civil liberties 112
civil rights 121, 182, 205, 326, 350, 447
civil service
bureaucracy 317
Catholics in 175
and community schools debate 52–53
decentralisation 55–56
deputising for ministers at official openings 52
Devlin Report 19
and Fulton Report 19, 54–55
Higher Civil Service 19
independence of 149
lack of unity in 21
overspecialisation 54
policy creation 4, 20
prominent civil servants 9, 53
reform 8, 51
relationship with governing politicians 55
responsibilities 55
size of 19, 20, 51
static nature of 19
Civil Service Arbitration Board 522
Civil Service Commission 31
Civil Service (Employment of Married Women) Act (1973) 622, 666
Civil Service Executive Association 53, 666
Civil Service Football Club 318
Claddagh Records 286
Clann na Poblachta Party 70
Clannad 268
Clapton, Eric 271
Clare, Anthony 543
Clare Island 562, 563–64
Claremorris Ham Festival, Andy Creighton's Lounge 268
Clark, Austin 292
Clarke, Sr Sarah 329
Clarke, Thomas 238
Claudia (arms-running vessel) 113
Cleary, Fr Michael 655
Clerkin, Garda Michael 335
Clerkin family 335
clientelism 8, 17, 24, 26, 27, 33, 48, 55
Clifden, Galway 562
Clinton, Mark 41, 413
Clonard Monastery, Belfast 2, 217
Clondalkin, Dublin 369
Clones 165
Cluskey, Frank 45, 71–72, 97, 188, 207, 479, 517, 601
Coade, Noel 303
coalition governments
1948–51 70
1954–57 74
1973–77 2, 17, 32, 62, 68, 69, 76, 104, 290, 483, 499, 505, 600
de Valera on 76, 108
Coffey, Thomas 53
Colgan, Gerry 261
Colgan, Michael 260
collective bargaining 460, 514
College of Europe, Bruges 406
College of Europe Scholarships 404–5

College of Industrial Relations, Dublin 459
Colley, George 36–37, 50, 52, 79, 80, 86, 97, 104, 189, 403, 417, 446, 460, 466, 473, 474, 489, 502–4, 505, 509, 513, 520, 558–59, 564, 671, 672
Colley, Harry 502
Collins, Gerry 164, 289, 290, 296, 306, 343, 344, 351, 382, 580
Collins, Michael 233, 234
Collins, Stephen 198, 479
Combat Poverty Agency 72
Comhaltas Ceoltóirí Éireann (Society of Irish Musicians) 267
Comiskey, Fr Brendan 377
Commission on the Status of Women (CSW) 659–60, 664–65, 673
Committee Against Rape (CAR) 356
Committee of Public Accounts 142
Committee on Industrial Progress 490
Common Agricultural Policy (CAP) 388, 396, 410–11
Common Market 397, 398
Common Market Defence Campaign 399
Common Market Defence Committee (CMDC) 398
community associations 569
community festivals 571
Concern 430, 432
Condon, Attorney General Colm 362–63
Confederation of Irish Industry 399
Conference of the Major Religious Superiors of Ireland 377
conflict of interest 41–43
Congo 390
Connaughton, Paul 23–24
Connemara Gaeltacht 550
Connolly, Helen 599
Connolly, James 17, 69, 71, 216, 238, 239
Connolly, Jerome 431
Connolly, Joe 316
Connolly, Linda 658
Connolly, Nora 239
Connolly, Roddy 239
Connolly Station, Dublin 582
Conquest of Light (film) 303
Conradh na Gaeilge (the Gaelic League) 276
Conroy, Judge John Charles 326
Conroy, Roisín 670
Conroy Report 326
conservation 613
Conservation Year (1973) 314
Conservatism, power of 7
Conservative government: *Northern Ireland: Constitutional Proposals* 174
Constituency Revision Bill 40
Construction Industry Federation 595
Consumer Affairs Office 484–85
Consumer Information Act (1978) 484
consumerism 6, 7, 467, 597
consumption surveys 482–83
contraception 4, 62, 76, 77, 92, 189, 191, 192, 206, 293, 354, 355, 543, 544, 583, 622, 641, 646, 648, 652, 662, 664, 673–79
Control of Importation, Sale and Manufacture of Contraceptive Bill (1974) 673–74
Conway, Cardinal William, Archbishop of Armagh and Primate of All Ireland 82, 92, 206, 237, 370, 632–33, 647, 651
Coogan, Fintan 490
Coogan, Tim Pat 61, 65, 75, 81, 104, 106, 148, 163, 309, 311, 361, 655
Cook, Judith 212
Cooke, Eamon 299
Coolahan, John 627
Coole Park, near Gort, County Galway 452
Coolock, Dublin 363
Cooney, Patrick 76, 98, 103, 194, 205, 206, 207, 210, 329, 337–38, 341, 342, 348–49, 354, 358, 370, 443, 446, 592, 596, 605, 666, 674
Córas Tráchtála (Irish Export Board) 453
Corboy, Denis 394, 406, 423
Corish, Brendan 45, 67, 73, 76, 103, 176, 188, 377, 383, 398, 404, 496–97, 544, 601–2, 671, 678
Cork 285, 296, 628, 677
Cork airport 491
Cork Chamber of Commerce 521
Cork County Council 30, 644
Cork Examiner 104, 307
Cork International Choral and Folk Dance Festival 267
Cork International Film Festival 269
Cork Marriage Guidance centre 648
Cork Opera House 265
Corrigan, Máiréad 186
Corvin, Donal 270
Cosgrave, Taoiseach Liam 33, 74–78, 103, 132, 165, 250, 324, 497–98, 511, 647
  and 1972 Dublin bombings 198

admired for conservatism and perceived steadiness 61
Anglo-Irish Treaty anniversary 233
appearance 74, 75
and Arms Trial events 142, 149
in Australia 441
and capital taxation 472, 473
caricatured 23
castigates Fianna Fáil TDs 43
and Childers 110
and the civil service 53
and conflict of interest 41
and the constitution 193
and contraception 76, 77, 675
and Corish 76
on Costello 368
criticism of 62, 113
Daly and Conway 206
as a delegator 75
on the difference between Fianna Fáil and Fine Gael 61–62
and dual membership issue 420
and Dublin/Monaghan bombings 199, 200–201
and Edmond O'Connor 139–40
and education 630, 633, 634, 636
and Emergency Powers Act 345
and emigration 555, 556, 557
expectations for his administration 39
and government departments 49
and hare coursing 315
and health boards 601
and Heath 412
on John A. Costello 245
judges' dispute 266
Kelly's 'baboons' remark 59
licensing laws 454
London talks with Wilson (1976) 185–86
and marriage 370
meetings with Heath (1973) 175–76
and mining 534, 535
and Mountjoy prisoners 205
and Northern Ireland 135, 160
and Ó Dálaigh 112–17
and O'Connell 236, 237
and oil/gas exploration 527, 528
and opinion polls 106
opposes 'think tanks' idea 110
and parliamentary broadcasting 46
party funding 37
personal papers 9–10, 76
personality 75, 76
police and civil service reform 174
and the power-sharing assembly 124
and prisons/prisoners 206, 207, 208, 210
and 'rather quiet' Irish students 94
refuses a TV debate 107
and reunification 192–93, 194
and the SDLP 185
and sport 316, 317
and Stokes 265
and strikes 518
succeeded by FitzGerald 78
Sunningdale (1973) 176–79
UCD debating society 196
unpopularity 197–98
upholding of law and order 15
views on moral issues 192
visits US (1976) 438–39
votes against his own government's bill 76, 77, 645, 673
and women's status 622, 669
Cosgrave, Patrick 157
Cosgrave, William T. 15, 74–75, 245
cost of living 6, 395, 396, 483, 561
Costello, Attorney General Declan 41–42, 46, 113, 168–69, 193, 214, 245, 345–46, 366, 367–70, 441, 557, 674
Costello, Taoiseach John A. 53, 77, 244–45, 367
Costello, Séamus 344
Costelloe, Paul 586
Coughlan, Anthony 476, 478
Coughlan, Eamon 322
Coughlan, Stevie 98
Coulson, Marjorie 202
Coulter, Phil 269
Council for Research and Development 650
Council for Social Welfare 464
Council for the Status of Women 4, 356, 622, 665, 669
Council of Europe 346, 406
Council of Ireland 2, 124, 173–79, 194, 219
Council of Ministers 671
Council of State 214, 346
councillors
dual mandate 27
expected role of 26
and policy-making 26
Countess Markievicz Fianna Fáil *cumann*, Sligo 139
courts: independent of government 18
Coyle, Marian 203
Craig, William 162, 174, 176

Crane Bag (journal) 224, 256, 287, 294
Crawford, Sir Stewart 174
Cremin, Con 647
cricket 322–23
crime
armed robberies 336, 349, 352
'Bugsy Malone' gang 57
decrease in detection rate 349, 350
domestic violence 355–57
drug offences 350
illegal acquisition of property 328
increase in 328, 333, 349, 350
mixed messages from crime figures 336–37, 352
and security 352
smuggling 353
tax evasion 352–53
young offenders 348–49, 351, 572
'crime explosion' 328–29
Criminal Justice Bill 60
criminal justice system 330
Criminal Law Amendment Act (1935) 191–92, 662, 673
Criminal Law (Jurisdiction) Bill 97
Crinion, Brendan 43
Croke Park, Dublin: pitched battle between supporters (1973) 319
Cronin, Adrian 293
Cronin, Anthony 260, 477, 580, 589
Cronin, Gráinne 587
cronyism 55
Cross, Kevin 196, 639
cross-border cultural co-operation 215–16
Crossmaglen 209
Crotty, Raymond 117, 399
Crotty, Tom 423
Crowe, Catríona 378
Crowley, Jeananne 262
Crummey, Frank 380
Cuba 440
Cubbon, Brian 212, 213
Cullen, Louis 250
An Economic History of Ireland Since 1660 223
Cullen, Mary 658, 661, 662
Cullen, Cardinal Paul 648
cultural identity 8
cultural nationalism 277
Cumann na nGaedheal 31, 33
Cummins, Mary 583
Cunnane, Joseph, Archbishop of Tuam 557
Cunningham, John 676
Curley, Walter 438
Curragh Hospital 361
Curragh military prison 208, 358, 361
Curran, Johnny 173
Currie, Austin 124, 125, 133, 173, 178, 184, 185, 187
Curry, Patrick 156
Customs and Excise 216
Cyprus 390, 433

D

Dáil Committee on Procedure and Privilege 43
Dáil Éireann
control over public expenditure 28
sitting frequency 28
TDs prominent in academia and broadcasting 96
women TDs in 90, 91
Daily Record 159
Daily Telegraph 371
Daingean, County Offaly 351
Daley, Mayor Richard 439
Dalkey School Project 82, 630
Daly, Dr Edward Bishop of Derry 205–6, 207, 651
Daly, Mary 247, 489
Daly's pub, Dublin 199–200
Dana 271, 273, 276
Danaher, Gerry 639
D'Arcy, Dr Brian 308
Darcy, Eamon 324
Davey, Shaun 267
David Hendrick's Gallery, Dublin 279
Davis, Thomas 658
Davitt, Michael 237, 285
Davy Byrnes pub, Dublin 578, 580
Dawson, George W.P. 431
Day by Day programme 298
Day, Robin 159
de Barra, Eamon 240–41
de Burca, Mairín 92–93, 353, 365–66, 377, 619, 662, 667–68
de Burgh, Chris 271, 577
de Courcy Ireland, John 67, 69, 171–72, 247, 398, 433, 493
De Dannan 268–69
De Paor, Liam 1, 3, 549
de Paor, Máire 265
de Valera, Eamon 109, 152, 232–33, 234, 237, 309, 647, 670–71, 676
and Arms Trial events 147
and coalition government 76, 108
death and funeral 86–87, 244
founder and patriarch of Fianna Fáil 16
success of 65, 66
de Valera, Síle 152
de Valera, Major Vivion 309, 676
de Valera family 309
Deane, Raymond 267
Deane, Seamus 286, 287, 288
death penalty 335
decentralisation 25, 55–56
DeGroot, Gerard: *The Seventies Unplugged* 3
Delaney, Eamon 280
Delaney, Edward 280, 287

democracy 14–15, 92, 98, 103, 125, 253, 548, 639
Democratic Unionist Party (DUP) 174, 175, 190
Denmark
  joins EEC 386
  women in politics 91
  and Wood Quay excavations 252
dental care 606
Department of Agriculture 238, 574
Department of Communications 50
Department of Defence 56, 181, 232, 238
Department of Economic Planning and Development 21, 461, 629
Department of Education 9, 55–56, 232, 250, 277, 315, 316, 376, 619, 627, 628, 631
Department of External Affairs 120, 389
  Anglo-Irish section 121
Department of Finance 9, 20, 24, 49, 52, 53, 176, 225, 234, 259–60, 265, 317, 337, 362, 363, 377, 395, 413, 416, 418, 461, 466, 470, 495, 501, 510, 556, 562, 627, 628–29, 671, 672
Department of Fisheries 493
Department of Foreign Affairs (DFA) 9, 66, 133, 143, 152, 161, 176, 181, 209, 233, 238, 388, 389–90, 397, 406, 408, 409, 415, 416, 417, 421, 425, 429, 434, 435, 439, 441, 443, 444, 445, 647, 651, 652, 666
  Anglo-Irish section 653
  Cultural Relations Committee 237
  political division 401
Department of Health 376, 382, 496, 608, 610
  1976 report 378
  memorandum on non-accidental injury 377–78
Department of Industry and Commerce 159, 303, 304, 416, 418, 482, 528, 534
Department of Justice 52, 139, 142, 193, 201, 204–5, 250, 314, 336, 337, 342, 349, 356, 359–61, 369, 381, 442, 446, 579, 605, 674
Department of Labour 238, 369, 508, 556
Department of Lands 49, 55–56
Department of Local Government 18, 50, 95, 488, 496, 595, 615
Department of Posts and Telegraphs 20, 291, 296–99, 312, 519
Department of Public Service 20, 21, 49, 54, 56, 369
Department of Social Welfare 480, 568, 671–72
Department of the Environment 50, 56, 57, 615
Department of the Gaeltacht 49, 52, 55–56, 562
Department of the Taoiseach 9, 51, 52, 54, 56, 74, 106, 111, 114, 121, 132, 139, 153, 155, 159, 160, 176, 179, 182, 184, 187, 189, 197, 198, 199, 209, 210, 212, 232, 234, 250, 252, 253, 264, 265, 298, 306–7, 316, 317, 320–21, 361, 373, 382–83, 403, 410, 429, 439, 444, 445, 448, 451, 454, 463, 469, 471, 473, 480, 495, 497, 498, 504, 509, 518, 520, 534–35, 564, 570, 579, 580, 591, 595, 610, 615, 647, 659, 671, 676
Department of Tourism and Transport 447, 491
Department of Transport and Power 49, 453, 525
derogation 346, 668, 669, 670
Derry 215, 572
  Bloody Sunday (January 1972) 121, 127, 129–31, 134, 206
  civil rights demonstration (1968) 121
  disturbances (early 1970s) 121
  Irish army intervention in 171
  response to Stagg's death 211
Derrynane, County Kerry 452
Desmond, Barry 27, 67, 406, 445, 630, 644, 651
Devitt, John 264
Devlin, Barry 270
Devlin, Bernadette 64, 381, 445
Devlin, Paddy 163, 178, 182, 183, 184, 193
Devlin Report (Report of the Public Services Organisation Review Group) (1969) 19, 48, 49, 363, 660
Diamond, Harry 182
Dillon, Brendan 670
Dillon, Eilís 265
  Blood Relations 283
Dillon, James 245
Dimbleby, Jonathan 158
Diploma in Archival Studies 248
Director of Public Prosecutions: creation of the position 368
District Courts 291, 310
'divisive implications' 232
divorce 189, 192, 193, 236, 330, 371, 372, 373, 567, 645, 648, 660, 667, 672, 679
Dobbin's Bistro, Dublin 575
Doctrine and Life 620

Dodder River 613
Dolan, Joe 273
Donegal 215, 286, 452, 566
Donegal Gaeltacht 52
Donegal North East constituency 136, 144, 151
Donegan, Patrick 45, 47, 115–16, 233, 471
  insults Ó Dálaigh 10, 97, 112–16, 493
Donlon, Seán 9, 133, 176, 178, 180, 181, 183, 184, 185, 187, 208, 218, 220, 449
Donnelly, Carolyn 586
Donoghue, Denis 283
Donoughmore, Earl and Countess of 139
Dooge, Jim 55
Doolan, Lelia 17, 261, 303, 662
Doolin, Lelia, Dowling, Jack and Quinn, Bob: *Sit Down and Be Counted* 303
Dorgan, Theo 285
Dorr, Noel 9, 416, 425, 434
Dowling, Brendan 55, 170, 494
Dowling, Jack 303
Downey, James 20, 38, 109, 114, 124, 149–50, 183, 308, 548
Doyle Hotel Group 473
Doyle, John 253
Doyle, Maurice 416
Doyle, P.V. 473
Drew, Ronnie 270
drink driving 548–49
Drogheda 85
drugs
  anti-drugs campaign 608
  offences 350
  prescription 599, 600
Druid Theatre Company 262
'Drumcondra Mafia' 28
Drumm, Marie 211
Dublin
  air pollution 612
  anti-rape protest (1978) 356–57
  bombings (1974) 124, 178, 198–201, 279, 517
  Friel on 256–57, 549–50
  Geldof on 272
  inner-city tenements 571–72
  letter-bomb scare 213
  lord mayor of 253
  Loyalist bombing (1972) 112, 197–98, 518
  Montessori schools 303
  population 320, 565, 570
  prostitution 356
  pubs and bars in 580–81
  stores in 484
  theatre in 257, 259–62
  third highest incidence of heart attacks among young males 597
Dublin airport 142, 145, 146, 147, 209, 211, 428, 432, 436, 437, 440, 550, 587
Dublin Area Rapid Transit (DART) 591–92
Dublin Castle 232, 401, 411
Dublin Central constituency 28, 64
Dublin Chamber of Commerce 570
Dublin City Council 348, 349, 572
Dublin City Marathon (1980) 315, 322
Dublin Corporation 252, 253, 315, 332, 572, 583–84, 594, 595, 614
  archives 249
Dublin Council of Churches 138
Dublin Council of Trade Unions 508, 509
Dublin County Council 42, 44
Dublin Diocesan Council of Priests 642
'Dublin Disco fever' 271
Dublin Festival of Twentieth Century Music 267
Dublin Finglas Constituency Council 68
Dublin Folk Festival 268
Dublin Fusiliers 248
Dublin Grand Opera Society 275
Dublin Health Authority 598
Dublin Horse Show 269, 324, 454
Dublin Housing Action Group 92–93
Dublin Itinerant Settlement Committee 383
Dublin North Central constituency 71
Dublin North West constituency 97
Dublin Ports and Docks Board 526
Dublin Rape Crisis Centre (DRCC) 357
Dublin Regional Tourism 592
Dublin South East constituency 68
Dublin South West constituencey 367
Dublin Theatre Festival 255, 259–60, 265
Dublin Women's Aid organisation 355
Dubliners 269–70
Dudley Edwards, Owen 290
Dudley Edwards, Robert 239, 246, 248, 250
  A New History of Ireland 247
  'Rescue the Records' (lecture) 248
Dudley Edwards, Ruth 239, 583
Dugdale, Rose 203, 204, 344
Duggan, Richard 604
Duignan, Clare 300
Dundrum, south Dublin 644

Dunlop, Frank 81, 86, 105–6, 344, 838
Dunne, Aidan 280
Dunne, Derek 3
Dunne, Lee: *Paddy Maguire is Dead* 284
Dunne, Rory 405, 406
Dunnes stores 484
Dunphy, Eamon 321, 444
Dunquin, West Kerry 277
Durcan, Paul 285
'Making Love Outside Áras an Uachtaráin' 285–86

E
Easkey, County Sligo 530
East Belfast 194
East Munster 552
Easter Rising (1916) 47, 69, 109, 205, 234, 238, 239, 247
Eastern Health Board 377, 600, 607
eating out 574–77
Eblana Theatre, Dublin 260
ecclesiastical law 370
Economic and Social Research Institute 329, 373, 405, 477, 494
survey (1978) 216
Economic and Social Review (journal) 460
economic reform 16
Economist, The (magazine) 100, 114, 158
ecumenism 315, 642, 643
Eddery, Pat 324
education
academic 631
class size 627–28
community schools 52, 618, 619, 631–34
compulsory full-time 189, 542
expansion of 5, 625
funding 626, 630
Gaeltacht schools 618
higher 94, 634
industrial schools 331, 374, 378, 379, 380, 381
inner-city levels 571
Intermediate Certificate examination 631
investment in 8
liberal 631
Montessori schools 303
neglect at St Patrick's 360
neglect of arts in 288
power distribution 5
primary schools 618, 619, 629, 630, 637
Protestant schools 140, 644
pupil statistics 567
regional technical 635
religious 621
remedial 628
school transport 629
second-level 277, 619
secondary school teachers' strike (1971) 516
secondary schools 495, 619, 630–31, 634
static nature of 19
technology colleges 84, 634
third-level 48, 94, 337, 619, 625, 634, 635, 637, 638, 673
university 5, 634
vocational 631, 632
Education Times 309, 612, 618–19
Edwards, Hilton 261
Egon Ronay Guide 575, 576
Egypt: diplomatic relations with Ireland 432, 433
Eire Broadcasting Corporation 297
elderly, the
housing 568–69
old-age pensions 72, 479
and their families 606
Electricity Supply Board (ESB) 513, 516, 517, 525, 526, 530, 591, 613
Elizabeth II, Queen 214, 401, 432
Emergency Powers Act (1939) 214, 345
Emergency Powers Act (1976) 112, 116, 214, 345, 354, 368
emigration 5, 8, 459, 541, 542, 549, 554–60, 625
employment 191
creation of new 8, 523
health authorities 498
public service 498
Employment Equality Act (1977) 623
Employment Equality Agency 587, 622, 665
environment 612–16, 679
alternative fuel and energy supplies 6
natural resources 6
pollution 6
Epsom Derby 324
equal pay 622, 659, 669, 670
Equal Pay Act 668
Equal Pay ad hoc committee 670
Equus (film) 304
Ervine, Andy 268
Estadio Nacional, Santiago, Chile 444
Ethiopia 430
Eurobarometers 390, 406, 422, 423
Europe Day (5 May) 404
European Championships (Prague, 1978) 322
European Commission 92, 395, 399, 410, 415, 419, 421, 476, 492, 668, 670, 671
European Commission of Human Rights 367
European Communities Committee 412
European Council 217, 219, 410
Convention for the Protection of

Human Rights and Fundamental Freedoms (later Convention on Human Rights) 346, 668, 675
Secretariat 420
European Court of Human Rights 341, 668
European Court of Justice, Luxembourg 45, 363, 493
European Economic Community (EEC) 170, 369
Agricultural Fund 506
Britain joins 386, 393
cheese mountain 574
Committee of Irish Civil Servants 409
Council of Ministers 424
directives paramount in advancing equality 623
enlargement 407, 410, 415, 416, 417, 418, 433
farm modernisation scheme 507, 551, 552
and Fine Gael 62
first Irish presidency (1975) 410, 411, 412
implications of membership 10
Information Centre 394
Irish membership 4, 6, 160, 243, 282, 386–91, 393–402, 403, 406–8, 427, 459, 464, 467, 503, 551, 593, 668
meeting of EEC heads of government (Paris, 1974) 410
and nuclear power 530
pig export subsidies 353
and politics as a male preserve 91
Regional Development Fund 388, 409–10, 413–15, 419
social action programme 480
Treaty Rules 330
VAT implementation 480
European Investment Bank 312
European Monetary System (EMS) 420, 523
European Monetary Union 412–13
European Parliament 670
dual membership 420
first elections to (1979) 38, 86, 424
Lynch's address to inaugural meeting 420
and patronage 45
European Social Fund 388, 417
European Union
bailout of the Irish economy 8
Tindeman's Report 412
Europeanisation 7
Eurovision Song Contest 271, 276, 407
Evelyn Marie (trawler) 564
Evening Herald 75, 104, 199, 307, 365
Evening Press 48, 272, 583
Evening Standard 424
Ewart-Biggs, Christopher 125, 212–13, 304, 343
Ewart-Biggs, Henrietta 213
Ewart-Biggs, Jane, Baroness 213–14
Ewart-Biggs, Kate 213
Ewart-Biggs, Robin 213
Ewart-Biggs Foundation 134
Exposure (short film) 303
external trade figures 491

F

factionalism 67
Fahey, Jackie 29
Fallon, Deirdre 334–35
Fallon, Garda Richard 326, 334–35
Fallon, Richard, Jr 334–35
Family Home Protection Act 372
family law 370–73
Family Law Act (1976) 372, 622
family law reform 369–70
Family Planning Bill 663, 677
family planning clinics 227
Fanning, Aengus 249–50
farm modernisation scheme 551, 552
Farmer's Journal 398–99
farming 504–7
Farmleigh 425
Farrell, Brian 15, 91, 104, 122–23, 211
Farrell, J.G.: *Troubles* 283
Farrell, Michael: 'In Memoriam; exhibition (1975) 279
Farrell, Peggy 94
Farrelly, Patrick 300
fashion 585–86
Fastnet sailing tragedy (1979) 564
Faul, Fr Denis 165, 181, 205
Faulkner, Brian 125, 176, 178, 184, 186
Faulkner, Pádraig 248, 591, 627, 631–32, 634, 638, 652
FCA (army reserve) 171
Féach (Look) (current affairs programme) 295
Feakle, County Clare 136
Federated Union of Employers (FUE) 510
Feehan, Fanny 275
Feeney, John 597
Feldman, Marty 304
feminist movement, feminists 625, 654, 657–79
achievements of 4
Action Information Motivation starts 664
'Chains or Change?' sent to Jack Lynch 660–61
Commission on the Status of Women founded 659–60

Council for the Status of Women established 665
CSW report 664–65
divisions in the IWLM 663–64
empowerment of working-class women 663
IWLM founded 660
and macho roots of Irish politics 18
representation of women's rights 92
'second wave' feminists 658
social security 671–72
see also women

Fenelli, Vatican's Sostituto (Deputy Secretary) 208
Fenian Rising (1867) 237
Fennell, Nuala (née Campbell) 89–90, 355, 356, 370, 576, 664, 666, 667
Ferenka steel plant, Limerick 203, 204, 516, 520
Ferns Report (2005) 378
Festival of Modern Music 275
festivals 269, 286, 571
Fianna Fáil
1970s as a turbulent decade 16, 33
Árd Fheis (annual party conference) 34, 63, 143, 610
and Arms Trial 33, 141
Comhairle Ceantair (district executive) 34, 35
Dáil Ceantair (constituency executive) 34
EEC membership 394–95
election manifesto (1977) 50, 85, 108, 296, 461, 593, 675
electoral defeat (1973) 4, 32, 36, 38, 45, 80, 105
end of historic dominance (2011) 679
excels at organisation 10, 61
Finance Committee 36
and first elections to the European Parliament (1979) 38, 424
founded (1926) 36, 231
fundraising 36–37
Haughey wins the leadership 219–20
Kelly on 60, 61, 65
'manifesto crisis' 500
National Executive 34, 37, 85, 87, 151, 182
Ó Dálaigh controversy 114
Organisation Committee 34, 35
papers of 10
and patronage 30–31
and Pearse's centenary 241
and political reform 45
proportional representation referendum 60
rates issue 488
recruitment 61
referendum campaign (1972) 400
returns in triumph (1977) 4, 32, 34, 41, 106, 107–8, 217, 473
and RTÉ 290
ruthless pragmatism 60
skulduggery at local level 34–35
stance on Northern Ireland 16, 218–19
successful political party 10, 16, 33, 38
and the Sunningdale communiqué 177–78
support base 16
tensions in relation to its structures and large membership 10
and Tully's Constituency Revision Bill 40–41
well-organised volunteers 60
West Mayo by-election loss 35–36
youth conferences 61
youth vote 70

Field, John 274
film industry 302–6
Film Industry Bill 302, 303
Financial Times 149
Fine Gael
coalition government (1973–7) 2, 17, 32, 62, 69
and EEC entry 400
internal difficulties 10, 59, 197
Kelly's soul-searching 59–61
lack of knowledge about Northern Ireland 136
magazine published by parliamentary party 31
and Offences Against the State Bill 198
patronage 31, 45
and a strong authoritarian state 15
support base 16
upholding of law and order 15
youth group 53

Finland
women in politics 91
and Wood Quay excavations 252

Finlay, Mary 639
Finucane, Marian 300
First World War 248, 286
fisheries, fishing 216, 390, 407, 414, 416, 419, 492–93
Fisk, Robert 198–99
Fitt, Gerry 176, 178, 182, 183, 186, 220, 653
FitzGerald, Alexis 77, 241, 471

FitzGerald, Desmond 16, 78–79, 387
FitzGerald, Taoiseach Garret 60, 123, 126, 128, 132, 133, 164, 178, 274, 343, 395, 433, 471, 651
on 1969 survey 474
and access to Irish historical material 259
and aid 430, 431
and the Alliance Party 182
and Amnesty 340–41, 446–47
apartheid 447
and Arms Trial events 144, 149
assessment of 62
in Australia 441
bank debt 45–46
BBC interviewee 159
and Birmingham pub bombs 161
bored by local politics 29
and British media 167
and Casaroli 193
church-state relations 645
and civil service 55
commitment to reconciliation and tolerance 79
communication skills 79
and conflict of interest 41
and the constitution 191
and Cosgrave's delegation 75
and a Council of Ireland 124
and danger of civil war 131
and document destruction 250
and eastern Europe 428, 444
and the economy 190
EEC presidency 412
and emigration 555, 556, 557, 558
endorsement of IAAM 446
equal pay issue 670
a Europhile 387
and Ewart-Biggs's death 213
and Fianna Fáil's 'manifesto crisis' 500
gatecrashes *The Late Late Show* 662
on Haughey 87
and ignorance about Northern Ireland 135–36
international profile 78
and Irish newspaper coverage of the Troubles 162
Kissinger's 'favourite foreign minister' 156–57
leader of Fine Gael 29, 78, 107
and letter from de Burca 365, 366
Littlejohn affair 152
and marriage bar 666
Minister for Foreign Affairs 10, 38, 45, 78, 79, 390, 409, 427, 496, 501
move to the left 69
'Mr Europe' 424
and non-government organisations 428–29
and Nuala Fennell 89–90
and Offences Against the State Bill 198
opposes dialogue with IRA 207
papers 10, 536
police and civil service reform 174
on poverty levels 53
and prisoners 206
on the Regional Fund 413–14
resented by Ryan 469
rise of 16
and the SDLP 185, 187
and Stagg's hunger strike 210
succeeded by Dukes (1987) 59
supports EEC membership 399
talks with Vance 440
and telephone network 312
televised debate with Colley 503
'unity in diversity' notion 391
and violent incidents in Northern Ireland 160–61
Towards a New Ireland 79
Fitzgerald, Gene 520–21
FitzGerald, John 424–25
Fitzgerald, Chief Justice William 673
Fitzgibbon, Theodora 575
Fitzpatrick, David: *Politics and Irish Life, 1913–21: Provincial Experience of War and Revolution* 223–24
Fitzpatrick, Jim 440
Fitzpatrick, Tom 551
FitzSimons, Peter 586
Five Nations Championship 323
Flanagan, Oliver J. 77–78, 208, 629–30
Flanagan, Seán 613
Flannery, Fr Austin 651
Fleadhanna Cheoil (music festivals) 268
Fleetwood Mac 273
Fleischmann, Aloys 267
Flynn, Mannix 262, 381
Flynn, Pádraig 96, 97
Flynn, Phil 203
Focus Theatre, Dublin 263
Foley, Dermot 227, 540
Foley, Donal 309
'The Church Goes to Market' 399
Foley, Richard 52
food
access to wider choice of 5–6

exemption from VAT 470
hygiene 605
inflation 422
poor 597
popular brands 573
prices 399
restaurants 574–77
Foot, Paul 228
Football Association of Ireland 444
Foras Forbartha, An (the Institute for Physical Planning) 612
Foras Talúntais (the Agricultural Institute) 506
Forde, Fr Walter 621
Foreign and Commonwealth Office 174, 213, 214, 653
Forest and Wildlife Service 614
Fortune, Fr Seán 378–79
Forty Foot all-male bathing area, Sandycove, County Dublin 678
Foster, Roy 79, 81, 90, 222, 509–10, 640
Fota Park Island, Cork 452
Four Courts, Dublin 232, 663
Fox, Billy 139, 202–3
France: cultural agreement with Ireland 425
Francis, Dick 159
Fraud Squad 44
Free Legal Advice Centres (FLAC) 48, 354, 355, 363
free trade 8, 398, 467, 490
Freedom of Information Act 63
Freeman, John 158
Freeman, Spencer 604
Freld, Dr Raymond 380
French Second Republic 407
Friel, Brian 256–58, 259, 263–64, 286, 549–50
Aristocrats 257
Faith Healer 264
The Freedom of the City 257
The Gentle Island 226, 257
The Mundy Scheme 226, 408
Philadelphia Here I Come! 256
Translations 257, 258
Friends of Medieval Dublin 251, 252
Friends of the Earth 531
Frontline (RTÉ programme) 84
fuel crisis (1979) 480–81
Fulton Report 19, 54–55
Furey Brothers 273
Furrow, The 620
Furry Glenn nature park, Phoenix Park, Dublin 452

G
Gaddafi, Muammar 113
Gaelic Athletic Association (GAA) 80, 81, 108, 229, 318, 319, 320, 552, 578
Gaelic football 229, 319–20, 555
Gaelic League 276, 277
Gaeltacht (Irish-speaking districts) 49, 52, 56, 277, 550
Gageby, Douglas 162, 163, 308, 309, 310, 405, 655
Gaiety Theatre, Dublin 257, 260, 445
Gaj, Margaret 660
Gaj's restaurant, Baggot Street, Dublin 660
Gallagher, Eamonn 121
Gallagher, Eddie 203, 204, 344
Gallagher, Hughie 564
Gallagher, Redmond 472
Gallagher, Rory 270, 272
Gallup polls 16, 106, 217
Galsworthy, Sir Arthur 175
Galway 655, 677
by-election (1975) 344
Galway, James 275
Galway Corporation 40, 677
Galway Family Planning Association 677–78
Galway Race Committee 454
Galway Races 269, 454
Galway West constituency 563
Garda Commissioner 57
Garda Representative Association (GRA) 335
Garda Review 326, 327, 342
Garda Síochána (Gardaí) 7, 45, 139, 140, 142, 145, 148
and Amnesty 341, 342
anti-subversive section C3 342
baton charge at Lansdowne Road 195
belief that isolated in contrast to Irish army 326–27
brutality allegations 63, 340, 341, 345, 354, 356
and child abuse by priests 331
clashes with pickets 522
Clerkin's death 335
complaints 339, 353
and contraceptive possession 673, 674
cuts in expenditure 337–38
diversion of manpower due to the Troubles 333
and domestic violence 355
Drugs Squad 350
and Dublin/Monaghan bombings 198, 200
and Emergency Powers Bill 112
and Ewart-Biggs case fingerprint errors 343
Fallon's death 326, 334–35
golden jubilee (1972) 335–36
'heavy gang' 328, 340, 343

individuals take law into own hands 327–28
lack of Gardaí at night 348
land sale fraud investigation 44
and a local security force 201–2
and the media 339
and motor vehicle registration 352–53
and Mountbatten's death 214
murders 326
new disciplinary code 336
NFDA investigation 57
O'Brien on 348
and potential air attack on Thatcher 219
and the Provisionals 165
relations with the community 328
relationship with Department of Justice 336, 342
Reynolds's death 335
road check points 160
and RTÉ 354, 475
and Sallins train robbery 327–28, 344–45
and the security threat 328
and the *Seven Days* team 291
Sinn Féin headquarters in Dublin closed down 210
size of 160, 215, 327, 336, 337, 338, 342, 350, 352
special branch 146, 209, 343, 354
traffic duty 588–89
unarmed 333
Garden of Remembrance, Dublin 232
Garfunkel, Art 273
Garvey, Edmund 328, 341, 342–44, 449
Garvin, Tom 24–25, 46, 387, 425, 652
gas exploration 526–30
Gate Theatre, Dublin 225, 260, 261, 262, 265
Gaullists 420
Gavin, Frankie 269
Gay Byrne Hour, The (RTÉ radio) 297
Gay Byrne Show, The 300
Gay News 584
Gay Trip (horse) 324
Gaynor, Gloria 273
GDP (gross domestic product) 468, 469
Geldof, Bob 229, 271–72, 545
general elections
1938 65
1951 78
1957 78
1965 66
1969 15, 16, 32, 35, 59, 60, 64, 66, 73
1973 16, 32, 38, 45, 64, 79, 80, 82, 95, 96, 104, 105, 106, 110, 503
1977 28, 29, 32, 36, 47, 50, 76, 77–78, 82, 85–86, 89, 90, 96, 106, 107–8, 187, 217, 461, 593, 602
general mortality rates 567
General Post Office (GPO), Dublin 519, 663
Geoghegan-Quinn, Máire 93, 344
German Green movement 531
German Welfare Council 559
gerrymandering 40, 41, 191
Gibbon, Peter 26
Gibbons, James 142, 144, 145, 146, 149, 150, 505
Gibbons, Monk 286
Gibson, Mike 323
Giles, David 95
Giles, John 321–22
Gill, Vincent 307
Gillen, Gerard 275
Gilmore, Eamon 173
Giornale, Il (Italian newspaper) 453–54
Girvin, Brian 645–46, 648
Glasnevin cemetery 234
Gleeson, Dermot 602
Glennon, Chris 526
Glens of Antrim 171
Glenstal Abbey 107
Gmelch, George 560
GNP (gross national product) 460, 499, 505, 552, 605, 626
Goffs Bloodstock Sales 324, 454
Goldsmith, Oliver 654
golf 323–24, 447–48
Gorham, Maurice 292
Gorta 430–31
government departments
departmental secretaries 19
as 'development corporations' 20
Devlin Report 19, 49
increase in number of 19
the Minister as 'Corporation sole' 20
moving out of Dublin 55–56
promotions 53
self-maintenance 49
see also under Departments
Government Information Services 53, 105, 213
GPA 45
Grade, Sir Lew (later Baron Grade of Elstree) 233
Graham, Bill 95, 268, 272
Granard, Lord 527–28, 528
Grand Knight of Columbanus 208
Grant, Patrick 216
Grassby, Al 555
Gray, Simon: *Close of Play* 260
Great Train Robbery, The (film) 305

Green Paper on energy policy 536
Green Property Company 251
Greenhill, Lord 213–14
Greevy, Bernadette 274–75
Gregory, Lady 452
Gregory, Tony 571, 572
Gresham Hotel, Dublin 528
Griffith, Arthur 232, 237
Griffith, Kenneth 233
Gromyko, Andrei 428
Guardian 209
Guevara, Che 440
Guinness 582, 586
Guinness, John 526
Guinness family 131
Gulf Oil 530
Guthrie, Tyrone 261

H

H Block (album) 209
H. Williams and Company 574, 669
Hailsham, Lord Chancellor 130, 157–58
Hall, Frank 23, 308, 483
Halligan, Brendan 68, 97–98, 207
Hallowell, Tom 500
Hall's Pictorial Weekly (television programme) 23, 26, 82, 308
hamburger joints 576–77
Hamilton, Justice Liam 252, 345
Hamilton, Timothy 540
Hanafin, Des 37
Hand, Derek 283
Hand, Eoin 321
Hang Out Your Brightest Colours (film) 233
Hanley, Brian 153, 157
Hanley, Dáithí 550
Hardiman, Adrian 638–39
Hardiman, T.P. 105
hare coursing 314–15
Harp 582, 586
Harris, Eoghan 105, 172, 295, 582
Harte, Paddy 56–57, 136, 179, 198, 205
Hartnett, Michael 278
Anatomy of a Cliché 278
Hattersley, Roy 173
Haughey, Taoiseach Charles 80, 81, 83, 96, 501, 503, 582–83
accountancy practice 85
anti-intellectual and and anti-policy 66
Arms Trial crisis and sacking (1970) 10, 66, 84, 122, 126, 141–48
and child care 383
his comeback 66, 88, 97, 126, 219–20, 466
Family Planning Bill 677
and fisheries 493
'the golden boy' 102
interest in wealth creation and social justice 84
local authority spending 489
and the media 84, 104, 105
Mills on 103
Minister for Finance 84, 85
Minister for Health and Social Welfare 84, 599, 602–3, 609–10
Minister for Justice 16, 84
motivation for actions leading to Arms Trial events 141
and Northern Ireland policy 218
payments to 85
and Pearse 241
personal wealth and ostentation 84
and the presidency 110
televised address (1980) 523–24
Hayes, Joe 406
Hayes, Maurice 645
Hayes McCoy, G.A. 227
health 597–611
attempts to tackle shortcomings 7
dental care 606
discussions with consultants 601, 602–3
and excessive drinking 577, 582, 597
expenditure 600–601, 605–6
Labour seek elimination of two-tier system 601
lack of exercise 597
life expectancy 597
limited eligibility for free primnary care 602
medical profession 543–44, 599–601
mental 7, 598–99, 679
National Health Council reports 605–6
over-dependence on prescription medicines 599
poor food 597
smoking 544, 605, 607–11
sweepstakes 311, 604–5
Health Act (1970) 375, 543, 600
health boards 600, 601, 602, 606
health clubs 598
Health Education Bureau 544, 582, 597
health levy 487, 600
health questionnaire (1978) 597–98
Healy, John (Backbencher) 83, 101–2, 122, 367, 576
Death of an Irish Town 549
Nineteen Acres 549
Heaney, Seamus 225–26, 265, 284, 285, 287, 638
Wintering Out 284
heart attacks 597
Heath, Sir Edward 8, 116, 129–32, 156, 164, 175, 181, 412

Hederman, Mark Patrick 224, 287
Hederman, Tony 342, 372, 677
Hederman O'Brien, Miriam 406
Heffernan, Kevin 320
Hefferon, Colonel Michael 144, 145, 148
Hegarty, Paddy 504
Heighway, Steve 322
Henchy, Judge Séamus 485, 667
Herlihy, W. 578–79
Herrema, Dr Tiede 114–15, 203, 204, 343
Hibernia (current affairs magazine) 11, 43–44, 65, 72, 73, 80, 85, 86, 94, 100, 103, 127, 128, 149, 150, 162, 187, 227–28, 235, 251, 261, 275, 281, 284, 292–93, 294, 307, 309–10, 311, 339, 354, 355, 371, 374, 382, 394–95, 400, 446, 474, 483–84, 502, 503, 510, 528, 532, 533, 574, 587, 593, 594, 596, 612–13, 627, 632–33, 643, 650, 658, 673, 675
Hickey, Brendan 555
Hickey, Kieran 303
Hickey, Tom 263
Higgins, Michael D. 66, 677, 678
  and broadcasting 290
  elected president of Ireland (2011) 24
  and the environment 612
  housing examples 26–27
  study of clientelism and the Irish 'gombeen' man 26
  wins a Dáil seat 28
High Court 93, 95, 178, 252, 291, 344, 362, 371, 454, 532–35, 672
Higher Education Authority 243, 259, 407, 634, 635–36
Hillery, Patrick 118, 129, 133, 143, 150, 241, 389–90, 393, 397, 401, 424, 651, 670, 672
historical film 306
historical research 223
Historical Society 386
Hobson, Harold 258–59
Hochhuth, Rolf 259
Hogan, Desmond 17, 284
Hogan, Louis 322
holidays 6, 497, 586–87
Holland, Mary 2, 3, 11, 158, 163, 228, 310
Holles Street Maternity Hospital 41
Holloway, Joe 416–17, 528
Holloway, Joseph 189
Holy Ghost Fathers' College, Templeogue, Dublin 52
Home Office 329
homelessness 351, 556, 558, 650, 664
homosexuality 583–84, 646
Hoover, J. Edgar 328
Horgan, John 46–47, 72, 619, 634
Horslips 270
Hospital Development Plan (1975) 544
Hospital Trusts Ltd 605
hospitals 311, 501, 598–99, 601, 602, 604
Hot Press (music magazine) 11, 95, 254, 268, 271–74, 299–300, 585, 672–73
Houlihan, Con 310
Hourican, Bridget 642
Hourican, Liam 117
household budget reviews 481–82
housing
  corporation 571, 594
  discriminatory 191
  domestic comforts 594
  the elderly 568–69
  expenditure on 29, 593–96
  house prices 6, 467, 484, 596
  house size 541–42
  inner-city tenements 571–72
  Irish immigrants 558
  left-wing protests 61
  local authority 72, 474, 595
  mortgage rates 470
  poor 5
  private housing sector 594–95
  squatters 594
  suburban developments 569–70
Housing Act (1966) 42
Howth gun running (1914) 235
Hoyle, Douglas 212
human rights 341, 442
Hume, John 121, 133, 157, 163, 170, 173, 174, 182–85, 187, 193, 205, 217, 218, 220, 286, 403, 404
Humphries, Tom 319
Hungarian refugees in Ireland 442–43
hunger strikers 181, 198, 205–8, 210–11, 345, 358, 361
hurling 229, 318, 320, 563
Hussey, Gemma 91, 357, 520
Hutchinson, Bertram 462
Hynes, Garry 262

I

Ibsen, Henrik: *Rosmersholm* 263
Image magazine 586
imperialism 172
In Dublin magazine 253, 309
Income Tax Act 672
Independent Newspapers 104, 199, 311
Indo-China refugees 444
Industrial Development Authority (IDA) 159, 303, 444, 462, 463

infant mortality rates 567, 605
inflation 4, 101, 330, 419, 422, 459, 461, 467, 469, 470, 480, 483, 495, 499, 511, 522
Inglis, Brian: *Roger Casement* 235
Inishbofin island 564
Inisheer island 562
Inishturbot island 562, 564
Inishturk island, off the coast of Mayo 561–62
inner-city communities 569, 570
  Dublin's tenements 571–72
  government inter-departmental group 570, 571
Insights documentary 583
Institute of Certified Public Accountants 489
Institute of Higher Education, Limerick 635
Institute of Public Administration (IPA) 18, 20, 41, 463
Inter-Departmental Committee on the Implications of Irish Unity 188–90, 192
Inter-Departmental National Security Group 201
Inter-Departmental Unit on Northern Ireland 168, 169
International Golf Association 448
International Monetary Fund (IMF) 9
International Olympic Committee 454, 526
International Planned Parenthood Federation 676
International Women's Day 660
International Women's Year 622, 658
International Year of the Child (1979) 382
internment 125, 185, 225, 334
Intoxicating Liquor Act (1962) 578
Iraq: potential oil refinery 536–37
Ireland: A Television History 132
Ireland, 51st American State Foundation 156
Ireland's Own magazine 355
Irish Anti-Apartheid Movement (IAAM) 391, 445, 446, 448
Irish army
  artillery range accident 347
  border patrols 346
  Costello on 169
  dealing with civilian affairs 347
  in the Middle East 346
  peacekeeping duties 390
  strength 169–70, 199, 346
  UN service 346, 432
  under strength and under-equipped 145
Irish Association 209
Irish Association of Civil Liberty 334, 341, 349–50, 353
Irish Association of Non-smokers 608
Irish Association of Professional Archaeologists 251–52
Irish Association of Social Workers 375
Irish Auctioneers and Valuers 129
Irish Ballet Company 265
Irish Cancer Society 608
Irish Censorship Board 584
Irish Centre, Camden, London 556–60
Irish civil war (1922–3) 7, 15, 25, 32, 110, 138, 205, 232–34, 358
Irish Commission for Justice and Peace 431
Irish Committee for the Restoration of Democracy in Chile 442
Irish Communist Party 64
Irish Conference of Professional and Service Associations 509
Irish Congress of Trade Unions (ICTU) 19, 172, 446, 462, 470, 508–11, 515, 521, 522, 532, 670
Irish Council Against Blood Sports 314
Irish Council for the European Movement (ICEM) 10, 41, 394, 395, 397, 399, 401–7, 422, 423–24, 429, 668
Irish Council of Civil Liberties (ICCL) 353–54, 382
Irish Countrywomen's Association (ICA) 93–94, 490
'Irish dimension' 131
Irish Embassy, London 132, 174, 189, 192, 233, 260
Irish Embassy, Paris 670
Irish Embassy, Rome 647
Irish Embassy, Washington 220
Irish Emigrants Rights Association 554–55
Irish Episcopal Commission 556, 557
Irish Family League 676
Irish Family Planning Association 673
  Family Planning 675
Irish famine (mid nineteenth century) 132–33
Irish Farmers' Association 403, 472, 504

Irish Fishermen's Organisation 492
Irish Foundation for Human Development 572
Irish Free State: Cosgrave leads first government 74
Irish Gay Rights Movement 583
Irish Georgian Society 251
Irish 'gombeenism' 26
Irish Heart Foundation 608
Irish Historical Studies 246
Irish Home Rule movement 97
Irish Housewives Association (IHA) 470, 489, 665–66
Irish identity 222, 224, 243, 255, 278, 287, 399, 440
Irish Independence Party 217, 218
Irish Independent 56, 103, 106, 113, 142, 158, 162, 307, 337, 394, 432, 446, 452, 520, 526, 527, 594
Irish Institute for International Affairs 429
Irish Jurist 330
Irish Labour History society 69
Irish Land Commission 551, 552
Irish Land League 552
Irish language 225, 276–78, 640, 645
Irish Management Institute 400, 401
Irish Manuscripts Commission (IMC) 248, 250
Irish Medical Association (IMA) 517, 543, 601, 602, 608
Irish Medical Times 543, 648
Irish Medical Union 543, 601
Irish National Caucus (INC) 157, 220
Irish National Petroleum Corporation (INPC) 529, 530
Irish National Teachers Organisation (INTO) 619, 620, 627, 628, 629, 631
Irish naval service 113
Irish News 195
Irish Offshore Oil 526
Irish Overseas Agency Trust 450
Irish Petroleum group 528
Irish Planning Institute 615
Irish Pregnancy Counselling Centres 678
Irish Press 52–53, 61, 100, 102, 103–4, 106, 143, 162, 163, 195, 219, 284, 291, 307, 309, 350–51, 401, 434, 453, 582, 583, 652–53, 660
Irish Red Cross 180, 181, 444
Irish Republic
- 1960s regarded as a decade of progress 7–8
- constitution 30, 48, 102, 111, 122, 126, 178, 188–91, 193, 205, 214, 330, 370, 380–81, 382, 557, 643
- declared a republic (1949) 14, 33
- decline of importance of agriculture 388
- EEC membership *see under* European Economic Community
- GDP per capita 388
- joins UN 74
- marketing 449–55
- monetary costs of 'Northern violence' 215
- Protestants in 138–40
- refugees from Northern Ireland 137, 169
- rural population ceases to dominate 4
- US governors visit 439–40

Irish Republican Army (IRA)
- and Arms Trial events 145, 146
- Birmingham pub bombs 161
- Bloody Sunday 130
- 'Brits Out' slogan 219
- ceasefire negotiations 125, 181, 185
- Clerkin's death 335
- concern in Republic for English victims of IRA terrorism 134
- dialogue established 136
- and Emergency Powers Act 214, 346
- Four Courts occupation 232
- and *Hibernia* 162
- High Command 160
- internment in the Maze prison 167
- killing of Billy Fox 202
- killing of Ewart-Biggs 125, 343
- killing of Mountbatten 260
- La Mon massacre 218
- Loyalist resistance to 2
- Lynch tries to undermine support for 151, 152
- and NORAID 154
- opposed by constitutional Nationalists 133
- Pope John Paul II's appeal 655
- prisoner of war status 361
- prisoners 204–9
- and the RTÉ Authority 81, 166
- RTÉ interviews (1971) 163–64
- and Russia 64
- and Sallins train robbery 345
- split in 172

and Stagg's death 211
and Ulster Vanguard Alliance 197
under pressure 186
undermining of Irish American support 123, 153–57, 220, 438
in War of Independence 223
Warrenpoint 260
Irish Republican Army Veterans, New York City 154
Irish Republican Socialist Party (IRSP) 344, 345
Irish Rugby Football Union 323
Irish School of Ecumenics 645
Irish Society for Archives 248
Irish Society for the Prevention of Cruelty to Children 378, 383
Irish sweepstakes 311
Irish TAM Ltd 295
Irish Taxi Federation 592
Irish Theatre Company 259, 265
Irish Times 20, 38, 48, 69, 75, 83, 97, 101–2, 106, 113, 116, 122, 124, 128, 138, 150, 158, 162–63, 182, 211, 224, 235, 236, 248, 274, 291, 299, 307–10, 326, 336, 340, 354, 362, 364, 366, 380, 399, 405, 422, 437, 444, 575, 583, 655, 657, 663, 667, 679
Eyes of the Law columns 364–65, 663
'Thinking Aloud' column 645
Irish Times Trust 308
Irish Transport and General Workers' Union (ITGWU) 71, 399, 475, 489, 492, 520, 522, 531, 670
Irish United Nations Association 429
Irish University Club, London 161
Irish University Review 224
Irish Volunteer movement 235, 239
Irish War of Independence (1919–21) 79, 149, 154, 155, 223, 236, 244, 246, 248, 282, 387
Irish Women United 90
Irish Women's Liberation Movement (IWLM) 45, 89, 90, 94, 622, 641, 658, 660–64
'Chains or Change?' 658, 660–61
Irish Workers League 64
Irish Workers Party 64, 105
Irish-Americans 25, 81, 153–57, 438, 449, 451, 555
Irishwomen United 354, 672, 678
Irvine, John 292
Irwin, Jonathan 454
Isa bin Salman Al-Khalifa Amir, Sheikh 449
islanders 561–64
ITV 200, 291
Iveagh House, Dublin 143, 183, 416, 427, 436

J

Jacob's biscuit factory 396
James, Clive 285
Jammets restaurant, Dublin 575
Jeffrey, George 504
Jenkins, Roy 411, 419–20
Joe Walsh Tours (JWT) 586
John F. Kennedy Park (Slieve Coillte), Wexford 614
John XXIII, Pope 620
John Paul II, Pope 361, 622, 652–56
Johnson, Des 294–95
Johnston, Jennifer 283
How Many Miles to Babylon 226
The Gates 282
Jordan, John 282
Jordan, Kevin 418–19
Jordan, Neil 262, 291
journalism 227–28, 306–7
Judd, Frank 217
judiciary, women in the 93
Judt, Tony 3–4
junior ministers 40
Juries Act 365, 667
'Just Society' 60, 62, 112, 367, 670
Juventus FC 321

K

Kahn, Frank 87
Kaplin, Anatoli 428
Kavaja, Nikola 440
Kavanagh, John 257
Keane, John B. 265
Keane, Moss 323
Kearney, Richard 224, 226, 287
Translations 226–27
Keating, Justin 71, 97–98, 304, 343, 404, 496, 518, 528, 529, 532–35, 548, 614
Keating, Michael 63
Keating, Paul 9, 120, 218, 238, 409, 412, 437–38, 444–45
Keating, Seán 98
Keatinge, Patrick: *The Formulation of Irish Foreign Policy* 427
Keats, John 195
Kee, Robert 132
Keery, Neville 401–5
Kehoe, Emmanuel 307
Kelly, Dáithí 260
Kelly, District Justice 572
Kelly, Frank 23
Kelly, Captain James 142, 144, 145, 148
Kelly, Senator and TD, John 16, 128, 150–51, 256, 471
academic career 30

and AIM 667
'baboons' remark 58–59
and Bloody Sunday 130–31
and the Bula agreement 535
capturing a Senate seat 47
and crime issue 349
and EEC membership 394
elected to the Senate 30, 107
and energy conservation 536
and family law 370
on Fianna Fáil 60, 61, 65, 151
hubris of 65
an intellectual in Irish politics 65
Ireland's foremost constitutional expert 10, 30, 102, 111, 114
on Irish political power 27
and Lynch 149
and nuclear power 531
and patronage 30–31, 45
and the Press 101
prowess as an orator 65
soul-searching about Fine Gael 59–61
and stereotyping 63
and tourism 455
Kelly, John (a Belfast Republican) 142
Kelly, Luke 269
Kelly, Maeve 284
Kelly, Nicky 327, 345
Kelly, Oisín 234
Kelly, Pearse 105
Kelly, Petra 531
Kelly, William 453
Kennan, Austin 485
Kennan, Seán 389
Kennedy, Denis 150, 399, 403
Kennedy, Eamonn 120
Kennedy, Senator Edward 153, 156, 157, 220, 439
Kennedy, Senator Fintan 510
Kennedy, Geraldine 75, 310, 645
Kennedy, John F. 614
Kennedy, Kieran and Bruton, Richard: *The Irish Economy* 462
Kennedy, Sr Stanislaus 478
Kennedy Report (1970) 331, 375, 376
Kennelly, Brendan 451
Kenny, Enda 35
Kenny, Henry 35, 40
Kenny, John Joseph 596
Kenny, Mary 45, 195, 309, 424, 651, 660–61, 664
Kenny, Pat 298
Kenny Report (1974) 596
Keogh, Dermot 81, 147
Kerr, Muriel 586
Kerrigan, Gene 70, 195, 271, 293, 298, 327, 351, 520, 580
Kerryman, The 310
Kevin Street College of Technology, Dublin 483, 637
Kiberd, Declan 26, 136, 255, 278, 284, 287, 407, 651
Kiely, Benedict 283
Kiernan, Tom 323
Kildare 565
Kilkenny conference (1971) 464
Kilkenny Social Services 378, 478
Kilkenny Urban District Council 666
Killanin, Lord 454, 455, 526
Killarney National Park 491
Kilmainham Jail museum 236
Kilmichael ambush (1920) 244
Kilroy, Thomas: *Talbot's Box* 264
Kilrush, County Clare 530
King Sitric fish restaurant, Howth 575
Kinlen, Dermot 158, 653–54
Kinsale, Cork 527, 528, 576
Kinsella, Seán 575
Kinsella, Thomas 286
Butcher's Dozen 286
Notes from the Land of the Dead 286
Kirwan, Walter 9, 51, 412, 415–16, 421, 499, 520, 671
Kissinger, Dr Henry 438
Knatchbull, Nicholas 214
Knights of Columbanus 650
Knock 644, 655
Korda, Alberto 440

L

La Mon House hotel, County Down massacre 218
Labour Court 514–15, 520, 669
Labour Force surveys
1975 565
1977 492
1979 666
Labour Party (British) 173
Labour Party (Ireland)
annual conferences 68, 398
annual report (1972–3) 67
coalition government (1973–7) 2, 17, 32, 62, 68, 69, 70
commissions Gallup poll (1969) 106
European Affairs Committee 404
general election (1969) 15
intellectual stars and personalities of 17
internal tensions 66–70
and Irish EEC membership 387, 398, 404, 406
Kelly's 'baboons' remark 58, 59
Liaison Committee of the Left 68–69, 532, 533
and Offences Against the State Bill 198

oldest of the dominant Irish political parties 16–17, 32
'Poverty in Ireland' report (1973) 477
'purges' 68
refusal to countenance coalition (1960s) 17
support base 16
and voting age 94–95
Labour Women's National Council 669
Ladies Gaelic Football Association 319
Laffan, Michael 223
Lalor, Paddy 159, 526, 532
Lamartine, Alphonse de 407
land
evaluation 504
ownership 14
re-zoning 596
speculation 596
Land Commission 562, 563
Land of Ireland, The (BBC documentary) 450
Land Registry 249–50
Landlord and Tenant Law Bill (prposed) 596
Langan, Peter 576
Langan's restaurant, Piccadilly, London 576
Laois 335
Larkin, Denis 445, 470
Last Remake of Beau Geste, The (film) 304
Late Late Show, The (RTÉ programme) 183, 228, 293, 304, 380, 661–62
Lavery, Don 112, 113, 346
Lavin, Mary 253, 281
Law Library 363
law reform 369
Law Reform Commission (LRC) 330, 367, 368, 370, 372
le Brocquy, Louis 287
Le Monde newspaper 74
lead deposits 532, 533, 535
League of Nations 425–26
Leahy, Dr Patrick 293
leaked information 33, 56–57, 102, 149, 182–83, 436
Lean, David 451
Leavy, Pat 262
Lebanon 346, 390, 432
Lee, Joe 400, 461, 462, 468, 474–75, 500, 523, 528, 626
Leeds United FC 321
legal aid 362
legal profession, criticism of 330
legal system: need to redesign 330
Legion of Mary 444
Leigue cemetery, Ballina 211
Leinster 565
Leinster House, Dublin 49, 54, 66, 76, 86, 150, 163, 304, 446, 663
Leinster House Press Gallery 582–83
Leitrim 551
Lemass, Frank 526–27
Lemass, Taoiseach Seán 20, 71, 80, 96, 101, 189, 232–33, 388, 459, 527, 608
Lenehan, Senator Joe 663
Lenihan, Brian 48, 84, 96, 102, 177, 202, 420, 522
Lennon, Patrick, Bishop of Kildare and Leighlin 207
Leonard, Hugh
Da 263, 293–94
A Life 260, 263
The Patrick Pearse Motel 257
Time Was 263
Leopardstown races 311, 494
L'Escargot (horse) 324
Leslie, Desmond 175
L'Estrange, Gerry 554
Letterfrack Industrial School 381
Levine, June 662, 663–64
Levine, Les 279
Liberties Festival, Dublin 571
Libya 536
Licensed Vintners Association 579
licensing laws 454, 454–55, 578, 580
life expectancy 568, 597
Lillis, Michael 154
Limerick 348, 677
Lisdoonvarna Festival 269
Lisdoonvarna matchmaking festival, County Clare 450–51
Listowel Writers Week 269
Lithuania 445
Little Company of Mercy Nuns 647
Littlejohn affair (Kevin and Keith Littlejohn) 151–52
Living City group 590
living standards 8, 70, 315, 463, 511
Local Appointments Commission 31
local elections
1974 43, 91
1979 29
local government
election to local authorities 26
local elections 29
loss of political and economic autonomy 25
power limits 18, 26, 29
static nature of 19
Local Government Act (1946) 42
localism 55, 555
Loftus, Seán 526
Logan Airport 156
Logue, Hugh 126, 187
London School of Economics 427, 484
Long Island, off West Cork 564
Long Kesh, near Lisburn 156, 167, 209, 211, 218
Longford 80, 566
Longford Leader 307
Longford News 307

Longley, Michael 284–85
Loreto Convent, North Great George's Street, Dublin 675
Loughan House project 360, 383
Louth County Council 216
Loyalists 126, 127, 171, 172, 179, 184, 186, 197, 201, 202–3
Lucey, Bishop Cornelius 648
Luggala, County Wicklow 286–87
Lunny, Donal 268
LWT 158
Lynch, Taoiseach Jack 16, 50, 96, 101, 124, 133–34, 154–55, 164, 188, 193, 210, 461, 511, 582
  Anglo-Irish Treaty anniversary 233
  and apartheid 448
  and Arms Trial episode 141, 142, 145–50, 219
  and Bloody Sunday 129–30, 131
  broadcast at outset of the Troubles 143
  and burning of British Embassy 128–29
  on church and state 643–44
  and the civil service 53
  and the civil war 232–33
  and confidentiality breaches 33, 102
  and the constitution 190
  criticism of 36, 81, 231
  and de Valera 87
  disappointed with EEC progress 414
  and Dublin Theatre Festival 259
  and education 632, 633, 636
  EEC referendum 400
  and emigration 555
  and the environment 613, 615
  and film industry 302, 304, 306
  and the GAA 80, 81, 108, 318
  hands-off approach 80
  and inner-city problems 570
  on the IRA 218
  Irish-Americans' views of 155–56
  leads the Fianna Fáil government (1969–73) 2
  and legal aid 362
  Littlejohn affair 151–52
  loss of trust in people 103
  McGee case 675–76
  and the media 163
  meetings with Callaghan 187, 218
  meetings with Northern Irish politicians 181
  meets Brandt 139, 159–60
  and Molloy's allegation 43
  Mountbatten's death 214
  and the NFDA 56–57
  and nominations to the Senate 108
  and oil/gas exploration 527
  and O'Malley 86
  and Pan European Union anniversary 393, 397
  and the papal visit 652
  and party funding 37
  and pay agreements 470
  and Pearse commemoration 240, 241
  personal papers 9–10, 82, 83, 88
  personality 81, 82, 83, 320
  popularity 60, 79–80, 82
  and poverty 64
  and Protestant community in the Republic 138
  replaced by coalition government 3
  resignation 219
  response to the Northern crisis 81, 82
  and reunification 216
  secret meeting with Hume and Currie 187
  and smoking 607–8, 609
  speech to EEC heads of government (1972) 394
  and strikes 515–16, 521
  Suárez's visit to Dublin 417–18
  succeeds Lemass 80
  successor to 88, 97, 220
  and the Sunningdale communiqué 177–78
  and talking directly to those engaged in violence 136
  talks with Heath 129–30, 131–32
  and telephone network 311–12
  titular ICEM president 405
  tries to undermine support for the IRA 151, 152
  and unemployment 64–65
  and a united Ireland 217
  upbeat speech about the economy 522–23
  and visits abroad 449
  warned against meddling in the affairs of Northern Ireland 125
  and women TDs 90
  and women's status 659, 667
  and Wood Quay 252
  and young voters 95
Lynch, Judge Kevin 533, 534
Lynch, Mary 507
Lynch, Maureen 82, 83, 86, 676
Lynch, Patrick 133

Lynott, Phil 272
Lyons, Leland 117, 128, 132, 245–46
Ireland Since the Famine 92, 128, 223, 386
Lyons, Patrick 476
Lyric Theatre, Dublin 257

M
McAleese, Mary 105, 310
McAllister, Ian 187
Mac Anna, Tomás 261
MacAnthony, Joe 311, 604
Mac Aonghusa, Proinsias 84, 295, 374–75
McAteer, Eddie 120, 217, 218
McAteer, Fergus 218
McBride, Big Tom 268, 271
McBride, Willie John 323
Mac Bride, Seán 95, 434, 531
McCabe, Fergus 572
McCafferty, Nell 30, 195, 310, 355–56, 357, 366, 380, 583, 644, 654–55, 658, 659, 660, 662–63, 672, 673, 678
In the Eyes of the Law 310
'In the Eyes of the Law' column 364–65
McCann, Eamonn 121, 122
McCann, Hugh 120, 125, 152, 390, 397, 437
McCarthy, Charles 462, 522
The Distasteful Challenge 19
McCarthy, Dan 422
Mac Conghail, Muiris 77, 105, 175, 177, 291, 293, 295
McConnell, G.B. 138
McCormick, James 599–600
Mac Curtain, Margaret 18, 618, 621
Mac Curtain, Margaret and Ó Corráin, Donncha, eds: *Women in Irish Society: The Historical Dimension* 658–59
McDonagh, Bobby 401, 425
McDonagh, Fr Enda 620, 645
MacDonagh, Thomas 238
McDonald, Charlie 420, 421
McDonald's 577
McDonnell, Patrick 578, 579
McDonnell, Tim 263
MacEntee, Patrick 345
Mac Entee, Seán 87
McGahern, John 226, 638
The Dark 227, 282
The Leavetaking 283
Nightlines 283
The Pornographer 283
McGee, Jimmy 308
McGee, Mary 673
McGee case 622, 645, 646, 673, 674, 675–76
Mac Giolla Choile, Brendan 249
McGlinchey, Senator 139
McGonagles pub, Dublin 273
McGowan, John 154
McGowan's of Blackrock, County Dublin 581–82
McGrath, Joseph 604, 605
McGrath, Patrick 311, 605
McGreevy, Desmond 443
Mac Gréil, Fr Mícheál 571, 646
McGuinness, Jim 105, 166–67
McGuire, John and Ned 472
McGurk, Gerard 195
McInerney, Michael 38
McIvor, Basil 177
McKay, Susan 195
Macken, Eddie 324
Macken, Matthew 525
McLaren, Bill 323
McLaughlin, Hugh 308
McLaughlin, Patrick 328, 344
MacLiammóir, Micheál 261–62
The Importance of Being Oscar 261
Prelude in Kasbek Street 261
MacMahon, Bryan: *A Pageant of Pearse* 242
McMahon, Marie 354–55
Mac Mathúna, Ciarán 268
McNally, Brian 345
MacNeill, Eoin 239
McQuaid, John Charles, Archbishop of Dublin 191, 380, 620, 635, 641–42, 662
Macroom Mountain Dew Festival 272
MacSharry, Ray 97, 139
McSorley, Gerard 262
Mac Stiofáin, Seán 164, 198, 228
MacSwiney, Terence 282
McTernan, Fr Oliver 558
Mac Uistin, Liam: 'Rinneadh Aisling Dúinn' (We Saw a Vision) 232
McVerry, Fr Peter 351, 572
Madden, Aodhan 135, 248, 583, 585
magazines 309–10
Magee, Fr John 652
Magheramorne Presbyterians 165
Magill magazine 11, 30, 53, 63, 81, 147, 148, 159, 162, 195, 208, 228, 239, 280, 290, 298, 309, 312, 322, 344, 351, 356, 377, 382, 477, 481, 484, 485, 494, 505, 507, 511, 520, 571, 575, 580, 585, 597, 599, 609, 630, 664, 672
Magill national poll (1977) 216
Magill Book of Irish Politics 44
Maher, Denis 395, 409
Maher, Mary 622, 660, 663
Maher, T.J. 516
Mahon, Derek 225, 285
Maintenance Orders Act (1974) 371–72, 622, 666

Malahide shipyard, County Dublin 235
Maloney, Oliver 105, 228
Maloney, Paddy 287
Manning, Maurice 211
Mannion, Marie 563
Mansergh, Martin 9
Mansholt, Most Reverend Dr 399–400
Mansion House, Dublin 582, 662
Maoists 64
Marathon Oil 527, 528
Marcus, David 143, 284
Marcus, Louis 302–3
  Revival: Pearse's Concept of Ireland 242
Margaret, HRH Princess 310, 576
Margrethe of Denmark, Queen 252
Marketing Society 395
Markievicz, Constance 92, 93, 344
marriage 193
  average ages of bride and groom 566–67
  bad 355, 356
  born outside marriage 381, 382, 567
  break down 623, 649
  desertion 371, 667
  dowry 450–51
  ending in divorce 567
  fertility in 567
  minimal legal age 371, 373
  mixed 192, 240
  nullity of 370, 371, 372
  rise in marriage rate 541, 567
  violence in 330–31
marriage bar 464, 622, 661, 666
Marron, Monsignor Eamon 653
Martin, F.X. 251
Martin, Janet 355
Martin, Michael Craig 280
Marx, Karl 398
Mason, Roy 157, 217, 218
maternity leave 622
Matthews, Alan 430, 505, 552
Maudling, Reginald 157
Maume, Patrick 145, 203
Maxwell, Paul 214
May Day rally (1970) 63–64
Maynooth College 209, 640, 645, 648, 649
Mayo 549, 554, 566
  bishops' meeting (1974) 643
Mayo County Council 40, 644
Maze prison, Long Kesh, near Lisburn 156, 167, 209, 211, 218, 361
  H Blocks 209, 236
Meaney, Colm 262
Meath 565
media
  cabinet memorandum on relations with 103
  coalition's crackdown on media freedom 104
  coverage of the Troubles 158–59, 162–67
  growing distrust between media and politicians 124
  leftist bias in news reports 64
  magazines 309–10
  newspapers 307–9
  O'Brien dissects views of newspapers 103–4
  public service broadcasting 5, 46
  RTÉ 104–5
  see also broadcasting; Press, the
medical cards 600, 602, 603
medical profession 543–44, 599–601, 606
medical social workers 606
Medical Union 517
Medico-Social Research Board 348, 609–10
Meehan, Sylvia 665
Meenan, James 454, 458
  The Irish Economy Since 1922 458
Meeting Place pub, Dublin 268
Melody Maker (music paper) 279
mental health 598–99
Merlin Park, Galway 374
Merriman Summer School 286
Merry, Bruce 294
Metropole cinema, Dublin 304
Mhac an tSaoi, Máire 99
Miami Showband 203
Middle East crisis 4, 466
migration 541, 549, 554, 560, 566
Mills, Michael 49, 60, 102, 103, 108, 132, 178, 219, 310, 582–83
Millstreet, County Cork 314
Milton Bradley Company 521
minimum wage 463
mining 532–35
ministers
  conflict of interest 41
  private secretaries to 53–54
  salaries 101
Ministries and Secretaries Act (1924) 20
Ministry of Defence (British) 151
Mirabeau restaurant, Dún Laoghaire 575
Mirror Mirror fashion chain 586
Missionary Magazine 651
Misuse of Drugs Act (1977) 350, 605
Mitchell, Jim 521–22
Mitchell, John 407
Mitchell and Sons wine merchants 581

Mná na hÉireann (Women of Ireland) 676
Mollan, Charles 375, 382
Molloy, Bobby 40, 43–44, 487–88, 563, 588–89, 596
Molloy, Jack 500
Moloney, Ed 208–9
Monaghan 35, 139, 335
bombings (1974) 124, 178, 198, 202, 517
Monday Club 131
moneylenders 475, 476
Monkstown, Dublin 138
Montague, John 195, 285
'A Resigned President' 118
'The Rough Field' 1
Montessori schools 303
Montgomery, Niall 237
Moody, Janet 291
Moody, T.W. 246, 247
'Irish History and Irish Mythology' (an address) 246
Moondance (album) 270
Moore, Brian 286
Moore, Christy 136, 209, 268–69, 531, 560, 657–58
Moore, Dan 324
Moore, Bishop Edward 471, 486
Moore, John D. 109, 437, 439
Moore, J.P. 599
Moore, Seán 480
Moran's Hotel, Dublin 199, 273
Morash, Christopher 257, 299, 308
Morrison, George 306
Morrison, Van 270–71
Morrissey, Eamon 23
Mountbatten, Lord Louis 214, 219, 260
Mountjoy Prison, Dublin 204, 205, 359, 360, 361
Moyne, Lord 131
Moynihan, Patrick 157
MRBI survey (1973) 646
Muintir na Tíre (People of the Land) 552
Mulcahy, John 11, 227, 448
Mulcahy, Noel 401
Mulcahy, Richard 155, 244, 608
Mulcahy, Risteard 155–56, 543, 608, 609
Mulcahy, Vivian 579–80
Mullaghmore, County Sligo 214, 260
Mulligan's pub, Poolbeg Street, Dublin 580
Mullins, Denis 350
Mullins, Tom 36
Munster rugby team 323
Murphy, Annie 650
Murphy, Caroline 300
Murphy, Francis 672
Murphy, Gary 389
Murphy, John A. 25, 123–24, 134, 135, 236, 239, 243, 277, 299–300, 407, 547, 621, 644, 646, 657
Ireland in the Twentieth Century 25
Murphy, Johnny 263
Murphy, Mary 672
Murphy, Fr Pádraig 180–81
Murphy, Patsey 658
Murphy, Suzanne 274
Murphy, Tom
Conversations on a Homecoming 258
A Crucial Week in the Life of a Grocer's Assistant 657
The Morning After Optimism 257, 258
The Sanctuary Lamp 258
A Whistle in the Dark 258
Murphy Report (2009) 379, 643
Murray, Charles 9, 53, 363
Murray, Ciarán 570
Murray, David 378
Murray, Frank 9, 51, 140, 155, 159, 341–42, 610
Murray, Marie 211–12, 335
Murray, Noel 211–12, 335
Murray, Fr Raymond 179
Murray, Thomas 613
music 5, 229, 266–76
Myers, Kevin 164, 308, 590
Myrdal, Gunnar: *Beyond the Welfare State* 55

N

Nader, Ralph 383
Nairn, Ian 454
Nally, Dermot 9, 51, 54, 126, 176, 178, 185, 264–65, 373, 415, 419, 438, 439, 449, 473, 509, 511, 535, 569, 570, 591, 610–11
Nash, Dr John 348
National Archives Act (1986) 9
National Archives of Ireland 9, 76, 82, 123, 129, 390
National Association of Tenants Organisations 571
National Association of Widows 659
National Bank 513
National College of Art 279
National Concert Hall, Dublin 255
National Conference of Priests of Ireland 620–21
National Council for Civil Liberties 131
National Council for Sport and Physical Recreation (COSAC) 315
National Council of Priests 649
National Economic and Social Council (NESC) 426, 606–7
'Towards a Social Report' 566
National Environmental Council 613
National Farmers Association 399, 516, 550, 552

National Film Studios of Ireland 305
National Flat Dwellers' Association (NFDA) 56, 57
National Gallery of Ireland 281
National Health Council Reports 604, 605–6, 673
National Income Tax Reform Organisation 504
National Institute of Higher Education, Limerick 405, 637
National Land League 237, 422, 551
National Library of Ireland 227, 251
National Library of Ireland Society 251
National Museum 227
National Off Licence Traders Association 578
national parks 452
National Prices Commission 482
National Prices Committee 573
National Register of Voters 37
National Road Safety Association 589
National Stadium 263
National Theatre (London) 260
National Tourism Council 453
National Understanding for economic and social development (1979) 511, 521, 522, 523
National Union of Journalists 306, 334
National University of Ireland 48
National Wage Agreements 71, 462, 497, 509, 510, 511, 521
National Youth Council of Ireland 95, 383
nationalism 14, 223, 235, 236, 246, 247, 407, 458
Nationalist Party 120
nationalization 514
natural resources 8
Navan site 533, 534
Nealon, Ted 53, 104, 213
Neary, Peter 468
Neeson, Liam 262
New History of Ireland series 223
'New Republic' 73
New Right 7
New Unionist Movement 135
New York Times 117, 451
New Zealand: women in politics 91
Newman, Jeremiah, Bishop of Limerick 648
Newry 171
Newry and Mourne District Council 216
newspapers 307–9
Ní Bhríain, Doireann 300
Ní Dhomhnaill, Nuala 284, 285
Nightbus (radio programme) 298
Nixon, Pat 83
Nixon, Richard 83, 103, 436, 437, 448, 517
Nolan, John E. 297
Non Stop Connolly Show 17
Noonan, Arthur 142
NORAID (Irish Northern Aid Committee) 153–54, 156, 157
Norris, David 584
North Central Community Council 571, 572
North Clare Creamery, Ennistymon 540
Northern Executive 177
Northern Ireland
abolition of its domestic government (1972) 125
British withdrawal 169, 170, 171, 185, 190, 209, 217–20
cabinet subcommittee on 141, 144
Childers's comments on American television 111
and Fine Gael 62
FitzGerald on violent incidents in 160–61
ignorance about 135–36, 195
internment without trial 125
Labour Party's divisions over the Northern Ireland question 67
Lynch and Cosgrave defend Irish government's record 160
Lynch's response to the Northern crisis 81, 82
O'Brien unable to debate in Senate 47
O'Brien's pronouncements on 98
refugees from 137, 169
repartitioning 169, 170, 184
shipping of arms to 64, 157
Thornley's Republican stance 69–70
Northern Ireland Assembly 175, 219
Northern Ireland Civil Rights Association (NICRA) 121, 131
Northern Ireland Office 173, 174, 212, 213
northern nationalism 141
Northern Nationalists 122, 124, 133, 141, 145, 149, 163, 166, 170, 179, 180
Norway
cultural agreement with Ireland 425
oil and gas resources 529

Nowlan, Kevin B. 615
nuclear non-proliferation
treaty (1968) 433
nuclear power 525, 530,
531–32
Nuclear Safety Association
531
Nyerere, Julius 448

O

O Brádaigh, Ruairí 153, 211
Ó Briain, Justice Barra 345
O Briain, Colm 225, 265, 288
Ó Cinnéide, Séamus 463–
64, 477
Ó Conaill, Dáithi 158, 208
Ó Dálaigh, Judge Cearbhall
157, 316, 368, 425, 647
appointed a member of
the European Court
363–64
culturally sophisticated
117
on de Valera 244
and EEC entry 401
and Emergency Powers
Act 214, 346
and Herrema 114–15
inauguration 109
insulted by Patrick
Donegan (1976) 10,
17–18, 97, 112–14, 115,
116
and Murrays' death
sentence 212
papers of 10, 114–17, 363
resignation 10, 97, 112, 114,
116, 117
succeeded by Hillery 118
valued by the Arts
community 118
Ó Donnachadha, DJ 663
Ó Fiaich, Archbishop Dr
Tomás 209, 210, 218, 648,
652
Ó hEithir, Breandán 319
Ligh Sinn i gCathú 278
Ó hUiginn, Seán 653
Ó Móráin, Dónall 166, 290
Ó Móráin, Micheál 142, 145,
146, 148, 334, 362–63
Ó Riada, Ruth 266
Ó Riada, Seán 266–67, 306,
407
Ó Riada foundation 266
Ó Súilleabháin, Micheál 267
Ó Tuathagh, Gearóid 640
O'Brien, Conor Cruise 17,
123, 133, 149, 175, 188
accused of manufacturing
propaganda 158
agnosticism 645
appears in broadcasts of a
history series 290
and broadcasting of Dáil
proceedings 46
and burning of the British
Embassy 128
and Childers 110
and commemorations 233
a committed Unionist
98–99
Communist Party
membership 64
and Cosgrave 75, 76, 77
description of 1916 239
and Dublin/Monaghan
bombings 200
edits the *Observer* 98, 163
and EEC membership
399
elected to the Senate 47
encounter with Dr John
O'Connell 181
on Garda attitudes 348
hatred of Haughey 85–86
and Herrema affair 343
and *Hibernia* 162, 228
historian and diplomat 10
international profile 78
a Labour Party
intellectual 66, 96
and liberation movements
429–30
Máire Mhac an tSaoi
on 99
and the media 104, 124,
164, 165, 166, 182
opposes dialogue with
IRA 207
on Pearse 241
personality 98
preoccupied with religion
166
and private secretaries to
ministers 53, 54
pronouncements on
Northern Ireland 98
rejects call for an 'Ulster
Dominion' 174
revisionism 247
and the SDLP 125, 182,
183, 184
and telephone network
312, 519
two nations theory 191,
246
warns of possible civil
war 132
States of Ireland 98, 165,
183
O'Brien, Edna 281, 283, 424
The Country Girls 281
A Pagan Place 281
O'Brien, Lieutenant
Colonel Kevin 171
O'Brien, Vincent 324
O'Brien's pub, Leeson
Street, Dublin 580
O'Byrne, John 575
O'Carroll, John F. 475
O'Casey, Seán
Juno and the Paycock 257
The Plough and the Stars
257
The Shadow of a Gunman
257
O'Clery, Conor 162–63
O'Connell, Daniel 236–37
O'Connell, Deirdre 262–63
O'Connell, James (prison
chaplain) 204
O'Connell, Dr John 66–68,
181, 207, 208, 343, 543
O'Connell, Maurice 78
O'Connell Street Business
Association 518

O'Connor, Christy, Jr 324
O'Connor, Chub 28–29
O'Connor, Donough 527
O'Connor, Edmond 139–40
O'Connor, John 267
O'Connor, Seán 9, 619, 627
O'Connor, Thomas P. 20
O'Connor, Tim 90
O'Connor, Ulick 81, 228, 240, 261–62, 284, 312, 381, 575, 585
O'Conor, John 274
O'Doherty, Brian 279
O'Donnell, Anne 357
O'Donnell, Dr Brendan 377
O'Donnell, Catherine 253
O'Donoghue, Martin 50, 96, 461, 499–500, 501, 508
O'Donoghue's pub, Merrion Row, Dublin 268, 580–81
O'Dowd, H. J. (Bertie) 9, 51, 54, 114, 445, 450, 454
O'Dowd, Niall 555–56
O'Driscoll, Brian 212
O'Duffy, Eoin 344
O'Dwyer, Mick 320
O'Faoláin, Julia
  No Country for Young Men 283
  Not in God's Image 282, 658
O'Faoláin, Nuala 195, 286, 548, 598
O'Faoláin, Seán 47, 282, 290, 353
O'Flynn, Liam 268
O'Grady, Geraldine 275
O'Hanlon, Rory 522
O'Herlihy, Bill 292
O'Higgins, Tom 110, 395
O'Kelly, Kevin 228
O'Kelly, Seán T. 390
O'Kennedy, Michael 195, 218, 315, 316, 395, 417, 421, 447, 448, 536–37
O'Laoghaire, Liam 306
O'Leary, David 321
O'Leary, Michael 3, 71, 188, 351, 367, 425, 497, 498, 508, 510–11, 518, 577, 622, 668–69, 670
O'Leary, Olivia 300
O'Mahoney, David 405
O'Mahoney, T.P. 541, 651
O'Malley, Cormac 155
O'Malley, Desmond 46, 86, 106–7, 122, 132, 144, 147, 148, 163, 198, 250, 336, 480, 485, 529, 530, 531, 535, 536–37, 578, 579, 610, 667
O'Malley, Donogh 86, 248, 619, 635
O'Malley, Ernie 155, 236
  The Singing Flame 236
O'Malley, Joseph 62, 106
O'Maoláin, Tomás 381
O'Neill, Terence 120
O'Neill, Congress Speaker T.P. ('Tip') 156, 157, 220, 435
O'Neill's shoe shop, Dublin 199
O'Nualláin, Colm 20–21
O'Raifeartaigh, Terence 243, 259, 407
O'Reilly, Jean 586
O'Riordan, Michael 64
O'Rourke, Mícheál 274
O'Shannon, Cathal 75, 583
O'Sullivan, Dan 51, 250
O'Sullivan, Donal 159, 161, 173, 174, 557
O'Sullivan, Gilbert 271
O'Sullivan, Harold 510
O'Toole, Liam 312, 520
Observer newspaper 98, 163, 285
Offences Against the State Act 163, 198, 210, 362
Offences Against the State (Amendment) Bill (1972) 112
Office of Public Works 51, 129, 234, 235, 252, 452, 654
Office of the Minister for Labour 515
Office of the Minister for Public Service 49–50
Official IRA 141, 158, 172
Official Secrets Act 57
Official Sinn Féin 92, 93, 105, 172–73, 211, 344
oil 525–31
  exploration 526–31
  oil spillages in Bantry Bay 526
  proposed refinery in Dublin Bay 525–26
  reducing dependence on 525
oil crises 6, 466, 467–68, 479, 480, 510, 525, 529, 531
old-age pensions 72, 479
Oliver Dowling Gallery, Dublin 280
Olympia Theatre, Dublin 260, 262, 381
Olympic Games (Munich, 1972) 160, 315, 322, 400
Ombudsman
  Irish 31, 48, 49
  Northern Ireland 645
Opera magazine 275
opinion polls 106
Orange Lodge members 139
Organisation for Economic Co-operation and Development (OECD) 432, 433
Organisation for European Economic Co-operation (OEEC) 406
Orpen, Hilary 300
Osborough, Nial 330
Oscar Theatre, Dublin 260
Outlook (television programme) 294
Outukumpu 534
Ovett, Steve 322
Owens, Senator Evelyn 669
Oyster Tavern, Cork 575

P

Paisley, Ian 174, 176, 653
Páistí ag Obair (Children at Work) (film) 303

Pakenham, Thomas 214
Palestine Liberation Organisation 433
Pan American Airways 428, 437
Pan European Union 393, 397
Parent Concern 676
Parent School Movement 627
parking fines 353
Parkinson, Louise 446
parliamentary privilege 43, 64
parliamentary reform 8
parliamentary secretaries 40
Parnell, Charles Stewart 237
Parochial House, Armagh 179
parochialism 91, 416
Partition of Ireland 2, 219, 389
patronage 95
  Fianna Fáil 30–31, 103
  Fine Gael 31, 45
Patterson, Frank 274
Paul VI, Pope 620, 655–56
Paxman, Jeremy 136
Pay Related Social Insurance (PRSI) 72
PAYE workers 507, 508, 509
Peace Movement 186
Peacock Theatre, Dublin 264
Pearse, Patrick Henry 25, 114, 219, 237, 238–42, 583
Pearse Commemoration Committee 240, 241
Pearson, Noel 11, 228
Peck, Sir John 131, 216
Pender, Aidan 104, 394
Penguin Book of Irish Poetry, The 269
Penneys store 484
People before Profit 474
Perdue, R.G., Bishop of Cork 140
Period of Transition, A (album) 271
personality cult 79–80
Peters, Mary 322
Pfizer Chemical Corporation project 515
Phibsboro First National bank 294–95
Philbin, William Joseph, Bishop of Down and Connor 193
Philip, HRH Prince, Duke of Edinburgh 214
Phoblacht, An 308
Phoenix Park, Dublin 110, 452, 654
pig smuggling 353
Pinochet, General 444
Pioneer Total Abstinence Association 578
P.J. Carroll and Company 609
planning authorities 615
Planxty 268
Plunkett, James 17
  Strumpet City 17
Plunkett, Oliver, Catholic Archbishop of Armagh 237–38, 647
pluralism 540, 541
poetry 225–26, 284–86
Poitín (short film) 303
political reform 17, 46, 48
Pollak, Andy 171
pollution 612–16
population
  decline 554, 567
  growth 541
Port Harcourt, Nigeria 648
Portadown, Co. Armagh 203, 205
Portlaoise 89, 274
Portlaoise Prison 203, 206, 207, 208, 335, 359, 360, 361
Portmarnock Golf Club, County Dublin 323–24
poverty, the poor 5, 53, 64, 463–64, 475, 476, 477–78, 541, 649
power
  abuse of 679
  centralisation of 24
  of Conservatism 7
  cultural 8
  cynical approach to misusing 40
  distribution of 7
  economic 8
  knowledge as 28
  local government 18, 26, 29
  parent 629
  political 8
  power holders as control freaks 25
  Senate's limited powers 46
  sharing 2, 124, 131, 156, 163, 170, 174, 176, 178, 183, 184
  shift of political power 27
  social 8
Power, Anne: *Estates on the Edge: The Social Consequences of Mass Housing in Northern Europe Since 1850* 570
power cuts 517
Prendergast, Peter 312
Presbyterians 165, 192, 381
president
  Childers's campaign for a new style of presidency 110, 111
  inauguration 109
  largely ceremonial 109
  Ó Dálaigh's resignation 10, 97, 112, 114, 116, 117
  salary 111
  'sleepy president' stereotype 110
  tensions between president and government 110–11
  visibility and controversial profile 4
President for all the People, A (film) 112
Press, the
  censorship 104

commentary on politicians becomes more caustic 102–3
information leaked to 102
Kelly takes issue with newspapers and editors 101, 102
see also broadcasting; media
prices
coal 480
consumer 460, 467, 499
gas 150
grocery 482–83
house 6, 467, 484, 596
land 484, 596
oil 511, 525
petrol 496, 525
turf briquettes 480
war on 489
Prices Commission 482, 485
Prison Act (1970) 358
'Prisoner of Conscience' year 341
prisoners, prisons
after care 329
aiming at rehabilitation 358
alcoholic prisoners 359
amnesty issue 361
and clergy 205–8
complaints by prisoners 359
concessions 204
Cooney's tour of prisons 329
Daly on conditions 205, 651
demand for political status 204
'dirty protests' 208–9
hard core young offenders 348–49, 351
hunger strikers 181, 198, 205–8, 210–11, 345, 358, 361
increase in number of prisoners 358–59
increase in paramilitary prisoners 358
prisoner of war status 361
recidivism 329, 361
'siege mentality' in prisons 329
strip searches 207, 208, 358
young offenders 348–49, 360
Prisoners Rights Organisation 358, 571, 660
Prisons Bill (1972) 358
Proclamation (1916) 238, 239
Programme for Economic Recovery 466
Prohibition of Forcible Entry Bill 334, 663
Project Arts Centre, Dublin 262, 263, 584
proportional representation 60, 189
Prosecution of Offenders Act (1974) 368
Prosperous (album) 268
prostitution 354, 355, 356, 380, 592
protection 8, 20
Protestant Church 136
Protestantism: statistics 5
Protestants
Cosgrave on 194
in the Republic 138–40, 644–45
provincialism 407
Provisional IRA 105, 141, 142, 153, 154, 164, 165, 172, 202, 204, 209, 217, 228
Provisional Republican movement 172
Provisional Sinn Féin 172, 173, 186, 216
Psychiatric Nurses Association 520
Public Bodies Corrupt Practices Act (1889) 42
public health nurses 606
public holidays 497
Public Hospital Acts 604
Public Record Office 130
Public Record Office of Ireland 249, 250
Public Record Office of Northern Ireland 148
Public Service Advisory Council 20
public service reform 8, 20, 54
Purcell, Betty 300
Purcell, Jackie 586
Pyle, Fergus 106, 308

Q
Queen's University Belfast 31, 246, 284, 651
Quinn, Barney 515
Quinn, Bob 289, 303
Quinn, Brian 75, 104, 303, 365
Quinn, Feargal 473
Quinn, John 574
Quinn, Margaret 295
Quinn, Patricia 639–40
Quinn, Ruairí 72–73, 96, 349, 421, 615

R
Rabbitte, Pat 521
racing 324
radio 5, 46, 276, 295, 297
Radio Dublin 299
Radio Éireann 292
Radio Melinda 299
Radio na Gaeltachta 276, 289
Rafferty, Mick 572
Raftery, Mary 379, 599
rail travel 591
Rampling, Charlotte 304
rape 356–57, 623
Rás Tailteann (cycling race) 316
rate abolition issue 18, 616
rate collectors 44
Rathdrum Presbytery, County Wicklow 676
Rathlin O'Birne island 564
Rathmines 593

rating system 486–87, 488
Reagan, Ronald 436
Red Rag, The (student publication) 640
Red Rum (horse) 324
Redgrave, Michael 260
Rees, Merlyn 125, 173
regional family planning services 677
regional health boards 487
Reid, Alec 574–75
Report of the Commission on the Status of Women (1972) 622
Republican Labour Party 182
Republican News 308
republicanism 93, 98, 105, 231
  constitutional 123
resource transfers 413, 420
Resources Protection Campaign 172–73, 532
restaurants 574–77
reunification 173, 190, 192–93, 194, 216
Revenue commissioners 216
revisionism 247, 581
Reynolds, Albert 80, 97
Reynolds, David 95
Reynolds, Garda Michael 211–12. 335
Richard, Cliff 273
Ricoeur, Paul 287
Ring, Christy 320
Riordans, The (soap opera) 228, 293, 580
roads 29, 590
Roberts, Ruairí 659
Robinson, Senator Mary 18, 27, 92, 193, 253, 282, 353, 362, 381, 403, 406, 407, 428, 658, 662, 663, 664, 676–77
Roche, Thomas 532
Roche's stores 484
Rochfort, Sir Cecil Boyd 324
Rock, Patrick 225
Roe, Judge Frank 78
Roelofs, Helen Hooker O'Malley 236
Rogers, William 123
Rolling Stones 268, 271
Rory Gallagher Irish Tour 1974 (album) 270
ROSC exhibition of international contemporary art 279–80, 281
Roscommon 107, 552, 566
Rose of Tralee Festival, County Kerry 678
Rosenburg, Alfred 237
Rosenthal, Harold 275
Ross, Diana 273
Rossa, O'Donovan 240
Roundwood *cumann*, Wicklow 37
Royal Ascot 324
Royal College of Physicians 610
Royal Dublin Society 454
Royal family 214
Royal Hibernian Academy 265
  exhibition 281
Royal Hibernian Hotel, Dublin 417, 419
Royal Irish Constabulary (RIC) 201–2
Royal Opera House, Covent Garden, London 401
Royal Ulster Constabulary (RUC) 163, 167
RTÉ 41, 60, 64, 75, 84, 104–5, 112, 163–64, 166–67, 183, 212, 216, 217, 228, 229, 244, 261, 267–68, 274, 276, 289–303, 306, 318, 354, 380, 383, 475, 484, 519, 533, 582, 583, 655, 658, 661, 676
  RTÉ 1 station 296
  RTÉ 2 station 296, 297, 299, 322
  RTÉ Authority 81, 164, 198, 227, 228, 289, 301, 306, 476
  RTÉ Guide 300
  RTÉ Sport 296
  RTÉ symphony orchestra 274, 401
rugby 323
Russborough House, Wicklow 203
Rutland Street experiment, Dublin 628
Ryan, Declan 575–76
Ryan, Dermot, Catholic Archbishop of Dublin 191, 495, 630, 640, 642, 649, 650
Ryan, Dermot (hotelier) 88
Ryan, Senator Eoin 108, 395, 526
Ryan, James 387, 639
Ryan, Liam 559, 618
Ryan, Michael 575–76
Ryan, Richie 23, 48–49, 50, 53–54, 135, 152, 201, 233, 235, 276, 337, 338, 403, 413, 453, 461, 465–70, 473, 479, 483–84, 489–90, 495–96, 499, 504, 551, 563, 566, 579, 601, 602, 628, 630, 666
Ryan, Thomas, Catholic Bishop of Clonfert 189
Ryan Report (2009) 379
Ryan's Daughter (film) 251
Ryan's pub, Parkgate Street, Dublin 580

S

Sachs Hotel, Dublin 304, 580
Saffron, Inga 507, 592
St Brendan's Hospital, Grangegorman 598–99
St Enda's school, Dublin 240, 241
St John's church, Falls Road, Belfast 180
St Johnstone, Donegal 139
St Joseph's Industrial School 378

St Patrick's Cathedral, Dublin 198, 199, 212, 213, 335
St Patrick's College, Maynooth 111, 638
St Patrick's Day 233–34, 247, 438, 449
St Patrick's Hospital, Dublin 598, 599
St Patrick's Institution for Younger Offenders 359, 360, 380
St Paul's Cathedral, London 335
St Peter's College 379
St Vincent de Paul Society 563
St Vincent's Hospital, Dublin 593
St Vincent's Nursing Home, Dublin 213
Sallenstown, County Louth 530
Sallins train robbery (1976) 327–28, 344–45
Salmon, Revd T. 252
Salmon, Trevor 405
Salthill, Galway 44
Sandy Row area, Belfast 194, 195
Sandycove, County Dublin 286, 678
Sandyford, County Dublin 212
Sandymount, Dublin 593
Sanfrey, J.W. 150
Saor Éire (Free Ireland) 334
Saothar journal 69
Savage, Tom 83
Save the Equal Pay Act Committee 622–23, 664
Saville Report 131
Sayers, Peig 561
Scally, Séamus 69
Scandinavia: women in politics 91
Scarriff, Clare 90
Scheper-Hughes, Nancy: *Saints Scholars and Schizophrenics* 542
Schering Plough 514
Scott, Michael 253
Scott, Fr Patrick 217
Scott, Walter 334
Scott Medals 334
Scully, Seán 280
Seán Lemass Memorial Lecture, Exeter 459
Second Programme for Economic Expansion 475, 626
Second World War 205, 248, 308, 358, 362, 386, 470
sectarianism 126, 139, 140, 188, 648
secularism 7, 540, 679
security firms 352
Senate (Seanad Éireann)
 attitudes to 47
 effective use of 47
 enlarged 189
 restricted electorate and powers 46
 a truly representative 8
 vocationalism 46, 47
Seven Days (RTÉ programme) 84, 104, 105
 Tribunal of Inquiry 291–93, 475
sexual abuse 331, 378–80
sexual discrimination 622
Shakespeare, William 262
Shamrock Rovers 321
Shannon airport 211, 491
Shannon Free Airport Development Company 451, 491
Shannon Free Trade Industrial Zone 451
Shannon Industrial Estate 491
Share, Bernard 445
Shatter, Alan 355
Shaw, Fr Francis, SJ 239
 'The Canon of Irish History: A Challenge' 239
Shaw, George Bernard 236, 262
Sheehy, Hanna 47
Shelbourne Hotel 176
Sheridan, Jim 262, 381
Sheridan, Peter 262, 381
Sheridan, Peter and Flynn, Mannix: *The Liberty Suit – The Prison Life of Mannix Flynn* 262, 381
Sherkin Island Festival 269
Sherwin, Councillor Frank 583–84
Shiels, Brush 272
Shine, Brendan 273
Shovelton, Patrick 238
show jumping 34
Show Jumping World Championships 324
Shrimps Wine Bar, Dublin 581
Simmons, James 285
Simms, Anngret 252
Simms, George Otto, Church of Ireland Archbishop of Armagh 645
single mothers 558, 559
single transferable vote 24
Sinn Féin 190, 217, 223, 399
 Desmond FitzGerald prominent in 78–79
 and Fine Gael 62
 founded by Griffith 232, 237
 headquarters in Dublin closed down 210
 newspapers 307–8
 prisoners 205
 split in 172
Sinn Féin the Workers Party 172, 173
Sinnotts bar, Dublin 580
Sisters of Charity 593
Sisters of Mercy 376
Skeffington, Andrée Sheehy 398
Skeffington, Francis 47
Skeffington, Owen Sheehy 47–48, 353, 398

Skerries harbour, Dublin 564
Skid Row 272
Sligo 139, 566
Sligo/Leitrim Development Organisation 551
Slott, Susan 262
Smith, Brendan 255, 259, 260
Smith, Patrick 34
Smith, Sheamus 84, 105, 112, 292, 303–4
smoking 544, 605, 607–11
smuggling 353
Smyth, Ailbhe 93
soccer 321–22
social assistance services 478
Social Democratic and Labour Party (SDLP) 67, 121, 124, 125, 126, 133, 157, 163, 173–77, 179, 181–87, 188, 193, 205, 218, 220, 653
Social Fund 419
social reform 16, 60
social security 671–72
social services 476–77, 605
Social Studies (sociology journal) 542, 625
Social Welfare Act (1974) 622
social workers 331, 354, 374, 375, 378, 380, 476, 557, 559, 605, 606, 607
Socialist Labour Action Group 67
Socialist Labour Party (SLP) 70
Society of United Irishmen 231
Soul, David 273
South Africa 429, 445–46, 447
South County Dublin constituency 72
South Leinster 552
Spain: EEC membership application 417
Spanish Civil War 64
Spare Rib 354
Special Criminal Court 151, 160, 211, 212, 340, 345, 362
Special Defence Unit 210
Spike, The (television series) 295
Spillane, Liz 586
sports 6, 229, 296, 314–24
Spotlight (BBC Northern Ireland programme) 136
Springboks 445, 446
SPS steel factory, Galway 500
Stack, Tommy 324
Stage Struck (album) 270
'stagflation' 3
Stagg, Bridie 210
Stagg, Frank 210–11
Stagg family 211
Staines air crash (1972) 402
Stanislavski method 263
Stans, Maurice 515
State Paper Office (SPO) 249, 250
Statoil 529
Staunton, Fr Pádraig 562
Stembridge, Gerry 639
Stewart, Rod 273
Stiff Little Fingers 273
Stillorgan area, south County Dublin 472
Stokes, Niall 11, 95, 299
Stokes, Richard 9, 51–52, 54, 74, 101, 111, 187, 189, 201, 234–37, 241, 252, 264–65, 298, 303, 304–5, 317, 373, 417, 418, 440, 500, 530–31, 548, 646–47
Stormont parliament 130, 149, 178, 182
Strabane 171
Strand Hotel, Rosslare 453
strikes 6, 524
  banking 513–14, 515
  bus 513, 518
  cement industry 515
  dustmen 521
  milk 520
  post office 513, 517, 519, 521–22
  refuse-collection 513
  rent 569
  reputational damage 515–16
Stuart, Francis 224, 282
  Black List, Section H 282
  A Hole in the Head 282
  Memorial 282
  Who Dares to Speak 282
Studies (Jesuit publication) 239, 463, 540, 625, 626
Suárez, Adolfo 417
Succession Act 84
Sunday Independent 42, 58, 59, 104, 142, 307, 339, 489, 604, 633
Sunday Press 315
Sunday Times 132, 192, 454
Sunday Tribune 534
Sunday World 103, 307, 308, 586
Sunningdale conference and Agreement (1973) 2–3, 124, 163, 170, 173, 176–78, 179, 184, 194, 367
Superquinn supermarket company 473
Supreme Court 93, 109, 112, 115, 116, 212, 214, 344, 345, 346, 349, 363, 364, 368, 382, 485, 531, 596, 622, 667, 673, 675
Swan, Colonel 176
Sweden, and Wood Quay excavations 252
'sweetheart deals' 513
Sweetman, Gerard 60
Sweetman, Michael 395, 401, 402
  Challenge: Industry and Free Trade 395
Swift, Hugh 161
Switzers store 484
Synge, J.M. 260–61
  Playboy of the Western World 260–61

T

Taaffe, Pat 324

Taca 37, 60
Taisce, An (the National Trust) 252, 615
Taiwan 434, 435
Talbot, Venerable Matt 264
Talbot Hotel, Dublin 306
Tansey, Paul 484
Tanzania 448
Taoiseach, salary of 101
Tara Exploration and Development 72, 532, 533, 535
Tarbett, Alex 432
TASS 428
tax evasion 352–53
taxation 6, 136, 460, 465, 466, 467, 472, 473, 486, 496
capital 62, 471, 472
capital gains 471
central 488
direct 495, 498
of farmers 504, 505, 506
income 508
indirect 495
motor 83
Taxi Mauve, Un (film) 304
taxis 591, 592
Taylor, James 271
TDs (Teachtaí Dála)
advancement of careers 27
communications 24
dual mandate 27
and Gardaí complaints about Garvey 344
salaries 100–101
stress on constituency service 31
women 90, 93
telephone network 311–13
Telesis Report (1982) 462, 463
television 5, 8, 46, 79, 81, 84, 96, 105, 106, 107, 111, 228–29, 245, 267–68, 276, 277, 290, 293, 318
multichannel 296
survey (1978) 295–96
Temple, H.L. 669
Templemore, Tipperary 328, 644
Terenure, Dublin 593
First National bank 295
Texaco 528
Texaco Sportsmen of the Year awards 314, 316
Thalidomide victims 383–84
Thames TV 167
Thatcher, Margaret, Baroness 219
theatre 255–65
Thin Lizzy 272, 273
'think tanks' 110
Third Programme for Economic Expansion (1969–72) 474, 475
This Week (RTÉ programme) 217, 218
Thom, Kenneth 401
Thornley, David 17, 67, 172, 625
and Cosgrave 76, 77
death 96–97
empathy with Northern Republicans 216
and firearms 216–17
historian and broadcaster 10, 66, 96
as an MEP 422
and Nöel Browne 70–71
O'Brien on 217
Republican stance over Northern Ireland 69–70
temporary loss of party whip 216
Three Mile Island reactor meltdown (1979) 532
Thurles First National 295
Tiernan, Joe 200
Times, The 130, 159, 160
Timmins, Eugene 101
Tindemans, Leo 412, 413
Tindeman's Report 412
Tinney, Mary Catherine 427
Tipperary 246
two county councils 29
Tipperary South 85
Tipperary Town Council 437
Toal, Maureen 262
tobacco *see* smoking
Tobin, Liam 52, 562
Togher Tenants' Association, Cork 569
Tóibín, Colm 286
Tóibín, Niall 228, 582
tokenism 277
Tone, Theobald Wolfe 231, 237, 280
Toner's pub, Dublin 273
Tonight (BBC programme) 167
Tory island, off the coast of Donegal 564
Total 530
tourism 133, 215, 304, 408, 450–55, 580
Towers, Robert 543
Tracey, Ray 321
Trade Disputes Act (1906) 513
trade unions/unionism 6, 71, 171, 173, 211, 334, 347, 387, 396, 399, 461–62, 507, 509, 511, 512–13, 515–16, 519, 522, 619, 661, 662, 669, 672
Tralee Town Park 401
Tralee Urban District Council 401
travel agents 586
travellers 569, 651
Treacy, John 322
Treacy, Seán 246
Treasury 55
Trench, Bea 94
Trench, Brian 29–30, 32, 172, 346, 478, 494, 507–9, 593
Trevor, William: *Angels at the Ritz* 226
Trimble, Gary 240
Trinity College Dublin (TCD) 27, 47, 48, 92, 105, 128, 195, 241, 273, 328, 386, 391, 405, 427, 430, 431,

445, 476, 483, 484, 500, 583, 584, 639, 640, 654
Douglas Hyde Gallery 280
Faculty of Medicine 599
Maoists in 94
proposed merger with University College 635
recruits British academics in the post-war years 14
Students Representative Council 95
Trinity College History Society 246
Trocadero restaurant, Dublin 575
Trocaire 430, 431
Trotskyist groups 105
Troubles, the (1969–98) 4, 25, 65
British lack of understanding about 157–58
broadcasting coverage 289
casualties 1, 2
day trips over the border 137
defining the island of Ireland in the 1970s 2
diversion of Garda manpower due to the Troubles 333
and Emergency Powers Act (1976) 345
fear that they would spill over the border 7, 121
and feminists 93
increase in profile and professionalism of Irish army 346
journalistic coverage 158–59
Lynch's famous television broadcast 143
monetary cost to the Republic 215
outbreak of 120, 127
peace and stability since end of 9
permeating decision-making 15
prompts poems 1, 2
reactionary impact on the Republic 134
refugees 137
result in terror and tension 19
the state's attitude to 122
transformation of the political environment 15
and a united Ireland 2
Trudder House, Wicklow 378
Tucker, Brian 586
Tuesday Report, The (RTÉ programme) 75
Tulio, Paulo 576
Tully, James 40–41, 43, 72, 489, 496, 526, 533, 565, 594, 614, 615
Tunney, Jim 629
Turbot island 562, 563
Tweedy, Hilda 665, 669, 670

U

U2 272, 582
Uí Chribín, Míne Bean 670
Ulster Defence Association (UDA) 136, 174
Ulster Defence Regiment 203
Ulster Freedom Fighters 202
Ulster Unionist Party (UUP) 174, 175, 176, 182, 183, 186
Ulster Vanguard Alliance 197
Ulster Vanguard movement 163, 174, 175
Ulster Volunteer Force (UVF) 124, 198, 202, 203
Ulster Workers Council 178, 183
under-age drinking 578–79
Undertones 273
unemployment 7, 64–65, 70, 300, 399, 410, 443, 459, 461, 467, 469, 475, 492, 494, 496, 499, 571, 595, 651, 669, 671
anti-unemployment demonstration (Waterford, 1978) 347
youth 419
unemployment benefit 671
unemployment assistance 478
Unfair Dismissals Act 519
Unicef (Irish branch) 383
Union of Students in Ireland (USI) 173, 634
Unionists 163
and BBC coverage of the Troubles 167
conservative 192
and the Council of Ireland 176, 177, 178
dedicated to keeping Northern Ireland in the United Kingdom 2
distrustful of politicians from the Republic 125–26
and the DUP 174
FitzGerald's contacts 135
and Haughey 220
ignorance about northern Unionists 120
and Lynch 151
resistance to reunification 190
and the SDLP 185
United Kingdom (UK): women in politics 91
United Nations (UN) 74, 120, 141, 155, 168–69, 170, 346, 382, 390, 391, 425, 441, 446, 647
and Aiken 433
General Assembly 340, 434, 445, 447
Irish in emergency force 346, 432
Universal Declaration of Human Rights 675

United States
abuse of trust in political establishment 7
Bicentennial 438
dealing with the Irish-American lobby 154–56
Dublin landing rights issue 428, 436, 437
governors visit the Republic 439–40
Jewish lobby 428
joint statement by 'The Four Horsemen' 157
Nixon's visit to Ireland (1970) 436–37
NORAID 153–54
number of Irish-Americans 156
presidential race (1976) 107
Reagan's visit to Ireland (1972) 436
State Department 428
statement by Jimmy Carter (1977) 156
undermining of Irish American support for the IRA 123, 220, 438
visits by senior Irish politicians 438–39
University College Cork (UCC) 63, 267, 452, 636
Law Society 111
University College Dublin (UCD) 1, 30, 78, 111, 179, 195, 239, 330, 441, 458, 548, 565, 618, 636, 639, 640, 642, 650, 676
appointments officer 661
Archives Department 10, 211, 248, 250
Great Hall 274
Literary and Historical Debating Society 196, 638–39, 652
proposed merger with Trinity College 635
Psychology Department 572
University College Galway (UCG) 26, 550, 636, 640
University of Limerick 635
University of Ulster 151
unmarried mother's allowance 622
urban/rural divide 547–53
urbanisation 329, 542, 648
Uris, Leon: *A Terrible Beauty* 543
US State Department 154
Ustinov, Peter 304
UTV 158

V
Vaizey, Lord 133
Vance, Cyrus 157, 440
vasectomy 675
VAT 353, 484, 496
Vatican 193, 206, 620
Vatican II Council 620, 621, 622, 652
Vaughan, Emmet 319
Vietnam War 433, 437
Vignoles, Julian 269
Village People 273
Voluntary Health Insurance (VHI) 602, 603
voting age 94–95

W
wages
agricultural 566
in Dublin area 579
equal pay 622
industrial 566, 567
women's 661, 672–73
Wakefield prison 210
Walker, Brian 135, 322
Walker, Dorothy 279
Wallace, A.J. 379–80
Walsh, Brendan 567
Walsh, Judge Brian 363, 364, 366, 372–73
Walsh, Dick 97
Walsh, Ed 635
Walshe, Eibhear 244, 263, 549, 583, 608, 657
Ward, Brian 563
Warnock, William 436
Warrenpoint 260
water quality 613
Waterford 263, 608
trade union anti-unemployment demonstration (1978) 347
Waterford Courthouse 250
Waterford Glass 303, 439
Waters, George 296
Waters, John 38, 81, 84, 107, 309, 552–53
Waterville Course 448
Weathermen 211
Welcome Here Kind Stranger (album) 270
West, Harry 186
West, Trevor 126
West German Labour Market Institute 491
West Mayo by-election (1975) 35–36
Westminster Lobby correspondents 158–59
Wexford Chamber of Commerce 487
Wexford Corporation 487
Wexford Opera Festival 265, 275
Whale, John 132, 192
Whelan, Bill 267
Whelan, C.V. 174
Whelan, Noel 20, 462–63
Whiddy Island oil terminal, Cork: 1979 disaster 530
Whitaker, T.K. 9, 20, 50, 82, 83, 84, 143, 219, 387, 431, 459, 461, 465–66, 467, 500, 501
White, Harry 266–67
White, Jack 112, 290, 296–97
White, James 265, 281, 421
White Papers
'Accession to the European Communities' (1972) 395

capital taxation (1974) 471, 472, 473
local finance 487, 488
Whitelaw, William 190
Whiting Bay, County Waterford 530
Whitlam, Gough 441
Whyte, John H. 31, 101
Church and State in Modern Ireland 1923–70 650–51
Wicca (feminist publication) 678–79
Wicklow 565
Wicklow, Lady (Eleanor Butler) 132
Widgery, Lord Chief Justice 130
Widgery Report 131
Wilde, Oscar 261, 262
Wilkinson, Colm T. 107
Williams, Betty 186
Williams, Desmond 133, 388
Wilson, Brian 563
Wilson, Fr Des 207
Wilson, Harold (Baron Wilson of Rievaulx) 8, 124, 125, 173, 178, 185, 207
Wilson, John 628, 637
Windlesham, Lord 173
Windscale plant 531
Wogan, Terry 297
Wolfe Tones 136
women
in broadcasting 300–301
in cabinet 93
in the civil service and local authorities 93
domestic violence 355–57, 666, 668
emergence of women's political organisations 90
employment of married women 4, 542
journalists 310
in the judiciary 93
status of 8, 657–79
TDs 90, 93
women's rights 89, 91, 92, 656
writers 281–82
see also feminist movement, feminists
Women Today programme 300–301
Women's Aid 356, 666
Women's Political Association (WPA) 90–91, 406
Women's Representative Association 90
Women's Representative Committee 622, 665–66
Wood, Alan 159
Wood, Ernest 445
Wood, Richard 534
Wood Quay site, Dublin 227, 251–54, 255, 315
Woodburn Development, Rathfarnham 594
Woodfield, Philip 174
Woodham Smith, Cecil 132–33
Woods, Gerard 208, 238, 651–52
Woods, Michael 421–22
Woodworth, Paddy 440
Woolworth's 484
World at One (BBC programme) 158
World Communications Day 662
World Cross-Country Championships 322
World Health Organisation Report (1976) 597
World Ploughing Championships, Wexford 446
World Synod of Bishops, Rome 642–43
Woulfe, Tom 318
Wright, Patrick 532
Wright, Thomas, Jr 532
writers 225–27, 281–84
Wymes, Michael 326, 532
Wymes, Patrick 534
Wynne, Revd William 138

Y

Yeats, W.B. 285, 451
Youghal Carpets 594
'Young Ireland' rebellion (1848) 237
Young Socialists 64
Young Unionist Association 190
youth culture 6, 11, 95

Z

Zimmerman, Joseph 26
zinc deposits 532, 533, 535